# CASES, MATERIALS AND PROBLEMS ON GENERAL PRACTICE INSURANCE LAW

## Third Edition

By

**Kenneth H. York**
*Distinguished Professor of Law, Emeritus, Pepperdine University*
*Professor of Law, Emeritus, University of California, Los Angeles*

**John W. Whelan**
*Professor of Law, University of California, Hastings College of Law*

**Leo P. Martinez**
*Professor of Law, University of California, Hastings College of Law*

AMERICAN CASEBOOK SERIES®

WEST PUBLISHING CO.
ST. PAUL, MINN., 1994

610 Opperman Drive
P.O. Box 64526
St. Paul, MN 55164–0526
1–800–328–9352


**Library of Congress Cataloging-in-Publication Data**

York, Kenneth H.
Cases, materials, and problems on general practice insurance law / by Kenneth H. York, John W. Whelan, and Leo P. Martinez. — 3rd ed.
p. cm. — (American casebook series)
Includes index.
ISBN 0–314–02951–6
1. Insurance law—United States—Cases. I. Whelan, John W. II. Martinez, Leo P., 1949– . III. Title. IV. Series.
KF1163.Y64 1994
346.73'086—dc20
[347.30686] 93–40771
CIP

**ISBN** 0–314–02951–6

(Y., W. & M.) Ins. Law 3rd ACB

# Preface to the Third Edition

As stated in the second edition, insurance continues to lurch from crisis to crisis. These crises necessarily determine, sometimes apart from our desires, the direction of the casebook. Hence, the section on coverage disputes is expanded and includes a substantial discussion of pollution exclusions arising from environmental concerns and the seemingly unlimited exposure to liability. The section on the exclusion of intentional acts now contains cases dealing with sexual harassment and liability for various forms of discrimination. Other parts of the book demonstrate, in less dramatic fashion, the inevitable if not always imminent, evolution in insurance law. In short, we have attempted to keep pace.

The earlier characterization of insurance as one of the principal fuels for litigation seems even more inescapable. Our hope is that the casual reader or the serious student will remain challenged and intrigued, as we are, by this multifaceted subject.

KENNETH H. YORK
JOHN W. WHELAN
LEO P. MARTINEZ

March 1994

*

# Acknowledgments

The authors also wish to acknowledge the diligent and able research assistance of Daniel Howell, a second-year student at Hastings College of the Law and a refugee from the insurance industry prior to his law school studies, in the compilation of this third edition.

*

# Summary of Contents

# Table of Contents

## APPENDICES



*

# Table of Cases

**The principal cases are in bold type. Cases cited or discussed in the text are roman type. References are to pages. Cases cited in principal cases and within other quoted materials are not included.**

# CASES, MATERIALS AND PROBLEMS ON

# GENERAL PRACTICE INSURANCE LAW

## Third Edition

*

# Part A

# IN GENERAL

# Chapter 1

# GOVERNMENTAL REGULATION OF INSURANCE

Law students, facing for the first time problems of understanding the insurance industry and interpretation of insurance contracts are going to have trouble with certain terms, some of them especially used in insurance law, others having a more common legal coinage. We would like to recommend that, at an early point in the course (namely this one) that students of the enterprising sort undertake their own search for definitions of the terms listed below. This will, we think, achieve more than the objective of familiarization with definitions; it will also achieve familiarization with some of the major texts and treatises, for example: Couch, Cyclopedia of Insurance Law 2d (see the "words and phrases" entries in the Index volumes); Appleman, Insurance Law and Practice; Keeton and Widiss, Insurance Law–Basic Text. The statutes of the student's own State may also offer definitions of some of these terms. There are other sources of definitions. There are certainly other words to be defined, but the following will be a start on gaining a grasp on "insurance law".

a. all risks policy
b. adverse selection
c. block policy (jewelers')
d. CGL
e. claims-made policy
f. co-insurance
g. CQV
h. excepted causes v. exclusions
i. 15/30/5
j. first party insurance
k. floater
*l.* incontestability
m. loan receipt
n. no-fault insurance
*o.* omnibus clause
p. reciprocal insurance
q. risk distribution
r. subrogation
s. self insurance
t. stacking
u. surplus line brokers
v. term insurance
w. territorial rating
x. third party insurance
y. ultimate net loss
z. umbrella policy

## A. STATE GOVERNMENT REGULATION

### PURPOSE OF INSURANCE REGULATION

The purpose of insurance regulation is dictated by social, political and economic values within and without the insurance industry. This theme was promulgated by Professor Spencer L. Kimball in his article entitled "The Purpose of Insurance Regulation: A Preliminary Inquiry in the Theory of Insurance Law" (45 Minn.L.R. 471, 1961). Insurance provides security for policyholders and much regulation is directed to ensuring continued security. Requirements for levels of paid-in capital, for adequate premium rates, and for permissive investments are directed to the solidity of the company. Prohibitions against discriminatory classifications, excessive premium rates, and unfair distribution policies address questions of equitable treatment of policyholders.

Another purpose of insurance regulation is to satisfy the general goals of society at large. Notions of democracy and liberty and consumer protection are apparent in requirements for policyholder participation in management (not yet implemented in the U.S.), and adherence to notice, hearing, and contract rights. Economic values underlie regulations for free access to the market, local protectionism, and use of investment funds. There are many complex and interacting purposes of insurance regulation. As Professor Kimball states: "Insurance is a small world that reflects the purposes of the larger world outside it."

## GRIFFIN SYSTEMS, INC. v. OHIO DEPARTMENT OF INSURANCE

Supreme Court of Ohio, 1991.
61 Ohio St.3d 552, 575 N.E.2d 803.

SWEENEY, JUSTICE.

The determinative issue presented in this appeal is whether appellant's vehicle protection plans are contracts "substantially amounting to insurance" within the meaning of R.C. 3905.42. For the reasons that follow, we answer such inquiry in the negative, and therefore reverse the judgment of the court of appeals and reinstate the trial court's judgment.

R.C. 3905.42 provides as follows:

> "No company, corporation, or association, whether organized in this state or elsewhere, shall engage either directly or indirectly in this state in the business of insurance, or enter into any contracts substantially amounting to insurance, * * * unless it is expressly authorized by the laws of this state, and the laws regulating it and applicable thereto, have been complied with."

Appellee ODI argues that the vehicle protection plans offered and sold by appellant are "contracts substantially amounting to insurance," and, thus, should be subject to the full array of insurance regulations within R.C. Title 39. ODI contends, and the court of appeals below agreed, that the key element that subjects appellant's protection plans to insurance laws and regulations is that appellant is neither the seller nor the manufacturer of the product it purports to warrant. ODI essentially asserts that extended warranties offered by sellers and manufacturers are part of the inducement process of making the product more desirable to the prospective buyer. Since appellant is an independent third party to the transaction, ODI submits that the claimed warranty appellant offers and sells is in reality a contract "substantially amounting to insurance."

The appellant, on the other hand, citing State, ex rel. Duffy, v. Western Auto Supply Co. (1938), 134 Ohio St. 163, 11 O.O. 583, 16 N.E.2d 256, and State, ex rel. Herbert, v. Standard Oil Co. (1941), 138 Ohio St. 376, 20 O.O. 460, 35 N.E.2d 437, contends that since its vehicle protection plans cover only those repairs necessitated by mechanical breakdown of defective parts, the protection plans constitute warranties and not contracts of insurance. Appellant relies on *Duffy*, supra, and argues that the instant vehicle protection plans limit reimbursement to loss due to defects in the product, and do not promise to reimburse loss or damage resulting from perils outside of and unrelated to defects in the product itself. Appellant submits that the issue of whether the seller or manufacturer (as opposed to an independent third party) offers or sells the type of contract in issue is wholly irrelevant.

In *Duffy*, supra, this court was asked to determine whether written guarantees issued by Western Auto covering tires it sold constituted contracts "substantially amounting to insurance" under G.C. 665. The language of one of the Western Auto guarantees stated that it protected the tires " 'against blowouts, cuts, bruises, rim-cuts, under-inflation, wheels out of alignment, faulty brakes or other road hazards that may render the tire unfit for further service (except fire and theft).' It then provided that 'In the event that the tire becomes unserviceable from the above conditions, we will (at our option) repair it free of charge, or replace it with a new tire of the same make at any of our stores, charging ___th of our current price for each month which has elapsed since the date of purchase. The new tire will be fully covered by our regular guarantee in effect at time of adjustment. Furthermore: every tire is guaranteed against defects in material or workmanship without limit as to time, mileage or service.' " Id., at 165, 11 O.O. at 584, 16 N.E.2d at 257.

In finding that the Western Auto guarantees were contracts substantially amounting to insurance, this court held in *Duffy*, supra, at paragraphs three and four of the syllabus:

> "A warranty promises indemnity against defects in an article sold, while insurance indemnifies against loss or damage resulting from perils outside of and unrelated to defects in the article itself.
>
> "A contract whereby the vendor of automobile tires undertakes to guarantee the tires sold against defects in material or workmanship without limit as to time, mileage or service, and further expressly guarantees them for a specified period against 'blowouts, cuts, bruises, rim-cuts, under-inflation, wheels out of alignment, faulty brakes or other road hazards that may render the tire unfit for further service (except fire or theft),' or contracts to indemnify the purchaser 'should the tire fail within the replacement period' specified, without limitation as to cause of such 'failure,' is a contract 'substantially amounting to insurance' within the provisions of

Section 665, General Code, which requires such guarantor or insurer to comply with the laws of the state authorizing and regulating the business of insurance."

The foregoing syllabus language clearly indicates that the "guarantees" in *Duffy* were found to be contracts substantially amounting to insurance because such guarantees promised to indemnify for losses or damages to the product outside of and unrelated to defects inherent in the product itself. Several years later, in *Herbert*, supra, this court was faced with another tire warranty/guarantee that was challenged by the Attorney General of Ohio. Therein, the tire warranty offered by Standard Oil promised repair or replacement for a limited period under certain conditions and provided in pertinent part:

> " 'This Warranty and Adjustment Agreement does not cover punctures, tires ruined in running flat, tires injured or destroyed by fire, wrecks or collisions, tires cut by chains, or by obstruction on vehicle, theft, clincher tires, tubes used in any form, or tires used in taxicab or common carrier bus service.
>
> " 'This Warranty and Adjustment Agreement does not cover consequential damages.' " Id., 138 Ohio St. at 378, 20 O.O. at 461, 35 N.E.2d at 439.

In finding that the Standard Oil tire warranty was indeed a warranty, and not a contract substantially amounting to insurance, this court held in paragraphs four and five of the syllabus as follows:

> "A warranty or guaranty issued to a purchaser in connection with the sale of goods containing an agreement to indemnify against loss or damage resulting from perils outside of and unrelated to inherent weaknesses in the goods themselves, constitutes a contract substantially amounting to insurance within the purview of Section 665, General Code. (State, ex rel. Duffy, Atty. Genl., v. Western Auto Supply Co., 134 Ohio St., 163 [11 O.O. 583, 16 N.E.2d 256], followed.)
>
> "A written warranty delivered to a purchaser, representing that the articles sold are so well and carefully manufactured that they will give satisfactory service under ordinary usage for a specified length of time, and providing for an adjustment in the event of failure from faulty construction or materials, but expressly excluding happenings not connected with imperfections in the articles themselves, is not a contract substantially amounting to insurance within the meaning of Section 665, General Code."

In summarizing the law enunciated in both *Duffy* and *Herbert* it is readily apparent that a contract "substantially amounting to insurance" in this context is one that promises to cover losses or damages over and above, or unrelated to, defects within the product itself.

A careful review of the instant vehicle protection plans indicates that losses or damages sustained by the purchaser of the product which are unrelated to defects within the product itself are specifically excluded from coverage. Thus, it would appear that under both *Duffy* and *Herbert*, the instant vehicle protection plans are indeed warranties, and are not contracts substantially amounting to insurance.

However, as mentioned before, ODI asserts that the crucial distinction, as noted by the court of appeals below, is that warranties not sold by either the vendor or manufacturer of the product are not made to induce a purchase of the product, and therefore constitute contracts substantially amounting to insurance. While the foregoing assertion may appear to be facially valid, we find it to be unpersuasive. Obviously, the distinction made in this vein was of no apparent consequence in *Duffy*, supra, inasmuch as it was the seller of the product therein who issued the "warranty" that this court found to be a contract substantially amounting to insurance.

In our view, the crucial factor in determining whether a contract is a warranty or something substantially amounting to insurance is not the status of the party offering or selling the warranty, but rather the type of coverage promised within the four corners of the contract itself. Under the rule of law announced in both *Duffy* and *Herbert*, it is clear that warranties that cover only defects within the product itself are properly characterized as warranties (as was the case in *Herbert*, supra), whereas warranties promising to cover damages or losses unrelated to defects within the product itself are, by definition, contracts substantially amounting to insurance (as was the case in *Duffy*, supra).

The fact that appellant herein is not the manufacturer, supplier, or seller of the products it purports to warrant is, in our view, of little or no consequence in determining whether its protection plans are subject to R.C. Title 39. Common experience in today's marketplace indicates that a large number of consumer products carry a short-term warranty, but that agreements that extend the warranty beyond the period of time offered by the manufacturer may often be purchased for additional consideration. Certainly, it can be safely surmised that most people are not induced to buy a specific product based upon an extended warranty agreement that may be purchased at an extra cost. Carrying ODI's arguments to their logical extreme, however, a seller of consumer products can offer such extended warranties to cover losses or damages, while independent third parties would be subject to insurance regulations even if the extended warranties specifically exclude losses or damages unrelated to defects in the product. Under such circumstances, we reject the status-determinative approach urged by ODI and adopted by the appellate court below, in favor of the substance-of-the-contract approach urged by appellant. Such a substance-of-the-contract approach was implemented by the court in Mein v. United States Car Testing Co. (1961), 115 Ohio App. 145, 20 O.O.2d 242, 184 N.E.2d 489, and is abundantly more consonant with the law and analysis set forth in both *Duffy*, supra, and *Herbert*, supra.

Therefore, based on all the foregoing, we hold that a motor vehicle service agreement which promises to compensate the promisee for repairs necessitated by mechanical breakdown resulting exclusively from failure due to defects in the motor vehicle parts does not constitute a contract "substantially amounting to insurance" within the purview of R.C. 3905.42. Accordingly, the judgment of the court of appeals is hereby reversed.

Judgment reversed.

DOUGLAS, HERBERT R. BROWN and RESNICK, JJ., concur.

MOYER, C.J., and HOLMES and WRIGHT, JJ., dissent.

WRIGHT, JUSTICE, dissenting.

* * *

In this instance, Griffin had no relationship with the consumer whatsoever until after the consumer had purchased the automobile, at which point Griffin directly solicited the consumer by mail for sale of its VPP. Having signed up the consumer, Griffin reinsured its business with the Great Plains Insurance Company, a Nebraska corporation, which is a wholly owned subsidiary of Griffin and is unlicensed to sell insurance in the state of Ohio. Therefore, without considering whether the VPPs before us here insure against contingencies other than product defects, we have a contract that is totally distinguishable from the warranty we found in *Herbert*. It is perfectly apparent that the VPP is not a warranty proposed by a manufacturer-seller and used for the purpose of inducing or increasing sales of the product in question. In a word, we have a case of first impression here which is certainly not controlled by either *Herbert* or State, ex rel. Duffy v. Western Auto Supply Co. (1938), 134 Ohio St. 163, 11 O.O. 583, 16 N.E.2d 256. Indeed, the *Duffy* case seems to directly support the holding of the court of appeals.

Griffin has argued and the majority has inexplicably found that the VPPs involved here do not constitute contracts "substantially amounting to insurance" pursuant to R.C. 3905.42 and, thus, the superintendent has no authority to order a halt to these sundry violations of law. I must vigorously disagree. The majority appears to overlook the difference between the contract sold by Griffin and the warranty described in the *Herbert* case. Here, Griffin is not the warrantor of a product it has manufactured or sold but is rather the insurer of the performance of component parts in a product manufactured and sold by a third party. The *Herbert* case certainly did not exclude all warranties or guarantees from control by ODI but only those warranties guaranteeing "satisfactory service under ordinary usage" of products being sold to a purchaser by the manufacturer or seller of that product. Id. at paragraph five of the syllabus.

The Ohio General Assembly has given ODI the broadest authority to regulate all forms of insurance by way of R.C. 3905.42, which states in pertinent part: "No company * * * shall engage * * * in the business of insurance, or enter into any contracts substantially amounting to insurance, or in any manner aid therein, or engage in the business of guaranteeing against liability, loss, or damage, * * * unless it is expressly authorized by the laws of this state, and the laws regulating it and applicable thereto, have been complied with." In the *Duffy* case, we " '[b]roadly defined insurance * * * [as] a contract by which one party, for a compensation called the premium, assumes particular risks of the other party and promises to pay to him or his nominee a certain or ascertainable sum of money on a specified contingency. As regards property and liability insurance, it is a contract by which one party promises on a consideration to compensate or reimburse the other if he shall suffer loss from a specified cause, or to guarantee or indemnify or secure him against loss from that cause.' * * * " Id. at 168, 11 O.O. at 585, 16 N.E.2d at 258–259. In my view, the VPPs offered by Griffin are within this definition.

The appellee herein cites Vance, The Law of Insurance (3 Ed.1951) 2, Section 1, which lists the following five elements as distinguishing characteristics of insurance: (1) the insured possesses an insurable interest; (2) the insured is subject to loss through the destruction or impairment of that interest by the happening of some designated peril; (3) the insurer assumes the risk of loss; (4) such assumption is part of the general scheme to distribute actual losses among a large group of persons bearing similar risks; and (5) the insured pays a premium as consideration for the promise. There is no question that each of the above-described elements is present under Griffin's VPP.

Griffin can hardly be likened to a manufacturer, supplier or seller offering an extended warranty on one of its products. As stated above, Griffin is clearly not involved in the manufacture or sale of automobiles, and has no control over the risk of defects in those products. It is an independent, for-profit entity offering a contract insuring against the risk of mechanical breakdown of a motor vehicle—an insurable interest. Griffin, for consideration of a stated premium from the policyholder, assumes the risk of certain specified losses and presumably distributes that risk among a larger group of persons bearing similar risks. This case does not involve a warranty because a warranty is a statement or representation made by the seller or manufacturer of goods contemporaneously with and as a part of the contract of sale.

Appellee has drawn our attention to opinions from out of state and under federal law in support of its position. Griffin Systems, Inc. v. Washburn (1987), 153 Ill.App.3d 113, 106 Ill.Dec. 330, 505 N.E.2d 1121, examined the same VPPs at issue in this case and concluded that they are insurance contracts. That opinion distinguished Griffin's VPPs from a warranty or service contract. The court stated, " * * * the distinguishing feature which sets * * * [manufacturer's or seller's service contracts and warranties] apart from an insurance policy is the fact that the respective compan[ies] manufacture or sell the products which they agreed to repair or replace. No third parties are involved nor is there a risk accepted which the company, because of its expertise, is unaware of. * * * " (Emphasis sic.) Id. at 117–118, 106 Ill.Dec. at 333, 505 N.E.2d at 1124.

As further evidence that Griffin's VPP is insurance and not a warranty, appellee cites a Federal Trade Commission ("F.T.C.") regulation, Section 700.11, Title 16, C.F.R., promulgated pursuant to the authority granted to the F.T.C. to enact rules implementing the Magnuson–Moss Warranty Act, Sections 2301 et seq., Title 15, U.S.Code. See Sections 2309 and 2312(c), Title 15, U.S.Code. The rule is relevant to the issue before us today in that it determines that VPPs such as the ones offered by Griffin are policies of insurance. Part (a) of the rule reads as follows:

> "The [Magnuson–Moss Warranty] Act recognizes two types of agreements which may provide similar coverage of consumer products, the written warranty, and the service contract. In addition, other agreements may meet the statutory definitions of either 'written warranty' or 'service contract,' but are sold and regulated under state law as contracts of insurance. One example is the automobile breakdown insurance policies sold in many jurisdictions and regulated by the state as a form of casualty insurance. The McCarran–Ferguson Act, 15 U.S.C. 1011 et seq., precludes jurisdiction under federal law over 'the business of insurance' to the extent an agreement is regulated by state law as insurance. Thus, such agreements are subject to the Magnuson–Moss Warranty Act only to the extent they are not regulated in a particular state as the business of insurance." (Emphasis added.) Thus, the F.T.C. considers such contracts ripe for insurance regulation.

Griffin urges this court to focus on whether it would "make sense" to apply the insurance statutes and regulations to its VPPs. The real issue, however, is whether each VPP contains the requisite elements of insurance such that it is a contract that "substantially amount[s] to insurance." See Mein v. United States Car Testing Co. (1961), 115 Ohio App. 145, 20 O.O.2d 242, 184 N.E.2d 489. As shown above, Griffin's VPP contains those elements and is, therefore, insurance. Because it is insurance, under R.C. 3905.42, ODI has the authority to regulate it.[1]

1. I offer yet further support for the appellee's position. Webster's defines "insurance" in part as "coverage by contract whereby for a stipulated consideration one party undertakes to indemnify or guarantee another against loss by a specified contingency or peril[.]" Webster's Third New International Dictionary (1986) 1173. Black's defines "insurance" similarly: "A contract whereby, for a stipulated consideration, one party undertakes to compensate the other for loss on a specified subject by specified perils. * * *" Black's Law Dictionary (6 Ed.1990) 802. All forms of warranties and guarantees meet this definition on some level. A simple manufacturer's limited warranty that comes with the product protects a purchaser from a specified loss (usually the value of the product) from a specified contingency or peril (usually a manufacturing defect). In fact, looking at Black's definition of "insurance," I am sure an accountant with the relevant actuarial and financial data could specify the amount of the product's price traceable to the warranty. At the same time, however, a manufacturer's warranty included in the price of the product is also a refinement of the manufactured product purchased: you do not just purchase a toaster, but rather you purchase a toaster that works, and a breach of the warranty means the product you received was not the product for which you contracted. I subscribe to this latter view of manufacturers' warranties where they are received as part of the product price; they are not contracts "substantially amounting to insurance." However, any and all warranties sold apart from a product seem to fall into the definition of "in-

Accordingly, I strongly dissent.

## TRUTA v. AVIS RENT A CAR SYSTEM, INC.

Court of Appeal, First District, Division 2, 1987.
193 Cal.App.3d 802, 238 Cal.Rptr. 806.

BENSON, ASSOCIATE JUSTICE.

This is an appeal from a judgment of dismissal entered after a demurrer to the complaint of Marianne Truta (plaintiff) was sustained without leave to amend. Plaintiff instituted this action for herself personally and on behalf of a class of persons similarly situated. The defendants in whose favor judgment was rendered are Avis Rent A Car System, Inc., The Hertz Corporation, Budget Rent A Car Corporation, and National Car Rental System, Inc.

The substance of plaintiff's six-count complaint is that within the four years preceding the filing of the action, plaintiff and other California residents had rented automobiles from the various defendants. Incidental to the rental of these automobiles, plaintiff and the class she purportedly represents agreed to pay an additional fee to defendants for a "collision damage waiver" (hereafter "CDW").[1] The CDW, which plaintiff alleges to be essentially uniform for all car rentals in California, provided that for a fee of $6 per day defendants agreed to assume responsibility (subject to certain terms and conditions) for the term of one day for collision or upset damage or loss to the vehicle in an amount up to $1,000. * * * The pertinent provision of that contract states:

> "LOSS OR DAMAGE TO THE CAR. I'll pay you for all loss of and damage to the car regardless of who is at fault. My responsibility for accidental collision or upset damage won't exceed the amount shown in box 38 [the amount shown was $1,000] on the other side of this agreement. If I've accepted the 'collision damage waiver' option, I won't have to pay anything. But I will be responsible for the full amount of the damage if I violate any of the terms of this agreement or if I abuse the car or drive it recklessly or while under the influence of alcohol or drugs. I won't have to pay for accidental loss or damage from fire, theft, or other causes that are normally covered by a standard comprehensive physical damage insurance policy. I will report the loss of or any damage to the vehicle promptly by calling the phone number listed on the other side of this agreement."

The first cause of action of the complaint alleges that defendants are engaged in the business of insurance in violation of Insurance Code

surance." This is particularly apparent under the "modus operandi" before us. This form of insurance is ripe for abuse by the less than scrupulous and, as such, is ripe for regulation by ODI. The record in this case surely supports this premise.

1. Although plaintiff consistently refers to collision damage waiver as "the insurance contract" we will refer to the provision with the same language used in the agreement.

section 700 in that none of the defendants has been admitted to transact any class of insurance in California.[2] * * *

The second cause of action alleges that because defendants are charging excessive rates for insurance in violation of section 1852 of the Insurance Code, they are consequently engaged in unlawful business practices. * * *

The fifth cause of action alleges that the CDW is unconscionable for five reasons which we summarize as follows: 1) the provision provides no protection for most circumstances, a fact which defendants concealed; 2) its cost is excessive within the meaning of the California Insurance Code and far in excess of a price that would be determined in a competitive business environment; 3) the language of the provision is misleading; 4) the manner in which the rental contracts are printed, worded, packaged and presented disguises the existence of a major portion of the contractual provisions; and 5) defendants obtained unfair advantage by use of their superior bargaining position. * * *

[I]n support of defendants' demurrer to plaintiff's complaint, defendants submitted exhibits of four superior court decisions from foreign jurisdictions dismissing similar actions on the grounds that the CDW is not insurance.[4] Additional exhibits included five opinions from attorneys general or insurance departments in other states.[5] Each document opined that the CDW was not insurance.

After plaintiff filed her points and authorities in opposition to defendants' demurrer, defendants filed a request that the court take judicial notice of a memorandum, dated October 23, 1968, rendered by the California Department of Insurance * * * concerning Ford Rent–A–Car System. According to the memorandum, Ford Rent–A–Car leased automobiles to the public whereby the lessees of the automobiles were liable for the first $100 damages due to fire, theft and collision.[7] If a

2. Section 700 of the Insurance Code provides: "(a) A person shall not transact any class of insurance business in this state without first being admitted for such class. Such admission is secured by procuring a certificate of authority from the commissioner. Such certificate shall not be granted until the applicant conforms to the requirements of this code and of the laws of this state prerequisite to its issue."

4. The decisions were *Burrell v. Avis* (Fla.Cir.Ct., June 21, 1984) No. 83–6162 C–7; *Russell v. Hertz Co.* (Cir.Ct. Cook, Ill., Feb. 28, 1983) 82 CH 6632; *Korn et al. v. Avis et al.* (Pa.Ct. of Com.Pleas, Philadelphia Co., Feb. 10, 1977) No. 1670; *Klein v. National Car Rental* (N.Y.Supreme Ct., Spec.Term, May 4, 1983) No. 22720/82; affd., 100 A.D.2d 987, 474 N.Y.S.2d 160 (1984) leave to appeal den., 63 N.Y.2d 605, 481 N.Y.S.2d 1023, 471 N.E.2d 462 (1984).

5. Opinions from the Florida Attorney General, New York Attorney General, North Carolina Insurance Department, Texas State Board of Insurance and the Insurance Department of Iowa were included. However, a subsequently revised opinion by the New York Attorney General that the CDW is insurance was submitted at oral argument before this court. (See Ops. N.Y.Atty.Gen. 86–F9.)

7. The memorandum specifically describes the operation as follows: "The Ford Motor Company has a plan whereby, under separate franchise, they [sic] license any Ford dealer to operate a Ford Rent–A–Car System station. Cars are leased by Ford to the franchise holding dealer, who in turn leases them to members of the public. As part of the agreement between Ford and the dealer, insurance is provided including $100 comprehensive fire, theft and collision. By the separate agreements, the dealer in his lease of cars from Ford agrees to be liable for all damage, and in turn the dealer extracts the same agreement from lessees

lessee elected to pay for "collision protection," he was no longer liable for the $100 deductible amount. The author of the Department of Insurance memorandum opined as follows: "No insurance coverage is provided for this $100 amount. Rather, the lessor simply agrees not to hold the individual renting a car liable for either negligence or contractual liability for damage to the vehicle. The question here is whether this provision concerning the $100 deductible is doing an insurance business.

"My conclusion is that the Ford Rent–A–Car System operator is not involved in providing insurance. The subject charge is not accumulated to pay any liabilities or costs incurred by the rentor. Rather, the system operator has simply, by contract, released the lessee from responsibility for any damage to the property of the lessor. This is not a spreading of risk within insurance concepts, but is rather an allocation of risk by contractual agreement. As the parties can contract to place full responsibility for damage on the lessee, it seems no less reasonable that they can contract to place this responsibility on the lessor."

* * *

Without, at this point, determining whether we agree with the Department of Insurance's memorandum, it is clear that the agency has taken a position that a car leasing business may, by contract, relieve a lessee from liability for damage done to the leased vehicle without the agreement constituting insurance. * * *

We next consider the question of whether defendants, by virtue of the CDW provision of the rental agreement, are engaged in the insurance business and therefore in violation of Insurance Code section 700.

Section 22 of the Insurance Code defines insurance as "a contract whereby one undertakes to indemnify another against loss, damage, or liability arising from a contingent or unknown event." Case law has construed the statute as requiring two elements: "(1) a risk of loss to which one party is subject and a shifting of that risk to another party; and (2) distribution of risk among similarly situated persons." (*Metropolitan Life Ins. Co. v. State Bd. of Equalization* (1982) 32 Cal.3d 649, 654, 186 Cal.Rptr. 578, 652 P.2d 426.) While a persuasive argument can be made that the CDW transaction meets this criteria, the mere fact that a contract contains these two elements does not necessarily mean that the agreement constitutes an insurance contract for purposes of statutory regulation.

"A statute designed to regulate the business of insurance * * * is not intended to apply to all organizations having some element of risk assumption or distribution in their operations. The question of whether an arrangement is one of insurance may turn, not on whether a risk is involved or assumed, but on whether that or something else to which it is related in the particular plan is its principal object and purpose." (12

from him. Since the above insurance exists, this liability extends only to the $100 deductible amount. What is named 'collision protection' is sold by the lessor to cover the $100 deductible."

Appleman, Insurance Law and Practice (1981) § 7002, p. 14, footnotes omitted.) This is because "insurance regulatory laws are not properly construed as aimed at an absolute prohibition against the inclusion of any risk-transferring-and-distributing provisions in contracts for services or for the sale or rental of goods. In short, the presence of a small element of insurance, if one wishes to call it that, closely associated with the predominant element of the transaction—the element that gives the transaction its distinctive character—does not conclusively demonstrate that the transaction is within the reach of insurance regulatory laws." (Keeton, Insurance Law (1971) § 8.2(c), p. 552.)

In analyzing whether a contract constitutes insurance it is advised that two inquiries be made: "To what extent, in each case, did the specific transactions or the general line of business at issue involve one or more of the evils at which the regulatory statutes were aimed? And were the elements of risk transference and risk distribution, characteristic of transactions at which the regulatory statutes were aimed, a central and relatively important element of the transactions or instead merely incidental to other elements that gave the transactions their distinctive character?" (*Keeton, op. cit. supra.*)

A review of the California appellate decisions concerned with the question of whether a particular entity was engaged in the business of insurance within the meaning of the regulatory statutes of this state reveals that the analytical approach mentioned in Keeton has been utilized in this state. For instance, in *California Physicians' Service v. Garrison* (1946) 28 Cal.2d 790, 172 P.2d 4, professional medical services were rendered to low income patients who paid monthly membership dues to a non-profit corporation. Payment for these services was made through a fund created by the dues received by the non-profit corporation. In affirming the trial court's determination that the organization was not involved in the insurance business the Supreme Court stated: "Absence or presence of assumption of risk or peril is not the sole test to be applied in determining [the corporation's] status. The question, more broadly, is whether, looking at the plan of operation as a whole, 'service' rather than 'indemnity' is its principal object and purpose." (*Id.* at p. 809, 172 P.2d 4.) The *Garrison* court in reaching its conclusion also looked to the purpose and nature of the regulatory provisions arising under the Insurance Code, "* * * particularly those relating to the maintenance of reserves and to the regulation of investments and financial operations," and observed: "The extensive insurance regulations ... are designed to protect the insured, or the public, from the insurer. [Citation.] Such regulations become important only if the insurer has assumed definite obligations. Conversely, it is evident that they are not intended to apply where no risk is assumed and no default can exist. * * *"

Similar reasoning was employed in *Transportation Guar. Co. v. Jellins* (1946) 29 Cal.2d 242, 174 P.2d 625. In *Jellins,* the court was called upon to determine whether two truck maintenance contracts containing provisions that the contractor agreed to insure the vehicles for the owner in an authorized insurance company constituted insurance contracts. Recognizing that nearly every business venture entails some assumption of risk, the high court stated: "We are satisfied that a sound jurisprudence does not suggest the extension, by judicial construction, of the insurance laws to govern every contract involving an assumption of risk or indemnification of loss; that when the question arises each contract must be tested by its own terms as they are written, as they are understood by the parties, and as they are applied under the particular circumstances involved." * * *

After reviewing the entire contract, the *Jellins* court concluded that the major purpose of the underlying agreement was to supply labor. The court then stated: "Plaintiff's obligations (with their reciprocal contractual rights) to make repairs, to maintain the truck in good running order, and to keep a truck constantly available to the owner except for reasonable service periods, do not in our opinion, make the plaintiff an insurer. Such obligations are similar to those ordinarily undertaken by a lessor of motor vehicles and, unless we are prepared to hold that any lessor of such vehicles, entering into such a contract, is in the insurance business, then we should not hold that plaintiff is, on that account, in such business." * * *

The principal object and purpose of the transaction before us, the element which gives the transaction its distinctive character, is the rental of an automobile. Peripheral to that primary object is an option, available to the lessee for additional consideration, to reallocate the risk of loss (up to the sum of $1,000) to the lessor in the event the vehicle sustains damage during the rental term. Thus, as in *Jellins,* after reviewing the entire contract we are satisfied that this tangential risk allocation provision should not have the effect of converting the defendants as contracting lessors into insurers subject to statutory regulation.

We also give deference to the Department of Insurance's interpretation of the Insurance Code [citations omitted] and we find a clear expression that the CDW transaction does not lend itself to the insurance regulatory statutes. As previously stated, the Department's analysis of Ford Rent–A–Car System where the lessor had, by contract, released the lessee from responsibility for any damage to the vehicle, opined that * * * "If the situation were such that the lessor was agreeing to pay any monies to third parties, then this conclusion would be different. Such an agreement would be similar to the type of coverage which has been extended by some companies in the past to reimburse for expenses incurred by an individual as a result of a deductible provision. That type of service would clearly be insurance. Here, there is no interest of the public which would be protected by our assuming jurisdiction. Since the lessor is not agreeing to pay anybody anything, but is simply agreeing not to hold the lessee liable, there is no need for accumulating reserves. The solvency or insolvency of the lessor does not affect this contractual provision."

It is obvious from the above that the Department of Insurance does not consider the California Insurance Code as designed to regulate the type of practice contained in the CDW transaction before us. Thus, on the basis of existing case law, legal commentary and the memorandum of the regulatory agency entrusted to enforce this state's insurance statutes, we hold that the CDW provision contained in automobile rental agreements does not constitute an insurance contract for purposes of statutory regulation.

[The court thereupon sustained the demurrer as to the first and second counts of the complaint, but overruled the demurrer to the fifth count that alleged "unconscionability" of the lease agreements pursuant to Cal.Civ.Code § 1670.5—which, parenthetically, is identical with U.C.C. § 2–302. No opinion was expressed as to whether the $6 per day fee for CDW is in fact substantively unconscionable].

* * *

The judgment is reversed and the case remanded for further proceedings on the fifth cause of action.

### *Notes*

1. *Life Insurance*

Do any of the definitions of insurance in the foregoing cases cover life insurance? What would be a proper definition? As in other types, a "little bit" of life insurance may escape regulation as long as it is not the dominant element in the situation or there is no need for the accumulation of reserves. For example a merchant may promote the installment sale of furniture by promising to cancel the balance due upon the death of the customer. A little bit of credit life insurance to be sure, which on an advanced level of commercial development would deserve, and get, regulation.

Or there is the local service club that may automatically assess its members to create a fund for the spouse of any member who dies. At this level the life insurance aspect may be overlooked, but herein is the forerunner of the fraternal benefit insurance societies (The Royal Neighbors, The Woodmen of the World, etc.) who have a respectable share of the life insurance business and are duly regulated.

See Hellner, The Scope of Insurance Regulation: What Is Insurance for Purposes of Regulation?, 12 Am.J. of Comparative Law 494 (1963).

2. "Insurance" and "suretyship" need to be carefully distinguished. See United States v. Tilleraas, 709 F.2d 1088 (6th Cir.1983) which concerned a Federally insured student loan (FISL). The student (Tilleraas) made no payments, the lending bank obtained payment from the U.S. which then sued the student. The U.S. was regarded as the student's surety and the applicable statute of limitations began to run only when the U.S. had paid off the bank which had made the FISL to Tilleraas. The court said (709 F.2d 1088, 1091–92):

The use of the word "insurance" in the statute is not determinative in light of the realities existing between the relevant parties. The nature of the substantive rights and duties among the parties clearly reflects a surety-principal-lender relationship. Insurance is a contract where one undertakes to indemnify another against loss, damage or liability caused by an unknown or contingent event. Since the insured pays the insurer for the promise of indemnity, the insurer benefits to the extent that a contingency never occurs. Where a contingency does occur, the insurer can still be made whole, by virtue of subrogation, to the extent that the insured would be able to recover damages from a third party. Despite the presence of this right of subrogation it is clear that *when the contract is formed* all legal rights and obligations flow between the insurer and the insured. At this initial stage, there is no legal obligation owing from the third party to the insurer. In fact, it is unknown at that stage whether such a third party obligation will ever arise and, if so, who that third party will be.

A surety, on the other hand, promises to assume the responsibility for the payment of a debt incurred by another should he or she fail to repay the creditor. The arrangement is made to induce the creditor to deal with the borrower where there might otherwise be a reluctance to do so. Under this arrangement, the nature, size, and source of the possible loss to the creditor is known from the start. In addition, there is no payment from the creditor to the surety or guarantor for this "insured" payment. Rather, a kind of tripartite relationship is formed. The consideration running from the creditor to the debtor is deemed sufficient to support the surety's promise to make the debt good. In turn, the benefit flowing to the debtor by virtue of the surety's promise places that debtor under an implied legal obligation to make good any loss incurred by any payment the surety must ultimately make to the creditor. 74 Am.Jur.2d *Suretyship* § 171 (1974). It is clear then that the two contracts are materially distinguishable, as are the rights and duties of the parties involved. * * *

Under the FISLP the student contracts to borrow money with no collateral and upon favorable interest and repayment terms. The lender, in turn, contracts with the Department of Education to insure repayment should the student default. This has consistently been interpreted as creating a third-party surety contract, despite its nomenclature. * * * The only possible "contingency" from which the government protects the lending institution is the possibility that the named student (in this case Tilleraas) may ultimately default on all or part of the designated loan amount. The interdependencies between the three parties, in this case the Dakota National Bank & Trust Co., Tilleraas, and the United States government, "are a situational adaptation of long-recognized principles of guaranty." * * * At common law the nature of the relationship would have undoubtedly given rise to an implied obligation on the part of Tilleraas to make good the loss incurred by the government when forced to satisfy her debt, a loss arising when the monies were paid to the Dakota National Bank & Trust Co.

* * *

### *Note on State Regulation of Insurers*

The powers of the chief officers (commissioners or superintendents) of State insurance agencies are complex and far-reaching. Some useful discussion will be found in 2 Couch on Insurance 2d § 21:4– § 21:23; 19 Appleman, Insurance Law and Practice, § 10391 et seq. An intriguing study of the North Carolina Commissioner, rate-making and judicial review of the Commissioner's actions can be found in State ex rel. Com'rs of Ins. v. North Carolina Rate Bureau, 300 N.C. 460, 269 S.E.2d 538 (1980); id. 300 N.C. 381, 269 S.E.2d 547 (1980). See also Symposium: Insurance Regulation, 1969 Wis.L.Rev. 1019; Roddis, Limited Omnipotence: the Bases and Limitations of the Powers of Insurance Regulators, XIII Forum 386 (1978).

Normally, it is not a difficult task to identify an organization in the business of insurance or to identify a contract of insurance made by such an organization. Governmental regulation of insurance is aimed largely at those who are avowedly insurers, and "what is insurance?" for purposes of a given State statute is a problem which does not seem to confront *courts* very much these days.

Regulation of companies transacting business in California, for example, is accomplished under the Insurance Code by the Insurance Commissioner and the Department of Insurance. The Commissioner also licenses insurers to do business and can withhold or revoke licenses as well as take over and run an insurance company.

The Insurance Code contains provisions of varying scope concerning the contents of insurance policies. For example, the terms of the standard fire insurance policy are prescribed by law, Ins.Code § 2071; with respect to automobile insurance, only individual clauses (and not complete policy texts) are mandated, e.g., the "uninsured motorist clause", Ins.Code § 11580.2 or the "omnibus" (permissive use) clause, Ins.Code § 11580.1(b)(4). The statutes contain many other provisions which are prescribed in terms or mandated to comply with certain standards. The problem with respect to a given line of insurance is finding all of the statutory requirements in the elaborate but often disjointed Insurance Code.

### *Notes*

1. Would it be permissible for a legislature to require insurance companies to make premium rebates because premiums charged under a competitive system were deemed "too high"? American Manufacturers Mutual Insurance Co. v. Commissioner of Insurance, 374 Mass. 181, 372 N.E.2d 520 (1978). The result might be in the public interest, but how would it affect the solvency of insurers?

2. The business of insurance is, of course, conducted by many companies on an interstate basis. And insureds, particularly in their automobiles, are on the move not only intrastate but interstate. There may be some reason for Federal regulation of insurance with a heavy interstate impact; there may also be some Federal aspiration for such regulation.

A little-known but extremely influential agency of the Congress, the United States General Accounting Office, issued a report to Congress ("Issues and Needed Improvements in State Regulation of the Insurance Business", PAD 79–72, October 9, 1979). The report made a resume of State regulation, and examined financial and trade practice regulation, price regulation of automobile insurance, regulation of automobile risk classification, insurance availability (to consumers), and organizational issues. Comments of State insurance officials were noted. Without making any specific recommendations for Federal legislation, the General Accounting Office report stated in its digest:

> There are serious shortcomings in State laws and regulatory activities with respect to protecting the interests of insurance consumers in the United States. In particular, most State insurance departments do not have systematic procedures to determine whether insurance consumers are being treated properly with respect to such matters as claims payments, rate-setting, and protection from unfair discrimination.

## WILSON v. ALL SERVICE INSURANCE CORP.

Court of Appeal of California, Second District, 1979.
91 Cal.App.3d 793, 153 Cal.Rptr. 121.

LILLIE, ACTING PRESIDING JUSTICE.

Plaintiffs commenced this action for damages allegedly sustained by them as a result of defendant insurance broker's having obtained for them a policy of automobile insurance issued by an insurance carrier which subsequently became insolvent after the occurrence of an accident covered by the policy. Plaintiffs appeal from summary judgment entered in defendant's favor.

* * *

It [is] alleged that on September 3, 1974, while the Transnational policy issued to plaintiffs was in effect, Rona, minor child of plaintiffs Willie and Yvonne Wilson, sustained bodily injuries through the negligence of an uninsured motorist; as a result of such accident plaintiffs Willie and Yvonne Wilson suffered severe emotional distress and physical injuries; following the accident plaintiffs presented to Transnational, pursuant to the uninsured motorist coverage afforded by the policy, a claim of $15,000 on behalf of Rona and a claim of $15,000 on behalf of Willie and Yvonne; on September 4, 1975, while the claims were pending, Transnational was declared insolvent and placed in liquidation by the Insurance Commissioner; in a reasonable, good faith effort to mitigate damages, plaintiffs settled their claims against Transnational for a total of $10,000; this sum was less than the actual value of the claims; but was fair and reasonable in view of Transnational's insolvency and the pending of liquidation proceedings against it; prior to the commencement of such proceedings, plaintiffs placed Transnational on notice that it was acting in bad faith in connection with their claims under the policy; as a result of Transnational's bad faith, each plaintiff was entitled to punitive damages in excess of $50,000.

The first cause of action concluded that as a "direct and proximate" result of defendant's negligence in failing to select a solvent insurance carrier for plaintiffs, they were denied (1) a major portion of the benefits to which they were entitled under the policy's uninsured motorist coverage, namely: $15,000 for Rona and $15,000 for Willie and Yvonne jointly, less the $10,000 received from Transnational, or a net total of

$20,000; and (2) damages in the sum of at least $50,000 for each plaintiff arising out of the bad faith conduct of Transnational.

* * *

The complaint discloses the defendant's liability is predicated on a breach of its alleged duty to plaintiffs to investigate Transnational's financial condition before having placed automobile insurance for plaintiffs with that carrier. If no such duty exists, plaintiffs are not entitled to recover the damages sought herein.

* * * In order to determine whether defendant owed plaintiffs a duty to investigate Transnational's financial condition, it is necessary to consider provisions of the Insurance Code governing the financial qualifications of an insurer to conduct business in this state.

Insurance Code section 700 provides in pertinent part: "(a) A person shall not transact any class of insurance business in this state without first being admitted for such class. Such admission is secured by procuring a certificate of authority from the commissioner. Such certificate shall not be granted until the applicant conforms to the requirements of this code and of the laws of this state prerequisite to its issue. * * * [¶](c) After the issuance of a certificate of authority, the holder shall continue to comply with the requirements as to its business set forth in this code and in the other laws of this state."

Prior to admission, each insurer must file with the Insurance Commissioner a certified copy of its last annual statement or a verified financial statement disclosing its condition and affairs. (Ins.Code, § 706.) Before an incorporated insurer may lawfully transact business in this state, it must meet specified requirements as to paid-in capital. (Id., § 700.01.) In addition to the paid-in capital requirements certain requirements as to surplus must be met before an insurer will be issued a certificate of authority. (Id., § 700.02.) The Insurance Commissioner is required to examine the business and affairs of a domestic insurer before issuing to it an original certificate of authority. (Id., § 730.) In the case of a foreign insurer, the Commissioner may examine its affairs and business, or he may authorize such an investigation to be made by the insurance authorities of the state in which the insurer is organized. (Id., § 731.) The Commissioner may also examine the business and affairs of any admitted insurer whenever he deems it necessary, or when he is requested to do so by verified petition showing that the insurer is insolvent signed by 25 persons interested as shareholders, policyholders or creditors of the insurer. (Id., § 730.) In making such examination the Commissioner has free access to all books and papers of the insurer. (Id., § 733.) Every insurer doing business in the state is required to file a detailed financial statement with the Insurance Commissioner on or before March 1, of each year, showing its condition and affairs as of the preceding December 31 (id., §§ 900.900.7), and to publish a synopsis as adjusted by the Commissioner to show the true condition of the insurer (id., § 901). The statement must show the details relative to capital stock or paid-in capital (id., §§ 905, 906), property or assets owned

(§ 907), liabilities (§ 908), income (§ 909), expenditures (§ 910), and amount of premiums on insurance on subject matter in this state (§ 911). The Insurance Commissioner may suspend or revoke the certificate of authority of an insurer which knowingly files a false financial statement. (Id., § 900.8.) Whenever the Commissioner finds that the investments of an admitted insurer are not so made as to make available within a reasonable time sufficient moneys to meet promptly any demand which might in the ordinary course of business be properly made against the insurer, he may order it to cease to effect new contracts of insurance until its financial circumstances have changed sufficiently to remove such condition. If the insurer fails to comply with such order, the Commissioner may suspend or revoke its certificate of authority. (Id., § 706.5.)

Thus, the Insurance Code prescribes financial requirements both for the issuance of a certificate of authority admitting an insurer to transact business in this state, and for an admitted insurer's right to continue conducting business pursuant to its certificate. The code imposes on the Insurance Commissioner the continuing duty to oversee the financial condition of an insurer holding a certificate of authority, and gives the Commissioner the power necessary to execute such duty. It would be superfluous, and would create a conflict with the regulatory scheme outlined in the Insurance Code, to impose upon an insurance broker a similar duty to ascertain the financial soundness of an insurer. Moreover, the imposition of such a duty would be meaningless inasmuch as a broker has no power to compel an insurer to divulge information regarding its financial condition. Accordingly, we hold that an insurance broker, such as defendant, owes no duty to its clients to investigate the financial condition of an insurer before placing insurance with it on their behalf. If a broker places insurance with an insurer conducting business pursuant to a certificate of authority, the broker has fulfilled its duty to its clients.

In support of its motion for summary judgment, defendant submitted the declaration of Joe Morton, Deputy Insurance Commissioner, in which the declarant stated that a certificate of authority to conduct business as an insurer was issued to Transnational on November 2, 1956, and remained in effect until September 4, 1975, when the Insurance Commissioner was appointed liquidator of Transnational by order of the court. Thus, Transnational was authorized to conduct business on August 18, 1974, when it allegedly issued its policy of automobile insurance to plaintiffs.

The judgment is affirmed.

## CLASSIFICATION OF INSURANCE

Couch on Insurance 2d between § 1.17 and § 1.117 lists approximately 80 (give or take a dozen or so) specific types of insurance policies. This is a traditional method of classification which the California Ins. Code § 100, for instance, has reduced to about 20 slots including such items as boiler insurance, team and vehicle insurance as well as the ever useful "miscellaneous" insurance category.

The ultimate basic classification is simply third party insurance and first party insurance. Third party insurance insures against legal liability for damages to third parties, and first party insurance (with some qualifications as to life insurance) includes everything else. The nomenclature is not exactly felicitous, since there seems to be no such thing as second party insurance.

In this book, insurance is divided into three general categories: (1) Insurance against property and economic losses (all first party examples); (2) Insurance covering personal injuries or diseases (first party) and death (life insurance is sui generis); and Insurance against liability (all third party, of course). Among the most common policies now issued are auto and homeowners' forms which may actually incorporate all three categories. In fact these two varieties of policies could be treated as the basis for a classification of insurance for many purposes as useful as the framework adopted here. A preliminary comment on automobile insurance may be helpful. Note particularly how the current trends in auto insurance toward uninsured/underinsured motorist coverage and toward no-fault insurance reflect a shift from third party to first party coverage. What are the reasons behind this?

## AUTOMOBILE INSURANCE

Automobile insurance, perhaps more than any other form of insurance, seems to come to American public and personal attention in all sorts of intricate ways. The traditional automobile policy has been issued within the framework of what has been called the "fault" system. The basic meaning of this is that the insurer will pay (within the policy limits, of course) for amounts which the insured (the owner of the policy) is held liable to pay third persons injured by him. Automobile policies were not confined to protection against liability; as they evolved, they expanded to feature other coverages including collision coverage (the insurer's agreement to reimburse the insured for loss to his motor vehicle), comprehensive, medical payments, and other varieties of coverage.

So many personal interests are affected by American automobiles that their free-wheeling operation on the streets and highways has called forth an immense amount of legislation and regulation. Particularly important, of course, are the laws and regulations dealing with the liabilities of owners and operators of automobiles for injuries to persons and property. Of major relevance to such liability laws are interlocking and related laws and regulations dealing with automobile insurance.

Many States have laws (often called "Owners Financial Responsibility Acts") which require demonstration of financial responsibility after certain events (for example, an accident) involving the auto have occurred. Demonstration of ability to meet any ensuing judgment is most frequently accomplished by presenting proof that an insurance policy applies to the potential judgment liability. Other means of making the required demonstration of responsibility are often allowed although less frequently used; for example, a bond, or a deposit of money or other security may under a given State's laws be sufficient to meet the requirement. Statutes also commonly provide for minimum levels of coverage in auto policies, for example, "15–30–5" meaning $15,000 coverage for injuries to one claimant, $30,000 for all claimants in a given incident and $5,000 for property damage. Inflation and jury verdicts being what they are, these minimum figures may be regarded as unrealistic by an automobile owner; motorists very frequently buy policies with much higher liability ceilings.

The obvious gap is that some motorists (in California, we are told, an *extraordinary* number of motorists) won't buy liability insurance at all. This fact has led in California and elsewhere to a variety of statutory remedies. For example, a State may require that every car be covered by a policy (or other demonstration of financial responsibility) as a condition of registration of the motor vehicle. See the Massachusetts Compulsory Motor Vehicle Liability Insurance Act, Mass.Gen.Laws, Chapter 90, Sections 34A–34J; Chapter 175, Sections 113A–113H, as amended.

Another way in which State legislatures have sought to plug this gap is by the "uninsured motorist" acts. These acts require policies to contain provisions protecting the insured (that is, the automobilist owning the policy and certain other persons) against injuries inflicted on them by motorists without any insurance policies covering the event. Commonly, a ceiling is placed on this coverage by the statute. Some insurers today provide a related coverage against "underinsured" motorists.

A number of States have attempted a large scale revision of the whole compensation scheme by enacting the so-called "no-fault" laws. A fairly typical "no-fault" statute is that of New York as described in Goodkin v. United States, 773 F.2d 19, at 21–22 (2d Cir.1985).

*New York's No–Fault Scheme*

> No-fault laws were created to remedy a long recognized and serious problem—the inability of the tort system to rapidly, adequately and fairly compensate victims of automobile accidents. 12A Couch on Insurance 2d § 45:661 (rev. ed. 1981). In *Mongtomery v. Daniels,* 38 N.Y.2d 41, 378 N.Y.S.2d 1, 340 N.E.2d 444 (1975), upholding the constitutionality of New York's no-fault law, the New York Court of Appeals enumerated three particular problems that the legislature intended the Act to address: (1) the excessive and needless expense of the tort system; (2) the unfair and inequitable distribution of compensation among accident victims, including long delays in payment, and (3) the strain placed on the state judicial system by tort litigation. The Act sought to remedy these problems by, *inter alia,* removing minor claims from the courts, eliminating

fault as a required predicate for recovering certain losses from a predicate determination of liability based on fault, requiring payments to be made immediately on accrual of loss and requiring all owners of motor vehicles to carry no-fault insurance. The preeminent purpose of the no-fault law, according to the Court of Appeals, was "to assure the prompt and full reimbursement of the 'economic' losses those injured in automobile accidents may suffer." *Perkins v. Merchants Mutual Insurance Co.,* 41 N.Y.2d 394, 396, 393 N.Y.S.2d 347, 348, 361 N.E.2d 997, 998 (1977).

New York's no-fault legislation

> provides a plan for compensating victims of automobile accidents without regard to fault. In essence, it is a two-pronged, partial modification of the preexisting system of reparation for personal injuries suffered in automobile accidents under which system liability was grounded in negligence under classic principles of tort law. One prong deals with compensation; the other with limitation of tort actions.

*Montgomery,* 38 N.Y.2d at 46, 378 N.Y.S.2d at 4, 340 N.E.2d at 446. The Act partially but not completely eliminated the rights of automobile accident victims to recover in tort for their injuries. It replaced what it excised with a relatively simple and straightforward compensation system designed to quickly reimburse injured parties, up to certain limits, for the common, out-of-pocket expenses generated by their injuries.

Under the Act, every owner of a motor vehicle is responsible, regardless of fault, to a specified class of persons for any and all basic economic loss resulting from injuries occasioned by the use or operation of that vehicle. The class of persons includes the owner himself, operators and occupants of his vehicle and pedestrians. By definition, basic economic loss is limited to an aggregate maximum of $50,000 per person and includes the cost of professional health services ascertainable within one year, lost earnings and the cost of substitute services up to $1,000 per month for not more than three years and other expenses up to $25 per day for not more than one year. N.Y.Ins.Law § 5102(b), which are due and payable when the loss is incurred.

The Act imposes two limitations on recovery for personal injuries. By their terms, these limitations apply only to actions between covered persons: "[n]otwithstanding any other law," a covered person cannot recover against another covered person for basic economic loss, and a covered person who has not sustained serious injury as defined in section 5102(d) [1] cannot recover against another

1. Section 5102(d) provides as follows:

> "Serious injury" means a personal injury which results in death; dismemberment; significant disfigurement; a fracture; a loss of a fetus; permanent loss of use of a body organ, member, function or system; permanent consequential limitation of use of a body organ or member; significant limitation of use of a body function or system; or a medically deter-

covered person for non-economic loss. *Id.* § 5104. Non-economic loss is "pain and suffering and similar non-monetary detriment." *Id.* § 5102(c).

A covered person as defined by the Act is "any pedestrian injured through the use or operation of, or any owner, operator or occupant of, a motor vehicle which has in effect the financial security required * * * or which [is among the exceptions in N.Y.Veh. & Traf.Law § 321 (McKinney Supp.1984), which includes vehicles owned by the United States] or any other person entitled to first party benefits." N.Y.Ins.Law § 5102(j). With certain exceptions, the motor vehicle owner's liability carrier must pay first party benefits to any person, "other than occupants of another motor vehicle or a motorcycle," whose injury arises out of the use or operation of the owner's vehicle. *Id.* at § 5103(a)(1). It must also pay first party benefits to "[t]he named insured and members of his household, other than occupants of a motorcycle," for injuries arising from the use or operation of any insured vehicle outside of New York but in the United States or Canada or any uninsured vehicle in the United States or Canada. *Id.* § 5103(a)(2). Finally, it must pay first party benefits to any New York resident not otherwise entitled to such benefits whose injury results from the use or operation of the owner's vehicle outside of New York but in the United States or Canada. *Id.* § 5103(a)(3). Everyone not entitled to first party benefits is a noncovered person.

Intended to address only minor personal injury claims, the no-fault law leaves unaffected the right to recover in tort for economic loss in excess of the basic economic loss limitations and the right to recover for non-economic loss associated with serious injury. The Act by its terms and operation simply eliminates the right of an injured covered person to recover in tort against another covered person for basic economic loss. In most instances, of course, the practical result of this is that covered defendants will not be liable for any amounts attributable to basic economic loss.

One has to consult the State's law to find the exact dimensions of "no-fault" coverage in that State. A useful discussion can be found in Woodroof, Fonseca, and Squillante, *Automobile Insurance and No-Fault Law* (Lawyers Cooperative Publishing Company, and Bancroft–Whitney Company, 1974). The CCH Automobile Law Reporter ¶ 1944–1987 lists States with no-fault laws.

State legislation and regulation have affected the terms of auto policies although on a scale less broad than the fire policy (see Part B). One required provision commonly found in a State's law is the so-called "omnibus" or "permission" clause. When a State legislature has man-

mined injury or impairment of a non-permanent nature which prevents the injured person from performing substantially all of the material acts which constitute such person's usual and customary daily activities for not less than ninety days during the one hundred eighty days immediately following the occurrence of the injury or impairment.

dated such a provision and laid down what it is supposed to cover, what should be done with a clause that differs from the requirements? The next case takes up this issue. And the one following demonstrates how the public policy behind uninsured motorist statutes can be seized upon by the judiciary to change a legislative "miss" into a "hit".

## METZ v. UNIVERSAL UNDERWRITERS INSURANCE CO.

Supreme Court of California, 1973.
10 Cal.3d 45, 109 Cal.Rptr. 698, 513 P.2d 922.

[Metz was run into by Hamlin driving a car leased to him by National. After recovering from Hamlin's insurers the limit of the policies they had issued ($100,000), Metz sought to recover the balance of his judgment claim against Hamlin ($154,593.74) from Universal, the company which had issued a liability policy to Hamlin's lessor, National. Metz won. One contention made by Universal was that its policy excluded from coverage cars "while rented to others". State statutes required auto liability policies to extend coverage to "permissive users".] The court said: (10 Cal.3d 50–54).

2. *The policy's exclusion of vehicles "while rented to others" conflicts with the mandatory coverage of permissive users, imposed, as of the policy date, by Insurance Code section 11580.1, subdivision (d).**

In Wildman v. Government Employees' Ins. Co., (1957) 48 Cal.2d 31, 307 P.2d 359, we held that the required coverage of permissive users "must be made a part of every policy of insurance issued by an insurer since the public policy of this state is to make owners of motor vehicles financially responsible to those injured by them in the operation of such vehicles. * * * [F]or an insurer to issue a policy of insurance which does not cover an accident which occurs when a person, other than the insured, is driving with the permission and consent of the insured, is a violation of the public policy of this state." (48 Cal.2d at p. 39, 307 P.2d at p. 364.)

* * *

Although Universal's policy provides coverage for permissive users, it unambiguously excludes automobiles "while rented to others." The issue before us thus must be whether this exclusion conflicts with Insurance Code section 11580.1, subdivision (d). Universal concedes that a provision excluding coverage of renters would be an exclusion of a class of permissive users and hence void. * * * It maintains, however, that its policy does not exclude a class of users, but a class of automobiles, namely, those rented to persons other than the named insured.

Universal points out that no statute or public policy requires an insurer to cover all vehicles owned by the named insured. * * * It may agree to insure a car used principally by the named insured, while

* The full text of this statute is set forth in Part D.

excluding another car rented by the insured to another person. (See Pacific Indem. Co. v. Liberty Mut. Ins. Co. (1969) 269 Cal.App.2d 793, 796, 75 Cal.Rptr. 559.) The insurer, moreover, may agree to insure a vehicle for ordinary use, but refuse coverage of extraordinary use. (See Allstate Ins. Co. v. Normandie Club (1963) 221 Cal.App.2d 103, 34 Cal.Rptr. 280 [exclusion of "any automobile while used as a public or livery conveyance."] )

The right of the insurer to limit its coverage of automobiles, however, does not go so far as to permit the insurer by adroit wording to evade the statutory requirement for coverage of permissive users. (See Bonfils v. Pacific Auto. Ins. Co. (1958) 165 Cal.App.2d 152, 156, 331 P.2d 766.) For example, a policy which excluded automobiles "when operated by a permissive user" would be clearly seen as an exclusion of persons, not vehicles and void under section 11580.1, subdivision (d). Thus in Clark v. Universal Underwriters Ins. Co. (1965) 233 Cal.App.2d 746, 43 Cal. Rptr. 822 and Pacific Indem. Co. v. Universal Underwriters Ins. Co. (1965) 232 Cal.App.2d 541, 43 Cal.Rptr. 26, in which the policy provision offered coverage to permissive users only while the insured automobile "is operated by the named insured," the courts had no difficulty finding the provision an impermissible exclusion of permissive users.

The case most closely resembling the present one is Republic Indem. Co. v. Employers Liab. Assur. Co. (1968) 267 Cal.App.2d 121, 72 Cal. Rptr. 718, in which a policy issued to an automobile repair shop provided that "such insurance as is afforded by this policy does not apply to any automobile used by the insured for the purpose of loaning to customers." The insurer contended that its policy excluded *automobiles,* not permissive *users* —essentially the same argument as that presented by Universal in the present case. The court rejected this contention and held that "The endorsement is a restriction against permissive users such as has been continually held to be violative of public policy." (267 Cal.App.2d at p. 126, 72 Cal.Rptr. at p. 721.)

The exclusion of automobiles "while rented to others" in the instant case parallels the exclusion of cars "loaned to customers" held invalid in *Republic Indemnity.* In both cases the policies spoke superficially of excluding only a class of automobiles. But in both cases the definitive characteristic of the excluded class of vehicles lies in the fact that they are operated by a class of permissive users; hence, in practical effect the exclusion denies coverage to this class of permissive users.

We have uniformly held that "the entire automobile financial responsibility law must be liberally construed to foster its main objective of giving 'monetary protection to that ever changing and tragically large group of persons who while lawfully using the highways themselves suffer grave injury through the negligent use of those highways by others.' " (Interinsurance Exchange v. Ohio Cas. Ins. Co. (1962) 58 Cal.2d 142, 153, 23 Cal.Rptr. 592, 598, 373 P.2d 640, 646; Barrera v. State Farm Mut. Automobile Ins. Co. (1969) 71 Cal.2d 659, 671, 79 Cal.Rptr. 106, 456 P.2d 674.) Applying this principle of construction, we conclude that section 11580.1, subdivision (d), did not merely proscribe policy provisions which by their terms exclude coverage for permissive users, but also invalidated provisions which, by defining a class of excluded vehicles in terms of their operation by permissive users, serves effectively to deny coverage to those users. We hold that Universal's exclusion of automobiles "while rented to others" conflicts with Insurance Code section 11580.1, subdivision (d), and is therefore ineffective to limit coverage of Hamlin.

[The remaining portions of the opinion are omitted.]

### *Notes*

1. Although the complicated subjects of "excess" and "primary" coverage will be given attention in Part D of this book, students ought to realize at this point that more than one insurance policy may be applicable in the case of the driver of a rented car. His own policy and the lessor's policy may, at least, apply, except, of course as the law may restrict that result.

2. The *Metz* case has to be viewed in the light of subsequent developments in California statutory law. For example, § 11580.1(d) has been added and amended to read:

> (d) Notwithstanding the provisions of paragraph (4) of subdivision (b), or the provisions of Article 2 (commencing with Section 16450) of Chapter 3 of Division 7, or Article 2 (commencing with Section 17150) of Chapter 1 of Division 9, of the Vehicle Code, the insurer and any named insured may, by the terms of any policy of automobile liability insurance to which subdivision (a) applies, or by a separate writing relating thereto, agree as to either or both of the following limitations, such agreement to be binding upon every insured to whom such policy applies and upon every third party claimant:
>
> (2) That with regard to any such policy issued to a named insured engaged in the business of leasing vehicles for those vehicles which are leased for a term in excess of six months, or selling, repairing, servicing, delivering, testing, roadtesting, parking, or storing automobiles, coverage shall not apply to any person other than the named insured or his or her agent or employee, except to the extent that the limits of liability of any other valid and collectible insurance available to such person are not equal to the limits of liability specified in subdivision (a) of Section 16056 of the Vehicle Code. If the policy is issued to a named insured engaged in the business of leasing vehicles, which business includes the lease of vehicles for a term in excess of six months, and the lessor includes in the lease automobile liability insurance, the terms and limits of which are not otherwise specified in the lease, the named insured shall incorporate a provision in each vehicle lease contract advising the lessee of the provisions of this subdivision and the fact that this limitation is applicable except as otherwise provided for by statute or federal law.

In Premier Insurance Company v. MacDonald et al., 210 Cal.Rptr. 458 (DCA–2 1985), the quoted section was construed as allowing an insurer in its contract with a "six month" lessor of vehicles to limit its liability to the difference between the minimum amounts prescribed by the Financial Responsibility Law ($15,000/30,000/5,000) and lesser amounts actually available under the lessee's policy. Although this result seems to have justification, the California Supreme Court ordered the decision to be "depublished" under California Rule 976. This means it cannot be cited or serve as precedent (with certain exceptions not here relevant) in California, see California Rule 977.

3. In another and related section (§ 11580.9) of the Insurance Code the California Legislature enacted a provision consonant with that of West's Ann.Cal.Ins.Code 11580.1(d), above:

> (b) Where two or more policies apply to the same loss, and one policy affords coverage to a named insured engaged in the business of renting or leasing motor vehicles without operators, it shall be conclusively presumed that the insurance afforded by such policy to a person other than the named insured or his or her agent or employee, shall be excess over and not concurrent with, any other valid and collectible insurance applicable to the same loss covering the person as a named insured or as an additional insured under a policy with limits at least equal to the financial responsibility requirements specified in Section 16056 of the Vehicle Code. The presumption provided by this subdivision shall apply only if, at the time of the loss, the involved motor vehicle either:
>
> (1) Qualifies as a "commercial vehicle" as that term is used in Section 260 of the Vehicle Code.
>
> (2) Has been leased for a term of six months or longer.

4. In other words, under the apparent meaning of the statutes, the *Metz* result continues to obtain in cases involving leases under six months. E.g., a lessee of a car for a day will be protected by the *Metz* rule and will be covered as provided by 11580.1(b)(4). That is, the full limits of the lessor's policy will be available to him. And, as the result of a further provision in West's Ann.Cal.Ins.Code 11580.9:

> (d) Except as provided in subdivisions (a), (b), and (c), where two or more policies affording valid and collectible liability insurance apply to the same motor vehicle or vehicles in an occurrence out of which a liability loss shall arise, it shall be conclusively presumed that the insurance afforded by that policy *in which the motor vehicle is described or rated as an owned automobile* shall be primary and the insurance afforded by any other policy or policies shall be excess.—

it seems that a car renter for less than six months taps the lessor's policy first and his own policy second.

5. This may be complicated, but it is a good point to realize some of the complications introduced into insurance law by the interaction of economic forces.

### *Problem*

May the Legislature permit a nonadmitted Mexican insurance company to sell policies in California which provide coverage *solely* in Mexico (and auto accidents occurring therein) but which *exclude* liability for injuries to an occupant of a covered vehicle? Or is this a denial of equal protection to

California admitted insurance companies to whom the legislative permission does not extend? See West's Ann.California Insurance Code §§ 11580.05, 11580.1(g); Seguros La Provincial, S.A. v. Fremont Indemnity Co., 138 Cal.App.3d 923, 188 Cal.Rptr. 331 (1983) (Fremont and Seguros—the Mexican company—both had issued policies in California applicable to a vehicle involved in an accident in Mexico which led to a suit by injured occupants.)

### *Note*

One of the more interesting constitutional innovations of the late Nineteenth and early 20th centuries was the adoption in many States of the initiative, referendum and recall powers, allocating power directly to the voters. The "Progressives", a then influential political group were the principal sponsors. States adopted either all or some of the powers enumerated; California in 1911 adopted all three under the leadership of Governor Hiram Johnson, a "Progressive".

The *initiative* allows the voters of California to petition for inclusion of constitutional or statutory provisions on an election ballot. This is able to be done without the consent or approval of the Governor or Legislature. The ballot is usually the ballot at the next general election. If the initiative is approved by a majority of the people voting, it goes into effect on the day after the election. Art. II of the California Constitution (as in effect from 1976) contains the present statement of the initiative, referendum, and recall powers.

All this impinges upon the enactment of Proposition 103 at the general election of November 8, 1988. At that time the movement for "tort reform" (which tended at the time to mean all things to all men) had become very significant. Nothing seemed to be more clear that one of the principal fuels of the tort system was the presence of insurance, particularly in auto liability cases. The Legislature had proved itself incapable of dealing with the problem and various protagonists set about getting initiatives on the ballot which would deal with that and other issues (despite the fact that the Constitution restricts initiatives to "one subject"). There were five of these initiatives: (a) *Proposition 100* ("The Insurance Reform and Consumer Protection Act" one of whose major sponsors was the California Trial Lawyers' Association); *Proposition 101* (major support coming from the President of the Coastal Insurance Company); *Proposition 103* (leading advocates included Ralph Nader, Harvey Rosenfield and "Voter Revolt to Cut Insurance Rates"); *Proposition 104* (the "Insurance Cost Control Act of 1984" a no fault proposal which found its major proponents in the insurance industry); and *Proposition 106* (the "Lawyers Fair Fee Act" which did not propose legislation directly impacting insurance, but which would have had a major impact on insurance litigation). Millions of dollars were spent in support of, and in opposition to, these initiatives, the total nearing, we are told, almost 100 million dollars. If all, or even some, of these propositions, especially the first four had been enacted, the possibilities of fascinating and complex problems of statutory construction would have been enormous. The presentation of such problems would hardly appear to have been in the public interest. In any event, the initiative statute which passed was Proposition 103 and then only by 51%–49%. All the others failed.

Proposition 103 did a variety of things, among them: (a) it provided for an immediate roll back of property and casualty insurance rates (not just auto insurance rates, but including them); (b) it called for a system of "good driver" discounts, (c) it mandated advance approval by the Insurance commissioner of (future) rates; (d) it set up new standards for rates; (e) subjected the business of insurance (see the McCarran–Ferguson Act) to the Unruh Civil Rights Act and to the antitrust and unfair business practice laws of California; (f) placed new restrictions on the cancellation and non-renewal of auto insurance policies; (g) provided for public participation in the rate-making process; and (h) provided that the Commissioner of Insurance should be elected.

The climate was such that a court test of Proposition 103 would soon take place. As noted above, initiative Propositions go into effect the day after the election at which they are approved. This meant that November 9th, 1988 was the effective date of Proposition 103. Interested parties went immediately to the Supreme Court of California. That court, exercising its original jurisdiction, granted a stay of enforcement of Proposition 103 on November 10th, 1988. On December 7th, the Court issued a new order staying the enforcement of only portions of Proposition 103. Hearings were held on a final order in March, 1989, and the Court issued its final order on May 4th, 1989.

The decision, Calfarm Insurance Co. v. Deukmejian, 48 Cal.3d 805, 258 Cal.Rptr. 161, 771 P.2d 1247, had the important effect of declaring that rate-making could not be "confiscatory" and might not deny a "fair return". This laid the foundation for litigation which continues even at the date of this writing. And, among other things the Court upheld the right of the State to legislate against non-renewals of existing insurance policies as well as those not yet made. The Court further denied that Proposition 103 violated the "one subject" rule observed above. This astonished the writers (and others), although it should be observed that the Court seems always to have followed a latitudinarian approach to the meaning of "one subject". In more recent times the Court has recognized the right of insurers to withdraw from doing business in the State but subject to the somewhat stringent requirements of West's Ann.California Insurance Code. See Travelers Indemnity Co. v. Gillespie, 50 Cal.3d 82, 266 Cal.Rptr. 117, 785 P.2d 500 (1990).

## B. STATE VS. FEDERAL REGULATION

### *Note*

The United States Supreme Court in 1868 said that the making of a contract or policy of insurance was not a "transaction of commerce". Paul v. Virginia, 75 U.S. (8 Wall.) 168, 19 L.Ed. 357 (1868). This led to widespread conviction that Congressional regulation of the business of insurance was constitutionally improper. In United States v. South–Eastern Underwriters Association, 322 U.S. 533, 64 S.Ct. 1162, 88 L.Ed. 1440 (1944), the court held that insurance was subject to regulation by Congress including the anti-trust laws. Congress' countermeasure follows:

## THE McCARRAN–FERGUSON ACT

59 Stat. 33 (1945) as amended 15 U.S.C.A. §§ 1011–15.

### § 1011. Declaration of policy

Congress declares that the continued regulation and taxation by the several States of the business of insurance is in the public interest, and that silence on the part of the Congress shall not be construed to impose any barrier to the regulation or taxation of such business by the several States.

### § 1012. Regulation by State law; Federal law relating specifically to insurance; applicability of certain Federal laws after June 30, 1948

(a) The business of insurance, and every person engaged therein, shall be subject to the laws of the several States which relate to the regulation or taxation of such business.

(b) No Act of Congress shall be construed to invalidate, impair, or supersede any law enacted by any State for the purpose of regulating the business of insurance, or which imposes a fee or tax upon such business, unless such Act specifically relates to the business of insurance: *Provided,* That after June 30, 1948, the Act of July 2, 1890, as amended, known as the Sherman Act, and the Act of October 15, 1914, as amended, known as the Clayton Act, and the Act of September 26, 1914, known as the Federal Trade Commission Act, as amended, shall be applicable to the business of insurance to the extent that such business is not regulated by State law.

### § 1014. Applicability of National Labor Relations Act and Fair Labor Standards Act of 1938

Nothing contained in this chapter shall be construed to affect in any manner the application to the business of insurance of the Act of July 5, 1935, as amended, known as the National Labor Relations Act, or the Act of June 25, 1938, as amended, known as the Fair Labor Standards Act of 1938, or the Act of June 5, 1920, known as the Merchant Marine Act, 1920.

### *Note*

Race, color, creed, ethnicity, sex, age, and disability theoretically may affect insurance premiums and the terms of insurance coverage with discriminatory effect. There may be on occasion sound economic grounds for such discrimination. For example, a longer life expectancy would justify a different premium calculation for men and women based on easily determinable and verifiable differences in life expectancy. At the same time there may also be a very good social and political basis for refusing to enforce discriminatory schemes in computing premiums or providing coverage. Not surprisingly, the Civil Rights Acts cast a long shadow in any area like this. One early example was Spirt v. Teachers Insurance and Annuity Association ("TIAA"), and College Retirement Equities Fund ("CREF"), 475 F.Supp. 1298 (S.D.N.Y.1979), in which the Court distinguished between "insurance" and "annuity" for the purposes of deciding whether the McCarran–Ferguson Act exempted either insurance (TIAA) or annuities (CREF) from application of Title VII of the Civil Rights Act of 1964. It held that TIAA was controlled by the State Law in fixing premiums (the New York Insurance Law, of course, had non-discrimination provisions of its own) and that CREF was not.

All the while other similar cases were wending their way through the courts. The case selected for the ultimate decision by the U.S. Supreme Court was Arizona Governing Committee, etc. v. Norris, 463 U.S. 1073, 103 S.Ct. 3492, 77 L.Ed.2d 1236 (1983).

*Norris* concerned a proposed pension plan for employees of the state of Arizona. The proposal (which was put up for bids from insurance companies) would have men and women of the same age pay into the plan in equal monthly installments, but the monthly pay outs after retirement would be less for women than for men because actuarially they live longer. The contention was advanced that such a pay out practice would constitute employment discrimination against women in violation of Title VII of the Civil Rights Act of 1964. Again, as in *Spirt,* the role of the McCarran–Ferguson Act as a shield against federal regulation of the insurance industry is brought into question.

The majority (5 votes) in *Norris* took the McCarran–Ferguson Act out of the picture by a footnote observing that it had not been treated in the briefs, but going on to add:

> "All that is in issue in this case is an *employment practice:* the practice of offering a male employee the opportunity to obtain greater monthly annuity benefits than could be obtained by a similarly situated female employee. It is this conduct of the employer that is prohibited by Title VII. By its own terms, the McCarran–Ferguson Act applies only to the business of insurance and has no application to employment practices. Arizona plainly is not itself involved in the business of insurance, since it has not underwritten any risks. * * * Because the application of Title VII in this case does not supersede any state law governing the business of insurance * * * we need not decide whether Title VII 'specifically relates to the business of insurance' within the meaning of the McCarran–Ferguson Act.*"

The minority (4 justices) in *Norris* asserted that McCarran–Ferguson did indeed constitute a bar to applying Title VII unless Congress expressly intended Title VII to pre-empt state insurance legislation. But, said Justice Powell, "Nothing in the language of Title VII supports this pre-emption of state jurisdiction." The dissenters position on the effect of McCarran–Ferguson is detailed, also in a footnote:

> "The majority argues * * * that the McCarran–Ferguson Act is inappropriate because Title VII will not supersede any state regulation. Because Title VII applies to employers rather than insurance carriers, the majority asserts * * * Title VII will not affect the business of insurance * * * This formalistic distinction ignores self-evident facts. State insurance laws such as Arizona's, allows employers to purchase sex-based annuities for their employees. * * * It begs reality to say

* Footnote 17, 463 U.S. at 1087, 103 S.Ct. at 3501.

that a federal law that * * * denies the right to do what state insurance law allows does not 'invalidate, impair or supersede' state law." *

*Sex and the Single Mortality Table*

Having removed the McCarran–Ferguson Act from the picture, the majority in the *Norris* case proceeded to the issue of whether group annuity sales, calculated on the known fact that women live longer than men, applied to employee pension plans, is *sex-based* discrimination. A precedent decision was City of Los Angeles, Dept. of Water and Power v. Manhart, 435 U.S. 702, 98 S.Ct. 1370, 55 L.Ed.2d 657 (1978) holding that an annuity plan that required women employees to pay more into the plan monthly, but get only the same monthly pension pay out, was discriminatory compensation in employment and invalid). Obviously on the same reasoning (if accepted) there is sex-based discrimination where the pay in is the same, but the pay out is less, and the *Norris* majority so held. The minority's position was simply that the mortality tables in use actually reflect longevity, which is a nondiscriminatory factor, and on this well established phenomenon the average male and female pensioner would in the long run have equal benefits.

In any event, the next problem is to remove the sex-based discrimination which the *Norris* majority has perceived. One solution is to have the same pay-in to the deferred compensation plans by both men and women employees, to be followed by a single lump sum pay-out on retirement—a method of pay-out that most retirees do not prefer, and is, perhaps, socially undesirable as defeating the long term goal of a disciplined life-time support system for the aged.

The other alternative that has found favor is the adoption of the so-called *unisex* mortality tables, which is no more than a blending of the existing separate male and female tables. Obviously this may be objected to in the annuity cases as substituting for a fair system an unfair one. One that requires males to subsidize enhanced benefits accruing to females (all in the name of eliminating discrimination according to sex). This "fairness" argument was anticipated and rejected by Justice Stevens in the *Manhart* case:

> "[W]hen insurance risks are grouped, the better risks always subsidize the poorer risks. Healthy persons subsidize medical benefits for the less healthy; unmarried workers subsidize the pensions of married workers; persons who eat, drink or smoke to excess may subsidize pension benefits for persons whose habits are more temperate. Treating different classes as risks as though they were the same for purposes of group insurance is a common practice which has never been considered as inherently unfair." **

Therefore it is not unfair that shorter lived men subsidize longer lived women annuitants.

*Query:* Age discrimination is now the target of much prohibitory legislation. Must a 45–year old person hired on as an employee at the same time as a

* Footnote 6, 463 U.S. at 1100, 103 S.Ct. at 3508.

** 435 U.S. 702 at 710; 98 S.Ct. at 1376.

20–year old be legally entitled to subsidization of his or her annuity by the 20–year old by using mortality tables that eliminate any longevity factors?

*The Other Side of the Coin*

The required use of *unisex* mortality tables in effecting annuity programs, of course, cuts both ways. As applied to conventional life insurance the male benefits at the expense of the longer-lived female and the unfairness thus created falls upon the female. The foregoing decisions arise from Congressionally mandated non-sexist employment compensation programs and the funding of such programs by group insurance. Remove this special context and a sharp and discomforting fact appears. The pursuit of the goals of sex, age or other forms of absolute equality into insurance rate regulation automatically creates patent unfairness and other socially undesirable results. In weighing the considerations, states have gone both ways either by administrative fiat, legislative enactment, or judicial inclination.

In Hartford Accident and Indemnity Co. v. Insurance Commissioner, etc., 505 Pa. 571, 482 A.2d 542 (1984) the Hartford Co. filed a rate classification plan with differential charges applied to young males as compared to female drivers. The Commissioner approved; whereupon a 26 year old male questioned the validity of charging him a $360 premium, while charging a female $212 with no difference other than gender. The Commissioner changed his mind and disapproved the insurer's rating plan. The matter wound up in court, the young male taking the position that the sex-based distinction violated his constitutional rights. The court sustained his position and the authority of the Commissioner (supported by the Equal Rights Amendment incorporated into the Pennsylvania Constitution in 1971) to disapprove gender based rate plans as here.

On the other hand is a statute such as West's Ann. California Ins.Code § 790.03:

> "The following are hereby defined as unfair methods of competition and unfair and deceptive acts or practices in the business of insurance.
>
> * * *
>
> (f) Making or permitting any unfair discrimination between individuals of the same class and equal expectation of life in rates charged for any contract of life insurance or of life annuity or in the dividends or other benefits payable thereon.
>
> * * *
>
> "This subdivision shall be interpreted, for any contract of *ordinary* life insurance or *individual* life annuity * * * to *require* differentials based on the sex of the *individual* insured or annuitant in the rates or dividends or other benefits payable thereon [emphasis added]. * * *

[As a gesture toward the *Norris* decision, a 1983 amendment to the above section states sex based differentials in rates or dividends shall *not* be required for group life insurance or annuities as to terms, conditions or privileges of employment as such terms are used in Title VII of the Civil Rights Act of 1964].

For an economic overview see, Wortham, The Economics of Insurance Classification, etc., 47 Ohio St.L.J. 835 (1986).

As an example of modern anti-discrimination legislation affecting insurance, see West's Ann.California Insurance Code § 10140, as amended in 1990, which reads:

> (a) No admitted insurer, licensed to issue life or disability insurance, shall fail or refuse to accept an application for that insurance, to issue that insurance to an applicant therefor, or issue or cancel that insurance, under conditions less favorable to the insured than in other comparable cases, except for reasons applicable alike to persons of every race, color, religion, national origin, ancestry, or sexual orientation. Race, color, religion, national origin, ancestry, or sexual orientation shall not, of itself, constitute a condition or risk for which a higher rate, premium, or charge may be required of the insured for that insurance.
>
> (b) It shall be deemed a violation of subdivision (a) for any insurer to consider sexual orientation in its underwriting criteria or to utilize marital status, living arrangements, occupation, gender, beneficiary designation, zip codes or other territorial classification within this state, or any combination thereof for the purpose of establishing sexual orientation or determining whether to require a test for the presence of the human immunodeficiency virus or antibodies to that virus, where that testing is otherwise permitted by law. Nothing in this section shall be construed to alter, expand, or limit in any manner the existing law respecting the authority of insurers to conduct tests for the presence of human immunodeficiency virus or evidence thereof.
>
> (c) Any insurer that knowingly violates this section shall for each violation be assessed a civil penalty in an amount not less than one thousand dollars ($1,000) and not more than five thousand dollars ($5,000) plus court costs, as determined by the court.
>
> (d) This section shall not be construed to limit the authority of the commissioner to adopt regulations prohibiting discrimination because of sex, marital status, or sexual orientation or to enforce these regulations, whether adopted before or on or after January 1, 1991.

### *Questions*

Conceding that the McCarran–Ferguson Act applies to the "business of insurance" but does not provide any total immunity from Federal regulation:

(a) Can SEC disapprove a merger of two insurance companies approved by a State? See Securities & Exchange Commission v. National Securities, Inc., 393 U.S. 453, 89 S.Ct. 564, 21 L.Ed.2d 668 (1969);

(b) Does the Federal "Truth in Lending" Act, 15 U.S.C.A. § 1601 et seq., apply to credit financing of auto insurance premiums when insurance rates and premium financing are regulated by State law? See Lowe v. Aarco–American, Inc., 536 F.2d 1160 (7th Cir.1976). Cf. King v. Central Bank, 18 Cal.3d 840, 135 Cal.Rptr. 771, 558 P.2d 857 (1977);

(c) Would a private treble-damage action under the Federal Anti–Trust laws be precluded where damages are sought for a nation-wide violation of such laws on the ground that Missouri insurance laws provide anti-trust remedies? See Seasongood v. K & K Insurance Agency, 548 F.2d 729 (8th Cir.1977);

(d) Is an agreement between a health insurer and pharmacies under which drugs would be furnished health insurance subscribers within the "business of insurance" exemption or can it be said to be a part of the "business of insurers" which is not protected against the anti-trust laws by the exemption? Lest the question be summarily dismissed as hair-splitting, see Group Life & Health Insurance Co. v. Royal Drug Co., 440 U.S. 205, 99 S.Ct. 1067, 59 L.Ed.2d 261 (1979).

### *Note*

The McCarran–Ferguson Act continues to generate litigation. Its most recent appearance in the United States Supreme Court concerns the anti-trust exemption contained in the Act. In Hartford Fire Insurance Co. v. California, ___ U.S. ___, 113 S.Ct. 2891, 125 L.Ed.2d 612 (1993), certain domestic insurers and foreign insurers attempted, among other things, to pressure the Insurance Services Office (ISO), a trade association, to issue its standard comprehensive general liability form policies with a "claims made" provision. According to the court, the insurers either refused or tried to persuade others to refuse to reinsure policies written on the ISO forms until the desired changes were made. In an opinion by Justice Souter that defies accurate condensation, the Supreme Court held that the McCarran–Ferguson act did not bar state anti-trust prosecution of the insurers conduct.

Despite the initial thrust of the opinion, a majority of the court, not including Justice Souter, held that while the McCarran–Ferguson's anti-trust exemption does not apply to "boycotts," the Act's concept of boycott was a narrow one. It remains to be seen, on the remand of the case to the District Court, whether the initial restriction of the anti-trust exemption will be undone by the Court's narrowing of the boycott definition.

# Chapter 2

# JUDICIAL POLICIES AND INSURANCE CONTRACTS

## PRELIMINARY NOTE

Restatement, Contracts (2d) § 206 * embodies a principle long applied by our courts in the interpretation of contracts:

> "In choosing among the reasonable meanings of a promise or agreement or a term thereof, that meaning is generally preferred which operates against the party who supplies the words or from whom a writing otherwise proceeds."

The Comment to the section points out the reasons for the rule: that the party choosing terms is likely to protect his own interests first, that he is more likely to know about uncertainties in the words chosen, and that he may have deliberately left meanings obscure. The result ought to be that, when there is doubt, and other factors do not prevail, the meaning attached to the words by the *other* party ought to be the one employed in interpreting the contract. Very commonly the rule is said to apply when the contract or one of its provisions is "ambiguous". The rule has a special application in case of standardized contracts where the drafting party has the stronger economic position, "contracts of adhesion"; and the principle sometimes resembles that of "unconscionability". It has found a specially wide interpretation in insurance contracts. Sometimes it is known by the Latin: "contra proferentem".

Comment (b) is specifically pertinent to insurance policies:

> *b. Compulsory contract or term.* The rule that language is interpreted against the party who chose it has no direct application to cases where the language is prescribed by law, as is sometimes true with respect to insurance policies, bills of lading and other standardized documents. In some cases, however, the statute or regulation adopts language which was previously used without compulsion and was interpreted against the drafting party, and there is

normally no intention to change the established meaning. Moreover, insurers are more likely than insureds to participate in drafting prescribed forms and to review them carefully before putting them into use.

## INSURANCE LAW INTERPRETATION

By E. Neil Young, John R. Lewis and J. Finley Lee.

Extracts from Article, Insurance Law Journal, Feb. 1975, No. 625, p. 71.



### BACKGROUND TO THE PROBLEM

The burdensome language of contemporary insurance contracts can be attributed in part to legislatively imposed requirements and in part to the common law. The good intent of each molding force is not in question. The nature of the insurance product and legal nuances easily give rise to complex policy wording. It is generally recognized that policy language must be harmonized to satisfy technical, economic and legal requirements of insurance companies, regulators and the courts. Those standard forms mandated by statutes or administrative orders are typically reflections of or reactions to judicial decision. In effect, the courts have been the chief architects of a great bulk of the verbose and highly technical policy language.

A continuing legal conflict between insurance companies and policyholders has found contract drafters looking to judicial decisions to isolate legal words of art and phrases whose import could be predicted with a reasonable degree of certainty, with policyholders, in turn, fashioning imaginative arguments to combat the effects of unfavorable provisions. The courts, as arbiters of this conflict, have historically viewed insurance policies as but another form of contract, and consequently have, at least ostensibly, construed them according to rules of construction applicable to contracts generally. At the same time, the courts have increasingly recognized that an inflexible application of these rules would result in an "unjust" decision. In order to protect the weaker party, the policyholder, while purportedly following recognized principles of contract construction, courts have so twisted existing doctrines that new and possibly inconsistent doctrines have been conceived and applied solely to insurance contracts. In some jurisdictions, these doctrines have evolved from mere interpretive tools to "broader, more fundamental approaches to insurance policy construction." [12] In others, courts continue to maintain that, "There is no greater sanctity and no more mystery about a contract of insurance than any other. The same rules of construction apply to it as to other contracts." [13]

12. Rodman v. State Farm Mutual Automobile Insurance Co., 208 N.W.2d 903, 906 (Iowa 1973).

13. Parris and Son, Inc. v. Campbell, 1972–1974 Fire and Casualty Cases 411, 128 Ga.App. 165, 196 S.E.2d 334 (1973).

Given the proper combination of contract language and factual situation, the causes of "fairness" and "equity" can be equally served by either approach—application of an independent doctrine which largely ignores policy language or strained construction of existing policy language. The difficulty lies in the fact that the prevailing judicial rationales are often so camouflaged by reference to "established rules" that it is impossible to pair a given situation with the appropriate doctrine so as to achieve a high degree of predictability. The law is left in an untidy state where neither party to the insurance contract knows precisely what the contract does or does not provide until after the fact of litigation.

Critics of this judicial methodology have discovered some degree of order in the apparently inconsistent decisions by seeking a common, though unexpressed rationale running through the cases.[14] Others have advocated forsaking the attempt to interpret insurance contracts by the use of conventional doctrines.[15]

### Basic Approaches to Insurance Contract Interpretation

Over the years, courts have interpreted insurance policies utilizing a number of different approaches to the problem of contract construction. The doctrines that have been applied to the problem of insurance contract interpretation include: (1) the general rule of contract construction approach, (2) the doctrine of *contra proferentem,* (3) adhesion, (4) reasonable expectation, and (5) the "wayfaring fool" doctrine approach.[16] Each of these doctrines can be briefly explained.

Under the first approach, insurance contracts have often been interpreted under the general rules governing interpretation of all contracts. In pursuing this approach, the courts have assumed that both parties to the contract have a right and a capacity to negotiate equally with respect to the terms of the contract. Furthermore, the courts have attempted to ascertain the intent and expectations of all parties to the contract. In using this doctrine, the courts have concluded generally that, when they could determine intent, they should interpret the contract accordingly.

The second interpretative approach that has been used is that of *contra proferentem.* This doctrine suggests that ambiguities in a contract should be interpreted against the one putting the contract forth, the drafter of the contract, regardless of the relative bargaining strength of the parties. In using this doctrine, the courts interpret ambiguities in

**14.** See, for example, Keeton, "Insurance Law Rights at Variance with Policy Provisions," 83 Harvard Law Review 961 (1970); Perlet, "The Insurance Contract and the Doctrine of Reasonable Expectation," 6 Forum 116 (1971); Squires, "A Skeptical Look at the Doctrine of Reasonable Expectation," 6 Forum 252 (1971).

**15.** See for example, Slawson, "New Approach to Standard Forms," 8 Trial 49 (1972); Comment, "The Adhesion Contract of Insurance," 5 Santa Clara Lawyer 60 (1965).

**16.** The order in which these approaches are stated reflects a continuum from conservative to liberal from the insured's point of view—that is, the general rule of contract construction is least liberal from the insured's point of view, while the "wayfaring fool" approach is most liberal.

a plain, ordinary, and proper sense of what the language implies, without considering the intent of the drafter.

A third doctrine, that of "adhesion," is somewhat similar to that of *contra proferentem,* except that it is a more severe interpretation rule from the position of the insurance company. This doctrine suggests that there is not equal bargaining strength and that, as a result, all contract ambiguities should be interpreted against the insurer. In the words of Judge Hand, "* * * insurers who seek to impose upon words of common speech an esoteric significance intelligible only to their craft, must bear the burden of any resulting confusion." [17]

One step further, one encounters the doctrine of "reasonable expectation," which might be termed "super adhesion." This doctrine has been referred to by Professor Robert B. Keeton of the Harvard University Law School as more than a mere rule of construction and, in fact, "* * * a measure of judicial regulation of insurance contracts." [18] The doctrine of reasonable expectation suggests that "insurers should not be allowed to enforce restrictions of coverage or interpretation of terms that are inconsistent with the reasonable expectations of the insurance purchaser."

A final doctrine that has been utilized occasionally in interpreting insurance contracts is the "wayfaring fool" test. This rule is extremely harsh from the position of the insurance company in the sense that it seeks to protect the purchaser of an insurance policy from his own ignorance. Specifically, this doctrine, traceable to a 1937 opinion of the Supreme Court of Arkansas, states that an insurer must use language that is sufficiently plain and clear that a "wayfaring man, though a fool, might not be deceived."

While it should be clear that numerous approaches to the interpretation of insurance contract ambiguities exist, it should likewise be clear that the adhesion and reasonable expectation approaches are by far the most commonly applied. * * *

### Adhesion Contracts

Application of the adhesion concept is not as straightforward as one might assume. If one proceeds from the premise that the law of contracts provides a means for parties to formulate for themselves a kind of private, but enforceable, law through a process of mutual bargaining and agreement, it would be quite logical to conclude that insurance policies are not contracts at all. While it is true that the insured may, to a degree, tailor his policy to suit his needs—he may, for example, elect expanded coverage in exchange for additional premiums—he does not normally have the opportunity to write or bargain for his own contract provisions. Generally, he does not propose or draft a single clause or phrase in the policy. He accepts that which has been written by the

17. State Farm Mutual Automobile Insurance Co. v. Oliver, 406 F.2d 409 (CA–6 1969).

18. "Insurance Lawyers View 'Wayfaring Fool' Doctrine," Insurance Advocate, July 24, 1971, p. 21.

company or nothing at all. There is a likelihood, in fact, that the insured will not even see the document evidencing his "agreement" until after he has paid his first premium.

It does not necessarily follow, however, that the method utilized in arriving at a contract of insurance is unfair or undesirable. More than 30 years ago, it was noted that, "The development of large-scale enterprise with its mass production and mass distribution made a new type contract inevitable—the standardized mass contract. * * * The standard clauses in insurance policies are the most striking illustrations of successful attempts on the part of business enterprises to select and control risks assumed under a contract." [19] Furthermore, standardization probably never has been, and certainly is not now, unique to insurance contracts. Today, it is virtually impossible for an individual to go to the marketplace to buy, sell, borrow, lease, obtain a service, or enter into a myriad of other typical business transactions without encountering a contract which is, to some extent, standardized and mass-produced.

Insurance contracts do differ from most other standardized contracts in that the insurance consumer receives no present tangible benefit; he receives only the conditional promises of the policy itself for his premium dollar. Perhaps it is for this reason that insurance contracts have been singled out as having the inherent potential of being oppressive, of allowing the more powerful party to legislate by contract "in a substantially authoritarian manner without using the appearance of authoritarian forms.[20] The courts have acted—many would argue that they have overacted—to protect the consuming public from this potential abuse. Judicial action, though, has been restricted by the framework of the common law of contracts, which dictates the fictional conclusion that the parties to the contract have agreed upon all terms of the contract, and demands that the courts do no more than interpret those terms. It is this process of interpretation and construction that has produced the inconsistent doctrines which have been the cause of consternation among representatives of the insurance industry, the legal profession, and the policyholding public generally.

Judicial efforts to protect insured from oppressive provisions and unjust results are usually, although not always, founded upon the concept that a contract of insurance is a contract of adhesion, a " * * * standardized contract, which, imposed and drafted by the party of superior bargaining strength, relegates to the subscribing party only the opportunity to adhere to the contract or reject. * * * " [21] The implication of such a statement would seem to be that adhesion contracts are to be treated in some special manner. The employment of the term "adhesion contract," however, as the term is used by most American

**19.** Kessler, "Contracts of Adhesion—Some Thoughts About Freedom of Contract," 43 Columbia Law Review 631 (1943).

**20.** Id., at p. 640.

**21.** Neal v. State Farm Insurance Cos., 188 Cal.App.2d 690, 10 Cal.Rptr. 781 (1961).

courts, tells us how the contract was formed, but it tells us very little more about how the contract is to be interpreted than we would have known in the absence of the term. * * *

* * * Perhaps the significance of the employment of the term "adhesion contract" is that certain associated "well-established" rules of construction are thereby raised, which rules grant to the courts greater latitude in detecting and protecting policyholders from unclear provisions. Possibly the use of the term can accurately be seen as no more than a symptom that a court is searching more diligently for an ambiguity. * * *

### TOWARD REASONABLE EXPECTATION

* * * Mr. Perlet, in a 1971 article, pointed out that there are two similar but distinct lines of cases which have used the term "reasonable expectation."[22] One line of cases, extending backward to the early 20th Century, has established the rule that insurance contracts should provide that coverage which one would reasonably expect upon a reading of the policy. This doctrine is little more than a refinement of the well-established rule of construing ambiguous phrases more strongly against the author (that is, if the contract does not, in fact, include ambiguous language, the doctrine has no applicability).

The other line of more recent cases espouses a reasonable expectation doctrine which, it is inferred, "* * * begins with the premise that the insured is entitled to all the coverage he may reasonably expect to be provided under the policy and that only an unequivocably conspicuous, plain and clear manifestation of the company's intent to exclude coverage will defeat that expectation." Clearly, if this is an accurate statement of the holdings in the pertinent cases, the doctrine of reasonable expectation is a distinct approach to contract construction which could be utilized by the courts independent of, or in the total absence of, ambiguous contract language. Presumably, for example, if a policyholder reasonably expected that a comprehensive personal liability policy extended to the operation of his automobile, a court, applying the reasonable expectation doctrine, would hold that the policy afforded such coverage although automobile liability was not mentioned, or even if it had been specifically excluded in something less than "unequivocably conspicuous, plain and clear" language.

Professor Robert Keeton's concept of the doctrine goes a step further:

> "The objectively reasonable expectations of applicants and intended beneficiaries regarding the terms of insurance contracts will be honored even though painstaking study of the policy provisions would have negated those expectations."

This principle, which Professor Keeton finds to be implicitly controlling in many decisions, would mandate that a policy provide a reasonably expected coverage, even though that coverage is excluded by clear and

22. Perlet, cited at footnote 14.

unambiguous language in the policy. If an insurer, then, desired to exclude a coverage which a prospective insured might reasonably expect the policy of insurance to include, it would be necessary to advise the prospective insured of the exclusion, possibly by specifically pointing out the exclusionary language, before the contract is entered into, thereby negating the possibility of any objectively reasonable expectation of the coverage in question.

While this view of the doctrine of reasonable expectation may, as Professor Keeton suggests, provide a rationale for explaining and harmonizing many of the decisions which have cited ambiguous language, as well as equitable estoppel, waiver, and other associated doctrines, as controlling factors, still most of the courts have been hesitant to verbalize a doctrine which admits the judicial imposition of a coverage that has clearly been excluded by policy language. Those that have, * * * have generally done so where broad general language (or the implications of that broad language) has been restricted by "fine print" exclusions.

## STEVEN v. FIDELITY AND CASUALTY COMPANY OF NEW YORK.

Supreme Court of California, In Bank, 1962.
58 Cal.2d 862, 27 Cal.Rptr. 172, 377 P.2d 284.

TOBRINER, JUSTICE.

* * *

On March 3, 1957, Mr. George A. Steven purchased at Los Angeles, California, a round-trip airplane ticket to Dayton, Ohio. As part of the return trip Mr. Steven's itinerary included a flight from Terre Haute, Indiana, to Chicago, Illinois. Mr. Steven simultaneously purchased for a premium of $2.50 a $62,500 life insurance policy which named his wife, appellant, as the beneficiary.

Mr. Steven bought the policy by means of a vending machine. The policy set out across the top the following specifications: "DO NOT PURCHASE MORE THAN A TOTAL OF $62,500 PRINCIPAL SUM NOR FOR TRAVEL ON OTHER THAN SCHEDULED AIR CARRIERS. THIS POLICY COVERS ON ONE-WAY TRIP ONLY UNLESS ROUND TRIP TICKET IS PURCHASED BEFORE DEPARTURE." Below this printed statement a box form provided for the insertion on appropriate lines of the insured's name, the name and address of the beneficiary, the point of departure and destination, the extent of the trip as on a one-way or round-trip ticket, the date, the principal sum of insurance ($62,500), the amount of the premium ($2.50), and the insured's signature. The evidence does not clearly show whether at the time of purchase the aperture of the vending machine disclosed the entire top portion of the policy, including the printed warning as to amount and coverage for travel on "scheduled air carriers," or merely the form for the personal data and flight information to be furnished by the purchaser. After obtaining the policy, Mr. Steven, using the envelope provided by the machine, mailed it to his wife.

On March 6, 1957, on his return trip from Dayton, Mr. Steven, according to his original plan, stopped off at Terre Haute. He arrived there between 7 and 8 o'clock in the morning. His round-trip ticket scheduled him to take a Lake Central Airlines plane to Chicago at noon that day. At about that time the public address system at the airport announced that the Lake Central plane had been grounded in Indianapolis and that there would be some delay. After several further announcements of repeated delays, the scheduled Lake Central flight to Chicago was finally cancelled at 4:30 p.m.

The agent of Lake Central Airlines then attempted to arrange for Mr. Steven and three other men substitute means of transportation to Chicago. The agent phoned railroads, bus lines and even an automobile rental company. After concluding that he could not thereby arrange a connection with the scheduled Chicago flight to Los Angeles, the agent took Mr. Steven and the other three men to the office of the Turner Aviation Corporation (hereinafter designated Turner) at the Terre Haute airport and introduced them to the agent there in charge. The Lake Central agent indicated that a flight on a Turner plane provided the only means for Mr. Steven to make his scheduled connection with the Chicago plane, a connection which Mr. Steven particularly desired because an essential work project awaited him in Los Angeles the next morning. Turner agreed to fly the men to Chicago for $36 per person, or, if two more passengers could be obtained, for $21 a person. Two additional passengers were obtained and accordingly Mr. Steven and each of the other passengers paid Turner $21 for his ticket.

Mr. Steven boarded the Turner aircraft, a Piper Tri–Pacer airplane, which took off from the Terre Haute airfield at 5:55 p.m. Some time around 7 p.m. on March 6, 1957, near Grant Park, Illinois, the plane crashed. Mr. Steven suffered fatal injuries.

* * * The plane trip on which the accident occurred was not a regular and scheduled flight of Turner.

The trial court found that the deceased at the time of the accident "was not riding as a passenger on an aircraft operated by a scheduled air carrier, as defined in (the) policy, and further * * * that he was riding a charter plane from Terre Haute, Indiana, to Chicago, Illinois," and concluded that appellant could not recover on the policy.

The purpose and intent of the insured in taking out the insurance was to obtain insurance protection for the trip. The insured could fairly believe that the policy would cover a reasonable emergency substitution necessitated by the exigencies of the situation. Since weather conditions and mechanical failure upon not infrequent occasions require such substitution, the insured would not ordinarily expect that his insurance would fail in the event of these foreseeable contingencies. Since his contract covered the trip, he would not contemplate a hiatus in coverage; he bargained for protection for the whole, not part of, the trip.

A reasonable person, having bought his ticket for a fixed itinerary, and thus having at the moment of purchase of the policy gained insurance protection for the whole trip, would normally expect that if a flight were interrupted by breakdown or other causes, his coverage would apply to substitute transportation for the same flight. If, for instance, the scheduled plane crashlanded, he would certainly assume that the policy covered the emergency relief plane whether or not it were a scheduled air liner. The same normal expectation would apply to the substitution of an alternate plane because the scheduled one had been grounded by mechanical failure.

The risk of injury on the substitute conveyance in many cases will be no greater than the risk on the scheduled flight; in all cases it will be less than if the scheduled air line attempts to fly the scheduled flight despite bad weather or mechanical difficulty. Thus, both in the terms of occurrence and magnitude of risk, substitute emergency transportation falls well within the obligation undertaken by the insurer.

The language of the policy does not specifically exclude the expected coverage for the substituted flight. Neither the insuring clause, the definitions of a scheduled air carrier nor section 3(b) infra negates, without ambiguity, protection for the emergency substitute flight.

The insuring clause alludes to a loss occurring "during the first one-way or round airline trip taken by the Insured after the purchase of this policy on Aircraft Operated by a Scheduled Air Carrier as defined below * * *" and does not mention the subject of substitution of another carrier in the event of breakdown. Section 4, which defines 'aircraft operated by a scheduled air carrier' differentiates between the scheduled and nonscheduled carriers but likewise does not describe the accorded coverage if an emergency causes the use of a nonscheduled carrier. These sections provide that the policy applies, as the heading in the box states, to the "round trip ticket * * * purchased before departure." Mr. Steven complied with these requirements: he purchased the round trip ticket on the scheduled airliner, and, when initially ensconced upon his plane, enjoyed the protection of his policy.

The only allusion to substituted transportation in the policy, contained in clause 3(b), does not in and of itself exclude coverage for the Turner flight. This provision affirmatively extends coverage to injuries sustained "while riding in or on a land conveyance provided or arranged for, directly or indirectly, by such scheduled air carrier * * * for the transportation of passengers necessitated by an interruption or temporary suspension of such scheduled air carrier's service. * * *" It thus makes clear that, at least in some cases, substitute emergency transportation will be included in the policy, and that, despite the narrowing of the insuring clause of the policy to "Aircraft Operated by a Scheduled Air Carrier," coverage may be extended to a nonscheduled nonflying vehicle not operated by an air carrier.

The crucial issue resolves into whether the limitation of that extension to "land conveyances" sufficiently overcomes the normal expectation that coverage would extend to any reasonable form of substitute conveyance. The clause clearly does not specifically exclude substitute emergency aircraft; it does not mention nonland conveyances at all. An inference of such noncoverage could arise only with the aid of the rule of construction expressio unius est exclusio alterius; i.e., that mention of one matter implies the exclusion of all others.

We do not believe the application of the maxim can resolve the present case. The maxim serves as an aid to resolve the ambiguities of a contract. If we invoke the expressio unius approach, we must necessarily thereby recognize the ambiguity of the contract; in that event other legal techniques for the resolution of ambiguities, including the rule that they should be interpreted against the draftsman, also come into play. Thus McNee v. Harold Hensgen & Associates (1960) 178 Cal.App.2d 881, 3 Cal.Rptr. 377, holds that if the applicability of a contract provision can be determined only by use of the maxim expression unius, the contract is ambiguous, and extrinsic evidence is therefore admissible to prove the intent of the parties.

The rule of resolving ambiguities against the insurer does not serve as a mere tie-breaker; it rests upon fundamental considerations of policy. In view of the somewhat fictional nature of intent in standardized contracts, the considerations which support the rule that ambiguities in the policy are to be interpreted against the insurer are more compelling that those which prompt the application of the mechanical expressio unius maxim. We do not believe the maxim should serve to defeat the basic rule that the insurance contract should be interpreted against the draftsman.

In any event, the maxim of expressio unius, which is surely a legalistic concept, hardly enters into the thinking of the reasonable layman. As we have stated, we interpret an insurance contract in the light of that understanding. We could not logically conclude that when Mr. Steven, unversed in legal abstractions, boarded the Turner plane at Terre Haute, he invoked this maxim of interpretation.

The facts of this case buttress the above conclusion. Mr. Steven planned a round trip entirely on scheduled air carriers; he purchased his policy with the expectation that it would provide insurance against death or injury in such contingencies as might arise in the course of such a trip. In Terre Haute, Mr. Steven, upon learning that the Lake Central flight had been cancelled, exhausted all the possibilities of obtaining substitute land transportation. He could complete his original itinerary only by the Turner flight. Indeed, the Lake Central agent suggested the Turner substitution, took him over to the Turner office and introduced him to the Turner agent. While the policy specified coverage for injuries suffered in a land conveyance provided by the scheduled carrier, it contains no statement whatsoever as to such substituted air conveyance. We do not see how such verbal vacuity can serve as clear and plain notice to the insured of noncoverage.

We therefore conclude that section 3(b) should not be interpreted to restrict coverage exclusively to land conveyances. The policy did not clearly notify Mr. Steven that in spite of his expectation, and in view of the intention of the parties in entering into the contract, the coverage did not extend to a substitute flight in the event of emergency. The provision for substitute transportation did not clearly overcome the normal expectation that coverage would extend to any reasonable form of substitute conveyance.

Turning to the second aspect of the policy which affects the substituted Turner flight, that is, the definition of scheduled air carrier, we find that it, too, created an ambiguity and failed to apprise Mr. Steven of the asserted noncoverage. * * *

Since Turner did not file and publish regular schedules, nor possess a certificate of public convenience and necessity, Turner does not fall under the literal affirmative definition of scheduled air carrier in the policy. Neither does Turner qualify under the exclusionary language in the last sentence of clause 4; it was not a military airline and was not designated by government regulations as an irregular carrier. Thus the negative definition of the term in the exclusionary phrase may serve to extend coverage to all types of air transport except the two that were specifically excluded.

In summary, the air-taxi carrier constitutes a third category of aircraft under the federal regulations; the air-taxi is neither a scheduled carrier nor a non-scheduled carrier. So regarded, air-taxi carriers are neither included in, nor excluded from, the coverage for the policy; clause 4 creates an ambiguity. "(T)he burden in such a case as this is on the defendant to establish that the words and expressions used not only are susceptible of the construction sought by defendant but that it is the only construction which may fairly be placed on them." (Lachs v. Fidelity & Cas. Co., supra, 118 N.E.2d at p. 555; emphasis added.) This burden has not been met.

If the classic rules of interpretation lead to the conclusion that the policy afforded coverage here, we must point out additionally that they apply with special force in the circumstances of this case. We do not deal here with the orthodox insurance policy sold in the protective aura of the insurer's explanation and discussion of its terms. The vending machine emitted a complex stereotyped document, which, because of the short time elapsing before the start of Mr. Steven's flight, hardly afforded him an opportunity even to read the policy. The mass-made contract, sold by the machine under such conditions, symbolizes the kind of transaction that lends to the accepted rules a special gloss of interpretation. As we shall explain in more detail, the cases have held that in such contracts the expected coverage of the policy can only be defeated by a provision for limitation which has been plainly brought to the attention of the insured.

Nothing in the instant contract or transaction apprised the insured that the protection of the policy would not extend to the substituted emergency flight. The manner of sale of the policy negated any possibility of such notice. The inanimate machine told the purchaser nothing, and even if he had wanted to ask about the coverage in the event of emergency, the box could not have answered. While the testimony leaves us in some doubt as to whether Mr. Steven saw the words in the window of the machine stating "Nor for travel on other than Scheduled Air Carriers," we know that if he did see them, he could neither have read the definition of "scheduled air carrier" nor the clause concerning substitute emergency transportation on "land conveyances." These clauses lay hidden behind the mechanized face of the vendor. Even after Mr. Steven purchased the policy he would only have found such clauses among the many complexities of the instrument. They were inconspicuous clauses, and, as we have stated, they were unclear.

To assume that Mr. Steven read the provisions, or conceivably understood them, is to rest upon hypothesis rather than fact. The insurer instructed the purchaser to mail the policy to the beneficiary and provided envelopes for this purpose. Like most purchasers, Mr. Steven, before boarding the plane at the very commencement of the trip, did mail the policy to the beneficiary. The company provided no duplicate. Thus, when Mr. Steven found it necessary at Terre Haute to take the Turner flight he could not have consulted the policy to determine its applicability. Instead, even assuming that three days earlier he had read it carefully, he would have been compelled to rely upon his memory. The policy is about 2,000 words long. It is so tightly drawn that if Mr. Steven had forgotten a single word in clause 3(b) or a short phrase in clause 4 he might well have concluded that the policy covered the Turner trip.

Even upon the highly unrealistic assumption that Mr. Steven surmounted all of these obstacles, the policy still would not have notified him that he was not covered. The policy, in defining scheduled airlines, refers to an airline possessing certificates of public convenience and necessity and filing schedules. Later it attempts to exclude lines designated in government regulations as irregular or nonscheduled. These facts, important in determining whether the Turner flight were covered, obviously do not compose the facts a passenger typically knows. "(T)he average man * * * is (not) expected to carry the Civil Aeronautics Act or the Code of Federal Regulations when taking a plane." (Lachs v. Fidelity & Cas. Co., supra, 118 N.E.2d at p. 558.) Neither can he generally be expected to inquire into the nature of the certification of the airline.

The company so arranged this transaction that Mr. Steven could not possibly read the policy before purchase and could not practically consult the policy after purchase. The language of the policy in itself was insufficient to afford the necessary notice of non-coverage. The facts of the case foreclose any contention of the company that it afforded Mr. Steven plain warning of non-coverage of the Turner flight. While the insurer has every right to sell insurance policies by methods of mechanization, and present-day economic conditions may well justify such distribution, the insurer cannot then rely upon esoteric provisions to limit coverage. If it deals with the public upon a mass basis, the notice of non-coverage of the policy, in a situation in which the public may reasonably expect coverage, must be conspicuous, plain and clear.

Finally, the one provision that deals with substitution of transportation in the event of emergency, section 3(b) of the policy, was not only hidden beneath the machine before purchase, and, subject after purchase, to obscurity and ambiguity, but literally applied, tended toward the harsh and unconscionable. The section states that coverage for "the transportation of passengers necessitated by an interruption or temporary suspension of such scheduled air carrier's service before arrival at destination" is limited to "riding in or on a land conveyance provided or arranged for, directly or indirectly, by such scheduled air carrier" (emphasis added). Yet innumerable flights traverse bodies of water; if a plane were forced down at such point and the scheduled carrier arranged for conveyance by water, the language would not apply. Indeed, if the plane were forced down upon land or water and relief was afforded by a chartered non-scheduled carrier, which, of course, is a very likely contingency, the language again would not apply. Does not such a provision approach a trap for the unwary purchasing public?

In standardized contracts, such as the instant one, which are made by parties of unequal bargaining strength, the California courts have long been disinclined to effectuate clauses of limitation of liability which are unclear, unexpected, inconspicuous or unconscionable. The attitude of the courts has been manifested in many areas of contract.

* * *

The approach of the California courts to the exculpatory [sic] or exclusionary clause of the standardized contract finds a reflection in cases of other states and in the writings of the commentators. Indeed, some legal authorities categorize the instant contract and comparable agreements under the term "contract of adhesion" to give it a more definite place in the law and to emphasize the need for the strict judicial scrutiny of its terms. The term refers to a standardized contract prepared entirely by one party to the transaction for the acceptance of the other; such a contract, due to the disparity in bargaining power between the draftsman and the second party, must be accepted or rejected by the second party on a "take it or leave it" basis, without opportunity for bargaining and under such conditions that the "adherer" cannot obtain the desired product or service save by acquiescing in the form agreement.

In an exhaustive analysis of such contracts the New Jersey Supreme Court in the recent case of Henningsen v. Bloomfield Motors, Inc., (1960) 32 N.J. 358, 161 A.2d 69, 75 A.L.R.2d 1, held void as against public policy an exculpatory provision of an express warranty that excluded claims against a dealer or manufacturer for personal injuries resulting from a defective car. The court stated the rationale of its ruling in these words: "The task of the judiciary is to administer the spirit as well as the letter of the law. On issues such as the present one, part of that burden is to protect the ordinary man against the loss of important rights through what, in effect, is the unilateral act of the manufacturer. * * * From the standpoint of the purchaser, there can be no arms length negotiating on the subject. Because his capacity for bargaining is to grossly unequal, the inexorable conclusion which follows is that he is not permitted to bargain at all. * * *" (161 A.2d p. 94.) The court emphasizes the requirement for an *understanding consent* of the consumer to any limitation of liability. "Basically, the reason a contracting party offering services of a public or *quasi*-public nature has been held to the requirements of fair dealing, and, when it attempts to limit its liability, of securing the understanding consent of the patron or consumer, is because members of the public generally have no other means of fulfilling the specific need represented by the contract. * * *" (161 A.2d p. 92.)

The instant contract presents an even stronger case than Henningsen for the requirement that the exclusionary clause of the contract should not be enforced in the absence of plain and clear notification to the public. The disparity in bargaining power between the insured and the insurer here is so tremendous that the insurer had adopted a means of selling policies which makes bargaining totally impossible. The purchaser lacks any opportunity to clarify ambiguous terms or to discover inconspicuous or concealed ones. He must purchase the policy before he even knows its provisions.

Because of the special dangers inherent in the mechanized selling of air travel insurance, the New York Court of Appeals has insisted that the burden of giving clear notice of non-coverage rests with the insurer. In Lachs v. Fidelity & Casualty Co. of New York (1954) supra, 306 N.Y. 357, 118 N.E.2d 555, an "Airline Trip Insurance" vending machine stood near a ticket counter for sales of nonscheduled flights in the airport; a smaller placard limited coverage to "any scheduled airline"; the printed policy provided for coverage for "Civilian Scheduled Airlines." As in the instant case the insurer provided envelopes for the immediate mailing of the policy to the beneficiary. Unlike the passenger in the instant case the New York purchaser arranged for her trip to Miami on a nonscheduled flight, which subsequently crashed. The Court of Appeals held that the trial court properly denied the insurer's motion for summary judgment. The court points to the ambiguity of the term "Civilian Scheduled Airline" and to the ambiguity of the situation itself. It holds "* * * (T)he burden in such a case as this is on the defendant to establish that the words and expressions used not only are susceptible of the construction sought by defendant but that it is the only construction which may fairly be placed on them. The defendant in its large illuminated lettering and in its application could have added proper, unambiguous words or a definition or could have avoided allowing its vending machine to be placed in front of the ticket counter 'utilized by all nonscheduled airlines operating out of the Newark Airport', thus removing the ambiguity or equivocal character of the invitation to insure, of the application for insurance and the contract of insurance itself. * * * (118 N.E.2d p. 559)."

We must view the instant claim in the composite of its special and unique circumstances. To equate the bargaining table, where each clause is the subject of debate, to an automatic vending machine, which issues a policy before it can even be read, is to ignore basic distinctions. The proposition that the precedents must be viewed in the light of the imperatives of the age of the machine has become almost axiomatic. Here the age of the machine is no mere abstraction; it presents itself in the shape of an instrument for the mass distribution of standard contracts. The exclusionary clause of that contract, upon which the insurance company relies, is an unexpected one. Its application in some circumstances would be unconscionable. It is placed in an inconspicuous position of the document. In view of all these characteristics its rigid application would cast an unexpected burden upon the travelling public and would prefer formality of phrase to the reality of the transaction.

The judgment is reversed, and the cause is remanded to the trial court with directions to enter judgment for the plaintiff.

### *Notes*

1. California, like many states, recognizes that insurance policies are contracts to be governed by contact law principles. E.g. Bank of the West v. Superior Court, 2 Cal.4th 1254, 10 Cal.Rptr.2d 538, 833 P.2d 545 (1992); AIU Ins. Co. v. Superior Court, 51 Cal.3d 807, 274 Cal.Rptr. 820, 799 P.2d 1253 (1990). At the same time, as the introductory note indicates, there is an explicit recognition that the unique context of insurance policies as contracts demands attention to the area in which insurance sets itself apart, hence the *Steven* case.

Recently, however, California has subtly limited the reach of *Steven* or at least the reach of the *contra proferentem* doctrine. In *Bank of the West v. Superior Court,* the court notes that the doctrine of reasonable expectations is to be used as a tool which does not necessarily result in an interpretation of the contract in the insured's favor. 2 Cal.4th at 1264–65, 10 Cal.Rptr.2d at 544–45, 833 P.2d at 551–52. According to this formulation then, only if the doctrine of reasonable expectations does not resolve ambiguity does the *contra proferentem* principle apply. See John L. Romaker & Virgil B. Prieto, *Expectations Lost: Bank of the West v. Superior Court Places the Fox in Charge of the Henhouse,* 29 Cal.W.L.Rev. 83, 125 n. 326 (1992).

2. Courts have noted the reasonable expectation that coverage under a "Comprehensive General Liability" policy be comprehensive and that an "all risks" property policy cover all risks. Insurers now title these policies "Commercial General Liability" and "Special" form property coverage.

## PONDER v. BLUE CROSS OF SOUTHERN CALIFORNIA

Court of Appeal, Second District, 1983.
145 Cal.App.3d 709, 193 Cal.Rptr. 632.

JOHNSON, ASSOCIATE JUSTICE.

The central issue on appeal is whether a form insurance contract effectively excludes coverage through a clause couched in undefined technical language not highlighted by location, typesize or otherwise. Under the circumstances of this case, we hold that it does not.

In early May 1979, Mrs. Tommie Ponder was suffering earaches, throat pains, coughing and headaches. She sought treatment from Harvey S. Kulber, M.D. He initially diagnosed the problem as upper respiratory infection and blocked Eustachian tubes. By her next visit on May 13, the infection had subsided but the earaches remained. Dr. Kulber's examination including X-rays revealed "severe temporomandibular joint disease, especially on the left side."

A few months later, Mrs. Ponder was experiencing severe headaches with the pain radiating into the ears. Dr. Kulber and his associate, Dr. Seltzer, also a physician, diagnosed the cause as "temporomandibular joint syndrome and etiology of the pain coming from that syndrome." They referred Mrs. Ponder to a clinic at White Memorial Hospital which specialized exclusively in the treatment of temporomandibular joint disease.

During this period, Blue Cross honored payment of the bills for the services of Drs. Kulber and Seltzer including those which indicated the condition treated was temporomandibular joint disease.

The White Memorial Hospital TMJ Clinic is staffed by medical doctors and oral surgeons. Mrs. Ponder was assigned to one of the oral surgeons, Douglas H. Morgan, D.D.S., for screening. He diagnosed her condition as "osteo-arthritic condition of the right and left temporomandibular joints, as well as dysfunction of the left meniscus." According to Dr. Morgan's declaration, this condition is treated by medical doctors or oral surgeons, or both. Moreover, when he performs the surgery often required to cure temporomandibular joint disease, he is assisted by a medical doctor.

Dr. Morgan began treating Mrs. Ponder for this condition by non-surgical methods which also are helpful should surgery become necessary. From July 17, 1979, through March 13, 1980, Dr. Morgan submitted 23 claims to Blue Cross for these treatments.

These 23 disputed claims were filed under a non-group insurance contract the Ponders have held since July 1, 1976. This contract is called the "High Option Performance Plus Plan." The terms of the contract are spelled out in a "certificate" which Blue Cross issues to "subscribers." When Blue Cross chooses to modify coverage, its computer merely sends out a new certificate to replace the superseded version.

During the period Mrs. Ponder was receiving the disputed treatments, the Ponders were covered by two successive certificates. From January 1, 1979—January 1, 1980, the Ponders claimed reimbursement under certificate "Non-group series G 2863." This three page, eleven part, 5,750 word contract contained two provisions of special relevance to this case. * * *

On page two, under Part VI, *General Limitations,* this certificate reads:

> "Blue Cross shall not furnish benefits for:
>
> "* * *
>
> "J. *Dental Care:* Treatment on or to the teeth or gums or extraction of teeth except when necessitated by accident, or as otherwise specifically provided for under this Agreement; treatment of dental abscess or granuloma, treatment for or prevention of temporo-mandibular joint syndrome, treatment of gingival tissue other than for tumors, and dental examinations."

A new certificate, "Non-group series G–3823," became effective on January 1, 1980. This certificate modified the two key terms of the contract to read:

* * *

> "Blue Cross shall NOT furnish benefits for:
>
> "J. *Dental Care:* Treatment on or to the teeth and gums or any tooth extraction except when it is required because of an accident occurring while the Member is covered under this Agreement. Treatment of dental abscess, granuloma, gingival tissues or dental examinations. Also, medical or surgical care for or prevention of temporo-mandibular joint syndrome or disease."

Blue Cross initially paid four of the 23 disputed claims totalling $742.48 which were filed during August 1979. Thereafter, Blue Cross paid no further claims for treating Mrs. Ponder's condition. * * *

[In early 1980], Mrs. Ponder was diagnosed as requiring surgery—a bilateral temporomandibular joint arthoplasty—and temporomandibular joint therapy. On September 17, 1980, the Ponders filed their complaint against Blue Cross seeking declaratory relief and damages.

* * *

In granting [defendant] summary judgment, the trial court rested its decision on a finding that the language of the contract excluding coverage of "temporomandibular joint syndrome" was unambiguous. * * *

The trial court apparently assumed that if the language of the exclusion is "unambiguous" in the sense of being precise, that ends the inquiry. Continuing the logic of the court's decision, *temporomandibular joint syndrome* is a precise term and was included in the exclusions section of the contract. The appellant was being treated for *temporomandibular joint syndrome.* Consequently she was not entitled to coverage.

We find it unnecessary to determine whether the phrase *temporomandibular joint syndrome* is indeed an "unambiguous" term.[1] Instead we subject this exclusion to two other tests which also must be satisfied before this contract term can be enforced against an insured. Because of the nature of the contract and the contracting parties, the most *precise* language imaginable may prove insufficient to eliminate coverage.

In order to understand why additional requirements apply to this contract, we first begin with the proposition that any contract is construed against the party who prepared the contract. [Citations omitted.] No one questions that Blue Cross prepared and printed this contract. Hence every term must be construed in favor of appellant. Secondly, this is not an ordinary contract, but an *insurance* contract which imposes an even more stringent duty on the court to interpret in favor of the insured. [Citations omitted.] Thirdly, the contract term in dispute is an exclusion from coverage. And an exclusion is subjected to the closest possible scrutiny. [Citations omitted.] Finally, we find this is not just an insurance contract but an adhesion contract for insurance. * * *

Since we hold this is an adhesion contract, it is not enough the exclusionary clause could be deemed to be precise. It also must pass muster under two other independent tests. (1) The exclusion must be *conspicuous* and (2) the language of the exclusion must be *plain and clear.* We have chosen to divide the traditional statement of the requirement that insurance policy exclusions be "conspicuous, plain and clear" into separate tests. As a matter of logic, this brief clause imposes two very different demands on those who draft insurance policies. First, the exclusion must be positioned in a place and printed in a form which would attract a reader's attention. Secondly, the substance of the exclusion must be stated in words that convey the proper meaning to persons expected to read the contract.

Nor is an explicit finding of an "adhesion contract" absolutely essential to the imposition of these two tests. Many of the appellate cases interpreting insurance contracts designed for the general public neither make nor require a specific finding the agreement constituted an "adhesion contract." * * * Without bothering to make that finding, the

1. The term *temporomandibular joint syndrome* is defined in Dorland's Medical Dictionary (25th edition, 1974) as a "dysfunction of the temporomandibular joint marked by a clicking or grinding sensation in the joint and often by pain in or about the ears, muscle tiredness and slight soreness upon waking, and stiffness of the jaw or actual trismus; it results from mandibular overclosure, condylar displacement, or stress, with deforming arthritis an occasional factor." (Id. at p. 1527.) "Temporomandibular," in turn, is defined as "pertaining to the temporal bone and the mandible." (Id. at p. 1546.) The temporal bone is "one of the two irregular bones forming part of the lateral surfaces and base of the skull, and containing the organs of hearing." (Id. at p. 219.) And the "mandible" is "the bone of the lower jaw." (Id. at p. 907.)

courts apply the special rules of interpretation ordinarily reserved for adhesion contracts. They scrutinize the provisions of these standardized insurance agreements to insure any exclusions or limitations on coverage meet the twin tests of being "conspicuous" and "plain and clear." * * *

One possible reading of these cases is that all standard insurance policies aimed at the general public are considered adhesion contracts per se since by definition they have the principal attributes of such agreements. Thus it is redundant to continually characterize them as adhesion contracts. What is abundantly clear is that this issue is largely irrelevant. Whether characterized as an "adhesion contract" or as merely a "standard insurance contract marketed with the general public" this Blue Cross policy and its exclusions must pass all the tests ordinarily imposed on "adhesion contracts" in other contexts.

* * *

It is not altogether clear that the *conspicuous* and *plain and clear* requirements apply unless the exclusion "disappoints the reasonable expectations" of the insured. Some cases couple the two statements in such a way as to suggest that only disappointed expectations will activate the conspicuous, plain and clear requirements. * * * On the other hand, other decisions appear to require exclusions to comply with these requirements without any finding that implementation of the exclusion would "disappoint the reasonable expectations" of the insured. * * * We can imagine exclusions which are so consistent with the scope of coverage an ordinary policyholder expects that it would be unnecessary if not redundant to impose special requirements these clauses be *conspicuous* and *plain and clear*. Nonetheless many, and perhaps most, exclusionary clauses by their very nature deny coverage that consumers otherwise would personally anticipate to be provided under the policy.

In any event, we have no difficulty holding the exclusion of coverage for *temporomandibular joint syndrome* clearly "disappoints the reasonable expectations" of the purchasers of these Blue Cross contracts. It is reasonable to expect a health insurance policy, especially one labelled a "High Option Performance Plan," to cover the costs of treating any condition which impairs one's health.

Temporomandibular joint syndrome clearly is such a condition. As the leading medical text cited earlier reminds us, "Organic disorders of a temporomandibular joint are similar to disorders of any other joints of the body.... Likewise the type of pain in temporomandibular joint diseases is similar to afflictions of other joints." (See fn. 1, supra.) There is no more reason for an insured to anticipate that diseases of the bone, muscles and tissues adjoining the temporomandibular joint would be excluded from coverage than that diseases of the knee joint or the elbow joint were excluded. Nor would there be any reason to expect that diseases which cause temporomandibular pain were excluded while diseases causing headaches or earaches were covered.

Certainly there was nothing special in Mrs. Ponder's situation which would alert her that *temporomandibular joint syndrome* was the sort of medical problem excluded from coverage under her Blue Cross policy. The initial diagnosis was made by a physician not a dentist. And this physician was treating her for symptoms related to her ears and head, not her teeth or gums. The physician, in turn, referred her to a hospital clinic not a dentist's office. A member of that clinic staff, who happened to be an oral surgeon but could have been a physician, diagnosed and treated her. Neither the symptoms she was experiencing, the diagnosis she might have heard or read, nor the treatments she received had anything to do with her teeth or gums. Rather they were all consistent with the kinds of diseases of the bones, muscles, and nerves an ordinary person might reasonably expect to be categorized as "medical" not "dental" and within the coverage of a normal health insurance policy, especially one designated as "a High Option Performance Plus Plan."

The *temporomandibular joint syndrome* exclusion appears under lettered subheading J within the category "General Limitations," which is section VI of the contract. It is conspicuous only in the sense that it contains the longest word in the entire body of the contract.[6] The page on which this brief exclusionary clause appears contains no less than 2,056 words, as well as 17 numbers and 54 letters designating headings and subheadings. This gives new meaning to the words "dense pack." True, this page cannot be characterized as a "sea of print" found objectionable in Schmidt v. Pacific Mutual Life Ins. Co., supra, 268 Cal.App.2d 735, 737, 74 Cal.Rptr. 367. But that is only because it has been divided into three "rivers of print" by channeling the 2,056 words, 17 numbers and 54 letters into three columns. The section on "Exclusions from Coverage" alone packs 923 words into its slightly more than one-third page.

This is not to say that every exclusion contained in this Blue Cross contract must fail because of the density of its verbiage. That factor alone would not be enough to render an exclusion inconspicuous. But it does place a special burden on Blue Cross to highlight exclusions which an ordinary insured might not expect to be in a health insurance contract. The contract is dotted with provisions in bold-face or all capitals. Generally these clauses address limitations or conditions on coverage which a policyholder might not anticipate. However, the *temporomandibular joint syndrome* exclusion is not accorded this treatment.

* * *

This does not mean policyholders need never read beyond the bold-faced subheadings on the paragraphs which exclude coverage. But we do suggest it is difficult to characterize as "conspicuous" an exclusion

6. One has to look to the partial listing of Relative Value Studies units to find two longer words, "dacryocyslorhinotomy" (20 letters) and "procto-sigmoioscopy" (18 letters), and one of equal length, "parathyroidectomy" (17 letters). No attempt is made to define an exclusion from coverage with these technical terms, however.

which is located under a subheading whose ordinary meaning does not encompass the condition purportedly excluded. * * * We are inclined to hold this exclusion invalid on the single ground it fails to meet the first test that it be "conspicuous." But there is an additional, more serious infirmity which is sufficient by itself to render the exclusion unenforceable against the Ponders.

* * *

An exclusion in an adhesion contract of insurance must be expressed in words which are "plain and clear." This means more than the traditional requirement that contract terms be "unambiguous." Precision is not enough. Understandability is also required. To be effective in this context, the exclusion must be couched in words which are part of the working vocabulary of average lay persons.

* * *

The test for a health insurance contract cannot be whether it is understood by physicians, dentists, or other health professionals. The terminology used must be comprehensible to the persons purchasing the insurance and expecting to receive the benefits they are paying for. Blue Cross is not targeting health professionals nor some highly educated segment of the population. Rather Blue Cross markets its standard policies to the general public. * * *

On its face, the clause excluding coverage for *temporomandibular joint syndrome* scarcely appears "comprehensible to lay persons." It is a technical medical term which has meaning primarily for health professionals. True, it might be argued that some technical medical terms have entered the common lexicon. Pneumonia, carcinoma, and hernia come to mind. But *temporomandibular joint syndrome* is not one of this select few. Indeed although the key word "temporomandibular" does appear among the 460,000 entries in the 2,752 pages of Webster's Third International Dictionary (1981), it is not mentioned among the over 100,000 entries and 1,000 pages of the more common college version of that dictionary. (Webster's New Collegiate Dictionary, 1980.) Nor does it appear among the over 100,000 entries in the more than 1,000 pages of The American Heritage Dictionary (2d ed., 1982) nor the 170,000 entries and 1,568 pages of the Random House College Dictionary (Revised Ed., 1982). A fortiori, this term is not one which ordinary human beings with average vocabularies can be held accountable to know.

Significantly, Blue Cross has chosen to define 21 words and phrases used in this contract. *Temporomandibular joint syndrome* is not one of these. Moreover, the contract provides plain language translations of other technical medical terms such as "blepharoplasty," "meloplasty," "mammoplasty" and even "surgery." But again *temporomandibular joint syndrome* is left undefined.

* * *

Respondent's counsel was asked at oral argument why this exclusion had not been expressed in plain English, comprehensible to the average policyholder. Counsel replied that temporomandibular joint syndrome embraced too many conditions to define in ordinary language, some of which were covered under the policy and some of which were not. This response only serves to highlight the term's failure to supply a "plain and clear" warning of what was excluded.

* * *

Admittedly, once a policyholder went to a physician or oral surgeon, she might be informed she had *temporomandibular joint syndrome* by the health professional familiar with this technical terminology. If clairvoyant or inherently suspicious, she might even think to reexamine the 5,750 words in her policy to determine whether that condition was covered.

* * *

Respondent's counsel was unable to cite, and we have been unable to locate, any cases suggesting health insurance policy holders are under some duty to check the policy language each time a new disease is diagnosed to determine whether it is indeed covered under the policy. Nor was counsel able to cite, nor have we been able to find, any cases holding the "plainness and clarity" of an exclusion are to be judged as of the time the disease is diagnosed rather than when the contract is executed.

We fully understand the absence of authority on both of these propositions. To adopt rules of this nature would turn every health insurance policy into a trap for the consumer. Coverage could be defined and exclusions stated in technical terms which held no meaning for the average citizen. Policyholders could only discover what they had bought with their premiums as their diseases were diagnosed and they found out, often to their sorrow, the true meaning of those mysterious words in their health insurance contracts.

* * *

The critical time for judging whether an exclusion is "plain and clear" is at the time the insured accepts the contract not when the incident triggering coverage first arises. There is nothing in the record on which this summary judgment was based indicating that anyone from Blue Cross attempted to explain the plain language meaning of *temporomandibular joint syndrome* to appellant or her husband before they accepted the contract. Nor is there any extrinsic evidence that either of them appreciated the meaning of the term at that time because of some special knowledge in their background.

* * *

We hold that the *temporomandibular joint syndrome* exclusion in the Blue Cross contract fails the *conspicuous* test because of its placement, its fine print and the density of the entire contract. Whether that alone would be sufficient to rule this exclusion ineffective we need not decide. Instead we hold this exclusion also fails the *plain and clear* test because the *undefined* technical terminology is not calculated to be part of the working vocabulary of average lay persons. This defect would have been sufficient by itself to invalidate the exclusion. Moreover, in combination, and under the circumstances of this case, these two infirmities are enough as a matter of law to render this clause ineffective to exclude coverage for the services rendered Mrs. Ponder in this case.

We diagnose the exclusion in this contract to suffer from "complexified occultation clause syndrome." That malady alone is fatal and thus we need not rule on other possible infirmities. Accordingly, we find it unnecessary to reach the question of whether the term *temporomandibular joint syndrome* is inherently ambiguous in the sense of being imprecise or whether its placement under the sub-heading "Dental Care" renders it ambiguous in that same sense.

* * *

The summary judgment in favor of respondent Blue Cross is reversed. The action is remanded for further proceedings consistent with this opinion.

### *Notes*

1. "Plain and clear" meaning problems are not limited to technical or medical language. Consider whether the use of the word "nil" in a policy plainly and clearly meant that certain medical expense coverage was omitted. See Read v. Western Farm Bureau Mutual Insurance Co., 90 N.M. 369, 563 P.2d 1162 (App.1977). If "nil" fails the "plain and clear" test because it is a word not ordinarily used in common speech, then does it follow *a fortiori* "temporomandibular joint syndrome" fails the test? See Ponder, 145 Cal. App.3d at 725, 193 Cal.Rptr. at 642. [omitted from the main case]

2. *A Duty To Explain?* In the course of the *Ponder* opinion it is stated that "there is nothing in the record * * * indicating that anyone from Blue Cross attempted to explain the plain language meaning of temporomandibular joint syndrome to appellant or her husband before they accepted the contract." Is this a suggestion that an insurer has an affirmative duty to sit down and explain the existence and meaning of all coverage provisions that might conceivably escape the comprehension of the applicant? Such a proposal appears from time to time in the cases and on one occasion at least has received a short-lived judicial sanction. In 1974, an intermediate appellate court laid down the following rule in Hionis v. Northern Mutual Ins. Co., 230 Pa.Super. 511, 327 A.2d 363:

> "Even where a policy is written in unambiguous terms, the burden of establishing the applicability of the exclusion or limitation involves proof that the insured was aware of the exclusion or limitation and that the effect thereof was explained to him."

Numerous decisions are to be found following the "Hionis Rule," but reservations and doubts also began surfacing as to the practical application as well as the unfairness of this allocation of an essentially unsustainable burden of proof—although the "Hionis Rule" did allow of two exceptions: (1) where the parties were of equal bargaining power and (2) where the facts demonstrated that the insured clearly understood the terms of the exclusion independent of any explanation offered by the insurer.

The doubts became discredit (or the blinds were drawn) in Standard Venetian Blind Co. v. American Empire Insurance Co., 503 Pa. 300, 469 A.2d 563 (1983). The Pennsylvania Supreme Court said (469 A.2d 563, 566–67):

> "Venetian maintains that this Court should adopt this language [of *Hionis* ] as a rule of insurance law, as the Superior Court has done here and in other cases decided since *Hionis*. See, e.g., Kelmo Enterprises, Inc. v. Commercial Union Ins. Co., 285 Pa.Super. 13, 426 A.2d 680 (1981); Klischer v. Nationwide Ins. Co., 281 Pa.Super. 292, 422 A.2d 175 (1980). See also Brokers Title Company, Inc. v. St. Paul Fire and Marine Ins. Co., 610 F.2d 1174 (3d Cir.1979).
>
> "We believe that the burden imposed by *Hionis* fails to accord proper significance to the written contract, which has historically been the true test of parties' intentions. By focusing on what was and was not said at the time of contract formation rather than on the parties' writing, *Hionis* makes the question of the scope of insurance coverage in any given case depend upon how a factfinder resolves questions of credibility. Such a process, apart from the obvious uncertainty of its results, unnecessarily delays the resolution of controversy, adding only unwanted costs to the cost of procuring insurance. Thus, *Hionis,* which would permit an insured to avoid the application of a clear and unambiguous limitation clause in an insurance contract, is not to be followed."

But see Tonkovic v. State Farm Mut. Auto. Ins. Co., 513 Pa. 445, 521 A.2d 920 (1987) a 5–2 decision in which the dissenters objected, in effect, that the blinds drawn in *Standard Venetian* were being set ajar.

## FOREMOST INSURANCE CO. v. PUTZIER [including Evel Knievel]

Supreme Court of Idaho, 1980.

100 Idaho 883, 606 P.2d 987.

DONALDSON, CHIEF JUSTICE.

This action arose in connection with the events surrounding the September 9, 1974 attempt by Robert C. Knievel, a/k/a Evel Knievel, to jump the Snake River Canyon near Twin Falls, Idaho on a jet powered motorcycle. As a prerequisite to his use of the land required for the event, Knievel and Snake River Enterprises, Inc. (the entity by which Knievel undertook the event) were required to secure a land use permit from the State of Idaho and a license from Twin Falls County.

* * *

[Both the State and the County permits required Knievel to obtain liability insurance under which the State and County would receive protection.]

* * *

For the purpose of obtaining the insurance required by the permit and license, Knievel's attorneys entered into negotiations with one Cardell Smith, a vice-president of the Fidelity Marketing Corporation insurance brokerage. * * * These negotiations culminated in the issuance by Foremost Insurance Company to Knievel and Enterprises of an insurance policy, which policy was later superseded by a second policy, effective August 28, 1974. Attached near the middle of the 29 separate pages of the second policy was an exclusion designated G332 which provided:

> "It is agreed that the insurance does not apply to bodily injury or property damage arising out of riot, civil commotion or mob action or out of any act or omission in connection with the prevention or suppression of any of the foregoing."

There was conflicting testimony as to whether this was read by or discussed with Knievel's attorneys.

Knievel attempted the jump September 4, 1974. During the preceding day or two, numerous unknown individuals damaged or destroyed the goods and equipment of Harold Putzier and Bob Crandall, each of whom was a concessionaire at the time. Putzier and Crandall filed an action against Knievel and Enterprises to recover compensation for their damages. [Foremost responded with a suit for declaratory judgment that the exclusion barred recovery on the policy.] The trial court held the exclusion valid in all respects; that the damage sustained by Putzier and Crandall fell within the exclusion, thereby relieving Foremost of liability for the damage. * * * We affirm.

The first issue presented is whether the trial court erred in finding the exclusion valid and applicable, thereby defeating appellants' claim of policy coverage. Appellants initially contend the parties entered into a valid contract for comprehensive general liability coverage prior to the issuance of the policy itself. In their view, the exclusion in the subsequently issued policy was at variance with the contract earlier negotiated, and therefore constituted a modification to which there was no agreement. Respondent Foremost agrees that a contract for liability coverage was negotiated by its agent and Knievel's attorneys. However, the parties are in sharp disagreement on the question whether the riot exclusion was at odds with the coverage for which Knievel bargained. Foremost contends, and the trial court found, that before August 28, 1979 [sic] (the effective date of the coverage), all exclusions, including the riot exclusion, were read to Knievel's attorney over the telephone and a general discussion was had concerning the athletic, medical malpractice, and pollution exclusions. A week later, a meeting was had between Foremost's agent and Knievel's attorneys. At this meeting, the insurance agent inquired of one of Knievel's attorneys whether he was familiar with the policy and whether there were any questions concerning it. Knievel's attorney advised that the policy had been reviewed and that he had no questions about it. Discussion was then had on the procedures to be used in processing claims covered by the policy. No dissatisfaction with the policy was expressed until after the event. Foremost's agent testified that the riot exclusion was common to comprehensive general liability policies written for special events, and that removal of the exclusion could be had only upon payment of an additional premium. Knievel's insurance expert testified on direct examination that a standard comprehensive general liability policy would not contain such an exclusion. However, it was brought out on cross-examination that he had never written such a policy and did not deal in the type of coverage involved here. Based on the evidence before it, the trial court concluded the written policy, together with the four exclusions attached thereto, accurately reflected the agreement of the parties. Nothing in the record compels a different conclusion here.

Appellants next attack the validity of the exclusion on the ground it was in contravention of the public policy of this state. They contend that by requiring Knievel to maintain "comprehensive public liability insurance" as a condition precedent to the validity of the temporary land use permit issued to him, the State of Idaho, through the Department of Lands, has articulated a policy which precludes recognition of the riot exclusion. We disagree. An agreement voluntarily made between competent persons is not lightly to be set aside on public policy grounds. Whether the contract is against public policy is to be determined from all the facts and circumstances of each case. Stearns v. Williams, 72 Idaho 276, 240 P.2d 833 (1952). In our view, the requirement of the land use permit that Knievel carry comprehensive public liability coverage falls far short of any declaration of public policy against exclusions for damage occasioned by riot, civil commotion, or mob action. Nor do we find the exclusion inimical to any articulable public interest. Accordingly, we decline to hold the exclusion void as against public policy.

It is next argued the doctrine of estoppel should be applied to prevent Foremost from raising the exclusion at all. However, the purpose of the doctrine in insurance cases is to enforce the contract as originally agreed upon by the parties, and not to write a new contract. Lewis v. Continental Life and Accident Co., 93 Idaho 348, 461 P.2d 243 (1969). As we pointed out above, the trial court found, on substantial and competent evidence, that Knievel's attorneys were made aware of the exclusion before the effective date of coverage, and made no comment or inquiry concerning it. From this, it was proper for the court to conclude the policy, with the exclusions, represented the agreement of the parties. The doctrine of estoppel is inapplicable here.

In a related argument, appellants contend the doctrine of reformation should be applied to write the exclusion out of the policy. However, reformation is inapplicable where, as here, the writing is a true expression of the parties' agreement. See Bilbao v. Krettinger, 91 Idaho 69, 415 P.2d 712 (1966).

Appellants also urge application of the doctrine of reasonable expectations. The thorn of Corgatelli v. Globe Life & Accident Ins. Co., 96 Idaho 616, 533 P.2d 737 (1975), which made the adoption of that doctrine in Idaho a debatable question, was recently removed from the side of our jurisprudence. Casey v. Highlands, 100 Idaho 505, 600 P.2d 1387 (1979), decided after this appeal was brought, expressly rejected the doctrine of reasonable expectations in favor of traditional contract rules of construction. We therefore reject appellants' contention that the doctrine of reasonable expectations should be applied here.

Appellants next contend the exclusion must fall because it was inconspicuous and ambiguous. Both contentions are without merit. We need not discuss the question whether the exclusion was inconspicuous, and if it was what effect such a determination would have, because Knievel's attorneys were expressly made aware of its existence prior to the effective date of the coverage. Nor do we find any basis for the contention that the language used in the exclusion is subject to more than a single, plain meaning.

Finally appellants contend respondent Foremost failed to carry its burden of proving the damage sustained was caused by activity specified in the exclusion. We disagree. In the absence of ambiguity, the words used in an insurance policy are to be given their plain, ordinary and popular meaning. * * * The trial court entered the following findings of fact concerning the activities here involved:

> "12. An estimated ten to fifteen thousand people congested at the jump site on September 7, 1975, and sometime after dark some of the people present knocked down a number of temporary toilets or 'outhouses' and others, riding motorcycles, jumped over the downed toilets. At about the same time several hundred of the people present surrounded a large semi-trailer, and members of the crowd broke into it and removed its contents, consisting of cases of beer, which was distributed and drunk by a great number of those present.
>
> "13. Shortly after the beer was removed from the semi-trailer referred [to] in Finding [12], the crowd moved over to another large semi-trailer, surrounded it, and members of the crowd broke a hole through its roof and removed its contents, consisting of beer, watermelons, cantaloupes and meat, which was distributed to the people congregated thereabouts."

* * * [W]e conclude, as did the trial court, that the damages sustained by appellants Putzier and Crandall were caused by persons who formed or were part of a mob and arose out of civil commotion or mob action.

* * *

The judgment of the trial court is affirmed. Costs to respondent.

## FOREMOST INSURANCE CO. v. PUTZIER [including Antonio Guanche]

Supreme Court of Idaho, 1981.
102 Idaho 138, 627 P.2d 317.

BISTLINE, JUSTICE.

Antonio Guanche was named as a defendant in Civil Action No. 27353, Fifth Judicial District of the State of Idaho, which action produced two other appeals in addition to this. Those other two appeals, which were consolidated, were decided in Foremost Insurance Co. v. Putzier, 100 Idaho 883, 606 P.2d 987 (1980). In that opinion this Court upheld the trial court's determination as to the extent of *liability* coverage under the Foremost policy.

This appeal was taken by Foremost from the trial court's decision that Foremost is liable to Antonio Guanche, as a first party insured. The relationship of Foremost and Guanche is well stated in the trial court's findings of fact:

> "Insofar as the issues framed by the complaint and defendant Guanche's answer to that complaint are involved in these proceedings, the following additional findings and conclusions are made.
>
> "14. The defendant Antonio R. Guanche speaks English in a heavy French–Italian dialect, which makes communication in the English language difficult between Guanche and third parties. At all times material to this proceeding he was engaged as a chef and entrepreneur. He had permission of the defendant Snake River Canyon Enterprises to erect a food stand on the premises to be used in selling food and drink to the spectators attending the public spectacle. He was told by one Veccio, an agent of the defendants Knievel and Snake River Canyon Enterprises, that he was required to have insurance before he began the operation of his food concession, and that it was obtainable through the plaintiff. [Foremost]
>
> "15. Sometime prior to August 28, 1977 [sic], the defendant Guanche delivered his check in the amount of $300 to Cardell W. Smith in return for insurance coverage. Guanche's $300 was accepted by Smith on behalf of the plaintiff, and Smith told Guanche that he was 'covered.' The record will not support any finding that Guanche ever advised plaintiff of the type or kind of insurance he desired, nor will it support a find that Guanche was ever advised by plaintiff as to the specific insurance coverage his $300 was purchasing. He has never been provided with any insurance policy. He has not read any insurance policy purporting to evidence his insurance contract with the plaintiff. He simply paid his money and was told that he was 'covered.'
>
> "16. *The defendant Guanche intended to insure his property against loss caused by theft* or the elements, *and* at all times material to this action *believed that* upon payment of $300 to the

plaintiff *the property* located at the jump site in which he had an interest *was insured* by plaintiff *against loss by theft,* fire or other calamity. *This belief was a reasonable belief under the facts in this case.*

"17. Sometime prior to September 7, 1974, the defendant Guanche had purchased, and had delivered to the jump site, a large truckload of provisions consisting of beer, melons, meat and ice cream. The activity described in Finding 13 involved property owned by the defendant Guanche.[24] (Emphasis added.)

The trial court entered the following conclusions of law:

"F When the plaintiff accepted a premium from Guanche, it had a duty to provide him with the insurance policy or advise Guanche in detail of the risks it was assuming in return for the premium. Failure to do so makes Guanche's intentions and expectations paramount in interpreting the terms of any insurance contract existing between Guanche and the plaintiff.

"G *Under the theories expounded in* Corgatelli v. Globe Insurance, 96 Idaho 616 [533 P.2d 737], *a valid contract of insurance existed* between the plaintiff and the defendant Guanche, supported by ample consideration, *which provided Guanche with first party coverage* for loss of and damage to property in which Guanche had an interest, and which was located at the jump site between August 28, 1974 and September 10, 1974." (Emphasis added) * * *

"It is, therefore, ORDERED, ADJUDGED and DECREED that the defendant Antonio R. Guanche recover from the plaintiff Foremost Insurance Company $29,979.63 damages, together with his costs taxed at $3,746.10, and that the claims of Foremost against Guanche and Guanche against Foremost be severed from this action and the remainder of the case be proceeded with according to law."

* * *

On appeal Foremost challenges (1) the finding of the trial court that Guanche intended to and believed he had purchased first party coverage, and that this belief was reasonable, and (2) the legal theory of the doctrine of reasonable expectations, thought to have been utilized by the trial court.

We note at the outset that the doctrine of reasonable expectations has since been declared not to be the law in Idaho. Foremost Insurance Co. v. Putzier, 100 Idaho 883, 606 P.2d 987 (1980); Casey v. Highlands Insurance Co., 100 Idaho 505, 600 P.2d 1387 (1980). Rather, where there is an ambiguity in an insurance contract, special rules of construc-

24. Finding No. 13:

"Shortly after the beer was removed from the semi-trailer referred to in Finding 11, the crowd moved over to another large semi-trailer, surrounded it, and members of the crowd broke a hole through its roof and removed its contents, consisting of beer, watermelons, cantaloupes and meat, which was distributed to the people congregated thereabouts."

tion apply to protect the insured. Casey v. Highlands, supra. Under these special rules, insurance policies are to be construed most liberally in favor of recovery, with all ambiguities being resolved in favor of the insured. Abbie Uriguen Oldsmobile Buick, Inc. v. United States Fire Insurance Co., 95 Idaho 501, 511 P.2d 783 (1973). "Where language may be given two meanings, one of which permits recovery and the other does not, it is to be given the construction most favorable to the insured." Shields v. Hiram C. Gardner, Inc., 92 Idaho 423, 427, 444 P.2d 38, 42 (1968). Accord, Erikson v. Nationwide Mutual Insurance Co., 97 Idaho 288, 543 P.2d 841 (1975).

Moreover, although the doctrine of reasonable expectations is not the law in Idaho, there is the closely analogous rule of contract construction pointed out by Justice Donaldson in his opinion in Corgatelli v. Globe Life & Accident Co., 96 Idaho 616, 533 P.2d 737 (1975)[25] wherein, citing Shields v. Hiram C. Gardner, Inc., supra, he wrote:

> "*[t]he doctrine of probability or reasonableness has long been a rule of construction geared toward ascertaining intent in situations of ambiguity. The standard to be applied is what a reasonable person* in the position of the insured *would have understood* the language to mean." 96 Idaho at 622, 533 P.2d at 743. (Donaldson, J., dissenting.) (Emphasis added.)

Under this rule of construction, which utilizes an objective standard and which is used in the case of ambiguously written insurance policies, to effectuate the intent of the parties, the test is what a reasonable person in the position of the insured would have understood the language of the contract to mean. This test is not necessarily conclusive as to the intent of the parties, but is only one rule of construction to be considered in construing an ambiguous contract. This standard is, of course, in accord with the general rule of construing insurance contracts against those who write them. See, e.g., Dunford v. United of Omaha, 95 Idaho 282, 506 P.2d 1355 (1973).[26]

In the present case, however, we are faced with the unusual situation where Guanche was never given a policy at all; he had an insurance transaction wherein he was simply told by an agent of Foremost that, in exchange for $300, he was "covered." This is not a case where the insured challenges the terms of the written policy as being ambiguous, but rather a case where he relies upon the oral binder or contract made by the agent. Under these unique facts, we must recognize this transaction as creating a patently ambiguous oral contract of insurance.* It was Foremost's responsibility to provide Guanche with a copy of the policy which it believed it was selling to him, I.C. § 41-1824. By not

**25.** The rationale of this opinion was adopted by the Court in Casey v. Highlands, 100 Idaho 505, 600 P.2d 1387 (1979).

**26.** Under the doctrine of reasonable expectations, on the other hand, the controlling test is a purely subjective one as to what the insured believed he was purchasing, with the only restraint being that that belief be reasonable.

* [Editors' footnote: The editors considered requesting a copy of the oral contract to determine whether the ambiguity might be latent rather than patent—but decided, prudently, against it.]

delivering that contract or informing Guanche of its terms Foremost must be bound by the terms of the oral contract. We simply apply the above rules of construction to this oral transaction without regard to the terms of the actual written policy.

This Court was faced with an analogous problem in Toevs v. Western Farm Bureau Life Insurance Co., 94 Idaho 151, 483 P.2d 682 (1971). In that case, a purchaser paid the initial premium on a life insurance policy but died before having had the required physical examination. His widow testified, and the court so found, that there was no discussion as to the date the policy would become effective, and that she expected that it was effective immediately.

> "In view of this finding [that the agent did not explain or discuss the effective date of the policy], the unequal bargaining power of the two parties, the complex legalistic and ambiguous phrasing used throughout the contract, and the use by the insurance company of the procedure or device known as 'conditional premium receipt,' this Court holds that a contract of insurance was in existence on the date that the insured died. By this holding the Supreme Court of Idaho is subscribing to the theory known as 'temporary contract of insurance.' The conditional premium receipt created a temporary contract of insurance subject to a condition, i.e., rejection of Toevs' application by the insurance company. Since rejection did not occur prior to Toevs' death, the company is liable." 94 Idaho at 155, 483 P.2d at 686.

In that case, the fact that the agent did not tell the purchaser that he would not be covered until he had undergone the physical exam was one of the factors considered by the Court in holding that the insured was covered in spite of the provision in the policy to the contrary.

In the present case, as in *Toevs,* the agent did not tell Guanche of any limitations in his coverage. Further, there could be no more unequal bargaining situation than the present one where Foremost took Guanche's money and never even told (or asked) him what he had purchased. Foremost could easily have told Guanche what he was purchasing, but it did not. As stated in Roeske v. Diefenbach, 75 Wis.2d 253, 249 N.W.2d 555, 559 (1977), in regard to an oral contract of insurance, "[i]f insurers desire to incorporate the provisions of their usual policies that are in derogation of the rights of the insured, such provisions must be specifically brought to the attention of the person seeking insurance at the time of the oral agreement." It is the duty of the insurer to inform the insured of what he is obtaining; it is not the duty of the insured to seek out exclusions and limitations not revealed to him. Where an insurance company, or its agent, accepts a premium as was done here, without explaining at all what was being sold, the company does so at the risk of being bound by what a reasonable person in the position of the insured would have understood. We will not look to the terms of an unmentioned, undelivered written policy to defeat coverage in the absence of any attempt by the insurer at explaining to the insured the coverage with which he was being provided.

* * *

[W]e find it unnecessary on our part to pin down with exactitude which of the many theories, all of which have application to varying degrees, brought the trial court to its ultimate conclusion. This Court has many times stated that it will affirm on a correct legal theory utilizing the trial court's findings where those findings are substantiated. * * * Applying the standard rules of construction for insurance contracts (to which we add insurance transactions) that all ambiguities are to be resolved against the insurer, and that what a reasonable person in the position of the insured would have believed to be the meaning of the language used is the standard to be used in resolving ambiguities—we are not persuaded that the trial court erred in concluding that Guanche had first party coverage protecting him against the losses which he sustained.

The judgment is affirmed, with costs, including I.C. § 41–1839 attorney fees, to respondent.

* * *

BAKES, CHIEF JUSTICE, dissenting:

* * *

The majority fails to discuss some of the more salient facts of this case. State and county licensing authorities had required Knievel and Snake River Canyon Enterprises to obtain liability insurance covering the event in question. First party coverage was not required. Representatives of Foremost, Knievel and Snake River Canyon Enterprises then negotiated the same insurance policy at issue in both this appeal and in Foremost Insurance Co. v. Putzier, 100 Idaho 883, 606 P.2d 987 (1980). Foremost was informed that some of Knievel's concessionaires might be added as additional insureds on the policy.

Representatives of Knievel and Snake River Canyon Enterprises in turn informed Guanche that he, too, would need insurance. There is no indication that Guanche would have purchased any insurance but for the fact that Snake River Canyon Enterprises required it. Guanche testified that he was too busy to "take care of insurance," and that he thought representatives of Knievel and Snake River Canyon Enterprises would "take care" of him. They did. He was made an additional insured on Snake River Canyon Enterprises' liability policy.

Guanche's testimony does demonstrate that he thought he was "fully" covered. When asked who had informed him that he had "full" coverage, he answered that it was the representatives of Knievel and Snake River Canyon Enterprises, and not any agent of Foremost.

Guanche did testify that Foremost's agent informed him that he was "covered," although Guanche never asked the agent what for.[27]

The entire transaction is summarized neatly in Guanche's amended counterclaim.

> "Guanche contracted with Snake River Canyon Enterprises, Inc., to provide food and beverage concessions * * * and as a part of said contract, *was required to maintain certain liability insurance in force. Guanche contacted Foremost Insurance Company and asked to have the required insurance coverage provided.* Foremost agreed to provide the coverage and merely added Guanche's name as an additional named insured to the policy of insurance described in the Complaint." (Emphasis added.)

Finally, it is clear, although the majority refuses to recognize it, that the court below based its decision squarely upon the now discredited doctrine of reasonable expectations.[28] In Finding of Fact 16, the trial court stated that Guanche "intended" to insure his property; that he "believed" he had first party coverage; and that such belief was "reasonable * * * under the facts in this case." On the basis of these "facts" and the "theories expounded in Corgatelli v. Globe Insurance," the trial court concluded that there did indeed exist a contract for first party coverage between Foremost and Guanche. In so concluding the trial court held as a matter of law that "Guanche's intentions and expectations [are] paramount in interpreting the terms of any insurance contract existing between Guanche and [Foremost]."

The above legal conclusion was erroneous, the doctrine of reasonable expectations having been "expressly rejected * * * in favor of traditional contract rules of construction." Foremost Ins. Co. v. Putzier, 100 Idaho at 888, 606 P.2d at 992. That being the case, we ought to reverse and remand the case for a new trial in order to give the lower court an opportunity to correct its legal error. But in no event should this Court decide the case on a legal theory not even asserted by Guanche, and then

27. What are, I wonder, the outer limits of Guanche's oral contract for insurance "coverage"? If a Mrs. Guanche was blessed with a child during Knievel's jump, could Guanche recover maternity benefits? How about life insurance for any children, or Guanche's horse? I think the limits of Guanche's coverage should be established, not by his secret and unexpressed desires, but by the context in which the insurance was obtained. Thus, the trial court should consider the probability that Guanche intended to procure, and Foremost intended to sell, only that coverage which satisfied the county's requirements, which did *not* include first party coverage.

28. The majority quotes some language from the *Corgatelli* dissent in support of its assertion that an ambiguous insurance contract should be construed in accordance with the understandings of a reasonable person in the position of the insured. The majority failed to quote the preceding sentence in the *Corgatelli* dissent. "If the meaning of the contract is in doubt, it must be construed in the sense in which the insurer believed, at the time of making, the insured understood the terms." Corgatelli v. Globe Life & Accident Co., 96 Idaho 616, 622, 533 P.2d 737, 743 (1975) (Donaldson, J., dissenting). If that standard were applied to the instant case, there could be no doubt as to the end result. In Guanche's case, Foremost was merely adding an additional insured to a negotiated special policy of liability coverage. Any reasonable insurance agent would be mildly astonished to discover that Guanche's unexpressed desires would ripen into first party coverage.

make an appellate finding of fact that there was an oral contract of first party insurance. There is no evidence to sustain such an appellate finding, and it is directly contrary to the trial court's express finding that Guanche never "advised [Foremost] of the type or kind of insurance he desired * * *." I would reverse.

### *Note*

Interpretation is, of course, an enduring problem. Possibly the last generation's choice of words, thought then to be clear and simple, pass before the eyes of this generation's judges in muddy swirls. Nothing is clearer than that "readability" ought to be promoted, desperate a hope as this may hold out. One Rudolph Franz Flesch sought to help with his book Testing Readibility (1951). See Skarlat commenting on readability in 21 For the Defense (1980). Promoting "readibility" to a statutory mandate ought to do the job, ought it not?

Massachusetts General Laws Annotated

Chapter 175.

**§ 2B. Readibility of policy form; definition; approval; actions based on language**

1. No policy form of insurance shall be delivered or issued for delivery to more than fifty policyholders in the commonwealth until a copy of the policy form has been on file for thirty days with the commissioner, unless before the expiration of said thirty days the commissioner shall have approved the form of the policy in writing as complying with this section; nor shall any such policy be delivered or issued for delivery if the commissioner notifies the company in writing within said thirty days that in his opinion the form of said policy does not comply with the provisions of this section, specifying the reasons for his opinion, provided that such action of the commissioner shall be subject to review by the supreme judicial court, but during any such review the form shall not be delivered or issued for delivery in the commonwealth; nor shall any such policy form be so delivered or issued for delivery unless:

(a) The text achieves a minimum Flesch scale readibility score of fifty;

(b) It is printed, except for tables, in not less than ten point type, one point leaded.

(c) The style, arrangement and overall appearance of the policy give no undue prominence to any portion of the text of the policy and any endorsements or riders;

(d) It contains a table of contents or an alphabetical subject index;

(e) The width of margins and ink to paper contrast do not unreasonably interfere with the readability of the form; and

(f) The organization of the content of the policy and the summary of the policy is conducive to understandability of the form.

Nothing in this section shall be construed to require the affirmative approval of the commissioner before issuance of a policy form which has been on file for at least thirty days.

For the purposes of this section, a Flesch scale readability score shall be measured as hereinafter provided:

(1) For policy forms containing ten thousand words or less of text, the entire form shall be analyzed. For policy forms containing more than ten thousand words, the readability of two two hundred word samples per page may be analyzed in lieu of the entire form. The samples shall be separated by at least twenty printed lines.

(2)(a)(i) The number of words and sentences in the text shall be counted and the total number of words divided by the total number of sentences. The figure obtained shall be multiplied by a factor of 1.015.

(ii) The total number of syllables shall be counted and divided by the total number of words. The figure obtained shall be multiplied by a factor of 84.6.

(iii) The sum of the figures computed under subclause (i) and subclause (ii) subtracted from 206.835 equals the Flesch scale readability score for the policy form.

(b) For the purposes of clause (a) the following procedures shall be used:

(i) A contraction, hyphenated word, or numbers and letters, when separated by spaces, shall be counted as one word;

(ii) A unit of words ending with a period, semicolon, or colon, but excluding headings and captions shall be counted as a sentence; and

(iii) A syllable means a unit of spoken language consisting of one or more letters of a word as divided by an accepted dictionary. Where the dictionary shows two or more equally acceptable pronunciations of a word, the pronunciation containing fewer syllables may be used.

Every policy form filed with the commissioner under this section shall be accompanied by a certificate stating the Flesch scale readability score achieved by such form.

The term "text" as used in this section shall include all printed matter except the name and address of the insurer, name or title of the policy, the brief description if any, captions and subcaptions, and schedule pages and tables.

The commissioner may, after notice and hearing, designate other readability tests as acceptable alternative tests to the Flesch scale readability analysis if he finds that any other such tests are equivalent in function, result and understandability. This section shall apply to any domestic or foreign company, whether licensed or unlicensed by the commissioner to do business in the commonwealth.

2. For the purposes of this section the words policy form shall include, in addition to all policy forms of insurance, all certificates and subscription agreements or contracts of insurance issued pursuant to chapters one hundred and seventy-six, one hundred and seventy-six A, one hundred and seventy-six B and one hundred and seventy-six G, but shall not include any form for casualty or property insurance which is issued to insure a business,

professional or governmental operation or any form for life insurance, accident or health insurance, or annuities, (a) which is a security subject to federal jurisdiction, (b) which is issued in connection with any employee benefit plan which is either subject to Title I of the Employee Retirement Income Security Act of 1974, 29 United States Code, sections 1002 to 1144, inclusive, or described in 26 United States Code, sections 79, 105, 125, 401, 403(a) or 409A of the Internal Revenue Code, (c) which conforms to the requirements of 26 United States Code, sections 403(b), 408 or 457 of said Code, or (d) which is a form used in connection with, as a conversion form, or in exchange for a policy form approved or deemed approved prior to the date such forms must be approved under this section; policyholder shall include, in addition to all insurance policyholders, all subscribers and holders of certificates issued pursuant to chapters one hundred and seventy-six, one hundred and seventy-six A, one hundred and seventy-six B and one hundred and seventy-six G.

3. Where the requirements of this section are met, the commissioner may approve such policy form for use in the commonwealth notwithstanding those provisions of any other laws which specify the content of insurance policies, provided the approved policy assures to the policyholders and claimants protection no less favorable than they would be entitled to under such other law.

In any action brought by a policyholder or claimant arising out of a policy form approved pursuant to this section, the policyholder or claimant may base such an action on either or both the substantive language prescribed by such other statute or the wording of the approved policy form.

# Chapter 3

# NEGOTIATING THE INSURANCE CONTRACT

## A. FORMALITIES OF CONTRACT MAKING

### STEPS IN THE NEGOTIATION OF INDIVIDUAL POLICIES

Simply for the purposes of early familiarization, it is important at this time to give a rough outline of important steps in the negotiation of an insurance contract and some of the papers used to make a record thereof. More detailed coverage may be found in the portions of the book dealing with insurance of the person, property insurance and liability insurance.

(1) the *application* (sometimes "the app") made by the prospective insured. Previous to this, it's likely that there will have been some solicitation by an agent of the insurer. Applications are normally in writing and they will contain representations by the prospective insured which may later surface as alleged misrepresentations. The agent may also make the entries on a form application for the applicant or he may inform the prospective insured about the meaning of requests for information contained in the form. Or he may say the information is unimportant. This may later surface in the form of an asserted "waiver and estoppel". Applications yield litigation in most lines of insurance but perhaps no more colorfully than in life insurance cases.

(2) *a "binder"*. The agent may have the power or appear to have the power to bind the insurer immediately upon application to a policy obligation, the formal papers constituting the policy to follow at a later date. This may leave room for speculation as to what the policy provisions were intended to be. The binder may be oral or evidenced by a memorandum sent by the agent to the insured. In life insurance cases under so-called "conditional receipts," some special problems arise.

(3) *insurance company evaluation.* When the effectiveness of the policy is conditioned in any way on insurer "headquarters" approval, the company has an opportunity to check the application and use such means as it has to validate it. That may include an applicant's driving record (auto liability insurance), condition or use of the property (proper-

ty insurance), medical history (life and health insurance). Available information extrinsic to the application (including public records, computer data banks) may be of assistance to the insurer.

(4) *issuance of the policy.* The day of issuance or "effective date" is sometimes hard to ascertain (see the materials on insurance of the person, infra), but whatever the precise date, issuance of the policy means its establishment as an obligation of the insurer. The *documents evidencing the insurer's obligation* are complex and prolix and contain much fine print ("what the front page giveth, the back page taketh away"). Most of these documents are forms. The discussion of their terms and conditions will be a major part of the insurance law course based on this or any book. We have already looked at some of the principles of legal construction.

### *Note*
### *Methods of Marketing Insurance*

Insurance is variously solicited or sold by mail, by direct sales by employees of the insurance company, through independent agents, through brokers, or even machines. The legal problems associated with the negotiation and consummation of the insurance transaction necessarily center upon the actual or ostensible authority of the person (however described in lay terms) at the point of contact with the customer. Some such persons can conclude the contract and bind the company on the spot. Others may only be authorized to winkle an offer out of the applicant which will be transmitted upward to, say, vice presidents specifically authorized to countersign the acceptance. For purposes of dealing with the principles of "waiver" and "estoppel" (or "election") resort must be had to the legal rules of Agency, which in turn require a general comprehension of methods of marketing various forms of insurance. A standard textbook * on the general subject affords illuminating information:

> **Property and Liability Insurance.** Most types of property and liability insurance are regularly sold through general insurance agents. * * *
>
> A general insurance agent usually has authority, within specified limits, to make and modify contracts of insurance and to receive notices on behalf of his principal, and he may be given authority, formally or informally, to settle losses of small amounts.
>
> Typically, the general insurance agent handles all financial transactions with the insured, billing and collecting premiums and extending credit. He reports monthly to his insurers, who have no direct contact with the insured except, but not always, in the adjustment of losses. Following the success of many direct writers and exclusive-agency insurers whose representatives serve mostly to make the original sale, an increasing number of independent-agency insurers have turned to

* Mowbray, Blanchard and Williams, *Insurance, Its Theory and Practice in the United States,* 6th ed., 1979. Reprint edition. Printed and Published by Robert E. Krieger Publishing Co. Inc., New York.  [The above extracts have been abridged and the sequence slightly changed. Reprinted with permission.]

policy writing by the insurer and to *direct billing* and *automatic renewal,* with the insurer taking over the financial relationship, crediting the agent with commission at a lower rate than formerly. Insurers are seeking economy and identification by these practices; agents have tended to oppose these changes because of the expected weakening, under these practices, of their personal relationship with the insured.

**Life Insurance.** In life insurance the agent is primarily a salesman equipped with a rate book showing the rates, surrender values, and other features of policies issued by his company, as well as sample policies and application blanks. These correspond, respectively, to the price lists, samples, and order blanks of a merchandise salesman. The agent is expected diligently to canvass his field for his insurer, usually devoting his entire time to it, and canvassing only the type of person covered by his instructions. He is paid by a commission on the premiums for policies issued upon applications secured by him. The policy is sent to him for delivery, and his powers are limited to securing the application, delivering the policy, and collecting the premium. He cannot bind the company on the acceptance of risks or the settlement of losses. However, if the insured pays the premium at the time he submits his application, the agent can issue the binding receipt described in [Collister v. Nationwide Life Insurance Co. reprinted in Part C].

While his primary function is that of salesman, the life-insurance agent is becoming more and more an adviser to his clients.

Many life-insurance companies insist on full-time exclusive representation and will accept business only from agents who conform to this requirement. Others accept business freely from general insurance agents and brokers doing a general business (who for this purpose are generally licensed as agents).

**Health Insurance.** Health insurance is sold by specializing agents, by general insurance agents, by life-insurance agents, and, to a considerable extent, by mail. With life-insurance companies increasing their activities in this field, greater interest in it is being shown by their agents. Life insurance and health insurance are complementary, since both are primarily concerned with the problems of the individual and his family.

## GROUP-INSURANCE MARKETING

Group life * and health insurance underwritten by commercial insurers is sold by commissioned agents and brokers, with agents selling

* [Editor's Footnote]

According to the Life Insurance Fact Book for 1990 Group Life Insurance in force in 1989 totalled $3,469.5 billion. By comparison Ordinary Life Insurance in force in 1989 totalled $4,940.0 billion.

The remaining comparatively small volume of life insurance reported in the Fact Book is taken up by Credit Life Insurance and so-called Home Service Life Insurance (the latter consisting in small individually marketed policies serviced by agents calling at home weekly or monthly to collect the premiums. It includes the traditional working man's Industrial Life Insurance together with a more recent form called Monthly Debt ordinary).

Not included in the statistics are the death benefits potentially payable under ac-

the most contracts and brokers accounting for the most premium dollars because they tend to specialize in large accounts. These agents and brokers, however, receive considerable technical assistance from salaried insurer group representatives and other specialists in selling, installing, and servicing the plan. * * * Blue Cross plans, Blue Shield plans, and most independent plans are usually marketed by salaried employees.

Group property and liability insurance * * * currently accounts for considerably less than 10 per cent of the total property-and-liability-insurance premium volume and it has only recently become a topic of major concern. In a recent comprehensive study of group property and liability insurance, Dr. James Chastain cited several reasons why the group concept has developed much less rapidly in this field than in life and health insurance.[31] Because the employer is the source of income payments interrupted by poor health, death, or retirement, he feels obligated to provide some protection against these perils, but he feels no similar obligation with respect to potential property or liability losses. Pressures to compete with the expanding social-insurance system have likewise been limited to potential losses caused by poor health, death, or retirement. Until recently property-and-liability insurers have had much less need for alternative marketing channels, primarily because it is easier to sell the need for adequate property and liability insurance than for life and health insurance. Agents selling individual insurance are more prone to resist group property and liability insurance than group life and health insurance[32] because the market for property and liability insurance is more nearly saturated and because group coverages are more likely to eliminate the need for any individual coverages. Because of this near saturation, public pressures for a new marketing channel are also small. Post-sales servicing needs are greater under property and liability insurance because of more difficult loss adjustments and changing exposures. In addition to other effects, this post-sales servicing makes the choice of the insurer more important to the group member and may reduce his interest in a particular group. The tighter rate regulation applicable to property and liability insurance, has also been a retarding factor. Most state insurance departments are opposed in principle to group property and liability insurance because, among other things, they believe that it discriminates unfairly against nongroup members and the higher-quality members of the group, threatens the present marketing system—the destruction of which would be against the public interest—would create a chaotic rating system, and would lead to insolvencies. Finally, the tax incentives that have made group life and health insurance an attractive fringe benefit are not applicable to group property and liability insurance.

cident policies, nor such benefits which may accrue to survivors of pensioners, etc.

**31.** James J. Chastain, "An Evaluation of Group Property Insurance." See also J.J. Chastain, "Group Property and Liability Insurance," chap. 39 in R.D. Eilers and R.M. Crowe (eds.), "Group Insurance Handbook."

**32.** Group life and health insurance, however, was also violently opposed by several groups before it became commonplace. Its extension beyond certain limits is still opposed, particularly by agents selling individual insurance, but also by others who are concerned about possible unsound underwriting.

Nevertheless, ways have been found to write group property and liability insurance or related plans, and the demand for this coverage has increased. Intense competition in recent years has increased insurer interest in alternative marketing channels.

* * *

### *Note on Lloyd's of London*

Most people interested in insurance law sooner or later become interested in "Lloyd's of London" and the way brokers conduct business in that venerable institution. In a case (with an almost symbolic name) called Edinburgh Assurance Co. v. R.L. Burns Corp., 479 F.Supp. 138, 144–46 (D.C.Cal.1979), the court provided an enlightening discussion:

*The London Insurance Market*

The parties have contested whether Emett & Chandler in Los Angeles and Hogg Robinson in London were agents of the insurers or the insured for various purposes, viz., issuance and delivery of the policies, and the inclusion of a service of suit clause. This court must also examine the contract formation process to ascertain the intent of the parties as to the scope of coverage. These questions require examination of the custom and practice of the unique insurance market at Lloyd's of London and the London insurance market generally.

Lloyd's was originally an association of underwriters in London with a management committee. It was incorporated in 1871 by an Act of Parliament. The Corporation of Lloyd's provides a physical site for the sale of insurance by underwriters that are members of the Corporation, together with support and incidental services to member underwriters. Lloyd's corporate committee, elected by members from among their number, administers matters of common interest to members.

The Corporation of Lloyd's never sells insurance itself and is not at risk on the insurance sold on the floor at Lloyd's. Rather, the underwriter members subscribe to cover all or part of a proposed placement of insurance, at their own election. Numbers of individual underwriters, many in England but others scattered throughout the world, have joined together to form syndicates. Syndicates may have anywhere from two or three to hundreds of members. The individual members are known as the "names" on that syndicate. These syndicates are the entities which subscribe on behalf of their members to cover risks and percentage parts of risks. The actual potential liability of a given name depends upon his percentage share of the syndicate of which he is a member, as well as the percentage of the risk to which his syndicate has subscribed.

Purchase and sale of insurance takes place on the floor of the underwriting room at Lloyd's and also in the offices of individual insurance companies in London. The underwriting market at Lloyd's consists of the syndicates; a syndicate or group of syndicates is in turn managed by an underwriting agency. An underwriting agency employs a management staff, and maintains a box on the floor at Lloyd's with a representative. This representative is an underwriter, who evaluates, negotiates, and decides on proposed placements of insurance brought by brokers for the consideration of the syndicate or syndicates he represents. The underwriting agent contracts for the liability of his syndicate or syndicates, and assumes no risk himself except insofar as he is a name himself on the syndicate.

The recognized custom and usage of the London insurance market is that the broker is the agent of the potential assured for most purposes, including the placement of insurance. The potential assured is recognized as the broker's client. The recognized role of the broker is to obtain the best possible terms and quotation he can from the market for his client. In addition, the brokers in the London insurance market generally serve as coordinators of all parts of the insurance, negotiation, placement, claims presentation, and sometimes payment. Only brokers who have been approved by the Committee of Lloyd's are permitted to place risks with Lloyd's underwriters. Such brokers are known as "Lloyd's brokers." Because an applicant for insurance from Lloyd's must act through a Lloyd's broker, there will often be at least one other broker in the picture. An applicant for insurance may deal with an outside broker not a Lloyd's broker, who then must contact a Lloyd's broker. In the instant case, the applicant API used the services of Emett & Chandler in Los Angeles to arrange the insurance transaction through Hogg Robinson, a Lloyd's broker in London.

The underwriter agent, or underwriter, sits at his box on the floor waiting for brokers to approach him with possible insurance risks. The broker provides for the underwriter's consideration a document known as a broker's slip, which contains the details of the risk which the broker is trying to insure. The broker negotiates with the underwriter to obtain the latter's agreement to both the insurance terms and the rate of premium. The underwriter who structures the transaction with the broker and settles on terms becomes known as the lead underwriter. The lead underwriter's syndicate is called the market lead or leader of the market for that particular risk. The lead underwriter then subscribes his syndicate to a particular percentage of the risk, for example, five percent. The underwriter places his initials on the broker's slip together with the particular percentage to which he is subscribing. By placing his initials on the slip, the underwriter considers that he has created an insurance contract between the individual members of the syndicate and the insured.

The broker, having obtained the agreement of one underwriter to terms and premium, as well as a subscription to a percentage of the risk, retains the slip and approaches other syndicates or insurance companies both on the floor at Lloyd's and in the outside offices of insurance companies. The broker presents the slip to them for them to consider whether they desire to subscribe to the agreement as constituted between the broker and the lead underwriter. Each subsequent underwriter may express no interest, may agree to the terms on the same premium rate, require a higher premium rate, or require different terms. In the last two cases, underwriters who had already subscribed would be informed of new terms and their obligations normally amended to conform. In any event, the underwriter who agrees to subscribe his syndicate places his syndicate initials and the percentage of risk he desires to cover on the slip, and the broker moves on to other underwriters. In this manner the broker moves around the insurance market, both at Lloyd's and among the insurance companies, until he has obtained underwriters' commitments subscribing to one hundred percent of the risk on the slip. At that stage, the broker can confirm to the applicant for insurance or his contact with the applicant that the risk is fully subscribed, or "completed."

Once the broker has succeeded in completing the slip, that is, has obtained one hundred percent coverage, he retains the slip and returns it to his office. Participating underwriters on the risk receive a copy of that part of the slip containing terms and conditions for their files. From the information on the slip, the broker's policy department prepares the policy, using the appropriate printed forms and completing them with the appropriate terms and conditions from the slip. The completed policy and slip are then forwarded to the Lloyd's Policy Signing Office * * *.

The broker also has responsibilities in the event that the insured makes a claim. His role is to present his client's claim, and present it in the best way possible, to the underwriters. If the insured makes a claim, the broker endorses the policy with details of the claim and submits it to the underwriters for their consideration. Often the market lead among the underwriters handles the claim, and other insurers follow the lead unless they have a major disagreement.

### ADDENDUM

The Lloyds market has recently been in a state of crisis. Losses for the period from 1988 through 1991 have been estimated at $11.2 billion, with further deterioration possible. Much of the blame has been placed on poor results in the North American liability portfolio, and that is largely attributed to what underwriters regard as judicial expansion of the policies to include long–tail risks, such as asbestosis and pollution. As each name is personally liable for a share of the risks his or her syndicate has assumed, the names are outraged and have alleged fraud by the underwriters, the underwriting agencies and the Lloyds Corporation itself. The Corporation has taken unprecedented steps to right the "ship". A separate company has been formed to assume liabilities incurred in prior years, and, for the first time, corporate names have been admitted—with limited liability. Corporate names will account for 15% of Lloyds' $16.2 billion underwriting capacity in 1994. See National Underwriter 3, 17 (Feb. 14, 1994).

## B. NEGOTIATION AND AGENCY: INSURERS' PROBLEMS

### WASHINGTON NATIONAL INSURANCE COMPANY v. STRICKLAND

Supreme Court of Alabama 1985.
491 So.2d 872.

HOUSTON, JUSTICE.

* * * On January 15, 1981, Bruce Palmer met with Carol Strickland and members of her family to discuss medical insurance. Mrs. Strickland was five feet, two inches tall, and weighed 180 pounds. Palmer described plans for medical insurance with four different companies, including a plan with Washington National which Mrs. Strickland and her husband chose. She completed a Washington National application for insurance; Palmer tore from the application a detachable form called a "conditional receipt" and gave it to Mrs. Strickland. He took a check from Mrs. Strickland for $100. The receipt stated that the effective date of coverage was January 15, 1981.

Mrs. Strickland and members of her family testified that Palmer told them at the meeting that Strickland's insurance coverage would be effective as of that date, January 15, 1981, and that she would be covered if she had an accident going home from that meeting. As a result of these assurances, Mrs. Strickland cancelled an application for hospitalization insurance with another company. Palmer testified, to the contrary, that he told Strickland she would be covered as of that date only "if everything was in order." The application for insurance and a statement in the conditional receipt given to Mrs. Strickland provided that no agent was authorized to make or modify contracts, to waive any of the company's rights or requirements, or to bind the company by making or receiving representations.

Four days after the meeting with Palmer, Mrs. Strickland fell and hurt her ankle. At the time of the accident, Palmer had not yet submitted Mrs. Strickland's application for medical insurance to Washington National. Palmer testified that he submitted the application to John Martin, a general agent for Washington National, on January 22, 1981. Following subsequent underwriting review, Washington National declined to issue a policy of coverage for Mrs. Strickland on grounds that she was physically unfit.

Palmer testified that his authority with Washington National was limited to the solicitation of applications and the collection of initial premiums. Martin testified that Palmer could solicit applications, but had no authority to bind Washington National to coverage. He stated that Palmer was a broker for Mutual of New York, and was not an agent for Washington National. The record shows, however, that Bruce Palmer was a licensed agent for Washington National in the State of Alabama. * * *

Mrs. Strickland sued Washington National and Bruce Palmer for fraud and misrepresentation. The jury awarded Mrs. Strickland $22,500. The parties had stipulated that the amount of compensatory damages involved in the case was $1,369.14, so $21,130.86 of the verdict constituted punitive damages. * * *

The first issue before this Court is whether Washington National could properly be found liable for the misrepresentation by Palmer that Mrs. Strickland had insurance coverage as of January 15, 1981. This would depend upon whether Palmer was acting as a general or soliciting agent for Washington National or as an independent agent or broker. If Palmer were a general or soliciting agent, Washington National would be liable. If Palmer were an independent agent or broker, Washington National would not be liable. A discussion of the distinctions between brokers, agents, and soliciting agents will go far to allay any initial confusion.

A "general agent" is one who has authority to transact all of the business of the principal, of a particular kind, or in a particular case. *Southern States Fire Insurance Co. v. Kronenberg,* 199 Ala. 164, 170–71, 74 So. 63, 67 (1917). The powers of such an agent are coextensive with the business entrusted to his care, authorizing him to act for the principal in all matters coming within the usual and ordinary scope and character of such business. *Id.,* 199 Ala. at 171, 74 So. at 67. A general agent has full power to bind the insurer to the agent's contract of insurance or to issue policies or to accept risks. *McGhee v. Paramount Life Insurance Co.,* 385 So.2d 969 (Ala.1980). In fact, a general agent "stands in the shoes" of the principal for the purpose of transacting business entrusted to him. Since a general agent's powers are coextensive with the business entrusted to him, his fraudulent act is the fraudulent act of his insurer principal as well.

An insurance company also has the right to employ agents with limited authority. [Citation omitted.] A "special agent," as distinguished from a "general agent," is authorized to act for the principal only in a particular transaction, or in a particular way. [Citation omitted.] In the insurance context, the most prevalent type of special agent is the "soliciting agent." A soliciting agent is different from a general agent in that he has no power to bind his insurer principal in contract. [Citation omitted.] However, when a soliciting agent commits a fraud upon one who seeks insurance coverage, his insurer principal will be liable for that fraud, if the fraud was perpetrated by the agent within the scope of his employment. The liability of an insurer for the fraudulent acts of its soliciting agents is grounded in the doctrine of "respondeat superior," and not the doctrine of agency. *National States Insurance Co. v. Jones,* 393 So.2d 1361 (Ala.1980). Since a soliciting agent is regarded as the "servant" of the insurer "master," the insurer has the full right of control over the agent's actions. A general agent, however, stands in the shoes of the principal; his actions are regarded as those of the principal. The law deems the principal to have "participated" in the fraud of its general agent, and so subjects the principal to direct liability. Where a soliciting agent commits fraud the insurer's liability is vicarious, and the principal is liable in spite of the fact that he did not participate in the fraud, or even forbade it. [Citation omitted.]

An independent agent or broker is usually not an agent for the insurer at all; rather, he is the agent of the insured. See Code 1975, § 27-7-1. For example, this Court has held that when an independent agent or broker fails in his duty to obtain insurance coverage, the principal may sue either for a breach of contract, or, in tort, for breach of duty imposed on the agent or broker to [show] reasonable skill, care, and diligence in obtaining insurance. *Highlands Underwriters Insurance Co. v. Eleganté Inns,* 361 So.2d 1060 (Ala.1978). In *Highlands,* the principal was the insured.

Washington National contends that Palmer was an independent agent or broker and that it was not liable for Palmer's misrepresentation. It cites *Northington v. Dairyland Insurance Co.,* 445 So.2d 283 (Ala.1984). In the *Northington* case, it was undisputed that the person committing the fraud was an independent agent and broker. But the court properly analyzed Dairyland Insurance Company's liability for the fraud of the independent agent/broker in terms of actual and apparent authority, because the issue was whether the agent/broker, normally an agent of the insured, was also acting as an agent for Dairyland.

Although an independent agent or broker is normally an agent for the insured, for some purposes he may at the same time be an agent for the insurer as well. See *Mobile Insurance, Inc. v. Smith,* 441 So.2d 894 (Ala.1983). In such cases, if the insurer principal authorizes the agent to make representations, and the agent makes those representations within the scope of his authority to make them, the principal will be liable if those representations are false. In other words, an insurer's liability for the fraud of an independent agent or broker is predicated upon actual or apparent authority conferred upon the agent/broker by the insurer to make representations on the insurer's behalf. The doctrine of respondeat superior does not apply in the independent agent or broker situation because the insurance company does not exert sufficient control over the activities of the agent/broker to put him in the same position as a company employee. An independent agent or broker can never impose liability upon his principal for representations that are not authorized by the principal.

In the instant case, appellant Washington National relies upon the *Northington* case for the proposition that it is not liable for Palmer's misrepresentation to Mrs. Strickland. But whereas in *Northington* it was clear that the person committing the fraud was an independent agent and broker, in the instant case Palmer's status is the subject of dispute. The issue is whether the jury could properly have found Palmer to be a general or soliciting agent for Washington National so that Washington National would be liable for Palmer's misrepresentation to Mrs. Strickland. The evidence clearly shows that Palmer had no actual or apparent authority to make the representations, so if Palmer had been an independent agent or broker, Washington National would not be liable for the fraud. * * *

There is sufficient evidence in the record to support the jury verdict in favor of Mrs. Strickland. Even though Martin testified that Palmer was a broker, and even though the record shows that Palmer offered four different companies' policies to Mrs. Strickland for her consideration, there is evidence indicating that Palmer was a licensed agent for Washington National. Copies of Palmer's Alabama Department of Insurance license and license application were introduced at trial. The license application gives the applicant a choice of describing himself as "agent," or "broker," or "solicitor." Palmer was designated as "agent" in the license application. Although the application was dated November 16, 1981, ten months after Palmer's meeting with Mrs. Strickland and her family, it was admitted into evidence without objection. The license itself purports to cover the years 1980, 1981, and 1982, so it described Palmer's past, present, and future status with Washington National, including his status at the time he took Mrs. Strickland's application. Martin notarized Palmer's signature on the license application. Likewise, Washington National provided Palmer with applications, sales literature, and instructions. Martin knew that persons purchasing

Washington National insurance from Palmer would be relying on Palmer's representations about insurance coverage. In order to hold Washington National liable for Palmer's misrepresentation, the jury must have found that Palmer was either a general agent, thereby subjecting Washington National to direct liability, or that he was a soliciting agent, thereby subjecting Washington National to vicarious liability under the doctrine of respondeat superior. There is sufficient evidence in the record to support either finding by the jury. * * *

In this case, the evidence, when viewed in the light most favorable to the nonmoving party, shows that an award of punitive damages by the jury was proper. The evidence of fraud in this case consists of Palmer's verbal statement to Mrs. Strickland that coverage would be effective as of January 15, 1981, and Palmer's handwritten notation on the conditional receipt, to wit: "coverage effective 15 January 81 on Carol and children." These representations were obviously ineffective for contract purposes in light of the following language found in the conditional receipt:

> "This Conditional Receipt does not create any temporary or interim insurance and does not provide any coverage except as expressly provided herein. This payment is received subject to the agreements contained in part 1 of the application and to the following terms and conditions:
>
> > "1. If the Company shall be satisfied that on the date of the application or the date of the last of any required medical examinations, whichever is the later date, the person or persons proposed for insurance were insurable under the Company's rules governing the acceptance of risks at the classification and for the amount and plan of insurance applied for, and
> >
> > "2. if the amount paid with the application equals or exceeds a monthly premium for the insurance premium for the insurance applied for, then insurance under the terms of the policy applied for shall take effect on the latest of the following dates: (a) the date of the application, (b) the date of the last of any required medical examinations or (c) the policy date, if any, requested in the application.
>
> "Unless all of the preceding conditions are met, there shall be no liability on the part of the Company except to return this payment."

From the evidence introduced, the jury could reasonably have inferred that Palmer knew that Mrs. Strickland's height and weight were such that a medical examination was likely to be required before Washington National would determine whether or not to assume the risk of coverage; that Mrs. Strickland was relying on Palmer's representation that she was insured as of that moment and so cancelled her application for hospital insurance with another insurer based upon Palmer's representation; and that Palmer made the representation in order to make a sale, without concern for whether Mrs. Strickland received insurance coverage as of that moment as promised. All this constitutes sufficient evidence from which a jury could reasonably have inferred that the fraud was committed with an intent to deceive or defraud. Consequently, the jury's award of punitive damages was proper. * * *

## TALBOT v. COUNTRY LIFE INSURANCE CO.

Appellate Court of Illinois, Third District, 1973.
8 Ill.App.3d 1062, 291 N.E.2d 830.

DIXON, JUSTICE.

This is an appeal from a judgment of the Circuit Court of Rock Island County dismissing, for failure to state a cause of action, an amended complaint filed by Suzanne Talbot, the plaintiff, against Country Life Insurance Company, the defendant in Count I and against Roy Melody, the defendant in Count II.

Count I of the amended complaint alleges in substance that: on September 13, 1969 Larry L. Talbot the husband of plaintiff applied in writing to the company's agent, Roy Melody for a life insurance policy in the amount of $15,000.00 on his own life, designating plaintiff as beneficiary; a first premium was then and there paid; on Feb. 19, 1970 Larry Talbot died; defendant retained the first premium and made no attempt to return it until Feb. 21, 1970; between the time of application and death Larry L. Talbot was in good health, his life was an insurable risk; he would have been able to obtain and would have obtained a policy from another company if it had not been for the representations of defendant; that defendant failed to take action on the application within a reasonable time; failed to issue a policy in accordance with the application and; failed to give notice of the action, if any, taken on the application and; that as a direct and proximate result the plaintiff was damaged.

One of the steps necessary to effecting an insurance policy is the filing of an application by the prospective insured; the application, being a mere offer or proposal for a contract of insurance, is not a contract. The existence of a contractual relationship between the parties (absent a binder) depends upon the acceptance by the insurer of the application. In the instant case the appellant concedes that she has no action ex contractu (the original complaint was on that theory). Neither the application nor the premium receipt provisions, if any, were pleaded, no binder is claimed; so the issue (Count I) is whether an insurer may be liable in tort for damage resulting from unreasonable delay in passing on an application for insurance.

There are divergent views on the question. On the one hand, it has been said that the failure of an insurer to act upon an application for insurance within a reasonable time, with resultant damage is a breach of the insurer's duty subjecting the company to liability for negligence. On the other hand, it has been said that an application for insurance is a mere offer and the insurer is under no duty to act on the offer. 43 Am.Jur.2d Insurance, Secs. 214, 215; 14 Am.Jur.Pl. and Pr.Forms (Rev.)

Form 111; Couch on Insurance 2d, Sec. 7:29; 44 C.J.S. Insurance § 232(c)bb., page 986.

* * *

This court in Wille v. Farmers Equitable Ins. Co., 89 Ill.App.2d 377, 232 N.E.2d 468 recognized unreasonable delay and quoted Appleman, Insurance Law and Practice, vol. 12, Sec. 7226 where the author states, "The more liberal, and probably the better rule, is to the effect that an insurance company obtaining an application for insurance is under a duty to accept it or reject it within a reasonable time."

Appleman also states in Sec. 7232, "The better rule is to the effect that where application was made for a life policy with a beneficiary being designated to receive the proceeds, a cause of action lodges in such beneficiary, upon the applicant's death, for unreasonable delay on the part of the insurer, in accepting or rejecting such application."

Count II charges the agent Roy Melody with having failed to take action on said application within a reasonable time and failing to give notice of any action taken on the application. The complaint clearly alleges that Roy Melody was the agent of Country Life Insurance Company (as distinguished from being a broker). Brokers as distinguished from soliciting agents have long been held liable in tort, 22 I.L.P. Insurance Sec. 77, page 123. The agent here is not the agent of the applicant. He is the agent of the company and his primary responsibility is to the company.

It has been suggested that the duty of an agent to use care in dealing with the application may be based on the principle, familiar in negligence cases, that one who enters upon an affirmative undertaking, to perform a service for another, is required to exercise reasonable care in performing it, to avoid injury to the beneficiary of the undertaking. Insurance agents who take applications, particularly where they receive premiums, may be said to have entered definitely upon a course of affirmative conduct, and be liable for misfeasance if they unreasonably delay. Prosser, Delay in Acting on an Application for Insurance, 3 University of Chicago Law Review 39 (1935). This appears to us to be a salutary rule. The thought it stands for is that the agent or company owes an applicant for insurance what amounts to be a legal obligation to act with reasonable promptness on the application, either by providing the desirable coverage or by notifying the applicant of the rejection of the risk so that he may not be lulled into a feeling of security or put to prejudicial delay in seeking protection elsewhere. Coffey v. Polimeni, 9 Cir., 188 F.2d 539; 43 Am.Jur.2d Insurance, Sec. 175; Annotation 29 A.L.R.2d 171.

Those engaged in the insurance business understand perfectly the peculiar urgency of the need for prompt attention in these matters, and in fact many premium receipts provide for delay by inserting an express provision that if the application is not accepted within a definite time it shall be deemed to have been rejected; others provide for a definite termination date (where conditional insurance is expressly given from the date of the application provided the applicant is then insurable for the plan and amount and at the premium rate applied for). Meyer, Life and Health Insurance Law, p. 121.

* * *

Reversed.

## MARYLAND CASUALTY CO. v. J.M. FOSTER

Supreme Court of New Mexico, 1966.
76 N.M. 310, 414 P.2d 672.

MOISE, JUSTICE.

The facts of the case are generally undisputed and not complicated. Some time prior to July 2, 1962, Poynor's White Stores, Inc., hereinafter referred to as "Poynor's," had appellant Foster write all of their insurance. At that time appellant sent all Poynor's old policies to someone in Albuquerque, but the workmen's compensation policy was not included. On July 2, Poynor's informed appellant of two minor accidents involving their employees, and it was at that time that appellant first became aware that no workmen's compensation insurance had been written. Upon advising Poynor's of this fact, at some time before noon on July 2, appellant was told to "cover" them immediately, and appellant responded that he would and that they were covered. No particular insurance company was designated by Poynor's. Neither did appellant name the company that he would have issue the policy. The Poynors were told that they should check and give appellant the approximate amount of the payroll. Appellant returned to his office and picked up the phone to call Whyburn and Company, general agents for appellee, Maryland Casualty Company, in El Paso, but decided to wait for the payroll figures, and so hung up before completing the call. Appellant was then interrupted by a man who came to his office, and with whom he went out of the office. While out of the office, appellant met with an accident and, as a consequence, never completed the call. The next morning, July 3, appellant received a call from Poynor's and was told that the payroll was $25,000.00 and, at the same time, that a man had been seriously injured. Thereupon, appellant called Whyburn and Company and explained the situation to a Mr. Connell of that company who said he would determine if they "were on the risk or not."

Appellant had an agency contract with appellee which allowed him to bind appellee as a workmen's compensation insurer. He also was agent for three other companies for which he had similar authority. Prior to July 2, 1962, he had written only four workmen's compensation policies, all of which were with appellee. In each instance, it had been his practice to call the general agent and place the insurance. He had not actually written the policies himself. It was his intention to phone the general agent and place the insurance when he started to call on July

2. It was his purpose to have the insurance issued by appellee, but there was no statement made or disclosure of this fact.

This action was commenced by J.W. Mason, an employee of defendant Poynor's who was injured in the July 3rd accident. He brought suit against his employer and against appellee as his employer's workmen's compensation insurer. Pursuant to permission granted by the court, appellee was permitted to file a third-party complaint against appellant and the three other insurance companies for whom he was agent.

* * * [W]e are impressed that the only real question involved is whether an insurance company can be bound by an oral agreement of its agent to insure when that agent represents several other companies and has not outwardly indicated his intention to act for the particular company.

Since the decision in Harden v. St. Paul Fire & Marine Ins. Co., 51 N.M. 55, 178 P.2d 578, there can be no question that oral contracts of insurance are recognized in this state. This is in accord with the general rule. See note, 15 A.L.R. 995, 69 A.L.R. 559, 92 A.L.R. 232. In that case, it was said that an oral contract of insurance is effected when the parties have agreed upon "(1) the subject matter; (2) the risk insured against; (3) the duration of the risk; (4) the amount of insurance; (5) the rate of premium paid or agreed to be paid; and (6) the identity of the parties." No question is here raised concerning any of these elements except "(6) the identity of the parties." The trial court concluded that appellant's secret intention to write the insurance in appellee company was not effective to bind appellee company, particularly in view of the fact that appellant was agent for other companies.

There can be no question that the trial court's holding is in accord with the great majority of decisions in cases involving undisclosed intention to place insurance with a particular company. Grimes v. Virginia Fire & Marine Ins. Co. (Tex.Civ.App.1920) 218 S.W. 810, is such a case. We quote the following therefrom:

> "The controlling question in the case is whether or not the evidence was sufficient to show that a parol contract of insurance was made. The question must be answered in the negative. That a parol contract of insurance is ordinarily valid and enforceable seems to be well settled. But an agreement by a fire insurance agent to furnish insurance to a property owner in some company to be selected by the agent from a number of companies represented by him is not enforceable against a particular company in the absence of proof that such agent before the fire properly designated such company as the insurer. In other words, a parol contract of insurance, made with an insurance agent representing several companies—the company to take the risk not being specified—is not enforceable. * * *"

The following additional cases support the rule: [citing cases from Kentucky, Texas, Michigan, South Carolina, Washington and Mississippi]

* * * [W]e are in entire accord with the statement in Fire Ins. Co., Philadelphia County v. Sinsabaugh, 101 Ill.App. 55, 57, to the following effect:

> "* * * The observation and experience of business men are that where applications for insurance are made, and officers or agents, with authority to issue the policies of several companies, have promised to issue the same, it is frequently left to the agent to write the policy in such company as he chooses, and it is not the intention of either party that the representatives of these companies shall be considered the agent of the insured for any purpose. If an insurance company will make a person agent for it, who at the same time holds commissions from other companies, they must be held to know, from general observation, that it is the practice of such agencies to make selections of the insurer who is to assume a particular risk, and after loss they can not be heard to deny that such agent had authority to do so. * * *"

In that case, the agent had written but had not delivered the policy and it was the court's conclusion that the agent had effectively bound the principal. See also Milwaukee Bedding Co. v. Graebner, 182 Wis. 171, 196 N.W. 533. * * * If appellant at any time before the loss had, by the slightest act, indicated that he was placing the insurance with appellee, a different result might have followed.

* * *

It follows from what has been said that the judgment appealed from is free from reversible error. It is, accordingly, affirmed.

It is so ordered.

### *Note*

Compare the *Foster* decision with Julien v. Spring Lake Park Agency, 283 Minn. 101, 166 N.W.2d 355 (1969). Under the theory of the *Foster* decision are both the agent *and* the insurance company free from liability?

For a discussion of "oral binders" see Granco Steel, Inc. v. Workmen's Compensation Appeals Board, 68 Cal.2d 191, 65 Cal.Rptr. 287, 436 P.2d 287 (1968).

Even if it is true that there is no general "statute of frauds" for insurance policies, be careful to ascertain what legislatures may have provided. Statutes like West's Ann. California Insurance Code § 2071 (which adopts a standard form fire insurance policy) ought, for example, to be consulted. And see the *Metz* decision, *supra*, for a provision mandated for automobile liability insurance policies. But, whatever statutes or regulations may provide, the use of writings, especially the use of printed forms, is the general practice in the insurance industry. Some examples of forms are contained in the Appendix to this book.

## SOUTHEASTERN COLORADO HOMELESS CENTER v. WEST

Colorado Court of Appeals Div. I, 1992.
843 P.2d 117, certiorari denied Jan. 4, 1993.

Opinion by JUDGE HUME.

Willard West and his employer, The Southeastern Colorado Homeless Center, seek review of the final order of the Industrial Claim Appeals Panel, which ruled that the Colorado Compensation Insurance Authority was not liable to pay workers' compensation benefits to West because the Center's insurance coverage had lapsed before the industrial accident in which he was injured. We set aside the order.

The facts are undisputed. The Center applied to the Authority for workers' compensation insurance coverage in a letter received by the Authority on May 15, 1989. In a letter dated May 25, 1989, the Authority advised the Center that a binder had been issued in accordance with the Workers' Compensation Act and that the premium was due by June 12 for coverage to be effective from May 16. The letter further stated that if the Authority received payment after June 12, coverage would be effective the day after receipt of the premium. The Authority and the Center later agreed on payment of the premium in quarterly installments, but did not otherwise alter the terms of the May 25 letter.

The Authority received the payment on June 16, and issued a policy effective June 17. West, however, was injured in a job related accident on June 15.

The administrative law judge ruled that coverage began on May 16 and did not lapse because the Center paid the premium within the 30–day grace period provided by § 8–45–113, C.R.S. (1991 Cum.Supp.). The Panel reversed, concluding that the grace period did not apply to binders.

Section 8–45–112, C.R.S. (1991 Cum.Supp.) provides in part that: "No contract of insurance between the Colorado compensation insurance authority and any employer shall be in effect until a policy or binder has been actually issued by the board and the premium therefor paid as and when required by this article." (emphasis added)

Section 8–45–113 provides in relevant part that: If any employer is in arrears for more than thirty days in any payment or wage report required to be made by said employer to the Colorado compensation insurance authority as provided in articles 40 to 47 of this title for advance premium, deposit premium, additional audited premium, or periodic premium, the employer shall by virtue of such arrearage be in default of such payment or reporting and any policy issued to such employer by said authority shall thereupon be cancelled without notice as of the effective or renewal date in the case of a new or renewal policy or as of the due date in the case of an existing policy. (emphasis added)

The Panel based its conclusion that § 8–45–113 was inapplicable on the absence therein of a reference to binders following the express reference to both policies and binders in § 8–45–112. We reject the Panel's approach and agree with West and the Center that a binder is a policy within the scope of § 8–45–113.

The term, "any policy," is ambiguous. There is no statutory definition of "policy" or "binder," and the common law definitions are ambiguous. Depending on the definitions used, a binder may be a temporary policy, or it may be a contract preliminary to a policy.

Although technically the term, "insurance policy," means the formal written instrument evidencing a contract of insurance, it is often used interchangeably with the term, "contract of insurance." See 1 G. Couch, Cyclopedia of Insurance Law § 3:1 (R. Anderson rev. 2d ed. 1984); United Benefit Life Insurance Co. v. McCrory, 414 F.2d 928 (8th Cir.1969), cert. denied, 396 U.S. 1039, 90 S.Ct. 687, 24 L.Ed.2d 684 (1970).

A binder has been defined as a temporary or preliminary contract of insurance that protects the insured until issuance of a formal policy or as a written memorandum evidencing the existence of such a contract. See 1 G. Couch, supra, § 3:2; 2 G. Couch, supra, § 14:26.

In the absence of an express agreement to the contrary, a binder generally incorporates the terms of the contemplated policy. See 2 G. Couch, supra, § 14:35. A binder is therefore sometimes described as a temporary policy. See Great American Insurance Co. v. Fireman's Fund Insurance Co., 481 F.2d 948 (2d Cir.1973); Turner v. Worth Insurance Co., 106 Ariz. 132, 472 P.2d 1 (1970).

In light of these varied and overlapping meanings, inasmuch as § 8–45–113 does not expressly exclude binders, the specific mention of both policies and binders in § 8–45–112, but only of policies in § 8–45–113 *119 does not resolve the ambiguity inherent in the statutory reference to "any policy."

On the other hand, since § 8–45–113 expressly includes new policies, the grace period provided therein applies to the first premium. Therefore, since binders are commonly issued in connection with payment of the first premium for a new contract of insurance, application of the grace period to the first payment due under a binder would give effect to the express application of the statute to new policies.

Moreover, § 8–44–102, C.R.S. (1991 Cum.Supp.) provides that: "Every contract for the insurance of compensation and benefits" is "subject to all the provisions" of the Workers' Compensation Act. Thus, since, under a broad definition, a binder is a contract of insurance, § 8–44–102 would make the grace period of § 8–45–113 applicable to binders. Also, § 8–45–113 is intended to protect employers as well as employees from lapses in coverage resulting from late payment of premiums, including first premiums for new policies. Construing the statute broadly to include binders will serve that purpose. See B.B. v. People, 785 P.2d

132 (Colo.1990) (construction of ambiguous statute should give effect to its underlying purpose).

Furthermore, the ultimate object of compensation insurance is to assure payment of benefits to injured employees. 4 A. Larson, Workmen's Compensation Law §§ 92.00, 92.20 (1990). See § 8–44–101(1), C.R.S. (1991 Cum.Supp.); Travelers Insurance Co. v. Savio, 706 P.2d 1258 (Colo.1985).

That purpose is served if the statutory requirements for the cancellation of workers' compensation insurance policies is applied to binders, and such construction of the statute is consistent with holdings in other jurisdictions. See Ives v. Sunfish Sign Co., 275 N.W.2d 41 (Minn.1979); Moore v. Adams Electric Co., 264 N.C. 667, 142 S.E.2d 659 (1965). See also Red Cab Co. v. St. Paul Mercury Indemnity Co., 98 F.2d 189 (7th Cir.), cert. denied, 305 U.S. 646, 59 S.Ct. 148, 83 L.Ed. 417 (1938); T.H. Mastin & Co. v. Russell, 214 Miss. 700, 59 So.2d 321 (1952). Accordingly, we conclude that "any policy" in § 8–45–113 includes binders as well as formal policies. Thus, since the premium was paid within the 30–day grace period, coverage did not lapse, and West was entitled to receive benefits under the policy.

The order is set aside, and the cause is remanded with directions to reinstate the order of the administrative law judge.

Pierce and Rothenberg, JJ., concur.

## *Problem*

Georgia Code § 56–2420(1) states: "Binders or other contracts for temporary insurance may be made orally or in writing and shall be deemed to include all the usual terms of the policy as to which the binder was given * * * except as superseded by the clear and expressed terms of the binder." Insured held an automobile policy "limiting coverage to events taking place within 300 miles radius of the [insured's] place of business." The policy also contained a paragraph: "Changes: Notice to any agent * * * shall not effect a waiver or a change in any part of this policy estop the company from asserting any right under the terms of this policy; *nor shall the terms of this policy be waived or changed except by endorsement issued to form a part of this policy.*" [Emphasis added].

On May 18th the insured requested the soliciting agent to remove the mileage limitation. Apparently the soliciting agent orally agreed. The soliciting agent, however, also notified the general agent, which issued the requested endorsement effective May 31 at 5:05 p.m. At 3:05 p.m. on that date a covered auto was involved in a collision over 300 miles from insured's place of business. A federal district court in Canal Insurance Co. v. Aldrich, 489 F.Supp. 157 (S.D.Ga.1980), held for the insurer in a declaratory judgment suit: "[the soliciting agent] had no power to orally modify the terms of the policy * * *. The courts have no more right or power to extend coverage of a policy or to make it more beneficial to the insured than they do to rewrite the contract and insurance coverage."

Question: If the agent can orally bind why cannot he orally modify, as long as the modification produces a policy which he could have bound in the first place?

### *Note*

### *Assurances of "Full Coverage" and Equitable Estoppel*

The common assurances by insurance salespersons or by marketing brochures that the applicant is getting "full coverage" is an open invitation to claim estoppel against the insurance carrier when gaps in coverage later appear. The problem, which is dealt with in the cases immediately following is that a fairly well entrenched principle, "no estoppel into coverage" is obviously being challenged. A frequently cited case is Harr v. Allstate Ins. Co., 54 N.J. 287, 255 A.2d 208 (1969). Harr owned a house and contents, and held a homeowner's policy covering a broad range of risks including water damage. He also carried on a small business in the basement and realized that the H.O. policy would not apply to property used for business pursuits. Before leaving on a trip to Florida he contacted an agent of Allstate, which had issued the H.O. policy, for appropriate coverage. The agent orally assured him that the business property was "fully covered", and urged him to enjoy his trip. Thereafter the house was flooded and it was then discovered that the policy (one usually issued in such situations) while indeed containing very broad coverage of business risks, had a somewhat obscure exclusion for water damage. The court, on several grounds including a mention of reasonable expectations, held the exclusion unenforceable. The primary base for the holding was estoppel, adopted deliberately by the court while recognizing that this meant estoppel into coverage (and a bit more). But see Harmon v. American Interinsurance Exchange Co., 39 Mich.App. 145, 197 N.W.2d 307 (1972) (representation of "full coverage" held unenforceable).

## WAIVER, ESTOPPEL, ETC.—A COMMENT

"Waiver", "estoppel" and "waiver and estoppel" occur with bristling frequency in insurance decisions. The conduct of agents gives rise to the application of these doctrines so it is appropriate that attention be paid here to them. A good analysis is found in Morris, Waiver and Estoppel in Insurance Policy Litigation, 105 U.Pa.L.Rev. 925 (1957). A succinct statement of doctrine is found in Salloum Foods & Liquor, Inc. v. Parliament Insurance Co., 69 Ill.App.3d 422, 26 Ill.Dec. 399, 388 N.E.2d 23, 27–28 (1979): [Citations are omitted.]

An insurance company can waive the limitation provision of an insurance contract, or, by its conduct, become estopped from invoking the provision as a defense to an action on the policy. * * *

In the context of insurance law, and especially with regard to limitation provisions in insurance policies, the terms "waiver" and "estoppel" have often been used without careful distinction, and thereby abused and confused. * * * This doctrinal confusion, epitomized by the frequently echoed phrase "waiver by estoppel", is so deeply rooted some courts have suggested that the term waiver, as applied in Illinois to insurance cases, is simply another name for estoppel. * * *

Notwithstanding the confusion already engendered by many of these cases, it is elementary that waiver and estoppel are two separate and distinct doctrines. * * * The fact that these doctrines are closely akin and often may coexist does not mean they are identical in connotation.

Waiver encompasses either an express or an implied * * * voluntary and intentional relinquishment of a known and existing right * * *.

Waiver is essentially unilateral in character, focusing only upon the acts and conduct of the insurer. Prejudice to, or detrimental reliance by the insured is *not* required. * * *

Equitable estoppel, on the other hand, generally is based upon an insurance carrier's conduct and/or representations which mislead an insured to his detriment. * * * Thus, if an insurance carrier's investigation and/or negotiation of a policy claim reasonably induces within the insured a false sense of security—namely, that the claim will be settled without suit—and the insured, in reliance thereon, foregoes filing suit during the policy's limitation period, the insurance carrier is estopped from later raising the limitation provision as a defense to an action on the policy. * * *

It is not necessary that the insurer intentionally mislead or deceive the insured, or even intent by its conduct to induce delay. * * * All that is necessary is that the insured reasonably relies on the insurer's representations or conduct in forbearing suit.

### *Note*

### *Election*

Another word that purports to have conceptual significance in this context is "election", referred to in texts and used occasionally in the cases. It is defined as "a cross between waiver and estoppel," and described as a "difficult concept to cope with, even when dealt with candidly." * Presumably the opportunity to use it is when the insurer, in a position to keep the benefit of the deal or to take advantage of an opportunity to get out, waffles unnecessarily. E.g., the company has collected a premium, while an agent is aware of a breach of condition. The application of the doctrine does not require detrimental reliance or voluntary relinquishment of a right, and obviously is related to the necessary choice of substantive rights which accompanies the rescission of contracts in general.

In truth, the doctrine is rarely made the basis for decisions in recent times, and the use of the word is as a tag along ("the conduct of the insurer constitutes waiver, estoppel or election") without any substantive significance.

## REPUBLIC INSURANCE CO. v. SILVERTON ELEVATORS, INC.

Supreme Court of Texas, 1973.
493 S.W.2d 748, 91 A.L.R.3d 500.

* See R. Keeton, Basic Insurance Law § 6.1 for a full discussion of the doctrine.

DANIEL, JUSTICE.

This suit was brought by Respondents, Silverton Elevators, Inc. and Carl L. Tidwell, against Petitioner, Republic Insurance Company, to recover under a Texas Standard Fire Policy issued to Silverton Elevators by Republic Covering a residential dwelling and household goods contained therein. In a non-jury trial, Silverton was awarded $3,000 "for the use and benefit" of Carl L. Tidwell for the loss of the household goods. The Court of Civil Appeals affirmed. 477 S.W.2d 336. We affirm.

Carl L. Tidwell was at all times material to this controversy, an officer, director and the general manager of Silverton Elevators, Inc. Silverton owned and furnished to Tidwell a house near its elevators, together with the insurance on the house and on Tidwell's household goods, as part of his compensation as general manager. Since 1964, Republic's local agent had issued and renewed insurance policies in the name of Silverton covering the dwelling and its household goods. It is undisputed that the local agent, who had authority to issue the policies and receive the premiums, knew that the household goods belonged to Tidwell and that Silverton was carrying the insurance for the benefit of Tidwell. On April 17, 1970, a tornado destroyed the house and the household goods.

On the date of the tornado there was in effect a Texas Standard Fire Policy with Extended Coverage on DWELLING & HOUSEHOLD GOODS in the sum of $10,000 issued by Republic to Silverton for the period of April 20, 1969 to April 20, 1972, insuring against loss from windstorm the specifically described "occupied dwelling" for $7,000 and "household goods * * * while in the described building" for $3,000.00. It is undisputed that Silverton paid the $227.00 premium, and the local agent admitted that at the time he issued the policy he knew the facts heretofore mentioned with respect to actual ownership of the insured property. He testified that he wrote the policy to cover Tidwell's household goods located in the dwelling which Tidwell and his family occupied; that he knew Silverton was carrying the policy on the household goods for the benefit of Tidwell; that when he issued the policy he did not think it made any difference that it was in the name of Silverton because "they were paying the premium"; and that he told Tidwell that the policy covered his household goods both before and after the tornado.

Republic acknowledged coverage on the house and paid Silverton $7,000 for its damage, but it denied any liability to Silverton or Tidwell on the household goods. Thereupon, Silverton and Tidwell brought this suit against Republic claiming coverage to the limit of the policy ($3,000) on the household goods owned by Tidwell. Republic defended on the grounds that Silverton had no ownership and therefore no insurable interest in the household goods and that the policy as written was limited by its terms to household goods owned by Silverton Elevators, Inc., the named insured.

Silverton and Tidwell's pleadings asserted that they both had insurable interests; that the insurance was purchased by Silverton and extended to Tidwell as part of his compensation as manager and as "a legal representative of Silverton Elevators, Inc."; and that when Republic issued its policy and accepted premiums with full knowledge of the true ownership and relations between Silverton and Tidwell, it waived the right to complain about any lack of ownership or insurable interest of the named insured and was estopped from denying coverage on behalf of Tidwell. As heretofore indicated, the trial court awarded Silverton Elevators $3,000 "for the use and benefit of Carl L. Tidwell."

Since the policy refers to and clearly purports to cover the household goods located in the specifically described dwelling, we agree with the Court of Civil Appeals that the knowledge of Tidwell's ownership of the household goods by Republic's local agent and his actions with respect thereto were imputed to and binding upon Republic. Issuance of the policy and collection of the premiums with such knowledge operates as a waiver of any requirement that the named insured own or possess a beneficial interest in the insured property. [citations].

In the above cases, the named insureds were not the owners or sole owners of the insured properties. In each case, the true owner was known to the insurance agent and was allowed direct recovery, or recovery for his benefit, on the grounds that the insurance company had waived warranties of sole ownership or lack of insurable interest. There is no conflict between the above cases and those which hold that waiver and estoppel cannot operate to bring within the terms of a policy liabilities or benefits which were expressly excepted therefrom, such as liability from injuries due to gunshot wounds in Washington Nat. Ins. Co. v. Craddock, 130 Tex. 251, 109 S.W.2d 165 (1937); loss for injuries while in military service in time of war, as in Ruddock v. Detroit Life Ins. Co., 209 Mich. 638, 177 N.W. 242 (1920); or payment of benefits beyond a specified termination date at age 65, as in Great American Reserve Ins. Co. v. Mitchell, 335 S.W.2d 707 (Tex.Civ.App.1960, writ ref.). The latter cases recognize that waiver and estoppel may operate to avoid forfeiture of coverage and benefits stated in the policy, but not to add specifically excluded risks or to enlarge the benefits or risks therein set forth. In the present case, plaintiffs seek to recover only on the risk assumed by Republic under the terms of the written policy. Republic's policy insured against the destruction of precisely the same household goods identified in its policy and for which it collected its premiums. There is no evidence that its risk was enlarged because the household goods were owned by Tidwell rather than Silverton.

* * *

[A portion of the opinion dealing with policy construction has been omitted.]

It has been suggested, but not by Republic, that the building item provision contained in the "Mortgage or Trustee" clause at the bottom of the face of the policy, and particularly the last sentence thereof, limits liability for compensation to the "interest of the insured," and that this applies to personal property. Even though the provision does not speak of "named insured," and for all practical purposes Tidwell was the "insured" because the policy as to household goods was written for his benefit, there are other more compelling reasons why this provision is inapplicable to the personal property involved in this case. Clearly, the entire clause refers to loss on "building items," their value at the time of loss less depreciation, repair, replacement and reconstruction, etc. None of the language refers to personal property. Furthermore, the last sentence begins with the words, "Subject to Article 6.13 of the Texas Insurance Code," and this Article contains the specific provision that: "The provisions of this article shall not apply to personal property."

The above clause has been a part of the Texas Standard Fire Policy form prescribed by the Insurance Commission since 1943. * * *

Whether applicable to personal property or not, we hold that the portion of the clause relating to limitation of liability to "the interest of the insured" falls within the category of ownership provisions which may be waived; the insurer may be estopped from denying liability to the true owner on policies issued in the names of third parties covering the risks on identified property with full knowledge by the company that the property is actually owned by the one for whose benefit the policy was written or maintained. * * *

Republic insists that reformation of the policy is the only proper remedy, if any, for recovery by Silverton on behalf of Tidwell, because of failure of the written policy to identify the household goods as belonging to Tidwell. We disagree. As heretofore indicated, under the undisputed facts, the household goods described in the policy belonged to Tidwell and were insured by Silverton for his benefit in a policy drawn by Republic's agent for such purpose, with assurances from the agent that it would cover Tidwell's furniture. If this was a mistake, it was made by Republic's agent, and it was mutual, because Tidwell and Silverton took the agent's word that it expressed the true agreement. With this evidence being fully developed in the present record, there is no reason to require another trial for reformation of the written policy. It has been held that even without a plea for reformation, when the facts show the true agreement intended and a mutual mistake, or mistake of the agent, in preparing the written policy, the agreement intended will be enforced without going through the formal proceedings of reformation. Aetna Ins. Co. v. Brannon, 99 Tex. 391, 89 S.W. 1057; Aetna Ins. Co. v. Brannon, 53 Tex.Civ.App. 242, 116 S.W. 116 (Tex.Civ.App.1904, no writ). See also 25 A.L.R.3d 589 § 3; 25 A.L.R.3d 1239 § 3; and 32 A.L.R.3d 677 § 3.

Silverton and Tidwell made every proof in this case that would entitle recovery on the policy as written. Under the above cited authorities, the trial court and Court of Civil Appeals have properly held that Silverton is entitled to recover for the benefit of Tidwell on the written policy without seeking a reformation thereof.

Accordingly, the judgments of the lower courts are affirmed.

* * *

WALKER, JUSTICE (dissenting).

* * *

The net effect of the majority holding is to extend the policy coverage and create an entirely different contract by waiver or estoppel. That is contrary, of course, to the established rule in Texas and most other jurisdictions. * * *

> * * * Waiver and estoppel may operate to avoid a forfeiture of a policy, but they have consistently been denied operative force to change, re-write and enlarge the risks covered by a policy. In other words, waiver and estoppel can not create a new and different contract with respect to risks covered by the policy. This has been the settled law in Texas since the decision in Washington Nat. Ins. Co. v. Craddock, 130 Tex. 251, 109 S.W.2d 165, 113 A.L.R. 854.

None of the cases cited in support of the waiver holding is pertinent here. Most of them involved the so-called sole and unconditional ownership clause, which provided that the entire policy would be void if the interest of the insured was other than sole and unconditional ownership. Others involved a stipulation that the policy would be void in case of a change of ownership unless otherwise provided by agreement endorsed on the policy. The policy in Old Colony Insurance Co. v. Messer, Tex.Civ.App., 328 S.W.2d 335 covered the dwelling that was damaged by fire, but it contained a provision limiting liability to the interest of the insured and another making the policy void if the insured had concealed any material fact. These provisions as well as lack of insurable interest were pled by the insurance company in bar. Although the jury made findings tending to support an estoppel theory, the Court of Civil Appeals affirmed the trial court's judgment in favor of the true owner on the basis of its holding that the provisions in question had been waived by issuance of the policy and acceptance of the premiums with knowledge of the ownership of the property. Be that as it may, there was no question of coverage in the case, and the decision does not stand for the proposition that the limitation of liability may be waived out of the policy for the purpose of determining coverage.

* * *

It is my opinion that respondents are not entitled to recover on the policy as written, and that is all they have attempted to do thus far. Tidwell may show his right to recover by offering evidence and obtaining findings that establish mutual mistake and the terms of the true agreement. See Aetna Ins. Co. v. Brannon, 99 Tex. 391, 89 S.W. 1057. The trial court would then be in position to enter a judgment based on the coverage actually agreed upon and intended by the parties. It would also be in position to insure that petitioner receives the appropriate premium for the risk actually assumed. I would reverse the judgments of the courts below and remand the cause in the interest of justice.

### *Problem*

Father applied for a homeowners' policy on a house owned by himself and Mother and occupied by Son. Agent was told of the actual state of ownership, and suggested that the homeowners' policy be issued in Son's name as the insured; this was done and Father and Mother were listed as mortgagees. Father paid the premiums and the taxes as well as the cost of improvements. Title never changed hands. The house and its contents were destroyed by fire after Son had occupied it for several years. Putting aside the question of whether Son might have an insurable interest, is it possible to dispose of the case on the basis that the Insurance Company is *estopped* to deny liability? See McGehee v. Farmers Insurance Company, 734 F.2d 1422 (10th Cir.1984).

## CRITERION LEASING GROUP v. GULF COAST PLASTERING & DRYWALL

District Court of Appeal of Florida, First District, 1991.
582 So.2d 799.

PER CURIAM.

This cause is before us on appeal from a final order determining appellants' responsibility for compensation benefits. For the following reasons, we affirm.

On July 7, 1989, Robert Bruce was injured in a work-related accident when he tripped and suffered a broken coccyx bone. The incident occurred while working for Evans & Blount Stucco (hereinafter Evans Blount) at a construction project known as the Crescent Beach Club.

Sea Coast Towers Construction (hereinafter Sea Coast) was the general contractor on the Crescent Beach Club project. Gulf Coast Plastering & Drywall (hereinafter Gulf Coast) subcontracted with Sea Coast to provide plastering and drywall.[1] Thereafter, Gulf Coast subcontracted the stucco work to Evans Blount. Evans Blount provided proof of workers' compensation coverage which showed the coinsureds as Criterion Leasing Corporation (hereinafter Criterion) and Evans Blount.[2]

Criterion acts as a large personnel department for a number of small companies. Criterion handled the workers' compensation coverage and payroll for Evans Blount. On April 13, 1989, all personnel who had formerly been employees of Evans Blount were then considered employees of Criterion. However, new employees of Evans Blount did not become employees of Criterion until after Criterion was notified that a

1. Gulf Coast provided Sea Coast with a current certificate of workers' compensation coverage.

2. Gulf Coast requires subcontractors to provide proof of workers' compensation coverage. When a subcontractor does not have coverage, Gulf Coast provides coverage and pays the premium with a portion of the draw paid to the subcontractor.

new employee had been hired. Criterion was unaware that Evans Blount had hired claimant.

Gulf Coast and its carrier, Continental Loss Adjusting, accepted the claim as compensable but reserved its right to seek reimbursement from Criterion, Evans Blount, and Hartford.[3] After hearing, the judge of compensation claims (JCC) found that Hartford issued a certificate of insurance indicating that Evans Blount employees were covered. Gulf Coast and Continental relied on this certificate and were detrimentally damaged by this reliance. The JCC found all the elements of equitable estoppel had been established, and therefore Evans Blount, Criterion, and Hartford were estopped from denying coverage.

Initially, we determine that the JCC erred in finding that "all of the elements of equitable estoppel have been satisfied." (emphasis added). Equitable estoppel may not be used to affirmatively create or extend insurance coverage. However, "[a]n exception to the general rule is the doctrine of promissory estoppel, a qualified form of equitable estoppel which applies to representations relating to a future act of the promisor rather than to an existing fact." Crown Life Ins. Co. v. McBride, 517 So.2d 660, 661 (Fla.1987) (citations omitted). Because the JCC found the elements of promissory estoppel present and followed the dictates of Masonry v. Miller Construction, 558 So.2d 433 (Fla. 1st DCA 1990), we affirm.

A party will be estopped from denying liability under the principle of promissory estoppel when the party makes "[a] promise which the promisor should reasonably expect to induce action or forbearance of a definite and substantial character on the part of the promisee and which does induce such action or forbearance . . . [and] injustice can be avoided only by enforcement of the promise." Coral Way Properties, Ltd. v. Roses, 565 So.2d 372, 374 (Fla. 3d DCA 1990), citing 1 Restatement of the *801 Law Second, Contracts 2d § 90 at 242 (1987).

We find that it was foreseeable to Hartford that Evans Blount would use the certificate of insurance as proof of workers' compensation coverage. First, Hartford provided workers' compensation coverage to Criterion Leasing. The certificate of insurance listed both Criterion and Evans Blount as coinsureds. The certificate was presented to Gulf Coast as proof of workers' compensation coverage. If Evans Blount did not present proof of insurance, Gulf Coast would have obtained a policy providing workers' compensation coverage prior to Evans Blount's employment. Therefore, Hartford's promise to provide workers' compensation coverage to the coinsureds (Criterion and Evans Blount) induced Gulf Coast to allow Evans Blount to begin working at the job site. Claimant's injury constituted the detrimental result that followed Gulf Coast's reliance.

3. Hartford issued the workers' compensation policy listing Evans Blount and Criterion as coinsureds.

Second, Section 440.10(1), Florida Statutes, requires a general contractor to provide workers' compensation coverage for a subcontractor's employees except when the subcontractor already has obtained coverage. Therefore, Hartford should have reasonably expected that Gulf Coast would rely on the certificate of insurance naming Evans Blount as a coinsured. This promise of coverage induced Gulf Coast to subcontract with Evans Blount.

Accordingly, we affirm the order under the principle of promissory estoppel.

### *Note*

In Tate v. Charles Aguillard Ins. & Real Estate, 508 So.2d 1371 (La.1987), Tate, the insured, owned a horse, British Colonial which was insured for $100,000 for one year beginning October 30, 1980 for a $4,500 premium. The issuance of the policy was subject to the condition that British Colonial be in good health on the date of the policy. Unfortunately the horse became sick and was destroyed December 25, 1981. It was undisputed that the condition for coverage was not met.

Tate's claim was that failure to deny coverage promptly prevented him from seeking alternative coverage and that he delayed destruction of British Colonial missing the coverage period under a prior policy. Although Tate was successful in avoiding the "waiving into coverage" restriction, he was unable to show that the insurer had waived the condition of the policy. The Louisiana court noted that Tate could not show reliance inasmuch as no other insurer would have insured British Colonial and the prior insurer wouldn't have allowed destruction of the horse because the horse's health was not hopeless until November when the policy lapsed.

### *Problems*

1. Does an insurance agent have standing to seek reformation of the insurance contract between the insurer and the insured? B (insured) asked R (agent) to add coverage of a new endloader to B's existing policy with W (insurer). R never informed W of the request for coverage. B sued R and W. W settled with B and R asked that the policy be reformed to include the requested coverage. Biondo v. Ridgemont Insurance Agency, Inc., 104 Mich.App. 209, 304 N.W.2d 534 (1981). Why did the agent *want* reformation?

2. Insured (now deceased) indicated to Insurer's Agent when applying for a life policy that he had driven "60/45 zone" and disclosed that he had other driving offenses although he was not clear on all the details. Insurer's Agent said that was all right and that Insured's record would be checked with the Department of Motor Vehicles. Insured's application form disclosed only the "60/45 zone" offense. Is Insurer charged with knowledge of the other driving offenses such that it cannot disclaim liability for payment under the policy the insured having died in an auto accident? See Willetts v. Integon Life Insurance Corp., 45 N.C.App. 424, 263 S.E.2d 300 (1980).

3. Agent accepted Insured's application for an all risk policy on his boat, knowing that Insurance Company refuses to provide coverage for boats of that value and age without a survey. Without a survey, Agent stated to

Insured that the boat was covered. It does not appear that Insured knew anything about Insurance Company's refusal of coverage for boats like his. The boat is, naturally, sunk. Can Insured recover against *both* agent and Insurance Company? If Insured recovers from Insurance Company can it recover "over" against Agent? Crawford v. DiMicco, 216 So.2d 769 (Fla. App.1968).

## C. THE LAW OF MISREPRESENTATION: AN APPLICANT'S PROBLEM IN NEGOTIATION

### MERCHANTS FIRE ASSURANCE CORP v. LATTIMORE

United States Court of Appeals, Ninth Circuit, 1959.
263 F.2d 232.

HAMLEY, CIRCUIT JUDGE.

In this action, Miss Ann E. Lattimore, the insured under a policy of personal property insurance, recovered judgment against the insurer in the sum of $17,034. Of this sum $7,084 was for loss in connection with the disappearance of, or damage to, scheduled fine arts. The remaining $9,950 was for loss due to the disappearance of, or damage to, unscheduled personal property covered by a personal property floater provision of the policy.

Appealing to this court, defendant, Merchants Fire Assurance Corporation, contends that with regard to the scheduled fine arts the trial court should have found the loss to be $4,339.45 instead of $7,084. Concerning the $9,950 loss relating to unscheduled personal property, the company contends that it should have been relieved from all liability on its defense of concealment and misrepresentation of a material fact.[52]

* * *

The material concealment or misrepresentation upon which appellant relies has to do with the declarations which Miss Lattimore made in paragraph 4 of the policy concerning "the unscheduled personal property." Appellant argues that in this paragraph the insured was called upon to declare the approximate value of all the unscheduled personal property which she owned.

52. The first paragraph of the policy under the heading "Conditions" reads: "This policy shall be void if the Assured has concealed or misrepresented any material fact or circumstance concerning this insurance or the subject thereof or in case of any fraud, attempted fraud or false swearing by the Assured touching any matter relating to this insurance or the subject thereof, whether before or after a loss."

This provision in effect carries into the insurance contract the applicable sections of the West's Ann.California Insurance Code referred to in this opinion. Section 331 of that code provides: "Concealment, whether intentional or unintentional, entitles the injured party to rescind insurance."

The value which she declared in this paragraph under five of the fifteen listed categories of property was $9,950.[53] At the trial it was stipulated that when the policy was issued, and for many years prior thereto, the actual value of the unscheduled property was at least $36,500. The insured thus failed to disclose that, in addition to the property declared in paragraph 4, she owned unscheduled personal property of the approximate value of $27,000.

In determining whether the failure to disclose this information constitutes the kind of "concealment" which warrants avoidance of liability, we turn first to the West's Ann.California Insurance Code. Under § 330 of that code, "neglect to communicate that which a party knows, and ought to communicate, is concealment."

Miss Lattimore either had personal knowledge of the approximate value of all the unscheduled personal property owned by her, or is charged therewith by reason of the knowledge of her agents Langman and Raymond Armsby.[54] She is consequently presumed to know the approximate value of the portion thereof which was not declared in paragraph 4. It remains to be determined whether, within the meaning of § 330, this was information which appellee "ought" to have communicated to the company.

A party to an insurance contract "ought" to communicate to the other at least such information as he is under a statutory duty to

53. The pertinent part of paragraph 4 as filled in reads as follows:

"4. The following are the approximate values of the unscheduled personal property, other than jewelry, watches and furs, as estimated by the Assured, at the time of issuance of this policy:

| | Wherever Located |
|---|---|
| (a) Silverware and pewter | $3,000.00 |
| (b) Linens (including dining room and bedroom) | $ 500.00 |
| (c) Clothing (Men's, Women's, Children's) | $5,000.00 |
| (d) Rugs (including floor coverings) and draperies | $ Nil |
| (e) Books | $ Nil |
| (f) Musical Instruments (including pianos) | $ Nil |
| (g) Television sets, radios, record players and records | $ Nil |
| (h) China & Glassware (including bric-a-brac) | $ Nil |
| (i) Camera & Photographic equipment | $ Nil |
| (j) Golf, hunting, fishing and other sports & hobby equipment | $ Nil |
| (k) Paintings, etchings, pictures and other objects of art | $1,000.00 |
| (*l*) Refrigerators, washing machines, stoves, electrical appliances and other kitchen equipment | $ Nil |
| (m) Bedding (including blankets, comforters, covers, pillows, mattresses, and springs) | $ Nil |
| (n) Furniture (including tables, chairs, sofas, desks, beds, chests, lamps, mirrors, clocks) | $ Nil |
| (*o*) All other personal property (including wines, liquors, foodstuff, garden and lawn tools and equipment, trunks, traveling bags, children's playthings, miscellaneous articles in basement and attic) and professional equipment, if any, covered under paragraph 7(b) | $ 450.00 |
| Total | $9,950.00" |

54. The court made no finding as to whether Armsby was Miss Lattimore's insurance broker. In answer to interrogatories prior to trial, counsel for appellee acknowledged that Armsby was her broker. Armsby and other witnesses also so testified at the trial. There was no evidence to the contrary. Section 33 of the West's Ann.California Insurance Code defines "broker" as one who transacts insurance "on behalf of another * * * with, but not on behalf of, an insurer."

communicate. Section 332 of the West's Ann.California Insurance Code requires the parties to such a contract to disclose certain facts. The section reads:

> "Each party to a contract of insurance shall communicate to the other, in good faith, all facts within his knowledge which are or which he believes to be material to the contract. * * * "

As we have already indicated, the facts concerning the approximate total value of all unscheduled personal property owned by Miss Lattimore were within her knowledge, or that of her agents. Miss Lattimore, who testified at the trial, did not explicitly state whether at the time the contract was entered into she believed that information as to the value of all her unscheduled personal property was material to the contract. Nor did the trial court make an express finding of fact as to this. But the court noted in its findings that the policy conveyed no explicit information as to the materiality of the declaration to be made in paragraph 4.

These and other more general findings of fact may have been intended to reflect an implicit finding that when the contract was negotiated Miss Lattimore had no reason to believe that this information was material to the contract. We will so assume.

Belief in the materiality of the withheld facts, as referred to in § 332, is satisfied, however, if an authorized agent of the contracting party held such belief. This follows from the general rule which charges an insured with the knowledge and acts of his agent. See Gelb v. Automobile Insurance Co., 2 Cir., 168 F.2d 774. Armsby testified, without contradiction, that he was aware of the facts and circumstances which made such information material to the contract. In view of her broker's awareness of the materiality of the information in question, Miss Lattimore had a duty under § 332 to communicate that information to appellant.

But even if it be supposed that Armsby was not aware of the materiality of these facts, the same result must be reached. Section 332 placed upon Miss Lattimore the duty to communicate material facts to appellant regardless of whether she or her broker believed them to be material. This is made clear by the disjunctive "or" in the phrase of § 332 reading " * * * which *are* or which he believes to be material to the contract * * *." (Emphasis supplied.)

Application of this alternative provision, which does not require belief as to materiality, is dependent upon whether the undisclosed facts as to value were in fact material to the contract. There are three tests which the courts employ to determine the materiality of undisclosed facts. The test most frequently applied is whether a fact is regarded as material by all similar insurers.[54.5] A second test is what a reasonable

**54.5** John Hancock Mutual Life Ins. Co. v. Conway, Ky., 240 S.W.2d 644; Patterson, "Misrepresentation by Insured under New

and prudent insurer would regard as material.[55]

The third test is whether the particular individual insurer regarded the undisclosed facts as material to the contract. This test looks only to the evidence concerning the attitude or practice of the insurance company involved in the suit. The courts of California have determined that under § 334 of the West's Ann.California Insurance Code [56] they are required to adopt this third test in determining the materiality of concealed or misrepresented facts.[57]

The trial court made no finding as to whether the fact of total approximate value of the unscheduled personal property owned by Miss Lattimore was material to the contract. Appellant, however, submitted considerable evidence to the effect that under its practice, and also under the practice of similar insurers, this fact was material. Thus, appellant produced evidence which, under either the stringent California rule or the more generally used first test mentioned above, tended to show materiality.

According to this testimony, the reason why the fact of total approximate value of all such property owned by the insured is material is that it definitely affects the risk assumed. As the witnesses giving this testimony explained it, most losses under a personal property floater are partial rather than total, but the risk of partial loss increases with the total value and amount of property owned. The chance of a $2,000 loss occurring is thus much greater in the case of a person who owns $50,000 worth of property than in the case of one who owns only $2,000 worth.[58]

Because of this, it was uniformly testified, it is customary for companies writing such insurance, and appellant in particular, to ask that the insurance coverage be not less than eighty per cent of the total value of the property owned. Hence, had it been disclosed to appellant that the approximate value of all unscheduled personal property owned

York Insurance Law," 44 Col.L.Rev. 241, 248.

**55.** Standard Accident Ins. Co. v. Walker, 127 Va. 140, 102 S.E. 585. Both of these tests reflect the rule of contract law that the materiality of facts which are misrepresented depends on whether the misrepresentation would affect the conduct of a reasonable man. See Restatement, Contracts, § 470.

**56.** Section 334 reads as follows: "Materiality is to be determined not by the event, but solely by the probable and reasonable influence of the facts upon the party to whom the communication is due, in forming his estimate of the disadvantages of the proposed contract, or in making his inquiries."

**57.** Robinson v. Occidental Life Ins. Co., 131 Cal.App.2d 581, 281 P.2d 39; Cohen v. Penn Mutual Life Ins. Co., 48 Cal.2d 720, 312 P.2d 241.

**58.** There was testimony to the effect, and appellant concedes, that a declaration of value is not to be regarded as a warranty. An insurance man, called as a witness by appellant, testified that "companies generally like to get about eighty per cent insurance to value." It is true that he further testified: "* * * I have seen any number of cases where the declaration, for example, might show $2,000 estimated value for clothing, and when loss finally overtakes the assured there might be $3,000 [or] $4,000 in value of clothing. Now, if that $4,000 falls within the limit of liability for the unscheduled items there is no question of the company not paying the loss." This testimony did not relate to any practice of appellant. In any event, the decision of a company to be lenient, once a loss has occurred, does not mean that it would have entered into the contract on the terms stated had it known the facts which were concealed.

by Miss Lattimore was $36,500, appellant would have insisted on a coverage of at least $29,200. The premium on such a coverage would have been $548.02, instead of the actual premium of $316.89.

As against this evidence of materiality, appellee calls attention to other evidence which, in her view, shows that the undisclosed fact was not material. One such item of evidence relates to a letter which appellee's broker wrote to appellant's issuing agent in July 1950. In this letter it was stated that certain personal property was stored in a named warehouse. Among the items of property referred to was "household furniture." Appellee argues that this letter put appellant on notice that Miss Lattimore owned some furniture—hence knew that the declaration of "nil" for furniture in the policy then in effect was wrong. In spite of this knowledge, the company entered into the contract, thereby indicating, so appellee contends, that the total value of property owned was not considered to be a material fact.

The fact is, however, that the policy then in effect had no separate item declared as value of furniture. It follows that the 1950 letter did not show any inaccuracy whatever in the 1949 declarations. In the 1950 form, used after this letter was sent, a category of furniture was added for the first time. It was contained in the 1952 form involved in this suit. It is apparently appellee's view that the 1950 letter should have put the company on notice in 1952 that Miss Lattimore had some furniture.

We do not believe that either lack of materiality or estoppel can be shown by a process of reasoning as speculative as this. Moreover, appellee or her broker had been in possession of the 1952 policy for three years and had never advised appellant that the "nil" declaration on furniture was erroneous. Appellee thereby adopted and confirmed the declarations just as if she had personally repeated them to the insurer. Telford v. New York Life Ins. Co., 9 Cal.2d 103, 69 P.2d 835.

Another item of evidence upon which appellee relies to show that the fact of total value was not material has to do with a clothing loss in 1950. This was a loss of $2,800, at a time when the declaration in the 1949–52 policy stated only $2,000 for clothing. Despite this declaration, the full claim of $2,800 was paid.

At the time of this incident, the total value declared was $6,950, and the unscheduled insurance was $5,578. After paying the loss, appellant's agent suggested to Miss Lattimore's broker that perhaps the values and the insurance were too low. As a consequence, the declaration on clothing value was increased from $2,000 to $5,000. It therefore appears that when an under-declaration came to the attention of appellant, the insured was requested to raise the declaration, and this was done. We find nothing in this incident to indicate that appellant did not regard the declaration of total value material.

* * *

It would therefore appear that, either because of Armsby's belief that such information was material or because, in any event, it was material, appellee had a statutory duty under § 332 to communicate this information to appellant. Her neglect to do so, unless otherwise excused, was therefore "concealment" within the meaning of § 330. This, under the terms of the contract and of § 331 of the West's Ann. California Insurance Code (see footnote 52) would seem to void the policy.

But appellee contends that she is to be excused for failing to disclose total value of property owned because, in her view, the declaration form contained in paragraph 4 of the policy did not plainly call for a statement of approximate value of all unscheduled personal property owned by Miss Lattimore. In this connection it is pointed out that there was not, in that paragraph or elsewhere in the policy, any reference to the company's eighty per cent practice referred to above. It is argued that it was reasonable for her to believe that all that was called for by this provision was a declaration as to that part of her total property which she desired to have protected by insurance. Appellee contends that it was pursuant to this belief that a declaration of $9,950 was entered in paragraph 4.

The trial court did not enter an express finding to the effect that Miss Lattimore or her broker understood that paragraph 4 called only for a declaration of the value of property sought to be protected by insurance. If such a finding is implicit in other general findings, it is clearly erroneous. Miss Lattimore did not so testify. As a matter of fact, she testified that when in 1946 she examined a predecessor policy containing a similar paragraph of declaration, "I thought it covered whatever belongings I had." In any event, her then broker, Armsby, made it clear that he knew that all property owned was to be declared. The fact that the policy makes no reference to the company's eighty per cent practice is immaterial, since appellee's broker was aware of that practice.

That appellee, or at least her broker, did not so construe the declaration provision is also indicated by the fact that her claim against the company is not limited to the categories of property for which she declared a value. See footnote 5. She had no clothing loss, and only $525 was claimed on silverware and pewter. Adding this figure to the valuations declared on three other categories, only $2,475 insurance coverage would be available to satisfy appellee's claim. Yet her claim was for $9,950, the full amount.

A claim in this amount would be justified only if the $9,950 coverage specified in paragraph 3(a) on "unscheduled personal property" meant coverage to this extent on all the personal property which Miss Lattimore owned. But if those words had that meaning in paragraph 3(a), they must also have had that meaning in paragraph 4.

* * *

This is not a case where the company had conducted an independent investigation by reason of which it became aware of some falsity. DiPasqua v. California Western States Life Ins. Co., 106 Cal.App.2d 281, 235 P.2d 64. In California an insured may not escape the consequences of his deception by placing on the insurer the burden of investigating his verified statements. Robinson v. Occidental Life Ins. Co., 131 Cal. App.2d 581, 281 P.2d 39.

One of the essential elements of estoppel or waiver in an insurance case is knowledge of the pertinent facts. Rizzuto v. National Reserve Ins. Co., 92 Cal.App.2d 143, 206 P.2d 431. A waiver cannot be established by a consent given under a mistake regarding essential facts, or in ignorance of the facts the effect of which is claimed to have been waived. * * * Mere cause for suspicion is not a substitute for knowledge. * * *

It is our conclusion that, both as a matter of fact and law, appellant established the defense of concealment, entitling it to void the personal property floater provision of the policy. This being the case, it is unnecessary to discuss the facts and law relative to appellant's defense based on asserted misrepresentation of a material fact.

The judgment is reversed and the cause is remanded with directions to enter judgment for appellee in the sum of $7,084, with interest, and costs, as provided in the original judgment, additionally increased in a sum equal to the premium paid for the personal property floater, with interest thereon. Appellant will recover its costs on this appeal.

### *Notes*

1. The Dean of Educational Administration at an Illinois College was an art collector. In applying for coverage for his collection from Lloyds of London, he submitted an appraisal signed by X stating the value to be $275,800. The collection was burglarized and a claim for the appraised amount was submitted. The insurers refused payment, having discovered that the insured had purchased the stuff from X for $19,800 and that the appraisal was made contemporaneously with the purchase. The court ruled that the concealment of this information was grounds for rescinding the coverage. Stone v. Those Certain Underwriters at Lloyds, London, Subscribing To Cover Note No. SL 10001, 81 Ill.App.3d 333, 36 Ill.Dec. 781, 401 N.E.2d 622 (1980). Was the court justified in holding that the concealed information was material?

2. The subject of misrepresentation and concealment and fraud will also arise in subsequent portions of this book. E.g. see the *Barrera* case, post Part D (liability insurance). We have felt that some substantial treatment of the subject was warranted here, because misrepresentation, fraud and concealment cut across the law of insurance contracts (and, of course, of all contracts). The reader (having the courses in Contracts, Torts and Remedies fresh in mind) might ask himself or herself:

(a) what remedies are available for misrepresentation, concealment, mistake?

(b) is a remedy available in case of an innocent misrepresentation?

(c) what remedies are available in the case of fraudulent misrepresentation?

Although the subject comes up frequently enough in connection with claims under insurance policies, more of the decisions seem to deal with applications for policies. Because a good deal of money and important personal and public interests are at stake, considerable legislative attention has been attracted from time to time. There are large variations among the statutes, a fact that does not help clarification at the casebook level. Sometimes the statutes are not received with the utmost hospitality by the learned writers (e.g. see Patterson, Some Contracts Provisions of the California Insurance Code, 32 So.Cal.L.Rev. 227 (1959). Nonetheless we have reproduced the following sections to illustrate legislative attention to the subject.

NEW YORK (New York Insurance Law)

**§ 3105. Representations by the insured**

(a) A representation is a statement as to past or present fact, made to the insurer by or by the authority of the applicant for insurance or the prospective insured, at or before the making of the insurance contract as an inducement to the making thereof. A misrepresentation is a false representation, and the facts misrepresented are those facts which make the representation false.

(b) No misrepresentation shall avoid any contract of insurance or defeat recovery thereunder unless such misrepresentation was material. No misrepresentation shall be deemed material unless knowledge by the insurer of the facts misrepresented would have led to a refusal by the insurer to make such contract.

(c) In determining the question of materiality, evidence of the practice of the insurer which made such contract with respect to the acceptance or rejection of similar risks shall be admissible.

(d) A misrepresentation that an applicant for life, accident or health insurance has not had previous medical treatment, consultation or observation, or has not had previous treatment or care in a hospital or other like institution, shall be deemed, for the purpose of determining its materiality, a misrepresentation that the applicant has not had the disease, ailment or other medical impairment for which such treatment or care was given or which was discovered by any licensed medical practitioner as a result of such consultation or observation. If in any action to rescind any such contract or to recover thereon, any such misrepresentation is proved by the insurer, and the insured or any other person having or claiming a right under such contract shall prevent full disclosure and proof of the nature of such medical impairment, such misrepresentation shall be presumed to have been material.

CALIFORNIA (California Insurance Code)

**§ 330. Definition**

Neglect to communicate that which a party knows, and ought to communicate, is concealment.

### § 331. Effect

Concealment, whether intentional or unintentional, entitles the injured party to rescind insurance.

### § 332. Required disclosures

Each party to a contract of insurance shall communicate to the other, in good faith, all facts within his knowledge which are or which he believes to be material to the contract and as to which he makes no warranty, and which the other has not the means of ascertaining.

### § 333. Matters not required to be disclosed except upon inquiry

Neither party to a contract of insurance is bound to communicate information of the matters following, except in answer to the inquiries of the other:

1. Those which the other knows.

2. Those which, in the exercise of ordinary care, the other ought to know, and of which the party has no reason to suppose him ignorant.

3. Those of which the other waives communication.

4. Those which prove or tend to prove the existence of a risk excluded by a warranty, and which are not otherwise material.

5. Those which relate to a risk excepted from insurance, and which are not otherwise material.

### § 334. Determination of materiality

Materiality is to be determined not by the event, but solely by the probable and reasonable influence of the facts upon the party to whom the communication is due, in forming his estimate of the disadvantages of the proposed contract, or in making his inquiries.

### § 335. Presumed knowledge

Each party to a contract of insurance is bound to know:

(a) All the general causes which are open to his inquiry equally with that of the other, and which may affect either the political or material perils contemplated.

(b) All the general usages of trade.

### § 336. Waiver of right to information

The right to information of material facts may be waived, either (a) by the terms of insurance of (b) by neglect to make inquiries as to such facts, where they are distinctly implied in other facts of which information is communicated.

### § 337. Nature and amount of insured's interest

Information of the nature or amount of the interest of one insured need not be communicated unless in answer to an inquiry, except as prescribed by section 381, or by the provisions of the insurance contract if such provisions are prescribed by this code as part of a standard form.

**§ 339. Information of party's own judgment**

Neither party to a contract of insurance is bound to communicate, even upon inquiry, information of his own judgment upon the matters in question.

**§ 350. Nature**

A representation may be oral or written.

**§ 351. Time of making**

A representation may be made at the time of, or before, issuance of the policy.

**§ 353. As to future**

A representation as to the future is a promise, unless it is merely a statement of a belief or an expectation.

**§ 354. Effect upon policy**

A representation cannot qualify an express provision in a contract of insurance; but it may qualify an implied warranty.

**§ 355. Alteration or withdrawal**

A representation may be altered or withdrawn before the insurance is effected, but not afterwards.

**§ 356. Time referred to**

The completion of the contract of insurance is the same to which a representation must be presumed to refer.

**§ 357. Information of others**

When an insured has no personal knowledge of a fact, he may nevertheless repeat information which he has upon the subject, and which he believes to be true, with the explanation that he does so on the information of others; or he may submit the information, in its whole extent, to the insurer. In neither case is he responsible for its truth, unless it proceeds from an agent of the insured, whose duty it is to give the information.

**§ 358. Falsity defined**

A representation is false when the facts fail to correspond with its assertions or stipulations.

**§ 359. Effect of falsity**

If a representation is false in a material point, whether affirmative or promissory, the injured party is entitled to rescind the contract from the time the representation becomes false.

**§ 360. Materiality**

The materiality of a representation is determined by the same rule as the materiality of a concealment.

### *Notes on Materiality*

1. *The Standard for Testing the Materiality of a Non-deliberate Misrepresented Fact*

A subjective standard:

Vance, 3d ed. 1951 at p. 407

" **** Any statement is material which in any wise induced the issuer to make a contract which he otherwise would not have made or would have made only on different terms."

An objective standard:

Couch, Cyclopedia of Insurance Law, 2d ed., § 69.121.

"The question of the materiality to the risk of statements by the insured in an application for reinstatement is not to be determined by the jury on the basis of what the applicant may think as to materiality, but upon the basis of what those engaged in the life insurance business, acting reasonably and naturally, in accordance with the practice usual among such companies, under similar circumstances, would do. Otherwise stated, the test * * * depends not upon what the insurer or the insured may think about the materiality or the importance of the false information given or the true information withheld, but upon what those engaged in the insurance business, acting reasonably and naturally in accordance with the usual practice among insurance companies under such circumstances, would have done had they known the truth; that is to say, whether reasonably careful and intelligent men would have regarded the facts stated as substantially increasing the chances of the happening of the event insured against so as to cause a rejection of the application."

Numerous case citations are made available for both propositions.

The objective standard espoused by Couch more clearly tracks the general rule applicable outside of insurance cases. See § 538 Restatement of Torts, 2d adopting the reasonable man standard (the qualification in that section is not adaptable to the insurance situation). See also § 162 Restatement of Contracts (2d). A major objection to the subjective test (i.e. did *this* insurer consider the fact material) is that it duplicates the requirement that the insurer prove it was induced to issue the policy in *reliance* upon the misrepresentation, which is obviously also a purely subjective matter. What is the test of materiality stated in *Thompson,* infra? In the New York statute?

2. *Deliberate misrepresentations* of non material *facts.*

The general rule is that rescission and restitution may be had by an aggrieved party who was induced to enter into a contract as a result of deliberate misrepresentation regardless of materiality. See § 9 comment b, Restatement of Restitution. Sometimes this proposition is set forth in Insurance Codes—e.g.: § 186 Mass.Gen.Laws. However it will be a very rare case indeed when a sizeable insurance company is able to convince a trier of fact that it justifiably relied and was victimized by an immaterial misrepresentation.

3. *Materiality and Causation*

Suppose X on his insurance application has misrepresented his history of drug abuse, but his untimely death is from an accidental gun shot wound. Obviously there is no relationship between the fact misrepresented and his untimely death, so why should the insurer not pay? In Howard v. Aid Association for Lutherans, 272 N.W.2d 910 (Minn.1978), the court summarized the situation:

> In general, we have held that an insurer has the option to void an insurance contract once it discovers that the insured has wilfully made a false representation which is material and which increases the contractual risk undertaken by the insurer. Minn.St. 61A.11.[33] * * * Shaughnessy v. New York Life Ins. Co., 163 Minn. 134, 203 N.W. 600 (1925); * * *.
>
> A review of authorities analyzing the effect of an insured's misrepresentation upon the insurer's coverage obligation reveals two distinct approaches to materiality. Plaintiff urges our adoption of the minority position that coverage may only be defeated when the facts misrepresented specifically relate to the cause of death. See, e.g., Central National Life Ins. Co. v. Peterson, 23 Ariz.App. 4, 529 P.2d 1213 (1975), and National Old Line Ins. Co. v. People, 256 Ark. 137, 506 S.W.2d 128 (1974). He asserts that since there exists no causal connection between a failure to disclose a history of drug abuse and an accidental shooting death, it is consistent with public policy to enforce the terms of the insurance contract.
>
> However, a majority of jurisdictions, including this court, has measured the materiality of a misrepresentation by the extent to which the disclosure influenced the insurer's decision to initially assure the risk of coverage, not by the degree of causal connection between the false statement and the loss protected by the policy. Neither decisional nor statutory authority in this state requires more than that an insured wilfully misstate necessary information or intentionally mislead the insurer into issuing a policy for coverage. Minn.St. 61A.11. In Shaughnessy v. New York Life Ins. Co., supra, we concluded that false responses to insurance application inquiries precluded recovery under the policy. The facts presented indicated that the deceased insured failed to disclose conditions of anemia and headaches, the latter having been diagnosed as related to syphilis. We held that while the insured's death was caused by a brain tumor and had no relationship to the matters concealed, the insured was obliged to truthfully detail her medical condition. A breach of that fundamental obligation affects the very essence of the insurer's decision to offer coverage and was therefore held material.

4. A not uncommon statutory provision addresses the materiality-causation problem—e.g., Kansas Stat.Ann.: (see also, R.S.Mo. (1968) § 376.-580.)

**33.** Minn.St. 61A.11 provides: "In any claim upon a policy issued in this state without previous medical examination, or without the knowledge or consent of the insured, or, in case of a minor, without the consent of his parent, guardian, or other person having his legal custody, the statements made in the application as to the age, physical condition, and family history of the insured shall be valid and binding upon the company, unless *willfully false or intentionally misleading.*" (Emphasis supplied.)

**40–418. Materiality of misrepresentation in obtaining policy.** No misrepresentation made in obtaining or securing a policy of insurance on the life or lives of any person or persons, citizens of this state, shall be deemed material or render the policy void unless the matter misrepresented shall have actually contributed to the contingency or event on which the policy is to become due and payable.

*Query:* Why does the statute single out life insurance?

## FUNCHESS v. UNITED STATES LIFE INSURANCE CO.

Supreme Court of New York, Appellate Division, 1980.
77 A.D.2d 516, 430 N.Y.S.2d 77.

MEMORANDUM DECISION

* * * The decedent met his end at the point of a gun. So far as is pertinent to this appeal, two affirmative defenses sought rescission, upon tendered refund of premiums, because of misrepresentation of age, the age of thirty-seven having been stated in the application instead of forty-seven. The difference between the two, claimed defendant, was material because the actual age would have, under the company's rules, required a physical examination. Materiality of representation to provide a basis for rescission was not proven. There was no showing that coverage would have been refused had the truth been told, or that the insured suffered at any time from any condition whatever which would have increased the carrier's risk, nor was any reason whatever assigned for the misstatement. Certainly, it was not demonstrated that the incorrect information had anything whatever to do with the actual cause of death or that its happening was thereby accelerated. In the circumstances, the trial court properly invoked section 155(1)(d) of the Insurance Law, requiring a provision in every policy—and found in the subject contract—that, if the age of an insured has been misstated, the benefit payable would be limited to such as the premium would have bought at the proper age. * * *

All concur.

### *Questions*

Why the special treatment given to misrepresentations of age in life insurance policies? Why not allow the insured in all cases of misrepresentation to avoid rescission by paying the difference between the premium paid and the premium which the insurer would otherwise have charged particularly where there is no causal connection between the misrepresentation and the cause of loss?

### *Note on Concealment in Insurance Law*

a. *Meaning of the word "Concealment."*

In ordinary contract cases, the word "concealment" means an active intentional endeavor to prevent the other party from discovering the truth—e.g., papering over the hole in the wall in a house offered for sale. In this sense "concealment" is a form of fraudulent misrepresentation (complete with scienter) so that both rescission and damages are remedies available to the aggrieved party. Mere silence with regard to material facts unknown to the other party is, in the usual contract, characterized as "non-disclosure" which is remediable by rescission only under limited circumstances. In other words, mere "non-disclosure" is basically privileged conduct unless a special obligation to disclose exists. § 161 of the Restatement of Contracts 2d lists the standard instances in which such an obligation arises. Insurance law uses not only its own rules but its own nomenclature—i.e., "Concealment" in insurance law includes the "non-disclosure" of ordinary contract law.

b. *The Effect of Concealment*

Originally concealment, with or without intent to deceive, sufficed to avoid the policy. As with many other quirks in Insurance law, this has been attributed to the realities of maritime risks which comprised the bulk of British underwriting in the developing days of insurance. Risks in precarious water, thousands of miles away and virtually beyond the communication means of the times, could not be inspected, and their fair evaluation necessarily depended upon honest disclosure of all material information by the applicants. Reliance could be had on little else. The traditional description of a contract of Insurance as a contract "uberrimae fidei"—the utmost good faith—became both a label and a legal guide.

Yet it was not necessarily the good faith of the applicant alone which was determinative but the materiality of the information; and that was a matter for the underwriter to determine.

This rigorous rule as to concealment is still said to prevail in England in all branches of insurance. Horne v. Poland, [1922] 2 K.B. 364. In the United States, it is applied to marine risks, but has been widely relaxed in other areas (even so-called inland marine or floater policies) so that a good faith, unintentional non-disclosure even of a material fact will not avoid the policy. The relaxation no doubt is influenced by the comparative ease with which an underwriter can investigate a risk should it be considered important in this modern age of data storage and retrieval, and also by a tendency to assume that the failure of the insurer to make inquiry as to a specific facet of a risk suggests that it did not regard the information as material.

Nevertheless there are still echoes to be found in American law of the strict application of the concealment rule in non-marine cases—in California, for instance, as may be discerned in the preceding statutes.

## THOMPSON v. OCCIDENTAL LIFE INSURANCE CO.

Supreme Court of California, 1973.
9 Cal.3d 904, 109 Cal.Rptr. 473, 513 P.2d 353.

[The *Thompson* case covered a number of important issues including the effect of a conditional receipt and agent's authority. Included below are only the facts and the portion of the case dealing with the effect of alleged misrepresentation. Attention is invited particularly to the circumstances relating to medical examination. The decision went for Thompson, 4–3.]

BURKE, JUSTICE.

We are asked to decide whether, under the particular facts of this case, a contract of life insurance existed between plaintiff's deceased spouse and defendant insurance company, and if so, whether decedent's alleged misrepresentations regarding the state of his health and past medical history rendered that contract void and unenforceable. The trial court, aided by an advisory jury, found in plaintiff's favor and awarded her $200,000, plus interest. Defendant appeals. We have concluded that the judgment should be affirmed.

Donald L. Thompson, husband of plaintiff Ruth M. Thompson, was insured by defendant Occidental Life Insurance Company of California ("Occidental") under a $15,000 life insurance policy which provided for double indemnity for accidental death. Concerned about the adequacy of his medical and life insurance, Thompson contacted John Kelly, the Oakland manager of Occidental, for the purpose of increasing his insurance coverage. Kelly then met with Thompson's accountant to determine what type of policy Thompson should purchase and decided upon a five-year convertible term policy for $100,000 with double indemnity for accidental death. On August 5, 1964, Thompson signed an application for the recommended policy and on August 11 submitted to a medical examination.

* * *

Thompson's application was received by Occidental's underwriters on August 17. The underwriters decided to require an additional medical examination. On August 24, before he was informed of this decision, Thompson sustained an accident (falling into his bathtub and nearly suffocating) which resulted in his death four days later. Occidental determined that Thompson's death was accidental and paid plaintiff, as beneficiary, $30,000 as double indemnity under the $15,000 life insurance policy. However, Occidental notified plaintiff on September 4 that it would neither issue nor make payment under the $100,000 life insurance policy because the additional medical examination had not been completed. Thereafter, Occidental returned to plaintiff the first premium by a check drawn on its own account. Plaintiff retained the check and sued to recover $200,000 as double indemnity under the $100,000 policy and, as indicated above, judgment was entered awarding plaintiff $200,000 and $82,108.60 as interest. Defendant appeals.

* * *

2. MISREPRESENTATION

Occidental's second contention is that, even if a contract of insurance were formed, it was rendered unenforceable by reason of misrepresentations by Thompson concerning his medical history. It is true that under certain circumstances material misrepresentations regarding the medical history of an applicant may justify the rescission of a life insurance contract. * * * In the instant case, however, both the advisory jury, answering a special interrogatory, and the trial judge, exercising his independent judgment, found that Thompson did not misrepresent or conceal the state of his health and past medical history to Occidental. That finding is supported by substantial evidence.

The alleged misrepresentations occurred during the insurance medical examination on August 11, 1964, and pertain to matters set forth in Thompson's insurance application. The record discloses that Thompson did not fill out the application himself; instead, his oral responses were recorded by the examining physician, Dr. Epstein, a private practitioner on Occidental's "approved" list of physicians, who, by prior arrangement with Occidental, performed medical examinations of insurance applicants. Dr. Epstein read the questions on the application to Thompson during a Friday afternoon session which included both a physical examination and completion of the questionnaire; since Epstein could perform three or four such examinations in an hour, Thompson's session may have lasted only 15 to 20 minutes. Occidental contends that Thompson misrepresented or concealed the answers to questions 5 and 6. Question 5 asked:

"During the past five years have you:

"A. Consulted, been examined or been treated by any physician or practitioner?

"B. Had an X-ray, electrocardiogram or any laboratory test or study?

"C. Had observation or treatment at a clinic, hospital, or sanitarium?

"D. Had or been advised to have a surgical operation?"

Dr. Epstein entered an affirmative answer to each portion of question 5 and noted the following on the portion of the application which requested details of affirmative answers: "5 ABCD—Vein ligation—Hernia, Providence Hosp. Oakland, 1963, M.C. Green MD 330 Elm St., Oakland, Cal." The "vein ligation" was a surgical operation involving the tying of the patient's veins; evidently, Thompson suffered from varicose veins, and the ligation was necessary to relieve this condition.

The pertinent portions of question 6 asked:

"Have you ever had or been told you had: * * *

"B. * * * pain or pressure in the chest, or any disorder of the heart, blood or blood vessels?

"C. * * * any disorder of the lungs, bronchial tubes, throat or respiratory systems?

"* * *

"I. Any disease, condition or disorder not indicated above?"

Epstein entered negative answers to each of these questions.

The alleged misrepresentations consist of Thompson's apparent failure to report to Epstein approximately 10 medical consultations he had at Kaiser Hospital with five different doctors which commenced on June 3, 1964, two months before the insurance medical examination, and ended only the day before the examination took place. During these consultations he (1) had complained of chest pain, (2) had an electrocardiogram performed, (3) was treated for "phlebitis" (vein inflammation), (4) was advised to keep off his feet to avoid the possibility that a clot in a leg vein might break off and travel to his lungs, (5) had his legs X-rayed for "intermittent claudication" (leg pain), and (6) was advised to undergo a "chemical sympathectomy" (injection of local anesthetic) to relieve the foregoing leg pain.

We first review the rules of law applicable in appraising a claim of misrepresentation in procuring insurance. It is generally held that an insurer has a right to know all that the applicant for insurance knows regarding the state of his health and medical history. * * * Material misrepresentation or concealment of such facts are grounds for rescission of the policy, and an actual intent to deceive need not be shown. * * * Materiality is determined solely by the probable and reasonable effect which truthful answers would have had upon the insurer. * * * The fact that the insurer has demanded answers to specific questions in an application for insurance is in itself usually sufficient to establish materiality as a matter of law. * * *

On the other hand, if the applicant for insurance had no present knowledge of the facts sought, or failed to appreciate the significance of information related to him, his incorrect or incomplete responses would not constitute grounds for recission. * * * Moreover, "Questions concerning illness or disease do not relate to minor indispositions but are to be construed as referring to serious ailments which undermine the general health." * * * Finally, as the misrepresentation must be a material one, "An incorrect answer on an insurance application does not give rise to the defense of fraud where the true facts, if known, would not have made the contract less desirable to the insurer. [Citations.]" * * * And the trier of fact is not required to believe the "post mortem" testimony of an insurer's agents that insurance would have been refused had the true facts been disclosed. * * *

Although there are several items on Occidental's list of alleged "misrepresentations," many items appear to relate to the ailment which Thompson affirmatively disclosed in answering question 5, namely, his varicose vein problem which led to the vein ligation surgery. As we shall see, the remaining items seemingly pertained to minor matters likely to have been of no interest to Occidental. Since Thompson disclosed his basic problems with his veins and circulation, the trial court might have concluded that it was the responsibility of the examining doctor to elicit additional details as to causes, consultations, treatments, diagnosis and prognosis.

It is suggested by the dissent, however, that Thompson knowingly concealed from Occidental that he suffered from *two* major problems, namely, varicose veins and arteriosclerosis, that the two conditions were unrelated, and that the latter condition had substantially reduced Thompson's life expectancy. Yet this theory (which was not raised in defendant's briefs in this case) finds no support in the record. The dissent relies primarily upon testimony by one of defendant's witnesses, Dr. Thompson, who never examined decedent Thompson during his life, and who consequently never discussed the arteriosclerosis condition with him. Contrary to the suggestion in the dissenting opinion (Circ. opn., p. 486), none of the physicians with whom decedent consulted testified that decedent was ever advised that he had arteriosclerosis, that this condition was unrelated to the past varicose vein problem disclosed to Dr. Epstein, or that this new "malady ... would shorten his life span by one-half to two-thirds." (Circ. opn., p. 490.) In fact, with respect to the intermittent claudication (leg pain) which Thompson was experiencing, Dr. Pellegrin told Thompson merely that it had "something to do with circulation * * *." According to Dr. Pellegrin, "You don't want to get somebody all wound up and alarmed and concerned about themselves and find out it isn't bad at all, and they are tense and anxious for no reason at all." From this testimony, the judge and jury could reasonably conclude that Thompson believed that he had a single leg circulation problem, related to his varicose vein condition. Accordingly, the finding that Thompson did not misrepresent his medical condition is supported by the evidence and the reasonable inferences which could be drawn from that evidence. As we have often stated, our reviewing power begins and ends with the determination whether there is any substantial evidence to support the trial court's findings. (E.g., Green Trees Enterprises, Inc. v. Palm Springs Alpine Estates, Inc., 66 Cal.2d 782, 784, 59 Cal.Rptr. 141, 427 P.2d 805.) On the present record, we cannot say that the trial court's finding is wholly unsupported by substantial evidence when viewed in the light of the foregoing legal principles.

There are at least four additional possible bases to support the finding that Thompson did not misrepresent or conceal the facts. (1) The court may have found that, in addition to disclosing his leg vein problems and surgery, Thompson also mentioned to Dr. Epstein the additional consultations regarding vein inflammation and leg pain but Epstein, in the course of hurrying to complete the brief examination, intentionally or inadvertently failed to record the information.[34] (See

**34.** Dr. Epstein could not recall what information Thompson in fact disclosed, although Epstein did testify that he customarily recorded all information furnished by the applicant in response to the questionnaire. The latter testimony may have been questioned by the trial court, for the record discloses that Epstein entered a negative response to the question calling for "evidence of past or present diseases or disorders of the * * * blood vessels," even though Thompson's legs bore visible scars of the vein ligation. Epstein also failed to indicate whether there was evidence of varicose veins, despite Thompson's disclosure of that problem to Epstein.

It is true that Thompson signed the application himself, thereby certifying to the accuracy of the questionnaire. Although some cases have emphasized that applicants for insurance must read the application and

Rutherford v. Prudential Ins. Co., 234 Cal.App.2d 719, 726–729, 44 Cal.Rptr. 697.) (2) The court may have believed that Thompson, as an ordinary layman, failed to recollect or appreciate the significance of the subject matter of the various Kaiser consultations. For example, the terms "phlebitis," "intermittent claudication," and "chemical sympathectomy" might well have been meaningless jargon to him. (3) Next, the court may have found that most of Thompson's undisclosed problems related to "minor indispositions" rather than serious ailments undermining the general health. For example, the chest pain of which he had complained was diagnosed as mild pneumonia and pleurisy caused by the pneumonia from which Thompson recovered in a single day following office treatment by a doctor. The electrocardiogram performed on Thompson showed no significant or abnormal tracings, and the X-rays of Thompson's legs were likewise negative. (4) Finally, the court may have determined that the subject matter of the Kaiser consultations would not have affected Occidental's decision to issue a policy; the court was not required to accept the contrary testimony of Occidental's officer.

Occidental asserts that there is no substantial evidence in the record to explain the incomplete responses on the insurance application. Yet we must remember that Thompson himself was unavailable for direct interrogation, and Dr. Epstein, who recorded Thompson's responses, was unable to remember the substance of their conversation. Under such circumstances, were the burden of proof upon them, the insured's beneficiaries would have a nearly insurmountable proof problem in establishing a satisfactory explanation for the various omissions in decedent's application for insurance. Yet under the authorities, the burden of proving misrepresentation rests upon the insurer. * * * Some cases have even assumed that fraud must be proven by "clear and convincing" evidence. * * * [preponderance of evidence sufficient].

report any misstatements or omissions (see Telford v. New York Life Ins. Co., 9 Cal.2d 103, 107–108, 69 P.2d 835), other cases have indicated that even if the applicant has signed the application, his omissions may be excused if it can be inferred that the examining doctor gave him the impression that additional written responses were unnecessary (see Rutherford v. Prudential Ins. Co., 234 Cal.App.2d 719, 728, 44 Cal.Rptr. 697; Boggio v. Cal.–Western States Life Ins. Co., 108 Cal.App.2d 597, 239 P.2d 144). Moreover, the fact that Thompson signed the application does not foreclose the argument that the information was immaterial to Occidental, or pertained to minor indispositions, or that Thompson failed to recall the facts or appreciate their significance.

Occidental's officer, Mr. Ryan, testified that Occidental would have declined to issue a policy had Thompson fully disclosed his medical history. Ordinarily, "the direct evidence of one witness who is entitled to full credit is sufficient for proof of any fact." (Evid.Code, § 411; see Hicks v. Reis, 21 Cal.2d 654, 659–660, 134 P.2d 788; Camp v. Ortega, 209 Cal.App.2d 275, 281–285, 25 Cal.Rptr. 873; Krause v. Apodaca, 186 Cal.App.2d 413, 417–419, 9 Cal.Rptr. 10.) Yet the trial court was entitled to withhold "full credit" from Ryan's testimony, either on the basis of his relationship with Occidental (see Witkin, Cal.Evidence, § 1113), or his manner of testifying (id., § 1115). (See McAuliffe v. John Hancock Mut. Life Ins. Co., supra, 245 Cal.App.2d 855, 858, 54 Cal.Rptr. 288; Hicks v. Reis, supra, 21 Cal.2d, p. 660, 134 P.2d 788.) This same reasoning could apply to Dr. Epstein's testimony; in addition, that testimony was not "direct evidence" (see Evid. Code, § 410) of Thompson's misrepresentation. Since Epstein could not recall Thompson's words, the court would have been required to infer that Epstein correctly and completely recorded Thompson's responses, an inference which the court could refuse to draw.

Thus, the burden was on Occidental to negate to the satisfaction of the trier of fact the various plausible explanations for the incomplete answers on Thompson's application.

Under the facts in this case, it is conceivable the court could have found that Thompson withheld pertinent information and to that extent misrepresented the facts. Yet, as we have pointed out, the court was entitled to find to the contrary based upon its appraisal of the testimony, the credibility (or lack thereof) of Occidental's witnesses, and the fair inferences arising from the evidence. It is not our function to second guess the trier of fact in such matters.

### *Note*

In Life Insurance Company of North America v. Capps, 660 F.2d 392 (9th Cir.1981), Mrs. Capps answered "no" to the question on her application:

> "Have you * * * ever had heart trouble, high blood pressure, chest pains * * * or other health impairments?"

In fact Mrs. Capps had within recent years suffered symptoms of a heart condition of which she was aware. She had consulted cardiologists and had been in a hospital coronary care unit on an emergency basis within the past year. All this was not revealed in response to another question as to whether she had consulted a physician. She died of heart failure within six months of the issuance of the policy. The beneficiaries, relying on *Thompson* supra, argued that Mrs. Capp's physician and husband misled her about the seriousness of her condition and that she believed it was insubstantial. The trial court granted summary judgment for the insurance company. Based on *Thompson* how would you have decided the appeal?

## LETTIERI v. EQUITABLE LIFE ASSURANCE SOCIETY OF UNITED STATES

United States Court of Appeals, Ninth Circuit, 1980.
627 F.2d 930.

GOODWIN, CIRCUIT JUDGE.

California beneficiaries of a life insurance policy appeal a judgment in favor of the insurer. The district court ruled that the substantive law of New York, rather than that of California, governed the questions of the enforceability of the policy. Because the plaintiffs had no legal theory upon which to proceed under New York law, they saved their objection to the choice-of-law ruling and judgment was entered.

The decedent, Alfredo Lettieri, a resident of New Jersey, while in poor health, bought a $400,000 five-year term life insurance policy from an agent Alfredo met in a New York City bar. Alfredo named his estate and his son Anthony, a California resident, as beneficiaries. His wife Becky later was substituted for the estate.

Alfredo obtained his required medical examination in New York City from a Dr. Martin, a physician on the insurer's approved medical examiner list. Neither Alfredo's medical history nor medical examination reports, which were completed and signed by Dr. Martin, revealed Alfredo's current or past ailments (save for an early appendectomy). Alfredo had been addicted to heroin as a youth, had been hospitalized for alcohol-related treatment, was at the time of the examination suffering from liver disease and alcoholism, and had other abnormalities that should have been obvious to a medical examiner.

The company issued the insurance policy in reliance upon Alfredo's application, which included the medical reports. Alfredo's signature certified the truthfulness of the application's contents. Within four months, Alfredo died of a bleeding ulcer in part caused by excessive use of alcohol. The insurer conducted an investigation of the claim and uncovered the falsehoods and omissions in the insurance application. The insurer then denied liability on the policy, asserting a right to rescind the policy upon discovery of the concealment or misrepresentation of material fact by the insured with respect to his medical history and state of his health when he applied for the policy. The beneficiaries brought this action in California where the choice of law appeared to be more favorable than that of other possible venues.

Under the substantive laws of both California and New York, an insurer may avoid liability on a policy procured through material misrepresentations by the insured. Where the laws arguably differ is in the method by which the factual issues are determined.[35]

Under New York law the insurer has an absolute right to rescind a life insurance policy if the application, signed by the insured and attached to the policy, contains false statements or omissions about medical history which the insured failed to correct. Under New York law, then false statements or omissions about health are conclusively presumed to be material misrepresentations. Minsker v. John Hancock Mut. Life Ins. Co., 254 N.Y. 333, 173 N.E. 4 (1930). See John Hancock Life Ins. Co. v. Yates, 299 U.S. 178, 180, 57 S.Ct. 129, 130–131, 81 L.Ed. 106 (1956). Thus, the district court's choice of New York law effectively precluded plaintiffs from pursuing their theory that the decedent had in fact disclosed the whole truth to Dr. Martin, and that Dr. Martin, or one of his employees, acting as the insurer's agent, or the company itself, had negligently or otherwise kept Alfredo's true medical history from reaching the insurer's files.[36]

**35.** We are not concerned with proof of materiality. In this case, the omissions and misstatements in the insurance application were material. The only triable questions are whether Alfredo in fact misrepresented his health history and under what substantive law that issue should be determined.

**36.** Plaintiffs' theory was that Alfredo had disclosed his health history but had wished to hide it—particularly his earlier heroin addiction and present alcoholism—from his family. They then surmise that Alfredo had requested that the attached report not reveal his actual history and condition, but that a second confidential and accurate report be forwarded separately to the insurer. No such confidential report is in the file. Plaintiffs assert that this failure is due to the negligence of either the doctor or the insurer. The ultimate credibility of this theory is not before us. Alfredo had obvious physical abnormalities at the time of his medical examination but none were noted on the report. Dr. Martin testified that although he could recall nothing about Alfredo or the examination, he

As we have already noted, California law also permits the insurer to avoid liability on a life insurance policy issued to an applicant who made material misrepresentations about health history. However, the parties disagree over whether the question of misrepresentation under that state's law remains one for the trier of fact even in the face of untrue statements or omissions in an application. Plaintiffs maintain that California law permits them to offer a plausible explanation for the falsehoods appearing in the insurance application, an explanation which the insurer then may rebut in order to avoid liability on the policy. They cite Thompson v. Occidental Life Ins. Co., 9 Cal.3d 904, 109 Cal.Rptr. 473, 513 P.2d 353 (1973), to support this position. The defendant, on the other hand, argues that *Thompson* is limited to its peculiar facts, and that California would apply a conclusive presumption similar to New York's in the instant situation. The insurer relies on the old case of Telford v. Occidental Ins. Co., 9 Cal.2d 103, 69 P.2d 835 (1937).

We agree with plaintiffs' interpretation of California substantive law. In *Thompson,* the California Supreme Court upheld the trial court's finding that the insurer was liable on a life insurance policy despite obvious misstatements and omissions concerning the insured's medical history in the signed application. The court reached this result through a broad willingness to engage in speculation concerning plausible reasons—other than actual misrepresentations by the insured—for the falsehoods, speculations for which as the dissent in *Thompson* points out, there was little supporting evidence in the record. Although the insured in that case had answered truthfully about his basic medical problem, the court indicated that misstatements or nondisclosures could be excused even absent some minimal disclosure. For example, the court suggested that the trial court may have concluded that the insured forgot or did not appreciate the significance of the undisclosed facts, or that he did, in fact, disclose the truth to the medical examiner but that the latter inadvertently or intentionally failed to record it. The court went on to hold that, in order to avoid liability based on material misrepresentation, the insurer must negate, to the trier's satisfaction, the plausible explanations offered by the beneficiary-plaintiff for the false or incomplete answers in the application. Although the case represents a departure from the earlier ruling of *Telford,* which was similar to current New York law, *Thompson* states the most recent California law on the issue to be resolved here. Because California case law differs from that of New York, we must address the choice of law question raised on appeal.

A federal court applies the choice of law rules of the state in which it sits, here California, to determine the substantive law to apply in a diversity action. Klaxon Co. v. Stentor Co., 313 U.S. 487, 496, 61 S.Ct.

signed the reports; therefore, he assumed that he must have conducted the examination as he normally did. He stated that if those abnormalities were present, he would have detected them. He further testified, consistently in part with plaintiffs' theory, on how he might have handled a request for a confidential report.

1020, 1021–1022, 85 L.Ed. 1477 (1941). The parties agree that California uses governmental interest analysis as its choice of law rule, supplemented by the doctrine of comparative impairment in cases posing a true conflict. Travelers Ins. Co. v. Workmen's Comp. App. Bd., 68 Cal.2d 7, 11–15, 434 P.2d 992 (1967); Bernhard v. Harrah's Club, 16 Cal.3d 313, 128 Cal.Rptr. 215, 546 P.2d 719 (1976). They disagree, however, on the result that application of these rules yields in the present case.

New York law and California law implement competing governmental interests in the context of this case. The defendant is a New York insurer. New York has an interest in protecting its resident insurance companies from fraudulent claims and is also interested in regulating the conduct of parties forming insurance contracts within its borders. California has an interest in the rights of local plaintiffs, and while California law does not purport to demand for its resident-beneficiaries an absolute right to collect proceeds in the face of actual misrepresentation or fraud against insurers, it has economic, and, as the forum, judicial interests, in protecting its residents from an erroneous denial of insurance proceeds. Plaintiffs' theory here is that their claims are, in fact, valid despite what appear to be errors, omissions, or misstatements in the decedent's application. Without the opportunity that California law provides its residents to pursue such a theory, these residents might become an economic burden to the state.

Competing interests of two interested states direct the next inquiry, therefore, thus: As between California and New York, "whose interest would be the more impaired if its law were not applied"? Bernhard v. Harrah's Club, supra, 16 Cal.3d at 320, 128 Cal.Rptr. at 219, 546 P.2d at 723.

If California law is applied, the New York insurer still receives some protection against fraud, although at the additional cost of having to submit the issue of the insured's misrepresentation to the hazards of local triers of fact.

Assuming, as we must, that triers do their work impartially, and can discern fraudulent claims from those which are only apparently fraudulent, the insurer has all the protection insurers in interstate business are entitled to expect. The extra litigation expense occurs only when the beneficiaries reside in, or move to, a jurisdiction like California. That additional economic burden can be spread actuarially among policy purchasers across the nation as a cost of doing business nationwide. Thus, even if New York has an interest in protecting its resident insurers from those litigation costs, even that interest is not unreasonably impaired by application of California law. In theory, truly culpable conduct will still be deterred. The effect of the California rule will be to protect the legitimate claims of local beneficiaries while permitting the insurer to prevail if the decedent's conduct was as culpable as the paper record on its face tends to prove.

We conclude that New York interests would not be greatly impaired if California law were applied in this case. On the other hand, some significant California policy or interest would be impaired if New York law were applied. By virtue of their position, beneficiaries cannot protect their own interests at the insurance contract formation stage. Thus, if they are to be denied proceeds because of fraud at the time the insurance contract is entered into, beneficiaries have a strong need for protection from an erroneous denial—that is, denial when in fact the insured did not withhold material facts from the insurer. California affords its resident beneficiaries greater protection than does New York by leaving the question of actual misrepresentation to the trier rather than by resorting to a conclusive presumption. If New York law were to govern, then some California beneficiaries with valid claims might be denied the policy proceeds without any concomitant furtherance of New York's interests in protecting its insurers against invalid or fraudulent claims. Application of the doctrine of comparative impairment in this case, then, should lead to the adoption of California law.

The insurer seeks to avoid this result by arguing, among other things, that denial of the force of New York law would lead to forum shopping and nonuniformity of result on the same policy if beneficiaries should reside in different jurisdictions. Neither of these possibilities is present under the facts of this case. The insurer knew from the time the policy was issued that one beneficiary was a California resident. It thus had notice that a claim might arise from that state and the insurer could have protected itself better at the onset by conducting an investigation appropriate to the risk being underwritten. Both individual plaintiffs here are bona fide residents of the same state. There is no evidence that Becky Lettieri took up her residence for the purpose of forum shopping, and we express no opinion on the effect of such evidence if it were present.

The judgment is vacated and the case is remanded for further proceedings under the guidance of California law to the extent that it applies in federal diversity litigation within the district.

Remanded.

### *Problems*

1. (a) An agent reads the questions propounded in the insurance application to the applicant who truthfully answers the questions. Since such answers would preclude the issuance of the policy (and mean the loss of a commission by the agent), the agent enters a false answer. Is the insurance company estopped from denying liability under the policy on the grounds of false statements in the application? (Bear in mind the *Minsker* rule cited in the main case.)

(b) Suppose the applicant read the "doctored" application containing the false entries before signing the application. Is the insurer estopped?

(c) Suppose the agent tells the applicant that his truthful answers will mean he can't get insurance whereupon the applicant changes his truthful answers. Is the insurer estopped?

Variations on this situation are common. For a typical (and divided) decision see Liberty National Life Insurance Co. v. Houk, 248 Ga. 111, 281 S.E.2d 583 (1981).

2. X applied for life insurance and was examined and interviewed by the insurer's doctor who asked a series of questions set forth in a form entitled "Declarations to Medical Examiner" and wrote down X's answers. One question (# 44) asked the applicant to identify any attending physicians consulted in the last 5 years and the results of the examination. X had mentioned only his regular physician for a routine physical in response to another question. No answer was entered as to question # 44. In fact X had had several medical examinations during the past 5 years for gonorrhea of the throat, swollen lymph glands, etc. X signed the "Declaration" and the policy was issued with it attached. X died of AIDS within a year. The beneficiary asserts that the examining doctor failed to ask X question # 44 and it may be assumed this is true. Does the insurer have to pay (1) under New York law? (2) under California law? See Zachary Trading Inc. v. Northwestern Mut. Life Ins. Co. 668 F.Supp. 343 (S.D.N.Y.1987) where the decision was in favor of the insurer.

# Chapter 4

# THE DUTY OF GOOD FAITH AND FAIR DEALING

---

## A. THE ORIGINS—THIRD PARTY CASES

### PRELIMINARY NOTE

The Restatement, Contracts, (2d) § 205 * states:

"Every contract imposes upon each party a duty of good faith and fair dealing in its performance and its enforcement."

The comments following the section provide some enlightenment for interpretation:

"*d. Good faith performance.* Subterfuges and evasions violate the obligation of good faith in performance even though the actor believes his conduct to be justified. * * * A complete catalogue of types of bad faith is impossible, but the following types are among those which have been recognized in judicial decisions: evasion of the spirit of the bargain, lack of diligence and slacking off, willful rendering of imperfect performance, abuse of a power to specify terms, and interference with or failure to cooperate in the other party's performance."

"*e. Good faith in enforcement.* The obligation of good faith and fair dealing extends to the assertion, settlement and litigation of contract claims and defenses. * * * The obligation is violated by dishonest conduct such as conjuring up a pretended dispute, asserting an interpretation contrary to one's own understanding, or falsification of facts. It also extends to dealing which is candid but unfair, * * *. Other types of violation have been recognized in judicial decisions: harassing demands for assurances of performance, rejection of performance for unstated reasons, willful failure to mitigate damages, and abuse of a power to determine compliance or to terminate the contract. * * *"

Insurance students ought to distinguish two situations: (a) *first party claims,* where the insured person alleges failure of good faith and fair dealing by the insurer in handling the insured's claims under the policy (e.g., to disability benefits), and (b) *third party claims,* where the insurer fails to practice good faith and fair dealing in discharging his obligations to the insured with respect to claimants against the insured (e.g., fails to defend or to negotiate a settlement when a third party claims the insured is liable to the third party and the insured can claim that his insurance applies).

## CRISCI v. SECURITY INSURANCE COMPANY

Supreme Court of California, In Bank, 1967.
66 Cal.2d 425, 58 Cal.Rptr. 13, 426 P.2d 173.

PETERS, JUSTICE.

In an action against The Security Insurance Company of New Haven, Connecticut, the trial court awarded Rosina Crisci $91,000 (plus interest) because she suffered a judgment in a personal injury action after Security, her insurer, refused to settle the claim. Mrs. Crisci was also awarded $25,000 for mental suffering. Security has appealed.

June DiMare and her husband were tenants in an apartment building owned by Rosina Crisci. Mrs. DiMare was descending the apartment's outside wooden staircase when a tread gave way. She fell through the resulting opening up to her waist and was left hanging 15 feet above the ground. Mrs. DiMare suffered physical injuries and developed a very severe psychosis. In a suit brought against Mrs. Crisci the DiMares alleged that the step broke because Mrs. Crisci was negligent in inspecting and maintaining the stairs. They contended that Mrs. DiMare's mental condition was caused by the accident, and they asked for $400,000 as compensation for physical and mental injuries and medical expenses.

Mrs. Crisci had $10,000 of insurance coverage under a general liability policy issued by Security. The policy obligated Security to defend the suit against Mrs. Crisci and authorized the company to make any settlement it deemed expedient.[1] Security hired an experienced lawyer, Mr. Healy, to handle the case. Both he and defendant's claims manager believed that unless evidence was discovered showing that Mrs. DiMare had a prior mental illness, a jury would probably find that the accident precipitated Mrs. DiMare's psychosis. And both men believed that if the jury felt that the fall triggered the psychosis, a verdict of not less than $100,000 would be returned.

An extensive search turned up no evidence that Mrs. DiMare had any prior mental abnormality. As a teenager Mrs. DiMare had been in a Washington mental hospital, but only to have an abortion. Both Mrs.

1. Mrs. Crisci's own attorney, Mr. Pardini, was consulted by the counsel for the insurance company, but Mr. Pardini did not direct or control either settlement negotiations or the defense of Mrs. DiMare's suit.

DiMare and Mrs. Crisci found psychiatrists who would testify that the accident caused Mrs. DiMare's illness, and the insurance company knew of this testimony. Among those who felt the psychosis was not related to the accident were the doctors at the state mental hospital where Mrs. DiMare had been committed following the accident. All the psychiatrists agreed, however, that a psychosis could be triggered by a sudden fear of falling to one's death.

The exact chronology of settlement offers is not established by the record. However, by the time the DiMares' attorney reduced his settlement demands to $10,000, Security had doctors prepared to support its position and was only willing to pay $3,000 for Mrs. DiMare's physical injuries. Security was unwilling to pay one cent for the possibility of a plaintiff's verdict on the mental illness issue. This conclusion was based on the assumption that the jury would believe all of the defendant's psychiatric evidence and none of the plaintiff's. Security also rejected a $9,000 settlement demand at a time when Mrs. Crisci offered to pay $2,500 of the settlement.

A jury awarded Mrs. DiMare $100,000 and her husband $1,000. After an appeal (DiMare v. Cresci,[2] 58 Cal.2d 292, 23 Cal.Rptr. 772, 373 P.2d 860) the insurance company paid $10,000 of this amount, the amount of its policy. The DiMares then sought to collect the balance from Mrs. Crisci. A settlement was arranged by which the DiMares received $22,000, a 40 percent interest in Mrs. Crisci's claim to a particular piece of property, and an assignment of Mrs. Crisci's cause of action against Security. Mrs. Crisci, an immigrant widow of 70, became indigent. She worked as a babysitter, and her grandchildren paid her rent. The change in her financial condition was accompanied by a decline in physical health, hysteria, and suicide attempts. Mrs. Crisci then brought this action.

The liability of an insurer in excess of its policy limits for failure to accept a settlement offer within those limits was considered by this court in Comunale v. Traders & General Ins. Co., 50 Cal.2d 654, 328 P.2d 198, 68 A.L.R.2d 883. It was there reasoned that in every contract, including policies of insurance, there is an implied covenant of good faith and fair dealing that neither party will do anything which will injure the right of the other to receive the benefits of the agreement; that it is common knowledge that one of the usual methods by which an insured receives protection under a liability insurance policy is by settlement of claims without litigation; that the implied obligation of good faith and fair dealing requires the insurer to settle in an appropriate case although the express terms of the policy do not impose the duty; that in determining whether to settle the insurer must give the interests of the insured at least as much consideration as it gives to its own interests; and that when "there is great risk of a recovery beyond the policy limits so that the most reasonable manner of disposing of the claim is a settlement which can be made within those limits, a consideration in good faith of

2. In the prior litigation plaintiff was sued as "Rosina Cresci."

the insured's interest requires the insurer to settle the claim." (50 Cal.2d at p. 659, 328 P.2d at p. 201.)

In determining whether an insurer has given consideration to the interests of the insured, the test is whether a prudent insurer without policy limits would have accepted the settlement offer.

Several cases, in considering the liability of the insurer, contain language to the effect that bad faith is the equivalent of dishonesty, fraud, and concealment. Obviously a showing that the insurer has been guilty of actual dishonesty, fraud, or concealment is relevant to the determination whether it has given consideration to the insured's interest in considering a settlement offer within the policy limits. The language used in the cases, however, should not be understood as meaning that in the absence of evidence establishing actual dishonesty, fraud, or concealment no recovery may be had for a judgment in excess of the policy limits. Comunale v. Traders & General Ins. Co., supra, 50 Cal.2d 654, 658–659, 328 P.2d 198, makes it clear that liability based or an implied covenant exists whenever the insurer refuses to settle in an appropriate case and that liability may exist when the insurer unwarrantedly refuses an offered settlement where the most reasonable manner of disposing of the claim is by accepting the settlement. Liability is imposed not for a bad faith breach of the contract but for failure to meet the duty to accept reasonable settlements, a duty included within the implied covenant of good faith and fair dealing. Moreover, examination of the balance of the Palmer, Critz, and Davy opinions makes it abundantly clear that recovery may be based on unwarranted rejection of a reasonable settlement offer and that the absence of evidence, circumstantial or direct, showing actual dishonesty, fraud, or concealment is not fatal to the cause of action.

Amicus curiae argues that, whenever an insurer receives an offer to settle within the policy limits and rejects it, the insurer should be liable in every case for the amount of any final judgment whether or not within the policy limits. As we have seen, the duty of the insurer to consider the insured's interest in settlement offers within the policy limits arises from an implied covenant in the contract, and ordinarily contract duties are strictly enforced and not subject to a standard of reasonableness. Obviously, it will always be in the insured's interest to settle within the policy limits when there is any danger, however slight, of a judgment in excess of those limits. Accordingly the rejection of a settlement within the limits where there is any danger of a judgment in excess of the limits can be justified, if at all, only on the basis of interests of the insurer, and, in light of the common knowledge that settlement is one of the usual methods by which an insured receives protection under a liability policy, it may not be unreasonable for an insured who purchases a policy with limits to believe that a sum of money equal to the limits is available and will be used so as to avoid liability on his part with regard to any covered accident. In view of such expectation an insurer should not be permitted to further its own interests by rejecting opportunities to settle within the policy limits unless it is also willing to absorb losses which may result from its failure to settle.

The proposed rule is a simple one to apply and avoids the burdens of a determination whether a settlement offer within the policy limits was reasonable. The proposed rule would also eliminate the danger that an insurer, faced with a settlement offer at or near the policy limits, will reject it and gamble with the insured's money to further its own interests. Moreover, it is not entirely clear that the proposed rule would place a burden on insurers substantially greater than that which is present under existing law. The size of the judgment recovered in the personal injury action when it exceeds the policy limits, although not conclusive, furnishes an inference that the value of the claim is the equivalent of the amount of the judgment and that acceptance of an offer within those limits was the most reasonable method of dealing with the claim.

Finally, and most importantly, there is more than a small amount of elementary justice in a rule that would require that, in this situation where the insurer's and insured's interests necessarily conflict, the insurer, which may reap the benefits of its determination not to settle, should also suffer the detriments of its decision. On the basis of these and other considerations, a number of commentators have urged that the insurer should be liable for any resulting judgment where it refuses to settle within the policy limits. (Note (1966) 18 Stan.L.Rev. 475, 482–485; Note (1951) 60 Yale L.J. 1037, 1041–1042; Comment (1949) 48 Mich.L.Rev. 95, 102; Note (1945) 13 U.Chi.L.Rev. 105, 109.)

We need not, however, here determine whether there might be some countervailing considerations precluding adoption of the proposed rule because, under Comunale v. Traders & General Ins. Co., supra, 50 Cal.2d 654, 328 P.2d 198, and the cases following it, the evidence is clearly sufficient to support the determination that Security breached its duty to consider the interests of Mrs. Crisci in proposed settlements. Both Security's attorney and its claims manager agreed that if Mrs. DiMare won an award for her psychosis, that award would be at least $100,000. Security attempts to justify its rejection of a settlement by contending that it believed Mrs. DiMare had no chance of winning on the mental suffering issue. That belief in the circumstances present could be found to be unreasonable. Security was putting blind faith in the power of its psychiatrists to convince the jury when it knew that the accident could have caused the psychosis, that its agents had told it that without evidence of prior mental defects a jury was likely to believe the fall precipitated the psychosis, and that Mrs. DiMare had reputable psychiatrists on her side. Further, the company had been told by a psychiatrist that in a group of 24 psychiatrists, 12 could be found to support each side.

The trial court found that defendant "knew that there was a considerable risk of substantial recovery beyond said policy limits" and that "the defendant did not give as much consideration to the financial interests of its said insured as it gave to its own interests." That is all that was required. The award of $91,000 must therefore be affirmed.

We must next determine the propriety of the award of Mrs. Crisci of $25,000 for her mental suffering. In Comunale v. Traders & General Ins. Co., supra, 50 Cal.2d 654, 663, 328 P.2d 198, 203, it was held that an action of the type involved here sounds in both contract and tort and that "where a case sounds both in contract and tort the plaintiff will ordinarily have freedom of election between an action of tort and one of contract. Eads v. Marks, 39 Cal.2d 807, 811, 249 P.2d 257. An exception to this rule is made in suits for personal injury caused by negligence, where the tort character of the action is considered to prevail (citations), but no such exception is applied in cases, like the present one, which relate to financial damage (citations)." [3] Although this rule was applied in Comunale with regard to a statute of limitations, the rule is also applicable in determining liability. Insofar as language in Critz v. Farmers Ins. Group, supra, 230 Cal.App.2d 788, 799, 41 Cal.Rptr. 401, might be interpreted as providing that the action for wrongful refusal to settle sounds solely in contract, it is disapproved.

Fundamental in our jurisprudence is the principle that for every wrong there is a remedy and that an injured party should be compensated for all damage proximately caused by the wrongdoer. Although we recognize exceptions from these fundamental principles, no departure should be sanctioned unless there is a strong necessity therefor.

The general rule of damages in tort is that the injured party may recover for all detriment caused whether it could have been anticipated or not. (Civ.Code, § 3333; see Hunt Bros. Co. v. San Lorenzo etc. Co., 150 Cal. 51, 56, 87 P. 1093, 7 L.R.A., N.S., 913.) In accordance with the general rule, it is settled in this state that mental suffering constitutes an aggravation of damages when it naturally ensues from the act complained of, and in this connection mental suffering includes nervousness, grief, anxiety, worry, shock, humiliation and indignity as well as physical pain. The commonest example of the award of damages for mental suffering in addition to other damages is probably where the plaintiff suffers personal injuries in addition to mental distress as a result of either negligent or intentional misconduct by the defendant. Such awards are not confined to cases where the mental suffering award was in addition to an award for personal injuries; damages for mental distress have also been awarded in cases where the tortious conduct was an interference with property rights without any personal injuries apart from the mental distress.

3. Comunale v. Traders & General Ins. Co., supra, 50 Cal.2d 654, 328 P.2d 198, was mainly concerned with the contract aspect of the action. This may be due to the facts that the tort duty is ordinarily based on the insurer's assumption of the defense and of settlement negotiations (see Keeton, Liability Insurance and Responsibility for Settlement (1954) 67 Harv.L.Rev. 1136, 1138–1139; Note (1966), supra, 18 Stan.L.Rev. 475), and that in Comunale the insurer did not undertake defense or settlement but denied coverage. In any event Comunale expressly recognizes that "wrongful refusal to settle has generally been treated as a tort." (50 Cal.2d at p. 663, 328 P.2d at p. 203.)

We are satisfied that a plaintiff who as a result of a defendant's tortious conduct loses his property and suffers mental distress may recover not only for the pecuniary loss but also for his mental distress. No substantial reason exists to distinguish the cases which have permitted recovery for mental distress in actions for invasion of property rights. The principal reason for limiting recovery of damages for mental distress is that to permit recovery of such damages would open the door to fictitious claims, to recovery for mere bad manners, and to litigation in the field of trivialities. (Prosser, Torts (3d ed. 1964) § 11, p. 43.) Obviously, where, as here, the claim is actionable and has resulted in substantial damages apart from those due to mental distress, the danger of fictitious claims is reduced, and we are not here concerned with mere bad manners or trivialities but tortious conduct resulting in substantial invasions of clearly protected interests.[4]

Recovery of damages for mental suffering in the instant case does not mean that in every case of breach of contract the injured party may recover such damages. Here the breach also constitutes a tort. Moreover, plaintiff did not seek by the contract involved here to obtain a commercial advantage but to protect herself against the risks of accidental losses, including the mental distress which might follow from the losses. Among the considerations in purchasing liability insurance, as insurers are well aware, is the peace of mind and security it will provide in the event of an accidental loss, and recovery of damages for mental suffering has been permitted for breach of contracts which directly concern the comfort, happiness or personal esteem of one of the parties. (Chelini v. Nieri, 32 Cal.2d 480, 482, 196 P.2d 915.)

It is not claimed that plaintiff's mental distress was not caused by defendant's refusal to settle or that the damages awarded were excessive in the light of plaintiff's substantial suffering.

The judgment is affirmed.

### *Notes*

1. In *Comunale v. Traders & General Ins. Co.,* 50 Cal.2d 654, 328 P.2d 198 (1958), cited in *Crisci,* plaintiffs were struck in a marked pedestrian crosswalk by a truck driven by Percy Sloan, who was insured by defendant. Sloan's policy provided for maximum liability of $10,000 for each person injured and $20,000 for each accident, but when Sloan notified the defendant of the accident, he was told that the policy did not provide coverage because he was driving a truck that did not belong to him. Defendant repeatedly refused to defend Sloan against a suit brought by plaintiffs, despite being informed that a judgement was likely to exceed the policy limits, and refused to accept an offer of settlement within the policy limits. A judgment in excess of the policy limits was subsequently entered. Plaintiff obtained an assignment of Sloan's rights against defendant and commenced any action to recover the portion of the judgment that was in excess of the policy limits.

4. Nor are we here concerned with the problem whether invasion of the plaintiff's right to be free from emotional disturbance is actionable where there is no injury to person or property rights in addition to the inflicted mental distress.

The California Supreme Court stated that "[t]here is an implied covenant of good faith and fair dealing in every contract that neither party will do anything which will injure the right of the other to receive the benefits of the agreement. This principle is applicable to insurance." The court further stated that the implied obligation of good faith and fair dealing requires the insurer to settle in an appropriate case even though the express terms of the policy do not impose such a duty. When there is a great risk of recovery in excess of the policy limits, a consideration in good faith of the insured's interest requires the insurer to settle the claim. "The insurer, in deciding whether a claim should be compromised, must take into account the interest of the insured and give it at least as much consideration as it does its own interest." Finally, the court held that "an insurer, who wrongfully declines to defend and who refuses to accept a reasonable settlement within the policy limits in violation of its duty to consider in good faith the interest of the insured in the settlement, is liable for the entire judgment against the insured even if its exceeds the policy limits."

In analyzing whether the duty of good faith and fair dealing was a contract or a tort action, the court stated "[a]n action for damages in excess of the policy limits based on an insurer's wrongful failure to settle is assignable whether the action is considered as sounding in tort or in contract." In dealing with a statute of limitations issue, the court indicated that "where a case sounds both in contract and tort the plaintiff will ordinarily have freedom of election between an action of tort and one of contract."

2. In *Gruenberg v. Aetna Ins. Co.,* 9 Cal.3d 566, 108 Cal.Rptr. 480, 510 P.2d 1032 (1973), decided after *Crisci,* the court recognized the insurer's duty of good faith and fair dealing toward its insured (*Comunale* and *Crisci* both considered the duty of the insurer to act in good faith in handling the claims of third persons). In *Gruenberg,* the plaintiff owned a restaurant which was destroyed by fire. Plaintiff was charged with arson and defrauding an insurer, both charges of which were dismissed at a preliminary hearing. Plaintiff alleged that the defendant insurer acted to falsely imply that plaintiff had motive to deliberately burn down his place of business. Further, when plaintiff refused to appear at an examination conducted by defendant on the advice of his attorney (pending the outcome of the criminal charges), defendant denied liability.

In its analysis, the court cited *Comunale* and *Crisci,* stating that an insurer has a duty to deal fairly and in good faith with its insured, a duty which sounds in both contract and tort and is imposed because there is an implied covenant of good faith and fair dealing in every contract. The duty not to unreasonably withhold payment due an insured are "merely two different aspects of the same duty."

"An insurer owes to its insured an implied-in-law duty of good faith and fair dealing that it will do nothing to deprive the insured of the benefits of the policy." The court went on to say that, as in *Crisci,* the violation of that duty sounds in tort notwithstanding that it also constitutes a breach of contract. The court concluded that "it is manifest that a common legal principle underlies all of the foregoing decisions; namely that in every insurance contract there is an implied covenant of good faith and fair dealing." This duty applies equally whether the insurer is dealing with the claims of third persons against the insured or with the claims of the insured. "Accordingly, when the insurer unreasonably and in bad faith withholds payment of the claim of its insured, it is subject to liability in tort."

## BETTS v. ALLSTATE INSURANCE COMPANY

Court of Appeal, Fourth District, 1984.
154 Cal.App.3d 688, 201 Cal.Rptr. 528.

[Ed. Note: A good part of the elaborate statement of facts by the Court has been summarized. Summarized portions are placed in brackets.]

STANIFORTH, ASSOCIATE JUSTICE.

In an earlier (underlying) lawsuit for damages arising out of an automobile intersection accident (*Gallucci v. Betts* ), Anne E. Gallucci obtained a jury verdict-judgment against Debra Betts for damages of $450,000, $350,000 in excess of Betts' automobile insurance policy issued by Allstate Insurance Company (Allstate). Allstate assumed the Betts defense, furnished the law firm of Ruston and Nance (Ruston) to represent Betts in the underlying lawsuit, but flatly denied liability and adamantly refused during the entire course of litigation and up to and including the motion for new trial to accept Gallucci's offer to accept its policy limits in settlement.

In the present action Betts sued Allstate, alleging breach of covenant to deal fairly and in good faith. She charges a "bad faith" refusal to accept a settlement offer within the policy limits. Betts alleges Ruston was negligent in conducting the defense of her lawsuit. A jury returned special verdicts awarding (1) compensatory damages against Allstate of $500,000 (to which the trial court added prejudgment interest and costs) and (2) punitive damages of $3,000,000. The jury found Ruston was also negligent and awarded $500,000 jointly and severally against the lawyers and Allstate for emotional distress. A motion for new trial was conditionally granted as to the latter $500,000 award of damages unless Betts accepted a reduction of the award of $500,000 to $50,000. Betts accepted that condition and a new trial was denied in its entirety. Allstate and Ruston appeal the respective portions of the judgment against them. Betts cross-appeals the order which conditionally granted the partial new trial.

[Gallucci, the victim, was it appears also insured by Allstate. After the accident, Allstate made several estimates of liability, at one point concluding that the case was 95–5 against liability. Because the accident involved two cars colliding in an intersection, Allstate hired Truesdale Laboratories, an accident reconstruction firm, to investigate and report. Truesdale filed three reports serially, each meeting with dissatisfaction at Allstate, (201 Cal.Rptr. at 534): "Thereafter from Allstate's head office to the district level the hiding of the Truesdale reports became a focus of activity." It was suggested at one juncture that the reports be put in the hands of a law firm where, after deletion of references to

Allstate, the firm could assert the attorney's work product privilege. The Ruston firm refused to cooperate. Allstate obtained from another of its District offices Gallucci's medical records (held there because she had filed her claim for medical payments under her own Allstate policy) and relabelled it to indicate that it had originated in connection with Gallucci's claim against Betts. One of the witnesses to the accident (Pamela Thayer) seemed initially favorable to Betts but later revised her version of the collision which at first had Gallucci at fault. Allstate came to regard her as "flaky" and "unreliable" and unable to substantiate Betts' version of the accident.

Allstate's appointed lawyers (the Ruston firm acting through attorney Powers) did not report an initial settlement offer at the policy limits to Betts, but did report a succeeding pre-trial offer (the "Bahan demand") to her. Strowmatt, an Allstate employee notified her of this and she was subsequently summoned to a conference at the Ruston office where: (201 Cal.Rptr. at 536) ]

* * *

Nineteen-year-old Betts went to Ruston's office to participate in the meeting concerning Bahan's demand. Betts said she relied entirely on Dragonette, Allstate's trial attorney. She had no reason to doubt that he was advising her or making a decision other than in her best interest. She did not understand the reference to a *settlement* conference nor did she understand what was meant by the Strowmatt letter saying that *her policy limits were being demanded.* At that meeting there was no discussion of a possible conflict of interest arising because of the settlement demand. *Betts was told nothing about the known liability problems arising from the Truesdale findings, Gallucci's employment of a specialist on traffic signals, or Thayer's dismissal,* not as a favorable witness, but *as "a flake."* Betts was not informed of the settlement recommendation of Dragonette and Strowmatt.

The jury could draw a rational inference the lawyers assured Betts she would win at trial. Typical of the statements made to her were: "You had a green light and you got to give that a try. You shouldn't have someone else in the wrong get the money. They're trying to get the money and you had a green light and you should try it. We can win. While we admire you Ms. Betts there is not too many people like you who stand behind what they say and feel the right and take action upon it." Myers recounted Betts and her father had met with the defense attorneys and they "both tell us to try the case." Betts maintained she had done nothing wrong and should *the verdict exceed the limits she would "just file bankruptcy."*

Dragonette signed a letter to the insurance company (actually written by Strowmatt) asserting Betts was *virtually judgment proof.* He noted *her understanding that should the jury not believe her and should a substantial verdict result she would file bankruptcy to discharge the obligation.* Most important to the lawyer was this: Betts was positive she had the green light and the other party was entirely at fault. He stated Betts understood the law of comparative negligence but simply did not feel the accident was one percent her fault.

Pursuant to instructions from Allstate's office, Dragonette's response (August 4, 1977) to Bahan's demands was to continue the "deny/defend" posture of the insured.

A judicial settlement conference was held on August 10, 1977; Allstate refused to *pay one cent in settlement.* The conference occurred without any notice to Betts. Strowmatt was present and the court questioned him at the outset as to any offer. He stated that he had "zilch" or "zip" (no money) to offer. Thereupon the court terminated the conference.

[Apparently evidence began to point more strongly toward liability on Betts' part. Gallucci's attorney, Trotter, hired a specialist in accident reconstruction, Krueper, who after a study concluded that Betts had run a red light at the intersection. At the trial, the defense made no effective rebuttal of evidence pointing to liability. Defense counsel refused to stipulate Gallucci's incompetence (she was diagnosed as having a brain stem injury with coma) and Trotter brought her into the courtroom where an Allstate employee said that she was one of the "most pathetic pieces of humanity" he had observed. Nonetheless, Allstate continued to refuse to pay and rejected all offers from Gallucci's side to settle within the policy limits.

At the end of the trial (Dragonette representing Betts) the jury returned a verdict for Gallucci in the amount of $450,000.]

* * *

Immediately after the excess verdict a senior claims attorney for Allstate, Wathen, took over active control of the case from Ruston. Allstate's posture, however, remained the same regarding settlement. At this late date Ruston engaged in a series of acts (which will be explored later in connection with the negligence claim against the Ruston firm), in failing to look after Betts' obligation arising from the excess verdict. For example, Trotter wished, in exchange for an assignment of Betts' rights, to release her from personal liability. Powers advised her not to assign; Trotter was described as the "enemy."

Allstate filed a motion for new trial. Pending its hearing, Allstate failed to explore the possibility of paying the $100,000 limits immediately in exchange for an offer of a full satisfaction. Although initially authorizing $100,000 for that purpose Allstate lawyer Wathen reversed himself. Wathen feared the money, if offered, would be irretrievably lost in the event the motion for new trial was granted or Allstate prevailed on appeal.[6] At no time during this period was Betts ever advised by anyone she might have to sue Allstate. Moreover, there was an attempted manipulation of Betts to keep her from seeking independent counsel.

6. The good faith of this position may be questioned. An appeal was not seriously considered because a bond would be necessary; in the event of affirmance Trotter would be able to obtain a full satisfaction of judgment without a bad faith lawsuit.

*Only after Betts was examined at a debtor's examination by Trotter and his offer to pay the cost of such consultation with an independent attorney did Dragonette give Betts the name of a lawyer to consult.*

In the post-judgment period Allstate attempted to change its files by the inclusion of a suggestion had Allstate known of Krueper's testimony in time the matter would have been settled, but *the opposition's tactics had prevented such knowledge.* After the judgment, Ruston continued to cooperate with Allstate. Powers wrote to Allstate: The verdict was "not supported by the evidence."

DISCUSSION

ALLSTATE APPEAL

*A.*

In addition to the duties imposed upon the parties to a contract by the express terms of their agreement the law implies in every contract a covenant of good faith and fair dealing. * * * The implied promise requires each contracting party to refrain from doing anything to impair the right of the other to receive the benefits of the agreement. * * * And as was pointed out in Egan v. Mutual of Omaha Ins. Co., supra, 24 Cal.3d at 818, 169 Cal.Rptr. 691, 620 P.2d 141: "The precise nature and extent of the duties imposed by such implied promise will depend upon the contractual purposes."

The California Supreme Court in Comunale v. Traders & Generals Ins. Co., [50 Cal.2d 654, 328 P.2d 198] addressed the nature and extent of duties imposed by this implied covenant in liability insurance policies. There the Supreme Court held an insurer in determining whether to settle a claim must give at least as much consideration to the welfare of the insured as it gives to its own interest. The governing standard is whether a prudent insurer would have accepted the settlement offer if it alone were to be liable for the entire judgment. * * * An insurer may be held liable for a judgment against the insured in excess of its policy limits where it has breached the implied covenant of good faith and fair dealing by unreasonably refusing to accept a settlement offer within the policy limits. * * * Allstate's argument that liability for an excess judgment is not imposed unless there is a "bad faith" breach of the contract is unsound. Liability is imposed "for failure to meet the duty to accept reasonable settlements, a duty included within the implied covenant of good faith and fair dealing." (Crisci v. Security Ins. Co., 66 Cal.2d 425, 430, 58 Cal.Rptr. 13, 426 P.2d 173.) "[R]ecovery may be based on an unwarranted rejection of a reasonable settlement offer and * * * *the absence of evidence, circumstantial or direct, showing actual dishonesty, fraud, or concealment is not fatal to the cause of action.*" (Ibid.; italics added; see also Gruenberg v. Aetna Ins. Co., 9 Cal.3d 566, 573, 108 Cal.Rptr. 480, 510 P.2d 1032.)

The duty to deal in good faith with the other party to the contract of insurance "*is a duty imposed by law, not one arising by the terms of the contract itself.*" (Gruenberg v. Aetna Ins. Co., supra, at p. 574, 108 Cal.Rptr. 480, 510 P.2d 1032; italics added.) In other words this duty of dealing fairly and in good faith is nonconsensual in origin rather than consensual.

The obligation of good faith and fair dealing requires the insurer to settle a claim in an appropriate case although the express terms of the policy do not impose such a duty. (Murphy v. Allstate Ins. Co., supra, 17 Cal.3d at p. 941, 132 Cal.Rptr. 424, 553 P.2d 584.) *The insurer must settle "within policy limits where there is a substantial likelihood of recovery in excess of those limits."* (Ibid. italics added.) This duty to settle is implied in law to protect the insured from exposure to liability in excess of coverage as a result of the insured's gamble on which only the insured might lose. (Ibid.; Shapero v. Allstate Ins. Co., 14 Cal. App.3d 433, 92 Cal.Rptr. 244.) "[I]n deciding whether or not to compromise the claim, the insurer must conduct itself as though it alone were liable for the entire amount of the judgment." (Johansen v. California State Auto. Assn. Inter–Ins. Bureau, supra, 15 Cal.3d at p. 16, 123 Cal.Rptr. 288, 538 P.2d 744.)

Thus, the permissible considerations in evaluating the reasonableness of the settlement offer are whether in light of the victim's injury and the probable liability of the insured the ultimate judgment is likely to exceed the amount of the settlement offer. Such factors as the limits imposed by the policy, a desire to reduce the amount of future settlements, or a belief that the policy does not provide coverage do not affect a decision as to whether the settlement offer in question is a reasonable one.

*B.*

A key factual question put to the jury was: Were the repeated offers made by the Trotter firm reasonable in the light of all of the circumstances of this case? If reasonable, their rejection by Allstate became unreasonable, therefore imposing on Allstate responsibility for the excess judgment.

The judgment was four and one-half times the offer of settlement. It is a rational inference the value of Gallucci's claim was the equivalent of the amount of the judgment. An acceptance of an offer within the policy limits was a most reasonable method of dealing with her claim.

These conclusions do not just arise by hindsight. There is uncontradicted evidence Allstate, whether blindly or purposefully, accepted the statement of the 17–year–old Debra Betts and upon that basis and that basis alone proclaimed its "no pay/defend stance" and refused to make any offer whatsoever. There was a mountain of available evidence which put Allstate on notice that this was a case of enormous liability. The findings of the Truesdale expert are the most significant. They demonstrate the Allstate prediction of 95–5 exposure had no rational basis.

Allstate failed to question the accuracy and soundness of its own client's conclusion. Gallucci's expert was able to take Betts' exact words and make out a prima facie case for Betts' liability. Betts' first account, if *facts* not conclusions, are the measure, would support at least an offer of the policy limits once the enormous Gallucci damages were known. These facts warrant the rational inference of either a willful or negligent failure by Allstate to investigate the facts surrounding Betts' liability.

In Egan v. Mutual of Omaha Ins. Co., supra, 24 Cal.3d 809, 817, 169 Cal.Rptr. 691, 620 P.2d 141, it was held an insurer may breach the covenant of good faith and fair dealing by failing to properly investigate its insured's claim. By equal parity of reasoning a failure to investigate and fairly appraise the third party's claim against the insured would breach the covenant of good faith and fair dealing. (Ibid.) Allstate's figurative hiding its head in the sand (or hiding adverse reports) is not a law-sanctioned approach to reasonable investigation and performance of its duty.

There is more than substantial evidence to support the jury's conclusion Allstate unreasonably rejected the policy limits offer made on several occasions by Gallucci's attorney. The compensatory money award, the excess over the policy limits plus interest, is affirmed.[7]

*C.*

The next question is: Was Allstate's breach of duty accompanied by oppression, fraud and/or malice warranting exemplary damages? In an action for breach of an obligation not arising from contract, Civil Code section 3294, subdivision (a), provides for sanctions by way of exemplary damages "where the defendant has been guilty of oppression, fraud, or malice." The plaintiff, in addition to the actual damages, "may recover damages for the sake of example and by way of punishing the defendant." (Civil Code § 3294, subd. (a).)

Under subdivision (c)(1) of the same section, "malice" means "conduct which is intended by the defendant to cause injury to the plaintiff or conduct which is carried on by the defendant with a conscious disregard of the rights or safety of others." The term "oppression" means "subjecting a person to cruel and unjust hardship in conscious disregard for that person's rights" (Civil Code § 3294, subd. (c)(2)) and the term "fraud" means "an intentional misrepresentation, deceit, or concealment of a material fact known to the defendant with the intention on the part of the defendant of thereby depriving a person of property or legal rights or otherwise causing injury." (Civil Code § 3294, subd. (c)(3); see Johns, California Damages (2d ed 1977) at pp. 394–395.) Thus an insurer's bad faith may not only breach the implied covenant of good faith and fair dealing but also can be treated for tort purposes as a basis for exemplary damages where it occurs in a context of malice, fraud or oppression. * * *

7. Allstate now challenges the sufficiency, competency, adequacy of the Gallucci offers. Allstate summarily rejected these offers without any attempt to seek clarification—it felt them ambiguous or incomplete. Allstate cannot now in good conscience use its own failure to explore the settlement offer as a defense of its own breach of duty to tender the policy limits—exactly what the Gallucci attorneys were willing to accept.

As summarized above, there was more than substantial evidence before the jury to support a finding Allstate had breached its duty to deal reasonably and in good faith with Betts, rendering Allstate liable to pay compensatory damages for all detriments caused by the breach. However, such a determination does not in itself establish Allstate acted with the quality of intent which is requisite to an award of punitive damages. * * *

To find the requisite intent for an award of punitive damages, it is necessary to search beyond the facts of [un]reasonable response to those adducing motive and intent. * * * There must be substantial evidence of an intent to vex, injure and annoy, a conscious disregard of the plaintiff's rights, before punitive damages may be awarded. (Silberg v. California Life Ins. Co., 11 Cal.3d 452, 462, 113 Cal.Rptr. 711, 521 P.2d 1103.)

A brief highlighting of the evidence demonstrates the substantial evidence that warranted the jury in making a finding Allstate's intended to vex, injure, and annoy. From almost the day of commencement of its duty to represent, defend and indemnify Betts, Allstate adopted an objectively unreasonable "no liability/no pay/defend" stance. This obstinate attitude-intent grew in strength in face of evidence piled upon evidence pointing to liability and ultimately to a verdict far in excess of policy limits.

There is much more here than Allstate's unwillingness to accept its responsibility to defend its insureds. Evidence abounds of an irrational refusal to face up to adverse evidence. The Truesdale reports disclosed Betts liability. The jury could draw a rational inference that Allstate deliberately concealed these adverse reports, not only from the other side but from their own insured.

Attorney Dragonette's failure for some unknown reason to pursue the cross examination of Gallucci's expert to determine his opinion and its fact basis gives rise to a whole series of rational adverse inferences suggesting Allstate's attorneys, as well as Allstate were unwilling to develop a record which would require abandonment of their "no liability/no pay/defend" policy.

The highly questionable practice of Allstate not putting adverse facts in writing—the "use the telephone" directive—indicates a lack of good faith in dealing with, an intent to vex, injure, and annoy, their client. Allstate's disreputable practice of violating its duty to one insured by "backdooring"—examining into the cross-file of another—suggests an intent to defraud or oppress its own clients.

The jury could reasonably conclude Allstate wilfully manipulated its own client through the process of coaching, encouraging a patently unreasonable belief in 17-year-old Betts that she had not run the red light—contrary to a whole series of developing facts. It is a further reasonable inference that Allstate, through its counsel, attempted to instill in Betts the determination, if there was an excess judgment, to go bankrupt. The post-trial manipulation of Betts again evidences an intent to vex, injure, and annoy. The moment of the excess verdict (if not before) there arose a duty to offer Betts independent counsel. Ruston, the Allstate-hired law firm, was at that moment placed in a position of open conflict of interest. Yet neither Allstate nor its attorneys bothered to inform the client. It was not until Betts was examined by opposing counsel, Trotter, at the debtor's examination, that she was advised of the necessity of and thereafter tendered independent counsel.

The foregoing evidence supports a conclusion of callous indifference to, an intent to vex, injure and annoy its insured. Allstate's counsel, even on this appeal, seek to minimize the disturbing practice by Allstate claiming "only by a handful of disgruntled former employees" does this evidence appear.

Many of the actions by Allstate could be, with myopic charity, described as negligent failures to investigate the claim against their insured. However, from these same facts a more sinister conclusion appears—an intent to vex, injure, and annoy Betts.

Finally, the almost irrational refusal to authorize any settlement even after an excess judgment and denial of a motion for new trial is hard evidence of malice, a willful intent to vex, injure, and annoy Betts.

The Supreme Court in Egan v. Mutual of Omaha Ins. Co., supra, 24 Cal.3d 809, 820, 169 Cal.Rptr. 691, 620 P.2d 141, shed light on the duties owed to an insured in context of a claim of exemplary damages:

> " '[A]s a supplier of a public service rather than a manufactured product, the obligations of insurers go beyond meeting reasonable expectations of coverage. *The obligations of good faith and fair dealing encompass qualities of decency and humanity inherent in the responsibilities of a fiduciary. Insurers hold themselves out as fiduciaries, and with the public's trust must go private responsibility consonant with that trust.' [Citation.] Furthermore, the relationship of insurer and insured is inherently unbalanced;* the adhesive nature of insurance contracts places the insurer in a superior bargaining position. *The availability of punitive damages is thus compatible with recognition of insurers' underlying public obligations and reflects an attempt to restore balance in the contractual relationship.* [Citation.]" (Italics added.)

More than substantial evidence warrants the conclusion that Allstate was guilty of oppression and malice and acted with an intent to vex, injure, and annoy and with a conscious disregard of Betts' rights. * * *

The judgment in all respects is affirmed.

### *Note*

The extensive comments of the court about the liability of the Ruston law firm to Betts have been omitted from the edited version of the case reproduced above. Because they are interesting for their separate bearing on insurance litigation, these comments are reproduced in this note. They follow, 201 Cal.Rptr. 544–46:

* * *

The Ruston Appeal

A.

Betts sued the Ruston firm, charging these lawyers negligently conducted themselves in defense of the Gallucci personal injury action. The jury awarded $500,000 joint and severally against both Ruston and Allstate for emotional distress (as well as a separate $3 million in punitive damages against Allstate alone). The trial court remitted the $500,000 amount to $50,000 as a condition of not granting a new trial. Ruston appeals the $50,000 judgment.

Ruston contends in light of the special findings of the jury, judgment must be entered in favor of Ruston. The first issue in the special verdict was posed by this question, "Was defendant Ruston and Nance negligent?" The jury answered, "Yes." Issue number two tendered the question, "Was the negligence of defendant, Ruston and Nance, a proximate cause of the excess verdict being rendered against the plaintiff?" The jury answered this question, "No." Issue number five was the question, "If your answer to issue number one is 'yes,' was the negligence of defendant, Ruston and Nance, a proximate cause of damage to plaintiff for fears, anxiety and other mental and emotional distress?" The jury answered, "Yes."

Thus the jury found the total dollar value of Betts' humiliation, emotional distress, and chagrin amounted to half a million dollars. It also found the conduct of the Ruston lawyers proximately caused, at least in part, that humiliation and emotional distress. The jury was most perceptive. While finding the negligent conduct of Ruston was not a proximate cause of the excess judgment, it found their conduct was so egregious in concert with Allstate as to cause Betts to suffer humiliation, emotional distress, chagrin, worry and nervousness to her damages of $500,000.

In accepting employment to render legal services, an attorney impliedly agrees to use such skill, prudence, and diligence as lawyers of ordinary skill and capacity commonly possess, and he is subject to liability for damage resulting from failure so to perform. (Lucas v. Hamm, 56 Cal.2d 583, 591, 15 Cal.Rptr. 821, 364 P.2d 685.) Furthermore, it is an attorney's duty to "protect his client in every possible way," and it is a violation of that duty for the attorney to "assume a position adverse or antagonistic to his client without the latter's free and intelligent consent given after full knowledge of all the facts and circumstances." The attorney is "precluded from assuming any relation which would prevent him from devoting his entire energies to his client's interests." (Anderson v. Eaton, 211 Cal. 113, 116, 293 P. 788; Klemm v. Superior Court, 75 Cal.App.3d 893, 901–902, 142 Cal.Rptr. 509.)

These traditional obligations of an attorney are in no way abridged by the fact that an insurer employs him to represent an insured. Typically, in such a situation, the attorney in effect has two clients, to each of whom is owed a "high duty of care." To the insured, the attorney owes "the same obligations of good faith and fidelity as if he had retained the attorney personally." (Lysick v. Walcom, 258 Cal.App.2d 136, 146, 65 Cal.Rptr. 406.)

Provided there is full disclosure and consent, an attorney may undertake to represent dual interests. However, whether in the insurer-insured context or otherwise, the attorney who undertakes to represent parties with divergent interests owes the "highest duty" to each to make a "full disclosure of all facts and circumstances which are necessary to enable the parties to make a fully informed decision regarding the subject matter of litigation, including the areas of potential conflict and the possibility and desirability of seeking independent legal advice." (Klemm v. Superior Court, supra, 75 Cal.App.3d at p. 901, 142 Cal.Rptr. 509; American Mut. Liab. Ins. Co. v. Superior Court, 38 Cal.App.3d 579, 590, 113 Cal.Rptr. 561; Lysick v. Walcom, supra, 258 Cal.App.2d at pp. 147–149, 65 Cal.Rptr. 406.)

The loyalty owed to one client by an attorney "cannot consume that owed to the other." (Ishmael v. Millington, 241 Cal.App.2d 520, 526, 50 Cal.Rptr. 592.) Thus a lawyer who, while purporting to continue to represent an insured devotes himself to the interests of the insurer without notification or disclosure to the insured breaches his obligations to the insured and is guilty of negligence. (Lysick v. Walcom, supra, 258 Cal. App.2d at pp. 150–152, 65 Cal.Rptr. 406.) Ruston mischaracterizes its duty as the obligation to achieve reasonable settlements before judgment, rather than the wider-reaching lawyer's obligation to exercise due care to protect a client's best interests in all ethical ways and at all stages.

Ruston asserts expert testimony was indispensable to a showing of its breach of duty. Expert testimony is not required to establish legal malpractice in all cases. (Wright v. Williams, 47 Cal.App.3d 802, 810, 121 Cal.Rptr. 194.) This is not a case in which the question of breach turned on legal technicalities requiring the fine exercise of professional judgment. The issue was simply whether Ruston did or did not abandon Betts' best interests in deference to the conflicting interest of Allstate. The proof on that issue was clear in its inculpatory impact. It speaks for itself without the aid of expert opinion.

Nevertheless, if the law requires expert testimony, there was expert testimony probative of Ruston's breach of duty. The opinions of several lawyers pointed to the wisdom of settlement for policy limits. Although attorney Powers acknowledged the policy limits should have been paid in settlement after Krueper testified and it would have been a "good step" to demand such payment in Betts' best interests, he did not so advise her. Instead he told her not to worry.

Powers and the head of the Ruston firm joined Trotter in testimony to the effect that at minimum Betts should have been advised of her right to consult independent counsel after the settlement demands and certainly after the excess verdict. According to Dragonette and Wathen, Ruston's obligations, after the excess verdict, were owed only to Betts, not Allstate; other attorneys would "likely" have advised Betts to assign to Gallucci or institute her own direct action against Allstate. Trotter condemned the advice to go into bankruptcy as "egregious." That Ruston kept Betts entirely ignorant of essential facts is not disputed.

Ruston admitted to the impropriety of meeting with a representative of the insurer in advance of meeting with the insured; Allstate lawyer Carzoli was of the opinion Ruston should have obtained a waiver from Betts before allowing Strowmatt to attend Ruston's meetings with her after the verdict. The Ruston firm also recognized Betts' best interests required that, while the motion for new trial was still pending, efforts be made to negotiate full satisfaction of the excess judgment by offering the policy limits.

B.

When the facts are viewed in the light most favorable to the judgment, the record compels affirmance of the finding that *Ruston breached the duty owed Betts in several respects.* The lawyers failed Betts by (1) lack of disclosure and sound advice, (2) after the excess verdict, when the conflict of interest was unmistakable, actively working to protect Allstate and persisting in manipulating Betts against her own best interests; (3) assisting in manufacturing a false record against the time when a bad faith lawsuit might be instituted; (4) rather than advising consultation of independent counsel as possible or desirable, resisting the efforts of such counsel to become informed when finally retained; (5) discouraging Betts' assignment of rights in exchange for personal release and influencing her instead in the direction of bankruptcy.

General money damages for the negligent infliction of emotional distress are authorized by law. (Molien v. Kaiser Foundation Hospitals, 27 Cal.3d 916, 167 Cal.Rptr. 831, 616 P.2d 813.) The jury was so instructed and so found. Does substantial evidence support the jury verdict? Ruston's counsel asked this question on the motion for new trial: "Kline: What in the world is the emotional distress theory [the jury] assessed against Ruston and Nance the result of?"

The shock of the substantial damage judgment alone would be sufficient to uphold a verdict for nervousness, shock, humiliation, chagrin, worry, etc. Betts was 19 years old when this half million dollar judgment was assessed against her. She could reasonably see no possibility of ever being debt free except through bankruptcy. She *was* concerned about her father's house being taken, about losing her car, etc.

Aside from the excess judgment horror, Betts was put through several years of unnecessary harassment, emotional distress, as a result of the various lawyer delicts. This 17-year-old had for over five years lived on the edge of financial volcano. The excess judgment was but a momentary single incident in many years of substantial emotional trauma caused at least in part by the negligent failure of the Ruston firm to attend reasonably to the interests of its client.

Counsel for Ruston was asked "what the damage should be" for the fear, anxiety etc. caused Betts. Ruston's answer "to your specific question—[was] no more than $50,000." Here the reduction from $500,000 to $50,000 was made by the trial court after the response by Ruston's lawyer.

Finally the trial court recognized this was not *mere negligence* in failing to properly depose an expert witness but rather it was "*not the type of conduct to be condoned in the legal profession* as far as this court is concerned." (Italics added). In short, the host of ethical/legal improprieties in the treatment of Betts caused her emotional damage separate and distinct from the excess verdict trauma and authorize the $50,000.00 award. We find no legal or factual basis for upsetting the trial court's remittitur of $500,000.00 to $50,000.00.

## MURPHY v. ALLSTATE INSURANCE COMPANY

Supreme Court of California, 1976.
17 Cal.3d 937, 132 Cal.Rptr. 424, 553 P.2d 584.

CLARK, JUSTICE.

* * *

The complaint alleges plaintiff sued Pollard—insured by Allstate Insurance Company—for wrongful death of her nine-year-old son. Allstate rejected settlement demands of $23,500 and $25,000, the latter being the maximum coverage provided by Pollard's policy. Plaintiff thereafter received a verdict of $85,000, but on motion for new trial, accepted a reduction in judgment to $42,000.

Subsequent to entry of judgment, Allstate advised it would pay the policy limit of $25,000 and, if that were rejected, would appeal. The offer was rejected, and Allstate appealed contending the award was excessive. As Allstate posted no bond on appeal, plaintiff obtained writ of execution ordering immediate payment by Pollard of the judgment plus interest. In supplemental proceedings pursuant to Code of Civil Procedure section 717, Allstate denied obligation owing to either Pollard or to plaintiff.

Plaintiff brought the present action against Allstate alleging breach of the duty of good faith to its insured by having refused to settle within policy limits. There is no allegation Pollard has assigned any cause of action.

In her first cause of action, plaintiff seeks recovery under Insurance Code section 11580, subdivision (b)(2) authorizing direct action against the insurance company by a judgment creditor. In her second, plaintiff alleges direct action is permitted by Code of Civil Procedure section 720 by creditors' suit. Allstate moved for judgment on the pleadings, first on the ground there is no allegation Pollard assigned to plaintiff his cause of action for failure to settle and, secondly that Allstate is not indebted to Pollard within the meaning of section 720.[2] The motion was granted.

### THE DUTY TO SETTLE

* * * "[T]he implied obligation of good faith and fair dealing requires the insurer to settle in an appropriate case although the express terms of the policy do not impose such a duty" (*Comunale v. Traders & General Ins. Co.* (1958) 50 Cal.2d 654, 659, 328 P.2d 198, 201).

2. Plaintiff's memorandum of points and authorities in opposition to the motion for judgment on the pleadings recites Allstate has paid Murphy $27,464.77 (policy limits plus interests and costs).

More specifically, the insurer must settle within policy limits when there is substantial likelihood of recovery in excess of those limits. [citations omitted]

The duty to settle is implied in law to protect the insured from exposure to liability in excess of coverage as a result of the insurer's gamble—on which only the insured might lose. * * *

The insurer's duty to settle does not directly benefit the injured claimant. In fact, he usually benefits from the duty's breach. Instead of receiving an award near policy limits, he stands to obtain judgment exceeding policy coverage. For instance, in the present case plaintiff has already received an amount equal to her highest settlement demand, holding an unsatisfied judgment for an additional $17,500.

The insurer's duty to settle—running to the insured and not to the injured claimant—is also demonstrated by *Shapero v. Allstate Insurance Co.,* 14 Cal.App.3d 433, 92 Cal.Rptr. 244. The insured died leaving no asset other than the insurance policy. Thus, a judgment in excess of policy limits presenting no risk to the insured or to his heirs, the insurer had no duty to settle within policy limits.

When the carrier does breach its duty to settle, the insured has been allowed to recover excess award over policy limits (*Comunale v. Traders & General Ins. Co., supra,* economic loss, physical impairment, emotional distress and punitive damage.[3] [citations omitted]

The insured may assign his cause of action for breach of the duty to settle without consent of the insurance carrier, even when the policy provisions provide the contrary. (*Comunale v. Traders & General Ins. Co., supra.*) However, part of the damage arises from the personal tort aspect of the bad faith cause of action. * * * And because a purely personal tort cause of action is not assignable in California, it must be concluded that damage for emotional distress is not assignable. (See *Reichert v. General Insurance Company of America* (1968) 68 Cal.2d 822, 834, 69 Cal.Rptr. 321, 442 P.2d 377; 7 Cal.Jur.3d, Assignments, § 5 at pp. 12–13.) The same is true of a claim for punitive damage. * * *

In *Purcell v. Colonial Ins. Co.* (1971), 20 Cal.App.3d 807, 814, 97 Cal.Rptr. 874, an insured assigned his cause of action for breach of the duty to settle, the assignee suing on the assignment. Subsequently, the insured sued for mental distress. The second action was held to violate the rule against splitting a cause of action. The court suggested the insured should have brought a single action in his own name for all damage, agreeing to pay part of the recovery to the assignee.

**3.** Unlike other damages listed in the text, punitive damage may not be recovered for mere breach of the covenant without more: "While we have concluded that defendant violated its duty of good faith and fair dealing, this alone does not necessarily establish that defendant acted with the requisite intent to injure plaintiff." (*Silberg v. California Life Ins. Co.,* 11 Cal.3d at 462–463, 113 Cal.Rptr. at 718, 521 P.2d at 1110.) Defendant must act with intent to vex, injure or annoy, or with a conscious disregard of plaintiff's rights. (*Id.*)

INSURANCE CODE SECTION 11580, SUBDIVISION (b)

Insurance Code section 11580 lists provisions to be included in every liability insurance policy issued or delivered in this state.[4] Subdivision (b), subpart (1) provides insolvency or bankruptcy of the insured will not release the insurer from payment, and subpart (2) of the subdivision permits the judgment creditor of the insured to maintain an action "against the insurer on the policy and subject to its terms and limitations * * * to recover on the judgment."

Subpart (2) makes the judgment creditor a third party beneficiary of the insurance contract between the insurer and the insured. * * *

A third party beneficiary may enforce a contract expressly made for his benefit. (Civ.Code, § 1559.) And although the contract may not have been made to benefit him alone, he may enforce those promises directly made for him. * * *

A third party should not [however] be permitted to enforce covenants made not for his benefit, but rather for others. He is not a contracting party; his right to performance is predicated on the contracting parties' intent to benefit him. * * * As to any provision made not for his benefit but for the benefit of the contracting parties or for other third parties, he becomes an intermeddler. Permitting a third party to enforce a covenant made solely to benefit others would lead to the anomaly of granting him a bonus after his receiving all intended benefit. Because, as we have seen, the duty to settle is intended to benefit the insured and not the injured claimant, third party beneficiary doctrine does not furnish a basis for the latter to recover. Moreover, Allstate having paid plaintiff the policy limits, she has already received all benefit contemplated by the policy.

Next, the Financial Responsibility Law does not require plaintiff be permitted to sue for breach of the duty to settle. Again, the duty is based not on the Financial Responsibility Law but rather on the implied covenant of good faith and fair dealing found in every contract. Unlike a failure to investigate the representations of the insured, a breach of the duty to settle does not involve the risk that a person injured by a negligent motorist will fail to receive the compensation called for by that law. Breach of the duty to settle will, if anything, allow the injured party to recover the amount of the offered settlement, perhaps an additional sum to the extent of the policy limits, and sums in excess of those limits from the negligent motorist. Because an insurer's refusal to accept a reasonable settlement does not diminish the injured claimant's

4. Insurance Code section 11580, subdivision (b): "Such policy shall not be thus issued or delivered to any person in this State unless it contains all of the following provisions: (1) A provision that the insolvency or bankruptcy of the insured will not release the insurer from the payment of damages for injury sustained or loss occasioned during the life of such policy. (2) A provision that whenever judgment is secured against the insured or the executor or administrator of a deceased insured in an action based upon bodily injury, death, or property damage, then an action may be brought against the insurer on the policy and subject to its terms and limitations, by such judgment creditor to recover on the judgment."

recovery, the policy of compensating persons injured by negligent motorists is not frustrated.

Having concluded section 11580 does not authorize plaintiff to proceed against Allstate for the excess of the judgment over policy limits, we next consider whether Code of Civil Procedure section 720 permits plaintiff to proceed by way of creditors' suit.

### Code of Civil Procedure Section 720

A cause of action is not subject to levy and execution sale. * * * Code of Civil Procedure sections 714–723 provide for supplemental proceedings for a judgment creditor when his writ of execution against the judgment debtor has been returned unsatisfied.

Section 719 states that in supplemental proceedings, property of the judgment debtor may be ordered applied toward satisfaction of the judgment provided that no such order may be made as to property or money in the hands of another who also claims an interest in the property adverse to the judgment debtor or who denies the debt.

When the judgment debtor's alleged debtor denies owing the judgment debtor or denies holding property in which the judgment debtor claims an interest, the judgment creditor must proceed by creditors' suit under section 720. (*Bond v. Bulgheroni* (1932) 215 Cal. 7, 10, 8 P.2d 130.) * * *

"Whether choses in action founded upon torts are subject to creditors' suit must depend upon whether they are, by the law of the state, assignable. If they are not, then they are not subject to such suits, otherwise they are so subject." (Freeman, Executions (3d ed. 1900) § 425 at pp. 2290–2291.) Because causes of action for tort committed to property are assignable (Code Civ.Proc., § 954), they may be reached by proceedings under section 720. On the other hand, section 720 should not be applied so as to render the nonassignable assignable. And nonassignable tort actions may not be reached in proceedings pursuant to section 720. The language of the section referring to "debt" and "interest in property," reinforces this conclusion.

We are confronted with a hybrid cause of action, assignable—yes—but comprising potential damage unassignable and unrecoverable in section 720 proceedings.

No case has been cited or found determining whether a hybrid cause of action may be enforced in proceedings under section 720. Even assuming other hybrid causes of action might be subject to section 720 proceedings, the policy reflected by the cases establishing the duty to settle and the direct action statute (Ins.Code, § 11580), compels us to conclude the cause of action before us may not be reached under section 720. As we have seen, in view of the potential conflicts among injured party, insured and insurer, the courts imposed the duty to settle to protect the insured—not the injured party. Permitting the injured party to proceed under section 720 would substantially defeat the very purpose of the cause of action and again, because it may not be split, the insured could be deprived of substantial recovery.

Requiring assignment before the claimant may proceed would of course insure notice to the insured that the claimant wished to proceed against the insurer. At that point the insured would have the choice of partially assigning and then joining in the action, or of bargaining for a release from liability in excess of coverage. The release would permit the insured to protect himself from continued exposure to personal liability. Further, because the judgment creditor would then both own and control the cause of action against the insurer, he could attempt to satisfy his judgment thereby. Finally, the insured could protect his right to nonassignable claims for punitive, emotional and personal injury damage.

The judgment is affirmed.

### *Notes*

1. May a court *order* an insured to assign his bad faith claim to his judgment creditor? See Nicholson v. St. Anne Lanes, Inc., 158 Ill.App.3d 838, 111 Ill.Dec. 223, 512 N.E.2d 127 (1987) (not, so far as appears, involving personal claims of the sort discussed in Murphy, above.).

2. Suppose F is injured by an automobile driven by C who is insured by R. F offers to settle for the policy limits but R has refused the offer. F then executed a release of the insured (C) from any liability for damages above the policy limits and took an assignment of C's cause of action for bad faith failure to settle against R. What did F get under the assignment? Apparently nothing. Since C can no longer be hurt by an excess judgment because of the release, the assignment is valueless. See Clement v. Prudential Property & Cas. Ins. Co. 790 F.2d 1545 (11th Cir.1986). What tactical lessons in insurance practice are to be learned here?

### *Problem*

If bad faith failure to settle is a hybrid "contort", which statute of limitation should apply? Suppose the tort statute has run? May the action be continued under the contract statute?

## B. THE EXTENSION—FIRST PARTY CASES

## BECK v. FARMERS INSURANCE EXCHANGE

Supreme Court of Utah, 1985.
701 P.2d 795.

ZIMMERMAN, JUSTICE:

Beck injured his knee in a hit-and-run accident on January 16, 1982, when his car was struck by a car owned by Ann Kirkland. Ms. Kirkland asserted that her car had been stolen and denied any knowledge of or responsibility for the accident. Beck filed a claim with Kirkland's insurer, but liability was denied on April 20, 1982.

At the time of the accident, Beck carried automobile insurance with Farmers. Under that policy, Beck was provided with both no-fault and uninsured motorist insurance benefits. On February 23, 1982, while his claim against Kirkland was pending, Beck filed a claim with Farmers for no-fault benefits. Sometime prior to May 26, 1982, Farmers paid Beck $5,000 for medical expenses (the no-fault policy limit) and $1,299.43 for lost wages.

On June 23, 1982, Beck's counsel filed a claim with Farmers for uninsured motorist benefits, demanding the policy limit, $20,000, for general damages suffered as a result of the accident. His counsel alleges that the brochure documenting Beck's damages, submitted to Farmers with the June 23rd settlement offer, established that his claim was worth substantially more than $20,000. Farmers' adjuster rejected the settlement offer without explanation on July 1, 1982.

Beck filed this lawsuit one month later, on August 2, 1982, alleging three causes of action: first, that by refusing to pay his uninsured motorist claim, Farmers had breached its contract of insurance with him; second, that by acting in bad faith in refusing to investigate the claim, bargain with Beck, or settle the claim, Farmers had breached an implied covenant of good faith and fair dealing; and third, that Farmers had acted oppressively and maliciously toward Beck with the intention of, or in reckless disregard of the likelihood of, causing emotional distress. Under the first claim, Beck sought damages for breach of contract in the amount of the policy limits; under the second, he asked for compensatory damages in excess of the policy limits for additional injuries, including mental anguish; and under the third, he sought punitive damages of $500,000.

Sometime in August of 1982, Beck's counsel contacted Farmers' counsel and offered to settle the whole matter for $20,000. This offer was rejected. Farmers filed an answer on September 1, 1982, and at the same time, moved to strike the prayer for punitive damages on the ground that they were unavailable for a breach of contract. Farmers' motion was granted. On September 29th, the trial court bifurcated the case and agreed to try the claim for failure to pay uninsured motorist benefits independent of Beck's claim alleging breach of an implied covenant of good faith and fair dealing.

Immediately after the trial judge bifurcated the case, Beck's counsel expressly revoked the previously rejected offer to settle the whole matter for $20,000. Instead, Beck offered to settle only the failure to pay the uninsured motorist benefits claim for $20,000, reserving the implied covenant or "bad faith" claim for separate resolution.

On October 20, 1982, Farmers apparently counteroffered. Negotiations proceeded, and sometime in late November, the parties agreed to settle the uninsured motorist claim for $15,000. On December 6, 1982, the parties stipulated to dismissal of that claim and specifically reserved the bad faith claim for later disposition.

In mid-December, Farmers moved to dismiss the reserved bad faith claim on two theories. First, Farmers asserted that under *Lyon v. Hartford Accident and Indemnity Co.,* 25 Utah 2d 311, 480 P.2d 739

(1971), it "had no duty to bargain with or settle plaintiff's uninsured motorist claim and, therefore, [could not] be held liable" for breach of contract or bad faith. Second, Farmers argued that even if it had some duty to bargain or to settle the claim, the facts set forth in the pleadings on file did not establish that it had breached the duty. No memoranda or factual affidavits supported this motion.

Farmers' motion was opposed by affidavits of Beck, his counsel, and a former insurance adjuster who worked for Beck's counsel as a paralegal. In his affidavit, Beck's counsel recited the dates and terms of the various settlement offers and the fact that they had been rejected without counteroffer. Beck's affidavit stated that he had accepted the $15,000 offer only because of financial pressures caused by the substantial expenses he had incurred in the ten months since the accident. The paralegal's affidavit stated that he had been an insurance adjuster for 19 years and that he had reviewed the settlement documentation submitted to Farmers in June when the claim was first filed. He expressed the opinion that a reasonable and prudent insurance company would have valued the claim at between $30,000 and $40,000 and attempted to settle the matter within weeks after the initial offer. The paralegal charged that the "only reason for such a substantial delay in settling this claim would be to put Mr. Beck in a situation of financial need and stress so that he would accept the first settlement offer," a tactic he characterized as acting in bad faith. Farmers filed no rebuttal affidavits, and the trial court granted Farmers' motion without specifying the basis for its holding.

Beck asks this Court to overrule *Lyon* and permit an insured to sue for an insurer's bad faith refusal to bargain or settle. * * *

Our ruling in *Lyon* left an insured without any effective remedy against an insurer that refuses to bargain or settle in good faith with the insured. An insured who has suffered a loss and is pressed financially is at a marked disadvantage when bargaining with an insurer over payment for that loss. Failure to accept a proffered settlement, although less than fair, can lead to catastrophic consequences for an insured who, as a direct consequence of the loss, may be peculiarly vulnerable, both economically and emotionally. The temptation for an insurer to delay settlement while pressures build on the insured is great, especially if the insurer's exposure cannot exceed the policy limits. *See Lawton v. Great Southwest Fire Insurance Co.*, 118 N.H. 607, 392 A.2d 576, 579 (1978); Harvey & Wiseman, *First Party Bad Faith: Common Law Remedies and a Proposed Legislative Solution,* 72 Ky.L.J. 141, 146, 167–69 (1983–84) (hereinafter cited as "First Party Bad Faith"); Note, *The Availability of Excess Damages for Wrongful Refusal to Honor First Party Insurance Claims—An Emerging Trend,* 45 Fordham L.Rev. 164, 164–67 (Oct. 1976) (hereinafter cited as "Availability of Excess Damages").

In light of these considerations, we now conclude that an insured should be provided with a remedy. However, we do not agree with plaintiff that a tort action is appropriate. Instead, we hold that the good faith duty to bargain or settle under an insurance contract is only one aspect of the duty of good faith and fair dealing implied in all contracts and that a violation of that duty gives rise to a claim for breach of contract.[1] In addition, we do not adopt the limitation suggested by Farmers, but hold that the refusal to bargain or settle, standing alone, may, under appropriate circumstances, be sufficient to prove a breach.

We recognize that a majority of states permit an insured to institute a tort action against an insurer who fails to bargain in good faith in a "first-party" situation,[2] adopting the approach first announced by the California Supreme Court in *Gruenberg v. Aetna Insurance Co.*, 9 Cal.3d 566, 510 P.2d 1032, 108 Cal.Rptr. 480 (1973). *See, e.g., Bibeault v. Hanover Insurance Co.*, R.I., 417 A.2d 313 (1980); *Craft v. Economy Fire & Casualty Co.*, 572 F.2d 565 (7th Cir.1978) (applying Indiana law); *MFA Mutual Insurance Co. v. Flint,* Tenn., 574 S.W.2d 718 (1978). Apparently, these courts have taken this step as a matter of policy in order to provide what they perceive to be an adequate remedy for an insured wronged by an insurer's recalcitrance. These courts have reasoned that under contract law principles, an insurer who improperly refuses to settle a first-party claim may be liable only for damages measured by the maximum dollar amount of the insurance provided by the policy, and such a damage measure provides little or no incentive to an insurer to promptly and faithfully fulfill its contractual obligations. Accordingly, these courts have adopted a tort approach in order to allow an insured to recover extensive consequential and punitive damages, which they consider to be unavailable in an action based solely on a breach of contract. *See Availability of Excess Damages, supra,* at 168–77; *First Party Bad Faith, supra,* at 158.

We conclude that the tort approach adopted by these courts is without a sound theoretical foundation and has the potential for distorting well-established principles of contract law. Moreover, the practical end of providing a strong incentive for insurers to fulfill their contractual obligations can be accomplished as well through a contract cause of action, without the analytical straining necessitated by the tort approach and with far less potential for unforeseen consequences to the law of contracts.

The analytical weaknesses of the tort approach are easily seen. In *Gruenberg,* the California court held that an insurer has a duty to deal in good faith with its insured and that an insured can bring an action in tort, rather than contract, for breach of that duty because the duty is imposed by law and, being nonconsensual, does not arise out of the

1. The Court in *Lyon* considered only the question of whether a claim of bad faith gave rise to a tort cause of action; however, to the extent that *Lyon* is philosophically inconsistent with our recognition today of a cause of action in contract, it is overruled.

2. We use the term "first-party" to refer to an insurance agreement where the insurer agrees to pay claims submitted to it by the insured for losses suffered by the insured. The present case involves such a first-party situation. In contrast, a "third-party" situation is one where the insurer contracts to defend the insured against claims made by third parties against the insured and to pay any resulting liability, up to the specified dollar limit.

contract. Glossing over any distinctions between first- and third-party situations, the court concluded that the duty imposed upon the insurer when bargaining with its insured in a first-party situation is merely another aspect of the fiduciary duty owed in the third-party context. *Gruenberg v. Aetna Insurance Co.*, 9 Cal.3d at 573–74, 510 P.2d at 1037, 108 Cal.Rptr. at 485.

Although this Court, in *Ammerman v. Farmer's Insurance Exchange,* 19 Utah 2d 261, 430 P.2d 576 (1967), recognized a tort cause of action for breach of an insurer's obligation to bargain in a third-party context, we cannot agree with the *Gruenberg* court that the considerations which compel the recognition of a tort cause of action in a third-party context are present in the first-party situation. In *Ammerman,* we stated that because a third-party insurance contract obligates the insurer to defend the insured, the insurer incurs a fiduciary duty to its insured to protect the insured's interests as zealously as it would its own; consequently, a tort cause of action is recognized to remedy a violation of that duty.

However, in *Lyon v. Hartford Accident and Indemnity Co.,* we held that a tort cause of action did not arise in a first-party insurance contract situation because the relationship between the insurer and its insured is fundamentally different than in a third-party context:

> In the [third-party] situation, the insurer must act in good faith and be as zealous in protecting the interests of the insured as it would be in regard to its own. In the [first-party] situation, the insured and the insurer are, in effect and practically speaking, adversaries.

* * *

This distinction is of no small consequence. In a third-party situation, the insurer controls the disposition of claims against its insured, who relinquishes any right to negotiate on his own behalf. * * * An insurer's failure to act in good faith exposes its insured to a judgment and personal liability in excess of the policy limits. * * * In essence, the contract itself creates a fiduciary relationship because of the trust and reliance placed in the insurer by its insured. * * * The insured is wholly dependent upon the insurer to see that, in dealing with claims by third parties, the insured's best interests are protected. In addition, when dealing with third parties, the insurer acts as an agent for the insured with respect to the disputed claim. Wholly apart from the contractual obligations undertaken by the parties, the law imposes upon all agents a fiduciary obligation to their principals with respect to matters falling within the scope of their agency. * * *

In the first-party situation, on the other hand, the reasons for finding a fiduciary relationship and imposing a corresponding duty are absent. No relationship of trust and reliance is created by the contract; it simply obligates the insurer to pay claims submitted by the insured in accordance with the contract. *Santilli v. State Farm Life Insurance Co.,*

278 Or. at 61–62, 562 P.2d at 969. Furthermore, none of the indicia of agency are present. * * *

Clearly, then, it is difficult to find a theoretically sound basis for analogizing the duty owed in a third-party context to that owed in a first-party context. And wholly apart from any theoretical problems, tailoring the tort analysis to first-party insurance contract cases has proven difficult. The pragmatic reason for adopting the tort approach is that it exposes insurers to consequential and punitive damages awards in excess of the policy limits. However, the courts appear to have had difficulty in developing a sound rationale for limiting the tort approach to insurance contract cases. This may be because there is no sound theoretical difference between a first-party insurance contract and any other contract, at least no difference that justifies permitting punitive damages for the breach of one and not the other. In any event, the tort approach and the accompanying punitive damages have moved rather quickly into areas far afield from insurance. *See, e.g., Seaman's Direct Buying Service, Inc. v. Standard Oil Co.,* 36 Cal.3d 752, 686 P.2d 1158, 1166–67, 206 Cal.Rptr. 354, 362–63 (1984); *Wallis v. Superior Court,* 160 Cal.App.3d 1109, 207 Cal.Rptr. 123, 127–29 (1984); *Gates v. Life of Montana Insurance Co.,* Mont., 668 P.2d 213, 214–16 (1983).

Furthermore, the courts adopting the tort approach have had some difficulty in determining what degree of bad faith is necessary to sustain a claim. *E.g., Anderson v. Continental Insurance Co.,* 85 Wis.2d 675, 692–94, 271 N.W.2d 368, 376–77 (1978). From a practical standpoint, the state of mind of the insurer is irrelevant; even an inadvertent breach of the covenant of good faith implied in an insurance contract can substantially harm the insured and warrants a remedy.

We therefore hold that in a first-party relationship between an insurer and its insured, the duties and obligations of the parties are contractual rather than fiduciary. Without more, a breach of those implied or express duties can give rise only to a cause of action in contract, not one in tort.[3] This position has not been widely adopted by other courts, although a "respectable body of authority" is developing. *See Duncan v. Andrew County Mutual Insurance Co.,* 665 S.W.2d at 18–19, and cases cited therein; *Lawton v. Great Southwest Fire Insurance Co.,* 118 N.H. 607, 392 A.2d 576 (1978); *Kewin v. Massachusetts Mutual*

3. We recognize that in some cases the acts constituting a breach of contract may also result in breaches of duty that are independent of the contract and may give rise to causes of action in tort. *Hal Taylor Assoc. v. UnionAmerica,* 657 P.2d at 750; *Lawton v. Great Southwest Fire Ins. Co.,* 392 A.2d at 580. For example, the law of this state recognizes a duty to refrain from intentionally causing severe emotional distress to others. *Samms v. Eccles,* 11 Utah 2d 289, 358 P.2d 344 (1961). Thus, intentional and outrageous conduct by an insurer against an insured, coupled with a failure to bargain, could conceivably result in tort liability independent of (and concurrent with) liability for breach of contract. Additionally, the facts that give rise to a breach of the duty to bargain in good faith could also amount to fraudulent activity, rendering an insurer independently liable for damages flowing from the fraud. *See Wetherbee v. United Ins. Co.,* 265 Cal.App.2d 921, 71 Cal.Rptr. 764 (1968). Also, under various unfair practices acts, there may be statutory requirements that give rise to independent causes of action. *E.g.,* U.C.A., 1953, §§ 31–27–1 to –24.

*Life Insurance Co.*, 409 Mich. 401, 295 N.W.2d 50 (1980); *Availability of Excess Damages, supra* p. 4, at 168–71. We further hold that as parties to a contract, the insured and the insurer have parallel obligations to perform the contract in good faith, obligations that inhere in every contractual relationship. *State Automobile & Casualty Underwriters v. Salisbury*, 27 Utah 2d 229, 232, 494 P.2d 529, 531 (1972); *Leigh Furniture & Carpet Co. v. Isom*, Utah, 657 P.2d 293, 306 (1982).[4]

Few cases define the implied contractual obligation to perform a first-party insurance contract in good faith. However, because the considerations are similar, we freely look to the tort cases that have described the incidents of the duty of good faith in the context of first-party insurance contracts. From those cases and from our own analysis of the obligations undertaken by the parties, we conclude that the implied obligation of good faith performance contemplates, at the very least, that the insurer will diligently investigate the facts to enable it to determine whether a claim is valid, will fairly evaluate the claim, and will thereafter act promptly and reasonably in rejecting or settling the claim. *See Anderson v. Continental Insurance Co.*, 85 Wis.2d at 692–93, 271 N.W.2d at 377; *Egan v. Mutual of Omaha Insurance Co.*, 24 Cal.3d 809, 818–19, 620 P.2d 141, 145–46, 169 Cal.Rptr. 691, 695–96 (1979). The duty of good faith also requires the insurer to "deal with laymen as laymen and not as experts in the subtleties of law and underwriting" and to refrain from actions that will injure the insured's ability to obtain the benefits of the contract. * * * These performances are the essence of what the insured has bargained and paid for, and the insurer has the obligation to perform them. When an insurer has breached this duty, it is liable for damages suffered in consequence of that breach.

In adopting the contract approach, we are not ignoring the principal reason for the adoption of the tort approach—to provide damage exposure in excess of the policy limits and thus remove any incentive for breaching the duty of good faith. Despite what some courts have suggested, *e.g.*, *Santilli v. State Farm Insurance Co.*, 562 P.2d at 969, and what some commentators have asserted, *e.g.*, J. Appleman, *Insurance Law & Practice* § 8878.15 at 424–26 (1981), there is no reason to limit damages recoverable for breach of a duty to investigate, bargain, and settle claims in good faith to the amount specified in the insurance policy.[5] Nothing inherent in the contract law approach mandates this narrow definition of recoverable damages. Although the policy limits define the amount for which the insurer may be held responsible in performing the contract, they do not define the amount for which it may be liable upon a breach. * * *

Damages recoverable for breach of contract include both general damages, *i.e.*, those flowing naturally from the breach, and consequential

4. The duty to perform the contract in good faith cannot, by definition, be waived by either party to the agreement.

5. In *Ammerman*, we suggested in dicta that in an action for breach of an insurance policy, the damages could not exceed the policy limits. 19 Utah 2d at 264, 430 P.2d at 578. We expressly disavow this dicta.

damages, *i.e.,* those reasonably within the contemplation of, or reasonably foreseeable by, the parties at the time the contract was made. *Pacific Coast Title Insurance Co. v. Hartford Accident & Indemnity Co.,* 7 Utah 2d 377, 379, 325 P.2d 906, 907 (1958), *citing Hadley v. Baxendale,* 9 Exch. 341, 156 Eng.Rep. 145 (1854). We have repeatedly recognized that consequential damages for breach of contract may reach beyond the bare contract terms. *See, e.g., Pacific Coast Title Insurance Co. v. Hartford Accident & Indemnity,* 7 Utah 2d at 379, 325 P.2d at 908 (attorney fees incurred for settling and defending claims were foreseeable result of contractor's default); *Bevan v. J.H. Construction Co.,* Utah, 669 P.2d 442, 444 (1983) (home purchasers entitled to damages for loss of favorable mortgage interest rate resulting from builder's breach of contract).

In an action for breach of a duty to bargain in good faith, a broad range of recoverable damages is conceivable, particularly given the unique nature and purpose of an insurance contract. An insured frequently faces catastrophic consequences if funds are not available within a reasonable period of time to cover an insured loss; damages for losses well in excess of the policy limits, such as for a home or a business, may therefore be foreseeable and provable. *See, e.g., Reichert v. General Insurance Co.,* 59 Cal.Rptr. 724, 728, 428 P.2d 860, 864 (1967), *vacated on other grounds,* 68 Cal.2d 822, 442 P.2d 377, 69 Cal.Rptr. 321 (1968) (because bankruptcy was a foreseeable consequence of fire insurer's failure to pay, insurer was liable for consequential damages flowing from bankruptcy). Furthermore, it is axiomatic that insurance frequently is purchased not only to provide funds in case of loss, but to provide peace of mind for the insured or his beneficiaries. Therefore, although other courts adopting the contract approach have been reluctant to allow such an award, *Lawton v. Great Southwest Fire Insurance Co.,* 392 A.2d at 581–82, we find no difficulty with the proposition that, in unusual cases, damages for mental anguish might be provable.[6] *See Kewin v. Massachusetts Mutual Life Insurance Co.,* 409 Mich. at 440–55, 295 N.W.2d at 64–72 (Williams, J., dissenting). * * * The foreseeability of any such damages will always hinge upon the nature and language of the contract and the reasonable expectations of the parties. * * *

With the foregoing principles in mind, we return to a consideration of the present case. * * *

Under [the] circumstances and resolving all doubts in Beck's favor, we cannot say that a jury could not find that Farmers breached its duty of good faith in rejecting Beck's claim without explanation and in failing to further investigate the matter. Therefore, we remand the matter to the trial court for further proceedings.

Affirmed.

6. Clearly, damages will not be available for the mere disappointment, frustration, or anxiety normally experienced in the process of filing an insurance claim and negotiating a settlement with an insurer.

### *Notes*

1. *Standards for Establishing "Bad Faith." First Party Compared to Third Party Cases.*

Extracts from Travelers Ins. Co. v. Savio, 706 P.2d 1258 at 1274–1276 (Colo.1985):

> Courts in California, the first jurisdiction to recognize the existence of a bad faith tort action in a first-party insurer context, have long recognized significant differences between first-party and third-party cases. *See, e.g., Austero v. National Casualty Co. of Detroit, Michigan,* 84 Cal.App.3d 1, 148 Cal.Rptr. 653 (1978). In defining the standard of care applicable in a first-party context, these distinctions should not be ignored. *See Employers Equitable Life Insurance Co. v. Williams,* 282 Ark. 29, 665 S.W.2d 873 (1984) (standard of care in third-party insurance tort action is negligence, while first-party cause of action requires "dishonest, malicious, or oppressive conduct").
>
> In *Anderson v. Continental Insurance Co.,* 85 Wis.2d 675, 271 N.W.2d 368 (1978), the Supreme Court of Wisconsin recognized the peculiar characteristics of first-party insurance claims and concluded that the appropriate standard for determining the presence or absence of bad faith dealing by an insurer with regard to a claim of its insured consisted of two parts: "the absence of a reasonable basis for denying benefits of the policy and the defendant's knowledge or reckless disregard of the lack of a reasonable basis for denying the claim." The court made the following observations concerning the applicability of this standard in first-party cases:
>
> > It is appropriate, in applying the test, to determine whether a claim was properly investigated and whether the results of the investigation were subjected to a reasonable evaluation and review. * * *
>
> While we have stated above that, for proof of bad faith, there must be an absence of a reasonable basis for denial of policy benefits *and* the knowledge or reckless disregard of a reasonable basis for a denial, implicit in that test is our conclusion that the knowledge of the lack of a reasonable basis may be inferred and imputed to an insurance company where there is a reckless disregard of a lack of a reasonable basis for denial or a reckless indifference to facts or to proofs submitted by the insured.
>
> Under these tests of the tort of bad faith, an insurance company, however, may challenge claims which are fairly debatable and will be found liable only where it has intentionally denied (or failed to process or pay) a claim without a reasonable basis.
>
> * * *
>
> The first element of this test—unreasonable conduct—was recognized in *Trimble* [Farmers Group, Inc. v. Trimble, 691 P.2d 1138 (Colo.1984) ] as the sole standard for the tort of bad faith dealing by an insurance carrier with its insured in a third-party setting. Whether an insurer has acted reasonably in denying or delaying approval of a claim

> will be determined on an objective basis, requiring proof of the standards of conduct in the industry. The second element of the test reflects a reasonable balance between the right of an insurance carrier to reject a non-compensable claim submitted by its insured and the obligation of such carrier to investigate and ultimately approve a valid claim of its insured. If an insurer does not know that its denial of or delay in processing a claim filed by its insured is unreasonable, and does not act with reckless disregard of a valid claim, the insurer's conduct would be based upon a permissible, albeit mistaken, belief that the claim is not compensable. While the distinction is subtle, recognition of the permissible scope of an insurer's right to refuse invalid claims requires the conclusion that in the context of a first-party claim the insured must establish the insurer's knowledge or reckless disregard of the fact that a valid claim has been submitted. * * * The conclusion of the Court of Appeals that the tort of bad faith conduct by an insurer in a first-party context requires proof only of simple negligence is erroneous.
>
> [See also deVries v. St. Paul Fire & Marine Ins. Co., 716 F.2d 939 (1st Cir.1983) ].

2. Decisions as to "bad faith" in first party cases continue to range across a broad spectrum. A body count of opinions may be found in the *Savio* case (note 1 above), 706 P.2d 1258 at 1273, and in Caruso v. Republic Ins. Co., 558 F.Supp. 430 (D.Md.1983). Some jurisdictions continue to join the so-called "majority" in recognizing the tort of "bad faith"—see, Justin v. Guardian Ins. Co. 670 F.Supp. 614 (D.Virgin Islands 1987). Others approach it but back away—e.g. Federal Kemper Ins. Co. v. Hornback, 711 S.W.2d 844 (Ky.1986). Others may hold fast to a conservative position—e.g. Northwestern National Ins. Co. v. Pope, 791 F.2d 649 (8th Cir.1986), following Iowa law.

Even in the many jurisdictions that judicially reject the tort of bad faith, the effect is softened by the rather open encouragement of consequential contract damages and other side benefits. The main case is an example. Another is Murphy v. Cincinnati Ins. Co., 772 F.2d 273 (6th Cir.1985), applying Michigan law, and extending the reach of consequential damages under Hadley v. Baxendale to the insured's attorneys' fee. Indiana claims to not need a tort of bad faith because it offers special contractual remedies (including punitive damages), Liberty Mut. Ins. Co. v. Parkinson, 487 N.E.2d 162 (Ind.App.1985). Of course, if the "bad faith" consists in a cognizable tort, such as deceit, punitive damages, if allowed at all, are to be expected.

3. *Punitive Damages*

The lure of punitive damages unquestionably provides the strong drive to inflate the breach of an implied contract promise of fair dealing into a full fledged "tort" of bad faith. The "tort" thus created usually causes moderate actual economic damages and only problematical emotional or physical distress. It is one which leaves behind no shattered bodies or brains, no destroyed reputations or environmental pollution. But by computing the deterrent and factors of the award as a miniscule fraction of the extraordinary "gross (or net) worth" of insurance companies—even those with cash flow difficulties—a sensational guaranteed funded prize is offered. Bitter controversy is also generated, and in the overall commotion about tort reform, the punitive awards against insurers for bad faith have provided a major disturbing element. Only a few cases from a mountain of material are needed to highlight the ongoing debate. *Betts v. Allstate Ins. Co.* supra at p. 119 will do for starters.

In Mississippi, Mr. Crenshaw lost his leg, whether by accident as he claimed or by pre-existing disease as his accident insurer contended. A jury sided with Mr. Crenshaw and awarded $20,000 in actual damages plus $1,600,000 punitive damages for bad faith handling of the claim. The Supreme Court of Mississippi affirmed the award in Bankers Life and Cas. Co. v. Crenshaw, 483 So.2d 254 (Miss.1985) and it survived before the U.S. Supreme Court on a constitutional challenge to punitive damages as such. Bankers Life and Casualty Co. v. Crenshaw, 486 U.S. 71, 108 S.Ct. 1645, 100 L.Ed.2d 62 (1988).

In Arizona, Mr. Hawkins quarreled with his insurer over the value of the replacement car he received for the destroyed insured vehicle (which had a blue book value of about $6,500). A jury found $15,000 compensatory damages and $3,500,000 in punitives. An intermediate appellate court eliminated the punitives but the Arizona Supreme Court reinstated the jury verdict, in part because "the jury could have rationally concluded that Allstate engaged in deceptive claims practices spanning 18 years * * * by deducting small innocuous amounts * * * under the guise of cost savings."

Allstate was revealed to have had in 1981 total assets of $8.6 billion and net income of $346.7 million. The award was therefore only 1/25 of 1% of total assets or 3½ days net income. A dissenting judge ventured the observation that the award was 3½ times the maximum fine allowed for any felony under the state's penal code.

One prominent aspect of tort reform is to place a cap on punitive damages. In Montana in 1985 a statute was passed to tighten up on the proof required for punitive damages and to put a limit of $25,000 or 1% of the defendant's net worth which ever is greater (except in cases of actual fraud or actual malice). Consider how little effect such a law has on the potential liability of an insurance company the size of Allstate. See the case of Safeco Ins. Co. v. Ellinghouse, 223 Mont. 239, 725 P.2d 217 (1986). In that case a trial court awarded $25,000 in economic damages, $200,000 emotional damages and $5,000,000 in punitives for the mishandling of the defense in a 3rd party case. A remittitur of $4,000,000 was ordered. The above statute was not yet in effect, but it will be observed that even the $5,000,000 award would probably have been under the statutory cap when Safeco had "amassed assets" of $3,414,715,000.

Finally there is the notorious case of Aetna Life Ins. Co. v. Lavoie, 475 U.S. 813, 106 S.Ct. 1580, 89 L.Ed.2d 823 (1986), which should be read on the point of judicial misconduct. The case was returned to the Alabama Court where the original award of $3,500,000 in punitive damages was reduced by $3,000,000. See Aetna Life Ins. Co. v. Lavoie, 505 So.2d 1050 (Ala.1987) (per curiam naturally).

4. Many cases using the rationale of "good faith and fair dealing" to aid the insured will be encountered in the course of this book, and assuredly in the advance sheets of newly published opinions in the years ahead. The parameters of the doctrine are not yet set, and some of the applications may

seem rather extraordinary. Consider, for example, Davis v. Blue Cross of Northern California, 25 Cal.3d 418, 158 Cal.Rptr. 828, 600 P.2d 1060 (1979), involving claims made against Blue Cross, a health insurer. Blue Cross' policies contained an unambiguous (but not particularly conspicuous) provision that if the Subscriber (i.e. insured) did not agree with Blue Cross' determination not to pay, "then such determination shall be made by arbitration under the laws of the State of California" [California has a strong public policy in favor of arbitration]. Certain subscribers (this was a class action) sued Blue Cross, which invoked the arbitration clause. In a 4–3 decision the California Supreme Court held that the failure to make the arbitration clause more conspicuous or to advise the subscribers when a claim was filed that arbitration was available was a breach of the duty of good faith, etc. Therefore Blue Cross had waived the arbitration provision and could not now compel arbitration.

Query: In what possible way were the subscribers harmed by this "breach" of the duty of good faith and fair dealing? And what about the public policy favoring arbitration?

## C. STATUTORY CREATION

### *Note*

The Unfair Practices Act, a version of which is the subject of interpretation in the following case, was originally formulated by the National Association of Insurance Commissioners. The California version of the Act is found in the Insurance Code beginning at § 790. California adopted the Act in 1959; it has been amended several times. But one thing stands out: the Act was adopted to fill in the ground renounced by Congress in the McCarran–Ferguson Act. Ins. Code § 790 makes explicit reference to McCarran–Ferguson (using the Public Law citation):

Of all the sections of the Unfair Practices Act, § 790.03 seems to have attracted the most interest in recent times. This section provides in part:

> The following are hereby defined as unfair methods of competition and unfair and deceptive acts or practices in the business of insurance, * * *
>
> "(h) Knowingly committing or performing with such frequency as to indicate a general business practice any of the following unfair claims settlement practices:
>
> "(1) Misrepresenting to claimants pertinent facts of insurance policy provisions relating to any coverages at issue.
>
> "(2) Failing to acknowledge and act reasonably promptly upon communications with respect to claims arising under insurance policies.
>
> "(3) Failing to adopt and implement reasonable standards for the prompt investigation and processing of claims arising under insurance policies.
>
> "(4) Failing to affirm or deny coverage of claims within a reasonable time after proof of loss requirements have been completed and submitted by the insured.

"(5) Not attempting in good faith to effectuate prompt, fair, and equitable settlements of claims in which liability has become reasonably clear.

"(6) Compelling insureds to institute litigation to recover amounts due under an insurance policy by offering substantially less than the amounts ultimately recovered in actions brought by the insureds, when the insureds have made claims for amounts reasonably similar to the amounts ultimately recovered.

"(7) Attempting to settle a claim by an insured for less than the amount to which a reasonable man would have believed he was entitled by reference to written or printed advertising material accompanying or made part of an application.

"(8) Attempting to settle claims on the basis of an application which was altered without notice to, or knowledge or consent of, the insured, his representative, agent, or broker.

"(9) Failing, after payment of a claim, to inform insureds or beneficiaries, upon request by them, of the coverage under which payment has been made.

"(10) Making known to insureds or claimants a practice of the insurer of appealing from arbitration awards in favor of insureds or claimants for the purpose of compelling them to accept settlements or compromises less than the amount awarded in arbitration.

"(11) Delaying the investigation or payment of claims by requiring an insured, claimant, or the physician of either, to submit a preliminary claim report, and then requiring the subsequent submission of formal proof of loss forms, both of which submissions contain substantially the same information.

"(12) Failing to settle claims promptly, where liability has become apparent, under one portion of the insurance policy coverage in order to influence settlements under other portions of the insurance policy coverage.

"(13) Failing to provide promptly a reasonable explanation of the basis relied on in the insurance policy, in relation to the facts or applicable law, for the denial of a claim or for the offer of a compromise settlement.

"(14) Directly advising a claimant not to obtain the services of an attorney.

"(15) Misleading a claimant as to the applicable statute of limitations.

"(16) Delaying the payment or provision of hospital, medical, or surgical benefits for services provided with respect to acquired immune deficiency syndrome or AIDS-related complex for more than 60 days after the insurer has received a claim for those benefits, where the delay in claim payment is for the purpose of investigating whether the condition preexisted the coverage. However, this 60–day period shall not include any time during which the insurer is awaiting a response for relevant medical information from a health care provider."

Other provisions of the Act prohibit unfair practices (§ 790.02), grant authority to the Commissioner of Insurance to fix a penalty not exceeding $5,000 for negligent violations, and $10,000 for willful violations (§ 790.035), prohibit advertising of insurance not available (§ 790.036), provide for investigation by the commissioner (§ 790.04), authorize cease and desist orders and court orders against unfair practices (§§ 790.05, 790.06), suspend or revoke the violator's license (§ 790.07), establish that action taken under the Act does not affect an insurer's liability to other administrative action or to civil liability or to criminal penalty under the laws of California. The purpose of the Act is "to regulate trade practices in the business of insurance in accordance with the intent of Congress" as expressed in the McCarran–Ferguson Act, 15 U.S.C.A. §§ 1011–1015.

## STATE FARM MUTUAL AUTOMOBILE INSURANCE COMPANY v. REEDER

Supreme Court of Kentucky, 1988.
763 S.W.2d 116.

WINTERSHEIMER, JUSTICE.

This appeal is from a decision of the Court of Appeals which reversed the circuit court and held that KRS 304.12–230, the Unfair Claims Settlement Practices Act, creates a private right of action against an insurance company by third-party claimants. The Court of Appeals affirmed the denial by the circuit court of prejudgment interest because it was based on unliquidated damages.

The principal issue is the enforceability of a private cause of action under the unfair claims settlement practices statute.

Reeder and the parents of Paul Hampton are next door neighbors and share a common driveway. While visiting his parents, Hampton accidentally drove his car into the support for the Reeder carport which collapsed. The impact damaged the roof, the home and demolished a ladder and boat in the carport. Hampton's parents were insured by State Farm and the company was promptly notified. State Farm obtained an estimate of repair for $8,471. The lowest estimate Reeder obtained was $13,392. Having declined the insurance company's subsequent offer of $8,961, Reeder sued for the amount he claimed for property damage and expenses, plus $15,000 for his attorney fees as well as $250,000 for violation of KRS 304.12–230. The circuit judge dismissed the unfair practice claim but the remainder of the case was tried by a jury which returned an $11,000 verdict which has been satisfied.

On appeal, Reeder argued a violation of KRS 304.12–230, and also sought prejudgment interest which had been denied by the circuit court. State Farm contends that the statute does not create a private right of action, but only gives the Commissioner of Insurance authority to perform a regulatory function. They claim the statute applies to a frequency of incidences indicating a general practice and that the statute lists 14 types of unfair claims settlement practices. They also argue that the Commissioner of Insurance may take action to prevent unfair practices when they are performed with such frequency as to indicate a general business practice.

KRS 304.12–230 does not specifically provide that any individual may maintain a claim for damages for violation of the act. However, the statute does not state that a violation of its terms is enforceable only by the insurance commissioner, and it does not prohibit a claim by an individual for damages for its breach. In our view, a person may maintain an action for damages resulting from the commission of such unfair practices only as a result of KRS 446.070. The right of a private citizen to maintain an action for violation of the Unfair Claims Settlement Practices Act is clearly supported by KRS 446.070 which provides: A person injured by the violation of any statute may recover from the offender such damages as he sustained by reason of the violation although a penalty or forfeiture is imposed for such violation.

Grzyb v. Evans, Ky., 700 S.W.2d 399 (1985) held that "Where the statute both declares the unlawful act and specifies the civil remedy available to the aggrieved party, the aggrieved party is limited to the remedy provided by the statute." Id. at 401. Here there was not only a contractual dispute over the amount of damages, for which the plaintiff has been awarded damages, but there is also a claim of a violation under the Unfair Claims Settlement Practices Act. This statute does not provide the aggrieved party with a civil remedy and therefore KRS 446.070 applies to such a violation. Reeder belongs to the class intended to be protected by the Insurance Code. Although the Insurance Code prescribes the remedy for its enforcement by the Insurance Commissioner, it does not provide a remedy for those individuals intended to be protected by the act.

This statute is very old; it was cited in City of Henderson v. Clayton, Ky., 57 S.W. 1, 22 K.L.R. 283 (1900). It has been part of the statutory law of Kentucky for at least 88 years. It has been frequently cited by this Court. See Hackney v. Fordson Coal Co., 230 Ky. 362, 19 S.W.2d 989 (1929). There is no reason why it should not be applied to third party claims. It creates a private right of action for the violation of any statute so long as the plaintiff belongs to the class intended to be protected by the statute.

It can be assumed that the General Assembly was aware of the existence of this statute when it enacted KRS 304.12–230. See Haven Point Enterprises, Inc. v. United Kentucky Bank, Inc., Ky. 690 S.W.2d 393 (1985). It can easily be harmonized with the unfair claims act. We find no reason to excuse this matter because it is brought by a third party claimant. The action results from the bad faith in adjusting the claim. If a first-party carrier can be sued for bad faith, there is no reason why a third party carrier cannot also be sued.

The Kentucky Unfair Claims Settlement Practices Act enumerates 14 specific practices which, if performed with such frequency as to indicate a general business practice, can amount to unfair claims settlement practices. It should be noted that this statute has been amended, effective July 15, 1988, so as to eliminate the requirement that the prohibited conduct be performed "with such frequency as to indicate a general business practice * * *." This amendment was after this cause of action accrued and so on remand Reeder must prove frequency of acts.

The Kentucky law is similar to those adopted by thirty-eight other states and is based on the 1971 amendment that the National Association of Insurance Commissioners made to its model "act relating to unfair methods of competition and unfair and deceptive acts and practices in the business of insurance." This statute is intended to protect the public from unfair trade practices and fraud. It should be liberally construed so as to effectuate its purpose. KRS 446.080; DeHart v. Gray, Ky., 245 S.W.2d 434 (1952).

There is a substantial split in authority among other states as to whether individuals can maintain an action under their respective state laws. Whether other states permit private individuals to maintain claims is based upon their particular statutory system and is of no consequence here. Our decision must be based on the language of the Kentucky law.

There is no common law cause of action in Kentucky for first party bad faith. Federal Kemper Ins. Co. v. Hornback, Ky., 711 S.W.2d 844 (1986). However, the legislature can enact a law creating a cause of action where none existed at common law. The act in question indicates a definite intention to prohibit unfair claims settlement practices and constitutes the public policy of Kentucky.

It is the holding of this Court that private citizens are not specifically excluded by the statute from maintaining a private right of action against an insurer by third party claimants. KRS 446.070 and KRS 304.12–230 read together create a statutory bad faith cause of action.

We must now turn to the question of prejudgment interest which was disallowed by the trial court and the Court of Appeals on the basis of Atlantic Painting & Contracting, Inc. v. Nashville Bridge 119 Company, Ky., 670 S.W.2d 841 (1984). Our opinion has been misapplied. This case holds that interest shall be awarded on a claim, or that portion of a claim that constitutes an uncontested "liquidated" amount, even though the balance due is in litigation.

Prejudgment interest may be awarded where justified by the facts of a particular case. See 22 Am.Jur.2d Damages § 179. A careful reading of Atlantic Painting, supra, indicates that as to what is admittedly due, the claimant is entitled to interest. The evidence here indicates the portion of the claim for damages in the amount of $8,471.14 was undisputed. If an item of damages is fixed or ascertainable with reasonable certainty and is not contested and the defendant fails or refuses to timely pay it unconditionally, or at least to tender it into court where it may be withdrawn unconditionally, he should be charged with interest on that item in the judgment. We believe the circuit court and the Court of Appeals have misinterpreted the application of Atlantic Painting.

Therefore, this matter is remanded to the circuit court to award interest at the statutory rate on the admitted amount of $8,471.14 from June 30, 1985.

The decision of the Court of Appeals is affirmed in regard to the private right of action under the Unfair Claims Settlement Practices Act but reversed in regard to the question of prejudgment interest.

The case is remanded to the trial court for further proceedings consistent with this opinion.

### *Notes*

1. In 1979 the California Supreme Court announced that West's Ann.California Insurance Code § 790.03, prohibiting unfair claims practices, created a private right of action that can be used by insureds and by third parties. In *Royal Globe Insurance Co. v. Superior Court,* 23 Cal.3d 880, 153 Cal.Rptr. 842, 592 P.2d 329 (1979), the plaintiff filed an action for personal injuries sustained when she slipped at a food market. She joined as defendants the Royal Globe Insurance Company, which had issued a policy of liability insurance to the market. The plaintiff claimed that defendant had violated subdivision (h)(5) of section 790.03 of the Insurance Code, a provision of the Unfair Practices Act that requires insurers to attempt in good faith to effectuate prompt settlement of claims when liability is reasonably clear.

The court first held that a private litigant may bring an action to impose civil liability for violation of § 790.03. In making this decision, the court focused on the language of the act "Section 790.03 provides that a cease and desist order issued by the commissioner * * * shall not absolve an insurer from 'civil liability or criminal penalty under the laws of this State arising out of the methods, acts or practices found unfair or deceptive.' " The court reasoned that "[t]his provision appears to afford to private litigants a cause of action against insurers which commit the unfair acts or practices defined in subdivision (h)." The court concluded that the fair construction of that language is that a person to whom the civil liability runs has the right to enforce an action against the insurer.

The court further held that the insurer's duty runs not only to the insured, but also to third party claimants. The court analyzed the language of the statute and the legislative history to conclude that creating a distinction between insureds and third party claimants would be contrary to the law's purpose, which is the prevention of unfair claims practices by insurers.

Nine years after *Royal Globe,* the California Supreme Court reversed itself in *Moradi–Shalal v. Fireman's Fund Insurance Companies,* 46 Cal.3d 287, 250 Cal.Rptr. 116, 758 P.2d 58 (1988). In *Moradi–Shalal,* the court held that "the Royal Globe court incorrectly evaluated the legislative intent underlying the passage of section 790.03, subdivision (h), and that accordingly *Royal Globe* should be overruled." In concluding that there is no private cause against insurers engaging in unfair practice, the court used the following factors to support its decision: stare decisis, the rejection of *Royal Globe* by other state courts, scholarly criticism, the 1980 report of the National Association of Insurance Commissioners, additional legislative history, adverse social and economic consequences resulting from the *Royal*

*Globe* decision and analytical difficulties caused by the insufficient guidance provided by the *Royal Globe* court.

2. Although some version of the Unfair Insurance Practices Act is in place in all jurisdictions (save perhaps the District of Columbia), few states have held that the Act creates a private cause of Action. See Pekular v. Eich, 355 Pa.Super. 276, 513 A.2d 427 (1986) which holds that a private cause of action can be brought according to consumer and fair trade laws, but no private cause of action exists under the state's unfair insurance practices act. Some states such as South Dakota and Tennessee have passed statutes specifically prohibiting such private causes of action.

On the other hand even fewer states have held that their version of the Act preempts common law bad faith actions that might otherwise exist. Kinney v. St. Paul Mercury Ins. Co., 120 Ill.App.3d 294, 75 Ill.Dec. 911, 458 N.E.2d 79 (1983); but see Calcagno v. Personalcare Health Management, Inc., 207 Ill.App.3d 493, 499, 152 Ill.Dec. 412, 419, 565 N.E.2d 1330, 1337 (1991) (questioning the holding in Kinney and limiting preemption to punitive damages); see also Emerson v. American Bankers Ins. Co. of Florida, 223 Ill.App.3d 929, 166 Ill.Dec. 293, 298, 585 N.E.2d 1315, 1320 (1992) (criticizing the holding in Kinney).

Some states have held that a private cause of action can be implied though unfair trade practices statutes rather than through unfair insurance practices. See Mead v. Burns, 199 Conn. 651, 509 A.2d 11 (1986) holding that a private cause of action exists through the Connecticut Unfair Trade Practices Act to enforce violation of the Connecticut Unfair Insurance Practices Act, but that there is no private cause of action under the latter act.

Meanwhile, a few states have passed laws specifically creating a statutory bad faith cause of action. See Jones v. Continental Ins. Co., 670 F.Supp. 937 (S.D.Fla.1987) upholding the constitutionality of such a statute in Florida and Russell v. Protective Ins. Co., 107 N.M. 9, 751 P.2d 693 (1988) discussing a new act which specifically grants a private cause of action.

A thorough compendium of the cases appears in Theisin, Recent Developments in Private Rights of Action Under the Unfair Claims Settlement Act, 28 Tort & Ins. L.J. (1987).

3. *"Final determination of liability"*

Nationwide Ins. Co. issued a $25,000 auto liability policy to Ms. Johnson. Ms. Calzada was injured in an accident in which Ms. Johnson was the other driver. A jury returned a verdict of $93,000 against Ms. Johnson in a personal injury action. Ms. Johnson appealed from the ensuing judgment. While the appeal was pending, Ms. Calzadc sued Nationwide under West's Ann.Cal.Ins. Code § 790.03 for bad faith in failing to negotiate a settlement within the policy limit. Nationwide demurred and moved for judgment on the pleading. The appellate court ruled the trial court erred in not sustaining the demurrer and granting the motion, stating that *Royal Globe* holds "the injured third party may not institute [a direct] action [under the statute] until a judgment establishing liability of the insured has been secured. * * * When a court speaks of final judgment of liability it has reference to a judgment that is final for res judicata purposes, not for purpose of appeal." Nationwide Insurance Co. v. Superior Court for County of San Bernardino, 128 Cal.App.3d 711, 180 Cal.Rptr. 464 (1982).

Bodenhamer Jewelers was burglarized. Lost in the burglary were items of jewelry belonging to customers of the store. Bodenhamer's insurer, St. Paul Fire & Marine Ins. Co., despite advice of counsel that it was liable under its policy, delayed payments for a substantial time and advised Bodenhamer's customers who had lost property that its position was that the policy provided no coverage. Nonetheless, by about three and one-half years after the burglary most (but not all) of the customers' claims had been paid by St. Paul. Bodenhamer alleged that it had lost customers due to ill will developed during and on account of the delays in payment of claims. Bodenhamer sued asserting both violations of the general law principles of good and fair dealing and of Ins. Code 790.03(h). The Superior Court granted St. Paul's motion for a summary adjudication of issues adverse to Bodenhamer explaining that neither the general law claim nor the 790.03(h) claim could be asserted absent a determination of liability against Bodenhamer by the third party (customer) claimants. The right result? See Bodenhamer v. Superior Court, 192 Cal.App.3d 1472, 238 Cal.Rptr. 177 (1987).

4. *Statutory Controls on Insurance Company Settlement Practices*

(a) *Schedule of Penalties for Delay in Payment of Claims*

The question arises as to whether or not a statutory schedule of penalty payments (if stiff enough) to the insured for dilatoriness in handling his or her claim might not be as effective, and at the same time easier to enforce, than the somewhat ad hoc punishment meted out in the name of "good faith and fair dealing" at the whim of a particular jury.

A number of states do have such statutes usually providing for additional interest payments on the award plus attorneys' fees (see, Vance, 3d ed. p. 46). A notable example is Louisiana (L.S.A.-R.S.) which imposes an 8% penalty for failure to pay within 60 days "without just cause" on a life policy (§ 656); or 100% penalty on health and accident contracts where payment is not made within 30 days "unless just and reasonable grounds, such as would put a reasonable and prudent businessman on his guard" are shown (§ 657); and the greater of 10% or $1,000 "damages" for failure to pay other types of insurance claims (25% "damages" in case of fire or theft of an auto) within 60 days "when such failure is found to be 'arbitrary, capricious or without probable cause' " (§ 658). See, Lombard v. Manchester Life Insurance Co., 406 So.2d 742 (La.App.1981) as into which category a claim under a "Student Accident Insurance" policy should fall.

Whereas the Louisiana statute (in common with most others) makes allowance for nonpayment on reasonable grounds, the Arkansas statute (§ 23-79-208 Ark.Stat.Rev.) imposes flat 12% "damages" together with attorneys' fees upon the amount of the loss in all cases of delay in payment beyond the time stipulated in the policy even though refusal is in good faith and on reasonable grounds. This statute withstood constitutional attack in Life and Casualty Insurance Co. v. McCray, 291 U.S. 566, 54 S.Ct. 482, 78 L.Ed. 987 (1934). However, a 1991 addition to this statute deters an insured's unreasonable failure to settle a claim, providing, "(d) Recovery of less than the amount demanded by the person entitled to recover under the policy shall not defeat the right to the twelve percent (12%) damages and attorneys' fees provided for in this section if the amount recovered for the loss is within twenty percent (20%) of the amount demanded or which is sought in the suit."

### *Questions*

The California Vehicle Code allows any person who is the registered owner of 25 or more vehicles to qualify as a self-insurer by obtaining a certificate of self insurance from the Department of Motor Vehicles. Should such a self insurer be subject to the Unfair Claims Practice Act (Ins.Code § 790.03(b) when conducting settlement negotiations? Likewise should an uninsured motorist who balks at settling a tort claim against him be subject to the act? See, Nathanson v. Hertz Corp., 183 Cal.App.3d 78, 227 Cal.Rptr. 799 (1986).

## D. THE FUTURE

*The Arise of Erisa*

What has been said so far about good faith and fair dealing indicates that it is pretty largely a matter of judge-made law with some statutory interventions. One might casually infer that the doctrine is also exclusively a matter of *State* law and preserved in that status by the McCarran–Ferguson Act, above. But, of course, Federal protection may be once given, may be pro tanto removed, or relieved by the Federal Congress.

The Employee Retirement Income Security Act (ERISA) was enacted in 1974 to serve the purpose indicated in its title that is, to protect the rights of employees and their beneficiaries in employee benefit plans. Such protection also included civil remedies for employees and their beneficiaries; the Act gave U.S. District Courts exclusive jurisdiction over such civil actions. This exclusivity was mitigated only by a grant to State courts of concurrent jurisdiction over actions to recover benefits due, to enforce rights, or to clarify rights to future benefits. See 29 U.S.C. 1132. But ERISA also provides for *pre-emption* of State law remedies, 29 U.S.C. 1144(a):

> "Except as provided in subsection (b) of this section, the provisions of this subchapter and subchapter III of this chapter shall supersede any and all State laws insofar as they may now or hereafter relate to any employee benefit plan described in section 1003(a) of this title and not exempt under section 1003(b) of this title. This section shall take effect on January 1, 1975."

29 U.S.C. 1144(b)(2)(A) provides in turn:

> "(2)(A) Except as provided in subparagraph (B), nothing in this subchapter shall be construed to exempt or relieve any person from any law of any State which regulates insurance, banking, or securities."

And 29 U.S.C. 1144(b)(2)(B) goes on to state:

> "(2)(B) Neither an employee benefit plan described in section 1003(a) of this title, which is not exempt under section 1003(b) of this title (other than a plan established primarily for the purpose of providing death benefits), nor any trust established under such a plan, *shall be deemed to be an insurance company or other insurer, bank, trust company, or investment company or to be engaged in the business of insurance or banking for purposes of any law of any State purporting to regulate insurance companies, insurance contracts, banks, trust companies, or investment companies.*"

Two important opinions of Justice O'Connor (writing for the Court) explore some of the implications of these provisions and describe them as "not a model of legislative drafting". The first decision was Pilot Life Ins. Co. v. Dedeaux, 481 U.S. 41, 107 S.Ct. 1549, 95 L.Ed.2d 39 (1987).

*PILOT LIFE: Good Riddance to Bad Faith?*

It is already clear that the "doctrine" of good faith and fair dealing is largely judge made (and controlled). But it also has to be recognized that some states view the Unfair Practices Act, e.g., California Insurance Code 790.03(h)(5), as a premise for actions by private parties such as third parties who assert bad faith by a defendant insured's insurance company. See the Reeder case, *supra*. All of this might seem purely a matter of State law, untramelled ala McCarran–Ferguson Act, p. 28, above, and subject to the varying points of view and different perceptions of the purpose of the doctrine and the statute which is normal for the judiciary. And it seems to further the regulation of the business of insurance as contemplated by the McCarran–Ferguson Act.

But this does not insure that Federal law may not enter the play. In Pilot Life Insurance Co. v. Dedeaux, 481 U.S. 41, 107 S.Ct. 1549, 95 L.Ed.2d 39 (1987), the court dealt with the impact of the Employee Retirement Income Security Act of 1974 (ERISA) upon the common law rights under State law of an employee to sue for "bad faith" in the first-party context. The employee, Dedeaux, claimed permanent disability benefits under a group disability policy obtained by his employer from Pilot. Dedeaux had a disabling accident in 1975 which he alleged to be permanent, but Pilot terminated his benefits after two years. In the three years following that termination, Dedeaux' benefits were reinstated and terminated several times. Dedeaux sued in 1980 asking damages for failure to pay benefits, for mental and emotional distress ($250,000) and punitive damages ($500,000).

Pilot Life argued that ERISA pre-empted Dedeaux' common law claim for failure to pay benefits. The Court (per Justice O'Connor) said:

> In ERISA, Congress set out to
>
> > protect * * * participants in employee benefit plans and their beneficiaries, * * *
>
> ERISA comprehensively regulates, among other things, employee welfare benefit plans that, "through the purchase of insurance or otherwise," provide medical, surgical, or hospital care, or benefits in

the event of sickness, accident, disability or death. § 3(1), 29 U.S.C. § 1002(1).

Congress capped off the massive undertaking of ERISA with three provisions relating to the pre-emptive effect of the federal legislation:

> "Except as provided in subsection (b) of this section [the saving clause], the provisions of this subchapter and subchapter III of this chapter shall supersede any and all State laws insofar as they may now or hereafter relate to any employee benefit plan. * * *" § 514(a), as set forth in 29 U.S.C. § 1144(a) (pre-emption clause).

> "Except as provided in subparagraph (B) [the deemer clause], nothing in this subchapter shall be construed to exempt or relieve any person from any law of any State which regulates insurance, banking, or securities." § 514(b)(2)(A), as set forth in 29 U.S.C. § 1144(b)(2)(A) (saving clause).

> "Neither an employee benefit plan * * * nor any trust established under such a plan, shall be deemed to be an insurance company or other insurer, bank, trust company, or investment company or to be engaged in the business of insurance or banking for purposes of any law of any State purporting to regulate insurance companies, insurance contracts, banks, trust companies, or investment companies." Section 514(b)(2)(B), 29 U.S.C. § 1144(b)(2)(B) (deemer clause).

To summarize the pure mechanics of the provisions quoted above: If a state law "relate[s] to * * * employee benefit plan[s]," it is pre-empted. § 514(a). The saving clause excepts from the pre-emption clause laws that "regulat[e] insurance." § 514(b)(2)(A). The deemer clause makes clear that a state law that "purport[s] to regulate insurance" cannot deem an employee benefit plan to be an insurance company. § 514(b)(2)(B).

* * *

We have observed in the past that the express pre-emption provisions of ERISA are deliberately expansive, and designed to "establish pension plan regulation as exclusively a federal concern." *Alessi v. Raybestos–Manhattan, Inc.,* 451 U.S. 504, 523, 101 S.Ct. 1895, 1906, 68 L.Ed.2d 402 (1981). * * *

The House and Senate sponsors emphasized both the breadth and importance of the pre-emption provisions. * * *

In *Metropolitan Life,* [Metropolitan Life Ins. Co. v. Massachusetts, 471 U.S. 724, 105 S.Ct. 2380, 85 L.Ed.2d 728 (1985) ] this Court, noting that the pre-emption and saving clauses "perhaps are not a model of legislative drafting," 471 U.S., at 739, 105 S.Ct., at 2389, interpreted these clauses in relation to a Massachusetts statute that required minimum mental health care benefits to be provided Massachusetts residents covered by general health insurance policies. The appellants in *Metropolitan Life* argued that the state statute, as applied to insurance policies purchased by employee health care plans regulated by ERISA, was pre-empted.

The Court concluded, first, that the Massachusetts statute did "relate to * * * employee benefit plan[s]," thus placing the state statute within the broad sweep of the pre-emption clause, § 514(a). * * * However, the Court held that, because the state statute was one that "regulate[d] insurance," the saving clause prevented the state law from being pre-empted. In determining whether the Massachusetts statute regulated insurance, the Court was guided by case law interpreting the phrase "business of insurance" in the McCarran–Ferguson Act. * * *

There is no dispute that the common law causes of action asserted in Dedeaux's complaint "relate to" an employee benefit plan and therefore fall under ERISA's express pre-emption clause, § 514(a). * * *

Unless these common law causes of action fall under an exception to § 514(a), therefore, they are expressly pre-empted. Although Dedeaux's complaint pled several state common law causes of action, before this Court Dedeaux has described only one of the three counts—called "tortious breach of contract" in the complaint, and "the Mississippi law of bad faith" in respondent's brief—as protected from the pre-emptive effect of § 514(a). The Mississippi law of bad faith, Dedeaux argues, is a law "which regulates insurance," and thus is saved from pre-emption by § 514(b)(2)(A).

In *Metropolitan Life,* we were guided by several considerations in determining whether a state law falls under the saving clause. First, we took what guidance was available from a "common-sense view" of the language of the saving clause itself. 471 U.S., at 740, 105 S.Ct., at 2390. Second, we made use of the case law interpreting the phrase "business of insurance" under the McCarran–Ferguson Act, 15 U.S.C. § 1011 *et seq.,* in interpreting the saving clause. Three criteria have been used to determine whether a practice falls under the "business of insurance" for purposes of the McCarran–Ferguson Act:

> "*[F]irst,* whether the practice has the effect of transferring or spreading a policyholder's risk; *second,* whether the practice is an integral part of the policy relationship between the insurer and the insured; and *third,* whether the practice is limited to entities within the insurance industry." *Union Labor Life Ins. Co. v. Pireno,* 458 U.S. 119, 129, 102 S.Ct. 3002, 3009, 73 L.Ed.2d 647 (1982) (emphasis in original).

In the present case, the considerations weighed in *Metropolitan Life* argue against the assertion that the Mississippi law of bad faith is a state law that "regulates insurance."

* * *

Certainly a common-sense understanding of the phrase "regulates insurance" does not support the argument that the Mississippi law of bad faith falls under the saving clause. A common-sense view of the word "regulates" would lead to the conclusion that in order to regulate insurance, a law must not just have an impact on the insurance industry, but be specifically directed toward that industry. Even though the Mississippi Supreme Court has identified its law of bad faith with the insurance industry, the roots of this law are firmly planted in the general principles of Mississippi tort and contract law. Any breach of contract, and not merely breach of an insurance contract, may lead to liability for punitive damages under Mississippi law.

Neither do the McCarran–Ferguson Act factors support the assertion that the Mississippi law of bad faith "regulates insurance." Unlike the mandated-benefits law at issue in *Metropolitan Life,* the Mississippi common law of bad faith does not effect a spreading of policyholder risk. The state common law of bad faith may be said to concern "the policy relationship between the insurer and the insured." The connection to the insurer-insured relationship is attenuated at best, however. In contrast to the mandated-benefits law in *Metropolitan Life,* the common law of bad faith does not define the terms of the relationship between the insurer and the insured; it declares only that, whatever terms have been agreed upon in the insurance contract, a breach of that contract may in certain circumstances allow the policyholder to obtain punitive damages. The state common law of bad faith is therefore no more "integral" to the insurer-insured relationship than any state's general contract law is integral to a contract made in that state. Finally, as we have just noted, Mississippi's law of bad faith, even if associated with the insurance industry, has developed from general principles of tort and contract law available in any Mississippi breach of contract case. * * *

Considering the common-sense understanding of the saving clause, the McCarran–Ferguson Act factors defining the business of insurance, and, most importantly, the clear expression of congressional intent that ERISA's civil enforcement scheme be exclusive, we conclude that Dedeaux's state law suit asserting improper processing of a claim for benefits under an ERISA-regulated plan is not saved by § 514(b)(2)(A), and therefore is pre-empted by § 514(a).

### *Notes*

1. *Pilot Life* has been followed as to state common law causes of action for delay in processing insurance claims, Belasco v. W.K.P. Wilson & Sons, Inc., 833 F.2d 277 (11th Cir.1987). Lower federal courts have held that claims of unfair settlement practices arising under West's Ann.Cal.Ins.Code § 790.03(h) are pre-empted under ERISA, Roberson v. Equitable Life Assurance Society Soc. of U.S., 661 F.Supp. 416 (C.D.Cal.1987), and Lee v. Prudential Ins. Co. of America, 673 F.Supp. 998 (N.D.Cal.1987).

On *Pilot Life,* see R. Egelko, Losing Faith in Bad Faith, 7 Cal.Lawyer 27, Oct. 1987.

2. *Pre-emption of Bad Faith Claims by FEHBA.* For the reasons given in *Pilot Life,* the tort claims of federal employees insured under the Federal Employee Health Benefits Act for common law bad faith or violation of Cal.Ins.Code § 790.03(h) have been held to be pre-empted by that Act (5 U.S.C.A. §§ 8901ff, 8902(m)(i)), Hayes v. Prudential Insurance Co. of America, 819 F.2d 921 (9th Cir.1987). Also Hartenstine v. Superior Court, 196 Cal.App.3d 206, 241 Cal.Rptr. 756 (1987).

## DISTRICT OF COLUMBIA v. GREATER WASHINGTON BOARD OF TRADE

Supreme Court of the United States, 1992.
___ U.S. ___, 113 S.Ct. 580, 121 L.Ed.2d 513.

JUSTICE THOMAS delivered the opinion of the Court.

The District of Columbia requires employers who provide health insurance for their employees to provide equivalent health insurance coverage for injured employees eligible for workers' compensation benefits. We hold that this requirement is pre-empted by the Employee Retirement Income Security Act of 1974 (ERISA), 88 Stat. 829, as amended, 29 U.S.C. § 1001 et seq.

I

ERISA sets out a comprehensive system for the federal regulation of private employee benefit plans, including both pension plans and welfare plans. A "welfare plan" is defined in § 3 of ERISA to include, inter alia, any "plan, fund, or program" maintained for the purpose of providing medical or other health benefits for employees or their beneficiaries "through the purchase of insurance or otherwise." § 3(1), 29 U.S.C. § 1002(1). Section 4 defines the broad scope of ERISA coverage. Subject to certain exemptions, ERISA applies generally to all employee benefit plans sponsored by an employer or employee organization. § 4(a), 29 U.S.C. § 1003(a). Among the plans exempt from ERISA coverage under § 4(b) are those "maintained solely for the purpose of complying with applicable workmen's compensation laws or unemployment compensation or disability insurance laws." § 4(b)(3), 29 U.S.C. § 1003(b)(3).

ERISA's pre-emption provision assures that federal regulation of covered plans will be exclusive. Section 514(a) provides that ERISA "shall supersede any and all State laws insofar as they may now or hereafter relate to any employee benefit plan" covered by ERISA. § 514(a), 29 U.S.C. § 1144(a). Several categories of state laws, such as generally applicable criminal laws and laws regulating insurance, banking, or securities, are excepted from ERISA pre-emption by § 514(b), 29 U.S.C. § 1144(b), but none of these exceptions is at issue here.

Effective March 6, 1991, the District of Columbia Workers' Compensation Equity Amendment Act of 1990, 37 D.C.Register 6890, amended several portions of the District's workers' compensation law, D.C.Code Ann. §§ 36–301 to 36–345 (1981 and Supp.1992). Section 2(c)(2) of the Equity Amendment Act added the following requirement: "Any employer who provides health insurance coverage for an employee shall provide health insurance coverage equivalent to the existing health insurance coverage of the employee while the employee receives or is eligible to receive workers' compensation benefits under this chapter." D.C.Code Ann. § 36–307(a–1)(1) (Supp.1992). Under § 2(c)(2), the employer must provide such health insurance coverage for up to 52 weeks "at the same benefit level that the employee had at the time the employee received or was eligible to receive workers' compensation benefits." § 36–307(a–1)(3).

* * *

II

We have repeatedly stated that a law "relate[s] to" a covered employee benefit plan for purposes of § 514(a) "if it has a connection with or reference to such a plan." This reading is true to the ordinary meaning of "relate to," see Black's Law Dictionary 1288 (6th ed. 1990), and thus gives effect to the "deliberately expansive" language chosen by Congress. Under § 514(a), ERISA pre-empts any state law that refers to or has a connection with covered benefit plans (and that does not fall within a § 514(b) exception) "even if the law is not specifically designed to affect such plans, or the effect is only indirect," Ingersoll–Rand, supra, 498 U.S., at 139, 111 S.Ct., at 483, and even if the law is "consistent with ERISA's substantive requirements," Metropolitan Life, supra, 471 U.S., at 739, 105 S.Ct., at 2389.[1]

Section 2(c)(2) of the District's Equity Amendment Act specifically refers to welfare benefit plans regulated by ERISA and on that basis alone is pre-empted. The health insurance coverage that § 2(c)(2) requires employers to provide for eligible employees is measured by reference to "the existing health insurance coverage" provided by the employer and "shall be at the same benefit level." D.C.Code Ann. § 36–307(a–1)(1) and (3) (Supp.1992). The employee's "existing health insurance coverage," in turn, is a welfare benefit plan under ERISA § 3(1), because it involves a fund or program maintained by an employer for the purpose of providing health benefits for the employee "through the purchase of insurance or otherwise." § 3(1), 29 U.S.C. § 1002(1).[2]

1. Pre-emption does not occur, however, if the state law has only a "tenuous, remote, or peripheral" connection with covered plans, Shaw, 463 U.S., at 100, n. 21, 103 S.Ct., at 2901, n. 21, as is the case with many laws of general applicability, see Mackey, 486 U.S., at 830–838, and n. 12, 108 S.Ct., at 2185–2190, and n. 12; cf. Ingersoll–Rand, 498 U.S., at 139, 111 S.Ct. at ___.

2. In Fort Halifax Packing Co. v. Coyne, 482 U.S. 1, 107 S.Ct. 2211, 96 L.Ed.2d 1 (1987), we construed the word "plan" to connote some minimal, ongoing "administrative" scheme or practice, and held that "a one-time, lump-sum payment triggered by a single event" does not qualify as an employer-sponsored benefit plan. Id., at 12, 107 S.Ct., at 2217–2218. Petitioners do not contend that employers in the District of Columbia provide health insurance for

Such employer-sponsored health insurance programs are subject to ERISA regulation, see § 4(a), 29 U.S.C. § 1003(a), and any state law imposing requirements by reference to such covered programs must yield to ERISA.[3] This conclusion is consistent with Mackey v. Lanier Collection Agency, which struck down a Georgia law that specifically exempted ERISA plans from a generally applicable garnishment procedure. 486 U.S., at 828, n. 2, and 829–830, 108 S.Ct., at 2184, n. 2, 2185–2186. It also follows from Ingersoll–Rand, where we held that ERISA § 514(a) pre-empted a Texas common-law cause of action for wrongful discharge based on an employer's desire to avoid paying into an employee's pension fund. Even though the employee sought no pension benefits, only "lost future wages, mental anguish and punitive damages," 498 U.S., at 136, 111 S.Ct., at 481 (internal quotations omitted), we held the claim pre-empted because it was "premised on" the existence of an ERISA-covered pension plan. Id., at 140, 111 S.Ct., at 482.

It makes no difference that § 2(c)(2)'s requirements are part of the District's regulation of, and therefore also "relate to," ERISA-exempt workers' compensation plans. The exemptions from ERISA coverage set out in § 4(b), 29 U.S.C. § 1003(b), do not limit the pre-emptive sweep of § 514 once it is determined that the law in question relates to a covered plan. See Alessi v. Raybestos–Manhattan, Inc., 451 U.S. 504, 525, 101 S.Ct. 1895, 1907, 68 L.Ed.2d 402 (1981) ("It is of no moment that New Jersey intrudes indirectly through a workers' compensation law, rather than directly, through a statute called 'pension regulation' "). Shaw v. Delta Air Lines, Inc., 463 U.S. 85, 103 S.Ct. 2890, 77 L.Ed.2d 490 (1983), does not support petitioners' position. Shaw dealt, in relevant part, with a New York disability law that required employers to pay weekly benefits to disabled employees equal to " 'one-half of the employee's average weekly wage.' " Id., at 90, n. 4, 103 S.Ct., at 2896, n. 4 (quoting N.Y.Work.Comp.Law § 204.2 (McKinney Supp.1982–1983)). We held that this law was not pre-empted by § 514(a) because it related exclusively to exempt employee benefit plans "maintained solely for the purpose of complying with applicable * * * disability insurance laws" within the meaning of § 4(b)(3), 29 U.S.C. § 1003(b)(3). See 463 U.S., at 106–108, 103 S.Ct., at 2904–2905. The fact that employers could comply with the New York law by administering the required disability benefits through a multibenefit ERISA plan did not mean that the law related to such ERISA plans for pre-emption purposes. See id., at 108, 103 S.Ct., at 2905. We simply held that as long as the employer's disability plan, "as an administrative unit, provide[d] only those benefits required by" the New York law, it could qualify as an exempt plan under

their employees without thereby administering welfare plans within the meaning of ERISA, and petitioners concede that the existing health insurance sponsored by respondent constitutes an ERISA plan. Tr. of Oral Arg. 14.

3. ERISA does not pre-empt § 2(c)(2) to the extent its requirements are measured only by reference to "existing health insurance coverage" provided under plans that are exempt from ERISA regulation, such as "governmental" or "church" plans, see ERISA §§ 4(b)(1) and (2), 29 U.S.C. §§ 1003(b)(1) and (2).

ERISA § 4(b)(3). Id., at 107, 103 S.Ct., at 2905. Thus, unlike § 2(c)(2) of the District's Equity Amendment Act, the New York statute at issue in Shaw did not "relate to" an ERISA-covered plan.

Petitioners nevertheless point to Metropolitan Life Ins. Co. v. Massachusetts, 471 U.S. 724, 105 S.Ct. 2380, 85 L.Ed.2d 728 (1985), in which we described Shaw as holding that "the New York Human Rights Law and that State's Disability Benefits Law 'relate[d] to' welfare plans governed by ERISA." Id., at 739, 105 S.Ct., at 2388–2389. Relying on this dictum and their reading of Shaw, petitioners argue that § 514(a) should be construed to require a two-step analysis: if the state law "relate[s] to" an ERISA-covered plan, it may still survive pre-emption if employers could comply with the law through separately administered plans exempt under § 4(b). See Tr. of Oral Arg. 16–17. But Metropolitan Life construed only the scope of § 514(b)(2)(A)'s safe harbor for state laws regulating insurance, see 471 U.S., at 739–747, 105 S.Ct., at 2388–2393; it did not purport to add, by its passing reference to Shaw, any further gloss on § 514(a). And although we did conclude in Shaw that both New York laws at issue there related to "employee benefit plan[s]" in general, 463 U.S., at 100, 103 S.Ct., at 2901, only the Human Rights Law, which barred discrimination by ERISA plans, fell within the pre-emption provision. See id., at 100–106, 103 S.Ct., at 2901–2905. As we have explained, the Disability Benefits Law upheld in Shaw—though mandating the creation of a "welfare plan" as defined in ERISA[4]—did not relate to a welfare plan subject to ERISA regulation. Section 2(c)(2) does, and that is the end of the matter. We cannot engraft a two-step analysis onto a one-step statute.

The judgment of the Court of Appeals [holding that the District's worker's compensation law is preempted] is accordingly Affirmed.

Justice STEVENS dissent is omitted.

### *Final Note*

### *Reverse Bad Faith*

There is a measure of ironic consistency in the fact that the state in which bad faith first reached full flower is also the point of origin of cases suggesting the counter use of the doctrine. In California Casualty General Ins. Co. v. Superior Court, 173 Cal.App.3d 274, 218 Cal.Rptr. 817 (1985), the insured sued for bad faith in the handling of her uninsured motorist claim. During the proceedings the insurer moved to amend its answer to assert the theory of "comparative" bad faith based on the manner in which the insured and her attorney prosecuted, handled, and managed her first party claim. The insured protested that this was a "disfavored" defense because it had never before been recognized. The trial court refused to allow the amendment and the insurer appealed. In issuing a mandate to the lower court to vacate its order the appellate court stated:

4. "Welfare plans" include plans providing "benefits in the event of sickness, accident, [or] disability." § 3(1), 29 U.S.C. § 1002(1).

"[A] duty of good faith and fair dealing in an insurance policy is a two-way street, running from the insured to his insurer as well as vice versa [citation]." * * * The specific content of each party's duty "is dependent upon the nature of the bargain struck between the insurer and the insured and the legitimate expectations of the parties which arise from the contract." * * *

There can be little question but that an insurer which provides uninsured motorist coverage has a reasonable expectation that if the insured suffers a loss claimed to be covered under the uninsured motorist provisions of the policy, the insured will promptly and accurately furnish it with all the information and evidence pertinent to the claim that is known to the insured. If a failure of the insured to do so results in delaying or impeding the investigation of the claim by the insurer or delays or makes improvident the insurer's payment of the claim, any economic loss and emotional distress caused the insured by virtue of any such nonpayment or delay in investigation or payment will have been caused either wholly or in part by the conduct of the insured. We perceive no sound reason, nor is any suggested, why the doctrine of comparative fault enunciated and applied to negligent conduct by the California Supreme Court in *Li v. Yellow Cab Co.* (1975) 13 Cal.3d 804, 119 Cal.Rptr. 858, 532 P.2d 1226, and later applied as between a strictly liable defendant and a negligent plaintiff (*Daly v. General Motors Corp.* (1978) 20 Cal.3d 725, 144 Cal.Rptr. 380, 575 P.2d 1162) and as between two tortfeasors one of whose liability was based on strict products liability and the other on negligence (*Safeway Stores, Inc. v. Nest–Kart* (1978) 21 Cal.3d 322, 146 Cal.Rptr. 550, 579 P.2d 441) should not be applicable to bad faith cases. While the duty of good faith and fair dealing arises out of a contractual relationship between the parties, breach of the duty and ensuing damages are governed by tort principles.

In a later case, Handel v. United States Fidelity & Guaranty Co., 192 Cal.App.3d 684, 237 Cal.Rptr. 667 (1987) the insurer cross-complained in a fire loss case, alleging fraud and false swearing on the part of the insured and requesting punitive damages. These were awarded at trial. The Appellate Court reversed because of failure to prove reliance—a necessary element in a common law deceit action. By dicta, however, the court recognized the existence of an independent "reverse bad faith" cause of action, but avoided the issue because it was neither pled nor tried in the case.

In theory an insurer has always been entitled (in addition to avoiding the policy) to sue its patrons for damages for common law fraud plus punitives, but this has not been commonly done. However to categorize as "bad faith torts" the breach of contractual conditions by the insured (or his or her attorney) such as "non-cooperation" or "failure to give prompt notice of a claim" or "false swearing as to the value of destroyed property" (to be dealt with shortly in this book) would bid fair to open new vistas in tort and contract law in general, and require a reappraisal of commonly employed legal strategies. And what about an affirmative defense asserting that the tactical moves made by the insured to "set up" a bad faith claim against the insured constitutes "reverse" bad faith? See Shipstead and Thomas, Comparative and Reverse Bad Faith, etc., 28 Tort & Ins.L.J. 215 (1987).

*

# Part B

# PROPERTY INSURANCE

# Chapter 5

# PRESENTATION OF CLAIMS

— **timeliness**
— **honesty**
— **filing suit**

## GARDNER-DENVER CO. v. DIC-UNDERHILL CONSTRUCTION CO.

United States District Court, Southern District of New York, 1976.
416 F.Supp. 934.

MOTLEY, DISTRICT JUDGE.

Plaintiff in this diversity action seeks to recover from defendants the value of an air compressor which it allegedly rented to defendants Dic-Underhill on or about August 3, 1973 for their use on the construction site of the World Trade Center in New York, owned by defendant Port Authority. This compressor was not returned to plaintiff, according to defendants, because it was stolen from the construction site. Defendants, in turn, seek indemnity for any possible loss in this action from Dic-Underhill's insurer, St. Paul, with the Port Authority basing its claim upon a subrogation clause in the contract between itself and Dic-Underhill. In response, St. Paul has moved for summary judgment pursuant to Rule 56, Fed.R.Civ.P., and the court grants this motion.

The facts are not disputed. Dic Concrete Corp. and Underhill Construction Corp. were parties to a contract with the Port Authority for the performance of concrete construction in connection with the construction of the World Trade Center. Prior to the date of the alleged theft, St. Paul issued to defendants Dic-Underhill a Contractors' Equipment insurance policy, numbered 365 JD 4974, insuring certain portable equipment[4] against "all risks of [p]hysical loss or damage from any external cause", with certain enumerated exceptions.

4. The contract of insurance provides coverage for "contractor's equipment, as listed below, the property of the Insured or the property of others in the custody or control of the Insured, for which they may be liable." An attached endorsement indicates that the coverage included, *inter alia,*

On or about August 16, 1973, the mobile compressor was allegedly stolen from the World Trade Center jobsite and was never returned. By letter of the same date, Dic–Underhill Joint Venture notified Armitage & Co., Inc. of the loss, since Armitage was the agent for American Home Assurance Co., the insurance carrier of the Port Authority and its contractor, Dic–Underhill, for all work at the World Trade Center. Subsequently, on August 20, 1973, Armitage forwarded the claim to Edward D. Weinstock, Inc. for adjustment.

From August 16, 1973 until March 31, 1975, Dic–Underhill and the Port Authority believed in good faith that the claim would be covered by American Home Assurance Co. However, by letter dated March 27, 1975 and received March 31, 1975, Dic–Underhill was informed by the Weinstock firm that the loss of the compressor was outside the scope of property covered under defendant's policy of builder's risk insurance, and that the claim would therefore be disallowed.

On April 29, 1975, Dic–Underhill Joint Venture notified its own insurance broker, John C. Vorbach Company, of the loss. By letter dated April 30, 1975, the Vorbach Company notified St. Paul's agent, The Maloy Agency, Inc., and the agent forwarded the letter of notification to St. Paul, which received it on May 3, 1975.

On September 2, 1975, St. Paul wrote to Dic–Underhill Joint Venture and informed them that "after careful consideration", St. Paul had concluded that the loss did not fall within the protection of the policy. Finally, on December 2, 1975, the instant suit was commenced by Gardner–Denver.

On the basis of the above chronology, St. Paul moved for summary judgment, arguing that defendants (Dic–Underhill, as the insured, and the Port Authority, as subrogee) have failed to comply with that provision of their insurance contract which requires that the insured notify St. Paul of any loss "as soon as practicable".[5] On the authority of a number of New York cases, St. Paul contends that the interval between the alleged theft in August of 1973 and the notification given to its agent in April of 1975 is unreasonable and amounts to a contractual violation as a matter of law.[6]

It is established New York law that compliance with the notice provision of an insurance contract is a condition precedent to an insurer's liability, and that an insurer need not show prejudice before it can

"all portable equipment usual to Insured's concrete construction operations, [etc.]"

**5.** "Notice of Loss. The Insured shall as soon as practicable report in writing to the Company or its agent every loss, damage or occurrence which may give rise to a claim under this Policy and shall also file with the Company or its agent within ninety (90) days from the date of discovery of such loss, damage or occurrence, a detailed sworn proof of loss."

**6.** Dic–Underhill and the Port Authority do not appear to question that the time for purposes of judging the reasonableness of the notification, is to be measured from the date of the alleged theft. They only argue that such notification was "as soon as practicable", in view of the circumstances. They specifically do not argue that they are not, even yet, obliged to give notice, since the "occurrence" upon which their claim would be based is an adjudication of their liability to plaintiff in the instant suit.

assert the defense of noncompliance. Security Mutual Insurance Company of New York v. Acker–Fitzsimons Corp., 31 N.Y.2d 436, 340 N.Y.S.2d 902, 293 N.E.2d 76 (Ct.App.1972). Absent a valid excuse, a failure to satisfy the notice requirement vitiates the policy. Id. at 905, 293 N.E.2d at 78. A provision that notice be given "as soon as practicable" after an occurrence merely requires that notice be given within a reasonable time under all the circumstances. * * *

Since it is not disputed that St. Paul's agent did not receive notice until April 30, 1975, the question is whether this delay of some twenty months after the date of the theft is unreasonable as a matter of law.

Absent some excuse or mitigating circumstances, courts have passed judgment on the insured's compliance with notice provisions, and have found much shorter delays to be unreasonable. (51 days, Deso, supra; 27 days, Reina v. United States Casualty Co., 228 App.Div. 108, 239 N.Y.S. 196 (App.Div., 1st Dept. 1930), aff'd 256 N.Y. 537, 177 N.E. 130 (1931); 30 days, Mason v. Allstate Insurance Co., 12 A.D.2d 138, 209 N.Y.S.2d 104 (App.Div., 2d Dept. 1960)). However. "[m]itigating circumstances may arise if the insured lacks, or is incapable of acquiring, knowledge of the occurrence; or the insured is out of the state; or in good faith reasonably believes there is no policy coverage or that the insured was not liable on the main action. [citations omitted]." Kason v. City of New York, 83 Misc.2d 810, 373 N.Y.S.2d 456, 459 (Sup.Ct., N.Y.Cty.1975). Where these excuses are asserted by the insured in mitigation of his failure to provide prompt notice to the insurer, the New York courts have apparently allowed the jury to evaluate the reasonableness of the insured's conduct. * * *

However, defendants do not rely on any of these accepted mitigating theories. Rather, they argue that their twenty-month delay in notifying St. Paul is excused by their good faith belief that their loss would be reimbursed by the American Home Assurance Company. Although it appears possible that there might be a serious question as to the reasonableness of their delay from the end of March, 1975 to the end of April, 1975 which could properly be entrusted to a jury for decision, defendants have cited no case, nor has the court's research discovered any case, in which notification of the "wrong" insurer has excused a failure to promptly notify the insurer being sued.

As a matter of fact, the law in New York seems to be that timely notification to another insurer does not excuse failure to notify the insurer being sued as soon as practicable. Mason, supra; Reina, supra. In *Mason,* the insured had inadvertently notified the wrong insurer concerning an automobile accident, and the proper insurer was not notified until a substantially later time. After reviewing the circumstances which may be legally sufficient to excuse a failure to promptly notify the proper insurer, the Appellate Division found "no extenuating circumstances in the instant case." "[N]egligence in notifying the wrong insurer does not excuse failure to give notice to the proper one." 209 N.Y.S.2d at 113.

The facts of this suit seem to present an even stronger case for application of the principle established by *Mason* and *Reina*. In this case, there seems to be no doubt that the defendants knew that they had a policy of insurance with St. Paul and suspected that they might be held liable for the compressor's loss. Their decision to look to American Home Assurance for reimbursement was apparently not based on any confusion as to the identity of the insurer, but rather reflected an election between those insurers whose policies might arguably cover the loss. No circumstance has been brought to the attention of the court which would have prevented defendants from notifying St. Paul at the time of loss in order that that insurer might investigate the occurrence—whether or not a claim might later be filed.[7]

Accordingly, the court finds that Dic–Underhill failed to notify St. Paul "as soon as practicable" after discovery of the loss of the compressor, and that that failure constitutes a breach of a material condition precedent to St. Paul's liability under its contract of insurance. Accordingly, both Dic–Underhill and its subrogee, the Port Authority, are contractually barred from recovery against St. Paul.

The only remaining question is whether St. Paul waived its defense to Dic–Underhill's claim by considering the claim after it was finally filed,[8] and by rejecting the claim in its letter dated September 2, 1975.[9] In support of their argument that St. Paul waived its policy defense based on lack of timely notice, Dic–Underhill and the Port Authority merely note that over four months elapsed between filing of the claim and final rejection, and that, during that period, St. Paul did not indicate to any representative of the insured that the claim was improper for failure to give the requisite notice. In these circumstances, the court finds neither that "manifested intention to release a right" necessary to infer a waiver, nor any legal prejudice to the insured necessary for a finding of estoppel against the insurer. See Allstate Insurance Company v. Gross, 27 N.Y.2d 263, 317 N.Y.S.2d 309, 314, 265 N.E.2d 736, 739 (Ct.App.1970); 31 N.Y.Jur., Insurance § 1589 [10] (1963). The letter from

**7.** The contract of insurance does, after all, require notification of any "loss, damage or occurrence" which "*may* give rise to a claim." (emphasis added)

**8.** Counsel for Dic–Underhill and the Port Authority has not vigorously advanced the waiver argument. No authorities are cited in support of the argument. Moreover, counsel at one point in argument withdrew the waiver point entirely, but then decided to stand by his assertion of waiver.

**9.** The entire text of that letter is as follows:

> "We have completed our investigation in connection with the above captioned claim and after careful consideration we feel that this loss does not fall within the protection of the policy."

**10.** "In general, to operate as a waiver by the company of, or an estoppel to assert, a condition in the policy limiting the time in which suit shall be brought after the loss, the act or declaration relied upon must be done or made during the running of the period of limitation, or at least commenced during such period, since acts taking place entirely after the expiration of the period cannot be said to have induced the insured not to bring action within the period." While this quotation pertains most directly to provisions, such as that in the instant policy, which require that suit be brought within a specified time after discovery of the loss or occurrence giving rise to the claim, the rationale is equally applicable to provisions requiring notification to the insurer "as soon as practicable". In this case, the claim itself was filed with St. Paul

St. Paul disallowing the claim is by no means an unequivocal statement that the loss at issue simply was not covered by the policy; it is also susceptible of a construction whereby the claim was disallowed due to lack of timely notice. Had the letter based the disallowance on some other ground, then there might be some basis for inferring that the insurer had chosen to waive the defense of improper notice. However, such does not appear to be the case here.

* * *

The motion for summary judgment is granted.

### *Notes*

1. Here Dic–Underhill held two policies:

a. a bailee's policy

b. a builders risk policy

The loss fell under (a) whereas a claim was made under (b). Whether or not bailees' policies cover bailed goods "for which they may be liable" is not an easy question to answer as will be seen in cases on the point later in this Part. E.g.: Was Dic–Underhill "liable" for the theft of the compressor? or did the policy apply to the compressor simply because Dic–Underhill was generally "liable" as a bailee? That issue, in fact, actually underlies the basic action here.

Isn't it natural for laymen to put in a claim under (b)? The contractors for one of the biggest buildings in the world as well as the directors of the Port Authority of New York (not exactly innocents in the industrial arena) mistakenly thought so. Shouldn't the insured at least have the opportunity to prove that its mistaken delay did not cause any detriment to the insurer?

On the point of estoppel or waiver, could an insurance company ever be held estopped to deny a claim which has been filed late? What sort of conduct would have to be shown? As to a claimed waiver, would not additional consideration be necessary to re-establish the coverage? See Petrice v. Federal Kemper Insurance Co., 163 W.Va. 737, 260 S.E.2d 276 (1979).

Should a distinction be made between ignorance of a cause of loss and ignorance of the fact that a loss has occurred for the purpose of excusing the filing of a late claim? The opinion in USLIFE Savings and Loan Association v. National Surety Corp., 115 Cal.App.3d 336, 171 Cal.Rptr. 393, 398 (1981) says so, but why? Which type of ignorance was it in the principal case?

2. *The present status of the prejudice to the insurer requirement*—(unsettled).

Cf. the statement in the principal case as to the necessity of showing prejudice with the flat assertion that "California law does not require strict compliance with insurance notice clauses, unless the insurer can show actual prejudice." Fidelity Savings & Loan Association v. Aetna Life & Casualty Co., 647 F.2d 933 (9th Cir.1981).

long after the expiration of a "reasonable time" after the loss, and any action or inaction by St. Paul could not have prevented the insured from correcting that fact.

3. *A step by step judicial rewrite of the notice requirements of standard fire policy. The Rhode Island gambit.*

Back in 1917 the rule was declared in Sherwood Ace Co. v. United States Casualty, 40 R.I. 268, 100 A. 572 (1917), that whether an insurer was prejudiced by the insured's neglect to give the notice required in the policy was wholly immaterial.

In 1971, the plaintiff, holding an automobile policy, filed a late notice and proof of a claim against an uninsured motorist. Employing the "contract of adhesion" rationale the Rhode Island Supreme Court rejected the *Sherwood* holding and adopted the rule that "an insurer could not rely on the so-called 'notice' provision of its policy unless it could demonstrate that it had been prejudiced by lack of notice." Pickering v. American Employers Insurance Co., 109 R.I. 143, 282 A.2d 584 (1971).

In 1980 it was decided that the same rule would apply to the legislatively mandated 60 day notice provision in the standard fire policy. Naturally the company questions its applicability to a policy not characterized as a contract of adhesion. The answer according to the court is simple: failure to give notice as required results in a forfeiture and, of course, the legislature would not intend to mandate a forfeiture. Q.E.D. the standard policy is not changed—only interpreted. (Siravo v. Great American Insurance Co., 122 R.I. 538, 410 A.2d 116 (1980)).

4. Where property insurance (crime, flood, etc.) is obtained from a Federal Agency, the applicant should be aware that there is little or no give in the procedural requirements of notice and proof of loss. Cohen v. Federal Insurance Administration, 654 F.Supp. 824 (E.D.N.Y.1986); Spratlin v. Federal Crop Ins. Corp., 662 F.Supp. 870 (E.D.Ark.1987). Why?

5. *Failure to give notice and breach of the co-operation clause*

The former, says the Florida Supreme Court in Bankers Insurance Co. v. Macias, 475 So.2d 1216 (1985), is a condition precedent with a presumption (rebuttable) of prejudice (a position it admits may be out of step with the modern trend). On the other hand the failure to co-operate in a P.I.P. case is a condition subsequent and the burden is on the insurer to show prejudice. An intermediate appellate court decision confusing the two was reversed. Query: Is the distinction really all that clear?

## SCHREIBER v. PENNSYLVANIA LUMBERMAN'S MUTUAL INSURANCE COMPANY

Supreme Court of Pennsylvania, 1982.
498 Pa. 21, 444 A.2d 647.

ROBERTS, JUSTICE.

* * * Appellants' sole contention throughout these proceedings has been that the one-year limitation of suit provision contained in their policy of fire insurance should not bar appellants from bringing suit on the policy over two years and two months after their alleged loss unless appellee insurance company can demonstrate that it has been prejudiced by appellants' delay. We find this contention to be without merit and, accordingly, affirm. * * *

In Brakeman v. Potomac Insurance Co., 472 Pa. 66, 371 A.2d 193 (1977), this Court held that a policyholder's failure to abide by a provision in an automobile insurance contract requiring timely notice of claims would not bar suit on the policy absent a showing of prejudice by the insurer. Appellants argue that *Brakeman* mandates a similar conclusion with regard to the statutory limitation of suit provision at issue here.

Contrary to appellants' assertion, the rationale of our decision in *Brakeman* is not applicable to the present case. In *Brakeman,* the insurer had chosen to include in its automobile insurance policy a provision requiring that,

> "[i]n the event of an accident, occurrence or loss, written notice * * * shall be given by or for the insured to the company or any of its authorized agents as soon as practicable."

* * *

* * * Because the above provision requiring notice "as soon as practicable" was included at the exclusive discretion of the insurer, this Court found the provision to be in the nature of a contract of adhesion. Thus this Court departed from precedent and held that an insurer must prove that it has been prejudiced by an insured's late notice before it can successfully invoke such a provision as a defense to a claim.

In contrast, the limitation of suit provision in appellants' fire insurance policy was not "dictated by the insurance company to the insured." Rather, the Legislature has mandated that every policy of fire insurance issued in this Commonwealth shall contain the proviso that

> "[n]o suit or action on this policy for the recovery of any claim shall be sustainable in any court of law or equity * * * unless commenced within twelve months next after inception of the loss."

* * * Such a statutory requirement can hardly be termed a "contract of adhesion," imposed unfairly by the stronger party upon the weaker. Rather, it represents a legislative determination of a reasonable period within which suits must be brought, a careful balancing of the interests of both insurers and insured. The validity of this statutorily mandated limitation of suit provision has been consistently upheld. See, e.g., General State Authority v. Planet Insurance Co., 464 Pa. 162, 346 A.2d 265 (1975); Lardas v. Underwriters Insurance Co., 426 Pa. 47, 231 A.2d 740 (1967).

We have recognized that in certain circumstances, a limitation of suit provision will not be permitted to bar a delayed suit: "a provision of this nature may be extended or waived where the actions of the insurer lead the insured to believe the contractual limitation period will not be enforced." General State Authority v. Planet Insurance Co., supra, 464 Pa. at 165 n. 6, 346 A.2d at 267 n. 6. * * * Here, however, despite ample opportunity to do so, appellants have at no time alleged that any conduct of appellee, either active or passive, was in any way responsible for appellants' delay of over two years in commencing their action on the policy. In these circumstances, the court of common pleas properly granted appellee's motion for judgment on the pleadings, and the Superior Court properly affirmed. * * *

Order affirmed.

## CLOSSER v. PENN MUTUAL FIRE INSURANCE CO.

Supreme Court of Delaware, 1983.
457 A.2d 1081.

HORSEY, JUSTICE:

This appeal raises a single issue—the timeliness of an insured's suit against his insurer to recover his portion of policy benefits from a fire loss on covered property owned in part by the insured.

Plaintiff, Raymond Closser, appeals Superior Court's grant of summary judgment to defendant, Penn Mutual Fire Insurance Company (hereafter "Penn Mutual" or "the insurer"). Summary judgment was granted on basically two grounds: (1) that the suit was time barred by the policy's twelve month suit limitation provision; and (2) that Closser had failed to meet his burden of proving either misleading or fraudulent conduct by Penn Mutual sufficient to toll the running of the policy's suit limitation.

On September 22, 1979, a fire of suspicious origin destroyed the home of Raymond Closser and his wife, not a party to this action. The property was titled in the Clossers' joint names and was insured by Penn Mutual against fire loss. The fire was determined to have been the result of arson.

In January, 1980, Closser, through his attorney (his wife was represented by other counsel), first contacted Penn Mutual's area representative as to a policy settlement. They communicated with each other through at least March of 1980. Sometime before July, 1980, Closser's brother-in-law admitted responsibility for the fire but implicated Closser; and Closser was indicted for arson in July, 1980. However, in November, 1980, the State nolle prossed the criminal charges against Closser.

In December, 1980, when Closser's attorney attempted to resume settlement negotiations with Penn Mutual, it rejected Closser's claim and denied liability.

Meanwhile, Closser's wife had reopened negotiations with Penn Mutual on her policy claim; and Penn Mutual paid her $40,000 in settlement of her interest in March, 1981. Closser then sought to reopen settlement negotiations with Penn Mutual but failed. Closser then filed the pending suit against Penn Mutual on May 5, 1981. As previously stated, Superior Court found the suit to be time barred and granted Penn Mutual's motion for summary judgment. Closser then docketed this appeal.

Closser's first ground for reversal relates to the accrual of the policy's suit limitation provision. The policy provides:

> No suit or action on this policy for the recovery of any claim shall be sustainable in any court of law or equity unless all the requirements of this policy shall have been complied with, and unless commenced within twelve months after inception of the loss.

It is settled Delaware law, as Closser concedes, that a one year limitation on suit on an insurance contract is reasonable and binding on an insured. Brooks v. Insurance Placement Facility of Delaware, Del. Supr., 456 A.2d 1226 (1983); Wesselman v. Travelers Indemnity Company, Del.Supr., 345 A.2d 423 (1975); Ottendorfer v. Aetna Insurance Company, Del.Supr., 231 A.2d 263 (1967). * * *

Closser argues that since the suit is for breach of contract, the twelve month limitation period should not begin to run until Penn Mutual disclaims coverage or denies liability. And since Penn Mutual did not reject Closser's claim until December, 1980, Closser says his suit filed five months later was timely filed. Closser relies for this result upon (a) Allstate Insurance Company v. Spinelli,[1] Del.Supr., 443 A.2d 1286 (1981) and (b) case law in other jurisdictions.

*Spinelli* does not control this case for two reasons: (1) a claim by an insured against his insurer on a fire policy is substantially different from a claim for uninsured motorist coverage benefits; and (2) a different event triggers each claim. In *Spinelli,* Allstate's insured had no assertable claim against Allstate for uninsured motorist benefits until he established his right to recover damages from the uninsured tortfeasor *and* the latter's insurer denied the claim or determined that the tortfeasor had no coverage. See, *Spinelli,* 443 A.2d at 1291.

Unlike *Spinelli,* Closser in this case had an immediately ascertainable and assertable claim against Penn Mutual from the date of the fire loss; and the controlling limitation provision of the policy plainly relates the running of the twelve month limitation from the "inception of the loss." In contrast, as we noted in *Spinelli,* "an uninsured motorist claim is only indirectly related to the accident itself." 443 A.2d at 1291. * * *

Under the fire insurance contract before us, we conclude that the language of the suit limitation clause, "after inception of the loss", must be construed to mean the date of the fire or other casualty causing the loss. * * *

Closser next argues that the reasonableness of the twelve month suit limitation running from date of fire is effaced by the policy's additional compliance "requirements" imposed on an insured. Appellant refers to the policy's preceding limitation language barring "[any] suit ... unless all the requirements of [the] policy shall have been

1. In *Spinelli,* an insured sued his automobile insurance carrier (Allstate) to recover uninsured motorist benefits provided under his policy. This Court held that such a cause of action did not accrue until the carrier of the third-party tortfeasor had denied coverage and notified Allstate's insured of the rejection of his claim for such third-party coverage benefits. * * *

complied with and unless commenced [within twelve months of] loss."
* * *

* * *

The particular provisions of the policy that Closser claims render a twelve month suit limitation unenforceable because unreasonable are: (1) the requirement that an insured file a loss claim within sixty days of the loss; (2) the requirement that an insured provide further documentation of property loss, whenever requested; (3) the appraisal procedures' lack of time limitations on their being invoked and carried through to an award; and (4) the sixty day hiatus under the "loss payable" clause between the determination of an appraisal award and the date the loss becomes payable by the insurer. Closser criticizes these provisions, claiming: (1) that a suit may not be brought by an insured until *all* of these steps have been "completed"; (2) that these requirements reduce an insured's time for filing suit to considerably less than twelve months from inception of loss; and (3) that the insured has no control over the time limitations of an appraisal. As a result, Closser argues that the suit limitation provision is "one-sided and ambiguous."

These criticisms appear to be more theoretical than real; for the insured has made no *prima facie* showing that compliance with these requirements in fact delayed the filing of his suit beyond the anniversary date of the fire loss. Absent such a showing, we decline to rule as a matter of law that the existence of such policy provisions *requires* either a tolling of the limitation from the date of the fire or a reinterpretation of the limitation words "inception of the loss" to mean the insurer's denial of coverage.[2]

While there is authority for either of these two results,[3] there is also

2. As will be seen, given our standard of review, this is not to say that a *prima facie* case of estoppel may not have been made against Penn Mutual of misleading conduct and reliance thereon by Closser to his detriment.

3. Authority for tolling an insurance contract limitation from running from the date of loss is found in Peloso v. Hartford Fire Insurance Company, N.J.Supr., 56 N.J. 514, 267 A.2d 498 (1970); Tom Thomas v. Reliance Insurance Company, Mich.Supr., 396 Mich. 588, 242 N.W.2d 396 (1976) and Phoenix Insurance Co. v. Brown, Tenn.Ct. App., 53 Tenn.App. 240, 381 S.W.2d 573 (1964). The *Peloso* court recognized that the majority of courts ruling on the question had held to the contrary [computing the limitation period from date of the loss where the limitation is clear and unambiguous]. But the Court opted to follow the reasoning of the "few" jurisdictions that had adopted a concept of tolling. See, Finkelstein v. American Insurance Company of Newark, N.J., La.Supr., 222 La. 516, 62 So.2d 840 (1952) and *Phoenix Ins. Co. v. Brown,* supra. However, *Finkelstein* was overruled by Gremillion v. Travelers Insurance Company, La.Supr., 256 La. 974, 240 So.2d 727 (1970), which then returned Louisiana to the majority view that "inception of the loss" must be taken to mean "time of the fire"—rather than "time of the ascertainment of the loss from fire damage." 240 So.2d at 731.

A few courts have also simply read an insurance contract limiting suit to one year from inception of loss to mean one year from the insurer's denial of coverage. Fireman's Fund Insurance Company v. Sand Lake Lounge, Inc., Alaska Supr., 514 P.2d 223 (1973). The Alaska court reached this result by analogy to the Uniform Commercial Code and by concluding that to enforce the insurance contract limitation provision as written would given an insurer an unfair advantage over insured claimants who have an inferior bargaining position. But here, no showing having been made that the contract was inherently unfair or unconsciona-

substantial authority to the contrary.[4] And the latter appears to be the majority rule. 44 Am.Jur.2d, *Insurance,* §§ 1884 and 1911. Annot. 95 A.L.R.2d 1023. While our prior insurance policy limitation case law has not specifically addressed the accrual issue, *Ottendorfer,* supra, and *Wesselman,* supra clearly lean towards the majority rule. * * *

* * *

Returning once more to the particular "requirements" of the policy before us, we are not persuaded that these provisions render unreasonable and unfair the twelve month suit limitation accruing from the occurrence of a fire loss. We find no unfairness in any of the "Requirements in case loss occurs" imposed upon the insured. Clearly, there is no unfairness in requiring an insured to give prompt notice of loss and to file a proof of loss claim within sixty days of the occurrence of a loss. Nor is there any inherent unfairness in the requirement that an insured provide such further documentation of a loss, "as may be reasonably required." As to the sixty day hiatus under the "loss payable" clause between the determination of an appraisal award and the insurer's obligation to pay the award, since no such award was made in this case, the clause has no relevance. Finally, the policy cannot be reasonably construed as either barring suit by an insured until all of the requirements and procedures have been completed nor as barring suit against Penn Mutual pending its review of the insured's proof of loss claim.

However, with respect to the policy's appraisal provisions, we cannot agree with Superior Court's conclusion that they have "nothing at all to

ble to the insured, we decline to rewrite the policy's limitation provision to read other than as accruing from the date of the fire loss. See, Tulowitzki v. Atlantic Richfield Co., Del.Supr., 396 A.2d 956 (1978).

Other courts applying a tolling concept have done so: (1) on the basis of policy language barring an insured from suing until after submission of proof of loss, Parker v. American Surety Company of New York, N.Y.Supr., 176 Misc.2d 985, 29 N.Y.S.2d 414 (1941); (2) based on a conflict between the contract limitation provision and statutes governing insurance policy clauses. *Peloso,* supra; and (3) if the insured cannot determine the existence of a claim until the rights or liability of third party in interest are resolved. Sassi v. Jersey Trucking Service, Inc., N.Y.App., 283 A.D. 73, 126 N.Y.S.2d 389 (1953) and Zurn Engineers v. Eagle Star Insurance Company, Ltd., Cal. App., 61 Cal.App.3d 493, 132 Cal.Rptr. 206 (1976).

**4.** Jurisdictions following the majority rule (that a contract limitation related to "inception of loss" runs from the time of the loss, absent waiver or estoppel and not from denial of coverage), include: Adams v. Northern Ins. Co., Ariz.App., 16 Ariz.App. 337, 493 P.2d 504 (1972); General State Authority v. Planet Insurance Co., Pa. Supr., 464 Pa. 162, 346 A.2d 265 (1975); Proc v. Home Insurance Co., N.Y.App., 17 N.Y.2d 239, 270 N.Y.S.2d 412, 217 N.E.2d 136 (1966); Bollinger v. National Fire Insurance Co., Cal.Supr., 147 P.2d 611 (1944); Chambers v. Atlas Ins. Co., Conn.Supr., 50 Am.Rep. 1, 51 Conn. 17 (1883); Appel v. Cooper Ins. Co., Ohio Supr., 76 Ohio St. 52, 80 N.E. 955 (1907); Ramsey v. Home Insurance, Va.Supr., 203 Va. 502, 125 S.E.2d 201 (1962).

Compare, *Proc v. Home Insurance Co.,* supra, wherein Judge Fuld of the New York Court of Appeals rejected in essence the rationale for the minority rule.

> "Nor do we perceive anything unfair in reaching the result we do. If conduct or action on the part of the insurer is responsible for the insured's failure to comply in time with the conditions precedent, injustice is avoided and adequate relief assured, without doing violence to the plain language used by the Legislature, by resort to traditional principles of waiver and estoppel." 270 N.Y.S.2d at 416, 217 N.E.2d at 139.

do with establishing liability, limitation of action, or filing suit for a loss." Assuming that the appraisal provisions are invoked by either party, it is clear that they lack time limitations on their being either initially invoked or being carried through to an award. If invoked, the carrying out of such provisions could obviously impinge on an insured's determination to file suit. Thus, while the policy's appraisal provisions and its suit limitation provisions may well serve entirely different purposes, the former provisions amount to an alternative form of dispute resolution, short of litigation. Further, since the policy states that "an award in writing, so itemized, of any two when filed with this Company shall determine the amount of actual cash value and loss", we construe the appraisal provisions of the policy, if invoked, to provide a mandatory form of arbitration, precluding recourse to the courts. Thus, we cannot agree with the position taken by the insurer that the appraisal provisions of the policy, even if invoked by either party, have no bearing upon the issue of whether Closser's suit is time barred under the policy's suit limitation provisions.

Having found the policy appraisal procedures, if invoked, to be relevant to the issue of whether Closser's suit is time barred, we reach the insured's further contention that Penn Mutual is estopped by its conduct from invoking its twelve month suit limitation provision as a bar to this action.

Closser contends that at the very least a factual issue exists as to whether Penn Mutual should be so estopped. * * *

The pertinent facts are: that the insured's attorney initiated settlement negotiations with Penn Mutual's area representative on January 9, 1980. The following day, the representative received a notarized proof of loss claim from the insured and forthwith rejected it with letter response to the insured. On January 29, 1980, the insured's attorney wrote Penn Mutual's area representative, stating in part:

> We have selected David Wilson of Wilson Auctions, Route 113, Lincoln, Delaware, to appraise the property pursuant to lines 123–140 of page 2 of the policy. Please notify me of the name of the appraiser upon whom you will be relying.

The lines of the policy referred to incorporate the provisions of the policy relating to "Appraisal". Under those provisions, Penn Mutual was required to select its own appraiser and to so notify the insured within twenty days. Penn Mutual did nothing. Thereafter, the insured's attorney arranged for a conference between the parties to be held in the middle of February. He asked that, "all necessary documents and written appraisals of my clients home" be brought. The scheduled meeting took place; and nine days later the insured's attorney forwarded a third real estate "estimate" to Penn Mutual's representative. However, no specific mention was made in follow-up correspondence to an appraisal proceeding as such. In late February, the insured submitted a third "estimate", made "demand" for the face value of the policy and requested a prompt reply. The insurer's only response to the

February 22 letter and two follow-up letters over the ensuing ten days was the following terse reply:

I acknowledge receipt of your letters of:

22 February, 1980
27 February, 1980
3 March, 1980

From March to July there is no record of any further communication between the parties.

* * *

Closser was indicted for arson on July 21, 1980. Those charges remained pending through the anniversary date of the fire in September and until late November, 1980, when the State entered a *nolle prosequi.* Shortly thereafter, the insured's attorney telephoned Penn Mutual's area representative and stated, in effect, "now that criminal charges [have been] dropped, let's get on and settle." The insurer responded by denying liability "at this time." In the meantime, the insurer reached a settlement with the insured's wife as to her claim under the policy. As previously stated, the insured filed suit in May, 1981, and the insurer then raised for the first time the twelve month suit limitation as barring the claim.

On this record we conclude that a rational trier of fact could conclude: (a) that the insured effectively invoked the appraisal provisions of the policy; (b) that the insurer was obligated under the policy to proceed with the appraisal "option" to litigation; (c) that the insurer did not thereafter deal fairly with the insured in responding to his several requests for the insurer's position on his "demand" for the policy coverage; and (d) that the insured was thereby misled to his detriment in assuming there was no need to file suit within the time limitations of the policy. * * * *See,* 18 Del.C. § 2304(16), The Delaware Unfair Claims Settlement Practices Act, providing:

No person shall commit * * * any of the following:

* * *

(b) Failing to acknowledge and act reasonably promptly upon communication with respect to claims arising under insurance policies;

* * *

(e) Failing to affirm or deny coverage of claims within a reasonable time after proof of loss statements have been completed.

* * *

Since a triable issue of estoppel exists, Superior Court erred in granting summary judgment for Penn Mutual. * * *

### *Note*

See Plant v. Illinois Employers Insurance of Wausau, 20 Ohio App.3d 236, 485 N.E.2d 773 (1984) holding that the 12 months limitation on bringing suit on the policy will bar the breach of contract claim but not a tort claim based on the insurer's duty to act in good faith, as the claim is independent of the insurance policy. Cf. Hearn v. Rickenbacker, 428 Mich. 32, 400 N.W.2d 90 (1987).

## NAGEL–TAYLOR AUTOMOTIVE SUPPLIES, INC. v. AETNA CASUALTY & SURETY CO.

Appellate Court of Illinois, Fourth District, 1980.
81 Ill.App.3d 607, 37 Ill.Dec. 412, 402 N.E.2d 302.

GREEN, JUSTICE:

The principal issue in this case is whether under the evidence a jury could properly find that coverage under a fire insurance policy had not been voided by fraud and false swearing when the insured submitted a verified proof of loss containing an unreasonably high estimate of its business interruption loss.

The suit was brought in the circuit court of Sangamon County by plaintiffs Marvin C. Taylor (Taylor) and Nagel–Taylor Automotive Supplies, Inc., a corporation of which Taylor was the sole owner and principal officer. It was brought against defendant Aetna Casualty & Surety Company of Illinois to recover for a fire loss occurring on May 13, 1976, when a building near Litchfield, owned and operated by plaintiffs as a nightclub, burned. After a trial by jury a verdict was returned for plaintiff allowing $125,000 for damage to the building, $50,000 for damages to its contents and nothing for business interruption loss.

The trial court granted defendant's motion for judgment n.o.v. ruling that defendant had proved as a matter of law that plaintiffs had committed fraud and false swearing in the proof of loss statement. * * *

Plaintiffs appeal and defendant has filed notice of cross appeal.

Defendant's affirmative defense of fraud and false swearing was based on a policy provision which stated:

> "*Concealment, fraud.* This entire policy shall be void if, whether before or after a loss, the insured has willfully concealed or misrepresented any material fact or circumstance concerning this insurance or the subject thereof, or the interest of the insured therein, or in case of any fraud or false swearing by the insured relating thereto."

Under the terms of the policy plaintiffs were insured for actual business interruption losses such that they would be reimbursed for the amount by which their profits decreased (or losses increased) during the interruption, "but not exceeding the reduction in gross earning less charges and expenses which do not necessarily continue during the interruption of business * * *." The policy limited payment for this type of loss to the sum of $50,000. A written proof of loss verified by Taylor and timely mailed to defendant stated, "Gross earnings—estimated loss in excess of $100,000 for twelve month period."

The insured property was located on U.S. Route 66 south of Litchfield, a municipality of some 7,000 population. Prior to its purchase and remodeling by plaintiffs, the building had been used as a fast food franchise restaurant. The evidence indicated that the location became undesirable for that purpose when Interstate Route 55, passing Litchfield farther to the west, was opened to traffic. The strongest evidence in support of the affirmative defense of fraud and false swearing were the financial records of the operation. They indicated a deficit exceeding $17,000 to have accumulated in the eight months of the club's operation on total receipts of about $95,000. The cost of goods sold was about $14,000.

Charles T. Baker, a certified public accountant specializing in business interruption claims testified on behalf of defendant concerning his examination of the club's records. He described the business as being "in very poor financial condition" and stated that liabilities exceeded current assets by 16 to 1 but he did not state the seemingly more important ratio of current liabilities to current assets. He described the records as somewhat unreliable but concluded from his examination of them that no business interruption loss was sustained.

Taylor testified, attempting to justify his optimistic expectations by explaining how entertainment expenses had been drastically cut prior to the fire. He described how previously he had hired expensive entertainers such as those used in expensive Las Vegas nightclubs but due to small weeknight crowds he had recently begun to hire cheaper performers who would appeal to younger crowds.

Taylor presented a profit and loss statement for nine months, the figures for the last month having been lost. When this statement was compared with the records for the eight months as contained in the books it was shown that a profit of $4,500 would have had to have been made in the last month in order for the statement to reconcile with the books. Taylor apparently obtained the results shown on the statement by crediting expense accounts which previously listed as expense, rent theoretically owed, but not paid by the corporation to Taylor or vice versa. The business was run and the records kept in such a way that one could not readily tell the respective functions of Taylor and the corporation.

We consider Taylor's estimate to be unreasonably high, but in determining whether the jury could have properly determined that fraud and false swearing did not exist we deem it important that the estimate contained no assertion of an existing fact nor even an opinion concerning the quality or value of an existing object. It was merely a projection of future earnings.

* * * [T]he most analogous fraud and false swearing cases are those involving proof of loss claims which greatly overestimate the value of physical objects. In Tenore v. American and Foreign Insurance Co. of N.Y. (7th Cir.1958), 256 F.2d 791, cert. denied 358 U.S. 880, 79 S.Ct. 119, 3 L.Ed.2d 110, an insured had submitted a proof of loss statement claiming $78,000 for a destroyed gun collection. At the trial undisputed evidence showed many guns were old and missing parts. The insured's own expert testified to the collection being worth no more than $20,000. Similarly in Saks & Co. v. Continental Ins. Co. (1968), 23 N.Y.2d 161, 295 N.Y.S.2d 668, 242 N.E.2d 833, an insured's proof of loss statement that clothing destroyed by fire had been worth $985,000 was held to be false swearing as a matter of law. The holding was based largely upon the jury's having found the actual value to have been only $104,316 and plaintiffs having shown no explanation for this great disparity. The court noted that the insured was an expert in the clothing field and reasoned that the gross disparity caused an unrebutted presumption of fraud. In American Home Fire Assurance Co. v. Juneau Store Co. (7th Cir.1935), 78 F.2d 1001, a disparity between a proof of loss valuation estimate of $73,000 for certain goods and a subsequent jury determination that they were only worth $33,000 was held sufficient to make the proof of loss estimate fraudulent as a matter of law. The court concluded that the disparity showed that claim was made for goods that had not in fact been destroyed because no dispute existed as to the value of individual items.

In other cases where fraud and false swearing have been held to exist as a matter of law additional factors have been present. In Kavooras v. The Insurance Company of Illinois (1912), 167 Ill.App. 220, an insured's proof of loss statement claimed that destroyed groceries had a value of $4,114. However, the insured admitted that these groceries consisted of $714 worth recently salvaged from a fire and $450 worth recently purchased. In Folk v. National Ben Franklin Ins. Co. (1976), 45 Ill.App.3d 595, 4 Ill.Dec. 104, 359 N.E.2d 1056, plaintiff's proof of loss statement included items he had sold after the fire. In Harold J. Warren Co. v. Federal Mutual Ins. Co. (1st Cir.1961), 386 F.2d 599, uncontradicted evidence showed that the contractor engaged to repair damaged air conditioning units had told the insured that only $3000 worth needed to be replaced because of the fire but nevertheless the insured submitted an $8750 proof of loss statement which included replacement of undamaged air conditioning units. Although holding fraud to have been proved as a matter of law there, the court stated:

> "Intent to defraud is not to be presumed and the trier of facts should make all reasonable allowance for lack of knowledge or sound judgment or for honest mistake on the part of the insured as well as for the tendency to believe that which is to one's own interest * * *." 386 F.2d 579, 581.

Reviewing courts have refused to find fraud or false swearing despite substantial discrepancies between the amount claimed in the proof of loss and the jury's verdict in Commercial Insurance Company of

California v. J. Friedlander (1895), 156 Ill. 595, 41 N.E. 183 ($9,840 vs. $1,278); Badger Mutual Ins. Co. v. Morgan (1963), 313 F.2d 783 ($95,-000 v. $35,400); and C–Suzanne's Beauty Salon, Ltd. v. General Ins. Co. (2nd Cir.1978), 574 F.2d 106. * * * See also Annot., 16 A.L.R.3d 774, "Insurance—Over-valuation of Loss" (1967).

Even in regard to the making of estimates of *existing* values of personal property, the court in *Harold J. Warren Co.* warned of the necessity for courts to make "reasonable allowances for lack of knowledge or sound judgment" on the part of the insured. That is even more applicable when applied to the making of *future* projections of earnings in a relatively new establishment in a volatile type of business. Many such businesses lose for a while and then become profitable. Taylor indicated an intention to change his method of operation. The jury could have believed that he thought that he could start operating at a substantial profit. Defendant points to the club's poor location and lack of surrounding population to support it. But these factors existed from the beginning, and the jury could have concluded that Taylor originally thought he could succeed because he was an overly optimistic person and this, rather than fraudulent design, accounted for his inflated proof of loss claim. This is especially true when we consider the dictum of *Harold J. Warren Co.* which noted that natural tendency "to believe that which is to one's own interest."

* * * We consider the inherently speculative nature of future profits to account for the lack of precedent. The more speculative an estimate is, the more difficult it becomes to find fraud or false swearing as a matter of law, especially where the estimate is made by a nonexpert.

Even though the jury rejected plaintiff's claimed business interruption loss and, even though Taylor's estimate of the loss was clearly unreasonable, neither prevented the jury from being able to properly conclude that Taylor actually had such an unrealistic view of the future. The jury's verdict was neither wrong as a matter of law nor contrary to the manifest weight of the evidence.

Defendant has properly called to our attention the damage to society resulting from fraud, false swearing, and arson by insureds. We recognize the seriousness of the problem but we do not think that our decision here, which may have the effect of permitting insureds to be imprecise in estimates of future earnings, will enlarge the problem. We recognize that an insurer need not be defrauded in order for the defense of false swearing to be established (16 A.L.R.3d 774, 798, sec. 10[b] ), but we deem it appropriate to note that insurers are unlikely to give any significant weight to an assertion by an insured, as speculative as the instant one, without an examination of facts upon which it might be based.

As we now turn to the arson issue, we also note that defendant has stated that we should consider the evidence of arson as bearing upon the proof of fraud and false swearing. We consider the evidence of arson to have some probative value as to plaintiff's *modus operandi* and intent. But, whether plaintiff committed arson was a question of fact. * * *

Defendant's theory that the fire was caused by plaintiff's arson is based upon the strong and unrefuted testimony of two experts in the fire and arson investigation field which would indicate that someone purposefully set the building on fire by use of gasoline. Taylor testified, by way of alibi, that he spent the night of the fire in a motel in Jacksonville with his girlfriend while on a business trip. This testimony was supported by strong corroboration but there was also substantial circumstantial evidence that the fire was set at his direction. He had the obvious motive to set the fire to recoup his investment in a failing business. Evidence also showed that at the time of the fire all of the keys to enter the building were in Taylor's possession or that of those friendly to him. Firemen arriving on the scene found the building locked. Thus it could have been difficult for anyone else to have gotten into the building to set the fire. The jury could also have inferred that by controlling all of the known sets of keys, Taylor hoped that firemen answering the fire call would be impeded in getting in the building to put it out.

Other circumstantial evidence also inferred Taylor's complicity. He had left very little liquor in the store at the time of the fire and had recently moved out several pinball and cigarette machines. The alibi testimony could have been considered to be so perfect as to be likely contrived. Taylor had obtained a very detailed receipt from the motel. Nevertheless, the evidence was all circumstantial and, in view of the alibi testimony, did no more than to create a question of fact which the jury resolved in plaintiff's favor.

The result of our determination is that the jury verdict should be reinstated.

### *Notes*

1. The principal case took considerable pains to distinguish a 1979 opinion of the 7th circuit applying Illinois law, i.e. Lykos v. American Home Insurance Co., 609 F.2d 314 (7th Cir.1979). Factually the cases are somewhat similar—a restaurant-bar burned by arsonists, and a jury verdict for the insureds overturned by the trial judge n.o.v.

Lykos, the insured, employed a public insurance adjuster at a fee of 10% of the total recovery. Together the two came up with demonstrably inflated figures for damage to the building and for the food, liquor and other equipment (e.g. a clock, cost $200 was claimed as damaged to the extent of $2,200). A modest sum of $39,703 for business interruption was claimed—an amount apparently so low that the court of appeals did not bother to consider the special problem of evaluating business interruption losses. The over-valuations on the tangible items sufficed to defeat *all* claims. Some observations from the *Lykos* opinion are notable:

> "The plaintiffs not only claimed a loss $395,805 in their sworn statement in proof of loss, but later brought suit for the entire amount. It is

clear * * * that the plaintiffs submitted the claim with the intent of receiving the entire amount." * * *

"The plaintiffs attempt to dismiss some of the misrepresentations as mere estimates for purposes of negotiation, and they suggest that the exaggerated claims would have been ironed out had the insurance company been willing to negotiate. They contend that the evidence, therefore, does not establish the requisite intent to defraud. Even assuming that the plaintiffs did not intend to recover more than their actual losses and merely exaggerated the extent of loss with an eye to settling, we think the proper rule is that

> 'a design on the part of the insured to gain a position of advantage in the settlement of the loss through false representations is a fraudulent design and the making of such representations knowingly for that purpose is an attempt to defraud * * *, even though the insured may not have expected or intended ultimately to obtain more than compensation for actual loss.'

14 Couch on Insurance 2d § 49:556 (1965).

"This court has previously stated that the insured, if he suffers a loss, must honestly state, under oath, the extent of his loss and give this information to the insurer. He must not make false proofs of loss with intent to defraud the insurer. Although the penalty is heavy and seemingly harsh, it is one way of stopping the presentation of false, fictitious or inflated claims. False and exaggerated claims seemingly go hand in hand with incendiarism. The court should therefore unhesitatingly act to prevent attempted frauds on the part of the insured."

Relying upon the abbreviated outline of *Lykos* are the distinctions between the cases to be found in the facts or the basic attitudes of the opinion writers? What practical lessons in settlement negotiations of property claims can be extracted here?

2. *Don't lie and we mean it!*

## California Penal Code

### § 550. False or fraudulent claims; prohibited acts

(a) It is unlawful to do any of the following:

(1) Knowingly present or cause to be presented any false or fraudulent claim for the payment of a loss, including payment of a loss under a contract of insurance.

(2) Knowingly present multiple claims for the same loss or injury, including presentation of multiple claims to more than one insurer, with an intent to defraud.

(3) Knowingly cause or participate in a vehicular collision, or any other vehicular accident, for the purpose of presenting any false or fraudulent claim.

(4) Knowingly present a false or fraudulent claim for the payments of a loss for theft, destruction, damage, or conversion of a motor vehicle, a motor vehicle part, or contents of a motor vehicle.

(5) Knowingly prepare, make, or subscribe any writing, with the intent to present or use it, or to allow it to be presented in support of any false or fraudulent claim.

(6) Knowingly assist, abet, solicit, or conspire with (A) any person who knowingly presents any false or fraudulent claim for the payment of a loss, including payment of a loss under a contract of insurance; (B) any person who knowingly presents multiple claims for the same loss or injury, including presentation of multiple claims to more than one insurer, with an intent to defraud; (C) any person who knowingly causes or participates in a vehicular collision, or any other vehicular accident, for the purpose of presenting any false or fraudulent claim; and (D) any person who knowingly prepares, makes, or subscribes any writing, with the intent to present or use it, or to allow it to be presented in support on any claim.

(7) Knowingly make or cause to be made any false or fraudulent claim for payment of a health care benefit.

(8) Knowingly submit a claim for a health care benefit which was not used by, or on behalf of, the claimant.

(9) Knowingly present multiple claims for payment of the same health care benefit with an intent to defraud.

(10) Knowingly present for payment any undercharges for health care benefits on behalf of a specific claimant unless any known overcharges for health care benefits for that claimant are presented for reconciliation at that same time.

(b)(1) Every person who violates paragraph (1), (2), (3), (4), (5), or (6) of subdivision (a) is punishable by imprisonment in the state prison for two, three, or five years, or by a fine not exceeding fifty thousand dollars ($50,000), or by both that imprisonment and fine, unless the value of the fraud is fifty thousand dollars ($50,000) or more. Whenever the value of the fraud is fifty thousand dollars ($50,000) or more, the fine may be double the amount of the value of the fraud. Except in the interest of justice, a person placed on probation for violating any provision of this section shall be required by the court to perform some community service, specifically, the removal of graffiti.

(2) Every person who violates paragraph (7), (8), (9), or (10) of subdivision (a) is guilty of a public offense.

(A) Where the claim or amount at issue exceeds four hundred dollars ($400), the offense is punishable by imprisonment in the state prison for two, three, or five years, by a fine not exceeding fifty thousand dollars ($50,000), or by both that imprisonment and fine, unless the value of the fraud exceeds fifty thousand dollars ($50,000), in which event the fine may not exceed the value of the fraud, or by imprisonment in a county jail not to exceed one year, by a fine of not more than one thousand dollars ($1,000), or by both that imprisonment and fine.

(B) Where the claim or amount at issue is four hundred dollars ($400) or less, the offense is punishable by imprisonment in a county jail not to exceed six months, by a fine of not more than one thousand dollars ($1,000), or by both that imprisonment and fine unless the aggregate amount of the claims or amount at issue exceeds four hundred dollars ($400) in any 12 consecutive month period, in which case the claims or amounts may be charged as in subparagraph (A).

(c) Notwithstanding any other provision of law, probation shall not be granted to, nor shall the execution or imposition of a sentence be suspended for, any adult person convicted of felony violations of this section who previously has been convicted of felony violations of this section as an adult under charges separately brought and tried two or more times. The existence of any fact which would make a person ineligible for probation under this subdivision shall be alleged in the information or indictment, and either admitted by the defendant in an open court, or found to be true by the jury trying the issue of guilt or by the court where guilt is established by plea of guilty or nolo contendere or by trial by the court sitting without a jury.

Except where the existence of the fact was not admitted or found to be true or the court finds that a prior felony conviction was invalid, the court shall not strike or dismiss any prior felony convictions alleged in the information or indictment.

This subdivision shall not prohibit the adjournment of criminal proceedings pursuant to Division 3 (commencing with Section 3000) of, or Division 6 (commencing with Section 6000) of, the Welfare and Institutions Code.

(d) Any person who violates subdivision (a) and who has a prior felony conviction of the offense set forth in that subdivision or in Section 548 shall receive a two-year enhancement for each prior felony conviction in addition to the sentence provided in subdivision (b). The existence of any fact which would subject a person to a penalty enhancement shall be alleged in the information or indictment and either admitted by the defendant in open court, or found to be true by the jury trying the issue of guilt or by the court where guilt is established by plea of guilty or nolo contendere or by trial by the court sitting without a jury.

(e) This section shall not be construed to preclude the applicability of any other provision of criminal law that applies or may apply to any transaction.

3. *Arson and False Swearing*

Arson, of course, is an implicitly excluded risk, but it may be hard to prove even with the most suggestive circumstantial evidence as the principal case would indicate. However, arsonists have a tendency to lie when presenting proofs of loss and this may avoid the necessity of proving the arson defense. E.g. Duke v. Hartford Fire Insurance Co., 617 F.2d 509 (8th Cir.1980), the insurer received a directed verdict, not on proof of arson, but because the insured admitted misrepresenting that he had no knowledge of the cause of the fire, that he was on a trip when the fire occurred, and that he had received no medical treatment for burns.

Insurance companies are said to be wary of undertaking arson investigations and defenses because of the prospect of exposure to extra-contractual damages where such investigations have been flubbed or simply failed to support the original suspicions with admissible evidence. See FTD, September 1982 at p. 20 citing such cases as Gruenberg v. Aetna Ins. Co., 9 Cal.3d 566, 108 Cal.Rptr. 480, 510 P.2d 1032 (1973) and Chavers v. National Security Fire & Cas. Co., 405 So.2d 1 (Ala.1981), reversed, 456 So.2d 293 (1984), among others. See also Dempsey v. Auto Owners Ins. Co., 717 F.2d

556 (11th Cir.1983) and deVries v. St. Paul Fire & Marine Ins. Co., 716 F.2d 939 (1st Cir.1983).

4. Ordinarily false swearing enables the insurer to recover *all* payments not just overpayments, Northwestern National Ins. Co. v. Barnhart, 713 P.2d 1360 (Colo.App.1985). (In that case the insurer paid and sued for restitution. A precaution against a bad faith claim perhaps?). Following a minority course is Johnson v. South State Ins. Co., 288 S.C. 239, 341 S.E.2d 793 (1986), holding that a fraudulent claim as to personalty did not avoid entire coverage on realty and living expenses.

5. *Refusal to Produce Records.*

Read lines 107–116 of the Standard Fire Policy, Appendix A. Here lies, not in peace, another requirement that may waylay the insured. Must the insured, to recover for the theft of an auto (with jewelry worth, it is said, about $130,000 in it) submit to interrogation as to his sources of income, whether or not he has been convicted of a crime, and to produce his income tax returns for the last 5 years? Yes indeed, suggests the Supreme Court of Georgia in response to questions certified by the U.S. Court of Appeals, 11th Circuit. Halcome v. Cincinnati Ins. Co., 778 F.2d 606 (11th Cir.1985). See also Stover v. Aetna Casualty & Surety Co., 658 F.Supp. 156 (S.D.W.Va. 1987). But see Chavis v. State Farm Fire & Cas. Co., 317 N.C. 683, 346 S.E.2d 496 (1986) reversing a lower court ruling upholding the right of an insurer, suspecting arson, to have the insured produce for examination all his bank records.

On the other hand, does the co-operation clause give the company the right to insist upon the examination of multiple claimants separately and apart from one another? See, United States Fidelity and Guaranty Co. v. Hill, 722 S.W.2d 609 (Mo.App.1986).

## FINE v. BELLEFONTE UNDERWRITERS INS. CO.

United States Court of Appeals, Second Circuit, 1984.
725 F.2d 179, cert. denied, 469 U.S. 874, 105 S.Ct. 233, 83 L.Ed.2d 162 (1984).

IRVING HILL, SENIOR DISTRICT JUDGE:

In June 1978, Plaintiff, Fine, purchased three contiguous parcels of land in New York City for a total price of $1,300,000. Each parcel had a building on it. Though the buildings had separate addresses (649, 653 and 657 Broadway), they were also contiguous and were operated as a single economic unit. The three buildings had a single heating system which employed a single boiler.

Following the purchase, Fine, through a broker, obtained a policy of fire insurance covering the three buildings (and other properties) from defendant Bellefonte Underwriters Insurance Co. (hereinafter "Bellefonte"). The policy was in the standard New York form.

At the time of Fine's purchase, the buildings were occupied by commercial tenants, some artists, and others who conducted light manufacturing and warehousing businesses. Fine desired to convert the buildings to residential use. Toward that end, after buying the buildings, he did not renew most expiring leases and he engaged in a "freeze-out" policy designed to minimize expenses and discourage tenants from remaining. The heat timer which controlled operation of the boiler, based in part on outside temperature, was set so that it would not start up the heating system until a sub-freezing temperature was reached. Additionally, the superintendent was told to turn off the heating system entirely from 11 a.m. to 2 p.m. each day regardless of the outside temperature. By February 1979, when the fire occurred, only about one-third of the premises remained occupied.

On February 14, 1979, a fire of unknown origin occurred which started in the 649 and 653 Broadway buildings and spread to 657 Broadway. The buildings at 649 and 653 Broadway were totally destroyed except for their facades and the building at 657 Broadway was substantially damaged.

On the night of the fire the sprinkler system in the buildings, which was the main fire protection device, did not operate. The sprinkler system was of the so-called wet pipe constant pressure type. In this type of system, pipes within the building are filled with water which is under pressure from gravity tanks. In addition, there are fittings outside the buildings at street level to enable the Fire Department to pump water from city mains into the system. The trial judge found that on the night of the fire, none of the sprinkler heads in the system worked. The Fire Department was unable to pump water into the system due to blockage in the pipes which the trial court found was "presumably" caused by ice. The trial court found that had the sprinklers functioned normally, the fire could have been controlled.

Fine submitted claims on the policy which Bellefonte, after investigation, denied. Bellefonte based its denial of liability on the assertion that three separate provisions of the policy had been breached, claiming that a breach of any one of the three would relieve it of liability. The three provisions were:

1. The so-called "Protective Maintenance Clause",[1] which is a warranty that "protective systems and warning devices" will be maintained in complete working order and will not be altered.

2. The so-called "Increased Hazard Clause",[2] which voids coverage if "the hazard is increased by any means within the knowledge of the insured."

**1.** The language of this policy provision is as follows:

*Protective Maintenance.* It is warranted that the insured shall maintain in complete working order such protective systems and warning devices as existed at time of attachment of this policy, or which the insured has agreed to install, insofar as it is under the insured's control or supervision, and that no change shall be made in the said protective systems and warning devices without the consent in writing of this company.

**2.** The language of this policy provision is as follows:

Conditions suspending or restricting insurance. Unless otherwise provided in writing added hereto this Company shall not be liable for loss occurring (a) while the hazard is increased by any means within the control or knowledge of the insured. * * *

3. The so-called "False Swearing Clause",[3] which provides that coverage is voided if, before or after a loss, the insured has willfully concealed or misrepresented any material fact concerning the insurance or the insured property, or in the event of any "fraud or false swearing by the insured" relating to any such material fact.

Fine filed the instant action against the insurer for payment of the loss. After a lengthy court trial, the trial court found in favor of Fine and against the insurance company and awarded a judgment of $1,214,-221 for damage to the buildings[4] plus additional sums of $150,000 for loss of rental and $170,446.60 for debris removal. Bellefonte appeals. * * *

We reverse on the ground that Fine violated the false swearing provision of the policy, thus voiding the coverage and the trial court's conclusion to the contrary cannot stand. It is therefore unnecessary for us to reach the other issues raised in connection with the appeal or the cross-appeal.

THE FALSE SWEARING ISSUE

The fire occurred during an extended period of extremely cold weather. Outside temperatures averaged 10° Fahrenheit on the day of the fire. Bellefonte quickly learned, as reported by the Fire Department, that the sprinkler system in the buildings had failed to operate during the fire. The rapid spread of the fire and much of the loss was attributed to the non-operation of the sprinklers.

Bellefonte also became aware, early on, of Fine's decision to rid the buildings of the existing commercial tenants and of the tenants' complaints that he had instituted a freeze-out policy. Bellefonte was naturally very interested, not only in what caused the fire, but also whether a freeze-out policy was in effect and, if so, whether Fine's actions in pursuit of the freeze-out might have contributed to the failure of the sprinkler system. An obvious theory suggested itself, i.e., that there had been extremely low temperatures in the buildings before the fire which caused the pipes in the sprinkler system to freeze and that this was the result of conduct by the insured. The facts of which Bellefonte became quickly aware suggested the possibility that further investigation might establish a material breach of the protective maintenance clause or the increased hazard clause, or both.

With this in mind, Bellefonte conducted extensive examinations under oath of Mr. Martin Fine (the one owner, among the group of owners, in charge of operating the buildings), and of Mr. George Peters,

3. The language of this policy provision is as follows:

> *Concealment, fraud.* This entire policy shall be void if, whether before or after a loss, the insured has wilfully concealed or misrepresented any material fact or circumstance concerning this insurance or the subject thereof, or the interest of the insured therein, or in case of any fraud or false swearing by the insured relating thereto.

4. Four months after the fire the three properties were sold in their fire-damaged condition for $2 million with the sellers apparently retaining all rights to recovery under the policy.

managing agent for the owners. The examination of both dealt to a large extent with the instructions given and the provisions made for inspection and maintenance of the boiler heater and the sprinkler system, and particularly with the temperature setting employed on the heat timer that controlled the operation of the boiler.

The district court found that Fine and Peters each answered falsely during examination under oath. Both Fine and Peters stated in the examinations that they had charged the superintendent, a Mr. Aloisio, with the responsibility for inspecting and maintaining the sprinkler systems as he had been charged under the prior ownership. The trial court found such testimony to be false and that Aloisio had not been so charged or instructed.

During his examination, Mr. Fine testified that the nighttime setting for the heat timer controlling the boiler was 40 degrees and Mr. Peters testified that he had instructed superintendent Aloisio to set the heat timer at 40 degrees for nighttime operation. The trial court found that the testimony of both men was false in this respect. The court found that Aloisio had been instructed by Peters personally to set the heat timer at 25 degrees for nighttime and that Aloisio had, despite such instruction, set it for 30 degrees.

Despite the aforesaid findings of falsity, the trial court rendered judgment for Plaintiffs on the false swearing defense on the ground that the false statements were not material.

Under the heading, "Conclusions of Law", the trial court said:

> "Here the statements were not material to the investigation. Given the extreme temperatures during the period from February 5th to February 14 as noted above, whether the heat timer setting was 25 degrees, 30 degrees or 40 degrees would not have affected the operation of the heating system. Further there was no testimony that a 25 degree or 30 degree setting would have constituted a practice which would have reasonably been foreseen to result in a freezing condition, which, in turn would have made the sprinkler system inoperative."
>
> "Similarly with respect to the sprinkler maintenance issue, whether Aloisio was instructed to perform maintenance on the sprinkler system or not, in fact he did take the action necessary to repair the system, and there is no indication in this record that any failure of record keeping or regular maintenance was in any way responsible for the freeze-up. Since the Fine policy of freeze-out has not been proved to be the cause of the freeze-up, the false statements, viewing them as such, were not material as contemplated under section 168 [of New York Insurance Law]." [5]

* * *

5. Section 168(6) of the New York Insurance Law prescribes the exact language to be used in a standard fire insurance policy in New York state, including the

The trial judge regarded the materiality of the false statements as being dependent upon the ultimate determination of the facts concerning the fire as they were finally revealed to the court after a trial lasting many weeks. As the trial judge analyzed it, if it turned out, after a trial, that the sprinkler system would have been inoperative anyway on the night of the fire for reasons unrelated to the subject of the false statements, false statements about the setting of the heat timer and about maintenance and inspection of the sprinkler system made during the company's earlier investigation became immaterial. To make such statements material, the trial judge appears to reason, the insurer would have had to prove at the trial that the setting of the heat timer or a failure of maintenance of the sprinkler system caused the pipes to freeze and the sprinklers to be inoperative on the night of the fire.

In our view, the trial judge's definition of materiality was far too restrictive and not in accordance with long-established case law.

The issue is: Is a false statement material only if it relates to a matter or subject which ultimately proves to be decisive or significant in the ultimate disposition of the claim, or is it sufficient that the false statement concerns a subject reasonably relevant to the insurance company's investigation at the time? The law is clear that the materiality of false statements during an insurance company investigation is not to be judged by what the facts later turn out to have been. The purpose of a provision requiring an insured to submit to an examination under oath is to enable the insurance company to acquire knowledge or information that may aid it in its further investigation or that may otherwise be significant to the company in determining its liability under the policy and the position it should take with respect to a claim. Thus the materiality requirement is satisfied if the false statement concerns a subject relevant and germane to the insurer's investigation as it was then proceeding.

* * *

> If the plaintiffs knowingly and wilfully, with intent to defraud the defendants, swore falsely in making the proofs of loss, such act amounted to a fraud upon the defendants which avoided the policies, irrespective of the ultimate effect upon the defendants.

Meyer v. Home Insurance Co., 127 Wis. 293, 299–300, 106 N.W. 1087, 1089 (1906).

* * *

exact language of the section on false swearing. The statutory language was followed in the instant policy. Insurance statutes in all or nearly all of the states prescribe a standard fire insurance policy including the exact language to be employed therein. R. Keeton, *Basic Text on Insurance Law* 70 (1971). Of those who do, almost all use the New York form, including its exact "False Swearing Clause". Ins. L.Rep. Fire & Casualty Cas. (CCH) pp. 2002 (Dec. 6, 1972), 2003–04 (Nov.1982), 2007–10 (Apr.1982).

It thus appears that materiality of false statements is not determined by whether or not the false answers deal with a subject later determined to be unimportant because the fire and loss were caused by factors other than those with which the statements dealt. False sworn answers are material if they might have affected the attitude and action of the insurer. They are equally material if they may be said to have been calculated either to discourage, mislead or deflect the company's investigation in any area that might seem to the company, at that time, a relevant or productive area to investigate.

* * * Bellefonte was investigating a plausible theory reasonably derived from the available facts, one which would result in the voiding of its coverage. The questions were material to that investigation. It is irrelevant whether Bellefonte was ultimately able to muster sufficient evidence to prove its theory at trial.

* * * The judgment of the district court is therefore REVERSED. The case is remanded to the district court with instructions to enter judgment for the defendant.

### *Questions*

1. Is the standard of "materiality" different when the false statement is made on the proof of loss than when it is made on the application? Should the state statutes as to the effect of "misrepresentations" be also applied to "false swearing" during post loss investigations?

2. The principal case does not address the issues of whether the insured breached a warranty or violated the "increase of the hazard" provision. Using the facts as related, how would you rule on these issues?

# Chapter 6

# POTENTIAL DEFENSES BY THE INSURER

## A. THAT THERE IS NO CONTRACT

**— illegal because of lack of insurable interest**

### INSURABLE INTEREST: A SEARCH FOR CONSISTENCY

[Extracts from an article by Robert Stuart Pinzur in the INSURANCE COUNSEL JOURNAL, Jan. 1979, p. 109].

*Reprinted with permission.*

To avoid the evils inherent in wagering contracts of insurance, the concept of insurable interest developed i.e., the insured was required to have an interest in the subject matter, at some time, as a prerequisite for recovery.

Two basic theories arose as guides for application of the insurable interest doctrine. The "legally enforceable right" theory required that the insured have some valid and recognizable property right in the subject matter. In contrast, the "factual expectations" view is based on the notion that the insured must suffer some actual loss or detriment from the damage, loss or destruction to the insured property, and maintain some gain, benefit or advantage from its continued existence. Courts have been inconsistent in the application of these two viewpoints. In fact, courts have created analytical problems by attempting to place an insured loss in one category or the other. The better view encourages courts to return to the underlying rationale and ask whether or not the particular contract of insurance constitutes a wager. The resolution of this controversy is best achieved by the application of the factual expectations approach, with a limitation that the insured be denied recovery to the extent such interest was created as a means to profit by wager.

The major issues regarding the nature of insurable interest were well-represented in Lucena v. Crauford,[12] an early nineteenth century English case. *Lucena* arose out of the capture of a foreign ship. Royal commissioners were authorized, in time of war, under a Parliamentary act, to take possession of certain ships and cargo brought into the territory of the United Kingdom. These commissioners procured insurance on several ships and cargo which were subsequently lost by perils of the sea on voyage from the port of seizure, but before reaching the Kingdom's port. The voyage's purpose was to put the ships and cargo in the commissioners' possession. The issue was whether or not the commissioners held an insurable interest in the ships, cargo and anticipated profits from the voyage. The commissioners, eventually, were awarded a verdict at a later trial. Nevertheless, the views of the Justices on the first appeal considerably influenced the development of insurable interest theory.

Lord Eldon spoke for the view that some legally enforceable property right was a prerequisite for an insurable interest and found that the commissioners lacked an insurable interest. Among other matters, he noted that the commissioners did not have good title to the property because the necessary condemnation by the court had not been formalized.

There was no question that an insured required an "interest" in the subject matter pursuant to 19 Geo. II, ch. 37. Lord Eldon believed that such interest had to be a legally enforceable property right because a mere expectation was inadequate.

The fact that the insurer had admitted the interest by issuing the insurance, but subsequently discovered there was no interest, was of no consequence to Eldon.

Lord Eldon cautioned that the Commissioners were not acting in a trustee capacity. A trustee has a legal interest in the trust property and, therefore, has an insurable interest. Furthermore, Eldon recognized that a consignee could insure for the principal's benefit, but such beneficial interest had to be expressed.

Lord Eldon was concerned with the earlier era's equivalent of a "parade of horribles". If the commissioners held an insurable interest, he reasoned, any warehouseman or remotely interested party could insure. Thus, there would be nothing preventing "the West India Dock Company from insuring all the ships and goods which came to their docks". Numerous persons would then be entitled to insure. Here, Lord Eldon was referring to an insured who took the proceeds for his own benefit, rather than on behalf of another. The benefit would include fees and charges for prospective services, or the like, to be rendered along Eldon's horribles' parade. Furthermore, the insurance would be effective prior to the insured's possession.

12. Bos. & Pul. 269, 127 Eng.Rep. 630 (1806).

Lord Eldon's dichotomy between an expectation, though a moral certainty, and a legally enforceable property right was best-illustrated by his own formulation:

> Suppose A. to be possessed of a ship limited to B. in case A. dies without issue; that A. has 20 children, the eldest of whom is 20 years of age; and B. is 90 years of age; it is a moral certainty that B. will never come into possession, yet there is a clear interest. On the other hand, suppose the case of the heir at law of a man who has an estate worth 20,000 £ a-year, who is 90 years of age; upon his death-bed intestate, and incapable from incurable lunacy of making a will, there is no man who will deny that such an heir at law has a moral certainty of succeeding to the estate; yet the law will not allow that he has an interest, or anything more than a mere expectation.

Lord Eldon added that irrespective of the expectation of profit, upon the loss of a ship of cargo, the "expectation is defeated" and no interest ever arose in such unascertained profits, other than a mere expectancy. Nonetheless, Lord Eldon's approach did not limit the insurable interest doctrine to a contract recognizing only one possible named insured for any insurable subject matter. A property interest is an expanding concept. It may be legal or equitable, a present possessory right or future interest, vested or contingent and may exist regardless of the likelihood that its possessor will ever realize and actually enjoy the specific property.

Vance also supports the view that an insurable interest is only maintainable when the insured has some legally enforceable relationship to the property.[13] Citing Lord Eldon's *Lucena* opinion, Vance stated his own interpretation:

> While it is not necessary that the person insured shall have any title to the property insured, either legal or equitable, yet an expectation of benefit, to be derived from its continued existence, however likely and morally certain of realization it may be, will not afford a sufficient insurable interest unless that expectation has a basis of legal right. If such legal basis exists, an expected benefit, however remote, constitutes an insurable interest.

Graham, B. and six others, in *Lucena,* represented a second view of insurable interest—i.e., an expectancy coupled with an interest. First, it was contended that the commissioners were not claiming a beneficial interest for themselves, but as consignees, agents or trustees for others, namely the Crown. Furthermore, upon the ships' arrivals, the commissioners would have acquired a vested right to the whole legal interest, though held in trust.

* * *

**13.** Vance 3d at 156.

It is unclear why an "expectancy coupled with an interest" does not fall within the two major interpretations: a legally enforceable right or a factual expectancy. If the interest is an enforceable property right, the former view would be sufficient. If the interest is less than an enforceable property right, it is an expectancy and, therefore, the latter theory would apply. Presumably, Graham was searching for some middle ground. However, a right is either legally enforceable or an expectancy, and nothing lies between.

Graham admitted that the commissioners' interest was inchoate and revocable, but compared it to a consignee whose interest is subject to alteration or revocation by the consignor. However, alteration of a consignee's interest results in a change of a legal and enforceable property relationship. In contrast, the commissioners did not change any property right or relationship.

Graham distinguished *Lucena* from LeCras v. Hughes,[14] the latter being "a case of mere expectations, and the circumstances were not near so strong in favor of the assured". Nevertheless, Graham maintained that some expectations were insurable. Furthermore, he posited that the commissioners might have sold the ships while at sea, subject to a contingency, and "it would then be most extraordinary if they could not insure them". Lord Eldon, presumably, would simply respond that a contract arose at the time of the sale, thereby creating the necessary legal interest.

Attempting to simplify the issue, Graham said the question must be whether or not the contract was one of gaming. Graham believed that *LeCras* was more likely to violate the policy against wagering contracts, whereas the commissioners, in *Lucena,* had a duty to preserve the property and, therefore, were not just "any number of persons" who might insure the ships.

Vance's view of a legally enforceable property right includes the so-called "expectancy coupled with an interest". He explained that an insurable interest exists if the insured maintains such relations to the subject property that:

> he has a reasonable expectation, resting upon a basis of legal right, of benefit to be derived from its continued existence, or of loss or liability from its destruction.[15]

**14.** 3 Dougl. 81, 99 Eng.Rep. 549 (1789). *LeCras* is noted for Lord Mansfield's formulation of the factual expectations doctrine. In *LeCras,* part of a ship's cargo was lost at sea. The ship had been seized during war. Insurance had been procured to protect the interests of the Captain, his officers and the crew. The insurer contended that the profits were a "mere expectancy" and, therefore, were not insurable prior to condemnation. Lord Mansfield recognized that some interest was necessary in a contract of indemnity, "but no particular kind of interest" was mandated. The court held that the Captain, officers and crew properly insured their profits, though they were contingent. Id. at 86, 99 Eng.Rep. at 552. Lord Mansfield added that such insurance prevented the risks of neutral claims and guards against a loss arising from the disappointment of an expectation which hitherto has never been disappointed.

**15.** Vance on Insurance, 124 (2d Ed. 1930) (cited as "Vance").

Vance then specified the type of cases where an insurable interest would be present.

(a) Where the insured possesses a legal title to the property insured, whether vested or contingent, defeasible or indefeasible.

(b) When he has an equitable title, of whatever character and in whatever manner acquired.

(c) When he possesses a qualified property or possessory right in the subject of the insurance, such as that of a bailee.

(d) When he has mere possession or right of possession.

(e) When he has neither possession of the property, nor any other legal interest in it, but stands in such relation with respect to it that he may suffer, from its destruction, loss of a legal right dependent upon its continued existence.[16]

The primary criticism of Vance's examples are that they are overly broad. Nonetheless, the list comports with Vance's requirement of a legally enforceable relationship. Vance says a mere possessor of property has an insurable interest therein, e.g., a thief or otherwise wrongful possessor. Vance explained that such person

> has a possessory right good as against all the world except the true owner or one having a prior right of possession.

Lawrence, J. spoke for the other major view of insurable interest in *Lucena,* known as the factual expectations doctrine. This theory was first articulated by Lord Mansfield in LeCras v. Hughes, twenty-four years earlier. It is based on the insured's interest in the preservation of the insurance subject matter. That is, the insured will suffer a detriment or loss, of some kind, if the property is lost or destroyed, but receives some benefit, gain or advantage by its continued existence.

Following from his definition of insurance, Lawrence stated that it is available to protect persons against uncertain events which may be disadvantageous to them,

> not only those persons to whom positive loss arise by such events, occasioning the deprivation of that which they may possess, but those also who in consequence of such events may have intercepted from them the advantage or profit, which but for such events they would acquire according to the ordinary and probable cause of things.[17]

Lawrence found it obvious that a title owner is harmed by property loss. The property is important to the owner and he is concerned to avoid exposures to its damage. Yet, he admits it may be difficult to prove that the nonoccurrence of the event would have resulted in the realization of advantage. However, this difficulty was not sufficient proof to Lawrence that insurance, as an abstract concept, must be

**16.** Vance 3d at 161.

**17.** 2 Bos. & Pul. at 301, 127 Eng.Rep. at 643.

limited to property rights where it is impossible to measure the profitability of gain being intercepted by such risks. Nevertheless, Lawrence admitted that "an interest so uncertain" may not be insurable. The obvious dilemma arises in attempting to distinguish between an insurable interest and one too uncertain. Yet, one must realize that most legal distinctions and standards are inherently vague, but still subject to resolution.[18]

Lawrence was concerned about the moral hazard and enforcement of wagering agreements. However, he found a sufficient interest in the insured, which overcame the wager question, based on an advantage from continued existence or prejudice from nonexistence. Yet, Lawrence did qualify that the advantage or benefit must be morally certain.

Discussing the context of *Lucena,* Lawrence said the commissioners would have "no existing concern" in the property and, therefore, could suffer no loss until their authority and duty as commissioners would attach. Furthermore, Lawrence noted that the commissioners' incapacity to abandon the property, where capable of abandonment, was indicative of a lack of interest at the time of loss.

Patterson also recognized the factual expectations view. He wrote that an insurable interest was not restricted to property rights, but that some "substantial loss or injury" to the insured was necessary.[19] In fact, Patterson suggested the importance of a factual expectancy:

> (I)t is believed that a carefully drawn policy explicitly covering a genuine factual expectation interest, valued by the policy at a fair sum or measured by any fair scale clearly defined, would not be declared unenforceable on the ground of wagering.

* * *

### *Notes*

1. Almost thirty years later, the Parliament enacted a statute concerning insurable interest in *lives,*—14 Geo. III, c. 48 (1778).

2. For additional discussion of the development of insurable interest requirements see Robert E. Keeton & Alan I. Widiss, Insurance Law (West, 1988), 3.2–3.5. See also Robert H. Jerry, Understanding Insurance Law (Matthew Bender 1987), Ch. 4.

## SILBERMAN v. ROYAL INSURANCE COMPANY

Supreme Court, Appellate Division, Second Department, 1992.
184 A.D.2d 562, 584 N.Y.S.2d 625.

MEMORANDUM BY THE COURT.

In an action to recover the value of a stolen vehicle under a policy of automobile insurance, the plaintiff appeals from an order of the Supreme

18. See, e.g., Bird v. St. Paul Fire & Marine Insurance Co., 224 N.Y. 47, 55, 120 N.E. 86, 88 (1918).

19. Patterson, Essentials of Insurance Law 109 (2d Ed.1957).

Court, Nassau County (Henderson, J.), dated August 2, 1990, which granted the defendants' motion for summary judgment.

ORDERED that the order is affirmed, with costs to the respondent Royal Insurance Company.

In order to recover under a policy of insurance, the insured must show that he or she has an "insurable interest" in the property. We find no triable issue as to the plaintiff's insurable interest in the vehicle, which he concedes was owned solely by his wife. The plaintiff's payment of the purchase price and insurance premiums on the vehicle did not give rise to any equitable or other interest within the meaning of Insurance Law § 3401 that could be insured. Nor is the insurer estopped from raising the defense of lack of an insurable interest by events occurring after the loss. Accordingly, the complaint was properly dismissed.

## G.M. BATTERY & BOAT COMPANY v. L.K.N. CORP.

Supreme Court of Missouri, En Banc, 1988.
747 S.W.2d 624.

BLACKMAR, JUDGE.

LKN Corporation (LKN) leased a commercial building from G.M. Battery and Boat Co. (GMB) for a term of two years commencing March 1, 1982 at a rental of $1,500 per month. The lease granted the lessee an option to purchase the property during the term for $145,000 with a credit on the purchase price of one-half of the rental paid during the second year. The lease also contained the following provision: No. 11. Insurance. Tenant agrees to maintain at his expense throughout the term of this Lease an all hazard insurance policy in the amount of $75,000.00 payable to and acceptable to Landlord. Tenant further agrees to deliver to the landlord a certificate of the insuring company certifying that such insurance is in full force and effect. (L.F. 195–196).

LKN did not obtain an insurance policy which complied with the requirements of the lease. It instead purchased a policy from St. Paul Fire and Marine Insurance Co., effective June 1, 1983, covering the building on the leased premises for $125,000 and the contents for $70,000. GMB was not named as a loss payee under this policy, but Mark Twain State Bank, which had lent money secured by inventory, was so named.

On August 23, 1983, the building and contents were totally destroyed by fire. GMB collected $75,000 on a policy which it had obtained on the building from an insurer other than St. Paul. St. Paul denied liability for any part of the building loss, claiming that LKN had no insurable interest in the building. It admitted liability for the contents coverage, subject to determination of the proper claimant, and for business interruption, to the extent that loss could be proved. These latter coverages are not in issue in this phase of the litigation.

GMB filed suit against LKN, St. Paul, and others. It sought $75,000 in damages from LKN for breach of the lease contract in failing to procure insurance on the building. LKN cross-claimed against St. Paul for the entire proceeds of its policy. St. Paul paid the $70,000 contents coverage into court, seeking to interplead possible claimants, and filed an answer denying liability on the building coverage because of LKN's lack of insurable interest. Other claims in the somewhat complicated litigation are not material to this appeal and need not be discussed.

The trial court entered summary judgment for GMB against LKN for $75,000 for failure to provide insurance, and for LKN against St. Paul for $125,000, this being the entire building coverage under its policy. Both of these judgments were declared to be final and appealable as authorized by Rule 81.06. St. Paul appealed, but LKN did not. The court of appeals reversed, finding that LKN did not have an insurable interest in the building. We granted transfer to consider possible conflict with DeWitt v. American Family Insurance Co., 667 S.W.2d 700 (Mo. banc 1984). Taking the case as on initial appeal, we conclude that DeWitt indeed states the proper rule of decision and affirm the judgment of the circuit court. The case comes to the writer on recent reassignment.

St. Paul urges a single point for reversal, as follows: THE TRIAL COURT ERRED IN FINDING THAT THE LESSEE L.K.N. CORP. WAS ENTITLED TO THE PROCEEDS OF THE INSURANCE FOR THE BUILDING FOR THE REASON THAT THE LESSEE WITH ONLY AN UNEXERCISED OPTION TO PURCHASE HAD NO INSURABLE INTEREST IN THE PLAINTIFF OWNER'S BUILDING SUCH THAT IT COULD OBTAIN COVERAGE FOR THE BUILDING AS THE NAMED INSURED.

* * *

The controlling rule, perhaps borrowed from elsewhere, but expounded in numerous Missouri cases, is as follows:

In general, a person has an insurable interest in the subject matter insured where he has such a relation or concern in such subject matter that he will derive pecuniary benefit or advantage from its preservation, or will suffer pecuniary loss or damage from its destruction, termination, or injury by happening of the event insured against. The substance of this rule, interestingly, is set out in Crossman v. American Insurance Co., supra, 164 N.W. at 429. It was emphatically applied in DeWitt, supra, which is the latest pronouncement of our Court on the subject of insurable interest in property. In DeWitt a husband and wife held real property which was awarded to the husband on dissolution of their marriage. The husband then died and his former wife took possession of the property, which she used to make a home for herself and a child of the marriage. She insured the property against fire in her own name. We held that, inasmuch as she was liable on the note secured by a deed of trust on the property, she had an insurable interest in spite of her lack of title, and that, when the property was totally destroyed, she was entitled to recover the entire face amount of the policy.

In Wrausmann v. Kansas City Fire and Marine Insurance Co., 477 S.W.2d 741 (Mo.App.1972), a person liable on a mortgage note, apparently as a "straw party," was held to have an insurable interest in property. A familiar quotation used by the court, reading as follows, is pertinent: It is not necessary, to constitute an insurable interest, that the interest would be such that the event insured against would necessarily subject the insured to loss; it is sufficient that it might do so, and that pecuniary injury would be the natural consequence * * * although a person has no title, legal or equitable, in the property, and neither possession nor a right to possession, yet he has an insurable interest therein if it is primarily charged in either law or equity with a debtor obligation for which he is secondarily liable.

Graves v. Stanton, 621 S.W.2d 524 (Mo.App.1981), involved an insurance policy taken out by the lessee of a trailer. The lessee had an option to purchase, with rental payments to be credited on the option price, and was required by the lease to maintain insurance on the trailer. The court found that the lessee had an insurable interest. St. Paul seeks to distinguish this case on the ground that the lessee had given notice of his intention to exercise the option before the trailer was destroyed. The attempted distinction is not total, for by established law an insurable interest must exist both when the insurance is written and at the time of the loss. The case is inconsistent with the existence of any categorical rule in Missouri that the holder of an unexercised option does not have an insurable interest. The optionholder has an insurable interest if there is potential for loss in the destruction of the subject property.

Other Missouri cases are consistent with our conclusion. In Farmers Mutual Fire & Lightning Co. v. Crowley, 354 Mo. 649, 190 S.W.2d 250 (1945), the court held that a life tenant could insure property for its full value and could collect the entire proceeds to the exclusion of the remainderman if there is a total loss. A holding of the court of appeals that the insurance would redound to the benefit of the remainderman, 187 S.W.2d 346 (Mo.App.1945), was expressly rejected. In M.F.A. Mutual Insurance Co. v. Gulf Insurance Co., 445 S.W.2d 829 (Mo.1969), we held that a building contractor had an insurable interest in an uncompleted house which he was required by contract to complete. The material circumstance in determining insurable interest is not title, but possibility of loss. Our courts make every effort to find insurable interest, and to sustain coverage, when there is any substantial possibility that the insured will suffer loss from the destruction of the property. Other supporting cases are cited in DeWitt.

St. Paul cites Puritan Insurance Co. v. Yarber, 723 S.W.2d 98 (Mo.App.1987). This is the most recent of a line of court of appeals cases holding that nobody but the holder of a certificate of title (or, no doubt, a duly endorsed lienholder) has an insurable interest in a motor vehicle. The result is deemed necessary by reason of § 301.210, RSMo 1986, which establishes a strong policy against informal transfers of title to motor vehicles and provides that any attempted transfer is void unless accompanied by delivery of a duly endorsed certificate of title. Policy reasons attend the titling of motor vehicles which are not present when the insurance covers real property.

Likewise distinguishable is Lumberman's Mutual Insurance Co. v. Edmister, 412 F.2d 351 (8th Cir.1969), applying Missouri law. There the owner of real property sold the property but maintained the existing insurance in force in his own name. He then sought to collect the proceeds when the property was destroyed by fire. The court found that he had misled the insurance company as to the state of his title. This finding is sufficient to support the denial of recovery.

Here it is patent that LKN could suffer loss if the building on the leased premises were destroyed. It had bound itself to furnish insurance payable to GMB, and has actually been held to pay damages for the breach of this covenant. There is no reason why its failure of literal compliance with the lease term should redound to the benefit of St. Paul, by relieving it of a liability which it voluntarily assumed for a loss actually suffered by its insured. LKN also stood to lose the remaining six months of the term of its lease, as well as the utility of the option and the rent credit on the option price. These very real possibilities for loss establish LKN's insurable interest.

Inasmuch as insurable interest is manifest, LKN is entitled to recover the full face amount of the policy for the total loss. The insurer makes no claim of depreciation, and so full recovery is mandated by Section 379.140, RSMo 1986, which places the risk of overinsurance on the insurer rather than on the insured. The insurer may protect itself by strictly defining the interest covered by its policy, or by obtaining representations or warranties about the state of the title, if it deems this information important. What it cannot do is to issue a policy, collect the premiums, and then argue that the value of the insured's insurable interest in the property is less than the coverage it underwrites. See DeWitt v. American Family Insurance Co., supra; Farmers Mutual Fire & Lighting Co. v. Crowley, supra.

Inasmuch as we reject the only point urged by St. Paul for reversal, the judgment appealed from is affirmed and the case is remanded for further proceedings not inconsistent with this opinion.

## HUNTER v. STATE FARM FIRE AND CASUALTY COMPANY

Supreme Court of Alabama, 1989.
543 So.2d 679.

PER CURIAM.

This is an appeal from a summary judgment in favor of State Farm Fire and Casualty Company ("State Farm") and its agent, Bobby Baker, in an action by Ida Mae Hunter based on breach of contract and negligence. We reverse.

Ida Mae Hunter and her husband, Howard K. Hunter, acquired their house in Fultondale, Alabama, by warranty deed in 1962. Mr. Hunter died in 1969. In 1970, Mrs. Hunter purchased a homeowner's insurance policy from State Farm through its agent Bobby Baker. This policy insured Mrs. Hunter's interest in the home and the personal property in the home. The policy was renewed each year and was in effect on October 7, 1985, when the insured premises was destroyed by fire.

Mrs. Hunter did not live in the house after her hospitalization in 1982. After staying with a daughter and then living in Florida for a short time, Mrs. Hunter, in 1984, established her residence in an apartment complex for senior citizens. Mrs. Hunter informed State Farm of her change of residence in a letter dated June 1984; State Farm forwarded this letter to Baker, who put it in Mrs. Hunter's file. Mrs. Hunter, however, continued to pay the policy premiums when they were due. Mrs. Hunter's son suffered a theft loss at the house in February 1985, and the claim for this loss was paid by State Farm.

State Farm denied Mrs. Hunter's claim for the loss of the house, contending that Mrs. Hunter did not have legal title to the house. State Farm based its conclusion on the fact that in 1982, while hospitalized after a heart attack, Mrs. Hunter had signed a warranty deed transferring legal title to the house to her children. Mrs. Hunter claims, however, that she was misinformed about the nature of the instrument and that she thought the document she signed in the hospital provided that her home would go to her children upon her death. In addition, Mrs. Hunter continued to pay taxes on the home. Her grandson lived in the house and apparently paid her rent "once or twice." He also agreed to keep up the house for her. She kept most of her belongings, other than personal effects, in the house while she lived in the apartment. Part of the reason she moved into the apartment was that it was thought the house had too many stairs for someone in her condition, and it can be inferred that when her health improved the stairs would not be an obstacle. She maintained that she always intended to return to the house and that she had begun fixing it up for her return.

Mrs. Hunter sued her children, seeking a declaration of rights in the subject property, claiming in particular that the children held the property in a constructive trust. Mrs. Hunter sued State Farm for breach of the terms of the contract of homeowner's insurance. She also sued State Farm and its agent, Bobby Baker, for negligently failing to maintain the insurance to protect her interest in the home and the personal property in it. In its answer, State Farm asserted that Mrs. Hunter did not have an insurable interest in the property damaged by the fire and that State Farm was not guilty of negligence. Bobby Baker's answer denied Mrs. Hunter's claim of negligence on his part. The trial court granted Baker's motion for summary judgment.

The trial court also granted State Farm's motion for summary judgment, except as to Mrs. Hunter's claim for the value of her personal property that had been destroyed by the fire. * * *

On appeal, Mrs. Hunter first claims that State Farm was negligent in failing to provide her with insurance coverage for the subject property. The record is clear, however, that the insurance policy that Mrs. Hunter had purchased for her home was in full force and effect at the time the home was destroyed by fire. The question remains, and was raised by Mrs. Hunter as her second issue on appeal, whether State Farm was justified, under the terms of the policy and the law of Alabama, in refusing to honor Mrs. Hunter's claim for loss.

Alabama Code 1975, § 27–14–4, provides: "(a) No contract of insurance of property or of any interest in property, or arising from property, shall be enforceable as to the insurance except for the benefit of persons having an insurable interest in the things insured as at the time of the loss. "(b) 'Insurable interest,' as used in this section, means any actual, lawful and substantial economic interest in the safety or preservation of the subject of the insurance free from loss, destruction or pecuniary damage or impairment. "(c) The measure of an insurable interest in property is the extent to which the insured might be damnified by loss, injury or impairment thereof."

The statute is a codification of the longstanding rule in Alabama that, in order to receive benefits for a loss under a contract of property insurance, an insured must have an "insurable interest" in the insured property. National Security Fire & Casualty Co. v. Newman, 53 Ala. App. 614, 303 So.2d 113 (1974). This principle of law is also made part of the language of insurance contracts, such as the instant policy, by words to the effect that the "insured" must be the resident of the insured property.

The Court of Civil Appeals in Ex parte Granite State Ins. Co., 362 So.2d 241 (Ala.1978), correctly held that Alabama law recognizes an insurable interest based upon a "factual expectation" theory as opposed to a "legal interest" theory: "That view is that an insurable interest exists if the insured will gain economic advantage from the continued existence of the property or will suffer economic disadvantage upon damage to or loss of the property. Harnett & Thornton, Insurable Interest in Property: a Socio–Economic Reevaluation of a Legal Concept, 48 Colum.L.Rev. 1162 (1948); Vukowich, Insurable Interest: When It Must Exist in Property and Life Insurance, 7 Williamette L.J. 1 (1971). "We believe Alabama by statute and court decision has already espoused the 'factual expectation' theory of insurable interest. "Our supreme court has stated that one can have an insurable interest, although he has no property in the thing insured, but any limited or qualified interest, equitable right or expectation of advantage is sufficient. Put another way, insurable interest exists where insured would suffer a loss from the property's destruction." Id. at 241. "[S]ince the requirement of an insurable interest arose merely to prevent the use of insurance for illegitimate (gambling) purposes, it should not be extended beyond the reasons for it by an excessively technical construction. And a right of property is not an essential ingredient of insurable interest; any limited or qualified interest, whether legal or equitable, or any expectancy of advantage, is sufficient. It does not matter in what way such benefit arises or the reason loss would occur thereby, limited presumably by dictates or public policy—if such benefit would be lost by destruction of the subject matter, that interest is insurable. "Thus, it may safely be said that a fee title is clearly not required of the insured, nor even a direct property interest, the test of exposure to financial loss being all important. An equitable title or interest or other qualified property right would clearly be sufficient * * *. And a person who had made himself responsible for property may insure it against loss." 4 Appleman, Insurance Law and Practice § 2123 (1969).

In Luchansky v. Farmers Ins. Co., 357 Pa.Super. 136, 515 A.2d 598 (1986), the court found an insurable interest in a house destroyed by fire, notwithstanding the fact that the insureds had given an unconditional deed of conveyance to their son. The insureds continued to pay taxes, made mortgage payments, collected all or some of the rent, and made repairs.

Mrs. Hunter undertook most of the same activities as the Luchanskys, albeit on a more limited scale. In addition, it is interesting to note, that as in Luchansky, the grantees in this case subsequently reconveyed the property to the insured. This after-the-fact conveyance gives some credence to Mrs. Hunter's claim that the original conveyance was not intended to be an unconditional fee simple transfer.

A mere expectancy that the owner will make a testamentary disposition of the property to the insured is insufficient to establish an insurable interest. Brewton v. Alabama Farm Bureau Mutual Casualty Ins. Co., 474 So.2d 1120 (Ala.1985). However, both the life tenant and the remaindermen have insurable interests. Dickerson v. Stewart, 473 So.2d 1078 (Ala.Civ.App.1985). There is evidence to support Mrs. Hunter's claim that the conveyance was intended to create a life estate in her. "A constructive trust is a creature of equity which prevents unjust enrichment. It will be applied when property has been acquired by fraud or where it would be inequitable to allow it to be retained by him who holds it." Seals v. Seals, 423 So.2d 222 (Ala.1982).

In light of the above and the fact that the trial court's order does not expressly address the viability of Mrs. Hunter's claim that a constructive trust should be established, we hold that summary judgment on the "insurable interest" issue was improperly granted to the defendant.

REVERSED AND REMANDED.

## TUBLITZ v. GLENS FALLS INSURANCE CO.

Superior Court of New Jersey, Law Division, Essex County, 1981.
179 N.J.Super. 275, 431 A.2d 201.

BAIME, J.D.C. (temporarily assigned).

This case presents a question of first impression in New Jersey. Defendant is the insurer of three buildings owned by plaintiff. On November 14, 1979 plaintiff entered into a contract for demolition of the buildings. The contract was to be performed within ten days. On November 18, 1979 one of the buildings was destroyed by fire. At issue is whether the accidental destruction of the building is a loss for which defendant must indemnify plaintiff under the fire insurance policy. The carrier has denied coverage on the ground that plaintiff has suffered no loss since it was the latter's intention to demolish the building in any event. Plaintiff maintains that defendant is liable for the actual cash value of the building. Plaintiff now seeks summary judgment as to liability only.

* * *

No New Jersey court has had occasion to determine the effect of impending demolition upon the insurable interest in a building. This issue has been considered in other jurisdictions, however. It is generally held that the existence of an executory contract for demolition of a building does not deprive the owner of an insurable interest in the property. Garcy Corp. v. Home Ins. Co., 496 F.2d 479, 481 (7 Cir.1974); Knuppel v. American Ins. Co., 269 F.2d 163, 166 (7 Cir.1959); Dubin Paper Co. v. Insurance Co. of North America, 361 Pa. 68, 63 A.2d 85, 93 (Sup.Ct.1949); Eagle Square Mfg. Co. v. Vermont Mut. Fire Ins. Co., 125 Vt. 221, 212 A.2d 636, 639 (Sup.Ct.1965).[1]

The mere fact that an executory contract exists for demolition does not render a structure worthless nor deprive it of its value as a matter of law. * * * The existence of such a contract does not deprive the owner of an insurable interest in his building. Gendron v. Pawtucket Mut. Ins. Co., 384 A.2d 694, 697 (Me.Sup.Ct.1978). A finding that an insurable interest in the building no longer exists typically involves a situation in which the demolition work has begun at the time of the fire. Aetna State Bank v. Maryland Cas. Co., 345 F.Supp. 903 (N.D.Ill.1972); Board of Education v. Hartford Fire Ins. Co., 124 W.Va. 163, 19 S.E.2d 448 (Sup.Ct.1942).[2]

The reasonable expectations of the insured must be considered in determining coverage. * * * In this case the fire occurred before any

1. An exception to this rule is recognized in cases where the executory demolition contract is subject to specific performance. See Royal Ins. Co. v. Sisters of the Presentation, 430 F.2d 759 (9 Cir.1970); Lieberman v. Hartford Ins. Co., 6 Ill.App.3d 948, 287 N.E.2d 38 (Ct.App.1970). This exception is inapplicable to the case at bar.

2. An insurable interest has been recognized even in situations where demolition has begun, however. See Eagle Square Mfg. Co., supra, 212 A.2d at 637; Irwin v. Westchester Fire Ins. Co., 58 Misc. 441, 109 N.Y.S. 612 (Sup.Ct.1908).

demolition work had begun. Despite the fact that the demolition contract was scheduled to be performed within ten days, it cannot be stated with certainty that it would, in fact, be commenced within that period. Performance of the contract may have been delayed by a number of factors, both within and beyond the control of the parties. So too, plaintiff could have chosen to repudiate the contract prior to demolition. Therefore, it is reasonable to infer from all the surrounding circumstances that plaintiff expected his fire insurance coverage to be in force until demolition was actually begun.

* * * Therefore, partial summary judgment is granted in favor of plaintiff on the issue of liability. An appropriate order should be submitted.[3]

### *Notes*

1. *The Mortgagor–Grantor. Does the Insurable Interest Cease Upon Sale?*

Quote from Reid v. Hardware Mutual Insurance Co. of the Carolinas, 252 S.C. 339, 166 S.E.2d 317 (1969):

> "Many cases hold that a mortgagor who has sold the premises, being still liable for the mortgage debt, has an insurable interest in the property. Lumberman's Nat. Bank v. Corrigan, 167 Wis. 83, 166 N.W. 650; Farmers & Merchants Bank v. Hartford Fire Ins. Co., 43 Idaho 222, 253 P. 379; Hanover Fire Ins. Co. v. Bohn, 48 Neb. 743, 67 N.W. 774; American Ins. Co. v. Dean, Mo.App., 243 S.W. 415; Baughman v. Niagara Fire Ins. Co., 163 Minn. 300, 204 N.W. 321. In the Baughman case it was held that because of the plaintiff's liability on the mortgage note to the bank he had an insurable interest in the property, even though his grantee had assumed the mortgage. In the Dean case it was held that where an owner had conveyed the insured premises and was not released from the payment of the mortgage indebtedness thereon he retained an insurable interest in the property conveyed, as a loss thereof would affect his liability on the note."

But see Sander v. Hartford Fire Ins. Co., 637 S.W.2d 793 (Mo.App.1982), contra.

2. *Insurable Interest in Stolen Property—(Almost Always Autos)*

Applying the rubric that there can be no bona-fide purchaser from a thief, a number of cases have held that the luckless possessor of stolen property, however personally innocent, cannot recover on a theft policy when, say, an automobile is in turn stolen from him. Such a result is virtually compelled if one follows the analysis of Lord Eldon in the *Lucena* case. However, a number of re-stolen auto cases have been decided the other way. Reznick v. Home Insurance Co., 45 Ill.App.3d 1058, 4 Ill.Dec. 525, 360 N.E.2d 461 (1977), summarizes the situation:

3. I have no occasion to decide the applicable measure of damages or whether the executory demolition contract will be admissible at a hearing to determine damages. See Elberon Bathing Co. v. Ambassador Ins. Co., 77 N.J. 1, 389 A.2d 439 (1978). Resolution of those issues must await a plenary hearing.

> While some jurisdictions hold a good faith purchaser of a stolen automobile has no insurable interest in such vehicle (Ernie Miller Pontiac, Inc. v. Home Ins. Co., supra; Ins. Co. of N. Am. v. Cliff Pettit Motors, Inc. (Tenn.1974), 513 S.W.2d 785, 787; Herrington v. American Secur. Ins. Co. (1971), 124 Ga.App. 617, 184 S.E.2d 673, 674), others have held that a good faith purchaser has an insurable interest since he has good title against all but the true owner (Scarola v. Ins. Co. of North America (1972), 31 N.Y.2d 411, 340 N.Y.S.2d 630, 292 N.E.2d 776; Barnett v. London Assur. Corp. (1926), 138 Wash. 673, 245 P. 3, 4). Plaintiff is not involved in a dispute with the true owner, but rather with the insurance company which has accepted premium payments by plaintiff in consideration for comprehensive insurance coverage on the Ford. Plaintiff had a right of possession of the car against any contrary assertion, except that of the true owner.
>
> We find that plaintiff has established in his pleadings and his deposition admitted as part of the record that he would have profited by continued possession of the Ford, and that he suffered an economic loss by its confiscation. We agree with those courts which, under similar facts, hold that a good faith purchaser of a stolen automobile has an insurable interest in such vehicle.

Perhaps these auto cases should be viewed narrowly, because of the practice of using state issued certificates of title in connection with auto transfers. These "pink slips" furnish a source for reasonable reliance by purchasers not applicable as to other chattels. Cf. Horton v. State Farm Fire & Casualty Co., 550 S.W.2d 806 (Mo.App.1977), in which the court found the victimized buyer had no insurable interest because the state's registration statute mandated literal compliance, whereas the application to transfer title to the previously stolen car did not contain the true I.D. number of the auto.

### *Problem*

Insured was the owner of a building and the franchisor of the retail hardware business conducted on the premises. His fire policy covered both the building and the inventory belonging to the franchisee. The whole thing was burnt. The insurer paid for the building but not for the inventory, claiming that the insured had no insurable interest in it. What ruling? See Seals, Inc. v. Tioga County Grange Mut. Ins. Co., 359 Pa.Super. 606, 519 A.2d 951 (1986).

## B. THAT THERE IS NO CONTRACT

**___ because there is no coverage of the claimant. (the personal nature of the insurance contract)**

### CHRIST GOSPEL TEMPLE v. LIBERTY MUTUAL INSURANCE CO.

Superior Court of Pennsylvania, 1979.
273 Pa.Super. 302, 417 A.2d 660.

MONTGOMERY, JUDGE:

* * *

The record shows that for many years, the congregation of Westminster Presbyterian Church (hereinafter referred to as "Westminster") owned and occupied a church building at Green and Reily Streets in the City of Harrisburg. In May, 1968, Westminster purchased a fire insurance policy on this building from the Appellee, Liberty Mutual Insurance Co. (hereinafter referred to as "Liberty"). The policy was written for an initial term of three years, and in May, 1971, was renewed for an additional three years. Premiums were paid annually and the last premium was paid by Westminster to cover the period from May, 1972 through May, 1973. Apparently for reasons of declining membership, in August, 1972, Westminster merged into another Presbyterian organization, the Appellant Presbyterian Church of Harrisburg (hereinafter referred to as "Presbyterian"). In the merger, Presbyterian acquired the former Westminster property at Green and Reily Streets. On December 19, 1972, Presbyterian conveyed that property for $9,000 to the Appellant Christ Gospel Temple (hereinafter referred to as "Christ Gospel"). Presbyterian also made a written assignment to Christ Gospel of Westminster's insurance policy with Liberty, for a separate consideration of $750. That amount apparently represented that part of the policy premium paid in advance for the remainder of the annual policy term. In its deed to Christ Gospel, Presbyterian retained an option, for a period of ten years, to repurchase the property for the original sale price if the premises ever ceased to be used for Christian services.

Liberty was not notified by the parties of the merger of Westminster and Presbyterian nor of the sale by Presbyterian of the property to Christ Gospel. Also, Liberty was not notified by the parties of the purported assignment of the fire insurance policy on the property from Presbyterian to Christ Gospel. On February 9, 1973, an agent of Liberty, as a result of a visit to the church, learned of the merger and the later sale of the property and reported these facts to Liberty. Ten days later, on February 19, 1973, fire substantially damaged the church structure.

Liberty denied coverage and Christ Gospel thereafter filed suit against Liberty for the fire loss. * * * Presbyterian, an additional defendant, then filed a cross-claim against Liberty, asserting that if Christ Gospel was not covered under the policy, then Presbyterian could recover for the loss since it claimed a continuing insurable interest in the property.

* * * With respect to the purported assignment of the policy from Presbyterian to Christ Gospel, Liberty relied greatly in its defense upon a clause in the insurance policy which provided that: "Assignment of this policy shall not be valid except with the written consent of this Company."

* * *

We first address the rights of Christ Gospel against Liberty. Although Christ Gospel is an appellant in this action, no real emphasis is directed on this appeal to contentions that Christ Gospel has any arguable basis upon which it can recover against Liberty for any fire loss to the church building. Christ Gospel, if it had any rights against Liberty, would enjoy those rights by virtue of the purported assignment to it by Presbyterian of the latter's rights under the Liberty policy. Even if we assume that Presbyterian held the position of an insured on the policy, after Presbyterian's merger with Westminster, the original insured, we cannot ignore the import of the provision on the front page of the policy which provides that "Assignment of this policy shall not be valid except with the written consent of this Company."

Although the Appellants argue on several grounds, that we must ignore that clear prohibition against assignments without Liberty's consent, we can find no legal basis for doing so. The provision in question is not simply a self-protective clause inserted at the whim of the Appellee, but rather is a legislatively mandated provision, *specifically required* to be included in fire insurance policies such as the one in issue in the instant case. In view of the lack of consent of Liberty to the assignment of the policy by Presbyterian to Christ Gospel, the latter has no rights under the policy.

We find no merit to the proposition that Liberty is estopped from contesting the assignment on the basis that its agent inspected the premises just a few days before the fire and was aware of the sale of the property to another congregation. It is well settled that a fire insurance policy is a *personal* contract of indemnity, and is on the insured's *interest* in the property, *not on the property itself.* Gorman's Estate, 321 Pa. 292, 184 A. 86 (1936).[22] Therefore, we find no basis for the claim asserted by Christ Gospel against Liberty in the instant case.

We reach a similar conclusion with respect to Presbyterian's claim, but on a different rationale. Although Liberty contends that the merger of Westminster into Presbyterian afforded the latter no rights on the policy, since Liberty did not consent to afford coverage on the policy to Presbyterian, for purposes of this appeal we will assume that Presbyterian succeeded to all the legal rights of Westminster on the policy at the time of the fire loss. Even with that assumption in favor of Presbyterian, however, we cannot find that it enjoyed the required *insurable*

**22.** On this point see Donovan v. New York Casualty Company, 373 Pa. 145, 94 A.2d 570 (1953); Spires v. Hanover Insurance Co., 364 Pa. 52, 70 A.2d 828 (1950); 43 Am.Jur.2d, Insurance, § 687; 16 Couch on Insurance 2nd, §§ 63:14 and 63:160; 5A Appleman on Insurance, § 4325.

*interest* in the property at the time of the fire as to allow it to recover any amount as a result of the fire loss on February 19, 1973.

Presbyterian conveyed the property to Christ Gospel on December 19, 1972. Its only remaining legal interest in the property was an option to repurchase, at the original selling price within a ten year period, in the event that the property was used for purposes other than for the holding of Christian services. Thus, on the date of the fire loss, Presbyterian had a mere possibility of the expectancy that it might exercise its option to repurchase upon the happening of a contingency. Under prevailing law, this does not amount to an insurable interest. An excellent case on point is Van Cure v. Hartford Fire Insurance Co., 435 Pa. 163, 253 A.2d 663 (1969). In *Van Cure* the Court recognized the long-established principle that an insurable interest in the property is demanded prior to recovery for a fire loss in Pennsylvania, and that a mere expectancy of an option to purchase is " * * * insubstantial and incapable of qualifying as an insurable interest." * * * While the *Van Cure* case involved the rights of a condemnee when a fire damaged the insured property after condemnation, we find the rationale directly applicable in our analysis of Presbyterian's claims on this appeal.[23] Plainly, Presbyterian's claim must fail because it lacked a legally required insurable interest in the building on the date of the fire loss. Thus, we can discern no error in the action of the lower court in dismissing the claims of both Appellants.

### *Notes*

1. Who is to blame for the fact that there was no one who could recover for the damages to the church despite a policy that had been duly paid for over the years? Christ Gospel's lawyer it would seem. At any rate, his professional responsibility insurer settled the church's claim against him for $125,000.

2. *Another interpretation of the "no valid assignment without written consent of insurer" clause: Good faith and fair dealing to the rescue.*

University of Judaism v. Transamerica Insurance Co., 61 Cal.App.3d 937, 132 Cal.Rptr. 907 (1976). [The Flegelmans conveyed property to the plaintiff university and assigned the insurance policies, but did not obtain the insurer's endorsement at the time. Since the premises were in a troubled urban area, the insurers apparently were contemplating cancellation. The fire occurred during a riot on February 1. On February 2, defendant notified Flegelman's agent of intent to cancel. It was not until February 12 that the insurers were notified of the loss and that the property had been sold and the policies assigned. The defense is grounded upon the same statutorily mandated provision as to assignment set forth in the principal case. The California court however allowed recovery by the grantee, stating:]

**23.** In *Van Cure,* supra, the condemnee was still living in the property at the time of the fire, making her claim of an insurable interest much more compelling, on an equitable basis, than that asserted by Presbyterian in this case.

"The purpose of this provision is apparent. It is "to prevent an increase of risk and hazard of loss by a change of ownership without the knowledge of the insurer." (16 Couch on Insurance (2d ed. 1966) § 63:31, p. 677; fn. omitted.) As stated in Bergson v. Builders' Ins. Co., 38 Cal. 541, 545, "The insurer has a right to know, and an interest in knowing, for whom he stands as insurer. He may be willing to insure one person and unwilling to insure another, while the owner of a particular parcel of property. He may have confidence in the honesty and prudence of the one in protecting the property and thereby lessening the risk, and may have no confidence in the other.

"In this case, had notice been promptly given prior to the loss, defendants would have routinely approved the assignment of the policy to plaintiff. There was no change in the nature of the activity carried on at the premises. There is no evidence that the change of ownership in any way increased the risk to defendants. Since the change of ownership did not increase the risk to defendants, and they would have routinely approved the assignment, they cannot claim they suffered any prejudice from the late notice. (See Sly v. American Indemnity Co., 127 Cal.App. 202, 208, 15 P.2d 522 (1932).)

"In effect defendants are asserting that even though they would have approved the assignment as a matter of course, they should have the arbitrary right to disapprove it when the only apparent reason for doing so is that an intervening loss has occurred. The arbitrary refusal of consent in such circumstances would be inconsistent with the insurer's duty of good faith. (See Gruenberg v. Aetna Ins. Co., 9 Cal.3d 566, 573, 575, 108 Cal.Rptr. 480, 510 P.2d 1032 (1973).)

"The language of the provision is consistent with plaintiff's theory that defendants should be deemed to have consented to the assignment, and that such consent relates back to the time of the assignment. Unlike prior versions of the standard form, which stated that '* * * this entire policy shall be void * * * if this policy be assigned before a loss', the present provision merely states that assignment shall not be valid 'except with' the written consent of the company. To avoid a forfeiture, plaintiff may, in lieu of express approval, show that the assignment would have been routinely approved."

3. To avoid litigation such as that in the *University of Judaism* an endorsement like the following should be immediately processed when a contract of sale is entered into.

CONTRACT OF SALE CLAUSE

CF 12 44
(Ed. 05 77)

| COMPANY | POLICY NO. | AGENCY |
|---|---|---|
| | | |

A contract for sale of the property described in this policy having been made between the Insured and ______

the interest of said last named party is also insured hereunder, but without any increase in the amount of insurance, and subject to all other terms, provisions and conditions of this policy, including any Mortgage Clause forming a part of this policy.

If there is other insurance upon the property described in this policy, this Company shall not be liable for a greater proportion of any loss hereunder than the amount hereby covered bears to the whole amount of insurance on said property, in favor of any party or parties having an insurable interest therein, whether collectible or not.

**This Endorsement must be attached to Change Endorsement when issued after the Policy is written.**

## C. THAT THERE IS NO COVERAGE OF THE RISK

- **because the loss was not established by required evidence (evidentiary conditions)**
- **how coverage is defined in property insurance**
- **because the insured event has not occurred (herein such matters as proximate causation, "exclusions", "exceptions", etc.)**
- **implied exceptions (hostile fires, etc.)**

## COCHRAN v. MFA MUTUAL INSURANCE CO.

Supreme Court of Nebraska, 1978.
201 Neb. 631, 271 N.W.2d 331.

CLINTON, JUSTICE.

This is an action upon a homeowner's insurance policy to recover the value of certain tools allegedly stolen from the insured's locked motor vehicle. The policy contained the following exclusion: "c. Theft Exclusions applicable to property away from the described premises: This policy does not apply to loss away from the described premises of: * * *

> "(2) property while unattended in or on any motor vehicle or trailer, other than a public conveyance, unless the loss is the result of forcible entry into such vehicle while all doors, windows or other openings thereof are closed and locked, provided there are visible marks of forcible entry upon the exterior of such vehicle or the loss is the result of the theft of such vehicle which is not recovered within 30 days, but property shall not be considered unattended when the Insured is required to surrender the keys of such vehicle to a bailee."

The evidence shows that there were no visible marks of forcible entry on the exterior of the vehicle. The car had been removed from the place where the owner testified he had parked it. The owner reported the vehicle stolen and it was recovered the same afternoon a few miles from the place where it had been parked. The owner testified that the car was locked when he left it and that all windows were closed. When found, tools were missing from the car and a "jiggle" key was found in the ignition switch. The insured, a locksmith and hardwareman by occupation, testified as an expert witness that a jiggle key is a type of key by which entry may be gained into many cars by proper and knowledgeable manipulation of the key. He gave his opinion that entry to and removal of the car had been gained by use of the jiggle key.

The case was tried in the municipal court of the city of Omaha and judgment was rendered for the defendant insurer. On appeal to the District Court the judgment was affirmed.

The defendant pled and relied upon the exclusion earlier set forth. The District Court found that there had been a forcible entry by use of a jiggle key, that there were no "visible marks of forcible entry upon the exterior of the vehicle," and that the defendant was entitled to rely upon the exclusion.

The plaintiff on this appeal urges that forced entry by use of a jiggle key comes within the coverage of the policy and urges that we so construe it.

The plaintiff relies principally upon the case of C & J Fertilizer, Inc. v. Allied Mut. Ins. Co. (Iowa), 227 N.W.2d 169, in which the Iowa court construed similar language in a policy covering losses through burglary. The court held, among other things, that under the particular facts of that case such a provision was unconscionable and would not be enforced where, although there were no marks of forced entry on the exterior of the building, there was other clear evidence of burglary on the interior door of the particular room from which the theft was made. Plaintiff also relies upon a line of cases which hold that such exclusions are ambiguous and establish a mere rule of evidence and that the exclusion will not be literally enforced if it is clear that the burglary is not an inside job. Ferguson v. Phoenix Assurance Co., 189 Kan. 459, 370 P.2d 379; Rosenthal v. American Bonding Co., 124 N.Y.S. 905.

This court has had prior occasion to consider similar exclusions in policies insuring against burglary and we have upheld the exclusion. Only a few years ago, in Hazuka v. Maryland Cas. Co., 183 Neb. 336, 160 N.W.2d 174, we said: "In a policy indemnifying insured for loss by burglary for 'the felonious abstraction of insured property within a vault or safe * * * by a person making felonious entry into such vault or safe * * *, when all doors thereof are duly closed and locked by all combination locks thereon, provided such entry shall be made by actual force and violence, of which force and violence there are visible marks made by tools, explosives, electricity or chemicals upon the exterior of (a) all of said doors of such vault or such safe and any fault containing the safe, if entry is made through such doors, * * *,' such visible marks requirement was intended to be and is a limitation on liability and not an attempt to determine the character of evidence to show liability.

"Such limited liability provision is not ambiguous and there is no room for the rule that insurance contracts will be construed most favorably to the insured."

We hold that [the] theft exclusion * * * is unambiguous and the provision requiring visible marks of forced entry is not unconscionable. We thus adhere to our former opinion in Hazuka v. Maryland Cas. Co., supra.

* * *

Affirmed.

### *Notes*

1. A store owner, suspicious that someone was using a pass key, put strips of transparent tape around the door frame. The next day the tape was broken and items were missing from the stock. Was the breaking of the tape "physical damage" so as to allow recovery on a burglary policy? See Hopson v. Southern American Insurance Co., 618 S.W.2d 745 (Tenn.App. 1980).

2. "Felonious exit" may be an alternative provision to "felonious entrance." In Norman v. Banasik, 304 N.C. 341, 283 S.E.2d 489 (1981) there were no entry marks, but a bolt was removed from inside a window which allowed it to be pushed outward so that property could be removed. The policy required "physical damage to the interior of the premises at the place of such exit." The court allowed recovery stating that extraction of the bolt "damaged" the security system by which intruders were denied entry.

3. Another form of "evidentiary condition" is to be found in policies covering losses by fraudulent or dishonest acts by employees, but "excluding" from that coverage any losses "the proof of which, either as to its factual existence or as to its amount is dependent upon an inventory computation or a profit and loss computation."

## NOTE: HOW COVERAGE IS DEFINED IN PROPERTY INSURANCE

The general idea of what is meant by "coverage provisions" has appeared here and there in Part A. Now is the time to get down to specifics.

Basically there are two ways of describing what the insured thinks of as coverage and what the insurance company thinks of as exposure.

1. *Specific designation of risks* with "add ons" or "wrap arounds" to extend coverage as desired. The obvious example in property insurance is the STANDARD FIRE POLICY which simply insures against "direct loss by fire, lightning and by removal from premises endangered". Additional coverage is obtainable for other risks, such as windstorm, earthquake, flood, vandalism, etc. by endorsements or separate policies—for, of course, additional premiums. Depending upon the

special circumstances of the property owner, this approach can result in a policy tailored to need and pocketbook.

The drawbacks to this method of coverage definition lie in the requirement that the insured has the burden of proving that the insured event has occurred—or in other words, that a specifically designated risk, e.g. fire, was the cause of the loss.

2. *"All risks"* or *"all physical loss"* (APL) or "special causes of loss" *policies* with listed exclusions or exceptions or excepted causes.

This approach traces to the ancient policy form whose archaic language survives embedded in the British Marine Insurance Act 1906.

> "Touching the adventures and perils which we the assurers are contented to bear and do take upon us in this voyage: they are of the seas, men of war, fire, enemies, pirates, rovers, thieves, jettisons, letters of mart and countermart, surprisals, takings at sea, arrests, restraints, and detainments of all kings, princes, and people, of what nation, condition, or quality soever, barratry of the master and mariners, and of all other perils, losses, and misfortunes, that have or shall come to the hurt, detriment, or damage of the said goods and merchandises, and ship, & c., or any part thereof."

Thereafter the insurer is at liberty to limit this broad coverage (announced up front so as to elevate the assured's expectations of utter security) by exclusions, exceptions, and "this policy does not cover" paragraphs, unfortunately too often relegated to the nether regions of the policy.

This method of defining coverage has the advantage to the insured of merely requiring proof of the casualty, with the burden shifting to the company to effect an escape via an applicable exclusion.

An instructive case on the interpretation of "all risks" policies is Pan American World Airways v. Aetna Casualty & Surety Co., 505 F.2d 989 (2d Cir.1974).

On September 6, 1970 Pan American Flight 093, while on a regularly scheduled flight from Brussels to New York, was hijacked in the sky over London about 45 minutes after it had taken off from an intermediate stop in Amsterdam. Two men, Diop and Gueye, acting for the Popular Front for the Liberation of Palestine [the "PFLP"], forced the crew of the aircraft to fly to Beirut, where a demolitions expert and explosives were put on board. The aircraft, a Boeing 747, was then flown to Egypt still under PFLP control. In Cairo, after the passengers were evacuated, the aircraft was totally destroyed.

Pan American obtained policies from a number of companies each insuring against all physical loss of or damage to the aircraft save for any loss "due to or resulting from 'certain exclusions' ". These exclusions included damage by military or usurped power, war, warlike operations, insurrection, strikes, civil commotion or riot. Perhaps such disasters at one time encompassed the known range of human villainy, but "hi-jacking" is only in more current lexicons. Hence the issue evolves: (a) do the carriers have the burden of bringing "hi-jacking" within the scope of the named exclusions; and, if so, (2) can this burden be actually carried off—in other words can "hi-jacking", by any stretch of argument, be equated with a war, insurrection, riot, etc.? The 2d Circuit in affirming judgment against the insurers stated:

> The all risk insurers, if they were to prevail, had the burden of proving that the proximate cause of the loss of the 747 was included within one of the terms of exclusion. The all risk insurers' task is made even more difficult by the rule that exclusions will be given the interpretation which is most beneficial to the insured. * * *
>
> In the district court the insured had the burden of proving the existence of the all risk policies, and the loss of the covered property. Neither of these elements is disputed. Thus Pan American began the action with a prima facie case for recovery which the all risk insurers could meet only by proving that the cause of the loss came under one of the terms of exclusion.
>
> *Contra Proferentem.*
>
> The loss in this case is covered by the all risk policies if Pan American or the war risk insurers can formulate a reasonable interpretation of the terms of exclusion to permit coverage. On the other hand, it is not sufficient for the all risk insurers' case for them to offer a reasonable interpretation under which the loss is excluded; they must demonstrate that an interpretation favoring them is the only reasonable reading of at least one of the relevant terms of exclusion. Sincoff v. Liberty Mutual Fire Insurance Co., 11 N.Y.2d 386, 390, 230 N.Y.S.2d 13, 15, 183 N.E.2d 899, 901 (1962). Sincoff states the well-established New York rule for all types of insurance.
>
> > Contra proferentem has special relevance as a rule of construction when an insurer fails to use apt words to exclude a known risk. The evidence indicates that the risk of a hijacking was well known to the all risk insurers. Between 1960 and 1970 over 200 commercial aircraft were hijacked, eight of which belonged to Pan American. International hijacking is the subject of the Tokyo Convention of 1963 and the Hague Convention of 1970. Hijacking is forbidden by a federal statute, 49 U.S.C. § 1472 (1970).
>
> Various exclusionary terms in use or being considered for use prior to the present loss would have excluded the loss had they been employed. The war risk insurers have demonstrated that "hijacking," "act for political or terrorist purposes," "irregular warfare," "intentional damage," "forceful diversion" and "theft" enjoyed some currency. For example, in 1969 underwriters in the London all risk aviation market began to consider various alternative wordings for a hijacking exclusion. In November, 1969, an organization of such underwriters adopted the text of an exclusion called "AV-48," which excluded the following:

"(f) Unlawful seizure or wrongful exercise of control of the Aircraft or crew in flight (including any attempt at such seizure or control) made by any person or persons on board the Aircraft acting without the consent of the Insured."

The text of AV–48 was known to the USAIG by June, 1969. Had AV–48 been employed by the present all risk insurers, they might well have avoided liability for the loss of the 747.

On September 12, 1969, the London all risk market revised AV–48 to make it even more specific. The revised exclusion, AV–48A, includes the following language:

"This Policy does not cover claims directly or indirectly occasioned by, happening through or in consequences of:—

* * *

"(d) Any act of one or more persons, whether or not agents of a sovereign Power, for political or terrorist purposes and whether the loss or damage resulting therefrom is accidental or intentional.

"(e) Any malicious act or act of sabotage.

* * *

"(g) Hi-jacking or any unlawful seizure or wrongful exercise of control of the Aircraft or crew in flight. * * *"

Any of these three AV–48A clauses, if employed by the appellant all risk insurers, might well have excluded the present loss.

The current practice of packaging diverse insurance coverages in but a single policy naturally produces a mixture of the above basic approaches to coverage definition. The homeowners' (H.O.) policy is an example at hand—using the language of a standard fire policy at one point, and that of an "all risks" plus exclusions at another point. Homeowners' policies are of recent development (roughly in the last 50 years) and the differences in language composition may have been influenced by the type of insurance that the underwriter was accustomed to marketing when the decision was made to branch out into multiple risks coverage. Thus the regular fire insurers (of fixed objects) would tend to build their H.O.s with basic plus specific extended coverages. Those whose business had been primarily in the writing of inland marine or floater policies would be likely to produce a predominantly "all risks" H.O. form.

## BIRD v. ST. PAUL FIRE & MARINE INSURANCE CO.

New York Court of Appeals, 1918.
224 N.Y. 47, 120 N.E. 86.

CARDOZO, J., delivered the opinion of the court:

On September 12, 1915, the defendant, a fire and marine insurance company, issued to the plaintiff its policy of insurance covering the body, tackle, apparel, and other furniture of the canal boat, the Henry Bird, Jr. "Touching the adventures and perils which the said company are content to bear and take upon themselves by this policy, they are of the sounds, harbors, bays, rivers, canals, and fires, that shall come to the damage of the said boat, or any part thereof." There was no express exception of damage from explosion.

On the night of July 30, 1916, a fire broke out from some unknown cause beneath some freight cars in the Lehigh Valley Railroad Company's freight yards at Black Tom, in the harbor of New York. The cars were loaded with explosives, and, after the fire had burned at least thirty minutes, the contents of the cars exploded. This explosion caused another fire, which in turn caused another and much greater explosion of a large quantity of dynamite and other explosives stored in the freight yard. The last explosion caused a concussion of the air, which damaged plaintiff's vessel, about 1,000 feet distant, to the extent of $675. No fire reached the vessel, the damage being solely from the concussion caused by the second explosion. The question is whether the loss is covered by the policy. * * * The appellate division gave judgment for the plaintiff.

There is no doubt that when fire spreads to an insured building and there causes an explosion, the insurer is liable for all the damage. * * * We assume that, in the absence of some exception in the policy, a like liability follows when an explosion caused by fire occurs in neighboring buildings. Hustace v. Phenix Ins. Co., 175 N.Y. 292, 302, 303, 62 L.R.A. 651, 67 N.E. 592. But the question here is whether space is a factor in the solution of the problem. The appellate division says that it is not; no matter how great the distance, the insurer remains liable. Other courts have held otherwise. The question came before the English court of common pleas in Everett v. London Assurance Co., 19 C.B.N.S. 126, 144 Eng.Reprint, 734. There gunpowder ignited and exploded. The plaintiff's building, half a mile away, was damaged by concussion. The court (Erle, Ch.J., and Willes and Byles, JJ.) gave judgment for the defendant. "Speaking of this injury, no person would say that it was occasioned by fire. It was occasioned by a concussion or disturbance of the air caused by fire elsewhere." A like ruling was made in Louisiana by a divided court. Caballero v. Home Mut. Ins. Co., 15 La.Ann. 217. In Tennessee, the ruling was the same: "Legal conclusions cannot always be safely reached by pressing the processes of logical illation to their ultimate results." Hall v. National F. Ins. Co., 115 Tenn. 513, 521, 112 Am.St.Rep. 870, 92 S.W. 402, 403, 5 Ann.Cas. 777, 19 Am.Neg.Rep. 553.

The problem before us is not one of philosophy. Pollock, Torts, 10th ed. p. 37. If it were, there might be no escape from the conclusion of the court below. General definitions of a proximate cause give little aid. Our guide is the reasonable expectation and purpose of the ordinary business man when making an ordinary business contract. It is his intention, expressed or fairly to be inferred, that counts. There are times when the law permits us to go far back in tracing events to causes. The inquiry for us is how far the parties to this contract *intended* us to go. The causes within their contemplation are the only causes that concern us. A recent case in the House of Lords gives the true method of approach. Leyland Shipping Co. v. Norwich F. Ins. Co. [1918] A.C. 350, 369. Lord Shaw refers in his opinion to the common figure of speech which represents a succession of causes as a chain. He reminds us that the figure, though convenient, is inadequate. "Causation is not a chain, but a net. At each point, influences, forces, events, precedent and simultaneous, meet, and the radiation from each point extends infinitely." Ibid. From this complex web, the law picks out now this cause and now that one. The same cause producing the same effect may be proximate or remote as the contract of the parties seems to place it in light or shadow. That cause is to be held predominant which they would think of as predominant. A common-sense appraisement of everyday forms of speech and modes of thought must tell us when to stop. It is an act of "judgment as upon a matter of fact." Ibid.

This view of the problem of causation shows how impossible it is to set aside as immaterial the element of proximity in space. The law solves these problems pragmatically. There is no use in arguing that distance ought not to count, if life and experience tell us that it does. The question is not what men ought to think of as a cause. The question is what they do think of as a cause. We must put ourselves in the place of the average owner whose boat or building is damaged by the concussion of a distant explosion, let us say a mile away. Some glassware in his pantry is thrown down and broken. It would probably never occur to him that, within the meaning of his policy of insurance, he had suffered loss by fire. A philosopher or a lawyer might persuade him that he had, but he would not believe it until they told him. He would expect indemnity, of course, if fire reached the thing insured. He would expect indemnity, very likely, if the fire was near at hand, if his boat or his building was within the danger zone of ordinary experience, if damage of some sort, whether from ignition or from the indirect consequences of fire, might fairly be said to be within the range of normal apprehension. But a different case presents itself when the fire is at all times so remote that there is never exposure to its direct perils, and that exposure to its direct perils comes only through the presence of extraordinary conditions, the release and intervention of tremendous forces of destruction. Tilton v. Hamilton F. Ins. Co., 14 How.Pr. 363, 372, 373. A result which in other conditions might be deemed a mere incident to a fire, and therefore covered by the policy, has ceased to be an incident, and has become the principal. Briggs v. North American & M. Ins. Co., 53 N.Y. 446, 449. The distinction is no less real because it involves a difference of degree. In such a case, the damage is twice removed from the initial cause. It is damage by concussion; and concussion is not fire nor the immediate consequence of fire. * * * But there is another stage of separation. It is damage by concussion traveling over a distance so remote that exposure to peril is not within the area of ordinary prevision,—the range of probable expectation. The average man who speaks of loss by fire does not advert to the consequences of this play of catastrophic forces.

Precedents are not lacking for the recognition of the space element as a factor in causation. This is true even in the law of torts, where there is a tendency to go farther back in the search for causes than there is in the law of contracts. Smith, Legal Cause in Actions of Tort, 25 Harvard L.Rev. pp. 126, 127, 326. Especially in the law of insurance, the rule is that, "you are not to trouble yourself with distant causes." Willes, J., in Ionides v. Universal M. Ins. Co., 14 C.B.N.S. 289, 143 Eng.Reprint, 457, * * * Leyland Shipping Co. v. Norwich F. Ins. Soc. [1917] 1 K.B. 873, 883, 893. "In an action on a policy, the causa proxima is alone considered in ascertaining the cause of loss; but in cases of other contracts and in questions of tort the causa causans is by no means disregarded." Fenton v. J. Thorley & Co., [1903] A.C. 443, 454, * * * The rule "is based," it is said, "on the intention of the parties." Reischer v. Borwick [1894] 2 Q.B. 550, * * * But even in tort, where responsibility is less dependent on intention, space may break the chain of causes. The wrongdoer who negligently sets fire to a building is not liable without limit for the spread of the flames. In our own state, there is a fixed and somewhat arbitrary restriction. Hoffman v. King, 160 N.Y. 618, 46 L.R.A. 672, 73 Am.St.Rep. 715, 55 N.E. 401. But even in jurisdictions where the liability is broader, its bounds are the reasonable and the probable. The wrongdoer may be charged with those consequences, and those only, within the range of prudent foresight. * * *

The case comes, therefore, to this: Fire must reach the thing insured, or come within such proximity to it that damage, direct or indirect is within the compass of reasonable probability. Then only is it the proximate cause, because then only may we suppose that it was within the contemplation of the contract. In last analysis, therefore, it is something in the minds of men, in the will of the contracting parties, and not merely in the physical bond of union between events, which solves, at least for the jurist, this problem of causation. In all this, there is nothing anomalous. Everything in nature is cause and effect by turns. For the physicist, one thing is the cause; for the jurist, another. Even for the jurist, the same cause is alternately proximate and remote, as the parties choose to view it. A policy provides that the insurer shall not be liable for damage caused by the explosion of a boiler. The explosion causes a fire. If it were not for the exception in the policy, the fire would be the proximate cause of the loss and the explosion the remote one. By force of the contract, the explosion becomes proximate. St. John v. American Mut. F. & M. Ins. Co., 11 N.Y. 516; Louisiana Mut. Ins. Co. v. Tweed, 7 Wall. 44, 19 L.Ed. 65. A collision occurs at sea, and fire supervenes. The fire may be the proximate cause and the collision the remote one for the purpose of an action on the policy. The collision remains proximate for the purpose of suit against the colliding vessel. New York & B. Despatch Exp. Co. v. Traders' & M. Ins. Co., 132 Mass. 377, 382, 42 Am.Rep. 440. There is nothing absolute in the legal estimate of causation. Proximity and remoteness are relative and changing concepts.

It may be said that these are vague tests, but so are most distinctions of degree. On the one hand, you have distances so great that, as a matter of law, the cause becomes remote; on the other, spaces so short that, as a matter of law, the cause is proximate. The boat moored to the pier is damaged by fire when dynamite about to be loaded from the pier is ignited by a falling match. Fire destroys the city building when the wall of an adjoining building, weakened by the flames, collapses. * * * Between these extremes, there is a borderland where juries must solve the doubt. * * *

In this case, the facts are not disputed. The inferences to be drawn from them are not doubtful. The damage was not a loss * * * by fire within the meaning of the policy.

The judgment should be reversed, and judgment ordered for the defendant, with costs in the Appellate Division and in this court.

* * *

## PAN AMERICAN WORLD AIRWAYS, INC. v. AETNA CASUALTY & SURETY CORP.

United States Court of Appeals, Second Circuit, 1974.
505 F.2d 989 at 1006–1007.

The Facts are set forth on pages 230–32

* * *

B. Proximate Cause.

The all risk policies exclude "loss or damage due to or resulting from" the various enumerated perils, a phrase that clearly refers to the proximate cause of the loss. Remote causes of causes are not relevant to the characterization of an insurance loss. In the context of this commercial litigation, the causation inquiry stops at the efficient physical cause of the loss; it does not trace events back to their metaphysical beginnings. The words "due to or resulting from" limit the inquiry to the facts immediately surrounding the loss. Standard Oil Co. v. United States, 340 U.S. 54, 58, 71 S.Ct. 135, 95 L.Ed. 68 (1950); Airlift International, Inc. v. United States, 335 F.Supp. 442, 449 (S.D.Fla.1971), aff'd, 460 F.2d 1065 (5th Cir.1972) (mem.). Thus, in Queen Insurance Co. v. Globe & Rutgers Fire Insurance Co., 263 U.S. 487, 492, 44 S.Ct. 175, 176, 68 L.Ed. 402 (1924), Mr. Justice Holmes wrote:

> "[T]he common understanding is that in construing these policies we are not to take broad views but generally are to stop our inquiries with the cause nearest to the loss. This is a settled rule of construction, and if it is understood, does not deserve much criticism, since theoretically at least the parties can shape their contract as they like."

New York courts give especially limited scope to the causation inquiry. The leading case is Bird v. St. Paul Fire & Marine Insurance Co., 224 N.Y. 47, 120 N.E. 86 (1918) (Cardozo, J.). * * *

Britain S.S. Co. v. The King, [1919] 2 K.B. 670 (C.A.), aff'd, [1921] 1 A.C. 99 (1920), illustrates how this principle has been applied by the English courts in the context of war-related losses. While on a voyage from England to Alexandria in the company and under the orders of a British escort, the *Matiana* went aground and was lost, because the convoy had taken a more northerly route than usual to avoid German submarines. The Court of Appeals held that the loss was due to a marine peril, running aground, rather than to a "warlike operation." It held that the warlike activity of the escorts did not proximately cause the loss: The Crown's naval authorities ordered the ship to take a general course fraught with maritime perils, but they did not actually order the *Matiana* aground. [1919] 2 K.B. at 699–700 (per Atkins, L.J.). The House of Lords agreed. [1921] 1 A.C. at 1121–22 (per Atkinson, L.J.).

Decisions in a variety of other jurisdictions follow the same approach. When the *Linwood* went aground as a result of the Confederates putting out the Hatteras light, the loss was a "consequence" of a marine peril, rather than "hostilities." Ionides v. Universal Marine Insurance Co., 143 Eng.Rep. 445, 456 (C.P.1863) (per Erle, C.J.). When the *John Worthington* collided with a minesweeper that was clearing the channel approaches to New York harbor in 1942, the loss was due to the collision, a marine peril, rather than the warlike reason for the minesweeper's presence in the harbor. Standard Oil v. United States, 340 U.S. 54, 71 S.Ct. 135, 95 L.Ed. 68 (1950). When the *Napoli* was lost in a head-on collision with another ship because it was sailing without running lights under British order, the loss was due to a marine peril, the collision. Queen Insurance Co. v. Globe & Rutgers Fire Insurance Co., 282 F. 976 (2d Cir.1922), aff'd, 263 U.S. 487, 44 S.Ct. 175, 68 L.Ed. 402 (1924). When an insured aircraft was lost over Vietnam in a collision with a military aircraft, the loss was due to an aviation peril, notwithstanding that the two aircraft were flying over Vietnam only because there was a war. Airlift International, Inc. v. United States, 335 F.Supp. 442, 449 (S.D.Fla.1971), aff'd, 460 F.2d 1065 (5th Cir.1972) (mem.).

These cases establish a mechanical test of proximate causation for insurance cases, a test that looks only to the "causes nearest to the loss." Queen Insurance Co. v. Globe & Rutgers Fire Insurance Co., supra at 492, 44 S.Ct. 175. This rule is adumbrated by the maxim contra proferentem: if the insurer desires to have more remote causes determine the scope of exclusion, he may draft language to effectuate that desire. Id.; Fleeney & Meyers v. Empire State Insurance Co., 228 F.2d 770, 771 (10th Cir.1955). In the present case, events drawn from the general history of unrest in the Middle East did not proximately cause the destruction of the 747. Of course, in some attenuated "cause of causes" sense, the loss may have resulted from the Fedayeen or PFLP pattern of military operations against Israel, from the domestic unrest in

Jordan, or from the most recent of the three wars which prior to 1970 had convulsed the Middle East. But for insurance purposes, the mechanical cause of the present loss was two men, who by force of arms, diverted Flight 093 from its intended destination.

* * *

## GRAHAM v. PUBLIC EMPLOYEES MUTUAL INSURANCE CO.

Supreme Court of Washington, En Banc, 1983.
98 Wn.2d 533, 656 P.2d 1077.

DORE, JUSTICE.

This appeal arises from a dispute which erupted between two insurance companies and their insureds following the May 18, 1980 explosion of Mt. St. Helens. The early pyroclastic flows from the eruption, along with hot ash and debris, began melting the snow and ice flanking the mountain and the broken glacial ice blocks within the Toutle River valley. This water, combined with torrential rains from the eruption cloud, existing ground water, water displaced from Spirit Lake, and ash and debris, created mudflows which began moving down the valley shortly after the eruption began. * * * Approximately 10 hours after the eruption began, the appellants' homes, 20–25 miles away from Mt. St. Helens, were destroyed by a mudflow or a combination of mudflows preceded by water damage from flooding.

At the time of the eruption, homeowners insurance policies issued by Public Employees Mutual Insurance Company (hereafter PEMCO) to appellants * * * provided in pertinent part as follows:

> SECTION 1—EXCLUSIONS
>
> We do not cover loss resulting directly or indirectly from:
>
> * * *
>
> 2. Earth Movement. Direct loss by fire, explosion, theft, or breakage of glass or safety glazing materials resulting from earth movement is covered.
>
> 3. Water damage, meaning:
>
> a. flood, * * *

Of the seven exclusions listed in the PEMCO policy, "earth movement" is the only one not specifically defined in the policy.

Prior to March 1980, PEMCO utilized insurance forms containing this exclusionary language:

> This policy does not insure against loss:
>
> * * *
>
> 2. caused by, resulting from, contributed to or aggravated by any earth movement, including but not limited to earthquake, volcanic

> eruption, landslide, mudflow, earth sinking, rising or shifting; unless loss by fire, explosion or breakage of glass constituting a part of the building(s) covered hereunder, including glass in storm doors and storm windows, ensures, and this Company shall then be liable only for such ensuing loss, but this exclusion does not apply to loss by theft;

This language was deleted by PEMCO in an overall effort to simplify the policy language.

The homeowners filed claims against the insurance companies under their homeowners policies, but the insurance companies rejected their claims on the basis that the damage was excludable as "earth movement" in the form of mudflows or a combination of earth movement and water damage. * * * [Summary judgment in favor of the insurance company was entered by the trial court].

For the purpose of ruling on the summary judgment motion, the trial court assumed the movement of Mt. St. Helens to be an "explosion" within the terms of the insurance policies. The trial court noted this issue was a factual issue to be determined by a jury. We agree, as the true meaning of "explosion" in each case must be settled by the common experience of jurors. * * * Because direct loss from an explosion resulting from earth movement is not excluded from coverage, the jury must also determine the factual issue of whether the earth movements were caused by the earthquakes and harmonic tremors which preceded the eruption.

If the jury determines the volcanic eruption was an explosion resulting from earth movement, it will then be necessary to reach the issue of whether the loss was a direct result of the eruption. The trial court held that the causation analysis of Bruener v. Twin City Fire Ins. Co., 37 Wash.2d 181, 222 P.2d 833 (1950) precluded the plaintiffs' claims.

In *Bruener,* the insured's vehicle skidded on icy pavement and collided with an embankment. The insurance policy contained a collision exclusion to the comprehensive coverage. This court held that the loss was a "collision" for insurance purposes, reasoning as follows at 183–84, 222 P.2d 833:

> In tort cases, the rules of proximate cause are applied for the single purpose of fixing culpability, with which insurance cases are not concerned. For that purpose, the tort rules of proximate cause reach back of both the injury and the physical cause to fix the blame on those who created the situation in which the physical laws of nature operated. The happening of an accident does not, in itself, establish negligence and tort liability. The question is always, why did the injury occur. Insurance cases are not concerned with why the injury occurred or the question of culpability, but only with the nature of the injury and how it happened.

The *Bruener* court expressly overruled Ploe v. International Indem. Co., 128 Wash. 480, 223 P. 327 (1924), a case involving a driver who lost control of an automobile while rounding a curve on a mountain road. The car left the highway and traveled 25 feet before striking a stump along the road. Holding that the insurer was not liable, the court characterized the proximate cause of the accident to be the skidding of the car and not the collision with the stump. *Ploe,* at 483, 223 P. 327. The court reasoned that the destruction of the car was imminent from the time it left the highway, whether it struck the stump or not. In overruling the *Ploe* decision, the *Bruener* court, 37 Wash.2d at 185, 222 P.2d 833 replaced this proximate cause analysis with one of "direct, violent and efficient cause".

In Dickson v. United States Fidelity & Guar. Co., 77 Wash.2d 785, 466 P.2d 515 (1970), the plaintiff's boom crane was insured under a policy which excluded coverage for latent defects. The boom crane was damaged when earth, collapsing onto an "H" beam that was being removed, caused a sudden stoppage of the hoist. This stoppage put an increase in load on the boom structure, causing a defective weld to break and the boom to collapse. This court affirmed the trial court's ruling that the earth collapse was the external and responsible cause of the failure of the weld and the collapse of the boom, stating at 793, 466 P.2d 515:

> The trial court regarded the collapsing earth as the external and responsible cause of the failure of the weld and the collapse of the boom. He did not thereby rule in contradiction to our rule on insurance causation, as set forth in Bruener v. Twin City Fire Ins. Co., [37 Wash.2d 181, 222 P.2d 833 (1950) ] wherein we stated that, for the purposes of insurance litigation, the responsible cause of a loss is that which is the "direct, violent and efficient cause of the damage."

In reviewing the foregoing cases, we conclude the immediate physical cause analysis is no longer appropriate and should be discarded. The *Bruener* rule is an anomaly, inconsistent with the rule in the majority of other jurisdictions.[1] We have defined "proximate cause" as that cause "which, in a natural and continuous sequence, unbroken by any new, independent cause, produces the event, and without which that event would not have occurred". Stoneman v. Wick Constr. Co., 55 Wash.2d 639, 643, 349 P.2d 215 (1960). Where a peril specifically insured against sets other causes in motion which, in an unbroken sequence and connection between the act and final loss, produce the result for which recovery is sought, the insured peril is regarded as the "proximate cause" of the entire loss. * * *

1. 18 G. Couch, *Insurance* § 74:693 (2d ed. 1968) states the majority rule as:

"When loss is sustained by the insured it is necessary that the loss be proximately, rather than remotely, caused by the peril insured against."

It is the efficient or predominant cause which sets into motion the chain of events producing the loss which is regarded as the proximate cause, not necessarily the last act in a chain of events. * * * The mechanical simplicity of the *Bruener* rule does not allow inquiry into the intent and expectations of the parties to the insurance contract. Sears, Roebuck & Co. v. Hartford Accident & Indem. Co., 50 Wash.2d 443, 313 P.2d 347 (1957). We now specifically overrule the *Bruener* case.[2]

* * *

In the present case, the mudflows which destroyed the appellants' homes would not have occurred without the eruption of Mt. St. Helens. The eruption displaced water from Spirit Lake, and set into motion the melting of the snow and ice flanking the mountain. A jury could reasonably determine the water displacement, melting snow and ice and mudflows were mere manifestations of the eruption, finding that the eruption of Mt. St. Helens was the proximate cause of the damage to appellants' homes. This issue is not a question of law but a question of fact, to be determined by the trier of facts.

CONCLUSION

The *Bruener* decision is hereby overruled. We remand to the trial court for a jury determination of whether the movement of Mt. St. Helens was an "explosion" within the terms of the insurance policies; whether that "explosion" was preceded by earth movement, and whether appellants' damages were proximately caused by the eruption of Mt. St. Helens on May 18, 1980.

BRACHTENBACH, CHIEF JUSTICE (dissenting).

* * *

The obvious flaw in the majority's opinion is that it improperly applies the terms of the policy to the chain of events. The facts of this case reveal the following possible chain of events which should result in a denial of coverage regardless of proximate cause analysis. As suggested by the majority, on May 18, 1980, earthquakes and moving lava caused earth to move, which caused an eruption (explosion?), which caused earth movement in the form of mudflows. The majority concludes that the exclusion operates to exclude the initial earth movement which preceded the eruption but that the exception for explosion contained in the exclusion brings the incident back within the potential terms of the policy. But if that result is correct, the majority neglects a necessary additional inquiry—that is—should the earth movement exclusion be applied a second time to exclude coverage for mudflows? This last question presents strictly a legal issue involving the proper interpre-

**2.** In Frontier Lanes v. Canadian Indem. Co., 26 Wash.App. 342, 346, 613 P.2d 166 (1980), the Court of Appeals read Bruener v. Twin City Fire Ins. Co., 37 Wash.2d 181, 222 P.2d 833 (1950) to require that a loss could be attributed to vandalism or malicious mischief only if "the immediate physical cause of that loss was the vandalistic or malicious act itself or an instrumentality employed directly by the wrongdoer to carry out that act". We decline to follow the *Frontier* analysis insofar as it is inconsistent with our holding in the present case.

tation of policy terms. I submit that the only logical resolution of this issue is that the earth movement exclusion must be considered a second time. This answer requires, unfortunately, that we deny coverage. To do otherwise, however, would be to use proximate cause analysis to circumvent the clear terms of the policy. In addition, the majority appears to stop its inquiry at a point on the causation chain where coverage would be provided. * * *

* * *

The interpretation I suggest is necessary to give effect to the expectations that the parties had at the time they contracted for insurance coverage.[3] I would therefore deny coverage and affirm the trial court.

DOLLIVER and DIMMICK, JJ., concur.

## *Notes*

### *Concurrent Proximate Causes—Earthquakes and Negligence*

Beginning with State Farm Mutual Auto. Ins. Co. v. Partridge, 10 Cal.3d 94, 109 Cal.Rptr. 811, 514 P.2d 123 (1973), California courts have applied a rule that where two proximate causes join in causing an injury one of which is insured against, the insurer is liable under the policy irrespective of the eventuality that there is another concurrent proximate cause which constitutes an uncovered risk. In *Partridge,* the insured while driving a car was injured by his negligent discharge of a pistol. He was allowed recovery under a homeowner's policy which excluded injuries arising out of the use, etc. of a vehicle. A federal court applied the same principle in Safeco Ins. Co. v. Guyton, 692 F.2d 551 (9th Cir.1982) in holding that a homeowner's policy excluding flood to nevertheless cover the flooding of the insured's property where the concurrent proximate cause was the negligence of third parties in maintaining flood control facilities. The court observed that it made no difference that neither of the two causes could be characterized as the "prime," "moving" or "efficient" cause. And in a similar vein the owner of a home which slid down the hill along with the hillside itself recovered under an "all risks" policy expressly excluding earth movement because a concurrent cause could be found in a subdrain that had been negligently damaged so that the ground became saturated and moved, Premier Ins. Co. v. Welch, 140 Cal.App.3d 720, 189 Cal.Rptr. 657 (1983). Although the court recognized that the holding could also be based on the existence of a nonexcluded cause setting in motion the immediate excluded cause, it chose to adopt the *concurrent cause* doctrine of the preceding cases.

All of this might not seem earthshaking, but California is an earthquake prone state, although only about 5% of the property owners carry earthquake coverage. It follows however that if a negligently constructed building falls down in an earthquake, the *concurrent cause* rationale can be applied. It is reported that after the 1983 Coalinga earthquake, insurers paid out over $10,000,000 to owners of property whose insurance excluded or

3. The fact that the Grahams made a claim and recovered under their Federal Flood Insurance policy for this damage demonstrates that they at least viewed the primary cause of the damage as unrelated to the explosion. Transcript at 43.

otherwise did not cover earthquakes. It is also reported that one insurer, refused to pay a $10,000 claim somewhat similar to the *Welch* case, supra, and thereby incurred a trial court judgment of $47,000 actual and $1 million in punitive damages. As a result the insurer revised between 6 and 7 million of its Homeowners' policies to avoid the negation of "earth moving" exclusions by citing negligent acts or construction as a concurrent cause. Of course, if your well-designed and constructed house collapses in an earthquake it is too bad. Legislation now requires insurers in California to advise policy holders of the availability of earthquake insurance.

In the near future California courts will have the opportunity to evaluate more recently drafted concurrent causation exclusions in the context of the 1989 Loma Prieta Earthquake, the 1991 Oakland Hills Firestorm and the 1994 Northridge Earthquake. In addition, the severe hurricanes in 1992 (Andrew and Iniki) and the 1993 Midwest floods should yield refinements in other states. Each of the disasters will generate litigation concerning problems with insurable values, increased costs due to operation of building code or ordinance, bad faith, etc.—issues which affect many subjects in this course. None of the litigation from these massive losses has matured as this edition goes to print. However, the case that follows is the touchstone on which many concurrent causation decisions will rely.

## GARVEY v. STATE FARM FIRE AND CASUALTY COMPANY

Supreme Court of California, In Bank, 1989.
48 Cal.3d 395, 257 Cal.Rptr. 292, 770 P.2d 704.

LUCAS, CHIEF JUSTICE.

We granted review to consider the Court of Appeal's reversal of a directed verdict of coverage in favor of Jack and Rita Garvey (hereafter plaintiffs). We sought to resolve some of the confusion that has arisen regarding insurance coverage under the "all-risk" section of a homeowner's insurance policy when loss to an insured's property can be attributed to two causes, one of which is a nonexcluded peril, and the other an excluded peril.

In recent years, some courts have misinterpreted and misapplied our decisions in Sabella v. Wisler (1963) 59 Cal.2d 21, 27 Cal.Rptr. 689, 377 P.2d 889, and State Farm Mut. Auto. Ins. Co. v. Partridge (1973) 10 Cal.3d 94, 109 Cal.Rptr. 811, 514 P.2d 123. In so doing, they have allowed coverage in first-party property damage cases under our holding in Partridge by inappropriately using the Partridge concurrent causation approach as an alternative to Sabella's efficient proximate cause analysis. This extension of the analysis in Partridge, a third-party liability case, allows coverage under a first-party property insurance policy whenever a covered peril is a concurrent proximate cause of the loss, without regard to the application of specific policy exclusion clauses.[1] Such

1. As we explain in greater detail below, the distinction between first- and third-party claims can be summarized as follows: if the insured is seeking coverage against loss or damage sustained by the insured, the claim is first party in nature. If the in-

reasoning ignores the criteria set forth in Insurance Code sections 530 and 532, the relevant analysis in Sabella and the important distinction between property loss coverage under a first-party property policy and tort liability coverage under a third-party liability insurance policy. Indeed, because a covered peril usually can be asserted to exist somewhere in the chain of causation in cases involving multiple causes, applying the Partridge approach to coverage in first-party cases effectively nullifies policy exclusions in "all risk" homeowner's property loss policies, thereby essentially abrogating the limiting terms of insurance contracts in such cases. We cannot believe Partridge intended such a sweeping result in first-party property loss cases. To the contrary, as we explain below, we must put Partridge, in its proper perspective, i.e., that decision should be utilized only in liability cases in which true concurrent causes, each originating from an independent act of negligence, simultaneously join together to produce injury. Therefore, as will appear, we conclude this case should be remanded to the Court of Appeal with directions to remand to the trial court for a jury determination of causation pursuant to Sabella, supra, 59 Cal.2d 21, 27 Cal.Rptr. 689, 377 P.2d 889.

## I.

## Facts

Plaintiffs bought their house in the mid–1970's. In 1977, plaintiffs purchased from State Farm Fire and Casualty Company (hereafter defendant) an "all risk" homeowner's policy of insurance which was in effect at all times relevant. Section I of the policy in question provided coverage for "all risks of physical loss to the property covered" except as otherwise excluded or limited. Losses excluded by this portion of the policy included those "caused by, resulting from, contributed to or aggravated by any earth movement, including but not limited to earthquake, volcanic eruption, landslide, mudflow, earth sinking, rising or shifting," and losses caused "by * * * settling, cracking, shrinkage, bulging or expansion of pavements, patios, foundations, walls, floors, roofs or ceilings * * *."

In August 1978, plaintiffs noticed that a house addition, built in the early 1960's, had begun to pull away from the main structure. They also discovered damage to a deck and garden wall. There ensued numerous phone calls, letters, meetings and investigations as plaintiffs tried to determine from defendant whether the damage was covered by their homeowner's property insurance policy.

In October 1979, after receiving from its counsel an opinion that the loss was not covered, defendant notified plaintiffs by letter that the "policy excludes coverage for the loss herein. Normally, such a denial of coverage would leave you to your remedies. However, because the company wishes to resolve the coverage issue in an atmosphere free from extraneous matters such as bad-faith and class action issues, the compa-

sured is seeking coverage against liability of the insured to another, the claim is third party in nature. The present case is a first-party property loss case.

ny is prepared to advance you the claimed sum of $11,550 subject to a reservation of rights as authorized by Johansen v. CSAA, [1975], 15 Cal.3d 9 [123 Cal.Rptr. 288, 538 P.2d 744] * * *." Under the agreement proposed, defendant would make the advance and file a declaratory relief action on the issue of coverage; plaintiffs would pay back the advance if the court ruled in defendant's favor, would waive "any claim of consequential or punitive damages arising out of any allegation of bad-faith, mental distress, oppression, fraud or insurance-related tort," and would not "institute any class-action against defendant on account of the facts and issues involved in this loss and claim."

After refusing to sign the foregoing agreement, plaintiffs sued, claiming that although their policy excluded coverage for losses caused or aggravated by earth movement, it implicitly provided coverage for losses caused by contractor negligence because negligence was not a specifically excluded peril under the policy. Plaintiffs also argued that defendant denied their claim before adequately investigating the damage to the structure, and that subsequent investigations were undertaken merely to confirm the original denial. In addition, plaintiffs asserted, defendant's denial of coverage constituted a breach of the implied covenant of good faith and fair dealing and violated various provisions of the Insurance Code. Plaintiffs sought as relief (i) policy benefits, (ii) general damages for economic detriment and emotional distress, and (iii) punitive damages. Defendant rested on the 12th day of trial, and the court granted a directed verdict for plaintiffs on the coverage issue. The court informed the parties it was following the decisions in Partridge, supra, 10 Cal.3d 94, 109 Cal.Rptr. 811, 514 P.2d 123, and Sabella, supra, 59 Cal.2d 21, 27 Cal.Rptr. 689, 377 P.2d 889, and that plaintiffs were covered under the policy because negligent construction, a covered risk, was a concurrent proximate cause of the damage. Specifically, the trial court stated: "[The Supreme Court] told me in Sabella that negligent construction can be a proximate cause. They told me in Partridge there may be coverage whenever an insured risk constitutes simply a concurrent proximate cause of the injuries. Now, to me that is crystal clear, putting those two causes together, that if negligent construction is a concurrent proximate cause of the loss, there is coverage." The court continued, "The key witness for the defense, Mr. Nelson, conceded in his testimony, as I heard it and understood it, that the negligent construction was a cause of the room falling away. He did not use the word 'proximate.' He said a causative factor at one time. I don't recall the exact language when he answered a question. In substance, that it was a cause on another occasion. As a matter of law, based upon the evidence, it was a proximate cause."

The jury subsequently found defendant liable for $47,000 in policy benefits and general damages, and $1 million in punitive damages. The court denied defendant's motions for judgment notwithstanding the verdict and for a new trial, and declined to issue a remittitur with respect to the punitive damages award. The court entered judgment in accordance with the verdict. Defendant appealed, and the Court of

Appeal reversed the judgment in a divided opinion. Before reviewing the Court of Appeal holding, and in order to provide sufficient background information that will aid in the understanding of this case, we first discuss the development of multiple and concurrent causation insurance analyses, and the important distinction between property and liability policies.

## II.

## Discussion

### A. *Development of Multiple Causation Insurance Coverage Analyses*

#### 1. The efficient proximate cause standard

Our courts have long struggled to enunciate principles that determine whether coverage exists when excluded and covered perils interact to cause a loss. Initially, the courts attempted to reconcile section 530 (which provides for coverage when a peril insured against was the "proximate cause" of loss) with section 532 (which provides, that "If a peril is specifically excepted in a contract of insurance, and there is a loss which would not have occurred but for such peril, such loss is thereby excepted [from coverage] even though the immediate cause of the loss was a peril which was not excepted").

In our 1963 Sabella decision, supra, 59 Cal.2d 21, 27 Cal.Rptr. 689, 377 P.2d 889, we faced a difficult property loss coverage question arising after a building contractor constructed a house on uncompacted fill and negligently installed a sewer line; negligent installation was a covered peril. Eventually, the sewer line ruptured causing water to saturate the ground surrounding the insureds' house, resulting in subsidence, an excluded peril. The insureds brought a first-party action against their insurer, seeking recovery for property loss under their homeowner's property policy. (Id., at p. 26, 27 Cal.Rptr. 689, 377 P.2d 889.) The trial court found the loss was not covered because subsidence was a specifically excluded peril under the policy. The insureds appealed this ruling and we reversed.

On its face, section 532 would have precluded coverage because the loss would not have occurred "but for" the excluded peril of subsidence. We recognized, however, that such a result would be absurd because it would deny coverage even though an insured peril "proximately" caused the loss simply because a subsequent, excepted peril was also part of the chain of causation. We reasoned that sections 530 and 532 were not intended to deny coverage for losses whenever "an excepted peril operated to any extent in the chain of causation so that the resulting harm would not have occurred 'but for' the excepted peril's operation * * *." (Sabella, supra, 59 Cal.2d at p. 33, 27 Cal.Rptr. 689, 377 P.2d 889.) Rather, we explained that when section 532 is read along with section 530, the "but for" clause of section 532 necessarily refers to a "proximate cause" of the loss, and the "immediate cause" refers to the cause most immediate in time to the damage. (Id., at pp. 33–34, 27 Cal.Rptr. 689, 377 P.2d 889.)

Thus, Sabella held that: " '[I]n determining whether a loss is within an exception in a policy, where there is a concurrence of different causes, the efficient cause—the one that sets others in motion—is the cause to which the loss is to be attributed, though the other causes may follow it, and operate more immediately in producing the disaster.' " (Id., at pp. 31–32, 27 Cal.Rptr. 689, 377 P.2d 889, quoting from Couch on Insurance (1930) § 1466; Houser & Kent, Concurrent Causation in First–Party Insurance Claims: Consumers Cannot Afford Concurrent Causation (1986) Tort & Ins.L.J. 573, 575.)

Furthermore, in characterizing the "but for" clause of section 532 as referring to the efficient proximate cause of the loss, we impliedly recognized that coverage would not exist if the covered risk was simply a remote cause of the loss, or if an excluded risk was the efficient proximate (meaning predominant) cause of the loss. On the other hand, the fact that an excluded risk contributed to the loss would not preclude coverage if such a risk was a remote cause of the loss.

We relied heavily in Sabella, supra, 59 Cal.2d 21, 27 Cal.Rptr. 689, 377 P.2d 889, on our earlier decision in Brooks v. Metropolitan Life Ins. Co. (1945) 27 Cal.2d 305, 163 P.2d 689, in which recovery was allowed on a homeowner's policy insuring against death by accidental means. In Brooks, the insured, who was suffering from incurable cancer, an excluded peril, died in a fire. We held, "recovery may be had even though a diseased or infirm condition appears to actually contribute to cause the death if the accident sets in progress the chain of events leading directly to death, or if it is the prime or moving cause." (Id., at pp. 309–310, 163 P.2d 689.) Brooks thus defined efficient proximate cause in the first-party loss context as the "prime or moving cause." (Ibid.)

The Court of Appeal here replaced the Sabella term "efficient proximate cause" with the term "moving cause." Sabella defined "efficient proximate cause" alternatively as the "one that sets others in motion" (59 Cal.2d at p. 31, 27 Cal.Rptr. 689, 377 P.2d 889), and as "the predominating or moving efficient cause." (Id., at p. 32, 27 Cal.Rptr. 689, 377 P.2d 889.) We use the term "efficient proximate cause" (meaning predominating cause) when referring to the Sabella analysis because we believe the phrase "moving cause" can be misconstrued to deny coverage erroneously, particularly when it is understood literally to mean the "triggering" cause. Indeed, we believe misinterpretation of the Sabella definition of "efficient proximate cause" has added to the confusion in the courts and, in part, is responsible for the erroneous application of Partridge, supra, 10 Cal.3d 94, 109 Cal.Rptr. 811, 514 P.2d 123, to first-party property loss cases.

By relying on Brooks, supra, 27 Cal.2d 305, 163 P.2d 689, and construing sections 530 and 532, Sabella, supra, 59 Cal.2d 21, 27 Cal.Rptr. 689, 377 P.2d 889, set forth a workable rule of coverage that provides a fair result within the reasonable expectations of both the insured and the insurer whenever there exists a causal or dependent relationship between covered and excluded perils. In multiple cause cases, a proximate cause analysis, focusing on the efficient proximate cause, could be employed to determine whether or not the insured was covered for the loss under the property portion of the homeowner's insurance policy. Indeed, for 10 years following Sabella, the Court of Appeal applied the efficient proximate cause analysis in resolving multiple-cause property-coverage questions under all-risk homeowner's property policies. (See, e.g., Gillis v. Sun Ins. Office, Ltd. (1965) 238 Cal.App.2d 408, 415–420, 47 Cal.Rptr. 868 [coverage afforded under policy insuring loss by windstorm but excluding loss from water damage; wind, causing gangway to fall on and sink a dock, was deemed efficient proximate cause of loss]; Sauer v. General Ins. Co. (1964) 225 Cal. App.2d 275, 278–279, 37 Cal.Rptr. 303 [coverage afforded when water leaking from plumbing system (covered peril) was the efficient proximate cause of subsidence damage (excluded peril) ].)

2. The doctrine of concurrent causation

In 1973, we were faced with a third-party tort liability situation that presented a "novel question of insurance coverage" and did not fit the Sabella analysis because no single peril could be labeled the predominant cause of the loss. In Partridge, supra, 10 Cal.3d 94, 109 Cal.Rptr. 811, 514 P.2d 123, the insured was covered under both an automobile liability policy and a homeowner's liability policy with comprehensive personal liability coverage. (The latter liability policy excluded losses "arising out of the use" of a motor vehicle.) The insured, after filing the trigger mechanism of his pistol to create a "hair-trigger" action (such negligence was a covered risk under the homeowner's property policy), hunted jackrabbits at night from his vehicle. As he drove over rough terrain while waving the gun in his hand (negligent driving was an excluded risk under homeowner's liability policy), the gun fired and injured a passenger.

First-party property coverage issues were not involved. The case concerned the personal liability of the insured who was sued by his injured passenger. Both policies were issued by the same insurer, which conceded the accident was covered under the automobile liability policy. The parties, however, disputed whether coverage was also afforded under the homeowner's liability policy, which excluded coverage for injuries "arising out of the use of motor vehicles." As in Sabella, supra, 59 Cal.2d 21, 27 Cal.Rptr. 689, 377 P.2d 889, we relied on Brooks, supra, 27 Cal.2d 305, at pages 309–310, 163 P.2d 689, to find coverage under the homeowner's policy. In analyzing the liability coverage, we explicitly recognized, "the 'efficient cause' language [of Sabella] is not very helpful, for here both causes were independent of each other: the filing of the trigger did not 'cause' the careless driving, nor vice versa. Both, however, caused the injury * * *. If committed by separate individuals, both actors would be joint tortfeasors fully liable for the resulting injuries. Moreover, the fact that both acts were committed by a single person does not alter their nature as concurrent proximate causes. (Cf., Flournoy v. State of California (1969) 275 Cal.App.2d 806, 811 [80 Cal.Rptr. 485].)" (Partridge, supra, 10 Cal.3d at p. 104, fn. 10, 109

Cal.Rptr. 811, 514 P.2d 123.) We concluded by stating, "Although there may be some question whether either of the two causes in the instant case can be properly characterized as the 'prime,' 'moving' or 'efficient' cause of the accident we believe that coverage under a liability insurance policy is equally available to an insured whenever an insured risk constitutes simply a concurrent proximate cause of the injuries." (Id. at pp. 104–105, 109 Cal.Rptr. 811, 514 P.2d 123, fns. omitted, second italics added.)

Because Partridge dealt with causation in the context of third-party liability insurance, we did not address, nor did we contemplate, the application of our decision to the determination of coverage in the first-party property insurance context. Indeed, Partridge asserted only that the "concurrent cause" standard was "consistent with Insurance Code sections 530 and 532, as authoritatively construed in Sabella v. Wisler. . . ." (Partridge, supra, at p. 105, fn. 11, 109 Cal.Rptr. 811, 514 P.2d 123.)

Furthermore, Partridge never considered in what manner concurrent causation could apply in the first-party property insurance context. Rather, by recognizing in Partridge the "novel question" of liability coverage presented because two separate acts of negligence simultaneously joined together to cause an injury, we also impliedly recognized the limited scope of our holding. We did not extend our holding to first-party property insurance cases. Accordingly, we should not apply the decision to such cases merely because it appears to simplify the coverage analysis.

*B. The Distinction Between Liability and Property Insurance*

As we will demonstrate, the decision of the Court of Appeal, in applying the Partridge concurrent causation analysis to property damage cases, like other recent insurance cases involving all-risk homeowner's policies, failed to differentiate between property loss coverage under a first-party policy and tort liability coverage under a third-party policy of insurance. First- and third-party coverage is today typically provided in a single policy, and under both types of coverage, once the insured shows that an event falls within the scope of basic coverage under the policy, the burden is on the insurer to prove a claim is specifically excluded. (See Clemmer v. Hartford Ins. (1978) 22 Cal.3d 865, 880, 151 Cal.Rptr. 285, 587 P.2d 1098; Royal Globe Ins. Co. v. Whitaker (1986) 181 Cal.App.3d 532, 537, 226 Cal.Rptr. 435; Strubble v. United Services Auto. Assn. (1973) 35 Cal.App.3d 498, 504, 110 Cal.Rptr. 828.) Moreover, exclusionary clauses are interpreted narrowly, whereas clauses identifying coverage are interpreted broadly. (See Reserve Ins. Co. v. Pisciotta (1982) 30 Cal.3d 800, 808, 180 Cal.Rptr. 628, 640 P.2d 764.)

The scope of coverage and the operation of the exclusion clauses, however, are different in the separate policy portions and should be treated as such. As one commentator has recently stated: "Liability and corresponding coverage under a third-party insurance policy must be carefully distinguished from the coverage analysis applied in a first-party property contract. Property insurance, unlike liability insurance, is unconcerned with establishing negligence or otherwise assessing tort liability." (Bragg, Concurrent Causation and the Art of Policy Drafting: New Perils for Property Insurers (1985) 20 Forum 385, 386.)

For these reasons it is important to separate the causation analysis necessary in a first-party property loss case from that which must be undertaken in a third-party tort liability case. The following quotation summarizes the distinction that must be drawn: "Property insurance * * * is an agreement, a contract, in which the insurer agrees to indemnify the insured in the event that the insured property suffers a covered loss. Coverage, in turn, is commonly provided by reference to causation, e.g., 'loss caused by * * *' certain enumerated perils. The term 'perils' in traditional property insurance parlance refers to fortuitous, active, physical forces such as lightning, wind, and explosion, which bring about the loss. Thus, the 'cause' of loss in the context of a property insurance contract is totally different from that in a liability policy. This distinction is critical to the resolution of losses involving multiple causes. Frequently property losses occur which involve more than one peril that might be considered legally significant. If one of the causes (perils) arguably falls within the coverage grant—commonly either because it is specifically insured (as in a named peril policy) or not specifically excepted or excluded (as in an "all risks" policy)—disputes over coverage can arise. The task becomes one of identifying the most important cause of the loss and attributing the loss to that cause." (Bragg, supra, 20 Forum at pp. 386–387, italics added.)

On the other hand, the right to coverage in the third-party liability insurance context draws on traditional tort concepts of fault, proximate cause and duty. This liability analysis differs substantially from the coverage analysis in the property insurance context, which draws on the relationship between perils that are either covered or excluded in the contract. In liability insurance, by insuring for personal liability, and agreeing to cover the insured for his own negligence, the insurer agrees to cover the insured for a broader spectrum of risks. In order to further demonstrate the differences between property loss and liability coverage, we compare two sections of a typical homeowner's policy—the all-risk property loss coverage section of the policy in this case and the personal liability section at issue in Partridge.

Each policy section is governed by separate exclusions. For example, the all-risk first-party property loss coverage section in this case provides for coverage against "all risk of physical loss" except: losses "caused by * * * settling cracking, shrinkage, bulging or expansion of pavements, patios, foundations, walls, floors, roofs or ceilings * * *." In comparison, in Partridge, "The coverage clause of the 'Personal Liability' section of the 'Homeowner's Policy' provides in relevant part: 'This Company agrees to pay on behalf of the Insured all sums which the Insured shall become legally obligated to pay as damages because of bodily injury or property damage, to which this insurance applies, caused by an occurrence.' * * *." (10 Cal.3d at p. 99, fn. 5, 109 Cal.Rptr. 811,

514 P.2d 123.) Moreover, "[t]he applicable exclusionary clause reads: 'This policy does not apply: 1. Under Coverage E—Personal Liability * * * (a) To Bodily Injury or Property Damage Arising Out of the Ownership, Maintenance, Operation, Use, Loading or Unloading of: * * * (2) Any Motor Vehicle Owned or Operated By, or Rented or Loaned to, any Insured * * *.' " (10 Cal.3d at p. 99, fn. 6, 109 Cal.Rptr. 811, 514 P.2d 123.)

As the two provisions cited above illustrate, under the all-risk first-party property policy, because generally "all risk of physical loss" is covered, the exclusions become the limitation on loss coverage. Under the liability portion of the policy, on the other hand, the focus is, at least initially, on the insured's legal obligation to pay for injury or damage arising out of an "occurrence."

In the property insurance context, the insurer and the insured can tailor the policy according to the selection of insured and excluded risks and, in the process, determine the corresponding premium to meet the economic needs of the insured. On the other hand, if the insurer is expected to cover claims that are outside the scope of the first-party property loss policy, an "all-risk" policy would become an "all-loss" policy. (Friedman, Concurrent Causation: The Coverage Trap (1985) 86 Best's Rev.: Prop./Casualty 50, 58.) In most instances, the insured can point to some arguably covered contributing factor. As we shall discuss, if the rule in Partridge, supra, 10 Cal.3d 94, 109 Cal.Rptr. 811, 514 P.2d 123, were extended to first-party cases, the presence of such a cause, no matter how minor, would give rise to coverage.

Finally, as we explain, the reasonable expectations of the insurer and the insured in the first-party property loss portion of a homeowner's policy—as manifested in the distribution of risks, the proportionate premiums charged and the coverage for all risks except those specifically excluded—cannot reasonably include an expectation of coverage in property loss cases in which the efficient proximate cause of the loss is an activity expressly excluded under the policy. Indeed, if we were to approve of the trial court's directed verdict, we would be requiring ordinary insureds to bear the expense of increased premiums necessitated by the erroneous expansion of their insurers' potential liabilities. (See Hartford Fire Ins. Co. v. Superior Court (1983) 142 Cal.App.3d 406, 417, 191 Cal.Rptr. 37.)

*C. The Court of Appeal Holding*

In reversing the directed verdict, the Court of Appeal rejected defendant's argument that although third-party negligence is not specifically excluded in an all-risk policy, it is not a covered peril because it is technically not considered a "risk of physical loss" within the policy terms. We agree and find defendant's claim is not supported by authority. (See e.g., Sabella, supra, 59 Cal.2d 21, 31, 27 Cal.Rptr. 689, 377 P.2d 889.)

Next, the court recognized that recent first-party property loss cases (discussed below) have forsaken the efficient proximate cause analysis developed in Sabella, supra, 59 Cal.2d 21, 27 Cal.Rptr. 689, 377 P.2d 889, and have looked instead to the holding in Partridge, supra, 10 Cal.3d 94, 109 Cal.Rptr. 811, 514 P.2d 123, to allow coverage for property damage simply because a nonexcluded risk is an independent proximate cause of the loss. Although the Court of Appeal refused to confine the application of Partridge to liability cases, the court did attempt to limit the scope of Partridge's concurrent causation standard in both liability and property cases by requiring the included and excluded perils to be independent of origin and independent in operation. Specifically, the Court of Appeal interpreted Partridge, supra, 10 Cal.3d 94, 109 Cal.Rptr. 811, 514 P.2d 123, as holding that "because each act could have caused the loss regardless of the existence of the other act [citation], they were independent of each other." According to the Court of Appeal: "Neither [cause in Partridge] can be said to have necessarily acted upon a condition created by the other, or to have propelled the other, or to have brought to fruition the potential for damage inherent in the other." The Court of Appeal believed the "Partridge court would not have found the covered risk to be 'independent' if that risk (negligence) existed only in relation to, [or was dependent on] an excluded risk." Thus, the Court of Appeal determined that in order for coverage to be found under Partridge, the concurrent event alone must have been a "sufficient condition" of the loss—i.e., capable of producing damage itself.[2]

In its effort to interpret and apply the Partridge decision in the present case, however, the court followed the lead of other Court of Appeal decisions and assumed, without discussion, that Partridge should apply to first-party property insurance policies. In so doing, the court relied on both Partridge, and Sabella, supra, 59 Cal.2d 21, 27 Cal.Rptr. 689, 377 P.2d 889, and announced the following two-tiered rule for determining coverage: "[W]hether the covered risk and excluded risk are causes in fact should be a court's threshold inquiry in cases such as this. If (i) they both are causes in fact and if the two risks are independent of each other, Partridge analysis is triggered: the insured is covered if the covered risk was a concurring proximate cause of the loss. If (ii) the two risks are dependent on each other, Sabella analysis is triggered: the insured is covered only if the covered risk was the moving cause of the loss." The Court of Appeal determined that the jury in the present case must decide the coverage issue because it was not clear, as a matter of law, whether the two risks were dependent on or independent of each other.

The Court of Appeal's formulation was an attempt to provide trial courts with an analytical framework from which to determine property insurance coverage when a loss is arguably caused by concurrent causes. The court was on the right track in attempting to reconcile first- and

2. The term "sufficient condition" as used by the Court of Appeal missapplied the Partridge holding because it implied that negligent driving alone could have caused plaintiff's injury in that case. Although we point out the court's analytical error for purposes of clarifying any confusion the term may have caused, we leave the application of Partridge in the liability context to a future liability case that raises the concurrent causation issue.

third-party cases that use the Partridge analysis in determining coverage. We believe, however, as set forth above, that the court erroneously failed to limit at the threshold the application of Partridge to the third-party liability context.[3]

*D. The Misapplication of Partridge in The First-party Property Insurance Context*

In Safeco Ins. Co. of America v. Guyton, supra, 692 F.2d 551, 553, the insurer sought declaratory relief against several insureds after flooding damaged their homes. The trial court rejected the policyholders' claim that the water district's negligence in failing to provide adequate flood control facilities (a covered risk) caused the damage, and held under Sabella there was no coverage because the excluded peril—flooding—was the efficient proximate cause of the property damage. The Ninth Circuit Court of Appeals reversed on the basis that the insureds should be allowed to seek coverage under Partridge, supra, 10 Cal.3d 94, 109 Cal.Rptr. 811, 514 P.2d 123. The court determined that in order for Partridge to apply, the covered peril must have existed independently of the excluded peril. The court reasoned, however, that the requirement was met because two independently created conditions interacted to cause the flood damage. Indeed, Guyton specifically stated that "the twin causes in Partridge were independent only in the sense that each cause had an independent origin, not that they did not interact with one another to cause the loss." (692 F.2d at p. 555.)

As amici curiae for defendant point out, however, Guyton, supra, 692 F.2d 551, was actually "a classic case of dependent causation" requiring use of a Sabella analysis. Because the damage caused by the defective flood control system was necessarily dependent on flooding, the Ninth Circuit misapplied Partridge to find coverage. It should have looked to Sabella for resolution to determine whether the defectively maintained flood control system was the efficient proximate cause of the property losses even though the flood was the "immediate" cause of the losses, or whether the trial court correctly denied coverage in determining that flooding was the efficient proximate cause of the loss. The Ninth Circuit specifically ignored the effect of the express policy exclusion contained in the Safeco policy that excluded loss "caused by,

3. As we explained above, Partridge, supra, 10 Cal.3d 94, 109 Cal.Rptr. 811, 514 P.2d 123, should be limited to the third-party tort liability context. In the unusual event that analysis under Sabella, supra, 59 Cal.2d 21, 27 Cal.Rptr. 689, 377 P.2d 889, would not be useful in a first-party property loss case because separate excluded and covered causes simultaneously join together to produce damage—a situation we have yet to address—we may then consider developing an appropriate doctrine of concurrent causation to apply in the property loss context. For example, if property loss were to result from the simultaneous crash of an aircraft into a structure (a covered peril in a typical all risk homeowner's policy) during an earthquake (typically excluded from coverage when it operates alone to cause a loss), it might be impossible to determine (under a Sabella analysis) which cause was the efficient proximate cause of the loss. In that "novel" case, we might consider developing a doctrine similar to the present Court of Appeal's independent concurrent causation standard in analyzing coverage under the policy. It would be imprudent to reach such a hypothetical issue here, however, and hence we leave discussion of such a doctrine to a future first-party property loss case, should one arise.

resulting from, contributed to or aggravated by any of the following: a. Flood, surface water * * *." (Guyton, supra, 692 F.2d at pp. 552–553.)

In Premier Ins. Co. v. Welch (1983) 140 Cal.App.3d 720, 728, 189 Cal.Rptr. 657, a third party's negligence (a covered peril) damaged a subdrain. After a heavy rain, the house slid from its foundation. Water damage was an excluded peril. The trial court relied on Sabella, supra, 59 Cal.2d 21, 27 Cal.Rptr. 689, 377 P.2d 889, and determined that coverage should be denied because the efficient proximate cause of the loss was the rainfall. The same Court of Appeal division that decided the present case reversed and awarded coverage, concluding under a Sabella analysis that the efficient proximate cause of the loss was the damaged subdrain. Notwithstanding this conclusion, the court continued by stating that the insured would be covered in any event under Partridge, supra, 10 Cal.3d 94, 109 Cal.Rptr. 811, 514 P.2d 123, because "as a matter of law * * * the damage to the drain was a concurrent proximate cause of the loss." (Premier, supra, 140 Cal.App.3d at p. 728, 189 Cal.Rptr. 657.)

In its opinion in the present case, the Court of Appeal correctly acknowledged that its earlier interpretation (in Premier) of Partridge's independence requirement was wrong. Reviewing the facts of Premier, the court stated that the property loss caused by the negligently damaged subdrain was dependent on the existence of rainfall, but that nonetheless, the slide would not have occurred if the drain had not been severely damaged. Thus, the Court of Appeal recognized, "Premier was simply a Sabella situation." As the court admitted, it had reached a satisfactory result under Sabella, supra, 59 Cal.2d 21, 27 Cal.Rptr. 689, 377 P.2d 889; the Partridge analysis was simply unnecessary in Premier.

*E. The Trial Court Erred in Directing the Verdict*

Finally, because we believe the Partridge analysis should be limited to third-party liability cases, we cannot sustain the directed verdict in this case. Plaintiffs argue the directed verdict was proper because there was no evidence of sufficient substantiality to support a determination other than the following: the included risk of negligent construction and the excluded risk of earth movement in the form of soil creep, if any, were independent, concurrent proximate causes of the loss plaintiffs sustained to their property.

We disagree. * * *

This case presents a classic Sabella situation. Coverage should be determined by a jury under an efficient proximate cause analysis. Accordingly, bearing in mind the facts here, we conclude the question of causation is for the jury to decide. If the earth movement was the efficient proximate cause of the loss, then coverage would be denied under Sabella, supra, 59 Cal.2d 21, 27 Cal.Rptr. 689, 377 P.2d 889. On the other hand, if negligence was the efficient proximate cause of the loss, then coverage exists under Sabella. These issues were jury questions because sufficient evidence was introduced to support both possibilities.

The judgment of the Court of Appeal is affirmed with directions to remand the cause to the trial court for further proceedings consistent with the opinion of this court.

PANELLI, EAGLESON and ARGUELLES, JJ. [sitting under assignment by the Chairperson of the Judicial Council], concur.

The separate concurring opinion by KAUFMAN, J., concurred in by PANELLI, J., and the dissenting opinions by MOSK, J., and BROUSSARD, J. are omitted.

### *Comment*

On balance it appears that tort notions of proximate causation have overcome the attempted contractual restrictions on "causation" as drafted by the insurers in the policies scrutinized in the *Graham* case and the like. But basically Justice Cardozo was correct in the *Bird* decision—ultimately "causation" in insurance is a matter of contract not tort lore. In obvious counteractions to the results in the "earthquake" and "earth movement" cases when other concurrent covered causes were brought forth to effect coverage, the following redraft of the basic "Dwelling Property Form" furnished by the Insurance Services Office was made in the California version as of 1983:

GENERAL EXCLUSIONS

The first sentence:

> "We do not cover loss resulting directly or indirectly from:" (a list of exclusions follows including "water damage")

is deleted and the following substituted:

> "We do not insure for loss directly or indirectly by any of the following. Such loss is excluded regardless of any other cause or event contributing concurrently or in any sequence to the loss."

**Question:** Is there any way around this language?

## AN EXERCISE IN ANALYSIS

Using the foregoing materials as a guide along the "causation" path running through the policy provisions defining coverage, how *should* these problem examples be resolved? (How they *were* resolved is indicated).

1. *Coverage provision:* "Perils NOT included: * * * loss by * * * smoke * * * caused by * * * order of any civil authority."

*Sequence of events:* agricultural chemicals in warehouse vaporized and penetrated cartons of salad dressings belonging to insured and deposited residue thereon. Government agents condemned the food products. Henri's Food Products Co. v. Home Insurance Co., 474 F.Supp. 889 (E.D.Wis.1979). [Held: for insured. "The loss was not caused by condemnation but, instead, by the chemical residue." (To hold that "vapor" = "smoke" gave the court no difficulty.) ]

Compare Blaine Richards & Co. v. Marine Indemnity Ins. Co., 635 F.2d 1051 (2d Cir.1980) where the coverage provision excluded losses from detention by customs officials. Insured was importing beans from France and in the process a forbidden fumigant had been improperly applied by the supplier. The customs officials detained the beans for six weeks until F.D.A. approved clean-up measures. In consequence of the delay the insured lost sales contracts. Held: the proximate cause was the fumigation although the immediate cause was the detention. (Notice that the 2d Circuit had to modify the position taken in *Bird* and *Pan–American World Airlines,* supra.)

2. *Coverage provision:* direct loss by windstorm.

*Sequence of events:* insured livestock exposed to cold wind in high country took shelter in lower warmer area and drowned in pond when ice broke. Lydick v. Insurance Co. of North America, 187 Neb. 97, 187 N.W.2d 602 (1971). (Held: for insurer).

3. *Coverage provision:* direct loss by windstorm, but excluding coverage for loss caused by, contributed to, or aggravated by, surface water or waves, wind driven or not.

*Sequence of events:* wind blew a gangway onto the insured docking facility puncturing supporting pontoons which filled with water sinking the structure. Gillis v. Sun Insurance Office, Limited, 238 Cal.App.2d 408, 47 Cal.Rptr. 868, 25 A.L.R.3d 564 (1965). (Held: for insured).

4. *Coverage provision:* loss by windstorm

*Sequence of events:* wind blew down power lines, meat in insured's cold storage plant spoiled because freezer went off. Federal Insurance Co. v. Bock, 382 S.W.2d 305 (Tex.Civ.App.1964). (Held: for insured)

5. *Coverage provision:* loss by windstorm

*Sequence of events:* because of high wind the insured owner of a horse brought it in and stabled it next to the feed bin. Horse broke through the partition and died of overeating. Lorio v. Aetna Insurance Co., 255 La. 721, 232 So.2d 490 (1970). (Held: for insurer).

6. *Coverage provision:* "direct loss resulting from actual physical contact of * * * vehicle * * * with a building containing the property covered."

*Sequence of events:* an automobile deposited by a flood onto the sidewalk in front of the insured's shop diverted the floodwaters against the door which thereupon broke, letting in the water to cause damage to the property covered. Habaz v. Employers' Fire Insurance Co., 243 F.2d 784, 64 A.L.R.2d 1184 (8th Cir.1957). (Held: for insurer).

7. *Coverage provision:* Covers damage from: "accidental discharge of water * * * from within a household appliance." Does not cover damage from: "water below the surface of ground which leaks through a building "(or foundation)."

*Sequence of events:* Insured put a sump pit in below the basement level the purpose being to pump out ground water before it reached basement level. Unfortunately the sump pump hose broke flooding the basement. Stone v. Royal Ins. Co., 211 N.J.Super. 246, 511 A.2d 717 (A.D.1986) (Held: for insured. The sump pump was a household appliance).

8. *Coverage provision:* Federal flood policy (designed to provide insurance at affordable price) covered flood but excluded loss "by landslide or other earth movement, such as mudslide or erosion."

*Sequence of events:* Tropical storm Dennis hit Florida with exceptionally heavy rainfall. No water entered the insured's house, but did saturate sand fill on which house was built. The resulting soil compaction caused house to crack. Quesada v. Director, Federal Emergency Management Agency, 753 F.2d 1011 (11th Cir.1985). (Held: for insured (2–1 decision)).

## COASTAL PLAINS FEEDERS, INC. v. HARTFORD FIRE INSURANCE CO.

United States Court of Appeals, Fifth Circuit, 1977.
545 F.2d 448.

LEWIS R. MORGAN, CIRCUIT JUDGE:

Plaintiff-appellee Coastal Plains Feeders, Inc. operates a commercial feed lot near Samson, Alabama where it holds cattle for their owners and fattens them for market. Defendant-appellant insurance companies issued "floater" policies to Coastal Plains insuring the cattle it held against loss by "theft, but excluding escape or mysterious disappearance." In this diversity action Coastal Plains sued the companies on the insurance contracts to recover the value of 512 cattle that vanished from its feed lot. * * *

After trial a six person jury found for Coastal Plains on the contractual claims in the amount of $172,657.48. The district court entered judgment for that amount plus $9,064.54 interest.

The insurance companies appeal the judgment, arguing (1) that the district court incorrectly instructed the jury as to the elements that Coastal Plains had to prove to recover; (2) that there was insufficient evidence of theft to present a jury question on liability; * * *

### I. FACTS

Coastal Plains put on evidence showing that in late 1973 and early 1974 it held about 7,000 cattle in its feeder pens near Samson. * * *

In late January of 1974 Coastal Plains became concerned because the amount of feed the cattle were consuming was abnormally low. Its nutritional and veterinary consultants found nothing wrong with the feed or cattle, however, and the drop in consumption was attributed to rainy weather. When consumption continued to be low through February, some owners became worried. On March 10 Coastal Plains conducted an exact head count of all the cattle at the lot. This count revealed, and the parties stipulated, that 512 cattle were missing.

Searches of the surrounding countryside, investigation by law enforcement officers, and offer of a $5,000 reward turned up neither hide nor hair of the missing cattle. Some light was shed on their disappearance, however, by three members of a family who lived on a lonesome dirt road leading to the back pens of the feed lot. They testified that on a number of occasions between December and March they saw an unmarked empty double-decker ("possum belly") cattle truck going up the road toward the lot at dusk without headlights. They also heard a heavy diesel truck return down the road in the early hours of morning. None of them ever saw such a large truck on the road before or since.

The back pens to which the dirt road led were not locked, and the heaviest loss of cattle was from those pens. The night watchman, who quit in February, could not see or hear anything happening at the back pens. Two men could load as many as 70 cattle into the kind of truck the family saw in a short time. Coastal Plains' fences were in good repair, and it had never had a problem with cattle straying or escaping.

## II. THE INSURANCE COMPANIES' APPEAL

A. *Instructions on theft and mysterious disappearance.* The insurance policies provided that the companies would be liable for the loss of cattle "through theft, but excluding * * * mysterious disappearance." The insurance companies contend that, under Alabama law, Coastal Plains carried both the burden of proving that theft was the cause of the loss, and the burden of proving that mysterious disappearance was not the cause of the loss. They further contend that the district court erred in failing to instruct the jury that Coastal Plains carried the latter burden as well as the former. We find it unnecessary to decide whether the burden of disproving mysterious disappearance was on Coastal Plains rather than the insurance companies; for assuming that it was on Coastal Plains,[41] the district court's instructions sufficiently apprised the

**41.** We recognize that there is some Alabama authority for the broad proposition that, where the general liability clause of an insurance policy itself contains an exclusion, the insured bears the burden of pleading and proving that he is not within the exclusion; although where an exclusion is stated in a separate clause, the insurer bears the burden of pleading and proving the applicability of the exclusion. E.g., New York Life Ins. Co. v. Beason, 229 Ala. 140, 141–142, 155 So. 530, 531–32 (1934); Protective Life Ins. Co. v. Swink, 222 Ala. 496, 498, 132 So. 728, 729 (1931); see Ruffalo's Trucking Serv., Inc. v. Nat'l Ben-Franklin Ins. Co., 243 F.2d 949, 952–53 (2d Cir.1957) (accord) (New York law). We note, however, that some states which have considered policies of the precise kind under consideration here, insuring against "theft, but excluding mysterious disappearance," have concluded that the insurer bears the burden of proving applicability of the exclusion. Lovas v. St. Paul Ins. Cos., 240 N.W.2d 53, 62 (N.D.1976); see Long v. Glidden Mut. Ins. Ass'n, 215 N.W.2d 271, 274 (Iowa 1974). This court, interpreting under Florida law an "all-risks" policy with a liability clause that excluded recovery for mysterious disappearance, reached the same conclusion. Jewelers Mut. Ins. Co. v. Balogh, 272 F.2d 889, 891–92 (5th Cir. 1959); see Betty v. Liverpool and London and Globe Ins. Co., 310 F.2d 308, 310–11 (4th Cir.1962) (accord). At least one other court, though, has suggested that it would place the burden of negating mysterious disappearance under policies like the one

jury that Coastal Plains was required to disprove mysterious disappearance in order to recover.

The district court did not just tell the jury that Coastal Plains must carry the burden of proving theft to recover under the policy. Rather, it told the jury repeatedly that Coastal Plains must prove that theft, *and not mysterious disappearance,* was the cause of its loss:

> "[D]efendants deny that Coastal Plains suffered any loss covered under these insurance policies since Coastal Plains has by the evidence shown nothing more than a mysterious disappearance of cattle and * * * a mysterious disappearance of cattle is not covered or compensable under these policies.
>
> * * *
>
> "[The i]nsurance policies * * * provide that Coastal Plains is insured against theft, but not escape or mysterious disappearance.
>
> * * *
>
> "The policies of insurance here in question provide insurance for theft, * * * but exclude escape or mysterious disappearance * * *. The burden of proof of theft, as I have told you, is on Coastal Plains, the plaintiff. That burden of proof is to reasonably satisfy you from the evidence that the loss in fact resulted from a theft or thefts."

[Later] the district court defined "mysterious disappearance" as "disappearance under unknown, puzzling, and baffling circumstances which arouse wonder, curiosity, or speculation, or under circumstances which are difficult or hard to explain." Thus, although the district court correctly charged that Coastal Plains could prove theft through circumstantial evidence,[43] it also made it clear to the jury that Coastal Plains had to prove something more than "mysterious disappearance," so defined, to make out a circumstantial case of theft. This amounted to an instruction that under the policy, Coastal Plains had to "negate mysterious disappearance" to prove "theft."

The district court rejected the insurance companies' request to charge explicitly that Coastal Plains carried two burdens—that of proving theft, *and* that of negating mysterious disappearance—on the ground that this could confuse the jury. The court apparently wanted to avoid misleading the jury into thinking that it was logically possible for

here on the insured. See Baugher v. Hartford Fire Ins. Co., 214 Kan. 891, 900–901, 522 P.2d 401, 409 (1974) (by implication).

**43.** Even under policies insuring against "theft, but excluding mysterious disappearance," it is accepted universally that the insured may prove theft by proving that circumstances surrounding the disappearance of property support an inference that theft probably was the cause of the disappearance. Long v. Glidden Mut. Ins. Ass'n, 215 N.W.2d 271, 273 (Iowa 1974); Baugher v. Hartford Fire Ins. Co., 214 Kan. 891, 902–903, 522 P.2d 401, 410–11 (1974); Gifford v. M.F.A. Mut. Ins. Co., 437 S.W.2d 714, 717 (Mo.Ct.App.1969); Raff v. Farm Bureau Ins. Co., 181 Neb. 444, 447–448, 149 N.W.2d 52, 55 (1967); Lovas v. St. Paul Ins. Cos., 240 N.W.2d 53, 60–61 (N.D.1976). If the insured were required to prove theft by so-called direct evidence—production of the thief or of eyewitnesses to the theft—"[t]his would be tantamount to denial of coverage for theft because theft is generally carried on in a secretive manner * * *" *Lovas,* supra, 240 N.W.2d at 60.

Coastal Plains to prove theft *without* negating mysterious disappearance, as it had defined that term.[44] We think this was a proper concern. The fact that the insurance contracts were drawn in confusing language does not justify instructing the jury in confusing terms—especially at the instance of the parties responsible for the source of the confusion. We hold that to inform the jury adequately that Coastal Plains carried the "burden of negating mysterious disappearance" as well as of proving theft, it was necessary only to define "mysterious disappearance" in the generally accepted manner, * * * and then to emphasize that Coastal Plains would be entitled to recover only if it proved theft, as distinguished from mysterious disappearance so defined.

* * *

Coastal Plains presented evidence tending to show that the disappearance of the cattle was not due to death, sale or reclamation by owners, straying, or miscounting. We need not decide whether this evidence by itself would support an inference that the cattle were stolen, compare Lovas v. St. Paul Insurance Companies, 240 N.W.2d 53 (N.D. 1976) (evidence of theft of hogs held sufficient) with Baugher v. Hartford Fire Insurance Company, 214 Kan. 891, 522 P.2d 401 (1974) (evidence of theft of cattle held insufficient); Gifford v. M.F.A. Mutual Insurance Company, 437 S.W.2d 714 (Mo.Ct.App.1969) (evidence of theft of cattle held insufficient); Raff v. Farm Bureau Insurance Company, 181 Neb. 444, 149 N.W.2d 52 (1967) (evidence of theft of hogs held insufficient); for here Coastal Plains also showed that an unmarked cattle truck was seen at night near the inaccessible back pens of the feed lot during the period in which the cattle disappeared, adding strength to the theory that the cattle in fact were stolen. See Wiley v. United Fire & Casualty Company, 220 N.W.2d 635, 636–37 (Iowa 1974) (evidence of theft of cattle held sufficient on facts nearly identical to instant case); Gifford v. M.F.A. Mutual Insurance Company, supra, 437 S.W.2d at 717 (suggesting that evidence of theft would have been sufficient if someone had seen "a strange truck traveling to or from where the cattle were kept," or had "heard any unusual activity at night near the pasture" where the cattle were kept; or if there was "evidence of [someone] being at or near the cattle under suspicious circumstances"). To hold that the jury could not reasonably infer from this evidence that the cattle were stolen would render meaningless the rule that Coastal Plains could prove theft through circumstantial evidence. * * * We hold that the district court did not err in submitting the case to the jury on the issue of liability.

44. In denying the companies' request to instruct, the district court stated, * * *

> I think this whole argument as to who has the burden of negating [mysterious disappearance] is nothing except confusing, because if the plaintiff sustains their burden of proving theft, they have automatically negated mysterious disappearance, and they can't establish loss by theft without negating mysterious disappearance or escape; and I have told the jury if that is all that happened, if it is just a mysterious disappearance or if it is an escape, then plaintiff can't recover.

### *Notes*

1. *The Background of the Mysterious "Mysterious Disappearance" Provision*

The North Dakota Supreme Court as of 1976 (Lovas v. St. Paul Insurance Companies, 240 N.W.2d 53 (N.D.1976)—a case frequently cited in the main opinion) furnishes us with an elaborate review of the history of the "mysterious disappearance" expressions in theft and burglary policies. Portions are here quoted:

"Early theft insurance policies merely provided for coverage for loss by theft but did not include or exclude or make reference to mysterious disappearance. The measure of proof required of the insured varied, but as a general rule it was held that a logical inference of a felonious taking might be drawn from circumstances surrounding a mysterious disappearance. * * *

"Occasionally, provisions were added to the effect that mere disappearance of the insured object would not be deemed sufficient evidence of its loss by theft or burglary.

"Under the old policies it was not necessary for the insured to offer direct proof of the theft. Circumstantial evidence could be relied on and if the insured was able to prove facts and circumstances sufficient to justify the inference of theft as the more rational hypothesis the case would go to the jury. Proof of the mysterious disappearance of property alone was insufficient to support a verdict; 'and if there was no evidence of a breaking and entry or other circumstance pointing to theft as the more probable cause of the loss, a recovery under the policy was not permitted. Thus, the insured, under the old policies, often-times found his claim contested and encountered difficulty in making out a case for the jury.' Davis v. St. Paul Mercury & Indemnity Co., 227 N.C. 80, 40 S.E.2d 609 (1946)."

In 12 A.L.R.3d 866, 867, Theft Insurance—Disappearance, we find the following:

> "§ 2. Background and summary
>
> "Pre–1943 burglary and theft insurance policies occasionally contained provisions to the effect that disappearance of the insured object would not be considered evidence of theft or burglary. Generally, these provisions were interpreted as not preventing the insured from proving his loss through theft or burglary by the use of circumstantial evidence. And since a mysterious disappearance was one circumstance from which a theft might be deduced, the courts readily accepted proof of disappearance of insured property under mysterious circumstances as adequate to support recovery under a policy in which the insurer agreed to pay for loss by theft.
>
> "Prior to 1943, however, the insurance companies varied widely in their requirements as to proof of theft, and in order to bring about a greater uniformity in adjustment practices and thereby eliminate a source of policyholder dissatisfaction, and motivated not so much by a sense of resignation as by a desire to make the policy more informative in this respect, both to insurance companies and policyholders alike, a

clause specifically covering the 'mysterious disappearance' contingency was introduced into the standard form theft policy, on April 19, 1943.

"Such a clause, as originally introduced, usually read: "The word "theft" includes larceny, burglary and robbery. Mysterious disappearance of any insured property shall be presumed to be due to theft.' This presumption clause had the effect of creating a contractual rule of evidence which facilitated proof of 'theft' by the insured in the absence of evidence either affirmatively establishing or clearly negating the existence of a theft in fact.

"Many persons thought that the presumption clause was designed to broaden the coverage of the policy so as to make it extend to losses which would not otherwise be covered. It was reasoned that, something new having been added to the policy, something additional in the way of protection must have been intended. As noted, however, the clause was not intended to give more coverage but rather was designed to reflect what had, by 1943, long been the judicial view as to what kind of evidence it takes to prove a loss within the coverage of a theft policy.

"The unmistakable trend has been toward an expansion of theft coverage to include loss from mysterious disappearance. Some policies actually include the term 'mysterious disappearance' within the definition of 'theft,' while others simply co-ordinate the contingencies covered by offering protection against loss by 'theft or attempt thereat or mysterious disappearance.' The general rule in either instance has been that proof of mysterious disappearance alone suffices to enable the insured to recover, even absent a showing as to the probability of theft."

It has been occasionally held or recognized that policies insuring property against burglary or theft containing the provision that the mere disappearance of the insured object shall not be deemed evidence of theft does not prevent the insured from establishing theft by circumstantial evidence. This is so even though the policy contained a provision requiring the production of direct or affirmative evidence. See 12 A.L.R.3d 865.

It has also been recognized by some jurisdictions that an insurance policy making mysterious disappearance a presumption of theft has the effect of creating a rule of evidence by contract. Such provision has been held to raise only a rebuttable presumption but does not broaden the coverage itself to include losses by mysterious disappearance. See 12 A.L.R.3d 865, and cases cited thereunder.

In 5 Appleman, Insurance Law and Practice, § 3173.25, at pages 506–08, the statement is made that the insured, under a presumption provision, does not have to produce evidence excluding the probability that the property was not stolen or prove that larceny was the more rational inference, or prove who stole the article. Accordingly, under this provision, the mysterious disappearance of the insured property without explanation may be sufficient to allow recovery.

In Davis v. St. Paul Mercury & Indemnity Co., supra, the Court stated that such a mysterious disappearance clause was designed to afford the insured a larger measure of protection than under the old theft policies. Theft is presumed until the presumption is rebutted, but the burden of proof is at all times on the plaintiff. If the jury finds from the evidence that the property did mysteriously disappear, such finding compels the inference of theft, unless the facts and circumstances surrounding the disappearance are such as to rebut the presumption. * * *

The presumptive provision, however, does not change the policy from a theft policy to one covering every loss due to mysterious disappearance. Appleman, supra, p. 508.

The trend has been to give more certain coverage to the insured through expansion of theft coverage by including loss from mysterious disappearance. Instead of inserting a presumption provision, policies have either provided for coverage for "theft or mysterious disappearance" or coverage for theft which is defined to include mysterious disappearance. See, Conlin v. Dakota Fire Insurance Company, 126 N.W.2d 421 (N.D.1964).

2. *An opposing trend—to exclude "mysterious disappearance" coverage*

Contrary to the concluding paragraph from the A.L.R. annotation which dates from 1960, it appears that most policies are now excluding coverage not only for mysterious disappearance, but also escape, inventory shortages, wrongful conversion and embezzlement. See, Anderson v. Farm Bureau Ins. Co. of Nebraska, 219 Neb. 1, 360 N.W.2d 488 (1985), and Ward Cattle Co. v. Farm Bureau Ins. Co., 223 Neb. 69, 383 N.W.2d 89 (1986). The urge to exclude "mysterious disappearance" from theft coverage appears particularly strong as to jewelry items and ambulatory live stock. Why? Note that the Coastal Plains policy also excluded "escape."

3. *Bringing it together*

Would this be an accurate summation of the various aspects of the "mysterious disappearance" phenomenon?

a. Theft only coverage. Here insured must prove theft according to the pre–1943 case analysis.

b. Theft with mysterious disappearance presumed to be theft. The presumptive provision aids the insured, but does not necessarily change the policy from a theft policy to one covering every loss due to mysterious disappearance.

c. An "all risks" policy with a *separate* "mysterious disappearance" exclusion. The insured here need only establish a loss, the burden being cast upon the insurer to bring it within the exception. (see particularly this interpretation applied to the standard jewelers' block policy in Jewelers Mutual Insurance Co. v. Balogh, 272 F.2d 889 (5th Cir.1959)).

d. "Theft, but excluding mysterious disappearance", this is a hybrid—neither unqualified theft, nor on the other hand a separately listed exclusion. The insured here has the burden of proving theft, but may do so by circumstantial evidence.

# ENGEL v. REDWOOD COUNTY FARMERS MUTUAL INSURANCE CO.

Supreme Court of Minnesota, 1979.
281 N.W.2d 331.

KELLY, JUSTICE.

* * *

The issue presented on appeal is whether a loss caused by excessive heat from a fire intentionally kindled and wholly confined to the furnace wherein it was intended to burn is covered under an insurance policy providing coverage for all losses or damage by fire.

The facts are not in dispute. The plaintiff was insured under a "Minnesota Standard Township Mutual Fire Insurance Policy" issued by defendant. In 1973, the plaintiff constructed a hog barn on his farm for use in farrowing hogs. The barn was heated by an L.B. White furnace which was located just outside the building and which blew hot air into the barn by means of a fan. The furnace was controlled by a thermostat which could be adjusted to shut off the fan and furnace at a pre-set temperature.

On January 1, 1976, the plaintiff discovered that 15 of the 16 sows then in the hog barn were dead. Subsequent investigation revealed that the sows died from an inadequate supply of oxygen in the hog barn, caused by increased temperature. The high temperatures resulted from a "short" which rendered the thermostat inoperable allowing the furnace to blow hot air into the barn until the high limit control, set at 120°, shut down the furnace. The thermostat was set at 75° and this was normally as high as temperatures inside the building would rise. At all times the fire inside the furnace burned and produced heat at its usual rate and was confined within the furnace causing no damage to the hog barn or to the furnace nor producing any soot or other foreign material.

Defendant refused to compensate plaintiff, claiming that the loss was not recoverable under his policy as it was the result of a so-called "friendly" rather than "hostile" fire.

The hostile fire doctrine is said to have originated in the early English case of Austin v. Drew, 4 Campb. 360 (1815).[46] In that case, sugar being refined in plaintiff's factory was damaged by excessive heat and smoke. The sugar was contained in various rooms of an 8–story building through which ran a flue supplying the heat necessary for the refining process. At the top of the flue was a register which was normally kept open when the fire was high. An employee started the fire without opening the register. As a result, the fire overheated,

**46.** Although this case is often cited as first originating the hostile fire doctrine, the terms hostile and friendly fire first appeared in the case of Way v. Abington Mutual Fire Ins. Co., 166 Mass. 67, 43 N.E. 1032 (1896).

smoking up the rooms containing the sugar and causing the damage complained of. The court, in denying recovery, stated:

> "I am of the opinion that this action is not maintainable. There was no more fire than always exists when the manufacture is going on. Nothing was consumed by fire. The plaintiff's loss arose from the negligent management of their machinery. The sugars were chiefly damaged by the heat; and what produced that heat? Not any fire against which the company insures, but the fire for heating the pans, which continued all the time to burn without any excess. The servant forgot to open the register by which the smoke ought to have escaped and the heat to have been tempered." 4 Campb. 361.

From this opinion has emerged a rule of law known as the hostile fire doctrine. It is recognized in a majority of jurisdictions where the issue has been raised, 44 Am.Jur.2d, Insurance, § 1348; 5 Appleman, Insurance Law and Practice, § 3082, although it has been criticized by many commentators. See Vance, Friendly Fires, 1 Conn.Bar J. 284; Reis, The Friendly Versus Hostile Fire Dichotomy, 12 Vill.L.Rev. 109; Morrison, Concerning Friendly Fires, 3 Boston C.Indus. & Com.L.Rev. 15. In brief, the rule generally states that a fire which is intentionally kindled and which remains at all times confined to the place where it was intended to be will be characterized as friendly and will not subject the insurer to any liability for the resulting loss. By adopting this doctrine, courts have in effect established a presumption, seemingly irrebuttable, that the parties to the transaction, particularly the prospective insured, were aware of this doctrine and contemplated its inclusion in the policy. Common sense tells us that this is more than likely not the case. When an insured buys a fire insurance policy which "covers all losses or damage by fire" his expectation is that it will cover all unintentional losses from fire, except listed exclusions, regardless of the nature or character of the fire. The doctrine thus seems to protect the insurer at the expense of the unwitting insured.

In Minnesota, this problem is avoided because of the judicially created limitations on friendly fires. In L.L. Freeberg Pie Co. v. St. Paul Mutual Insurance Co., 257 Minn. 244, 100 N.W.2d 753 (1960), we joined a minority of courts which require that a friendly fire, in addition to the elements listed above, be non-excessive. In the *Freeberg* case, the thermostat on a bake oven failed and, as a result, the flame inside the oven continued to build up to such a degree as to seriously warp and damage the oven. The lower court determined that, because the fire in the oven was intentionally kindled and only burned in its intended place, it was a friendly fire and recovery was precluded.

On appeal, we reexamined the *Austin* decision and aligned ourselves with the minority, reasoning as follows:

> "As has been stated, the rule originated with Austin v. Drew, 4 Campb. 360. However, a reading of that case will disclose that Lord Chief Justice Gibbs did not base the distinction between what is now

called a 'friendly' fire and a 'hostile' fire only on the locus or the place where the fire was burning. He stated in the opinion (4 Campb. 361):

> "'* * * There was no more fire than always exists * * * which [the fire] continued all the time to burn without any excess. * * *
>
> * * *
>
> "'* * * Had the fire been brought out of the flue, and any thing had been burnt, the Company would have been liable. But can this be said, where the fire never was at all excessive, and was always confined within its proper limits? '

> The rule as stated in the texts above cited and in the decided cases ignores entirely these references to the nature of the fire in question, that it continued 'to burn without any excess' and 'never was at all excessive.' The excessiveness of the fire, however great and destructive it might be if confined to the place where it was intended to be, has been considered immaterial in determining whether a fire was 'friendly' or 'hostile.' Although the result we are reaching is contrary to the great majority of decided cases, there is a respectable minority supporting it." 257 Minn. at 248, 100 N.W.2d at 755.

Under the *Freeberg* case, a fire may be found to be hostile although it was intentionally kindled and never escaped its confines if it was excessive or uncontrolled. * * *

In the case before us defendant argues that even under the minority rule it should not be held liable because the fire was in no way excessive. In support of this contention, defendant points to the stipulated facts which state:

> "The fire inside the furnace burned and produced heat at its usual rate."

Defendant reasons that if the furnace burned only at its usual rate it could not possibly be excessive. We disagree. A fire which causes damage by burning for a greater length of time than intended is no less uncontrolled merely because it continues to burn at its usual rate. See, generally, Morrison, Concerning Friendly Fires, 3 Boston C.Indus. & Com.L.Rev. 15.

Returning to the facts before us, the malfunctioning thermostat caused the furnace to burn continuously until the temperature reached 120°—well beyond the pre-set temperature of 75°. We do not believe that under these circumstances this fire can be described as controlled. It burned for an excessive period of time resulting in temperatures much greater than those intended, causing the loss complained of. By characterizing this fire as hostile we are in no way departing from our prior decisions. We merely hold that a fire may be hostile although burning at its usual rate if it burns substantially longer or in some fashion other than expected. For the above reasons, we affirm the decision of the trial court.

Affirmed.

### *Questions*

1. In Schulze and Burch Biscuit Co. v. American Protection Insurance Co., 96 Ill.App.3d 350, 51 Ill.Dec. 823, 421 N.E.2d 331 (1981) a bakery oven was left on during a shift change without any contents to dissipate the heat. The temperature rose from the normal 450° to 1600° causing nearly $150,000 damage to the oven. The court rejected the hostile/friendly dichotomy and allowed recovery using the ambiguity approach, the adhesion approach, as well as the doctrine of reasonable expectations. It suggested that the implied exclusion could be easily made express. Assuming an inclination to permit the insured to recover, is this technique as justifiable as the one used in the principal case? Are fire insurers in a position to insert express exclusions in statutorily mandated policies as casually as suggested in *Schulze and Burch Biscuit?*

2. Another question: Should the standard fire policy cover the loss of the dinner turkey burned because the cook inadvertently set the thermostat too high?

### *Notes*

*Implied Exception—Destruction of Property by Co-insured.*

1. This is an implied exception which seems to be breaking down. An initial step in this process was to hold that when the interests of the co-insureds were several rather than joint—e.g., partnerships or tenants in common, the destruction of the property by one would not void the policy as to the interest of the others. Hoyt v. New Hampshire Fire Insurance Co., 92 N.H. 242, 29 A.2d 121, 148 A.L.R. 484 (1942). This still leaves the situation where the interests of the co-insureds are joint—particularly when they are spouses. Here, too there are recent cases refusing to imply the exception. See, McCracken v. Government Employees Ins. Co., 284 S.C. 66, 325 S.E.2d 62 (1985) and American Economy Insurance Co. v. Liggett, 426 N.E.2d 136 (Ind.App.1981). (Co-insured wife recovers full amount of property insurance when her husband, who died in the fire, committed arson.) The latter court sets forth the wording of a possible express exclusion.

Comment: If the implied exclusion is contrary to public policy it would seem to follow that an express exclusion would also be so. Cf. the arguments of a similar nature in accident cases—e.g., *Wetzel v. Westinghouse Corp.* post at Chapter 9, section D.

2. What if one spouse intentionally destroys insured community property in a community property state? Is the innocent spouse protected? The answer is not at the moment absolutely certain. In Kulubis v. Texas Farm Bureau Underwriters Ins. Co., 706 S.W.2d 953 (Tex.1986) the court overruled previous decisions to now permit the innocent coinsured of property *jointly held* to be protected, but added: "Texas courts are faced with an additional problem because we are a community property state * * *. We are not to be understood as holding that an innocent spouse is barred from recovering under an insurance policy covering community property. We do

not have that fact situation before us and therefore do not address the problem of how to compensate the innocent spouse and yet not permit benefit to the wrongdoing spouse. That problem will be addressed when and if presented to us." In Norman v. State Farm Fire & Cas. Co., 804 F.2d 1365 (5th Cir.1986) the question was presented in federal court, and, while agreeing that it was not the "custodian of Texas's community property law" and that possibly legislative or even judicial initiatives could remove the obvious incentive to fraud, the federal court could not countenance a result that would do so in the circumstances presented.

## D. THAT INSURED HAS BREACHED CONDITIONS OF POLICY

**___ warranties and similar conditions (to be distinguished from coverage conditions if possible)**

### INTRODUCTORY NOTE

*No Coverage vs. Breach of Warranty*

There is a sharp difference between the insurer's defenses that there is no contract (because a condition precedent, such as payment of the premium, has not been met) or that there is no coverage (because the condition precedent that the event insured against simply never happened) and the defense that an express term of the policy itself—e.g., a warranty made by the insured—has been broken.

The defense of "no contract" or "no coverage" once established is abruptly terminal to the insured's claim and virtually impregnable as indicated by the repeated insistence (in most cases anyway) that there can be no estoppel into coverage.

The consequences of a breach of warranty, as originally inflicted, were hardly less drastic. Vance on Insurance, 4th ed. 1952 § 71, includes the consequences of breach in his definition of "warranty" itself:

> "A warranty is a statement or promise set forth in the policy * * * the untruth or unfulfillment of which in any respect and without reference to whether the insurer was in fact prejudiced by such untruth or unfulfillment, renders the policy voidable by the insurer wholly irrespective of the materiality of such statement." [47]

An implacable rule voiding purchased insurance protection for trivial or inconsequential breaches invites its own destruction. As will be seen, the effect of warranty breaches have been much softened by judicial interpretation, by moderating statutes, and by a liberal application of waiver or estoppel principles.

**47.** Cf. the California statutory definition of a warranty. § 441 Calif.Ins.Code. "A statement in a policy of a matter relating to the person or thing insured or to the risk, as a fact, is an express warranty." § 445, "A statement in a policy which imports that there is an intention to do or not to do a thing which materially affects the risk, is a warranty that such act or omission will take place."

The problem thus becomes the usual one of categorization. Is the policy provision on which the company's defense rests a fatal "coverage" provision or the less terminal, though still dangerous, "warranty"? The problem is enhanced because of the prevalent use of the word "condition" in insurance policies. What, for instance, is suggested by the phrase "Conditions Restricting Insurance"? Or the frequent couplet "Warranties and other conditions"?

Probably intelligent laymen, who have not been exposed to a law school course in Contracts where the topic of "Conditions" is dissected at chapter length, would understand, and be comfortable with, the label "precedent condition" applied to coverage and the description "subsequent conditions" applied to warranties (and "similar conditions", to overburden the word still further) written into a contract with the understanding that a breach may bar the insured's accrued claims. Accrued, that is, in the sense that at this point the insured has proven a binding policy covering a loss which has in fact occurred. Naturally the insurer should carry the burden of proving the breach.

*An Academic Analysis*

Legally trained persons, however, are aware that texts on the Law of Contract confine the notion and scope of "conditions subsequent" to a small area. (See, e.g., Corbin on Contracts, § 739ff.) The argument is that virtually all conditions—including warranties—must be satisfied, *before* the insured may recover on his policy. Hence, warranties are "conditions precedent", which must be distinguished from "conditions precedent to coverage" in some other fashion than by label.

Prof. Edwin Patterson, late professor of law at Columbia University, and an eminent authority on Contracts, Restitution and Insurance undertook in his influential book, Essentials of Insurance Law (2d ed. 1957), § 60, to make the distinction in this fashion: "the difference between warranty conditions and other conditions is that the former relate to *potential causes* of the insured event." Thus the condition precedent that the loss be "caused by windstorm" applies to the *actual cause* of loss and is therefore a coverage clause; whereas warranties such as that the premises are protected by an automatic sprinkler system, or that the ship is "copper clad" are conditions (precedent likewise) dealing only with *potential* rather than the actual causes of loss.

Since Prof. Patterson was at one time Deputy Superintendent of Insurance of New York his concepts as to coverage clauses (relating to *actual* cause of loss) versus other conditional clauses, such as warranties (relating to *potential* causes of loss) were embodied in the unique New York statutory definition of a warranty:

*Insurance Law § 3106*

(a) In this section "warranty" means any provision of an insurance contract which has the effect of requiring, as a condition precedent of the taking effect of such contract or as a condition precedent of the insurer's liability thereunder, the existence of a fact which tends to diminish, or the non-existence of a fact which tends to increase, the risk of the occurrence of any loss, damage, or injury within the coverage of the contract. The term "occurrence of loss, damage, or injury" includes the occurrence of death, disability, injury, or any other contingency insured against, and the term "risk" includes both physical and moral hazards.

### *Question*

Which definition of a "warranty"—Vance's, the California statutory, or the New York statutory would be easiest to explain to an applicant for insurance?

## VIOLIN v. FIREMAN'S FUND INSURANCE COMPANY

Supreme Court of Nevada, 1965.
81 Nev. 456, 406 P.2d 287.

THOMPSON, JUSTICE:

This is an action by the insureds on a policy of insurance covering a Guadagnini violin of the agreed value of $10,000. Following loss of the violin, the insurer Fireman's Fund Insurance Company canceled the policy, tendered return of the premium paid and denied liability on the ground that the insured had made a fraudulent, material misrepresentation in their application for insurance. The lower court ruled in favor of the insurer, and this appeal by the insureds followed. The sole question is whether, on the facts here disclosed, the insurer waived its right to cancel the policy or is estopped to deny liability. We have concluded that factors favoring the application of the doctrine of waiver against the insurer are here present, thus precluding avoidance of liability. Accordingly, we reverse.

The question asked on the application for insurance with which we are concerned was, "Has any company ever refused or canceled insurance?"[1] The applicants answered, "No." The answer was false. Four years earlier the same insurer, Fireman's Fund, had canceled a policy which it had issued to the same insureds covering musical instruments. The lower court found that this misrepresentation was material to the risk against which the applicants sought coverage and was not innocently made. Notwithstanding this fact the insureds insist that the insurer may not avoid liability as it was chargeable with knowledge of the prior cancellation because of information in its own records and chose to write the present policy anyway.

1. It is, of course, true that one has an obligation not to speak falsely when inducing another to make a bargain. This worthy rule is recognized both by statute and case law in Nevada. NRS 686.190: Poe v. La Metropolitana Compania Nacional De Seguros, S.A., Havana, Cuba, 76 Nev. 306, 353 P.2d 454 (1960); Smith v. North American Ins. Co., 46

1. The question is poorly phrased. However, it was not contended below, or here, that its meaning is obscure and the applicants misled.

Nev. 30, 205 P. 801 (1922). Thus, absent factors favoring the application of the doctrines of waiver or estoppel, an insurer is not bound by an insurance contract that he was induced to make by the fraudulent misrepresentations of the insured. The application for insurance in the instant matter contained the following language, "Signing this form does not bind the Proposer or the Company to complete the insurance, but it is agreed that this form shall be the basis of the contract, should the policy be issued. If any of the above questions have been answered falsely or fraudulently the entire insurance shall be null and void and all claims thereunder shall be forfeited." Cf. Poe v. La Metropolitana Compania Nacional De Seguros, S.A., Havana, Cuba, supra, where similar language was used in the application for insurance and noted by this court in affirming a judgment for the insurer. Relying upon the quoted clause of the application for insurance, the claims superintendent of Fireman's Fund, after notice of loss, advised the insureds that the application was incorrectly filled out "resulting in a non-disclosure of information material to our acceptance of the risk," rescinded the policy and tendered return of the premium paid.

The application for insurance was not made a part of the insurance contract by incorporation by reference, i.e., a statement in the policy that the application is made a part of the policy, Phoenix Mutual Life Insurance Co. v. Raddin, 120 U.S. 183, 7 S.Ct. 500, 30 L.Ed. 644 (1887), or by endorsement on the policy itself. Smith v. North American Insurance Co., supra; cf. Universal Underwriters v. Snyder, 81 Nev. ___, 402 P.2d 483 (1965). Thus the answers in the application did not become warranties or conditions, but are representations collateral to the contract of insurance. The distinction between a warranty and a representation is sometimes of controlling significance in insurance litigation * * *. In general terms a warranty in insurance law is a term of the insurance contract which does not create an obligation on the part of the warrantor, but which creates a condition of the insurer's duty to pay the loss. The traditional view is that a warranty must be strictly complied with and, once a breach of warranty has occurred, the insurer may avoid the policy. The ancient Nevada case of Healey v. Imperial Fire Insurance Company, 5 Nev. 268 (1869), is an example of the traditional, orthodox view. On the other hand, a representation is not a term of the insurance contract and, though it may also, if false, and material to the risk, supply the basis for a rescission of the insurance contract by the insurer, courts tend to be less strict in their treatment of a representation than is the case when a warranty is involved. Here the insurer's rescission rests solely upon a false representation by the applicants which was collateral to the contract of insurance, though perhaps an inducement to its issuance, and not upon any claim that a term of the insurance contract was breached.[2] With these preliminary

2. The distinction between a warranty and a representation disposes of an alternative argument offered by the insurer on this appeal. The insurer seeks to sustain the judgment in its favor by the "non-waiver" provision of the insurance contract. That provision denies power to an agent or representative of the insurer to waive any condi-

observations in mind we turn to discuss the question presented by this appeal.

2. The insureds do not challenge the finding below, that they fraudulently misrepresented a fact material to the risk when applying for coverage. However, they do contend that the insurer may not rely upon that misrepresentation to avoid liability, for it had in its possession full information about the prior cancellation, and elected to issue the present policy in spite of such knowledge.

The insurer's claims department, Los Angeles office, did have a record of the prior loss and subsequent cancellation. However, no agent of that department of the insurance company was in any way connected with the solicitation or issuance of the present policy, and neither the insurer's application-taking agent nor its policy-writing agent was aware that the applicants had misrepresented a material fact in requesting coverage. It is also apparent that, because of the expense, volume and complexity of its business, the insurer in this and related situations believed itself free to rely upon the representations of fact contained in an application for insurance, and had not instituted a program for communicating information in the files of the claims department to those in the production end of the business. Pointing primarily to these circumstances the insurance company argues that it would be improper to invoke the doctrines of waiver or estoppel against it and authorize a policy liability, for we would be rewarding claimants who are not in court with clean hands.

This argument is not without persuasion. Yet it finds only meager support in case law. See Rhode v. Metropolitan Life Ins. Co., 129 Mich. 112, 88 N.W. 400 (1901); Great Northern Life Ins. Co. v. Vince, 118 F.2d 232 (6th Cir.1941), which stand for the principle that earlier records do not necessarily put the company on notice unless there is some circumstances to direct its attention to them. See also Schrader v. Prudential Ins. Co., 280 F.2d 355 (5th Cir.1960), dealing with group insurance. The overwhelming body of authority favors the insured and holds that the insurer, as a matter of law, is chargeable with knowledge of the misrepresentation, because of full information about it present in its own files. The rationale employed is not always clear. Some courts speak in terms of waiver. Others invoke estoppel. On occasion both doctrines are used interchangeably and without differentiation. Whatever the theory, a fact of overriding significance exists in every case—the insurer's ability to promptly discover the misrepresentation after the loss has occurred. We prefer that diligence to be exercised at an earlier time—when the application for insurance is taken. The Rhode Island Court in O'Rourke v. John Hancock Mutual Life Ins. Co., 23 R.I. 457, 50 A. 834, 57 L.R.A. 496, expressed the same view in the following words, "The defendant argues that it is unreasonable to hold that a company is bound to have present knowledge of all that appears on its previous files. To this

tion or provision of the policy. As the representation here involved is not a term of the policy, the non-waiver clause is inapplicable.

suggestion at the trial the judge asked the pertinent question: 'Any more so than it was to ascertain that fact just after the boy died? They have taken the money. Now, just as soon as the boy died, and the beneficiary asks to be paid, then their records are looked up; then they saved the record.' The company had exactly the same information in its possession at the time the contract was made that it has now. If it is available at one time, it ought to be imputable at the other."

We agree that in these peculiar circumstances the insurer, as a matter of law, is chargeable with actual knowledge of the misrepresentation and may not avoid liability. Our conclusion rests upon waiver. In the law of insurance waiver is defined as the giving up of a known privilege or power. It may be express or implied from circumstances and always involves consent, express or implied, but does not necessarily rise to the level of contract. Specifically we hold that the insurer waived its power to rescind the insurance contract by issuing the policy with knowledge that the insureds had fraudulently misrepresented a material fact in their application for insurance.

The judgment below is reversed, with direction to enter judgment in favor of the appellants and against the respondent for $10,000 with interest from July 24, 1961, until paid, and taxable costs below and here.

ZENOFF, DISTRICT JUDGE (dissenting):

I respectfully dissent. There should not be a reward for a knowing and wilful misrepresentation * * *. "[T]he insured should observe the utmost good faith and deal honestly and fairly with the company in respect to all material facts inquired about, and as to which he had or should be presumed to have had knowledge, and make a full, direct, and honest answer, without evasion or fraud, and without suppression, misrepresentation, or concealment of material facts which the parties themselves deemed material to be disclosed."

* * *

In the case before this court, the information deemed by the majority to be knowledge to the insurer are facts from an inactive file. A distinction should be made between files used periodically by an insurer to record premiums paid, changes in beneficiaries and addresses, and renewals, and files containing records of rejections for coverage, claims from former policies, and cancellations.

It appears from the evidence that all current policies are on file at the head office and that inactive files are destroyed according to a specified company policy. The evidence also shows that destruction of records in various branch offices, while subject to the same policy, is not coordinated with the destruction at the head office due to different storage facilities. It seems inequitable to hold an insurance company to knowledge of what is contained in the files of one isolated outpost. Since all active files are maintained at the head office, it seems that the only workable rule is to hold an insurer cognizant of the active files.

* * * In the present case the loss of the violin occurred slightly more than two months after issuance of the policy. The trial court here found that the company did not have knowledge of the prior experience with the insured at the time of the issuance of the policy, and since there was such a short period between issuance of the policy and the loss, and only one premium had been paid, there is not sufficient evidence in the record to have alerted the insurer to search its dead files to upset the determination of the trial judge that the company should be held to be without knowledge, actual or presumed.

* * *

This was not a case where the agent of the company who had written the first policy also wrote the second. Nor was this a situation where there was another evidence file with the company that would cause it to be aware on a periodic basis that something unusual existed between the insured and the company. Nor am I satisfied that the language of the application and the policy did not sufficiently refer to each other so as to make the false inducement a part of the policy itself. And since NRS 686.190 requires that applications be attached to policies only in the life insurance and health and accident insurance classifications in order for the insured to be bound by the written statements in the application, it is clear that actual attachment of the application is not necessary in this instance. See NRS 681.030(3)(c) for the separate classification of personal property floaters. The application form itself referred to the policy and provided that, " * * * this form shall be the basis of the contract should policy be issued. If any of the above questions have been answered falsely or fraudulently the entire insurance shall be null and void and all claims thereunder shall be forfeited."

The policy as issued contained the following condition: "1. Misrepresentation and Fraud. This policy shall be void if the assured has concealed or misrepresented any material fact or circumstances concerning this insurance or the subject thereof or in case of any fraud, attempted fraud or false swearing by the assured touching any matter relating to this insurance or the subject thereof, whether before or after a loss. 'THIS POLICY IS MADE AND ACCEPTED SUBJECT TO THE FOREGOING STIPULATIONS AND CONDITIONS AND TO THE CONDITIONS PRINTED IN THE BACK HEREOF, WHICH ARE HEREBY ESPECIALLY REFERRED TO AND MADE A PART OF THIS POLICY, together with such other provisions, agreements or conditions as may be endorsed hereon or added hereto, and no officer, agent or other representative of this company shall have power to waive or be deemed to have waived any provision or condition of this policy unless such waiver, if any, shall be written upon or attached hereto, nor shall any privilege or permission affecting the insurance under this policy exist or be claimed by the assured unless so written or attached.' " (Emphasis added.)

While there is a split of authority in the state courts as to the validity of non-waiver agreements, many state courts and the Federal courts hold that these agreements are a valid limitation to the policy.

Healey v. Imperial Fire Ins. Co., 5 Nev. 268, 5–6–7 Nev. 215, seems to lend support to strictly enforcing these provisions. "There is but one safe rule, and that is to take the contract as written, subtracting nothing therefrom, adding nothing thereto. * * * The court is to enforce contracts which the parties have made, but has no power to make new contracts for them, or to alter or vary in any essential particular, those they have mutually agreed to be bound by." Id. at 220–221. Therefore, since there was no waiver written upon or attached to the policy, the insurer should not be deemed to have waived the condition requiring forfeiture for misrepresentations. * * *

### *Note*

For the cynic who notes the coincidence of the name of the insured and the subject matter of the case, Mischa Violin was a concert violinist and conductor of world renown. He made his professional debut at age 12 with the Berlin Philharmonic and he had concert appearances with many symphony orchestras throughout the world during his career. *Music and Dance in California and the West* (Drake–Williams 1948, Richard Drake Saunders ed.)

## REID v. HARDWARE MUTUAL INSURANCE CO. OF THE CAROLINAS

Supreme Court of South Carolina, 1969.
252 S.C. 339, 166 S.E.2d 317.

MOSS, CHIEF JUSTICE.

Hardware Mutual Insurance Company of the Carolinas, Inc., the appellant herein, on May 22, 1964, issued a fire insurance policy to Zelphia H. Reid and W.C. Reid, in the amount of $5,000.00, insuring against loss or damage by fire, for a five year period, a one story frame dwelling located in Conestee, South Carolina, owned by Zelphia H. Reid, the respondent herein, with a mortgagee clause payable to the Peoples National Bank of Greenville, South Carolina, as trustee for the Pickens Mill Profit Sharing Fund, which held a first mortgage on the lot on which the insured dwelling was located. The building insured was described in the policy as being one story frame constructed, approved roof, owner occupied, one family dwelling. [The building was occupied by a tenant at the time of loss.] The appellant was notified of the loss of said dwelling by fire and demand for payment by the insureds under the aforesaid policy was made and such was refused.

* * *

The final question for determination is whether the designation, at the time the policy was issued, that the insured dwelling was "owner occupied" was a continuing warranty.

A warranty, in the law of insurance, is a statement, description, or undertaking on the part of the insured, appearing in the policy of insurance or in another instrument properly incorporated in the policy, relating contractually to the risk insured against. Generically, warranties are either affirmative or promissory. An affirmative warranty is one which asserts the existence of a fact at the time the policy is entered into, and appears on the face of said policy, or is attached thereto and made a part thereof. A promissory warranty may be defined to be an absolute undertaking by the insured, contained in a policy or in a paper properly incorporated by reference, that certain facts or conditions pertaining to the risk shall continue, or that certain things with reference thereto shall be done or omitted. 29 Am.Jur., Insurance, Sections 708 and 709. While it is generally recognized that a warranty may be "promissory" or "continuing", the tendency is to construe a statement in the past or present tense as constituting an affirmative rather than a continuing warranty. Thus, a description of a house in a policy of insurance, as "occupied by" the insured, is a description merely and is not an agreement that the insured should continue in the occupation of it. Joyce v. Maine Ins. Co., 45 Me. 168. O'Niel v. Buffalo Fire Ins. Co., 3 N.Y. 122. A statement in an insurance policy that the property is occupied by the insured as a dwelling for himself and family, is not a warranty that it shall continue to be so occupied but is only a warranty of the situation at the time the insurance is effected. German Ins. Co. v. Russell, 65 Kan. 373, 69 P. 345, 58 L.R.A. 234.

There is no provision in the policy contract that the dwelling would be "owner occupied" during the term of the insurance contract nor any requirement that if the premises are otherwise occupied than by the owner, notice of such change of occupancy or use would be given to the insurer.

The insurance contract here involved contained a description of the dwelling insured as being "owner occupied". This was an affirmative warranty, not a continuing warranty, by the respondent that the dwelling was so occupied by him at the time the contract of insurance was made. The appellant argues that a breach of the warranty as to occupancy at the time the contract of insurance was made would defeat a recovery by the respondent. Even though this question is argued in the brief it is not supported by an exception and raises no issue for determination by us.

Affirmed.

## VLASTOS v. SUMITOMO MARINE & FIRE INS. CO. (EUROPE), LTD.

United States Court of Appeals, Third Circuit, 1983.
707 F.2d 775.

ADAMS, CIRCUIT JUDGE.

Evelyn Vlastos appeals from a judgment denying her recovery on an insurance policy for a fire that occurred in a commercial building that she owned. Applying Pennsylvania law, the district court declared that Vlastos had unambiguously warranted that the third floor of her building was occupied exclusively as a janitor's residence. Based on this ruling by the court, the jury found that Vlastos had breached the warranty, and the court declined to set aside the jury verdict. Inasmuch as we hold that it was error to determine that the warranty clause in question is unambiguous, the order of the district court will be vacated and the case remanded for further proceedings.

Vlastos owned a 20′ × 80′ four-story building at 823 Pennsylvania Avenue, Pittsburgh, Pennsylvania. Prior to a fire on April 23, 1980, Vlastos and her son operated a luncheonette and a bar on the first floor of the building. The second and third floors were leased to Spartacus, Inc., which conducted a massage parlor on the second floor. Evidence was introduced at trial tending to show that the massage parlor also utilized at least a portion of the third floor. At the rear of the third floor there was a section variously described as a padlocked room or a section partitioned off from the remainder of the floor. It was in this area that Philip "Red" Pinkney, Vlastos' handyman and janitor, is alleged to have lived. Vlastos kept supplies on the fourth floor, and maintained a small office there as well. She occasionally remained overnight on the fourth floor rather than return to her residence. Vlastos was not staying there the night of the fire, but two friends of hers were residing there temporarily and were killed. A third person was also killed in the fire.

All of Vlastos' insurance matters were handled by her broker, John Mitchell. Mitchell obtained insurance for Vlastos from a group of European insurance companies through two sub-brokers. The policy in question, dated November 22, 1979, provided $345,000 of fire insurance with a $1,000 deductible provision. It contained a section, Endorsement No. 4, expressly incorporated into the policy, which stated in part: "Warranted that the 3rd floor is occupied as Janitor's residence."

After the building and its contents were destroyed by the fire, the insurers refused to pay the claim, citing an alleged breach of the warranty. * * * Vlastos has appealed, [from the adverse judgment], raising numerous points, including the contention that the jury was incorrectly instructed that the warranty was unambiguous.

Vlastos objects that "no proof was offered that the provision in Endorsement No. 4 actually was a warranty." Although her brief does not specify an alternate characterization of the provision, presumably she means to assert that it was a representation. If, as Vlastos implies, it was a representation, then the insurers would be under an obligation to show that the provision was material to the risk insured against in order for the insurers to avoid their obligations under the contract.

A representation, unlike a warranty, is not part of the insurance contract but is collateral to it. If a representation is not material to the risk, its falsity does not avoid the contract. On the other hand, the materiality of a warranty to the risk insured against is irrelevant; if the fact is not as warranted, the insurer may deny recovery. [Citations of

Pennsylvania cases.] In case of doubt, courts normally construe a statement in an insurance contract as a representation rather than a warranty. * * * But no reason has been advanced for doubting that the provision in question here—which by its terms "warrant[s]" a fact and is part of the insurance contract—is a warranty. Accordingly, we cannot hold that it was improper for the trial judge to read this provision as a warranty. The district court therefore did not err in ruling that evidence of materiality would not have been relevant to the question whether Vlastos can recover on the policy.

The parties agree that the provision in question concerned a state of affairs existing at the time the contract was signed, and was not a promise that a janitor *would* occupy the third floor in the future. In other words, the provision is satisfied if a janitor occupied the floor on Nov. 22, 1979, the date the policy was issued, even if the situation had changed by the time of the fire several months later.[1] The district court erroneously instructed the jury on this issue at two points. It stated that Vlastos agreed that the floor "*would be* occupied as a janitor's residence" * * * and that the warranty was breached if "*at the time of the fire* " a massage parlor occupied any significant portion of the floor. * * * If the district court on remand decides that the case must be retried * * *, then it should instruct the jury that the relevant time for purposes of the warranty is the time at which the parties entered into the contract.

Having established that Vlastos did warrant that at the time she entered into the contract "the 3rd floor [was] occupied as Janitor's residence," it must be determined what the language of the warranty should be construed to mean. * * *

* * *

Applying Pennsylvania law to the facts of this case, we conclude that the warranty here was ambiguous. Although the view of the insurance companies—that Vlastos stated that the floor was to be the janitor's exclusive province—is a possible construction, a reasonable person could have understood Vlastos to have warranted merely that her janitor lived on the third floor.

Even if one takes the warranty clause in isolation, it is questionable that the reading proffered by the insurance companies is the only plausible one. If Pinkney resided on the third floor, then it is not simply and unambiguously false to say that he occupied that floor, even assuming the existence of a significant competing or concurrent use. In response to the query "does a janitor occupy the third floor?" a categorical "no" surely would be misleading at best, and even a qualified "no" ("no, he occupies only part of it" or "no, a massage parlor occupies it as well") is strained. It seems that the most appropriate reply, making the

**1.** Thus there is no contention that this provision was a so-called "promissory warranty."

relevant factual assumptions, would be a qualified affirmative ("yes, although he occupies it along with a massage parlor").[3]

When the relevant language is examined in the context of the remainder of the policy, and in light of the alleged purposes for the insertion of the warranty, it becomes even more difficult to say that Vlastos unambiguously warranted that her janitor alone occupied the third floor.

It is significant that the warranty was not made in the course of a description of the various uses to which the building was being put. The policy did not make any warranties as to any other floors of the building. Thus, it would be reasonable to infer that the warranty evinced a concern that there be a resident janitor rather than an intent that the various floors of the building, such as the third floor, be put to relatively safe uses.

Although the actual reasons for the insertion of the warranty are not clear from the record, the insurers represented at trial that one reason was that a resident janitor decreases the risk of losses due to fire. * * * This purpose of the provision would be fulfilled if Pinkney lived on the third floor, regardless of the proportion of this floor that was reserved for his sole use. Occupancy of the premises by a janitor might increase the likelihood that fire hazards would be taken care of promptly. It also might mean that there is a good chance that if a fire were to begin a responsible person would be on the scene to put it out or call the fire department, thus minimizing the damage from fires that do occur. A full-time resident janitor might also deter prowlers and vandals from entering the building. For reasons such as these, Vlastos could have assumed that the insurance companies looked kindly upon her having a resident janitor, without understanding that the insurance companies had any interest in whether the janitor occupied all or only part of the floor.

It is true that a second reason has been proposed for the insertion of the warranty. If a janitor occupied all of the third floor, then no occupant more dangerous—as a massage parlor perhaps is—would be there. Viewed in light of this possible motive, the warranty would have been intended to contemplate the occupancy of the entire third floor. Although this suggestion as to the purpose of the warranty is plausible, it is less obvious than the first suggested reason, especially when it is recalled that the insurers did not request any assurance that extremely dangerous usages were absent from the other three floors of the building.

The conclusion that the warranty is ambiguous is buttressed by the consideration that the insurers easily could have precluded doubt by the addition of one word. Had the provision read: "Warranted that the 3rd Floor is occupied solely as Janitor's residence," then the question wheth-

3. Cf. 45 C.J.S. *Insurance* § 556 at 304 (1946) ("The mere fact that only one room in the house is actually used by the occupant does not render the building vacant or unoccupied.")

er there would be a breach if a massage parlor operated in some of the space would have been unlikely to arise. * * *

Because the provision is ambiguous, under Pennsylvania law it must be construed in a manner favorable to insurance coverage. We therefore hold that Vlastos warranted only that a janitor resided on the third floor, not that there was no other occupancy of the floor.

If any jury issue existed at all, it was simply whether or not a janitor resided on the third floor at the time of the contract. The district court at several points indicated that the insurers had presented no evidence that Pinkney did not live on the third floor, and that it would not let the insurers go to the jury on this question. On the other hand, the district court did instruct the jury that it could find "that nothing occupied the space at all * * *." * * *. There also is some uncertainty whether the district court, in considering the sufficiency of the evidence that Pinkney did not occupy the third floor, focused on the time of the fire as distinguished from the time that the parties entered into the contract. * * * Accordingly, on remand the district court should clarify whether, in its view, there was a jury question whether Pinkney lived on the third floor at the time the contract was made. If it determines that there was sufficient evidence to go to the jury on this issue, then a new trial on the liability issue should be held. If there is no jury question, then under the facts of this case a new trial would be unwarranted, and the district court should enter judgment for Vlastos on liability.

* * *

## AMERICAN HOME ASSURANCE CO. v. HARVEY'S WAGON WHEEL, INC.

United States District Court of Nevada 1975.
398 F.Supp. 379, (aff'd without opinion, 554 F.2d 1067).

BRUCE R. THOMPSON, DISTRICT JUDGE.

This is a consolidated action brought by two insurers * * * against defendant, Harvey's Wagon Wheel, Inc. (Harvey's) for a declaration that the insurers are not liable for a fire loss under the business interruption policies that were issued to defendant by plaintiffs. * * *

* * *

Both policies contained automatic sprinkler warranties which provided:

"AUTOMATIC SPRINKLER WARRANTY

"THIS POLICY BEING WRITTEN AT A REDUCED RATE BASED ON THE PROTECTION OF THE PREMISES BY AN AUTOMATIC SPRINKLER SYSTEM, IT IS A CONDITION OF THIS POLICY THAT SO FAR AS THE SPRINKLER SYSTEM AND THE WATER SUPPLY THEREFOR ARE UNDER THE CONTROL OF THE INSURED, DUE DILIGENCE SHALL BE USED

BY THE INSURED TO MAINTAIN THEM IN COMPLETE WORKING ORDER, AND THAT NO CHANGE SHALL BE MADE IN SAID SYSTEM OR IN THE WATER SUPPLY THEREFOR WITHOUT THE CONSENT IN WRITING OF THIS COMPANY." * * *

At the time the policies were issued, the restaurant and casino areas of Harvey's were equipped with operative automatic sprinkler systems. Prior to the issuance of the policies. Harvey's had begun to reconstruct the casino and restaurant areas. * * *

On May 15, 1973, the insured building was damaged by fire and Harvey's business was interrupted for more than sixty days. At the time of the fire, the sprinkler system in the casino was inoperative. The sprinkler system in the restaurant was operative. The casino was damaged by fire; the restaurant was not. * * *

It is a well established principle of insurance contract interpretation that if the language in a policy may be interpreted in two or more ways, it is to be construed in favor of the insured. Defendant attempts to use that principle to establish that the automatic sprinkler provisions are not warranties and therefore are not determinative of underlying coverage but rather are conditions concerned only with a reduced premium rate allowable for sprinklered building risks. Thus, defendant argues, its breach of the automatic sprinkler warranty should not affect coverage but should result only in an increase in the premium rate. * * *

Specifically, defendant argues that the phrases "written at a reduced rate based on the existence * * * of an automatic sprinkler system" and "due diligence shall be used by the insured to maintain them in complete working order" imply that the parties intended that there would always be coverage.

* * *

The instant automatic sprinkler warranty provides clearly and unequivocally that "no change shall be made in said system * * * without the consent in writing of this company." Since defendant shut off the water supply without obtaining written consent, defendant breached the warranty. See Buehler Corporation v. Home Insurance Company, 358 F.Supp. 15 (S.D.Ind.1973), aff'd, 495 F.2d 1211 (7th Cir.1974). There plaintiff's building was insured by a policy containing a provision essentially identical to the instant automatic sprinkler warranty. Because of a broken valve, the sprinkler system was shut off for a period of about four months. After a fire damaged the building, the insurers disclaimed liability. The Court held that since the plaintiff did not advise the Rating Bureau that the sprinkler system was shut off, it had violated a condition of the policy and could not recover from the insurer. * * *

It may be observed in a general way that in the area of insurance law, hardship cases produce exceptions to established contract principles. Sometimes there is plain evidence that the insurance company is taking unfair advantage of the insured by relying on technical provisions of the policy, the so-called "fine print." In such cases, the courts are naturally eager to find exceptions and doctrines of waiver and estoppel and the like are stretched to the outermost limits. This is not such a case. The automatic sprinkler endorsement was of the essence of the policy. It resulted in a premium rate approximately one-eighth the rate for non-sprinklered business premises. It was specifically bargained for by the insured and was discussed at about the time the policy was delivered. It was again called to the insured's attention when construction was underway. The unsprinklered areas were damaged by fire while the sprinklered areas were not. Law and equity require that the insurers be permitted the protection of the unambiguous policy warranty under these circumstances.

* * *

*It hereby is ordered* that judgment shall be entered in favor of plaintiffs and against defendant.

## A SAMPLING OF STATUTES WHICH LIMIT THE CONSEQUENCES OF BREACHES OF WARRANTY AND SIMILAR CONDITIONS

Mo.Ann.Stat.

**379.170. Construction of warranties of fact incorporated in policy**

The warranty of any fact or condition hereafter incorporated in or made a party of any fire, tornado or cyclone policy of insurance, purporting to be made or assented to by the assured which shall not materially affect the risk insured against, shall be deemed, taken and construed as representations only in all suits at law or in equity brought upon such policy in any of the courts of this state.

California Insurance Code

**§ 447. Violation of material warranty**

The violation of a material warranty or other material provision of a policy, on the part of either party thereto, entitles the other to rescind.

**§ 448. Breach of immaterial provision**

Unless the policy declares that a violation of specified provisions thereof shall avoid it, the breach of an immaterial provision does not avoid the policy.

Smith–Hurd Illinois Statutes, Chap. 215

**§ 5/154. Misrepresentations and false warranties**

No misrepresentation or false warranty made by the insured or in his behalf in the negotiation for a policy of insurance, or breach of a condition of such policy shall defeat or avoid the policy or prevent its attaching unless such misrepresentation, false warranty or condition shall have been stated in the policy or endorsement or rider attached thereto, or in the written application therefor, of which a copy is attached to or endorsed on the policy, and made a part thereof. No such misrepresentation or false warranty shall defeat or avoid the policy unless it shall have been made with actual intent to deceive or materially affects either the acceptance of the risk or the hazard assumed by the company. This section shall not apply to policies of marine or transportation insurance.

Massachusetts General Laws

**§ 186. Misrepresentations by insured; effect**

No oral or written misrepresentation or warranty made in the negotiation of a policy of insurance by the insured or in his behalf shall be deemed material or defeat or avoid the policy or prevent its attaching unless such misrepresentation or warranty is made with actual intent to deceive, or unless the matter misrepresented or made a warranty increased the risk of loss.

New York Insurance Law § 3106

(b) A breach of warranty shall not avoid an insurance contract or defeat recovery thereunder unless such breach materially increases the risk of loss, damage or injury within the coverage of the contract. If the insurance contract specified two or more distinct kinds of loss, damage or injury which are within its coverage, a breach of warranty shall not avoid such contract or defeat recovery thereunder with respect to any kind or kinds of loss, damage or injury other than the kind or kinds to which such warranty relates and the risk of which is materially increased by the breach of such warranty.

(c) This section shall not affect the express or implied warranties under a contract of marine insurance in respect to, appertaining to or in connection with any and all risks or perils of navigation, transit, or transportation, including war risks, on, over or under any seas or inland waters, nor shall it affect any provision in an insurance contract requiring notice, proof or other conduct of the insured after the occurrence of loss, damage or injury.

Michigan Compiled Laws Annotated

**500.2836. Losses**

Sec. 2836. (1) An insurer shall not base a defense under the terms of a fire insurance policy permitted to be used in this state, upon a breach of warranty or condition occurring before loss, unless the breach exists at the time of the loss or contributes to the loss or to the amount of the loss.

Iowa Code Annotated

**515.101 Invalidating stipulations—avoidance**

Any condition or stipulation in an application, policy, or contract of insurance, making the policy void before the loss occurs, shall not prevent recovery thereon by the insured, if it shall be shown by the plaintiff that the failure to observe such provision or the violation thereof did not contribute to the loss.

Nebraska Revised Statutes (1943)

44.358. **Policy provisions; misrepresentations; warranties; conditions; effect.** No oral or written misrepresentation or warranty made in the negotiation for a contract or policy of insurance by the insured, or in his behalf, shall be deemed material or defeat or avoid the policy, or prevent its attaching, unless such misrepresentation or warranty deceived the company to its injury. The breach of a warranty or condition in any contract or policy of insurance shall not avoid the policy nor avail the insurer to avoid liability, unless such breach shall exist at the time of the loss and contribute to the loss, anything in the policy or contract of insurance to the contrary notwithstanding.

## Note

*Word Play—Disguising Warranties as "Conditions Precedent."* Sometimes this ploy has had the desired effect; sometimes not.

A leading case is Fidelity–Phenix Fire Insurance Co. v. Pilot Freight Carriers, 193 F.2d 812, 31 A.L.R.2d 829 (4th Cir.1952), wherein the insured sought recovery on a theft policy when a truck containing 630 cartons of cigarettes was hi-jacked while the driver was having coffee. The insurer defended on grounds that the truck was left unattended without the alarm system on. The policy contained six paragraphs concerning the installation, maintenance, and use of anti-theft devices comprising the Babaco Alarm System. Two of the paragraphs started with the words: "It is a condition precedent to the liability of the insurer * * *" Others began with the phrase, "It is further warranted * * *"

> Paragraph 5 was one of the others: "It is further warranted by the Assured that the Babaco Alarm System on the cargo compartment of each trailer and the 'Parker' device on each trailer will be in the 'on' position when such vehicles are parked unattended * * *"
>
> Paragraph 6 stated: "The assured agrees, by acceptance of this policy, that the foregoing conditions precedent relate to matters material to the risk by the Insurer. Failure of the insured to comply with any of the foregoing conditions precedent in any instance shall render policy null and void as respects theft coverage for vehicles."

The insured asserted that paragraph 5 was a warranty and that a mere breach of warranty did not void the policy.

The court after noting the intertwining use of the expressions "condition precedent" and "warranties" concluded that they both involved a forfeiture and meant the same thing—in short the term "condition precedent" was here used as the equivalent of a "warranty."

Ironically, the plaintiff lost anyway because the court held the breach of warranty to have been material. At least the insured came closer to recovery than did the plaintiff in Blue Ridge Textile Co. v. Travelers Indemnity Co., 407 Pa. 463, 181 A.2d 295 (1962), where a similar Babaco alarm provision was held really to be a condition precedent to coverage rather than a warranty.

On the other hand, the "condition precedent" technique was successful in the Massachusetts case of Charles, Henry & Crowley Co. v. Home Insurance Co., 349 Mass. 723, 212 N.E.2d 240 (1965). In its proposal form for a "Jewelers' Block Policy" against theft, the plaintiff represented that the maximum value of the jewelry displayed in the windows during business hours "would not exceed $14,500 where the window or case was protected by swinging shatterproof glass, and $500 where the window or case was not protected." The policy itself provided: "It is a condition precedent to any recovery hereunder that the values of property displayed will not exceed the amount represented in * * * the Proposal forms attached to this policy." Thieves broke a window and stole $13,620 worth of jewelry at a time when $18,512 was displayed in the protected window and $1,118.40 in the unprotected one. The appellate court reversed a lower court holding which had allowed plaintiff to invoke the mitigating Massachusetts statute relating to representations and warranties. Said the court, "A statement made in an application for a policy of insurance may become a condition of the policy rather than remain a warranty or representation if: (1) the statement made by the insured relates essentially to the insurers' intelligent decision to issue the policy: and (2) the statement is made a condition precedent to recovery under the policy, either by using the precise words 'condition precedent' or their equivalent."

### *Problem*

A law firm has a policy with the following endorsement:

> "4. Protection of Valuable Papers and Records. Insurance under this policy shall apply only while valuable papers and records are contained in the premises described above, it being a condition precedent to any right of recovery that such valuable papers and record be kept in [steel cabinets] at all times when the premises are not open for business except when such valuable papers and records are in actual use."

A partner in the firm left the files on a class action bad faith insurance case (against insurers of the manufacturer of a defective drug) on his desk late Saturday night expecting to resume work on Sunday morning. A fire occurred in the firm's office at 2 a.m. Sunday morning destroying the papers. Does the insurance cover this loss? Cf. American Indemnity Co. v. Lancer, Vandroff and Sudakoff, 452 So.2d 594 (Fla.App.1984).

## AN EXERCISE IN ANALYSIS

*Cheaper Auto Insurance in Lower Risk Areas—The problems of draughtsmenship. Coverage provisions? Warranty–Conditions? Representations?*

There is no question that the insurance industry is willing to accommodate owners whose vehicles are largely operated in areas where the accident experience is low by lowering their rates. The obvious problem is to be sure that the vehicles are indeed operating within the prescribed zone, usually defined with reference to the "place of garaging," without making the policies unmarketable or unacceptable to regulatory authority.

There follows a sampling of various forms of "place of garaging" provisions. In each case it is conceded that the cost of the insurance would have been appreciably higher without the provision. This sample affords an opportunity to review the various clauses by which insurers control their risks. In each item the policy provision is set forth with the description title used in the case, followed by an abbreviated statement of facts. The exercise is to categorize the provision—as a coverage provision, warranty-condition or representation, then to determine whether the insured should be paid—taking into consideration the common law and statutory constraints applicable to the type of provision it is determined actually to be. Additional factors entering into the analysis might include whether the vehicle was a commercial or private car, and whether the claim was for damage to the insured vehicle or for liability against the owner or driver. (The citations with an indication of the holding—sometimes surprising—are given at the end).

1. Declaration: "The vehicle will be principally garaged in the above town [Puenta, California], county and state unless otherwise specified herein."

Insured's family moved to Oklahoma, where son was involved in an accident.

2. Warranty: "The automobile described herein will be principally used and garaged at Bakersfield Kern County California."

Within 8 hours after policy became effective, insured had an accident. The record disclosed that the car was continuously used and garaged in Los Angeles where rates were higher.

3. Geographical limitation endorsement: " * * * insurance applies only while the respective vehicles are operated within radius indicated for each vehicle [here 400 miles]. It is further agreed that the radius is measured from the garage location indicated on this endorsement [Boston, Georgia] * * * and that no vehicle is covered if operated beyond its radius * * * It is expressly understood that occasional trips beyond the radius specified are not permitted."

An accident involving the insured commercial truck occurred on the last leg of a 2000 mile round trip from Boston, Ga. to Huntspoint, N.Y. and at a point only 15 miles from Boston, Ga.

4. Commercial radius endorsement: " * * * it is agreed that the automobile described in the policy will be used and operated entirely within a radius of 500 miles of the place where such automobiles are principally garaged."

Also: "The company shall not be liable for, nor will it pay any loss occurring while the automobiles * * * are being operated outside the radius of 500 miles."

The accident occurred on a trip beyond radius, but at a point on the return portion within the radius.

5. Endorsement: " * * * it is agreed that the automobile described * * * will be operated and used within 50 miles from the place of garaging, and it is further understood and agreed that no coverage is provided * * * if such equipment is proceeding to or returning from a point beyond 50 miles from Philadelphia, Penn. regardless of where such piece of equipment may be involved in an accident."

No additional facts.

6. Limitation of use endorsement: [on policy issued to a trucking concern]. " * * * it is represented by the insured that no regular or

frequent trips of commercial vehicles described in Policy are, or will be, made beyond a (______) radius from the limits of city or town [Exira, Iowa] of principal garaging of such vehicle."

Varying radius limits were fixed on different vehicles. The radius limitations on the one demolished was 150 miles and it was wrecked in Memphis, Tenn. over 500 miles from Exira, Iowa. Of 53 trips made by this vehicle, 9 had been beyond the radius (including some to Canada). Overall 400 trips had been made by the covered fleet of vehicles and 27 of these exceeded the radius limitation.

7. Endorsement: "The cotton pickers insured under this policy are limited to custom farming within a radius of 50 miles from the principal place of garagement."

Insured was engaged in custom farming 150 miles from place of garaging when machines were damaged by fire.

8. Condition defining coverage: "Commercial truck excluding regular or frequent use beyond 100 miles from principal place of garaging (Boswell, Indiana) or into the City of Chicago."

Truck operated on a regular basis more than 100 miles from Boswell and the accident occurred outside the radius.

9. Exclusion clause in liability policy limits coverage of tractor-trailer to within 150 miles radius of McCrory, Ark. where vehicle is garaged. Plaintiff was injured by insured in Mississippi outside of 150 mile limit.

*What the courts seem to have held:*

1. Treated as a warranty, but insured recovered under the protection of Calif. Insurance Code Sections 447, 448. "Besides the policy contained no provision that the car insured was covered only when located and garaged at the place designated in the declaration." Republic Indemnity Co. v. Martin, 222 F.2d 438 (10th Cir.1955).

2. For the insurer; a breach of warranty. Purcell v. Pacific Automobile Insurance Co., 19 Cal.App.2d 230, 64 P.2d 1114 (1937).

3. For the insured. Coverage was suspended during the time the vehicle was outside the perimeter. Insurance reattached to cover the incident within the geographical area. (Query: Would it make better sense for the insured to limit the mileage per trip rather than within a geographical circle? The court suggests a trip of virtually unlimited length could be accomplished within the circle). Canal Insurance Co. v. Baldree, 489 F.2d 1393 (5th Cir.1974).

4. For insurer. "* * * a promissory warranty on part of plaintiff which when violated by him in sending his vehicle on a trip to Miami, Florida, beyond that radius, entitled defendant to declare the policy, for purposes of that trip, or operation, in its entirety void." Wallace v. Virginia Surety Co., 80 Ga.App. 50, 55 S.E.2d 259 (1949).

5. For insured. A coverage provision, but not in fact broken. (Where is 50 miles from Philadelphia anyway?) Exchange Insurance Association v. Miller, 249 F.2d 530 (3d Cir.1957). cf. Person v. Tyson, 215 N.C. 127, 1 S.E.2d 367 (1939).

6. For insurer; a warranty which was breached. No citation was made to Iowa Code § 515.101, although the insured claimed recovery could not be prevented unless it is shown that a violation of the condition contributed to the loss. The court said, "the correct statement of the mile is that a breach of condition must be shown to have contributed to the loss or in fact made the risk more hazardous (citing Iowa case). There can be no doubt that Haley's breach * * * increased the risk for the company." Commercial Standard Insurance Co. v. Haley, 282 F.Supp. 16 (S.D.Iowa 1968).

7. For insured. "This endorsement is no more than an agreement. It is not a limitation of coverage or a warranty." Texas Farm Bureau Mutual Insurance Co. v. Carnes, 416 S.W.2d 863 (Tex.Civ.App.1967).

8. Summary judgment for insurer. "The provision clearly excludes coverage" Carlile v. United Farm Bureau Mutual Insurance Co., 419 N.E.2d 1021 (Ind.1981).

9. For the injured party in a garnishment action against insurer. The "exclusion" was void as against the public policy of Arkansas since it did not cover the entire state, and therefore some injured Arkansas victims might not be protected whereas others would. An exclusion void under Arkansas law would not be given effect by Mississippi courts. Nichols v. Anderson, 788 F.2d 1140 (5th Cir.1986). Query: would the exclusion be void as to 1st party property damage coverage?

## E. THAT INSURED HAS BREACHED CONDITIONS OF THE POLICY

**___ reporting conditions**

**___ common policy conditions suspending coverage**

- **___ increase of the hazard**
- **___ vacancy or unoccupancy**
- **___ other insurance**

## MIDWEST OFFICE TECHNOLOGY, INC. v. AMERICAN ALLIANCE INS. CO.

Supreme Court of Iowa, 1989.
437 N.W.2d 555.

SCHULTZ, J.

This appeal arises out of a dispute over the amount of insurance policy coverage provided for inventory. The insurer maintains the extent of coverage is limited by a reporting provision in the policy * * *. [T]he trial court ruled in favor of the insured, awarding the face amount of the policy. We reverse.

Midwest Office Technology, Inc. (Midwest) purchased a business protection insurance policy from the American Alliance Insurance Company (American) covering losses of inventory up to $600,000. Because its inventory fluctuated, Midwest selected a policy that provided variable coverage corresponding to the amount of inventory Midwest reported. Although the policy had a stated limit, the premiums were determined from the average inventory which the insured was required to report on a monthly basis. If a report was delinquent at the time of a loss, the coverage was limited to the amount listed in the last report filed prior to the loss.

After purchasing the policy, Midwest made inventory reports occasionally, but less often than the monthly requirement. It had not filed its monthly report when a fire destroyed Midwest's inventory. The loss was valued at over $600,000. Midwest sought the entire policy limits of $600,000. American, relying on its policy provision, paid only $478,-619.00, the amount of inventory claimed by Midwest in its most recent report prior to the fire.

* * *

* * * [Midwest] claims that a technical breach which neither contributed to the loss nor increased the risk of the insurer does not permit American to limit the inventory coverage below the actual loss sustained, subject to the policy limit.

* * * [American] insists that the reporting requirement merely sets the coverage amount, rather than serving as a forfeiture provision that voids the entire policy or portions thereof.

The clause in dispute provides: At the time of any loss, if the insured has failed to file with the Company reports of values as above required, this policy, subject otherwise to all its terms and conditions, shall cover only at the locations and for not more than the amounts included in the last report of values filed prior to the loss * * *. (Emphasis added.)

Midwest first contends that [Iowa Code] section 515.101 invalidates the limitation of coverage clause. This section states: Any condition or stipulation in an application, policy, or contract of insurance, making the policy void before the loss occurs, shall not prevent recovery thereon by the insured, if it shall be shown by the plaintiff that the failure to observe such provision or the violation thereof did not contribute to the loss.

The trial court found section 515.101 inapplicable to the reporting clause. The disputed clause does not abrogate the policy. It only sets the limits of coverage. We agree that the reporting clause simply does not fall within the section's terms of a "condition * * * making the policy void."

This conclusion is consistent with our previous statement that this statute becomes operative only when the breach of contract by the insured would void the insurance policy. See Carr v. Iowa Mut. Tornado

Ins. Ass'n, 242 Iowa 1084, 1090, 49 N.W.2d 498, 501 (1951). "It is only when there has been sufficient proof of some act of the insured which would ordinarily abrogate the contract, that section 515.101 has any effect or meaning." Id. at 1090, 49 N.W.2d at 501. It is also consistent with the federal court conclusion that this section is "ordinarily applied to a case where the defense of 'increase of hazard' was relied upon by the insurer to avoid coverage." Hawkeye Chem. Co. v. St. Paul Fire & Marine Ins. Co., 510 F.2d 322, 326 (7th Cir.), cert. denied, 421 U.S. 965, 95 S.Ct. 1955, 44 L.Ed.2d 452 (1975). In this case, the trial court correctly concluded that section 515.101 is inapplicable.

In ruling against American, the trial court relied upon language found in Commercial Standard, which stated, "the rule is that breach of a condition must be shown to have contributed to the loss or in fact make the risk more hazardous." Commercial Standard, 282 F.Supp. at 24–25. In so doing, the trial court greatly expanded the language of Commercial Standard and erred as a matter of law.

In Commercial Standard, the federal court was interpreting Iowa law. * * * Here, the trial court correctly recognized that the rule in Commercial Standard is nothing more than a restatement of [the predecessor statute to section 515.101]. However, its ruling went on to expand the rule to also apply to a policy condition prescribing a limitation on the extent of coverage after a breach. This is inconsistent with our statement in Carr which limited the statute's application to breaches of policy conditions that abrogated or avoided coverage. Because the Commercial Standard rule is directly derived from cases grounded on this statute, we find the trial court's conclusion is faulty. Just as section 515.101 speaks to "making the policy void," the court in Commercial Standard prefaces its discussion of the rule by speaking of a condition "making the policy void." 282 F.Supp. at 24. We believe, as we did in Carr, that the application of section 515.101 and the language in Commercial Standard is limited to situations in which an insured's breach of a condition voids the policy and forfeits the insured's coverage. Such is not the case here.

Other jurisdictions have addressed the issue of whether a breach of the value reporting clause causes forfeiture or merely sets limits of coverage. These cases have evolved from the insureds' claims of waiver and estoppel. Estoppel is a defense to a forfeiture of a policy, but does not extend coverage. Northern Assurance Co. v. Stan–Ann Oil Co., 603 S.W.2d 218, 223 (Tex.Civ.App.1979). The cases uniformly reject these claims because a breach of the value reporting clause creates only a limitation of coverage rather than a forfeiture of rights. Although these cases examine the clause for a different purpose, the analysis is relevant to our inquiry of whether the breach voids coverage or merely sets its limits.

Additionally, other jurisdictions interpreting clauses similar or identical to this one have concluded they are clear and unambiguous on their faces, requiring the policy language be given full effect. Watchung Pool

Supplies, Inc. v. Aetna Casualty & Sur. Co., 169 N.J.Super. 474, 486, 404 A.2d 1281, 1287 (Law Div.1979). The uniform rule is that an insured who is delinquent on its reports is limited on the amount of coverage to the amount shown on the last report filed prior to the loss. * * *

We have also considered Midwest's suggestion that the policy clause should be held invalid on public policy grounds citing Lakeside Plywood & Building Materials, Inc. v. Aetna Casualty & Surety Co., 75 Wis.2d 484, 250 N.W.2d 1 (1977). However, the Wisconsin court's holding was based on a statutory provision and determined that it was "not necessary to consider [the insured's] claim based upon general public policy." Id. at 497, 250 N.W.2d at 7. Such a provision is not against public policy. Cordeiro v. American Home Assurance Co., 409 F.2d 205, 206 (9th Cir.1969); 6 J. Appleman, Insurance Law and Practice § 3866.25 (1972). We find no merit in this contention.

In summary, we believe that neither section 515.101 nor Commercial Standard provides aid to Midwest. The rule announced in Commercial Standard applies only to policy conditions that would completely avoid coverage. The rule was directly derived from the predecessor to section 515.101 that speaks to "making the policy void." When the value reporting clause is breached, liability is not avoided, but merely limited. Value reporting clauses are standard in the insurance industry and have been often construed by litigation. The applicable case law uniformly supports our position.

The policy unambiguously provides that the insured's coverage is limited to the amount of inventory reported on the last report filed prior to any loss. The trial court erred when it concluded to the contrary.

REVERSED.

### *Note*

Watchung Pool Supplies v. Aetna Cas. & Surety Co., 169 N.J.Super. 474, 404 A.2d 1281 (1979), cited in the principal case and typical of the problem, dealt with a multi-peril policy which required the insured to advise Aetna within 30 days of the value of its inventory subject to a policy limit of $100,000. The insured was consistently late in reporting and when a fire occurred in July when the latest inventory value reported was in April with a $65,000 value. After the fire, an inventory of $87,000 was reported for May and $101,000 was reported for June. The policy provided that liability was limited to the last reported value before loss.

In upholding a limit of liability to $65,000, the court noted that the purpose of the provision was both to save the insured money by not overinsuring the inventory and to protect the insurer against fraud. According to the court, the language of the limitation was clear, the provision was reasonable and material.

### *Problem*

Quality Foods, Inc. held a monthly reporting form insurance policy covering its inventory. The relevant facts are:

1. The inventory value report, filed on July 31 showed the amount of $1,000,000.

2. The actual total value of the inventory on the date was $2,299,592.

3. The value of the inventory on Aug. 31, as reported in October was $2,529,554.

4. During September a hurricane caused damage to the goods to the amount of $247,164.

Question: How much can Quality Foods recover? See, Quality Foods, Inc. v. United States Fire Ins. Co., 715 F.2d 539 (11th Cir.1983).

## MYERS v. MERRIMACK MUTUAL FIRE INSURANCE COMPANY

United States Court of Appeals, Seventh Circuit, 1986.
788 F.2d 468.

CUMMINGS, CHIEF JUDGE.

This appeal comes to us from the district court's grant of summary judgment, in favor of the defendant Merrimack Mutual Fire Insurance Company. * * * For the reasons set out below, we affirm the judgment of the district court.

In 1977, plaintiff Walter Myers purchased a fully occupied ten-unit apartment building in Lacon, Illinois. Subsequently he began to convert the units from oil to electric heat and charge the tenants for the fuel. As a result, the tenants began to leave. The last tenant moved out of her apartment in October or November of 1981. From that time until April 3, 1983, when the apartment building was severely gutted by fire, there were no tenants living there.

Beginning in November 1981, plaintiff began renovating the building. In addition to changing the heating system, plaintiff took steps to rewire the entire building, install drywall and insulation, and convert the building from ten rental units to nine rental units. However, these renovations proceeded somewhat slowly. Plaintiff's job as a railroad signal worker required him to be on call at all times, and he was also busy building his Missouri retirement home. As a result, plaintiff worked on the apartment building only on weekends when he was not away from Lacon on business for the railroad or at work on his new home in Missouri. Plaintiff conceded that he would be at the apartment building only about once a month, and he was last there in late February 1983.

The apartment building during this time was deserted and unsecured. There was no water or electricity. The apartments were empty, except for some stoves and refrigerators. [There were few locks and the plaintiff had no keys anyway.]

The apartment building was insured against loss from multiple perils, including fire, under a policy issued by defendant. The relevant portions of the policy for purposes of this appeal are as follows:

* * *

"17. *Vacancy, Unoccupancy and Increase of Hazard.*

(a) This Company shall not be liable for loss occurring while a described building, whether intended for occupancy by owner or tenant, is vacant beyond a period of sixty (60) consecutive days. 'Vacant' or 'Vacancy' means containing no contents pertaining to operations or activities customary to occupancy of the building, but a building in process of construction shall not be deemed vacant.

(b) Permission is granted for unoccupancy. * * *

Defendant contends that plaintiff violated the vacancy clause contained in ¶ 17(a). Plaintiff counters that the contract is ambiguous. . . . [H]e maintains that ¶ 17(b), which grants permission for unoccupancy, is ambiguous when read together with ¶ 17(a) in that it is difficult for a layman like himself to distinguish between "unoccupied" and "vacant."

* * *

The * * * ambiguity alleged by plaintiff is that what the policy gives with one hand (permission for unoccupancy in ¶ 17(b)) it takes away with the other (vacancy exclusion in ¶ 17(a)), creating an apparent nullity. However, there is no such ambiguity in our case. The terms "vacant" and "unoccupied" are not synonymous: "vacant" means entirely empty (*i.e.,* lack of animate or inanimate objects), while "unoccupied" means the lack of habitual presence of human beings (*i.e.,* lack of animate objects). * * * *Foley v. Sonoma County Farmers' Mutual Fire Insurance Co.,* 18 Cal.2d 232, 115 P.2d 1, 2 (1941) (Traynor, J.). * * * This well-accepted definition of vacant conforms to the definition explicitly given in the contract; unoccupancy is not defined in this contract. A dwelling may thus be unoccupied but not vacant. * * * Perhaps the paradigm example of an unoccupied but not vacant house would be a fully furnished Palm Springs home owned by a Chicago resident who resides in Palm Springs for only three months during the winter. Such a home would be unoccupied for the remainder of the year, yet since the house is filled with all the inanimate objects customarily found in a home, it would not be classified as vacant.

It is a bit more difficult to imagine an unoccupied but not vacant dwelling in a rental context. Most apartments (including those in the instant case) are rented unfurnished, and so when the animate objects (*i.e.,* the tenants) leave, the inanimate objects tend to follow. Thus, if one tenant leaves a month before the new tenant moves in, the apartment (though of course not the entire building) might well be classified as vacant and not merely unoccupied. Moreover, a tenant in a rental apartment, as opposed to an owner of a home, is less likely to leave the unit for a sufficient length of time [1] for the apartment to be classified as

1. A dwelling is not "unoccupied" when the owners are only temporarily absent for a reasonable time, since if the absence is temporary they are still "habitually present" in the dwelling. *Foley,* 115 P.2d at 2 (not unoccupied where temporary thirteen-day absence); *Hemenway v. American Ca-*

unoccupied, since the tenant must still pay rent during his absence. It would have been preferable for defendant to define both of these terms in the contract and how they interact. Nevertheless, the presence of these two terms in the contract does not create an ambiguity; it merely means that a grant of permission for unoccupancy but not vacancy appears to be less valuable to the policyholder when the insured dwelling is an apartment building with unfurnished apartments.

Given this distinction between the terms vacant and unoccupied, there can be no doubt that the apartment building in the instant case was vacant and not merely unoccupied. These apartments were entirely empty for approximately eighteen months, lacking both tenants and inanimate objects. Plaintiff at oral argument noted that there were some stoves and refrigerators in the apartments, but such minimal items, without more, do not prevent us from concluding that the building was vacant. *Dunton v. Connecticut Fire Insurance Co.,* 371 F.2d 329, 330 (7th Cir.1967) ("It is well-settled that the use of a building to store a few articles does not show that the building is still occupied."); *Jelin,* 72 F.2d at 327 (fifteen-room house that contained a few items (an old brass bed, old straw mattress, and a chair) and that no one had lived in for several months, is vacant). * * *

The district court's grant of summary judgment in favor of defendant is affirmed.

### *Notes*

1. *When is a Commercial Rental Vacant or Unoccupied?* Knight v. United States Fidelity & Guaranty Co., 123 Ga.App. 833, 182 S.E.2d 693 (1971):

> "It is undisputed that the property was insured as a service station and restaurant and was closed for business by the plaintiff in June, 1964. The fire occurred on November 13, 1966. Initially, we point out that a breach of these insurance contracts by reason of vacancy or unoccupancy for more than a 60 day period does not render the policies void. This provision merely suspends the insurance and the policy coverage may be revived by compliance with its terms before loss. Athens Mutual Ins. Co. v. Toney, 1 Ga.App. 492, 57 S.E. 1013. No definition of the terms 'vacant' or 'unoccupied' are contained in the policies. Our research reveals the lack of any Georgia cases construing the meaning of these terms. However, these words have been the subject of many decisions in other jurisdictions. The general definition of 'vacant' is that it means empty or deprived of contents or without inanimate objects. Couch on Insurance 2d, § 37:845, 848; Black's Law Dictionary, 4th Ed. The meaning of the term 'unoccupied' can vary depending upon the nature of the property insured, i.e., whether it is a dwelling house, a store, restaurant, school or a church. It should be construed with reference to the nature and character of the building for the use contemplated by the parties. See Annot. 158 A.L.R. 894. When these terms are used in the disjunctive, as they are here, they cannot be

*sualty Co.,* 215 F.Supp. at 104 (not unoccupied where temporary two-week absence).

considered to be synonymous or complimentary. The testimony of the plaintiff shows that at the time she closed her business in 1964 all of the restaurant equipment, fixtures, booths, stools, coffee urn and stove were left in the building. In August, 1966 she decided to reopen. In connection with her intention to reopen, she testified she had purchased and installed a new refrigerator on the premises, installed a music box, electrical service was reconnected and she had the kitchen area painted. These activities according to her testimony all occurred at varying times, ranging from two weeks to not later than one month prior to the fire. From the plaintiff's testimony that there was restaurant equipment within the premises at the time of the fire, it cannot be concluded as a matter of law that the premises were vacant for the period specified by the policies so as to preclude recovery on the ground of vacancy. Notwithstanding this, if the evidence on motion for summary judgment conclusively shows that the property was unoccupied for more than 60 days prior to the fire, then the defendants are of course entitled to summary judgment. However, as we construe the evidence, it does not conclusively show that the property was unoccupied for more than 60 days prior to the fire. Her testimony concerning installing new equipment, painting the interior, and reconnecting the electrical service are all activities consistent with making the premises ready for use for the very purpose for which it was insured. These activities are also all reasonably consistent with occupancy within the meaning of the policies. See Limbaugh v. Columbia Ins. Co. (Mo.App.), 368 S.W.2d 921; Rainwater v. Maryland Cas. Co., 252 S.C. 370, 166 S.E.2d 546. There is nothing in the policies from which it can be construed that the insured premises had to be open to the public in order to be occupied. Thus, there are issues of material fact for jury resolution. The judgments granting summary judgments were erroneous. * * * "

2. *Vacancy and Unoccupancy of House Under Construction and for Sale.*

Houses under construction are always unoccupied and builders' risk insurance covering such projects stipulate that a building in the course of construction shall not be deemed vacant. After completion, however, many houses remain unsold for some time. In one case, the builder was insured against vandalism of the house in question, with an exclusion "if the described dwelling had been vacant beyond a period of 30 days." The house was a model house for a tract and the realtor had been using the building as a sales office, coming in at least 4 days a week. However the only furnishings were a telephone, desk and some chairs. Vandals damaged the place after it had been on the market for more than 30 days. Was the "dwelling" vacant? Ellmex Const. Co., Inc. v. Republic Ins. Co., 202 N.J.Super. 195, 494 A.2d 339 (A.D.1985) held no.

3. *Fire insurance in the deteriorating inner cities.*

Here the "vacancy" clauses go hand in hand with the "increase of the hazard" clauses. The insured absentee owners profess lack of knowledge. For a graphic description of the situation in Chicago, see Chicago Title & Trust Co. v. Illinois Fair Plan Association, 90 Ill.App.3d 1061, 46 Ill.Dec. 483, 414 N.E.2d 205 (1980), wherein the court avoided the policies for breach of the above conditions. "The question was not whether the buildings would burn, but when."

### *Problems*

1. Assume a standard fire policy with a 60 day vacancy or unoccupancy provision. The agent issuing the policy was aware that the premises were vacant and unoccupied at the time the policy took effect. They burned 107 days later, still vacant and unoccupied. Is the company estopped from denying liability because it knowingly issued a broken policy? See Zweygardt v. Farmers Mutual Insurance Co. of Nebraska, 195 Neb. 811, 241 N.W.2d 323 (1976).

2. *What constitutes an increase of the hazard? Any or all of the following?*

a. Putting up a warning sign on premises insured against fire that the house is protected by a spring loaded gun? Boyd v. Aetna Insurance Co., 192 F.Supp. 435 (S.D.Fla.1960).

b. Telling the fuel supplier to discontinue service in the dead of winter to a Michigan house insured against direct loss by freezing? See Smith v. Lumbermen's Mutual Insurance Co., 101 Mich.App. 78, 300 N.W.2d 457 (1980) (dissenting opinion). Compare with Newmont Mines Ltd. v. Hanover Ins. Co., 784 F.2d 127 (2d Cir.1986) involving the collapse of the roof of a major mining complex in Canada under the weight of snow. The area received 100 feet of snow annually and the buildings and roofs were designed so that the heat of the buildings combined with the pitch of the roof would cause the snow to slide off. Operations ceased, the heat was turned off, and the collapse of the roof caused over $6,000,000 damage. The insurer had not been informed of the change.

c. Storing gasoline in plastic trash cans in the hall closet during gas shortage? (How many fire insurance policies may have been suspended during the 1978 gas crunch?)

d. An illegal liquor still concealed in a floor closet under the eaves of the roof? Good v. Continental Insurance Co., 277 S.C. 569, 291 S.E.2d 198 (1982).

## F. THAT INSURED OBTAINED THE ISSUANCE OF THE POLICY BY CONCEALMENT OR MISREPRESENTATION

*(Refer back to Part A, Chapter 3, C)*

### MERCHANTS FIRE ASSURANCE CORP. v. LATTIMORE

United States Court of Appeals, Ninth Circuit, 1959.
263 F.2d 232.

Supra at p. 101.

## G. THAT THE POLICY HAS BEEN CANCELLED (WITH OR WITHOUT CAUSE)

One of the expectable phenomena of the various insurance "crises" arising during the 1960s–1990s was the reliance by insurance companies on cancellation of, or refusals to renew, insurance policies. This is reflected by legislators' concern with the subject. Both property and automobile insurance have been the subjects of legislation (although not the only subjects) on cancellation and/or non-renewal. The present day coverage is quite extensive in those two areas and is rather too long to quote. Even a sampling of the California statutes would not be appropriate because its incompleteness might be misleading. Nonetheless, the reader concerned with these subjects should consult West's Ann.Cal.Insurance Code §§ 660ff (automobile policies) and 675ff (property policies). Worth remembering is the extensiveness and complexity of these statutes.

Worth observing is the impact of Initiative Proposition 103 on auto policies. The new West's Ann.Cal.Insurance Code § 1861.03(c) provides (and only in part):

> (c)(1) Notwithstanding any other provision of law, a notice of cancellation or nonrenewal of a policy for automobile insurance shall be effective only if it is based on one or more of the following reasons: (A) nonpayment of premium; (B) fraud or material misrepresentation affecting the policy or insured; (C) a substantial increase in the hazard insured against.
>
> (2) This subdivision shall not prevent a reciprocal insurer, organized prior to November 8, 1988, by a motor club holding a certificate of authority under Chapter 2 (commencing with Section 12160) of Part 5 of Division 2, and which requires membership in the motor club as a condition precedent to applying for insurance, from issuing an effective notice of nonrenewal based solely on the failure of the insured to maintain membership in the motor club. * * *

This section might well be taken to be additive to (but not superseding) West's Ann.Cal.Insurance Code § 661:

**§ 661. Grounds for valid notice of cancellation**

(a) A notice of cancellation of a policy shall be effective only if it is based on one or more of the following reasons:

(1) Nonpayment of premium.

(2) The driver's license or motor vehicle registration of the named insured or of any other operator who either resides in the same household or customarily operates an automobile insured under the policy has been under suspension or revocation during the policy period or, if the policy is a renewal, during its policy period or the 180 days immediately preceding its effective date.

(3) Discovery of fraud by the named insured in pursuing a claim under the policy provided the insurer does not rescind the policy.

(b) This section shall not apply to any policy or coverage which has been in effect less than 60 days at the time notice of cancellation is mailed or delivered by the insurer unless it is a renewal policy.

(c) Modification of automobile physical damage coverage by the inclusion of a deductible not exceeding one hundred dollars ($100) shall not be deemed a cancellation of the coverage or of the policy.

(d) This section shall not apply to nonrenewal.

## MID-CENTURY INSURANCE CO. v. NORGAARD

Supreme Court of South Dakota, 1979.
273 N.W.2d 191.

WOLLMAN, CHIEF JUSTICE.

In this declaratory judgment action, Mid-Century Insurance Company (Company) sought a determination that the Company was under no duty to provide coverage for the Norgaards' liability arising out of an accident that occurred on July 27, 1976. The trial court found that the policy of insurance issued to appellant Norgaard had expired by its terms on July 26, 1976, and had been effectively cancelled April 17, 1976, for nonpayment of premium, and that hence the Company was under no duty to defend nor was it liable on the policy. We affirm.

Appellant Ken Norgaard is the teenage son of appellant Leo Norgaard. On July 27, 1976, Ken was involved in an accident that entailed bodily injuries. Ken and his father were sued in federal court for damages from that accident. Respondent Company commenced a defense of this action under a unilateral reservation of rights. During that litigation the Company began this declaratory judgment action. * * *

Leo Norgaard had purchased insurance policies from respondent covering four different vehicles. The policy in question was issued January 26, 1976, contained an expiration date of July 26, 1976, and carried a premium of $150.30. The Norgaards apparently learned of a discount that was offered by the Company for policyholders having children who receive good grades and are licensed to drive. They therefore tendered $120.30 in payment of the premium less the "good student credit." Upon learning of the existence of a student driver, the Company reclassified the policy and raised the premium to $248.30. The Company then sent a premium notice showing a credit of $57.90 for the good student discount, a credit of $120.30 for the payment that had been made by the insured, and a balance due of $70.10. A second premium due notice was sent followed by a third, which notified the insured that the policy would be cancelled if the balance of the premium was not paid prior to April 17, 1976. A final notice of cancellation was sent by the Company on April 28, 1976. This final notice afforded the insured an opportunity to reinstate the policy by paying the remaining premium within sixty days and also included a refund of $37.08 for unearned premium. The refund check was retained by Mr. Norgaard and was cashed, apparently by his wife.

During April and May of 1976, the Norgaards began experiencing marital difficulties. Mrs. Norgaard left the home on June 13, 1976, and the Norgaards thereafter were divorced. Prior to the divorce, Mrs. Norgaard had handled the family finances under the direction of Mr. Norgaard. Mr. Norgaard believed that his wife had paid the premium due. Following his wife's departure, Mr. Norgaard was unable to find the insurance policies he held, and on July 9, 1976, he called his insurance agent to inquire about the policy on the 1973 Chevrolet Camero. According to Mr. Norgaard, the agent replied that "it would be covered until sometime in August." On August 3, 1976, Mr. Norgaard once again called the insurance agent to report the accident in which his son had been involved. Before reporting the accident, he asked the agent, "which cars we had covered * * * He named off my '75 Chevrolet pickup, '73 Chevrolet Impala, '66 Ford Mustang and the 1973 Camero." Mr. Norgaard then told the agent, "Well, you better be right about that Camero, because it was just in an accident that involved bodily injury."

Two insurance agents were involved with Mr. Norgaard's file. The agent who wrote Mr. Norgaard's policy had been discharged by the Company prior to the conversations noted above. The agent who spoke to Mr. Norgaard by phone was Frederick DeNeui. Mr. Norgaard's account was transferred to agent DeNeui on or about July 1, 1976. Prior to the July call from Mr. Norgaard, agent DeNeui had never reviewed any of the Norgaard files. Mr. DeNeui testified that when Mr. Norgaard called in July concerning the insurance on the 1973 Chevrolet Camero, he pulled all four files on the Norgaard vehicles. The evidence shows that there was an insurance contract on a 1973 Chevrolet with an expiration date of August 13, 1976. The policy on the 1973 Chevrolet Camero bore an expiration date of July 26, 1976.

* * * The trial court found that both on July 9 and on August 3, 1976, the agent told Mr. Norgaard that the policy was in force.

There is essentially one issue in this case, and that is whether an agent's statements will operate to revive a cancelled policy of insurance.

If there is a general rule, it is that an agent cannot revive a properly cancelled policy through mere representations that the policy is still in effect. Pearson v. General Casualty & Surety Co., 107 N.J.L. 509, 154 A. 739; Ingalls v. Commercial Insurance Co. of Newark, N.J., 18 Wis.2d 233, 118 N.W.2d 178. See Annot. 3 A.L.R.3d 1135, 1136 § 2.

In some of the cases the cancellation is held invalid because of the agent's statutory authority to bind the company or revoke cancellations, coupled with his assurances that coverage exists. See, e.g., Carlisle v. American Auto Insurance Co., 229 La. 717, 86 So.2d 683; Blakely v. American Employers' Insurance Co., 5 Cir., 424 F.2d 728. * * * In Sjoberg v. State Auto Ins. Ass'n of Des Moines, Iowa, 78 N.D. 179, 48 N.W.2d 452, the insured paid his premium with a nonsufficient funds check and although notice of cancellation was sent, the insurance company directed the agent to attempt collection of the check. The court held that the attempted collection of the check was inconsistent with an intention to cancel the policy and hence the company was held to have waived its notice of cancellation. No basis for such waiver can be found here. In many of the cases holding cancelled policies valid the crucial issue is whether there was in fact a cancellation. * * * Here there can be no question but that the policy was effectively cancelled prior to the July 9 telephone conversation, for Mr. Norgaard had received notice of cancellation together with the unearned premium, which he retained.

In a case with facts similar to those in the case now before us, the Minnesota Supreme Court held an insurance company liable, partially because the premium had not been returned to the insured. The court said: "[B]oth net premium and commission were retained by [the agent] and never returned to [the insured]. Had the full premium been returned to [the insured] when the alleged cancellation took place, he would undoubtedly have known that his insurance was terminated." Morrison v. Swenson, 274 Minn. 127, 142 N.W.2d 640, 646. Here, appellant knew beyond doubt that the policy had been cancelled. He could not reasonably believe that mere oral representations by the agent could revive the policy.

* * *

We hold only that when an insured has received notice of cancellation and a refund of his unearned premium, the cancelled policy may not be revived by representations of coverage on the part of the agent without a clear showing that the agent had express authority by statute or contract to revoke cancellations issued by the insurance company.

The judgment appealed from is affirmed.

# Chapter 7

# PAYMENT OF CLAIMS

## A. MEASURE OF RECOVERY

___ **valuation**
___ **co-insurance**

### TITUS v. WEST AMERICAN INSURANCE CO.

Superior Court of New Jersey, Law Division, 1976.
143 N.J.Super. 195, 362 A.2d 1236.

BEETEL, J.C.C., Temporarily Assigned.

Plaintiff is a young man who operates his own auto body repair shop and who has been an auto body mechanic all his working life. On March 16, 1972 he purchased a used 1966 Mustang convertible for a purchase price of $472.50 (including $22.50 in sales tax). About three weeks later he contacted his insurance broker, Robert Herdman, and requested that this vehicle be added to his current insurance policy underwritten by defendant. At this time he wanted only coverage for liability.

Plaintiff purchased this car with the idea of "customizing" it. He enjoys working with automobiles and wanted to make his 1966 Mustang something special. To this end he did extensive work on the automobile. During the first seven months he owned the car he repainted it, added new tires, installed a new canvas top and added several other small items to the automobile. Evidence was submitted by plaintiff showing that during these seven months he spent approximately $350 on parts alone, exclusive of his own labor.

In September 1972 he contacted his insurance broker again and requested that "comprehensive" (theft and property damage) coverage be added to his policy. The broker, Herdman, testified that when this coverage was added plaintiff never mentioned to him that the car was in the process of being extensively remodeled or customized. Herdman admitted that he knew from casual observation that plaintiff's car had been repainted and that new tires had been added, but he stated that this alone gave him no cause to suspect that the car was being customized or that these changes represented any increase in the insurable risk.

The broker duly purchased this additional coverage at a cost of $9.18 a year.

Thereafter, plaintiff continued to improve and customize his vehicle. In March 1973 he rebuilt the engine at a cost of $156.10 (including labor). In May 1973 he purchased a second set of tires and a set of "mag wheels" at a total cost of $293.52 (including wheel locks). He also spent nearly $450 on other parts and equipment. During this time his automobile insurance policy was automatically renewed semi-annually. At no time did plaintiff inform the company or his broker of the extensive modification he made on the automobile.

On February 23, 1974 plaintiff's automobile was stolen. To this date it has not been returned. Shortly thereafter plaintiff filed a claim with defendant insurance company giving a description of the car and indicating that the odometer read 89,000 miles at the time of the theft. Lengthy negotiations ensued which resulted in the instant suit and the failure of the appraisers and the umpire to agree upon the standard upon which value should be determined.

At trial each side adduced expert testimony regarding the question of value and the method of evaluating auto insurance losses. Like the court-appointed umpire and defendant's appraiser, these experts were in substantial agreement regarding the market value of plaintiff's customized 1966 Mustang convertible. Among afficionados of such vehicles, plaintiff's car would have sold for $2,000 on the date of the theft. Plaintiff introduced pictures of his late beloved vehicle into evidence, and from viewing these photos this court finds that there is no question that the car was in excellent, indeed "cream puff," condition. Thus, this court finds as a fact that the market value of plaintiff's car, with the special equipment he added, was $2,000 on February 23, 1974.

The experts could not agree on the value of a 1966 Mustang convertible with full standard options in excellent condition. Defendant's expert, an appraiser with many years of experience, testified that the "book value" of such a car was $375. "Book value," he explained, refers to two publications used throughout the auto and insurance industries to evaluate used automobiles, the *Red Book* published by National Market Reports, Inc., and the *N.A.D.A. Official* Used Car Guide published by the National Automobile Dealers' Association. He testified, further, that the maximum value of such a vehicle would be double the "book" price, or $750. Plaintiff's experts testified that such a vehicle would have sold for about $1,000. They rejected the book value method of evaluation as the only guide toward the determination of actual cash value. Berezny, the umpire, agreed with plaintiff's experts and thus iterated his previous findings made during arbitration.

If this court were to make independent findings of fact on this issue, it might place the value of a fully equipped "cream puff" 1966 Mustang convertible at something closer to the double book value standard espoused by defendant's expert. However, for the reasons which follow, this court finds that $1,000 was the actual cash value of such a vehicle on the date of the theft under the terms of the insurance contract in question.

* * * The pertinent paragraph of the policy states that:

> The limit of the company's liability for loss shall not exceed the actual cash value of the property, or if the loss is a part thereof, the actual cash value of such part, at time of loss, nor what it would then cost to repair or replace the property or such part thereof with other of like kind and quality, nor, with respect to an owned automobile described in this policy, the applicable limit of liability stated in the declarations * * *.

The policy does not define actual cash value, nor is there any reported decision in this State defining the term within the context of an automobile insurance contract. N.J.A.C. 11:3–10.2 defines the term as follows:

> "Actual cash value", unless otherwise specifically defined by law or policy, means the lesser of the amounts for which the insured or the designated representative can reasonably be expected to:
>
> 1. Repair the motor vehicle to its condition immediately prior to the loss; or
>
> 2. Replace the motor vehicle with a substantially similar vehicle. Such amount shall include all monies paid or payable as sales taxes on the motor vehicle repaired or replaced. This shall not be construed to prevent an insurer from issuing a policy where the amount of damages to be paid in the event of total loss is a specified dollar amount. * * *
>
> "Substantially similar vehicle" means a vehicle of the same make, model, year and condition, including all major options of the insured vehicle. Mileage must not exceed that of the insured vehicle by more than 4,000 miles. Mileage differences of more than 4,000 miles may, at the option of the insured, be exchanged for the presence or absence of options or a cash adjustment.

Even if this section were controlling (it was made effective on May 1, 1976 and thus post-dates the controversy here), it provides little assistance in resolving the meaning of ACV.

In determining the meaning of actual cash value generally, there appears to be a split to authority. See Annotation, "Test or Criterion of 'Actual Cash Value' under Insurance Policy Insuring to Extent of Actual Cash Value at Time of Loss," 61 ALR2d 711. Some courts adopt a market value test; others look to a formula reflecting reproduction or replacement cost; others have adopted the so-called "broad evidence rule" under which any evidence is received which logically tends to establish actual cash value, and some courts have held that actual cash value is an independent test to be applied without reference to other criteria.

* * *

Unrestrained by controlling precedent, this court is in the position to adopt what appears to be the better rule for determining the actual cash value of an automobile, and that is, its market value. See 15 Couch on Insurance 2d, § 54:232; 7 Am.Jur.2d, Automobile Insurance, § 190; Annotation: supra, 61 ALR2d 711, § 6. As these authorities point out, there is a readily determinable market value for used automobiles, and this value adequately compensates the insured and adequately reflects his reasonable expectations. The broad evidence rule, while helpful in indemnifying owners of property which might be unique or which, when sold on the market would not bring a reasonable return (e.g., used furniture or clothing), is too uncertain a standard to be applied to the day-to-day business of adjusting automobile insurance claims.

This conclusion is buttressed by the testimony of the witnesses in this action. They all assumed that when you talk of value, you are talking about market value. They disagreed over whether the industry guidebooks were the only evidence of market value, but they agreed that market value governs.

Thus, this court holds that actual cash value means market value. * * *

The final question to be resolved is what automobile is to be evaluated. Plaintiff argues strenuously that it is his car, as he had equipped it, which should be the subject matter of the evaluation. Defendant argues with equal intensity that the subject matter of the evaluation is an automobile of the same model, year and condition, equipped with standard options. Surprisingly, research has disclosed no case directly on point, nor do the commentators provide significant enlightenment.

Defendant insurer presented uncontradicted expert testimony by an experienced insurance underwriter regarding long-established industry custom and usage. He stated that comprehensive coverage is geared to insure the ordinarily equipped automobile and that this was widely known and employed by all insurers. He further opined that the insurance buying public is aware of this custom, and that the extremely modest premiums payable for such coverage should, at a minimum, put the insured on notice that what was being insured was an ordinary risk.

Testimony was also adduced regarding the manner in which comprehensive coverage is purchased. The potential insured contacts his insurance broker or agent and is then asked to provide certain information—the make, model, year and serial number of the car; whether standard optional equipment is present or absent, e.g., automatic transmission, "power options," air conditioning, etc. The broker then consults standard industry manuals to determine the applicable premium. This is based upon the average market value of a similarly equipped motor vehicle of the same model and year.

Based on the testimony defendant argues that the subject matter of this policy was a "1966 Mustang with standard options," not a "customized 1966 Mustang with a rebuilt high-powered engine, mag wheels, racing tires, a front sloping chassis, and special paint." To point to the logical absurdity of plaintiff's position, counsel for defendant advanced a "horrible hypothetical"—a solid gold 1966 Mustang with mink seat-covers studded with precious gems. Surely, he urges, such a vehicle could not be insured at full value for the paltry sum of $9.18 a year.

Defendant's logically extreme example is compelling. It would be patently unreasonable for the owner of such a vehicle to expect full coverage in case of loss. Plaintiff's vehicle is not, however, positioned at this extreme. Surely, an owner who maintains his car in excellent condition by regular servicing and the replacement of worn parts can reasonably expect to be covered for the full value of his automobile. In fact, by providing for arbitration in its policy, the insurer recognizes that individual automobiles of the same model year do vary in value, and thus makes allowance for these legitimate expectations. This plaintiff, however, did something more than merely maintain his car in excellent condition. He added equipment which did more than make the vehicle safe and convenient, and more than was necessary to make it a running car. Shapiro v. Security Ins. Co., 256 Mass. 358, 152 N.E. 370 (Sup.Jud. Ct.1926). It is undisputed that the special improvements placed on the vehicle more than doubled its value. Thus, plaintiff could not reasonably expect to receive full value for the addition of nonessential and nonstandard equipment.

In response to this, plaintiff cites State Auto. Mut. Ins. Co. v. Cox, 309 Ky. 480, 218 S.W.2d 46 (Ct.App.1949). In that case the insured purchased a new 1946 automobile for $1,398.93. Six months later the car was stolen. His policy insured the vehicle for "actual cash value." At trial the insured presented evidence that the car had a market value of $2,100 on the date of the theft. The inflated value was produced by the post-World War II shortage of automobiles. The court found in favor of the insured despite the fact that the insurance premium was calculated upon the purchase price of the car.

Cox is not dispositive. The increased risk was caused by market conditions, not by any unanticipated alterations of the vehicle by the insured. Insurance companies are expected to absorb, either by way of profit or loss, the economic fluctuations of the market place. This is an accepted risk of doing business.

Plaintiff also urges that notwithstanding the fact that modified vehicles may not be within the ambit of the insurable risk, the insurer is in a position to protect itself by asking the potential insured whether or not his vehicle is other than an ordinary one. In essence, plaintiff argues that the insurer has a duty to ask the insured the "magic question," and failing this, the insured may safely not disclose facts relevant to the risk. Reliance is placed upon the rule of law found in Harr v. Allstate Insurance, 54 N.J. 287, 255 A.2d 208 (1969):

> Average purchasers of insurance are entitled to the broad measure of protection necessary to fulfill their reasonable expectations; * * * it is the insurer's burden to obtain * * * all information

pertinent to the risk and the desired coverage before the contract is issued. * * * [at 304, 255 A.2d at 217]

This argument is not without merit. Assuming that the average purchaser of auto insurance reasonably expects that if his vehicle is customized he need not bring this to the attention of his carrier unless asked, then there might be a duty imposed on the insurer to obtain information relevant to this risk. However, defendant disputes the basic assumption upon which such a duty is premised. First, its experts asserted that the average consumer has no such justifiable and reasonable expectation; and second, that this particular plaintiff, an auto body mechanic with, at a bare minimum, peripheral involvement with claims adjustment, should have known the universal practice and custom within the insurance industry—that customized vehicles must be insured under a stated value policy.

This court need not decide whether to impose a duty on the insurance company to make inquiries in the case of an average consumer, because it is apparent that this plaintiff is not an average consumer. Given the undisputed testimony that it was clearly not the practice of the insurance industry to make inquiries regarding present or future modifications of the insured vehicle, the fact that this practice was sufficiently notorious in the trade to have put this insured plaintiff on notice and the fact that the plaintiff was in the best position to know the extent of the additional risk he was creating, plaintiff's claim for an additional $1,000 in damages must be denied. * * * It is clear that the increased value sought is attributable to parts which were not needed to make the car a working vehicle, but to parts designed to make the automobile more aesthetically pleasing. ACV coverage is not designed to insure such value.

The situation presented here may also be analogized to the long-recognized rule of law that:

> A misstatement or false declaration in the application or policy with respect to the description of the character of the insured vehicle may, if material to the risk, constitute a sufficient ground for avoidance or forfeiture of the policy, without regard to whether the misdescription was made intentionally or in good faith. [7 *Blashfield's Automobile Law and Practice* (3 ed.), § 302.1 at 331–332].

* * * Although this rule is not favored in this State, see, e.g., Merchants Indem. Corp. v. Eggleston, 37 N.J. 114, 179 A.2d 505 (1962), it does demonstrate the law's recognition of the actuarial consequences flowing from a proper or improper representation as to the identity of the risk to be insured. Here, plaintiff represented that his car was a "1966 Mustang convertible" when in fact it was (or became) a "customized 1966 Mustang convertible." Such a misstatement was certainly "material to the risk," since it both increased the potential liability of the insurer and the likelihood that the vehicle might be purloined. Had not defendant graciously admitted liability, it may well have been able to

advance the argument that the policy should have been avoided on this ground.

* * *

For the reasons stated above, this court finds in favor of plaintiff in the amount of $1,000 plus taxed costs and interest. Because of the novel questions of law involved and defendant's lack of bad faith, taxed costs shall not include an award of counsel fees.

## McANARNEY v. NEWARK FIRE INSURANCE CO.

Court of Appeals of New York, 1928.
247 N.Y. 176, 159 N.E. 902, 56 A.L.R. 1149.

KELLOGG, J. The plaintiff was the vendee of certain real estate, purchased in the year 1919 from the defendant, Lembeck & Betz Eagle Brewing Company, under written contract, for the sum of $8,000. Seven large buildings, designed for the manufacture of malt, stood upon the premises. Malt had been extensively manufactured therein prior to the year 1918. Owing to the passage of the National Prohibition Act (27 USCA) its manufacture was discontinued in March of that year and thereafter the buildings ceased to be employed for any useful purpose. In January, 1920, policies of insurance insuring the plaintiff and the Lembeck & Betz Eagle Brewing Company, as their interest might appear, against loss of the buildings by fire, in the aggregate sum of $42,750, were taken out. In April 1920, the buildings were destroyed by fire. Subsequently the plaintiff served proofs of loss wherein he valued the buildings at approximately $60,000 and made claim for the total amount of the insurance. * * * The action was tried before a jury, to which the trial judge submitted the written question, "What was the intrinsic or depreciated structural value of the buildings burned?" The jury returned a verdict specifying the value to have been $55,000. * * *

Complaint is made that the trial court in the course of the trial committed a variety of errors in ruling upon the admissibility of proof offered by the defendant. It refused to receive proof that the plaintiff, when a director of the Lembeck & Betz Company, in the year 1919 reported to that company that he had been unable to obtain a purchaser for the property; that in the same year the corporation had directed the plaintiff to erect a sign upon the premises advertising the property for sale for the sum of $12,000. It refused to receive in evidence an affidavit made by the plaintiff in the year 1919 which was filed with the local board of assessors. In this affidavit the plaintiff had stated that the property had no value except for the production of malt; that the production of malt upon the premises had entirely ceased; that the owners would accept for the property the sum of $15,000; that the best offer which had been received was $6,000. To the rulings made, excluding such proof and proof of a similar nature, the defendant duly excepted. Complaint is also made of the court's charge to the jury and of its refusals to charge. The court said to the jury:

> "Your answer shall not be the market value—shall not be the sum that the buildings would sell for, but what it cost to build them—what it cost to build the structures, less depreciation proven in the case."

It charged that the fact that the buildings because of the passage of the National Prohibition Act, could no longer be used for the manufacture of malt, and the fact that the buildings could no longer be employed for any useful purpose, were wholly immaterial. It further charged that the value of the buildings destroyed was to be measured solely by the cost of replacement less deductions for physical deterioration. The defendant duly excepted to the charges made. It requested the court to charge several propositions of law which were the direct converse of the charges thus made, and, to its refusal, duly excepted.

The policy in suit contained the standard clause, applicable alike to fire losses whether of chattels or buildings, reading as follows:

> "The insurance company does insure * * * and legal representatives to the extent of the actual cash value (ascertained with proper deductions for depreciation) of the property at the time of loss or damage, but not exceeding the amount which it would cost to repair or replace the same with material of like kind and quality within a reasonable time after such loss or damage."

We cannot agree with the defendant that, under this clause, the market value of the buildings destroyed was the exclusive measure of the plaintiff's loss. Insurance is thereby limited to "actual cash value (ascertained with proper deductions for depreciation) of the property at the time of loss or damage." Value ascertained by market price is necessarily expressive of a suitable deduction for depreciation. If "actual cash value" were synonymous with "market value," the words in parenthesis, to have force, would require depreciation to be twice subtracted. No such anomalous result could have been intended. In order that the parenthetical words should have force, therefore, "actual cash value" must be interpreted as having a broader significance than "market value." Moreover, if market value were the rule, property, for which there was no market, would possess no insurable value, a proposition which is clearly untenable. We think it manifest that the clause was not intended to restrict a recovery for this insurance loss to the market value of the insured buildings. We interpret "actual cash value" to have no other significance than "actual value" expressed in terms of money. For methods by which actual value may be ascertained, we must look beyond the terms of the policy to general principles of the law of damages.

No principle, obtaining in the law of damages, requires that the recovery be restricted to the market value of the buildings. True it is that articles of commerce destined for sale must be appraised, to measure loss through conversion or breach of contract, by the market prices at which such articles are bought and sold. The reason for the rule is this: The loser of the article, if awarded the prevailing price therefor, may enter the market and, with the sum awarded, replace the article lost with a substitute identical in kind and quality. Replacement in kind necessarily accomplishes complete indemnity. However, the rule presupposes the existence of a broad market with frequent trading in articles of an identical character with the article lost. * * * Self-evidently, the buildings which are the subject of this action had no "market value" in a strict sense. In the first place, buildings, independently of the land upon which they stand, are never the subject of market sales. In the second place, no two buildings are alike in size, proportion, ornamentation, or otherwise. Doubtless no buildings, duplicating those destroyed, could be found the world over. They are incapable of replacement from any market whatsoever. Therefore, the strict rule that market value or market price is an exclusive measure of damage does not apply.

We do not agree with the plaintiff that, under the standard clause, the sole measure of damage was cost of reproduction less physical depreciation. The words "not exceeding the amount which it would cost to repair or replace the same with material of like kind and quality within a reasonable time after such loss or damage," afford no remedy to the assured. They merely express a privilege granted to the insurer. The insurer might, if it so elected, reconstruct the destroyed buildings upon their ancient pattern with materials of like kind and quality, or pay the assured the necessary cost of such reconstruction. If the insurer so elected, it could be allowed nothing for the difference between the value of the old and the new buildings. Wood on Fire Insurance, § 472. The clause makes no allusion to depreciation, except as it provides for the recovery of "actual cash value" to be "ascertained with proper deductions for depreciation." This provision, while it doubtless comprehends cost of reproduction, does not restrict the field of investigation to such cost or provide that, with depreciation, it shall constitute an exclusive measure of recovery.

* * * The insurer, in our case, in its contract with the plaintiff stipulated that it "does insure" the plaintiff "to the extent of the actual cash value." Under our interpretation of the phrase, the insurer "does insure" to the limit of actual value. To insure is "to guarantee or secure indemnity for future loss or damage." The Century Dictionary. Where insured buildings have been destroyed, the trier of fact may, and should, call to its aid, in order to effectuate complete indemnity, every fact and circumstance which would logically tend to the formation of a correct estimate of the loss. It may consider original cost and cost of reproduction; the opinions upon value given by qualified witnesses; the declarations against interest which may have been made by the assured; the gainful uses to which the buildings might have been put; as well as any other fact reasonably tending to throw light upon the subject. * * *

In the case at bar the trier of fact, in considering cost of reproduction, was required by the policy to make proper "deductions for depreciation." "The word (depreciation) means, by derivation and common usage, a 'fall in value; reduction of worth.'" N.Y. Life Ins. Co. v. Anderson, C.C.A., 263 F. at p. 529. It includes obsolescence. Nashville,

C. & St.L.R.Co. v. United States, C.C.A., 269 F. 351, at p. 355; San Francisco & P.S.S. Co. v. Scott, D.C., 253 F. 855. An obsolete thing is a thing no longer in use. In determining the extent to which these buildings had suffered from depreciation, the trier of fact should have been permitted to consider that, owing to the passage of the National Prohibition Act, they were no longer useful for the purposes to serve which they were erected. It should have been permitted to consider their adaptability or inadaptability to other commercial purposes. The law of damages distinguishes between marketable chattels possessed for purposes of sale and chattels possessed for the comfort and well-being of their owner. In the instance of the former it judges their value by the market price. In the instance of the latter it measures their loss, not by their value in a secondhand market, but by the value of their use to the owner who suffers from their deprivation. The latter measure is employed in the case of household furniture, family records, wearing apparel, personal effects, and family portraits. * * * Doubtless the law should similarly discriminate between buildings used and usable for commercial purposes and buildings used and usable for residence purposes. "The considerations affecting the value of a family residence and of an apartment house or office building are not entirely the same." Citizens' Bank v. Fitchburg Fire Ins. Co., [86 Vt. 267, 84 A. 970]. It might well be held that handsomely carved woodwork or other ornamental features, when found in a private home, have insurable value; whereas, when found in a factory, since they are not useful for factory purposes, they have no such value. However, that may be, it is a self-evident proposition that factory buildings peculiarly adapted to the manufacture of malt must have depreciated in value when malt may no longer be manufactured; that buildings useful only for factory purposes have lost value when they are no longer used or usable for such purposes.

The foregoing discussion necessarily establishes that the trial judge committed reversible error in excluding the declarations against interest as to the value of the buildings, made by the plaintiff; in charging the jury that upon the question of value they must consider no other subject than cost of reproduction less depreciation; and in further charging that the obsolescence of the structures or their inutility for commercial or manufacturing purposes might not be considered. Accordingly, the judgment must be reversed.

### *Notes*

1. The so-called "broad evidence rule" seems to have been widely accepted in principle in recent years (see Annot. (1958) 61 A.L.R.2d 711, § 5), although the introduction of "broad" evidence when the usual legal standards of market value and replacement less deterioration are plainly provable may not be universally tolerated, perhaps because it unnecessarily complicates and prolongs a trial.

On the other hand, when there was no market for the property at instant of loss, and replacement less deterioration is unrealistic, the admission of broad evidence is virtually compelled. The most familiar illustrations are heirlooms (which should therefore be scheduled), growing fruit trees and crops, half grown feeder livestock, minks, chinchillas, etc. Here the evidence of the potential profit, depending upon the ultimate market price less the costs of bringing the crops or animals to maturity, may be shown as the A.C.V. See Strauss Brothers Packing Co., Inc. v. American Insurance Co., 98 Wis.2d 706, 298 N.W.2d 108 (1980).

2. Incidentally, property insurance policies currently in use have dropped the confusing qualification that actual cash value is to be "ascertained with proper deductions for depreciation."

3. Query: Does the insurer or insured benefit most from the allowance of "broad" evidence?

4. "Valued policies"

Many American States have enacted "valued policy laws" applicable to fire insurance policies in case there has been a total loss. In such cases, the laws generally provide that the face value of the policy must be paid no matter whether the "actual cash value" is less. The State laws vary a good deal and each one has to be consulted to ascertain its precise meaning and coverage. One motivation leading legislatures to the enactment of valued policy laws was the desire to deter insurance agents from selling high face value policies on lower value premises, thus collecting higher premiums. Absent such a statute, of course, the payout in case of loss would be based on the indemnity principle, that is, "actual cash value" lost by the insured. The suggestion that valued policy laws might also provide some temptation to arson and also to fraudulent overvaluation of property by insureds seems plausible.

5. "Full Replacement Insurance"

Travelers Indemnity Co. v. Armstrong, 442 N.E.2d 349 (Ind.1982):

> "Replacement cost insurance is not a pure indemnity agreement. It is an optional coverage that may be purchased and added to a basic fire policy by endorsement. It is more expensive because the rate of premiums is higher and the amount of insurance to which that rate applies is usually higher.
>
> "Replacement cost coverage is available on the insurance market to meet the need which troubled the plaintiff. That need may be expressed this way:
>
>> "Since fire is an unwanted and unplanned for occurrence, why can't the owner of an older home buy insurance to cover the full cost of repair even if those repairs make it a better or more valuable building? Since at the time of fire the homeowner may be least able to pay for improvements, why can't that hazard be insured too? Instead of apportioning the cost of repair after a fire between the actual cash value, to be paid by the insurer, and the betterment to be paid by the insured, why can't the policyholder simply pay a higher premium each year but not have to pay anything more to have his home fully repaired in the event of fire?

> "When the insurance industry adopted a standard extension of coverage endorsement to provide replacement cost, it took into account the one great hazard in providing this kind of coverage: the possibility for the insured to reap a substantial profit, if fire occurs. See Higgins v. Insurance Co. of North America, (1970) 256 Or. 151, 469 P.2d 766, 66 A.L.R.3d 871 and the annotation beginning at 66 A.L.R.3d 886.
>
> "The cost of repair may exceed the fair market value of the building, and in the case of very old or obsolescent buildings, the difference may be very substantial. To permit recovery of the cost of repair, without also requiring the repairs to be made usually provides an even greater windfall than is provided when repairs are made. In effect the insured sells his building not at its market value but at a much higher figure and for cash."

Consult Appendix B. (Property and Homeowners' Policy) under "3. Loss Settlement." Here provision is made for payment at full replacement *cost* if the insured has paid the premium for at least 80% of the full replacement *value* of the premises. Obviously this *is* expensive.

*Important.* Note carefully that this "80% provision" is different from the "80% Coinsurance Clause" set out in Note on Coinsurance on p. 314.

6. *Replacement value of goods, especially inventory*

Ordinarily the value of inventory will be the cost of replacement on the appropriate market, usually wholesale in the case of inventory. Of course market value tends to fluctuate and this causes problems when the insured has to make periodic reports under a "value reporting clause" as in Midwest Office Technology, Inc. v. American Alliance Ins. Co., reprinted *supra.*

For example in FSC Paper Corp. v. Sun Ins. Co., 744 F.2d 1279 (7th Cir.1984) the insured paper company maintained a huge inventory of waste paper in its warehouse. For over five years the insured had regularly made quarterly reports of the replacement value of the inventory (pursuant to the policy requirement quoted below), basing the estimates upon its "historical cost" of acquiring the paper. The premiums, of course, depended on these figures.

Further facts are given in the case (here from the dissenting opinion):

The policy was in full force and effect on July 8, 1979, when a fire destroyed 12,827 tons of the Special Pack inventory. According to FSC's amended value report, the Special Pack had a monetary value of $611,719.63, or $47.69 per ton, as of June 30, 1979, but following the fire that occurred just eight days later, FSC claimed that it was entitled to recover $91.15 per ton, or $1,169,197.00. Sun Insurance disputed FSC's inflated valuation of recovery and FSC, in turn, filed this lawsuit.

The immediate controversy stems from two provisions included within the insurance contract that must be read jointly. Endorsement 11 of the policy provides:

> "VALUATION: In case of loss the basis of adjustment for all property covered by this policy, * * * shall be replacement cost at time and place of loss. * * *

> When rendering reports as provided in Section 11, values are to be reported on an equivalent basis."

Section 11 of the policy provides in pertinent part:

> "REPORTS AND PREMIUMS: Within 60 days after the end of each quarter the Assured shall report to the Company the total values of all property at risk under this policy on the last business day of that quarter. Once during each calender year the Assured shall report to the Company the values of property at risk as of quarter September 30 by locations (as defined by Section 6 hereinabove)."

Based upon the extensive evidence presented at trial, the trial judge found that Endorsement 11 of the policy "constitutes a valuation provision which is intended to fix the value of destroyed property at a specific time and place. * * *" The trial judge further determined that "[t]he words 'equivalent basis' * * * are not clear when read in isolation, but their meaning is clarified when viewed in the light of evidence of the [prior] practices and procedures of the parties." According to the trial judge, the term "equivalent basis" means that "values of all property * * * are to be reported on the same basis as provided in Section 11 of the policy. Endorsement 11 then uses such reports for valuation reports for purposes of adjustment." The trial judge added that "Endorsement 11 provides for replacement cost at 'time and place of loss' which ... ties down the valuation figure to a specifically ascertainable amount when reported under Section 11." Based upon these findings, the trial judge concluded that "[u]nder the reasonable and businesslike interpretation of the policy, including the last sentence of Endorsement No. 11, Sun Insurance was required to determine 'replacement cost at time and place of loss' on the basis of the values reported by FSC under Section 11."

The Court of Appeals (2–1) rejected the District Court's conclusion and remanded for recalculation:

> "We agree with FSC's argument that the policy, * * * unambiguously provides for a measure of damages different from historical cost. * * *
>
> "While we understand the district court's concern for Sun Insurance's problem, we are compelled to conclude that FSC's recovery is not limited to amount [of its last report]. * * *
>
> "We believe that FSC's recovery must be measured in general by the amount it was reasonably required to expend to put itself in the position it would have occupied had the fine not occurred."

*Editorial Comments:*

a. The replacement of over 12,000 tons of waste paper on the open market immediately after a fire would naturally drive the price up considerably. The majority recognized this and rejected the *actual* replacement cost of $1,169,197 as the appropriate measure; instead cautioning the trial court on remand to consider the commercial reasonableness of immediately replacing the depleted inventory on a thin and volatile market.

b. Should not there be an adjustment of the premium, at least to accord with the difference between the last report and the actual value?

How about the previous five years during which the reports were based on the same calculations as the last one?

### *Problems*

1. An Argentine employee of an American corporation makes off with a billion or so pesos in Buenos Aires in 1977 when the rate of exchange is 350 pesos to $1. A claim on a fidelity bond is made in 1980 when the exchange rate is 290,720 pesos to $1. In 1984 when judgment for the insured entered the peso is really down. Which date should be used to calculate the insurer's liability in dollars. See Levi Strauss & Co. v. Aetna Cas. & Surety Co., 184 Cal.App.3d 1479, 229 Cal.Rptr. 434 (1st Dist.1986).

2. An insurance policy covers $100,000 property damage with $2,000 deductible. Damages amount to $105,000. How much is payable: $98,000, $100,000, $102,000, $103,000? Cf. Brinker v. Guiffrida, 629 F.Supp. 130 (E.D.Pa.1985).

3. The owner of a residence fronting on the ocean is insured for $1,000,000 by a policy covering "all risks of physical loss or damage" to the building. Heavy storms have caused the sand to wash away up to the foundation of the house. No physical harm has been done to the house, but unless a sea wall is built at the cost of $100,000, the house may collapse in another storm. How much can the owner recover under the policy? Nothing? $100,000? Diminution of market value?

### *Note on Coinsurance*

The term "coinsurance" (which can be used in a number of different ways) is most often used to signify a property insurance clause which provides a formula for loss-sharing between insurer and insured. The clause is widely used in policies covering commercial properties. The purpose of the clause is pretty clear. Most fires today cause less than total destruction because of fire prevention devices, fire protection services, or other reasons. Thus an insured may be inclined to insure only a relatively small portion of the value of his building at a small premium expecting enough coverage to meet any likely loss. If he insures his $100,000 building for $25,000 and his loss is $10,000, he is fully covered.

A common version of the clause illustrates how coinsurance deals with this inclination of insureds:

> The "percentage specified" is commonly enough 80%. Put in formula fashion the clause would say:
>
> $$\frac{\text{AMT of INSURANCE}}{\text{80\% of ACV}} \times \text{AMT of LOSS} = \text{AMT PAYABLE}$$
>
> Assuming that the amount of the insurance (face value of the policy) is $50,000, that the ACV is $100,000, that the amount of the loss is $8,000:
>
> $$\frac{\$50{,}000}{\$80{,}000} \text{ or } \frac{5}{8} \times \$8{,}000 = \$5{,}000$$
>
> If the amount of insurance varies, then the amount payable differs. E.g., if the amount of insurance is $90,000, then the policy would cover the entire loss.

If, however, the loss is total (that is, $100,000) then the whole amount of the policy becomes payable.

See, for some comment, Vance, Insurance (3d Ed., 1951), § 158; Keeton & Widiss, Insurance Law § 3.8 (1988).

## JEFFERSON INSURANCE CO. v. SUPERIOR COURT

Supreme Court of California, 1970.
3 Cal.3d 398, 90 Cal.Rptr. 608, 475 P.2d 880.

McCOMB, JUSTICE.

By this petition for a writ of mandate, petitioners (hereinafter referred to as "the insurers") seek to compel respondent court to set aside an order vacating an appraisal award. The matter is before us on an alternative writ issued by the Court of Appeal.

Real party in interest (hereinafter referred to as "the insured") is the owner of a hotel building, which has a fair market value, excluding the value of the land, of $65,000. Prior to the fire loss which resulted in this litigation, the insured had acquired from the insurers fire insurance policies written in the California standard form prescribed by section 2071 of the Insurance Code. The policies contained an "average clause," providing for a proportionate reduction of any loss unless the building was insured to 70 percent of its "actual cash value." [59] The policies were written in the total amount of $45,000, which is approximately 70 percent of the fair market value of the building.

The parties agreed that the amount of the loss was $24,102.05 ($25,702.05, the cost of repairs, less $1,600 betterment). The insurers, however, refused to pay that amount, contending that the property was substantially underinsured according to the average clause. Their theory was that "actual cash value," as used in the policy, does not mean fair market value, but means the replacement cost of the building less depreciation. The replacement cost less a reasonable depreciation factor is approximately $170,000. The insured contended that the building was sufficiently insured, asserting that the "actual cash value" referred to in the policy means fair market value.

Upon demand by the insurers, appraisers were appointed, pursuant to the statutory appraisal clause contained in the policy, for the purpose of having them determine the actual cash value of the building.[60] The

**59.** The "average clause" limits the liability of the insurers, as follows: "[T]his company shall be liable for no greater proportion of such loss than the amount of insurance specified in such item bears to the percentage specified in the first page of this policy [70%] of the *actual cash value* of the property. * * * " (Italics added.)

**60.** The appraisal clause in the policies is in the required statutory language of section 2071 of the Insurance Code, as follows: "In case the insured and this company shall fail to agree as to the actual cash value or the amount of loss, then, on the written demand of either, each shall select a competent and disinterested appraiser and notify the other of the appraiser selected within 20 days of such demand. The appraisers shall first select a competent and disinterested umpire. * * * The appraisers

appraisers, after some disagreement among themselves, accepted the insurers' contention that the term "actual cash value" means replacement cost less depreciation of the building, and determined on that basis that the actual cash value of the building was $169,547. One of the appraisers independently determined that the fair market value of the building was $65,000. From the appraisers' determination that the actual cash value was $169,547, the insurers offered to pay $10,154 as their proportion of the $24,102.05 loss sustained.[61] The insured rejected the offer and petitioned respondent court under section 1285 of the Code of Civil Procedure to vacate the appraisal award.

The evidence before respondent court established conclusively that the appraisers had determined as a matter of law that the issue before them was the "replacement cost less depreciation" of the building, and that in arriving at the value listed in their award as "cash value," they refused to consider income, location, or any other relevant factor tending to show the fair market value of the property, despite the fact that such evidence was made available for their use.

Based upon this showing, respondent court ordered that the award be vacated pursuant to section 1286.2, subdivisions (d) and (e), of the Code of Civil Procedure, thus finding by implication (1) that the appraisers had exceeded their powers by erroneously deciding a question of law (the meaning of "actual cash value"), which they had not been authorized to decide, and (2) that the insured had been substantially prejudiced by the refusal of the appraisers to consider material evidence. Respondent court, in ordering a second appraisal, directed that new appraisers "employ the standard definition of fair market value, which is synonymous with the 'actual cash value' in said insurance policy, namely, the price that a willing buyer would pay a willing seller, neither being under any compulsion to sell or buy."

*Questions:* First. *Did the appraisers, in determining the "actual cash value" of the insured's building, properly use "replacement cost less depreciation"?*

*No.* "Actual cash value," as used in section 2071 of the Insurance Code, is synonymous with "fair market value." (See Martin v. State Farm Mutual Auto. Ins. Co., 200 Cal.App.2d 459, 470, 19 Cal.Rptr. 364, 371; Hughes v. Potomac Ins. Co., 199 Cal.App.2d 239, 252–253, 18 Cal.Rptr. 650.) Thus, in *Martin,* the Court of Appeal, in construing the section, said: "The loss payable on an insurance policy is not the cost of the car to plaintiffs but its fair market value just prior to its destruction."

shall then appraise the loss, stating separately actual cash value and loss to each item; and, failing to agree, shall submit their differences, only, to the umpire. An award in writing, so itemized, of any two when filed with this company shall determine the amount of actual cash value and loss. * * *"

**61.** The figure of $10,154 is arrived at by taking the ratio of the $45,000 policy limit to 70 percent of the actual cash value, and applying that fraction to the amount of the loss.

It is clear that the Legislature did not intend the term "actual cash value" in the standard policy form, set forth in section 2071 of the Insurance Code, to mean replacement cost less depreciation. The term appears not only in the average clause, hereinabove referred to, but also in the insuring clause and must be given the same meaning in both. The latter clause insures "to the extent of the actual cash value of the property at the time of loss, but not exceeding the * * * cost to repair or replace the property. * * *" Since replacement cost less depreciation can *never* exceed replacement cost, it would not be logical to interpret this clause to mean "to the extent of the replacement cost less depreciation, but not exceeding the * * * cost to repair *or replace* the property." (Italics added.) If "actual cash value" had been intended to mean replacement cost less depreciation, the Legislature would not have used "the cost to * * * replace the property" as a limiting factor, and would have specified as a limiting factor only the cost to repair the property.

Second. *Did respondent court act properly in vacating the appraisal award because the appraisers based the award on a misconception of the law?*

*Yes.* Although *arbitrators* are frequently, by the terms of the agreement providing for arbitration, particularly in construction contracts, given broad powers (see, e.g., Olivera v. Modiano–Schneider, Inc., 205 Cal.App.2d 9, 11, 23 Cal.Rptr. 30, where the contract provided that any controversy or claims arising out of the contract were to be settled by arbitration), *appraisers* generally have more limited powers. As stated in Hughes v. Potomac Ins. Co., supra, 199 Cal.App.2d 239, 253[9], 18 Cal.Rptr. 650, 658: "The function of appraisers is to determine the amount of damage resulting to various items submitted for their consideration. It is certainly not their function to resolve questions of coverage and interpret provisions of the policy."

Thus, in the present case the appraisers were authorized to determine only a question of fact, namely, the actual cash value of the insured building.

Since the evidence shows that the appraisers misinterpreted the meaning of "actual cash value" and therefore failed to decide the factual issue submitted to them, the insured properly invoked the jurisdiction of respondent court to vacate the award and order a rehearing. * * *

The alternative writ is discharged, and the petition for a peremptory writ is denied.

## *Notes*

1. The coinsurance clause applied to partial losses puts the parties into unnatural postures—the owner depreciating the worth of his property and the insurer asserting whatever appraisal formula will most inflate the value. In Erin Rancho Motels v. United States Fidelity and Guaranty Co., 218 Neb. 9, 352 N.W.2d 561 (1984) a motel was insured for $247,000 with an 80% coinsurance clause. The owner's expert, using cost less depreciation, comparable sales, and income approaches came up with a figure of $253,700 as the

value of the damaged motel, which would require no deduction from the amount of the loss. The insurer's expert "insisted that replacement cost less depreciation was the only method suitable for use in arriving at 'actual cash value' for coinsurance purposes." He arrived at the figure of $376,000 which would reduce the owner's recovery to 82% of the actual loss. The jury came up with $300,700 as the value of the property. How much of the partial loss should the owner be paid?

2. If A takes out a $2,500 policy on property worth $2,500 and B takes out a $2,500 policy on property worth $10,000—each policy with an 80% Co-insurance clause—should A and B be charged the same premium? Why not require, as a matter of law, that all property insurance policies contain a 100% Co-insurance clause? See Procaccia and Shafton, Co–Insurance Clauses and Rate Equity, Ins.L.J. # 661 (February 1978) at page 69.

## APPAREL CITY SEWING MACHINE CO., INC. v. TRANSAMERICA INS. GROUP

Court of Appeal of California, First District, 1982.
129 Cal.App.3d 400, 181 Cal.Rptr. 64.

WHITE, P.J. * * *

On April 12, 1974, appellant purchased a policy of insurance from respondent which included coverage for a loss resulting from the interruption of business caused by a fire. On December 17, 1976, while said policy was in effect, there was a fire at appellant's premises which resulted in an interruption of its business affairs. "An accountancy firm hired to compute the loss, determined that [appellant's] gross earnings for the twelve months following the loss, had the loss not occurred, would have been $390,744.00." The net earnings loss resulting from the fire was computed by the same firm to be $41,603. The parties do not contest the accuracy of these figures.

Paragraph six of the business interruption form of the insurance policy issued by respondent provides: "CONTRIBUTION CLAUSE: IN CONSIDERATION OF THE RATE AND FORM UNDER WHICH THIS POLICY IS WRITTEN, THIS COMPANY SHALL BE LIABLE, IN THE EVENT OF LOSS, FOR NO GREATER PROPORTION THEREOF THAN THE AMOUNT HEREBY COVERED BEARS TO THE CONTRIBUTION (COINSURANCE) PERCENTAGE SPECIFIED ON THE FIRST PAGE OF THIS POLICY (OR ENDORSED HEREON) OF THE GROSS EARNINGS THAT WOULD HAVE BEEN EARNED (HAD NO LOSS OCCURRED) DURING THE 12 MONTHS IMMEDIATELY FOLLOWING THE DATE OF DAMAGE TO OR DESTRUCTION OF THE DESCRIBED PROPERTY." The amount of coverage under the policy at the time of the fire was $60,000. The coinsurance percentage specified in the policy is 50 percent.

Appellant filed a complaint in the Superior Court of San Francisco County alleging under the terms of the policy issued by respondent, it was entitled to $20,801.50 (one-half of the net earnings loss it sustained on account of the fire). In its answer, respondent alleges that the amount due appellant by virtue of the business interruption coverage provided by the policy issued by respondent "is and was $12,776.28, and this defendant issued and delivered to plaintiff its draft in said amount on or about July 27, 1977, * * * "

Based upon the pleadings and the trial briefs of the parties, the trial court concluded: "The contribution clause is valid and enforceable and is neither vague nor ambiguous" [and gave judgment for $12,776.28. The insured appealed].

* * *

Appellant contends that the policy at the time of the loss provided coverage in the amount of $60,000 "for loss of gross earnings subject to fifty (50%) percent coinsurance. As there was no other insurance it becomes apparent that Appellant became its own coinsurer to the extent of one-half (½) of any loss." Appellant claims the contribution clause merely provides that "the carrier shall not be responsible for a greater proportion of the loss than the amount covered bears to the contribution percentage specified on the first page of the policy. This would be the fifty (50%) percent.... Accordingly, it is submitted that as the Appellant was its own fifty (50%) percent coinsured, the Respondent carrier was responsible for one-half (½) of the afore referred to $41,603.00, to wit, $20,801.50, less the $12,776.28 already paid by Respondent to Appellant, thus now leaving $8,025.22 due to Appellant." Simply stated, appellant's position is that he is entitled to 50 percent of the loss not to exceed the amount of insurance ($60,000). Appellant contends that the trial court erroneously imposed "upon Appellant reductive formulas not expressed in the [policy]."

* * *

* * * [W]e are not bound by the trial court's interpretation of the insurance policy involved in this case, but our independent determination has resulted in an interpretation that is consistent with that of the trial court.

The full text of paragraph six of the business interruption form which is entitled "CONTRIBUTION CLAUSE" has been set out earlier in this opinion. If we were to adopt the interpretation of the contribution clause proposed by appellant, we would have disregarded most of the language of the clause. * * * Specifically, appellant would disregard the language which refers to the gross earnings as follows, "the gross earnings that would have been earned (had no loss occurred) during the 12 months immediately following the date of damage to or destruction of the described property."

It is clear that the amount owing under the policy in question is to be calculated using a ratio or fraction given the use of the words "proportion" and "bears." There is no dispute that the reference to the amount covered is to the maximum sum that can be collected under the policy ($60,000). Likewise there is no dispute that the contribution or coinsurance percentage is 50 percent. Appellant also does not contest the figures of the accountant and therefore agrees that his gross earnings for the 12–month period immediately following the fire would have been $390,744.

Accordingly, the individual phrases in paragraph six are not ambiguous or uncertain. However, we must still see whether the language in paragraph six is ambiguous or misleading or uncertain in explaining the ratio to be used in determining the coverage afforded under the policy in question. We do not regard the language setting out the ratio to be ambiguous, misleading or uncertain. Paragraph six merely provides that respondent was not liable for any greater sum than the maximum amount of coverage ($60,000) bears to the contribution percentage (50 percent) of the gross earnings ($390,744). The trial court determined that only $12,776.28 was due and owing under the insurance policy and set its calculations as follows: "Fifty (50%) percent of $390,744.00 equals $195,372 and the percentage of $60,000 to $195,372.00 equals 30.71% [¶] * * * The plaintiff was therefore entitled to 30.71% of his loss of $41,603.00 or $12,776.28, which has already been paid to plaintiff." The fact that the formula used in the policy to determine the coverage provided for a loss is not as simple as that considered in some cases, does not mean that the formula is ambiguous, uncertain or misleading. [Affirmed].

## B. ARBITRATION

### *Note*

If students will look at the fire insurance form in Appendix A, lines 117–33, they will find a substantial bit of clauseology dealing with "appraisal". In many fire or property insurance cases, the chief issue may be the amount of payment the insured can claim. There are all sorts of people qualified as "experts" on various property and these people are capable of serving as appraisers to determine the insured's amount of entitlement. That amount itself is not always a simple thing. The policy speaks of the "actual cash value" (or "ACV") of the property lost or damaged as a crucial factor. Incidentally, the language used in the form is founded on the New York standard fire form. See N.Y.Ins.Law § 3404. Many States have adopted this form in substance by statute or regulation. In California, see West's Ann.Cal.Ins.Code § 2071.

There follows a case discussing appraisal and referring to arbitration.

### SAFECO INSURANCE COMPANY OF AMERICA v. SHARMA

Court of Appeal, Second District, 1984.
160 Cal.App.3d 1060, 207 Cal.Rptr. 104.

SPENCER, PRESIDING J.

INTRODUCTION

Respondent Kendra P. Sharma appeals from a judgment denying his cross-petition to vacate an appraisal award and granting the petition of Safeco Insurance Company of America to confirm the award.

STATEMENT OF FACTS

Respondent purchased a homeowner's insurance policy from petitioner. The policy was written on the Standard Form Fire Insurance Policy, pursuant to Insurance Code sections 2070 and 2071, and provided coverage for loss resulting from theft.

Respondent's home was burglarized on November 1, 1978, after which respondent filed an insurance claim for items which were stolen in the course of the burglary. Respondent and petitioner were unable to agree as to the value of a set of 36 miniature paintings, which respondent described as a "set of 36 Rajput miniature paintings, Bundi School, India, late 18th Century." As a consequence, respondent demanded an appraisal in accordance with the pertinent provision of the insurance policy.

The policy provision relating to appraisal provides the following: "In case the insured and this company shall fail to agree as to the actual cash value or the amount of loss, then, on the written demand of either, each shall select a competent and disinterested appraiser and notify the other of the appraiser selected within 20 days of such demand. The appraisers shall first select a competent and disinterested umpire; and failing for 15 days to agree upon such umpire, then, on request of the insured or this company, such umpire shall be selected by a judge of a court of record in the state in which the property covered is located. The appraisers shall then appraise the loss, stating separately actual cash value and loss to each item; and failing to agree, shall submit their differences, only to the umpire. An award in writing, so itemized, of any two when filed with this company shall determine the amount of actual cash value and loss. Each appraiser shall be paid by the party selecting him and the expenses of appraisal and umpire shall be paid by the parties equally." This policy provision is mandated by Insurance Code sections 2070 and 2071.

Due to misconduct, the result of an initial appraisal was vacated. In the course of that appraisal, the paintings had been valued at $18,000. A second appraisal panel was not informed of the previous appraisal proceeding. The second panel valued the paintings at $14,000. The second arbitration award describes the items valued as "36 paintings."

Respondent's attorney wrote to the umpire, requesting clarification of the basis of the award. The umpire replied, "We were not convinced, by a preponderance of the evidence, that the artwork was of 'Rembrandt' quality, * * * but rather, that it was of average quality, assuming as we did, Mr. Sharma owned the art at the time of its loss."

CONTENTION

Respondent contends the lower court abused its discretion by confirming the appraisal award, in that the appraisers exceeded the scope of their powers. For the reasons set forth below, we agree.

## Discussion

In view of the similarity between arbitration and appraisal enforcement proceedings (Jefferson Ins. Co. v. Superior Court (1970) 3 Cal.3d 398, 401, 90 Cal.Rptr. 608, 475 P.2d 880), we apply to the appraisal proceeding at issue herein the general standard of review applicable to arbitration. Accordingly, "every presumption favors the arbitrator's award." (Lehto v. Underground Constr. Co. (1977) 69 Cal.App.3d 933, 939, 138 Cal.Rptr. 419.)

We note, however, one significant difference between the two proceedings. Generally an arbitration proceeding encompasses questions both of fact and of law; hence, "the merits of the award, either on questions of law or fact, are generally not subject to review." (Ibid.) In contrast, appraisers have the power only to determine a specific question of fact, "namely, the actual cash value of the insured [item]." (Jefferson Ins. Co. v. Superior Court, supra, 3 Cal.3d 398, 403, 90 Cal.Rptr. 608, 475 P.2d 880.) As stated in Hughes v. Potomac Ins. Co. (1962) 199 Cal.App.2d 239, 253, 18 Cal.Rptr. 650: "The function of appraisers is to determine the amount of damage resulting to various items submitted for their consideration." Accordingly, the merits of an appraisal award on the question of fact presented, i.e., the value or amount of loss, will not be reviewed on appeal. However, this court may examine the record to ascertain what the appraisers considered the factual issue to be, in order to determine whether they exceeded their powers. (Jefferson Ins. Co. v. Superior Court, supra, 3 Cal.3d 398, 403, 90 Cal.Rptr. 608, 475 P.2d 880.)

In essence, respondent contends that the appraisers improperly predicated their award on the existence of property other than that which he claimed to have lost. In other words, rather than assessing the value to be assigned to the paintings respondent described ("set of 36 Rajput miniature paintings, Bundi School, India, late 18th Century"), the panel exceeded its powers by making a factual determination that the set of 36 paintings was unmatched (i.e., from various schools). Our examination of the record discloses abundant support for respondent's position.

Facially, the umpire's letter suggests the award was based on the panel's opinion of the quality of respondent's paintings—a factor necessarily involved in an appraisal of value. Nevertheless, the statement, "we are not convinced, by a preponderance of the evidence, that the artwork was of 'Rembrandt' quality" must be evaluated in light of other factors appearing in the record. We have no record of the appraisal hearing itself; however, petitioner provided the lower court with ample indications of the scope of that hearing. In petitioner's opposition to respondent's cross-petition to vacate the award, petitioner phrased the issue thusly: "The only issue [before the appraisal panel] was the precise type of paintings involved and their value." (Emphasis added.)

Discussing the evidence presented at the appraisal hearing, petitioner's opposition states: "Right after the theft, the respondent reported to the police and the insurance company that the set of 36 paintings were Tibetan and were of the 14th century. Before litigation was commenced, respondent told an art appraiser, John Angus McKenzie, that they were from various schools, which would mean that they were an unmatched set." (Emphasis added.) The opposition continues: "An art expert from Sotheby's called by Safeco testified that a matched set of 18th century Bundi School would be of museum quality. He did not know of any such set on the west coast, and said there were perhaps no more than ten such sets in existence in the entire world, and to his knowledge, they would all be in museums or in very well-known private collections."

Petitioner argued the matter before the lower court in a similar vein. With respect to the appraisal panel itself, petitioner argued: "Judge Knight, as the neutral arbitrator, stated, 'I'm not considering whether he owned them or not. I assume he owned them.' He said the question before this panel is what were the nature of the paintings he owned." In referring to the evidence, petitioner recounted: "We had experts in this hearing. We had a man from Sotheby's that showed examples of what [respondent] described * * *. What he claims he had was of such museum qualities. The expert said he knows of no matched set Bundi that is in a museum or notable private collection. There is none on the West Coast, he said. So they didn't believe it was true."

Throughout the instant confirmation proceedings, as illustrated by each of the above examples, petitioner has conceded two points: (1) Petitioner placed at issue whether the paintings respondent actually owned were those he claimed to have owned; and (2) the determination of that issue—adversely to respondent—is inherent in the appraisal award. Hence, it is clear that the umpire's reference to a determination "that the artwork was [not] of 'Rembrandt' quality" is an acknowledgment that the panel did not believe the artwork respondent lost was that which he described. In simple terms, the panel concluded the paintings were an unmatched set, rather than a matched set.

That this determination exceeded the appraisers' powers is beyond question. The appraisal provision of the insurance policy, based on Insurance Code sections 2070 and 2071, speaks of the appraisers' duty to determine actual cash value or the amount of loss. Those cases dealing with appraisals focus on the same terminology. Hughes v. Potomac Ins. Co., supra, 199 Cal.App.2d 239, 18 Cal.Rptr. 650 expressly characterizes the duty of appraisers as the determination of "the amount of damage resulting to various items submitted for their consideration." (Id., at p. 253, 18 Cal.Rptr. 650; accord, Jefferson Ins. Co. v. Superior Court, supra, 3 Cal.3d 398, 403, 90 Cal.Rptr. 608, 475 P.2d 880.) Figi v. New Hampshire Ins. Co. (1980) 108 Cal.App.3d 772, 166 Cal.Rptr. 774 describes the appraiser's function thusly: "he only evaluates the loss * * *." (Id., at p. 777, 166 Cal.Rptr. 774.)

Nevertheless, petitioner relies on a variety of cases from other jurisdictions for the proposition that appraisal properly encompasses disputes as to the 'nature' of the property at issue, i.e., the identity of the property. None of these cases stand for that proposition. St. Paul Fire Marine Ins. v. Tire Clearing House (8th Cir.1932) 58 F.2d 610 and Second Society of Universalists v. Royal Ins. Co. (1915) 221 Mass. 518, 109 N.E. 384 simply state that it is proper for an appraisal to include a hearing at which evidence is taken. Aetna Ins. Co. v. Murray (10th Cir.1933) 66 F.2d 289 and Gregory v. Pawtucket Mutual Fire Ins. (1939) 58 R.I. 434, 193 A. 508 hold it is improper for appraisers to determine value without taking evidence thereon where they have no sufficient basis in experience or knowledge to do so independently. In no authority is it suggested that an appraisal panel is empowered to determine whether an insured lost what he claimed to have lost or something different.

When an insurer disputes an insured's description in identification of the lost or destroyed property, it necessarily claims the insured misrepresented—whether innocently or intentionally—the character of the loss in filing a proof of loss. In turn, this claim opens the door to allegations of fraud. Where an insurer permitted to include the former issue within the scope of an appraisal, a determination in the insurer's favor would foreclose a court from determining one essential element of fraud in any subsequent litigation. Certainly, an insurer is free to litigate whether the insured has misrepresented what he lost but it is beyond the scope of an appraisal. Petitioner repeatedly confuses the question of identity of the property with those questions relating to value, e.g., quality or condition.

An arbitration or appraisal award may be vacated when "[t]he arbitrators exceeded their powers and the award cannot be corrected without affecting the merits of the decision upon the controversy submitted * * *." (Code Civ.Proc., § 1286.2, subd. (d).) As noted in Jefferson Ins. Co. v. Superior Court, supra, 3 Cal.3d 398, 90 Cal.Rptr. 608, 475 P.2d 880: " ' * * * it is in the determination of whether a decided issue was properly before the arbitrator * * *, that the agreement or order of submission falls under the scrutiny of the court.' " (Id., at p. 403, 90 Cal.Rptr. 608, 475 P.2d 880; quoting from Meat Cutters Local No. 439 v. Olson Bros., Inc. (1960) 186 Cal.App.2d 200, 204, 8 Cal.Rptr. 789.) Since the instant appraisal panel clearly exceeded its powers by deciding a factual issue not properly before it, and the award cannot be corrected without affecting the merits of the decision, the lower court necessarily abused its discretion in granting the petition to confirm the award and denying the cross-petition to vacate.

The judgment is reversed and the superior court is directed to enter a new and different judgment vacating the appraisal award.

### *Notes*

1. Most states have arbitration statutes and provisions for appraisal such as the one involved in the *Sharma* case. The arbitration and appraisal processes withstood constitutional challenge in *Hardware Dealers' Mut. Fire Ins. Co. of Wisconsin v. Glidden Co.,* 284 U.S. 151, 52 S.Ct. 69, 76 L.Ed. 214 (1931), where the Court held that a statute regulating the insurance contract

remedy did not violate due process or the right to jury trial as long as it was, "not unreasonable or arbitrary, and the procedure it adopts satisfies the constitutional requirements of reasonable notice and opportunity to be heard." States vary as to whether the valuation is binding on both parties or only the party invoking the provision. See 46A Corpus Juris Secundum § 1355.

2. Can appraisal (or arbitration) fall afoul of state constitutional provisions? It appears that this can happen. Below is an excerpt from *Massey v. Farmers Insurance Group,* 837 P.2d 880 (Okl.1992):

SIMMS, JUSTICE.

Certified Question of Law from the United States Court of Appeals for the Tenth Circuit.

Appellees, Harold and Dorothy Massey, purchased a fire insurance policy on their home from appellant, Farmers Insurance Group d/b/a Truck Insurance Exchange/Truck Underwriters Association (Farmers). The policy conformed to the statutory requirements of a standard fire insurance policy as mandated by 36 O.S.1981, § 4803, and contained a clause permitting the amount of loss to be determined by an appraisal of the property by appointed experts. This clause reads as follows:

> "Appraisal. In case the insured and this Company shall fail to agree as to the actual cash value or the amount of loss, then, on the written demand of either, each shall select a competent and disinterested appraiser and notify the other of the appraiser selected within twenty days of such demand. The appraisers shall first select a competent and disinterested umpire; and failing for fifteen days to agree upon such umpire, then, on request of the insured or this Company, such umpire shall be selected by a judge of a court of record in the state in which the property covered is located. The appraisers shall then appraise the loss, stating separately actual cash value and loss to each item, and, failing to agree, shall submit their differences, only, to the umpire. An award in writing, so itemized, of any two when filed with this Company shall determine the amount of actual cash value and loss. Each appraiser shall be paid by the party selecting him and the expenses of appraisal and umpire shall be paid by the parties equally." 36 O.S.1981, § 4803(G).

After a fire damaged their home, the Masseys made claim upon Farmers under the policy. The parties could not reach an agreement upon the amount of the loss, and the Masseys filed an action against Farmers in Atoka County District Court. Farmers then invoked the appraisal provision, and both parties appointed appraisers who figured the estimate for repair.

Farmers moved the court to appoint an umpire pursuant to the appraisal clause, and the court appointed a local builder suggested by Farmers' appraiser and attorneys. The umpire surveyed the property and reviewed the recommendations of the appraisers determining the damage to be repairable for $49,146.00.

A supplemental record and a filed affidavit indicate that the umpire attempted to contact each of the appraisers to obtain further detailed information, and though he received such information from Farmers' appraiser, he could not reach the Massey's appraiser. A letter from the appraiser appointed by Farmers shows that they agreed with the umpire's determination. It is unclear whether the award was filed with Farmers per the requirement of the provision, however, it was apparently sent to the district court. The Masseys did not file a formal objection to the award. Rather, they discharged their attorney and filed a pro se Motion to Reconsider the appointment of the umpire. They then retained new counsel, dismissed the Atoka County action without prejudice, and filed a new action on the policy as well as a bad faith claim in the United States District Court for the Eastern District of Oklahoma. The federal suit went to trial over the objection of Farmers, and the jury returned a verdict for the Masseys exceeding $4,000,000.00 in actual, consequential and punitive damages.

On appeal to the United States Court of Appeals for the Tenth Circuit, Farmers asserted the umpire's damage appraisal was preclusive as to damages. In reviewing this assertion, the Tenth Circuit Court determined that it contained an issue not addressed by the courts of Oklahoma and certified the following question of law pursuant to the Uniform Certification of Questions of Law Act, 20 O.S.1981, § 1601 et seq.:

> "Under Oklahoma law, what is the preclusive effect of a court-appointed umpire's damage appraisal under a statutorily-mandated provision of a fire insurance policy, where the insured, as of right, dismisses without prejudice an initial lawsuit without challenging the umpire's appraisal and, thereafter, institutes a subsequent lawsuit on the same cause of action in another court?"
>
> We hold that the umpire's damage appraisal award made pursuant to the policy provision mandated by 36 O.S.1981, § 4803 has no preclusive effect upon issues raised and litigated by the party who did not make demand to enter into the appraisal process.

The legislature enacted § 4803 in 1957, and this Court has had little opportunity to interpret the appraisal portion of it. However, such appraisal clauses have been a part of standard fire insurance policies for well over one hundred years. See Appalachian Ins. Co. v. Rivcom Corp., 130 Cal.App.3d 818, 182 Cal.Rptr. 11 (1982) (citing Old Saucelito Land & Dry–Dock Co. v. Commercial Union Assurance Co., 66 Cal. 253, 5 P. 232 (1884)). Furthermore, this Court has approved of such appraisal provisions in fire insurance contracts since 1912. See Home Ins. Co. of New York v. Ballard, 32 Okla. 723, 124 P. 316 (1912); Rochester German Ins. Co. of Rochester, N.Y. v. Rodenhouse, 36 Okla. 378, 128 P. 508 (1912).

We construed the appraisal provision of § 4803 in Fidelity–Phenix Fire Ins. Co. of New York v. Penick, 401 P.2d 514 (Okla.1965), and though we did not determine the preclusive effect of appraisal awards, we did discuss the effect of an insurer calling for appraisal without admitting liability. We held that the appraisal clause of § 4803 does not constitute a condition precedent for maintaining an action on a policy where the insurer, in making demand for an appraisal, reserves the right to litigate the question of liability. Moreover, denial of liability by an insurer waives the right of the insurer to invoke the appraisal provision. Concordia Fire Ins. Co. of Milwaukee v. Barkett, 110 Okla. 177, 236 P. 890 (1925).

This holding finds support in the majority view concerning appraisal provisions, including the generally recognized rule that appraisal provisions permit appraisers or umpires to determine one issue, to wit, the amount of damage to the property. * * *

The majority view also concludes that although appraisal awards generally cannot determine the cause of a loss and do not discharge a cause of action on the policy, they are conclusive as to the amount of damages, and a confirmed award has the same preclusive effect as a judgment in a civil action. * * * The award in the case at bar was not confirmed by the state district court.

In joining the majority of jurisdictions, this Court recognized that awards made under the appraisal clauses of insurance contracts are conclusive as to the amount of loss. Aetna Ins. Co. v. Jester, 37 Okla. 413, 132 P. 130 (1913). After an award was made, plaintiff objected to it on several grounds and brought an action on the policy. The jury found that the appraisal was invalidated by the misconduct of the appraisers. On review, we held as follows:

> "Where an appraisal has been fairly conducted in accordance with the law and the terms of the policy, the finding of the appraisers is binding upon the parties, and the insured cannot disregard the appraisal and offer independent evidence of the amount of his loss. His rights, so far as the extent of the loss is concerned, are limited by the award of the appraisers. It would seem, therefore, that [insured] should have an opportunity to make the same proof before the appraisers that he would have if the matter were being litigated in a court of justice, because the action of the appraisers will keep him from litigating the question again."

(Emphasis added) 132 P. at 132. * * *

However, these cases were concerned with whether the appraisal clause was binding on the parties to the contract and were written long before the appraisal provision became mandatory in § 4803. In other words, those contracts were entered into by both parties without any mandate from the Legislature to include an appraisal clause, and this Court approved of the clause as a part of that contract. The significant difference between those appraisal provisions and the one before us now is that the latter is imposed upon both the insurer and the insured by statute, and neither party can negotiate its inclusion or exclusion. Moreover, when one party demands that the appraisal process begin, the other party is compelled to submit to it whether they want to or not.

This distinction was significant to the Oregon Supreme Court when they considered a question almost identical to the one before this Court. In Molodyh v. Truck Ins. Exch., 304 Or. 290, 744 P.2d 992 (1987), the court held, as this Court did in Penick, supra, that a statutorily-mandated appraisal provision is not a condition precedent to litigation. Thus, the statute does not require compliance with the provision in order to litigate a claim. The court further held that once the appraisal process is demanded by one of the parties, the procedure of the statute and policy becomes mandatory. Hence, to the demanding party, the appraisal process is permissive because they have chosen to invoke it. However, once that party invokes it, the process becomes mandatory to the other party.

As a result, the provision compels one party to submit to appraisal upon the other party's demand. The court in Molodyh concluded that the appraisal award that results is binding upon the party which demanded the appraisal because the provision is permissive to him and he chose the appraisal tribunal as his forum. However, where a statute requires mandatory compliance with the appraisal provision, the appraisal award is not binding upon the party who did not demand the appraisal because such binding nature of the appraisal award would violate the non-demanding party's constitutional right to trial by jury. The court stated: "One party may not unilaterally decide to have someone other than a jury determine the issues and thereby destroy the other's right to a jury trial." 744 P.2d at 998.

The reasoning of the Oregon court is sound, and we embrace it in our analysis of the case at bar. At the time this action was filed, the Oklahoma Constitution, Art. 2, § 19, provided: "The right of trial by jury shall be and remain inviolate, except in civil cases wherein the amount in controversy does not exceed One Hundred Dollars ($100.00)."

Other than this monetary limit, no act of government may deny the right of trial by jury to a person. While as in the case of arbitration, a person may waive his right to jury trial, the legislature cannot waive it for him.[1]

Since the appraisal provision statutorily-mandated in § 4803 compels the Masseys to submit to the appraisal process upon Farmers demand, Farmers has unilaterally decided which forum the issue of the amount of loss would be decided, namely the appraisal tribunal. Hence, a construction of the statutory appraisal provision in the same manner as similar provision in contracts would run afoul of the Art. 2, § 19 right of jury trial.

The Masseys urge this Court to strike down the appraisal provision as unconstitutional. However, we are constrained to construe statutes whenever possible so as to uphold their constitutionality. St. Paul Fire & Marine Ins. Co. v. Getty Oil Co., 782 P.2d 915, 918 (Okla.1989). Therefore, we hold, as the court in Molodyh did, that § 4803(G) makes appraisal awards binding upon the party invoking the appraisal process,

1. Arbitration differs from the subject appraisal process in that arbitration is not forced upon the parties by statute. This Court noted in Voss v. City of Oklahoma City, 618 P.2d 925, 927 (Okl.1980), that arbitration is "the referral of a dispute by the voluntary agreement of the parties to one or more impartial arbitrators for a final and binding decision as a determination of their dispute." (Emphasis added) The appraisal provision in the case at bar was not agreed to voluntarily, but rather, was required by statute.

yet makes those same awards non-binding upon the party compelled to participate due to the other party's demand. * * *

The illuminating concurring opinion of Chief Justice Opala has been omitted. It is lengthy, too lengthy for inclusion here, but it adds valuable information, particularly on some of the background factors in the case.

## C. APPORTIONMENT AMONG PARTIAL INTERESTS

- **co-tenants**
- **mortgagor—mortgagee**
- **vendor—purchaser**
- **seller—buyer of goods**
- **bailor—bailee**

### RUSSELL v. WILLIAMS

Supreme Court of California, 1962.
58 Cal.2d 487, 24 Cal.Rptr. 859, 374 P.2d 827.

THE COURT. * * *

The issue on this appeal is whether a surviving joint tenant may recover from the estate of a deceased joint tenant the proceeds of a fire insurance policy covering improvements on their joint-tenancy property, the policy having been issued to and paid for by the joint tenant who now is deceased, and the loss having occurred prior to his death.

This case was decided upon a stipulation of facts that: Dorothy Mouser, now Dorothy Russell, the plaintiff and appellant herein, and John Mouser, now deceased, whose estate is being administered by the defendant and respondent herein, while husband and wife, owned the subject property as joint tenants; in October 1957, Mrs. Mouser separated from Mr. Mouser and went to Nevada where she obtained a divorce on November 13th of that year; the divorce decree so obtained made no provision respecting any property rights of the parties and they did not enter into any property settlement agreement; the title to the subject property continued in joint tenancy and Mr. Mouser continued to live thereon until his death on June 3, 1958; in the interim, i.e., on November 29, 1957, he obtained a policy of fire insurance covering the improvements on that property, which was issued to him as the sole insured, the premiums being paid from his separate funds; no agreement existed between Mr. and Mrs. Mouser respecting the placing of any fire insurance upon the premises nor concerning the disposition of the proceeds of any such policy, and the subject policy was issued without her knowledge; about six weeks prior to Mr. Mouser's death, the improvements in question were destroyed by fire, and thereafter the proceeds of the policy, representing the full value of the destroyed premises, were paid to the administrator of his estate.

Mrs. Mouser became the sole owner of the property and brought this action to recover the proceeds in question, alleging that the defendant estate became "indebted to plaintiff for moneys had and received for the use and benefit of plaintiff."

Primarily, the plaintiff's claim is based on the contention that the moneys paid by the insurance company under the subject policy constituted proceeds of the property that was destroyed and retains the character of that property. This is a false premise.

It is a principle of long standing that a policy of fire insurance does not insure the property covered thereby, but is a personal contract indemnifying the insured against loss resulting from the destruction of or damage to his interest in that property. * * * This principle gives rise to the supplemental rule that, in the absence of a special contract, the proceeds of a fire insurance policy are not a substitute for the property the loss of which is the subject of indemnity. * * * As a consequence, the plaintiff has no claim to the proceeds of the insurance paid to Mr. Mouser's estate upon the ground that they are proceeds of the joint-tenancy property of which she now is sole owner.

There are instances where, because of contractual provisions or equitable considerations, the insured holds the proceeds of a fire insurance policy in trust for or otherwise subject to the claim of others who have an interest in the property covered by the subject policy. * * * However, unless the insured has an obligation to insure, or equitable considerations are present, the proceeds of a policy issued to and paid for by the named insured on his separate insurable interest are not subject to the claims of others who also have an interest in the property covered by the policy. * * *

There is no obligation upon the part of one cotenant to insure the other cotenant against loss of the latter's interest in their jointly owned property. * * * As to this matter there is no distinction between the various types of cotenancy. Analogously it has been held that there is no duty upon a life tenant to insure for the benefit of the remaindermen. * * * Cases to the contrary from other jurisdictions, which have been cited by the plaintiffs, are not controlling.

Following the rules heretofore stated, the right of one cotenant to recover the proceeds of a policy of insurance issued to another cotenant has been denied. [citations] The same ruling has been applied as between a life tenant and a remainderman [citations]; mortgagor and mortgagee [citations]; builder and owner; and vendor and vendee, subject to certain equitable considerations. [citations].

It has been held that where the policy of insurance purports to cover the interest of all cotenants, the question of the right of the noninsuring cotenant to a part of the proceeds, upon occurrence of a loss, is dependent upon equitable circumstances. [citations]. On the other hand, it also has been held that the mere fact that the proceeds of a fire insurance policy equal the full value of the property destroyed does not entitle the owners of noninsured interests in that property to recover a part of those proceeds. [citations]. In the instant case, even though the amount of the proceeds obtained from the policy of insurance represented the full value of the property destroyed, no equitable considerations exist which require a determination, as a matter of law, that the plaintiff was entitled to any portion thereof. She separated from Mr. Mouser and left him in full possession of the property; he obtained a policy which insured his interest therein and paid the premium thereon; and she had no knowledge or agreement with respect thereto. It may not be assumed that the policy in question covered the plaintiff's interest. Under the statutes of this state a fire insurance policy must specify the "interest of the insured in property insured, if he is not the absolute owner thereof" (Ins.Code, § 381); and, pursuant to the requirements of the standard form prescribed therefor, must recite that the amount payable thereunder, in any event, shall not be "for more than the interest of the insured" (Ins.Code, § 2071). Under the circumstances, the plaintiff's claim is wholly without foundation.

In support of her position, plaintiff cites the decisions in Hawes v. Lathrop [1869] 38 Cal. 493 and Estate of MacDonald [1955], 133 Cal. App.2d 43 [283 P.2d 271]. In the former, * * * property was transferred in trust for school purposes with a remainder reserved to the grantor; the trustees caused a policy of fire insurance covering the same to be issued to them; a fire and consequent loss resulted; the trustees decided to terminate the trust and return the property to the grantor; and the court determined that the trustees held the insurance proceeds "in their fiduciary, and not in their private capacity," were not entitled thereto, and the disposition thereof should be governed by the terms of the trust which required a return of the trust corpus to the grantor upon termination. In the latter case, i.e. Estate of MacDonald, the policy of insurance, which covered an automobile, provided that in the event of damage thereto, the insurance company might either repair the damage or purchase the automobile and pay the insured its value prior to loss; the insured was killed in an accident which resulted in damage to the subject automobile; it had been bequeathed by a will previously executed; the insurance company exercised its option to purchase the automobile and pay the value thereof rather than repair the same; and the court held that the legatee to whom the automobile had been bequeathed was entitled to the insurance proceeds in question upon the ground that she would have received the damaged automobile if the insurance company had not exercised its option to purchase, that the automobile so bequeathed was subject to the insurance contract which contained this option, and that the legatee should receive the benefits of that contract upon the exercise of that option. The decisions in the cited cases are not in conflict with the views heretofore expressed in this opinion.

It may further be noted that in Estate of MacDonald the decedent had by her will demonstrated an intent that her legatee should receive the automobile, whereas in the present case decedent Mr. Mouser by purchasing with his *separate funds* fire insurance payable *to himself alone* evidenced an intent to protect only his own interest in the property and not that his cotenant should share in any proceeds of the insurance contract to which she was not a party and for which she gave no consideration.

Plaintiff suggests that if the parties had wished to dissolve the joint tenancy by partition or other means, they could have done so; that in such event plaintiff would have been entitled to one-half of the property or its value; that to permit defendant to retain the proceeds of the fire insurance on the destroyed improvements "frustrates the parties' intent by allowing the non-survivor to receive the full value of the joint tenancy"; that "the equities" therefore require that plaintiff prevail herein. This contention is without merit either in fact or at law. In the first place the nonsurvivor here does not "receive the full value of the joint tenancy." To the contrary, plaintiff is now the sole owner, free from any claim of interest therein by Mr. Mouser's estate, of all the subject real property which was held in joint tenancy at the time such tenancy terminated. The stipulated facts show that such real property comprises 13 acres of land in the County of San Bernardino, and that the fire insurance proceeds paid to defendant administrator pursuant to decedent's contract amounted to $8,084.30. No showing has been made as to the value of the 13 acres of land received by plaintiff, and for aught that appears from the record such land may have a value in excess of the insurance money received by Mr. Mouser's estate under the personal insurance contract with him which, it is stipulated, he purchased with his separate funds. Under the circumstances plaintiff has not shown that either legal or equitable considerations support her claims.

The judgment is affirmed.

## MANN v. GLENS FALLS INSURANCE CO.

United States Court of Appeals, Ninth Circuit, 1976.
541 F.2d 819.

GOODWIN, CIRCUIT JUDGE:

Glens Falls Insurance Company appeals from a judgment requiring it to pay a disputed insurance claim, plus interest, and general damages flowing from the initial refusal to pay. This diversity case was tried under Nevada law.

In 1969, the company insured Mrs. Mann's house for $15,000. The policy was a standard-form fire policy with a "mortgage clause" making the insurance proceeds partially payable to a local bank which then held a mortgage on the property. In 1971, Mrs. Mann paid off the mortgage and the bank lost its insurable interest in the property.

Mrs. Mann subsequently sold the house for $25,000. The buyers, Mr. and Mrs. Bates, paid $2,000 cash and agreed to pay $23,000 secured by a purchase-money mortgage [62] payable to Mrs. Mann.

**62.** For the ease of the reader and because the parties have argued in terms of "mortgage", we will use the term "mortgage" and its derivations throughout the

The Bateses agreed orally to insure the house against fire loss and to name Mrs. Mann as loss-payable mortgagee. However, before the Bateses purchased any insurance, the house burned to the ground. At the time of the loss, Mrs. Mann's 1969 policy had not expired.

The company's claims adjuster estimated that the house was a total loss and that the actual damage exceeded the policy limits. The adjuster recommended payment of $15,000, the policy limit.

Because of the change in the character of Mrs. Mann's insurable interest (from owner to mortgagee), the company asked her to sign a "partial, subordinated assignment" of the mortgage and the mortgage debt. This partial, subordinated assignment would have allowed Mrs. Mann to receive $15,000 in cash, plus pro rata mortgage payments to be made by the Bateses (if any) or the first $8,000 realized from the foreclosure of the mortgage, if it were foreclosed. If the foreclosure sale netted proceeds in excess of $8,000 the partial, subordinated assignment would then entitle the company to the next $15,000.

Mrs. Mann refused the offer. She desired to use all $15,000 of the insurance proceeds to reestablish the status quo ante the fire—to rebuild the house, place the Bateses back in possession, and then receive her monthly mortgage payments from the Bateses.[63] Mrs. Mann did not want to foreclose or permit the insurer to foreclose the Bateses. On the advice of counsel, she refused to sign. The company refused to pay on her terms, and this litigation is the result.

I

Fire insurance on mortgaged property ordinarily is underwritten with the owner as "insured". The mortgagee, in such cases, is named as the person to whom a part of the proceeds will be paid in the event of loss. In the standard mortgage situation, the mortgagor is the named insured; the mortgagee may be an additional insured with rights in the policy, or it may be a third-party beneficiary. However, should the mortgagor fail to insure, the mortgagee can buy insurance to protect its insurable interest in the property. Despite some criticism,[64] the widely accepted rule is that the mortgagor is not entitled to insurance protection under the mortgagee-only type insurance policy.

The parties in this case never decided what sort of policy was involved. Mrs. Mann bought the policy when she owned the house. During the policy term, she sold the house and took back a security interest. Her rights to the proceeds depend in part upon whether her

opinion. The document actually executed was a deed of trust, but the differences between the two instruments do not affect the outcome of the case.

**63.** Mrs. Mann's attorney attempted to create a legally binding arrangement which would ensure that the insurance proceeds actually went back into the property. He did this to counter the company's concern that Mrs. Mann might get a "double recovery"—from the insurance company and from the Bateses payments.

**64.** See generally, King, Subrogation Under Contracts Insuring Property, 30 Tex. L.Rev. 62, 72–76 (1951); e.g., In re Future Mfg. Coop., 165 F.Supp. 111 (N.D.Cal. 1958); Note, 72 Harv.L.Rev. 1380 (1959).

policy is treated as a standard owner-mortgagee policy or a mortgagee-only policy.[65]

The language of the contract states that the company insures Mrs. Mann against fire loss up to the policy limit, but not "in any event for more than the interest of the insured". Her insurable interest at the time of the fire[66] was that of a mortgagee. The Bateses were in possession. They had received no assignment of the policy. The policy does not name the Bateses as insureds nor create any rights in them. Mrs. Mann, the former owner, now mortgagee, is the only insured. We conclude that the policy, by operation of law, had become a mortgagee-only type policy.

The policy had a subrogation clause which stated that the company "may require from the insured an assignment of all right of recovery against any party for loss to the extent that payment therefor is made by this company". Subrogation against a person other than an insured is common to fire insurance contracts[67] and includes all claims which the subrogor may have against third parties for the loss in question.

Mrs. Mann asserts that the company was not entitled to subrogation of her debt claim against the Bateses and that she did not have to assist in that subrogation by signing the partial, subordinated assignment.

Mrs. Mann first contends that the subrogation clause refers only to tort claims. It is true that most subrogation cases involve third-party tortfeasors. But the paucity of nontort subrogation litigation is better explained by the rarity of mortgagee-only policies[68] than by a doctrinal barrier. We have unearthed examples of subrogation to contract claims[69] and the company cites examples of subrogation to a mortgage.[70]

We do not read the subrogation clause in this policy as referring to tort claims only. The company is entitled to be subrogated to the claims the mortgagee Mann may have had against the mortgagor Bateses. If one were to substitute a bank for Mrs. Mann in this case the relations of

**65.** These definitions ordinarily are spelled out in writing. But here, the owner changed her insurable interest without the knowledge of the company; and it becomes necessary to construe the language of their contract with reference to a new factual situation not specifically covered in the written contract.

**66.** 4 J. Appleman, Insurance Law and Practice § 2122, at 34 (relevant insurable interest is the one at the time of the loss) (1969).

**67.** R. Keeton, Insurance Law, § 3.10, at 147–148. At p. 187, Keeton traces the doctrine that an insurer cannot have subrogation against its own insured.

**68.** In the standard policy, the mortgagor is an insured; so, when the insurer pays the mortgagee, any subrogation right to the mortgage could only be asserted against the mortgagor, who, as an "insured", is protected from the insurer.

**69.** See, e.g., Atlantic Mutual Insurance Co. v. Cooney, 303 F.2d 253 (9th Cir.1962); cf., Employers Mutual Casualty Co. v. Shepherd–Vineyard Motors, Inc., 189 Kan. 525, 370 P.2d 388 (1962). But see, Levit, Court Denies Subrogation to Contractual Rights, 1968 Ins.L.J. 105 (comment on Patent Scaffolding Co. v. William Simpson Construction Co., 256 Cal.App.2d 506, 64 Cal.Rptr. 187 (2d Dist.1967). Also, mortgagee subrogation is almost universally allowed. 6A J. Appleman, Insurance Law and Practice § 4071, at 195 n. 8 (1969).

**70.** Commercial Standard Insurance Co. v. Hitson, 73 N.M. 328, 388 P.2d 56 (1963); Wriedt v. Beckenhauer, 183 Neb. 311, 159 N.W.2d 822 (1968).

the parties would be more conventional, and perhaps easier to deal with as matters of insurance law.

Mrs. Mann next asserts that the right to subrogation arises only after payment is made by the company. She states that since the company did not make payment, it was not entitled to subrogation.

The company offered to pay Mrs. Mann her $15,000 immediately upon her signing of the partial, subordinated assignment. Her refusal was undoubtedly reinforced by advice of counsel that she was entitled to the insurance proceeds free of the company's claim as a subrogee. Mrs. Mann left no doubt that she disputed the company's subrogation rights when she refused to sign. But her motive—to confer a benefit upon the Bates family at the expense of her insurance carrier—however generous it may have been, was not a motive the insurance company had any duty to share.

The order of performance by the parties—when the company was to pay, either before or after Mrs. Mann signed the partial, subordinated assignment—was simply not an issue in the original dispute. We have no basis for deciding the case on that ground. The company's insistence on the assignment before it made payment may have been a breach; but then Mrs. Mann's intransigence about the company's subrogation rights also may have been a breach. We need not grade the magnitude of these blunders. The center of the dispute was the subrogation right, not the order of performance.

Mrs. Mann also recites the policy's "mortgagee obligations clause" and argues that it requires the company to discharge her *entire* mortgage interest before she must assign the mortgage or part of it to the company. Her reliance on this clause is misplaced. By its own terms, the clause applies to the former mortgagee, Mrs. Mann's bank, not to Mrs. Mann herself. That clause refers only to the mortgage in existence when the policy was written, not to any subsequent mortgage interest. Westchester Fire Ins. Co. of N.Y. v. Norfolk Bldg. & Loan Assn., 14 F.2d 524 (8th Cir.1926). The general subrogation clause, not the mortgagee obligations clause, governs the rights of the parties. And that clause clearly authorizes the company to require pro tanto assignments.[71]

II

While this litigation was pending, the Bateses defaulted on their mortgage payments. Mrs. Mann, again on advice of counsel, took back a deed in lieu of foreclosure. Because Nevada has no antideficiency legislation, a foreclosure action would have preserved her rights against the Bateses. But when Mrs. Mann chose to take a deed in lieu of

71. The subrogation clause states that the company "may require" an assignment of rights "to the extent" payment is made by the company. The company here took a subordinated position in the outstanding claim against the Bateses and the Bates property. This position has the greatest support in precedents. See citations collected in R. Keeton, Insurance Law at 161 n. 11. See also, 6A J. Appleman, Insurance Law and Practice § 4071, at 192 (1969).

foreclosure, the deed discharged the Bateses and the mortgage debt entirely.[72]

The company asserts that Mrs. Mann's destruction of the rights to which the company would have been subrogated destroys its obligation to pay her as mortgagee. An insured's violation of the insurer's subrogation rights does serve as a defense which the insurer can use to avoid payment of benefits to the insured. In a mortgagee-subrogation context, our court has held that destruction of the mortgage by the mortgagee defeats the mortgagee's right to recover from the insurance company. Rosenbaum v. Funcannon, 308 F.2d 680 (9th Cir.1962). See also Insurance Co. of North Amer. v. Citizens Ins. Co. of N.J., 425 F.2d 1180 (7th Cir.1970). Mrs. Mann, by accepting the deed, discharged the Bateses of their debt and at the same time wiped out her insurable interest. Her claim against the insurance company could rise no higher than her claim against the Bateses. When that claim expired, her insurable interest and her rights under the policy expired.

The judgment is reversed.

### *Problem*
### *(with a reverse twist)*

Rocky Mountain Helicopters has a fleet of these machines and has bought another under a conditional sales contract from Bell Helicopters (manufacturer, seller and lienholder). The purchase agreement called upon the purchaser to insure for the benefit of the purchaser and seller as their interest may appear. The policy obtained named the purchaser as insured and the seller as loss payee, with the proviso that the interest of the lienholder "shall not be invalidated ... by any act or neglect of the insured." Because of a breach of warranty by the lienholder, the chopper crashed. The insurer paid the purchaser and seeks subrogation against the seller, who protests that there can be no subrogation against an insured under the policy. What should be the decision? See Rocky Mountain Helicopters, Inc. v. Bell Helicopters Textron, a Div. of Textron, Inc., 805 F.2d 907 (10th Cir.1986).

*Hint.* Said the court: "There are limits to this fiction that a mortgage clause operates as an independent contract."

## WHITNEY NATIONAL BANK OF NEW ORLEANS v. STATE FARM FIRE AND CASUALTY CO.

United States District Court, Eastern District of Louisiana, 1981.
518 F.Supp. 359.

CHARLES SCHWARTZ, JR., DISTRICT JUDGE.

* * *

On May 27, 1979 a fire damaged or destroyed property of Foreign Car Parts, Inc., 4921 Airline Highway, Metairie, Louisiana. This fire

72. The Deed in Lieu of Foreclosure stated that Mrs. Mann gave as consideration $10 plus "full satisfaction of all obligations secured by the Deed of Trust * * *."

was caused by arson instigated by Robert Bradford Smith * * *. At the time of the fire Robert Bradford Smith was President, Registered Agent and General Manager and supervised all the operational activities of Foreign Car Parts, Inc. * * *

The actual value of the contents, inventory and other chattels (or movable property) located at Foreign Car Parts, Inc. as of the date and time of the fire was $264,565.00. After the fire the aforesaid property had a value of $35,000.00 and therefore the loss insofar as it pertains to contents amounted to $229,565.00.

* * *

* * * Whitney is the mortgagee as to the movable property, that is the contents, inventory and other chattels of Foreign Car Parts, Inc. as holder of a collateral mortgage note in the sum of $1,000,000.00 * * *. The mortgage indebtedness to Whitney far exceeds the fire loss and damage to the movable property, contents, inventory and other chattels of Foreign Car Parts, Inc. Attached to and forming part of the policy are endorsements MLB–100 entitled "SMP General Property Form," * * * and MLB–101 entitled "SMP Special Building Form," * * *. It is obvious that said endorsement MLB–101 cancels and replaces any coverage on buildings provided under any other form made a part of the policy.

State Farm also issued a separate "Loss Payable Clause" Form LPC 17 (attached hereto as Appendix C) to CIT Financial Service Corporation. Both Endorsements MLB–100 and MLB–101 at Section 9 entitled "Conditions" provide in pertinent part as follows:

> "C. *Mortgage Clause:*
>
> Applicable to buildings only (this entire clause is void unless name of mortgagee (or trustee) is inserted in the Declaration): Loss, if any, under this policy shall be payable to the mortgagee (or trustee), named on the first page of this policy, as interest may appear under all present and future mortgages upon the property herein described in which the aforesaid may have an interest as mortgagee (or trustee) in order of precedence of such mortgages, and this insurance as to the interest of the mortgagee (or trustee) only therein, shall not be invalidated by any act or neglect of the mortgagor or owner of the within described property * * *"
>
> * * *

The sole issue in this case is whether the arson of Foreign Car Parts, Inc. bars Whitney's claim as the holder of the aforesaid chattel mortgage on the contents of Foreign Car Parts, Inc.[73] In order to resolve

73. The parties have also stipulated that Smith's arson is imputable to Foreign Car Parts, Inc., and thus, that company is barred from recovery pursuant to the policy.

the dispute it is necessary to determine whether Whitney is entitled to the protection of the "New York Standard" or "Union Mortgage Clauses" [74] of the policy or whether Whitney is otherwise to be treated as a party entitled to unconditional recovery. Whitney in part argues that the rights set forth in Declaration "C" are applicable to chattel mortgages and/or contents as well as to buildings, and thus claims the benefit of the standard or union mortgage clause.

Louisiana law is in accord with the law in almost all jurisdictions to the effect that where there are loss payees in a policy of insurance pursuant to an open mortgage clause, i.e. without inclusion of a standard or union mortgage clause, their right to recover is contingent upon, and purely derivative of the right of the mortgagor to recover from the insurer. [Citations.] [75]

The inclusion in State Farm's policy of both endorsements MLB–100 and MLB–101 demonstrates that the parties intended MLB–101 to be the coverage afforded by the policy on the buildings, and MLB–100 to be the coverage for the contents. The language in MLB–100 which provides for application of the union or standard mortgage clause clearly

**74.** The distinction between the rights of a mortgagee protected by the standard or union mortgage clause and the mortgagee under the open mortgage clause is set forth in Appleman, Insurance Law and Practice, § 3401 at pp. 292–296.

"A distinction which is rather important to grasp is that the policy terms are themselves not nullified by a standard mortgage clause. It is rather, that a new contract containing those provisions is made with the mortgagee personally; and the mortgagee is not bound by the mortgagor's contract which, while it may be identical in language, may be breached by the mortgagor's act. In other words, the indemnity of the mortgagee is not at the whim of his debtor, and is subject only to breaches of which the mortgagee is, himself, guilty. It has been properly stated that in some instances, certain of the provisions of the fire policy are modified and, under certain conditions, even omitted by the new agreement which springs from the mortgage clause and the insurance policy.

"This is the important distinction between the standard or union mortgage clause and the open loss payable clause in which the mortgagee could not recover where the insured was barred from recovery. In the open form, the indemnity of the mortgagee is subject to the risk of every act and neglect of the mortgagor which would avoid the original policy in the mortgagor's hands. The rights of the mortgagee in that type of contract are purely derivative, and if the mortgagor would have no right to recover, neither would the mortgagee. Under a standard mortgage clause, the liability of the insurer is prospective, and is to be determined by the rights of the mortgagee as of the time of loss. A clause providing that the loss should be payable to a mortgagee requires that such party have a mortgage on the property, and where the mortgagee had no interest in the insured property not owned by the mortgagor, a standard mortgage clause attached to the policy has been held invalid. Nor would it generally be valid where there was no mortgage debt owed by the named insured at all. Furthermore the insurer cannot be considered to have assumed payment of the mortgage debt by issuance of a policy with such a clause attached."

**75.** To the same effect, although not a Louisiana case, Paskow v. Calvert Fire Insurance Co., 579 F.2d 949 (5th Cir.1978), contra J.B. Kramer Grocery Co., Inc. v. Glenns Falls Ins. Co., 497 F.2d 709 (8th Cir.1974) which is distinguishable because plaintiff sought to insure contents only and building coverage was not intended to be included.

states "Applicable to buildings only." [76]

* * *

* * * The mortgagees as to buildings have the benefit of the standard or union mortgage clause and others do not.

The claim of Foreign Car Parts, Inc. to recover from State Farm is barred by its arson and since Whitney is a conditional payee not entitled to protection of the standard mortgage or union clause, its claim is likewise barred. * * *

Thus, in summary, the Court concludes that Whitney only has an equitable lien on any proceeds which might become due to Foreign Car Parts, Inc. * * *

As the holder of an equitable lien on insurance proceeds payable to Foreign Car Parts, Inc., Whitney's recovery is solely contingent upon the insured's rights to recover. * * *

Accordingly, plaintiff is not entitled to any recovery herein and its suit is DISMISSED with prejudice, at plaintiff's cost.

### *Problems*

1. Suppose a mortgagee, insured under a standard union mortgage clause, accepts a deed to the premises in satisfaction of the secured indebtedness. The insurance is still in effect. The premises are thereafter damaged by fire. May the mortgagee recover the amount of the loss? See, 495 Corp. v. New Jersey Insurance Underwriting Association, 86 N.J. 159, 430 A.2d 203 (1981).

2. Suppose a mortgagee, insured lender under a standard union mortgage clause, *after* a fire loss forecloses on the mortgage and bids in the property for the amount of the debt. Is the insurer now liable to the mortgagee for the damages to the property? See Farmers & Merchants Savings Bank v. Farm Bureau Mut. Ins. Co., 405 N.W.2d 834 (Iowa 1987).

3. Suppose premises are insured under a standard union mortgage clause. After a fire loss the mortgagor immediately effects repair of the premises. The insurer now declines to pay the mortgagee on the ground that the mortgagee has sustained no loss. What result? See Talman Federal Savings & Loan Ass'n v. American States Insurance Co., 468 So.2d 868 (Miss.1985).

## KRESHEK v. SPERLING

Court of Appeal of California, Second District, 1984.
157 Cal.App.3d 279, 204 Cal.Rptr. 30.

* * *

In May, 1968, Saul S. Kreshek, Elise Nina Kreshek, Henry Fox and Fay G. Fox (hereafter sellers) sold a piece of property located at 54th and

76. The collateral mortgage which Whitney relies upon to secure its indebtedness and which we must assume was either prepared by it and/or approved by its attorneys, with reference to insurance provides in pertinent part: "The policies of insurance to contain a clause that in the event of loss if any, payment shall be made to the mortgagee as his interest may appear." It does not provide that insurance policies shall contain the standard or union mortgage clause.

Avalon in the City of Los Angeles to Jacob and Zvi Sperling (hereinafter buyers). Under the sales agreement, sellers took back an all inclusive promissory note and second trust deed in the sum of $400,000, as a part of the purchase price. The note terms provided for monthly payments at eight and one-half percent interest. One of the provisions of the deed of trust was as follows:

"A. To Protect the Security of this Deed of Trust, Trustor Agrees:

"* * *

"(2) To provide, maintain and deliver to the Beneficiary fire insurance satisfactory to and with loss payable to Beneficiary. The amount collected under any fire or other insurance policy may be applied by Beneficiary upon any indebtedness secured hereby and in such order as Beneficiary may determine, or at option of Beneficiary the entire amount so collected or any part thereof may be released to Trustor. Such application or release shall not cure or waive any default or notice of default hereunder or invalidate any act done pursuant to said notice."

On or about May 24, 1982, a fire occurred on the premises destroying 22,840 square feet of improvements. However, approximately 103,000 square feet were left unaffected by the fire. Buyers spent about $50,000 of their own money conducting repairs on the property, but were undecided about rebuilding the portion destroyed by fire. After the fire, the property including the destroyed portion was worth in excess of $2 million.

Buyers filed a claim with their insurance company which issued a check in the sum of $420,992.00. Sellers then sought declaratory relief as to how those proceeds should be distributed under the terms of the deed of trust. At the time of the hearing, $319,375.60 was due to sellers under the terms of the note. Of this amount $130,908.74 was due to the holders of the first deed of trust. The trial court ruled that the first $319,375.60 would be given to the trust deed holders with the remainder given to buyers. * * *

A Beneficiary of a Deed of Trust Is Only Entitled to Insurance Proceeds to the Extent the Security Interest Has Been Impaired.

Although this case is one of first impression, the result appears to be preordained by the developing body of law in this state. (See, e.g., Miller, *Valuation of the Mortgagee's Interest Upon Partial Condemnation* (1982) 15 Loyola L.A.L.Rev. 227; Leipziger, *The Mortgagee's Remedies for Waste* (1976) 64 Cal.L.Rev. 1086.) Recent cases take the position that the beneficiary of the deed of trust only has an interest in insurance proceeds or condemnation proceeds when his security is impaired. Even then, his interest extends only to the extent of the impairment. (See, e.g., Schoolcraft v. Ross (1978) 81 Cal.App.3d 75, 146 Cal.Rptr. 57; People ex rel. Dept. of Transportation v. Redwood Baseline, Ltd. (1978)

84 Cal.App.3d 662, 149 Cal.Rptr. 11; Milstein v. Security Pac. Nat. Bank (1972) 27 Cal.App.3d 482, 103 Cal.Rptr. 16.)

This philosophical change also exists in other associated areas. It has partially resulted from the court's imposing a covenant of good faith and fair dealing on both parties to a land sale contract. (See, e.g., Schoolcraft v. Ross, supra, 81 Cal.App.3d 75, 146 Cal.Rptr. 57.) Thus, in cases involving "due on sale clauses," the Supreme Court has held that these may be enforced only when it is necessary to protect the lender's legitimate interests. * * *

The court in Milstein v. Security Pac. Nat. Bank, supra, 27 Cal. App.3d at page 487, 103 Cal.Rptr. 16, pointed out: "The purpose of the note and deed of trust is that respondents shall have the use of the funds loaned on the terms and at the interest rate specified in the note, and that appellant shall have the security provided by the deed of trust. To carry out that purpose, the implied covenant of good faith and fair dealing requires that appellant beneficiary exercise its discretion with respect to the condemnation fund in such fashion that it distribute to respondent borrowers all proceeds in excess of those necessary to recoup any impairment in security caused by the eminent domain proceeding. Since the trial court concluded on substantial evidence that appellant's [seller's] security is not impaired, respondents [buyers] are entitled to all of the proceeds of the eminent domain action."

Here, all sellers could expect from the note terms was to receive the agreed upon interest rate for the note's duration. The trial court by its judgment allowed sellers to accelerate payment on this note even though there was no showing that sellers security interest had been impaired. In fact, only contrary evidence was presented on the issue, i.e., that the value of the land and buildings were worth in excess of $2 million and the amount of the remaining debt was about $320,000. This action, urged by sellers, violated the implied covenant of good faith and fair dealing, which requires that neither party impair the other's right to receive the benefits from the agreement. * * *

* * * Sellers further contend that *Schoolcraft v. Ross,* supra, is distinguishable because there the buyer intended to rebuild whereas here, there is no showing of any such intent. Their argument misses the point. The whole purpose of the fire insurance policy under paragraph A(2) of the trust deed was to provide additional security for the deed of trust. To the extent the security was unimpaired, sellers had no right to keep the proceeds.

However, the trial court did not determine whether sellers' security interest was impaired. Thus, the case will be remanded for a hearing to determine the extent, if any, of impairment. * * *

* * *

The judgment is reversed.

## GRAIN PROCESSING CORPORATION v. CONTINENTAL INSURANCE CO.

United States Court of Appeals, Eighth Circuit, 1984.
726 F.2d 403.

FAGG, CIRCUIT JUDGE.

Continental Insurance Company (Continental) appeals from the district court's grant of summary judgment in favor of Grain Processing Corporation (GPC) and Glenmore Distilleries Company (Glenmore). Continental claims the district court committed error in finding that it was liable under a policy of marine cargo insurance it issued to GPC. Finding, as did the district court, that Glenmore has an insurable interest covered under the policy, we affirm.

This dispute involves the interpretation of a contract of insurance issued to GPC, a merchant dealing in grain alcohol, by Continental. In April of 1981, GPC contracted to sell a substantial quantity of grain alcohol to Glenmore. In May, the cargo was shipped F.O.B. Muscatine, its point of origin, to Owensboro, Kentucky, its point of destination. While en route to Owensboro, by way of the Mississippi River, the barge carrying the alcohol was destroyed. After Continental denied liability for the losses suffered, GPC and Glenmore instituted this diversity action in district court.

There is no question that the policy issued to GPC specifically covers the type of loss sustained, i.e., loss resulting from the transportation of alcohol on the Mississippi River. The question, rather, is whether GPC or Glenmore has an insurable interest mandating coverage under the specific terms of the policy. Continental maintains that GPC cannot recover under the policy because the cargo was shipped F.O.B. from Muscatine. Risk of loss having passed to Glenmore once the cargo was loaded, Continental claims that GPC did not have an insurable interest at the time the accident occurred. Continental further argues that although Glenmore had an insurable interest in the lost cargo, it was not an insured party under the specific terms of the policy. The district court held that Glenmore has an insurable interest to which the policy extends coverage. We agree; thus, it is unnecessary to decide whether GPC, too, has an insurable interest covered under the policy.

Continental rightfully contends that although paragraph 1 of the policy provides for the possibility of extending coverage to other than the named insured, i.e., "1. For account of whom it may concern.", GPC, the policyholder, must intend that the unnamed party be covered. * * * Continental argues that 1) the lack of any provision respecting insurance in the contract of sale; 2) the fact that the cargo was shipped F.O.B. rather than, for example, C.I.F. (meaning the price includes a lump sum cost of the goods and the insurance and freight to the named destination); and 3) the fact that in declaring the shipment as required by paragraph 22 of the policy, GPC declared for itself rather than for

Glenmore, makes clear that GPC had no intention of extending coverage of the policy to Glenmore. We cannot agree.

We believe, as did the district court, that the language of the policy itself evinces GPC's intent to cover a consignee with an insurable interest in the cargo. The policy was issued for the "account of whom it may concern." Paragraph 17 of the policy provides that "[t]his insurance to be of the same force and effect as if issued separately to each individual owner, shipper or consignee." Because Glenmore is the consignee of the cargo, and has an insurable interest in it, Glenmore is a concerned party within the meaning of paragraph 1 and is clearly covered under the terms of the policy.

Continental contends that in order for a particular shipment to be covered under the policy, there must be compliance with the provisions in paragraph 3(A). Paragraph 3(A) provides in relevant part:

> 3(A) To cover all shipments not otherwise insured * * * made by *this Assured,* and/or their subsidiary or affiliated companies or by others for their account, in which they have an insurable interest or on which they, prior to attachment of risk, receive written instructions to insure, in consideration of premium as agreed. (Emphasis added.)

Continental takes the position that Glenmore does not fit within the coverage of 3(A) because it is not the "Assured" or a subsidiary or affiliated company. Continental also argues that paragraph 17 does not create coverage, but rather makes clear "that for each owner, shipper or consignee named as an assured or intended to be insured as per paragraph 3, the policy will provide full protection for their interest." Although Continental concedes that any manifestation of intent by GPC that Glenmore be covered would ensure coverage for Glenmore under the policy, it contends that paragraph 17 does not serve as evidence of GPC's manifestation of intent to insure Glenmore but rather is included in the policy for the purpose of clarifying paragraph 3(A). We cannot agree.

Under Continental's interpretation of paragraph 17, the provision accomplishes no more than saying that the interests of those who are covered under paragraph 3(A) are really covered. Such a superfluous interpretation of paragraph 17 will not withstand analysis. In reading the policy as a whole, we reiterate our view that paragraph 17 evinces GPC's intent to cover a consignee with an insurable interest in the cargo.

* * *

In conclusion, we have no difficulty holding Continental liable under its policy of marine cargo insurance provided to GPC. Continental accepted a premium to provide coverage for the precise type of loss which occurred. The policy specifically undertakes to extend coverage to individual consignees. Glenmore, being an individual consignee with an insurable interest in the cargo, is entitled to recovery under the policy.

Affirmed.

### *Note*

### *Insurable Interest and the Uniform Commercial Code*

UCC 2–501 provides:

**§ 2–501. Insurable Interest in Goods; Manner of Identification of Goods**

(1) The buyer obtains a special property and an insurable interest in goods by identification of existing goods as goods to which the contract refers even though the goods so identified are non-conforming and he has an option to return or reject them. Such identification can be made at any time and in any manner explicitly agreed to by the parties. * * *

(2) The seller retains an insurable interest in goods so long as title to or any security interest in the goods remains in him and where the identification is by the seller alone he may until default or insolvency or notification to the buyer that the identification is final substitute other goods for those identified.

(3) Nothing in this section impairs any insurable interest recognized under any other statute or rule of law.

## INSURANCE OF DUAL INTERESTS UNDER EXECUTORY LAND SALE CONTRACTS—PRELIMINARY NOTE

In order to isolate the insurance law problems in the vendor-purchaser cases, it is first necessary to determine which party bears the risk of destruction of the premises between the time of the making of the contract and the time at which the legal title is deeded to the buyer. This is a point at which the law of contracts, legal rules as to damages awardable against non-wilfully defaulting vendors, real property doctrines as to title, the equity doctrine of "equitable conversion" together with the equitable remedy of specific performance, plus the lay person's notions as to who ought to have the responsibility of protecting property from casualty loss all rub somewhat incompatibly together. The obvious result has been sharply conflicting views, much legal writing and wide divergence of authority from state to state. For present purposes, an extract from a single case summarizing the several discrepant "risk of loss" rulings, together with the Uniform Vendor–Purchaser Risk Act, will do.

Judge Hyde in SKELLY OIL CO. v. ASHMORE, 365 S.W.2d 582 (Mo.1963):

* * *

"The contract of sale here involved contained no provision as to who assumed the risk of loss occasioned by a destruction of the building, or for protecting the building by insurance or for allocating any insurance proceeds received therefor. When the parties met to close the sale on April 16, the purchaser's counsel informed vendors and their attorney he was relying on Standard Oil Co. v. Dye, 223 Mo.App. 926, 20 S.W.2d 946, for purchaser's claim to the $10,000 insurance proceeds on the building. * * * It is stated in 3 American Law of Property, § 11.30, p. 90, that in the circumstances here presented at least five different views have been advanced for allocating the burden of fortuitous loss between vendor and purchaser of real estate. We summarize those mentioned: (1) The view first enunciated in Paine v. Meller (Ch. 1801, 6 Ves.Jr. 349, 31 Eng.Reprint 1088, 1089) is said to be the most widely accepted, holding that from the time of the contract of sale of real estate the burden of fortuitous loss was on the purchaser even though the vendor retained possession. (2) The loss is on the vendor until legal title is conveyed, although the purchaser is in possession, stated to be a strong minority. (3) The burden of loss should be on the vendor until the time agreed upon for conveying the legal title, and thereafter on the purchaser unless the vendor be in such default as to preclude specific performance, not recognized in the decisions. (4) The burden of the loss should be on the party in possession, whether vendor or purchaser, so considered by some courts. (5) The burden of loss should be on the vendor unless there is something in the contract or in the relation of the parties from which the court can infer a different intention, stating "this rather vague test" has not received any avowed judicial acceptance, although it is not inconsistent with jurisdictions holding the loss is on the vendor until conveyance or jurisdictions adopting the possession test. As to the weight of the authority, see also 27 A.L.R.2d 448; Tiffany, Real Property, 3rd ed., § 309".*

---

## UNIFORM VENDOR AND PURCHASER RISK ACT

### § 1. Risk of Loss.

Any contract hereafter made in this State for the purchase and sale of realty shall be interpreted as including an agreement that the parties shall have the following rights and duties, unless the contract expressly provides otherwise:

(a) If, when neither the legal title nor the possession of the subject matter of the contract has been transferred, all or a material part thereof is destroyed without fault of the purchaser or is taken by eminent domain, the vendor cannot enforce the contract, and the purchaser is entitled to recover any portion of the price that he has paid;

(b) If, when either the legal title or the possession of the subject matter of the contract has been transferred, all or any part thereof is destroyed

* See also: Friedman, Contracts and Conveyances of Real Property, 3d ed. Sec. 4.11, Practicing Law Institute, 1975.

without fault of the vendor or is taken by eminent domain, the purchaser is not thereby relieved from a duty to pay the price, nor is he entitled to recover any portion thereof that he has paid.

---

Note in each of the vendor-purchaser cases which follow where the court has laid the risk of loss. From that strong point the insurance aspects of the case can be attacked.

## ACREE v. HANOVER INSURANCE CO.

United States Court of Appeals, Tenth Circuit, 1977.
561 F.2d 216.

BREITENSTEIN, CIRCUIT JUDGE.

In this diversity case the question is whether the seller or the buyer is entitled to the proceeds of insurance policies covering damage which occurred when the insured property was under an executory sales contract later consummated by the parties. The trial court gave summary judgment for the buyer. The seller appeals. We affirm.

On March 8, 1974, plaintiff-appellant Acree, Seller, contracted to sell his home in Chickasha, Oklahoma, to Donald R. and Joyce Martin, Buyer, for $125,000. The sale was to be completed and possession delivered to Buyer on July 8, 1974. On June 18, 1974, Seller renewed two insurance policies on the premises. On June 23, the premises were damaged by fire and vandalism.

The contract provided that if the property should be damaged to any appreciable extent by fire, Buyer could "at his option, refuse to complete said sale, and said escrow money shall be returned to him and this contract shall be null and void." The contract did not mention any obligation on the part of either party to keep the premises insured. After the fire, Buyer elected to complete the contract, paid the full purchase price, and took possession. Buyer claims, and Seller denies, that the sale was completed with the understanding that Buyer would receive the proceeds from the insurance policies.

Defendants Hanover Insurance Company and Fireman's Fund Insurance Company insured the premises. They refused to pay Seller, who then sued them in federal court. Buyer intervened. The material facts are not disputed. The district court gave judgment for Buyer against the insurors [sic] for $13,000. The insurors paid that amount into the court registry and do not participate in this appeal by Seller.

The parties agree that Oklahoma law governs the disposition of the controversy and that there is no Oklahoma decision directly in point. Seller contends that the insurance policies are personal contracts of indemnity for the benefit of the insured. He says that Buyer has not bargained for the benefit of Seller's insurance and is not entitled to the proceeds arising from the fire damage. Buyer says that the insurance is to indemnify for damage to the insured property and that, because he has paid the full purchase price, recovery of the insurance proceeds by Seller would inequitably and unjustly enrich Seller.

Two opposing lines of cases have dealt with the right to insurance proceeds when the damaged property was under an executory sales contract. One line holds in essence that insurance is a personal contract of indemnity to protect the interest of the insured. See e.g. Brownell v. Board of Education of Inside School District, 239 N.Y. 369, 146 N.E. 630, 632. The other line recognizes an insurable interest in both the seller and buyer and holds that when a seller has received insurance proceeds for damage to property covered by an executory sales contract and the seller has later received the full purchase price, the seller holds the proceeds in trust for the buyer. See e.g. Brady v. Welsh, 200 Iowa 44, 204 N.W. 235, 236. The existence of these two lines of authority has long been recognized. In addition to Brady v. Welsh, see Glens Falls Insurance Company v. Sterling, 219 Md. 217, 148 A.2d 453, 455–456, and Annotation in 64 A.L.R.2d 1402, 1404–1414. Oklahoma has no cases decisive of the issue.

The liability of the insurors is not before us. They have paid the loss. Our concern is whether Buyer or Seller is entitled to the amount paid. The sale has been consummated and Seller has been paid in full. The fact that before consummation each party claimed the insurance proceeds is irrelevant. No agreement was reached. The contract provision permitting Buyer to rescind in the event of appreciable fire damage did not convert the contract into an option to purchase. Rather, it gave Buyer a choice of remedy. * * *

At the time of the fire, Buyer had equitable title to the property, and Seller, as legal title owner, held the property in trust for Buyer, see Western Assur. Co. v. Hughes, 179 Okl. 254, 66 P.2d 1056, 1058, and as security for the payment of the purchase price. It may be that Buyer was entitled to have the purchase price diminished by the amount of the fire loss. See Alabama Farm Bureau Mutual Insurance Service, Inc. v. Nixon, 268 Ala. 271, 105 So.2d 643, 646. In the case at bar, Buyer paid the full price and Seller seeks the insurance proceeds in addition thereto.

Seller asserts that Welch v. Montgomery, 201 Okl. 289, 205 P.2d 288, supports his position. That case related to a claim by a lienor to the proceeds of insurance obtained by the lienee. The claim was disallowed. The court said, Ibid. 205 P.2d at 291: "Equity will not take rights acquired by one who has been vigilant and give their benefit to one who has lost by reason of nonaction." The position of a lienor, however, is significantly different from that of a buyer. A lienor has neither equitable title to the property nor a right to demand specific performance. In the instant case Buyer held equitable title and had the right to require performance.

The effect of Welch v. Montgomery is somewhat dissipated by High Hill Rural Development Club v. Great American Ins. Co., Okl., 428 P.2d 249. There, because of annexation of school districts, a school building was no longer used for school purposes and was occupied by a club which secured insurance, naming itself as beneficiary. The building was destroyed by fire and the club claimed the insurance proceeds. The court ruled that the proceeds were held in trust for the school districts, explaining, Ibid. 428 P.2d at 251, that "* * * when the building was destroyed by fire, there was an involuntary conversion of the property and the proceeds of the insurance policy represent or stand in the place of the property destroyed." Although the case differs from that at bar because the building was public property, the quoted statement is pertinent here.

The Uniform Vendor and Purchaser Risk Act, adopted by Oklahoma in 16 O.S.A. § 202, has no applicability. The provisions of its subsection (a) apply "unless the contract expressly provides otherwise". In the instant case the sales contract has an express provision relating to the right of Buyer if the property is appreciably damaged by fire. At the time of the fire the contract was executory, but it gave Buyer the option of completion. The completion of the contract extinguished whatever risk had previously been borne by Seller. In the circumstances, the time of the fire is not determinative of the rights of the parties.

A fire insurance policy indemnifies the holder of an insurable interest against actual loss. 4 Appleman, Insurance Law and Practice, 1969 ed. § 2107, 16–17. Seller sustained no loss. He has received the full sale price. He is not entitled to a partial double payment. See Republic Insurance Company, Dallas, Texas v. French, 10 Cir., 180 F.2d 796, 799, a case arising under Oklahoma law. If the insurors had exercised their policy options of repairing and restoring the property, Buyer would have suffered no loss. Insurors paid rather than repaired. The insurance proceeds stand in place of the damages to the property.

The line of decisions which holds that in the circumstances presented here the Seller holds the legal title in trust for the equitable title of the Buyer is well reasoned. The legitimate contractual expectations of all parties are realized. Seller receives the price for which he bargained. The insurors pay the damage within the coverage of their policies. Buyer gets the property for the price which he agreed to pay and receives the benefits of the insurance as recompense for the damage to the property. * * * We are convinced that the trial judge reached the correct conclusion.

Affirmed.

### *Note*

Of course, under the general rule, the seller is entitled to recoup the premiums paid before crediting the proceeds against the purchase obligation. Berlier v. George, 94 N.M. 134, 607 P.2d 1152 (1980).

### *Problem*

Plaintiff leased a house with option to purchase and took out property insurance in her own name on the premises. A fire destroyed the house and she exercised her option to purchase. How much can plaintiff recover under the policy? See Kelly v. Iowa Valley Mut. Ins. Ass'n, 332 N.W.2d 330 (Iowa 1983).

## PARAMOUNT FIRE INSURANCE CO. v. AETNA CASUALTY & SURETY CO.

Supreme Court of Texas, 1962.
163 Tex. 250, 353 S.W.2d 841.

GREENHILL, JUSTICE.

This case is an appeal from a summary judgment. The question is one of first impression in Texas and involves the liability of two insurance companies, each issuing a policy covering improvements which were destroyed by fire.

On July 17, 1957, the heirs of Mrs. R.L. Cameron entered into a written agreement labeled "Contract of sale and receipt for earnest money," whereby the seller(s) "sells and agrees to convey" and the purchaser(s), Mr. and Mrs. Sterling D. Holmes and Pauline Reece, "agrees to consummate the sale within fifteen days from date title company approves title" of a tract of land upon which were situated the improvements later destroyed. The contract specified the total purchase price, a down-payment, and terms of $125 monthly until the final closing date one year later, July 17, 1958, when the balance was due. Both seller and purchaser were given the right of specific performance. Purchasers had the right to occupy the premises from the inception of the contract, which they did, and had the right to make all desired improvements on the property.

On October 12, 1957, sellers procured from petitioner, Paramount Fire Insurance Company, an insurance policy for $15,000 covering improvements on the contracted land and payable only to sellers. A clause extending protection to purchasers under this policy was specifically rejected by sellers.

The fire involved occurred on July 7, 1958. By this time, the title company had issued the title insurance policy. The sellers had prepared a warranty deed conveying the property to the purchasers. Some, but not all of the sellers had already signed the deed, and it was being sent to the others for their signatures and acknowledgments. Purchasers had made the monthly payments of $125 and had procured a sufficient loan from Richardson Savings and Loan Association to pay the balance of the purchase price. Purchasers had also procured an $18,000 fire insurance policy from respondent, Aetna Casualty & Surety Company, in their favor with loss payable clause to the mortgagee as its interest might appear. This policy was dated June 25, 1958. All these and related papers, including the Aetna policy, were deposited in escrow with National Title & Abstract Company for final closing of the transaction on July 8, 1958. Because of the July 7 fire, this meeting was postponed until September 3, 1958. At the latter date, purchasers paid the contract price and received the warranty deed. Sellers, at the same time, assigned all their rights and claims under the Paramount policy to the purchasers.

Thereafter, purchasers and their mortgagee filed suit against both insurance companies, claiming property loss of $14,000. This suit was settled as to the plaintiffs by each insurance company's contributing a prorata share of the loss based on the amount of its respective policy, reserving its rights against the other. The suit then proceeded between the two insurance companies to determine liability as against each other. The trial court rendered summary judgment against Aetna, awarding Paramount the amount of money it contributed in the settlement with purchasers. Aetna's motion for summary judgment was consequently denied. On appeal, the judgment was reversed and the loss prorated between both companies in proportion to the face amount of the respective policies. 347 S.W.2d 281.

Both companies filed applications for writ of error to this Court. Paramount, of course, seeks to have the trial court's judgment affirmed. Aetna asks that the full loss be imposed upon Paramount, or, alternatively, that the judgment of the Court of Civil Appeals be affirmed.

* * *

* * * Aetna being the insurer of purchasers in possession under a contract of sale, it must bear all the loss unless it has a right to require Paramount to bear a prorata share as held by the Court of Civil Appeals.

Paramount's application attacks this proration holding, arguing that the vendors suffered no actual pecuniary loss from the fire and that, therefore, the vendees' insurance company should incur the total liability. Paramount's position is based on the generally accepted principle that:

> "Since a contract for insurance against fire ordinarily is a contract of indemnity * * * insured is entitled to receive the sum necessary to indemnify him, or to be put, as far as practicable, in the same condition pecuniarily in which he would have been had there been no fire; that is, he may recover to the extent of his loss occasioned by the fire, but no more, and he cannot recover if he sustained no loss." 45 C.J.S. Insurance § 915, p. 1010.

Aetna does not challenge this principle. Instead, the controversy is as to whether or not the insureds of Paramount suffered any "loss" in a legal sense.

The Court of Civil Appeals regarded the date of the fire as controlling and found that the vendors did incur a loss, despite the fact that they received the full contract price from the vendees after the fire. There is a line of cases which supports this viewpoint; e.g., State Mutual Fire Insurance Co. v. Updegraff, 21 Pa. 513; Dubin Paper Co. v. Insurance Co. of North America, 361 Pa. 68, 63 A.2d 85, 8 A.L.R.2d 1393; Insurance Co. of North America v. Alberstadt, 383 Pa. 556, 119 A.2d 83; Milwaukee Mechanics Insurance Co. v. Maples, 37 Ala.App. 74, 66 So.2d 159; First National Bank of Highland Park v. Boston Insurance

Co., 17 Ill.2d 147, 160 N.E.2d 802; Kahn v. American Insurance Co., 137 Minn. 16, 162 N.W. 685. See generally 8 A.L.R.2d 1416, § 6. The rationale of these cases is that an insurance company contracts to protect an insured against destruction by fire of his property and that liability is fixed if such fire occurs, all other contract terms being met. Any compensation to the insured from their parties, such as payment from the vendees here, is regarded as being unrelated to the insurance contract, of no concern to the insurance company, and in the nature of a windfall to the insured.

On the other hand, there is also a line of cases which supports Paramount's argument that its insureds ultimately suffered no pecuniary loss from the fire and are therefore not entitled to recover on their insurance contract. In Ramsdell v. Insurance Company of North America, 197 Wis. 136, 221 N.W. 654, it was said:

> "The court looks to the substance of the whole transaction rather than to seek a metaphysical hypothesis upon which to justify a loss that is no loss. This is not a case where a stranger to the transaction, out of charity, or for other reasons, might make good the loss * * *. The loss has been made good out of a related transaction * * *."

Accord, Tauriello v. Aetna Insurance Co., 14 N.J.Super. 530, 82 A.2d 226; Smith v. Jim Dandy Markets, 172 F.2d 616 (9th Cir.). We are inclined toward this latter view.

The complexity of the present problem is heightened, however, by another widely accepted principle upon which the Court of Civil Appeals relied in ordering a proration between Paramount and Aetna. In 64 A.L.R.2d 1406, § 4, it is said:

> "Where the purchaser as equitable owner will bear the loss occasioned by a destruction of the property pending completion of the sale, and the contract is silent as to insurance, the rule quite generally followed is that the proceeds of the vendor's insurance policies, even though the purchaser did not contribute to their maintenance, constitute a trust fund for the benefit of the purchaser to be credited on the purchase price of the destroyed property, the theory being that the vendor is a trustee of the property for the purchaser."

The difficulty is that in some jurisdictions, even where the vendor is regarded as having suffered no loss from a fire, he is allowed to collect on his insurance policy subject to a constructive trust for the vendee's benefit. E.g., Wm. Skinner & Sons' Ship-Building and Dry-Dock Co. v. Houghton, 92 Md. 68, 48 A. 85. Obviously, this result does violence to the indemnity theory of insurance, but as one commentator observed, it represents an attempt by the courts to "accommodate the contract to lay expectation without tarnishing the ideal of freedom of contract." Young, Some "Windfall Coverages" in Property and Liability Insurance, 60 Colum.L.Rev. 1063. The rationale is that if a vendee pays the full contract price for property which has been damaged or destroyed by fire, it is only equitable to allow him the benefit of any insurance proceeds rather than to give the vendor both the insurance proceeds and the proceeds of sale.

Paramount concedes that it is difficult to quarrel with the equity of this rule, but strenuously argues that the rule should have no application when the vendees have secured their own insurance policy. We agree.

Although none of the decisions applying the constructive trust theory purport to base the result on the fact that the vendee had no insurance, yet it appears that such was the situation in all but two cases. The two exceptions are Vogel v. Northern Assurance Co., 219 F.2d 409 (3rd Cir.), and Insurance Company of North America v. Alberstadt, 383 Pa. 556, 119 A.2d 83. In these cases, the vendee was allowed to benefit from both his and the vendor's policies, even to the extent of being allowed to profit from the fire in the Vogel case. It must be observed, however, that both cases applied Pennsylvania law that an insured's loss is determined as of the date of the fire regardless of any subsequent developments. See Dubin Paper Co. v. Insurance Company of North America and State Mutual Fire Insurance Co. v. Updegraff, supra.

We believe the better result to be that if a vendor is entitled to specific performance under a contract of sale and thereby collects the full purchase price despite fire damage to improvements, he has suffered no legal loss. As it is not before us here, we leave open the question of whether, where the vendee has no insurance, there can be recovery on the vendor's policy subject to a constructive trust for the vendee, who is often ignorant of his legal liability in such a situation. We believe that there is nothing in the present case, however, which would require such an exception to the principle that an insurance policy is basically a personal, indemnity contract.

Here we are not dealing with an unwitting risk bearer, but rather with vendees who are protected by their own insurance. Also, we do not have a situation where the vendors originally intended for their policy to protect the vendees, for they specifically rejected such a provision. Further we note that in the vendors' own policy there is a provision that Paramount's liability should not exceed "the interest of the insured." After the contract of sale, the interest of Paramount's insured became the amount of the unpaid purchase price and, as to that interest, they suffered no loss. Accordingly, there is no liability under the Paramount policy, and Paramount's insureds had no rights to assign to the vendees.

* * *

For the reasons stated herein, the judgment of the Court of Civil Appeals is reversed and the judgment of the trial court is affirmed.

GRIFFIN, JUSTICE (dissenting).

I do not agree that all of the loss from the destruction of the improvements by fire should fall on Aetna. I believe the law requires that the loss be prorated between Aetna and Paramount as decreed by the Court of Civil Appeals.

The majority opinion recognizes that Paramount's insured had an insurable interest in the property at the time of the issuance of that policy. The majority reasons that the liability of Paramount to the insurer is to be determined by events happening after the loss by fire has occurred. * * *

Such a holding is in direct violation of and contrary to the language of the policy. The policy provides: "Loss on building items shall be payable to ASSURED address ______ as Mortgagee or Trustee, as their *interest may appear at time of loss,* subject to Mortgage Clause (without contribution) printed elsewhere in this policy." (Emphasis mine.) Clearly the loss of the building and the time of the fire are contemporary and simultaneous. The mortgage clause referred to above has no application to our cause. Further, the policy also contained a provision that the liability of the company "shall not exceed the actual cash value of the property *at the time of loss.*" (Emphasis mine.) Thus again this clearly fixes the date of the fire as the date on which liability is to be determined.

Let us apply the majority reasoning that Paramount only insured the vendor for the unpaid balance of his purchase price to the fact situation in this cause. Take the date fixed by the policy for determining this interest—which is the "time of loss"—we find that on the date of the loss, which is the date of the fire, the purchaser owed the vendor $12,675.00, plus the contract interest. This figure is computed by subtracting from the total contract price of $15,250.00 the sum of $1,200.00 paid at the time the contract was signed, less eleven monthly payments of $125.00 each totalling $1,375.00. By the terms of the policy contract between the vendor and Paramount, Paramount's liability became fixed to vendor for this sum of $12,675.00. Purchasers hold an assignment from vendor of all his rights against Paramount. Paramount has never paid this liability. Therefore, I maintain that Paramount is still liable on its policy to the assignees of vendor, and its liability is to be prorated in accordance with the terms of the policy.

No public policy is violated; no statute is offended by the parties to the insurance contract making the contract which they did make. Suppose the vendor and purchaser had entered into a contract providing for $5,000.00 cash payment, the balance to be paid in monthly instalments of $125.00 each due on the 10th day of each successive succeeding month. This would require 82 months, or approximately seven years, to pay the deferred payments. Vendor could not be forced to take his balance in one lump sum. He could insist on the monthly payments as set out in the contract in order to earn the interest. Under the majority holding Paramount's liability would not be known until the last payment had been made. This example illustrates very clearly the fallacy of the reasoning of the majority opinion.

* * *

I would affirm the judgment of the Court of Civil Appeals.

WALKER and NORVELL, JJ., join in this dissent.

## *Notes*

1. *Two types of land sale contracts.*

Most land sale contracts are simply "cash" sales or "sales through escrow" where conveyance by deed is made at the close of the transaction. If the deal is financed, the purchaser becomes the owner-mortgagor. Not infrequently the vendor, himself, will "carry the paper" and become transformed into the mortgagee. The rules as to the allocation of insurance, between mortgagee-mortgagor have been discussed in the preceding group of cases.

The principal case is an example of another type of land sale contract—the installment sale where the vendor retains title as a security device (vendor's lien) until the land installment is made. Although described as a vendor-purchaser situation its function is as a security device equivalent to a mortgage. The modern trend indeed is to treat the device as such for practical purposes. See Nelson and Whitman, The Installment Land Contract—A National Viewpoint, 1977 Brigham Young Univ.L.Rev. 541. If the current attitude is to be adopted it would seem that, on the mortgagee-mortgagor analogy, the vendor's insurer in the principal case should be subrogated to the vendor's right to the unpaid purchase price. (But, of course, it wasn't.)

2. *Risk of loss on the uninsured purchaser. Recent cases.*

Two recent cases have held that a land purchaser who took possession *prior* to closure of the escrow or contract cannot claim the benefit of the vendor's insurance proceeds. McGuire v. Wilson, 372 So.2d 1297 (Ala.1979) and Long v. Keller, 104 Cal.App.3d 312, 163 Cal.Rptr. 532 (1980). (Applying Uniform Vendor–Purchaser Risk Act.). But, cf. Gilles v. Sprout, 293 Minn. 53, 196 N.W.2d 612 (1972).

3. *Problem:* Assume the risk of loss is on the vendor and a *material* portion of the premises have been destroyed by fire. The vendor collects on his insurance policy. Should the purchaser seek to have the proceeds held in trust for his benefit, or sue for specific performance with abatement of the price? Cf. World Exhibit Corp. v. City Bank Farmers Trust Co., 186 Misc. 420, 59 N.Y.S.2d 648 (1945), affirmed 270 App.Div. 654, 61 N.Y.S.2d 889 (1946), affirmed 296 N.Y. 586, 68 N.E.2d 876.

## INSURANCE OF WAREHOUSING AND OTHER BAILMENT RISKS

Extracts from an article by CLARENCE R. CONKLIN in the University of Illinois Law Forum. Vol. 1957, page 560.*

### "IN TRUST AND ON COMMISSION"

As has been previously noted, some policies of insurance are frequently procured by bailees to cover only the property of their bailor

* [Copyright 1957 by the Board of Trustees of the University of Illinois].

customers, but generally bailees cover their own property as well. In development of the various forms of such coverage, certain language of the older forms has been retained. Thus, many policies continue to use language which contains the so-called "in trust and on commission" clauses. An excellent example is the standard form of fire insurance policy, the language of which is usually required to be uniform. The Illinois approved contents fire policy contains the following clause: "* * * and provided the Insured is liable therefor, personal property of others held in trust, or on commission or consignment, in storage or for repairs, sold but not delivered or removed." Some variation of this language is to be found in many of the different inland marine forms of coverage, as for example, in contractor's equipment floater forms principally covering property belonging to others: "This policy also covers materials, equipment, supplies, and temporary structures of all kinds incident to the construction of said building, and (when not otherwise insured) builder's machinery, tools and equipment belonging to the insured *or similar properties belonging to others for which the insured is liable,*" or "for which the assured are or may be liable," or "and provided the assured is legally liable therefor, this policy shall also cover such property sold but not delivered, held in trust or on consignment or for storage." Other similar combinations of language are employed.

One of the landmark cases where various aspects of the problem inherent in the "in trust" and "on commission" conditions were before the court, is B.N. Exton & Co. v. Home Fire and Marine Ins. Co.[77] The New York Court of Appeals, opinion by Justice Crane, unanimously concurred in by Justices Cardozo, Pound, Andrews, Kellogg, and O'Brien, cited with approval the statement from Waring v. Indemnity Fire Ins. Co.[78] as follows:

> " 'The phrases describing property "as held in trust," or "on commission," and kindred terms, in a policy to an agent, factor or the like, have been held as giving to the owner of the property a right to take the place of the insured, to adopt the contract. * * *' "[79]

In Burke v. Continental Ins. Co.[80] the court said:

> "* * * The words 'in trust' may, with entire propriety, be applied to any case of bailment where the goods belonging to one person are entrusted to the care of another, for which the bailee is responsible to the owner."[81]

In Southern Cold Storage & Produce Co. v. A.F. Dechman & Co.[82] the court said:

> "The expression 'held in trust,' as used in insurance policies, means simply that the goods or property are in the custody of the

77. 249 N.Y. 258, 164 N.E. 43 (1928).
78. 45 N.Y. 606 (1871).
79. 249 N.Y. at 261, 164 N.E. at 44.
80. 184 N.Y. 77, 76 N.E. 1086 (1906).
81. Id. at 82, 76 N.E. at 1087.
82. 73 S.W. 545 (Tex.Civ.App.1903).

insured." [83]

The phrases which have been most widely misinterpreted are "for which the insured is liable," "provided the insured is liable," "legally liable," or such similar phrase. There has been much litigation with respect to the intent of these phrases. The majority rule is that such language should properly be interpreted to refer to the responsibility of the bailee to account for property and that such phrase is merely descriptive of the property covered by the policy. In view of the importance of this point and because it is unfortunately true that there is still some misunderstanding or disagreement on the part of some, including insurance men, it may be helpful to examine and cite at some length from certain of the leading authorities which are representative of the majority rule.

* * *

## FOLGER COFFEE CO. v. GREAT AMERICAN INSURANCE CO.

United States District Court, Western District of Missouri, 1971.
333 F.Supp. 1272.

WILLIAM H. BECKER, CHIEF JUDGE.

* * *

The following facts, pertinent to the issue under consideration, have been admitted by the parties:

> "On or about September 14, 1966, defendant made and delivered its policy of insurance, number 1-00-91-31 to Ar-Ka-Mo Sporting Goods, Inc., a Missouri corporation. * * *
>
> "In June and July, 1969, Ar-Ka-Mo Sporting Goods, Inc., was a warehouseman of property owned by the plaintiff and others.
>
> "On or about the date set out in plaintiff's Complaint, the plaintiff did sustain damage to certain of its property which was warehoused and bailed with Ar-Ka-Mo Sporting Goods, Inc., however, the extent of that loss is not admitted.

According to the true copy of the insurance policy attached to the complaint herein, the following is the clause which is relied upon by plaintiff as bringing its losses within the coverage of the policy:

> "III. Property covered
>
> The policy covers:
>
> A. Personal property usual to the conduct of the Insured's business, consisting principally of Premiums for Prizes, the property of the Insured, or similar property of others held by the insured *for which the insured is liable,* except as provided elsewhere in this policy." (Emphasis added.)

83. Id. at 546.

* * * Defendant relies on the emphasized language, contending that the word "liable" in the provision means "legally liable" and that plaintiff must therefore show the negligence of the bailee Ar–Ka–Mo Sporting Goods, Inc., before it can recover under the policy.

In cases like that at bar, however, the courts have almost uniformly held that if, from the contract construed in its entirety, the fair interpretation and construction of the insurance contract is that it was intended primarily to cover the property held by the insured, then "liable," as used within the policy, does not refer to any fixed legal liability of the insured to respond in damages, but should be construed more broadly to mean "responsible." This view is well developed in the leading cases of Penn v. Commercial Union Fire Ins. Co., 233 Miss. 178, 101 So.2d 535, 67 A.L.R.2d 1238, and United States v. Globe & Rutgers Fire Ins. Co. (N.D.Tex.) 104 F.Supp. 632, affirmed (C.A.5) 202 F.2d 696. * * * See also Anno., 67 A.L.R.2d 1241 at pages 1254 and 1255, subparagraph (c); 4 Appleman, Insurance Law and Practice, § 2345, p. 341, note 53.75. * * *

In the *Globe & Rutgers* case, supra, the Government sued the defendant insurance companies for the loss of certain cotton seed which was destroyed by fire at the premises of the McCoy Gin Company, Inc., on November 18, 1949. The policies sued upon all contained the following provision, concerning the property insured:

> "On cotton, ginned and unginned, baled and unbaled, seed cotton, cotton seed, supplies of sacks and other packaging material containing or to contain cotton seed, and bagging and ties, their own, and provided the insured is legally liable therefor, this policy shall also cover such property sold but not delivered, held in trust, or on consignment or for storage."

The Government sued for the loss of cotton seed which it had contracted to buy under price support programs and which was destroyed by fire. In holding that the Government could recover without any showing of negligence on the part of the McCoy Gin Company, Inc., the Court stated as follows:

> "The contention of the defendants is that the plaintiff cannot recover under the present policies without showing that the insured is legally liable for the fire loss of the cotton seed. That view is quite arguable. The pertinent provision of the policies has been quoted in full above and the central phrase thereof reads 'provided the insured is legally liable therefor'. The words 'liability' and 'liable' have manifold meanings in law and that nuance makes 'liable' fit as well in respect to one bound to respond in duty as to one bound to respond in damages. The gin company under its caretaker duty as bailee for hire certainly was responsible for the cotton seed and obligated to keep and deliver same safely, subject to exoneration only if performance be prevented without negligence on its part. That was a present and positive liability, and in fact no other liability ever supervened. In other words that liability in

being was complete, and adequately answers the terms of the policy provision. Nothing novel is being stated. In the typical instance of bailment relationship a proper delivery of the property thereupon satisfies the right of the bailor and discharges the liability of the bailee, but that does not gainsay the fact that the bailee bore a legal liability during the period of the bailment.

"Of course when construing flexible language the best key usually is the context. The entire language of the relevant policy provision in its ordinary sense consistently points to insurance on *property,* not on the insured's *liability* for a fire loss on such property. A strained construction is required to say that 'legally liable therefor' in the central phrase defines the thing insured. Instead the more natural reading is that it defines a selective condition on the thing being insured. A simpler statement perhaps is that said central phrase is really some of the descriptive language identifying the property insured. This viewpoint may draw question on the theory that it renders such phrase sterile, presupposing the insured would necessarily and without more be legally liable in the sense herein stressed for all property 'held in trust or on consignment or for storage', but for one thing that contention would overlook the frequent tendency of bailees to attempt contractual stipulations against their common law liability. [Emphasis in original.]

"If the policy provision in fact read 'on the liability' of the insured then to be sure it could only mean liability for fire loss of the property, and the plaintiff would fail in the suit. This is true for the simple reason that a fire insurance policy, like many forms of insurance, is a contract of pecuniary indemnity. Its subject matter must have a money measure. Such insurance on *liability* cannot become payable apart from an incurred liability of the insured for money damages or at least a pecuniary obligation. The present policies however plainly purport to insure *property,* not only property of the specified kinds belonging to the insured, but also property of like kind, for which insured is liable, belonging to another owner, and the reasonable construction of the insurance contract is that the central phrase of the policy provisions means liability of the insured already present and not contingent liability ushered in by a fortuitous fire. If the contrary meaning had been intended it would have been easy to state same in unmistakable terms. This construction makes for certainty instead of contingency. The protection of the bailor is on a dependable footing. Bailor and bailee are spared the vexation of controversy as to liability of the bailee for the fire loss. No violence is done to the language of the policies. Even any fair doubt should be resolved in favor of the insured. The plaintiff has a good claim under the policies." [Emphasis in original.] 104 F.Supp. at 634–635.

In affirming the judgment, the United States Court of Appeals for the Fifth Circuit held as follows:

> "In applying the policy provisions, the trial Court properly gave great weight to the fact that the entire tenor and effect of the contracts was insurance against property loss by fire and not insurance only against the legal liability of the named insured for the fire loss. The policies provide property insurance,—not indemnity or liability insurance. Whether the described commodities were owned by the insured, or 'held in trust or on consignment or for storage', in either and all events it is provided that the policy shall cover 'property'. It was likewise correctly determined by the trial Court that the phrase 'provided the insured is legally liable therefor, when considered in connection with these policy provisions providing insurance on property, should be considered to refer to the present and existing liability of the custodian generally and not restricted to liability which was the consequence alone of a fire." 202 F.2d at 697.

* * * Defendant relies on the cases of Millers' Mutual Fire Insurance Association v. Warroad Potato Growers Ass'n (C.A.8) 94 F.2d 741; * * * McCoy v. Home Ins. Co., 170 Pa.Super. 38, 84 A.2d 249; In re Podolsky (C.A.3) 115 F.2d 965; and Orient Insurance Co. v. Skellet Co. (C.A.8) 28 F.2d 968. But those cases either applied the minority view recognized in Minnesota or involved contracts of insurance which specifically and precisely covered only the legal *liability* of the insured to respond in damages. In Orient Ins. Co. v. Skellet Co., supra, the insurance contract contained a provision insuring the owners of the public storage warehouse against loss on merchandise not owned by the insured "for which they may be *legally* liable" (emphasis added), as in United States v. Globe & Rutgers Fire Ins. Co., supra, but as the Court in the latter case noted, 104 F.Supp. at 635:

> "This [Orient Ins. Co. v. Skellet Co., supra] would be a formidable decision in behalf of the present defendants, but for the fact that the court also said that if the policy had recited that the goods were held in trust, or in similar custody then there could be no doubt that the insurance was for the benefit of the real owners." [4]

Similarly, the contract involved in In re Podolsky, supra, (applying Minnesota law, following the minority view) insured only the insured's "*legal interest in* and * * * legal liability for * * * property held by him." (Emphasis added.) And, in Millers' Mutual Fire Insurance Association v. Warroad Potato Growers Ass'n, supra, (applying Minnesota law, following the minority view), the policy again purported only to cover legal liability on the loss of the property. The policy was written

4. In the *Orient* case, the Court was very explicit on this point, saying:

> "Concededly, Skellet Co.'s relation to the owners of the stored goods and its interest in them was such as entitled it to take out insurance for their protection. Any expression in an insurance contract signifying that intent and purpose is sufficient. To that end the clause 'for which they may be legally liable' should have been omitted, or there should have been a statement that the goods described were held in trust, or a similar expression of like import should have been used,—and then there could be no doubt that the contract was made in the name of Skellet Co. for the benefit of the real owners." 28 F.2d at 970.

to make "liability" modify only the word "loss" by making liability contingent upon loss. All of these cases, therefore, are consistent with the theory of United States v. Globe & Rutgers Fire Ins. Co., supra, insofar as that case recognized that if the policy provision expressly reads or otherwise indicates that the insurance is "on the liability," then a recovery cannot be had by the "real owners" of the property without a showing of negligence of the bailee. Thus, the contract must be interpreted and construed to determine whether it was intended to cover the liability of the insured to respond in damages or his responsibility for the property. With this proposition, none of the cases are in conflict.

* * *

* * * Applying the rule that the meaning of the word "liable" must be construed according to "its true intent and purpose from the terms used in the contract" to the case at bar leads to the firm conclusion that the policy was intended to insure property for which Ar–Ka–Mo Sporting Goods, Inc., was responsible, rather than legal liability of Ar–Ka–Mo to plaintiff. The opening paragraph of the policy provides that:

> "In consideration of the provisions and stipulations herein or added hereto and of the premium above specified, this Company, for the term of years specified from inception date shown above at Noon (Standard Time) to expiration date shown above at Noon (Standard Time) at location of *property* involved, to an amount not exceeding the amount(s) above specified, does insure the insured named above and legal representatives, to the extent of the actual cash value of the *property* at the time of loss, but not exceeding the amount which it would cost to repair or replace the property with material of like kind and quality within a reasonable time after such loss, without allowance for any increased cost of repair or reconstruction by reason of any ordinance or law regulating construction or repair, *and without compensation for loss resulting from interruption of business or manufacture,* nor in any event for more than the interest of the insured, against all direct loss by fire, lightning and by removal from premises insured against in this policy, except as hereinafter provided, to the *property* described herein while located or contained as described in this policy * * *." (Emphasis added.)

An endorsement attached to the policy insures the insured "against all risks of direct physical loss of or to the *property* covered" (emphasis added) including, to a limit of $200,000.00, to "*[p]roperty* at locations owned, leased, operated, regularly used or specifically declared by the Insured" at "1531 Vernon, North Kansas City, Missouri." (Emphasis added.) Then, the policy goes on to cover the *personal property* of the type which plaintiff had bailed with Ar–Ka–Mo Sporting Goods, Inc. From the words and phrases used in the contract, viewed in its entirety, including its repeated use of the word "property" to define the subject matter of the insurance and specifically excluding business interruption and other insurance, the conclusion is that the policy in this case was meant to insure property rather than legal liability. * * *

* * *

In the case at bar, the true meaning of the contract, properly construed in light of the admitted facts, is that it covers *property* rather than *liability*. Under the law of Missouri, as under the law generally, as noted above, this has the effect of including property of others possessed by the insured.

* * *

It is therefore

Adjudged that judgment be, and it is hereby, entered for plaintiff and against defendant on the issue of defendant's liability to plaintiff on the insurance policy of defendant. * * *

### *Note*

### *Other Ramifications of the Bailor–Bailee Coverage Situation*

*Bailments and Co–Insurance*

[Further extracts from CONKLIN, Insurance of Warehousing and Other Bailment Risks, Univ. of Ill.L.Forum, Vol. 1957, p. 560ff.]

* * *

It is of some interest to contrast the decision in [United States v. Globe & Rutgers Fire Insurance Co. (as well as the principal case and others there cited) ] with the later case of Texas City Terminal Railway Co. v. American Equitable Assurance Co.[86] In this decision, the court concluded that the policy language was distinguishable from the conditions contained in the policy involved in the *Globe & Rutgers* case. The litigation arose by reason of the very substantial damage occasioned in the Texas City explosion of 1947. The American Equitable carried an explosion policy for plaintiff which covered plaintiff's buildings, tanks, sheds, trestles, platforms, equipment, rolling stock, and the like. The policy contained a ninety per cent co-insurance clause and an "in trust and on commission" clause, as follows: "It is understood and agreed that this insurance also covers the interest of the assured in and/or liability for similar property belonging in whole or part to others, and held by the assured either sold but not removed on storage or for repairs, or otherwise held." The property damage involved in this case was great. The loss to plaintiff's property was some $4,500,000 and the damage to property of others stored on plaintiff's premises ran to some $19,600,000. On the other hand, plaintiff carried one blanket explosion policy with defendant insurer with limits of $2,300,000. The insurer contended that its policy extended coverage to all property on plaintiff's premises, including the property of others, and that the ninety per cent co-insurance clause should be applied to this total amount, even though the owners of the other property were making no claims of liability against plaintiff. If the position

86. 130 F.Supp. 843 (S.D.Tex.1955).

of the insurer was correct, the effect would limit plaintiff's recovery for its own loss to about ten per cent.

The opinion considers many of the leading cases on both sides of the question of whether the "in trust and on commission" clause should be interpreted as coverage on property or construed as liability insurance. The court disallowed the insurer's claim and held that the defendant's policy constituted liability insurance and did not cover the property of others in the possession of the insured. The soundness of the court's reasoning on this point would appear to be subject to question. It has been suggested that the court may have been influenced in its decision in concluding that the language of the policy should be distinguished from that involved in the *Globe & Rutgers* case to avoid what it believed to represent an inequitable or unjust result. Regardless of whether the court was right in denying the position of the insurer on the foregoing premise, the court also found another reason for denying the insurer's position that the goods of others were covered under its policy. The court referred to the fact that plaintiff's property covered buildings, tanks, sheds, etc., whereas the property of others referred to includes the "interest of the insured and/or liability for *similar property* belonging in whole or in part to others."

The court then said:

> "* * *. The property of others on the Terminal premises was not 'similar property' within the terms of the above provision. The word 'similar' has been variously defined as exactly alike, * * * or as a synonym for the word 'like,' * * * or being like in quality, nature, degree, purpose, or other characteristics. * * * The Terminal's business was the operation of a terminal railroad. * * * [T]he property insured consisted of the Terminal's operating facilities, equipment and supplies used or to be used in the maintenance and operation of the facilities and business of the Terminal. 'Similar property' within the meaning of American Equitable Group's 'liability' clause would necessarily mean and be limited to property in the nature of operating facilities, equipment and supplies for use in connection therewith. The goods of others which American Equitable Group contends are similar property consist of cargo in course of commerce such as bagged flour, tin bullion, tin ore, bullion racks, knocked down French box car parts, bagged rice, bagged fertilizer, bagged sulphur, wool, mohair, wheat, carbon black and jute bagging. These goods stored on the premises are not 'similar' to the operating facilities, equipment and supplies of the Terminal but are entirely dissimilar in quality, nature, degree, purpose and other characteristics." [87]

An important point which the court, for the reasons expressed, was not required to decide was whether the co-insurance clause was applicable to the total value of all the property of the insured as well as the value of the property of others in the possession of the insured. There has been little or no litigation which has reached the higher courts with respect to this controversial question. It is obvious that this is of great importance because

**87.** Id. at 860. See Krakowski v. United States, 161 F. 88 (2 Cir.1908), where "similar" is defined as "exactly alike."

the value of property of others in the possession of bailees may fluctuate from time to time from a very small quantity to values running into millions, as in the *Texas City* case. The intent of each policy of insurance must be determined by consideration of the specific language employed. Where it is clear that the policy extends specific insurance coverage to property of others which is similar to the property of insured, which otherwise represents the principal coverage under the policy, and assuming, of course, that there is no other language which requires a contrary intention, it appears sound to conclude that co-insurance is contemplated with respect to the total values of all property covered by the policy regardless of ownership. The *Texas City* case, of course, illustrates the other extreme, where the property of others is not only dissimilar but, assuming the court to have been correct, the policy language is in other respects interpreted to provide protection against liability and is not held to be descriptive of the property covered. The troublesome cases lie in the area between the two extremes, where confusing or ambiguous language has been employed. As indicated, each case must stand on its own merits.

The case of Miller's Mut. Fire Ins. Ass'n v. Warroad Potato Growers Ass'n [88] is frequently cited as upholding a minority view. On the other hand, it may be contended that the decision can be distinguished by reason of the language employed. There, insurance was extended "On stock consisting of potatoes and all other merchandise and supplies not otherwise insured and not more hazardous, handled or used by the insured in their business, their own or held by them in trust or on storage, *if in case of loss the insured* is legally liable therefor, while contained in the insured's warehouse." A fire occurred and destroyed potatoes owned by members of the plaintiff association. Defendant denied liability on the premise that plaintiff was not "legally liable" for the destroyed property. The trial court held for the plaintiff and the court of appeals reversed and said:

> "The policy in suit, by its terms, insured potatoes handled or used by the insured, its own or held by it in trust or on storage, 'if in case of loss the insured is legally liable therefor.' If the quoted words were omitted, the policy would undoubtedly have covered all potatoes in storage contained in the warehouse, although not owned by the insured and although it was not legally liable for their loss. California Insurance Co. v. Union Compress Co., 133 U.S. 387, 10 S.Ct. 365, 33 L.Ed. 730; Home Insurance Co. v. Baltimore Warehouse Co., 93 U.S. 527, 23 L.Ed. 868. The presence of these words, however, negatives any intention on the part of the insurers to cover potatoes in storage for the loss of which the insured was not legally liable. It is plain, therefore, that this policy did not insure potatoes in storage, but covered only the liability of the insured to the owners in case of loss by fire."

* * *

### *Problem*

The following is given to persons hiring driver/guides from PESONALIZED TOURS OF TEXAS. Suppose the hired driver negligently backs into a brick wall causing $1000 damage to the tourist's car. What is the effect, if

88. 94 F.2d 741 (8 Cir.1938).

any, of this "agreement" on the tourist's property insurance covering his car.

GENERAL INFORMATION

The self-employed guides, and driver/guides, supplied by PERSONALIZED TOURS OF TEXAS are well-trained, experienced, and courteous. They have excellent driving records and are thoroughly familiar with the rules, regulations and driving conditions of Texas. Each has been certified by the American National Red Cross as having completed the Standard Course of Instruction, Multimedia System, of First Aid to the Injured. Furthermore, each is trained and equipped to prevent and treat problems related to high altitude, heat, and sunstroke.

LIABILITY WAIVER

While every effort is made to assure the well-being of our clients, the impossibility of our insuring each vehicle for liability, collision, bodily injury, etc., requires that *this responsibility rest with the person supplying the vehicle used on the tour.* Therefore, tour participants agree that tour owners, guides, and driver/guides will not be held liable for any accident, injury or loss during the tour.

## D. SUBROGATION

"Subrogation," a term which occurs many times in this book, seems sometimes to be a enigma within a puzzle (to borrow part of a phrase). However, it is *very* important to understand the term as well as possible. The term is, of course, defined and discussed in the texts and treatises as well as in the *Frost* case that follows; nonetheless, it is worthwhile to essay a simple, short analysis at this point.

The word "subrogation" derives from the Latin "subrogare" which could be used to mean "to put one person in the place of another." Subrogation can be agreed on in a contract (called "conventional" subrogation) and is commonly included in many policies. See the Basic Standard Fire Policy, Appendix A lines 154–57. Subrogation, even absent express contractual provision, would be likely allowed in any event by operation of law (called "legal" subrogation and really "equity" as used by the courts).

Whether legal or conventional, subrogation places an insurer in the place of the insured with respect to any claim the insured has against a third party for causing the loss. To reach this point, the insurer is required to have paid its insured under the terms of the policy. The insurer gets no greater rights than the insured had to give so far as a claim against the third party is concerned. The loss is thus charged to the negligently or wilfully acting responsible party. In a sense the principle of unjust enrichment is involved; if the insurer pays the insured and makes her whole, then the third party is in a position to extricate himself without economic loss unless the law intervenes to give an insurer a right to recover what it has paid the insured.

So much for a "homespun" definition of subrogation. The definition leaves much unanswered. Can subrogation be waived? If the insured settles independently with the third party, can the insured still make a claim against the insurer on the basis that the insurer has been adequately compensated for such payment? What if the amount recovered from the third party plus the amount payable under the policy are together insufficient to compensate the insured for her loss? Will subrogation be available where the wrong committed by the third party is "only" to breach his contract with the insured?

One or two insurance bromides can be stated that are of general application: (a) there is no subrogation against an insured, and (b) the insurer will not be recognized to have subrogation rights if it "volunteers" payment to the insured (this bears a resemblance to the maxim "equity does not aid a volunteer").[a]

## FROST v. PORTER LEASING CORP.

Supreme Judicial Court of Massachusetts, Middlesex, 1982.
386 Mass. 425, 436 N.E.2d 387.

HENNESSEY, CHIEF JUSTICE.

* * *

Frank F. Frost was injured in a motor vehicle accident. At the time, he was a beneficiary of a group insurance policy issued to a union health plan and paid for by his employer. Frost submitted medical expense claims totalling $26,566.04, and the insurer, The Union Labor Life Insurance Company (Union Labor), paid benefits of $22,679.57.[1]

The present case began as a tort action by Frost and his wife, Rilla Frost, against the owner and driver of the other vehicle involved in the accident. Frank Frost claimed damages for the medical expenses he had incurred, as well as for pain and suffering, impaired earning capacity, and future medical expenses. Rilla Frost claimed damages for loss of consortium.

Union Labor intervened in the Frosts' action, asserting a right of subrogation. Specifically, it claimed that, to the extent of the benefits it had paid to Frost, it was entitled to any damages Frost might recover from the defendants for medical expenses. Union Labor did not assert any claims directly against the tortfeasors.

Subsequently, the Frosts negotiated a settlement with the owner and driver of the other car. Frank Frost demanded $500,000, and Rilla

a. We have not found good case examples which directly support this proposition, presumably because it is the rare insurer who will actually make payments without some reason to believe legal responsibility exists to make them, i.e. no insurer would ever truly volunteer payment. Many cases, though, invoke the principle saying it doesn't apply.

1. The difference between Frost's claims and Union Labor's payments reflects a $2,000 deduction for no-fault benefits Frost received under a separate policy, and a $1,886.47 deduction according to limitations in the group insurance policy. Frost does not claim that the $2,000 deduction for no-fault benefits was improper.

$100,000. The parties agreed to a lump-sum settlement of $250,000, the limit of the defendants' liability insurance policy. The case was dismissed as against the defendants, leaving the Frosts and Union Labor to dispute over the proceeds of the settlement. The judge then allowed the parties' motion for a report to the Appeals Court, see Mass.R.Civ.P. 64, 365 Mass. 831 (1974), and entered a memorandum of decision, in which he concluded that Union Labor enjoyed a right of subrogation in the proceeds to the extent of the benefits it had paid, less a share of the costs the Frosts had incurred in obtaining a settlement. We granted the Frosts' application for direct appellate review.

Subrogation is an equitable adjustment of rights that operates when a creditor or victim of loss is entitled to recover from two sources, one of which bears a primary legal responsibility. If the secondary source (the subrogee) pays the obligation, it succeeds to the rights of the party it has paid (the creditor or loss victim, called the subrogor) against the third, primarily responsible party. The doctrine of subrogation applies, within limits to be discussed shortly, to payments under policies of insurance. Upon payment, the insurer is entitled to share the benefit of any rights of recovery the insured may have against a tortfeasor for the same loss covered by the insurance. If the insured recovers from the tortfeasor, the insurer's right becomes a right to the proceeds in the hands of the insured.

An insurer's right of subrogation may be reserved in an agreement between the insurer and the insured, or may arise by implication, as a matter of general law. Here, Union Labor admits that Frost's insurance policy contained no provision for subrogation. Union Labor's claim is one of implied subrogation, and we express no opinion on the ability of parties to fix their rights by contract.

The reason for implied subrogation under contracts of insurance is to prevent an unwarranted windfall to the insured. If the insured recovers from both the insurer and the tortfeasor, his compensation may exceed his actual loss. Duplicative recovery is "a result which the law has never looked upon with favor." It is contrary to the indemnity purposes that underlie many insurance contracts, and produces a form of unjust enrichment. Further, duplicative recoveries by particular accident victims cause an inefficient distribution of the overall resources available for accident compensation. Subrogation returns any excess to the insurer, who can then recycle it in the form of lower insurance costs.

Nevertheless, rights of subrogation do not arise automatically upon payment of benefits under any contract of insurance. The availability of subrogation has generally depended on the type of coverage involved. Courts have readily implied rights of subrogation under policies covering property damage. The insurer's obligation under a policy of property insurance is viewed only as a duty to indemnify the insured for actual loss, and not as an absolute liability to pay a certain sum of money upon the happening of an event. Moreover, the insured's loss is generally liquidated, and tort recovery is comparable, if not identical, to insurance coverage. Therefore, the insured's actual loss, and the amount of any excess compensation from the combination of insurance proceeds and tort recovery, can be determined with certainty.

On the other hand, courts have not recognized implied rights of subrogation in the area of "personal insurance," a category that has included medical expense benefits as well as life insurance and other forms of accident insurance. Personal insurance is said to be less a contract of indemnity than a form of investment, imposing on the insurer an absolute duty to pay if the named condition occurs. Further the insured's receipt of both tort damages and insurance benefits may not produce a measurably duplicative recovery. The insured is likely to have suffered intangible losses that are insusceptible to precise measurement, and the two sources of his recovery may cover different ranges of loss and be differently affected by considerations such as fault.

Commentators have objected to the courts' classification of medical expense policies with other forms of personal insurance, and have argued that subrogation rights should be implied upon payment of benefits for medical and hospital expenses. They point out that medical coverage, like property insurance, is designed to indemnify the insured for quantifiable economic losses, and bears little similarity to an investment.

Although we recognize the indemnity character of medical and hospital expense benefits, we do not feel that the principles that support subrogation under policies of property insurance would be served by extending implied rights of subrogation into the field of insurance for personal injuries. Subrogation rights, as we have said, are implied to prevent unwarranted compensation and to facilitate sound distribution of compensation resources. If medical expenses are isolated from the other consequences of an accident, excess compensation of an insured accident victim may appear definite and quantifiable. However, when subrogation is based on broad principles of equity and efficiency, rather than on the contract of the parties, isolation of medical expenses is artificial, and the accident victim's position should be viewed as a whole. Subrogation played no part in the bargain between insurer and insured,[2] and in this circumstance, the courts should not intervene to adjust the rights of the parties unless all the adverse consequences of the accident have been offset.

When the insured's losses are viewed in their entirety, duplicative compensation is both uncertain and unlikely. The insured may be faced with property damage, pain and suffering, and diminished earning capacity, in addition to medical bills. The costs of litigation, or the decision to settle, may reduce his overall recovery. Yet the insured's implied right of subrogation must be limited to excessive recovery if it is

2. Union Labor points out that the premiums for Frost's policy were paid by Frost's employer rather than by Frost himself. The fact that the benefits do not flow to the party who has paid premiums, however, should not detract from the force of legitimate expectations, both of the beneficiary and of the one who has paid. This is particularly true when, as here, the policy is an employment benefit, bargained for by the insured's union.

to conform to the purposes that justify it. Further, when the insured has not agreed to subrogation, doubt should be resolved in his favor.

Perhaps a formula could be devised by which subrogation could be confined to recapture of duplicative compensation. The insurer might, for example, be permitted to recover if it could demonstrate that the insured's net recovery (insurance proceeds and tort recovery, less costs of collection) exceeded fair compensation for the insured's losses. However, the costs of implementing the formula could well undercut its justifications, particularly when, as here, the insured had reached a lump-sum settlement with the tortfeasor. If the inquiry covered the insured's overall loss from the accident-as in fairness it should-determination of the extent of excess recovery could be equally as complex as the personal injury trial the original parties sought to avoid by settlement. Thus, litigation over subrogation would impose additional burdens on the insured, and cut into his overall compensation for injury. Moreover, this added step in the adjustment of rights would detract from any generalized benefits that subrogation might bring to the sound use and distribution of resources available to compensate loss. Much of the "windfall" produced by overlapping coverage would be absorbed by the costs of dividing it, rather than recycled to reduce the costs of insurance.

For these reasons, we conclude that, in the absence of a subrogation agreement between the insurer and the insured, an insurer that has paid medical or hospital expense benefits has no right to share in the proceeds of the insured's recovery against a tortfeasor. Accordingly, we answer the reported question in the negative.

So ordered.

* * *

### *Note*

Is subrogation a good idea or a windfall for insurers who are compensated to assume all or some of the insured's risk? Although subrogation clauses are generally accepted in the context of property coverage, jurisdictions are split over their enforceability in personal injury policies, with a minority disallowing subrogation. For a cogent and concise argument urging adoption of the minority position through anti-subrogation legislation applicable to non-property damage claims, see Roger M. Baron, Subrogation in Medical Expense Claims: The "Double Recovery" Myth and the Feasibility of Anti-Subrogation Laws, 96 Dick.L.Rev. 581 (1992).

## RICHARD D. BREW & CO. v. AUCLAIR TRANSPORTATION, INC.

Supreme Court of New Hampshire, Hillsborough, 1965.
106 N.H. 370, 211 A.2d 897.

The following reserved case was transferred by Grant, J.

"Assumpsit to recover damages to personal property delivered by the plaintiff to the defendant for carriage by the latter to the plaintiff's consignee at Reno, Nevada. The plaintiff paid for the carriage of the goods which were delivered in a damaged condition. * * * The 'goods' in question were a high temperature electric furnace consigned to the U.S. Bureau of Mines with a value of some $15,817.00 and a so-called pyrometer of a value of some $2800.00.

* * *

"Just before the conclusion of the trial it became known to the Court that this was a subrogation case, Brew having been paid its loss by its own insurer who was seeking to recover from Auclair. The plaintiff paid an annual premium of $150.00 to Employers' Liability Assurance Corp., Ltd. and collected benefits thereunder for the loss herein described."

The contract of insurance provided in part as follows: "6. Benefit of Insurance. It is agreed by the Insured that this insurance shall not inure directly or indirectly to the benefit of any carrier, bailee, or other party, by stipulation in bill of lading or otherwise, and any breach of this agreement shall render this policy null and void."

"The Uniform Straight Bill of Lading delivered to Brew by Auclair Sec. 2, (c) reads:

" 'Any carrier or party liable on account of loss of or damage to any of said property shall have the full benefit of any insurance that may have been effected upon or on account of said property, so far as this shall not avoid the policies or contracts of insurance, provided that the carrier reimburse the claimant for the premium paid thereon.' The defendant argues that the limit of its liability is $150.00, the amount of the annual premium paid by Brew.

"Whether this portion of the Uniform Straight Bill of Lading, only whose legal effect is disputed, relieves the defendant of all damages except the $150.00 premium is reserved and transferred to the Supreme Court."

PER CURIAM.

The defendant carrier emphasizes the provisions of s. 2(c) of the bill of lading and contends according to its terms that it is liable only for the amount of the premium on the insurance policy procured by the plaintiff shipper. The insurance company, which is subrogated to the rights of the plaintiff shipper, emphasizes the provisions of the insurance policy that the insurance shall not "inure directly or indirectly to the benefit of any carrier," and contends that it is not subject to the limitation of liability contained in the bill of lading. These contentions are neither novel nor new and there is some logical support for each. The struggle between insurer and carrier as to which will bear the ultimate burden when the insured goods are damaged or lost in transit has been a protracted one. Phoenix Ins. Co. v. Erie & Western Transportation Co., 117 U.S. 312, 6 S.Ct. 750, 29 L.Ed. 873; Luckenbach v. W.J. McCahan Sugar Refining Co., 248 U.S. 139, 39 S.Ct. 53, 63 L.Ed. 170; The Turret Crown, 297 F. 766 (2d Cir.1924); Note, Subrogation of an Insurer: The

Burden of the Loss of Insured Goods in Transit, 37 Harv.L.Rev. 901 (1924); Vance, Insurance 794–796 (3d ed. 1951). "In the beginning, the insurer of goods in transit was, on paying the insured, subrogated to the insured's claim, as shipper, against the carrier. Then the carrier inserted a stipulation in the bill of lading requiring the shipper to give it the benefit of any insurance that he might have, and this clause was held to cut off the insurer's right of subrogation even though the loss was due to the carrier's negligence. [Phoenix Ins. Co. v. Erie & Western Transp. Co., 117 U.S. 312 [6 S.Ct. 750, 29 L.Ed. 873] (1886) ] This decision, which caused all the trouble, was an erroneous application of the perfectly sound principle that the insurer is subrogated only to the extent of the insured's claim against the third party. The carrier did not and could not by stipulation extinguish his liability to the shipper; and if the idea of subrogation is sound, the loss should ultimately fall upon the person who had the greater measure of control over it. However, the decision stood, and the insurers countered by inserting a condition, in policies on goods in transit, that the policy should be void if the insured should contract with the carrier that the latter should have the benefit of the insurance. The carrier has not been successful in counteracting the effect of these stipulations; and under most recent decisions, the ultimate loss falls upon the carrier." Patterson, Essentials of Insurance Law 150 (2d ed. 1957).

Contradictory provisions and stipulations in contracts of insurance and carriage must be resolved in spite of logical difficulties. "The apparent circularity of expression may be resolved by interpreting the provision in the bill of lading as entitling the carrier to the insurance if there is no opposing *stipulation* in the policy or contract of insurance, that is, no warranty or provision for avoidance; and not, if there is. Consequently, the insured may recover from the insurer; the insurer is effectively subrogated to his cause of action against the carrier; and the carrier is not entitled to the insurance." Campbell, Non-Consensual Suretyship, 45 Yale L.J. 69, 85 (1935). * * *

The result of the decisions was succinctly stated in Patterson, Cases and Material on Insurance 305 (1955) as follows: "The legal impasse created where the insurer of goods in transit stipulated that it should be subrogated to the shipper's right to hold the carrier liable for the loss of the goods, and the carrier in its bill of lading issued to the shipper stipulated that it should be entitled to the benefit of the shipper's insurance, seems finally to have been resolved in favor of the insurer." * * *

We conclude that the answer to the question transferred by the Trial Court without ruling is that the bill of lading does not relieve the defendant of all damages and the liability is not limited to the insurance premium. It follows, on the authorities cited above, that the insurer is effectively subrogated to the shipper's cause of action against the carrier for the damages he sustained. King, Subrogation under Contracts Insuring Property, 30 Tex.L.Rev. 62, 78–81 (1951).

* * *

Defendant's exceptions overruled.

## SUTTON v. JONDAHL

Court of Appeals of Oklahoma, 1975.
532 P.2d 478.

BRIGHTMIRE, JUDGE.

Landlord's fire insurance carrier sued a tenant and his 10–year–old son (in the name of the property owners) to recover a $2,382.57 fire loss. A jury returned a verdict favoring the insurance company against only the father. * * *

* * * Once upon a time the elder Jondahl rented from the Suttons a home for his family in Ponca City, Oklahoma. For Christmas 1968 he gave an inexpensive chemistry set to his 10–year–old son—a co-defendant—who performed experiments for about a year without mishap.

Then, on January 11, 1970, the budding scientist took an electric popcorn popper to his bedroom and while using it to heat some chemicals a flame suddenly flared upward igniting nearby curtains causing damage to the house in the amount of $2,382.57.

Central Mutual Insurance Company which covered subject premises with fire insurance, paid the loss, and then, as subrogee, brought this suit against John Jondahl and his boy, alleging, in substance, that the father contributed to the cause of the fire by breaching a duty to prohibit his son from carrying on unsupervised chemical experiments in the bedroom.

* * *

Later, at the request of defendants, the court required Central to substitute itself for the Suttons since it paid the full loss and therefore the landlords were not real parties in interest.

* * *

We hold here the instructions improperly directed the jury to return a verdict for plaintiff unless it found defendants had borne the burden of proving themselves blameless or of presenting proof otherwise sufficient to exonerate themselves from a legal presumption of negligence. Failure of the trial court on the foregoing fundamental error, we think, was prejudicial to defendant and therefore warrants a new trial.

Defendant's other proposition is that the verdict is not supported by evidence and is contrary to law. The argument is that the evidence fails to establish negligence on the part of the defending father pitched as it was on a failure to properly perform his duty to supervise his son whom the jury found innocent of negligence. While evidence bearing on the breach of such duty was indeed scarce we cannot say there was an absence. What we do say, however, is that there is no evidence to establish Central Mutual Insurance Company has been actionably damaged by such breach. The reason is that under the circumstances thus far disclosed by the record here, the insurance company has no subrogational rights against the tenant of its policyholder.

The principle of subrogation was begotten of a union between equity and her beloved—the natural justice of placing the burden of bearing a loss where it *ought to be*. Being so sired this child of justice is without the form of a rigid rule of law. On the contrary it is a fluid concept depending upon the particular facts and circumstances of a given case for its applicability. To some facts subrogation will adhere—to others it will not. Home Owners' Loan Corp. v. Parker, 181 Okl. 234, 73 P.2d 170 (1937).

Under the facts and circumstances in this record the subrogation should not be available to the insurance carrier because the law considers the tenant as a co-insured of the landlord absent an express agreement between them to the contrary, comparable to the permissive-user feature of automobile insurance. This principle is derived from a recognition of a relational reality, namely, that both landlord and tenant have an insurable interest in the rented premises—the former owns the fee and the latter has a possessory interest. Here the landlords (Suttons) purchased the fire insurance from Central Mutual Insurance Company to protect such interests in the property against loss from fire. This is not uncommon. And as a matter of sound business practice the premium paid had to be considered in establishing the rent rate on the rental unit. Such premium was chargeable against the rent as an overhead or operating expense. And of course it follows then that the tenant actually paid the premium as part of the monthly rental.

The landlords of course could have held out for an agreement that the tenant would furnish fire insurance on the premises. But they did not. They elected to themselves purchase the coverage. To suggest the fire insurance does not extend to the insurable interest of an occupying tenant is to ignore the realities of urban apartment and single-family dwelling renting. Prospective tenants ordinarily rely upon the owner of the dwelling to provide fire protection for the realty (as distinguished from personal property) absent an express agreement otherwise. Certainly it would not likely occur to a reasonably prudent tenant that the premises were without fire insurance protection or if there was such protection it did not inure to his benefit and that he would need to take out another fire policy to protect himself from any loss during his occupancy. Perhaps this comes about because the companies themselves have accepted coverage of a tenant as a natural thing. Otherwise their insurance salesmen would have long ago made such need a matter of common knowledge by promoting the sale to tenants of a second fire insurance policy to cover the real estate.

Basic equity and fundamental justice upon which the equitable doctrine of subrogation is established requires that when fire insurance is provided for a dwelling it protects the insurable interests of all joint owners including the possessory interests of a tenant absent an express agreement by the latter to the contrary. The company affording such coverage should not be allowed to shift a fire loss to an occupying tenant even if the latter negligently caused it. New Hampshire Ins. Co. v. Ballard Wade, Inc., 17 Utah 2d 86, 404 P.2d 674 (1965). A parallel effect was reached in Hardware Mut. Ins. Co. v. Dunwoody, 194 F.2d 666 (9th Cir.1952). For to conclude otherwise is to shift the insurable risk assumed by the insurance company from it to the tenant—a party occupying a substantially different position from that of a fire-causing third party not in privity with the insured landlord.

Failure of either the pleadings or the evidence to show the landlords' insurance carrier possesses a right of subrogation against the Jondahls furnishes another reason why it was fundamental error to instruct the jury that they should return a verdict for the insurance company unless "defendants prove * * * they * * * [were] not negligent."

The judgment below is therefore reversed and the cause remanded for a new trial.

### *Notes*

1. It has been suggested that "lessees should first attempt to be covered as an additional insured on the lessor's policy * * * but if for various reasons this is not permissible, the lessee should at least obtain a mutual waiver of subrogation, such as: 'Insofar as permitted under their respective policies of insurance the lessor and lessee waive all rights, each against the other, for damage caused by fire or other perils which are covered by insurance.'" What might be the reaction of the risk manager of a prospective insurer when shown such a provision in the lease? See Lindblad, Risk Implications in Lease Agreements, Ins.L.J. # 677 (June 1979) at page 307.

2. If the tenant is by implication, or by the terms of the lease, liable for negligent harm to the demised premises, a familiar problem may then arise if the tenant repairs the premises before the insurance is paid. Is the tenant discharged because the insured landlord has sustained no loss? In this landlord-tenant area the two disparate lines of cases have been designated as the *New York rule* (holding to the principle that events subsequent to the loss do not affect the insurers' liability) exemplified in Foley v. Mfrs' and Builders' Fire Ins. Co., 152 N.Y. 131, 46 N.E. 318 (1897); and the contrary *Wisconsin rule* of Ramsdell v. Insurance Co. of North America, 197 Wis. 136, 221 N.W. 654 (1928). The Wisconsin rule was followed in Mission Nat'l Ins. Co. v. Schulman, 659 F.Supp. 270 (D.Conn.1986).

## DUELL v. GREATER NEW YORK MUTUAL INSURANCE CO.

Supreme Court, Appellate Division, First Department, 1991.
172 A.D.2d 270, 568 N.Y.S.2d 93.

MEMORANDUM DECISION.

* * *

Plaintiffs (collectively "Landlord") of a building known as 949 Park Avenue in Manhattan, brought this action to recover damages against defendant-attorneys arising from alleged malpractice committed by them in defense of an action brought by an art gallery tenant ("Tenant") in Landlord's building who recovered a judgment against Landlord upon a jury verdict in the approximate sum of $77,000. That recovery was based upon Landlord's negligence in causing or permitting an infusion of water into Tenant's art gallery. Numerous acts of professional negligence in the unsuccessful defense of that lawsuit are alleged, many of which appear to raise triable issues. One of these acts consists of allegations that although the lease between Landlord and Tenant (par. 36) required Tenant to provide $100,000 of property damage insurance naming both Landlord and Tenant as the insured, Tenant never performed this obligation. Because defendants omitted to allege this breach of lease by Tenant in Landlord's answer, the trial court precluded any testimony or other reference thereto throughout the trial. Another specification of negligence is that counsel carelessly elicited misleading testimony that Landlord was insured for the loss (which it was not); because of Tenant's breach, Landlord had only excess coverage for property damage over $100,000 at the time Tenant's cause of action accrued.

The motion court recognized the principle that a plaintiff in a legal malpractice action must show that but for his attorney's negligence he would have prevailed on the underlying claim, citing Romanian American Interests, Inc. v. Scher, 94 A.D.2d 549, 464 N.Y.S.2d 821. In that connection, the motion court did not hold that this defense relating to Tenant's breach of lease could not have prevailed as a matter of law (cf. N.A. Kerson Co. Inc. v. Shayne, 45 N.Y.2d 730, 408 N.Y.S.2d 475, 380 N.E.2d 302). (Clearly a jury, if such proof were adduced before it, might have rationally concluded that the proximate cause of Tenant's loss was its own default, irrespective of Landlord's negligence). Nonetheless the court erroneously concluded that the defense, even if properly interposed, would have made no difference, inasmuch as the insurance carrier, after paying Tenant's judgment, would have had the right to recover its loss against Landlord by way of subrogation and indemnification.

This was error. "It is a well-established principle of insurance law, however, that the right of subrogation exists only with respect to the rights of the insured against third persons and that there is no right of subrogation in favor of the insurer against its own insured (16 Couch, Insurance 2d, § 61:133; 6A Appleman, Insurance Law and Practice, § 4055; 2 Richards, Insurance [5th ed.], s 185)." (New York Board of Fire Underwriters v. Trans Urban Construction Co., 91 A.D.2d 115, 120, 458 N.Y.S.2d 216, aff'd 60 N.Y.2d 912, 470 N.Y.S.2d 578, 458 N.E.2d 1255). Here, of course, had the lease been complied with, Landlord would have been a named insured under the policy, with no exposure to a subrogation action by its own carrier.

Thus plaintiffs' malpractice claim is not subject to defeat as a matter of law on the ground that the alleged negligence bears no relation to the loss sustained. The question presents a triable issue, requiring reversal of the order appealed from.

## REEDER v. REEDER

Supreme Court of Nebraska, 1984.
217 Neb. 120, 348 N.W.2d 832.

PER CURIAM.

This appears to be a case of first impression in this jurisdiction and presents the question of whether one who occupies the home of another with the owner's permission, and who negligently causes damage to the home, may be sued by the owner's insurance carrier under a right of subrogation after the insurance carrier has paid the owner for the damages. The trial court concluded that the cause of action did not lie. We believe that the trial court was correct, and, accordingly, we affirm. Theodore N. Reeder and Rosalie M. Reeder, husband and wife, were the owners of a residence located in Omaha, Nebraska. In August of 1979 they moved to Arlington, Texas, still owning the home in Omaha. Reeder's brother, Bernard Reeder, who lived in Omaha, was in the process of constructing a new home for himself and his family. The brothers agreed that Bernard Reeder and his family could occupy the Theodore Reeder home in Omaha while the Bernard Reeders were awaiting the completion of their new home. As one would anticipate in arrangements of this type, there was no formal agreement and little discussion regarding the informal agreement. Theodore Reeder testified: We didn't have a lease, he did not lease it from me, he was only living in it. He was building a house of his own in the neighborhood, and he wanted to get his children in Christ the King School as soon as possible, and my house was sitting there vacant and he asked me if he could move in while he was completing his house and be closer to it, and get his kids in the school district right away. And I said that is fine, because it is sitting there vacant, and I can sell it with furniture in it just as easy as I can without; and you move in, and that is fine. Further, Theodore Reeder testified that "there was no rent paid and no agreement. He was to just take care of it and shovel the snow, live in it. Pay the utility bills, which I wouldn't have to pay." The brothers understood that Theodore Reeder, the owner, would pay the taxes, but no rent was to be paid by Bernard to Theodore. Additionally, Theodore Reeder testified that he specifically told his brother, "that I would leave my insurance policy that I had on it on it while he was in there, and I didn't really discuss any part of his homeowner's or anything else. I just assumed he would take care of that. But we did discuss that I would leave my policy on it."

On March 4, 1980, while occupying the house, Dana Reeder, Bernard's daughter, ignited the gas fireplace in the family room of the house. Allegedly, she failed to open the damper, which caused a fire resulting in substantial destruction to the home.

Cornhusker Casualty Company, Theodore Reeder's carrier, paid the sum of $139,760 to Theodore Reeder and obtained in return a subrogation receipt. Cornhusker then filed suit against Bernard Reeder and Patricia Reeder, parents of Dana Reeder, as well as against Dana Reeder herself. The parents were dismissed from the action, and no appeal has been taken from that order. It is therefore final and binding and not at issue in this appeal. Following the order dismissing the parents, Dana Reeder filed a motion for summary judgment. On May 11, 1983, the trial court sustained the motion for summary judgment and dismissed the action as against the remaining defendant, Dana Reeder.

It is from that order, dismissing the petition against Dana Reeder, that Cornhusker appeals, assigning as error, in essence, the following claims: (1) That the granting of the summary judgment was inappropriate under the facts of the case; (2) That the trial court erred in finding that the relationship between the parties was that of landlord/tenant; (3) That the trial court erred in finding the majority rule prohibits a landlord's insurer from subrogating against a negligent tenant.

While we believe that the order of the trial court was correct, we should at this point note that nothing in either the motion for summary judgment or in the trial court's order sustaining the motion for summary judgment indicates the basis upon which the trial court rendered its judgment. There are no findings in the trial court's order that the relationship between the parties was that of landlord/tenant, nor any finding that the trial court was adhering to any particular rule, majority or minority. The motion for summary judgment simply asks that judgment be granted "for the reason that the pleadings, including all discovery pleadings filed herein, and the depositions filed herein establish that there is no genuine issue as to any material fact, and defendant is entitled to a judgment as a matter of law." And the order of the trial court sustaining the motion for summary judgment simply recites: "Motion of defendant Dana Reeder for summary judgment is sustained."

The issue whether the relationship between Theodore Reeder and his brother, Bernard Reeder, was that of landlord/tenant, as urged by appellee, or that of licensor/licensee, as urged by appellant, is raised in part by Dana Reeder's amended answer and by the briefs of the parties to this court. It is not, however, a part of either the motion for summary judgment or the court's order. Nor do we believe that attempting to categorize this relationship is either material or helpful. One of the difficulties we too often encounter in the law is our effort to attempt to force every situation into a known and recognized relationship, hoping that by doing so the answer to our question may of necessity automatically follow.

In the instant case, we believe the facts would disclose that the relationship created between Theodore Reeder and his brother, Bernard Reeder, was neither landlord/tenant nor licensor/licensee in the full legal sense. To be sure, the relationship has characteristics of both landlord/tenant and licensor/licensee, but of a separate and unique kind, and in this instance meriting a different treatment. In Friend v. Gem International, Inc., 476 S.W.2d 134, 137–38 (Mo.App.1971), it was noted: The status of landlord and tenant is defined, generally, to arise from contract, express or implied, under the terms of which a person designated as "tenant" enters into possession of land of another, known as "landlord", with the rights of the tenant subordinate to the landlord. "The essentials of that relationship are said to be (1) a reversion in the landlord, (2) the creation of an estate in the tenant, either at will or for a term less than that for which the landlord holds, (3) the transfer of exclusive possession and control of the premises to the tenant, and (4) a contract, either express or implied, between the parties." Johnson v. Simpson Oil Company, Mo.App., 394 S.W.2d 91, 96[4] [1965]. On the other hand, the condition of licensor and licensee has also been defined, generally, to arise when one who owns or possesses land known as the "licensor" grants to another known as "licensee" the privilege of going onto land for a certain purpose without passing an estate in the land. (Emphasis supplied.) See, also, Bentley v. Palmer House Company, 332 F.2d 107 (7th Cir.1964); Gage v. City of Topeka, 205 Kan. 143, 468 P.2d 232 (1970). As noted in 49 Am.Jur.2d Landlord and Tenant § 6 at 47 (1970), the legal status of parties in their relationships one to the other "is a question of which direction the general effect of the various tests that have been applied, after weighing opposing ones against each other, can be said to take."

An express agreement to create a landlord/tenant relationship is not necessary; nevertheless, the evidence must indicate that the parties intended to impliedly create such an arrangement, including the fact that by entering into this arrangement the tenant acquired certain rights and the landlord assumed certain obligations. See Bodie v. Epler, 132 Neb. 442, 272 N.W. 249 (1937). We believe that when one examines the relationship and discussion between the parties, it is clear that Theodore Reeder did not intend to assume any obligations, nor did Bernard Reeder obtain any "rights" other than the opportunity to occupy his brother's home for such time and under such conditions as Theodore Reeder might impose arbitrarily from day to day. It is clear, for instance, that there was no intention of any payment of rent by Bernard to Theodore, nor was Theodore precluded from occupying the house any time he might return to Omaha.

Additionally, the relationship of licensor/licensee has been thought to exist with regard to the use of land and not the occupancy of a house. See, Matter of Daben Corp., 469 F.Supp. 135 (D.Puerto Rico 1979); Moore v. Chesapeake & O. Ry. Co., 493 F.Supp. 1252 (S.D.W.Va.1980), aff'd 649 F.2d 1004 (4th Cir.1981); Wenner v. Dayton–Hudson Corp., 123 Ariz. 203, 598 P.2d 1022 (1979); Ulan v. Vend–A–Coin, Inc., 27 Ariz.App. 713, 558 P.2d 741 (1976); Union Travel Assoc. v. International Assoc., 401 A.2d 105 (D.C.App.1979).

The arrangement, for whatever difference placing titles on it may be, was really that of a host and guest. The word [guest] is descriptive of a relationship known to the common understanding. Besides its somewhat narrow technical significance in statutes, it has a broad, general meaning, implying both a social relationship and the existence of a host; and has been defined in general, as meaning a person entertained in one's house or at one's table, a visitor entertained without pay; a person received and entertained at the house of another, a visitor; * * * hence a person to whom the hospitality of a home, club, etc., is extended. 39 C.J.S. Guest at 447 (1976). In Stadelmann v. Glen Falls Ins. Co., 5 Mich.App. 536, 147 N.W.2d 460 (1967), the Michigan court said a guest is a person who is received at one's home.

The reason that we make this distinction is not to simply find our own "pigeonhole" in which to force the answer. Rather, it is to clarify the question presented by this case. This question is not whether the relationship between the brothers was that of landlord/tenant or licensor/licensee, but whether the carrier, by seeking to recover from Theodore Reeder's "guest," is, in effect, seeking to recover from the insured himself for the very risk that the carrier insured and for which it received premiums.

We should note that the question presented to us is not whether a landlord may sue his tenant for negligent destruction to the landlord's property or whether a licensor may sue a licensee for negligent destruction of the licensor's property, absent agreements to the contrary. Rather, the question is whether the relationship between the host and the guest, under the facts in this case, is such that if the carrier is permitted to sue the guest under a claim of right of subrogation, in effect the carrier is recovering from the insured himself on the very risk which the insurer agreed to take upon payment of the premium. Therefore, in this case, the issue is not whether, absent insurance, Theodore Reeder could sue his brother or his niece, but whether the relationship between the insured and his brother was such, however characterized, that by permitting the carrier to sue the brother, in effect the carrier is suing the insured. This we believe the carrier may not do.

In Cagle, Inc. v. Sammons, 198 Neb. 595, 602, 254 N.W.2d 398, 403 (1977), we noted: The doctrine of subrogation is not administered by courts of equity as a legal right, but the principle is applied to subserve the ends of justice and to do equity in the particular case under consideration.... The facts and circumstances of each case determine whether the doctrine is applicable. While it is true that the right of an insurance company to recover against a wrongdoer whose negligence has subjected the insurance company to a liability, whether the company's right be based on an equitable subrogation or an express assignment is traced through the insured, see Omaha & R.V.R. Co. v. Granite State Fire Ins. Co., 53 Neb. 514, 73 N.W. 950 (1898), it is also true that an insurer cannot recover against its own insured, see Midwest Lumber Co. v. Dwight E. Nelson Constr. Co., 188 Neb. 308, 196 N.W.2d 377 (1972).

In Stetina v. State Farm Mut. Auto. Ins. Co., 196 Neb. 441, 451, 243 N.W.2d 341, 346 (1976), we said: "No right of subrogation can arise in favor of an insurer against its own insured since, by definition, subrogation exists only with respect to rights of the insurer against third persons to whom the insurer owes no duty. 16 Couch on Insurance 2d, § 61:133; see also 46 C.J.S. Insurance § 1209(b); 16 Couch on Insurance 2d, § 61:136. This principle is succinctly stated in Chenoweth Motor Co. v. Cotton, 2 Ohio Misc. 123, 207 N.E.2d 412, 413 [1965]: "'* * * it is axiomatic that [an insurance company] has no subrogation rights against the negligence of its own insured.' (Bracketed material paraphrased.) To allow subrogation under such circumstances would permit an insurer, in effect, to pass the incidence of the loss, either partially or totally, from itself to its own insured and thus avoid the coverage which its insured purchased * * *." (Emphasis supplied.) In Alaska Ins. Co. v. RCA Alaska Commun., 623 P.2d 1216, 1218 (Alaska 1981), the court said: Absent an express provision in the lease establishing the tenant's liability for loss from negligently started fires, the trend has been to find that the insurance obtained was for the mutual benefit of both parties, and that the tenant "stands in the shoes of the insured landlord for the limited purpose of defeating a subrogation claim." Rizzuto v. Morris, 22 Wash.App. 951, 592 P.2d 688, 690 (1979), citing Rock Springs Realty, Inc. v. Waid, 392 S.W.2d 270, 278 (Mo.1965); Monterey Corp. v. Hart, 216 Va. 843, 224 S.E.2d 142, 146 (1976). See, also, West American Ins. Co. v. Pic Way, 110 Mich.App. 684, 313 N.W.2d 187 (1981); Gift Box v. Scott, 272 Ark. 256, 613 S.W.2d 395 (1981); Liberty Mut. Fire Ins. Co. v. Auto Spring Supply Co., 59 Cal.App.3d 860, 131 Cal.Rptr. 211 (1976). The undisputed evidence is that Theodore Reeder testified that he told his brother, Bernard, that he would "leave my insurance policy that I had on it on it while he was in there." It is difficult to see how the insurance was not for the benefit of the Bernard Reeders to the same extent as it was for the Theodore Reeders.

In the case of Rizzuto v. Morris, 22 Wash.App. 951, 955–56, 592 P.2d 688, 690 (1979), the Washington Court of Appeals reasoned: [I]nsurance companies expect to pay their insureds for negligently caused fire, and they adjust their rates accordingly. In this context, an insurer should not be allowed to treat a tenant, who is in privity with the insured landlord, as a negligent third party when it could not collect against its own insured had the insured negligently caused the fire. In effect, a tenant stands in the shoes of the insured landlord for the limited purpose of defeating a subrogation claim. It occurs to us that if the reasoning underlying the denial of a subrogation claim applies between a landlord and a tenant, then we conclude that this reason is even more compelling when the relationship is that of host and guest, particularly when the host has assured the guest that there is insurance coverage. It may be presumed that the insured bought this policy so that he would not have to look to his guest for payment in the event of damage caused by the negligent act of the guest. We are persuaded that the relationship which existed between the brothers in this case was such that, regardless of how their relationship is characterized, a right of subrogation in the insurer against the insured's niece should not lie as a matter of law.

Having therefore concluded as a matter of law that the carrier was not entitled to maintain the right of subrogation, and, further, in view of the fact that there is no dispute as to the facts, this was a case in which there existed no genuine issue as to any material fact, the ultimate inferences to be drawn from those facts were clear, and the moving party was entitled to judgment as a matter of law. Under such circumstances the court was obligated to enter summary judgment. See Interholzinger v. Estate of Dent, 214 Neb. 264, 333 N.W.2d 895 (1983). The judgment of the trial court granting summary judgment in favor of the appellee and against the appellant was correct, and the judgment is affirmed.

AFFIRMED.

### *Note*

### *Subrogation to Contract Rights. Equitable Contribution.*

Some years ago the court in Patent Scaffolding Co. v. William Simpson Construction Co., 256 Cal.App.2d 506, 64 Cal.Rptr. 187 (1967) laid down the rule that an insurance company which pays a property damage claim is not subrogated to the insured's rights against third parties (other than different insurance companies) also contractually liable to indemnify the insured unless the loss involved is *causally* related to a breach of duty by that third party. In that case a prime contractor (Simpson) agreed to procure fire insurance on the subcontractor's (Patent's) equipment at the jobsite. Patent already had insurance on its gear. When fire destroyed Patent's property it was discovered that Simpson had not procured the agreed coverage. Patent's insurer therefore paid and sought subrogation against Simpson based on Patent's claim for breach of contract. Subrogation was denied because there was no evidence that Simpson caused the fire, and therefore the loss was not causally connected with the breach of the agreement to procure insurance. The court observed however that the principle of equitable contribution (not raised in the case) might apply.

In an analogous case involving a sub-lessee's contractual liability in event of loss, California Food Service Corp. v. Great American Ins. Co., 130 Cal.App.3d 892, 182 Cal.Rptr. 67 (1982), the court followed the principle of *Patent Scaffolding* and denied subrogation to the sub-lessor's insurer, but moderated the result by applying "equitable contribution" "based on the common sense notion that where two indemnitors share equal contractual responsibility for a loss, the selection of which indemnitor is to bear the loss should not be left to the sometimes arbitrary choice of the loss claimant. * * * More importantly, the indemnitor should not be given the incentive to avoid paying a just claim in hopes that the claimant will obtain payment from the co-indemnitor. * * *" 130 Cal.App.3d at 901, 182 Cal.Rptr. at 72–73. Thus the insurer, although denied subrogation, recoups ½ of the loss.

## E. POST PAYMENT MATTERS

— **much more on subrogation**

— **consequences of interference with insurer's subrogation rights**

— **loan receipts**

## WIMBERLY v. AMERICAN CASUALTY COMPANY OF READING, PENNSYLVANIA (CNA)

Supreme Court of Tennessee, 1979.
584 S.W.2d 200.

FONES, JUSTICE.

The Wimberly's restaurant was destroyed by fire, and they sustained an undisputed loss of $44,619.10. The fire was caused by Shelia McLemore's driving her automobile into the restaurant. Her insurance carrier paid the policy limits of $25,000. The Wimberlys had a total of $15,000 fire insurance coverage with defendant insurance companies.

The single question for determination is what are the subrogation rights of the two fire insurance companies when the total recovery of the insured from the tortfeasor and the fire insurance policies is less than the casualty loss.

The chancellor ruled that the insureds must be paid in full for their loss before subrogation rights arose in favor of their insurance carriers. The Court of Appeals reversed and held that the insureds and the insurers were entitled to an equal distribution of the proceeds received from the tortfeasor's insurance company. * * *

The fire insurance policies that the Wimberlys had with American Casualty and New Hampshire Casualty both contained the standard subrogation clause, which read:

> "This company may require from the insured an assignment of all rights to property against any party for loss to the extent that payment therefor is made by this company."

On February 18, 1975, the Wimberlys signed a proof of loss and subrogation receipt, by which they subrogated their insurers "to all of the rights, claims and interests which the undersigned may have against any person or corporation liable for the loss" and agreed to cooperate with their insurers in litigating or compromising their claims. On February 27, the insurers issued checks to the Wimberlys for $7,000 and $8,000, the full amount of the respective policies, for a total of $15,000. On April 16, 1975, Hartford Insurance Company, the insurer of McLemore, issued a check for $25,000, payable to Robert R. and Evelyn M. Wimberly, American Casualty Company and New Hampshire Insurance Company. In late May all of the payees of the $25,000 check executed a joint release of McLemore in consideration of the settlement with her insurer.

The American Casualty Company received $3,921.53 and the New Hampshire Insurance Company received $4,482.94, for a total of $8,404.47 as a pro rata share, and the Wimberlys received $16,595.53 of the settlement payment. Subsequently, since they had to bear an uninsured loss of $13,023.57, the Wimberlys sued to recover the $8,404.47 received by their insurers * * *.

The Court of Appeals reversed the trial court judgment in favor of the plaintiffs and held that both the insured and the insurers were entitled to a pro rata share of the sum recovered from the third-party tortfeasor. * * * The Court of Appeals appears to have bottomed its decision on its conclusion that "[b]oth the plaintiffs and defendants were legally entitled to recover all of their loss from the tortfeasor but were prevented from making a complete recovery due to the inadequacy of funds received from tortfeasor. All had an equal right to recovery, and the standing of one was not greater than the other."

Defendants contended at trial that under the stipulated facts and applicable law, they are entitled to priority because of their subrogation rights against the recovery from the third-party tortfeasor. In support of this position, defendants relied on cases from other jurisdictions which have allowed the insurer to be first indemnified out of the proceeds recovered from the third-party tortfeasor when the insured had assigned to his insurer all rights of recovery against the tortfeasor to the extent of payment, even when the insured suffered a fire loss only partially covered by his policy. *See Peterson v. Ohio Farmers Ins. Co.,* 175 Ohio St. 34, 191 N.E.2d 157 (1963); *accord, Ervin v. Garner,* 25 Ohio St.2d 231, 267 N.E.2d 769 (1971); *Travelers Indemnity Co. v. Ingebretsen,* 38 Cal.App.3d 858, 113 Cal.Rptr. 679 (1974). * * *

In *Peterson v. Ohio Farmers Ins. Co., supra,* the Ohio Supreme Court considered a factually similar case, in which the insured also executed an assignment of all of the insured's rights of recovery against the third-party tortfeasor to the extent of the insurer's payment to the insured. The Court held that the outcome of the case was determined by the subrogation provisions of the insurance policy and the subrogation receipt signed by the insured upon settlement of the claim for loss, both of which had language identical to that found in the Wimberly's policy and subrogation receipt. The Court reasoned:

> "The insured's conveyance of all right of recovery up to a certain limit, viz., the extent of the insurer's payment in settlement of the insured's claim, can mean only that the assignee is the owner of all the insured's rights of recovery until he is paid. The assignee, being the owner of all of the insured's right of recovery, must have priority in payment out of the funds recovered. Otherwise, the words 'all right of recovery' are without meaning." *Id.,* 191 N.E.2d at 159.

Although the Ohio Court gave weight to the fact that the insurer had cooperated and assisted in proceedings against the wrongdoer, the clear holding of the case was that the specific subrogation provision and the assignment of "all right of recovery" was interpreted to give the insurer priority to the proceeds received in the judgment recovery from the third party tortfeasor. In a subsequent case, *Ervin v. Garner, supra,* moreover, the Ohio Court indicated that it would not concede that cooperation and assistance are prerequisites under the *Peterson* rule. *Id.,* 267 N.E.2d at 773. Rather, as in *Peterson,* the Ohio Court found, "we fail to see how the insured can specifically assign *each and all claims and demands* to the insurer concerning the single cause of action, limited only by the monetary amount which the insured has paid, and yet still retain any part of his claim or demand."

We disagree with the position taken by the Ohio Court and find the results of these cases at odds with the principles of equitable subrogation. * * * The question for decision in this case * * * is whether the equitable operation of subrogation is modified by the terms of the underlying contract, so-called conventional subrogation.

In *Castleman Constr. Co. v. Pennington,* 222 Tenn. 82, 432 S.W.2d 669 (1968), this Court, speaking through Chief Justice Burnett, rejected the contention made by an insurance company that conventional subrogation is not governed by the same tests applied to find subrogation which arises by operation of law. The Court quoted with approval from Couch on Insurance 2d § 61:20 (1966):

> " 'The doctrine of subrogation in insurance does not arise from, nor is it dependent upon, statute or custom or any of the terms of the contract; it has its origin in general principles of equity and in the nature of the insurance contract as one of indemnity. The right of subrogation rests not upon a contract, but upon the principles of natural justice.' " * * *

The Court viewed the distinction between legal and conventional subrogation only dispositive of "whether there is a right of subrogation in the first instance, rather than in the enforcement of such right." * * * Consequently, we believe our resolution of this case must be guided by general principles of equity, to wit, that the insured must be made whole before subrogation rights arise in favor of the insurers.

The purpose of insurance subrogation is to prevent either the unjust enrichment of the insured through a double recovery or a windfall benefit to the principal tortfeasor by allowing the insurer to stand in the shoes of the insured once the insurer has fully indemnified the insured. * * * It is obvious that the insureds will not be unjustly enriched by recovering from their insurers on their fire policies as well as from the tortfeasor's insurer because the total indemnity of $40,000 will not cover the casualty loss of $44,619.10. The principal tortfeasor has not reaped a windfall, but rather has been released by the parties in consideration of a $25,000 settlement with her insurer. Finally, although defendant insurers must pay the full limits of their policies without reimbursement by way of subrogation, the insured loss was a risk that the insureds paid for them to assume. Had the tortfeasor been judgment-proof and uninsured, defendants would still have been required to bear the loss to the full extent of the policies.

In *Garrity v. Rural Mut. Ins. Co.,* 77 Wis.2d 537, 253 N.W.2d 512, 516 (1977), the Supreme Court of Wisconsin refused to follow the *Peterson* rationale and held that "we regard the differentiation between subrogation and assignment in this situation as purely procedural." The Court correctly isolated the pivotal question, not considered by the Ohio Court in *Peterson,* whether the insurance contract had changed the rule that the surety's right of subrogation does not arise ordinarily until the debt is paid in full, and held that "because the contract here contains no language to the contrary, the normal rule of subrogation applies and the subrogee has no right to share in the funds recovered from the tortfeasor until the subrogor is made whole." * * * The Court simply recognized that the assignee under the subrogation receipt is a subrogee, and nothing more. As a subrogee, the insurer does not acquire the rights of its insured until the latter is made whole. "The assignment adds nothing to the rights vested in the surety by the doctrine of subrogation." *Id.* at 516, *quoting from Couch, supra,* § 61:105.

We believe that the rule followed in *Garrity* comports with the doctrine of subrogation as applied under Tennessee law and represents the approach followed in a plurality of jurisdictions. [Citations from Montana, Utah, N. Car., Mich., Miss., Texas, and Kansas]

The judgment of the Court of Appeals is reversed and that of the trial court reinstated. Costs are adjudged against appellees.

## MURPHY v. AETNA INSURANCE COMPANY

Supreme Court, Appellate Division, Fourth Department, 1983.
96 A.D.2d 99, 468 N.Y.S.2d 265.

BOOMER, JUSTICE.

* * *

Plaintiff is the sole stockholder of Top Choice Foods, Inc., which operated a grocery store. Top Choice was the named insured in a fire insurance policy issued by the defendant Aetna, which insured the contents of the store. Tripi Foods, Inc., a wholesale food broker, sold groceries to Top Choice on credit and, as security for the outstanding balance, Top Choice gave Tripi a chattel mortgage on the contents of the store and caused Tripi to be named as "loss payee" in the mortgage clause of the fire insurance policy. Also as security for Top Choice's debt, the plaintiff co-signed a note payable to Tripi and gave Tripi a second mortgage on his residence.

Fire broke out at the store and destroyed the contents. Top Choice was unable to recover its loss under the fire insurance policy because the policy had been cancelled for non-payment of premiums, and it defaulted on its debt to Tripi. Faced with the prospect of losing his residence, plaintiff paid Tripi the amount owed by Top Choice and took an assignment of Tripi's rights under the fire insurance policy.

Plaintiff claims that, as against Tripi, the cancellation of the policy was not effective because defendant Aetna neglected to send Tripi a notice of cancellation. Defendant Aetna contends that Tripi, as a "loss payee" under the policy, was not entitled to notice of cancellation (see Dyer v. Great Eastern Ins. Co., 41 A.D.2d 581, 340 N.Y.S.2d 3). Plaintiff rejoins, however, that Tripi was not merely a "loss payee" but was a mortgagee, entitled to notice under the mortgage clause contained in the

New York State standard fire insurance policy (Insurance Law, § 168). The first part of that clause provides: If loss hereunder is made payable, in whole or in part, to a designated mortgagee not named herein as the insured, such interest in this policy may be cancelled by giving to such mortgagee a ten days' written notice. The policy issued by Aetna to Top Choice Foods, Inc. insured the contents of the grocery store and contained the printed notation: "Mortgage Clause: Subject to the provisions of the mortgage clause attached hereto, loss, if any, on building items, shall be payable to:" Immediately following was typewritten: "Loss Payee: Tripi Food, Inc., 1427 William St. Box 1107, Buffalo, New York." The court found these notations to be ambiguous and determined that a question of fact existed since "the parties may or may not have intended said loss payee to assume all the statutory rights of a mortgagee including notice of cancellation."

We find it unnecessary to decide whether Tripi should have received notice of cancellation. Assuming that Tripi is entitled to be treated as a "mortgagee" under the terms of the policy, neither Tripi nor plaintiff, as assignee, is entitled to recovery because the debt owed to the mortgagee, Tripi, has been paid and discharged (see Whitestone Sav. & Loan Ass'n v. Allstate Ins. Co., 28 N.Y.2d 332, 321 N.Y.S.2d 862, 270 N.E.2d 694; Heilbrunn v. German Alliance Ins. Co., 150 App.Div. 670, 135 N.Y.S. 769; Meyers v. Norwich Union Fire Ins. Soc., 47 Misc.2d 353, 262 N.Y.S.2d 579). The standard mortgage clause in a fire insurance policy creates a separate contract between the insurer and the mortgagee in which the owner has no interest (1 Jones on Mortgages, § 506; Heilbrunn v. German Alliance Ins. Co., 150 App.Div. 670, 671, 135 N.Y.S. 769, supra; Meyers v. Norwich Union Fire Ins. Soc., 47 Misc.2d 353, 355, 262 N.Y.S.2d 579, supra). The contract with the mortgagee is one of indemnity and is measured by the amount of loss incurred by the mortgagee. The insurable interest of the mortgagee in the property extends only to the amount of the mortgage debt and where the mortgage has been paid and the debt satisfied, whether before or after the fire, the mortgagee suffers no loss and no longer has an insurable interest in the property (Heilbrunn v. German Alliance Insurance Co., 150 App.Div. 670, 672, 135 N.Y.S. 769, supra). Here, since Tripi had been paid and thus suffered no loss, it was not entitled to payment from the insured under the policy. Plaintiff, as assignee of the insurance policy, has no greater right than his assignor, Tripi.

Plaintiff cannot claim that his payment to Tripi did not discharge the mortgage and satisfy the debt, but acted only as assignment of the mortgage and debt to him. At an examination before trial he testified that he "satisfied the indebtedness to Tripi Foods." Moreover, there is no showing that he took an assignment of the chattel mortgage or the debt it secured. Absent a formal assignment, a mortgage or mortgage debt may be kept alive after payment in full to the mortgagee under the principles of subrogation or equitable assignment (Arnold, et al. v. Green, 116 N.Y. 566, 571, 23 N.E. 1), but those principles have no application here. Although the doctrine of subrogation or equitable assignment applies where it is equitable that a person furnishing money to pay a debt should be substituted for the creditor (57 N.Y.Jur., Subrogation, § 4), it will not apply where it will adversely affect the rights of a party having a superior claim (57 N.Y.Jur., Subrogation, § 14). Here, the defendant Aetna has the superior claim to be subrogated to the rights of the mortgagee.

Aetna derives its right of subrogation from the second part of the mortgage clause in the policy, which provides: If this company shall claim that no liability existed as to the mortgagor or owner, it shall, to the extent of payment of loss to the mortgagee, be subrogated to all of the mortgagee's rights of recovery, but without impairing mortgagee's right to sue; or it may pay off the mortgage debt and require an assignment thereof and of the mortgage. Under this clause, if Aetna had paid the fire loss to Tripi, it would have been subrogated to all of Tripi's rights to collect the mortgage debt, including the right to sue plaintiff on the note he co-signed and to foreclose the lien of the mortgage on his residence. Thus, Aetna, if it had paid the mortgagee, could have collected the mortgage debt from plaintiff just as did the mortgagee.

The case of Home Ins. Co. v. Bishop, 140 Me. 72, 34 A.2d 22, illustrates this right of the insurer, as subrogee, to proceed against persons, other than the mortgagor, liable for the mortgage debt. There, defendant, Bishop, was an accommodation endorser on a note given by the O'Rileys for the balance of the purchase price of an automobile. The O'Rileys deliberately set fire to the automobile and were thereby precluded from recovering under the automobile insurance policy issued by plaintiff, Home Insurance Company, which provided coverage for loss by fire. After the fire, Home Insurance Company paid Commercial Credit Corporation, the holder of the note and of the security interest in the automobile, for its loss as mortgagee. The policy contained a mortgage clause similar to that contained in the New York standard fire insurance policy and, as required by the subrogation provision of that clause, Commercial Credit Corporation, the mortgagee, assigned the security interest in the automobile, together with the note endorsed by Bishop, to plaintiff, Home Insurance Company.

Home Insurance Company sued Bishop on the note. The court dismissed the complaint holding that Home Insurance Company was entitled to be subrogated to all of the rights of the mortgagee against the mortgagors, the O'Rileys, but not against defendant, Bishop, the accommodation endorser of the note. On appeal, the Supreme Judicial Court of Maine reversed, stating that the right of subrogation stated in the policy was essentially the same as that arising by operation of law; that under the law of subrogation, the insurance company was substituted for the mortgagee and was entitled to all of the remedies available to the mortgagee, including the right to sue Bishop, as endorser of the note. Quoting from 25 Ruling Case Law, Subrogation, § 10, the court wrote (140 Me. at p. 78, 34 A.2d at p. 24): "The right of subrogation is not restricted to the remedies which the creditor had against the principal debtor but extends to all the remedies which he had against the principal and others liable for the debt." Citing American Bonding Co. v. National Mechanics' Bank, 97 Md. 598, 55 A. 395, 99 Am.St.Rep. 466 and note. See also, National Surety Co. v. State Savings Bank, 8 Cir., 156 F. 21, 14 L.R.A., N.S., 155, 13 Ann.Cas. 429.

Here, under the principles of subrogation, if Aetna had paid the fire loss to Tripi, it could have proceeded against plaintiff on the note he signed for the accommodation of his corporation, Top Choice, and it could also have instituted an action to foreclose the lien of the mortgage on his residence. Thus, the right of the defendant Aetna to subrogation is superior to that of the plaintiff and, under these circumstances, plaintiff can claim no right to equitable assignment or subrogation.

Instead of discharging the debt owing by his corporation to Tripi, plaintiff might have kept the debt alive by taking an assignment of the chattel mortgage and of the debt it secured. This, however, would have been to no avail. In order to recover under the insurance policy, the plaintiff would be compelled to comply with the subrogation provisions of the insurance policy by assigning to the insurer the chattel mortgage, together with all of the remedies the mortgagee, Tripi, had against the mortgagor, Top Choice Foods, and against "others liable for the debt," which "others" would include the plaintiff, who had co-signed the note for the mortgage debt. Thus, any money owing by defendant Aetna to plaintiff under the policy would be offset by the amount of plaintiff's obligation on the note. It would not be necessary for defendant Aetna to admit its liability and then counterclaim against plaintiff for a like amount (see Heilbrunn v. German Alliance Ins. Co., 150 App.Div. 670, 672, 135 N.Y.S. 769, supra).

In summary, plaintiff has no cause of action under the mortgage clause of the fire insurance policy. As assignee of the policy it has no greater rights than its assignor, Tripi, and Tripi, as mortgagee, had no rights under the policy because the mortgage debt was satisfied and thus it suffered no loss. Nor can plaintiff claim that the debt should be kept alive under the principles of equitable assignment or subrogation since the defendant Aetna has the superior right of subrogation. Accordingly, the order should be reversed and the complaint dismissed.

Order unanimously reversed with costs, motion granted, and complaint dismissed as against defendant Aetna Insurance Company.

## HOME INSURANCE CO. v. HERTZ CORP.

Supreme Court of Illinois, 1978.
71 Ill.2d 210, 16 Ill.Dec. 484, 375 N.E.2d 115.

UNDERWOOD, JUSTICE:

* * *

Plaintiff-insurer alleged that on August 2, 1974, defendant Gary L. Gardner, an employee of defendant Ingram Barge, Inc., negligently drove an automobile owned by defendant Hertz Corporation so as to injure plaintiff's insured and damage his auto. Plaintiff also alleged that it paid its insured's property damage and medical payments policy claims in the amount of $2,082.36 and that it thereby became subrogated to the interests of the insured to the extent of those payments. Ingram submitted in support of its motion to dismiss a full and final release of all personal injury and property damage claims arising from the accident, which release was executed by the insured in consideration of the payment to him of $6,000. It is not disputed that this release had been executed by the insured in connection with the settlement of his separate suit against the defendants here for personal injury damages and the $100 property damage paid by him under his deductible clause, and that no recovery had been sought in that suit for the property damage paid by the insurer. It is also undisputed that defendants had notice of plaintiff's subrogation rights prior to the settlement of the insured's suit and the signing of the release.

The precise question before us is whether an unlimited general release by an insured of all claims against a tortfeasor bars a subrogation action by an insurer-subrogee against that tortfeasor, where the tortfeasor procures the release from the insured-subrogor with knowledge of the insurer's interest.

It is true as defendants contend that the appellate court authority in this State supports their position. The appellate court here relied on Inter Insurance Exchange of Chicago Motor Club v. Andersen (1947), 331 Ill.App. 250, 73 N.E.2d 12, * * * In *Andersen,* the insurer, after paying its insured under a collision policy, brought a subrogation action against the tortfeasor for property damage to the insured's automobile; it also joined the insured as a defendant, alleging that, by executing the release, he failed to protect the insurer's subrogation rights as required by the insurance contract. The tortfeasor invoked a release, signed only by the insured, as a bar to the insurer's action. Faced with deciding whether the tortfeasor or the insured should protect the insurer's subrogation interest, the appellate court chose the insured because he had a contractual relationship with the insurer while the tortfeasor did not. The court in *Andersen* acknowledged that "[t]he general rule seems to be that where the wrongdoer procures a release from the insured with knowledge that the insurance has been paid, the release is no bar to an action by the subrogee insurer against the wrongdoer" (331 Ill.App. 250, 254, 73 N.E.2d 12, 14), but it found that "[t]he goal of prudence in one's conduct would seem to be reached more truly by making the insured duty bound to refrain from executing a release except with the approval of the insurer" (331 Ill.App. 250, 256, 73 N.E.2d 12, 15).

While our appellate court has adhered to this position, authority elsewhere is to the contrary, allowing the insurer to recover from the tortfeasor. [Citations from 21 states omitted.]

The difficulty with the *Andersen* rule, in our opinion, is that its application in the circumstances here is fundamentally unfair to both the insured and his insurer. Denied enforcement of its subrogation rights against the real wrongdoer, the insurer must instead seek recovery from its own insured, an obviously unpalatable alternative. Thus the tortfeasor and his own liability insurer, if any, escape payment for damage caused by the tortfeasor, while the tort victim is effectively denied payment from his own insurance carrier *and* from the tortfeasor. The *Andersen* rule in these circumstances constitutes a trap for the unwary insured plaintiff. While no fraud is alleged here, the rule itself encourages fraud or, at the very least, sharp practice on the part of the tortfeasor or his insurance carrier. The insured may be an unsophisticated, unrepresented party presented with a full and final release which he is told he must sign in order to effect a needed settlement. To require him to execute a release of all claims, even though the tortfeasor has knowledge of the insurer's interest and the probable existence of a standard insurance policy provision obligating the insured to protect the insurer's subrogation rights, is simply not consistent with fair dealing and ought not to be encouraged. In short, adoption of the *Andersen* rule would (1) permit the tortfeasor to escape liability for the amounts paid by the insurer, (2) require the tort victim to go uncompensated as to the amounts paid by the insurer even though he has paid insurance premiums and has also suffered loss at the hands of the tortfeasor defendant, (3) force the insurer to sue his own injured insured, and (4) place a premium on sharp practice and dishonesty. Simply put, the *Andersen* rule produces, in our judgment, an inequitable result and ought not to be applied in the circumstances before us.

* * *

Reversed and remanded.

### *Note*

### *Co-operation and Subrogation*

PAXTON NATIONAL INS. CO v. BRICKAJLIK, 513 Pa. 627, 522 A.2d 531 (1987):

> "* * * Mr. William Brickajlik, [is] the owner of a truck which was stolen while in the possession of a service station. Based on a written policy insuring against theft, the insurance company reimbursed Mr. Brickajlik for his loss. The reimbursement was $3,350. The insurance company then attempted to bring a third-party action against the service station, but despite three written requests by the insurance company and similar requests by the insurance company's counsel, Mr. Brickajlik refused to sign the complaint. The insurance company then commenced an action against Mr. Brickajlik to recover the $3,350 paid on account of Mr. Brickajlik's loss, plus interest. [Lower courts held that Mr. B's refusal to sign the complaint constituted a breach of both the subrogation and co-operation clauses in the policy].

"The question then remains whether Mr. Brickajlik's breach was a material one. * * *

"By the strict rules of the common law, the right to subrogation could only be enforced in the name of the creditor, 73 Am.Jur.2d, Subrogation, § 139; however, in Pennsylvania we have long recognized the right of a subrogee to sue in either his own name or the name of the subrogor to recover monies paid. Slack v. Kirk, 67 Pa. 380, 385, 5 A. 438 (1871). Thus, the insurance company could properly assess its prospects for success and, in accordance with its assessment, elect to bring the third-party action in either its name or the name of its insured.

"The general rule in Pennsylvania is that evidence of insurance is irrelevant and prejudicial and justifies grant of a mistrial. The reason is obvious: fact-finders should not be tempted to render decisions based upon the extraneous consideration that an insurance company will actually pay the bill. In view of the potential for prejudice to the insurance company if its presence were made known to the fact-finder, the insurance company properly elected to proceed against the third party in the name of its subrogor. As noted by the trial court, '[T]he insurance company's case would almost certainly be stronger if filed in the name of the insured.' We cannot, consistent with the general policy of excluding evidence of insurance coverage, conclude that Mr. Brickajlik was reasonably requested to sign the complaint in the third-party action and his refusal to do so constituted a material breach of the agreement justifying a return of the proceeds paid under the policy.

"Reversed."

## EXECUTIVE JET AVIATION, INC. v. UNITED STATES

United States Court of Appeals, Sixth Circuit, 1974.
507 F.2d 508.

PHILLIPS, CHIEF JUDGE.

* * *

On July 28, 1968, one of Executive Jet's aircraft crashed on take-off from the Cleveland, Ohio, airport after its engines had ingested a large number of seagulls that had been roosting on the runway. The plane was covered by a $1,300,000 policy of aircraft hull insurance issued by a group of British insurance companies. On October 17, 1968, Executive Jet received $1,300,000 from the insurers pursuant to a typical loan receipt agreement, under which Executive Jet was obligated to make repayment only out of any net recovery it might obtain from those liable for the crash. In addition, the agreement required that Executive Jet stand ready to institute suit in its own name for the purpose of effecting such a recovery. The insurers, however, were to bear the expense and to assume direction and control of any such litigation.

By letter dated May 6, 1969, Executive Jet submitted to the Federal Aviation Administration a written claim in the amount of $1,763,643.64. The letter made no reference to the insurers or to the loan receipt agreement.

On May 12, 1969, Executive Jet filed a complaint against the United States in the action out of which this appeal arises, alleging negligence on the part of the FAA air traffic controllers in not warning of the presence of seagulls on the runway and praying for $1,763,643.64 in damages. In an answer filed July 24, 1969, the Government raised several issues, including the defense that Executive Jet was not the real party in interest.

In an unreported opinion rendered on November 2, 1973, the District Court looked to the law of Ohio as stated in Cleveland Paint & Color Co. v. Bauer Manufacturing Co., 155 Ohio St. 17, 97 N.E.2d 545 (1951), and concluded that the loan receipt arrangement was a mere fiction that would not avoid subrogation. Thus the insurers, rather than Executive Jet, were held to be the real parties in interest. The court noted in passing that even if federal law were to control the effect of the loan receipt, the same result would be achieved under what the court considered the better federal rule announced in City Stores Co. v. Lerner Shops, Inc., 133 U.S.App.D.C. 311, 410 F.2d 1010 (1969). Further, the District Court held that because the insurers had not filed an administrative claim within two years of the accident as required by 28 U.S.C.A. § 2401(b), the insurers could not be joined as plaintiffs. Therefore, the court dismissed the complaint with prejudice, and Executive Jet perfected this appeal.

In the view that we take of this case, we need not decide whether the effect of the loan receipt arrangement is governed by state or federal law. It is conceded that under the law of Ohio payment pursuant to a loan receipt is considered outright payment and does not avoid subrogation of the insurer. Cleveland Paint & Color Co. v. Bauer Mfg. Co., supra, 155 Ohio St. 17, 97 N.E.2d 545 (1951). In our opinion the federal courts should follow the same rule. Thus we would reach the same result on the subrogation issue regardless of whether we apply the State law of Ohio or federal law.

Executive Jet insists that the federal practice has been to respect the form of loan receipts and to find no subrogation when this device is employed. Principal reliance is placed on Luckenbach v. W.J. McCahan Sugar Refining Co., 248 U.S. 139, 39 S.Ct. 53, 63 L.Ed. 170 (1918), an admiralty case in which the Supreme Court considered a loan receipt transaction and found "no good reason * * * either for questioning its legality or for denying it effect." Id. at 148, 39 S.Ct. at 55. *Luckenbach,* however, is distinguishable because of its unusual factual setting. In that case the insurer was liable only contingently—it would have incurred liability to the insured shipper only after it had been established that recovery against the carrier for the lost cargo was impossible. Furthermore, if the insurer had paid the shipper outright before the carrier's liability had been determined, the carrier would have become liable to no one. Therefore, the loan receipt device was used so that the insured would not be deprived of the use of the money for which either the insurer or the carrier eventually would incur liability.

Thus in *Luckenbach* there were present at least some of the indicia of a true loan. In the case at bar, not only were the insurers absolutely liable to Executive Jet, but the terms of the loan did not require repayment of a definite sum at a definite time and did not assess any interest charges. Nor is it mere coincidence that the amount loaned was precisely equal to the aircraft's agreed value in the insurance policy. Further, we note that under the loan receipt agreement the insurers assumed the expense, control, and direction of litigation against any third parties who might be liable for the plane crash. This, of course, is precisely the result that would be achieved in the ordinary case of payment and subrogation. These circumstances lead us to conclude that the transfer of $1,300,000 to Executive Jet was a loan in name only. In fact it was an outright settlement of a loss covered under the insurance policy, and we are unwilling to permit the form of the transaction to control its substance.

Executive Jet insists, however, that it does not rely solely upon *Luckenbach* and that subsequent federal cases have given literal effect to loan receipt agreements in circumstances similar to those in the case at bar. Executive Jet refers us particularly to Augusta Broadcasting Co. v. United States, 170 F.2d 199 (5th Cir.1948), a case under the Tort Claims Act in which the court held "that the giving of the loan receipt did not affect [the insured's] right to sue * * *." Id. at 200. However, the court in that case stated its conclusion without any reasoning or analysis. Moreover, it appeared to rely only on *Luckenbach* and a decision by the Georgia Court of Appeals. Obviously the Georgia case can provide no support for Executive Jet's position, and insofar as *Augusta Broadcasting* relies on *Luckenbach,* its theoretical underpinnings seem weak.

In many of the other cases cited by Executive Jet as authority for giving literal effect to loan receipts, the court looked for guidance to *Luckenbach* or to state law or to both. See, e.g., Sanders v. Liberty Mut. Ins. Co., 354 F.2d 777 (5th Cir.1965); Export Leaf Tobacco Co. v. American Ins. Co., 260 F.2d 839 (4th Cir.1958); Dixey v. Federal Compress & Warehouse Co., 132 F.2d 275 (8th Cir.1942); First Nat'l Bank v. Lloyd's of London, 116 F.2d 221 (7th Cir.1940). These cases would seem subject to the same observations we made about *Augusta Broadcasting.* In any event, we do not find the reasoning in this line of cases to be compelling in the case at bar.

On the other hand, we note that our conclusion is supported by the relatively recent case of City Stores Co. v. Lerner Shops, Inc., supra, 133 U.S.App.D.C. 311, 410 F.2d 1010 (1969). In this case the court first analyzed *Luckenbach* and found it not controlling. It could discern only one purpose for the use of a loan receipt—to avoid subrogation and thereby to circumvent the requirement of the Federal Rules that "[e]very action shall be prosecuted in the name of the real party in interest." Fed.R.Civ.P. 17(a). The court summed up its views about loan receipts as follows:

> "It does not seem sensible to say that an insured who has been paid in full by his insurer is nevertheless the real party in interest merely because of a sham 'loan agreement' which is a transparent subterfuge to avoid subrogation and to evade a federal rule." 410 F.2d at 1015.

We agree with the reasoning and with the decision in the *City Stores* case, and we note that it does not stand alone among federal cases in refusing to give literal effect to a loan receipt. See Potomac Elec. Power Co. v. Babcock & Wilcox Co., 54 F.R.D. 486, 489 (D.Md.1972) (concluding that a loan receipt "hardly amounts to a bona fide loan"); Condor Inv. Co. v. Pacific Coca–Cola Bottling Co., 211 F.Supp. 671 (D.Or.1962) (finding outright payment despite use of loan receipt).

We hold, then, that despite the use of the loan receipt, when the insurers in this case transferred $1,300,000 to Executive Jet, they became subrogated to Executive Jet's claims against the Government. That being so, the insurers are real parties in interest under Federal Rule 17(a) to the extent of the payment. United States v. Aetna Cas. & Sur. Co., 338 U.S. 366, 380–382, 70 S.Ct. 207, 94 L.Ed. 171 (1949).

### *Note*

Notwithstanding the principal case, the loan receipt is commonly used in many states. The following form for a loan receipt is taken from Pennsylvania Lumbermens Mutual Insurance Co. v. Thomason, 178 F.Supp. 382 (D.C.N.C.1959):

> "$______ *[Place]* *[Date]*
>
> "Received from ______ Insurance Company ______ Dollars as a loan and repayable only to the extent of any net recovery I/We may make from any person or persons, corporation or corporations, on account of loss by ______ to our property on or about ______ 19__.
>
> "As security for such repayment I/We hereby pledge to said ______ the said recovery and deliver to it all documents necessary to show my/our interest in said property, and we agree to enter and prosecute in my/our name, suit against such person or persons, corporation or corporations, on account of said claim for said loss, with all due diligence, at the expense and under the exclusive direction and control of said insurance company.
>
> "I/We certify that no settlement has been made by me/us with any person or persons, corporation or corporations, who may be responsible for said loss. Any money paid me/us by any other participant in loss is held in trust pending instructions by Insurance Company.
>
> "______________________________
>
> "By ______________________________
>
> "President"

*

# Part C

# INSURANCE OF THE PERSON

# Chapter 8

# METHODS OF MARKETING

- ___ **more details on the negotiation of contracts insuring the person; and on the function of agents**
- ___ **conditional binder receipts**
- ___ **insurance on the run (trip insurance and machine issued policies)**

## *Comment*

Insurance of the person provides for payment upon the occurrence of death, personal injury or sickness. Coverages include life insurance, accident insurance, and health insurance. Policies can also provide for annuities; that is, the policy may provide for the payment of a fixed monthly or annual sum after the insured has reached a certain age. Most commonly, annuities are purchased separately by people who earn very large sums during a short period of their lives, e.g. movie stars, baseball players, boxers, etc.

Life insurance policies can be organized into two main types of products: "term" insurance and "whole-life" or "ordinary life" insurance. An example of the latter can be found in Appendix C.

Term policies provide a specified amount (the "face value" of the policy) to the designated beneficiaries if the person whose life is insured dies during the coverage period which can be one, five or more years, while the insured is employed by a given employer, or while the insured is on a trip. "Convertible" term policies give the insured the right to change the contract to a whole-life one, often without requiring proof of insurability. Term policy premiums are calculated according to life expectancy ascertained from actuarial tables. Very often, employers provide policies to be effective during the period of employment. These policies vary, but commonly they are of the "group" insurance variety whereby an employer's work force may elect to become members of the group. Especially common among larger employers are "group health" and "accident" policies under which coverage may extend into the employee's retirement. The broad subject of health care insurance is a matter of national concern at the time this is written.

Whole-life or ordinary life policies are quite different. The intent behind these policies is that the insured will by monthly or yearly premium payments provide the insurance company with a sum of money to cover losses (that is, death benefits) and expenses, and build up equity. Insurers invest the premium such that the sum will grow. Naturally, enough money has to be produced to pay the company for its costs of doing business, and, if the insurer is a stock company, a hoped for profit.

The making of a whole-life policy is considerably different from the making of a term policy. Whole-life policies are solicited from prospective insured by salesmen. A sometimes complicated application disclosing such matters as the applicant's health and other factors has to be filed, and the insured is normally required to have a physical exam given by a physician selected by the insurer. The results of the physical and the revelations in the application are then evaluated by the company, which, if it approves, issues the policy.

A number of parties may be associated with the making of a whole-life policy, the insured and the insurer, of course. But the applicant and owner of the policy may not be the person whose life is covered; among other possibilities, the latter may be the spouse, parent, child, or employer. The person whose life is covered is sometimes called the "cestui que vie". If the policy is payable to a third party, that party is called the "beneficiary". Obviously, questions of insurable interest will arise, although it is ordinarily said that a person has an unquestionable interest in his own life. Indeed, a frequently issued policy is one taken out by "John Jones" on his own life, payable to his own estate.

One of the most interesting features of the whole-life policy is the accumulation of equity, which, as time passes may amount to a considerable asset. Protection of this asset against forfeiture (by non-payment of premium, let us say, when the policy is in its twentieth year) has been a concern of lawmakers. As a result, several financial features are noteworthy. Policyholder rights include the right to obtain a loan against the policy, the right to "cash it in" by surrendering the policy in return for payment of a stipulated value, and the right to have the policy's equity applied to premiums in case the policyholder is no longer able to make payments. Certain other rights are interesting: the insured benefits by a "grace period" (for late payments, e.g. 30 days), and the policy becomes "incontestable" after a given period. "Incontestability" applies primarily to the insurer's right to rescind the policy for fraud or mistake.

There are numerous variations on the whole-life policy. For example, some allow insured directed investment strategies and others are structured to meet the insured's cash-flow profile. "Participating" policies include plans under which the insured is entitled to dividends which may be used to offset premium payments or increase the coverage by adding to the cash value. For additional information on the coverage and variations see Keeton and Widiss, *Insurance Law,* § 1.5(c) (1988), Appleman, *Insurance Law and Practice,* §§ 1–90 (1981), Couch, *Couch on Insurance 2d,* §§ 1:73–1:78 (1984).

As a preliminary matter, a fundamental tension in marketing life insurance products is the insurer's desire to delay coverage until after it has had an opportunity to evaluate the risk, while simultaneously emotionally binding the applicant at time of application by securing payment of part or all of the first premium. The cases that follow explore the twilight zone created by the conditional receipt and the familiar complication of agency and fraud or mistake.

## COLLISTER v. NATIONWIDE LIFE INSURANCE CO.

Supreme Court of Pennsylvania, 1978.
479 Pa. 579, 388 A.2d 1346.

MANDERINO, JUSTICE.

On or about September 24, 1972, appellant's husband applied to appellee Nationwide Life Insurance Company for life insurance in the amount of $10,000.00, with double indemnity for accidental death, plus $22,500.00 level term insurance. Appellee, through its agent, accepted $60.66 from appellant's husband at the time of the application. This amount represented a two-month premium payment on the above described insurance. In exchange for this payment appellee's agent gave appellant's husband a "conditional receipt."

On November 4, 1972, appellant's husband, was killed in an automobile accident. At the time of appellant's husband's death Nationwide had neither issued the policy applied for nor had it rejected the application. Nor had appellant's husband taken the medical examination required by the wording of the application. Subsequent to appellant's husband's death, Nationwide denied liability, asserting that certain conditions contained in the application and in the conditional receipt (namely the taking of the medical examination) had not been fulfilled by the applicant.

[The trial court granted the insurance company's motion for summary judgment.]

Appellant argues before us, as she did below, that a contract of insurance came into being between appellant's husband and Nationwide at the time Nationwide accepted the application form and the first premium payment. This transaction, urges appellant, created a temporary insurance contract that provided insurance coverage for the period of time extending from acceptance of the premium deposit until Nationwide either rejected the application because of the applicant's uninsurability or accepted the application and issued the policy applied for. For the reasons that follow, we agree with appellant.

At the outset, we note that temporary contracts of insurance affording coverage pending issuance of the formal policy by the insurer are well known in the insurance industry. See 12 Appleman, Insurance Law and Practice, §§ 7221–7233 (1943); 1 Couch on Insurance 2d, §§ 14:26–14:46 (1959). * * * [I]n McAvoy Vitrified Brick Co. v. North America Life Assurance Co., 395 Pa. 75, 149 A.2d 42 (1959), we held that an application for insurance coverage, a deposit premium receipt, and an "interim assurance certificate," constituted a contract to provide temporary insurance for the period of time between the delivery of the certificate and the subsequent decision of the insurer at its home office of whether to issue the policy applied for or reject the application. Like

Nationwide here, the insurer in *McAvoy,* argued that its liability was subject to a condition precedent; in that case the alleged condition precedent was the insurer's good-faith determination that the applicant was an insurable risk.

The *McAvoy* court considered the conflicting points of view before arriving at its conclusion that a contract of temporary insurance existed. Quoting from the California Supreme Court's decision in Ransom v. Penn Mutual Life Ins. Co., 43 Cal.2d 420, 274 P.2d 633 (1954), we said,

> " 'The courts in several jurisdictions have construed clauses similar to the one involved here. A number of decisions have held, in accordance with defendant's view, that no contract of insurance exists until the insurer has been satisfied as to an applicant's acceptability, and that the provisions that the insurance shall be in force from the date of the application means that, if and when the company is satisfied, the contract shall be considered to relate back and take effect as of that date. (Citations omitted.)
>
> On the other hand, a number of courts have held that the provisions to the effect that the insurance shall be in force from the date of the application if the premium is paid gives rise to a contract of insurance immediately upon receipt of the application and payment of the premium, and that the proviso that the company shall be satisfied that the insured was acceptable at the date of the application creates only a right to terminate the contract if the company becomes dissatisfied with the risk before a policy is issued.' " (Citations omitted.)

* * *

The courts of several other jurisdictions have also recognized the validity of temporary insurance contracts. [citations].

The rationale of these cases is succinctly stated in Smith v. Westland Life Ins. Co., supra, 123 Cal.Rptr. at 655, 539 P.2d at 439:

> "We chose to align California with those jurisdictions recognizing temporary insurance, for a number of reasons: First, we found the language of the conditional receipt to be ambiguous and susceptible of the interpretation that coverage would be provided immediately subject to the insurance company's right to terminate coverage if it did not choose to issue the policy applied for. Resolving this ambiguity against the insurer, we held that coverage arose immediately upon completion of the application and payment of the premium. Second, noting that the insurance company drafted the language of the conditional receipt, we reasoned that if the insurer intended to condition its liability under the policy upon its prior approval of the application, it could have easily used clear and unequivocal language to indicate its intention. Third, we concluded that an ordinary person paying the premium at the time he applied for insurance and receiving in return a receipt which stated that coverage was to be effective as of the date of application, had a

reasonable expectation that he would secure the benefit of immediate coverage. Finally, we noted the obvious advantage gained by the insurance company in receiving payment of the premium at the time of application. We therefore concluded that it would be unconscionable to allow the insurer, who had required from the applicant payment of the first premium, to escape the obligation of coverage which the applicant could reasonably assume and expect that the insurer was thereby undertaking."

* * *

To accept the insurer's argument that its liability is contingent on a condition precedent permits the insurer to hold itself immune from liability while it considers whether to accept or reject the risk, as in *McAvoy,* or, as in the instant case, during the period between receipt of the application and premium deposit and the date of the medical examination, while at the same time enjoying the benefits that flow from immediate collection of the premium. See Turner v. Worth Ins. Co., 106 Ariz. 132, 472 P.2d 1 (1970). Viewing insurance contracts (including contracts for temporary insurance) as contracts of adhesion, the courts have accordingly imposed more stringent requirements upon the insurer. For example, some courts have ruled that because of the adhesionary nature of insurance documents (including conditional receipts similar to that at issue here) an insurer who wishes to avoid liability must not only use clear and unequivocal language evidencing its intent to limit temporary coverage, but it must also call such limiting conditions to the attention of the applicant. Absent proof of such disclosure, coverage will be deemed to be that which would be expected by the ordinary layperson, namely, complete and immediate coverage upon payment of the premium. In Smith v. Westland Life Ins. Co., supra, 15 Cal.3d 111, 123 Cal.Rptr. 649, 539 P.2d 433 (1975), the court stated:

> "[T]he applicant [in Young v. Metropolitan Life Ins. Co., 272 Cal. App.2d 453, 77 Cal.Rptr. 382] applied for life insurance under a plan providing double indemnity in the event of accidental death. He paid the premium at the time of application and received a conditional receipt which expressly and unambiguously stated that if the applicant died before the company had approved the policy, the company would pay the benefits provided by the policy, *not including accidental death benefits.* Young died before his application was approved. The insurer claimed that its liability under the policy was limited by the terms of the conditional receipt.
>
> While the court found that the language of the application and receipt clearly made company approval a condition precedent to the insurer's full liability under the policy, the court nevertheless ruled that the company must be held liable to the full extent under the policy applied for, including accidental death benefits, unless it satisfied the burden of proving that the provisions limiting the company's liability were called to the applicant's attention or that the applicant had read them. In so holding, the court reasoned that

> *'the very acceptance of an advance premium by the carrier tends naturally toward an understanding of immediate coverage though it be temporary and terminable * * *. In short, to the ordinary layman, payment of the insurance premium constitutes payment for immediate protection,* and it is unlikely that he would carefully read the fine print contained in a receipt unless he was given the incentive to do so by the carrier's agent." (Citations omitted.) (Emphasis in original.)

In an analogous situation, we have also concluded that the adhesionary nature of insurance documents is such that the insured is under no duty to read the policy sent by the company. Rempel v. Nationwide Life Ins. Co., 471 Pa. 404, 370 A.2d 366 (1977).

* * * [T]he reasonable expectations of the insured clearly became the important consideration once the courts had decided that normal contract principles were no longer applicable in insurance transactions. * * *

Recognition of the reasonable expectations of the insured forms the basis of the New Jersey court's decision in Allen v. Metropolitan Life Ins. Co., supra, 44 N.J. 294, 208 A.2d 638 (1965):

> "Although he knew that his application might ultimately be rejected, he undoubtedly assumed there was interim coverage in the event he died, for that was the very reason he had paid the $576.42 in advance. Indeed, if he was not so covered what justification could the company fairly advance for having taken that large sum from him; surely not the insubstantial collateral advantages which it now asserts or the protection against accidental death which he could have purchased separately for a relatively insignificant amount." * * *

Furthermore, conditional receipts, such as was used in the instant case, tend to encourage deception. As stated by the court in Toevs v. Western Farm Bureau Life Ins. Co., 94 Idaho 151, 154, 483 P.2d 682, 685 (1971),

> "We do not mean to imply affirmative misconduct by the soliciting insurance agent. We suggest only that if nothing is said about the complicated and legalistic phrasing of the receipt, and the agent accepts an application for insurance together with the first premium payment, the applicant has reason to believe that he is insured. Otherwise, he is deceived." * * *

* * *

We believe that the proper resolution of questions such as that presented by the instant appeal depends upon an analysis of the totality of the transaction involved. It is not enough simply to say that a contract for temporary insurance coverage is subject to the same rules of interpretation as any other insurance contract. To be sure, any ambiguity in the written words will be construed liberally in favor of the insured and against the insurer, * * * and if the language of the application and conditional receipt, when so read, indicates an intent on the part of the insurer to provide interim insurance, then such benefits will be awarded by the court. That, however, is not the end of the examination. In situations where the circumstances of the transaction do not indicate that the insurer intended to provide interim insurance, but nevertheless show that the insurer accepted payment of the first premium at the time it took the application, it is then up to the insurer to establish by clear and convincing evidence that the consumer had no reasonable basis for believing that he or she was purchasing immediate insurance coverage.

The reasonable expectation of the insured is the focal point of the insurance transaction involved here. * * * Thus, regardless of the ambiguity, or lack thereof, inherent in a given set of insurance documents (whether they be applications, conditional receipts, riders, policies, or whatever), the public has a right to expect that they will receive something of comparable value in return for the premium paid. Courts should also keep alert to the fact that the expectations of the insured are in large measure created by the insurance industry itself. Through the use of lengthy, complex, and cumbersomely written applications, conditional receipts, riders, and policies, to name just a few, the insurance industry forces the insurance consumer to rely upon the oral representations of the insurance agent. Such representations may or may not accurately reflect the contents of the written document and therefore the insurer is often in a position to reap the benefit of the insured's lack of understanding of the transaction.

* * *

Turning then to the factual circumstances surrounding the instant appeal, we hold that the insurer has failed to establish by clear and convincing evidence that appellant's husband could not have entertained a reasonable expectation that appellee was obligating itself to provide insurance coverage beginning with appellee's acceptance of the first premium payment. Appellee has argued that the language of the "conditional receipt" gave notice to appellant's husband that no insurance was to take effect until successful completion of the required medical examination. (The receipt is attached as an appendix to this decision). The conclusion we reach here is not determined by the language of the conditional receipt, but by the dynamics of the transaction viewed in its entirety.

In the instant situation, appellant's husband could reasonably have believed that the "conditional receipt" was what it purported to be; i.e., a receipt given to evidence that he had paid the first two months premium. Placement on a "receipt" of contract terms and conditions is not a procedure calculated to inform the customer of the content of those terms and conditions, but rather, tends to lull the customer into a failure to observe them. To the ordinary consumer, a receipt is considered only to be evidence that money has been paid as part of the insurance purchasing transaction, and as such is often not taken note of when signed by a trusted advisor in the presence of the consumer. At best, the consumer may possibly glance at the receipt to ascertain that the correct dollar amount has been entered on the blank space provided or that the document is signed by the person receiving the money. Frequently, the customer is given such a receipt while still engaged in conversation with the agent, and always, the receipt is given after, or simultaneously with, payment of the initial premium. Any conditions which the insurer has placed within the body of the receipt are therefore irrelevant to the transaction that has already been completed. The payment of money does not indicate a continuation of contract negotiations, but rather their completion. The payment marks the beginning of performance, which generally occurs after the contract has been entered into. At that point, the consumer is put in a position, of either accepting the receipt as a receipt and nothing more, or put in a position in which he must ask the insurance agent to remain silent so that he, the consumer, might have an opportunity to read and study the document. Furthermore, the consumer might be reluctant to read the document aware that such conduct might imply a mistrust of the person with whom he has already made an agreement, generally after lengthy and personal discussions.

Appellee also contends that their agent informed appellant's husband that a medical examination was necessary. Appellee has not established by clear and convincing evidence, however, that their agent told the decedent that he was paying money upon application for insurance coverage that would not begin until successful completion of the medical examination. The fact that he informed appellant's husband that a medical examination was required by the insurer does not affect our conclusion therefore.

An often stated objection to construing a "conditional receipt" so as to create interim or temporary insurance is that affording such present insurance coverage may allow one who is in fact an uninsurable risk to secure coverage for as long a period of time as it takes the insurer to discover that the applicant is not an acceptable risk. Citing Prudential Ins. Co. of America v. Lamme, supra, 83 Nev. 146, 425 P.2d 346 (1967), the court in Damm v. National Ins. Co. of America, 200 N.W.2d 616 (N.D.1972) dismissed this objection stating that insurance companies have a choice either to accept the risk sometimes involved in the use of conditional receipts, or the insurance company could forego the advantages derived from the customer's payment of a premium deposit upon application, and write "C.O.D." insurance. The court in *Prudential,* supra, explained "C.O.D." insurance as follows:

> "Absent a contrary agreement (the conditional receipt, for example) payment of the initial premium and delivery of the policy are usually concurrent acts, thereby creating a period between the signing of the application by the applicant and the delivery of the policy during which no money has been advanced to the insurance company, and no insurance is in effect. This is called 'COD', or 'cash on delivery' insurance. * * *

* * * If insurers wish to protect themselves from liability during the interim period between the taking of the application and approval (or between the application and successful completion of a required medical examination), all that need be done is to delay acceptance of the applicant's money until that time. If, on the other hand, the insurer wishes to enjoy the substantial benefits it receives by securing the customer's cash at the time of the taking of the application, it must return what the customer can reasonably expect that the insurer is selling: i.e., immediate coverage. Alternatively, the insurer could inform the prospective applicant, *before any money changes hands,* that it does not intend to give the customer anything in return for advance payment, and that the customer is actually paying money now for nothing because no insurance will take effect until approval. Such notification would have to be given *before* the consumer paid the initial premium in order to avoid placing that consumer at the psychological disadvantage of having to ask for a return of the premium if he or she is dissatisfied with such terms. Furthermore, any such notice must be made in a manner calculated to bring the facts of the transaction—that the customer is paying money now, but getting nothing until later—to the customer's attention in no uncertain terms. As such, the notice could not be printed on a receipt.

* * * [W]e therefore vacate the order of the Superior Court, reverse the order of the trial court, and remand the matter to the trial court with instructions that it enter an order in favor of appellant.

* * *

## APPENDIX TO OPINION

### FRONT

This receipt must not be detached unless settlement of the first full premium has been made by the Applicant at the time of application and such premium amount meets the Company's minimum Premium rules.

CONDITIONAL FIRST LIFE PREMIUM RECEIPT: NO INSURANCE WILL BECOME EFFECTIVE PRIOR TO POLICY DELIVERY UNLESS THE ACTS REQUIRED BY THIS RECEIPT ARE COMPLETED. NO AGENT OF THE COMPANY IS AUTHORIZED TO CHANGE ANY ACT REQUIRED.

**NO 308531** Received from ____________ this ______ day of __________, 19__, the sum of ______________ Dollars ($__________) in connection with an application for Life insurance in NATIONWIDE LIFE INSURANCE COMPANY, Columbus, Ohio which application bears the same date and printed number as this receipt.

If the sum indicated above equals the first full premium on the premium payment basis selected in the application for the insurance applied for and if the following acts are completed. (a) receipt by the Company of a fully completed application which includes fully completed medical examinations, if any required by the Company's published underwriting rules because of the age of the insured or the amount of insurance applied for and (b) completion of all investigation by the Company and the Company is satisfied that the Proposed insured and (without prejudice to the Proposed insured) each person proposed for coverage under the Family Rider or the Children's Rider (whichever is applicable and if applied for) is insurable and qualified under the Company's published rules, limits and standards on the plan and for the amount applied for and at the premium specified herein, the said insurance shall take effect and be in force subject to the provisions of the policy applied for from the date of the last medical examination, or if no medical examination is required, the insurance shall take effect on the application date. Unless all acts required are completed, no insurance shall take effect hereunder.

In any event, the amount of insurance becoming effective under the terms of this receipt is hereby limited to the extent that in the event of the death of the Proposed insured the total liability of the Company shall not exceed $100,000, said amount to include any life insurance then in force with the Company and any benefits payable by the Company as a result of accidental death.

If the application is declined the amount evidenced by this receipt shall be refunded.

(Agent must sign here) ______________________________ Agent

NOTICE: This receipt is not valid for any premium for the insurance applied for except the first full premium thereon which in no event shall exceed one annual premium for such insurance together with the premium for interim term insurance, if any.

REVERSE

**IMPORTANT**

The Company reserves the right to require a medical examination. Until you can provide proof that you are insurable, the Company provides no insurance.

If you are requested to have an examination, don't delay. Make arrangements promptly. There is no insurance until a satisfactory medical examination has been made and all the conditions of this receipt are completed.

### *Note*

#### *Termination of "Temporary" Insurance*

In jurisdictions such as the principal case which hold that the conditional binder receipts create a temporary contract of life insurance, it might be assumed that a rejection of the application by the insurer would terminate the temporary contract. However in one of the more debatable aspects of the case of Smith v. Westland Life Insurance Co., 15 Cal.3d 111, 123 Cal.Rptr. 649, 539 P.2d 433 (1975), the majority held that a notice of rejection delivered while the insured was still alive did not alone terminate the temporary policy; rather an actual return of the premium was also essential. Does such a requirement comport with the usual mechanical practices as to rescission of contracts?

Should *Collister* be extended to provide temporary insurance to an employee under a group policy where the employer pays the premium along with the submission of the application, and the insurer never issues a conditional receipt anyway? See Blair v. Manhattan Life Insurance Co., 516 F.Supp. 759 (W.D.Pa.1981).

## THOMAS v. THOMAS

Supreme Court of Kansas, 1992.
824 P.2d 971, 250 Kan. 235.

HERD, J.

This is a breach of contract action arising out of an application for life insurance. Richard I. Thomas applied for life insurance from Monumental Life Insurance Company (Monumental) through its agent, Ronald Thomas, who was also Richard's brother. Richard applied for the insurance on July 2, 1986, and died January 28, 1987 without being issued an insurance policy or being refunded the first month's premium he had paid at the time of application. Grover Thomas (Grover), the beneficiary of Richard's life insurance, brought this action against Ronald and Monumental contending they owed him the proceeds of Richard's insurance because Richard was covered at the time of his death by the temporary coverage provided by the conditional receipt given to Richard at the time of application. The trial court entered judgment in favor of Grover and against Monumental. Monumental appeals.

Let us examine the controlling facts. On July 2, 1986, Richard applied for $50,000 of life insurance coverage from Monumental through its agent, his brother Ronald. Richard named his father, Grover Thomas, as the beneficiary. At the time the application was written, Richard paid the initial monthly premium of $16.45 in cash. Because of Richard's age, he was not required to get a medical physical before being issued insurance.

In exchange for the application and premium payment, Ronald signed and gave Richard a conditional receipt, which stated in part:

> "IMPORTANT: THIS CONDITIONAL RECEIPT DOES NOT PROVIDE ANY INSURANCE UNTIL ALL CONDITIONS ARE MET. * * *. "(1) If all the following conditions are met the insurance applied for shall become effective as of the date of this receipt or the latest required medical examination, whichever is later, subject to the terms and conditions of the policy applied for. The conditions are: (a) payment of an amount equal to the first full premium for the benefits applied for to the Agent at time of signing the application. (b) completion of the application; provided, however, that if the Company makes any change as to amount, classification, plan of insurance, age, benefit, or adds any restrictive rider, the applicant's written acceptance of such change is necessary before any insurance becomes effective. (c) all required medical examinations have been completed. (d) and the Company is satisfied that on the date of the application each person to be insured is a risk insurable and acceptable under its rules, limits and standards for the plan and amount applied for at its standard rate of premium. "(2) If within 45 days from the date hereof a policy has not been issued to the applicant, then the application shall be deemed to have been declined by the Company and any deposit paid will be refunded. "(3) No agent has the authority to modify the application or this receipt, or to bind the Company by making any promise or representation contrary to the provisions hereof." (Emphasis added.)

Monumental has a company policy against agents acting as witnesses for applications by the agent's relatives. The company's policy states: "Applications upon your life, members of your immediate family or your relatives must be written by an unrelated licensed agent or member of management, who will also witness the signature. Your name, of course, is to be inserted in the space for placement and commission credit." Despite this policy, Ronald had taken applications from his family members on numerous prior occasions, including applications by his wife, two daughters, an uncle, a sister, a niece, and his father. None of these applications had been written or witnessed by an unrelated agent. All these applications, however, had been accepted by Monumental and policies had been issued without inquiry by the company.

On July 2 or 3, 1986, Ronald submitted Richard's application, along with the $16.45, to Monumental. Richard's application was first given to an assistant district administrator, Lisa Florez, at Monumental's office in Kansas City. She questioned the validity of the application because it was written in violation of the company's policy. Florez, therefore, brought it to the attention of the district manager, P.J. West, rather than following the normal procedure of forwarding the application to the home office for consideration. Florez also gave West the $16.45 cash deposit which had been submitted with the application.

Upon review of the application, West determined Ronald had violated Monumental's policy against writing applications for relatives and witnessing relatives' signatures. On July 3, 1986, West rejected Richard's application and put it and the cash deposit in an envelope in Ronald's mail slot at the company office. West also enclosed a note asking Ronald to see West.

Although West and Ronald attended meetings twice a week at Monumental's office, they never discussed Richard's application. At trial, Ronald testified he never received the envelope with Richard's application and premium payment with West's note. Monumental did not issue a policy to Richard. Richard paid no additional monthly premiums to Monumental. Monumental received no inquiries about the status of Richard's application from Richard or Ronald.

Richard died January 28, 1987, 165 days after the expiration of the conditional receipt. Upon denial of coverage by Monumental, Grover brought this action to recover the $50,000 proceeds from Richard's life insurance. The parties could not produce Richard's application at trial. The parties stipulated to the following facts: "1. Grover Thomas is the father of Ronald Thomas and Richard I. Thomas, now deceased. Ronald Thomas and Richard I. Thomas are brothers. "2. Ronald Thomas submitted an application for $50,000 life insurance on the life of Richard I. Thomas with the initial monthly premium of $16.45 on or about July 2 or 3, 1986, to Monumental General's Kansas City, Kansas, office. "3. Ronald Thomas was employed as an insurance agent by Monumental General Life Insurance Company on or about July 2 or 3, 1986. "4. On July 2, 1986, Ronald Thomas signed a 'Conditional Receipt.' "5. No policy of life insurance was issued in 45 days nor was any policy of life insurance ever issued. "6. After the initial payment of $16.45 no monthly insurance premiums were ever paid to Monumental General Life Insurance Company. "7. Richard I. Thomas died on January 28, 1987."

* * *

The jury returned the following verdict: "1. Was Ronald Thomas acting within the scope and course of his authority as an insurance agent of Monumental Life Insurance Company when he took the application of Richard I. Thomas for life insurance with that company and witnessed his signature on that application? Answer yes or no: yes "2. Did P.J. West review the application for insurance and reject it? Answer yes or no: yes "3. Did P.J. West put the application and $16.45 in an envelope and place the envelope in Ronald Thomas' mail slot? Answer yes or no:

yes "4. Did Richard Thomas, during his lifetime receive notice that his application for insurance had been rejected and receive a refund of the $16.45? Answer yes or no: no "5. Was Grover Thomas the named beneficiary in the application for insurance? Answer yes or no: yes"

Based upon the jury's verdict, the trial court entered a partial journal entry of judgment in favor of Grover and against Monumental. Monumental filed a motion to alter and amend the partial journal entry of judgment; the motion was denied. On March 21, 1991, the trial court entered a journal entry dismissing Monumental's cross-claim against Ronald and finalizing the judgment against Monumental. Monumental appealed.

The first issue is whether Richard's life insurance was in effect at the time of his death because of the temporary coverage provided by the conditional receipt.

Monumental argues Tripp v. Reliable Life Insurance Co., 210 Kan. 33, 499 P.2d 1155, should be overruled or in the alternative its application should be narrowed. * * *

The receipt given to Tripp provided in part: "'* * * The insurance under the policy for which application is made shall be effective on date of this receipt or the date of completion of the medical examination (if, and when required by the Company), whichever is the later date, * * *.' 'Company shall have 60 days from date of application to consider and act upon the application. Failure of the Company to offer a policy within such 60 days shall be deemed a declination.'" 210 Kan. at 34, 499 P.2d 1155.

Tripp was never contacted by Reliable within the 60–day declination period. On May 23, 1969, the company's home office instructed its local agent to refund the premium deposit and retrieve Tripp's receipt. 210 Kan. at 39–40, 499 P.2d 1155. On June 1, 1969, Reliable's agent tendered Tripp's initial premium and requested return of the conditional receipt. Tripp's daughter had died on May 29, 1969, 51 days after the 60–day conditional receipt expired. Tripp refused to return the receipt, claiming coverage. He then brought suit against Reliable for his daughter's life insurance benefits.

The trial court determined the company was estopped to deny insurance coverage and entered judgment against the company. 210 Kan. at 35, 499 P.2d 1155. On appeal, this court held Reliable owed Tripp the life insurance proceeds despite the 60–day limit on temporary coverage found in the application and receipt. We stated: "The only reason for failure to return the premium at the end of the sixty days would be that the company was still contemplating issuing the policy. We cannot support a rule which would permit an insurance company to make a decision on an application after the insured's death. We conclude under the facts disclosed in this record that when an application for life insurance is made and the company receives the initial premium and issues a receipt therefor, a policy of temporary insurance is created and said policy of temporary insurance continues in effect until the insurance company declines the application, notifies the insured, and returns the premium, notwithstanding the provisions of the application and the receipt to the contrary." 210 Kan. at 38, 499 P.2d 1155. (Emphasis added.)

Monumental argues the dissenting and concurring opinion written by Justice Fontron and joined by Justice Fromme is better reasoned. Justice Fontron contended the prior Kansas cases cited by the majority were not applicable to the facts presented in Tripp. He further stated no notice was required to terminate coverage because the application and receipt clearly stated the temporary coverage would not extend beyond 60 days. Justice Fontron, referring to the rule that insurance contracts are construed against the insurer, wrote: "[T]he rule of strict construction does not relieve a tentative insurance purchaser of the obligation to read the papers which govern the transaction, nor was the rule intended to rewrite insurance contracts when they are fairly expressed and untainted by fraud." 210 Kan. at 41–42, 499 P.2d 1155.

* * *

In Tripp, we relied upon Waldner v. Metropolitan Life Ins. Co., 149 Kan. 287, 87 P.2d 515 (1939). * * *

It is worth noting that in Waldner there was no written instrument with a specified expiration date. It involved an application for reinstatement after cancellation for nonpayment of premium, a clearly distinguishable fact situation from Tripp.

The Tripp opinion also relied upon the reasoning found in Harvey v. United Ins. Co., 173 Kan. 227, 245 P.2d 1185 (1958). * * *

Here again, there was no specific expiration date on the application.

Finally, Tripp relied upon the reasoning of Service v. Pyramid Life Ins. Co., 201 Kan. 196, 440 P.2d 944 (1968). Unlike Waldner and Harvey, the Service case did involve a provision for the automatic declination of insurance 60 days after application. * * *

In Service we thoroughly discussed temporary insurance created by the conditional receipt and the reasons for insurers to offer temporary coverage. If the insurer did not offer temporary coverage upon application the applicant would have the power to revoke the offer made in his application, thereby causing the company to risk losing what it has expended for the investigation and medical examination of the applicant. By offering binding receipts, the applicant has the obligation to perform and the insurer has the use of the premium money at the earliest possible date. 201 Kan. at 210, 440 P.2d 944.

* * *

Monumental further argues that following the rule in Tripp will allow a conditional receipt of insurance to provide coverage ad infinitum with no further premium from the insured.

We have carefully considered all of the available cases, particularly Service, upon which Tripp relied. In Service, the insured died during the conditional receipt period, making it completely distinguishable from Tripp. From our consideration of all the cases, we conclude Tripp should be overruled. The conditional receipts in Tripp and in this case state clearly and unequivocally that if no insurance policy is delivered to the applicant within a specified period, there is no insurance. Thus, the contract expired by its own terms. Such does not represent a new principle of law. Most contracts have termination dates. We are mindful of the rule that contracts drafted by one of the parties should be strictly construed against the party who drafted it. Monumental drafted this contract, but because it is clear and unambiguous it requires no construction by this court. Fast v. Kahan, 206 Kan. 682, Syl. P 2, 481 P.2d 958 (1971). Thus, the strict construction rule is inapplicable.

It is a cardinal rule of construction that courts will not rewrite a contract by construction if it is clear and unambiguous. See Havens v. Safeway Stores, 235 Kan. 226, 231, 678 P.2d 625 (1984). This contract falls into that category. Richard applied for a policy of life insurance. He was issued 45 days of coverage by the conditional receipt. His premium paid for the coverage. If Monumental desired to terminate the temporary coverage before the 45 days expired, it was required to notify him and return his premium. If, however, it did not so notify him, he received 45 days of insurance, but no more, with his premium used for that coverage. In this case the insured died after the coverage under the conditional receipt expired and, therefore, Monumental is not liable. We hereby overrule Tripp v. Reliable Life Insurance Co., 210 Kan. 33, 499 P.2d 1155 (1972).

In light of the foregoing holding, we need not discuss the remaining issues.

The judgment of the district court is reversed, and this case is remanded with instructions to enter judgment for Monumental Life Insurance Co.

## ROHDE v. MASSACHUSETTS MUTUAL LIFE INSURANCE CO.

white

United States Court of Appeals, Sixth Circuit, 1980.
632 F.2d 667.

JOHN W. PECK, SENIOR CIRCUIT JUDGE.

This is a diversity action under Ohio law in which the district court entered judgment for the defendant insurance company declaring that no insurance contract existed on the life of plaintiff's deceased husband. Plaintiff contends that defendant's bad faith determination that her husband was an unacceptable risk entitles her, as beneficiary, to recover the full value of the insurance policy applied for by her husband. We agree and reverse the judgment of the district court.

I

Plaintiff is the widow of a man who applied for life insurance, arranged for payment of the initial premium, and took the required physical examination all on the same day. In exchange for these acts, defendant's agent completed a form designated as a "Conditional Receipt."[1] This form contained a promise by the defendant to insure the applicant under the policy sought, effective the latest date on which the applicant completed the application and physical examination. The receipt further stated that defendant had no obligation except to return payment unless the company determined that as of the completion of the physical and application the applicant was an acceptable risk under its "limits, rules, and standards."

The same day that the defendant applied for life insurance he died of an apparent heart attack. Acting under the condition of the receipt requiring the defendant to determine whether the applicant was an acceptable risk, the defendant investigated the application of plaintiff's husband and determined that the deceased had been uninsurable for the policy sought. Accordingly, defendant denied liability under the agreement with the decedent and returned the premium payment to plaintiff.

II

An application for life insurance is an offer to purchase a policy and the insurer must accept before a contract exists. During the time the offer is outstanding and unaccepted the applicant has the power to revoke the offer. Such revocation would not only deny the insurer the right to accept and complete a sale, but also would be likely to cause the insurer to lose the expense of processing and investigating an application.

Insurers discourage or prevent the revocation of offers by use of conditional receipts or "binders" that give the insurer the option of ultimately accepting or rejecting the offer while making the offer irrevocable by conditionally accepting it. The most straightforward of these binders accept the offer and, as consideration for the applicant's promise to purchase insurance, create immediate insurance for the applicant while reserving a right of the insurer to cancel all insurance after an opportunity to investigate the application.

**1.** The portions of defendant's receipt relevant to this appeal read as follows:

> *This Conditional Receipt does not create temporary or interim insurance, and does not provide any coverage except as provided herein. This payment is made and accepted subject to the limits provision on the reverse side and to the following terms and conditions:*
>
> If: * * *
>
> 2. the Company determines that, as of the latest of the dates of all required parts of the application, initially required medical examination * * * and tests, each person proposed for insurance was a risk acceptable under the limits, rules and standards of the Company for the basic policy plan and sum insured * * * then the insurance under the terms of the policy * * * applied for shall take effect as of the latest of the dates of all required parts of the application, [and] medical examinations. * * * *Unless all of the preceding conditions are met, there shall be no liability on the part of the Company except to return payment.*

The more prevalent form of binder, however, seeks to make the applicant's offer irrevocable without giving the applicant interim insurance in exchange. See 7 *Williston on Contracts,* § 902A, pp. 197–203 (3d ed. 1963). In this form insurance is promised to begin as of the date of the application or receipt subject to the qualification that the application must first be accepted or approved before any coverage begins. With these two provisions standing side-by-side in the binder, all that the applicant actually receives in exchange for his promise to purchase is the possibility of interim insurance. If the insurer does not approve the application, then no coverage ever exists. Of course, by the time the insurer approves or rejects, it will be likely to know whether the applicant has incurred a covered loss and can exercise its option to reject. Thus, the possibility of interim coverage is largely illusory under this type of binder. Recognizing that such binders are confusing to applicants and that applicants generally would be unlikely to enter such bargains if they actually understood them, courts have tended to find that binders that condition liability on "approval" of the insurer are ambiguous and that the parties to such contracts actually intend interim insurance as consideration for the applicants' promises to purchase insurance if the insurer approves. E.g., Leube v. Prudential Life Insurance Company of America, 147 Ohio St. 450, 453, 72 N.E.2d 76 (1947).

Plaintiff in this case argues that the condition contained in defendant's receipt is ambiguous and that the receipt should be liberally construed to provide interim insurance for the applicant pending the defendant acting on the condition. We agree with the finding of the district court that this condition is unambiguous and cannot be construed to provide the applicant with coverage prior to defendant's determination that the applicant is "insurable."

Unlike conditions which make an insurer's liability depend solely on the insurer's approval of the application, the condition contained in defendant's receipt requires that the defendant determine whether the applicant meets limits, rules and standards of the defendant company regarding the policy sought by the applicant. This condition does not involve judgments based on subjective factors, but rather considerations of actuarial and medical prediction balanced against the company's ordinary risk assignment practices. The defendant's satisfaction or dissatisfaction with the risk represented by the applicant's offer must be based on a reasonable examination of the application. [citations] The defendant's liability under the contract represented by the conditional receipt does not depend on the defendant's subjective approval. Rather, the defendant promised to be liable for a covered loss if the applicant was qualified on the date his application was completed. This promise was the consideration agreed to by the applicant for his promise to purchase the policy. Since the defendant's promise was not illusory and thus not inherently ambiguous, the cases cited by the plaintiff in arguing that defendant's receipt should be construed as a promise of interim insurance are inapposite. The defendant's receipt clearly stated that no interim insurance was provided and that coverage would become effective as of the date of the application only if the defendant found the applicant an acceptable risk under objective standards.

This conclusion is also responsive to plaintiff's argument that the condition of insurability is a condition subsequent, the occurrence of which terminates insurance arising upon completion of the application. Under Ohio law insurers may attach conditions precedent to liability. See Gregg v. Insurance Co., 43 Ohio St.2d 119, 123, 330 N.E.2d 913 (1975). Cases cited by plaintiff finding conditions in insurance receipts to be conditions subsequent involve situations where sufficient ambiguity existed in the language of the receipt to warrant findings that the applicant could have believed that he received immediate temporary insurance. Defendant's receipt in the present case clearly states that no interim insurance is provided until the occurrence of the condition that the defendant determine the applicant to be an acceptable risk. We agree with the district court that the second condition in defendant's conditional receipt is a condition precedent to liability of the defendant. There is no ambiguity either in the language of the agreement or in the consideration given by the defendant sufficient to warrant a finding that temporary insurance in fact existed upon completion of the application.

III

Based on trial testimony and considering the entire record, the district court found that the defendant acted in bad faith and was without reasonable grounds in determining that plaintiff's husband failed to meet the requirements for the policy sought. The issue of defendant's good or bad faith is primarily a question of fact requiring an examination of defendant's intent or state of mind. * * *

Having found defendant's determination that the applicant was uninsurable to have been made in bad faith, the district court proceeded to determine what conclusion the defendant would have reached had it acted in good faith. Deciding that the defendant in good faith would have determined that the applicant was uninsurable under the standard policy applied for, the district court concluded that the defendant was not liable. This analysis fails to give defendant's bad faith determination of the applicant's uninsurability proper legal effect under Ohio law.

The defendant's good faith determination that the applicant meet the defendant's standards of insurability was a condition precedent to defendant's liability under the contract represented by the conditional receipt. When the defendant acted in bad faith and determined that the applicant failed to meet the defendant's standards, then the defendant's own act prevented the occurrence of the condition precedent. The nonoccurrence or nonperformance of a condition is excused where that failure of the condition is caused by the party against whom the condition operates to impose a duty. [citations] Defendant's failure to honor its obligation of good faith in exercising its right to examine the application deprives defendant of any benefit it might obtain from that condition. The fact that the defendant might have found the applicant uninsurable had the defendant acted in good faith is not relevant under Ohio law.

With the condition precedent of determining the applicant to be insurable deleted from the contract, all conditions precedent to defendant's liability were satisfied. By the terms of the contract agreed to by the defendant and the applicant when the receipt was completed the policy applied for became effective as of the day the applicant died and prior to his death. The defendant is therefore liable to the plaintiff in the full amount of the policy.

For these reasons we conclude that the judgment of the district court must be reversed and the case is remanded to the district court for further proceedings consistent herewith.

### *Note*

The open question here is whether Massachusetts Mutual Life Insurance Co. has devised a conditional binder receipt so explicitly a condition precedent that it cannot be transmogrified into a condition subsequent by even the linguistic ingenuity of a Pennsylvania or California Supreme Court.

If the conditional receipt is apt to be turned into a temporary policy anyway, the obvious solution is for the insurer to substitute a specific term insurance policy, for 60–90 days perhaps, covering the period during which the application is being reviewed (charging, of course, an appropriate premium for the particular risk). Such policies are now available.

Other decisions have declared the "insurability" or "satisfaction" type of receipt, composed in the rather emphatic fashion of the *Massachusetts Mutual* example, to be unambiguous as a list of conditions precedent, but at the same time insist that the company's determination of "insurability" be exercised objectively and in good faith. The question of whether the applicant was indeed insurable under the company's standards is one to be answered by the trial court. See e.g. Hemenway v. MFA Life Ins. Co., 211 Neb. 193, 318 N.W.2d 70 (1982); Ford v. Lamar Life Ins. Co., 449 So.2d 1204 (Miss.1984) and Hildebrand v. Franklin Life Ins. Co., 118 Ill.App.3d 861, 74 Ill.Dec. 280, 455 N.E.2d 553 (1983). The *Hildebrand* opinion clarifies the standard of proof (455 N.E.2d at 565):

> "* * * [T]he necessary standard of insurability will be supplied by the company's own underwriting rules, limits, and standards [citation]. A standard prevalent in the industry but not shared by the company in question is irrelevant to the company's defense, yet the plaintiff may introduce it if that evidence shows that the company's evidence of its own standard is improbable. (See Simpson v. Prudential Insurance Co. of America (1962), 227 Md. 393, 177 A.2d 417 (insurability receipt implies the existence of an objective standard of insurability; beneficiary must present a *prima facie* case of insurability and may rely on general industry standards; insurer may rebut with proof of its own standards).) The company's control over its own underwriting standards and its access to instant witnesses—its underwriters—entitle the plaintiff to present evidence of general underwriting standards for this limited purpose."

## STEVEN v. FIDELITY & CAS. CO.

*Supra*

### *Note*

In Mutual of Omaha Ins. Co. v. Russell, 402 F.2d 339 (10th Cir.1968), the insured tried to buy a life insurance policy in an airport machine. The machine issued a round-trip policy labelled "T–20" policy but the insured lacked the change to purchase the machine policy. He went to the insurer's airport booth and was unwittingly sold a "T–18" policy which was more generous in benefits but was of a shorter term. The insured died in plane crash 12 hours after the T–18 policy expired but before the T–20 policy would have expired. The court, noting the tension between guarding against fraud (despite the lack of fraud in the case) and upholding contract law held that the contract entered into should be the one enforced. The court further declined to create an obligation by insurers to inform insureds of policy differences.

### *Note on Machine Issued Policies (and an outside of class research assignment)*

Air travelers hurrying through airports are generally aware of the existence of vending machines dispensing some form of short term trip insurance. Usually a selection of forms, 10″ × 12″ in size, printed on both sides, but folded 3 times to a size of 3⅛″ × 6½″ is available on racks. The detachable application takes up much of the outside of the folded form on which is also stated the general nature of the insurance such as "Scheduled Airline Trip Insurance"; "Air Trip Accident Insurance" or "Nonrenewable Accident Policy." On the inside folds are the policy terms. Presumably the applicant should unfold the form, read the coverage, refold, fill out the application, and insert the form in the machine together with a sum of money equal to the premium for the desired amount of coverage. The machine keeps the money and the application, while the insured, now given the policy, may mail it to the designated beneficiary if one is named.

*Assignment*

Obtain from your friendly neighborhood air terminal, a sampling of the available vending machine policies. Without unfolding the form, but examining the application side only, consider the following problems:

1. Who is the offeror and who is the offeree?
2. Is the policy an accident policy, a life insurance policy, or a hybrid—e.g. an accident policy with special death benefits? What difference would it make anyway?
3. One of the samples you may find states that it is "SCHEDULED AIR LINE TRIP INSURANCE" and "that the insured is the owner unless checked here: [ ] Beneficiary is owner."

Suppose the applicant checks the box, strikes out the word "Beneficiary", writes in your name and inserts the application in the machine which stamps the policy as validated. Do you have any rights in the policy?

4. How do you change the beneficiary on a machine issued policy?

# Chapter 9

# POTENTIAL DEFENSES BY THE INSURER

## A. NO CONTRACT—BECAUSE OF FAILURE TO MEET CONDITIONS PRECEDENT

— **delivery of policy (delivery in good health)**
— **payment of premiums**

### MEGEE v. UNITED STATES FIDELITY AND GUARANTY CO.

Supreme Court of Delaware, 1978.
391 A.2d 189.

HERRMANN, CHIEF JUSTICE:

* * *

On May 14, the plaintiff, a self-employed contractor, filed an application for disability income insurance with the defendant United States Fidelity and Guaranty Company (USF & G). The agent through whom the plaintiff filed the application was the defendant Chandler T. McEvilly, an agent of the defendant Vertex Insurance Agency, Inc. of Newark, Delaware (Vertex). The plaintiff did not choose to remit the premium at the time because Vertex could not assure the plaintiff that he would qualify for coverage at the desired level under USF & G's standard of eligibility. The plaintiff preferred to withhold the first premium until he knew the specific amount of benefits provided by the policy.

The application was received in the Philadelphia office of USF & G on May 20 and forwarded to its home office in Baltimore where it was received May 21. A credit investigation of the plaintiff was completed May 25 and a physical examination of the plaintiff was conducted on June 1 at plaintiff's convenience. Thereupon, a policy was issued, dated June 1. The policy was sent from the Baltimore office to the Philadelphia office of USF & G on June 2, and received there on June 4. It was received by Vertex in Newark on Saturday, June 5.

On that same day, June 5, the plaintiff was accidentally injured and has been unable to work ever since. Upon learning on Monday, June 7, that the plaintiff was injured, McEvilly asked USF & G for instructions. USF & G directed McEvilly not to deliver the policy and not to accept the first premium. On June 10, the plaintiff mailed a check for the first premium, but it was returned uncashed on June 30, with a letter declining coverage.

The plaintiff brought an action against USF & G for breach of contract and negligent failure to deliver the policy, and an action against Vertex and McEvilly for negligent failure to forward the application to USF & G and negligent failure to deliver the policy to the plaintiff. The Superior Court granted the defendants' motion for summary judgment. * * *

The plaintiff contends that the Trial Court erred in granting summary judgment for the defendants upon the ground that there was no contract for insurance in existence at the time of the accident.

Under the plaintiff's theory, the policy was in effect at the time of the injury because it had been constructively delivered to him on the morning of June 5th in that it had been delivered to the agent McEvilly, at that time, with no condition precedent to delivery, the advance payment of the premium having been waived, and the first premium having been tendered later in accordance with the terms of the application.

We find no error in the Trial Court's conclusion that no contract was in existence at the time of the accident. Immediately above the plaintiff's signature on the application, the following appeared:

> "It is agreed that USF & G's liability shall only be as specified in the policy, A & H 1381, applied for, beginning (a) when the policy is issued and full first policy premium paid during the lifetime of and while the health of the person(s) proposed for insurance is as here described on the policy date, or (b) if the premium is paid with this application, as specified in the conditional receipt."

Manifestly, neither condition set forth for the commencement of USF & G's liability was met in the instant case: no premium was paid with the application; nor was the first full premium proffered while the health of the plaintiff was the same as on June 1, 1977.

* * *

The plaintiff further contends that the contract for insurance should have been interpreted in accordance with his reasonable expectations, citing State Farm Mutual Automobile Insurance Co. v. Johnson, Del. Sup., 320 A.2d 345 (1974). Such reasonable expectations, according to the plaintiff, were that the policy became effective when the credit check and physical examination were completed and approved, and not when the premium was paid. Assuming, *arguendo,* the applicability of *State Farm* to the instant facts, in view of the clear language of the application which he signed and presumably read, regarding payment of premium, we are of the opinion that the plaintiff's asserted expectations were unreasonable.

* * *

For these reasons, we find no reversible error in the Trial Court's decision on the contract facet of the summary judgment.

On the negligence facet of the case, the plaintiff contends that the defendants were negligent in not processing the application within a reasonable time.

The cases allowing recovery for violation of the duty to act upon an application for insurance within a reasonable time generally involve payment of the first premium with the application. See Anno., "Insurance Application—Delay", 32 A.L.R.2d 487 at 511. The rationale is that the insurance company has received consideration and has a duty to act promptly; that acting otherwise would prejudice the defendant because he would believe he is insured and not seek insurance elsewhere. E.g., Pohorily v. Kennedy, Del.Super., 269 A.2d 240 (1969). Such is not the situation here. Because no premium had been paid by the plaintiff under the explicit terms of the application, neither USF & G nor Vertex had a duty to act within a time certain. Moreover, delay created by compiling information as to an applicant's health and other material facts cannot be considered unreasonable delay, 43 Am.Jur.2d Insurance § 215, especially where, as here, the physical examination was scheduled to suit the convenience of the plaintiff.

Thus, it is clear that the Trial Court was correct in finding no negligence as a matter of law on the part of the defendants.

Affirmed.

## FRIEZ v. NATIONAL OLD LINE INSURANCE CO.

United States Court of Appeals, Ninth Circuit, 1983.
703 F.2d 1093.

Moberly

SCHROEDER, CIRCUIT JUDGE:

Old Line Insurance Company appeals from the district court's judgment allowing recovery on a $12,000 life insurance policy. The policy application, completed on December 15, 1977, contained the following health question: "Do you know of any impairment, disease or disorder now existing in your health or physical condition?" The insured, Mr. Friez, answered "no." The application also contained a "good health" clause which provided: "I understand and agree that there shall be no insurance in force until the policy hereby applied for is issued and delivered to me during my lifetime and good health and the first premium is paid by me in which event the insurance shall be effective as of the Date of issue stated in the policy." The policy was issued on January 5, 1978.

When Mr. Friez died on February 21, 1978, Old Line refused to pay the death benefits specified in the policy; it returned the premiums paid by Friez and cancelled the policy. The company argues that the policy was void under Montana law on two grounds. First, Old Line argues that pursuant to the above "good health clause," the insured's good health at the time the policy was delivered was a condition precedent to coverage and that, because at the time the policy was issued the insured was suffering from an undiagnosed terminal cancer, the policy was void. Second, Old Line argues that Friez made a misrepresentation in his answer to the health question because, nine years prior to the time of application, he had been treated for ulcers. We uphold the district court's rejection, under Montana law, of both arguments.

Appellant's first argument fails because there was no fraud in connection with the "good health" clause. The insured did not know he had cancer when the policy was delivered. The relevant language of the insurance application here is similar in all material respects to the language construed in Pelican v. Mutual Life Insurance Company, 44 Mont. 277, 119 P. 778 (1911). The court in *Pelican* refused to void a policy issued to a terminally ill insured, stating that once "the premium had been paid and retained" by the insurance company, the insured was entitled to judgment "in the absence of evidence of fraud." * * *. The *Pelican* court further stressed that a warranty or condition precedent, as opposed to a representation, must be made a part of the contract by "express agreement of the parties on the face of the policy."

Here, it is not apparent on the face of the policy that the parties intended the good health clause to be a condition precedent to coverage. The district court held, and the dissent disputes, that the provision is ambiguous. In the district court's view, the policy could be construed either to require good health at the time the policy is issued, or merely to establish that no insurance coverage is provided until the policy issued. Resolving such an ambiguity in favor of the insured, the district court concluded that the provision did not create a bar to coverage under the insurance policy.

* * *

As appellee stresses, there is a more apparent ambiguity in the "good health" clause which requires upholding recovery under the policy. Whether or not the clause is a condition precedent, the term "good health" may be construed to mean "objective good health," in which case the insured's knowledge of the existence of bad health at the time of application is immaterial, or it may be construed to mean "subjective good health," in which case the clause is satisfied if the insured has no knowledge or reason to believe that he is in bad health. *See* G. Couch, *Couch On Insurance* §§ 11:7–11:8 (R. Anderson 2d ed. 1959).

This ambiguity must also be construed in favor of the insured. No Montana court has ever held that an insured who is unaware of a serious illness is not in "good health" within the meaning of a provision like this one. In both McDonald v. Northern Benefit Association, 113 Mont. 595, 131 P.2d 479 (1942), and Schroeder v. Metropolitan Life Insurance

Company, 103 Mont. 547, 63 P.2d 1016 (1937), the cases upon which appellant relies, the insured knew when the policy was issued that he suffered from the illness which eventually caused his death. These cases cannot stand for the proposition, suggested by the dissent, that knowledge of bad health is "irrelevant" under Montana law. Cf. *Pelican v. Mutual Life Insurance Company,* supra (objective evidence coupled with subjective belief of ill-health allows avoidance of policy). The import of Montana case law is that if the validity of an insurance policy is to be conditioned upon the insured's objective good health, irrespective of what he knew or should have known, the condition must be clearly and conspicuously set forth. Since the "good health" clause was not so clearly expressed in this policy, we are required to hold that it cannot bar recovery.

Old Line's second argument is that the policy should have been voided because Mr. Friez's failure to reveal treatment for ulcers nine years earlier amounted to a material misrepresentation under Montana Revised Code § 33–15–403.[1] This argument also fails. Mr. Friez's misstatement did not affect the validity of the policy within the meaning of the Montana statute. The district court found that had the insured answered "yes," Old Line would have asked only for additional information. There is no showing that his statement was material to Old Line's acceptance of the risk or that the company would not have issued the policy had he responded otherwise. Further, the court found no intent to mislead on the part of the insured and no prejudice to the insurer, because the cause of death was not related to an ulcer. See Pelican v. Mutual Life Insurance Co., 44 Mont. at 289, 119 P. at 781; McDonald v. Northern Benefit Assoc., supra, 113 Mont. at 606, 131 P.2d at 485 (to prove fraudulent misrepresentation which will prevent recovery, party must show intention to mislead). These findings are not clearly erroneous and the district court's conclusions were therefore proper.

Affirmed.

WALLACE, CIRCUIT JUDGE, dissenting:

* * * We are bound to follow decisions of the highest state court in resolving diversity cases. * * *

* * *

1. Montana Revised Code § 33–15–403 provides:

> Representations in applications—recovery precluded if fraudulent or material. (1) All statements and descriptions in any application for an insurance policy of annuity contract or in negotiations therefor by or in behalf of the insured or annuitant shall be deemed to be representations and not warranties.
>
> (2) Misrepresentations, omissions, concealment of facts, and incorrect statements shall not prevent a recovery under the policy or contract unless either:
>
> (a) fraudulent;
>
> (b) material either to the acceptance of the risk or to the hazard assumed by the insurer; or
>
> (c) the insurer in good faith would either not have issued the policy or contract or would not have issued a policy or contract in as large an amount or at the same premium or rate or would not have provided coverage with respect to the hazard resulting in the loss if the true facts had been made known to the insurer as required either by the application for the policy or contract or otherwise.

Two Montana Supreme Court decisions dictate a finding that the good health clause is not ambiguous and that it is a condition precedent which must be strictly fulfilled. In Schroeder v. Metropolitan Life Insurance Co., 103 Mont. 547, 63 P.2d 1016 (1937) (*Schroeder*), the Montana Supreme Court held an insurance policy void because the clause "the Insured is not alive or is not in sound health" was a condition precedent. The insured had not fulfilled the condition because she had a serious heart affliction on the date the policy was issued. In McDonald v. Northern Benefit Association, 113 Mont. 595, 131 P.2d 479 (1942) (*McDonald*), the Montana Supreme Court, relying on *Schroeder,* construed a provision that "there will be no liability on the part of the Ass'n. unless and until the certificate of membership is issued and delivered to me while I am ... in good health, free from disease" as a condition precedent to liability of the insurer. The insured was not in good health on the date the insurance certificate issued. The language in the policy in the case before us is substantially identical to the language held to constitute a condition precedent by the Montana Supreme Court in *Schroeder* and *McDonald.* These decisions by the highest state court require us to hold that the good health clause in this case is not ambiguous. * * *

Pelican v. Mutual Life Insurance Co., 44 Mont. 277, 119 P. 778 (1911) (*Pelican*), relied on by the majority, is distinguishable. *Pelican* focused on whether the insured made a fraudulent representation to the insurer. The inquiry was relevant because the policy stated that "[a]ll statements made by the insured shall, in the absence of fraud, be deemed representations and not warranties." 44 Mont. at 287, 119 P. at 780 (summary of action). In the absence of this policy language, fraud would not have been relevant to a determination whether the good health clause was a warranty or condition precedent. In the case before us, the policy contains a statement similar to that quoted above from *Pelican.* The district court, however, correctly separated its discussion of this language from its discussion of whether the good health clause was a condition precedent.

I would reverse the judgment of the district court and hold that the "good health" clause was a condition precedent. I would remand for consideration of whether the condition precedent was met.

### *Note*

In Life Ins. Co. of North America v. Commonwealth of Pennsylvania Insurance Dept., 43 Pa.Cmwlth. 282, 402 A.2d 297 (1979) the Court sustained the decision of the Insurance Commissioner who had disapproved certain policy forms for group long-term salary continuance insurance because of an objectionable provision—i.e., exclusion of "pre-existing conditions." This exclusion is "designed for individual not group policies because the chances of adverse selection in a group policy are minimal."

# FURTADO v. METROPOLITAN LIFE INSURANCE CO., INC.

District Court of Appeal of California, Fourth District, 1976.
60 Cal.App.3d 17, 131 Cal.Rptr. 250.

KAUFMAN, ASSOCIATE JUSTICE.

* * *

On February 12, 1973, Metropolitan issued a policy of life insurance with a face value of $15,000 to and on the life of plaintiff's son Vincent E. Furtado, then 18 years of age. Plaintiff was designated as beneficiary.

Premium payments of $26.45 each were to be paid on or before the 12th day of each month commencing February 12, 1973. A total of six monthly premiums were paid, the last payment being that of July 12, 1973. The payment due August 12, 1973, was not paid.

Plaintiff's son died on October 26, 1973, 75 days after August 12, 1973, the due date of the August premium. Plaintiff claimed that the insurance policy was still in effect on the date of death. Metropolitan claimed that the policy had lapsed for nonpayment of premiums. [Following a trial by the court, judgment was rendered in favor of Metropolitan. Plaintiff appeals from the judgment.]

The controversy revolves around three policy provisions. On page 6 of the policy under the large-lettered heading "PREMIUM PAYMENT AND REINSTATEMENT" and a bold-face subheading entitled "Payment of Premiums and Grace Period" the policy provides:

> "A grace period of 31 days will be granted for the payment of each premium after the first, during which period the policy will continue in force. If the Insured dies during such period, any unpaid premium will be deducted from the amount otherwise payable under this policy."

For purposes of identification we designate this provision "provision one."

On page 7 of the policy under a large-lettered heading entitled "INSURANCE OPTIONS ON NONPAYMENT OF PREMIUMS" the policy provides:

> "The insurance options provided below are available if a premium is in default beyond the grace period. The option for Extended Term insurance will be automatically effective if premiums have been paid for at least a number of years for which a period of Extended Term insurance is first shown in the Table on page 8." (Italics added.)

For purposes of identification we shall refer to this provision as "provision two."

Immediately following provision two, under the bold-face heading "Extended Term Insurance" the policy provides:

> "Under this option, the policy will be continued as nonparticipating paid-up Extended Term insurance.
>
> "For a policy without any paid-up additions, dividend accumulations, or indebtedness, the amount of such insurance will be the Face Amount of Insurance and *the term of the insurance, measured from the due date of the premium in default,* will be as specified in the Table on page 8." (Italics added.)

For purposes of identification we shall refer to this provision as "provision three."

The table on page 8 of the policy clearly specifies that for a policy in force six months the period of extended term insurance is to be 60 days.

CONTENTIONS

In a somewhat overlapping presentation plaintiff contends:

(1) The grace period of 31 days and the 60–day period of extended term insurance should run consecutively and not concurrently;

* * *

(4) Provision three constitutes an exclusion from or limitation upon coverage and is not stated in language that is conspicuous, plain and clear.

DISCUSSION AND DISPOSITION

*Exclusion From or Limitation Upon Coverage*

Plaintiff is correct that exclusions or limitations upon coverage must be "conspicuous, plain and clear." * * * Plaintiff is incorrect in asserting, however, that policy provision three dealing with the duration of extended term insurance constitutes an exclusion from or limitation upon coverage. Plaintiff is further mistaken in asserting that the language of provision three is not clear, plain and conspicuous.

Treating the last assertion first, the language of provision three plainly and clearly specifies that the term of the extended term insurance is "measured from the due date of the premium in default," August 12, 1973. The provision is not inconspicuous; it appears in quite readable print under the bold-face caption "Extended Term Insurance," which, in turn, appears under the large-lettered heading "INSURANCE OPTIONS ON NONPAYMENT OF PREMIUMS."

Provision three does not constitute an exclusion from or limitation upon coverage. On the contrary, provision three constitutes a nonforfeiture provision in compliance with, and indeed more liberal than, the requirements of the Standard Nonforfeiture Law (see Ins.Code, §§ 10159.1–10167).

Section 10160 of the Insurance Code mandates certain standard provisions for life insurance policies issued or delivered in California. In relevant part, that section provides:

> "Except as provided in Section 10165, no policy of life insurance shall be issued or delivered in this State unless it shall contain in substance the following provisions, or corresponding provisions which are at least as favorable to the defaulting or surrendering policyholder;
>
> "(a) Nonforfeiture benefit. That, in the event of default in any premium payment after premiums have been paid for at least one full year the insurer will grant, upon proper request not later than 60 days after *the due date of the premium in default,* a paid-up nonforfeiture benefit on a plan stipulated in the policy, *effective as of such due date,* of such value as may be hereinafter specified." (Italics added.)

Thus, that part of provision three which provides that the term of the extended term insurance is to be "measured from the due date of the premium in default" is fully authorized by Insurance Code section 10160.

### Consecutive or Concurrent Running of the Grace Period and the Term of Extended Term Insurance

In urging that the 31–day grace period and the 60–day period of extended term insurance should run consecutively and not concurrently, plaintiff correctly asserts that under policy provision two the extended term insurance option does not become operative or available unless and until "a premium is in default beyond the grace period." It does not follow, however, that the grace period and the period of extended term insurance should run consecutively and not concurrently. Policy provision three is the only provision dealing with the commencement of the term of extended term insurance, and it clearly and unmistakably specifies that, once the extended term insurance provision takes effect, the term of such insurance is to be "measured from the due date of the premium in default." Thus, the grace period and the period of extended term insurance run concurrently, not consecutively. Plaintiff's contention to the contrary is based upon the mistaken notion that policy provision one providing a grace period of 31 days affords a free month of insurance and that the concurrent running of the grace period and the period of extended term insurance would deprive him of the benefit of the prescribed grace period. To the contrary, the grace period does not afford a free period of insurance coverage. It simply allows for reinstatement of the policy by payment of the premium in default without a showing of insurability. (See Schick v. Equitable Life Assur. Soc., 15 Cal.App.2d 28, 33, 59 P.2d 163; 6 Couch, Insurance (2d ed.) § 32:133, pp. 348–349.)

Apparently the question whether the grace period and period of extended term insurance run concurrently or consecutively has not heretofore been decided in California. However, there is ample authority from other jurisdictions for the proposition that the grace period and the period of extended term insurance may both commence on the due date of the payment in default and, thus, run concurrently when the language of the policy clearly so provides [citations]. [S]ee generally, Annot., 106 A.L.R. 1276; 45 C.J.S., Insurance, § 638. As previously noted, the commencement of the period of extended term insurance at the due date of the payment in default is expressly authorized by section 10160 of the Insurance Code.

In support of his argument that the grace period and the period of extended term insurance should be construed to run consecutively, plaintiff cites Mitchell v. Southern Union Life Insurance Company (Tex.Civ.App.) 218 S.W. 586 and Prudential Insurance Company v. Devoe, 98 Md. 584, 56 A. 809, in both of which it was held that periods of extended term insurance commenced at the end of the respective grace periods. In *Mitchell,* the policy failed to prescribe the date of commencement of the period of extended term insurance. The *Mitchell* court observed that the absence of any clear provision as to the inception point of the period of extended term insurance rendered the provisions uncertain and held "* * * the policy is at least ambiguous, and * * * it admits of [plaintiff's] construction, and it being that most favorable to the insured, will be enforced." (218 S.W. at p. 590.) In *Devoe* the policy provided: " 'In the payment of any premium under this policy, except the first, a grace of one month will be allowed, during which time the policy will remain in force. If the policy, after being in force one full year, shall *lapse* for nonpayment of premium the company will continue in force the insurance under the policy for a period of sixty days *from the date of the lapse.*' " (56 A. at p. 809.) (Italics added.) The *Devoe* court, relying on the literal import of the quoted language, held that, inasmuch as the policy did not lapse until the end of the grace period, the extended term insurance would not commence until the end of the grace period. Both *Mitchell* and *Devoe* are thus distinguishable. In the case at bench policy provision three clearly and unequivocably provides that the period of extended term insurance is to be "measured from the due date of the premium in default."

* * *

Affirmed.

## *Note*

### *Anti–Forfeiture Provisions in Life Insurance Policies*

Life insurance in the form of whole life or endowment policies whereby the insured pays the premiums on a level term basis, i.e. the same periodic payments throughout, means that during their youthful years the policy holders are paying premiums that are actuarialy far in excess of the risk of their deaths assumed by the insurer. In other words such policies build up sizeable "cash values", which may be advantageously used by the insured, but which at the same time might be lost in the event of termination of the policy for failure to make a premium payment. Indeed such forfeitures were once tolerated but the unfairness was so manifest—particularly with respect to the so called Industrial Life policies marketed to the low income urban working class—that legislative pressures built to mandate anti-forfeiture provisions in policies that have cash values (in contrast with term insurance policies that do not.)

These statutes, are usually referred to as the Guertin Laws, named after a committee chaired by Alfred N. Guertin which was appointed in 1937 and which devised model legislation approved by National Association of Insurance Commissioners. The applicable mortality tables have been periodically revised. The California statute (§ 10160 ff. West Ann.Ins.Code) cited in the principal case is typical of the legislation.

Essentially the policy forms thus mandated give the insured who stops paying the premiums, the alternative of accepting the cash surrender value, extended term insurance, or reduced paid up insurance in accordance with specified tables (see Appendix C). Absent any deliberate choice, the insured is automatically afforded paid up term insurance. For extended discussion, see Griede and Beadles, *Law and the Life Insurance Contract,* 4th ed. 1979; Meyer, *Life and Health Insurance Law,* 1972 § 10.9 ff.

## B. NO CONTRACT—BECAUSE ILLEGAL FOR LACK OF INSURABLE INTEREST

### STATUTES

### CALIFORNIA INSURANCE CODE

**§ 10110. Insurable interest**

Every person has an insurable interest in the life and health of:

(a) Himself.

(b) Any person on whom he depends wholly or in part for education or support.

(c) Any person under a legal obligation to him for the payment of money or respecting property or services, of which death or illness might delay or prevent the performance.

(d) Any person upon whose life any estate or interest vested in him depends.

**§ 10110.1. Insurable interest; employers; time of requirement; charitable organizations**

(a) An insurable interest, with reference to life and disability insurance, is an interest based upon a reasonable expectation of pecuniary advantage through the continued life, health, or bodily safety of another person and consequent loss by reason of that person's death or disability or a substantial interest engendered by love and affection in the case of individuals closely related by blood or law.

(b) An individual has an unlimited insurable interest in his or her own life, health, and bodily safety and may lawfully take out a policy of insurance on his or her own life, health, or bodily safety and have the policy made payable to whomsoever he or she pleases, regardless of whether the beneficiary designated has an insurable interest.

(c) An employer has an insurable interest, as referred to in subdivision (a), in the life or physical or mental ability of any of its directors, officers, or employees or the directors, officers, or employees of any of its subsidiaries or any other person whose death or physical or mental disability might cause financial loss to the employer; or, pursuant to any contractual arrangement with any shareholder concerning the reacquisition of shares owned by the shareholder at the time of his or her death or disability, on the life or physical or mental ability of that shareholder for the purpose of carrying out the contractual arrangement; or, pursuant to any contract obligating the employer as part of compensation arrangements or pursuant to a contract obligating the employer as guarantor or surety, on the life of the principal obligor. The trustee of an employer or trustee of a pension, welfare benefit plan, or trust established by an employer providing life, health, disability, retirement, or similar benefits to employees and retired employees of the employer or its affiliates and acting in a fiduciary capacity with respect to those employees, retired employees, or their dependents or beneficiaries has an insurable interest in the lives of employees and retired employees for whom those benefits are to be provided. The employer shall obtain the written consent of the individual being insured.

(d) An insurable interest shall be required to exist at the time the contract of life or disability insurance becomes effective, but need not exist at the time the loss occurs.

(e) Any contract of life or disability insurance procured or caused to be procured upon another individual is void unless the person applying for the insurance has an insurable interest in the individual insured at the time of the application.

(f) Notwithstanding subdivisions (a), (d), and (e), a charitable organization that meets the requirements of Section 214 of the Revenue and Taxation Code may effectuate life or disability insurance on an insured who consents to the issuance of that insurance.

(g) This section shall not be interpreted to define all instances in which an insurable interest exists.

**§ 10110.2. Representations of insurable interest; reliance of insurer**

An insurer shall be entitled to rely upon all statements, declarations, and representations made by an applicant for insurance relative to the insurable interest that the applicant has in the insured, and no insurer shall incur any legal liability except as set forth in the policy, by virtue of any untrue statements, declarations, or representations so relied upon in good faith by the insurer.

New York Annotated Insurance Law

**§ 3205. Insurable interest in the person; consent required; exceptions**

(a) In this section:

(1) The term, "insurable interest" means:

(A) in the case of persons closely related by blood or by law, a substantial interest engendered by love and affection;

(B) in the case of other persons, a lawful and substantial economic interest in the continued life, health or bodily safety of the person insured, as distinguished from an interest which would arise only by, or would be enhanced in value by, the death, disablement or injury of the insured. (2) The term "contract of insurance upon the person" includes any policy of life insurance and any policy of accident and health insurance. (3) The term "person insured" means the natural person, or persons, whose life, health or bodily safety is insured.

(b)(1) Any person of lawful age may on his own initiative procure or effect a contract of insurance upon his own person for the benefit of any person, firm, association or corporation. Nothing herein shall be deemed to prohibit the immediate transfer or assignment of a contract so procured or effectuated.

(2) No person shall procure or cause to be procured, directly or by assignment or otherwise any contract of insurance upon the person of another unless the benefits under such contract are payable to the person insured or his personal representatives, or to a person having, at the time when such contract is made, an insurable interest in the person insured.

(3) If the beneficiary, assignee or other payee under any contract made in violation of this subsection receives from the insurer any benefits thereunder accruing upon the death, disablement or injury of the person insured, the person insured or his executor or administrator may maintain an action to recover such benefits from the person receiving them.

(c) No contract of insurance upon the person, except a policy of group life insurance, group or blanket accident and health insurance, or family insurance, as defined in this chapter, shall be made or effectuated unless at or before the making of such contract the person insured, being of lawful age or competent to contract therefor, applies for or consents in writing to the making of the contract, except in the following cases:

(1) A wife or a husband may effectuate insurance upon the person of the other.

(2) Any person having an insurable interest in the life of a minor under the age of fourteen years and six months or any person upon whom such minor is dependent for support and maintenance, may effectuate a contract of insurance upon the life of such minor, in an amount which shall not exceed the limits specified in section three thousand two hundred seven of this article.

## *Note*

Gertrude Berg was the star of the Broadway play, "Dear Me, The Sky is Falling". The producers took out a policy which provided: "This insurance is to pay the insured in the event of inability of the insured artist to appear in the insured production, directly in consequence of her suffering any personal accident or sickness or in the event or occurrence of her death or total disability during the period of insurance". The amount of insurance payable was $1,500 per missed performance up to a certain amount. Gertrude Berg became ill and the producer sought recovery. The insurance company conceded limited liability so the following remarks by the court may be considered pure dicta:

> "Plaintiff's insurable interest derived from employment of Gertrude Berg as star of the production (Ins. Law § 146 subdiv. 2, now § 3205). The economic success of the production depended on the effective appearance and performance of Gertrude Berg."

After referring to Berg as the "insured artist", the court then turned to other issues and decided in plaintiff's favor. Theatre Guild Productions v. Insurance Corp. of Ireland, 25 A.D.2d 109, 267 N.Y.S.2d 297 (1966).

*Query:* Is this a case of the insurance of another person's life or health? Or is it simply business interruption insurance in which the insurable interest is not particularly debatable? (The lower court's decision was affirmed by the New York Court of Appeals; the point as to insurable interest was not brought up.) 19 N.Y.2d 656, 278 N.Y.S.2d 625, 225 N.E.2d 216 (1967).

## MUTUAL SAVINGS LIFE INSURANCE CO. v. NOAH

Supreme Court of Alabama, 1973.
291 Ala. 444, 282 So.2d 271, 60 A.L.R.3d 81.

HEFLIN, CHIEF JUSTICE.

[William Noah drowned. His brother, Donald, had taken out insurance policies on William's life, naming himself as beneficiary. Donald filed a claim on the policies which was refused by the insurer. This case originated as a declaratory judgment action by Donald. The trial court found in his favor.]

The most divisive issue with which this court is faced is presented by appellant-respondent's contention that Donald R. Noah has no insurable interest in the life of the insured, and that each of the three policies was invalid by reason thereof. It may be well to note at the outset that this court holds the burial policy not to be subject to the insurable interest requirement. * * *

Under the evidence the two life policies were procured or "taken out" (an expression used in our cases) by the beneficiary, and thus the long-established rule that the insurance is invalid unless the beneficiary has an "insurable interest" in the life of the insured applies. This rule is to the effect that a person has an unlimited insurable interest in his own life and may designate any person as his beneficiary so long as the insurance was procured or taken out by the insured and the premiums paid by him, but one taking out a policy of insurance for his own benefit, on the life of another person, must have an insurable interest in the continuance of the life of such insured. National Life & Accident Ins. Co. v. Alexander, 226 Ala. 325, 147 So. 173; Tit. 28A, § 316, Code of Alabama, 1940 (Recomp.1958).[22]

**22.** Although the Insurance Code, i.e., Title 28A, became effective after all relevant times for purposes of the instant case, this court is of the opinion that the result obtained in the instant case would not be altered by the application of section 316, which provides as follows:

"§ 316. Insurable interest; personal insurance.—(1) Insurable interest with reference to personal insurance is an in-

Several reasons have been assigned as the basis for the insurable interest requirement, both of which are grounded upon public policy considerations: a policy taken out by one for his own benefit on the life of another, in whom he has no insurable interest is, in substance, a wagering contract; and such a policy may hold out a temptation to the beneficiary to hasten by improper means the death of the insured. * * *

Certain blood relationships have been held sufficient, in and of themselves to negate the supposition that the beneficiary would take out such a policy for the purpose of wagering on the insured's death, or that such a policy would entice the beneficiary to take the insured's life, and in such cases the relationship alone is said to create an insurable interest. This is true notwithstanding the fact that the beneficiary may have no reasonable expectation of pecuniary advantage through the continued life of the insured or consequent loss by reason of his death, which would otherwise be required in order to find an insurable interest.

The relationship of husband and wife has been held to be sufficiently close to give either an insurable interest in the life of the other. Jennings v. Jennings, 250 Ala. 130, 33 So.2d 251. The parent-child relationship has been accorded the same status as that given to husband and wife in *Jennings*. Warnock v. Davis, 104 U.S. 775, 26 L.Ed. 924; 44 C.J.S. Insurance § 204.

On the other hand, the following relationships have been held not to create an insurable interest on the basis of such relationship alone. Cousin and cousin, National Life & Accident Ins. Co. v. Alexander, 226 Ala. 325, 147 So. 173; beneficiary has no interest in the life of the wife of his wife's brother, National Life & Accident Ins. Co. v. Middlebrooks, 27 Ala.App. 247, 170 So. 84; aunt and niece, Commonwealth Life Ins. Co. v. George, 248 Ala. 649, 28 So.2d 910; aunt-in-law and niece, Liberty National Life Ins. Co. v. Weldon, 267 Ala. 171, 100 So.2d 696; niece and uncle, Bell v. National Life & Accident Ins. Co., 41 Ala.App. 94, 123 So.2d 598.

The specific issue presented in the case under review is whether one has an insurable interest in the life of his brother by virtue of the relationship alone. While realizing that this issue is one of first impression in Alabama, and that other jurisdictions are in conflict on this matter, a review of the holdings of other states has convinced this court that the vast majority [23] and best reasoned holdings support the proposi-

terest based upon a reasonable expectation of pecuniary advantage through the continued life, health or bodily safety of another person and consequent loss by reason of his death or disability, or a substantial interest engendered by love and affection in the case of individuals closely related by blood or by law."

**23.** This court's research has disclosed that of the nineteen jurisdictions which have written to this issue, fourteen have stated that one has an insurable interest in the life of his brother by virtue of the relationship alone.

tion that the brother-brother relationship will, in and of itself, support an insurable interest.

* * *

The reason most often assigned as the basis of a holding that such relationship will, in and of itself, support an insurable interest is that the natural love and affection prevailing between the two and the expectation that one will render the other aid in time of need is sufficient to overcome any wagering contract argument, as well as any impulse to hasten the death of the insured. This rationale was well stated in Century Life Ins. Co. v. Custer, 178 Ark. 304, 10 S.W.2d 882 (1928), as follows:

> "Brothers are so closely related that they are naturally interested in the preservation of the life of each other. Generally, they will lay down their life for each other. As a rule they care for each other in illness to the extent, if necessary, of furnishing all needed comforts and medicinal aid. It would be contrary to human nature for them to speculate on the death of each other, so it may well be that their contracts for insurance on the life of each other should not be classed as wagering contracts."

* * *

Perhaps the facts of the instant case tend to contradict the closeness and mutual love and affection which the above holdings attribute to the brother-brother relationship, but this court does not write for this case alone. The holding of this court today will govern all future cases, not just the exceptional one where the natural love and affection common to the brother-brother relationship may be missing.

* * *

Affirmed.

JONES, JUSTICE (dissenting).

I must disagree with the majority holding that one has an insurable interest in the life of his brother (or sister) on the basis of their relationship alone.

* * * We know that the relationship of husband and wife constitutes such a relationship per se, Jennings v. Jennings, 250 Ala. 130, 33 So.2d 251; and while I do not find that this Court has been specifically called upon to decide whether in every case the relationship of parent and child, or child and parent, in and of itself, with a presumption that is not even rebuttable, gives rise to an insurable interest in either, the overwhelming weight of authority is that this relationship is sufficient to constitute an insurable interest by one in the life of the other (44 C.J.S. Insurance § 204, at 907). But is the relationship of brothers in the same category, or does it depend upon the circumstances of the particular case?

* * *

In any case, I think that the relationship alone is not sufficient, that the rule requiring something other than the relation is the sound one and I would so hold. This is based on the rationale that there is but one test for insurable interest—that of a pecuniary interest or some reasonable expectation of monetary benefit from the continuance of the insured's life; and within certain blood or affinity relationships this pecuniary interest or benefit is conclusively presumed. Such relationships are that of husband and wife, parent and child, grandparent and grandchild, and under certain conditions loco parentis relationships. This "conclusive presumption" rule with respect to these relationships does not violate the public policy necessitating insurable interest aimed at preventing homicide and wager contracts. While an extension of this rule to the brother relationship might be permissible as to the homicide aspect, to so extend this rule would facilitate the violation of the second evil which the aforementioned public policy seeks to prevent; vis., wager contracts.

Having adopted the above view, I would hold that the line must be drawn short of the brother relationship, and that insurable interest in such cases should depend upon a pecuniary benefit, or advantage to be gained from the continued life of the insured, which cannot be conclusively presumed, but is subject to proof. * * *

## NEW ENGLAND MUTUAL LIFE INSURANCE CO. v. NULL

United States Court of Appeals, Eighth Circuit, 1979.
605 F.2d 421.

HEANEY, CIRCUIT JUDGE.

Shirley Ann Null appeals from an order of the District Court which declared void a personal insurance policy issued by New England Mutual Life Insurance Company (New England) on the life of Victor Null. Shirley Ann Null contends that the District Court erred in finding that Victor Null contracted for the insurance solely because Ronald and James Calvert required it as security for their investment in the development of Victor Null's invention. * * *.

Ronald Calvert planned to obtain several insurance policies on the life of Victor Null, an inventor who sought Calvert's financial backing, and then arrange Null's murder and obtain the insurance proceeds. After an unsuccessful attempt at procuring a $500,000 policy from Prudential Insurance Company, Calvert discussed with New England agents the possibility of obtaining a $500,000 policy on Null's life. New England's underwriter, however, refused to issue more than $150,000 in "business insurance," or insurance for the benefit of Calvert. After consultation with Calvert and Victor Null, the insurance agent requested a $100,000 personal life insurance policy which the company agreed to issue. On Friday, July 21, 1972, Mr. Null executed an application designating as beneficiary the "Estate of Insured." The following Monday, Null and Calvert arrived at New England's St. Louis office and

Null executed an "Absolute Assignment and Change of Beneficiary Request" in favor of James Calvert, Ronald Calvert's father and his straw man and agent in the scheme.

Also on Monday, July 24, Calvert paid the premiums for both the $150,000 business policy and the $100,000 personal insurance policy by a check of his father in the amount of $5,616. New England issued the policies and the agent delivered them to Ronald Calvert.

The parties have stipulated that

> "The Calverts" at all times pertinent and prior to the issuance of the policy in question, had a preconceived intent to engage in criminal conduct which would and did result in the murder of Victor Null on November 8, 1972, which intent was unknown to Null and the company (plaintiff).

* * *

The appellant contends that New England could not prove it was defrauded because it had knowledge of the underlying business transaction between Mr. Null and Calvert and specifically solicited the insurance to effectuate that transaction. The evidence shows that New England's agent originally contacted Calvert regarding life insurance for Null after learning of Calvert's unsuccessful application with Prudential. The agent first attempted to obtain a $500,000 policy on Victor Null's life from New England for Calvert's benefit. The company refused to issue more than $150,000 of such insurance. Calvert then told the agent that his business transaction with Null could not go forward with such a small amount of insurance. The agent discussed the situation with several other agents and suggested to Calvert and Victor Null the possibility of obtaining a personal insurance policy which Victor Null would be able to assign to Calvert. The agent, therefore, sought to contravene the company's directive by offering an alternative means of obtaining insurance which would be payable to the Calverts on Victor Null's death. The appellant argues that under these circumstances, New England cannot prove that it was in any way defrauded by the policy application. New England was aware of the business transaction between Calvert and Victor Null. New England, through its agents, supplied Calvert with the incentive to kill Victor Null by issuing insurance in an amount that exceeded Victor Null's worth to Calvert. New England allowed this in spite of its awareness of this risk, which it demonstrated by its refusal to issue more than $150,000 in business insurance. The appellant contends that New England may not show it was defrauded when its eagerness to sell the policy created the risk that resulted in Victor Null's death.

This argument is not unappealing. Historically, the law has looked with disfavor on insurance contracts which create a risk of death to the insured.

> [I]t is contrary to a sound public policy to permit one, having no interest in the continuance of the life of another, to speculate upon

> that other's life—and it should be added that to permit the same might tend to incite the crime of murder * * * and that the rule is enforced, and the defense permitted, not in the interest of the defendant insurer, but solely for the sake of the law, and in the interest of a sound public policy[.]

Henderson v. Life Ins. Co. of Virginia, 176 S.C. 100, 179 S.E. 680, 692 (1935).

> It is well settled that "to allow the creditor to procure insurance greatly exceeding the amount of the debt might be to tempt him to bring the debtor's life to an unnatural end, and thus contravene the principle of public policy which has been seen to lie at the very basis of the doctrine of insurable interest[.]" (Citation omitted.)

Lakin v. Postal Life and Casualty Insurance Co., 316 S.W.2d 542, 551 (Mo.1958).

The courts have, therefore, voided life insurance policies which have encouraged the murder of the insured. E.g., Henderson v. Life Ins. Co. of Virginia, supra; Lakin v. Postal Life and Casualty Insurance Co., supra. These decisions have served the purpose of discouraging beneficiaries who plan a murder, but they do not have the effect of discouraging insurance companies from negligently issuing policies in contravention of the public interest. To reach this problem, the Supreme Courts of Alabama and South Carolina have allowed negligence actions against an insurer who negligently issues a life insurance policy which creates the risk of murder. Liberty National Life Insurance Company v. Weldon, 267 Ala. 171, 100 So.2d 696 (1957); Ramey v. Carolina Life Insurance Company, 244 S.C. 16, 135 S.E.2d 362 (1964). In *Weldon,* the court allowed a wrongful death action by the father of a minor child against three insurance companies which issued life insurance policies to the insured's aunt. The aunt, who had no insurable interest in the child's life, murdered the child. In *Ramey,* the South Carolina court allowed a suit against an insurance company by an insured who was severely injured by his wife, the owner-beneficiary of a life insurance policy, who attempted to poison him. The insurance company issued the policy without the insured's consent and with knowledge that his wife had forged his signature on the application. In both cases, the courts allowed proof of allegations that the negligent issuance of the policies was the proximate cause of the murders.

We have been unable, however, to find a decision in any state, including Missouri, which has permitted the estate of the insured to recover on the policy itself from an insurer which has negligently issued a policy. In Lakin v. Postal Life and Casualty Insurance Co., supra, the Missouri court held a life insurance policy obtained under somewhat similar circumstances void for want of an insurable interest. Although the argument the appellant makes here was not raised in *Lakin,* its facts support an inference that the agent solicited the policy with knowledge of the owner-beneficiary's true relationship with the insured and the lack of any insurable interest. We find no indication in that opinion, or in any other case, that the Missouri court would permit the estate of the insured to recover on the policy itself. In view of the fact that no Missouri decision is precisely on point, we would be prepared to distinguish *Lakin* if persuasive authority for a recovery by the estate on the policy could be discovered elsewhere. Since we find no such authority, we rely on the accepted rule that a life insurance policy is void *ab initio* when it is shown that the beneficiary thereof procured the policy with a present intention to murder the insured. * * *

* * *

* * * [T]he remaining issue is whether the beneficiary or the insured "procured" the insurance policy; i.e., whether Victor Null executed the application for his own purposes or was merely a pawn in the Calverts' plan. The District Court sitting without a jury found from the evidence that he did not execute the application for his own purposes. * * *

* * *

Shirley Ann Null does contend, however, that the District Court erred in failing to consider whether Victor Null had a business purpose in obtaining the insurance. She argues that Victor Null desired the insurance policy so that he could assign it for the protection of the investors he so desperately needed, and that this furthered his own purposes as much as would benefiting his estate. The District Court heard the evidence offered on this issue, however, and found that "[t]he only reason that Null applied for the insurance was to obtain the coverage deemed necessary by the Calverts for their investment." We cannot say that the court clearly erred in making this finding. New England's insurance agent testified that he communicated his idea of obtaining the assignable personal insurance to Calvert and Victor Null after Calvert indicated to him that the underlying business transaction would not go forward if only the $150,000 business insurance policy were issued. There was no evidence that Victor Null applied for the insurance for a business purpose unrelated to the Calverts' secret objective. There was no evidence that Victor Null applied for the insurance with a plan to assign it to any backers other than the Calverts, nor was there any evidence that Victor Null intended to obtain such insurance prior to his negotiations with Calvert. The agent testified that at the time of Null's policy application, it was clear to Victor Null that the policy was to be assigned to James Calvert. On this evidence, we must affirm the District Court's factual finding that Victor Null's only reason for obtaining the insurance was because the Calverts deemed it necessary for him to do so. In so doing, we do not imply that Victor Null possessed no motivation for obtaining the insurance, or that he did not believe that he would benefit by so doing. That, however, is not determinative of the question because Victor Null had no motivation other than that supplied by the beneficiary who planned his murder. Victor Null, therefore, was not elevated beyond the status of a "mere instrumentality" in the Calverts' scheme.

* * *

For the foregoing reasons, the judgment of the District Court is affirmed.

### *Notes*

1. *Another duty of life insurers; to notify the beneficiary that he or she will not be paid if he or she murders the insured.*

An insurance company issued to Lopez's wife (who "clearly had an insurable interest") a policy on her husband's life in the amount of $130,000 plus double the amount for accidental death. The annual premiums were $7,644 although the family's total annual income was but $9,000. Mr. Lopez signed the forms but claimed he was tricked into doing so by his wife's misrepresentation that it was health insurance. When Lopez overheard his wife and brother-in-law plotting to kill him, he notified the insurer which did nothing about it. Later the conspirators were interrupted in the process of drowning Mr. Lopez, who survived to sue the insurance company for negligence. Life Ins. Co. of Georgia v. Lopez, 443 So.2d 947 (Fla.1983) held that the facts stated a cause of action in tort:

"[Insured's] notice should have triggered an investigation which would have * * * uncovered the disproportion between the insured's economic worth to the beneficiary dead and alive, the insured's lack of consent to the issuance of the policy, and the financial impossibility of the couple meeting the premium payments for any extended period of time. Such an aggregation of suspicious circumstances must surely impose on the insurance company a duty to eliminate any motive for effecting the insured's death, if not by withdrawing the coverage as void for reasons of public policy, then at least by warning the beneficiary that no proceeds would be payable if she in fact murdered the insured."

2. The *Null* case is discussed in Burton v. John Hancock Mut. Ins. Co., 164 Ga.App. 592, 298 S.E.2d 575 (1982) but the opinion holds that the Georgia insurable interest statute absolutely precludes holding the company liable in *tort* for wrongful death when the C.Q.V. has named his murderer as beneficiary.

## C. NO COVERAGE OF PARTICULAR PERSONS BECAUSE OF STATUS QUALIFICATIONS

— **incontestability clauses**

— **enrollment qualifications in group policies**

## CRAWFORD v. EQUITABLE LIFE ASSURANCE SOCIETY OF UNITED STATES

Supreme Court of Illinois, 1973.
56 Ill.2d 41, 305 N.E.2d 144.

WARD, JUSTICE.

This appeal presents the question whether an incontestability clause contained in a group life insurance policy bars the insurer from defending against a claim on the ground that the insured was not an employee eligible for insurance under the terms of the policy. The question is one of first impression in this court.

The plaintiff, Harvey A. Crawford, brought an action in the circuit court of Rock Island County against the defendant, The Equitable Life Assurance Society of the United States, to recover the sum of $10,000 as the beneficiary of his wife under a group insurance policy issued by the defendant. * * * The circuit court granted [a] motion for summary judgment, and the appellate court affirmed. We granted the defendant's petition for leave to appeal. Leave was also granted to three other life insurance companies to file a joint brief *amici curiae.*

The undisputed facts are that effective January 1, 1965, the defendant issued a group life insurance policy to the Warm Air Heating and Air Conditioning Group Insurance Trust. The trust was established by the Warm Air Heating and Air Conditioning Association, for the purpose of providing insurance on the lives of employees of companies which were members of the association, as authorized by section 230(2)(e) of the Insurance Code Ill.Rev.Stat.1971, ch. 73, par. 842(2)(e).

One of the members of the association was the Crawford Heating and Cooling Company, Inc., whose president was the plaintiff. In December, 1964, shortly prior to the issuance of the policy, the plaintiff executed and delivered to the association an enrollment form which requested insurance for three persons, each of whom he represented to be employees of his company. Among the three were the plaintiff himself and his wife, Rose A. Crawford. A certificate of insurance was thereafter issued to Mrs. Crawford in the face amount of $10,000. The certificate also provided for certain hospital and medical expense benefits. The plaintiff was named as the beneficiary. The premiums were paid by the Crawford Heating and Cooling Company. Mrs. Crawford died in February, 1969.

The master policy contained a provision that only a "full time employee" would be eligible for insurance, subject to a proviso that any employee "whose work week calls for a schedule of less than 32 hours shall not be eligible for insurance hereunder."

The insurance certificate issued to the decedent, while stating that the insurance provided under the policy was effective "only if the Employee is eligible for insurance," did not contain the specific full-time employment requirement found in the master policy. The enrollment form executed by the plaintiff, however, did state that an employee must work at least 32 hours a week, and the plaintiff marked the form in such fashion as to indicate that each of the three persons listed did meet that requirement. The same representation was made in regular monthly statements submitted by the plaintiff to the trustee with his premium payments from February, 1965, until February, 1969.

An individual application for insurance executed by the decedent also included a representation by her that she worked 32 hours a week or more. She stated further in her application that her position with the company was that of Secretary–Treasurer, and that she earned $7500 or more a year. Information as to position and salary was significant under the policy because these factors affected the amount of death benefits payable.

In point of fact the representations made by the plaintiff and by the decedent were false. Neither at the time when the policy issued nor at any time thereafter did the decedent ever complete a week in which she worked 32 or more hours. According to the complaint the extent of her duties was to spend several hours a month in assisting the plaintiff in drawing up proposals for contracts, and in taking night telephone calls when he was on a job or out of town. She received no compensation for these functions.

It is admitted that the defendant made no inquiry into the circumstances of the decedent's employment until after her death. The facts came to light when the plaintiff submitted his claim to the trustee accompanied by a death certificate, which listed the decedent's occupation as that of housewife. The trustee notified the defendant, and requested it to verify the decedent's eligibility. An employee of the defendant then made a single call to the bookkeeper of the plaintiff's company, from whom the decedent's employment status was ascertained. The defendant thereafter wrote to the plaintiff denying the latter's claim.

The master policy contains an incontestability clause which reads as follows:

> "The validity of this policy shall not be contested, except for the non-payment of premiums, after it has been in force for two years from the date of issue; and no statement made by any employee insured under this policy relating to his insurability shall be used in contesting the validity of the insurance with respect to which such statement was made, after such insurance has been in force prior to the contest for a period of two years during such employee's lifetime nor unless it is contained in a written application signed by such employee and a copy of such application is or has been furnished to such employee or his beneficiary."

The provision quoted above incorporates portions of section 231 of the Illinois Insurance Code (Ill.Rev.Stat.1971, ch. 73, par. 843), which specifies certain provisions which must be contained in any policy of group life insurance issued or delivered in this State. Subsection (a) of section 231 requires inclusion of "A provision that the policy shall be incontestable after two years from its date of issue during the lifetime of the insured, except for nonpayment of premiums and except for violation of the conditions of the policy relating to military or naval services in time of war." Subsection (b) requires inclusion of "A provision * * * that all statements made by the employer or trustee or by the individual employees shall, in the absence of fraud, be deemed representations and not warranties, and that no such statement shall be used in defense to a claim under the policy, unless it is contained in a written application."

As presented by the parties, the basic issue in this case is whether the eligibility of an employee relates to the "coverage" of the policy and may, therefore, be challenged notwithstanding the incontestability clause. Each party apparently considers that only the first portion of the incontestability clause in the policy, reading "The validity of this policy shall not be contested, except for non-payment of premiums, after it has been in force for two years from the date of issue," is relevant in determining this issue. This view is presumably based on the assumption that the succeeding portion of the clause is intended only to deal with cases where proof of individual insurability is required. See Gregg, Group Life Insurance (2d ed.) 92.

* * *

An incontestability clause was considered in Baker v. Prudential Insurance Company of America, 279 Ill.App. 5, where recovery was sought under a group life insurance policy for the death of a former employee who had been discharged shortly prior to his death. The master policy specified that insurance should cease upon the termination of employment. Despite the incontestability clause, the appellate court held that the insurer was not liable, stating (279 Ill.App. 5, 10).

> "The incontestable provision did not prevent the defendant insurance company from showing the policy was no longer in effect because Baker had been discharged a month before death. That provision of the policy would prevent the defendant in the instant case from contending that the policy was obtained by fraud or misrepresentation or upon any other ground, going to the original validity of the policy."

Historically the incontestability clause arose in the context of individual life insurance policies, and typically involved situations where the insured, in connection with his application for insurance, made statements respecting his health. In the absence of an incontestability clause, the insurer, upon the death of the insured, would be entitled to resist payment of the claim upon a showing that there had been a material misrepresentation of fact made by the insured or on his behalf, and that the contract of insurance was therefore voidable. * * * The insurer, if he had no knowledge of the misrepresentation, was not ordinarily barred by the passage of time from making this defense, but might preserve it for use at such time as the insured died and the claim was presented for payment. The resulting situation was described by this court in Powell v. Mutual Life Insurance Company of New York, 313 Ill. 161, 164–165, 144 N.E. 825, 826, in the following language:

> "In the earlier development of insurance contracts it not infrequently occurred that, after the insured had paid premiums for a large number of years, the beneficiaries under the policy found, after the maturity thereof by the death of the insured, that they were facing a lawsuit in order to recover the insurance; that in certain answers in the application it was said by the insurer, the insured had made statements which were not true, and the beneficiaries were not entitled to recover on the policy. It is needless to call attention to the fact that this situation gave rise to a widespread suspicion in the minds of the public that an insurance contract was designed largely for the benefit of the company. Recognizing this fact and seeing the effect of it on the insurance business, numerous insurance companies inserted in their policies what is now known as an incontestable clause."

Whatever the manner of its origin, in most States, as in Illinois, the matter of incontestability is now covered by statute. (See Keeton, Basic Text on Insurance, sec. 6.5(d) (1971).) It is evident that one effect of an incontestability clause is to permit recovery in cases of false or even fraudulent representations, simply because these had not been discovered prior to the expiration of the contestable period. Balanced against this undesirable result, however, was the social desirability of assuring a beneficiary that his claim could not be put to a challenge at some remote future time when the insured was dead and when others who might have testified in the beneficiary's behalf might also be unable to do so. See Flanigan v. Federal Life Insurance Co., 231 Ill. 399, 83 N.E. 178; Williston, Contracts, sec. 745 (3d ed. 1961); Holland, The Incontestable Clause, in Krueger and Waggoner, The Life Insurance Policy Contract, 57–58 (1953).

The conventional incontestability clause contains certain exceptions, most commonly one for the nonpayment of premiums. It is clear, however, that there are other, unenumerated grounds on which an insurer may refuse to pay a claim after the period of contestability has run. The clause obviously does not preclude a refusal based on the fact that the particular event insured against has not taken place, and the insurer is thus not barred from "contesting" the claim or the interpretation of the coverage provisions advanced by the claimant. This point of distinction was described by Justice Cardozo, then the Chief Judge of the New York Court of Appeals, in the often cited case of Metropolitan Life Insurance Co. v. Conway (1930), 252 N.Y. 449, 169 N.E. 642. It was urged in that case that a rider in a policy excluding from protection death resulting from travel in an aircraft (except as a fare-paying passenger) conflicted with the incontestability provision contained in the New York insurance laws. The Court of Appeals held to the contrary, stating: "The provision that a policy shall be incontestable after it has been in force during the lifetime of the insured for a period of two years it not a mandate as to coverage, a definition of the hazard to be borne by the insurer. It means only this, that within the limits of the coverage the policy shall stand, unaffected by any defense that it was invalid in its inception, or thereafter became invalid by reason of a condition broken."

While the broad distinction drawn in *Conway* between a policy's limits of coverage and its validity has been quite generally recognized, differences of opinion have arisen as to its application, particularly with respect to group life insurance. (See, e.g., Keeton, Basic Text on Insurance, sec. 6.5(d); Young, "Incontestable—As to What?", 1964 U.Ill. L.F.) With individual life insurance the policy identifies a specific individual by name, and it is relatively easy to distinguish between a question of coverage (the death of the insured or his death from some specific cause) and a question of validity created by antecedent misrepresentations on the part of the insured. In the case of group life insurance, however, the master policy undertakes to provide insurance for a collection of unnamed persons defined only in terms of membership in a class, such as the employees of a certain company. To ascertain whether a person is insured necessitates a determination of whether he is in fact a member of the class. To the extent that that determination is based upon information furnished by the employer or by an employee or alleged employee, the question whether coverage exists tends to become intertwined with the question whether the coverage was obtained by false representations.

The courts of other States have considered a number of factual situations relating to eligibility, such as whether the insured is an employee at all, whether he was actively employed, whether he exceeded a specific maximum age, whether he was disqualified for some other reason, and whether he was incorrectly classified as to position. The decisions, which are collected in an annotation appearing in 26 A.L.R.3d 632, are not uniform in result.

[Citations.]

* * * [T]he New York view, as first expressed in a Federal decision, was that the insurer might raise the defense of ineligibility (Fisher v. United States Life Insurance Co. (4th Cir.1957), 249 F.2d 879), but a subsequent decision in 1969 by the New York Court of Appeals holds to the contrary (Simpson v. Phoenix Mutual Life Insurance Co. (1969), 24 N.Y.2d 262, 299 N.Y.S.2d 835, 247 N.E.2d 655). It is the *Simpson* * decision on which the appellate court principally relied in the case now before us.

We, however, consider that the question of eligibility is one which relates to the risk assumed and that a defense based on lack of eligibility is therefore not foreclosed by an incontestability clause.

* [Editors' Footnote.] In *Simpson,* the Phoenix Mutual Life Ins. Co. issued a master policy through the trustees of the Cemetery and Funeral Service and Supply Industry Group Insurance Fund. Simpson was an officer and attorney in the Lebanon Cemetery Association of Queens, Inc., a participating employer. He completed an enrollment card and was included in the list submitted to the insurer. However he never satisfied the eligibility provision that he work 30 hours per week at the employer's place of business. Over two years later he was killed by a robber.

It is, of course, true that eligibility may relate to circumstances existing at the inception of the contract (although it may also arise subsequently because of a change in employment status). It is also true that it may have been determined initially upon the basis of statements made by the insured or by his employer. And it may be assumed that whether a person is an employee or is a full time employee is a matter affecting the willingness of the insurer to assume the defined risk at the defined premium charge, since employment or active or full-time employment may protect the insurer against adverse selection. See Gregg, Group Life Insurance (2d ed.) 34–36.

A challenge to eligibility does not, however, involve an attack by the insurer on the validity of the master policy. The defendant is not seeking to set aside the policy because of the misrepresentations made and the only aspect of the insurance plan which is affected is the payment sought by a single beneficiary. Moreover, even as to that beneficiary, while the defendant may have relied on his representations as well as those of the decedent, the defendant's success in this litigation does not require that the defendant establish the falsity of those representations as such. Had the plaintiff alleged that the decedent had been a full-time employee, instead of admitting that she was not, the defendant would of course have been put to his proof of ineligibility. But it would be the fact of eligibility or ineligibility which would be decisive, not what prior representations had been made on the subject.

As we read *Simpson,* it represents a basic departure from the distinction announced in *Conway* between matters concerning validity, to which the incontestable clause applies, and the risk assumed, to which it does not. The court in *Simpson* takes the position that some matters which relate only to the risk assumed are nevertheless covered by the incontestable clause, namely those risks which could have been discovered at the time the contract was entered into. (See 24 N.Y.2d 262, 267, 299 N.Y.S.2d 835, 247 N.E.2d 655, 658.) We consider that conclusion both inapplicable to the policy we consider here as well as unsuitable to the group insurance situation with its constantly changing body of insured employees.

The incontestability clause of the policy, to begin with, provides only that the validity of the policy may not be contested, and, as we have seen, its validity is not disputed.

A further factor which we deem significant was expressed in Rasmussen v. Equitable Life Assurance Society of the United States, 293 Mich. 482, 487, 292 N.W. 377, 380, in connection with a group policy excluding employees over a certain age: "[A] greater social good is served by enabling employed groups to obtain the most advantageous protection that their status warrants by restricting the invitation to particular age groups. Those who deliberately misstate their age and thus tend to lower the experience record of the group should not be placed by construction within the aegis of the incontestability provision."

Similarly, in the present case we can envisage the possibility of an adverse effect upon other employers if, by virtue of the incontestability clause, claims must be paid out upon the death of persons not meeting the standards of eligibility contained in the policy, in that actuarial calculations upon which the premium rate had been determined could be distorted, with the consequence of increased rates being imposed as the result of experience rating. See Gregg, Group Life Insurance (2d ed.) 220–229.

We do not mean to intimate that the occasions in which an employer would intentionally make a misrepresentation as to the eligibility of an employee would be of frequent occurrence. In the ordinary case the employer, who is paying all or a portion of the premiums, would not appear to have any incentive to create a supply of fictitious employees. The risk does exist, however, as indicated by the facts of this case and the somewhat similar facts in such cases as Fisher v. Prudential Insurance Co. (1966), 107 N.H. 101, 218 A.2d 62.

A third consideration underlying the decision we reach lies in the possibility that an employee who is eligible at the time when the policy is issued might, at some point more than two years after the issuance date, cease to be a full-time employee, or, indeed, even terminate his employment. Were the incontestability clause to be applied in such a situation, there would appear to be no manner in which payment of a claim could be resisted if the employer or employer group had failed to notify the insurer of the change in the status of the employee. We think that the termination of employment is clearly a matter which the insurer may raise, as was held by the appellate court in Baker v. Prudential Insurance Company of America, 279 Ill.App. 5. On the same reasoning we believe that raising the question whether a person ever became an employee or became an employee of the type eligible for insurance is also not barred by an incontestability clause.

The principle of discoverability which governed the *Simpson* decision would put the insurer to an election between the risk of making payment on unwarranted claims or conducting an investigation, in some manner not dependent upon information provided by the employer or employee, into the employment status of every person purportedly insured. The contention is made here that the latter course of action would cause substantial expense and the unnecessary duplication of records. It would undermine group life insurance which is customarily conducted on a "self administrative" fashion with the employer or employer group maintaining the record of individual employees, thus reducing the cost of premiums. (Cf. General American Life Insurance Co. v. Charleville (Mo.1971), 471 S.W.2d 231, 236.) The record made in this case does not supply us with evidence as to what overall method of administration was followed under the insurance plan involved or as to what the costs of some alternative method might be, and we therefore do not consider this contention in reaching our decision.

* * *

Reversed and remanded, with directions.

GOLDENHERSH, JUSTICE (dissenting).

I dissent. The incontestability clause provides:

> "[A]nd no statement made by any employee insured under this policy relating to his insurability shall be used in contesting the validity of the insurance with respect to which such statement was made, after such insurance has been in force prior to the contest for a period of two years during such employee's lifetime * * *."

As used in this policy the term "insurability" does not refer solely to the condition of the employee's health; it means "capable of being insured" or the "quality or condition of being insurable" (Kahn v. Continental Casualty Co., 391 Ill. 445, 63 N.E.2d 468), and the only contention made by defendant of her ineligibility or lack of insurability is her failure to be regularly employed. Defendant accepted premiums covering Mrs. Crawford for 52 months, and admittedly, if she had been afflicted with some incurable malady at the time the policy was issued, her "insurability" could not, after two years, have been contested. Neither logic nor the authorities cited support the drawing of a distinction between noninsurability based on illness and noninsurability based on failure to be employed for a minimum number of hours during each week. Indeed, if any distinction were to be drawn it should serve to more rigidly apply the incontestability clause to the latter situation for the reason that it is so easily discoverable.

The reason for the inclusion of the incontestability clause in policies of this type is obvious, and the fixing of the two-year period is clearly for the purpose of providing ample time for the insurer to investigate the veracity of the representations made. It is naive to believe that group insurers are trusting souls who accept, without question, the representations of the groups whom they insure, and the fact is that the policies provide for, and the insurers make, periodic inspections and audits. I cannot share the majority's apprehension with regard to the hypothetical case of the terminated employee. If the insurer failed to learn of the termination, and accepted premiums for a period of two years after its occurrence, that too should be governed by the incontestability clause. Under the terms of this policy the defendant was entitled to inspect and audit payroll records, and its failure to discover within the two-year period that Mrs. Crawford was not employed should not permit it to invoke a defense in clear violation of the express provisions of its policy. The rationale of Simpson v. Phoenix Mutual Life Insurance Co., 24 N.Y.2d 262, 299 N.Y.S.2d 835, 247 N.E.2d 655, which the appellate court followed, is preferable to the grounds upon which the majority rests its decision, and I would affirm the judgment.

### *Notes*

1. A group life policy covered "Employee's legal spouse residing with the employee." In 1973, the employee listed Beulah as his dependent spouse on the enrollment card. Premiums were deducted from his paycheck. In

1979 Beulah died. In fact she was not his wife but had lived with him for 35 years as a "concubine" or common law wife. May the insurer refuse payment in the face of the incontestable clause? Held: yes in Jackson v. Continental Casualty Co., 402 So.2d 175 (La.App.1981).

2. For an excellent review and analysis of the problem, see Words, Coverage Clauses and Incontestable Statutes: The Regulation of Post Claim Underwriting, 1979 Ill.L.Forum 809.

### *Note*

### *Group Insurance and Conflicts of Law*

It is the nature of the group policies that the beneficiaries, and even the insureds, are apt to be scattered over a number of jurisdictions, each possibly different from the corporate domicile of the insurer. § 192, comment h of the Restatement (Second) of Conflicts of Law provides that, "the rights against the insurer are usually governed by the law which governs the master policy."

Krauss v. Manhattan Life Insurance Co. of New York, 643 F.2d 98 (2d Cir.1981), however, indicates that the choice of law problem may not be that easily resolved. In that case a New York insurer issued and delivered in New York a group policy covering the employees of an Illinois concern. As in the *Crawford* case the plaintiff (a lawyer) was included in the plan, although "ineligible" because he was only a part-time employee. His death occurred after the expiration of the "Incontestable" period. Illinois law under the *Crawford* decision would not allow the Illinois beneficiary to recover, whereas New York under the *Simpson* rule would. The 2d Circuit using New York choice of law doctrine held that Illinois law applied in this situation.

> "Because certificate holders in other states under the same master policy are apt to be governed by other states' laws, we recognize that the rule formulated by the Second Restatement might offer greater uniformity than the interest-analysis and center of gravity approach used by New York courts. This does not, however, compel a different result. Uniformity and predictability were undeniably compromised when the classical territorial approach to choice of law problems was abandoned [in New York] * * *. Moreover, this outcome retains substantial uniformity as to the [employer] all of whose employees are in Illinois."

*Query:* What if the certificate holders were not all in Illinois?

## D. NO COVERAGE OF THE PARTICULAR LOSS CLAIMED

__ **no occurrence within time limits of policy**

__ **semantic questions:**

- __ **what is "disability"?**
- __ **what is "accident or occurrence"?**
- __ **what is "accidental means"?**

# MASSACHUSETTS CASUALTY INSURANCE CO. v. FORMAN

United States Court of Appeals, Fifth Circuit, 1975.
516 F.2d 425.

GODBOLD, CIRCUIT JUDGE:

The appellant, Massachusetts Casualty Insurance Company, filed suit against appellee Forman seeking to rescind and cancel a disability insurance policy it had issued to him and to recover $5,500 disability benefits already paid. Forman counterclaimed for enforcement of the policy. Following a nonjury trial, the District Court entered judgment in favor of Forman for $30,800 accrued benefits plus specific enforcement of the policy (which if Forman lived to life expectancy would produce total benefits of around $400,000), * * * Relief to the company was denied. We reverse the award of benefits * * * and direct that the policy continues in effect but without coverage for diabetes, the specific condition here in question. Also we hold that the company is entitled to repayment of the $5,500 previously paid.

Forman, a resident of Florida and formerly a chiropractor in New York, applied for the policy in October 1969. He had been hospitalized in New York September 7–20, 1968, and November 14–December 20, 1968. At least as early as December 2, 1968, his condition had been diagnosed as diabetes and he had been informed of the diagnosis. Despite these facts, now not disputed, the application for insurance contained numerous and egregious false statements concerning prior illness, treatment and hospitalization, including specific denials that the applicant had ever had diabetes.

After receipt of the application, the company procured an independent report from the Retail Credit Company verifying certain of Forman's factual statements concerning income and employment and supplying information on his military service and general life style. This report contained virtually no information on Forman's health, aside from the statement "Health is good." Relying on the application and on the Retail Credit report, Massachusetts Casualty issued to Forman on November 20, 1969, a sickness and accident policy insuring against (emphasis added):

(1) Accidental bodily injury *occurring during* the term of this Policy.

(2) Sickness which *first manifests itself during* the term of this policy.

Among the benefits were total disability payments of $1,000 per month for a period up to the life of the insured.

On June 24, 1971, Forman executed a proof of loss and filed a claim alleging total disability as a result of diabetes which he claimed had been first diagnosed approximately one year earlier. The company began making disability payments, then discontinued them, and on November

16, 1971, filed suit against Forman seeking rescission and cancellation of the policy and return of benefits paid on the ground that in his application Forman had misstated his earned monthly income. In May 1972 the company learned of the preexistence of Forman's diabetic condition, and, with leave of court, amended its complaint to add this ground.

The District Court found that Forman had not misrepresented his earned income. This disposed of the sole ground for cancellation and denial of benefits asserted in the original complaint. With respect to the additional ground raised for the first time by the amended complaint, the court found that the incontestable clause of the policy became effective November 20, 1971, two years after the policy was issued. The portion of the policy headed "Incontestable" is as follows:

> INCONTESTABLE: A. After this Policy has been in force for a period of two years during the lifetime of the Insured, it shall become incontestable as to the statements contained in the copy of the application. B. No claim for loss incurred or disability (as defined in the Policy) commencing after two years from the date of issue of this Policy shall be reduced or denied on the ground that a disease or physical condition not excluded from coverage by name or specific description effective on the date of loss had existed prior to the effective date of coverage of this Policy.

Both of the quoted provisions are required by F.S.A. § 627.607.

The court erred in what appears to have been its view that the effect of these provisions was to bring Forman's diabetes within the policy although it had "first manifested" itself before the policy was issued.

"First manifest" provisions shelter insurers from claims arising from conditions which exist, and which are known by the insured to exist, before coverage commences. See Continental Casualty Co. v. Robertson, 245 F.2d 604, 606–608 (CA5, 1957); Fuller v. Aetna Life Ins. Co., 259 F.2d 402 (CA5, 1958). In this case the condition for which Forman claimed benefits had "first manifested" itself almost a year before the policy became effective. Thus disability resulting from diabetes was never within the scope of policy coverage, and Forman cannot now claim diabetes-related disability benefits unless the incontestability provisions of the policy caused this prior-existing illness to become covered. We conclude that they did not have that effect.

Incontestable clauses protect both insurer and insured. Winer v. New York Life Ins. Co., 140 Fla. 534, 190 So. 894 (1938). An incontestable clause safeguards an insured from excessive litigation many years after a policy has already been in force and assures him security in financial planning for his family, while providing an insurer a reasonable opportunity to investigate. Simpson v. Phoenix Mut. Life Ins. Co., 24 N.Y.2d 262, 267–269, 299 N.Y.S.2d 835, 839–841, 247 N.E.2d 655, 657–58 (1969). See also Prudential Ins. Co. of America v. Prescott, 130 Fla. 11, 176 So. 875, 878 (1937).

The great weight of authority, including decisions of this court, holds that an incontestable clause in a disability policy does not deprive the insurer from defending on the ground that the particular disability was never within the policy coverage.

> Where loss is claimed by reason of disability covered by the policy, it is necessary, under the average policy, that the cause of such disability arise within the policy terms and after the insurance has been effected. This is a condition of liability, a condition of the insurance. * * * The incontestable clause does not apply under those circumstances, and there can be no recovery unless the cause of disability arose within the time designated.

1 Appleman, Insurance Law and Practice § 333 at 600 (1941). See also 18 Couch on Insurance § 72:16 at 79–80 (2d Ed.1968). In United States v. Kaminsky, 64 F.2d 735 (CA5, 1933), a war risk insurance case, the incontestable clause was one imposed by federal statute. The beneficiary claimed benefits for a total disability commencing while the insured was in the army, and subsequent death benefits. This court held that the insurer was not barred from defending on the ground that the disability existed before the insured entered the service and was therefore, not covered.[24] This result is but a precisely targeted application of the general rule that incontestable clauses do not cut off defenses going to coverage. Then Chief Judge Cardozo of the New York Court of Appeals has drawn this distinction:

> The provision that a policy shall be incontestable after it has been in force during the lifetime of the insured for a period of two years is not a mandate as to coverage, a definition of the hazards to be borne by the insurer. It means only this, that within the limits of the coverage the policy shall stand, unaffected by any defense that it was invalid in its inception, or thereafter became invalid by reason of a condition broken.

Metropolitan Life Ins. Co. v. Conway, 252 N.Y. 449, 452, 169 N.E. 642 (1930). *Metropolitan Life* refers to the opinion of this circuit in Sanders v. Jefferson Standard Life Ins. Co., 10 F.2d 143 (CA5, 1925), in which we had held that an incontestable clause which provided that the policy "shall be incontestable for any cause except for nonpayment of premiums" did not bar the insurer from asserting the exception to the double indemnity provision that excluded death arising from bodily injury inflicted by another person. Other Fifth Circuit cases are: Metropolitan Life Ins. Co. v. Shalloway, 151 F.2d 548 (CA5, 1945), and Equitable Life Assur. Society v. First National Bank, 113 F.2d 272 (CA5, 1940) (incontestable clause does not bar inquiry into actual age for purposes of applying an age adjustment clause); Washington National Ins. Co. v. Burch, 270 F.2d 300 (CA5, 1959) (eligibility of the insured under a group

**24.** For a survey of other cases which, with respect to disability policies, permit the defense of preexisting disability despite incontestable provisions, see 13 A.L.R.3d 1383.

policy and proper classification within the group may be inquired into despite an incontestable clause).

Here, where coverage is framed in terms of first manifestation and the misrepresentation of no prior history of diabetes goes to the heart of the definition of coverage, the principle of not permitting incontestability to broaden the scope of coverage attains especially strong force. There is little reason to decline to give it full effect. The policy of protecting the insured from belated discovery that he has no coverage loses much of its vitality.

Our conclusion is not inconsistent with the two statutorily-required provisions of the incontestable clause in this policy. Subparagraph A provides that after two years the policy "shall become incontestable as to the statements contained in the copy of the application." Applying this plain and straightforward statement as written, it would appear to bar defenses that spring from—and only from—statements in the application. So read, subparagraph A has no application to the issue of whether diabetes was outside the coverage of the policy because it first manifested before the policy was issued. Applying subparagraph A as written is consistent with the general law, discussed above, concerning interplay of incontestable clauses and questions of coverage.

* * *

Subparagraph B * * * only prohibits denials of claims based on the prior *existence* of a disease. Such denials are irrelevant here because a disease is covered no matter when it existed, so long as it was not first manifested prior to the policy date. Thus subparagraph B has no effective field of operation. Giving it some scope of operation by reading "existed" as "existed and manifested" goes beyond the language of the clause and is contrary to the general principle that incontestable clauses do not operate to extend coverage beyond that contracted for. Moreover, such a reading would not promote the purpose or policy of § 627.607. The statutory clause protects both parties from uncertainty where coverage turns on when a disease first existed, occurred or arose. Under such policies coverage may be uncertain even long after the policy was procured because a disease may exist but not be discoverable by reasonable medical investigation. This clause resolves the uncertainty in favor of coverage beginning two years after the policy date. Where coverage turns on *manifestation* rather than existence, the insurance policy itself eliminates this uncertainty since manifestation is normally discoverable by reasonable medical investigation.

Florida requires that incontestable clauses be included in several other types of insurance policies. The provision required in life insurance policies, § 627.455, excludes from incontestability, at the option of the insurer, "provisions relative to benefits in event of disability." Section 627.463 provides that a clause in any life insurance policy providing for incontestability after a specified period "shall preclude only a contest of the validity of the policy, and shall not preclude the assertion at any time of defenses based upon provisions in the policy which exclude or restrict coverage, whether or not such restrictions or exclusions are excepted in such clause." For group life insurance policies, § 627.560 requires a provision that "the validity of the policy shall not be contested, except for nonpayment of premium" after two years. The succeeding section, § 627.561, requires an additional provision that no statement made by an insured shall be used in any contest unless a copy of the instrument containing the statement has been furnished to him or to his beneficiary. Group disability policies must provide that in the absence of fraud misrepresentations for the purpose of effecting insurance shall not avoid the policy or reduce benefits unless contained in a written instrument signed by the insured (or policyholder), a copy of which has been furnished to the policyholder or insured or beneficiary. § 627.657. Certain endowment and annuity contracts, and industrial life policies, must contain a provision for incontestability after two years except for nonpayment of premiums, but at the option of the insurer the contract may also except provisions relating to benefits in the event of disability and provisions relating to accidental death. §§ 627.466 and 627.506. While these provisions do not present a wholly consistent pattern, they reveal at least that the legislature does not consider incontestability to be plenary in nature. Also, several sections provide for reduced benefits where the age or sex of the insured has been misstated, § 627.456 (life insurance), § 627.468 (annuity and endowment contracts), § 627.507 (industrial life policies), § 627.620 (disability policies). None of these sections purports to limit its application to the period of time during which the particular policy is contestable.[25]

Thus the law concerning incontestable clauses in general, the specific language of the incontestability provisions of this policy, and the Florida statutory scheme, lead us to the decision that the fact that Forman suffered from diabetes which had become manifest before the policy was issued excluded diabetes-related disability from coverage.[26]

We conclude, however, that the company is not entitled to cancellation and rescission. A generalized incontestable clause, i.e., one providing that the policy is incontestable after a specified number of years except for nonpayment of premiums, bars assertion of fraudulent misstatements in an application as the basis for invalidity of the policy. Winer v. New York Life Ins. Co., 130 Fla. 115, 177 So. 224 (1937) and 140 Fla. 534, 190 So. 894 (1938). That conclusion is even more clearly required where the clause is more specific, as is subparagraph A. Though incontestability is often cast in terms of defenses it applies also to efforts by the insurer to obtain the affirmative relief of cancellation

**25.** See Metropolitan Life Ins. Co. v. Shalloway, 151 F.2d 548 (CA5, 1945), supra, and Equitable Life Assur. Society v. First National Bank, 113 F.2d 272 (CA5, 1940), supra, holding that an incontestable clause does not prevent giving effect to an age adjustment clause.

**26.** Our approach has been through the rubric of incontestability because that is the one most often employed, and the two policy provisions that we have discussed were labeled "Incontestable." More accurately, part B is not an incontestable clause, properly so called, but a legislative expansion of coverage, having a field of operation wholly independent of statements made in the application. Under such an approach the result is the same.

and rescission. Prudential Ins. Co. v. Prescott, 115 Fla. 365, 156 So. 109 (1933); *Winer,* supra. Though the policy continues in effect it, of course, does not cover diabetes.

The company is entitled to the $5,500 of benefits that it paid to Forman under the erroneous understanding that his diabetic condition had initially manifested itself after the policy was issued. Restatement of Restitution § 16 (1937).

* * *

Reversed in part; affirmed, as modified, in part; and remanded for further proceedings consistent with this opinion.

## WILLDEN v. WASHINGTON NATIONAL INSURANCE CO.

Supreme Court of California, 1976.
18 Cal.3d 631, 135 Cal.Rptr. 69, 557 P.2d 501.

TOBRINER, JUSTICE.

This case involves the interpretation of an accident and disability policy. As a result of injuries caused by an automobile accident in 1966, the record indicates that plaintiff began to suffer debilitory [sic] effects of multiple sclerosis, finally becoming totally disabled in February of 1969. After receiving special verdicts, the trial court denied plaintiff's claim for accident disability benefits. * * * We affirm the judgment.

Defendant issued plaintiff a "Disability Income Policy for Realtors and Real Estate Salesmen" in 1965. Part 2 of the policy provides 60 months' coverage for injuries which "totally and continuously disable the Insured within thirty days of the date of the accident so as to prevent him from performing each and every duty pertaining to his occupation." [27] If, after payment of disability benefits for 60 months, the insured is unable to perform "each and every duty pertaining to any gainful occupation," the policy provides additional benefits for as long as the disability continues. The policy also extends one year of benefits for total disability caused by sickness.

Plaintiff, a real estate salesman, was injured in an automobile accident on February 11, 1966. He experienced tremors in his leg the following day; numbness in the leg by April of 1966; and on October 10, 1966, his condition was diagnosed as multiple sclerosis. Unemployed from April of 1966 to April of 1967, he obtained a business license and worked as a real estate and business opportunity broker until 1972. His condition continued to deteriorate, and he was unable to resume any

27. The portion of part 2 providing occupational disability benefits reads as follows: "If injury shall totally and continuously disable the Insured within thirty days from the date of the accident so as to prevent him from performing each and every duty pertaining to his occupation, the Company will pay at the rate of the Monthly Accident Indemnity for the period of such total disability beginning with the day of total disability specified in the Policy Schedule, but not exceeding sixty months during any one period of disability."

gainful employment until May 1, 1973. The duration of plaintiff's total disability was disputed at trial, but partially resolved by a special verdict that plaintiff was not totally disabled between April 21, 1967, and February 25, 1969, but was totally disabled thereafter.

Defendant paid plaintiff one year of sickness benefits, terminating on April 21, 1967. Plaintiff then sued for accident benefits accruing after that date. At trial, plaintiff, appearing in propria persona, presented expert testimony that his multiple sclerosis was precipitated by the trauma of the automobile accident. The jury returned a special verdict finding plaintiff's "disability resulted directly and independently of all other causes from the accident of February 11, 1966." * * * The trial court then requested additional special verdicts, and the jury rendered a finding that plaintiff was not totally and continuously disabled within 30 days of the accident. * * * On the basis of these special verdicts the trial court entered judgment for defendant, and plaintiff appealed.

As we have observed, part 2 of the policy (see fn. 27) provides occupational disability benefits if the injury "shall totally and continuously disable the Insured *within thirty days from the date of the accident* so as to prevent him from performing each and every duty pertaining to his occupation." (Italics added.) Consequently the special verdict that plaintiff was *not* totally and continuously disabled within 30 days of the accident appears to bar his claim for accident disability benefits.

Plaintiff contends, however, that the special verdict rests upon a construction of the policy which is inconsistent with the judicially recognized "process of nature" rule. The "process of nature" rule holds that, within the meaning of policy provisions requiring disability within a specified time after the accident, the onset of disability relates back to the time of the accident itself whenever the disability arises directly from the accident "within such time as the process of nature consumes in bringing the person affected to a state of total [disability]." (Schilk v. Benefit Trust Life Ins. Co. (1969) 273 Cal.App.2d 302, 307, 78 Cal.Rptr. 60, 39 A.L.R.3d 1019.)

The process of nature rule, created by judicial decision in other states in response to the efforts of insurers to enforce arbitrary limitations on coverage, was first established in California in Frenzer v. Mutual Ben. H. & A. Assn. (1938) 27 Cal.App.2d 406, 81 P.2d 197. In *Frenzer,* the insured became disabled from blood poisoning and later died; medical testimony opined that the blood poisoning resulted from a minor injury incurred several hours before any symptoms became evident. Rejecting the insurer's contention that recovery was barred by a provision limiting benefits to injuries which are "immediately and totally disabling," *Frenzer* stated that "While courts are not altogether in accord in the interpretation of the meaning of the words 'immediately and totally disabling' as used in the policy, the weight of authority is toward the so-called process of nature rule; that is, that when a disability follows from an accidental injury within such time as the processes of nature consume in bringing the affected person to the state of total incapacity to prosecute every kind of business pertaining to his occupation such disability is immediate under the terms of the policy." (27 Cal.App.2d at p. 413, 81 P.2d at p. 201.)

The Court of Appeal decision in Schilk v. Benefit Trust Life Ins. Co., supra, 273 Cal.App.2d 302, 78 Cal.Rptr. 60, confirmed the process of nature rule and applied that rule to interpret a policy essentially identical to the policy at issue here. Schilk sustained a whiplash injury on September 27, 1961, and became totally disabled as of February 2, 1962. In denying benefits, the insurer relied on a provision limiting coverage to injuries which "within twenty days of the date of the accident, totally and continuously disable the Insured." The Court of Appeal, however, upheld the trial court's conclusion that under the process of nature rule *Schilk* was deemed disabled within the policy's 20–day period. Rejecting the insurer's attempt to distinguish *Frenzer,* the court stated that "The reasoning applied to the word 'immediately' in *Frenzer* has equal force when the language of a policy provides a specific number of days, as here." (273 Cal.App.2d 302, 307, 78 Cal. Rptr. 60, 64.)

On the facts of this case the jury should have been instructed concerning the process of nature rule. Plaintiff, however, bears the fault for the court's failure to so instruct the jury. * * * Plaintiff proposed no instruction concerning the process of nature rule, and consequently cannot complain of the court's failure to instruct on that subject. (Barrera v. De La Torre (1957) 48 Cal.2d 166, 170, 308 P.2d 724.)

Plaintiff further contends that the 30–day provision of the policy is unconscionable and hence, invalid as a matter of law. No authority supports this contention; the cases clearly indicate that similar provisions, *if* interpreted in accord with the process of nature rule, are not unconscionable. (See Schmidt v. Pacific Mut. Life Ins. Co. (1969) 268 Cal.App.2d 735, 740, 74 Cal.Rptr. 367; Schilk v. Benefit Trust Life Ins. Co., supra, 273 Cal.App.2d 302, 307–308, 78 Cal.Rptr. 60.) The harsh and arguably unconscionable application of the 30–day provision [28] to bar plaintiff's claim in the present case is the result of plaintiff's failure to seek a jury instruction based upon the more liberal process of nature rule.

* * *

The judgment is affirmed.

**28.** As Justice Taylor pointed out in Schilk v. Benefit Trust Life Ins. Co., supra, 273 Cal.App.2d 302, 78 Cal.Rptr. 60, in discussing a similar limitation "* * * [S]erious internal injuries often do not manifest themselves until long after the accident happened and the injured person may be completely oblivious of his condition, although the process of nature may be actively engaged in developing the latent hurt into a severe or even fatal injury. The fact that respondent, under such circumstances, pursued his usual occupation * * * ought not, in all fairness, militate against him when the more serious but hidden injury subsequently manifests itself." (pp. 307–308, 78 Cal.Rptr. p. 64.) "The strict interpretation of the clause here," Justice Taylor concluded, "would lead to an unjust result * * *. Such a very limited and highly technical construction of an insurance contract cannot be foisted onto a layman nor does it make any sense in terms of the risks insured against." (p. 308, 78 Cal. Rptr. p. 64.)

## EMOND v. STATE FARM MUTUAL AUTOMOBILE INSURANCE CO.

Court of Appeals of Georgia, 1985.
175 Ga.App. 548, 333 S.E.2d 656.

CARLEY, JUDGE.

The facts relevant to this appeal are as follows: Appellant-plaintiff was injured in an automobile collision in 1979. Appellant was insured by appellee-defendant. Although the policy specifically purported to provide only basic PIP coverage, appellant had "the right to demand and receive the benefit of $50,000 [optional PIP] coverage upon [her] tender * * * of such additional premium as may be due and filing of proof of loss * * *." Flewellen v. Atlanta Cas. Co., 250 Ga. 709, 712, 300 S.E.2d 673 (1983). However, since Jones v. State Farm Mut. Auto. Ins. Co., 156 Ga.App. 230, 274 S.E.2d 623 (1980) and Flewellen v. Atlanta Cas. Co., supra, had yet to be decided at the time, appellant received only her $5,000 basic PIP benefits. Appellant's policy with appellee also provided $5,000 medical payment coverage for the "payment of medical expenses incurred for services furnished within one year from the date of the accident." The policy also provided that medical payment coverage "shall be excess insurance over any Personal Injury Protection benefits paid or payable under this or any other automobile insurance policy because of bodily injury sustained by an eligible injured person." After appellant was paid $5,000 in basic PIP benefits, she was paid the full $5,000 of her excess medical payment benefits.

Subsequent to the decision in Flewellen v. Atlanta Cas. Co., supra, appellant paid a premium for $50,000 optional PIP coverage. Appellee agreed that appellant was entitled to that coverage. Appellee, having already paid $10,000 of appellant's claims in the form of $5,000 basic PIP and $5,000 excess medical payments, paid $40,000 more, bringing its total payments to $50,000. Appellant then submitted a claim for medical expenses, all of which she had incurred more than one year after the collision. Appellee refused to pay this claim.

Appellant then instituted the instant civil action against appellee. Under the allegations of the complaint, appellant asserted that she had been paid only $45,000 in PIP benefits and that she was entitled to an additional $5,000 in such benefits. Appellee answered, and among its other defenses, asserted that appellant "has been paid all benefits available under [the] terms of the applicable policy."

Cross motions for summary judgment were filed. The trial court concluded that the $5,000 that had originally been paid to appellant under the excess medical payment coverage of the policy should, as the result of appellant's subsequent invocation of Flewellen v. Atlanta Cas. Co., supra, be reallocated so as to be considered as payment under her optional PIP coverage. Thus, rather than $45,000 in PIP benefits and

$5,000 in excess medical payment benefits, the trial court determined that $50,000 in PIP benefits had already been paid to appellant. The trial court further concluded that appellant would not be afforded excess medical payment coverage under the terms of the policy until her full $50,000 in PIP benefits had first been exhausted. The trial court's final conclusion was that appellant was not entitled to any additional benefits for her medical expenses under the policy. According to the trial court's analysis, appellant was not entitled to recover pursuant to the PIP coverage, which had already been exhausted at $50,000, or pursuant to her excess medical payment coverage, which required that medical expenses be incurred within one year of the collision. Summary judgment was granted in favor of appellee. Appellant's motion for summary judgment was denied. Appellant appeals, asserting that appellee was erroneously granted summary judgment and that she was erroneously denied partial summary judgment as to liability for the $5,000 in additional benefits.

1. The trial court was correct in holding that appellant was not entitled to excess medical payment benefits under the terms of her policy until her full $50,000 in PIP benefits had first been exhausted. Hall v. State Farm Mut. Auto. Ins. Co., 254 Ga. 633, 331 S.E.2d 530 (1985.)

2. The issue thus becomes whether the trial court erred in determining that the $5,000 which was originally paid as excess medical payment benefits should now be deemed reallocated so as to have constituted payment under appellant's PIP coverage.

OCGA § 13–1–13 provides, in relevant part, as follows: "Payments of claims made through ignorance of the law or where all the facts are known and there is no misplaced confidence and no artifice, deception, or fraudulent practice used by the other party are deemed voluntary and cannot be recovered unless made under an urgent and immediate necessity therefor or to release person or property from detention or to prevent an immediate seizure of person or property." Although appellee does not seek a $5,000 judgment against appellant, it does seek to have the $5,000 that it originally paid as excess medical payment benefits now applied against its liability to appellant for optional PIP benefits. Under these circumstances, we believe that OCGA § 13–1–13 is applicable. Cf. Mitchell v. Holden, 58 Ga.App. 712, 713(3), 199 S.E. 835 (1938). "An insurer cannot recover the payment of a claim made by mistake without showing a valid reason for failing to ascertain the truth." 658 Barker v. Federated Life Ins. Co., 111 Ga.App. 171, 141 S.E.2d 206 (1965).

"While money voluntarily paid may not ordinarily be recovered, this rule is not without exception. [Cits.]" Greene v. McIntyre, 119 Ga.App. 296, 298, 167 S.E.2d 203 (1969). "If [payment] was made in ignorance of law, recovery is barred; if in mistake of law, recovery is permitted. [Cits.]" American Surety Co. v. Groover, 64 Ga.App. 865, 870, 14 S.E.2d 149 (1941) (On Motion For Rehearing). As noted above, appellant in the instant case was paid the $5,000 in excess medical payment benefits after she had exhausted her basic PIP benefits but prior to the determination that she was entitled to an additional $45,000 in optional PIP benefits. Compare Hawkins v. Travelers Ins. Co., 162 Ga.App. 231, 235, 290 S.E.2d 348 (1982). Appellee contends that, but for its mistaken interpretation of the no-fault law prior to the Jones and Flewellen decisions, appellant would not have been paid any excess medical payment benefits until such time as her full $50,000 in optional PIP benefits had been exhausted. In our opinion, this would constitute payment under a mistake of law rather than through ignorance of the law. "While it is true that we held in Flewellen that 'the mandate of the law was clear' * * *, its interpretation by the bench, bar, insurers and insureds were obviously less so." Cotton States Mut. Ins. Co. v. McFather, 251 Ga. 739, 743, 309 S.E.2d 799 (1983). Where one acts "under a mistake of what the law was as applicable to [the] state of facts, or was requiring of it, we think that the mistake, though a product of ignorance, would be such a mistake of law * * * as would come within the rule." (Emphasis in original.) American Surety Co. v. Groover, supra 64 Ga.App. at 871, 14 S.E.2d 149 (On Motion For Rehearing).

Moreover, it does not appear that, in good conscience, appellee should not be allowed to reallocate the $5,000 towards its payment of PIP benefits to appellant. Appellant is not thereby deprived of any benefits to which she would otherwise be entitled. The payment of benefits already received is merely being redesignated to conform strictly with the terms of the contract, the enforcement of the terms of which appellant herself initiated by invoking Jones and Flewellen.

Accordingly, we find that the trial court did not err in holding that appellee was not a "volunteer" as to the original $5,000 payment and is now entitled to have that payment reallocated as payment of PIP benefits. Appellant has thus received her full $50,000 in PIP benefits.

3. It is undisputed that the medical expenses for which appellant seeks coverage were incurred more than one year after the collision. Citing Strickland v. Gulf Life Ins. Co., 240 Ga. 723, 242 S.E.2d 148 (1978), appellant contends that that provision of the policy which limits excess medical payment coverage to those expenses incurred within one year is unconscionable and unenforceable.

In Strickland, the policy provided coverage for loss of a limb only in the event that the loss occurred within 90 days of the injury to the limb. Our Supreme Court held that "[w]here loss of a limb is involved at an arbitrary point in time, here 90 days, the insured under these cases is confronted with the ugly choice whether to continue treatment and retain hope of regaining the use of his leg or to amputate his leg in order to be eligible for insurance benefits which he would forego if amputation became necessary at a later time. We find an insurance limitation forcing such a gruesome choice may be unreasonable and thus may be void as against public policy." Strickland v. Gulf Life Ins. Co., supra at 725, 242 S.E.2d 148.

Unlike Strickland, the policy provision in the instant case does not provide for a short-term period after the occurrence of a potentially insured event, within which period the insured faces a gruesome choice determinative of whether coverage will or will not be afforded. Under the instant policy, it is clear that appellant was being afforded coverage for excess medical payments, the only limitations on eligibility being the exhaustion of her PIP coverage and the consequent incurring of payments within one year of her injury. In our opinion, this provision specifically defines the coverage being afforded (see Hawkins v. Travelers Ins. Co., supra 162 Ga.App. at 236(2), 290 S.E.2d 348) and is not analogous to the provision under consideration in Strickland, supra. Nothing in the record would authorize a finding that appellee has waived enforcement of the one-year limitation on coverage, or that such provisions are so unreasonable as to violate public policy. Cf. Porter v. Allstate Ins. Co., 172 Ga.App. 657, 658, 324 S.E.2d 515 (1984).

Judgment affirmed.

### *Notes*

1. With *Emond* in mind, consider the following coverage limitations: (1) accidental loss of limb provided there is dismemberment within 90 days, and (2) life insurance with double indemnity if death occurs within 90 days. The *Strickland* case cited in Emond is a variation of the first type wherein the victim's dilemma is so obviously acute as to tempt an emotional resolution. However, the *Strickland* opinion relies upon a case from Pennsylvania and one from New Jersey which are based on the second type and which are stated to represent the minority view. In National Life and Accident Insurance Co. v. Edwards, 119 Cal.App.3d 326, 174 Cal.Rptr. 31 (1981), the insured had an $8,000 life insurance policy with double indemnity ($16,000) in case death ensued within 90 days after an auto accident. The insured was rendered a quadriplegic in an auto crash but lived for two years before dying of complications. The insurer tendered the face amount of the policy but resisted the double indemnity claim. In the course of the majority opinion it was frankly stated:

> "Although there is a substantial and growing body of law applying the process of nature rule to disability policies the courts have shown reluctance in extending this concept to time limitations in double indemnity provisions in life insurance policies."

Nevertheless the majority held the insurer liable for double indemnity citing the same two cases from Pennsylvania and New Jersey as did *Strickland.* The dissenting justice asserted that it is inappropriate to classify such policies as "adhesive". The insured could have procured $16,000 ordinary life coverage from a variety of competing policies and a variety of competing companies, but chose a cheaper one with $8000 coverage in any event and double indemnity only under exceptional and well understood circumstances.

2. In Alvarado v. Pilot Life Ins. Co., 663 S.W.2d 108 (Tex.App.1983) the company was granted summary judgment on insured's claim for accidental loss of a foot badly mangled by a gunshot but not amputated until 59 days after the "90 day" period specified in the policy. The court found no violation of public policy in the provision nor any ambiguity in the word "severance." See Annot. (1971) 39 A.L.R.3d 1311.

3. As a result of the AIDS epidemic, a growing number of insurance companies and other corporations are buying life insurance policies to make cash available to terminally ill persons. With these accelerated death benefits, the terminally ill insured can receive anywhere between 25% and 95% of the value of the policy. Rather than simply purchasing the policy from the insured, some insurance companies are offering riders or separate policies to guarantee accelerated payment of a portion of the policy upon diagnosis of a terminal illness. These riders tend to come at a substantial extra charge, although the nation's largest insurance company has established a program that pays full benefits minus only the interest the company would have earned by holding the money an extra six months. See Taxation for Accountants, Volume 49, Number 1, Life Benefits from Insurance May Be Taxable, Kathryn Sullivan and Joann Canning, July, 1992; Death and Taxes: The Taxation of Accelerated Death Benefits for the Terminally Ill, Wayne M. Gazur, 11 Virginia Tax Review Association 263, Fall, 1991; New York Times, Section 1, Page 1, Column 3, Terminally Ill Can Collect Death Payout While Alive, Tamar Lewin, January 27, 1990.

The growing use of accelerated death benefits currently poses a tax problem; while the Internal Revenue Code excludes from gross income insurance benefits paid by reason of death of the insured, the Internal Revenue Service has not yet ruled whether accelerated benefits get the same treatment. A proposed IRS rule is currently being commented on and should be decided by the end of 1993. If promulgated, the proposed regulations would recognize the needs of individuals who become terminally ill and would allow the payment of benefits prior to death without any income tax liability to the recipient if death is expected to occur within 12 months. See Proposed Rules, Department of the Treasury, Internal Revenue Service, 26 CFR Part 1 (FI–25–92), RIN 1545–AQ70.

### *Problem*

A group accidental death and dismemberment policy provides for payment of $100,000 for loss of "life," "two hands," "two feet," etc. but specifically provided that "with regard to hands and feet, loss shall mean dismemberment by severance at or above wrist or ankle joints respectively * * *." An insured under the policy sustained a severed spinal cord which has resulted in total loss of control and sensation in his legs. Could it be reasonably argued that functional loss of use of legs by severance of the spinal cord was within the policy coverage? See: in Cunninghame v. Equitable Life Assurance Society of United States, 652 F.2d 306 (2d Cir. 1981).

## CHALMERS v. METROPOLITAN LIFE INSURANCE CO.

Court of Appeals of Michigan, 1978.
86 Mich.App. 25, 272 N.W.2d 188.

BEASLEY, JUDGE.

After long service as an airplane pilot for General Motors Corporation, plaintiff suffered a severe heart attack on January 17, 1971.

Although he recovered, his pilot's license was permanently suspended as a result of the heart attack. Plaintiff claimed benefits under an extended disability benefit section of a group insurance policy issued by defendant Metropolitan Life Insurance Company for the reason that he is totally disabled to perform his job as an airplane pilot. Defendant denied extended disability benefits on the basis that, although plaintiff is no longer able to get a pilot's license, there are many jobs that he is physically qualified to do. * * * The trial court granted plaintiff a partial summary judgment for benefits payable as of that time based on a finding that plaintiff was totally disabled within the meaning of the language of the insurance policy. Defendant appeals as of right.

* * *

Essentially, the question here involves interpretation of the disability provisions of the group life insurance policy issued by defendant. The key provision in the policy reads:

> "If, while insured * * * the Employee is both under age 65 and *totally disabled so as to be unable to engage in any gainful occupation or employment for which he is reasonably qualified by education, training or experience,* the amount of Extended Disability Benefit Insurance (Monthly Benefits) then in force on account of the Employee shall be paid to the Employee each month during the period the Employee is so disabled, as set forth herein." (Emphasis added.)

Generally, two aspects or elements are involved in defining "total disability". First, there is the element of *quality,* which involves the question of whether the insured must be unable to work in his particular occupation, or whether he must be unable to work in other occupations as well. Then, there is the element of *quantity,* which is concerned with the amount of work an insured can be capable of performing and still be considered "totally disabled", that is, whether the insured need be absolutely helpless, or whether he may be able to perform minor acts only, or whether he may be able to perform substantial acts.[32]

It should be noted that since plaintiff in the instant case is one hundred percent disabled from performing within his former occupation of airplane pilot, the question of what quantity of work he is capable of performing within his given occupation is not at issue. The question is: Does the fact that plaintiff could possibly pursue some occupations other than that of licensed airplane pilot preclude a conclusion that he is totally disabled as the term is used in the insurance policy?

* * *

There is an ambiguity in the provision * * * The policy provides that a person is totally disabled if he is unable to engage in any gainful occupation or employment for which he is *reasonably qualified* by education, training or experience. Careful reading indicates the policy

**32.** 21 A.L.R.3d 1155, 1158–1159.

language covers "any gainful occupation or employment" but that the words "any gainful occupation or employment" are modified by the clause, and limited to those, "for which he is reasonably qualified by education, training or experience". Thus, the ambiguity arises from and the question then is as to the meaning, under the policy, of "reasonably" qualified.

In general, there are three views relating to the interpretation of "total disability" provisions in insurance policies. They are:

1) the *extreme view in favor of the insured* that total disability exists whenever the insured is unable to perform the duties of his particular occupation;

2) the *extreme view in favor of the insurer* that total disability exists only when there is incapacity to pursue any occupation whatever, and

3) the *intermediate view,* which regards total disability as a relative term, which rejects both of the two extreme views and which employs differing language to explain the degree of incapacity required to constitute total disability.[33]

We interpret the Michigan cases to follow the so-called intermediate view.

In Ebert v. Prudential Ins. Co. of America,[34] the Michigan Supreme Court utilized the above terminology and affirmed a judgment in favor of plaintiff who was an undertaker. The evidence indicated that plaintiff injured his back in an automobile accident suffering what was described as hypertrophic arthritis. The Court said that while he could do some light work he could not perform the embalming and lifting required of an undertaker. The Court concluded that he was permanently and totally disabled so as to be entitled to benefits under a provision contained in his life insurance policies. The *Ebert* Court made it clear that where there is ambiguity, insurance policies are to be liberally construed in favor of the insured. Technical construction to defeat claims is not favored.

We recognize that the language of the insurance policies involved in the Michigan cases tends to vary, but within those varying provisions, the Michigan Court has indicated a strong commitment to a liberal construction of such insurance policies that does not permit defeat of a reasonable expectation of payment of benefits. See Crowell v. Federal Life & Casualty Co.[35]

Applying that view to the facts of the instant case, we note that the record reveals beyond dispute that plaintiff is totally disabled from pursuing his former occupation of airplane pilot. There is considerable evidence of record to indicate that all significant education, training and experience accumulated by plaintiff was geared to his preparation for the

**33.** Id. at 1161; See also, 21 A.L.R.3d 1383, 1393–1394.

**34.** 338 Mich. 320, 330, 61 N.W.2d 164 (1953).

**35.** 397 Mich. 614, 247 N.W.2d 503 (1976).

specialized occupation of airplane pilot. It is this particular occupation for which plaintiff is reasonably qualified.

Defendant argues that prior to his heart attack plaintiff had experience in sales and aviation-related jobs such as maintenance, scheduling and flight operations. Defendant says this experience compels the conclusion that plaintiff is reasonably qualified for such jobs and that, therefore, since plaintiff is now physically capable of doing that kind of work, he is *not* totally disabled within the meaning of the term as delineated in the insurance policy. In support of this argument, defendant cites Przbylinski v. Standard Pressed Steel Co.[36]

In *Przbylinski,* this Court affirmed a directed verdict for defendant where plaintiff failed to offer evidence that "he suffered a disability which prevented him from engaging in any occupation for which he was reasonably fitted" and also failed to offer evidence that he was being treated by a physician for the disability as required under that insurance policy. In fact, the evidence showed that plaintiff, a supervisor, believed he was still physically able to do the work and did similar work for another employer for 4½ months subsequent to his alleged disablement. We conclude, *Przbylinski* is, on its facts, readily distinguishable from this case and is not controlling precedent here.

In the within case, the trial judge said:

> "Now it would seem to me that to say that this man now is reasonably qualified by education, training, or experience to do anything but fly is stretching it a little bit far. Clearly his whole adult life for all practical purposes has been devoted to flying, and to say now that at age 51 he is reasonably qualified by education, training, or experience to undertake something else, real estate or some other type of employment, seems to me stretching the language a little bit."

We do not believe his finding was clearly erroneous.

To hold as defendant contends would be to interpret the policy as extending very limited coverage. We believe the coverage afforded under this group policy looked to the work performed by the employee for this employer. We also note that the work experience relied upon by defendant as a basis to attempt to defeat liability occurred many years ago. The trial judge's ruling is consistent with the Michigan cases.

Affirmed.

### *Problems*

1. One of the more troublesome provisions in accident policies has concerned the loss of sight. "With respect to eyes", reads this provision, " 'loss' means the entire and irrecoverable loss of sight." Suppose the insured who had 20/20 vision in both eyes accidentally sustains an injury to one eye reducing vision to 2/200. The other eye is unaffected. By the use of a contact lens the visual acuity of 20/25 can be obtained in the injured eye.

**36.** 62 Mich.App. 461, 233 N.W.2d 614 (1975).

Should the insured recover? This question split the Missouri Supreme Court 4–3 in Crim v. National Life and Accident Insurance Co., 605 S.W.2d 73 (Mo.1980).

2. Would a lawyer who sustained an injury rendering one hand useless be considered as totally disabled? See Laidlaw v. Commercial Insurance Co., 255 N.W.2d 807, 6 A.L.R.4th 413 (Minn.1977), and the annotation following on the effect of other injuries on a lawyer's ability to perform his or her work.

## ARATA v. CALIFORNIA-WESTERN STATES LIFE INSURANCE CO.

District Court of Appeal of California, First District, 1975.
50 Cal.App.3d 821, 123 Cal.Rptr. 631.

TAYLOR, PRESIDING JUSTICE.

* * * [T]he insured, who died on November 3, 1971, was a member of the State Bar of California, had been actively engaged in the practice of law and was insured under a group policy issued by the insurer. The pertinent portion of the policy provided double indemnity accidental death benefits if the insured dies as a result of accidental bodily injury, directly and independently of all other causes, within 90 days after the date of injury, but also stated that the benefit was not payable "* * * if death * * * is contributed to by:

"(1) disease or bodily or mental infirmity * * *." The court found the facts as follows:

At all pertinent times, the insured had hemophilia type 8, a congenital condition present since his birth. On October 30, 1971, the insured slipped and fell to the floor, an accidental occurrence. The bodily injuries sustained by the insured in his fall proximately caused a subdural bleeding that commenced at the time of the fall. This subdural bleeding, due to his preexisting condition of hemophilia, continued from the time of the fall until his death several days later. The subdural bleeding or subdural hematoma was the direct and immediate cause of his death. If the preexisting condition of hemophilia type 8 did not exist, the accident and the resulting subdural bleeding alone would not have caused the death of the insured. A person who did not have hemophilia type 8 would not have died from the accident or from the subdural bleeding. In the absence of the accident, the insured would not have died from his preexisting condition of hemophilia.

The court concluded that the death of the insured occurred within the 90-day period and did not result from and was not contributed to, by disease within the intent or meaning of the exclusionary provision and entered its judgment in favor of the widow for the double indemnity death benefit of $36,000 provided by the policy.

* * * [T]he main question is whether the court below properly interpreted the exclusionary clause of the insurance policy. The insurer argues that the language "* * * is contributed by" excluded the in-

sured's preexisting hemophilia, which was the cause of his death. The trial court held otherwise pursuant to Brooks v. Metropolitan Life Ins. Co., 27 Cal.2d 305, 163 P.2d 689. In *Brooks,* the insured, afflicted with debilitating cancer, was covered by an accident policy that, so far as here pertinent, excluded death caused wholly, partly, directly or indirectly by disease. After the insured died in a fire, his widow sought to recover the double indemnity benefits payable under the policy for death by fire. The Supreme Court held that under such circumstances, "the presence of preexisting disease or infirmity will not relieve the insurer from liability if the accident is the proximate cause of death * * * [R]ecovery may be had even though a diseased or infirm condition appears to actually contribute to cause the death if the accident sets in progress the chain of events leading directly to death, or if it is the prime or moving cause." The *Brooks* rule has been consistently followed by the courts of this state, as we indicated in Shafer v. American Casualty Co., 245 Cal.App.2d 1, 4–7, 53 Cal.Rptr. 446.

The insurer contends that the *Brooks* rule has no application here because the "contributed to" language of its exclusion is different from that of the policy in *Brooks,* and relies on Miller v. Life & Casualty Insurance Co. of Tenn., 102 Ga.App. 655, 117 S.E.2d 237, 238, and some dicta of this court in Shafer v. American Casualty, supra.[37] It is not necessary to discuss in detail *Miller* or the numerous other out-of-state authorities cited by the insured that do not follow the California and majority rule.

In State Farm Mut. Auto. Ins. Co. v. Partridge, 10 Cal.3d 94, 109 Cal.Rptr. 811, 514 P.2d 123, our Supreme Court recently reaffirmed the rule of interpreting exclusionary clauses narrowly against the insurer and held, as follows, at pages 104–105: "The rationale of the *Brooks* decision equally applies to the instant case. Here, as in *Brooks,* an insured risk (the modification of the gun) combined with an excluded risk (the negligent use of the car) to produce the ultimate injury. Although there may be some question whether either of the two causes in the instant case can be properly characterized as *the* 'prime,' 'moving' or 'efficient' cause of the accident we believe that coverage under a liability insurance policy is equally available to an insured whenever an insured risk constitutes simply *a* concurrent proximate cause of the injuries. That multiple causes may have effectuated the loss does not negate any single cause; that multiple acts concurred in the infliction of injury does not nullify any single contributory act."

While no California court has construed policy provisions identical to those here, the Illinois Appellate Court did so in Carlson v. New York Life Insurance Co., 76 Ill.App.2d 187, 222 N.E.2d 363 and held that a

**37.** The insurer relies on the quotation in *Shafer* by this court of certain dicta in Stokes v. Police & Firemen's Ins., 109 Cal. App.2d Supp. 928, 243 P.2d 144, stating that the insurer could avoid liability by a "contributed" clause as in Evans v. Metropolitan Life Ins. Co. (1946) 26 Wash.2d 594, 174 P.2d 961. As pointed out in the insured's brief, both this court and the *Stokes* court overlooked the fact that in *Evans,* two different policies were involved: one contained the "contributed to" provision; the other did not, and the court denied recovery under both.

preexisting disease or illness, although contributing to the loss resulting from the accident, does not relieve the insurer of liability where the accident is the proximate cause of the loss. We think an identical result is compelled here under the *Brooks* rule and that the slightly different wording of the policy provisions here is not controlling.

We think the application of the rule is particularly apt here, where the insured was suffering from a condition that in and of itself would not have caused his death, but had to be set in motion by the accident. Thus, contrary to the insurer's contention, the evidence supports the conclusion of law that the insured died as a result of accidental bodily injury and was entitled to the double indemnity death benefits.

The judgment is affirmed.

## VALLEY DENTAL ASS'N, P.C. v. THE GREAT–WEST LIFE ASSURANCE CO.

Court of Appeals of Arizona, 1992.
173 Ariz. 327, 842 P.2d 1340.

EHRLICH, JUDGE.

The issue presented in this case is whether Gregory S. Christensen's death was "accidental" for purposes of his beneficiaries' recovery under the double indemnity portion of a life insurance policy. We hold that his death was not an accident and therefore reverse the summary judgment granted to the beneficiaries.

### I. FACTS AND PROCEDURAL HISTORY

#### A. *The Insurance Policy*

The Great–West Life Assurance Company ("Great–West") issued a group insurance policy to the American Dental Society, of which Christensen was a member. Named as the beneficiaries of the policy issued on Christensen's life were Valley Dental Association and Amalgamated Investment Resources ("the beneficiaries"). The policy amount was $350,000, with a provision for double indemnity in case of accidental death. The accidental death provision read: If a Member sustains bodily injury which: (1) is caused solely by accidental means; and (2) is sustained while he is insured under the Group Policy; and (3) results in his death; then the Company will pay an additional amount of insurance. Payment will be made only if death: (a) occurs within 90 days after the accident; (b) is a direct result of an accident; and (c) is unrelated to any other cause. The word "accident" is undefined.

#### B. *Christensen's Death*

The material facts are undisputed for purposes of this appeal. On September 27, 1987, Christensen picked up a 15–year–old female hitchhiker. After starting to take the girl in her intended direction, Christensen drove the car off the road in a remote area. He forced the girl at knife-point to perform oral sex on him and sexually assaulted her. He then grabbed her throat, announced "I have to kill you" and began choking her. The girl resisted and, in the struggle, they both fell out of the car, onto the ground. She grabbed the knife, but Christensen knocked it from her hand. He then got on top of her and placed both hands around her throat, choking her as he banged her head against the ground. She managed to kick Christensen in the face, knocking off his glasses. As he turned to get his glasses, the girl again picked up the knife. Christensen, having retrieved his glasses, approached the girl. She stabbed him in the leg. He backed away and the girl escaped. Christensen, whose left femoral artery had been severed, bled to death at the scene.

### C. *The Insurance Claim*

Following Christensen's death, the beneficiaries filed a claim with Great–West, seeking the death benefit of $350,000 plus the additional $350,000 accidental death benefit. Great–West paid the death benefit but denied the accidental death benefit, asserting that the death was not an accident. The beneficiaries then filed this suit under breach of contract and bad faith theories. On cross-motions for summary judgment, the trial court awarded the beneficiaries judgment on the breach of contract claim and awarded Great–West summary judgment on the bad-faith claim.

Great–West appealed. The interpretation of the insurance contract is a question of law for this court to decide independently of the conclusions of the trial court. Thomas v. Liberty Mutual Insurance Co., 173 Ariz. 322, 334, 842 P.2d 1335, 1337 (App.1992).

## II. Discussion

The insurance policy states that extra benefits will be paid if the insured dies of "accidental means." In Landress v. Phoenix Mutual Life Insurance Co., 291 U.S. 491, 497, 54 S.Ct. 461, 463, 78 L.Ed. 934 (1934), the Supreme Court held that, in such a policy, the mechanism or action causing the injury or death must have been accidental; it is not enough that the result was accidental or unintended.

Justice Cardozo dissented in Landress, decrying the court's distinction between means and results. 291 U.S. at 498–501, 54 S.Ct. at 463–464. In Knight v. Metropolitan Life Insurance Co., 103 Ariz. 100, 103–04, 437 P.2d 416, 419–20 (1968), our supreme court adopted the dissent:

> In an oft-quoted dissent which has now become the majority rule throughout the states, Justice Cardozo said: "The attempted distinction between accidental results and accidental means will plunge this branch of the law into a Serbonian Bog. Probably it is true to say that in the strictest sense and dealing with the region of physical nature there is no such thing as an accident. On the other hand, the average man is convinced that there is, and so certainly is the man who takes out a policy of accident insurance * * *. When a man has died in such a way that his death is spoken of as an accident, he has died because of an accident, and hence by accidental means. If there was no accident in the means, there was none in

the result, for the two were inseparable. There was an accident throughout, or there was no accident at all." [Citation omitted.]

* * *

[W]e are going to clarify our position and determine along with the growing majority rule that an accident is an accident whether it be in the "means" or the "result." [Footnote omitted.]

Knight died following a dive from the top of Coolidge Dam. An experienced diver, who indeed had jumped from this dam before, he nonetheless seemingly misjudged the distance and rolled onto his back from a swan dive before hitting the water. The court, after discussing the "average man" approach taken by Justice Cardozo in Landress, held that this was an accident, stating:

> One paying the premium for a policy which insures against "death by accidental means" * * * *intends to insure against the fortuitous, the unintentional, and the unexpected, that which happens through mishap, mischance or misjudgment.* When he pays that premium month after month he does not intend that any act committed by him, no matter how daring, reckless or foolhardy, be adjudged by a court under "reasonable man tests" or "natural and probable consequence" standards to deprive his beneficiary of contractual rights arising out of his unintended and unexpected and, therefore, accidental death. [Emphasis added.] The term "accidental means" as used in this policy should not be construed in a technical sense but should be given its ordinary and popular meaning according to common speech and usage and the understanding of the average man. [Citation omitted.] 103 Ariz. at 104, 437 P.2d at 420.

In urging that the "ordinary and popular meaning" be applied to the term "accident" in determining whether a death is covered by the accidental death provision of a policy, the court in Knight again acted in consonance with the then-growing majority of jurisdictions in applying the common understanding of "accident" as an event that is at least unexpected. As applied to an insured such as Christensen, [t]he general rule to be gleaned from the cases is that if the insured threatens to kill, or inflict serious bodily injury on, another person or assaults another person under circumstances making it likely the other person will respond with deadly force, and does so and kills the insured, the insured's death is not accidental. Hoffman, 669 P.2d at 417. See e.g., Howard, 474 So.2d at 1111; Cockrell v. Life Ins. Co., 692 F.2d 1164, 1168 (8th Cir.1982); James v. Aetna Life Ins. Co., 161 Ga.App. 64, 289 S.E.2d 290, 291 (1982); Butcher, 290 S.E.2d at 375–76; Byrd v. Life Ins. Co., 219 Va. 824, 252 S.E.2d 307, 310 (1979); Rodolph v. New York Life Ins. Co., 412 P.2d 610, 611–12 (Wyo.1966); Henry, 217 N.E.2d at 486; Perringer, 244 S.W.2d at 617; Meister, 179 P. at 916; Annot., 26 A.L.R.2d at 402; Couch on Insurance, § 41:204 at 300 ("essential" to coverage that insured not have provoked act). When there have been differing interpretations, the division "seems to arise from the courts' varying ideas regarding the degree of foresight which should be required of the insured. Cf. R. Keeton, Insurance Law § 5.4(f) (1971)." Carlyle, 551 P.2d at 666. The court in Knight, by referring to "the understanding of the average man," sought to strike a balance between focusing exclusively on the insured and the subjective state of mind that cannot comprehend death and the artificial "reasonable man" who would declare not an accident any "daring, reckless or foolhardy" act. 103 Ariz. at 104, 437 P.2d at 420.

Here, by any definition, Christensen's death was not an accident.[1] He created a situation in which another person had to fight for her life in order to survive. It was he who was armed with a knife and the intent to kill and, as was certain, the victim struggled against death and seized the weapon to defend herself. Christensen's resulting death cannot be classified as "fortuitous" or "unexpected," or as having occurred through "mishap, mischance or misjudgment." Knight, 103 Ariz. at 104, 437 P.2d at 420.

If there was no accident in the means, there was none in the result, for the two were inseparable. There was an accident throughout, or there was no accident at all. Id. at 103, 437 P.2d at 419 (quoting Landress, 291 U.S. at 501, 54 S.Ct. at 464 (Cardozo, J., dissenting)).

Accordingly, Great–West need not pay accidental death benefits under the policy.

* * *

The judgment in favor of the beneficiaries is reversed. The case is remanded to the trial court for further proceedings.

### *Notes*

1. In Knight v. Met Life Ins. Co., 103 Ariz. 100, 437 P.2d 416 (1968), cited in the principal case, the insured's death after swan dive off Coolidge Dam on Gila River was held covered given evidence that the insured was experienced at dare devil dives. Is Knight consistent with *Valley Dental*?

2. Should there be a criminal act exclusion in the policies discussed?

## WETZEL v. WESTINGHOUSE ELECTRIC CORP.

Superior Court of Pennsylvania, 1978.
258 Pa.Super. 500, 393 A.2d 470.

CERCONE, JUDGE:

Willy C.J. Wetzel died on March 16, 1975 at the hand of his son, Roy Wetzel. Roy Wetzel was tried by a jury for murder and voluntary

1. We are not in this opinion creating a criminal act exclusion in Christensen's insurance policy. It is for the insurance company, and not the court, to write its policy and the fact that an insured was engaged in criminal conduct does not in every case preclude a finding that a death or injury was accidental. Roque, 467 A.2d at 1129; Hoffman, 669 P.2d at 417.

manslaughter in the Court of Common Pleas of Beaver County and was found not guilty. Mary Margaret Wetzel, appellant and widow of Willy Wetzel, then brought this suit to recover the insurance proceeds from an accidental death policy issued on her husband's life. * * * The lower court found that Willy Wetzel's death did not occur through accidental means and therefore there could be no recovery under the insurance policy. The court granted defendant's motion for summary judgment and it is from that order this appeal comes to us. We reverse the decision of the lower court.

Willy Wetzel and his son, Roy Wetzel, were experts in the martial arts, including karate, and operated a school in Beaver County. On the day of Willy Wetzel's death, Roy had been working on his father's income tax return. Willy visited his son and began reading the completed tax forms. The testimony of Roy, admitted through an excerpt from the transcript in the criminal proceedings in Beaver County, describes the events that ensued. As Willy Wetzel started to sign the tax forms, he threw the pen against the drapes and began to scream obscenities. He walked toward the front door mumbling that he was going to lose his house, car and everything. Grabbing a Hawaiian sword, Willy Wetzel turned and let out a battle cry called a "kewah." The fight began.

Willy began to remove the sword from its case when Roy attempted to grab the case. Willy kicked Roy and the sword was bent in half. The hand-to-hand fight continued for approximately twenty-five minutes. Roy made several attempts to reach the telephone to call for help, but was stopped each time by his father's tactics. Finally, Roy placed nanchukas sticks, used in karate, around his father's head to try to render him unconscious. Shortly after that Roy realized his father was dead.

Based on these facts, we are faced with deciding whether the death of Willy Wetzel occurred through accidental means under the insurance policy in question. The Benefit Provisions of the Certificate of Insurance in this case read in part:

> "If, while insured under the Group Policy for Personal Accident Insurance, the Employe sustains bodily injuries solely through violent, external and accidental means, and within ninety days thereafter suffers any of the losses specified in Section C hereof as a direct result of such bodily injuries independently of all other causes, the Insurance Company shall pay the amount of the insurance specified for such loss * * * provided, however, that in no case shall any payment be made for death or any other loss which is:
>
> * * *

> (D) caused by or resulting from intentional self-destruction or intentionally self-inflicted injury, while sane or insane."

* * * The lower court opinion correctly stated that subsection (D) of the benefit provisions of the insurance contract in this case does not apply where the death was due to the acts of another. The difficult question arises when the policy does not contain a violation of law clause "or the commission of a crime exception and the injury is as a result of the insured's culpable conduct." Mohn v. American Casualty Co., 458 Pa. at 579, 326 A.2d at 348.

In Mohn v. American Casualty Co., supra, a father sued for expenses incurred when his son was fatally wounded by a police bullet while he was fleeing from a burglary. The insurance policy did not contain a violation of law clause, just as is the case with the policy before us. The *Mohn* case aptly discusses the split of authorities in this kind of case. One view is to preclude recovery when the insured's injury is the direct result of his own criminal conduct. However, even these jurisdictions that base the view on public policy involved grant an exception where the suit for recovery is brought by an innocent beneficiary.[40] Other jurisdictions refuse relief on the grounds that the occurrence was the foreseeable consequence of the acts of the insured and therefore not accidental.[41] This was the reasoning given in the opinion of the lower court and argued by appellee in the case before us. However, the Pennsylvania cases have expressly rejected the public policy reasoning as well as the use of the reasonably foreseeable test in denying recovery where the insured was involved in culpable conduct. Eisenman v. Hornberger, 438 Pa. 46, 264 A.2d 673 (1970); Beckham v. Travelers Ins. Co., 424 Pa. 107, 225 A.2d 532 (1967). Thus the *Mohn* court permitted recovery by the father.

In justifying its decision, the court in *Mohn,* supra, cited with approval Eisenman v. Hornberger, supra. There, two persons broke into a home and stole liquor. In the course of their crime, they lit matches in order to see their way. One of the matches lodged in a chair and caused a fire that destroyed the home. The insurance contract involved did not contain a "violation of law" clause and therefore recovery could not be denied. The court further explained that it was not convinced of any overriding public policy which would deny recovery.

> "There is no evidence whatsoever that the policy was procured *in contemplation* of the crime. Nor can the insurance policy be said to have *promoted* the unlawful act. Moreover, it seems equally implausible that denying coverage would serve as a crime *deterrent.* Finally, the insurance policy in no way saves the insured from the consequences of his criminal act." 438 Pa. at 50, 264 A.2d at 675.

When applying the factors used by the *Eisenman* court to the case before us, we reach the same result. Although stealing liquor is distinguishable from the criminal assault Willy Wetzel committed upon his

**40.** See 43 A.L.R.3d 1125 et seq. (1972).

**41.** See Id. at 1132–34.

son, Roy, both involved criminal conduct not covered by a violation of law clause in the policy. The facts of the case before us show Willy's rage was due to his income tax return and was in no way related to the procurement of the accidental insurance policy. Nor would denying recovery to an innocent beneficiary in this case deter this type of culpable conduct on the part of the insured.

The *Mohn* case explains that recovery must be placed on the actions of the insured and not on the acts of a third party. From this view it may be argued that it was reasonably foreseeable to Willy Wetzel that his son could have killed him due to his skill in the martial arts. However, "the modern legal trend is to abandon the former 'reasonably foreseeable' rule and treat the occurrence as accidental even though it resulted from the insured's criminal conduct." Mohn v. American Casualty Co., 458 Pa. at 585, 326 A.2d at 351. Our Supreme Court adhered to the modern trend in allowing recovery on an insurance policy in the *Mohn* case and in *Eisenman.*[42] In following this reasoning, we find that the death of Willy Wetzel was due to "violent, external and accidental means" within the meaning of the policy, and appellant, as an innocent beneficiary, must recover.

Order of the lower court reversed.

* * *

VAN DER VOORT and HESTER, JJ., dissent. * * *

### *Note*

The *Wetzel* case finds no overriding public policy which would *imply* the felony exclusion clause in all accident policies. But, what about an insured arsonist for hire who is burned to death by the premature explosion of his gasoline cans because a pilot light was on in the targeted house? See, Taylor v. John Hancock Mutual Life Insurance Co., 11 Ill.2d 227, 142 N.E.2d 5 (1957). Should professional criminals be allowed to provide this sort of family protection against the hazards of their trade as part of their estate planning?

Compare a later decision by the Pennsylvania Supreme Court, Roque v. Nationwide Mut. Ins. Co., 502 Pa. 615, 467 A.2d 1128 (1983), involving the same type of policy as in *Wetzel.* The insured trapped by police when he was burglarizing a home called out a warning to the policeman to get out or he would kill him. The insured carrying a gun emerged from a bedroom and was shot dead. The lower courts relying on *Wetzel* granted summary judgment for the insured's beneficiary. The Supreme Court reversed: "In *Mohn* [discussed at length in the Wetzel opinion] * * * there was nothing * * * to indicate that the insured had threatened or otherwise provoked the

**42.** See also Beckham v. Travelers Ins. Co., 424 Pa. 107, 225 A.2d 532 (1967). In *Beckham,* the mother of the insured sued to collect the insurance proceeds under the policy issued on the life of her son who died due to a self-administered overdose of narcotics. The court expressly abandoned the artificial distinction between accidental means and accidental results, as well as stating that the determination of what was "foreseeable" would be just as troublesome for the courts. Recovery under the policy was allowed.

officer who fired the fatal shot * * *. In this case, unlike *Mohn,* the insured repeatedly told police officers that he had a gun and intended to shoot to kill * * *. In these circumstances, it must be concluded that insured's conduct provoked the shooting and that the insured's death was thus not accidental." [*Wetzel* was not even cited.]

### *Notes, Examples and a Problem on Accidents, Etc.*

The expressions "accident," "accidental result" and "accidental means" must certainly be considered among the most intractable in the legal lexicon. Synonyms are hard to come by; impossible, indeed, for a straight "accident" policy, and seemingly useless in property or liability insurance where the substitution of "occurrence" for the word "accident" has led only to the redefinition of occurrence as an accident. Justice Cardozo's simplistic (as critics describe it) attempt to take "accidental means" out of the Serbonian Bog by equating it with "accidental result" may not have accomplished much more than to have moved the problem to another, albeit shallower, part of the Bog. The continuing inability to obtain a judicial consensus on the meaning of these expressions invites litigation which in turn affords numerous recent examples of situations which have reoccurred so often as to make possible rough categorizations. (The actual holdings in the examples are summarized at the conclusion of the notes.)

I. *Provocation Cases:*

1. Smith v. Equitable Life Assurance Society, 614 F.2d 720 (10th Cir.1980). Accidental means policy. Insured was killed by neighbor in a heated altercation over the location of the boundary line out west near Pinedale, Wyoming.

2. Floyd v. Equitable Life Assurance Society, 164 W.Va. 661, 264 S.E.2d 648 (1980). Accident policy. Husband was killed in a marital fight by his wife (the beneficiary). He was a 240 lb. ex-Marine who had on occasion beaten his wife, Elsie, who weighed 80 lbs. She had never fought back previously but on this occasion she took a knife and stabbed him. He said: "You can't hurt me. Stab me again." She did. Contrast with Funchess v. Metropolitan Life Insurance Co., 94 Ill.App.3d 871, 50 Ill.Dec. 598, 419 N.E.2d 706 (1981).

3. Davis v. Continental Cas. Co., 560 F.Supp. 723 (N.D.Miss.1983). Accidental means provision in a group life policy. Wife, Jimmie Nell, was the insured. H, the beneficiary claimant, was a classic instance of the battered husband, no doubt because of his philandering activities during which he sired children by at least two different paramours. Despite a history of her violent assaults by firearms and knives, Jimmie Nell never experienced that H would fight back except to disarm her. On the fatal occasion, according to the only testimony (H's), Jimmie Nell came after him with a shotgun, which he took away from her; she then confronted him with a knife, which he took away from her; thereupon she obtained a rifle, which discharged and killed her as they struggled.

II. *Aberrant Behavior of a Risky Nature—Flirting with Death*

a. *Over-Indulgence in Drugs or Alcohol.* "Glue Sniffing".

4. Patch v. Metropolitan Life Ins. Co., Inc., 733 F.2d 302 (4th Cir. 1984). A straight uncomplicated over-dose of heroin situation.

5. Pollard v. Metropolitan Life Insurance Co., 598 F.2d 1284 (3d Cir.1979). Accidental means policy, excluding "intentional self destruction and self inflicted injury while sane or insane." Insured died while attending a business conference. An autopsy showed acute alcohol and drug intoxication although immediate cause of death was asphyxiation brought on by choking on vomit.

6. Jones v. Prudential Insurance Co. of America, 24 D.C.R. 683; 10 O.R. 101 (1972). Accidental result policy. Insured put a plastic bag over his head and inhaled fumes from a bottle of Cutex nail polish.

7. Vihstadt v. Travelers Insurance Co., 103 N.M. 465, 709 P.2d 187 (1985). Health policy covering expenses "incurred on account of an accident" or "incurred as a result of accidental injury or sickness." A 14 year old girl quarreled with her natural mother and deliberately ingested 50 aspirin to "commit suicide or scare her mother." She recovered. Her step-mother sued on the policy to recover the medical expenses to treat the girls aspirin poisoning.

b. *Auto-erotic Cases*

8. Sigler v. Mutual Benefit Life Insurance Co., 506 F.Supp. 542 (S.D.Iowa 1981) (Aff'd 663 F.2d 49 (1981)). Accidental result policy. This phenomenon, as described by the court, involves the participant "hanging himself by the neck creating an asphyxial state in an attempt to stimulate nerve centers in the brain and heighten the masturbation experience." Insured was found dead in the noose he had placed on his neck.

9. International Underwriters v. Home Insurance Co., 500 F.Supp. 637, (E.D.Va.1980) (Rev'd 662 F.2d 1084 (4th Cir.1981)). Accidental result policy. Here the insured rigged an elaborate fail-safe pulley system which failed.

c. *Miscellaneous*

10. Ray v. Federated Guaranty Life Insurance Co., 381 So.2d 847 (La.App.1980). Accidental means policy. Insured was insane and under the delusion he had supernatural powers and could come to no harm. He held his head under water in bathtub and drowned. (The 2–year suicide expulsion in the policy had expired so only question was whether death was by accidental means.)

d. *Russian Roulette Variations*

11. Linder v. Prudential Insurance Co. of America, 39 N.C.App. 486, 250 S.E.2d 662 (1979). Accidental means policy. Husband (insured) and wife (beneficiary) were driving home from the airport. He expressed a desire to go to a movie, W demurred because of a headache. When they reached home H got out a pistol and tossed from hand to hand. The following conversation ensued.

H. "We are still not going to a movie?"

W. "No"

H. "Do you want me to do this?" (Raising pistol toward head)

W. (Looking away). "No"

At this point the gun discharged.

III. *Pre-existing Disease Cases*

a. *Over-exertion by cardiovascular victims*

12. Kasper v. Provident Life Insurance Co., 285 N.W.2d 548, 1 A.L.R. 4th 1305 (N.D.1979). Accident policy with pre-existing disease exclusion. Insured had heart condition and was obese but went hunting with friends. He collapsed and died while fighting a prairie fire started by his hunting party.

13. Gottfried v. Prudential Insurance Co. of America, 82 N.J. 478, 414 A.2d 544 (1980). Accidental result policy which excluded "loss which results * * * directly or indirectly from bodily infirmity." 44 year old insured with known arterio-sclerotic condition died of a heart attack playing basketball. (No autopsy was requested by the insurer. The beneficiary testified that her rabbi informed her that an autopsy was forbidden by her religion.)

b. *Pre-existing diseases and immediate causes*

14. Orman v. Prudential Insurance Co. of America, 296 N.W.2d 380 (Minn.1980). Accident policy excluding any loss caused or contributed to by infirmity or disease. Insured had a cerebral aneurism (classified as a disease) which burst. He toppled into a bathtub and drowned.

15. Nagel v. Continental Casualty Co., 498 F.Supp. 265 (D.C.Cal.1980). Group policy for bodily injury caused by an accident resulting directly and independently of all other causes in loss of life. Insured had a dismaying array of medical problems including epilepsy, cancer, emphysema, nephritis, acute colitis, diverticulitis. She had undergone an hysterectomy, mastectomy, removal of her adrenal glands, and had been given chemotherapy for her cancer because it was thought to be spreading into her bones. One evening she went out with the family for dinner, became ill, vomited, and was placed in a hospital where she was put on a soft diet and fed intravenously. A couple of mornings later she was found dead due to aspiration of gastric contents as a consequence of diverticulitis, coli or colitis—i.e., strangulation on her own vomit.

16. Doettl v. Colonial Life and Accident Ins. Co., 539 F.Supp. 176 (D.Mont.1982). Policy covered "bodily injuries effected solely through accidental means." Insured, a nurse, had arthritis. A male patient grabbed her and applied a "full nelson" wrestling hold. A flare-up of the arthritis left her totally disabled.

17. Williams v. Hartford Accident and Indemnity Co., 158 Cal.App.3d 229, 204 Cal.Rptr. 453 (1984). Policy covered injury caused by an accident which results directly and independently of other causes in the loss. Loss from disease was excluded. Insured while suffering from a retinal tear went jogging. The jog aggravated the original tear by inducing an additional amount of subretinal fluid which in turn caused other retinal tears. Corrective surgery failed and he lost all sight in the eye.

*Holdings in the Example Cases:*

1. For beneficiary—plus attorney's fee for late payment under a Wyoming statute. "Accidental nature of death is determined from the perspective of the insured. * * * Generally intentional killing of insured during a fight is deemed accidental when insured did not provoke such and was not the aggressor."

2. Summary judgment for insurer reversed. "We do not believe (Floyd's) statement at the time of stabbing compels the conclusion as a matter of law that the deceased could have reasonably foreseen his conduct would result in his death." (Note that the only evidence here was the deposition of Elsie, the beneficiary).

3. Held: for H, beneficiary. "It is generally held that when the insured is the aggressor and is armed with a deadly weapon his resulting death is not accidental. * * * In a family quarrel, however, courts are more inclined to find the death is an accident despite aggression by the insured with a deadly weapon." 560 F.Supp. at 729. Incidentally H had married one of his paramours before the verdict was handed down.

4. For insurer. "No mischance, misstep or mishap". But see: O'Toole v. New York Life Insurance Co., 671 F.2d 913 (5th Cir.1982).

5. Judgment for insurer sustained on appeal (2–1). The burden of proof on beneficiary to show that death was by accidental means was not met.

6. For insurer. (The English digest heading for this is: "Death by stupid act.")

7. For insurer. No suicide exclusion and no accident either.

8. For insurer. "* * * a reasonable person would foresee that placing a noose about his neck for the purpose of inducing asphyxia could result in his death. Certainly (he) did not intend to cause his own death, but * * * he should have expected that his actions could be fatal." In addition, the death was within an exclusion for injuries intentionally self-inflicted. But see: Connecticut General Life Insurance Co. v. Tommie, 619 S.W.2d 199 (Tex.Civ.App.1981).

9. For beneficiary. The trial court held this to be an "unnatural and unintentional death." The Fourth Circuit reversed, applying Virginia law.

10. For beneficiary. In Louisiana "death is accidental when shown to result from violent and external means where the injury is unforeseen by the victim."

11. For insurer.

12. For insurer. "No intervening means."

13. By divided vote, the Supreme Court reversed two lower court decisions and held for the beneficiary. A classic presentation of both views.

14. For beneficiary.

15. For beneficiary. (Note the similarity to the proximate cause rationale in the property insurance cases, Part B. In each of the last two examples the *immediate* cause of death was not excluded).

16. Held: for beneficiary. The opinion notes that Montana has overruled previous decisions in this area, e.g. one denying recovery for the death of an insured suffering from heart disease whose aorta ruptured causing him to fall off a chair and strike his head, the latter blow resulting in his death.

17. Held: for insurer. "[A] tautological review of the various opinions will tend to incline the analyst first to one view of the case and then the other. * * * [I]t is not true * * * that recovery may be had because the jog set in progress the events directly leading to loss of appellant's vision since that activity, except for the result, was not of such nature as properly to be characterized an "accident."

### *Note*

*Eliminating the More Esoteric Variety of "Accidents" by Policy Exclusions*

Justice Udall admonished in *Knight v. Met Life* (see *Valley Dental* ) that, if the accident insurers desire to exclude "reckless and foolhardy acts," they may do so with "simplicity and clarity of expression. It is an invitation which has been accepted (with limitations) by the industry. However, achieving simplicity and clarity of expression is not easy when attempting to circumscribe bizarre human behavior. It is quite doubtful that any court would accept a blanket exclusion of the results of "reckless and foolhardy (or stupid) acts" from coverage under an accident policy. At the same time, the attempt to extend by specific exclusion the catalogue of foolhardy behavior begun by Justice Udall would produce a policy of such length as to invite judicial derision.

Current policies (see Rider below) do seek to exclude some of the forms of aberrant behavior which have been particularly troublesome. Consider how some of these exclusions (such as "intentional self inflicted injury"; "medicine, drug or sedative * * * except when prescribed"; and the absorption or inhalation of toxic matter under any circumstances) might affect the decisions in the example cases set forth in the preceding note.

The exclusion from coverage of accidents incurred while committing or attempting to commit a felony certainly operates to deny recovery for many instances of foolhardy behavior. Note its potential applicability to the situation in the *Wetzel* case.

---

## RIDER

## ACCIDENTAL DEATH BENEFIT (ADB)

[*Reprinted with permission of Provident Mutual Life Insurance Company of Philadelphia* ]

**BENEFIT.** The Company will pay this benefit upon receipt of due proof that the Insured's death was the direct and independent result of accidental bodily injury. Such death must have occurred:

1. within one year after the injury was sustained; and
2. while this rider was in force.

The amount of this benefit, shown on page 3, will be paid as a part of the proceeds of this policy.

**EXCLUSIONS FROM COVERAGE.** This benefit will not be payable if the Insured's death was the result of:

1. a physical or mental disease or ailment;
2. suicide while sane or insane;
3. intentional, self-inflicted injury while sane or insane;
4. medicine, drug or sedative voluntarily taken or administered, except those prescribed by a duly licensed physician;
5. poison, chemical, chemical compound, gas or fumes voluntarily taken, administered, absorbed or inhaled;
6. committing or attempting to commit assault or a felony;
7. travel in or descent from an aircraft of any kind if the Insured;
   a. was a pilot, officer or member of its crew;
   b. was giving or receiving any training or instruction;
   c. had any duty aboard; or
   d. had any duty requiring descent from the aircraft;
8. war, declared or not, or any act incident to a war or to a conflict involving the armed forces of any country.

**AUTOPSY.** The Company at its own expense will have the right to examine the Insured's body and to perform an autopsy unless prohibited by law.

**INCONTESTABILITY.** The Company will not contest this rider after it has been in force during the Insured's lifetime for 2 years from the issue date of this policy, except for nonpayment of premiums.

**TERMINATION.** This rider will terminate:

1. upon written request;
2. 31 days after the due date of any unpaid premium for either this rider or the policy to which it is attached;
3. at attained age 70; or
4. upon the surrender, maturity, expiry or other termination of this policy.

Attached by PROVIDENT MUTUAL LIFE INSURANCE COMPANY OF PHILADELPHIA on the issue date of this policy.

---

### *Note*

Some current forms, while framed as "accidental result" policies, add the equivalent of the evidentiary conditions observed in property insurance cases—i.e. the "injury must cause either a visible mark on the exterior of the body or an internal injury revealed by an autopsy.

Does not such a provision revive, at least in part, the much criticized "accidental means" requirement?

As to internal injuries the above rider provides that the company has the right to an autopsy unless prohibited by law. What if religious objections are raised? Cf. Life Investors Insurance Co. of America v. Heline, 285 N.W.2d 31 (Iowa 1979).

Another express exclusion has been drafted successfully to forestall recovery where a pre-existing disease is connected with the insured's accident, to wit:

> "no payment shall be made for any loss resulting from any injury caused or contributed to by, or as a consequence of, any of the following excluded risks, *even though the proximate or precipitating cause of loss is accidental bodily injury* (emphasis added):
>
> (a) bodily or mental infirmity; or
>
> (b) disease * * *."

This provision was held to preclude recovery in the common situation where the insured with cardiovascular disease passes out and hits head on floor, the blow being the immediate cause of death. See Sekel v. Aetna Life Ins. Co., 704 F.2d 1335, 1336–1337 (5th Cir.1983) (applying Texas law).

### *A Problem*

X and Y engage in sport called "chicken" consisting of driving their respective cars at each other to see who will be the first to turn aside. For several passes Y gives way, but at last decides not to be "chicken". Both are killed. X has an accidental result type of policy. Y an accidental means variety. Should the respective insurers have to pay?

### *Problem*

### *The Burden of Proof in Suicide Cases*

Assume a life policy for $100,000 with double indemnity for accidental death. An exclusion exists as to intentionally self inflicted bodily injury or suicide. The CQV locked himself in a room and is later found dead from a gun shot wound. His gun is found nearby. Suppose the beneficiary files a claim on the life policy and the insurer asserts the exclusion. Suppose, instead, the beneficiary files a claim for double indemnity. Who has the burden of proof (persuasion) on the issues? See Evans v. National Life and Accident Ins. Co., 22 Ohio St.3d 87, 488 N.E.2d 1247 (1986).

## E. THAT THERE ARE GROUNDS FOR RESCINDING THE POLICY (MISREPRESENTATION OR CONCEALMENT)

See Cases and Materials in Part A.

# Chapter 10

# RIGHTS TO THE PROCEEDS OF THE POLICY

— **proving the loss**
— **beneficiary's rights**
— **change of beneficiary**
— **beneficiary as owner**
— **murder of the insured by the beneficiary**
— **multicoverages (subrogation in medical policies)**

## NORTH AMERICAN LIFE & CASUALTY CO. v. WOLTER

United States Court of Appeals, Fifth Circuit, 1979.
593 F.2d 609.

JAMES C. HILL, CIRCUIT JUDGE:

* * *

This case was initiated in the district court when North American Life and Casualty Company (North American) and the Minnesota Mutual Life Insurance Company (Minnesota Mutual), appellees herein, filed separate actions for declaratory judgment, alleging that they had issued certain insurance policies on the life of Rutheled B. Wolter who died from gunshot wounds to the neck soon after purchasing these policies. North American and Minnesota Mutual further alleged that certain information in their possession indicated that the death of Rutheled B. Wolter was possibly suicide and that access to other information regarding the insured's death had been denied them so as to prevent their complete investigation of the cause of death. The insurance companies requested the district court to declare their rights and liabilities to the beneficiaries of these life insurance policies which provided that if within two years from the date of issue, the death of the insured occurred by suicide, the liability of the companies would be limited to the return of premiums paid. The beneficiaries in the same actions filed counter-claims against North American and Minnesota Mutual for the face value of the life insurance policies.

* * * The jury, at the conclusion of testimony and evidence at trial, deliberated as to whether the death of Rutheled B. Wolter was an accident or a suicide, and returned with a verdict that the death was by accidental means. Based upon this verdict, the trial court * * * held that the face value of the life insurance policies was due to the beneficiaries with interest from the date of judgment. A final judgment was entered, and this appeal ensued over the issue of the court's award of interest.

Appellees contend that an award of interest is discretionary and that there is no evidence that the district court abused its discretion in failing to award interest to appellants. We disagree. Where a debt is certain in amount and payable at a certain time, interest follows recovery of the money due as a matter of law. * * * Relying principally on Edwards v. John O. Evans Construction Co., 155 Fla. 263, 19 So.2d 799 (1944), appellees argue that a court may refuse to award interest in extraordinary cases. While this may be true in some cases, under Florida law the award of interest is discretionary *only* in cases in equity. * * * The present case involves an action at law, notwithstanding the fact that the insurance companies beat the beneficiaries to the courthouse door by filing a declaratory judgment action. * * *

The only question remaining for us to resolve is the date upon which interest should commence to run. In actions *ex contractu* interest runs from the date the debt becomes due. * * * In the case of insurance contracts, the debt is "due" on the date the loss becomes payable under the terms of the policy. * * * The policies drafted in this case by North American and Minnesota Mutual provided that the loss became payable upon receipt of "due proof" of the insured's death. Minnesota Mutual received claim reports in September of 1976 and the death certificate in December of 1976; North American received claim forms and the death certificate on September 16, 1976. Appellants contend that they are entitled to interest dating from the receipt of the death certificates since that is the date the loss became due and payable.

Appellees argue that "due proof" of the insured's death was not furnished by simply supplying them with a copy of the death certificate. Relying primarily on Washington v. Metropolitan Life Insurance Co., 363 N.E.2d 683, 685 (Mass.1977), appellees contend that "the beneficiaries should have supplied information sufficient for the insurer to form an intelligent estimate as to whether the death came within the terms of the policy." * * * But in *Washington* the insurance policy required due proof of *death by accidental means,* a proof requirement much stricter than the one involved in the present case. In the absence of a requirement in the policy obligating the beneficiary to furnish proof of the *cause of death,* the insurer may only insist that the fact of death be shown with reasonable certainty.

Therefore, we reverse and remand this case to the district court with directions to amend the final judgment so as to allow interest to commence upon the date of receipt of the death certificates.

## VICTOR v. MANHATTAN LIFE INSURANCE CO.

Missouri Court of Appeals, Eastern District, Division Two, 1989.
772 S.W.2d 826.

KAROHL, J.

This action involves a suit by plaintiffs, David Victor, Betty Victor, Richard Victor and Deborah Victor, in their capacity as named beneficiaries of Morris Victor in a group life insurance policy issued by defendant Manhattan Life Insurance Company. Morris Victor died on September 23, 1981. Plaintiffs filed a claim for benefits in September, 1983, and promptly received the face amount of the policy. They ultimately sued for loss of use of proceeds occasioned by an eighteen month delay in payment, interest thereon and vexatious delay damages under § 375.420 RSMo 1978. The policy was procured from Manhattan Life by Thrifty Drug Company, Inc., an Illinois corporation, on behalf of Morris Victor, a retired officer of Thrifty, and other employees * * *.

* * *

The group life insurance policy was an exhibit incorporated in the stipulated facts. Resolution of the appeal issues largely depends on the provisions of Section 8, the insuring clause. It reads, "[u]pon receipt by the Insurance Company of *due proof in writing* that an Individual insured hereunder *shall have died*, the Insurance Company shall pay, subject to the terms hereof, to the Beneficiary of record of such Individual, the amount of life insurance, if any, enforce [sic] hereunder on account of any such Individual in accordance with Section 7, at the date of death." (Our emphasis).

The parties do not dispute the face amount of the coverage, or, plaintiffs' status as beneficiaries. The provision in the insuring clause, "subject to the terms hereof" is not relied on as a defense. The policy contains no provision defining or detailing elements of "proof of loss." Particularly, there is no provision in the policy that requires the named beneficiaries, or any of them, to personally perform any function, including notification that the insured died, in order to obtain the proceeds of the policy. All that is required, per Section 8, is the above emphasized written proof that the insured has died. Joseph Victor filed such proof of death with Manhattan Life in March, 1982. At that time Manhattan Life had in its own records the names of all beneficiaries and the address of at least one of them.

* * *

We first dispose of defendant's claim that nothing it did or failed to do was vexatious. According to the terms of its own policy Manhattan Life required only a proof of death to create an obligation to pay to the named beneficiaries the face amount of the policy. It received proof of death of Morris Victor in March, 1982. At that time it had in its own records the names of the beneficiaries and a means to directly contact them for the purpose of payment. However, payment was not made until September, 1983. The narrow question is whether the eighteen month delay in payment of life insurance proceeds was, as a matter of fact, vexatious delay.

Although Joseph Victor [insured's nephew and executor of the estate] filed a claim for benefits this competing claim was not, as a matter of fact, sufficient to overcome the legal duty under the insurance contract to make payment. "The existence of a litigable issue, either factual or legal, does not preclude a vexatious penalty where there is evidence the insurer's attitude was vexatious and recalcitrant." DeWitt v. American Family Mutual Insurance Co., 667 S.W.2d 700, 710 (Mo. banc 1984). DeWitt also says direct and specific evidence to show vexatious refusal is not required. Id. It instructs that the issue of vexatious is a factual matter and the fact finder "may find vexatious delay upon a general survey and a consideration of the whole testimony and all the facts and circumstances in connection with the case." Id. In the present case Manhattan Life's reliance on the competing claim of Joseph Victor and on its instructions given to its general agent to obtain a claim filed by plaintiffs as beneficiaries and the withdrawal of Joseph Victor's claim, was found by the trial court to be insufficient to avoid a finding of vexatious delay. We find no error in that finding of fact.

DeWitt considered the same point of law but in the context of a claim for fire insurance benefits. What the court said in DeWitt is equally applicable to a § 375.420 RSMo 1978 claim under a life insurance policy. Plaintiffs' evidence was sufficient to support a finding that Manhattan Life's failure to timely process payment was willful and without reasonable cause. In Handly v. Lyons, 475 S.W.2d 451 (Mo.App. 1971) the court considered a vexatious delay penalty claim in addition to life insurance benefits. The court noted that the insurance company "had received all information it had sought concerning the policy * * * more than six weeks before paying the policy benefits to Maxwell Lyons, the executor." Id. at 461. The trial court there found that during the entire six week period the company "did absolutely nothing to determine the circumstances of the document's disposition and whereabouts, except to inquire of the executor if there was a carbon copy in the deceased's personal effects." Id. The court then concluded: "Metropolitan's failure to contact and communicate with, and seek information from plaintiffs is significant in the instant question, as is Metropolitan's failure to follow an alternative procedure such as interpleader, which would have relieved it of responsibility to plaintiffs." Id.

Manhattan Life Insurance Company's actions in the present case were similar to those of Metropolitan in the Handly case. Handly affirmed a finding that failure to promptly process and pay life insurance benefits was vexatious. We find, as Handly found, that the evidence was sufficient to support a finding of vexatious delay.

Even if the facts support a finding of vexatious delay, for two related reasons Manhattan Life claims it was entitled to judgment and is now entitled to a reversal. Both are matters of law. First, Manhattan claims that plaintiffs have no claim under § 375.420 RSMo 1978 because they were paid the face amount of the policy in September 1983, and filed suit on that section in Count VIII on March 5, 1986. It argues that payment and receipt of the face amount of the policy removed any possibility that plaintiffs had a "loss," as that word is used in § 375.420, and in the absence of a loss no interest or penalty damages are authorized. Second, in the event the statute does apply, by accepting payment plaintiffs either waived any further claim under the policy, or their claim is barred by the doctrine of payment.

* * *

We held in State ex rel. United States Fidelity & Guaranty Company v. Walsh, 540 S.W.2d 137 (Mo.App.1976) a judgment under § 375.420 RSMo 1969, must be for an aggregate sum of a balance due on the insurance contract and penalties. Id. at 141. In Walsh the claimant had recovered a judgment in a separate suit for his entire claim with interest against a construction contractor. Claimant was paid and satisfied the judgment. We prohibited a judge from proceeding in a separate suit where the suit involved only a claim for statutory penalty and attorney's fees against a surety. The satisfaction of judgment "eliminated the debt or loss to which vexatious damages must be appended." Id. Here the face amount of the policy was paid but an obligation for policy damages remained. Penalty damages are authorized only if appended to "loss and interest." However, a penalty is allowable only as a percentage of the loss. Gosnell v. Camden Fire Insurance Ass'n of Camden, N.J., 109 S.W.2d 59, 72 (Mo.App.1937). The judgment here on appeal awarded penalties together with a judgment for the damages. There was no independent judgment for the loss with interest and no satisfaction of such judgment. In the present case the payment of face value after vexatious delay was only a partial payment of Manhattan's debt, not full payment. The partial payment did not eliminate the debt. Here the court could have entered a judgment for an unpaid balance under the policy without only penalty award or attorney's fees. That was not possible in Walsh.

* * *

Nor do we find plaintiffs' acceptance of the face amount of the policy in September 1983, constitutes either a waiver or payment in full. The facts support a finding plaintiffs received payment of the face amount of the policy before they learned Joseph Victor had filed a proof of death of Morris Victor in March 1982, and they were entitled to payment eighteen months earlier. Accordingly, when they accepted payment they were not informed that they might be entitled to damages based upon the payment provisions of the policy and a previous filing of notice of death. Under these circumstances no waiver occurred. Acceptance of the face amount of the policy, was payment by Manhattan Life of less than the sum owed. Such payment was not consideration for an accord and satisfaction or the defense of payment in full.

Manhattan Life also argues plaintiffs settled their claims against Joseph Victor; they thereby recovered from Joseph Victor exactly the same damages for which the trial court granted plaintiffs' judgment against Manhattan Life; but, plaintiffs are entitled to only one satisfaction of the loss of use damages, hence, the court erred in allowing plaintiffs to twice recover the same claim. This argument has merit. On April 21, 1986, plaintiffs settled with Joseph Victor their "claims" against Joseph Victor. At that time they settled Count I, a contest of the will of Morris Victor, and Counts III–V premised on common law claims which resulted from the actions of Joseph Victor in filing a proof of death with Manhattan Life and requesting payment as beneficiary and, at the same time, not notifying plaintiffs of their rights as beneficiaries under the policy. According to plaintiffs' settlement agreement it is clear that Joseph Victor settled with plaintiffs in April 1986, for their loss of use of the proceeds of the life insurance policy from March 1982, until payment in September 1983. Joseph Victor paid plaintiffs $55,000 in April 1986, to settle the will contest and the loss of use claims. The settlement agreement did not assign a separate value to those claims.

The court justified awarding plaintiffs judgment for the same damages against Manhattan Life as follows:

> Defendant is not entitled to a set-off against any judgment rendered against it herein on the basis of a settlement previously reached between Plaintiffs and Joseph Victor. This court has found, supra, that the policy proceeds were due and owing to Plaintiffs in March 1982; nothing Joseph Victor subsequently did or did not do altered that legal liability. (In addition, Joseph Victor and Defendant were not liable in tort for the same injury as is required under § 537.060, R.S.Mo.)

The difficulty with the finding of the court lies in the observation, "nothing Joseph Victor subsequently did or did not do altered that legal liability." If we construe the word liability to mean obligation to pay, the statement is correct. However, that is not responsive to the defense which correctly claims plaintiffs can only have one satisfaction for the same demand. See, State ex rel. United States Fidelity & Guaranty v. Walsh, 540 S.W.2d 137 at 141. In the sense of credit, something Joseph Victor did after March 1982, has, as a matter of law, altered plaintiffs' right to recover judgment for loss of use damages on late payment of the policy proceeds. What Joseph Victor did was repay plaintiffs, by payment under a settlement, the same and only "loss" plaintiffs now claim under § 375.420. Plaintiffs are not entitled to recover a loss from Joseph Victor and also recover the same loss under the statutory claim against Manhattan Life. This appeal does not involve any claims for contribution between Joseph Victor and Manhattan Life. Accordingly, the provisions of § 537.060 RSMo 1986, relating to tort-feasor contribution, are not relevant to Manhattan Life's defense. The defense is based upon Manhattan Life's affirmative defense that plaintiffs have been paid the "loss" they claim. Plaintiffs' loss was the direct result of acts of Joseph Victor which led to the statutory liability of Manhattan Life.

Accordingly, the trial court properly determined the amount of loss to be $12,825 but erred in granting judgment against Manhattan Life for this amount as it was previously recovered in the settlement. The judgment must be reversed, in part, to withdraw from the judgment a claim previously satisfied, after suit but before judgment.

Plaintiffs' respond that the settlement with Joseph Victor involved both the will contest and the loss of use claims and Manhattan Life has not proven plaintiffs' claim has been satisfied. However, the judgment in the present case determined plaintiffs' loss of use damages to be $12,825. Plaintiffs did not appeal and do not contest the amount or manner of calculation of that sum. The settlement expressly settled the loss of use claims. This sum is much less than the total settlement of $55,000. The record is devoid of any evidence that the $55,000 settlement paid less than all of the "loss of use" damages. The documentary evidence, especially the settlement agreement, requires a finding that the settlement, in excess of the loss of use damages, fully compensated plaintiffs for such damages. Plaintiffs are not entitled again to recover by judgment against Manhattan Life $12,825 as "loss of use" damages.

The prejudgment interest must be recalculated from September 1983, to April 21, 1986, (the recovery date) not to the date of judgment in July 1988. By using the legal rate of interest of nine percent the proper amount is $2,981.81. It is not clear from the settlement of the claims against Joseph Victor that pre-judgment interest was included in the settlement. Further, § 375.420 expressly creates a statutory right to prejudgment interest. In the absence of any evidence presettlement interest was paid in the settlement, Manhattan Life is not entitled to a finding such interest is improper as a double recovery.

The penalty awards must be recalculated. The attorney's fees, were found by the court to be one-third of the damages, plus prejudgment interest, plus penalty. By applying the formula adopted by the trial court and the percentage used we find the attorney's fees authorized by statute to be $5,746.44. The award of $1,432.50, under the penalty provisions as set forth in § 375.420, remains unchanged because it was calculated only on the loss of use figure as determined by the trial court, $12,825.

Summarizing the above, the judgment of the trial court is affirmed in part and reversed in part so as to be as follows:

| | |
|---|---|
| 1. Damages, late payment of proceeds from March 1982 to September 1983: | |
| ($95,000 × .09 × 18/12) | $12,825.00 |
| 2. Pre-judgment interest on damages from September 1983 to April 21, 1986: | |
| ($12,825 × .09 × 31) | 2,981.81 |

| | |
|---|---|
| 3. Penalty: | |
| (10% of $12,825 after first $1,500, 20% of first $1,500) | 1,432.50 |
| 4. Attorney's fees: | |
| (33⅓% of total of 1, 2 and 3 above) | 5,746.44 |
| TOTAL: | $22,985.75 |
| Less the same damages previously recovered by plaintiffs by settlement with another | 12,825.00 |
| Judgment for plaintiffs | $10,160.75 |

We affirm the judgment in part and reverse in part. We remand for entry of judgment in accord with this opinion.

### *Notes*

1. Despite certain language in the Wolter case, is it not true that the beneficiary of a life insurance policy should *always* have the burden of establishing the "fact" of the policy holder's death, as distinct from the burden of showing the "cause" of death as in accident policies.

2. Allowance of pre-judgment interest is a matter of much divergence in state law. In any event the query arises here as to whether it should date from:

a. time of death?

b. time of presentation of claim?

c. time of "proof" of death?

What argument could be made for each of these?

3. Mo.R.S. 375.420 reads:

**Sec. 375.420. Vexatious refusal, to pay claim damages for, exception**

In any action against any insurance company to recover the amount of any loss under a policy of automobile, fire, cyclone, lightning, life, health, accident, employers' liability, burglary, theft, embezzlement, fidelity, indemnity, marine or other insurance except automobile liability insurance, if it appears from the evidence that such company has refused to pay such loss without reasonable cause or excuse, the court or jury may, in addition to the amount thereof and interest, allow the plaintiff damages not to exceed twenty percent of the first fifteen hundred dollars of the loss, and ten percent of the amount of the loss in excess of fifteen hundred dollars and a reasonable attorney's fee; and the court shall enter judgment for the aggregate sum found in the verdict.

## LEONARD v. OCCIDENTAL LIFE INSURANCE CO.

Court of Appeal of California, 1973.
31 Cal.App.3d 117, 106 Cal.Rptr. 899.

DEVINE, PRESIDING JUSTICE.

Selma Leonard, individually and as administratrix of the estate of Andrew Leonard, deceased, appeals from a summary judgment for respondent, Occidental Life Insurance Company of California. By her complaint, plaintiff sought recovery of her alleged community property interest in two life insurance policies on the life of her deceased husband. Defendant answered, setting up the affirmative defense that, pursuant to the terms of the policies, it had paid the designated beneficiaries, Andrew Leonard, Jr., Joseph Leonard, Juanita Belec, and appellant, all of the benefits payable under the policies.

Appellant is the widow of Andrew Leonard, who died on July 8, 1969. Andrew and Selma were married in 1962. Andrew then had two sons and a daughter by a prior marriage. All were adults and married. At the time of his death, Andrew left two paid-up life insurance policies with respondent company. The beneficiaries in Group Life Insurance Policy 9134–LD were the three adult children; the beneficiaries in Group Life Insurance Policy 5500–K were appellant Selma Leonard and the three children. On August 28, 1969, full benefits pursuant to the terms of policy 9134–LD were paid the beneficiaries, the three children. On September 17 and 18, 1969, full benefits pursuant to the terms of policy 5500–K were paid to appellant and the three children. It was not until September 23, 1969, that appellant gave written notice to respondent of her claim to community interest in these policies. For present purposes, it is conceded that the premiums had been paid by the husband with community funds.

The trial court granted the motion for summary judgment because of Insurance Code section 10172, holding that respondent had discharged its obligations under the policies by making payment to the beneficiaries before having received notice of claim by the widow. Section 10172 provided, in pertinent part: "Notwithstanding the provisions of Sections [5105] and [5125] of the Civil Code, when the proceeds of, or payments under, a life insurance policy become payable and the insurer makes payment thereof in accordance with the terms of the policy, or in accordance with the terms of any written assignment thereof if the policy has been assigned, such payment shall fully discharge the insurer from all claims under such policy unless, before such payment is made, the insurer has received, at its home office, written notice * * *."

The contention on appeal is that because Insurance Code section 10172, construed literally, did not allow appellant, as the widow of the insured, a reasonable time within which to assert her claim, the court's reliance on the statute resulted in depriving her of due process of law and that the statute as so interpreted is unconstitutional.

In Blethen v. Pacific Mut. Life Ins. Co., 198 Cal. 91, 243 P. 431, it was recognized that the insurance company, having contracted with the husband and having promised to pay the proceeds of the policy to whomsoever he designated, could do nothing but fulfill its contract in the absence of notice of any adverse claim. This was even before the Legislature gave specific approval and assurance to life insurance companies by enacting section 10172. The court balanced the interests of wives who are ignorant of their husbands' affairs and those who may be defrauded by connivance with officials of the insurer against serious impairment of the usefulness of life insurance policies which would result from the almost intolerable burden of determining in each instance prior to payment whether or not the premiums were paid out of community funds and, if so, what proportion was so paid, as well as the burden of investigating any change in the marital situation and relations of the insured. The court ruled as it did "in harmony with a sound public policy having for its purpose the promotion of the free writing of life insurance". The *Blethen* case has remained intact and its ruling has been reinforced by the enactment of section 10172. The reasons given by the Supreme Court in *Blethen* remain equally valid today. * * *

It is contended by appellant that in order to save its constitutionality section 10172 must be regarded as allowing a reasonable time for a widow to give the written notice at the home office. But what is a reasonable time? Appellant asserts that the 72–day period is a reasonable one. If this were so even in a single case, probably few insurers would deem it prudent to make payment until at least that time had expired, and probably more. But one of the prime purposes of life insurance is to place money at the ready disposal of the beneficiaries soon after the death of the insured. The policy in the instant case, as in many others, calls for immediate payment. At first blush, it might seem that a widow's rights, if she be a named beneficiary, would not be subjected to delay by requiring a reasonable time for a wife to appear. But this does not follow. The insurer would have to find, at its peril, that the lady named as beneficiary truly was the wife of the insured at the moment of his death. Although in most cases it is likely that she would be, an insurer could not well take the chance of paying and discovering that there had been a change in the marital situation. But this is not all. The company, in order to avoid possible double payment, would have to postpone honoring the named beneficiary, even if she be described as wife, until the company has made itself sure that none of the premiums had been paid from community property of the decedent and a former wife, if the policy were not covered by dissolution decree or agreement, as in Grimm v. Grimm, 26 Cal.2d 173, 157 P.2d 841. The interpretation contended for by plaintiff would likely be of disadvantage to a vast majority of wives who are named as beneficiaries and who survive their husbands, because of the compulsion placed upon insurers to investigate marital situations to a considerable extent before making payment.

Other complications which suggest themselves are those relating to those life insurance policies, the purpose of which is the carrying on of a business. Payment could not safely be made to partners or associates named as beneficiaries until that vague period known as a "reasonable time" for a wife or possibly a former wife to appear had expired. Then, there is the matter of interest. If the policy calls for an immediate payment, as the one in this case does, interest must be paid from the time the application becomes due and payable. (Nesbit v. MacDonald, 203 Cal. 219, 222, 263 P. 1027; Flynn v. California Casket Co., 105

Cal.App.2d 196, 208, 233 P.2d 131.) Apparently the insurer would be obliged to pay interest, although it could not safely make payment to the named beneficiary. It is not a sufficient answer to these difficulties to say that the insurer would have the right to interplead. Interpleader takes time and money. The Legislature has decided, by enactment of section 10172, that the balance of necessities or convenience is in favor of prompt payment. Recovery from beneficiaries who have been paid something to which they were not entitled is provided for by section 10175 of the Insurance Code. No doubt this provision is not effective in some cases and is less ready in all where widows seek to enforce their claims. But again, the Legislature was not obliged to provide the best possible remedy for some widows who were not informed of their husbands' affairs, at the expense of delayed payments to a multitude of beneficiaries, including widows among them.

Appellant argues that although there is nothing in the record to show that the insurer at all times had knowledge of her standing as a wife, it must be assumed that within its file it would be disclosed that the decedent did have a wife and that premiums were deducted from his earnings. But even if it were so assumed, these facts would not diminish the protection given to the insurer by section 10172. The insurer need not make an examination or establish a cross-index system in order to inform itself of possible claimants other than the named beneficiaries. In Morrison v. Mutual L. Ins. of N.Y., supra, it was held that the mere fact of receipt of premiums from the wife could not establish knowledge of the company that she was the owner of plaintiff's policy (15 Cal.2d 587, 103 P.2d 963).

It is further argued by appellant that the company surely knew that the decedent had a wife because it made payment under policy 5500–K, not only to decedent's three children, but also to her as fourth beneficiary. Here again, because of section 10172 the company was not obliged to make inquiry. It is, of course, possible for a wife to agree with her husband that others may be named as beneficiaries. The company need not investigate the relationship, whether cordial or hostile, of those persons to whom by the terms of the policy it must make payment.

* * *

The judgment is affirmed.

## *Notes*

1. *Pay now and regret later. When to interplead*

According to Leonard the insurer is reasonably secure in paying immediately to the beneficiary of record. But, if the company receives notice of a claim adverse to that of the named beneficiary before disbursement of the proceeds, should it invariably interplead (a litigational process quite detrimental to the named beneficiary in any event)? Or, in the interest of prompt distribution of the monies, should it be given considerable discretion, leaving it to the intervening claimant to proceed directly against the beneficiary in doubtful cases? Consider the insurer's problem in Butler v. Metropolitan Life Ins. Co., 500 F.Supp. 661 (D.C.D.C.1980). The insurer issued a policy on Kitrell pursuant to the Federal Employees Group Life Insurance Act (FEGLIA). FEGLIA mandates that, when an insured fails to name a beneficiary and is not married, the proceeds be paid to the "parents" of the insured. Kitrell's insurance situation at death seemed to meet these specifications, so the insurer paid one half of the proceeds to his mother and the other one-half to the "biological" father. However, the "biological" father had never married his mother, and had deserted Kitrell before birth. Holding that under the D.C.Code a biological father is not treated as a "parent" for all purposes, the court held that the insurer had paid at its peril and should have interpleaded. Metropolitan's assertion that this conclusion will work an administrative nightmare in the processing of FEGLIA claims was brushed aside as "without merit".

2. When insurer is made aware that the named beneficiary may have been involved in the murder of the insured an obligation of good faith requires a reasonable and prudent prepayment investigation. Otherwise the insurer also will have to pay the contingent beneficiary. Harper v. Prudential Ins. Co. of America, 223 Kan. 358, 662 P.2d 1264 (1983). The potential of dual exposure to bad faith claims suggests interpleader in such cases.

California Insurance Code

### § 10172. Discharge of insurer by payment

Notwithstanding Sections 751 and 1100 of the Family Code, when the proceeds of, or payments under, a life insurance policy become payable and the insurer makes payment thereof in accordance with the terms of the policy, or in accordance with the terms of any written assignment thereof if the policy has been assigned, such payment shall fully discharge the insurer from all claims under such policy unless, before such payment is made, the insurer has received, at its home office, written notice by or on behalf of some other person that such other person claims to be entitled to such payment or some interest in the policy.

### § 10172.5. Failure to pay within 30 days of death of insured; interest; notice to beneficiaries

(a) Notwithstanding any other provision of law, each insurer admitted to transact life insurance in this state which fails or refuses to pay the proceeds of, or payments under, any policy of life insurance issued by it within 30 days after the date of death of the insured shall pay interest, at a rate not less than the then current rate of interest on death proceeds left on deposit with the insurer computed from the date of the insured's death, on any moneys payable and unpaid after the expiration of such 30–day period. This section shall apply only to deaths of insureds which occur on or after January 1, 1976.

(b) Nothing in this section shall be construed to allow any insurer admitted to transact life insurance in this state to withhold payment of money payable under a life insurance policy to any beneficiary for a period longer than reasonably necessary to transmit such payment. Whenever possible payment shall be made within 30 days after the date of death of the insured.

(c) In any case in which interest on the proceeds of, or payments under, any policy of life insurance becomes payable pursuant to subdivision (a), the insurer shall notify the named beneficiary or beneficiaries at their last known address that interest will be paid on the proceeds of, or payments under, such policy from the date of death of the named insured. Such notice shall specify the rate of interest to be paid.

(d) This section shall not require the payment of interest in any case in which the beneficiary elects in writing delivered to the insurer to receive the proceeds of, or payments under, the policy by any means other than a lump sum payment thereof.

## IN RE THE MARRIAGE OF O'CONNELL.

Court of Appeal, Sixth District, 1992.
8 Cal.App.4th 565, 10 Cal.Rptr.2d 334.

COTTLE, ACTING PRESIDING J.

INTRODUCTION

John O'Connell died on December 25, 1990, leaving two life insurance policies sponsored by his employer totaling $212,000, according to his widow, Nona O'Connell. At issue is whether John's ex-wife, Raytha O'Connell, and their son, Richard, are entitled to two-thirds of the insurance proceeds because of a court order requiring they be designated as beneficiaries of the policies. Nona, as an individual and as executrix of John's estate, appeals from an order denying her motion to vacate the order that John designate Raytha and Richard as joint life insurance beneficiaries with Nona. Nona contends the court lacked jurisdiction to make the original order because it was beyond the court's power, the life insurance was not properly before the court, and Nona received no prior notice of the request to modify the life insurance. Facts are stated where relevant. For the reasons stated below, we will affirm the order.

*Facts*

On July 15, 1985, John, a design specialist for Lockheed Missiles and Space Co., filed for dissolution of his 16–year marriage to Raytha. In July 1986 the parties stipulated to bifurcate the proceedings as to the issue of status. On November 12, 1986, their marriage was dissolved with the court reserving jurisdiction over "all other issues in this proceeding, including, but not limited to, division of property and debts, spousal support, child support and injunctive orders."

According to Nona, John married her on November 14, 1986, and designated her the beneficiary of life insurance provided through Lockheed.

On December 30, 1987, after trial of remaining issues, the court ordered John to pay monthly spousal support of $651 and child support of $912 for two minor children. This amended judgment also divided the parties' property and reserved jurisdiction over other issues. There was no disposition of John's life insurance.

By stipulation and order filed April 18, 1990, the parties agreed that child support would be reduced to $450 and spousal support to $200 monthly as of September 1, 1989.

On June 4, 1990, John filed a motion seeking a reduction in child and spousal support due to his disability. Raytha offered, by letter and telephone call but without a formal responsive pleading, to agree to reduction if she alone or she and their children were named beneficiaries of John's life insurance. According to Nona, John did not appear at the hearing on July 27, 1990, due to illness. At the hearing John's counsel objected to the request to modify the insurance because it was not made through formal pleadings, it would be unfair to Nona, John had no obligation to support his adult son, and both children would be entitled to social security benefits on John's death if he survived to the age of 62 on October 17, 1990. The court ordered reductions in monthly spousal support to nothing and child support to $125 during John's disability and, as child and spousal support, that John name Raytha and Richard, his minor son, as beneficiaries of his life insurance along with Nona. This order was served on John on September 20, 1990.

John died on December 25, 1990, without providing for his children in his will. According to Nona, John was covered by two life insurance policies purchased through his employer, a $112,000 basic policy and a $100,000 optional policy, the latter purchased by John's earnings without his employer's contribution.

On January 15, 1991, Raytha filed a motion seeking enforcement of the life insurance modification order and alleging John did not change beneficiaries before he died. On January 31, 1991, the court granted Nona's request to intervene in this action. Nona was appointed the executrix of John's estate on March 4, 1991.

On March 15, 1991, Nona filed a motion to vacate the order modifying the life insurance. The motion was denied at a hearing on May 10, 1991, for reasons partly quoted below.

## Discussion

1. Was the Marital Dissolution Court Empowered to Order the Designation of Life Insurance Beneficiaries as a Support Substitute?

In a dissolution action the court can order a spouse as a form of support to maintain life insurance to benefit either the other spouse or a minor child. Section 4801.4 of the Family Law Act (§ 4000 et seq.), cited in the trial court's statement of decision, provides in pertinent part: "For the purposes of Section 4801, where it is just and reasonable in view of the circumstances of the respective parties, the court, in determining the needs of a supported spouse, may include an amount sufficient to purchase an annuity for the supported spouse or to maintain insurance for the benefit of the supported spouse on the life of the spouse required to make the payment of support, * * * so that the supported spouse will not be left without means for support in the event that the order for support is terminated by the death of the party required to make the payment of support. Except as otherwise agreed to by the parties in writing, an order made under this section may be modified or terminated at the discretion of the court at any time prior to the death of the party required to make the payment of support."

As explained in In re Marriage of Ziegler (1989) 207 Cal.App.3d 788, 255 Cal.Rptr. 100: "[T]he Law Revision Commission comments to section 4801.4 * * * state: 'If insurance is already in force on the life of the support obligor, this section authorizes the court to order that the support obligor maintain some or all of the insurance in force and name the supported spouse as the beneficiary of the insurance.'" (Id. at p. 791, 255 Cal.Rptr. 100.) The statute authorized a court to require an ex-husband to maintain a military survivor benefit plan as a form of annuity for his ex-wife. (Ibid.)

* * *

Nona also contends this order violates the rule that a spousal support obligation ordinarily ends on the obligor's death. (§ 4801, subd. (b).) Ziegler, supra, 207 Cal.App.3d 788, 255 Cal.Rptr. 100, also rejected this contention. "Section 4801.4 does not change this rule. (Cal.Law Revision Com. com., 12A West's Ann.Civ.Code, supra, § 4801.4 * * *.)" (Id. at p. 792, 255 Cal.Rptr. 100.) The obligor's death still ends the obligor's support obligation, specifically to maintain the insurance or annuity, and creates a new obligation in the insurer or annuity provider to the supported spouse. (Ibid.)

On the same reasoning, provision of insurance for a minor does not extend the obligor's child support obligation beyond the obligor's death. Even if it did, a child support obligation survives the obligor's death and becomes the obligation of the obligor's estate. (Franklin Life Ins. Co., supra, 249 Cal.App.2d 623, 631, 57 Cal.Rptr. 652; In re Marriage of Gregory (1991) 230 Cal.App.3d 112, 115–116, 281 Cal.Rptr. 188.)

Thus, courts have the power in marital dissolutions to order maintenance of life insurance for the benefit of children and former spouses as a support substitute.

2. Was the Issue of Modifying John's Life Insurance Before the Court?

Nona contends this particular dissolution court had no jurisdiction to order modification of John's life insurance because Raytha did not formally bring the issue before the court by either a motion or a pleading responding to John's request to reduce support * * *.

* * *

We agree with the trial court that John's motion to reduce support put his life insurance in issue. When a support obligor pleads inability to maintain an existing level of spousal and child support from current income, it is reasonable to expect that the court will consider available support alternatives including modification of life insurance. The trial court found that local practice also justified this expectation. At the hearing John did not claim to be so surprised as to be unable to respond to the merits, nor could he in light of Raytha's informal requests to modify his life insurance. John in fact did respond to the merits, arguing that his children had other support alternatives, such as social security benefits. Under these circumstances, the trial court in ruling on John's motion to reduce support had jurisdiction over his life insurance.

3. Must an Order to Change Life Insurance Beneficiaries Be Preceded by Notice to the Current Beneficiary?

Nona contends that the dissolution court could not order her husband to add beneficiaries to his life insurance without notice to her as the existing beneficiary. This contention requires consideration of the nature of Nona's interests in John's life insurance as both the designated beneficiary and his surviving spouse.

It remains surprisingly unsettled whether the community interest in an insurance policy limits an insured spouse's ability to change beneficiaries. We will attempt to define this community interest after analyzing related interests. It helps to distinguish among four related interests: (1) the insured's contractual or statutory right to change beneficiaries (Ins.Code, § 10170) [1], (2) any community interest in that right, (3) the beneficiary's interest in remaining designated, and (4) the community interest in the policy proceeds.

A. The Insured's Right to Designate Beneficiaries and the Beneficiary's Interest in Remaining Designated

To an insured, the right to designate and change insurance beneficiaries may be a vested contractual right worthy of constitutional protection against impairment. (Frazier v. Tulare County Bd. of Retirement (1974) 42 Cal.App.3d 1046, 1051–1052, 117 Cal.Rptr. 386—beneficiary designation could not be overridden by Gov.Code amendment.) To the designated beneficiary, however, the insured's unfettered right to change beneficiaries trivializes the beneficiary's interest into a mere unvested expectancy unworthy of constitutional protection. (Wissner v. Wissner (1950) 338 U.S. 655, 661, 70 S.Ct. 398, 401, 94 L.Ed. 424—California community property law neither prevents federal insured from changing insurance beneficiary nor controls distribution of proceeds.) It has long been established, when the insured retains the right to change beneficiaries, the designated beneficiary's interest is a mere revocable expectancy vesting only on the insured's death, though the policy is acquired with community funds.

The insured can waive any right to change beneficiaries by appropriate agreement, such as by making an irrevocable beneficiary designation. An irrevocably designated beneficiary obtains a vested contractual right not dependent on any community interest. When an insured ignores a

1. Insurance Code section 10170, subdivision (e) provides that an agreement to pay life insurance "may be rescinded or amended by the parties thereto without the consent of any beneficiary therein designated unless the rights of any such beneficiary have been expressly declared to be irrevocable."

court order or contractual obligation to retain an irrevocable beneficiary, that beneficiary is entitled to recover the insurance proceeds.

*B. The Community Interest in Life Insurance Proceeds*

Acquisition by community funds does affect life insurance. Both spouses ordinarily have a community interest in the proceeds of an insurance policy to the extent it was acquired with community funds. Life insurance proceeds are subject to the general rule that a spouse cannot dispose of community personal property without either the other spouse's written consent or consideration. (§ 5125, subd. (b).) Thus, it is established that after the insured's death the surviving spouse can bring an action to set aside any unauthorized gift of insurance proceeds to the extent of his or her community interest, if this right has not been waived or released.

C. The Community Interest, If Any, in an Insured's Right to Change Beneficiaries

What remains unsettled is whether there is a community interest in the insured's right to change beneficiaries. Is this interest more like the community interest in the insurance proceeds or the designated beneficiary's mere expectancy?

On the one hand we find dictum stating a spouse can completely set aside an insurance beneficiary change during the insured's life if it amounts to an unauthorized gift of community property. None of those cases involved any challenge to a beneficiary change during the insured's life. Tyre, supra, and Polk, supra, actually applied the rule that after the insured's death the surviving spouse can set aside a beneficiary change to the extent of her community interest in the insurance proceeds. (54 Cal.2d at pp. 404–406, 6 Cal.Rptr. 13, 353 P.2d 725; 228 Cal.App.2d at pp. 782, 785, 39 Cal.Rptr. 824.) Benson, supra, merely discussed the community interest in life insurance in order to contrast it with public employee pension benefits. (60 Cal.2d at p. 363, 33 Cal.Rptr. 257, 384 P.2d 649.) None of these cases considered the effect of the provision in Insurance Code section 10170 that a beneficiary's consent to change life insurance is only necessary when the beneficiary is irrevocable. Polk, supra, expressly held this statute inapplicable because it postdated the insurance policies in issue. (228 Cal.App.2d at p. 787, 39 Cal.Rptr. 824.)

On the other hand, in addition to the unsettled scope of Insurance Code section 10170, we find dictum stating a spouse has no cause of action arising from an insurance beneficiary change until the insured's death, though meanwhile the spouse can notify the insurer of the community interest in a policy. (See Estate of Mendenhall (1960) 182 Cal.App.2d 441, 445–446, 6 Cal.Rptr. 45.) That opinion was filed four days after Tyre, supra, and does not discuss it. That case also involved no challenge to a beneficiary change during the insured's life. It involved the taxability to the surviving spouse's estate of insurance proceeds.

Thus, there is nonbinding, inconclusive support for concluding a spouse by virtue of his or her community interest in a life insurance policy has a somewhat greater interest in the insured spouse's right to change beneficiaries than the designated beneficiary's mere unvested expectancy.

*D. Nona's Entitlement to Notice of a Potential Court Order to Change her Husband's Life Insurance Beneficiary*

Applying the rules above to the facts of this case, we conclude, absent any evidence that Nona was an irrevocable life insurance beneficiary, her status as a designated beneficiary conferred no protection against John changing life insurance beneficiaries. However, her status as his spouse arguably enhanced her interest in his right to change beneficiaries to the extent the insurance was acquired by community funds of her marriage to John.

As Raytha points out, Nona's claim on appeal that the life insurance was purchased with her community funds is unwarranted. Nona merely declared, "The premiums on the optional life policy were paid entirely from John's earnings * * *." Based on this declaration, she asked the trial court to find "all premiums on the life insurance policies * * * were paid with the community property of John O'Connell and Nona O'Connell." The trial court made no finding on this issue, perhaps due to the following conflicting evidence. John's original declaration of income and expenses, filed May 30, 1986, reflected a deduction from income during his marriage to Raytha for life insurance. Later declarations filed June 9, 1987, April 12, 1989, and June 20, 1990, showed unspecified tax and insurance expenses but no life insurance deduction. We cannot assume the trial court implicitly resolved this factual dispute against Nona. (Code Civ.Proc., § 634.)

Even if we accept for the sake of discussion the questionable factual premise that the insurance policies were acquired with Nona's community funds and we apply the questionable legal premise that she therefore had a right during John's life to set aside his change of life insurance beneficiaries, Nona was not entitled to prior notice of the dissolution court's potential order to change John's life insurance beneficiaries. Any community interest in an insured's right to change beneficiaries is limited to avoiding gifts of community personal property. As Raytha contends and Nona disputes, there was no actual or potential unauthorized gift in this case.

John's remarriage created new community and separate property, both of which were subject to his existing spousal and child support obligations. A change in life insurance beneficiaries to fulfill existing support obligations is not a gift, particularly when ordered by a court. Thus, even if the life insurance policies were acquired with Nona's community funds, it was no gift for the court to order John to add Raytha and Richard as beneficiaries. (Cf. Burgart, supra, 5 Cal.App.3d at pp. 412–413, 85 Cal.Rptr. 122.)

Whatever the exact nature of Nona's interest as John's spouse in his right to change life insurance beneficiaries, it did not extend beyond the prevention of an unauthorized gift of community property. Raytha's request to designate herself and her child as additional beneficiaries of John's life insurance was made and considered by the dissolution court as a support substitute. This request did not propose a potential gift of Nona's community property and the resulting order did not effectuate such a gift. Therefore, Nona had no interest at stake justifying advance notice to her of the possibility of an order to change John's life insurance beneficiaries.[2]

Disposition

The order is affirmed.

### *Note*

As noted in the principal case, life insurers may have special administrative problems in community property states. In Texas, the insurer declined to effectuate a change of beneficiary from the ex-wife to the new wife of the insured on the grounds that the ex-wife had a community property right which could not be divested by the act of the insured. The Texas appellate court, however, held that the insurer was obliged to make the change although it would only apply to the insured's community property interest. Prudential Ins. Co. of America v. Burke, 614 S.W.2d 847 (Tex.App.1981).

## OCCIDENTAL LIFE INSURANCE CO. OF CALIFORNIA v. ROW

United States District Court, Southern District of West Virginia, 1967.
271 F.Supp. 920.

CHRISTIE, DISTRICT JUDGE:

This is an interpleader action (28 U.S.C.A. § 1335) brought by the Occidental Life Insurance Company of California to determine the conflicting claims to the proceeds of a policy of life insurance on the life of Ernest S. Allie, of Huntington, West Virginia. * * *

* * *

On December 1, 1957, a decreasing term insurance policy was issued on the life of Ernest S. Allie, the insured, to Mary K. Allie, his wife, as owner and beneficiary. On or about March 12, 1962, Mary K. Allie, as owner of the policy, executed a request for conversion. Thereafter plaintiff issued to her, as owner and beneficiary, a modified life at age 70 type policy, with an initial face amount of $40,000.00 on the life of Ernest S. Allie, and it is the proceeds of this policy which is the subject matter of this controversy.

2. A different conclusion might result if the court had attempted to adjudicate without notice to Nona the extent of her community interest in the life insurance proceeds or her right to reimbursement, if any (§ 5120.150; e.g., In re Marriage of Williams (1989) 213 Cal.App.3d 1239, 262 Cal.Rptr. 317), but these issues were not presented.

Mary K. Allie, the owner-beneficiary of the policy died May 19, 1966. On May 21, 1966, the insured, Ernest S. Allie, who was also the sole beneficiary under Mary K. Allie's will and the named executor thereof, contacted J. Hermansdorfer, a general agent of the insurer, located in Huntington, West Virginia, and advised him of a desire to change the beneficiary of the policy to his daughter, Margaret A. Row. The agent informed Mr. Allie that inasmuch as Mrs. Allie had been the sole owner and beneficiary of the policy it would be necessary to contact the home office regarding the procedure to follow. Nevertheless, Mr. Allie requested that he be allowed to complete a standard change of beneficiary form so that the company's preparation of the proper papers might be expedited. This was done. The agent also advised Mr. Allie that he was soon to be hospitalized for a serious operation and it was suggested that by the time he had recovered the necessary forms should be available. The executed form was forwarded by the general agent to the home office under a memorandum dated May 21, 1966. By a return memorandum from the home office dated May 27, 1966, the general agent was advised that the submitted form had been placed on file and marked "not used," since it had not been signed by the insured. The general agent was then confined to a hospital recovering from a major operation performed May 23, 1966, and he had not returned to work when Mr. Allie died on June 3, 1966. The memorandum also contained a list of steps the company considered necessary to effectuate the change.[44]

Prior to his death, Mr. Allie qualified, on May 24, 1966, as executor of his wife's will, which devised and bequeathed all her estate to him. Margaret Allie Row qualified as executrix of his will on June 7, 1966. After devising his home and the furniture and household goods therein to his daughter, Margaret Allie Row, he bequeathed the residue of his estate equally to his three children, Robert C. Allie, Margaret Allie Row, and Betty Allie DeBoer. On July 14, 1966, Margaret Allie Row qualified as administratrix c.t.a., d.b.n. of the estate of Mary K. Allie.

### Issue

The narrow issue for determination is the effect, if any, of Ernest S. Allie's attempt to change the beneficiary of the policy two days after the owner-beneficiary's death and prior to his qualification as executor of her will. * * *

* * *. The general West Virginia law on this subject is stated in Union Mut. Life Ins. Co. v. Lindamood, 108 W.Va. 594, 152 S.E. 321, 322, and is as follows:

**44.** "A. If owner's estate has not been distributed we should be furnished with:

"1. A certified copy of Letters Testamentary or Letters of Administration, as the case may be.

"2. An assignment by the representative of Mary K. Allie's estate, which is supported by a certified copy of a court order permitting him to execute the assignment.

"3. A beneficiary form signed by the new owner, in duplicate, after the assignment has been made."

"It is undoubtedly the general rule that the mode prescribed in a life insurance policy for changing the beneficiary must be at least substantially followed. To this general rule, however, exceptions are recognized in the following cases: (1) Where the insurer has waived compliance with the prescribed regulations, or estopped itself to assert noncompliance therewith. (2) Where it is beyond the power of the insured to comply literally with the regulations. (3) Where the insured has done all that he is required to do and only formal ministerial acts on the part of the insurer remain to be done in order to complete the change, equity will treat it as having been made. 'Equity will aid in attempted, but incomplete, change of beneficiaries; * * * when the insured in good faith has attempted to comply with the prescribed mode of change. Equity will, in such case, consider that done which ought to have been done, and will not require impossibilities.' Cooley's Briefs on Insurance, p. 6455. * * *

The factor which distinguishes the present controversy from the usual case in this area is that the beneficiary, rather than the insured, was the policy owner. As a result it is necessary to examine the rights that attached to these different capacities so that we may determine the effect of Mr. Allie's action. Under the terms of the policy,[45] Mrs. Allie, as owner, possessed the exclusive right to change the beneficiary. Nevertheless, it must be recognized that her interest as owner was separate and distinct from that possessed by her as the policy's named beneficiary. This latter interest gave her no absolute right to the proceeds, but rather it was a conditional interest subject to defeasance, which consisted merely of an expectancy during the life of the insured, contingent upon her remaining the beneficiary until the time of the insured's death. 29A Am.Jur.Insurance Sec. 1640 (1960). This expectancy ceased upon

**45.** The pertinent provisions of the policy in question are as follows:

"*Beneficiary Provisions* —The interest of any beneficiary who dies before the Insured shall terminate at the death of the beneficiary. The interest of any beneficiary who dies simultaneously with the Insured or dies within 30 days after the death of the Insured and before payment of any of the proceeds to that beneficiary shall also terminate. The proceeds will then be paid as though such beneficiary had died before the Insured. If the interest of all designated beneficiaries has terminated, any proceeds payable because of the death of the Insured will be paid to the then owner of this policy, if living, otherwise to the executor or administrator of the owner.

"*Owner of Policy* —Before the death of the Insured, the owner of this policy alone shall be entitled to all rights granted by this policy or allowed by the Company under this policy. If the owner is a partnership, all rights of the owner belong to the partnership as constituted at the time a right is exercised. If the owner is an individual and dies before the Insured, all rights of the owner belong to the executor or administrator of the owner unless otherwise provided in this policy.

"CHANGE OF BENEFICIARY

"A change of beneficiary may only be made by filing a satisfactory written notice with the Company. A beneficiary designated irrevocably may not be changed except with the written consent of that beneficiary. A change of beneficiary shall not be effective until recorded at the Home Office of the Company. When so recorded, even if the Insured is not then living, the change of beneficiary shall take effect on the date the notice was signed, subject to any payment made by the Company before recording the change."

her death and her rights as owner vested, under the terms of the policy, in her executor.

It is significant that upon the policy owner's death her husband became possessed, in his several capacities as the insured, sole legatee of her personal property, and executor of her will with every right and incident of ownership connected with the policy. As a result, any action he may have taken in any of these capacities would necessarily be deemed to have been taken in his best interest in the others.

* * *

It is * * * urged that, * * * he could not have legally named a beneficiary since this would constitute a diversion of the estate's assets. The fallacy of this argument is that while the ownership of the policy became an asset of the estate, the expectancy as beneficiary did not.

We believe that where the policy itself grants all the deceased owner's rights to an executor of the estate, the new owner-executor has the legal capacity to designate a new beneficiary. None of the assets available to the former owner's creditors are removed from the estate by such a step.

In view of this determination the question becomes: What * * * was the legal effect of Mr. Allie's action insofar as the rules regarding substantial compliance with change of beneficiary provisions are concerned?

The circumstances surrounding the present situation are strikingly analogous to those found in Provident Life & Accident Ins. Co. v. Dotson, 93 F.Supp. 538 (S.D.W.Va.1950). In that case an insured requested the agents of an insurance company to change the beneficiary in his policy from his wife to his mother. He was advised that the necessary forms were not available but that they would be procured. The insured returned a week or two later and was told that the forms had not yet been received. He was killed before they were received. The Court states, p. 541:

> "From the foregoing authorities it appears: (1) That the insured did everything within his power to effect the twice requested change in beneficiary; that strict compliance with the formal provisions of the policy was due entirely to the fault and neglect of the agent of the insurance company, and in such cases equity will consider that done which ought to have been done; and (2) Such provisions in the policy relating to the mode of change of beneficiary are for the benefit of the insurer alone, and the insurer has waived strict compliance with such provisions by bringing this interpleader action and paying the proceeds of the policy into court."

In the instant case it is seen that Mr. Allie advised the insurance company's general agent of his desire to change the beneficiary and filled out the standard form to effect this. In short he, at the time, did everything within his knowledge and power to bring about the desired change. If this did not comport with the company's requirements, it then became its responsibility to promptly advise him of the formal procedure to be followed and to furnish him with the necessary forms. There can be little doubt that had this been done Mr. Allie could and would have complied with the requirements, whatever they might have been. No dereliction on his part is indicated or suggested, rather it was the untimely illness of the company's general agent and the company's failure to otherwise advise him of the procedure that accounted for the delay.

* * * The theory underlying the equitable rule of substantial compliance with change of beneficiary provisions is, of course, to prevent the thwarting of an insured's wishes because of technicalities designed for the protection of the insured, and the courts must keep this in mind in considering cases of this sort. It is conceded that, insofar as the proceeds of the insurance policy are concerned, had Mr. Allie chosen some other method to make his daughter the recipient of his generosity he could have done so. Under the view we take, though other roads may have been less marred with legal chuckholes, in the eyes of the law the action taken was sufficient to reach the intended destination.

Under the terms of the policy the executor of the deceased owner's will became possessed of all the policy's rights. Mr. Allie was the executor, sole legatee of the deceased owner-beneficiary's personal property, as well as the named insured. There may be situations where such a combination of relationships must be dealt with separately; such would be the case where the executor and the legatee are different individuals. Under such circumstances it is doubtful that the executor would be permitted to designate a new beneficiary without the acquiescence of the policy's new owner. Those circumstances do not confront us here and there is no reason apparent—legal or equitable—requiring us to close our eyes to the realities of Mr. Allie's total relationship to this insurance policy.

Whatever his reason for doing so, Mr. Allie made an unequivocal attempt to effect a change of beneficiary to Margaret Allie Row. At the time he possessed every incidence of authority necessary to do so, save the bare formality of qualifying as executor of his wife's will. The letter of instruction from the Home Office, dated May 27, 1966, cannot be construed to be an outright or unequivocal rejection of the requested change. The fact that the executed form was simply marked "not used" rather than rejected and returned is significant. It indicates that the insurer was holding it in reserve for just such a contingency as Mr. Allie's death before the instructions could be complied with. Under such circumstances, the equitable rule of considering done that which ought to have been done applies with all its force and vigor.

* * * Therefore, Margaret Allie Row, in her individual capacity, is rightfully entitled to its proceeds and she will be awarded summary judgment accordingly.

## MANHATTAN LIFE INSURANCE CO. v. BARNES

United States Court of Appeals, Ninth Circuit, 1972.
462 F.2d 629.

PREGERSON, DISTRICT JUDGE:

The Manhattan Life Insurance Company [hereinafter "Manhattan"] brought this action in interpleader on March 11, 1968, pursuant to 28 U.S.C.A. § 1335, to determine the beneficiary of group life insurance policy # 1878 GL. Manhattan had issued the policy on April 14, 1960, on the life of one Victor H. Barnes. Barnes had died on December 22, 1967. In its complaint Manhattan admitted liability in the amount of $55,000 plus interest at the rate of 3.5% from the time of the insured's death. It paid that sum into the registry of the court below and asked that court to restrain defendants from instituting other actions to recover any part of the proceeds of the policy, to require defendants to interplead so that the beneficiary could be determined, and to discharge it from any additional liability in connection with the policy.

The complaint named five defendants: Margaret Ann Barnes, Mr. Barnes's former wife, who was named as beneficiary on Manhattan's records at the time of Mr. Barnes's death; Mr. Barnes's three daughters, Margaret Ann Smith, Victoria L. Bakke, and Barbara J. Thompson; and Mr. Barnes's estate, the administratrix of which was Mrs. Smith. On May 27, 1968, after the defendants had answered Manhattan's complaint, the court below dismissed Manhattan, discharging it from any additional liability in connection with the policy and restraining the defendants from instituting other suits against it in order to collect proceeds of the policy. On August 2, 1968, Mr. Barnes's estate was voluntarily dismissed. Mrs. Barnes filed a motion for summary judgment on October 9, 1969, and the court below granted the motion on January 22, 1970. Mrs. Smith and Mrs. Bakke have appealed from the judgment entered below.

Section VI of the policy provided, in part,

> "The Beneficiary for the Individual shall be the person or persons designated on the insurance records maintained in accordance with the Group Policy and the Beneficiary shall be in accordance with the Individual's selection. The Individual may change his Beneficiary at any time upon satisfactory written request."

Mrs. Smith and Mrs. Bakke concede that at the time of Mr. Barnes's death, Mrs. Barnes was the beneficiary designated on Manhattan's records in accordance with Section VI of the policy. They contend, however, that on February 21, 1966, twenty-two months before his death, Mr. Barnes executed a form in which he requested a change of beneficiary and named his three daughters as the new beneficiaries of the policy in question. Mrs. Smith allegedly found the change of beneficiary request card among some of her father's papers thirty-two days after his death. Along with the request card she also allegedly found a note, written in the hand of one of her father's employees, which read, "Change Manhattan, beneficiary of Manhattan policy." The daughters also submitted depositions that indicated that their father had believed that he had changed the beneficiary of the policy. This evidence was contradicted, however, by evidence offered by Mrs. Barnes.

The parties agree that California law governs this case; they disagree as to what that law is. Mrs. Smith and Mrs. Bakke argue that the formal requirements for changing a beneficiary that are specified in the insurance policy—i.e., written notice on a prescribed form—serve only to protect the insurer. They contend, therefore, that if the insurer institutes an action in interpleader, it waives its right to insist on compliance with these formalities, because after the insurer pays the funds that are the subject of the dispute into the registry of the court, the court will shield it from any additional liability. Since no other party has a right to invoke these formalities, the daughters conclude, a court of equity must determine whether or not the insured intended to change the beneficiary, and it must give effect to that intent. In this case, of course, there is considerable dispute over what Mr. Barnes's intent actually was. It is clear, therefore, that if Mrs. Smith and Mrs. Bakke accurately state the applicable law, material issues of fact remain unresolved, the summary judgment entered below was inappropriate, and the case should go to trial.

The California case law is not entirely free from ambiguity. Nevertheless, the Supreme Court of California has laid down the applicable rules of law in Pimentel v. Conselho Supremo, 6 Cal.2d 182, 57 P.2d 131 (1936). The Supreme Court stated in its decision,

> "While there is a division of authority on the question of whether interpleader and payment into court operates as a waiver of the insured's failure to comply with the policy provisions concerning change of beneficiary, *it is settled in this jurisdiction that it does not.* * * * Appellant concedes this to be the present rule in this state, but argues that it is against the weight of authority and asks that the cases so holding be overruled. We are satisfied that the better reasoning supports the rule adopted by our courts * * *. Nor are we convinced that the rules requiring certain formalities for the change of beneficiaries are solely for the benefit of the insurer and are not in any degree intended to protect the insured and the original beneficiary." 57 P.2d 132–133. [Emphasis added.]

The Supreme Court pointed out that the earlier decisions had recognized three exceptions to the general rule requiring strict compliance with the prescribed procedures. Two of those exceptions are not relevant to this case, but the third one is relevant: if an insured has pursued the prescribed course of action and has done all in his power to change the beneficiary, but has died before the formal procedures could be complied with in their entirety, a court of equity will treat the change of beneficiary as having been made.[46] See, e.g., McLaughlin v. McLaughlin, 104 Cal.

**46.** The other two exceptions are as follows: (1) If the insurer has waived strict compliance with its own rules by issuing a new certificate pursuant to a request by the

171, 37 P. 865 (1894); Supreme Lodge v. Price, 27 Cal.App. 607, 150 P. 803 (1915); Barbozo v. Conselho Supremo, 43 Cal.App. 775, 185 P. 1028 (1919); Johnston v. Kearns, 107 Cal.App. 557, 290 P. 640 (1930). The Supreme Court pointed out, however, that this exception

> "has been variously interpreted as meaning all that is required of the insured, leaving only ministerial duties to be performed by the insurer * * * or as all that it was possible for the insured to do under the circumstances under which he attempted to make the change." 57 P.2d at 134.

The Supreme Court resolved this conflict by concluding,

> "We think that where the insurer is not contesting the change the rule is not to be applied rigorously and where the insured makes every reasonable effort under the circumstances, complying as far as he is able with the rules, and there is a clear manifestation of intent to make the change, which the insured has put into execution as best he can, equity should regard the change as effected." 57 P.2d at 134.

Institution of an action in interpleader, in short, does not waive compliance with the prescribed procedures. It merely relaxes the requirements, and a court of equity may give effect to an intended change if "the insured [made] every reasonable effort under the circumstances, complying as far as he [was] able with the rules," and if there has been "a clear manifestation of intent to make the change."

Mrs. Smith and Mrs. Bakke cite a more recent decision by the California District Court of Appeal in support of their contention that California law regards the institution of an action in interpleader as a waiver of strict compliance with contractual requirements. In Saunders v. Stevers, 221 Cal.App.2d 539, 34 Cal.Rptr. 579 (1963), the court stated,

> "Where, as here, the company makes no contest but interpleads the contesting beneficiaries and pays the proceeds of the policy into court, a liberal rule obtains and courts of equity seek to do that which the insured intended to have done and to award the funds to the claimant who has the strongest claim under the facts of the case." 34 Cal.Rptr. at 581.

The only authority for this statement cited by the court was *Pimentel* and two cases decided by the District Court of Appeal prior to *Pimentel.* Examined in the light of this authority, the statement is ambiguous and may be read in two ways: it either does no more than loosely paraphrase the rule established in *Pimentel,* or it contradicts that rule and, as a result, finds no support in the California Supreme Court decision that purportedly stands as its authority.

insured, a court of equity will treat the change of beneficiary as complete; (2) if it was beyond the power of the insured to comply literally with the requirements—if, for example, he was unable to gain access to the policy itself or to prescribed forms—a court of equity will also treat the change as having been made. See, e.g., Pimentel v. Conselho Supremo, supra, 57 P.2d at 133.

The details of the *Saunders* case support the former interpretation. The relevant contractual provision stated,

> "The insured shall have the right at any time, and from time to time, to change the beneficiary, by written notice in form acceptable to the Company, which will be furnished on request."

The insured wrote to the insurer, notifying it of her intention to change beneficiaries. The insurer sent her its forms, the insured executed them, at least in part, but they were inadvertently destroyed before she could send them back to the insurer. She requested new forms, and they were sent. The insured died one month later, however, and never executed the second set of forms. The District Court of Appeal held that the beneficiary had been changed. The court did not hold that by instituting an action in interpleader the insurer had waived compliance with the contract. It emphasized, instead, the ambiguity of the contractual provision and reasoned that the institution of the action in interpleader constituted acceptance by the insurer of the insured's initial letter to it as "written notice in form acceptable to the Company." The court also stressed the fact that there was additional evidence of the insured's desire to change the beneficiary, while there was no evidence of any desire not to change the beneficiary. The decision, in short, was not necessarily inconsistent with *Pimentel.* The institution of an action in interpleader relaxed the ordinary rule requiring strict compliance. * * *

* * *

* * * California requires at least substantial compliance with the provisions of the insurance contract, even if the insurer has brought an action in interpleader. That requirement protects both the original beneficiary and the expressed intent of the insured from interference based on modest bits of evidence. * * * The evidence submitted by the daughters shows, at most, that during February 1966 Mr. Barnes executed a change of beneficiary request card and that on one occasion during the next twenty-two months he instructed an employee to change the beneficiary of the policy. There is no evidence that Mr. Barnes was incapacitated in any way during these twenty-two months; all the evidence shows that he continued to conduct his business. Under these circumstances, he could certainly have done more to insure that the contractual requirements were complied with. It cannot be said that he made "every reasonable effort" to change the beneficiary. The insured in *Saunders* twice wrote to the insurer in regard to her desire to change beneficiaries. The insured in *Pimentel* gave instructions for changing beneficiaries from his deathbed, repeatedly asked whether his wishes had been followed, but received mistaken assurances. In Johnston v. Kearns, supra, the insured wrote a letter to the insurer while on his deathbed, gave instructions that the letter be mailed, but died before it could be deposited in the mail. The efforts allegedly made by Mr. Barnes do not approach what was done in these cases.[47] Summary

**47.** Our decision is based on the inadequacy of Mr. Barnes's efforts to change the beneficiary; we have not considered whether or not there has been a "clear manifestation of intent to make the change," within the meaning of *Pimentel.*

judgment for Mrs. Barnes was appropriate, and the district court's decision will be affirmed.

## Notes

1. *"Every Reasonable Effort"—Suppose beneficiary has the policy?*

Evelyn Jenkins was named beneficiary of a policy on the life of her husband, Hercules Jenkins. The policy permitted a change of beneficiary which "shall be effective only if written notice thereof is received by the company at its Home Office and if such designation is accepted by the Company; * * * except that the Company may at its discretion, waive this requirement." After 19 years of marriage the Jenkins' in April 1976, separated unamicably and an annulment action was begun. On June 23, 1976, Jenkins, using forms supplied by the insurance company, requested a change of beneficiary to his nephew. Included was a "declaration of lost policy" form with the explanation that Mrs. Jenkins had removed it without authorization and had it in a bank vault. (The testimony was in conflict as to whether Mr. Jenkins had actually requested its return). On July 8, 1976, the Company wrote Mrs. Jenkins that Mr. Jenkins desired to change the beneficiary of the policy which was not available to him, and stated: "we must consider waiving presentation of the policy to the company. Therefore, unless within 30 days of the date of this letter we receive a claim of sufficient interest in the policy that would stand in the way of the insured's request, we must proceed in waiving presentation of the policy and grant the insured's request."

Jenkins died on August 5, 1976. Mrs. Jenkins called the company with the somewhat ambiguous explanation for not responding, "because I was going to bury my husband."

Was every reasonable effort made? See Haynes v. Metropolitan Life Insurance Co., 166 N.J.Super. 308, 399 A.2d 1010 (1976) Held: for the nephew.

2. In Horne v. Gulf Life Ins. Co., 277 S.C. 336, 287 S.E.2d 144 (1982) the insured desired to change the beneficiary (his ex-wife) of a policy apparently in the beneficiary's possession. He certified (falsely) that the original was lost, stolen or destroyed and thereby obtained duplicates from the insurer and formally changed the beneficiary by endorsement with the company's consent. The ex-wife sued on the policy when the insured died but was denied recovery. Two dissenting justices objected that the agent of the company knew all along that the policy was not lost.

3. *More beneficiary problems for the insurer. Inadequate records and computer foul-ups.*

Mr. Collins joined the Exxon Travel Club. One of the side benefits was an accidental death policy issued by Travelers Ins. Co. payable to his estate in the absence of a specific beneficiary designation. Some years later the Collins' divorced and Mrs. Collins remarried three days later. Mr. Collins changed or attempted to change the beneficiaries of a number of other policies to his two children. As to the Travelers policy the situation is murky. The Travel Club's records indicated a beneficiary had been named. Unfortunately, the beneficiary's name was not identified and could not be retrieved: "They [Travelers], through mistake, pushed a button on a computer that destroyed the evidence that Dr. Collins had made to name the beneficiary." The court held that since "a beneficiary" had been named, the estate of Dr. Collins was excluded. As to the ex-wife and children the court held that *both* should be paid the *full* amount of the policy—for breach of the insurer's duty to maintain proper records. Travelers Insurance Co. v. Collins, 484 F.Supp. 196 (E.D.Va.1980).

*Query:* Why not give *each* child the full amount of the policy? How many potential beneficiaries did Dr. Collins have to whom the Company owes a duty to maintain proper records?

4. *Change of Life Insurance Beneficiaries—Its Role in Family Wealth Transference*

Every generation succeeds to the accumulated personal wealth of its predecessors. As to that portion of such wealth as passes by intestate succession or by will the transfer has been supervised through tight legal controls. Intestate succession follows rigid statutory guidelines obviously drafted to confine the disposition as far as possible within the nuclear family. Testate succession requires formalities amounting almost to ritual.

But with regard to methods of transferring the legal right of access to life insurance proceeds (always in negotiable cash), which represent a very large proportion of the wealth passing from one generation to the next,* the controls are comparatively casual. The matter of formulating the ground rules for designating the recipients and changing them back and forth has been left to the life insurance companies in drafting their policy forms. Even such formal requirements as are laid down (and these vary widely from insurance company to insurance company) may be casually waived by the insurers, since the judicial attitude is that the change of beneficiary provision is primarily for the convenience of the party which drafted it. The only other controls provided by the judicial system to this wealth transferral process is the loose and variable case by case review of the equally loose and variable practices of the insurance companies in switching beneficiaries around. In analyzing the opinions it is proper to ask if the same court would allow the interest of a specific legatee of $10,000 to be cancelled in quite as informal fashion as allowed in the case of the named beneficiary of the same amount of insurance. Consider, for example, a case such as Lemke v. Schwarz, 286 N.W.2d 693 (Minn.1979). The insured had been married three times. He had been married to his named beneficiary for a little over a year, of which the last six months had been a period of marital strain. She indicated intent to leave, whereupon the insured executed a letter, describing it as his "will" addressed to his daughter "bequeathing" the proceeds of his insurance under a company plan to them and admonishing "share nothing with Bernie [the wife-beneficiary] because she has not been willing to share her life with me." He died the next day, the letter being postmarked the day of his death. No copy was sent to the employer or the insurance company. Although it was conceded the document was not a will,

* The American Council of Life Insurance states that in 1989 the total amount of life insurance in force in the United States amounted to $8,694,015,000,000.

the daughters were nevertheless awarded the insurance proceeds. "We hold that where an insured has clearly and unambiguously demonstrated an intent to change the beneficiary of a life insurance policy, this intent should be given effect unless prejudice to the insurer would result."

5. As to whether a change of beneficiary can be effected by will, see Burkett v. Mott, 152 Ariz. 476, 733 P.2d 673 (App.1986).

6. *Government Sponsored Insurance. A Liberal Pragmatic Approach to the Change of Beneficiary Problem versus Bureaucratic Convenience.*

In 1940 the Congress passed the National Service Life Insurance Act affording low cost insurance for servicemen. Changes of beneficiary were to be accomplished by forwarding a completed form to the Veterans Administration. During the next several years the poignant scenario all too frequently arose of the 18 year old lad, who had originally signed a policy naming Mom as beneficiary, departing aboard a troopship and leaving on the dock a new bride, often pregnant.** The problem of obtaining forms and managing the final execution of a change of beneficiary during the hectic period before the youth's death in combat led to a liberal practice as to such policies of recognizing a change of beneficiaries on the basis of homesick and heartsick notes to the beloved. See Mac Farlane v. United States, 476 F.Supp. 787 (E.D.La.1979).

In the not too peaceful year of 1965 the government sponsored the Serviceman's Group Life Insurance Act giving servicemen free insurance (to be administered through private insurers). It was modeled after the Federal Employee's Group Life Insurance Act, which act in 1967 was interpreted to allow a change of beneficiary by means of a holographic will. Sears v. Austin, 292 F.2d 690 (9th Cir.1961). The *Sears* decision prompted Congress to amend the Act, because it was said: "The precedent established could if generally followed result in administrative difficulties for the Civil Service Commission and the insurance companies and, more important, seriously delay paying insurance benefits to survivors of Federal Employees". In consequence the enactments were amended to provide that the order of procedure in paying claims would be:

> "First to the beneficiary or beneficiaries designated by the employee in a signed and witnessed writing received before death in the employing office * * *. For this purpose, a designation, change or cancellation of beneficiary in a will or other document not so executed and filed has no force or effect."

This provision was held to preclude a liberal attitude toward change of beneficiaries as to this particular form of Servicemen's policy. Hill v. Hill, 23 Cal.App.3d 760, 100 Cal.Rptr. 458 (1972). Also, Prudential Ins. Co. of America v. Parker, 840 F.2d 6 (7th Cir.1988).

See also Huff v. Metropolitan Life Ins. Co., 675 F.2d 119 (6th Cir.1982): "1966 Amendments to Federal Employees Group Life Insurance Act abol-

** Another frequent, and only slightly less poignant, scenario was the 18–year old serviceman who married at the dock and effected NSLI insurance with his wife as beneficiary, only to discover sometime later that his bride was also the designated beneficiary of several other 18–year olds in the regiment.

ished manifest intent test for determining beneficiaries when policy is silent."

*Query:* Would not the statutory requirement of a standard policy provision for change of beneficiary in *all* life insurance policies, modeled on the Congressional enactment above, save a great deal of litigation?

7. *A Statutory Rule*

A Wisconsin statute (§ 632.48(1)(b) Stats.) provides that: "as between beneficiaries, any act that indicates an intention to make the change is sufficient to effect it." Suppose insured gives oral instruction to his attorney to change the beneficiary (his business) on his life policy, and "for the proceeds to go for the benefit of my family". The change of beneficiary forms were not completed before his death. Under the statute who gets the proceeds? See Empire General Life Ins. Co. v. Silverman, 135 Wis.2d 143, 399 N.W.2d 910 (1987).

## LEE v. AYLWARD

Supreme Court of Missouri, En Banc, 1990.
790 S.W.2d 462.

BLACKMAR, C.J.

Gary Lee was insured under a group policy written by Metropolitan Life Insurance Company. He named his wife Aubyn as primary beneficiary, and appellants Clarence Williamson, Emmannuel Williamson and Quentin Williams as contingent beneficiaries. Aubyn shot and killed Gary, after which she pleaded guilty to manslaughter. By reason of the ensuing conviction she is disabled from taking the proceeds. The question is whether the proceeds are payable to the contingent beneficiaries, or to Gary's estate. The trial court held in favor of the estate, under authority of Reliable Life Insurance Co. v. Spurgeon, 763 S.W.2d 674 (Mo.App.1988). The court of appeals reversed. We granted transfer to resolve the apparent conflict in decisions. We likewise reverse, and remand with directions to enter judgment for the contingent beneficiaries.

The applicable contract provision reads as follows: "If any designated Beneficiary shall die before the Employe, the rights and interest of such Beneficiary shall thereupon automatically terminate. If, at the death of the Employe, there be no designated Beneficiary as to all or any part of the Life Insurance payable, then the amount of Life Insurance payable for which there is no designated Beneficiary shall be payable to the estate of Employe."

In the "Employe's Designation of Beneficiary and Contingent Beneficiaries" form, the insured named Aubyn Lee as beneficiary, and also provided that "[i]n the event said beneficiary predeceases me, I designate as contingent beneficiaries: Emmannuel O. Williamson, Quentin R. Williams, and Clarence C. Williamson."

The beneficiaries of Gary's estate argue that, by the plain language of the provision, the contingent beneficiaries have no interest unless the named beneficiary predeceases the insured. They argue that the proceeds necessarily pass to the estate, because the only person who could claim to be a beneficiary has been disabled from taking by operation of law, and because of the expressed survivorship language.

The problem with this argument is that the law interdicts the performance of the contract in accordance with its "plain meaning." The courts, therefore, must determine how the problem they created is to be resolved. This is not an uncommon situation in the law of contracts. Courts have made use of concepts such as constructive trust, impossibility, frustration, and the like. These are but tools, which in and of themselves do not solve the basic problem.

We conclude that the insured has given a clear indication that he preferred the contingent beneficiaries to take, rather than his legatees or next of kin. He has designated the former as alternate takers, and has made no mention of those who would take from his estate. The insured was interested in having alternate takers, and it may be doubted that this purpose was limited to cases in which the primary beneficiary did not survive him. We reach this conclusion even though some of the contingent beneficiaries are children of the slayer. Any thought that he would exclude them if he had realized that their mother would kill him introduces inappropriate speculation. We believe that it is better to have a rule of general application.

Counsel for the estate point to the "slayer statutes" in effect in several states, but not in Missouri. A provision in favor of the contingent beneficiaries is included in the Model Probate Code, but not in our statutes, although they borrow frequently from the Model Code. We do not consider this circumstance significant. All the omission does is to deny us legislative guidance, so as to require us to decide the issue according to the principles of common law.

Our conclusion is supported by the substantial weight of authority. Numerous cases hold for the contingent beneficiaries.[1] The next of kin's position is supported by only a few cases.[2] We do not give Spurgeon

1. Cases from states not having "slayer" statutes are as follows: Beck v. West Coast Life Ins., 38 Cal.2d 643, 241 P.2d 544 (1952); Turner v. Prudential Ins., 60 N.J.Super. 175, 158 A.2d 441 (1960); In re Kaplan's Estate, 49 Misc.2d 335, 267 N.Y.S.2d 345 (N.Y.Sup.Ct.1966); Neff v. Massachusetts Mutual Life Ins., 158 Ohio St. 45, 107 N.E.2d 100 (1952); National Home Life Assurance v. Patterson, 746 P.2d 696 (Okla.Ct.App.1987); Lewis v. Lewis, 281 S.C. 388, 315 S.E.2d 816 (1984); Brooks v. Thompson, 521 S.W.2d 563 (Tenn.1975). Decisions by federal courts construing state law include Patton v. Lee, 394 F.Supp. 501 (D.C.Ky.1975); Continental Bank v. Maag, 285 F.2d 558 (10th Cir. 1960) (applying Utah law); United States v. Burns, 103 F.Supp. 690 (D.C.Md.1952); Metropolitan Life Ins. v. McDavid, 39 F.Supp. 228 (D.C.Mich.1941); Life Ins. Co. v. Cashatt, 206 F.Supp. 410 (D.C.Va.1962). See also Annotation, Killing of Insured by Beneficiary as Affecting Life Insurance or its Proceeds, 27 A.L.R.3d 794; J. Appleman, Insurance Law Practice § 482 (1981 & Supp.1989).

2. Bullock v. Expressmen's Mut. Life Ins., 234 N.C. 254, 67 S.E.2d 71 (1951); Crawford v. Coleman, 726 S.W.2d 9 (Tex. 1987). Webb v. Voirol, 773 F.2d 208 (8th Cir.1985); and Life and Casualty Insurance Co. v. Martin, 603 F.Supp. 281 (E.D.Mo. 1985), are cases governed by Missouri law.

particular weight, even though it is a Missouri case. We were not asked to review it.

The law of property furnishes an analogy. Section 240, Restatement of Property, reads as follows: "When a remainder is subject to a condition precedent, the termination, before such condition precedent is fulfilled, of all prior interests created simultaneously therewith, does not destroy the remainder."

The comment provides the following rationale: "When A transfers Blackacre to B for life, remainder to those children of B who attain 21, A does not thereby manifest a concern as to whether the children of B attain their majority in the lifetime of B, or thereafter."

The judgment is reversed and the case is remanded with directions to enter judgment for the appellant contingent beneficiaries.

## LEE v. STATE FARM MUTUAL INSURANCE COMPANY

Court of Appeal, Third District, 1976.
57 Cal.App.3d 458, 129 Cal.Rptr. 271.

EVANS, ASSOCIATE JUSTICE.

Plaintiffs appeal from that portion of a summary judgment which declared valid provisions in automobile insurance policies issued by defendant requiring plaintiffs to reimburse defendant for certain medical payments received by plaintiffs pursuant to the insurance agreement.

Defendant appeals from that portion of the judgment which required it to pay a pro rata share of attorney's fees incurred by plaintiffs in securing a settlement or recovery out of which the reimbursement was required.

The following facts are not in dispute: from May 1965, through and including February 1968, the automobile insurance policies issued by defendant contained the following provisions:

"COVERAGE C—Medical Payments. To pay reasonable medical expenses incurred within one year from the date of accident:

"* * *

"POLICY CONDITIONS—APPLICABLE TO ALL COVERAGES
UNLESS OTHERWISE NOTED

"* * *

"4. Subrogation. Upon payment under coverages A, B, D, D–50, F, G, H, and division 1 of W–1 and W–2 of this policy the company shall be subrogated to all of the insured's rights of recovery therefor and the insured shall do whatever is necessary to secure such rights and do nothing to prejudice them.

"Upon payment under coverages C, of this policy the company shall be subrogated to the extent of such payment to the proceeds of any settlement or judgment that may result from the exercise of any rights of recovery which the injured person or anyone receiving such payment may have against any person or organization and such persons shall execute and deliver instruments and papers and do whatever else is necessary to secure such rights. Such person shall do nothing after loss to prejudice such rights."

* * * During October 1968 and thereafter, all policies issued by defendant contained the following two separate provisions providing for reimbursement:

"POLICY CONDITIONS

"* * *

"4. Subrogation. Upon payment under this policy, except under coverages C, the company shall be subrogated to all the *insured's* rights of recovery therefor and the *insured* shall do whatever is necessary to secure such rights and do nothing to prejudice them.

"Upon payment under coverages C of this policy the company shall be subrogated to the extent of such payment to the proceeds of any settlement or judgment that may result from the exercise of any rights of recovery which the injured *person* or anyone receiving such payment may have against any *person* or organization and such *person* shall execute and deliver instruments and papers and do whatever else is necessary to secure such rights. Such *person* shall do nothing after loss to prejudice such rights.

"5. Trust Agreement–Coverages C, and U. In the event of payment to any *person* under coverage C,

"(a) the company shall be entitled to the extent of such payment to the proceeds of any settlement or judgment that may result from the exercise of any rights of recovery of such *person* against any *person* or organization legally responsible for the *bodily injury* because of which such payment is made;

"(b) such *person* shall hold in trust for the benefit of the company all rights of recovery which he shall have against such other *person* or organization because of the damages which are the subject of claim made under the coverages;

"(c) such *person* shall do whatever is proper to secure and shall do nothing after loss to prejudice such rights;

"(d) if requested in writing by the company, such *person* shall take, through any representative designated by the company, such action as may be necessary or appropriate to recover such payment as damages from such other *person* or organization, such action to be taken in the name of such *person;* in the event of a recovery, the company shall be reimbursed out of such recovery for expenses, costs and attorneys' fees incurred by it in connection therewith;

"(e) such *person* shall execute and deliver to the company such instruments and papers as may be appropriate to secure the rights and obligations of such *person* and the company established by this provision." (Emphasis in original.)

Pursuant to cross-motions for summary judgment, the trial court rendered its judgment in favor of defendant on the question of the validity of the subrogation or reimbursement provisions of the various insurance policies.

These cross-appeals ensued presenting for our determination the following questions: * * *

(1) Are the policy provisions requiring reimbursement of medical payments void as an attempt to assign a cause of action for personal injury; and (2) should the "common fund theory" extend to defendant, requiring it, under the reimbursement provisions, to bear a pro rata share of attorney's fees and costs incurred by its insured in securing a settlement or recovery against a third party tortfeasor.

* * * The Supreme Court of California has long adhered to the doctrine that if an injured party receives some compensation for his injuries from a source wholly independent of the tortfeasor, such payment should not be deducted from the damages which the plaintiff would otherwise collect from the tortfeasor. * * * [In] (*Helfend v. Southern Cal. Rapid Transit Dist.* (1970) 2 Cal.3d 1, 6, 84 Cal.Rptr. 173, 175, 465 P.2d 61, 63.) * * * the court in considering these circumstances said:

> "The collateral source rule as applied here embodies the venerable concept that a person who has invested years of insurance premiums to assure his medical care should receive the benefits of his thrift. The tortfeasor should not garner the benefits of his victim's providence.
>
> "The collateral source rule expresses a policy judgment in favor of encouraging citizens to purchase and maintain insurance for personal injuries and for other eventualities. Courts consider insurance a form of investment, the benefits of which become payable without respect to any other possible source of funds. If we were to permit a tortfeasor to mitigate damages with payments from plaintiff's insurance, plaintiff would be in a position inferior to that of having brought no insurance, because his payment of premiums would have earned no benefit. Defendant should not be able to avoid payment of full compensation for the injury inflicted merely because the victim has had the foresight to provide himself with insurance." * * *
>
> "[T]he plaintiff receives no double recovery; the collateral source rule simply serves as a means of by-passing the antiquated doctrine of nonassignment of tortious actions and permits a proper transfer of risk from the plaintiff's insurer to the tortfeasor by way of the victim's tort recovery. The double shift from the tortfeasor to the victim and then from the victim to his insurance carrier can normally occur with little costs in that the insurance carrier is often

intimately involved in the initial litigation and quite automatically receives its part of the tort settlement or verdict." * * *

[I]t is well established in California that an assignment of a cause of action for personal injuries is void and in the absence of statutory authority, a cause of action for personal injury is not subject to subrogation. (*Block v. Cal. Physicians' Service* (1966) 244 Cal.App.2d 266, 270, 53 Cal.Rptr. 51.) However, the court in *Block* stated, at page 273, 53 Cal.Rptr. at page 55: "By becoming a member of the plan under a Group Health Service agreement plaintiff has voluntarily associated himself with the public policy of this state. While he has a right to seek to be made whole, it is unfair for him to seek enrichment by double recovery which would result from retention of all proceeds of the settlement of his suit * * * and of all medical and hospital benefits paid to him by defendant Service under its [insurance] agreement—for the same injuries—all eventually at the cost of the participating members of the plan." It has been clearly established in California that insurance contract provisions, although classified as adhesion contracts, requiring reimbursement of medical payments under the label of subrogation but providing only access to the proceeds of settlement or judgment resulting from the exercise of rights of recovery by the injured person, are valid and enforceable. * * *

Plaintiffs place emphasis upon the fact that each of the challenged provisions is prefaced by the label "subrogation." Subrogation or assignment of a cause of action for personal injury operates to transfer from one person to another that cause against a third party. The reasons of policy against the assignment or subrogation of certain personal causes do not apply to insurance policy provisions that merely require the insured to reimburse the insurer out of any recovery or settlement. Plaintiffs have stressed the use of the word "subrogation" in the insurance agreement while arguing against the requirement that the insured execute and deliver instruments and papers and do whatever else is necessary in order to secure the insurers' rights labeled "subrogation." The right of subrogation contained in each contract is stated to be "* * * to the extent of such payment to the proceeds of any settlement or judgment that may result from the exercise of any rights of recovery which *the injured person or anyone receiving such payment* may have against any person or organization * * *." (Emphasis added.) The argument that the provision under attack is an assignment or true subrogation obviously fails. Substance rather than form is the determining factor. The right given to the insurer according to the terms of the policy is not to the chose in action but is to the proceeds of any settlement or judgment resulting from the exercise of the injured party's rights of recovery against a third party tortfeasor. The right of repayment, reimbursement or subrogation does not arise until the proceeds of settlement or judgment come into existence. * * *

The trial court properly held valid the so-called subrogation provisions of defendant's insurance policies.

Defendant State Farm Mutual Automobile Insurance Company appeals from that portion of the summary judgment awarding plaintiffs a pro rata share of their litigation costs and attorney's fees expended in procuring a settlement or recovery against possible third party tortfeasors. It is conceded that some of the plaintiffs were required to pay attorney's fees and costs in their process of securing settlement or recovery from which reimbursement was required. In support of its argument against the imposition of a pro rata share of such costs, defendant contends that its contracts of insurance do not provide for payment of any portion of its insureds' attorney's fees incurred while pursuing their personal right of recovery against third persons. Defendant asserts that in the absence of a controlling statute or an agreement between the parties, attorney's fees are generally not awarded to successful litigants. * * *

However, under certain circumstances, the inherent equitable powers of the court have been utilized to create exceptions to the basic rule on attorney's fees. The prime example is the "common fund" exception as described by the Supreme Court in *D'Amico v. Board of Medical Examiners* (1974) 11 Cal.3d 1, 112 Cal.Rptr. 786, 520 P.2d 10. The Court there, at page 25, 112 Cal.Rptr. at page 803, 520 P.2d at page 27, stated: "[W]hen a number of persons are entitled in common to a specific fund, and an action brought by a plaintiff or plaintiffs for the benefit of all results in the creation or preservation of that fund, such plaintiff or plaintiffs may be awarded attorneys fees out of the fund," * * * here, unless ordered to participate pro rata in plaintiff's attorney's fees and cost, defendant, as a passive beneficiary, would be unjustly enriched by reimbursement of medical payments as required by the provisions of the insurance contract.

The judgment is affirmed; each side shall bear its own costs.

FRIEDMAN, ASSOCIATE JUSTICE (concurring).

I concur, but with reluctance. My unwilling agreement results from the precedential force of *Block v. California Physicians' Service* (1966) 244 Cal.App.2d 266, 53 Cal.Rptr. 51, and *West v. State Farm Mutual Automobile Ins. Co.* (1973) 30 Cal.App.3d 562, 106 Cal.Rptr. 486. In composite, these two decisions represent a creeping erosion of the anti-subrogation principle established at common law * * *. The successive amendments of State Farm's "reimbursement" clauses illustrate how eagerly and quickly the disingenuous draftsmen of insurance policies move into the gaps created by decisional erosion.

Although I respectfully suggest that the *West* decision was unrealistic, it is possible that State Farm's draftsmanship goes beyond the limits staked out in that case. The *West* decision expressly abstained from considering the effect of a clause requiring the insured to bring suit against the third party. (30 Cal.App.3d at p. 565, 106 Cal.Rptr. 486.) The present policy contains such a clause. The cumulative effect of the policy provisions is to create the economic reality of subrogation to the personal injury claim without its language.

The defendant insurance company argues that these clauses prevent double recovery. A liability insurance policy is a piece of merchandise. (See 7 Williston on Contracts, § 900, p. 34.) In a free society an individual may go out and buy and keep all the merchandise he desires. The question is not whether the policyholder is recovering from two sources but whether the insurance company is supplying the merchandise for which it exacted a premium. The double recovery argument is singularly unmoving. * * *

### Notes

1. The above holding was further extended in Hartford Accident and Indemnity Co. v. Gropman, 163 Cal.App.3d Supp. 33, 209 Cal.Rptr. 468 (Super.1984) to apply to medical coverage in individual automobile policies as well as to group policies.

2. *Public policy and subrogation to medical claims*

When an auto insurer makes first party medical payments and then claims subrogation "to all of the insured's rights of recovery" (up to the amount of the payments) against the tort feasor, objections continue to be made. E.g. Maxwell v. Allstate Ins. Cos., 102 Nev. 502, 728 P.2d 812 (1986):

> "Assuming, without deciding, that a medical payments subrogation clause would now be statutorily permissable, we consider whether the subrogation clause violates public policy" [The court held that it does]. "Precluding subrogation does not result in double recovery, the insured is merely receiving the benefits for which he has already paid. * * * Further, the injured party may be unable to fully recover his actual damages * * *. [He] must often compromise because of liability problems or limited coverage carried by the tort feasor * * *. The injured party suffers 'out of pocket' losses such as loss of income or earning power and costs of asserting the claim and non-economic losses such as pain and mental anguish * * *. Yet under a subrogation for its medical expense payments, the insurer is assured full reimbursement for its medical expense payments regardless of whether the injured person's tort recovery fully covers his actual damages."
>
> Is there a flaw in this reasoning? What if premiums reflected anticipated subrogation recovery?

3. *Subrogation and settlements*

In Westendorf by Westendorf v. Stasson, 330 N.W.2d 699 (Minn.1983) a Health Maintenance Organization (HMO) paid the medical expenses of an enrollee who had been injured in an auto accident and sought "reimbursement" from a settlement effected between the enrollee and the tort feasor. The court held that the clause in question applied only to payments specifically collected by the enrollee for those medical expenses. It further held that although the word used was "reimbursement" the equitable principles that govern "subrogation" would apply. Therefore reimbursement "will not be allowed where the insured's total recovery is less than the insured's actual loss." [Note that this is the same rule laid down in *Wimberly v. American Casualty Co. of Reading, Pa. (CNA),* 584 S.W.2d 200 (Tenn.1979) reprinted as a main case *supra.*]

Questions remain:

a) is the "insured's actual loss" the medical expenses incurred by the enrollee in the HMO in the *Westendorf* case; or the more expansive concept of loss developed in the *Maxwell* case in note 2?

b) the settlement reached between the enrollee in the HMO and the tortfeasor in the *Westendorf* case was for $100,000. How do we know how much went for actual medical expenses? Suppose the parties (as in the actual case) do not say? Could they be trusted if they did say?

### *Problem*

The X insurance company issued an auto policy to D providing both personal injury protection (P.I.P.) up to $10,000 and uninsured motorist protection up to $35,000. A separate premium was paid for each coverage. The P.I.P. portion read: "If we (the insurer) make a payment under this coverage and the person to whom payment is made recovers damages from another, that person shall reimburse us to the extent of our payment."

D was badly injured in a collision with an uninsured motorist and the X insurance company immediately paid $10,000 in P.I.P. benefits. D settled her claim against the uninsured motorist for $25,000. The amount of her damages has been fixed at $45,000. D now claims an additional $35,000 under the uninsured motorist provision, asserting that the reimbursement provision is unenforceable. At least she claims it was contrary to her reasonable expectations. What decision? Suppose the amount of her personal injury damages was determined to be $60,000. Would that affect the decision? Cf. Keenan v. Industrial Indemnity Ins. Co., 108 Wash.2d 314, 738 P.2d 270 (1987).

## IN RE ESTATE OF SCOTT

Appellate Court of Illinois, Second District, 1991.
208 Ill.App.3d 846, 153 Ill.Dec. 647, 567 N.E.2d 605.

JUSTICE GEIGER delivered the opinion of the court:

The respondent estate (the estate) of William W. Scott, Jr. (Billy), appeals from the trial court's order awarding the claimant Sundstrand–Sauer (Sundstrand or the company) judgment on the subrogation provision of its Health and Disability Group Insurance Plan (the Plan). We affirm.

In March 1988, Billy, who was age 18, was seriously injured while riding as a passenger on a motorcycle. He was later declared a disabled adult and his estate brought suit based upon the accident. Sundstrand, Billy's father's employer, paid approximately $200,000 for Billy's injuries pursuant to the terms of the Sundstrand health plan. The Plan includes a subrogation clause which states: "*Subrogation, Assignment and Lien.* On payments of benefits hereunder as a result of Injury or Illness, the Fund shall be subrogated, to the extent of benefits made or to be made under This Plan, to all the rights of a Covered Individual against any person, firm or organization arising out of such Injury or Illness and the Covered Individual shall execute and deliver instruments and documents and do whatever is necessary to secure such rights to the Fund. The Covered Individual shall do nothing to prejudice such rights. Each Covered Employee hereby assigns to the Trustees of the Fund out of any amounts received or to be received by the Covered Individual as a result of Injury or Illness for which the Covered Individual has a claim against any person, firm or organization to the extent of benefits made or to be made under This Plan. In addition, the Covered Individual hereby grants a lien to the Trustees of the Fund out of any amounts received or to be received by the Covered Individual as a result of Injury or Illness for which the Covered Individual has a claim against any person, firm or organization to the extent of benefits made or to be made under This Plan."

In January 1989, the court signed an order approving the estate's settlement with the motorist who had struck Billy's motorcycle. That settlement was for the motorist's $121,000 insurance policy limit. After the payment of court-approved fees, there remained approximately $82,-000 in estate assets. In February 1990, after a hearing and receipt of written arguments regarding Sundstrand's claim for subrogation, the court entered its order finding that under the Plan's subrogation clause, the company was entitled to the remainder of the estate's assets from the settlement. The estate brought this appeal.

The estate's first argument on appeal is that either Sundstrand's claim should be denied or it should be allowed only on a pro rata basis because Billy did not receive full compensation for his injuries. It notes that the trial court observed that Billy's damages could be worth $3 to $5 million and that the settlement did not make him whole. The argument's focus is that the subrogation award, by depleting the estate's assets, is inequitable.

Sundstrand responds to this argument by asserting that the estate, through Billy, is an intended third-party beneficiary of the Plan and that Sundstrand's clear contractual rights should not be overridden by inapplicable equitable analysis.

Rights to subrogation originated in equity, and they may now arise in common-law, or through statute or contract. (See Dworak v. Tempel (1959), 17 Ill.2d 181, 190–92, 161 N.E.2d 258.) Medical subrogation clauses in insurance contracts are generally enforceable; furthermore, if such a clause is enforceable, it is not common-law concepts of subrogation but the contract terms that control. See Spirek v. State Farm Mutual Automobile Insurance Co. (1978), 65 Ill.App.3d 440, 449, 21 Ill.Dec. 817, 382 N.E.2d 111.

In this case, it is clear that, in the fashion that Billy was named as a covered dependant under his father's health plan with Sundstrand, the parties manifested their intent to confer third-party beneficiary status upon him so that he was a direct contract beneficiary. (See Altevogt v. Brinkoetter (1981), 85 Ill.2d 44, 54–55, 51 Ill.Dec. 674, 421 N.E.2d 182.) It is also clear that based on that coverage, Sundstrand extended some $200,000 in payments on account of Billy's accident and the resulting disability. The insurance contract that obligated Sundstrand to cover Billy's expenses also included a clear right to subrogation. It provided that the company's insurance fund would be subrogated, to the extent of benefits extended, to all amounts received by or due a covered individual because of an injury creating a claim under the Plan. Billy's insurance settlement following the injury was for a lesser amount than the benefits already extended by Sundstrand on account of that same injury.

We find that the trial court's careful analysis was correct and that the company was entitled to the full subrogation ordered. This is not a case based in equity, but rather on contractual terms. Furthermore, courts have recognized the equity of subrogating insurers to their insureds' rights against tortfeasors who had caused an insurance claim. (See Dworak v. Tempel (1959), 17 Ill.2d 181, 190–92, 161 N.E.2d 258.) Further, we note that it is not determinative that the subrogation order depletes the estate's assets. To the extent, if any, that the estate's settlement did not accurately compensate the estate, Sundstrand is not at fault. We note, also, that, to the extent that the estate's resources are less than the claim payments made by Sundstrand, the company is also disadvantaged by the estate's small settlement.

We are not persuaded by the estate's foreign authority (see Rimes v. State Farm Mutual Automobile Insurance Co. (1982), 106 Wis.2d 263, 275, 316 N.W.2d 348, 353), where the court held that an insurer may not be subrogated unless the insured has been made whole for his loss. In Illinois, also, the doctrine of subrogation will be applied or not applied, according to the dictates of equity, good conscience, and public policy considerations. (Reich v. Tharp (1987), 167 Ill.App.3d 496, 501, 118 Ill.Dec. 248, 521 N.E.2d 530.) However, its use is encouraged in appropriate circumstances. (See In re Estate of Schmidt (1979), 79 Ill.App.3d 456, 458, 34 Ill.Dec. 766, 398 N.E.2d 589.) We are not aware that Illinois has ever made a statement analogous to that of the Rimes court.

As Sundstrand points out, this case is distinct from the wrongful death cases upon which the estate partially relies. There, courts noted a public policy against subrogation in the case of wrongful death. (See In re Estate of Schmidt (1979), 79 Ill.App.3d 456, 458, 34 Ill.Dec. 766, 398 N.E.2d 589; National Bank v. Podgorski (1978), 57 Ill.App.3d 265, 14 Ill.Dec. 951, 373 N.E.2d 82.) In Hardware Dealers Mutual Fire Insurance Co. v. Ross (1970), 129 Ill.App.2d 217, 262 N.E.2d 618, also a wrongful death case, the court found no full recovery by the injured insured and no right to subrogation by the plaintiff insurer. The absence of full recovery by the injured insured, however, was not determinative in Ross. There, importantly, the insurer had sought to avoid liability for the insured's claim, and only after the insured had received a third-party insurance settlement had it stipulated to its coverage.

Here, where Sundstrand's insurance contract with Billy through his father included an unambiguous applicable subrogation clause, and where Sundstrand apparently has made all payments which it was obligated to make under that contract, we find no reason to deny subrogation. Furthermore, we find no Illinois authority to support the estate's alternative argument that Sundstrand should receive only a pro rata share of settlement proceeds.

The estate also argues that Sundstrand's subrogation interest amounts to an assignment of a personal tort, which is void as against public policy. According to the estate, the enforcement of the subrogation to Sundstrand, when Billy had not been made whole by the settlement, would operate as an assignment of all Billy's rights. As a consequence, Billy would not be compensated for his injuries, disability, pain and suffering, and lost earnings.

We agree with Sundstrand that the estate has improperly characterized the subrogation claim as an "assignment." Sundstrand neither sought nor received Billy's rights to make full claims for his injury. Rather, it merely sought and was awarded the right to recoup payments advanced to the estate which had been recovered from a third-party source. (See Remsen v. Midway Liquors, Inc. (1961), 30 Ill.App.2d 132, 144, 174 N.E.2d 7.) Contrary to the estate's assertion, the language of the Plan's subrogation provision does not call for the full assignment of the insured's rights but, rather, mere reimbursement of amounts forwarded by the Plan.

The estate's concluding argument is that allowance of Sundstrand's claim would violate article 1, section 12, of the Illinois Constitution (Ill. Const.1970, art. I, § 12), or be a denial of due process under the United States Constitution. Article 1, section 12, provides that "[e]very person shall find a certain remedy in the laws for all injuries and wrongs which he receives to his person * * *. He shall obtain justice by law, freely, completely, and promptly." Ill. Const.1970, art. I, § 12.

We agree with Sundstrand's response that there is no merit to this argument. Sundstrand was awarded subrogation only after a full hearing in which the estate fully participated. We find no basis for a due process claim. (See Mathews v. Eldridge (1976), 424 U.S. 319, 96 S.Ct. 893, 47 L.Ed.2d 18.) Also, we reiterate that, to the extent that Billy was not fully compensated for damages beyond his medical expenses, that is a result of the limited settlement to which the estate agreed; Sundstrand, which has a valid claim to recovery of its insurance expenses in Billy's behalf, is not responsible for that agreement.

Based upon our conclusions above, we need not consider Sundstrand's argument that ERISA (Federal Employee Retirement Income Security Act) provisions preempt any Illinois limitations upon Sundstrand's right to subrogation.

Accordingly, we affirm the judgment of the circuit court of Stephenson County.

Affirmed.

McLaren, J., concurs.

Presiding Justice Reinhard, specially concurring:

I would affirm the trial court, but I do not agree with the entire analysis of the majority opinion.

In its principal contention the estate asks us, under principles of equity and public policy, to either deny or restrict Sundstrand's contractual right to recoup up to the full amount of its medical expense payments from the settlement. Sundstrand responds that the Employee Retirement Income Security Act of 1974 (ERISA) (29 U.S.C. § 1001 et seq. (1988)) preempts State judicial or statutory limitations on subrogation provisions in self-insured employee benefit plans. Although the estate acknowledges that there is authority for Sundstrand's position (see, e.g., Reilly v. Blue Cross & Blue Shield United (7th Cir.1988), 846 F.2d 416), the estate asks us to rely on contrary authority (see, e.g., FMC Corp. v. Holliday (3d Cir.1989), 885 F.2d 79).

The Supreme Court recently addressed these conflicting decisions on this issue and ruled that States may not restrict contractual subrogation provisions contained in self-insured employee benefit plans. (FMC Corp. v. Holliday (1990), 498 U.S. ___, 111 S.Ct. 403, 112 L.Ed.2d 356.) The estate concedes in its reply brief that, if ERISA's preemption provisions are applied, "then all state laws including Illinois common law of subrogation and equity are preempted." Thus, the Supreme Court's decision in Holliday preempts judicial modification of the contractual subrogation provision. The majority's analysis of the validity of the subrogation provision under Illinois law is unnecessary, and I do not partake in it. I concur in the balance of the majority opinion regarding the other issues raised.

## *Notes*

1. By 1975, when the numbers of medical malpractice lawsuits in California had swollen to what many thought were unbearable numbers, the Legislature, in extraordinary sessions, enacted a number of Code sections [known collectively as the Medical Injury Compensation Reform Act or "MICRA"] which it was hoped would alleviate the "crisis". Extracts follow (for brevity definitions and certain other materials are omitted):

### *Business and Professions Code*

**§ 6146. Limitations; periodic payments**

(a) An attorney shall not contract for or collect a contingency fee for representing any person seeking damages in connection with an action for injury or damage against a health care provider based upon such person's alleged professional negligence in excess of the following limits:

(1) Forty percent of the first fifty thousand dollars ($50,000) recovered.

(2) Thirty-three and one-third percent of the next fifty thousand dollars ($50,000) recovered.

(3) Twenty-five percent of the next five hundred thousand dollars ($500,-000) recovered.

(4) Fifteen percent of any amount on which the recovery exceeds six hundred thousand dollars ($600,000).

The limitations shall apply regardless of whether the recovery is by settlement, arbitration, or judgment, or whether the person for whom the recovery is made is a responsible adult, an infant, or a person of unsound mind.

(b) If periodic payments are awarded to the plaintiff pursuant to Section 667.7 of the Code of Civil Procedure, the court shall place a total value on these payments based upon the projected life expectancy of the plaintiff and include this amount in computing the total award from which attorney's fees are calculated under this section.

(c) * * *.

*Code of Civil Procedure*

### § 667.7. Action against health care provider; periodic payments of future damages; contempt; legislative intent

(a) In any action for injury or damages against a provider of health care services, a superior court shall, at the request of either party, enter a judgment ordering that money damages or its equivalent for future damages of the judgment creditor be paid in whole or in part by periodic payments rather than by a lump-sum payment if the award equals or exceeds fifty thousand dollars ($50,000) in future damages. In entering a judgment ordering the payment of future damages by periodic payments, the court shall make a specific finding as to the dollar amount of periodic payments which will compensate the judgment creditor for such future damages. As a condition to authorizing periodic payments of future damages, the court shall require the judgment debtor who is not adequately insured to post security adequate to assure full payment of such damages awarded by the judgment. Upon termination of periodic payments of future damages, the court shall order the return of this security, or so much as remains, to the judgment debtor.

(b)(1) The judgment ordering the payment of future damages by periodic payments shall specify the recipient or recipients of the payments, the dollar amount of the payments, the interval between payments, and the number of payments or the period of time over which payments shall be made. Such payments shall only be subject to modification in the event of the death of the judgment creditor.

(2) In the event that the court finds that the judgment debtor has exhibited a continuing pattern of failing to make the payments, as specified in paragraph (1), the court shall find the judgment debtor in contempt of court and, in addition to the required periodic payments, shall order the judgment debtor to pay the judgment creditor all damages caused by the failure to make such periodic payments, including court costs and attorney's fees.

(c) However, money damages awarded for loss of future earnings shall not be reduced or payments terminated by reason of the death of the judgment creditor, but shall be paid to persons to whom the judgment creditor owed a duty of support, as provided by law, immediately prior to his death. In such cases the court which rendered the original judgment, may, upon petition of any party in interest, modify the judgment to award and apportion the unpaid future damages in accordance with this subdivision.

(d) Following the occurrence or expiration of all obligations specified in the periodic payment judgment, any obligation of the judgment debtor to make further payments shall cease and any security given, pursuant to subdivision (a) shall revert to the judgment debtor.

(e) * * *.

### § 1295. Contract for medical services; mandatory provision; waiver of right to sue; form of notice; nature of contract

(a) Any contract for medical services which contains a provision for arbitration of any dispute as to professional negligence of a health care provider shall have such provision as the first article of the contract and shall be expressed in the following language: "It is understood that any dispute as to medical malpractice, that is as to whether any medical services rendered under this contract were unnecessary or unauthorized or were improperly, negligently or incompetently rendered, will be determined by submission to arbitration as provided by California law, and not by a lawsuit or resort to court process except as California law provides for judicial review of arbitration proceedings. Both parties to this contract, by entering into it, are giving up their constitutional right to have any such dispute decided in a court of law before a jury, and instead are accepting the use of arbitration."

(b) Immediately before the signature line provided for the individual contracting for the medical services must appear the following in at least 10–point bold red type:

"NOTICE: BY SIGNING THIS CONTRACT YOU ARE AGREEING TO HAVE ANY ISSUE OF MEDICAL MALPRACTICE DECIDED BY NEUTRAL ARBITRATION AND YOU ARE GIVING UP YOUR RIGHT TO A JURY OR COURT TRIAL. SEE ARTICLE 1 OF THIS CONTRACT."

(c) Once signed, such a contract governs all subsequent open-book account transactions for medical services for which the contract was signed until or unless rescinded by written notice within 30 days of signature. Written notice of such rescission may be given by a guardian or conservator of the patient if the patient is incapacitated or a minor.

(d) Where the contract is one for medical services to a minor, it shall not be subject to disaffirmance if signed by the minor's parent or legal guardian.

(e) Such a contract is not a contract of adhesion, nor unconscionable nor otherwise improper, where it complies with subdivisions (a), (b) and (c) of this section.

(f) * * *

(g) * * *

*Civil Code*

### § 3333.1. Negligence of health care provider; evidence of benefits and premiums paid; subrogation

(a) In the event the defendant so elects, in an action for personal injury against a health care provider based upon professional negligence, he may introduce evidence of any amount payable as a benefit to the plaintiff as a result of the personal injury pursuant to the United States Social Security Act, any state or federal income disability or worker's compensation act, any health, sickness or income-disability insurance, accident insurance that provides health benefits or income-disability coverage, and any contract or agreement of any group, organization, partnership, or corporation to provide, pay for, or reimburse the cost of medical, hospital, dental, or other health care services. Where the defendant elects to introduce such evidence, the plaintiff may introduce evidence of any amount which the plaintiff has paid or contributed to secure his right to any insurance benefits concerning which the defendant has introduced evidence.

(b) No source of collateral benefits introduced pursuant to subdivision (a) shall recover any amount against the plaintiff nor shall it be subrogated to the rights of the plaintiff against a defendant.

(c) * * *

**§ 3333.2. Negligence of health care provider; noneconomic losses; limitation**

(a) In any action for injury against a health care provider based on professional negligence, the injured plaintiff shall be entitled to recover noneconomic losses to compensate for pain, suffering, inconvenience, physical impairment, disfigurement and other nonpecuniary damage.

(b) In no action shall the amount of damages for noneconomic losses exceed two hundred fifty thousand dollars ($250,000).

(c) * * *.

2. For purposes of the above sections, the definition in Civil Code Sec. 3333.1(c)(2) will suffice as illustrative:

"Professional negligence" means a negligent act or omission to act by a health care provider in the rendering of professional services, which act or omission is the proximate cause of a personal injury or wrongful death, provided that such services are within the scope of services for which the provider is licensed and which are not within any restriction imposed by the licensing agency or licensed hospital.

3. The term "collateral source" (see sec. 3333.1(b) above) deserves emphasis. A classic discussion of it in California is found in Helfend v. Southern California Rapid Transit District, 2 Cal.3d 1, 84 Cal.Rptr. 173, 465 P.2d 61 (1970) in which the collateral source doctrine was employed to deny the tortfeasor defendant the right to offset the plaintiff's hospitalization benefits against the plaintiff's claim. The court noted that the collateral source rule which was applied in the case "embodies the venerable concept that a person who has invested years of insurance premiums to assure his medical care (in the case Blue Cross) should receive the benefit of his thrift." 2 Cal.2d 1, 9–10. The court observed that the policy concerned provided for a "refund of benefits" to the insurer out of any recovery made by the plaintiff. Subrogation and "collateral source" are opposite sides of the same coin. This makes the provision of Sec. 3333.1 doubly interesting.

## BLUE CROSS AND BLUE SHIELD OF KANSAS, INC. v. RIVERSIDE HOSPITAL

Supreme Court of Kansas, 1985.
237 Kan. 829, 703 P.2d 1384.

McFarland, Justice:

The facts are not in dispute and may be summarized as follows. Leslie Stadalman is an employee of defendant Riverside Hospital and, as such, is a "covered person" under that institution's employee health care plan. Leslie Stadalman is the wife of Gregory Stadalman. Mr. Stadalman is employed by the City of Wichita and is covered under his employer's Blue Cross–Blue Shield group health plan. The Blue Cross–Blue Shield plan provides coverage for Mr. Stadalman's dependents. In the Fall of 1982, Leslie Stadalman incurred medical expenses in the amount of $1,963.19. The Riverside plan refused to pay the claims on the basis it provided only secondary coverage. Blue Cross–Blue Shield (plaintiff) initially refused to pay the claims for the same reason—that its plan provided only secondary coverage. Ultimately, Blue Cross–Blue Shield paid the claims, expressly reserving the right to seek contribution and indemnity from Riverside. This action resulted.

Blue Cross–Blue Shield Plan

The Blue Cross–Blue Shield plan contains the following provisions:

Non-Duplication of Benefits.

"M.1 *The Plans will not duplicate benefits for covered health care services for which You are eligible under any of the following Programs:*

*Group, blanket, or franchise insurance.*

* * *

"Individual health insurance contracts are not included as Programs.

"M.2 To avoid duplicate benefit payments, one Program will be 'Primary' and others will be 'Secondary'.

"a. *When the Plans are Primary, benefits will be paid without regard to other coverage.*

"b. *When the Plans are Secondary, the benefits under this Certificate may be reduced. The benefits for Covered Services will be no more than the balance of charges remaining after the benefits of other Programs are applied to Covered Services.*

"M.3 Under this Certificate, the *Plans are Secondary when:*

a. *You are covered as a dependent under this Certificate but are covered as an employee, union, or association member under another Program;* or

* * *

c. The other Program does not have a non-duplication of benefits provision; or

* * *

"In all other instances, the Plans are Primary under this Certificate." (Emphasis supplied.)

RIVERSIDE PLAN

The Riverside Plan contains the following provisions:

"1. ELIGIBILITY FOR COVERED PERSONS: The following persons will be eligible for coverage under the Plan;

(a) All permanent full-time employees in Active Service at their customary place of employment who work a minimum of 30 hours per week for the Employer.

(b) All other persons are excluded."

The Riverside plan contains the further provision:

NON-DUPLICATION OF BENEFITS

"This *Plan* has been *designed* by specific action of the Board of Directors of Osteopathic Hospital *to coordinate payment of benefits with other plans so as to avoid overpayments. This Plan requires that if any person covered hereunder is also covered under any other plan* (as defined below), *the other plan shall be primary and this Plan shall pay the balance of expenses up to the total eligible charges.* In no event shall the combined payments exceed 100%.

"However, it is the intent of the Plan to be primary as regard to any participant who is not covered under any other Plan as defined below.

"*Plan means any plan providing benefits or services for any health or dental care under any group, franchise, blanket insurance,* health maintenance plan, union welfare, governmental plan, or any coverage required by statute." (Emphasis supplied.)

The district court held the non-duplication of benefits provisions of the two plans to be conflicting and mutually repugnant and directed that the Stadalman claim be paid 50% by each plan. Both Blue Cross–Blue Shield and Riverside were aggrieved by this determination and duly appealed therefrom.

* * *

As applicable to the narrow issue raised herein, both plans have quite similar purposes. They are group health care plans provided by employers to their employees without cost to the employees where only the employee is covered (single coverage). If the employee desires family coverage, he or she must contribute to the cost of the coverage. These plans seek to provide adequate financially responsible coverage at the lowest cost. In keeping with this goal, benefits should not be duplicated where an individual has coverage under more than one such plan—hence the need for non-duplication of benefits clauses, or as sometimes referred to, "coordination of benefits" clauses.

* * *

If both plans are studied side by side, as equals, it would appear Leslie Stadalman has two secondary coverages and no primary coverage. This is an untenable position to maintain, and this led the district court to hold the plans to be mutually repugnant. This approach was followed (relative to automobile liability policies) in *Western Cas. & Surety Co. v. Universal Underwriters Ins. Co.,* 232 Kan. 606, 657 P.2d 576, wherein we held:

> " '[W]here two or more policies provide coverage for the particular event and all the policies in question contain "excess insurance" clauses—it is generally held that such clauses are mutually repugnant and must be disregarded, rendering each company liable for a pro rata share of the judgment or settlement, since, if literal effect were given to both "excess insurance" clauses of the applicable policies, neither policy would cover the loss and such a result would produce an unintended absurdity.' 7A Am.Jur.2d, Automobile Insurance § 434, pp. 87–88.

* * *

The difficulties of such a proration procedure when applied to employee health care group plans has been pointed out by Blue Cross–Blue Shield—the two plans have different deductibles, covered services, and coinsurance provisions.

Leslie Stadalman is an employee of Riverside and coverage was provided to her as a "covered person" as defined by the plan. Mrs. Stadalman, as a "covered person" (as opposed to a covered dependent), received the coverage as a part of her employment, and, as required by ERISA, was fully advised of the plan in writing. The Riverside plan was intended to provide her coverage but would not pay duplicate benefits with those she would have under another group employee plan. We believe the logical approach is to look to her own plan first in determining the effect of non-duplication of benefits provisions. The Riverside plan (repeated for convenience) provides:

> "This Plan has been designed by specific action of the Board of Directors of Osteopathic Hospital to *coordinate payment of benefits with other plans so as to avoid overpayments.* This Plan requires that if any person covered hereunder is also covered under any other plan (as defined below), the other plan shall be primary and this Plan shall pay the balance of expenses up to the total eligible charges. In no event shall the combined payments exceed 100%." (Emphasis supplied.)

If Mrs. Stadalman had held two jobs with primary coverage provided by the two respective employers, the Riverside plan would intend to avoid duplication of benefits by becoming secondary. As a dependent of

Gregory Stadalman under his Blue Cross–Blue Shield family plan, Leslie Stadalman has Blue Cross–Blue Shield coverage that is only excess (secondary) in nature. Her own group plan is primary unless another group plan provides primary coverage. The Blue Cross–Blue Shield plan does not provide primary coverage to Mrs. Stadalman by virtue of the fact she is a covered employee in her own group plan. Therefore, there is no potentiality for duplication of benefits or overpayment. In such circumstances, generally, the primary coverage of Riverside should pay all benefits due thereunder on the claims, and the excess claims should be submitted to Blue Cross–Blue Shield for determination of benefits due under its secondary coverage. On the specific claims involved herein, the parties do not directly address the matter of whether the Riverside plan, as the provider with primary coverage, would provide full coverage therefor. There are inferences that such is the case, but we are not satisfied that the parties have agreed such is true. Therefore, we decline to reverse and enter judgment against Riverside for the entire amount of the claims paid by Blue Cross–Blue Shield. This aspect of the case must be determined by the district court.

The judgment of the district court is reversed and the case is remanded with directions to enter judgment against defendant consistent with this opinion.

## O'BAR v. MFA MUTUAL INSURANCE COMPANY

Supreme Court of Arkansas, 1982.
275 Ark. 247, 628 S.W.2d 561.

HICKMAN, JUSTICE.

The only issue on appeal is whether a reduction clause in an automobile insurance policy that provides for $5,000 in accidental death benefits is void because it violates public policy. The trial court held that the clause which reduced payment by any amounts paid under worker's compensation law was valid. We disagree and find such a provision void as against public policy.

The appellant's husband, Jeweral Wayne O'Bar, was killed in a vehicle accident while driving his employer's truck. His widow, Reba Faye O'Bar, the appellant, and his child received over $5,000 for his death from worker's compensation. O'Bar had an automobile insurance policy with the appellee, MFA Mutual Insurance Company, and it provided $5,000 in benefits for accidental death. MFA refused to pay, relying on a clause in the policy which reads:

> REDUCTION OF AMOUNT PAYABLE—Any amount payable under the terms of this coverage on account of death of an insured shall be reduced by the amount paid and the present value of all amounts payable on account of such death under any workmen's compensation law, disability benefits law or any other similar law.

The case was submitted to the trial court for summary judgment and the court ruled for MFA. Both parties relied to an extent on our decision in Aetna Ins. Co. v. Smith, 263 Ark. 849, 568 S.W.2d 11 (1978), which held such a reduction clause for medical and disability benefits was not void. *Aetna* interpreted Arkansas's no fault insurance law, enacted in 1973. Ark.Stat.Ann. §§ 66–4014—66–4021 * * *. The no fault law was enacted "* * * to make an insured whole on relatively minor automobile injury damage claims without regard to fault * * *" * * *. It provided that policies must give an insured the right to certain minimum medical and hospital benefits, income disability benefits and accidental death benefits. * * * But the insured has the right to reject in writing any one or all of such benefits. * * *.

More importantly, an insurance company has the *right* to reduce, or claim reimbursement for any medical hospital benefits or income disability benefits paid out. Ark.Stat.Ann. § 66–4019. No such right was granted in regard to accidental death benefits. Therein lies the crux of this case. While requiring automobile insurance policies to provide for three different types of benefits, the General Assembly granted the insurer the right to reduce only medical and income disability benefits by any amount recovered by the insured from another source. Obviously medical or income disability benefits if not so reduced would allow double recovery to certain beneficiaries. Accidental death benefits are like life insurance and life insurance is treated differently from medical and income disability benefits so far as double coverage is concerned. Life insurance is more in the nature of an investment and is actually a contract to pay a sum certain upon the death of the insured. 43 Am.Jur.2d *Insurance* §§ 3, 1594 (1969).

There is no convincing reason such a benefit should be reduced simply because an insured also receives worker's compensation and since the General Assembly made no such provision, we hold such a clause to be in violation of public policy.

Reversed.

## *Note*

### *Coordination of Private Medical Coverage with Medicare*

A common provision in private medical insurance policies is called the Medicare Care "Carve out" provision of which the following is a sample:

INTEGRATION WITH MEDICARE

1. Any benefits payable under the medical expense insurance provisions of this policy will be reduced by the amount of any benefit to which the insured is entitled under Medicare. The reduction will apply whether or not the individual has received, or made application for, such other benefits.

2. An insured is deemed "entitled" to all Medicare benefits for which he or she is or has become eligible.

One Hanton was insured under a medical policy containing that provision. He became 65 years of age on Aug. 11, 1982. He was hospitalized on Aug. 13 and on Aug. 18 called the Social Security Administration to apply for

Medicare, but was unable to complete the processing of his application before his death on Aug. 20. His estate got around to filing the application in June 1983, but it was rejected by the Social Security Administration because it violated its rule that written application had to be filed within 6 months of the original contact with the office to be entitled to retirement insurance benefits. Therefore no benefits were payable. In the meantime Hanton's private insurer has refused to pay anything on the ground that he was "entitled" to Medicare under the Integration provision.

Who should pay, if anyone? See Jeczala v. Lincoln Nat. Life Ins. Co., 146 Ill.App.3d 1043, 100 Ill.Dec. 536, 497 N.E.2d 514 (1986).

### *Addendum*

Because health care and workers' compensation insurance costs continue to outpace other expenses, employers and insurers have sought to ensure that "double recovery" be prevented through increasing coordination of all benefits. One proposal is "24–Hour Care", a plan which would combine workers' compensation coverage with health care coverage in a single package. It is likely that thorough coordination of benefits will be included in any changes adopted in state or national healthcare reform.

# Chapter 11

# LIFE INSURANCE FOR BUSINESS PURPOSES, SPECIAL PROBLEMS

___ **debtor-creditor relationship**

___ **rights of assignee vis-a-vis beneficiary (the insurable interest resurfaces)**

___ **employer-employee relationship (keyperson insurance)**

___ **funding buy-sell agreements**

## WELLS v. JOHN HANCOCK MUTUAL LIFE INSURANCE CO.

Court of Appeal of California, Second District, 1978.
85 Cal.App.3d 66, 149 Cal.Rptr. 171.

KAUS, PRESIDING JUSTICE.

Plaintiff, Ruth Wells, appeals from judgment in favor of defendant John Hancock Mutual Life Insurance Company (John Hancock) after John Hancock's demurrer to her first amended complaint was sustained with leave to amend, but she failed to do so.

FACTS

The various causes of action which plaintiff has attempted to allege against John Hancock, arise out of these basic facts:

One Robert S. Parker, who died on March 11, 1975, had been plaintiff's accountant and financial adviser for over twenty years. Between May 1, 1973 and August 1, 1974, plaintiff loaned Parker a total of $31,000.[57] On September 1, 1974—one month after the last loan had been made to him—Parker assigned to plaintiff as security for these loans a life insurance policy which John Hancock had issued to him on

**57.** The loans were evidenced by three promissory notes. The first, in the amount of $15,000, was executed on May 1, 1973 and payable on May 1, 1976; the second in the amount of $6,000 was executed on December 6, 1973 and repayable in installments; the third note in the sum of $10,000 was dated August 1, 1974 and payable in full on August 1, 1977.

January 20, 1972. The policy in question was a ten-year decreasing term policy, which at no time had any surrender or nonforfeiture value. The initial sum insured was $100,000. At the time of the assignment to plaintiff it was $85,900. At the time of issue, Parker had been 46 years old.

The assignment was executed on a printed form furnished by John Hancock. It recites the amount of the loan which the policy purportedly secures—$31,000. A duplicate of the assignment was filed at John Hancock's home office on October 3, 1974. On that date John Hancock in fact acknowledged receipt of the assignment as follows: "The John Hancock Mutual Life Insurance Company, without assuming any responsibility for the validity or the sufficiency of the foregoing assignment, has, on this date, filed a duplicate thereof at its Home Office." This acknowledgment is itself part of John Hancock's printed form.[58]

On May 22, 1974, however, Parker had assigned the same policy to First Los Angeles Bank to secure a loan of $35,000. This assignment had also been filed with John Hancock's home office on June 14, 1974, but John Hancock at no time advised plaintiff of its existence.

Another blemish of the assignment was that at the time John Hancock received and acknowledged the assignment, the policy did not really exist—it had in fact lapsed for nonpayment of premiums and the passage of the grace period.[59] John Hancock at no time advised plaintiff of the fact that the policy had lapsed.

### The First Amended Complaint

The first amended complaint contains five causes of action, only four of which concern John Hancock, the first being directed against the administrator of Parker's estate. The second cause of action, labeled "FRAUD AND DECEIT," alleges that John Hancock fraudulently represented to plaintiff that there had been no prior assignment of the policy and that it was in full force and effect and that John Hancock made these misrepresentations intending to defraud plaintiff in various respects.[60] Had plaintiff been advised of the true condition of the policy she would have taken "necessary action to obtain other, more adequate, security for the * * * three notes." In addition, John Hancock's nondisclosure of the lapse of the policy prevented plaintiff from attempting to

**58.** Right below the John Hancock signature line appears a 6-part "notice," the first part of which reads as follows: "The company furnishes this form of assignment for the convenience of the parties, and it assumes no responsibility for its sufficiency or validity."

**59.** The policy could, however, have been reinstated on evidence of insurability satisfactory to John Hancock and payment of overdue premiums with interest.

**60.** "* * * with the intent to defraud and deceive plaintiff, to lull her into an unwarranted sense of security, to induce her not to pay premiums due or require ROBERT S. PARKER to submit evidence of insurability, to induce her to forbear making an investigation into ROBERT S. PARKER's financial condition or to otherwise take any action calculated to obtain other, more adequate, security for the aforementioned three notes."

revive it by paying the overdue premiums and submitting proof of insurability.[61]

The third cause of action, labeled "NEGLIGENCE," omits the allegations of intentional fraud and pleads more benignly that John Hancock negligently failed to inform plaintiff that there had been a prior assignment and that the policy had lapsed.

Plaintiff's fourth cause of action repeats the gist of the second and third counts and adds the conclusion that by reason of the pleaded facts John Hancock "is estopped to claim that the subject policy was not in full force and effect" at the time of Parker's death.

The fifth cause of action seeks declaratory relief against all defendants. It adds no relevant allegations, but does contain the intriguing news that on January 20, 1975, Parker had once more assigned the policy to one Phyllis Bracker as security for a loan of $15,000.

DISCUSSION

Of course, if anybody connected with the litigation had taken seriously plaintiff's allegations of actual, intentionally misleading fraud, we would not be here, for no court would have sustained defendant's general demurrer to the entire complaint. In truth, plaintiff has always made it clear that in spite of the liberal use of pejoratives in her pleadings, her grievance is not any hardcore lie by John Hancock, but its failure to advise her, in connection with its acknowledgment of having received a copy of the assignment, that the policy had lapsed and that there had been a previous assignment to another creditor of Parker.

What it boils down to is simply this: When a life insurance company is advised that a policy issued by it has been assigned as security for a loan and acknowledges in writing that it has received a duplicate of such assignment, is it under a duty to inform the assignee that it has been advised of other assignments of the same policy, that the policy has lapsed for nonpayment of premiums, or both?

*The Previous Assignment:* Plaintiff gives us neither authority nor persuasive reason for holding that John Hancock was under any obligation to advise her of the previous assignment of which it had notice.[62] John Hancock had no way of knowing whether the debt secured by that assignment had been paid off in whole or in part or whether the Los Angeles Bank had accepted different security for the loan due to it. John Hancock's books are not like the records of a county recorder, where satisfaction of mortgages and reconveyances of deeds of trust are

**61.** See footnote 59, supra. Plaintiff does not allege that proof of Parker's insurability could have been furnished. We note again that Parker died only six months later; we are not told, however, whether his death was accidental or the result of an illness which made him uninsurable in October 1974. One can, of course, speculate that his proven ability to borrow large sums of money on a term policy suggests that he did not look well.

**62.** It so happens that under the facts of this case the previous assignment was the least of plaintiff's worries. As noted, the sum insured at the time of Parker's death was $85,900 and the previous assignment secured a loan of $35,000, leaving plenty to satisfy plaintiff's three notes.

recorded. To advise plaintiff that Parker had made a previous loan on the strength of the policy could have been an officious betrayal of confidential information, serving possibly no useful purpose.

In brief, we are satisfied that John Hancock was under no duty to reveal previous assignments known to it.

*The Lapse of the Policy.* The fact that at the time John Hancock acknowledged receiving a copy of the assignment the policy had actually lapsed, presents an entirely different problem. Unlike a previous assignment—which may or may not be still in effect as far as the insurer knows—the fact that a policy has lapsed and that, therefore, the insurer is under no legal obligation if the insured dies, is, of course, a fact of which the insurer must be fully aware.

The simple question to be decided by us is, therefore, whether under all of the circumstances John Hancock was under a duty to advise plaintiff that the policy which she had accepted as security for a $31,000 loan was, in fact, worthless?

Several considerations are relevant to a correct answer:

First: this is not a case of a former obligor who has casually learned that a former obligee has purported to assign the extinguished obligation for value and who would have to go out of his way to tell the assignee that he has bought the Brooklyn Bridge. Since John Hancock was returning the duplicate assignment form to plaintiff anyway—precisely as was contemplated by its own procedures—it would not even have had to buy an extra stamp to advise plaintiff that the assignment was worthless.

Second: John Hancock is not entirely a disinterested third party in connection with assignments of the policies it sells. Life insurance companies conduct business of a "quasi-public nature." (Barrera v. State Farm Mut. Automobile Ins. Co. (1969) 71 Cal.2d 659, 673, 79 Cal.Rptr. 106, 456 P.2d 674). The life insurance industry as a whole and—according to the allegations of the complaint—John Hancock in particular, have quite properly emphasized the role of life insurance policies as convenient security devices. In order to regularize assignment procedures with respect to its own policies and to keep itself advised, John Hancock has devised a useful form on which such assignments for security purposes can be made and which does double-duty as a means of notifying John Hancock of the assignment and, in turn, of notifying the parties that John Hancock has been so notified. By thus involving itself in the transaction, John Hancock acts in part in its own interest: it not only promotes the efficiency of life insurance policies as a security device, but also keeps itself informed concerning the changing interests of owners and creditors of owners in the policies which it has issued.[63]

**63.** The policy provides: "The Company will not be on notice of any assignment unless it is in writing, nor until a duplicate of the original assignment has been filed at the Home Office of the Company. The

Third and most vitally: As between the creditor who accepts a life insurance policy as security for a debt and the life insurance company itself, knowledge concerning the legal status of the policy is peculiarly that of the insurer. A long unbroken line of California decisions recognizes that such disparity of knowledge may result in an imperative of disclosure. (Massei v. Lettunich (1967) 248 Cal.App.2d 68, 73, 56 Cal.Rptr. 232 [duty to disclose that lots were on filled land]; Rothstein v. Janss Inv. Corp. (1941) 45 Cal.App.2d 64, 68, 113 P.2d 465 [ditto]; Curran v. Heslop (1953) 115 Cal.App.2d 476, 480, 252 P.2d 378 [failure to disclose violation of State Housing Act, not discoverable on casual inspection]; Barder v. McClung (1949) 93 Cal.App.2d 692, 697, 209 P.2d 808 [failure to disclose violation of zoning ordinances]; Witkin, Summary of Cal.Law (8th ed. 1974) Torts, § 462.) We think the present situation easily falls within the principle of these decisions.

In sum since the processing of assignments of policies was part of John Hancock's regular business, since its involvement served a business purpose of its own and, finally, since it was fully aware of a vital fact—the lapse of the policy—unknown to the plaintiff, we hold that it was under a duty to disclose that fact.[64]

John Hancock makes much of the disclaimer of responsibility which appeared just above the signature on the printed form and the "notice" just below that signature. It argues in its brief that these caveats indicate that it was not warranting the "*validity or sufficiency* of the policy as collateral." (Emphasis ours.) This argument rests, with all respect, on a total misunderstanding or misreading of the two provisions. In one John Hancock declares that it assumes no responsibility for the validity or the sufficiency of "the foregoing assignment. * * *" In the "notice" it again assumes no responsibility "for *its* sufficiency or validity." (Emphasis ours.) In context, the "it" may be the form of assignment or the assignment itself. (See fn. 58, supra.) Certainly, neither disclaimer has anything to do with the validity or sufficiency of the policy itself. The point has no merit.

To support its claim that it had no duty to notify plaintiff of the lapse of the policy, John Hancock relies on a series of cases which stand for the proposition that the insurer is under no obligation to notify an assignee that premiums are coming due and that the policy is about to lapse.[65] (See 2A Appleman, Insurance Law & Practice, § 1315, 5 Couch, Insurance 2d, p. 677, § 30.143.) The validity and good sense of these

company assumes no responsibility for the validity or sufficiency of any assignment."

**64.** Actually a layman may think that it would have been so natural for John Hancock to note that the assignment of which it was notified and which it formally acknowledged was, in fact, worthless, that a jury might reasonably infer that the failure to do so amounted to more than mere nondisclosure: that it was an implied representation that the policy was valid. We need not and do not go that far in our holding. We merely cite the reasonableness of such a conclusion in support of what we do hold: that there was a duty to speak.

**65.** This apparently general rule of law was changed by the 1975 enactment of section 10173.2 of the Insurance Code, obligating the insurer to give the assignee not less than ten days notice before "the final lapse of the policy, * * *" It permits the insured to charge $2.50 for each such notice.

authorities need not be questioned. They are, however, not in point. Plaintiff does not contend that she would have been entitled to continuous nudges from John Hancock concerning matters that had to be done in order to keep the policy alive. All that she claims is that if the company is notified in writing that the insured has purported to assign the policy and the company acknowledges that it has received such notification and knows that the policy has, in fact, lapsed, it should advise the assignee of that fact. We think that simple fairness demands nothing less.

If we are correct so far, and John Hancock was under an obligation to advise plaintiff what it knew for a fact—that the policy had lapsed—our holding really swallows up plaintiff's purported cause of action for negligence: there is no point in asking whether John Hancock was negligent in failing to inform plaintiff about the true status of Parker's policy when it was under a positive obligation to do so.

*Estoppel:* In plaintiff's fourth cause of action she claims that by reason of all of the facts previously pleaded, John Hancock is "estopped to claim that the subject policy was not in full force and effect at the time of Robert S. Parker's death." If that pleading was intended as nothing but another way of asserting that John Hancock should have revealed that the policy had lapsed, it presumably does no harm. If, as seems more likely, the claim of estoppel is intended to dispense with the proof of damages, some remarks are in order.

All that we have held so far is that John Hancock should have informed plaintiff that the policy had lapsed. Although plaintiff sanguinely pleads that, had she been so informed, she would have taken "necessary action to obtain other, more adequate security," the general impression one gets from the few facts pleaded in the complaint is that no such security would have been available, that Parker was barely one step ahead of his creditors and that John Hancock's failure to inform plaintiff that her security was worthless probably caused no damage. If, on the other hand, it were the law that John Hancock is estopped to claim that the policy was not in full force and effect, plaintiff would find herself in a creditor's paradise: there would be $85,900 in insurance, plenty to satisfy her and all the other assignees who have surfaced so far. Yet, at least as far as this plaintiff is concerned an estoppel to deny full coverage would be an undeserved windfall: it should be recalled that plaintiff had parted with her $31,000 long before there were any communications from John Hancock. By no stretch of the facts, therefore, can she claim that whatever John Hancock did or did not do caused her to relinquish $31,000. Her loss is measured by the "other, more adequate, security" she was led not to demand and obtain. The burden of proving the exact amount of such loss cannot be swept under the rug by a glib slogan: that John Hancock is estopped to deny full coverage.

The judgment is reversed.

### *Note*

In Estate of Coate v. Life Insurance Company of California, 98 Cal. App.3d 982, 156 Cal.Rptr. 794 (1979), the court extended the obligation to notify an assignee of policy lapses to include prospective lapses.

## RYAN v. TICKLE

Supreme Court of Nebraska, 1982.
210 Neb. 630, 316 N.W.2d 580.

BRODKEY, RETIRED JUSTICE.

Lois M. Ryan, the plaintiff and appellant herein, is the widow of Eugene Ryan and the executrix of his estate. She commenced this action to recover the proceeds of a life insurance policy which were paid to the decedent's former business partner, appellee Gerald L. Tickle. After a trial in the District Court of Lincoln County, Nebraska, the appellee demurred to the evidence presented by the appellant and moved to dismiss appellant's petition. In its judgment entered on June 4, 1980, the trial court sustained the appellee's motions and dismissed the appellant's petition with prejudice. We affirm.

The facts as revealed in the record disclose that the decedent, Eugene Ryan, was a licensed mortician doing business in North Platte as the manager and president of Ryan Funeral Home, Inc. Tickle was licensed as a mortician doing business in Arnold, Nebraska, as owner of the Quig–Tickle Funeral Home. It appears that the two men had known each other since 1964, and in October 1971 they went into business together. The Ryan Funeral Home, Inc., had 477 outstanding shares of stock distributed among 12 shareholders. Ryan owned 50 shares of the company and Tickle purchased 25 shares. The two men also obtained an option to purchase the remaining outstanding stock in the Ryan Funeral Home from the other shareholders. The 5–year option was to expire on September 2, 1976, and granted Ryan and Tickle, or the survivor of them, the right to exercise the option.

In March 1972 Ryan and Tickle were offered an opportunity to purchase the Mullen Funeral Home located in nearby Mullen, Nebraska. They purchased the funeral home together for $20,000, as equal partners. They borrowed $7,000 for the downpayment and arranged to finance the balance over a period of 5 to 6 years.

Shortly after the purchase of the Mullen Funeral Home, Ryan and Tickle decided to purchase life insurance policies on each other's lives, their ultimate business goal being to acquire ownership of the Ryan and Mullen funeral homes and to provide a fund by which the survivor could purchase the homes upon the death of one of the partners. It was their estimate that if one died, the survivor would need $20,000 to $25,000 to purchase the other's interest in the Mullen Funeral Home and an additional $75,000 to purchase the outstanding stock of the Ryan Funeral Home from the owners thereof under the option agreement.

Ryan and Tickle thereupon purchased decreasing term life insurance policies on their joint lives in the total amount of $100,000. Tickle was designated the owner of one policy which had a face value of $50,000, and Ryan was designated the owner of a second policy, also valued at $50,000. Both policies insured the joint lives of Ryan and Tickle so that the entire proceeds were payable to the survivor of them. The premiums for the insurance were paid by an automatic bank withdrawal arrangement through a partnership bank account maintained for the Mullen Funeral Home.

In early 1973 it was discovered that Ryan had cancer from which he subsequently died on October 25, 1975. Following Ryan's death, Tickle collected a total of $88,000 as the beneficiary of the two life insurance policies. On September 22, 1976, Tickle and the appellant entered into a settlement agreement in which Tickle purchased the decedent's interest in the Mullen Funeral Home for the sum of $15,000. In addition, Tickle agreed to pay an additional $3,000 to the appellant in full and complete distribution of any sum of money claimed to be distributable to the decedent as undistributed earnings from the Mullen partnership. Tickle also agreed to assume and pay the unpaid balance due on the Mullen Funeral Home in the amount of $9,000. He also purchased all the assets of the Ryan Funeral Home from the board of directors and shareholders of the corporation for the sum of $147,000.

On November 7, 1977, the appellant, as executrix of the estate of Eugene Ryan, instituted this action alleging that the estate was entitled to all insurance proceeds paid upon the death of the decedent. In her brief on appeal to this court, appellant makes two principal arguments, to wit: That Tickle did not have an insurable interest in the life of the deceased, Eugene Ryan, and hence was not entitled to receive the proceeds of the insurance policies as the surviving partner of the deceased; and that the proceeds paid under the insurance agreement on decedent's life exceeded by $73,000 the amount of decedent's insurable interest in the Mullen Funeral Home, thus creating a wagering contract which is void as against public policy.

We note at the outset that the evidence in the record clearly indicates that the agreement between the partners had a dual purpose: not only to acquire for the survivor the Mullen Funeral Home but also to acquire the outstanding shares of stock in Ryan Funeral Home, Inc. The trial court found, and we conclude that the record sustains such finding, that the parties made a good faith estimate that the amount of money necessary to accomplish both such purposes would be approximately $100,000. That being so, appellee argues that the insurance contract was not a "wagering" contract but, rather, was a valid and enforceable contract of insurance. Also, with regard to appellant's contention that appellee did not have an insurable interest in the life of the decedent, appellee points out that the term "insurable interest" is defined in Neb.Rev.Stat. § 44–103(13) (Reissue 1978) as follows: "Insurable interest, in the matter of life and health insurance, exists when the beneficiary because of relationship, either pecuniary or from ties of blood or marriage, has reason to expect some benefit from the continuance of the life of the insured." In view of their avowed purpose in obtaining the insurance in question, in addition to the fact that evidence in the record discloses income tax returns showing increased profits from the operation of the funeral homes since the association of the parties as partners, appellee argues that there was clearly an expectation of benefit from the continuance of the life of the insured, and that therefore Tickle had an "insurable interest" in the life of the decedent Ryan.

We conclude, however, that we need not, and indeed may not, decide these issues, for the reason that the appellant herein has no standing or right to bring this lawsuit.

The law is well established throughout the country that only the insurer can raise the objection of want of an insurable interest. "The question of the lack of insurable interest in a life insurance policy may be raised only by the insurance company, and, where the company recognizes the validity of the policy, as by paying the amount thereof to the person named therein or into court, ordinarily adverse claimants to the fund may not raise the objection of lack of insurable interest." 44 C.J.S. Insurance § 212 at 915 (1945). See, also, Poland v. Fisher's Estate, 329 S.W.2d 768 (Mo.1959); Ryan v. Andrewski, 206 Okla. 199, 242 P.2d 448 (1952); Edgington v. Equitable L. Assur. Soc., 236 Iowa 903, 20 N.W.2d 411 (1945). "The heirs of the insured have no cause of action against the insurer upon a policy the proceeds of which have been paid by the insurer to a third person who was the beneficiary designated in the policy, on the ground that the insurer could have refused to make the payment for want of an insurable interest on the part of the beneficiary." 3 Couch on Insurance 2d, Insurable Interest, § 24:6 at 76 (1960).

The above-cited authorities make it clear that only an insurer has standing to complain of a lack of insurable interest and that the heirs of the insured may not proceed on such cause of action against the designated beneficiary. This position was recently discussed in an excellent opinion by the Michigan Court of Appeals in Secor v. Pioneer Foundry, 20 Mich.App. 30, 173 N.W.2d 780 (1969). In that case Pioneer Foundry obtained a $50,000 life insurance policy on Secor, who was a 9–year employee of the company. Three years later Secor terminated his employment; however, the company paid the 1964 policy premium 8 months after Secor had terminated his employment. Secor died a month later, and the company collected the proceeds of the insurance. Secor's widow filed suit, alleging that Pioneer Foundry had no insurable interest in Secor's life and sought a constructive trust to be imposed in favor of Secor's estate. The trial court dismissed Mrs. Secor's suit.

On appeal, the Michigan court, citing Hicks v. Cary, 332 Mich. 606, 52 N.W.2d 351 (1952), held: " 'We hold to the rule that lack in the beneficiary of an insurable interest equal to the full amount of the insurance policy, to the extent that it thereby renders the policy a wagering contract, constitutes a barrier to the beneficiary's right to receive and retain the full amount of the insurance proceeds, but that it is one which may be raised by and for the benefit of the insurer alone.' " Id. 20 Mich.App. at 33, 173 N.W.2d at 781. The court concluded that it was the insurer alone who had standing to complain of a lack of insurable interest and noted that the insurance company had paid the proceeds of the policy to Pioneer Foundry without raising the issue. The court affirmed the dismissal of the plaintiff's action based on a lack of standing to complain.

In Secor the court at 33, 173 N.W.2d at 782, stated: "The rule that only the insurer can raise the question of lack of insurable interest appears to be well supported in other jurisdictions," and cites in support thereof, 3 Couch on Insurance, supra; 2 Appleman, Insurance Law & Practice, § 765 (1966); Vance on Insurance, § 31 at 199 (3d ed. 1951). In the opinion, the court at 34, 173 N.W.2d at 782, states: "In recognition of these considerations the almost universal rule of law in this country is that if the insurable interest requirement is satisfied at the time the policy is issued, the proceeds of the policy must be paid upon the death of the life insured without regard to whether the beneficiary has an insurable interest at the time of death." The court in Secor also recognized that there are cases that hold that a creditor who acquires insurance on his debtor's life may not recover more than the amount of the debt and the premiums he paid. In this connection, however, the court at 37, 173 N.W.2d at 784, stated: "This analysis has been rejected in the better-reasoned cases; it is contrary to the principle that the termination of an insurable interest does not affect the rights of an owner-beneficiary in a life policy." The court also noted at 35, 173 N.W.2d at 783: "Life insurance is not meant to assuage grief; its primary function is monetary. It serves fundamentally the same purpose whether the beneficiary is a widow or a business; it seeks to replace with a sum of money the earning capacity of the life insured." The court concluded at 36, 173 N.W.2d at 783: "We also decline to limit Pioneer Foundry's recovery to the amount of its investment in the policy and its financial loss (probably nil) upon Secor's death. Pioneer Foundry's investment in the policy was large both quantitatively and relatively."

The holding and reasoning of the Michigan Court of Appeals is persuasive in the instant case, and we conclude that appellant is without standing to object that no insurable interest existed between the decedent and the appellee, or that the parties had entered into an illegal wagering agreement. The judgment of the District Court dismissing appellant's cause of action must be, and hereby is, affirmed.

AFFIRMED.

## *Note*

In American Casualty Co. v. Rose, 340 F.2d 469 (10th Cir.1964), Rose had a $50,000 accidental death policy for a thirty day term. The named beneficiary was Rose's employer, King. Upon Rose's death, insurer initially denied liability but ultimately settled for $24,000 in return for King's release. Rose's widow brought action on theory that King held the policy in trust for benefit of the insured's family largely on evidence that of letters from Rose to his wife. In holding for the insurer, the court noted that the rights of the family had to flow from King. Other than the letters, nothing in the record supported the proposition that Rose intended to deny the effect of naming King as beneficiary. Moreover, there existed reasonable grounds to believe that naming King as beneficiary was appropriate because of Rose's form of employment arrangement and existing employee loans.

California Insurance Code

**§ 286. When insurable interest required**

An interest in property insured must exist when the insurance takes effect, and when the loss occurs, but need not exist in the meantime; and interest in the life or health of a person insured must exist when the insurance takes effect, but need not exist thereafter or when the loss occurs.

### *Problems*

1. A agreed to let B in on a sort of partnership-franchise of a highly dubious enterprise to publish a "TV Journal." The whole affair was woefully underfinanced and neither of the parties, B in particular, had much in the way of qualifications. B nevertheless was expected to do the work while A was to provide the capital. In a sanguine mood B, whose annual income at the moment was $7,800, agreed to pay A $1000 per month for the next 20 years for this golden privilege. B could however terminate the deal on 60 days notice.

A thereupon took out a $240,000 life insurance policy on B, naming himself as beneficiary. The policy was delivered in October although the first payment on B's debt to A was not due until the following April. In November B was killed while on a hunting party with A and a group of A's relatives. A brings an action to recover on the policy. One of the defenses is lack of insurable interest. What decision? See Rubenstein v. Mutual Life Ins. Co. of New York, 584 F.Supp. 272 (E.D.La.1984).

2. X (designated owner) was a farmer who named his wife as the beneficiary of a $200,000 life policy X had taken out on his life. X also had borrowed $200,000 from Bank to finance his farming operations and assigned the life policy as collateral security. X had also by will named various devisees and legatees other than his wife to share in his rather large estate. When X died, Bank applied the proceeds of the policy to the satisfaction of the debt. The wife now seeks subrogation to the claim Bank would have had against X's estate if there had been no insurance policy. What result? See, Matter of Estate of Winstead, 144 Ill.App.3d 502, 98 Ill.Dec. 162, 493 N.E.2d 1183 (1986).

### *Buy-Sell Agreements—Insurance Aspects*

Buy-sell agreements are contractual arrangements made by partners or by the shareholders in closely held corporations regarding the disposition to be made of the ownership interest of the partner or shareholder in the business entity upon such person's death (or withdrawal, which does not here concern us). There is a voluminous specialized body of literature dealing with these agreements mostly with regard to the tax and corporate law considerations. However, because life insurance is frequently the source of funding for the carrying out of the agreements, a brief outline of some of the insurance aspects is warranted. (For a full bibliography see O'NEAL, Close Corporations § 7.25). The main reasons for such agreements are to prevent the deceased's proprietary interest from going to unwelcome outsiders, thereby destroying the essential personalized nature of the small business entity; and, secondly, to provide an agreeable and predetermined formula for compensating the spouse or other next of kin of the decedent, who has by the agreement been bound to yield the business interest which would have passed to him or her. This means a sizeable cash sum will be needed at an undetermined time. Life insurance whose maturation will correspond precisely with this business need obviously offers a most convenient method of funding such agreements. Since there are different ways of setting up the insurance plan, some awareness of the existence of insurance law problems is essential. Let us consider a business partnership of A, B and C, or a closely held corporation of three equal shareholders, also A, B and C. Their buy-sell arrangements are motivated as stated above. Consider the problems (and how to avoid them) with these possible alternatives of insurance funding.

I

| | |
|---|---|
| A insures the life of | B<br>C |
| B insures the life of | A<br>C |
| C insures the life of | A<br>B |

Each pays the premiums on the policies held on the others' lives. In case of death (say of A), B and C collect and pay off the spouse of A according to the compensation formula set forth in the agreement and keep the balance of the proceeds.

**Questions:** Are we safe in assuming that a partner has an insurable interest in the life of another partner; or that a shareholder has an insurable interest in the life of another shareholder? (Is this question really likely to be raised?)

Suppose A is a young person and B and C are elderly, would this not be a costly arrangement for junior partners? Would this arrangement be suitable if there are 50 partners?

II

| | |
|---|---|
| A insures own life and names | B as beneficiaries. C |
| B insures own life and names | A as beneficiaries. C |
| C insures own life and names | A as beneficiaries. B |

Here if A dies and B and C receive proceeds and pay off A's spouse according to the plan formula and keep the balance of the proceeds. There is no problem as to insurable interest. Nor is there quite the bulk of policies needed as in I.

**Questions:** Suppose A, B or C is uninsurable or elderly? Suppose A failed to pay premiums?

III

The closely held corporation or partnership insures each individual A, B and C, deducting the premiums as a business expense.

Here if A dies the business entity collects the proceeds and pays off A's estate according to the agreed valuation formula and keeps any surplus.

**Questions:** Is there an insurable interest issue here? (Why should a *corporation* have an insurable interest in the life of a shareholder?) In most states a corporation cannot purchase its own shares except from retained earnings or earned surplus. Do the insurance proceeds qualify as corporate earnings for this purpose?

IV

A insures own life and names corporation or partnership as beneficiary or assignee of the policy.

B does same.

C does same.

Here A (say a shareholder) dies. The corporation will collect and use the proceeds to buy A's stock from his or her estate. (This is commonly done through a trustee).

**Question:** Suppose the insurance proceeds exceed the amount needed to purchase the stock, who would be entitled to the surplus? See Hamilton National Bank v. Graning Paint Co., 59 Tenn.App. 37, 436 S.W.2d 883 (1968).

## Addendum

State Farm Life Ins. Co. v. Fort Wayne National Bank, 474 N.E.2d 524 (Ind.App.1985).

Hoffman, Judge.

Fort Wayne National Bank, in the capacity of personal representative, filed suit against State Farm Life Insurance Company and Robert Houser, for failure to properly effect insurance on the life of its decedent, James Zimmerman. Following trial to the court, judgment was rendered in favor of the estate for $34,373.97, plus pre-judgment interest. State Farm and Houser appeal.

The record discloses that James owned 95% of Zimmerman Excavating Service, Inc., while his son, Steven, owned the remaining 5%. In 1975, James purchased insurance on his life from Robert Houser of State Farm Insurance. Steven was named beneficiary, and the undisputed purpose of this policy was to fund Steven's purchase of stock in the event of James' death. On April 1, 1980, James died. The insurance proceeds were paid to Steven, but because the policy named James as owner, the proceeds passed through his estate causing a $34,373.97 tax consequence.

The dispute between the parties centers around James' ownership of the policy. The trial court concluded that State Farm and Houser were negligent in that they knew the purpose of this policy, but failed to advise James of the consequences. Had Steven been named as owner, the estate would have saved $34,373.97 in state and federal taxes.

[Affirmed]

[There is no indication that an attorney had a role in this buy-sell arrangement.]

# Part D

# LIABILITY INSURANCE

## INTRODUCTORY NOTE

Persons who purchase liability insurance which they hope will "protect" them against liability to third persons want two things: (a) the insurer's promise to pay (within the policy limit) any amount adjudged against the insured and (b) the insurer's promise to defend the insured in an action to have such liability adjudged. Insurers are, of course, willing to sell such promises. The terms in which such promises are clothed are, after decades of judicial interpretation, less than simple. A fairly ordinary set of clauses (slightly adapted from ones in use) bearing on the insurer's liability to pay and to defend would include:

(a) Insurer will pay on behalf of an insured all damages which the insured shall be legally obligated to pay because of bodily injury sustained by any person, and injury to or destruction of property arising out of the ownership or use of the owned automobile. The Insurer will defend any lawsuit, however groundless, false or fraudulent, against any insured for such damages as are payable under this policy but the Insurer may make such settlement of any claim or suit as it thinks appropriate.

(b) No action shall lie against the Insurer until after full compliance with the terms of the policy and until the amount of the insured's obligation to pay shall have been finally determined by judgment against the insured or written agreement of settlement among the insured, the claimant and the Insurer.

(c) The insured shall cooperate with the Insurer by disclosing all pertinent facts known to him or her, and upon Insurer's request shall attend hearings and trials, shall assist in obtaining evidence and the attendance of witnesses and shall participate in effecting settlements and conducting suits.

Other policy terms will clearly be involved in determining when the insurer's promise to pay and promise to defend are to be performed. E.g., the terms of the policy concerning the extent and the amount of coverage, the meaning of "insured" under the policy, and clauses (or State statutes) prohibiting coverage of willful injuries inflicted by an insured. But the ones outlined above are thicket enough, e.g.: (a) who has real control over a lawsuit against the insured, (b) can the insurer refuse to defend the lawsuit if the insurer believes that the policy does not cover the underlying liability, (c) does the insurer breach its duties when it refuses to make a settlement on behalf of the insured within the policy limits and the settlement offer was a reasonable one, (d) when, if at all, do third parties have the right to sue the insurer directly, (3) what is the responsibility of the insurer when it has breached either its duty to pay or its duty to defend, (f) is the insurer's duty to defend conditional on the insured complying with his duty to cooperate, and (g) in any case of breach of duty, what is the measure of damages?

# Chapter 12

# PRESENTATION OF CLAIMS AND FILING SUIT

— notice requirements for liability claims
— actions against liability insurers

## SECURITY MUTUAL INSURANCE CO. OF NEW YORK v. ACKER-FITZSIMONS CORP.

Court of Appeals of New York, 1972.
31 N.Y.2d 436, 340 N.Y.S.2d 902, 293 N.E.2d 76.

JASEN, JUDGE.

The issue on this appeal is whether the insured complied with a liability insurance policy provision requiring notice to the insurer "as soon as practicable" after the "occurrence".[1]

On November 29, 1964, Security Mutual Insurance Company of New York (Security Mutual) issued its Owner's, Landlords' and Tenants' Liability Policy to Fernley Realty Corp. (Fernley) insuring it against liability for personal injuries arising from the operation of certain premises located at 2–10 East 196 Street, Bronx, New York. In addition to the named insured, the policy covered Norman Levy, president of Fernley, and Acker–Fitzsimons Corp. (Acker–Fitzsimons), managing agents of the property.

On May 23, 1965, a major fire occurred on the insured premises and three days later the New York City Department of Buildings lodged certain structural violations against them. The buildings were again swept by fire on October 4, 1965, during the course of which three firemen, defendants Adams, Harrington and Manning, were allegedly injured. The buildings were subsequently demolished.

Levy evidently learned of the second fire (but not the personal injuries) on the afternoon of its occurrence. On November 9, 1965, he

1. An occurrence is defined in the policy as "an event, or continuous or repeated exposure to conditions, which unexpectedly causes injury during the policy period."

heard "rumors" [2] that certain unnamed firemen had been injured in the October 4 fire. He then telephoned this information to James Kannar, Fernley's insurance broker, and followed up with a letter, also dated November 9, instructing him to notify the insurer of the claimed injuries. Kannar was of the view that until a more concrete claim was made, there was no obligation to report the incident to the insurer. He also opined that since firemen go at their own risk, there was no liability anyway.

In ordinary course, the plaintiff issued a renewal policy for the premises. But on November 15, 1965, before the effective date of the renewal policy, Kannar wrote to Security Mutual advising it of the contemplated demolition of the premises. Telephone conversations followed on November 16 between Kannar and Theodore Moschitta, an employee of Security Mutual, during which Moschitta was advised of the fire of October 4, but no mention was made of any personal injuries. The policy was subsequently canceled on January 6, 1966.

On December 19, 1965, the *Sunday News* reported that two firemen (Adams and Manning) had filed a claim for $1,500,000 against the City of New York for injuries allegedly sustained in the fire of October 4. Mention was also made of alleged liability of the owners and operators of the premises. The article was brought to Levy's attention, who, on December 27, 1965, forwarded a copy to Kannar, together with a letter stating that he believed it should be forwarded to the liability carrier. Kannar took no action, apparently believing that, absent some more substantial basis, there was nothing to report to the carrier.

In October, 1966, the firemen, Adams and Manning, now joined by Harrington, commenced the prime action by serving a summons and complaint on the City of New York only. Service upon Fernley and Acker–Fitzsimons was effected by service upon the Secretary of State on April 28, 1967. Levy was personally served on June 23, 1967. Upon receiving the summons, the defendant Acker–Fitzsimons promptly notified Security Mutual of the pendency of the action—some 19 months after the actual occurrence.

Notice provisions in insurance policies afford the insurer an opportunity to protect itself, and the giving of the required notice is a condition to the insurer's liability. (Rushing v. Commercial Cas. Ins. Co., 251 N.Y. 302, 167 N.E. 450.) Absent a valid excuse, a failure to satisfy the notice requirement vitiates the policy (Deso v. London & Lancashire Ind. Co., 3 N.Y.2d 127, 164 N.Y.S.2d 689, 143 N.E.2d 889; Insurance Law, Consol.Laws, c. 28, § 167, subd. 1, par. [d] ), and the insurer need not show prejudice before it can assert the defense of noncompliance. (31 N.Y.Jur., Insurance, § 1262.)

There may be circumstances, such as lack of knowledge that an accident has occurred, that will explain or excuse delay in giving notice and show it to be reasonable. (Rushing v. Commerical Cas. Co., 251

2. The "rumors" consisted of a phone call to Levy from an unnamed person.

N.Y. 302, 167 N.E. 450, supra; Woolverton v. Fidelity & Cas. Co. of N.Y., 190 N.Y. 41, 82 N.E. 745.) But the insured has the burden of proof thereon. (Rushing v. Commercial Cas. Co., 251 N.Y. 302, 167 N.E. 450, supra.) Moreover, he must exercise reasonable care and diligence to keep himself informed of accidents out of which claims for damages may arise.

Then, too, a good-faith belief of nonliability may excuse or explain a seeming failure to give timely notice. (875 Forest Ave. Corp. v. Aetna Cas. & Sur. Co., 37 A.D.2d 11, 322 N.Y.S.2d 53, affd. 30 N.Y.2d 726, 332 N.Y.S.2d 896, 283 N.E.2d 768; Woolverton v. Fidelity & Cas. Co. of N.Y., 190 N.Y. 41, 82 N.E. 745, supra; 31 N.Y.Jur., Insurance, § 1281.) But the insured's belief must be reasonable under all the circumstances, and it may be relevant on the issue of reasonableness, whether and to what extent, the insured has inquired into the circumstances of the accident or occurrence. (Haas Tobacco Co. v. American Fid. Co., 226 N.Y. 343, 123 N.E. 755, * * *

Finally, a provision that notice be given "as soon as practicable" after an accident or occurrence, merely requires that notice be given within a reasonable time under all the circumstances. (Deso v. London & Lancashire Ind. Co., 3 N.Y.2d 127, 164 N.Y.S.2d 689, 143 N.E.2d 889. * * *

The Appellate Division, 39 A.D.2d 34, 330 N.Y.S.2d 865, was of the view that the insureds had no direct knowledge that injuries had resulted from the fire of October 4, 1965, and that the insureds' belief of nonliability was reasonable. The majority concluded that the notice given upon receiving the summons in the prime action (some 19 months after the occurrence) was, therefore, given as soon as practicable. We disagree.

On December 19, the *Sunday News* reported that two firemen had filed claims against the City of New York for injuries allegedly sustained in the October 4 fire. Mention was also made in the article of the possible liability of the owners and operators of the premises. This article was brought to the attention of the insureds, Levy and Acker-Fitzsimons, in late December. While this information was, in our view, sufficient to apprise the insureds of the occurrence, of itself, it probably was not a sufficient predicate for giving immediate notice. However, it seems to us that such information would cause a reasonable and prudent person to investigate the circumstances, ascertain the facts, and evaluate his potential liability, particularly where there were, at the time of the alleged injuries, existent violations against the premises involving structural deficiencies caused by the first fire (May 23, 1965). Similarly, although the belief that firemen go at their own risk generally accords with the law, (see, e.g., McGee v. Adams Paper & Twine Co., 26 A.D.2d 186, 271 N.Y.S.2d 698, affd. 20 N.Y.2d 921, 286 N.Y.S.2d 274, 233 N.E.2d 289), under these circumstances, and absent an investigation of the facts, the insured's bare reliance on that belief would appear to be unreasonable.[3]

The recent case of 875 Forest Ave. Corp. v. Aetna Cas. Corp. (37 A.D.2d 11, 322 N.Y.S.2d 53, affd. 30 N.Y.2d 726, 332 N.Y.S.2d 896, 283 N.E.2d 768, supra), relied upon by the majority at the Appellate Division, is distinguishable. In that case a three-year-old child fell from a fourth floor apartment window and was killed. It was held that delayed notice of the accident did not breach the notice provision where the insured, acting as a reasonable and prudent person, believed he was not liable. That accident, however, simply was not one which would lead a reasonable person to envision any possible liability on the part of the insured corporate owner of the building. In fact, the circumstances (of which the insured apprised itself) indicated negligence on the part of the child's mother. Here, the insureds had information (the newspaper article) about personal injuries arising from a fire at their building against which certain structural violations had been posted—yet they failed to pursue the facts or reasonably evaluate their potential liability.

In sum, we conclude that the insureds failed to exercise reasonable care and diligence in ascertaining the facts about the alleged accident and in evaluating their potential liability. Thus, the otherwise unreasonable delay of 19 months in giving notice may not be excused or explained on the basis of "lack of knowledge" or a "belief of nonliability".

For the reasons stated, the order of the Appellate Division should be reversed and the judgment of the Supreme Court, Bronx County, reinstated.

### *Notes*

1. [In 1981 North Carolina reversed a long line of decisions to the effect that the requirement of notice by the insured "as soon as practicable" was a condition precedent to coverage under a liability policy so that it was immaterial whether the insurer was prejudiced by delay. After adopting a new rule requiring the showing of prejudice, the court then proceeded to the question of which party should have the burden of proof on the issue of prejudice.]

> The authorities are split on this issue. Some hold that because the insured is seeking relief from the literal meaning of the terms of the contract, he should bear the burden of showing that his delay has not materially prejudiced the insurer. E.g., Hartford Accident & Indemnity Co. v. Lochmandy Buick Sales, Inc., 302 F.2d 565 (7th Cir.1962); Dairyland Insurance Co. v. Cunningham, 360 F.Supp. 139 (D.Colo.1973). Other jurisdictions have reasoned that the burden of showing prejudice should be on the insurer because it is seeking to escape its obligation to

3. As we have previously noted, Levy was sufficiently concerned about the alleged injuries that he instructed his insurance broker to inform the carrier. But this did not constitute the notice contemplated by the policy since a broker is normally the agent of the insured and notice to the ordinary insurance broker is not notice to the liability carrier.

defend and indemnify, the very thing which it is paid to do. E.g., State Farm Mutual Automobile Insurance Co. v. Milam, 438 F.Supp. 227; Cooper v. Government Employees Insurance Co., 51 N.J. 86, 237 A.2d 870. "[A]lthough the policy may speak in terms of 'condition precedent' * * *, nonetheless what is involved is a forfeiture, for the carrier seeks, on account of a breach of that provision, to deny the insured the very thing paid for." Id. at 93–94, 237 A.2d at 873.

We believe the sounder rule to be that requiring the insurer to prove that it has been materially prejudiced by the delay. If the insurer has the burden of proving prejudice, then when it receives a delayed notification the rule will encourage the insurer to make a prompt preliminary investigation of the claim to protect its interests. An investigation may reveal that the delay has materially prejudiced the insurer, and, in that event, the insurer may deny coverage and either wait for a suit against it or file suit for declaratory relief. If, on the other hand, the preliminary investigation reveals that the ability of the insurer to investigate and defend has not been materially prejudiced, the insurer, presumably, will proceed with the claim and the question of coverage will never reach the courts. Additionally, the insurer, because it is an expert in investigation of accidents, is in a much better position to know what factors are relevant to its ability to investigate and to recognize prejudice. An insured would be in a far less enviable position if he had the burden of showing an absence of prejudice. Indeed, the insured would be forced to prove a negative. Placing the burden of showing prejudice on the insurer encourages an adequate investigation by the qualified party at the earliest possible time. These factors lead us to conclude that the burden of proof on the issue of prejudice is properly placed on the insurer.

The rule which we adopt today amounts to a reversal of a long line of previous cases upon which insurers have justifiably relied. Lest this decision be perceived as encouraging dilatory tactics in the notification of the insurer and, thus, as being unfair to insurers, we also now impose the requirement that any period of delay beyond the limits of timeliness be shown *by the insured* to have been in good faith. Anyone who knows that he may be at fault or that others have claimed he is at fault and who purposefully and knowingly fails to notify ought not to recover even if no prejudice results. Equity dictates that a bad faith delay in notifying an insurer, even though no material prejudice results, should bar the insured from enforcing the policy. This requirement is in accord with the common law principle that implicit in every contract is the obligation of each party to act in good faith.

The effect of this decision is to create a three-step test for determining whether the insurer is obliged to defend. When faced with a claim that notice was not timely given, the trier of fact must first decide whether the notice was given as soon as practicable. If not, the trier of fact must decide whether the insured has shown that he acted in good faith, e.g., that he had no actual knowledge that a claim might be filed against him. If the good faith test is met the burden then shifts to the insurer to show that its ability to investigate and defend was materially prejudiced by the delay.

Great American Insurance Co. v. C.G. Tate Construction Co., 303 N.C. 387, 279 S.E.2d 769 (1981) (a full review of authorities).

2. *Failure to give prompt notice and breach of co-operation clause.*

The line between these two may be vague, and the consequences equally detrimental to the insured and the third party, but a practical distinction was made in Miller v. Dilts, 463 N.E.2d 257 (Indiana, 1984) which held that prompt notice is condition precedent and the insurer need not show prejudice to invoke its lack; whereas the duty to co-operate is a condition subsequent and the insurer must show prejudice for its breach. The same distinction is drawn in Illinois Insurance Guaranty Fund v. Lockhart, 152 Ill.App.3d 603, 105 Ill.Dec. 572, 504 N.E.2d 857 (1987).

## EVANSTON INSURANCE CO. v. INTERNATIONAL MANUFACTURING CO.

United States District Court, D. Wyoming, 1986.
641 F.Supp. 733.

BRIMMER, CHIEF JUDGE.

* * *

The following facts are undisputed: An insurance policy for specified products and completed operations liability insurance was issued by plaintiff Evanston Insurance Company (Evanston), an Illinois corporation, to defendant International Manufacturing Company (International), a California corporation. The products and completed operations covered by the policy included automobile wheels manufactured and distributed by International. The insurance agreement provided that Evanston would pay "damages because of bodily injury * * * caused by an occurrence during the policy period." Bodily injury was defined as "bodily injury * * * which occurs during the policy period." An occurrence was defined as "an accident, including continuous or repeated exposure to conditions, which results in bodily injury * * * neither expected nor intended by the Insured." Nearly three pages of detailed exclusions are included in the policy. The policy period was from February 15, 1979 to February 15, 1980. The policy expired in February, 1980 and was not renewed by International.

On April 9, 1979, International manufactured a wheel it sold and shipped to defendant Subaru of America (Subaru). The wheel was thus manufactured and shipped to Subaru during the policy period. Subaru installed the wheel on one of its automobiles. Defendant Mark Miller Pontiac and Subaru (Mark Miller) sold the automobile in October, 1979. On November 22, 1982, defendant Chad Anderson attempted to place a new tire on the wheel. The wheel collapsed, striking Anderson in the head. Anderson filed suit against Subaru, Mark Miller, and International for injuries suffered in the accident. See Anderson v. Subaru of America, et al., No. C85–0296–B1, pending in the United States District Court for the District of Wyoming.

International demanded that Evanston defend and indemnify it against Anderson's suit. Evanston then filed this action under the Declaratory Judgment Act, 28 U.S.C. §§ 2201, 2202, seeking a declaration of its duties to provide coverage to International * * *.

* * *

Because the parties in this case agree on all material issues of fact, the question under Rule 56(c) is whether Evanston is entitled to judgment as a matter of law. Evanston contends that the controlling rule in this case is that "the time of an occurrence of an accident . . . is not the time the wrongful act was committed, but the time when the complaining party was actually damaged," citing Remmer v. Glens Falls Indem. Co., 140 Cal.App.2d 84, 88, 295 P.2d 19, 21 (1956), and Tijsseling v. General Acc. Fire & Life Assur. Corp., 55 Cal.App.3d 623, 626, 127 Cal.Rptr. 681 (1976). Evanston concludes that Chad Anderson's injury was not an occurrence resulting in bodily injury during the policy period. Under California law, Evanston argues, the time of the occurrence was when Chad Anderson was injured in 1982, not when the defective wheel was manufactured by International in 1979. International urges that the time of the occurrence was when the wrongful act occurred, not the time of injury. International also argues that the insurance policy is ambiguous and must therefore be construed in favor of International and in light of its reasonable expectation of coverage. See Gray v. Zurich Ins. Co., 65 Cal.2d 263, 54 Cal.Rptr. 104, 419 P.2d 168 (1966).

The parties also agree that California law controls the validity and effect of this contract * * *.

California's Supreme Court spoke to this issue on two occasions. In Gyler v. Mission Ins. Co., 10 Cal.3d 216, 110 Cal.Rptr. 139, 140, 514 P.2d 1219, 1220 (1973), an attorney sought indemnity under an expired "claims made" insurance policy for malpractice occurring during the term of the policy. The court construed the policy to provide coverage for claims maturing during the policy period regardless of whether the claim is asserted at that time. Id., 110 Cal.Rptr. at 141, 514 P.2d at 1221. The court first concluded that the language of the policy was ambiguous. In such cases, the court said, the meaning of the policy must be determined by the insured's reasonable expectation of coverage. Uncertainties and ambiguities must be resolved against the insurer. Notice of noncoverage must be conspicuous and clear. Because malpractice liability may continue long after the negligent act and injury, the court concluded that the insured would reasonably expect continuing coverage for negligent acts occurring during the policy period. Id. While factually distinguishable from the present case, Gyler demonstrates that California does not rigidly adhere to the rule that the time of the occurrence of an accident is the time the complaining party is actually injured.

In a case similar to the instant litigation, an insurer issued a liability policy protecting the insured from negligent maintenance of an aircraft and indemnifying the insured against "occurrences or accidents which happen during the policy period." Insurance Co. of North America v. Sam Harris Constr. Co., 22 Cal.3d 409, 149 Cal.Rptr. 292, 293, 583 P.2d 1335, 1336 (1978). The insured later sold the airplane, cancelled the policy and received a refund of the unearned premium. The airplane crashed, and the new owner sued the insured for negligent maintenance. Id. Although the craft was no longer covered by the insurer at the time of the accident, the California Supreme Court held that negligent maintenance of the airplane within the policy period was an accident or occurrence covered by the policy. Id., 149 Cal.Rptr. at 293, 583 P.2d at 1337.

The court first noted the trial court's reliance on the rule that the time of the occurrence of an accident is the time the complaining party was actually damaged. The court said that "[i]n our view that rule is not applicable to this case. The issue here turns on the meaning of 'occurrences or accidents ... during the policy period.' " Id., 149 Cal.Rptr. at 292, 583 P.2d at 1336. The court thus rejected Remmer v. Glens Falls Indem. Co., supra, and Tijsseling v. General Acc. Fire & Life Assur. Corp., supra, given the facts in Sam Harris.

Because "accident" and "occurrence" were undefined in the policy, the court concluded that the policy was ambiguous and that the insured could reasonably expect the insurer to provide a defense. Id. The court further noted that: "It is elementary in insurance law that any ambiguity or uncertainty in an insurance policy is to be resolved against the insurer * * *. [I]f the doubt relates to extent [sic] or fact of coverage, whether as to peril insured against [citations], the amount of liability [citations], or the person or persons protected [citations], the language will be understood in its most inclusive sense, for the benefit of the insured." Id., 149 Cal.Rptr. at 294, 583 P.2d at 1337 quoting Continental Cas. Co. v. Phoenix Constr. Co., 46 Cal.2d 423, 296 P.2d 801, 809–10 (Cal.1956).

The dissent argued that the majority's holding required the "insurance coverage to remain open-ended, indefinite in duration, and free." Sam Harris, supra, 149 Cal.Rptr. at 296, 583 P.2d at 1339 (Richardson, J., dissenting). Nevertheless, the dissent recognized this argument would be inappropriate in a products liability case. Justice Richardson stated that: "It must be kept in mind that the insured was not in the business of selling or repairing aircraft, and accordingly that the subject policy was neither a *products liability [policy]* nor professional (errors and omissions) policy which *reasonably might have been expected to provide extended coverage for liability based upon negligent conduct occurring during the policy period.* This fact clearly serves to distinguish such cases as Sylla v. United States Fid. & Guar. Co. * * * and Oil Base, Inc. v. Continental Cas. Co. * * * relied on by defendants herein." Id. (emphasis supplied). This shows that both the dissent and the majority would find that, in the case of products liability, mismanufacture is an occurrence during the policy period, even where injury to a consumer occurs after the policy expires.

The rule emerging from Sam Harris and Gyler is that, absent clearly expressed intent to exclude coverage, products liability coverage extends to defective products manufactured during the policy period but which cause injury after the policy terminates. If the language of the policy is obscure, the policy is interpreted based on the insured's reasonable expectations of coverage. Insurance Co. of North America v. Sam Harris Constr. Co., supra, 149 Cal.Rptr. at 293, 583 P.2d at 1336.

In Sylla v. United States Fidelity and Guar. Co., 54 Cal.App.3d 895, 897, 127 Cal.Rptr. 38 (1976), the intermediate court of appeals for the second district considered a policy defining "occurrence" as "an accident, * * * which results, during the policy period, in bodily injury or property damage * * *." The court decided that the failure to define "accident" created an ambiguity in the insurance policy leading to a reasonable expectation of coverage on the part of the insured. The court therefore held that the insurer was obligated to provide coverage for actions during the policy period which resulted in damage only after the policy expired. Id., 54 Cal.App.3d at 902, 127 Cal.Rptr. at 41. See also, Oil Base, Inc. v. Continental Cas. Co., 271 Cal.App.2d 378, 76 Cal.Rptr. 594 (1969).

Other lower courts of appeals disagree with this holding. Evanston cites Maples v. Aetna Cas. & Surety Co., 83 Cal.App.3d 641, 148 Cal.Rptr. 80 (1978); Employers Casualty Co. v. Northwestern Nat'l Ins. Group, 109 Cal.App.3d 462, 167 Cal.Rptr. 296 (1980); Wolf Machinery Co. v. Insurance Co. of North America, 133 Cal.App.3d 324, 183 Cal. Rptr. 695 (1982); and Highlands Ins. Co. v. Schrillo Co., 181 Cal.App.3d 766, 226 Cal.Rptr. 717 (1986). Each of these cases strongly criticize Sylla and Oil Base. The intermediate California courts of appeals are therefore split on the issue in this case.

The rule of *stare decisis* does not apply when appellate decisions conflict. Auto Equity Sales, Inc. v. Superior Court, 57 Cal.2d 450, 20 Cal.Rptr. 321, 324, 369 P.2d 937, 940 (1962). When more than one appellate court has decided an issue and the decisions conflict, the trial court can and must choose between the conflicting decisions. Id. The reasoning of Sylla seems in closer harmony with Gyler and Sam Harris than does that of Maples and the other cases cited by Evanston. Indeed, both the majority and the dissent in Sam Harris appear to endorse Sylla and Oil Base. The rule that the time of the occurrence of an accident *within the meaning of an indemnity policy* is the time the complaining party was actually damaged presupposes that "accident" has an agreed upon meaning within the terms of the policy. The failure to define "accident" renders the rule inapposite. Although the court in Maples found that the failure to define "accident" did not create an ambiguity in that case, this does not mean that no ambiguity exists in the present agreement. Maples v. Aetna Casualty & Sur. Co., supra, 83 Cal.App.3d at 630, 148 Cal.Rptr. 80.

Applying the rule in Sylla to this case, Evanston's failure to define the term "accident" in its policy creates an ambiguity requiring this

Court to construe the document in light of International's reasonable expectations. This Court, however, does not rely exclusively on Sylla.

The policy at issue in this case is inherently ambiguous. First, the definition of "occurrence" in this policy is even more obscure than that in Sylla. The policy in Sylla defined "occurrence" as "an accident, * * * which results, during the policy period, in bodily injury or property damage * * *." Sylla v. United States Fidelity and Guar. Co., supra, 127 Cal.Rptr. at 38. The agreement between Evanston and International defines an "occurrence" as "an accident, including continuous or repeated exposure to conditions, which results in bodily injury * * *." The definition does not say that the injury must occur during the policy period. This omission, coupled with the phrase "including continuous or repeated exposure to conditions," serves as a trap for an unwary insured. Only an extremely careful reading discloses that bodily injury must occur during the policy period.

The misleading nature of the policy is further demonstrated by Evanston's failure to exclude coverage for future injuries. The insurance policy in this case contains two pages of detailed exclusions. Nowhere does the policy reveal that injuries suffered in the future because of products manufactured during the policy period are uncovered. As the court in Gyler noted, "notice of noncoverage in a situation where coverage may be reasonably expected must be conspicuous, plain, and clear." Gyler v. Mission Ins. Co., supra, 110 Cal.Rptr. at 141, 514 P.2d at 1221. Because the policy is ambiguous, the next step is to determine whether International reasonably expected coverage.

Whether a party has a reasonable expectation of coverage is an issue of law, not of fact. Wolf Machinery Co. v. Insurance Co. of North America, supra, 133 Cal.App.3d at 329, 183 Cal.Rptr. at 697. A manufacturer buys products and completed operations liability insurance only for a specified time. But because liability based on defects in those products may continue long after the negligent act, a manufacturer would seek and, in the absence of clear language to the contrary, reasonably expect coverage for mismanufacture during the policy period. See Gyler v. Mission Ins. Co., supra, 110 Cal.Rptr. at 141, 514 P.2d at 1221. Thus, both an ambiguity and a reasonable expectation of coverage are present in the instant case. Therefore, it is

ORDERED that plaintiff's motion for summary judgment be, and the same hereby is, denied. It is further

ORDERED and ADJUDGED that plaintiff Evanston Insurance Company has the obligation to provide coverage to International Manufacturing Company under the policy of insurance between the parties and that defendant International Manufacturing Company has the right to expect defense and indemnity from plaintiff Evanston Insurance Company.

### *Notes*

1. In 1975, in response to Gyler v. Mission Insurance Co., 10 Cal.3d 216, 110 Cal.Rptr. 139, 514 P.2d 1219 (1973), cited in the above case, the

California legislature enacted section 11580.01 of the Insurance Code which requires that claims made policies contain on the face page of the policy a prominent and conspicuous notice of such limitation.

2. California courts have not unanimously followed *Evanston.* In Hallmark Insurance Company, Inc. v. Superior Court, 201 Cal.App.3d 1014, 247 Cal.Rptr. 638 (1988), the court found that similar coverage wording was unambiguous and refused to apply the doctrine of reasonable expectations. The *Hallmark* court held that the time of occurrence was the time when the accident occurred. In fact, the *Hallmark* opinion specifically rejected *Evanston,* stating that it was not the, "prevailing rule of the state." The time may have come for the state's supreme court to evaluate more recent policy wording.

### *Questions*

### *(As we move toward the next chapter)*

Assume an "occurrences" malpractice policy covering a lawyer. How does the lawyer know when to give notice of an occurrence?

On the other hand, assume a "claims made" malpractice policy covering a lawyer. A claim is made against the lawyer, but is not reported to the insurer until after the policy period has expired. Is there coverage? See Zuckerman v. National Union Fire Ins. Co., 100 N.J. 304, 495 A.2d 395 (1985). What is a claim, and when is it actually made? See, Phoenix Ins. Co. v. Sukut Construction Co., Inc., 136 Cal.App.3d 673, 186 Cal.Rptr. 513 (1982) and Hoyt v. St. Paul Fire & Marine Ins. Co., 607 F.2d 864 (9th Cir.1979). Examine Appendix F, below.

## ACTIONS AGAINST INSURERS

### PRELIMINARY NOTE

In general, the right to sue on a contract (including a contract of insurance) is possessed by the parties to a contract or third party beneficiaries. For many types of insurance policies, that is enough. In the case of liability and other policies where third party claims are likely a different problem exists: should a third party claimant against a liability insured (on an auto policy, for example) be able to sue the *insurer* without first suing the *insured*? The advantage to the claimant is obvious.

Most such policies, however, contain a "no-action" clause. The following language is a sample.

> No action shall lie against the company unless, as a condition precedent thereto, the insured shall have fully complied with all the terms of this policy, nor until the amount of the insured's obligation to pay shall have been finally determined either by judgment against the insured after actual trial or by written agreement of the insured, the claimant and the company.

In general, the law of the States recognizes the validity of such provisions, although it is common enough for State statutes to preserve the liability of insurers if the *insured* becomes insolvent or bankrupt and to allow third party claimants to sue insurers once the claimants have judgments against the insured. See, for example, California Ins.Code § 11580.

Some States have allowed direct actions to some third party claimants. Direct action statutes (varying considerably in their provisions) exist in: the Territory of Guam, Government Code § 43354; Louisiana, LSA Rev.Stat. 22:655, 22:983; Puerto Rico, Laws, Title 26, §§ 2001, 2003; Rhode Island, Gen.Laws 27–7–1, 27–7–2; Wis.Rev.Stat. 632.24, 632.34, 803.04 (formerly 204.30(4) and 260.11). See Watson v. Employers Liability Assurance Corp., 348 U.S. 66, 75 S.Ct. 166, 99 L.Ed. 74 (1954).

In Florida judicial action has made direct suits available in some cases, Beta Eta House Corp. v. Gregory, 237 So.2d 163 (Fla.1970).

### Uninsured Motorists' Claims

While there is some authority otherwise, the majority of courts have held that it is not a prerequisite to recovery for an insured under a statutorily mandated uninsured motorists provision to first obtain a judgment against the uninsured tort feasor before bringing suit against the insured's liability carrier. Lane v. State Farm Mutual Auto Insurance Co., 209 Neb. 396, 308 N.W.2d 503 (1981), Guess v. Gulf Insurance Co., 96 N.M. 27, 627 P.2d 869 (1981). See Annot. 73 A.L.R.2d 632 (1976).

### *Problem*

R and S are involved in an auto accident in Indiana. S was R's auto guest. R's auto policy was issued by State Farm in Indiana. Under Indiana statutes, S could not sue R. S moved to Minnesota where State Farm does business. Can S sue R and State Farm in Minnesota and garnish State Farm's policy obligation to R? R was not served in Minnesota. See Seider v. Roth, 17 N.Y.2d 111, 269 N.Y.S.2d 99, 216 N.E.2d 312 (1966); Rush v. Savchuk, 444 U.S. 320, 100 S.Ct. 571, 62 L.Ed.2d 516 (1980). See also Hoteles Camino Real S.A. v. Superior Court, 70 Cal.App.3d 367, 138 Cal. Rptr. 807 (1977).

## MARCHLIK v. CORONET INSURANCE CO.

Supreme Court of Illinois, 1968.
40 Ill.2d 327, 239 N.E.2d 799.

HOUSE, JUSTICE.

This is an appeal from an order of the circuit court of Cook County dismissing the complaint of plaintiff, Christine Marchlik, against two Illinois insurance companies, Coronet Insurance Company and State Farm Mutual Automobile Insurance Company. Constitutional questions are raised.

Plaintiff, a resident of Wisconsin, was injured when the automobile of Henry Tapio, in which she was riding, was involved in a collision with one driven by Edward Trombley on U.S. Highway 51 in Iron County, Wisconsin. She received hospital and medical care in Wisconsin. Tapio was a resident of Bessemer, Michigan, Trombley was a Wisconsin resident, and the automobile driven by him bore Wisconsin registration. Tapio's liability policy was issued by Coronet and Trombley's by State Farm. Each policy was issued in Illinois, and they contained practically identical "no action" clauses prohibiting direct action against the carrier until final judgment had been entered against the insured.

The action was commenced under the Wisconsin "Direct Action" statutes (Wisc.Stat.1965, sec. 204.30(4) and sec. 260.11(1),) which authorize original suits against insurance companies provided the injuries are sustained in Wisconsin.

* * *

The issues as stated by the parties are whether the public policy of Illinois precludes direct action against an insurer for tort liability of the insured where the policy has a "no action" clause and when the statutory law of the place where the tort occurs allows direct action and, if so, does the full-faith-and-credit clause of the constitution of the United States force a State to enforce a foreign statute.

The preliminary approach to these issues is whether Wisconsin's direct action statutes are procedural or substantive. If procedural or remedial, it is well settled that the *lex fori,* or law of the jurisdiction in which relief is sought, will govern. (15A C.J.S. Conflict of Laws § 9; 16 Am.Jur.2d, Conflict of Laws, sec. 76.) On the other hand, the *lex loci delictus* or law of the place of wrong generally governs where the substantive rights of the parties will be affected. But, even this is an oversimplification for, if entertaining a foreign cause (such as this direct action suit against casualty insurers) is contrary to the public policy of the forum, its courts may bar enforcement of the foreign remedy, provided, of course, such a bar is not in contravention of the full-faith-and-credit clause of the Federal constitution.

Section 260.11(1) of the Wisconsin statutes (Wisc.Stat.1963, sec. 260.11(1),) in pertinent part reads: "A plaintiff may join as defendants * * * any insurer of motor vehicles * * * in any action brought by plaintiff in this state on account of any claim against the insured. The right of direct action herein given * * * shall exist whether the policy of insurance sued upon was issued or delivered in the state of Wisconsin or not and whether or not the policy or contract of insurance contains a provision forbidding such direct action, provided the accident or injury occurred in the state of Wisconsin." Prior to its amendment in 1959 the section was held by the Wisconsin Supreme Court to be procedural. (Oertel v. Williams, 214 Wis. 68, 251 N.W. 465; Ritterbusch v. Sexsmith, 256 Wis. 507, 41 N.W.2d 611.) However, we read cases subsequent to the amendment, in which the right of direct action was limited to accidents occurring in Wisconsin, to hold that both sections of the direct action statutes be considered together and that the statutes create a substantive rather than a procedural right. See Snorek v. Boyle, 18 Wis.

202, 118 N.W.2d 132; Frye v. Angst, 28 Wis.2d 575, 137 N.W.2d 430; Koss v. Hartford Accident and Indemnity Co. (7th Cir.), 341 F.2d 472.

The other section (204.30(4)) reads in part: "Any bond or policy of insurance covering liability to others by reason of the operation of a motor vehicle shall be deemed and construed to contain the following conditions: That the insurer shall be liable to the persons entitled to recover for the death of any person, or for injury to person or property, irrespective of whether such liability be in praesenti or contingent and to become fixed or certain by final judgment against the insured, when caused by negligent operation, maintenance, use or defective construction of the vehicle described therein, such liability not to exceed the amount named in said bond or policy."

In commenting on the two sections the Wisconsin court said: "Sec. 204.30(4) is substantive and creates direct liability between the injured third person and the insurer while sec. 260.11(1) is procedural and determines when the insurer can be made a party to the action despite the presence of a no-action clause in the policy." (Miller v. Wadkins, 31 Wis.2d 281, 283, 142 N.W.2d 855.) While passing on the question of the effect of no-action provisions the Supreme Court of Minnesota in Kertson v. Johnson, 185 Minn. 591, 242 N.W. 329, held the Wisconsin direct action statute (now sec. 204.30(4)) to be substantive. In Oltarsh v. Aetna Insurance Co. (1965) 15 N.Y.2d 111, 256 N.Y.S.2d 577, 204 N.E.2d 622, it was said that the Puerto Rican direct action statute, which resembled section 260.11(1) of the Wisconsin statute, was substantive in character and even though New York had no similar statute the insured injured in Puerto Rico could maintain her action directly against the insurance carrier. Mr. Justice Traynor, speaking for the California court in Grant v. McAuliffe, 41 Cal.2d 859, 264 P.2d 944, recognized that the courts of that State determine substantive matters by adopting as their law the law of the place where the tortious acts occurred, unless contrary to the public policy of the State. The question of first impression there was whether survival of causes of action was procedural or substantive for conflict-of-laws purposes. It was carefully pointed out that survival statutes do not create a new cause of action and are analogous to statutes of limitations, whereas the wrongful death statutes do create new causes of action and are substantive.

We adopt the view that this direct action statute is substantive and, as such, is entitled to comity, provided there is no compelling public policy of this State to the contrary.

Public policy has been defined as "Judicial decisions, legislation and constitutions as well as customs, morals and notions of justice which may prevail in a state." (Speidel, Extra-territorial Assertion of the Direct Action Statute: Due Process, Full Faith and Credit and the Search for Government Interest, 53 Northwestern U.Law Review 179, 200.) The author in developing the thesis that the direct action statute contravenes Illinois public policy said: "An exclusionary policy which is directed at the nature of the right sought to be enforced and is predicated upon protecting the outcome of litigation from prejudice and error reflects a peculiar local interest * * *. This argument becomes even more compelling when it is realized that the direct action statute is an innovation which has been adopted by only three states [Wisconsin, Louisiana and Rhode Island]. While uniform enforcement in general may be a desirable goal, it should not foist the experimental whims of other states upon the place of trial." (P. 203.) An examination of Illinois law and customs will, we believe, demonstrate that entertaining direct action suits is contrary to a firmly-fixed public policy.

First, while there is no direct legislation prohibiting such actions as in Michigan (Lieberthal v. Glens Falls Indemnity Co. of Glens Falls, New York, 316 Mich. 37, 24 N.W.2d 547), section 25 of the Civil Practice Act (Ill.Rev.Stat.1967, chap. 110, par. 25(2),) which provided for the filing of a third party complaint, expresses a legislative policy by adding the admonition: "Nothing herein applies to liability insurers or creates any substantive right to contribution among tortfeasors or against any insurer or other person which has not heretofore existed." Section 388 of the Insurance Code (Ill.Rev.Stat.1967, chap. 73, par. 1000) provides that policies shall contain a privilege for suit against an insurer where the insured becomes insolvent or bankrupt and execution has been returned unsatisfied. These statutory provisions definitely indicate to us a legislative policy against direct actions against insurers before judgment.

In Pohlman v. Universal Mutual Casualty Co., 12 Ill.App.2d 153, 138 N.E.2d 848, section 388 was interpreted as expressing a legislative policy against direct action against insurers until after liability had been established and judgment rendered against an insured. In Mutual Service Casualty Insurance Co. v. Prudence Mutual Casualty Co., 25 Ill.App.2d 429, 166 N.E.2d 316, the appellate court refused to permit the plaintiff company to maintain an action to enforce a repayment of the amount it had to pay under Wisconsin's comparative negligence statute. The decision was based squarely upon the theory that public policy of this State prohibited direct actions against insurers. * * * Disclosure of liability coverage at a trial against an insured for injuries resulting from his negligence constitutes prejudicial error in this State, contrary to the rule prevailing in Wisconsin. (Kavanaugh v. Parret, 379 Ill. 273, 40 N.E.2d 500.) The Wisconsin direct action statute is in direct contravention of no action clauses in policies which are recognized in this State. Piper v. State Farm Mutual Automobile Insurance Co., 1 Ill.App.2d 1, 116 N.E.2d 86.

Foreign substantive law is not, of course, unenforceable as being contrary to public policy just because it differs from our own law, but the differences here are such as to be against our public policy. Our courts and juries would be hard put to cope with the complex problems posed by other aspects of Wisconsin law if these direct actions are permitted. Wisconsin's lack of a guest statute such as we have, and its interpretation of policy language, would result in confusion and possibly injustice. If this case is entertained by our courts, many more will follow with their attendant appeals. Eventually two bodies of law would be built up, one relating to domestic cases and the other based on our interpretation of Wisconsin law.

Public policy of Illinois precludes the use of our courts as the forum for cases under the Wisconsin direct action statutes and application of the exclusionary rule does not violate the full-faith-and-credit provisions of the Federal constitution.

The judgment of the circuit court of Cook County is affirmed.

### *Note*

Suppose a resident of state X, which has no direct action statute, is negligently injured by an insured tortfeasor in state Y, which does have a direct action statute. Can the injured party sue the other driver's insurance company directly in State X? Which public policy should prevail: the public policy against direct actions or the public policy of the state to advance the interest of its citizens? See, Myers v. Government Employees Insurance Co., 302 Minn. 359, 225 N.W.2d 238, 83 A.L.R.3d 328 (1974).

# Chapter 13

# POTENTIAL DEFENSES BY THE INSURER

## A. NO COVERAGE

___ **intentional or wilful acts**
___ **no "occurrence"**
___ **no loss within meaning of policy**
___ **not "arising out of use" of automobile**

### PACHUCKI v. REPUBLIC INSURANCE CO.

Supreme Court of Wisconsin, 1979.
89 Wis.2d 703, 278 N.W.2d 898.

COFFEY, JUSTICE.

This is an appeal taken from interlocutory judgments entered in favor of the defendant-respondents Underwriters Insurance Company (hereinafter Underwriters) and Republic Insurance Co. (hereinafter Republic.) Judgment was granted dismissing the plaintiff-appellant, Gary Pachucki's complaint and the cross-complaints against Underwriters and Republic after a bifurcated trial to the court on the issue of insurance coverage.

The plaintiff-appellant, Gary Pachucki, commenced this action seeking to recover damages for personal injuries suffered during an incident at work on September 10, 1972 when he was struck in the right eye. On the date of the accident, the plaintiff was employed as a printer at Steins Garden Center of Milwaukee. At approximately 5:30 p.m., co-employees and the defendants in this action, Dale Boschke, Bernard Halas and Anthony Anderson, entered the room where Pachucki was working and started a "greening pin war." A greening pin war is described as being comparable to the shooting of paper clips with rubber bands. The flying metal object that caused an injury to the cornea of the plaintiff's right eye was a greening pin, similar in size and weight to a bobby pin.

The plaintiff's complaint also named as defendants in this action Republic and Underwriters insurance companies. At the time of the accident, Republic had in full force and effect policies of homeowners insurance covering the parents of Dale Boeschke and Anthony Anderson, with their children named as additional insureds. Similarly, Underwriters had issued a homeowners policy to the parents of Bernard Halas, naming him as an additional insured. The original answers filed by the insurance companies were subsequently amended to allege certain defenses in coverage relying upon the "business pursuit" and the "intentional tort" policy exclusions. Each policy contained the following language in the coverage exclusionary provisions:

> "THIS POLICY DOES NOT APPLY:
>
> "1. Under Coverage E—Personal Liability and Coverage F—Medical Payments to Others: * * *
>
> "(d) to bodily injury or property damage arising out of business pursuits of any insured except activities therein which are ordinarily incident to non-business pursuits; * * *
>
> "(f) to bodily injury or property damage which is either expected or intended from the standpoint of the insured."

Republic and Underwriters moved for summary judgments of dismissal upon the above recited policy exclusions. In the alternative, the insurers requested a bifurcated trial with respect to the issue of policy coverage in the event that the motions for summary judgment were denied. The trial court denied the respective summary judgment motions but granted Republic's and Underwriter's requests for a separate trial on the issue of coverage.

At the trial on the issue of coverage, the defendant Boeschke stated that he did not mean to hit or hurt the plaintiff as he was taking haphazard aim. However, on cross-examination, Boeschke contradicted this testimony stating that although he had no intention of hitting the plaintiff in the eye, he had intended to strike Pachucki's body with the rubber band-propelled projectile. In his testimony, Boeschke stated "You do not have too much control" when shooting a greening pin; and admitted that the plaintiff could be hit in the eye because of the lack of control over the flying object's course of travel. Boeschke personally realized the danger of the flying object, testifying that on one occasion he had bled after being struck with a greening pin.

The defendant, Bernard Halas, testified that he was aiming in the plaintiff's general direction but was not trying to hit any particular part of his body. He explained that since a flying greening pin could strike anywhere on a person's body he realized there was a possibility that the pin could hit Pachucki in the face. The Defendants, as well as the plaintiff, stated that the "war" game was spontaneous and not the result of any provocation or animosity. During the 3–5 minute "game of war" the plaintiff and the defendants fired approximately 30 greening pins with only one other pin striking the plaintiff in the leg. It is undisputed in the record that the plaintiff returned the defendants' volleys and that

Boeschke was standing about 6 feet away when he fired the pin into the plaintiff's eye.

After trial, the court granted judgment in favor of the insurance companies and made the following pertinent findings of fact:

> "21. That the shooting of greening pins is an activity ordinarily associated with non-business pursuits.
>
> "22. That the defendants were shooting greening pins with the intent of hitting the plaintiff, although they had no intent to hit plaintiff in the eye and cause the specific injury which occurred.
>
> "23. That it was a substantial certainty that the plaintiff would sustain some kind of damage.
>
> "24. That from the standpoint of the actors, the shooting of the greening pins was an intentional act of the kind and character exempted from coverage pursuant to the exclusion contained in each of the three policies."

ISSUE:

Whether pursuant to the language contained in a homeowners insurance policy excluding coverage for bodily injury or property damage which is either expected or intended from the standpoint of the insured is coverage excluded only upon adequate proof that the insured specifically intended the resulting injury?

* * *

The appellant's principal argument is that the policy provision excluding coverage for " * * * bodily injury * * * which is either expected or intended from the standpoint of the insured" should be construed as requiring proof of a specific intent to cause injury. The appellant maintains that under this construction of the intentional tort exclusion, insurance coverage should be provided as it is virtually undisputed that none of the defendant co-employees intended to inflict injury to the plaintiff's eye.

To the contrary, the respondents support the trial court's analysis of the policy exclusion interpreting the provision to mean: where the insured intends to strike or hit a third party, the intent to injure may be inferred by the nature of the act as well as the reasonable foreseeability of the resulting harm, even though the actual injury is different in character or magnitude.

Home Insurance v. Neilsen, (Ind.App.1975), 332 N.E.2d 240 outlines three general rules that have emerged with respect to the construction of an intentional tort exclusion:

> (1) The minority view follows the classic tort doctrine of looking to the natural and probable consequences of the insured's act;
>
> (2) The majority view is that the insured must have intended the act *and* to cause some kind of bodily injury;

(3) A third view is that the insured must have had the specific intent to cause the type of injury suffered.[4]

The trial court denied coverage in the instant case with application of the majority view. The majority position is summarized in the following: (1) it is necessary that the insured intend both the act as well as intending to cause bodily injury in order for the exclusion to apply; (2) intent may be actual or may be inferred by the nature of the act and the accompanying reasonable foreseeability of harm; (3) once it is found that harm was intended, it is immaterial that the actual harm caused is of a different character or magnitude than that intended. See: Butler v. Behaeghe, 37 Colo.App. 282, 548 P.2d 934 (1976); Clark v. Allstate Ins. Co., 22 Ariz.App. 601, 529 P.2d 1195 (1975).

To date, there is no Wisconsin case law that has squarely met the issue of determining the interpretation of "* * * bodily injury or property damage which is either expected or intended from the standpoint of the insured." In Peterson v. Western Cas. & Surety Co., 5 Wis.2d 535, 93 N.W.2d 433 (1958) the court construed the phrase excluding coverage for "* * * injury * * * caused intentionally by * * * the insured" and affirmed the trial court's finding of coverage. Peterson was injured while standing next to the insured's open car door and was struck as the car moved away from its parked position. The court concluded that although the insured may have acted intentionally in an effort to escape from the police as he rapidly backed up his auto, his intentional acts were not directed toward the plaintiff. This court stated in regard to the trial court's finding that the insured's acts constituted gross negligence:

> "The law may treat gross negligence as equivalent to intentional wrongdoing for some purposes, but not for the purpose of excluding liability for gross negligence from the coverage of a liability insurance policy." supra at 542, 93 N.W.2d at 437.

Thus *Peterson* is interpreted as requiring proof of an intent to inflict harm in addition to an intentional act before coverage will be denied.

In Falk v. Whitewater, 65 Wis.2d 83, 221 N.W.2d 915 (1974) the court again pointed out that an intentional act is a separate legal consideration and must be distinguished from the intent to cause injury. In *Falk,* the defendants contended that a cause of action in negligence had not been stated as the plaintiff alleged the defendant intentionally made a fist and negligently struck him in the face. The defense argued "because the making of a fist in and of itself is an intentional act, * * * any further act resulting therefrom is likewise intentionally done." In rejecting this argument, the court stated:

> "Even assuming that the making of a fist is necessarily an intentional act, to reason that the striking of someone with that fist is therefore necessarily likewise intentional is a *non sequitur.* Al-

4. See: Annotation: Liability Insurance: Specific Exclusions of Liability Intentionally Caused by the Insured, 2 A.L.R.3d 1238 (1965).

most all negligent conduct is composed of individual intentional components; to constitute an intentional tort, however, the actor must intend the consequences of his acts, or believe that they are substantially certain to follow. Restatement, 1 *Torts* 2d, p. 15, sec. 8A. While a driver may intentionally step on the accelerator and intentionally steer his car into the passing lane, a resulting collision with an oncoming car is not ipso facto intentional on the driver's part.

The language in *Falk* defining intentional conduct as contrasted to negligent behavior is similar to the criteria set forth in Prosser, Law of Torts, 4th ed. (1971) and cited by the trial court. Professor Prosser, in defining the meaning of intent, stated:

> "The intent with which tort liability is concerned is not necessarily a hostile intent, or a desire to do any harm. Rather it is an intent to bring about a result which will invade the interests of another in a way that the law will not sanction. The defendant may be liable although he has meant nothing more than a good-natured practical joke, * * *
>
> * * *
>
> "Intent, however, is broader than a desire to bring about physical results. It must extend not only to those consequences which are desired, but also to those which the actor believes are substantially certain to follow from what he does. * * * The man who fires a bullet into a dense crowd may fervently pray that he will hit no one, but since he must believe and know that he cannot avoid doing so, he intends it. The practical application of this principle has meant that where a reasonable man in the defendant's position would believe that a particular result was substantially certain to follow, he will be dealt with by the jury, or even by the court, as though he had intended it. * * *" Id. at 31–32.

Thus, we note that in each case of this type, the intent to inflict injury is a question of fact, Peterson v. Western Cas. Ins. Co., supra, 5 Wis.2d at 341–43, 93 N.W.2d 433, and therefore the applicability of this decision is limited to the policy language and the facts presently before us. As the intent to cause injury is a question of fact, the test to be applied to the trial court's determination relating to the question of intent is whether or not the finding of intent is contrary to the great and clear preponderance of the evidence. Ehlers v. Colonial Penn. Ins. Co., 81 Wis.2d 64, 259 N.W.2d 718 (1977).

In the instant case, there is no dispute from the record that the defendants intentionally fired the greening pins. Despite some statements to the contrary, each of the defendants admitted to attempting to hit the plaintiff but not in the eye, and they further testified it is almost impossible to obtain any degree of accuracy when shooting a greening pin. We note there is no direct evidence that the defendants were intending to inflict any harm other than to "sting" the plaintiff.

Upon this evidence, the trial court found that none of the defendants specifically intended to inflict injury to the plaintiff's eye. * * *

The trial court's finding that the intent to inflict injury could be inferred from the nature of the defendants' intentional acts is not contrary to the great weight and clear preponderance of the evidence in the record. There was testimony supporting the fact that each of the defendants had prior knowledge that being struck with a greening pin will result in injury. Boeschke stated on one occasion after being hit by a greening pin he suffered an injury and bled.

In support of the trial court's finding, we examine Clark v. Allstate Insurance Co., supra. In that case, Clark struck another student in the face with his fist causing severe injuries. Allstate had issued a policy of homeowners insurance to Clark's parents and had denied coverage, interpreting similar contract language as contained in this exclusionary clause. Clark maintained that he never intended to hurt the other student even though he did intend to hit him in the face with a "short jab." Concluding that the injuries herein were intentionally caused, the court stated:

> "* * * an act may be so certain to cause a particular harm that it can be said that a person who performed such an act intended the harm." Id. 529 P.2d at 1196.

Some courts might characterize the defendants' conduct in this case as "horseplay" as there was no specific intent to do harm. However, the boys' actual knowledge based upon prior experience that a greening pin will cause harm when it strikes, especially when fired at the close range of six feet, distinguishes this appeal from the classic "horseplay" case of Morrill v. Gallagher, 370 Mich. 578, 122 N.W.2d 687 (1963). In *Morrill* the defendant Gallagher threw a cherry bomb into the plaintiff's office attempting to scare him but the result was a serious hearing impairment. The insurer, in its defense of the case, relied in part upon the intentional tort exclusion. The court rejected the defense position and stated:

> "There is nothing in this case to justify [the] conclusion that [the insured] intended to cause any physical harm to the plaintiff." Id., 122 N.W.2d at 691.

In *Morrill* the remote possibility of harm cannot be equated with the substantial certainty that harm would result under the facts of this case.

The present case is properly similar to Butler v. Behaeghe, supra, wherein the defendant's insurer refused to defend based on an identical exclusionary clause. The plaintiff and the insured got into an argument after an altercation between their two teen-aged sons. The insured ordered the plaintiff off his property and when the plaintiff refused to leave, the insured procured a steel pipe. Although he intended to strike the plaintiff in the stomach, he hit the plaintiff on the head and an injury ensued. Finding that the insured's conduct fell within the exclusionary provision, the court concluded:

> "Where coverage is excluded if bodily injury is 'intended or expected' by the insured, such exclusion is inapplicable if and only if the insured acts without any intent or any expectation of causing any injury, however slight. And conversely, such exclusion is inapplicable if the insured acts with the intent or expectation that bodily injury will result even though the bodily injury that does result is different either in character or magnitude from the injury that was intended." Id. 548 P.2d at 938.

Thus, we hold the applicable case law supports the trial court's findings that the facts and circumstances of this case bar recovery pursuant to the language contained in the intentional tort exclusionary sections in the respective policies. We affirm the trial court's finding that the defendants' intent to inflict injury to the plaintiff can be inferred from the evidence and circumstances in this case.

Judgments affirmed.

### *Notes*

1. The policy reasons for saying that an insurer should not be made to pay when the insured is held liable for an intentionally wrongful act seem clear. California Insurance Code § 533 provides:

> An insurer is not liable for a loss caused by the wilful act of the insured; but he is not exonerated by the negligence of the insured, or of the insured's agents or others.

> California Civil Code § 1668 provides:

> All contracts which have for their object, directly or indirectly, exempt anyone from responsibility for his own fraud, or willful injury to the person or property of another, or violation of law, whether willful or negligent, are against the policy of the law.

Messrs. W., L., and B. were each convicted on several (fraud) counts of violating the Federal securities laws. They belonged to an accounting firm which maintained a professional liability policy with St. Paul Fire & Marine Ins. Co. Civil suits for damages were filed against W., L., and B., some of these suits being based on negligence. St. Paul asks the court to declare that it need not provide W., L., and B. with a defense. It refers to clauses in the professional liability policy excluding liability for "dishonesty, misrepresentation, or fraud", to the statutes quoted above, and to "collateral estoppel." What result? See St. Paul Fire & Marine Insurance Co. v. Weiner, 606 F.2d 864 (9th Cir.1979). The criminal case is United States v. Weiner, 578 F.2d 757 (9th Cir.1978), certiorari denied 439 U.S. 981, 99 S.Ct. 568, 58 L.Ed.2d 651 (1978).

Insureds faced with the intentional acts exclusion do their best to find a crack in the policy through which they may squeeze some coverage. For a successful argument (subject to appeal), see Wong v. State Compensation Ins. Fund, 12 Cal.App.4th 686, 16 Cal.Rptr.2d 1 (1993) (allegation of *constructive* wrongful discharge may trigger duty to defend under workers' compensation policy).

2. Is the "BB gun game" by juveniles to be looked at in the same way as the "greening pin war"? See Allstate Insurance Co. v. Steinemer, 723 F.2d 873 (11th Cir.1984) and Bell v. Tilton, 234 Kan. 461, 674 P.2d 468 (1983).

3. Because society and the law are not static, new issues regularly arise. A legislative enactment may produce a new body of law to be applied, as the Congress did with passage of the Americans with Disabilities Act of 1990 (42 U.S.C.A. § 12101 *et seq.*). Beyond legislation, the changing attitudes of modern society have developed a new source of litigation with respect to intentional acts—sexual misconduct. While reading the cases that follow, keep in mind the policies embodied in prior contexts. Perhaps the questions presented are not as novel as they first appear.

## ANDOVER NEWTON THEOLOGICAL SCHOOL, INC. v. CONTINENTAL CASUALTY CO.

United States Court of Appeals, First Circuit, 1991.
930 F.2d 89.

COFFIN, SENIOR CIRCUIT JUDGE.

In 1987, a jury found that Andover Newton Theological School, Inc. (Andover) both violated the Age Discrimination in Employment Act (ADEA), 29 U.S.C. §§ 621–634, and breached an employment contract when it terminated a tenured professor. This court affirmed the jury's verdict in Linn v. Andover Newton Theological School, Inc., 874 F.2d 1 (1st Cir.1989). Andover thereafter made a claim on its insurance carrier, Continental Casualty Co. (Continental). When Continental refused to pay the claim, Andover filed suit, alleging breach of insurance contract and unfair and deceptive trade practices. The district court held that Continental was not obligated under the policy to reimburse Andover for damages arising from the Linn case because Massachusetts law precluded an insurance company from insuring a willful violation of the ADEA. See Mass.Gen.L. ch. 175, § 47 Sixth (b). The court also held that the policy language unambiguously excluded payments for amounts due under the terms of a contractual obligation. The court held, however, that the policy permitted recovery of costs associated with the defense of the Linn case, and awarded $102,748.85 for that loss.

On appeal, Andover challenges * * * the district court's determination that a willful violation of the ADEA fell within the public policy proscriptions of Mass.Gen.L. ch. 175, § 47 Sixth (b) * * *. Continental, in turn, appeals the award of litigation costs.

After hearing oral argument, this court concluded that a critical issue in this case turned on a question of Massachusetts law on which we could find no controlling precedent. We therefore certified a single question to the Massachusetts Supreme Judicial Court in accordance with Mass.S.J.C. Rule 1:03: "Does a finding of willfulness under the Age Discrimination in Employment Act (ADEA), if based on a finding of 'reckless disregard as to whether [defendant's] conduct is prohibited by federal law,' constitute 'deliberate or intentional * * * wrongdoing' such as to preclude indemnification by an insurer under the public policy of Massachusetts as codified at Mass.Gen.L. ch. 175, § 47 Sixth (b)?" Andover Newton Theological School, Inc. v. Continental Casualty Co., 901 F.2d 1, 3 (1st Cir.1990). The SJC answered that it did not. Andover Newton Theological School, Inc. v. Continental Casualty Co., 409 Mass. 350, 566 N.E.2d 1117 (1991). With that answer in hand, we now address the parties' contentions on appeal. Concluding that the district court erred, we reverse and remand the case for further proceedings consistent with this opinion.

## I. The ADEA Claim

Andover was insured by Continental for losses arising out of wrongful acts. The scope of the insured loss specifically was limited by policy language stating that: "such subject of loss shall not include * * * matters which shall be deemed uninsurable under the law pursuant to which this policy shall be construed."

In the underlying action, Andover was found by a jury to have violated the ADEA by discharging Dr. Edmund Linn from his tenured faculty position when he was 62 years of age. The jury also found Andover's conduct to have been willful under the ADEA. The jury's finding of willfulness was based on an instruction that "[a] defendant acts willfully if it knows its conduct was prohibited by federal law or if it acts in reckless disregard as to whether its conduct is prohibited by federal law. 'Prohibited' being age discrimination in this case."

The district court granted summary judgment to Continental, holding that the United States Supreme Court had defined "willful" under the ADEA to mean "voluntary," "deliberate" or "intentional" in McLaughlin v. Richland Shoe Co., 486 U.S. 128, 133, 108 S.Ct. 1677, 1681, 100 L.Ed.2d 115 (1988). The court then concluded that "willful" conduct was within the meaning of the Massachusetts provision precluding insurance coverage for "deliberate or intentional * * * wrongdoing."

The district court's reliance on this language from McLaughlin was misplaced. First, the controlling definition by the Supreme Court of the word "willful" in the liquidated damages provision of the ADEA, 29 U.S.C. § 626(b), appears in Trans World Airlines, Inc. v. Thurston, 469 U.S. 111, 128, 105 S.Ct. 613, 625, 83 L.Ed.2d 523 (1985), where the Court held that "a violation is 'willful' if 'the employer either knew or showed reckless disregard for the matter of whether its conduct was prohibited by the ADEA.' " Second, the language from McLaughlin quoted by the district court was preliminary discussion; the McLaughlin Court ultimately adopted the Thurston standard. Finally, regardless of the standard enunciated by the Supreme Court, what is significant here is the standard actually applied by the jury in reaching its finding of willfulness—knowing or reckless disregard of whether conduct is proscribed by federal law. And, answering our certified question, the SJC has held that an action taken in reckless disregard of the ADEA is not conduct uninsurable under Massachusetts law. It would seem, therefore, that Continental is obligated under the policy to reimburse Andover for the loss if the jury's finding of willfulness rested on a finding of recklessness.

Continental, however, advances one further reason why Andover's conduct falls within the Massachusetts statute's proscription. It argues that, in an individual disparate treatment case, a finding of liability constitutes a finding of intentional discrimination. See, e.g., Menzel v. Western Auto Supply Co., 848 F.2d 327, 329 (1st Cir.1988) ("finding of pretext is the equivalent of a finding that the employer intentionally discriminated"). Therefore, Continental suggests, once the jury found liability, coverage was illegal under the Massachusetts statute, and the finding of willfulness was unnecessary.

Continental relies for this argument on cases from other circuits adopting a standard of willfulness higher than the Thurston standard in actions alleging individual disparate treatment because, in such cases, a finding of liability requires a finding of intentional discrimination, and therefore willfulness will almost always be present. Those courts concluded that a more stringent willfulness standard must be applied in such cases to respond to the Thurston Court's understanding that "willfulness" was not intended to be interpreted so as to result in double damages in almost every case. See Thurston, 469 U.S. at 128, 105 S.Ct. at 625. But these cases do not state that every finding of liability in an individual disparate treatment case necessarily requires a finding of willfulness under the Thurston standard. More importantly, these cases do not even come close to suggesting that the standard for liability in individual disparate treatment cases is higher than the Thurston standard for willfulness—in other words, that a finding of discrimination precludes the employer's conduct from being merely reckless with regard to the Act—as defendant argues here.

In addition, the SJC's opinion expressly rejects the defendant's loose understanding of the word "intentional." As the court says, "[t]he fact that a wrongful act was committed intentionally * * * does not alone bar coverage. That bar arises only if an intentionally committed, wrongful act was also done deliberately or intentionally, in the sense that the actor knew that the act was wrongful." Andover Newton, 409 Mass. at 352, 566 N.E.2d 1117.[3]

There is no indication in this case that the jury made a determination about Andover's state of mind other than in its conclusion that Andover had acted willfully—a finding that would bar recovery only if the jury based its determination on a conclusion that Andover knew its actions were wrongful. Instead, the jury was asked to determine whether "age was a motivating factor in [Linn's] discharge in the sense that

3. In other words, Massachusetts law only proscribes coverage of acts committed with the specific intent to do something the law forbids. Cf. Loeb v. Textron, Inc., 600 F.2d 1003, 1020 n. 27 (1st Cir.1979) ("'An act is done "willfully" if done voluntarily and intentionally, and with the specific intent to do something the law forbids; that is to say, with bad purpose either to disobey or to disregard the law.'") (quoting E. Devitt & C. Blackmar, Federal Jury Practice and Instructions § 14.06, at 384 (3d ed. 1977)).

but for defendant's motive to discriminate against him because of his age he would not have been discharged." And the judge specifically instructed the jury that Andover legally could not consider the availability of a pension to Linn or make assumptions about the productivity of older persons in deciding which faculty member to terminate. The jury could have found that Andover considered these factors—and therefore discriminated—without consciously appreciating the illegality of its act. See Burlew, 869 F.2d at 1066 (" '[A]ge discrimination may simply arise from an unconscious application of stereotyped notions of ability rather than from a deliberate desire to remove older employees from the workforce * * *.' ") (quoting Syvock v. Milwaukee Boiler Mfg. Co., 665 F.2d 149, 154–55 (7th Cir.1981), overruled in part by Coston v. Plitt Theatres, Inc., 860 F.2d 834 (7th Cir.1988) (emphasis in original)). There is simply nothing inherent in the finding of age discrimination or in the instructions given the jury here that rendered a finding of willfulness superfluous.

We therefore conclude that Massachusetts public policy does not bar insurance coverage of an employment action solely because it is found to violate the ADEA in an individual disparate treatment case. Nor, according to the SJC, does a jury's determination that the violation was willful bar coverage, if the jury based that determination on a finding of recklessness. The district court therefore erred in granting summary judgment to Continental on this issue.

* * *

### III. Defense Litigation Costs

Continental argues that the district court erred in determining that it was liable under the policy to reimburse Andover for defense costs incurred in the Linn action. Continental asserted below that coverage for defense costs is limited to those situations in which there is underlying policy coverage for the act. The district court determined that, notwithstanding the fact that liability coverage was unavailable for willful discrimination under the ADEA, the policy failed to exclude coverage for defense costs associated with those claims. We agree.

The Continental policy covers losses the assured becomes legally obligated to pay, and "loss" is defined as: "any amount which the Assureds are legally obligated to pay * * * for a claim or claims made against the Assureds for a Wrongful Act and shall include but not be limited to damages, judgments, settlements and costs, cost of investigation and defense of legal actions, (excluding from such costs of investigation and defense, salaries of officers or employees of the School District or any other governmental body) claims or proceedings and appeals therefrom, * * * provided always, however, such subject of loss shall not include * * * matters which shall be deemed uninsurable under the law pursuant to which this policy shall be construed." Continental does not deny that discriminatory acts are "wrongful acts" within the meaning of the policy. Coverage for wrongful acts, however, is limited by a specific exclusion of those "subjects of loss" deemed uninsurable under Massachusetts law. The exclusion of defense costs therefore is dependent on whether Massachusetts would consider such costs uninsurable.

As we have discussed, Massachusetts law precludes an insurance company from insuring "any person against legal liability for causing injury, other than bodily injury, by his deliberate or intentional crime or wrongdoing." Mass.Gen.L. ch. 175, § 47, Sixth (b). As we read this language, while public policy proscribes insuring against *legal liability* for intentional wrongdoing, the language of the public policy prohibition expresses no intent with respect to insurance coverage for the costs of defending against such liability. Although an argument can be made that a public policy is to some extent subverted by insurance against defense costs, the basic fact is that this is not insurance against liability. Continental points to no authority for extending the public policy bar to these claims. Where the SJC has declined to interpret the scope of the public policy provision expansively, see Andover Newton, 409 Mass. 350, 566 N.E.2d 1117, we also are loath to do so.

As we have noted, exclusions must state clearly what items are to be excluded, see American Home Assur., 786 F.2d at 26. Continental, while it could have done so, made no attempt to exclude defense costs associated with uninsurable claims. The policy therefore allows such coverage. See Starkville Mun. Separate School Dist. v. Continental Casualty Co., 772 F.2d 168, 170 (5th Cir.1985) ("While punitive damages themselves may be uninsurable for reasons of public policy, that same public policy does not apply to costs and attorney's fees incurred in a defense against a plea for punitive damages * * *. If CNA intended to exclude these other costs from the policy's coverage, it needed to do so more explicitly * * *.").[6]

Continental, however, relies on an unpublished district court case, Continental Casualty Co. v. McAllen Indep. School Dist., No. B–86–007 (S.D.Tex. May 19, 1987), holding that with a reimbursement policy such as the one in this case, the reimbursement coverage obligation is limited to losses incurred with respect to "covered claims." But even were this decision of precedential value here, see Loc.R.App.P. 36.2 (citation to unpublished decisions limited to related cases), the case is inapposite. McAllen decided that the underlying acts did not fall within the scope of covered acts under the policy. It is therefore reasonable for reimbursement for defense costs to extend only as far as coverage for the acts. In this case, as we have observed, there is no dispute that the policy covers "wrongful acts" of the type that occurred here. It is only the scope of the *exclusion* that is at issue, and the exclusion language is narrow.

We therefore conclude that Continental is liable for defense costs incurred in the Linn action, regardless of whether the termination ultimately is found to have been taken in knowing violation of federal

6. Continental attempts to distinguish Starkville because the defense of the punitive damages claim in that case ultimately was successful, unlike in this case. But the Starkville court, while noting that this factor was an additional reason supporting coverage, did not rest its analysis on the distinction.

law. Continental does not dispute that defense costs associated with the contract action are recoverable if the ADEA defense costs are covered. Andover therefore is entitled to reimbursement for its defense costs associated with all claims.

* * *

## COIT DRAPERY CLEANERS, INC. v. SEQUOIA INSURANCE CO.

Court of Appeal, First District, 1993.
14 Cal.App.4th 1595, 18 Cal.Rptr.2d 692.

PETERSON, PRESIDING JUSTICE.

* * *

### I. FACTS AND PROCEDURAL HISTORY

We summarize the claims and evidence before the trial court as follows.

#### A. *Sexual Harassment*

During 1987, Linda Seahorn, who was about 28 at the time, interviewed for a telephone dispatcher and management trainee position at Coit Drapery Cleaners, Inc. She was interviewed by Dr. Louis J. Kearn, who had founded the company more than 40 years ago and was its president, a major stockholder, and chairman of the board of directors.

Kearn relished his reputation around the company as "a dirty old man." The evidence disclosed Kearn had a long history of sexually harassing young women employees, which was "common knowledge" at Coit. "[A]ny female employee who wanted to remain in Coit's employment, and particularly if she wanted to advance, * * * had to make herself available in some way to Lou Kearn. * * * Lou was very free to put his hands on the female employees." He invited female employees to share his bedroom on trips to Mexico, made sexual advances to female employees in his office, sexually fondled and groped female employees on the job, and offered to pay female employees thousands of dollars from corporate funds for sex. There was also evidence that Coit employees, including Dr. Kearn, jokingly referred to the corporate name Coit as short for "coitus."

If a female employee did not accede to Kearn's demands, she would be fired.

When Seahorn was interviewed by Kearn, he did not dwell upon her qualifications for the job or other business-related inquiries. Instead, he followed his usual practice in interviewing women applicants, by inquiring as to her attitudes toward sex, telling her that he took business trips with female employees and stayed in the same hotel room with them, asked if she had a boyfriend or was unattached, and inquired whether she would be willing to go to bed with prospective clients.

When Seahorn asked another Coit management employee, Sandra Park, whether such highly personal inquiries were "normal," Park told Seahorn not to " 'worry' " about Kearn, that he was " 'just a dirty old man.' " Park told Seahorn that Kearn, despite his sexual insinuations, was harmless. Although Seahorn felt Kearn's behavior in the interview was bizarre and upsetting, she very much needed the job and felt she could handle the situation for the 90 days she would be in Coit's California offices, near Kearn, before her promised position as a Coit manager in Chicago came through.

Seahorn testified Kearn made numerous unwelcome advances and propositions to her during the approximately two months she worked for Coit, before she was terminated for rejecting his advances. He tried to involve her in a game of strip poker, asked about her underwear, and tried to get her into a hot tub—with the aid of Park, who acted as Kearn's procuress in these efforts, and suggested to Seahorn that she should have sex with Kearn.

On one occasion, Kearn invited Seahorn into his private office during business hours—which was strange since there was no business reason requiring the president of the company to confer with a telephone dispatcher, who was separated from him by intermediate supervisors. Kearn asked Seahorn to pour him a drink, and she did so. He asked her to give him a hug, and she gave him a non-passionate hug. He asked for a passionate hug, and squeezed her tighter. He then pulled her into his office bathroom, put her hand inside his pants on his penis, and put his hand under her skirt and panties. He tried to push her down to the carpeted floor and demanded sex; but Seahorn resisted, pulled away, and left the office. Seahorn was afraid she would lose her job since she did not comply with Kearn's sexual demands.

Shortly thereafter, Kearn had Seahorn fired under the pretext of a reduction in force due to adverse economic conditions. However, the economic conditions in question had been the same two months previously when Seahorn was hired. Thereafter, Kearn called Seahorn on numerous occasions, offered her money, and tried to keep her quiet and away from lawyers.

Kearn's sexual harassment and termination of Seahorn caused her to suffer lost wages and serious psychiatric problems, including depression, chemical dependency, and suicidal thoughts.

### B. *Seahorn's Lawsuit and Its Tender to an Insurer*

Seahorn brought an action against Coit, Kearn, and Park, alleging theories of sexual harassment in violation of Government Code section 12940 et seq., invasion of privacy, wrongful termination, breach of public policy, infliction of emotional distress, fraud, and battery, with demands for punitive damages.

Several months later, Coit sought to tender defense of the Seahorn lawsuit to its insurer, respondent Sequoia Insurance Company, which had in force a policy of general liability coverage for Coit's dry cleaning business.

Sequoia referred the matter to its counsel for investigation and, on the advice of counsel, declined to accept the tender of the defense. Sequoia relied on the fact that, inter alia, the claimed sexual harassment and wrongful termination of Seahorn could not constitute an "occurrence" under its policy, since these events were expected or intended by the insured.

In March 1990, the action was settled by Seahorn and the defendants, without the participation of Sequoia, for slightly more than $1 million. The settlement agreement contains a number of rather unusual features designed to force respondent insurer Sequoia to pay the bulk of the settlement, despite its refusal to admit coverage for intentional acts of sexual harassment and wrongful termination. For instance, the total amount of the settlement was $1,055,000 ($750,000 plus costs and attorney fees of $305,000) of which Coit was to ultimately pay only $350,000, with nothing contributed by Kearn or Park, who were allegedly the actual wrongdoers. The settling parties agreed among themselves that Sequoia would have to pay the almost two-thirds of the settlement which was remaining—$705,000. Seahorn made an uncontested motion to determine that this settlement was in "good faith," and the trial court granted the unopposed motion. No judgment of dismissal was ever filed, so technically the Seahorn action is still pending.

### *C. Suit Against the Insurer*

Coit, Kearn, and Park then filed this action against respondent insurer Sequoia, alleging breach of contract and of the covenant of good faith and fair dealing for Sequoia's refusal to defend or indemnify against Seahorn's sexual harassment and wrongful termination claims under its general liability policy.

* * *

## II. Discussion

We affirm the trial court's ruling that the acts of sexual harassment and wrongful termination claimed here were intentional acts, for which coverage was excluded by the language of the relevant insurance policy and by Insurance Code section 533 (section 533). * * *

### *A. Section 533 Bars Coverage for Sexual Harassment*

California law and applicable precedents do not allow the recharacterization of such clearly intentional and willful sexual misconduct as merely negligent or nonwillful, so as to trigger insurance coverage. In the lead case of J.C. Penney Casualty Ins. Co. v. M.K. (1991) 52 Cal.3d 1009, 1020–1021, 278 Cal.Rptr. 64, 804 P.2d 689, our Supreme Court clarified the applicable legal principles by holding that section 533 bars recovery on an insurance policy for the "wilful act" of sexually molesting a child. In Fire Ins. Exchange v. Altieri (1991) 235 Cal.App.3d 1352, 1359–1360, 1 Cal.Rptr.2d 360, the Sixth District held that section 533 bars insurance recovery for an intentional battery, such as the one Seahorn allegedly suffered as a result of Kearn's attack on her in his office. In Studley v. Benicia Unified Sch. Dist. (1991) 230 Cal.App.3d 454, 281 Cal.Rptr. 631, Division One of this district held that section 533 bars insurance recovery for the death of a victim during an assault by her estranged boyfriend. In B & E Convalescent Center v. State Compensation Ins. Fund (1992) 8 Cal.App.4th 78, 9 Cal.Rptr.2d 894, the Second District held that section 533 bars insurance recovery for an employer's willful act in wrongfully discharging an employee.

* * *

"Section 533 is an implied exclusionary clause statutorily read into all insurance policies. (J.C. Penney [supra, 52 Cal.3d at p. 1019, 278 Cal.Rptr. 64, 804 P.2d 689.] ) It is subject to the rules of *statutory* construction, *not* to the rules governing contract interpretation, and must be construed in order to effect its purpose. [Citations.]" (California Casualty Management Co. v. Martocchio, supra, 11 Cal.App.4th at p. 1531, 15 Cal.Rptr.2d 277, emphasis in original.)

Quite apart from the plain meaning of section 533, and its obvious application to claims of intentional wrongdoing such as those in issue here, the purpose and public policy represented by the section, and the public and statutory policy of this state against sexual harassment of employees, would not be well served by a ruling which would exonerate a perpetrator from payment of damages for his own willful act of sexual gratification, by shifting such liability to an insurer. (See Bank of the West v. Superior Court (1992) 2 Cal.4th 1254, 1267, 10 Cal.Rptr.2d 538, 833 P.2d 545.) "If insurance coverage were available for monetary awards under the Unfair Business Practices Act, a person found to have violated the act would simply shift the loss to his insurer * * *." (Ibid.)

*B. The Unavailability of Coverage As to Coit*

We understand, but reject, the various arguments appellants make in an attempt to secure insurance coverage for these intentional and willful acts of its high managerial agents and policy makers.

1. Defamation

First, appellants claim coverage might be available, at least to the extent of creating a duty to defend, if a claim for defamation had been made against defendants. However, as the trial court aptly noted, no such claim for defamation was made, nor do the facts alleged in the complaint or put before the trial court support the existence of such a claim.

* * *

Further, we note that, after the parties to the Seahorn lawsuit did begin to discuss a potential claim for defamation, Sequoia agreed to defend the lawsuit, despite its objections. The Coit defendants refused that offer of a defense, because they had already decided to settle the case. These events do not support a claim of bad faith breach of covenant by an insurer for failure to defend a potential claim of defamation—rather the reverse.

2. Negligence

Moreover, despite the Coit defendants' latter-day contention that a claim for "negligent supervision" of the sex life of its president and chairman of the board might have somehow been covered, Seahorn never made such a claim in her complaint, and in fact disavowed any such claim. In her counsel's words: "This is not an action involving negligent supervision * * *." Review of the complaint confirms the truth of this statement: There are, in fact, no allegations at all of negligent supervision.

* * *

Our conclusion as to the duty to defend is consistent with that reached recently by our Supreme Court in Horace Mann Ins. Co. v. Barbara B. (1993) 4 Cal.4th 1076, 17 Cal.Rptr.2d 210, 846 P.2d 792. Horace Mann dealt with an unusual situation, in which a junior high school band teacher had had apparently nonforcible sexual contact with a 13–year–old student. The student alleged she was harmed by both the teacher's intentional conduct in carrying on his affair with a minor, and by his negligent conduct in publicly embarrassing her with the fact of the affair, through his inept statements and conduct in front of other students. (Id. at p. 1079, 17 Cal.Rptr.2d 210, 846 P.2d 792.) As to the sexual contact with the minor, our Supreme Court held there clearly was no duty to defend. (Id. at p. 1083, 17 Cal.Rptr.2d 210, 846 P.2d 792.)

The Supreme Court also recognized that the claimed negligent conduct could lie outside the scope of the duty to defend, if the alleged instances of negligent conduct "occurred in such close temporal and spatial proximity to the molestation as to *compel* the conclusion that they are inseparable from it for purposes of determining whether [the insurer] owed a duty to defend [the insured]." (Horace Mann Ins. Co. v. Barbara B., supra, 4 Cal.4th at p. 1084, 17 Cal.Rptr.2d 210, 846 P.2d 792, emphasis in original.) While rather unclear, we take the language "temporal and spatial proximity to the molestation" to mean that certain alleged conduct can be "inseparable" from intentional wrongful conduct and, therefore, not subject to any duty to defend, even where such conduct might have triggered such a duty when standing alone. For instance, if in the course of inseparably intentional sexual molestation or harassment of the victim, the wrongdoer so negligently behaved as to cause the victim additional physical or emotional harm, there is no duty to defend, even though mere negligence not occurring during an inseparable course of intentional conduct might theoretically be covered. (See ibid.)

However, as the Supreme Court noted in Horace Mann, it was dealing with the case "in somewhat of a factual vacuum." (4 Cal.4th at p. 1084, 17 Cal.Rptr.2d 210, 846 P.2d 792.) There were "unresolved factual disputes" concerning whether certain conduct, which the Court of Appeal and Supreme Court called " 'parasexual' " (hugging, kissing, and dandling the victim in front of other students) was either intentional or inseparable from intentional conduct; therefore, the duty to defend might still exist. (Id. at pp. 1083, 1084–1085, 17 Cal.Rptr.2d 210, 846 P.2d 792.) One might question the assumption that a teacher may unintentionally kiss, hug, and fondle a young student with whom the teacher is intentionally having an illicit affair. (See id. at p. 1088, 17 Cal.Rptr.2d 210, 846 P.2d 792 (conc. opn. of Baxter, J).) "On this record, that conclusion strains common sense." (Ibid.) However, our Supreme Court, dealing with the case in a "vacuum," apparently entertained this as at least a theoretical possibility.

In the present case, of course, the conduct of the defendants was inseparably intentional. It was part of a consistent course of sexual harassment of an unconsenting victim, in an employment setting. All of this conduct was harmful and wrongful, as a matter of law; there are no unresolved factual issues as to the intentionality of Kearn's harassing conduct, as appellants conceded at oral argument. There was no duty to defend. (See Horace Mann Ins. Co. v. Barbara B., supra, 4 Cal.4th at pp. 1083–1084, 17 Cal.Rptr.2d 210, 846 P.2d 792.)

In the present case, no claim for negligent supervision was made in the complaint and none was supportable by the facts; and the sexual abuse of female employees by Kearn was so widespread, well-known, and so ratified by the corporation as to constitute intentional corporate policy, which cannot be the subject of insurance coverage. (Loyola Marymount University v. Hartford Accident & Indemnity Co. (1990) 219 Cal.App.3d 1217, 1225, 271 Cal.Rptr. 528 [No coverage for damages caused by university's allegedly discriminatory policy of discharging married priests, despite claims that the university might have been merely negligent in failing to comply with federal anti-discrimination laws, because "an intentional discharge or application of an employment policy does not become an accidental occurrence even if it has only an unintended federally prohibited discriminatory effect."] ) * * *. Here, the trial court found Coit, its managers, and board of directors were well aware of, and ratified and condoned, the sexual harassment of female employees as a way to satisfy Kearn's urges for sexual domination of females. Coit should not receive insurance coverage for the liability it, thus, intentionally created.

For the same reasons, it is unavailing for appellants to suggest Coit was merely negligent in failing to enact and enforce corporate policies against sexual harassment, so as to prevent its president and major shareholder from attacking female employees. Coverage cannot be created by claimed negligence in failing to dissuade oneself from committing an intentional act, otherwise every intentional act would be covered and section 533 would have no meaning. (See J.C. Penney Casualty Ins. Co. v. M.K., supra, 52 Cal.3d at pp. 1019–1021, 278 Cal.Rptr. 64, 804 P.2d 689.) We are required to interpret section 533 so as to give effect and meaning to all its provisions; just as we cannot allow insurers to recharacterize negligent conduct as intentional, we cannot allow the insured to recast intentional conduct as merely negligent. (See ibid.)

* * *

Although we also believe the acts claimed in the Seahorn lawsuit would not in any event constitute an "occurrence" under the terms of the policy—since they were not unexpected or unintended from the standpoint of the insured, we base our holding more directly upon the statutory mandate of section 533 since, as our Supreme Court held in J.C. Penney, supra, section 533 forms part of the policy by operation of law, and the parties to an insurance contract cannot in any event agree, intend, or expect to create coverage which violates section 533.

* * *

4. The Public Policy Against Sexual Harassment Must Be Harmonized with Section 533

In light of the strong public policy against sexual discrimination and harassment in employment, as embodied in Government Code section 12940 et seq., we seriously question whether section 533 would ever permit insurance coverage for any intentional course of conduct, as evidenced by this record, consisting of a long pattern of behavior of sexual discrimination and sexual harassment by a corporation's high managerial agents which have been known, ratified, and condoned by the corporation. As Justice Croskey observed in B & E Convalescent Center, when considering the public policy against unlawful employment discrimination in light of the mandates of section 533: "Under any reasonable criterion, a termination in violation of such public policies must be held *wrongful as a matter of law.* As we have pointed out, such claim[s] can *only* be established by evidence of an employer's motive and intent to violate and frustrate the law(s) declaring or establishing fundamental public policy. It would be unreasonable, mischievous and improper if section 533, which reflects the 'fundamental public policy of denying coverage for willful wrongs' (J.C. Penney, supra, 52 Cal.3d at pp. 1019–1020, fn. 8 [278 Cal.Rptr. 64, 804 P.2d 689] ), were construed in any way other than to deny insurance coverage in the most certain and unambiguous terms for willful and intentional acts that contravene 'fundamental policies that are delineated in constitutional or statutory provisions' (Gantt, supra, 1 Cal.4th at p. 1095 [4 Cal.Rptr.2d 874, 824 P.2d 680] )." (8 Cal.App.4th at p. 99, 9 Cal.Rptr.2d 894, emphasis in original.)

In order to effectuate this public policy, corporate employers have been made liable for the acts of sexual harassment by their managerial agents in the workplace of which the corporation was aware and which it ratified or condoned; theories of negligent supervision are no longer even necessary to establish corporate liability for the intentional acts of managerial agents in this context. (See Fisher v. San Pedro Peninsula Hospital (1989) 214 Cal.App.3d 590, 608, fn. 6, 262 Cal.Rptr. 842.)

We are concerned here, however, not with corporate liability but with an insurer's responsibilities to defend and indemnify the corporation it insures when such intentional acts occur under the circumstances of this case. The sexual harassment complained of here occurred in the context of a policy of quid pro quo, where corporate funds, employment, and advancement were used or withheld, as a matter of common knowledge and routine, to coerce sexual favors for a high managerial employee. The corporation here, in allowing, condoning, and ratifying such intentional conduct as a matter of corporate policy, triggered the prohibition against insurance coverage for such intentional wrongful conduct embodied in section 533. Thus, the insurer had no duty to defend.

In words which our Supreme Court applied in denying insurance coverage under section 533 for sexual molestation of a child, and which are equally applicable to the actions of the insured corporation in the sexual harassment in issue here: "Section 533 precludes coverage in this case because [the wrongful act] is *always* intentional, it is *always* wrongful, and it is *always* harmful." (J.C. Penney Casualty Ins. Co. v. M.K., supra, 52 Cal.3d at p. 1025, 278 Cal.Rptr. 64, 804 P.2d 689, emphasis in original.)

### III. Disposition

The judgment of dismissal is affirmed. Costs are awarded to Sequoia.

### *Notes*

1. In a modification to the principal case on May 12, 1993, the court addressed the contention that though insurance coverage for intentional sexual harassment is barred by section 533 and by public policy there is no statute or public policy directly forbidding an insurer's provision of a defense to its insured. Despite, the absence of legislation regarding the duty to defend, the court noted that "it is well established, however, that where * * * both statute and public policy bar any possibility of indemnity for conduct which is inseparably intentional, there is also no duty to defend. Otherwise, an insurer would have a duty to defend actions alleging only intentional wrongful conduct outside the scope of any potential for coverage provided by the insurance policy itself or permitted by statute."

2. A number of recent cases arise out of sex contact situations where the contact was intended but the intent to harm is denied: e.g., Horace Mann Ins. Co. v. Independent School District No. 656, 355 N.W.2d 413 (Minn.1984) in which an adult school teacher-counselor engaged in sexual contact with a minor student. The court held that an intent to cause "bodily injury" may be inferred as a matter of law. In accord, Grange Ins. Ass'n v. Authier, 45 Wn.App. 383, 725 P.2d 642 (1986). Even a minor boy (the insured) who engages in sex with minor girls is subject to the inference, Illinois Farmers Ins. Co. v. Judith G., 379 N.W.2d 638 (Minn.App.1986). See State Auto Mut. Ins. Co. v. McIntyre, 652 F.Supp. 1177 (N.D.Ala.1987).

After Hollywood-star Rock Hudson's death from an AIDS–related illness, his partner prevailed in a lawsuit for damages in which the jury found that Hudson had concealed his HIV status and continued to have high risk sex. The jury awarded $14,500,000 in compensatory damages. The estate administrator sued Hudson's liability insurer for coverage, but the court held that high risk sex is an intentional act which is inherently harmful and therefore uninsurable. *Aetna Casualty and Surety Co. v. Sheft,* 989 F.2d 1105 (9th Cir.1993).

The position adopted by the Supreme Court of Wisconsin may differ with that of California. In *Loveridge v. Chartier,* 161 Wis.2d 150, 468 N.W.2d 146 (1991), the court held in part that statutory rape of a consenting sixteen year old female was not harmful as a matter of law, and that allowing insurance coverage for *negligent* transmission of a sexually transmitted disease would not violate public policy. In response to the nationwide increase in similar claims, many homeowners policies now include an "STD" exclusion.

3. Can the rule on insurability of intentional acts applied in *Coit* be reconciled with the position adopted by the Massachusetts Supreme Judicial Court in *Andover Newton?*

4. *Lack of capacity to have intent.*

Many policies exclude coverage for events caused "intentionally by or at the direction of the insured." Steven H. was an additional insured under his parents' homeowners' policy providing comprehensive personal liability coverage. He set fire to a wastebasket in a classroom of the synagogue he attended and the resulting fire caused property damage of nearly $50,000. Steven was under a psychiatrist's care prior to the fire and the issue of his mental capacity to cause damage intentionally was involved in litigation initiated to establish the responsibility of the homeowners' policy insurer for the fire loss. The policy contained the language quoted at the beginning of the paragraph. Is Steven's conduct to be deemed not intentional only if he could be deemed legally insane for purposes of criminal responsibility? Held, "no", in Congregation of Rodef Sholom v. American Motorists Insurance Co., 91 Cal.App.3d 690, 154 Cal.Rptr. 348 (1979) ("If Steven was suffering from a mental disease or defect which deprived him of capacity to intend to set the fire and cause the damage complained of, or which deprived him of the capacity to govern his conduct in accordance with reason, then he did not act intentionally as that word is used in the exclusionary clause, * * *.")

See also American Family Mutual Ins. Co. v. Mueller, 570 F.Supp. 348 (E.D.Mo.1983). Exclusion does not apply to insured suffering psychotic depression (as well as a pain in his foot) who shot his doctor in legs.

Voluntary drunkenness may reach the stage that insured lacks the requisite intent and the exclusion becomes inoperative. MacKinnon v. Hanover Ins. Co., 124 N.H. 456, 471 A.2d 1166, 1169 (1984). Contra is American Family Mut. Ins. Co. v. Peterson, 405 N.W.2d 418 (Minn.1987).

On the related issue of "self-defense" as a bar to the application of the exclusion, see Western Fire Ins. Co. v. Persons, 393 N.W.2d 234 (Minn.App. 1986).

5. *Collateral estoppel.*

On the collateral estoppel issue, see Clemmer v. Hartford Insurance Co., 22 Cal.3d 865, 151 Cal.Rptr. 285, 587 P.2d 1098 (1978) (Dr. Lovelace killed

Dr. Clemmer and was convicted of second degree murder after withdrawing a plea of not guilty by reason of insanity. The widow Clemmer obtained a judgment against Lovelace for wrongful death. In an action against Lovelace's comprehensive liability insurer, the widow was not to be estopped, said the Supreme Court, from litigating the issue of wilfulness because she lacked the requisite privity to Lovelace's criminal defense. The insurer had the burden of proving wilfulness.)

See also St. Paul Fire and Marine Ins. Co. v. Weiner, 606 F.2d 864 (9th Cir.1979), Country Mut. Ins. Co. v. Duncan, 794 F.2d 1211 (7th Cir.1986). (Plea of guilty to voluntary manslaughter does not collaterally estop insured from escaping the exclusion in a civil case).

On the other side, if the insured has been found not guilty of criminal conduct in a battery charge because of mental disease, the insurer is not precluded from litigating the intent issue in a civil case brought by victim against the insured, Rajspic v. Nationwide Mutual Ins. Co., 110 Idaho 729, 718 P.2d 1167 (1986), and State Farm Fire and Cas. Co. v. Poomaihealani, 667 F.Supp. 705 (D.Hawaii 1987).

6. Defendants in an action for malicious prosecution tendered defense to their Homeowner's policy insurer. The policy contained the intentional acts exclusion. Held: that the insurer could refuse the defense: Carrier need only show the nature of the alleged tort has an element of intentional wrongdoing. State Farm Fire & Casualty Co. v. Drasin, 152 Cal.App.3d 864, 199 Cal.Rptr. 749 (1984).

### *Comment (And a Problem or Two)*

### *Liability Insurance Limited to Bodily (Physical) Injury or to Tangible Property Damage*

In tort law the plaintiff is generally speaking, entitled to compensation for all personal injuries or property damage proximately caused by the defendants' conduct.

Liability insurers may (and commonly do) seek to avoid pay out on the more esoteric varieties of personal injury and to limit coverage to "bodily" or "physical" injuries. For example, the Homeowners policy in Appendix B covers bodily injury which it cautiously defines as "bodily harm, sickness or disease."

This language may be given literal effect to eliminate non economic damages such as emotional suffering from coverage (e.g. St. Paul Fire and Marine Ins. Co. v. Campbell County School Dist. No. 1, 612 F.Supp. 285 (D.Wyo.1985). Or at the other end of the spectrum, a court by liberal and expansive use of the canons of insurance policy interpretation may stretch "bodily injury" to embrace loss of consortium damages sustained by the spouse of a person injured in an auto accident (e.g. Abellon v. Hartford Ins. Co., 167 Cal.App.3d 21, 212 Cal.Rptr. 852 (1985)). [What the appropriate medical treatment may be for such "bodily injury" is not clear.]

To obtain additional insurance to pay the full amount of possible tort damages, the applicant may seek out excess or umbrella coverage. Many of these policies employ the new or simplified ["plain, easy to understand

English"] as in the Personal Liability Catastrophe Policy in Appendix G. The phraseology is of interest:

> "What do we mean by an accident or incident? Anything that causes property damage, personal injury or death without your expecting or intending it. If you could've expected the result you're not covered—."
>
> * * *
>
> "What do we mean by personal injury? Bodily injury, of course. But also injuries to a person's feelings or reputation. Like mental injury. Mental anguish. Shock. Wrongful eviction. Libel. Slander. Defamation of character. Invasion of Privacy. False arrest."

Now for a problem. Suppose the insured is sued for alienation of affections—and justifiably so. Is there coverage? How about false arrest? Can there be false arrest without intention or expectation of the result? How about malicious prosecution, etc.? For some insight on such issues see Smith v. St. Paul Guardian Ins. Co., 622 F.Supp. 867 (W.D.Ark.1985).

*Tangible property*

"What do we mean by property damage? Any damage to tangible property or its loss or destruction. Also the loss of its use—for instance the cost of having to rent a substitute car to go to work while the damaged car is being repaired."

The motivation for such limitation is the same as that for restricting personal injury damages to actual physical injuries. Although the majority rule as to tort damages for negligence refuses to impose liability for economic damages standing alone where no harm is done to plaintiff's property, the rule is not universal, and insurers are are naturally reluctant to extend, or to be interpreted as extending, coverages for what is potentially a vast amount of damages. For example, A, insured, hired to perform work on B's property does so negligently and interferes with customers' access to C's business. Obviously, the language quoted above is intended to preclude coverage of A's liability (if any exists in the jurisdiction anyway) to C. But see, Geurin Contractors, Inc. v. Bituminous Casualty Corp., 5 Ark.App. 229, 636 S.W.2d 638 (1982).

*A sample or two of disputes as to what is property damage:*

A T.V. dealer, with liability insurance, supplies unscramblers for sets and is sued by the pay T.V. people. Must the insurer defend or pay for the losses alleged sustained by the plaintiffs? See Nichols v. Great American Insurance Companies, 169 Cal.App.3d 766, 215 Cal.Rptr. 416 (1985).

In Montana, the Lindsay Drilling Co., with typical liability insurance, was in the business of drilling core samples and assaying the gold content. The owners of a placer claim hired Lindsay to drill test holes. The core samples showed a high gold content on which the owners relied to their later sorrow. It turns out the samples had been salted either by Lindsay's employees or by-standers whom Lindsay permitted to be present. The owners sue Lindsay for $2,000,000 in economic losses. Was there an accident causing tangible property damages? See Lindsay Drilling & Contracting v. United States Fidelity & Guaranty Co., 208 Mont. 91, 676 P.2d 203 (1984).

## LIABILITY INSURANCE AND PUNITIVE DAMAGES

The moral and legal arguments against permitting a person to insure against his or her liability for punitive damages, quite similar to those against allowing insurance for the consequences of intentional acts, need no belaboring here. A hard core of jurisdictions are adamantly opposed to it (even in these states, however, the insurer may have to defend a claim which includes punitive damages, Ohio Cas. Ins. Co. v. Hubbard, 162 Cal.App.3d 939, 208 Cal.Rptr. 806 (1984)). More and more jurisdictions are finding no objection to the practice, it being considered a matter of contract—if an insurer is willing to accept the consequences of such risky underwriting. Other states are tolerant of insurance for punitive damages imposed for vicarious acts, where the moral argument is of less weight. The cases have mainly arisen in the context of policies (usually C.G.L. policies) that simply did not refer to punitive damages at all. No one argues that coverage of punitive damage cannot be expressly excluded.

A concise article on the subject by Schumaier and McKinsey, 72 A.B.A.Journ. 69 (March 1986) provides a table of the various jurisdictional holdings. It has been updated with information from the treatise by Richard L. Blatt, Robert W. Hammesfahr and Lori S. Nugent, Punitive Damages, §§ 8.2–8.3 (West 1991).

| Insurable | Vicarious Only | Not Insurable |
|---|---|---|
| Alabama | California | Colorado |
| Alaska+ | Connecticut | Maine*** |
| Arizona | Florida | Missouri*** |
| Arkansas | Illinois | North Dakota*** |
| Delaware* | Indiana | Ohio |
| District of Columbia* | Kansas | Pennsylvania*** |
| Georgia | Minnesota | Rhode Island*** |
| Idaho | New Jersey | Virginia** |
| Iowa | New York | |
| Kentucky* | Oklahoma* | |
| Louisiana* | | |
| Maryland | | |
| Mississippi | | |
| Montana | | |
| New Mexico | | |
| North Carolina* | | |
| Oregon | | |
| South Carolina | | |
| Tennessee* | | |
| Vermont | | |
| West Virginia | | |
| Wisconsin | | |

| Insurable | Vicarious Only | Not Insurable |
|---|---|---|
| Wyoming | | |

| Not Recognized | Undetermined |
|---|---|
| Michigan | Hawaii |
| Nebraska | Massachusetts |
| New Hampshire | Nevada |
| Puerto Rico | South Dakota |
| Washington | Texas |
| | Utah |

* Based on negligence; undetermined in other contexts

** Based on property damage, insurable when based on bodily injury

*** Undetermined on vicarious

\+ Based on negligence; undetermined in other contexts

Insurable or otherwise, the United States Supreme Court has affirmed the constitutionality of punitive damage awards. See TXO Productions Corp. v. Alliance Resources Corp., ___ U.S. ___, 113 S.Ct. 2711, 125 L.Ed.2d 366 (1993); and Pacific Mutual Life Insurance Company v. Haslip, 499 U.S. 1, 111 S.Ct. 1032, 113 L.Ed.2d 1 (1991). Check your local listings!

*Uninsured Motorist: Coverage of Punitive Damages*

The uninsured motorist (first party) coverage in auto insurance has customarily provided merely that the company would pay "all sums which the insured * * * shall be legally entitled to recover as damages from the owner or operator of an uninsured vehicle." Does this include punitive damages? Are the legal and moral issues as to punitive damages in 3rd party cases the same? What if the "uninsured motorist" is of the hit and run variety who cannot be found? See Hutchinson v. J.C. Penney Cas. Ins. Co., 17 Ohio St.3d 195, 478 N.E.2d 1000 (1985) or Mullins v. Miller, 683 S.W.2d 669 (Tenn.1984). Both cases sustain the recovery of punitive damages under the U/M coverage, but both attracted strong dissents.

## OLSEN v. MOORE

Supreme Court of Wisconsin, 1972.
56 Wis.2d 340, 202 N.W.2d 236.

These are multiple actions arising out of a 1965 automobile accident or accidents occurring in Waukesha county. At about 5:30 p.m. on August 4th Thomas J. Moore of Milwaukee was driving east on Interstate Highway I–94 when his automobile left the highway, crossed the median strip, entered the westbound lane and hit two oncoming automobiles. One of the westbound autos was driven by plaintiff Nancy Rauwald, and the other by Bruno Janikowski, also a plaintiff. Moore was alone in his car. * * *

* * *

* * * His car collided with the Rauwald car in the right westbound lane, forcing that car into the ditch on the north side of the highway. The Moore car then glanced into the left westbound lane and collided with the Janikowski car. Both cars stopped almost immediately after this impact.

Defendant Moore was insured by the Badger State Mutual Casualty Company, also named as a defendant. The family combination automobile policy provided for bodily injury liability in the maximum of $10,000 per injured person, and $20,000 per occurrence.

The five cases started by the several plaintiffs were consolidated for trial which commenced on June 2, 1970. At the close of the trial, issues of negligence and scope of employment were submitted to the jury. The jury found Moore not to be acting within the scope of his employment at the time of the accident and totally causally negligent.

* * *

WILKIE, JUSTICE.

* * *

Was the impact between the Moore automobile and the Rauwald automobile a separate "occurrence" from the impact between the Moore and Janikowski autos within the terms of the policy of insurance?

* * *

*One v. two "occurrences."* The contract of insurance issued by Badger State Mutual Casualty Company provided the following limits of liability in its declarations:

| "Premiums | Limits of Liability | Coverages |
|---|---|---|
| $22.50 | $10,000.00 each person | Bodily injury liability |
| | $20,000.00 each occurrence | Bodily injury liability |
| $12.50 | $10,000.00 each occurrence | Property damage liability" |

Although the word "occurrence" is not defined in the policy, the limits of the company's liability are elaborated upon:

> "Limits of Liability. The limit of bodily injury liability stated in the declarations as applicable to 'each person' is the limit of the company's liability for all damages, including damages for care and loss of services, arising out of bodily injury sustained by one person as the result of any one occurrence; the limit of such liability stated in the declarations as applicable to 'each occurrence' is, subject to the above provision respecting each person, the total limit of the company's liability for all such damages arising out of bodily injury sustained by two or more persons as the result of any one occurrence."

Appellants' essential position is that Thomas Moore's negligent driving resulted in two accidents or "occurrences" rather than one. Appellants submit one occurrence or collision occurred when the Moore auto hit the Rauwald auto and another separate and distinct occurrence resulted when the Moore automobile collided with the Janikowski auto. This would result in raising Badger State Mutual's maximum exposure to $40,000.

The question of whether a collision of one automobile with two or more other automobiles constitutes one or several accidents or occurrences has not before been decided by this court.[5] The problem has been dealt with in several other jurisdictions. There is a split in authority on this question which the commentators say is due to a split in the theoretical approach of viewing the problem.[6] "An influential majority" of jurisdictions have utilized what has come to be known as the "cause theory" approach in analyzing whether one or more accidents or occurrences have occurred.[7] This approach was initially adopted in this country in Hyer v. Inter–Insurance Exchange,[8] and is best summarized in Truck Insurance Exchange v. Rohde,[9] involving an auto driving on the wrong side of a highway and successively hitting, with individual "thuds," three motorcyclists. In Truck Insurance Exchange v. Rohde the Washington Supreme Court held only one accident or occurrence had occurred and stated:

> "* * * Proximate cause is an integral part of any interpretation of the words 'accident' or 'occurrence,' as used in a contract for liability insurance which indemnifies the insured for his tortious acts. * * *
>
> "* * * There was but one proximate, uninterrupted, and continuing cause which resulted in all of the injuries and damage. We are of the opinion that the contract contemplated that the terms, 'accident' and 'occurrence,' included all injuries or damage within the scope of the single proximate cause. * * *"

A like result also occurred in Saint Paul–Mercury Indemnity Co. v. Rutland,[10] wherein a truck collided with a train causing its derailment and damage to 16 railroad cars belonging to 14 different owners, their contents and the railroad company roadbed. The Fifth Circuit Court of Appeals had initially sustained the insured's contention that there were as many accidents as insureds.[11] After motion for reargument was granted a new panel of judges reversed the original decision and stated:

5. This court has, however, defined the concept of a cause of action: "*The operative facts, not the consequences, are determinative of a cause of action.* * * * Applying these concepts, a cause of action must be viewed as a grouping of facts falling into a single unit or occurrence as a lay person would view them. This grouping of facts consists of 'the defendant's wrongful act.'" (Emphasis supplied.) The court went on to hold joinder of causes of action was not proper where the two accidents contributing to plaintiff's injuries occurred over five months apart. See Caygill v. Ipsen (1965), 27 Wis.2d 578, 582, 135 N.W.2d 284. See also: Fitzwilliams v. O'Shaughnessy (1968), 40 Wis.2d 123, 161 N.W.2d 242.

6. Annot. (1957). 55 A.L.R.2d 1300; 15 Couch, Insurance 2d, p. 696, sec. 56:20.

7. 1 Long, Law of Liability Insurance, sec. 2.11 at 2–20.

8. (1926), 77 Cal.App. 343, 246 P. 1055.

9. (1956), 49 Wash.2d 465, 303 P.2d 659, 55 A.L.R.2d 1288.

10. (5th Cir.1955), 225 F.2d 689.

11. The original case was recalled and, hence, can only be found in the Federal Reporter advance sheets, 217 F.2d 585; cf.

"The only limit expressed in the policy for automobile property damage liability is the disputed phrase '$5,000.00 each accident.' It can hardly be denied that when ordinary people speak of an 'accident' in the usual sense, they are referring to a single, sudden, unintentional occurrence. They normally use the word 'accident' to describe the *event,* no matter how many persons or things are involved.

"* * *

"* * * we think it clear that the word 'accident' as used in the disputed phrase was intended to be construed from the point of view of the cause rather than the effect." [12]

A small number of jurisdictions subscribe to the "effect theory" of liability. The origin of this view of the words occurrence or accident is found in an early English case, South Staffordshire Tramways Co. v. Sickness & Accident Assurance Asso. Ltd.,[13] wherein it was contended that each injury caused to a passenger on a tramcar which overturned constituted one accident: In this case the court stated:

"* * * If several persons were injured, I think, upon the true construction of this policy, there were several accidents."

This holding was first adopted in this country in a decision of the Federal Court of Appeals for the Fifth Circuit, Anchor Casualty Co. v. McCaleb,[14] and subsequently in several other jurisdictions.[15] None of these cases involves automobile accidents. *Anchor Casualty* involved a blown oil well which caused eruptions intermittently over two days. Each eruption caused quantities of oil, gas distillate, sand and mud to be deposited on the property of surrounding land owners. The court of appeals held that the term "each accident" was to be viewed from the point of view of the person whose property was injured. The court in *Anchor* extensively relied upon the definition of "accident" found in Bouvier's Law Dictionary, which defines an accident as an event which " 'is unusual and unexpected by the person to whom it happens.' " [16]

At least one author regards this theory as falsely premised. It is suggested in Long's treatise on liability insurance that courts must look at the policy's provision relating to the upper limits of liability "* * * the total limit of the company's liability for all such damages arising out of bodily injury sustained by two or more persons as the result of any one occurrence." * * * According to Long, it is "unparalleled non-

1 Long, Law of Liability Insurance, supra, footnote 4, at 2–25.

**12.** Saint Paul–Mercury Indemnity Co. v. Rutland, supra, footnote 8, at pages 691, 692. See also: Tri-State Roofing Co. v. New Amsterdam Casualty Co. (D.C.Pa. 1955), 139 F.Supp. 193: Denham v. La-Salle–Madison Hotel Co. (7th Cir.1948), 168 F.2d 576.

**13.** 1 Law Reports 402 (Q.B.1891).

**14.** (5th Cir.1949), 178 F.2d 322.

**15.** Pennsylvania Home Improvement Co. v. American Casualty Co. (1955), 4 Pa.D. & C.2d 516, 47 Berks County L.J. 285; Kuhn's of Brownsville v. Bituminous Casualty Co. (1954), 197 Tenn. (1 McCanless) 60, 270 S.W.2d 358.

**16.** Anchor Casualty Co. v. McCaleb, supra, footnote 13, 178 F.2d at page 324.

sense" to assert that two or more persons might ever be injured in one accident if each injury equals one accident.[17]

The issue thus before this court is whether an "accident" or "occurrence" in a liability insurance policy providing stated limits of liability "per accident" or "per occurrence," should be viewed from the perspective of *cause* or *effect.* If viewed from the point of view of a cause, it would appear that a single, uninterrupted cause which results in a number of injuries or separate instances of property damage is yet one "accident" or "occurrence." If, however, that cause is interrupted or replaced by another cause the chain of causation is broken and more than one accident or occurrence has taken place. Liberty Mutual Ins. Co. v. Rawls,[18] a case cited by appellants for their proposition that two rather than one accident occurred herein, fits into the cause theory of liability. The Fifth Circuit Court of Appeals in *Rawls* did find that two accidents had occurred when the insured's vehicle struck two successive automobiles. The reason two accidents occurred was due to the fact that the insured had not lost control of his vehicle after he hit the first auto. He had been traveling at a high rate of speed and was being pursued by two deputy sheriffs. After striking the first auto, the insured continued for approximately 30 to 300 feet and two to five seconds. While the insured's auto veered across the median strip and struck the second vehicle head on, the court found no evidence that the insured had ever lost control. The court noted, in concluding, that such a result could have been reached under either the cause theory or the effect theory.

The facts here are distinctly different from those in *Rawls.* Here Thomas Moore's vehicle struck both vehicles almost instantaneously. Witness Robert Perlick testified that he was in a car approximately six car lengths behind the Rauwald and Janikowski automobiles. He testified to the effect that the Moore auto crossed over the median strip, over the left lane and struck the first auto in the right lane; that the Rauwald auto was thrown into the ditch and the Moore car was deflected into the high-speed lane where it collided with the second (Janikowski) auto. On cross-examination Perlick testified that the collisions occurred almost instantaneously. According to Perlick, the whole incident occurred in less than a second. There was also testimony by defendant Thomas Moore that he remembered nothing of the accident:

> "I remember making a turn off onto Highway I–94, I remember passing a car, I remember rolling up the window so the wind wouldn't blow in, and I proceeded down the highway and that's the last I remember."

There was virtually no time or space interval between the two impacts. Moore never regained his control over the automobile prior to striking the second car as did the driver in *Rawls.* Viewed from the standpoint of the "cause theory" the situation here clearly would result in but one accident or occurrence.

**17.** 1 Long, Law of Liability Insurance, supra, footnote 7, at pages 2–31.

**18.** (5th Cir.1968), 404 F.2d 880.

The term "accident" has been defined in a workmen's compensation case as "a fortuitous event, unexpected and unforeseen by the injured person," [19] and, therefore, the term "accident" in these industrial cases is viewed from the perspective of the injured person. The distinction, of course, is that workmen's compensation is an insurance for the benefit of the insured—the injured person. Here, however, the liability insurance policy was not purchased to insure the injured plaintiffs but to give liability protection to the defendant—Thomas Moore. Among other reasons, this leads us to reject the "effect theory" in defining the term "occurrence."

Appellants further contend that the policy language is ambiguous and should, therefore, be construed against the insurer. But such rule of construction is not applicable unless there is ambiguity.[20] There is none here.

Furthermore, it has often been noted that no essential difference exists between the words "accident" and "occurrence." [21] The close parallel between these words is noted in Truck Insurance Exchange v. Rohde,[22] wherein it was held:

> " * * * However, in our opinion and for the purposes of this case, the terms, 'accident' and 'occurrence,' are synonymous." [23]

* * *

Affirmed.

## *Notes and Problems*

1. Rust Control, Inc. a spray painting contractor carried a liability policy with $250 deductible for each occurrence. It was hired to paint a couple of water towers on the premise of M–B, Inc., and in doing so also managed to spray the cars of about 40 employees of M–B. M–B thoughtfully paid for the damages which totalled $4000 (only one car was damaged beyond $250 and that for $350) and took an assignment from each car owner. It presented a bill for $4000 to the insurer. How much should it collect? [Held: $100 in Atlas Underwriters, Inc. v. Meredith–Burda, Inc., 231 Va. 255, 343 S.E.2d 65 (1986).]

**19.** Semons Department Store v. I.L.H.R. Dept. (1971), 50 Wis.2d 518, 523, 184 N.W.2d 871.

**20.** Leatherman v. American Family Mut. Ins. Co. (1971), 52 Wis.2d 644, 649, 650, 190 N.W.2d 904. See also: Westerman v. Richardson (1969), 43 Wis.2d 587, 591, 168 N.W.2d 851.

**21.** Annot. (1957), 55 A.L.R.2d 1300, 1301.

**22.** Supra, footnote 8.

**23.** Id. at page 469, 303 P.2d at page 661. See also: Aerial Agricultural Service of Montana, Inc. v. Till (D.C.Miss.1962), 207 F.Supp. 50, 57, 58. " * * * To begin with, the word 'occurrence', to the lay mind, as well as to the judicial mind, has a meaning much broader than the word 'accident'. As these words are generally understood, accident means something that must have come about or happened in a certain way, while occurrence means something that happened or came about in any way. Thus *accident* is a special type of *occurrence,* but occurrence goes beyond such special confines and, while including accident, it encompasses many other situations as well."

2. Insured under Homeowner policy went on a shooting spree, firing 3 shots in 2 minutes at two deputy sheriffs. How many occurrences? See American Indemnity Co. v. McQuaig, 435 So.2d 414 (Fla.App.1983).
3. S is a mini storage rental facility where storage spaces are housed in rows of buildings with individual doors. S hired the insured to clear a heavy snowfall from the premises with a tractor. Insured managed to damage 98 doors with the tractor over a 4 hour period. How many occurrences? Unigard Ins. Co. v. United States Fidelity and Guar. Co., 111 Idaho 891, 728 P.2d 780 (App.1986).
4. In USAA v. Baggett, 209 Cal.App.3d 1387, 258 Cal.Rptr. 52 (1989), the California Court of Appeal held that two consecutive collisions were one accident within the meaning of the policy.

## APPALACHIAN INSURANCE COMPANY v. LIBERTY MUTUAL INSURANCE COMPANY

United States Court of Appeals, Third Circuit, 1982.
676 F.2d 56.

CAHN, DISTRICT JUDGE.

* * *

This action involves the question of whether a liability insurer must provide coverage for losses its insured incurred in the settlement of class action litigation involving sex discrimination in employment where the insured's discriminatory conduct originated before the effective date of coverage but had an impact on class members both before and after that date. The material facts underlying this action are not in dispute.

I.

A.

In 1965, Liberty adopted certain employment policies applicable to female employees in its claims department. Several female employees in Liberty's claims department filed charges in May 1971 before the Equal Employment Opportunity Commission alleging that these employment policies discriminated against women. After satisfying certain administrative prerequisites, these claimants, on February 28, 1972, filed a complaint containing class action allegations in the United States District Court for the Western District of Pennsylvania. The plaintiffs alleged that Liberty committed sex discrimination in its claims department in hiring, promoting and compensating females. In due course the district court certified the class and found that Liberty's employment policy discriminated against female employees on the basis of sex.

After considerable additional activity in the district court, the court of appeals and the Supreme Court, the class action litigation was settled for an amount in excess of $5,500,000. In the September 20, 1978, Stipulation of Compromise and Settlement, the class was redefined to

> [I]nclude each of Defendant's [Liberty's] female technical employees who was employed in the Defendant's Claims Department anywhere in the United States as a Claims Representative, Claims Representative Supervisor or Supervising Claims Representative at any time between October 19, 1970, and January 8, 1974.

The terms of the settlement included a complicated scheme for distributing the proceeds of the settlement among the class members. For purposes of this proceeding all that need be noted is that the settlement compensated employees employed before August 1, 1971, for injuries allegedly sustained both before and after that date and compensated some employees who were hired after August 1, 1971.

B.

From August 1, 1971, through August 1, 1974, Liberty was insured by Appalachian under an umbrella liability policy. The Appalachian policy was part of an umbrella insurance package which in participation with the underwriters at Lloyds of London covered Liberty for ultimate net loss up to $15,000,000 in excess of a $25,000 retention for each occurrence.

After Liberty settled the class action case in September of 1978, it claimed indemnification under the Appalachian policy. Appalachian filed the within suit on October 10, 1978, seeking a declaratory judgment that it was not liable to Liberty under that policy. Appalachian did not contend that its policy excluded claims based on sex discrimination. Instead it alleged that the occurrence of the loss and the impact from that occurrence took place prior to the effective date of its policy. The parties filed cross-motions for summary judgment. The district court denied Liberty's motion for summary judgment and granted Appalachian's motion.[7] Liberty appeals from the grant of summary judgment contending that the district court erred in its resolution of the legal issue.

II.

In granting summary judgment for Appalachian the district court relied on its characterization—one undisputed by the parties—of the Appalachian policy as an "occurrence" policy as distinguished from a "claims made" policy.[8] Under an "occurrence" policy the insured is

7. The district court's opinion is reported at 507 F.Supp. 59 (W.D.Pa.1981).

8. Because it was part of a package, the Appalachian policy adopted the terms and provisions of a certain underlying policy written by the underwriters at Lloyds of London. Under the policy Appalachian agreed to indemnify Liberty (subject to certain limitations) for

> [A]ll sums which the Assured [Liberty] shall be obligated to pay by reason of the liability
>
> (a) imposed upon the Assured by law.
>
> * * *
>
> for damages on account of:—
>
> (i) Personal Injuries
>
> * * *
>
> caused by or arising out of each occurrence happening anywhere in the world.

The policy defined occurrence as

> [A]n accident or a happening or event or a continuous or repeated exposure to conditions which unexpectedly and unintentionally results in personal injury, proper-

indemnified for acts or occurrences which take place within the policy period while under a "claims made" policy the insured is indemnified for claims made during the policy period regardless of when the acts giving rise to those claims occurred.

Based on the characterization of the Appalachian policy as an occurrence policy the district court had to determine whether there was a single occurrence or multiple occurrences for which Liberty sought indemnification and when the occurrence or occurrences took place. The district court held that Liberty's claim for indemnification was based on a single occurrence. It ruled that whether losses are caused by a single occurrence or multiple occurrences is determined by reference to the cause of the loss. It found that a single occurrence took place in 1965 when Liberty adopted the employment policies which resulted in the imposition of liability for sex discrimination. The district court also looked to the date the cause of the loss took place to determine when the occurrence happened. "[I]t is the cause of the loss, and not the resulting injury that determines the incidents of liability under such policy." 507 F.Supp. at 62. Since the single occurrence took place before the effective date of the Appalachian policy the district court concluded that Appalachian was not liable to Liberty.

In so holding the district court rejected Liberty's contention that it was at least entitled to indemnification for damages paid to class members based on periods of employment after the Appalachian policy was in force. The district court said this contention could be sustained only if there were multiple occurrences. The district court observed that if there were multiple occurrences the $25,000 retention per occurrence would insulate the Appalachian policy from responding because no single class member received a distribution in excess of $25,000.[9] The district court relying on a single definition of "occurrence" in the policy, see note 8 supra, was unwilling to find, as Liberty urged it to do, multiple occurrences for the purpose of coverage but only a single occurrence for the purpose of applying the deductible retention.

III.

On this appeal Liberty maintains that the district court erred in determining when the occurrence took place. Liberty acknowledges that the determination of whether an occurrence is single or multiple properly depends on whether there is a single cause or multiple causes for the losses sustained. Liberty argues, however, that for the purpose of determining coverage under an "occurrence" policy an occurrence takes place not when the wrongful act is committed, but when the complaining party is actually damaged. Since the damages paid to female employees were in a number of instances based on periods of employment during

ty damage or advertising liability during the policy period. All such exposure to substantially the same general conditions existing at or emanating from one premises location shall be deemed one occurrence.

9. Implicit in this conclusion is the district court's view that multiple occurrences mean that each employee's injury constitutes a separate occurrence.

which the Appalachian policy was in effect, Liberty urges that the occurrence did not precede the effective date of the policy and it is entitled to indemnification at the very least for damages calculated during the policy period.

Appalachian contends that the district court correctly resolved the legal issue because both the cause of the injuries and the injuries themselves began in 1965. It argues that the accrual of damages into the period covered by the Appalachian policy is insufficient to require that policy to respond.

IV.

After considering the contentions of Liberty and Appalachian, we conclude that the judgment of the district court should be affirmed. Nevertheless, since our analysis of the issue presented by this appeal differs somewhat from that of the district court further explication is necessary.

As the court below observed the Appalachian policy is of the "occurrence" variety because coverage is provided only when there is an occurrence within the policy period. The policy states that the insurer will indemnify Liberty for "all sums" which it "shall be obligated to pay by reason of the liability imposed upon [Liberty] by law * * * for damages on account of:—(i) Personal Injuries * * * caused by or arising out of each occurrence * * *." Although this language is sufficient for us to classify the policy as an "occurrence" policy our conclusion is reinforced by the fact that under the policy the deductible of $25,000 is applied on a per occurrence basis. See Transport Ins. Co. v. Lee Way Motor Freight, Inc., 487 F.Supp. 1325, 1329 (N.D.Tex.1980).

In order to ascertain whether there was an occurrence within the policy period we must identify the occurrence and then determine when it took place.

The general rule is that an occurrence is determined by the cause or causes of the resulting injury. "[T]he majority of jurisdictions employes the 'cause theory'. [Citations omitted.] Using this analysis, the court asks if '[t]here was but one proximate, uninterrupted, and continuing cause which resulted in all of the injuries and damage.'" Bartholomew v. Insurance Co. of N. America, 502 F.Supp. 246, 251 (D.R.I.1980), aff'd. sub nom. Bartholomew v. Appalachian Ins. Co., 655 F.2d 27 (1st Cir. 1981), citing Olsen v. Moore, 56 Wis.2d 340, 202 N.W.2d 236 (1972); Transport Ins. Co. v. Lee Way Motor Freight, Inc., 487 F.Supp. 1325, 1330 (N.D.Tex.1980); contra, Elston–Richards Storage Co. v. Indemnity Ins. Co. of N. America, 194 F.Supp. 673, 682 (W.D.Mich.1960), aff'd., 291 F.2d 627 (6th Cir.1961).

Applying the general rule to the facts of this case we agree with the district court's finding that there was but one occurrence for purposes of policy coverage.[11] The injuries for which Liberty was liable all resulted

11. Because there was one occurrence the deductible retention of $25,000 would

from a common source: Liberty's discriminatory employment policies. Therefore, the single occurrence, for purposes of policy coverage, should be defined as Liberty's adoption of its discriminatory employment policies in 1965.

The fact that there were multiple injuries and that they were of different magnitudes and that injuries extended over a period of time does not alter our conclusion that there was a single occurrence. As long as the injuries stem from one proximate cause there is a single occurrence. Champion Int'l. Corp. v. Continental Casualty Co., 546 F.2d 502, 505–506 (2d Cir.1976), cert. denied, 434 U.S. 819, 98 S.Ct. 59, 54 L.Ed.2d 75 (1977). Indeed, the definition of the term "occurrence" in the Appalachian policy contemplates that one occurrence may have multiple and disparate impacts on individuals and that injuries may extend over a period of time.

We now reach the crucial issue of determining when the single occurrence took place because only if it took place within the policy period is Appalachian required to indemnify Liberty.

The district court concluded that the occurrence took place in 1965 when Liberty adopted its discriminatory employment policies. It placed the occurrence at that point by applying the same "cause" test it used in determining whether there was a single occurrence or multiple occurrences. Since the employment policies caused the resulting injuries to Liberty's employees the district court reasoned that the occurrence took place when the employment policies were adopted.

While the "cause" test is appropriate for determining whether there is a single occurrence or multiple occurrences, it is not applicable in determining when an occurrence takes place. We hold that the determination of when an occurrence happens must be made by reference to the time when the injurious effects of the occurrence took place. "There can be no question but that the aspect of the occurrence which must take place within the policy period * * * is the 'result,' that is, the time when the accident or injurious exposure produces personal injury." Eagle–Picher Indus., Inc. v. Liberty Mutual Ins. Co., 523 F.Supp. 110, 114 (D.Mass.1981); Deodato v. Hartford Ins. Co., 143 N.J.Super. 396, 363 A.2d 361, 365 (Law Div.1976); Peerless Inc. Co. v. Clough, 105 N.H. 76, 193 A.2d 444, 446 (1963).

Our adoption of the "effect" test for determining when the occurrence took place is dictated by the reasonable expectations of the insured in purchasing a policy of this type. Liberty could reasonably expect that it would be indemnified for damages paid on account of liability incurred during the policy period. Since injury is a prerequisite to liability, Liberty reasonably expected to be indemnified for injuries occurring during the policy period. The expectation is evidence in the language of

be applicable only once and not to the separate claims of each class member, none of which exceeded $25,000.

the policy which specifically defines occurrence as something that results in injuries during the policy period.

Application of the "effect" test to the instant case is not easy.[14] The "effect" test requires us to determine whether the injurious effects of Liberty's 1965 employment policies—the occurrence as previously defined—took place during the policy period. The problem here is that the injurious effects of Liberty's 1965 employment policies began immediately upon their adoption and continued at least to some extent into the period of coverage provided by the Appalachian policy.

We hold that in this type of a case the occurrence takes place when the injuries first manifest themselves. Bartholomew v. Insurance Co. of N. America, 502 F.Supp. 246, 254 (D.R.I.1980), aff'd. sub nom. Bartholomew v. Appalachian Ins. Co., 655 F.2d 27 (1st Cir.1981). In *Bartholomew* injuries to the plaintiff continued throughout a number of different policy periods but the court held that only the policy in effect when the injuries first manifested themselves had to respond.[16] Since the injuries to Liberty's employees occurred immediately upon the promulgation of Liberty's discriminatory employment policies the occurrence took place for purposes of coverage before August 1, 1971.[17] Appalachian need not indemnify Liberty because the occurrence preceded the effective date of the insurance policy.

A contrary result in this case would contravene the rule that an insured cannot insure against something which has already begun. Bartholomew v. Appalachian Ins. Co., 655 F.2d 27, 29 (1st Cir.1981); see Summers v. Harris, 573 F.2d 869, 872 (5th Cir.1978). The rule is based on the realization that the purpose of insurance is to protect insureds against unknown risks. When the Appalachian policy became effective, however, the risk of liability was no longer unknown because injuries resulted immediately upon Liberty's promulgation of its discriminatory policies. Also, the complaint to the EEOC preceded the effective date of the Appalachian policy.

**14.** This is not a case where an insured commits a tortious act and then after a lapse of time a claimant is injured by that act. See Travelers Ins. Co. v. C.J. Gayfer's & Co., 366 So.2d 1199 (Fla.App.1979) (no coverage under contractor's policy where contractor installed roof during policy period but roof leaked after expiration of policy). Here, Liberty's policy of sex discrimination had an immediate impact on its female employees in the claims department. Nor is this case akin to the litigation involving coverage of defendants involved in the asbestos litigation. In those cases it is not at all clear when the alleged tortious acts of the defendants first impacted on the health of a victim of asbestosis.

* * *

**16.** Our decision to follow the reasoning of the *Bartholomew* case is reinforced by other cases holding that when an injury manifests itself during a policy period the insurer remains liable after the expiration of the policy for the entire loss. E.g., Harmon v. American Casualty Co., 155 F.Supp. 612, 613–14 (S.D.Cal.1957).

**17.** The fact that under the Stipulation of Compromise and Settlement some class members who received damage awards did not begin their employment with Liberty until after August 1, 1971, is immaterial. Once we established there was but one occurrence it either took place before or after the effective date of the policy. To recover for damages accrued after August 1, 1971, Liberty would have to establish there were multiple occurrences which it did not attempt to do nor could it do under our analysis.

For the foregoing reasons the judgment of the district court will be affirmed.

### *Problems*

1. A large company with many employees carried liability insurance, including liability for discriminatory hiring practices, for damages "caused by or arising out of each occurrence happening anywhere in the world." The policy provides for a deductible amount of $25,000 per occurrence. In a federal civil action by the United States, the employer was found guilty of racially discriminatory practices in 47 cases and ordered to back-pay awards of between $3000 to $138,000 to the individuals involved (totalling $1,800,-000). Does the employer bear one $25,000 deductible or forty-seven? See Transport Insurance Co. v. Lee Way Motor Freight, 487 F.Supp. 1325 (N.D.Tex.1980).

2. The word "occurrence" also appears in some property insurance cases. An orthodontist took out an Inland Marine "Physicians' and Surgeons' Equipment Floater" policy which among other things, covered loss of currency, money and stamps on the premises "not exceeding $250 in any one occurrence." An employee embezzled $9000 but with no individual defalcation in excess of $250. Is the insurer liable for $9000 or $250? Slater v. United States Fidelity and Guaranty Co., 379 Mass. 801, 400 N.E.2d 1256 (1980).

3. Separate civil rights suits have been construed as one occurrence, though a separate police harassment suit was a distinct occurrence so that there were two occurrences for policy purposes. Mead Reinsurance v. Granite State Ins. Co., 865 F.2d 992 (9th Cir.1989).

## NOTE, ADJUDICATING ASBESTOS INSURANCE LIABILITY: ALTERNATIVES TO CONTRACT ANALYSIS *

97 Harvard Law Review 739, 739–43 (1984)

Recent surveys of the medical literature indicate that approximately 265,000 people will die from asbestos-related diseases between 1980 and 2015.[1] The potential tort liability is enormous.[2] The compensation of asbestos victims, however, may well turn on whether asbestos manufacturers or their insurers must ultimately bear the costs of providing such compensation. Asbestos manufacturers and their insurers have been



**1.** P. MacAvoy, J. Karr & P. Wilson, The Economic Consequences of Asbestos Related Disease 4–12 (July 1983) (unpublished working draft on file in Harvard Law School Library) [hereinafter cited as P. MacAvoy]; cf. Mansfield, *Asbestos, The Cases and the Insurance Problem,* 15 Forum 860, 865–66 (1980) (reporting projection of 20,-000 deaths per year for the years 1980–2000); Comment, *An Examination of Recurring Issues in Asbestos Litigation,* 46 Alb.L.Rev. 1307, 1308 n. 4 (1982) (projected deaths near three million); Note, *Asbestos Litigation: The Insurance Coverage Question,* 15 Ind.L.Rev. 831, 831 (1982) (200,000 deaths by the end of the century).

**2.** See P. MacAvoy, supra note 1, at 4–45 (total liability projections range from $7.6 billion to $87.1 billion).

engaged in extensive litigation[3] over whether the relevant products liability insurance policy, the Comprehensive General Liability (CGL) policy, provides indemnification for the tort claims of the victims of asbestos-related diseases.[4]

Four United States courts of appeals and several federal district courts have considered the problem of asbestos insurer liability.[5] Although all courts have held for the insureds (that is, the manufacturers),[6] they have adopted conflicting interpretations of how the CGL policy allocates liability between successive insurers and between the insurers and the insured manufacturers.[7]

Part I of this Note demonstrates why the contract and insurance law principles that have been applied to the asbestos insurance controversy will invariably produce such inconsistent results. Part II addresses the problems inherent in any attempt to maintain the impression of "contractual" adjudication through the supposed reconstruction of a "rational" bargain on behalf of the parties. Finally, Part III explores alternative criteria for evaluating solutions to the asbestos insurance issue—allocational efficiency, libertarian individualism, and communitarian pluralism—and suggests that only pluralism can provide a coherent rationale for a court's allocation of liability between asbestos manufacturers and their insurers.

## I. The Inescapable Ambiguity of the CGL Policy

### A. *Theories of Insurer Liability*

Under the CGL policy, an insurer is liable to the insured when "bodily injury," defined to include "sickness" or "disease," occurs during the policy period.[8] The heart of any contractual analysis of the

3. See, e.g., Rosow & Liederman, *An Overview to the Interpretive Problems of "Occurrence" in Comprehensive General Liability Insurance,* 16 Forum 1148, 1153–54 (1981) (listing 17 pending suits).

4. *See* Comment, *Liability Insurance for Insidious Disease: Who Picks Up the Tab?,* 48 Fordham L.Rev. 657, 666–67 (1980). The policies were revised and standardized in 1966, *see id.* at 667 n. 50, but no variations in the language of the original policies have been relevant to determining when bodily injury "occurs." See id. There are rare cases, however, involving nonstandard policies. See, e.g., Commercial Union Co. v. Pittsburgh Corning Corp., 553 F.Supp. 425 (E.D.Pa.1981).

5. See Eagle–Picher Indus. v. Liberty Mut. Ins. Co., 682 F.2d 12 (1st Cir.1982), cert. denied, 103 S.Ct. 1280 (1983); Keene Corp. v. Insurance Co. of N. Am., 667 F.2d 1034 (D.C.Cir.1981), cert. denied, 455 U.S. 1007 (1982); Porter v. American Optical, 641 F.2d 1128 (5th Cir. Apr. 1981), cert. denied, 454 U.S. 1109 (1981); Insurance Co. of N. Am. v. Forty–Eight Insulations, 633 F.2d 1212 (6th Cir.1980), clarified, 657 F.2d 814 (6th Cir.), cert. denied, 454 U.S. 1109 (1981). Asbestos cases are deemed to provide critical precedents for the interpretation of CGL policies in general. See, e.g., American Home Prods. v. Liberty Mut. Ins. Co., 565 F.Supp. 1485 (S.D.N.Y.1983) (CGL policy applied to drug manufacturers' products liability); see also Sandoz, Inc. v. Employer's Liability Assurance Corp., 554 F.Supp. 257, 263 (D.N.J.1983) (same). Two state courts have also adjudicated the asbestos insurance issue. See Zurich Ins. Co. v. Raymark Indus., No. 78–L–8760 (Cook County, Ill., Cir.Ct. Sept. 23, 1983); Crown Cork & Seal Co. v. Aetna Casualty & Sur. Co., No. 1292 (Philadelphia County, Pa., Ct.C.P. Aug. 2, 1983).

6. See American Home Prods., 565 F.Supp. at 1510.

7. See infra pp. 741–43.

8. The policy language reads:

> [The insurer] will pay on behalf of the insured all sums which the insured shall be legally obligated to pay as damages

CGL policy is therefore a determination of when bodily injury "occurs."[9] A manufacturer may have had several successive insurers during the period between the tort victim's exposure to asbestos and the manifestation of symptoms of asbestos-related disease. The manufacturer may also have been uninsured for long periods. Thus, a determination of when bodily injury "occurs" may establish who is responsible, in whole or in part, for providing compensation to the tort victim. But the beginnings of asbestos-induced disease are often hard to pinpoint,[10] and harm becomes inevitable long before it is readily detectable.[11] It is therefore not surprising that courts have adopted conflicting views about when "bodily injury" occurs and have come to different conclusions regarding when insurance coverage begins.[12]

> because of * * * bodily injury or * * * property damage to which this policy applies caused by an occurrence.
>
> "Bodily injury" means bodily injury, sickness or disease sustained by any person which occurs during the policy period, including death at any time resulting therefrom.
>
> "Occurrence" means an accident, including injurious exposure to conditions which results, during the policy period, in bodily injury. * * *

Comprehensive General Liability Policy (1966), cited in Insurance Co. of N. Am. v. Forty–Eight Insulations, 633 F.2d 1212, 1216 (6th Cir.1980), clarified, 657 F.2d 814 (6th Cir.), cert. denied, 454 U.S. 1109 (1981).

**9.** See American Home Prods. v. Liberty Mut. Ins. Co., 565 F.Supp. 1485, 1489 (S.D.N.Y.1983). Three different diseases have been linked to asbestos exposure. One is asbestosis, a cumulative fibrotic scarring of the lung tissue that results in pulmonary impairment and sometimes in death, usually after at least 10 years of fibrosis. Unlike related diseases such as silicosis, asbestosis is detectable by radiography only when the fibrotic process is quite advanced, and often only after symptoms (for example, shortness of breath) are already present. See generally I. Selikoff & D. Lee, Asbestos and Disease 144–78, 413–17 (1978) (describing etiology and pathology of asbestosis). A second disease is mesothelioma, a once-rare form of cancer of the linings of the chest cavity or abdominal cavity. The average time between exposure and development of a tumor is approximately 35–40 years. See id. at 263. The third disease is pulmonary carcinoma—malignant lung cancer. There is a long interval between exposure and the appearance of a tumor; deaths peak 25–34 years after exposure. Id. at 319–21. As with mesothelioma, scientists have only a limited understanding of the manner in which exposure to asbestos results in the malignancy. Id. at 423; see also Reply Brief of Appellant at 14a–15a, Keene Corp. v. Insurance Co. of N. Am., 667 F.2d 1034 (D.C.Cir.1981) (Nos. 81–1179, 81–1180, 81–1181 & 81–1182) (excerpting expert testimony discussing the scientific uncertainty in determining when or how the malignancy develops). Despite this uncertainty, courts have found that the same interpretive problems pertain to both asbestosis and the cancers linked to asbestos. See, e.g., Keene, 667 F.2d at 1038 n. 3; see also Insurance Co. of N. Am. v. Forty–Eight Insulations, 657 F.2d 814, 815 (6th Cir.) (the diseases are analytically identical for the purpose of determining when bodily injury "occurs"), cert. denied, 454 U.S. 1109 (1981).

**10.** See generally I. Selikoff & D. Lee, supra note 9, at 157, 295, 309.

**11.** See id. at 174, 263, 319. For judicial summaries of expert testimony, see for example, Keene Corp. v. Insurance Co. of N. Am., 667 F.2d 1034, 1045 (D.C.Cir.1981), cert. denied, 455 U.S. 1007 (1982); id. at 1058 (Wald, J., concurring in part); Porter v. American Optical, 641 F.2d 1128, 1133 (5th Cir. Apr. 1981), cert. denied, 454 U.S. 1109 (1981); Eagle–Picher Indus. v. Liberty Mut. Ins. Co., 523 F.Supp. 110, 115 (D.Mass.1981), modified in part, 682 F.2d 12 (1st Cir.1982), cert. denied, 103 S.Ct. 1280 (1983); Insurance Co. of N. Am. v. Forty–Eight Insulations, 451 F.Supp. 1230, 1237 (E.D.Mich.1978), aff'd, 633 F.2d 1212 (6th Cir.1980), clarified, 657 F.2d 814 (6th Cir.), cert. denied, 454 U.S. 1109 (1981).

**12.** Cf. Note, *The Fairness and Constitutionality of Statutes of Limitations for Toxic Tort Suits,* 96 Harv.L.Rev. 1683 (1983) (discussing similar alternative theories regarding the statutes of limitations).

1. *The Manifestation Theory: Reasonable Date of Diagnosis.* Under one such view, the manifestation theory, coverage is triggered (1) when the worker first learns that he has an asbestos-related disease, (2) when the worker first should know that he has such a disease, or (3) when the disease is first diagnosed in fact, whichever is earliest.[13] Some courts have also equated "manifestation" with the date on which the disease is "reasonably capable of medical diagnosis."[14] The manifestation theory tends to place liability on either (1) the narrow group of insurers who provided coverage at the time when diagnosis of asbestos-related disease became widespread, or (2) the insured, who may have been unable to obtain insurance without prohibitive deductibles once the wide incidence of asbestos-related disease became clear.[15]

2. *The Exposure Theory.* According to the exposure theory, the first inhalation of the asbestos fibers triggers coverage; all insurance companies that provided coverage during the period of exposure must pay the insured a pro-rated share of the insured's tort liability.[16] This view diffuses liability among the insurers who provided coverage during the period of exposure.[17] Unlike the manifestation theory, the exposure theory does not allow insurance companies to escape financial responsibility for the insured's liability,[18] as long as the manufacturer had insurance during the exposure period.[19]

3. *Actual Injury Theory.* The actual injury theory holds that coverage is triggered when the body's defenses are "overwhelmed" and impairment or premature death becomes inevitable; all insurers with policies in force after that date are liable.[20] This view diffuses liability

**13.** See Insurance Co. of N. Am. v. Forty–Eight Insulations, 633 F.2d 1212, 1216 (6th Cir.1980), clarified, 657 F.2d 814 (6th Cir.), cert. denied, 454 U.S. 1109 (1981); Mansfield, supra note 1, at 876.

**14.** Eagle–Picher Indus. v. Liberty Mut. Ins. Co., 682 F.2d 12, 24–25 (1st Cir.1982) (modifying district court's alternative formulation of the manifestation theory), cert. denied, 103 S.Ct. 1280 (1983). This formulation has been characterized as a departure from the orthodox manifestation theory. See American Home Prods. v. Liberty Mut. Ins. Co., 565 F.Supp. 1485, 1494, 1497 (S.D.N.Y.1983) (suggesting that the *Eagle–Picher* view is really an "actual injury" theory). A "capable of being diagnosed" test is equivalent to an actual injury test only if one assumes that the date of actual harm, determined ex ante, is the same as the date on which a doctor could have performed a diagnosis. This will rarely be the case. The actual injury rule, see infra p. 742, is thus distinct from this formulation of the manifestation rule. On the other hand, because the date a disease is reasonably diagnosable may be defined as the date the disease was "discoverable," this Note does not separately discuss the "discovery rule" theory proposed by Judge Merritt in his dissenting opinion in Forty–Eight Insulations, 633 F.2d at 1230–32 (Merritt, J., dissenting).

**15.** See Mansfield, supra note 1, at 876; R. Epstein, The Legal and Insurance Dynamics of Mass Tort Litigation 40 (Oct. 21, 1983) (unpublished paper prepared for the Conference on Policy Options for Catastrophic Personal Injuries, Hoover Institution, Stanford University).

**16.** See, e.g., Porter v. American Optical, 641 F.2d 1128, 1142, 1145 (5th Cir. Apr. 1981), cert. denied, 454 U.S. 1109 (1981); Insurance Co. of N. Am. v. Forty–Eight Insulations, 633 F.2d 1212, 1223 (6th Cir.1980), clarified, 657 F.2d 814 (6th Cir.), cert. denied, 454 U.S. 1109 (1981).

**17.** See Mansfield, supra note 1, at 877.

**18.** See R. Epstein, supra note 15, at 40.

**19.** See Keene Corp. v. Insurance Co. of N. Am., 667 F.2d 1034, 1044 (D.C.Cir.1981), cert. denied, 454 U.S. 1007 (1982).

**20.** See Insurance Co. of N. Am. v. Forty–Eight Insulations, 633 F.2d 1212, 1217 (6th Cir.1980), clarified, 657 F.2d 814 (6th

among all insurers who provided coverage after the date of "actual harm" had passed.[21]

4. *Continuous Injury Theory.* Under a continuous injury theory, all insurance companies who issued policies during the period between the victim's first exposure and the manifestation of his symptoms must provide coverage for his injuries.[22] This theory offers the broadest diffusion of liability: it makes all insurers who ever provided coverage to the insured potentially responsible for providing indemnification.[23]

### *B. The Limits of Traditional Contract Interpretation*

In determining which of the four possible approaches to insurer liability to apply, courts have employed a series of traditional techniques of contract interpretation, including analysis of the "plain meaning" of the policy language,[24] reference to the expressed intent of the drafters,[25] and reliance on trade custom.[26] Some courts have also employed insurance law construction rules, such as the interpretation of ambiguous

Cir.), cert. denied, 454 U.S. 1109 (1981); American Home Prods. v. Liberty Mut. Ins. Co., 565 F.Supp. 1485, 1497 (S.D.N.Y.1983); see also Brief of Amici Curiae Fireman's Fund and Federal Insurance Co. at 52–53, Forty–Eight Insulations, 633 F.2d 1212 (6th Cir.1980) (Nos. 78–1322, 78–1323, 78–1324, 78–1325 & 78–1326) (equating "overwhelming"-of-body's-defenses or "turning point" theories with the point at which harm becomes "irreversible"); Zurich Ins. v. Raymark Indus., No. 78–L–8760, slip op. at 14–15 (Cook County, Ill., Cir.Ct. Sept. 23, 1983) (body can heal itself only up to a point; thereafter scarring is irreversible).

**21.** See American Home Prods., 565 F.Supp. at 1497.

**22.** See Keene Corp. v. Insurance Co. of N. Am., 667 F.2d 1034, 1047 (D.C.Cir.1981), cert. denied, 455 U.S. 1007 (1982); see also Crown Cork & Seal Co. v. Aetna Casualty & Sur. Co., No. 1292, slip op. at 8–9 (Philadelphia County, Pa., Ct.C.P. Aug. 2, 1983) (adopting the *Keene* formulation). A modified version of the continuous injury rule was adopted in Zurich Ins. v. Raymark Indus., No. 78–L–8760, slip op. at 24 (Cook County, Ill., Cir.Ct. Sept. 23, 1983) (insurers providing coverage during period of exposure or during period of manifestation are liable; but whether insurers providing coverage after exposure yet before manifestation must also provide indemnity for the insured would be decided on a case-by-case basis).

**23.** See *Keene,* 667 F.2d at 1047. The *Keene* rule, however, bars the insured from obtaining payment from more than one primary policy for each injury; that is, the insured cannot "stack" the limits of successive primary policies. See Keene, 667 F.2d at 1049. But see Oshinsky, *Insurance Coverage for Asbestos Tort Liability Litigation,* 5 J.Prod.Liab. 69, 79 (1982) (suggesting that "stacking" might still be possible when a single injury claim exceeds the limits of any of the individual policies).

**24.** See Eagle–Picher Indus. v. Liberty Mut. Ins. Co., 682 F.2d 12, 19–20 (1st Cir. 1982), cert. denied, 103 S.Ct. 1280 (1983); Zurich Ins. v. Raymark Indus., No. 78–L–8760, slip op. at 6 (Cook County, Ill., Cir.Ct. Sept. 23, 1983); see also Patterson, *The Interpretation and Construction of Contracts,* 64 COLUM.L.REV. 833, 838–41 (1964) (under the "plain meaning" rule, extrinsic evidence will be excluded if the language "itself" is clear). But see *Eagle–Picher,* 682 F.2d at 18 (discussing Professor Corbin's view that extrinsic evidence should generally be admitted for purposes of clarification); Farnsworth, *Meaning in the Law of Contracts,* 76 YALE L.J. 939, 952–65 (describing modern trend toward Corbin's view). Courts sometimes use conflicting definitions of "ambiguity" and distinguish terms that are inherently ambiguous from terms that are ambiguous only as applied to the asbestos situation. See Comment, supra note 4, at 678–79; see also *Zurich Ins.,* No. 78–L–8760, slip op. at 16 ("The difficulty is not with the terms themselves but in how these terms apply to asbestos-related diseases * * * ").

**25.** See, e.g., American Home Prods. v. Liberty Mut. Ins. Co., 565 F.Supp. 1485, 1500–03 (S.D.N.Y.1983) (discussing drafters' intent).

**26.** See id. at 1503–08 (analyzing course of dealing).

policy language either against the drafter[27] or in accordance with the reasonable expectations of the insured.[28] These traditional techniques cannot produce a coherent result.

### *Notes*

1. The physical injury (as well as legal) ramifications of the asbestosis phenomenon were not clearly apparent to the insurers of the manufacturers, product handlers, etc. of the material at the various periods during which the so-called C.G.L. policies, under which coverage is asserted, were in use. These fairly standardized policies are drafted and periodically revised by joint committees within the industry. Over the course of years there have been changes in the policy language defining the insured event, and in reading the cases wherein there are multiple successive insurers, one becomes aware that the policies may not be exactly the same. As a rough guide:

a. pre 1967 policies provide for coverage with respect to bodily injury or property damage resulting from an "occurrence" which is defined as "an event or continuous exposure to conditions, which unexpectedly caused injury during the policy period."

b. from 1967 to 1973 the definition of occurrence was changed to: "an accident, including injurious exposure to conditions, which results, during the policy period, in bodily injury, property damage neither expected nor intended from the standpoint of the insured."

c. after 1973 the policies cover "bodily injury," meaning "bodily injury, sickness or disease, which occurs during the policy period."

The court in Keene Corp. v. Insurance Co. of North America (D.C.Cir. 1981) 667 F.2d 1034, which as the text notes is the primary example of the continuous injury (or "triple trigger") approach, has an elaborate appendix on the differences in policy language of the various insurers at risk, but concludes that none of the differences warrant different interpretation. (677 F.2d at 1039)

Is it not possible, (even likely), however, that the language of the pre–67 policies might lead at court to the conclusion that "exposure" is *the* trigger of coverage?

2. The leading case on the "Manifestation Theory: Reasonable Date of Diagnosis" is cited as Eagle–Picher Indus., Inc. v. Liberty Mut. Ins. Co., 682 F.2d 12 (1st Cir.1982). Exactly when does a disease become "reasonably capable of medical diagnosis"? This question came back to the First Circuit in the same case five years later. See, Eagle–Picher Indus., Inc. v. Liberty Mut. Ins. Co., 829 F.2d 227 (1st Cir.1987), which resulted in a further remand. Observe how the court in the next main case disposed of the "diagnosable" test.

**27.** See, e.g., Insurance Co. of N. Am. v. Forty–Eight Insulations, 633 F.2d 1212, 1221–22 (6th Cir.1980), aff'g 451 F.Supp. 1230 (E.D.Mich.1978), clarified, 657 F.2d 814 (6th Cir.), cert. denied, 454 U.S. 1109 (1981); *Forty–Eight Insulations,* 451 F.Supp. at 1237–38 (when policies are ambiguous, they are construed against the insurer).

**28.** See, e.g., Keene Corp. v. Insurance Co. of N. Am., 667 F.2d 1034, 1041 (D.C.Cir.1981), cert. denied, 455 U.S. 1107 (1982). * * *

3. The 9th Circuit has espoused the "exposure" test in Hancock Laboratories, Inc. v. Admiral Ins. Co., 777 F.2d 520 (1985).

4. Note that the policies issued after 1973 cover three items under the term "bodily injury"—bodily injury itself/sickness/disease. Should not a different trigger be applied to each? See Zurich Ins. Co. v. Raymark Industries, Inc., 118 Ill.2d 23, 112 Ill.Dec. 684, 514 N.E.2d 150 (1987).

## AMERICAN HOME PRODUCTS CORPORATION v. LIBERTY MUTUAL INSURANCE COMPANY

United States Court of Appeals, Second Circuit, 1984.
748 F.2d 760.

KEARSE, CIRCUIT JUDGE:

* * *

### A. THE INSURANCE POLICIES

The policies at issue here were the product of negotiation between AHP and Liberty and are variants of the Comprehensive General Liability Policy ("CGL"), a standard-form policy for liability coverage introduced by the insurance industry in the mid–1960's to deal with the problem of liability for injuries caused over a period of time. The question is what event triggers coverage.

During the relevant period, Article I of AHP's policies provided liability coverage for occurrences that result in "personal injury, sickness or disease, including death at any time resulting therefrom, sustained by any person." Article IV of the policy provided that "[t]his policy applies only to (1) personal injury, sickness or disease including death resulting therefrom * * * which occurs during the policy period." Effective in 1968, AHP's policies also contained a proviso ("Proviso") that "[t]he policy does not apply to such injury, death or destruction caused by such continuous or repeated exposure any part of which occurs after the termination of the policy."

### B. THE PROCEEDINGS BELOW

AHP, a manufacturer of drugs, foods, and household products, has been named a defendant in the 54 Underlying Suits which arose from its manufacture and sale of six pharmaceuticals: Ovral and L/Ovral (oral contraceptives), DES (Diethylstilbestrol), Mysoline (an anticonvulsant used to treat epileptic seizures), Atromid–S (an antilipidemic used to treat high levels of blood cholesterol), Premarin (used in estrogen replacement therapy), and Anacin (a nonprescription analgesic). In each suit, the injury complained of did not manifest itself until after termination of Liberty's insurance coverage on November 1, 1976. In each case, AHP requested that Liberty defend it; Liberty refused to defend and denied coverage. AHP then initiated this suit seeking a judgment declaring that Liberty is obligated under the policies to defend and indemnify it in each of the Underlying Suits.

After a period of discovery, AHP moved for summary judgment. It contended that the policies should be read as providing either (a) that coverage was triggered if exposure, or injury, or manifestation occurred during the policy period, or (b) that regardless of when the injuries occurred or became manifest, coverage was triggered if exposure occurred during the policy period. It argued, *inter alia,* that the policy language was ambiguous, that discovery had revealed no conclusive evidence of the parties' intent at the time the language was drafted, and that New York law therefore required the application of the doctrine of *contra proferentem,* which requires that all ambiguities in contract language be resolved against the drafter of the language.

Liberty opposed AHP's motion, arguing that the trigger-of-coverage clause was unambiguous and provided coverage only when an injury became manifest within the policy period. Liberty also moved for partial summary judgment on the ground that the Proviso unambiguously excluded coverage for all cases in which exposure to the allegedly injurious substance continued after the termination of Liberty's coverage on November 1, 1976, regardless of when the injury occurred or manifested itself.

The district court rejected both parties' interpretations of the policies. It found that the trigger-of-coverage clause was unambiguous; that it did not support either AHP's continuous trigger theory, or its exposure theory, or Liberty's manifestation theory; and that, construed "as * * * written," the clause plainly called for coverage upon the occurrence of an injury in fact during the policy period. The court stated that the policies required

> a showing of actual injury, sickness or disease occurring during the policy period, based upon the facts proved in each particular case. Thus, an occurrence of "personal injury, sickness, or disease" is read to mean any point in time at which a finder of fact determines that the effects of exposure to a drug actually resulted in a diagnosable and compensable injury.

565 F.Supp. at 1489. The court elaborated as follows:

> The most basic demand of the policy language is that to establish Liberty's liability the insured must prove that an "occurrence"—injury, sickness, or disease—arose during the policy period. The plain language demands that the insured prove the cause of the occurrence (accident or exposure), the result (injury, sickness, or disease), and that the result occurred during the policy period. An exposure that does not result in injury during coverage would not satisfy the policy's terms. On the other hand, a real but undiscovered injury, proved in retrospect to have existed at the relevant time, would establish coverage, irrespective of the time the injury became manifest.

*Id.* at 1497.

The court also rejected Liberty's interpretation of the Proviso as unsupported by any evidence or by any reasonable reading of the policy as a whole. Rather, the court found that the plain language of the Proviso supported its view of the plain meaning of the trigger-of-coverage clause:

> Liberty argues correctly that the provision is unambiguous, but its meaning is not the one Liberty suggests. Rather, on its face the provision removes from coverage only injury, death, or destruction that is caused by continuous or repeated exposure occurring in part after November 1, 1976, the date AHP terminated the policy. It does not remove from coverage harm caused wholly by exposure occurring prior to November 1, 1976. Nothing in the language of the provision takes such harm out of the policy simply because exposure to the same products continued after November 1, 1976, or indeed because further harm may have occurred from such continued exposure. If, in a particular case, pre-November 1, 1976 exposure is found to have caused a particular harm, no exposure after November 1, 1976 would be a cause of that particular harm; such harm is not "caused by * * * exposure any part of which" occurred after November 1, 1976, because all of that harm-causing exposure occurred before that date.

*Id.* at 1498–99.

Finally, the court ruled that the policies' broad language concerning Liberty's duty to defend requires that Liberty defend AHP in every suit in which the complaint permits proof of facts establishing coverage, until Liberty is able to exclude the possibility of any recovery for which it provided insurance. *Id.* at 1499–1500. The court declined, however, to determine Liberty's actual duty in any given Underlying Suit to defend and indemnify AHP because it concluded that those questions depended on the particular facts of each case, including what injury was alleged and what drug was alleged to have caused it. The court therefore concluded that a determination of whether the complaint in each of the Underlying Suits permitted proof of a recovery for which Liberty would be liable under the policies was an issue inappropriate for resolution in an action for a declaratory judgment.[1] These appeals followed.

1. The final judgment declared, in pertinent part, as follows:

> 1. Liberty is required by the provisions of its above policies to pay all sums which AHP has become, is, or becomes liable to pay by reason of liability of AHP for damages arising from the use of AHP products, insofar as such damages result from diagnosable and compensable injury, sickness, or disease to a claimant during the coverage period of such a policy; no such indemnification is required, however, with respect to any injury, sickness, or disease which Liberty can establish resulted solely from the use of AHP product after November 1, 1976.
>
> 2. Liberty shall bear the costs of defense of each lawsuit against AHP in which [ ] the complaint could be read to permit proof, or does not exclude the possibility, of the existence of any diagnosable, compensable injury, sickness or disease during any policy period. Liberty shall enter and defend, and shall bear the costs of defense, in every case brought against AHP for damages caused by any of the drugs at issue, from the time each case is brought, until and unless Liberty confines a particular plaintiff's claim so

## Discussion

* * *

We agree with the district court's conclusion, substantially for the reasons stated in its opinion, that the trigger-of-coverage clause unambiguously provides for coverage based upon the occurrence during the policy period of an injury in fact. We reject only so much of the court's decision as holds that "injury in fact" means an injury that was "diagnosable" or "compensable" during the policy period.

### *A. Coverage in General*

We agree with the district court that the plain language of the policies is quite inconsistent with any of the interpretations put forth by the parties. The provision that the policies give coverage for occurrences that cause injury, read with the provision that the policies apply only to "personal injury, sickness or disease * * * which occurs during the policy period," clearly supports the court's conclusion that coverage is triggered by injury in fact. Liberty's construction of "injury" as "manifestation of injury" is inconsistent with this language. Some types of injury to the body occur prior to the appearance of any symptoms; thus, the manifestation of the injury may well occur after the injury itself. There is no language in the policies that purports to limit coverage only to injuries that become apparent during the policy period, regardless of when the injury actually occurred. Therefore, we agree with the district court that Liberty's manifestation interpretation is not reasonable.

AHP's contentions that exposure alone is sufficient to trigger coverage are likewise contrary to the plain language of the policies. Injury cannot be read as the equivalent of exposure, because the policy contemplates injury caused by exposure; since a cause normally precedes its effect, it is plain that an injury could occur during the policy period although the exposure that caused it preceded that period. AHP's interpretations urging that exposure alone could trigger coverage are thus also not reasonable.

The same recognition of the sequence of cause and effect supports the court's rejection of Liberty's interpretation of the Proviso as eliminating its responsibility for injury that occurred during the policy period where exposure that commenced prior to or during that period continued thereafter. An effect never precedes its cause. The policies plainly give coverage for injury that occurred during the policy period and was caused by exposure to AHP products; injury occurring during the policy period could not have been caused by an exposure that occurred thereafter.

* * *

as to exclude the possibility of a recovery for which Liberty has provided insurance. Whether Liberty has so confined any particular claim shall be determined by the Court before which each such case is brought, based upon the facts developed in each litigation.

We find no basis, however, for a ruling that "injury in fact" means injury that is "diagnosable" or "compensable" during the policy period. First, no clause in the policies uses either of those terms or any equivalents. Second, compensability is a legal concept that is not material to the determination of whether an injury has in fact occurred. As the district court ruled, that determination must be made according to the facts of the particular case based on medical evidence as to which drug was used and what type of injury is claimed.

Finally, the requirement that the injury be diagnosable during the policy period, like Liberty's contention for a requirement that it be manifested during that period, presents the potential for imposing an unwarranted limitation on the injury-in-fact concept. *See generally* Dykhouse & Falik, *Trigger of Coverage: The Business Context, the Plain Language and American Home Products*, 16 Conn.L.Rev. 497, 504–12 (1984). For example, a person may suffer an injury or illness that does not become diagnosable until after some period of gestation; it may be possible after diagnosis to infer that the harm must have begun some time prior to diagnosability because of the stage of the illness at the time it is diagnosed and the fact that the type of illness that is diagnosed does not occur without a gestation period. Thus, diagnosability need not coincide with the actual occurrence of injury; to add the requirement that an injury be diagnosable limits the scope of the "injury-in-fact" trigger-of-coverage clause in a way that is not justified by the policies' language. To paraphrase the district court's analysis rejecting the manifestation theory, "a real but undiscovered injury, proved in retrospect to have existed at the relevant time, would establish coverage, irrespective of the time the injury became [diagnosable]." 565 F.Supp. at 1497.

Accordingly, we modify the district court's judgment, *see* note 1 *supra,* to eliminate from paragraphs 1 and 2 thereof the words "diagnosable" and "compensable."

### B. *Coverage in the 54 Underlying Suits*

We affirm the district court's refusal to issue a declaratory judgment as to the question of Liberty's duty to defend and indemnify AHP in the Underlying Suits. The issuance of declaratory relief is a matter committed to the discretion of the trial court; it is not a matter of right of the litigants. We see no basis for concluding that the court abused its discretion here.

* * *

The judgment of the district court is modified to eliminate the terms "diagnosable" and "compensable"; as modified, the judgment is affirmed.

### *Note*

The main case has become the exemplar of the "actual injury" approach to determining *when* the liability policy coverage is triggered. See also

Aetna Cas. & Surety Company v. Abbott Laboratories, Inc., 636 F.Supp. 546 (D.Conn.1986).

The diversity of theories in the federal courts is attributable in part to the necessity of applying state law in an area where the latter is likewise divergent, opaque, or non-existent. New York law is the purported authority for the "injury in fact" theory set forth here.

In Keene Corp. v. Insurance Co. of North American, 667 F.2d 1034, the D.C.Circuit, without authoritative guidance by state law developed the widely approved triple-trigger, continuous injury theory. Yet in Abex Corp. v. Maryland Casualty Co., 790 F.2d 119 (D.C.Cir.1986), the same court, obligated by the Erie doctrine, applied the New York "injury in fact" approach of the main case and produced an opinion virtually, if not literally, in antithesis to *Keene.*

### *Note*

### *The Pollution Exclusion*

During the last quarter-century or so, growing concerns with the environment and invasive "pollution" (including pollution by toxic material) grew rampant. Statutes were enacted, regulations under them were promulgated and enforced and, it became apparent, that liability for "pollution" was increasingly going to have to be borne by industrial and other enterprises. The public purse was not going to pay the entire bill. Naturally, insurance coverage was sought, particularly under the "Commercial General Liability" types of policy (for an example, see Appendix E). The insurance industry became aware of the immense potential for liability and sought by means of various exclusions to exercise some form of "damage control". The CGL policies generally provided, inter alia, coverage for "bodily injury" or "property damage" arising out of an "occurrence", but excluded therefrom, e.g.:

> This insurance does not apply: (f) to bodily injury or property damage arising out of the discharge, dispersal, release or escape of smoke, vapors, soot, fumes, acids, alkalis, toxic chemicals, liquids or gases, waste materials or other irritants into or upon land, the atmosphere or any watercourse or body of water; *but this exclusion does not apply if such discharge, dispersal, release or escape is sudden or accidental* (emphasis added).

This would appear to have considerable impact to what seems to have been a very common sort of pollution: the gradual escape of pollutants from one property to another. Many courts took the words "sudden or accidental" quite literally. (For an example of "sudden" as importing a strictly temporal condition, see Hybud Equipment Corp. v. Sphere Drake Ins. Co., Ltd., 64 Ohio St.3d 657, 597 N.E.2d 1096 (1992), rehearing denied 65 Ohio St.3d 1445, 600 N.E.2d 686 (1992), cert. denied ___ U.S. ___, 113 S.Ct. 1585, 123 L.Ed.2d 152 (1993). Other courts perceived ambiguity and held for coverage, see, e.g., Queens City Farms, Inc. v. Central National Ins. Co., 64 Wn.App. 838, 827 P.2d 1024, 1049, review granted 120 Wash.2d 1025, 847 P.2d 481 (1993). Another form of the exclusion reads:

> "We won't cover claims or damage caused by the *continuous or intentional* discharge or release of pollutants such as: Smoke, Vapors, Soot,

Fumes, Acids, Alkalis, Toxic Chemicals, Liquids or Gases, Or Waste Materials. But will cover sudden accidents involving pollutants."

This posed the same possibility of ambiguity as the first quotation (i.e., "sudden accidents" and added another, i.e., "intentional". Another formula may present the latter problem more clearly,—injuries are not covered when "neither expected nor intended from the standpoint of the insured". The interaction of these interpretational problems seem realized in the next case.

## CLAUSSEN v. AETNA CASUALTY & SURETY CO.

Supreme Court of Georgia, 1989.
259 Ga. 333, 380 S.E.2d 686.

CLARKE, PRESIDING J.

In this case we are called upon to interpret the meaning of the "pollution exclusion" clause of a comprehensive general liability insurance policy. For the reasons stated below, we hold that the insurance policy at issue does not preclude coverage for liability for environmental contamination caused by the discharge of pollutants over an extended period of time.

Briefly stated, the history of the case is as follows: Since 1966, Henry Claussen has owned, either individually or through corporate entities, fifty-two acres of land known as Picketville. In 1968, the City of Jacksonville, Florida contracted to use the site as a landfill. Beginning in 1971, the City dumped industrial and chemical waste there almost exclusively. The City closed the site in 1977, and returned it to Claussen completely filled, graded and seeded. Claussen claims he had no knowledge that the site was used for dumping hazardous wastes.

In 1985, the Environmental Protection Agency determined that the groundwater beneath the site had been contaminated by the release of hazardous substances. In a list ranking the 115 worst hazardous waste sites in the nation, Love Canal was ranked twenty-fourth, and Picketville was ranked twenty-sixth. The agency informed Claussen, the City and others that they were responsible for taking corrective action.

Henry Claussen then filed an action against Aetna Casualty & Surety Company and others seeking a declaratory judgment that the insurance company is obligated under a "comprehensive general liability" policy for the costs to be incurred in connection with the EPA's demand that the hazardous site be studied and cleaned up. Aetna denied coverage citing exclusion (f), commonly referred to as the "pollution exclusion" which states that coverage is excluded for: "* * * bodily injury or property damage arising out of the discharge, dispersal, or release or escape of smoke, vapors, soot, fumes, acids, alkalis, toxic chemicals, liquids or gases, waste materials or other irritants, contaminants or pollutants into or upon land, the atmosphere or any water course or body of water; but this exclusion does not apply if such discharge, dispersal, release or escape is sudden and accidental * * *."

The federal district court granted Aetna's motion for summary judgment, holding that the exclusion clause precludes coverage for Claussen's environmental liabilities. The court found the clause to be clear and unambiguous and decided that dumping of toxic wastes occurring over several years was not "sudden" within the policy language. Claussen appealed to the Eleventh Circuit Court of Appeals which certified the following question to this court: Whether, as a matter of law, the pollution exclusion clause contained in the comprehensive general liability insurance policy precludes coverage to its insured for liability for costs for liability for the environmental contamination caused by the discharge of pollutants at the site over an extended period of time? To put it another way, does the insurance policy in this case require the insurance company to provide a defense and coverage to the insured for liability for the discharge of pollutants that occurred over an extended period of time?

1. "The construction of a contract is a matter of law for the court." OCGA § 13–2–1. Extrinsic evidence to explain ambiguity in a contract becomes admissible only when a contract remains ambiguous after the pertinent rules of construction have been applied. Holcomb v. Ward, 239 Ga. 847, 238 S.E.2d 915 (1977). Under Georgia rules of contract interpretation, words in a contract generally bear their usual and common meaning. OCGA § 13–3–2(2). However, "if the construction is doubtful, that which goes most strongly against the party executing the instrument or undertaking the obligation is generally to be preferred." OCGA § 13–2–2(5). Georgia courts have long acknowledged that insurance policies are prepared and proposed by insurers. Thus, if an insurance contract is capable of being construed two ways, it will be construed against the insurance company and in favor of the insured. See, e.g., Richards v. Hanover Ins. Co., 250 Ga. 613, 299 S.E.2d 561 (1983); Cincinnati Ins. Co. v. Davis, 153 Ga.App. 291, 265 S.E.2d 102 (1980); American Casualty Co. v. Callaway, 75 Ga.App. 799, 44 S.E.2d 400 (1947); Massachusetts Benefit Life Ass'n v. Robinson, 104 Ga. 256, 30 S.E. 918 (1898).

What is the meaning of the word "sudden" as it is used in the insurance policy? Claussen argues that it means "unexpected"; Aetna asserts that the only possible meaning is "abrupt." This seemingly simple question has spawned a profusion of litigation. The majority of courts considering the issue have adopted the meaning asserted by Claussen. See Developments—Toxic Waste Litigation, 99 Harv. Law Rev. 1458, 1582 (1986). See also cases cited in Claussen v. Aetna Casualty & Surety Co., 865 F.2d 1217, 1218 (11th Cir.1989). Other courts have decided that "sudden" cannot be defined without its temporal connotation. See, e.g. Claussen v. Aetna Casualty & Surety Co., 676 F.Supp. 1571 (S.D.Ga.1987), and cases cited therein.

The primary dictionary definition of the word is "happening without previous notice or with very brief notice; coming or occurring unexpectedly; not foreseen or prepared for." Webster's Third New International Dictionary, at 2284 (1986). See also, Funk and Wagnalls Standard

Dictionary, at 808 (1980); Black's Law Dictionary, at 1284 (1979). The definition of the word "sudden" as "abrupt" is also recognized in several dictionaries and is common in the vernacular. Perhaps, the secondary meaning is so common in the vernacular that it is, indeed, difficult to think of "sudden" without a temporal connotation: a sudden flash, a sudden burst of speed, a sudden bang. But, on reflection one realizes that, even in its popular usage, "sudden" does not usually describe the duration of an event, but rather its unexpectedness: a sudden storm, a sudden turn in the road, sudden death. Even when used to describe the onset of an event, the word has an elastic temporal connotation that varies with expectations: Suddenly, it's spring. See also, Oxford English Dictionary, at 96 (1933) (giving usage examples dating back to 1340, e.g., "She heard a sudden step behind her"; and, "A sudden little river crossed my path As unexpected as a serpent comes.") Thus, it appears that "sudden" has more than one reasonable meaning. And, under the pertinent rule of construction the meaning favoring the insured must be applied, that is, "unexpected."

2. Aetna next argues that construing "sudden" to mean "unexpected" violates another pertinent rule of construction, which requires that the contract be read so as to give all parts meaning. The policy states: "The company will pay on behalf of the insured all sums which the insured shall become legally obligated to pay as damages because of property damage to which this policy applies, caused by an occurrence * * *." The policy goes on to define "occurrence" as "property damage neither expected nor intended from the standpoint of the insured." Aetna contends that if "sudden" is interpreted as "unexpected," it simply restates the definition of "occurrence." We do not agree. The pollution exclusion clause focuses on whether the "*discharge, dispersal or release*" of the pollutants is unexpected and unintended; the definition of occurrence focuses on whether the *property damage* is unexpected and unintended. The pollution exclusion clause therefore has the effect of eliminating coverage for damage resulting from the intentional discharge of pollutants.[3]

3. Aetna also argues that the construction proposed by Claussen violates the cardinal rule of contract interpretation because it is inconsistent with the intention of the parties. They assert that pollution liability is an enormous risk that was not assessed in the process of underwriting this policy.

Sixteen years ago when the policy at issue here went into effect, it is unlikely that either party anticipated the extent of potential liability for pollution damage. "The past two decades have seen an explosion of litigation seeking compensation for damage to the environment and

3. Other Courts have denied coverage under the policy to insureds that actively disposed of toxic or radioactive wastes in the regular course of business activity. See, e.g., American Motorists Ins. Co. v. General Host Corp., 667 F.Supp. 1423 (D.Kan.1987); American States Ins. Co. v. Maryland Casualty Co., 587 F.Supp. 1549 (E.D.Mich.1984); City of Milwaukee v. Allied Smelting Corp., 344 N.W.2d 523 (Wis. Ct.App.1983).

injuries arising from environmental pollution." Note, The Pollution Exclusion Clause Through the Looking Glass, 74 Geo.L.J. 1237 (1986). Moreover, the Federal Superfund Act, passed in 1980, imposed "retroactive strict liability" for the costs of cleaning up hazardous waste storage sites on the generators and transporters of hazardous wastes and on the owners and operators of the sites. Abraham, Environmental Liability and the Limits of Insurance, 88 Colum.L.Rev. 942, 957 (1988). Referring to the decade before CERCLA passed, one commentator noted:

> In the past, insurance was available at prices that did not reflect the full environmental risks of each insured firm. Insurers had little incentive to tailor premiums closely to an individual firm's risk profile, because such tailoring requires the expense of monitoring each firm and because insurers did not expect courts to impose significant waste-related liabilities. Developments—Toxic Waste Litigation, 99 Harv.L.Rev. 1458, 1575 (1986).

If Aetna had been aware of the yawning extent of potential liability, it almost certainly would have drafted its policy differently. However, the fact that it did not, cannot be construed to the detriment of the insured who purchased a "comprehensive general liability" policy. Under Georgia law, the risk of any lack of clarity or ambiguity in an insurance contract must be borne by the insurer. Ranger Ins. Co. v. Culberson, 454 F.2d 857 (5th Cir.1971), cert. denied 407 U.S. 916, 92 S.Ct. 2440, 32 L.Ed.2d 691 (1972).

Further, the interpretation of the policy advanced by Claussen is not contrary to the interpretation Aetna gave the clause when it was adopted. Documents presented by the Insurance Rating Board (which represents the industry and on which Aetna participated) to the Insurance Commissioner when the "pollution exclusion" was first adopted suggest that the clause was intended to exclude only intentional polluters. The Insurance Rating Board represented "the impact of the [pollution exclusion clause] on the vast majority of risks would be no change." See, Claussen, 676 F.Supp. at 1573.

4. Finally, Aetna argues that Claussen's proposed interpretation of the policy language contravenes public policy because it encourages the land owner to keep his head in the sand—to remain oblivious to ongoing polluting activities on his land. This argument would be somewhat persuasive, but for the many events that have taken place between the date of this policy and the present lawsuit. "Environmental liability insurance has recently undergone a shift from apparent under-deterrence to apparent over-deterrence of environmental damages." Developments 99 Harv.L.Rev. 1458, 1574 (1986). Federal and state laws now require waste treatment facilities to carry insurance for both short and long term environmental risks or to meet a financial test alternative. See, Georgia Department of Natural Resources, Environmental Protection Division v. Union Timber Corporation, 258 Ga. 873, 375 S.E.2d 856 (1989). Insurance companies have become wary of insuring against environmental risks and have either dropped out of the field or are

charging higher premiums. Id. In short, the situation has changed so that our decision is not likely to have any serious impact on prospective behavior.

In sum, we conclude that the pollution exclusion clause is capable of more than one reasonable interpretation. The clause must therefore be construed in favor of the insured to mean "unexpected and unintended."

Question answered.

HUNT, J., dissenting.

I respectfully dissent because in my view the Federal District Court was correct in finding the "pollution exclusion" clear and unambiguous. While "sudden" may have a number of meanings, and, over the years, may have been used in a number of contexts, in this context it clearly means abrupt and unexpected. Certainly, its use within this context does not encompass the gradual dumping of toxic wastes over a period of several years.

### *Note*

The tsunami of environmental litigation has washed much wreckage onto the shores of insurance law. One of the more prominent problems has been due to the provisions of CERCLA (the Federal "Comprehensive Environmental Response, Compensation and Liability Act of 1980", as amended, and similar statutes. For example Sec. 107 of CERCLA, 42 U.S.C.A. § 9607, provides in part:

> (a) Covered persons; scope; recoverable costs and damages; interest rate; "comparable maturity" date
>
> Notwithstanding any other provision or rule of law, and subject only to the defenses set forth in subsection (b) of this section—
>
> (1) the owner and operator of a vessel or a facility,
>
> (2) any person who at the time of disposal of any hazardous substance owned or operated any facility at which such hazardous substances were disposed of,
>
> (3) any person who by contract, agreement, or otherwise arranged for disposal or treatment, or arranged with a transporter for transport for disposal or treatment, of hazardous substances owned or possessed by such person, by any other party or entity, at any facility or incineration vessel owned or operated by another party or entity and containing such hazardous substances, and
>
> (4) any person who accepts or accepted any hazardous substances for transport to disposal or treatment facilities, incineration vessels or sites selected by such person, from which there is a release, or a threatened release which causes the incurrence of response costs, of a hazardous substance, shall be liable for—
>
> (A) all costs of removal or remedial action incurred by the United States Government or a State or an Indian tribe not inconsistent with the national contingency plan;

(B) any other necessary costs of response incurred by any other person consistent with the national contingency plan;

(C) damages for injury to, destruction of, or loss of natural resources, including the reasonable costs of assessing such injury, destruction, or loss resulting from such a release; and

(D) the costs of any health assessment or health effects study carried out under section 9604(i) of this title.

The amounts recoverable in an action under this section shall include interest on the amounts recoverable under subparagraphs (A) through (D). Such interest shall accrue from the later of (i) the date payment of a specified amount is demanded in writing, or (ii) the date of the expenditure concerned. The rate of interest on the outstanding unpaid balance of the amounts recoverable under this section shall be the same rate as is specified for interest on investments of the Hazardous Substance Superfund established under subchapter A of chapter 98 of Title 26. For purposes of applying such amendments to interest under this subsection, the term "comparable maturity" shall be determined with reference to the date on which interest accruing under this subsection commences.

(b) Defenses

There shall be no liability under subsection (a) of this section for a person otherwise liable who can establish by a preponderance of the evidence that the release or threat of release of a hazardous substance and the damages resulting therefrom were caused solely by—

(1) an act of God;

(2) an act of war;

(3) an act or omission of a third party other than an employee or agent of the defendant, or than one whose act or omission occurs in connection with a contractual relationship, existing directly or indirectly, with the defendant (except where the sole contractual arrangement arises from a published tariff and acceptance for carriage by a common carrier by rail), if the defendant establishes by a preponderance of the evidence that (a) he exercised due care with respect to the hazardous substance concerned, taking into consideration the characteristics of such hazardous substance, in light of all relevant facts and circumstances, and (b) he took precautions against foreseeable acts or omissions of any such third party and the consequences that could foreseeably result from such acts or omissions; or

(4) any combination of the foregoing paragraphs.

(c) Determination of amounts

(1) Except as provided in paragraph (2) of this subsection, the liability under this section of an owner or operator or other responsible person for each release of a hazardous substance or incident involving release of a hazardous substance shall not exceed—

(A) for any vessel, other than an incineration vessel, which carries any hazardous substance as cargo or residue, \$300 per gross ton, or \$5,000,000, whichever is greater;

(B) for any other vessel, other than an incineration vessel, $300 per gross ton, or $500,000, whichever is greater;

(C) for any motor vehicle, aircraft, pipeline (as defined in the Hazardous Liquid Pipeline Safety Act of 1979 [49 U.S.C.A. § 2001 et seq.] ), or rolling stock, $50,000,000 or such lesser amount as the President shall establish by regulation, but in no event less than $5,000,000 (or, for releases of hazardous substances as defined in section 9601(14)(A) of this title into the navigable waters, $8,000,000). Such regulations shall take into account the size, type, location, storage, and handling capacity and other matters relating to the likelihood of release in each such class and to the economic impact of such limits on each such class; or

(D) for any incineration vessel or any facility other than those specified in subparagraph (C) of this paragraph, the total of all costs of response plus $50,000,000 for any damages under this subchapter.

(2) Notwithstanding the limitations in paragraph (1) of this subsection, the liability of an owner or operator or other responsible person under this section shall be the full and total costs of response and damages, if (A)(i) the release or threat of release of a hazardous substance was the result of willful misconduct or willful negligence within the privity or knowledge of such person, or (ii) the primary cause of the release was a violation (within the privity or knowledge of such person) of applicable safety, construction, or operating standards or regulations; or (B) such person fails or refuses to provide all reasonable cooperation and assistance requested by a responsible public official in connection with response activities under the national contingency plan with respect to regulated carriers subject to the provisions of Title 49 or vessels subject to the provisions of Title 33 or 46, subparagraph (A)(ii) of this paragraph shall be deemed to refer to Federal standards or regulations.

(3) If any person who is liable for a release or threat of release of a hazardous substance fails without sufficient cause to properly provide removal or remedial action upon order of the President pursuant to section 9604 or 9606 of this title, such person may be liable to the United States for punitive damages in an amount at least equal to, and not more than three times, the amount of any costs incurred by the Fund as a result of such failure to take proper action. The President is authorized to commence a civil action against any such person to recover the punitive damages, which shall be in addition to any costs recovered from such person pursuant to section 9612(c) of this title. Any moneys received by the United States pursuant to this subsection shall be deposited in the Fund.

Pretty clearly, these provisions (which are actually only a small part of 42 U.S.C.A. § 9607) pose their own problems of interpretation. But just as obviously they impose liabilities on insureds. For example, the impact of subsec. (a)(4)(A) and (B) making persons subject to the Act liable for "all costs of removal or remedial action" by the U.S., a State, or an Indian tribe and for "any other necessary costs of response" sound minatory in the extreme. Can such costs come within the coverage of a CGL policy?

## AIU INSURANCE CO. v. SUPERIOR COURT

Supreme Court of California, 1990.
51 Cal.3d 807, 274 Cal.Rptr. 820, 799 P.2d 1253.

LUCAS, CHIEF JUSTICE.

We are called on to decide whether, under comprehensive general liability (CGL) insurance policies issued by petitioners (insurers) to real party in interest FMC Corporation (FMC), insurers are obligated to provide coverage to FMC for cleanup and other "response" costs incurred pursuant to the Comprehensive Environmental Response and Compensation and Liability Act (CERCLA) (42 U.S.C. § 9601 et seq.) and related state and federal environmental laws. FMC seeks review of the peremptory writ of mandate issued by the Court of Appeal, which directed the superior court to enter summary adjudication on this issue in favor of the insurers.

We reverse the decision of the Court of Appeal. The insurance policies at issue provide coverage to FMC for all sums FMC becomes legally obligated to pay as "damages" (under two policy forms) or "ultimate net loss" (under a third) because of property damage. Under established principles of contract interpretation, we construe policy language according to the mutual intentions of the parties and its "plain and ordinary" meaning, resolving ambiguities in favor of coverage. Applying these rules, we conclude that the policies cover the costs of reimbursing government agencies and complying with injunctions ordering cleanup under CERCLA and similar statutes. Although many of the policies contain exclusions arguably relevant to whether environmental cleanup costs are covered, we do not consider the applicability of exclusions in this case, which comes to us on motion for summary adjudication solely as to the coverage clauses.

### I. FACTUAL AND PROCEDURAL BACKGROUND

#### A. *The Insurance Policies*

FMC holds over 60 primary and excess CGL policies issued by the insurers. Each policy contains one of three coverage clauses:

1. Policies issued by the Liberty Mutual Insurance Company and others provide coverage to FMC for "all sums which [FMC] shall become legally obligated to pay as damages because of * * * property damage to which this policy applies."

2. Policies issued by the FMC Insurance Company and others provide coverage to FMC for "all sums which [FMC] shall become obligated to pay by reason of the liability * * * imposed upon [FMC] by law * * * for damages on account of * * * property damage * * *."[2]

3. Policies issued by the First State Insurance Company and others provide coverage to FMC for "all sums which [FMC] shall be obligated to

2. FMC Insurance Company is a subsidiary of FMC. As such, it is not named as a defendant in this suit, although it issued policies to its parent corporation identical to those under which FMC seeks coverage here.

pay by reason of the liability * * * imposed upon [FMC] by law * * * for damages, direct or consequential and expenses, all as more fully defined by the term 'ultimate net loss' on account of * * * property damages * * *."

These coverage provisions were adopted verbatim from standard CGL policies used by the insurance industry. (See Mountainspring, Insurance Coverage of CERCLA Response Costs: The Limits of "Damages" in Comprehensive General Liability Policies (1989) 16 Ecology L.Q. 755, 759; Chesler et al., Patterns of Judicial Interpretation of Insurance Coverage for Hazardous Waste Site Liability (1986) 18 Rutgers L.J. 9, 53.) They contain several common elements. Each provision covers only sums that FMC is "legally obligated" or "obligated * * * by law" to pay. They each require that the sums paid be the result of FMC's liability for "property damage[s]." The first two policies limit coverage to sums paid as or for "damages." None of these terms is defined in any of the policies. The only relevant definition contained in any of the policies is of "ultimate net loss" (covered by the third policy), which includes both "damages" and "expenses."

*B. The Third Party Suits Against FMC*

The United States and local administrative agencies (hereafter agencies) filed suits against FMC, seeking relief for alleged violations of CERCLA, the Resource Conservation and Recovery Act (RCRA) (42 U.S.C. § 6901 et seq.), the Clean Water Act (33 U.S.C. § 1251 et seq.), the Safe Drinking Water Act (42 U.S.C. § 300f et seq.), and California's Hazardous Substance Account Act (Health & Saf.Code, § 25300 et seq.). In sum, the suits allege that FMC is responsible for the contamination of 79 different hazardous waste disposal sites, groundwater beneath the sites, aquifers beneath adjoining property, and surrounding surface waters. The agencies seek two types of relief: (i) injunctions compelling FMC both to terminate disposal of further hazardous waste and to remove contaminants already present on and around the disposal sites, and (ii) reimbursement of their costs of investigating, monitoring, and initiating cleanup of hazardous waste for which FMC allegedly is responsible.

All of the statutes on which the third party suits are based expressly authorize injunctive relief. (See CERCLA, 42 U.S.C. § 9606(a); RCRA, 42 U.S.C. § 6973(a); Clean Water Act, 33 U.S.C. § 1364(a); Safe Drinking Water Act, 42 U.S.C. § 300i(a); Hazardous Substance Account Act, Health & Saf.Code, § 25358.3, subd. (a).) CERCLA and the Hazardous Substance Account Act, however, also authorize government recovery of the costs of removing hazardous waste and restoring affected property, providing the agencies with a choice (subject to judicial approval) of how to proceed with and finance cleanup efforts. (See CERCLA, 42 U.S.C. § 9607(a)(4)(A) [reimbursement of government costs of removal or remedial action]; Hazardous Substance Account Act, Health & Saf.Code, § 25360 [reimbursement of state cleanup expenses.].) In addition, CERCLA authorizes the federal government to recover sums for "damages to natural resources." (42 U.S.C., § 9607(a)(4)(C).) In their present suits against FMC, however, the agencies do not seek recovery under this last provision, although surface and groundwater nominally owned by the state (Wat.Code, § 102) has been damaged at many of the sites where remedial action is sought, and although CERCLA defines "natural resources" to include water and groundwater "belonging to, managed by, held in trust by, appertaining to, or otherwise controlled by" the federal or state government.[4] (See CERCLA, 42 U.S.C. § 9601(16).)

### C. *The Present Suit*

In the present suit, FMC seeks declaratory relief establishing that the CGL policies cover costs it may become obligated to pay as a result of injunctive relief and/or reimbursement ordered in the third party suits. The insurers moved for summary adjudication, asserting that, as a matter of law, the CGL policies do not cover costs of abating and cleaning up hazardous waste and reimbursing governmental agencies for their cleanup efforts. In response, FMC contended that (i) the policy language encompasses all of its costs resulting from the agencies' suits under CERCLA and the other statutes, (ii) the intent of the parties to the policies is a relevant and contested issue of material fact bearing on the issue of coverage, and (iii) FMC should be granted preliminary discovery of evidence bearing on such intent.

* * *

We granted review to determine whether the Court of Appeal correctly directed the superior court to enter summary adjudication for the insurers.

## II. Discussion

At issue here is whether, as a matter of law, the CGL policies cover either or both of the types of costs that FMC may be required to pay as a result of the third party suits. Specifically, we must determine whether (i) any adverse orders issued in those suits will "legally obligate" FMC to pay such costs, (ii) the costs will constitute "damages" or "ultimate net loss," and (iii) such costs will be incurred because of "property damage." Only if all three conditions are fulfilled will the insurers' duty to provide coverage arise under the policies.

Our task has two distinct parts. First, we must determine, under California law, what rules of insurance policy interpretation apply in this context. Second, we must interpret the CGL policies under applicable principles of insurance coverage. Although one can readily conceive of arguments for and against permitting insurance against the costs of

4. Because the agencies do not seek recovery under the CERCLA "damages to natural resources" provision, we do not here directly consider whether such recovery would be covered by CGL policies. We note the existence of the provision, however, because the insurers in part rely on its existence to support their argument that recovery of response costs is mutually exclusive from recovery of statutory "damages."

rectifying pollution, at the outset we note that such arguments are not pertinent to either of our inquiries in this case. Both CERCLA and the Hazardous Substance Account Act expressly permit responsible parties to insure against the costs of relief available under the legislation. Thus, because Congress and the Legislature already have made the relevant public policy determinations, the issue before this Court is not whether CGL policies *may* provide the coverage sought, but whether they *do* provide it according to their terms. The answer is to be found solely in the language of the policies, not in public policy considerations.

Numerous state and federal courts have addressed the issue presented in this case. Until the present Court of Appeal decision, nearly every state appellate decision has concluded that cleanup costs incurred under environmental statutes are covered by policies identical to those concerned here.

These decisions have generally held that the costs of reimbursing governments or third parties for their remedial and mitigative efforts are covered, either because such costs are plainly "damages" that the insured is "legally obligated" to pay as a result of "property damage", or because these phrases are ambiguous and therefore must be resolved in favor of coverage under ordinary rules of insurance policy interpretation. We have found only one state appellate decision holding to the contrary. (See Braswell v. United States Fidelity & Guar. Co. (1989) 300 S.C. 338, 387 S.E.2d 707.)

Similarly, state courts have consistently held costs of compliance with environmental injunctions covered, either because such costs fit within a broad definition of "damages", or because a contrary holding would unreasonably make coverage hinge on the "mere fortuity" of which recovery mechanism (injunction, reimbursement, or "damages to natural resources") the government selects in enforcing CERCLA. Again, only one state appellate decision, in dictum, reaches the opposite conclusion.

The federal courts, however, purporting to apply state law, are sharply divided on whether environmental cleanup costs are covered by CGL policies. Several courts have followed the majority of state decisions, concluding that both forms of relief sought by the government in statutory environmental suits constitute "damages" covered under the standard policies. (See, e.g., Avondale Industries, Inc. v. Travelers Indem. Co. (2d Cir.1989) 887 F.2d 1200 [insurers' duty to defend suits seeking reimbursement of response costs]; Intel Corp. v. Hartford Acc. and Indem. Co. (N.D.Cal.1988) 692 F.Supp. 1171, app. pending 9th Cir. (Intel).)

Other courts, however, have ruled that cleanup costs are not covered. These decisions all rely on one or more of four basic arguments. First, looking to the language of CERCLA itself, they often emphasize that because it contains separate provisions for government recovery of "damages" to natural resources (see 42 U.S.C. § 9607(a)(4)(C)) and of "remedial costs" compensating it for cleanup (id., § 9607(a)(4)(A)), the latter form of recovery cannot be classified as "damages," notwithstanding whether state law principles would permit such a characterization in the absence of the statutory distinction.

Second, some courts have held, as the Court of Appeal did in this case, that because the agencies may recover their response costs without having suffered harm to property or resources in which they have a proprietary interest, such recovery is not for "damages," as that term is defined at law.

Third, several decisions conclude that "damages," defined either in lay or legal terms, is an unambiguous term that does not include costs of complying with injunctive relief available under CERCLA and related statutes. Such costs, they reason, are not sums paid to another party to compensate it for wrongs committed by the insured; they are simply "sums which the insured becomes legally obligated to pay because of property damage," failing to fulfill the "as damages" qualifier on coverage under CGL policies. Relying on decisions holding that an insured's costs of complying with mandatory injunctions issued in suits asserting common law claims are not "damages" (see, e.g., Aetna Casualty and Surety Company v. Hanna (5th Cir.1955) 224 F.2d 499 (Hanna)), these courts have held that the costs of compliance with environmental injunctions should be treated no differently.

Fourth, several courts have reasoned that the costs of injunctions and reimbursement are not covered because, in the corporate "insurance context," insureds should not receive the benefit of insurance policy interpretation principles designed to protect unsophisticated, arguably disadvantaged policyholders. Under this view, courts should interpret CGL policies by affording them narrow legal meanings under which the terms "legally obligated" and "damages" exclude the costs of *equitable* relief from coverage. Classifying reimbursement of government cleanup costs as equitable "restitution" and costs of compliance with injunctions as a consequence of equitable relief, several courts have concluded for this reason that neither type of relief is covered.

As these decisions suggest, two general arguments underlie the insurers' position that expenses incurred under CERCLA and similar statutes are not covered by the CGL policies at issue. First, it is argued that established rules of insurance policy interpretation are inapplicable in this context, and that we should apply more restrictive principles that will preclude coverage of environmental response costs under these policies. Second, even under traditional principles of interpretation, the policies should be interpreted to unambiguously exclude coverage of the types of relief sought in the underlying suits. We examine these propositions in turn.

### A. *Principles of Insurance Policy Interpretation*

Under statutory rules of contract interpretation, the mutual intention of the parties at the time the contract is formed governs interpretation. (Civ.Code, § 1636.) Such intent is to be inferred, if possible, solely from the written provisions of the contract. (Id., § 1639.) The "clear and explicit" meaning of these provisions, interpreted in their "ordinary and popular sense," unless "used by the parties in a technical sense or a special meaning is given to them by usage" (id., § 1644), controls judicial interpretation. (Id., § 1638.) Thus, if the meaning a layperson would ascribe to contract language is not ambiguous, we apply that meaning. (See, e.g., Reserve Insurance Co. v. Pisciotta (1982) 30 Cal.3d 800, 807, 180 Cal.Rptr. 628, 640 P.2d 764; Crane v. State Farm Fire & Cas. Co. (1971) 5 Cal.3d 112, 115, 95 Cal.Rptr. 513, 485 P.2d 1129.)

If there is ambiguity, however, it is resolved by interpreting the ambiguous provisions in the sense the promisor (i.e., the insurer) believed the promisee understood them at the time of formation. (Civ. Code, § 1649.) If application of this rule does not eliminate the ambiguity, ambiguous language is construed against the party who caused the uncertainty to exist. (Id., § 1654.) In the insurance context, we generally resolve ambiguities in favor of coverage. (See, e.g., State Farm Mut. Auto. Ins. Co. v. Jacober (1973) 10 Cal.3d 193, 197, 110 Cal.Rptr. 1, 514 P.2d 953). Similarly, we generally interpret the coverage clauses of insurance policies broadly, protecting the objectively reasonable expectations of the insured. (See, e.g., Garvey v. State Farm Fire & Casualty Co. (1989) 48 Cal.3d 395, 406, 257 Cal.Rptr. 292, 770 P.2d 704). These rules stem from the fact that the insurer typically drafts policy language, leaving the insured little or no meaningful opportunity or ability to bargain for modifications. (See, e.g., Garcia v. Truck Ins. Exchange (1984) 36 Cal.3d 426, 438, 204 Cal.Rptr. 435, 682 P.2d 1100.) Because the insurer writes the policy, it is held "responsible" for ambiguous policy language, which is therefore construed in favor of coverage.

It follows, however, that where the policyholder does not suffer from lack of legal sophistication or a relative lack of bargaining power, and where it is clear that an insurance policy was actually negotiated and jointly drafted, we need not go so far in protecting the insured from ambiguous or highly technical drafting. (Garcia v. Truck Ins. Exchange, supra, 36 Cal.3d at p. 438, 204 Cal.Rptr. 435, 682 P.2d 1100 [refusing to resolve ambiguity against insurer when insured enjoyed "substantial bargaining power vis-a-vis the carrier," and actually negotiated and joined in drafting terms of coverage].)

FMC unquestionably possesses both legal sophistication and substantial bargaining power. For this reason, the insurers contend, we should neither construe the policy language at issue in this case in the broad sense understood by laypersons (as opposed to a narrower technical sense) nor resolve ambiguities in favor of coverage. There is some force to these arguments, particularly in light of the fact that FMC itself operates a subsidiary that drafts CGL policies identical to those at issue in this case. In the absence of evidence that the parties, at the time they entered into the policies, intended the provisions at issue here to carry technical meanings and implemented this intention by specially crafting policy language, however, we see little reason to depart from ordinary principles of interpretation. Similarly, in the absence of evidence that the insurers had cause to believe, at the time of formation, that FMC understood policy language in any technical or restrictive manner, we decline to depart from the settled rule that ambiguities are resolved against the party responsible for their inclusion in the policies.

We deem this party to be the insurers. They have presented no evidence suggesting that the provisions in question were actually negotiated or jointly drafted. (Compare Garcia v. Truck Ins. Exchange, supra, 36 Cal.3d at p. 434, 204 Cal.Rptr. 435, 682 P.2d 1100.) Indeed, the evidence that is before us reveals that such provisions, drafted by the insurers, are highly uniform in content and wording. For the above reasons, we interpret their contents, if ambiguous, in favor of coverage.

### B. *Interpretation of CGL Policy Language*

The CGL policies at issue in this case cover sums which FMC becomes "legally obligated" to pay as "damages" (or "ultimate net loss") incurred because of "property damage." We next consider whether, as a matter of law, the types of relief at issue in the third party suits satisfy these requirements.

1. "Legally Obligated"

The first requirement for coverage is that FMC be legally obligated to pay the costs at issue. Because it is clear that, if FMC is held liable in the third party suits, it will be "obligated" to pay for whatever relief the courts order, the only remaining question is whether that obligation may be considered "legal" under applicable rules of interpretation. The insurers contend it may not, for the simple reason that whether the courts award injunctive relief or order FMC to reimburse the agencies for their response costs, they will be exercising "equitable" rather than "legal" authority.

Both injunctions and awards of response costs under CERCLA reasonably can be viewed as equitable relief. (See, e.g., United States v. Northeastern Pharmaceutical (8th Cir.1986) 810 F.2d 726, 749, cert. den. (1987) 484 U.S. 848, 108 S.Ct. 146, 98 L.Ed.2d 102 [no right to jury trial in suit seeking reimbursement of response costs].) The mere characterization of relief under federal law, however, is not dispositive of the proper construction of insurance policies under state law. Because California has generally abandoned the traditional distinction between courts of equity and courts of law (see Code Civ.Proc., §§ 24, 30; Aerojet, supra, 211 Cal.App.3d at p. 230, fn. 8, 257 Cal.Rptr. 621, 258 Cal.Rptr. 684), even a legally sophisticated policyholder might not anticipate that the term "legally obligated" precludes coverage of equitably compelled expenses. Because the relief is ordered by a court of law, as that term is used in the modern sense, FMC could reasonably believe that its obligation to pay is legal. As the Court of Appeal noted in Aerojet, supra, 211 Cal.App.3d at page 228, 257 Cal.Rptr. 621, 258 Cal.Rptr. 684: "[P]etitioners would be surprised indeed to learn that coverage depended on whether the proceeding employed to obtain recompense was defined as 'legal' or 'equitable.' * * * It would come as an unexpected, if not incomprehensible, shock to the insureds to discover that their insurance coverage was being denied because the plaintiff chose to frame his complaint in equity rather than in law." Thus, as a matter of plain meaning, the term "legally obligated" covers injunctive relief and recovery of response costs.

Moreover, even if this phrase raises doubts in the minds of legally trained observers about whether a law-equity distinction was intended, it would be unreasonable to conclude that it unambiguously incorporates this sophisticated distinction into the policies. In this respect, whatever ambiguity it possesses in light of a party's legal knowledge is resolved in favor of coverage. Whether the term "legally obligated" is ambiguous or not, therefore, we conclude that it encompasses the types of relief sought in the third party suits.

2. "Damages"

We next consider whether FMC's prospective legal obligation in the third party suits is to pay "damages." Because the CGL policies do not define the word "damages," for interpretation purposes we look to its "ordinary and popular" definition. (Civ.Code, § 1644; Allstate Ins. Co. v. Thompson (1988) 206 Cal.App.3d 933, 938, 254 Cal.Rptr. 84.) Section 3281 of the Civil Code provides: "Every person who suffers detriment from the unlawful act or omission of another, may recover from the person in fault a compensation therefor in money, which is called damages." As our cases have pointed out, this provision is intended to represent the plain and ordinary meaning of the word "damages." Other lay and legal definitions are similar. [discussion of dictionary meanings is omitted]

We note, however, that CERCLA and the Hazardous Substance Account Act authorize alternative remedies—injunction and reimbursement—that are relatively interchangeable in a way perhaps not foreseen by the parties at the time they entered the CGL policies. As we discuss at greater length below, the policies necessarily present some ambiguity in light of statutory schemes that by their very operation tend to eliminate the formal distinction between compensation paid to an aggrieved party and sums expended by the insured under compulsion of injunction. For this reason, although we take the statutory and dictionary definitions described above to be the "ordinary and popular" definition of "damages" for interpretation purposes, we will not apply this definition inflexibly. To the extent that policy language is ambiguous in light of the way environmental statutes authorize relief, our goal remains to protect the objectively reasonable expectations of the insured.

With this background, we now examine whether the basic forms of relief at issue in the underlying suits are "damages."

(a) Reimbursement of government response costs

In numerous CERCLA suits seeking recovery from responsible parties, courts have routinely referred to reimbursement of response costs as "damages," regardless of the nature of the cleanup performed or property interest possessed by the plaintiff. (See, e.g., Pennsylvania v. Union Gas Co. (1989) 491 U.S. 1, ___-___, 109 S.Ct. 2273, 2284–2285, 105 L.Ed.2d 1) In the insurance context, this view is persuasive. The ordinary, nontechnical meaning of "damages," as stated by statute and dictionaries and used by the courts in related contexts, encompasses reimbursement of response costs. The agencies' expenditure of federal funds to investigate and initiate cleanup of hazardous waste constitutes "loss" or "detriment." Furthermore, reimbursement by responsible parties is monetary "compensation" for such loss.

The first element of the statutory and dictionary definitions of "damages" is fulfilled in this case. The agencies suffer "loss" or "detriment" in two separate ways when they incur response costs under CERCLA and similar statutes. First, release of hazardous waste into groundwater and surface water constitutes actual harm to property in which the state and federal governments have an ownership interest; this harm is "detriment" in statutory terms. (Civ.Code, § 3282; Wat. Code, § 102 ["All water within the State is the property of the people of the State, but the right to the use of water may be acquired by appropriation in the manner provided by law."]) Second, the agencies' out-of-pocket expenses of investigating and removing the waste as required by statute is "loss" incurred as a direct result of harm allegedly created through the unlawful act or omission of FMC.

Viewed in this second context, such expenditure constitutes "loss" or "detriment" even as to agency efforts specifically directed at cleaning up property in which neither the state nor the federal government has an ownership interest. Under statute, the agencies are charged with the duty of removing hazardous waste, whether or not their proprietary interests are harmed or they ultimately are compensated for their efforts. They are not mere contractors who act out of an expectation of recompense for their cleanup work; their expenses are incurred as a matter of public duty rather than hope of private gain. Thus, when they seek reimbursement of their response costs, the basis of the claim is harm done to the public fisc. In ordinary terms, such harm constitutes "loss" or "detriment."

The language of the CGL policies themselves supports this view. The clauses at issue here cover sums expended as damages "because of property damage." If "damages" is construed to include a requirement that the aggrieved party suffered harm to a proprietary interest in the damaged property, the latter phrase becomes redundant. The plain language of the policies therefore supports the conclusion that the agencies' out-of-pocket expenditures, irrespective of the government interest in the property sought to be cleaned up, constitute "loss" or "detriment."

The second element of the statutory and dictionary definitions of "damages" is also fulfilled in this case. FMC's reimbursement of government response costs is monetary "compensation" for the loss suffered by the agencies when they proceed with environmental cleanups. Moreover, because the compensable loss is all remedial out-of-pocket expenditures incurred by the agencies, the "compensation" sought from FMC includes reimbursement for costs of cleaning up existing contamination on and off the disposal site itself, investigating the extent of contamination or the viability of cleanup options, and monitoring the spread of waste from the site. (See, e.g., Intel, supra, 692 F.Supp. at p. 1192.) As long as some "property damage," as defined below, has already taken place, the agencies' expenses for responding constitute loss or detriment, whether or not the expenses are attributable to actual cleanup, mitigation of damage, or investigation and monitoring. When the agencies seek reimbursement of such expenses from the insured under CERCLA, their claim is for compensation for all their expenses, not merely those resulting from actual cleanup efforts on government property. Any other conclusion would be illogical as a matter of the reasonable expectations of the insured.

For three specific reasons not relating to the ordinary meaning of the word "damages," however, the insurers contend that a reasonable interpretation excludes reimbursement of response costs from coverage under the CGL "damages" provision. First, they argue that because CERCLA distinguishes response costs from damages, it mandates the same distinction in the insurance context because the agencies do not seek "damages" as prescribed by statute. Second, the insurers contend that because environmental statutes authorize the agencies to recover response costs even if they suffer no property damage or personal injury, such recovery is "a government-imposed cost of doing business" rather than compensation for loss or detriment. Finally, the insurers contend that reimbursement is best characterized as restitutive relief, the measure and purpose of which is sufficiently different from "damages" to render the two concepts mutually exclusive. None of these arguments is persuasive in the insurance context. [insurers' arguments are omitted]

The insurers' argument contains several flaws. First, recovery of tort damages is not invariably limited by the value of damaged property. The courts have recognized that recovery in excess of such value may be necessary to restore the plaintiff to the position it occupied prior to a defendant's wrongdoing. (See, e.g., Heninger v. Dunn (1980) 101 Cal. App.3d 858, 863, 162 Cal.Rptr. 104 [permitting recovery of reasonable repair costs in excess of value of damaged property, when plaintiff has personal reason for making repairs]; Dandoy v. Oswald Bros. Paving Co. (1931) 113 Cal.App. 570, 572–573, 298 P. 1030 ["To hold that appellant is without a remedy merely because the value of land has not been diminished, would be to decide that by wrongful act of another, an owner of land may be compelled to accept a change in the physical condition of his property, or else perform the work of restoration at his own expense. This would be a denial of the principle that there is no wrong without a remedy."]; see generally Rest.2d Torts, § 929.)

Second, even if the courts generally award tort "damages" in an amount limited to the lesser of the value of damaged property or the costs of repair, that does not mandate that a greater recovery authorized by state or federal statute therefore should be held to constitute something other than "damages" in conceptual terms. Even if a court applying common law might not award the full extent of such costs, the excess above what is awarded remains "damages" for insurance policy interpretation purposes. The whole recovery of response costs, not just the amount limited to the value of harmed property, constitutes loss or detriment for harm caused by FMC's allegedly unlawful act or omission.

This brings us to the alternative thrust of the insurers' argument: reimbursement of government response costs is not "damages" because it is a restitutive remedy that is "specific" rather than "substitutive" in character. The United States Supreme Court recently adopted this distinction in discussing whether a state's claim for "reimbursement" of federal Medicaid subsidies is a claim for "money damages" under the terms of the Administrative Procedure Act (APA) (5 U.S.C. § 702). Characterizing such a claim as one for "restitution," the high court held that it was therefore not a claim for money damages: "Our cases have long recognized the distinction between an action at law for damages—which are intended to provide a victim with monetary compensation for an injury to his person, property, or reputation—and an equitable action for specific relief—which may include an order providing * * * for 'the recovery of specific property *or monies* * * *.' " (Bowen v. Massachusetts (1988) 487 U.S. 879, 893, 108 S.Ct. 2722, 2732, 101 L.Ed.2d 749 [citation omitted, italics in original].)

We too have recognized a distinction between restitution and compensatory damages. Reimbursement can reasonably be labelled a restitutive remedy, either because it awards a plaintiff "the very thing to which he was entitled", or because it attempts to compensate a plaintiff for the cost of performing the duty of another (see Rest., Restitution, § 115 [providing that a person who performs the duty of another is entitled to "restitution"] ).

This label does not, however, preclude characterization of the amounts in question here as "damages" awarded to compensate a plaintiff for out-of-pocket expenditures. Indeed, restitution, to which the insurers analogize the reimbursement at issue here, is frequently denominated as one type of "damages" for descriptive purposes. Whatever technical distinctions we and other courts have drawn between restitution and compensatory damages in other contexts, in ordinary terms both concepts are within the definition of "damages." For the purposes of interpretation, this fact is dispositive.

Nonetheless, because reimbursement of response costs is restitutive in that it attempts to restore to the governments the value of a benefit constructively conferred on FMC, we consider one further argument. California courts have held that, as a matter of public policy, an insured's payment of certain types of restitution cannot be covered by insurance. (See, e.g., State Farm Fire & Cas. Co. v. Superior Court (1987) 191 Cal.App.3d 74, 236 Cal.Rptr. 216 [insurer has no duty to defend criminal prosecution of insured, because "restitution" to victims of criminal conduct is punitive remedy not coverable as "damages"]; Jaffe v. Cranford Ins. Co., 168 Cal.App.3d 930, 214 Cal.Rptr. 567 [insurer has no duty to defend insured against criminal prosecution for Medicaid fraud, despite fact that state could have sought civil reimbursement of fraudulently procured funds instead of prosecuting; such reimbursement would be "restitution," not "damages"].)

These cases are inapposite. Unlike State Farm Fire & Cas. Co. v. Superior Court, the relief sought in the underlying suits at issue here is not punitive. CERCLA, for example, is a strict liability statute that serves essentially remedial goals, irrespective of fault. Reimbursement of response costs, moreover, is not restitutive in the narrow sense identified by Jaffe as inappropriate for insurance coverage. (See Jaffe v. Cranford Ins. Co., supra, 168 Cal.App.3d at p. 935, 214 Cal.Rptr. 567 ["Although the concept of 'restitution' may have a broader meaning in other contexts, we limit our reference to it here to situations in which the defendant is required to restore to the plaintiff that which was wrongfully acquired."].) In short, we are not persuaded that the relief at issue here is of the narrow type identified by these cases as not a proper subject of coverage by insurance. We conclude that reimbursement of environmental response costs is "damages" under the terms of the insurance policies at issue here, and that public policy does not prevent coverage.

(b) Costs of compliance with injunctions

The statutes on which the third party suits are based provide that, in lieu of remedying contamination and seeking reimbursement, the agencies may obtain injunctions compelling responsible parties to both cease discharging hazardous waste and clean up damage already present. As courts and commentators have recognized, government cleanup efforts are generally considerably more expensive than cleanups performed by the responsible party. (See, e.g., Intel, supra, 692 F.Supp. at p. 1183; Chemical Applications Co. v. Home Indemnity Co. (D.Mass.1977), 425 F.Supp. 777, 778–779; Pendygraft et al., Who Pays for Environmental Damage: Recent Developments in CERCLA Liability and Insurance Coverage Litigation (1988) 21 Ind.L.Rev. 117, 151.) For this reason, federal and state governments generally seek voluntary and involuntary cleanup by the responsible party (pursuant to injunction if necessary) before performing it themselves and seeking reimbursement under CERCLA. We now examine whether any or all of the costs of complying with injunctions issued under CERCLA and similar statutes are "damages" under the CGL policies.

The costs of injunctive relief, whether incurred for prophylactic, mitigative, or remedial purposes, do not readily satisfy the statutory or dictionary definitions of "damages." Because such costs are paid to employees or independent contractors rather than aggrieved parties, they do not directly "compensate" aggrieved persons for "loss" or "detriment." To be sure, in economic terms it may make little difference whether cleanup is performed and paid for directly by the insured pursuant to injunction or undertaken by the agencies (who then seek reimbursement). Nonetheless, it is difficult to construe the two methods of payment as equally covered by the ordinary definition of the word "damages," as we have described it above. If the costs of injunctive relief may be deemed "damages," the "as damages" limitation contained in the policies seems to be rendered meaningless. The costs of injunctions are essentially "sums to which the insured becomes legally obligated to pay * * * because of property damage." Construing them also to be "sums to which the insured becomes legally obligated to pay as damages because of property damage" makes the italicized phrase redundant. Because we are obligated to give effect to every part of an insurance policy (Civ.Code, § 1641), we hesitate to reach this result.

It is unlikely, however, that the parties to CGL policies intended to cover reimbursement of response costs but not the costs of injunctive relief, at least where the latter costs are incurred—generally at a lower total cost—for exactly the same purposes addressed through governmental expenditure of response costs. In this respect, we note that the relationship between the remedies authorized by CERCLA and similar statutes is not the same as that between damages and injunctive remedies traditionally available at common law and in equity. In ordinary tort actions, injunctive relief is generally available only if legal remedies (e.g., monetary compensation) are inadequate. (Code Civ.Proc., § 526; Civ.Code, § 3422; see generally 6 Witkin, Cal.Procedure (3d ed. 1985) Provisional Remedies, § 276, p. 576, and cases cited therein.) Thus, a plaintiff ordinarily may seek to enjoin conduct that constitutes a nuisance, even though the activity complained of does not cause him any cognizable property or personal damage. In such a situation, the defendant's costs of complying with an injunction might not be covered by CGL policies.

In Hanna, supra, 224 F.2d 499, the leading case holding that the cost of complying with mandatory injunctions in tort actions is not "damages" under CGL policies, adjoining property owners brought suit against the insured, alleging trespass by boulders and debris from the insured's property. The owners sought no damages (and there was no evidence that the value of their property had decreased as a result of the encroachment). Instead, they sought, and obtained, an injunction ordering the insured to remove the debris. The Fifth Circuit Court of Appeals held the costs of complying with the injunction not covered under the insured's liability policy, which contained substantially the same coverage clause as those at issue here. Its reasoning, however, focused on the fact that, under Florida law, the owners' potential damages remedy was limited to the diminution in value of their property; injunctive relief, by contrast, required monetary payment whether or not the value of the owners' property had decreased. Because there was no evidence of any decrease in property value, the court reasoned, the costs of complying with the injunction were not "damages."

We need not here decide whether the reasoning of Hanna is persuasive as a matter of California law.[28] Unlike Florida, California does not, as is noted above, absolutely limit damages for trespass to the diminution in value of the plaintiff's property. Moreover, the basic foundation of the Hanna decision—the interplay of legal and equitable remedies in tort actions in which it is entirely speculative whether the plaintiff has suffered compensable harm—differs from the relationship between the various remedies authorized by CERCLA, under which injunctive relief may be available even though legal or restitutive remedies are adequate.

The mere fact that the agencies seek an injunction in an environmental protection action does not indicate an absence of cognizable property damage or personal injury. The prima facie case for injunctive relief is identical to that for reimbursement of response costs, with the single added element of "imminent and substantial endangerment" of public health or welfare or the environment. Moreover, in its remedial aspects, the injunction results in exactly the type of expenditures involved in reimbursement of response costs, whether or not the agencies have an adequate remedy in the form of reimbursement. (See, e.g., United States v. Price (D.N.J.1983) 577 F.Supp. 1103, 1112 [Congress intended injunctive relief under 42 U.S.C. § 9606 to be "a viable alternative or concurrent means of achieving the same goal" as reimbursement under 42 U.S.C. § 9607].)

For these reasons, it would exalt form over substance to interpret CGL policies to cover one remedy but not the other. Given the practical similarity of remedies available under the environmental statutes at issue here, we believe a reasonable insured would expect both remedies to fall within coverage as "damages." Insofar as injunctive relief is an equivalent substitute for the goal of government remedial action, the distinction relied on by Hanna is inapposite in the CERCLA context.

A majority of courts have also reached this conclusion. Some have reasoned that such costs are "damages" according to the reasonable expectations of the parties, even if they would not be "damages" under technical definitions. Others have stated this conclusion in terms of public policy: costs of compliance must be interpreted as "damages" in the environmental context, because to hold otherwise would make insurance coverage hinge on the "mere fortuity" of the way in which government agencies seek to enforce cleanup requirements, would un-

**28.** In this respect, we agree with the court in Aerojet, supra, 211 Cal.App.3d at page 234, 257 Cal.Rptr. 621, that Hanna, supra, 224 F.2d 499, is distinguishable from CERCLA cases. We note, however, that the approach taken in Aerojet to resolve the issue presented here may have unintended consequences in distinguishable cases. Because Aerojet applies an extremely broad definition of "damages" (i.e., "any economic outlay compelled by law to rectify and mitigate property damage caused by the insured's pollution"), it implicitly suggests that the costs of mandatory injunctive relief in all contexts, common law as well as statutory, may be covered by CGL policies. (Id. at p. 228, 257 Cal.Rptr. 621.) We find that a more debatable proposition than the limited one—based on the peculiar juxtaposition of injunctive and reimbursement remedies in CERCLA—we endorse here. The precise issue presented in Hanna remains unresolved as a matter of California law.

reasonably constrain the agencies' choice of cleanup mechanisms, and would introduce substantial inefficiency into the cleanup process.

We agree with the underlying rationale of these decisions. Under CERCLA and similar statutes, injunctive relief and reimbursement of response costs serve substantially the same purpose. For this reason, we find CGL policy language is ambiguous as applied to remedial and mitigative costs incurred pursuant to injunction under CERCLA and similar statutes, and therefore must be construed in favor of coverage to satisfy the reasonable expectations of the insured.

In contrast to our determination, two federal Courts of Appeals have concluded that the costs of injunctive relief under CERCLA and similar statutes are not covered by CGL policies. (See NEPACCO, supra, 842 F.2d at p. 986; Armco, supra, 822 F.2d at p. 1353.) One of these decisions essentially relies on an uncritical adoption of the Hanna result. (NEPACCO, supra, 842 F.2d at p. 986 [stating that "black letter insurance law holds that claims for equitable relief are not claims for 'damages' under liability insurance contracts," while citing four cases supporting the proposition and three challenging it in the environmental context].) The other decision supports its conclusion by referring to the "prophylactic," and therefore uninsurable, nature of injunctive relief. (See, e.g., Armco, supra, 822 F.2d at p. 1353.) Because the reasoning of the Hanna court is not compelling in the CERCLA context, and because it is incorrect to portray injunctive relief under CERCLA and related statutes as wholly prophylactic in nature, we decline to follow these decisions.[18]

It is true that some costs required under environmental injunctions are prophylactic in nature (e.g., altering dumping practices to prevent recurrences of leakage). As we discuss below, these costs are not incurred "because of property damage," and therefore are not covered by CGL policies. Nevertheless, environmental injunctions requiring remedial and mitigative action result in costs that constitute "damages" under CGL policies. Because an insured would reasonably expect equal coverage of the costs of equivalent or alternative remedies, the costs of injunctive relief under the statutes in question here are "damages" for CGL purposes.[19]

**18.** We again note that the additional justification offered by these decisions for their result—the fact that coverage of the costs of injunctive relief would render the "as damages" clause of CGL policies meaningless—possesses some merit. For the reasons stated above, however, it is our view that "damages" is ambiguous in the CERCLA context and therefore should be construed in favor of coverage and in accordance with the objectively reasonable expectations of the insured, regardless of any formal or technical difficulties this reading poses.

**19.** Our conclusion—that the costs of injunctive relief as well as reimbursement of government response costs constitute "damages"—applies equally to the policies covering "ultimate net loss." As defined by the policies, "ultimate net loss" includes "the *total sum* which [FMC] * * * becomes obligated to pay by reason of * * * property damage," including "expenses" as well as "damages." (Italics added.) The plain meaning of this definition encompasses reimbursement of response costs and the costs of compliance with injunctions ordering FMC to clean up hazardous waste. For this reason, such costs are "ultimate net

3. "Because of Property Damage"

Several courts have held that government claims for injunctive relief and reimbursement of costs incurred in cleaning up disposal sites and water surrounding them are not covered by CGL policies, because such claims do not allege "property damage." We disagree. As we note above, these decisions either misperceive the basic character of remedies available under environmental statutes or apply an unduly narrow definition of "property damage." CGL policies cover sums expended as damages not only because of "harm to human or animal life" (Armco, supra, 822 F.2d at p. 1354), but more generally because of "property" damage. Contamination of the environment satisfies this requirement.

We also hold that reimbursement of response costs and the costs of injunctive relief under CERCLA and related statutes are incurred "because of" property damage. As discussed above, the mere fact that the governments may seek reimbursement of response costs or injunctive relief without themselves having suffered any tangible harm to a proprietary interest does not exclude the recovery of cleanup costs from coverage under the "damages" provision of CGL policies. For similar reasons, in plain and ordinary terms such recovery is "because of" property damage. It is immaterial whether motivations other than protection of property—for example, protection of the health of persons living near hazardous waste sites—also contribute to the agencies' pursuit of statutory relief. The Court of Appeal's emphasis on the fact that the agencies' objectives may be regulatory rather than proprietary is misplaced. Whatever their dominant motive, the event precipitating their legal action is contamination of property. The costs that result from such action are therefore incurred "because of" property damage.

This is true, moreover, whether the cleanup at issue in the underlying suits takes place on property owned by FMC, the state or federal government, or third parties. The provisions at issue here do not specify that coverage hinges on the nature or location of property damage. We therefore construe them to encompass damages because of property damage in general, regardless of by whom it is suffered.

We do agree that prophylactic costs—incurred to pay for measures taken in advance of any release of hazardous waste—are not incurred "because of property damage." Until such damage has occurred, whether on the waste site itself or elsewhere, there can be no coverage under CGL policies. Beyond this limited circumstance, however, and because the agencies in this suit allege that the waste sites themselves and water on and surrounding the sites have already been contaminated by hazardous waste, we conclude that the reimbursement and the costs of injunctive relief sought here at least in part constitute "damages because of property damage."

loss" within the meaning of these policies, as we are compelled to interpret them. (Civ.Code, § 1638 ["The language of a contract is to govern its interpretation, if the language is clear and explicit, and does not involve an absurdity."].)

### III. Conclusion

For the foregoing reasons, we conclude that the Court of Appeal erred in directing the superior court to enter summary adjudication in favor of the insurers. It is not clear, as a matter of law, that all of the relief for which FMC is potentially liable in the underlying suits cannot be deemed sums which it will be "legally obligated to pay as damages because of property damage." Although the costs of compliance with injunctions ordering FMC to undertake prophylactic measures are not covered by CGL policies covering payment of damages "because of property damage," the remaining remedies sought by the agencies in the underlying suits are not precluded from coverage as a matter of law; such relief satisfies the plain and ordinary meanings of the phrases "legally obligated," "damages," "ultimate net loss," and "because of property damage." Accordingly, we reverse the decision of the Court of Appeal and vacate its order issuing a writ of mandate, and direct the Court of Appeal to remand this case to the superior court for further proceedings consistent with this opinion.

### *Note*

As the AIU case makes clear, the federal courts have not provided consistent treatment of coverage for "damages." An illustrative case is Maryland Casualty Co. v. Armco, 822 F.2d 1348 (4th Cir.1987), in which Armco mades claim against its insurer for coverage and defense of claims for injunctive relief and reimbursement of environmental damage caused by Armco. As in AIU, the policy provided coverage suits for injury seeking "damages." Noting that it is black letter law that damages are legal not equitable, the court held that the insurer has no duty to defend unless there is a possibility of recovery under the policy. Without an allegation of legal injury there is no coverage for the purely equitable claim.

## BANKERS TRUST CO. v. HARTFORD ACCIDENT AND INDEMNITY CO.

United States District Court, Southern District of New York, 1981.
518 F.Supp. 371.

Lasker, District Judge.

This case presents the question whether an insurance policy whose coverage includes damage to the property of third persons but excludes damage to the insured's property, covers work performed on the insured's property in order to prevent damage to the property of third parties.

Bankers Trust Company and Great Lakes Realty Corp. move for summary judgment in their favor for monies allegedly due under two insurance policies issued by Hartford Accident and Indemnity Company for work done to correct a pollution problem caused by a leaking fuel oil pipe located on property adjacent to the East River.

Bankers Trust acquired title to * * * (the "property") by foreclosing on a mortgage it issued to Great Lakes. The property is located in Long

Island City on the east shore of the East River, and is bordered on the north by Rainey Park, which is owned by the City of New York. A warehouse which has an oil-fired furnace and oil tanks beneath the boiler room to store the fuel oil is situated on the property.

Plaintiffs procured from Hartford two insurance policies: General Liability Insurance Policy * * * which was limited to $100,000, coverage, and Umbrella Liability Policy * * * which had a $5,000,000 limit. * * * The policies, the terms of which are set out in the margin,[24] exclude "first party" coverage, that is, they do not insure against damage to the plaintiffs' property.

On June 15, 1977, plaintiffs were orally notified by the United States Coast Guard that the property was suspected to be the source of fuel oil polluting the East River and its shores. * * * Excavation revealed that the source of the leaking fuel was a broken pipe beneath the warehouse on the property.

Clean-up operations ensued. Work was done both off the property (in the East River and Rainey Park), and on the property. * * *

* * *

Hartford was notified of the pollution problem and plaintiffs' claims under the policies on June 23, 1977. It subsequently retained the engineering firm John B. Drinan Associates, Inc. to inspect the site and review the work done. After Drinan was retained, the firm was consulted on each step subsequently taken to correct the pollution problem. Drinan concurred that the work was done correctly and that the costs were reasonable. * * *

Plaintiffs sue to recover their expenses incurred in cleaning the oil out of the river and its shores, and in preventing further seepage by removing the oil from the property.

Hartford does not dispute that the work done to clean up the East River and Rainey Park falls within the policies' coverage. It contends, however, that the work done to remove the oil from the soil in plaintiffs' property is excluded from coverage because it was done to correct

24. The General Liability Insurance policy provided:

"The company will pay on behalf of the *insured* all sums which the *insured* shall become legally obligated to pay as *damages* because of * * * property damage to which this insurance applies, caused by an *occurrence* * * *.

"This insurance does not apply:

* * *

(k) to *property damage* to

(1) property owned or occupied by or rented to the *insured,*

(2) property used by the *insured,* or

(3) property in the care, custody or control of the *insured* or as to which the *insured* is for any purpose exercising physical control * * *."

The Umbrella Liability Policy provided:

"The Company will indemnify the *insured* for *ultimate net loss* in excess of *underlying limits* or the *self-insured retention,* whichever is the greater, because of * * * *property damage* * * * to which this insurance applies, caused by an *occurrence* which takes place anywhere in the world.

"This insurance does not apply:

(f) to *property damage* to property owned by any *named insured* * * *"

damages to plaintiffs' own property and not to property of third persons. * * *

We agree with plaintiffs that the work done on the property to prevent further oil seepage was as a matter of law within the coverage of the policies. First, it was done to prevent damage to the property of third parties. There is no dispute that the oil seepage was not affecting the use of the property by its owners. Second, Hartford does not dispute plaintiffs' assertion that if the preventive work had not been done, the oil would have continued to seep into the river for a substantial period hereafter, and that plaintiffs—and that ultimately, Hartford—would have had to spend much more to clean up the resulting damage to the river and its shores. * * * Third, it is Hartford's burden to show that the exclusion applies here. Any ambiguity in an insurance policy—and the policies here are ambiguous as to whether they include costs for preventing third party property damage—must be construed against the insurer. * * * The insurer also bears the burden to show that an exclusionary clause applies. * * * Fourth, because the policies are ambiguous as applied to this situation, the proper construction is one that yields a reasonable result. * * * Here, the reasonable result follows plaintiffs' construction: As noted above, if the policy did not cover this situation, plaintiffs could have allowed the oil to continue to pollute the river and its shores, causing further social damage and damage to third parties, and ironically ultimately costing even Hartford more money.

No New York cases have been cited addressing the question whether an insurance policy covering damage to the property of third persons also covers costs to prevent damage to third persons. Plaintiffs rely mainly on American Economy Insurance Co. v. Commons, 26 Or.App. 153, 552 P.2d 612 (1976), in which the court held that an insurance policy covering property damage covered the costs by the State of Oregon to fight a forest fire on the insured's property (which had already spread to adjoining properties) to prevent damage to forests in the area. *Commons* held that fire suppression costs are for "property damage," but did not address whether the property damage was to the insured or third persons, and the opinion does not mention an exclusionary clause for damage to the insured's property, such as that involved here. See also Globe Indemnity Company v. People, 43 Cal.App.3d 745, 118 Cal. Rptr. 75 (1974). Although for this reason *Commons* is not directly applicable, it is consistent with the conclusion that work done on a first party's property to prevent property damage to third persons is a reasonable construction of the policies at hand.

* * *

The motion for summary judgment is granted to the extent indicated above.

[Vacated for unrelated reasons.]

### *Note*

Cf. Leebov v. United States Fidelity & Guaranty Co., 401 Pa. 477, 165 A.2d 82 (1960). Does this decision mean that an insured auto owner can recover under the liability portion of his policy for the cost of getting his brakes fixed, on the theory of preventing a huge liability claim against the insurer in the future?

### *Problem*

Arsenic appears in bottles of aspirin in isolated stores throughout the country. Two deaths are caused. The manufacturer issues a recall order of millions of bottles. Does its liability insurance cover the costs of the recall? Cf. McNeilab Inc. v. North River Ins. Co., 645 F.Supp. 525 (D.N.J.1986).

## EMCASCO INSURANCE CO. v. L & M DEVELOPMENT, INC.

Supreme Court of North Dakota, 1985.
372 N.W.2d 908.

GIERKE, J.

AID Insurance Company (AID) has appealed from a district court judgment in favor of the plaintiffs in an action to determine whether or not an insurance policy issued by AID to L & M Development, Inc., also known as Wyngate, Inc. (Wyngate), afforded coverage for a property damage claim against Wyngate. We affirm.

Wyngate hired independent contractors to construct townhomes which Wyngate later sold. After Wyngate sold the townhomes, shingles blown off the townhomes in a windstorm broke windows, damaged screens, and marred siding. Pursuant to homeowner's insurance policies issued by the plaintiffs to the owners of the townhomes, plaintiffs compensated their insureds for the damages to the townhomes.

The plaintiffs brought a subrogation action against Wyngate, alleging that Wyngate breached express and implied warranties that the townhomes were constructed in a good workmanlike manner, reasonably fit for continued habitation, and free from defects. During the pendency of that action, Wyngate tendered to AID the defense of the action. AID denied coverage and refused to defend. Wyngate and the plaintiffs entered into a settlement agreement providing that the plaintiffs would collect damages, if any, only under the insurance policy issued by AID to Wyngate.

The trial court determined that the insurance policy afforded coverage for the underlying property damage claim and judgment was entered in favor of the plaintiffs. The issue on appeal is whether or not the comprehensive general liability insurance policy issued by AID to Wyngate affords coverage for the underlying property damage claim.

The insurance policy in issue provides:

"The company will pay on behalf of the insured all sums which the insured shall become legally obligated to pay as damages because of

Coverage A. bodily injury or

Coverage B. property damage

to which this insurance applies, caused by an occurrence, * * *

"Exclusions

This insurance does not apply:

"(a) to liability assumed by the insured under any contract or agreement except an incidental contract; *but this exclusion does not apply to a warranty of fitness or quality of the named insured's products or a warranty that work performed by or on behalf of the named insured will be done in a workmanlike manner;* [Emphasis added.]

* * *

"(*o*) to property damage to work performed by or on behalf of the named insured arising out of the work or any portion thereof, or out of materials, parts or equipment furnished in connection therewith; * * *"

Of the identical underscored language in exclusion (a) in a similar policy, we said in Applegren v. Milbank Mut. Ins. Co., 268 N.W.2d 114, 118 (N.D.1978): " * * * This clearly means that the policy covered and applied to the insured's warranties that the work would be performed in a workmanlike manner. We can reach no other conclusion."

AID argues that exclusion (a) relates only to those situations where an insured assumes liability under a hold harmless or indemnity contract; that the two exceptions to the contractual liability exclusion relate to the exclusion only; and that exclusion (*o*) clearly excludes coverage for property damage to the work performed by the named insured.

We construed identical exclusions (a) and (*o*) in AID Ins. Services, Inc. v. Geiger, 294 N.W.2d 411 (N.D.1980). After adopting the reasoning and conclusion in Applegren v. Milbank Mut. Ins. Co., supra, we stated:

"What Aid Insurance gives to Geiger in the form of coverage pursuant to the exception to exclusion (a), it purports to take away through the provisions of exclusion (*o*), the 'business risk' exclusion. The two exclusionary clauses are irreconcilable and patently ambiguous * * *. We believe that exclusion (a) is in conflict with exclusion (*o*) and therefore an ambiguity exists.

" * * * [I]t is well-established in North Dakota that, because an insurance policy is a contract of adhesion, any ambiguity or reasonable doubt as to the meaning of the policy is to be strictly construed against the insurer and in favor of the insured. If the language in an insurance contract will support an interpretation which will impose liability on the insurer and one which will not, the former interpretation will be adopted. Section 9–07–19, N.D.C.C., provides in part:

> 'In cases of uncertainty not removed by the preceding rules, the language of a contract should be interpreted most strongly against the party who caused the uncertainty to exist. The promisor is presumed to be such party, * * * '

"We conclude that uncertainty does exist in the present case and the language of exclusion (a) is susceptible to a construction which will impose liability on the insurer, Aid Insurance, and afford coverage to the insured, Geiger. The coexistence of exclusionary provisions (a) and (*o*) creates, at the very least, an ambiguity which must be resolved in favor of the insured so as to provide coverage. Insurance contracts are unipartite in character. They are drafted by company experts learned in the law of insurance. Insurance policies should be written so that an ordinary layperson untrained in the field of insurance, can clearly understand them and know whether or not coverage is afforded. If they are not so written, the insurance company must assume the consequences of the ambiguity and resulting confusion." [Citations omitted.] AID Ins. Services, Inc. v. Geiger, 294 N.W.2d at 414–415.

Asserting that counsel in Geiger, supra, did not adequately inform us of the insurance industry's intent in exclusions (a) and (*o*), AID asks that we overrule Geiger. We decline the invitation and adhere to the rationale and conclusion adopted in Geiger.

Whether we construe the exception to exclusion (a) as granting coverage for breach of warranty or as excepting breach of warranty from the application of the exclusion for contractual liability, thereby leaving breach of warranty within the coverage grant, which is "broad enough to include the insured's obligation to pay damages for breach of contract as well as for tort," [G. Tinker, Comprehensive General Liability Insurance—Perspective and Overview, FIC Quarterly 217, 265 (Spring 1975) ], coverage of damages arising out of a breach of warranty is clearly and specifically provided and it is not overcome by the general language in exclusion (*o*), which does not mention warranties. "The insurer has the duty to define, in clear and explicit terms, any limitations or exclusions to coverage expressed by broad terms." 2 R. Long, The Law of Liability Insurance § 10.05 (1985).

If AID intended to exclude coverage for damages arising out of a breach of warranty, the language employed in exclusions (a) and (*o*) is not well suited for accomplishing that intention. While our construction of exclusions (a) and (*o*) may represent a minority position, we note that we are not alone in holding that damages arising out of a breach of warranty are covered by the policy. See e.g., Federal Ins. Co. v. P.A.T. Homes, Inc., 113 Ariz. 136, 547 P.2d 1050 (1976); Baybutt Constr. Corp. v. Commercial Union Ins. Co., 455 A.2d 914 (Me.1983); Fresard v. Michigan Millers Mut. Ins. Co., 97 Mich.App. 584, 296 N.W.2d 112

(1980); McRaven v. F–Stop Photo Labs, Inc., 660 S.W.2d 459 (Mo.App. 1983); Commercial Union Assur. Companies v. Gollan, 118 N.H. 744, 394 A.2d 839 (1978).

We disagree with AID's assertion that our construction of the liability policy in Geiger transformed a liability policy into a performance bond. The parties generally protected by liability insurance policies and performance bonds are different and the events giving rise to liability for payment are different. See Commercial Union Assur. Companies v. Gollan, supra.

AID argues that the liability policy involved in the instant case is fundamentally different from the one in Geiger because, unlike the policy in Geiger, the policy involved here does not include "completed operations hazard" coverage, and that this difference requires a different result. Our decision in Geiger did not turn on the presence of completed operations coverage. The meaning of the exception to exclusion (a) does not depend upon the availability of completed operations coverage, which might have been, but was not, purchased. Coverage for damages arising out of a breach of "a warranty of fitness or quality of the named insured's products or a warranty that work performed by or on behalf of the named insured will be done in a workmanlike manner" is clearly and specifically provided and is not overcome by a failure of the insured to also purchase completed operations coverage. Nor is clear and specific coverage for breach of the warranties recited in the exception to exclusion (a) overcome by an exclusion of property damage included within the "completed operations hazard", which is defined in the policy without mentioning the warranties recited in the exception to exclusion (a). Limitations or exclusions from broad coverage must be clear and explicit. 2 R. Long, supra. An insurance company must assume the consequences of ambiguity and confusion. Geiger, supra.

Judgment affirmed.

## USAA CASUALTY INSURANCE CO. v. SCHNEIDER

United States District Court, Eastern District of New York, 1985.
620 F.Supp. 246.

GLASSER, DISTRICT JUDGE:

USAA Casualty Insurance Company ("USAA") brings this action seeking a declaration that it is not obligated to insure John P. McEnroe, Jr. ("McEnroe") for damages that may arise from an incident during a match at the 1983 United States Open Tennis Championship. Specifically, USAA wishes to be absolved from responsibility with regard to a suit brought by Christopher Schneider ("Schneider"), a spectator at that match. McEnroe, in return, argues that he is covered by a homeowner's policy issued to him by USAA in April, 1983, to be effective for one year. This case is before me on cross-motions for summary judgment. Because "there is no genuine issue as to any material fact," Fed.R.Civ.P. 56(c), summary judgment will be granted in favor of the plaintiff.

The pertinent facts of this case are set forth adequately by McEnroe:

2. On August 30, 1983, McEnroe competed in a first round match of the men's singles against Trey Waltke. Throughout the match Schneider was pulling for McEnroe's opponent, Waltke. In the third set, the score stood at one set apiece and each had two games in the third set. Waltke had service in the fifth game. They played the first point which was won by Waltke so that the score stood at 15–0.

3. After play on the point had been concluded and in response to Schneider's repeated heckling, McEnroe departed from the playing court and approached the box in which Schneider was sitting. The two exchanged words. At the time of his departure, McEnroe's hand waved in the air and some grains of rosin (a material used by athletes to absorb perspiration), flew in Schneider's general direction. Schneider asserts he was touched by them. The altercation between the two men lasted several moments.

4. After conclusion of the incident, McEnroe returned to the playing court. The match resumed where it had left off in the fifth game of the third set, with Waltke leading McEnroe 15–0. Play continued for some time and McEnroe ultimately defeated Waltke in the five set match, by a margin of three sets to two.

Having bested Waltke on the tennis court that day, McEnroe was soon faced with two new court battles. In October, 1983 Schneider served McEnroe with a summons and complaint in a New York state court action, recounting the incident described above and seeking damages of $6,000,000.00. In November, 1983, USAA, having been notified by McEnroe of his upcoming match with Schneider for the purpose of having USAA defend and indemnify him, brought this action.

The sole legal issue presented is whether the facts just described entitle McEnroe to protection under the homeowner's policy mentioned earlier. The relevant portions of that policy are as follows:

SECTION II—LIABILITY COVERAGES

COVERAGE E PERSONAL LIABILITY

If a claim is made or a suit is brought against any *insured* for damages because of *bodily injury* * * * to which this coverage applies, [USAA] will:

a. pay up to [its] limit of liability for the damages for which the insured is legally liable; * * *

SECTION II—EXCLUSIONS

1. Coverage E—*Personal Liability* * * * do[es] not apply to *bodily injury* * * *:

* * *

b. arising out of business pursuits of any *insured* * * * This exclusion does not apply to:

(1) activities which are ordinarily incident to non-business pursuits * * *

USAA maintains that any injury that may have been sustained by Schneider "arose out of" McEnroe's "business pursuits", i.e., his competition in a professional tennis tournament, and is thus excluded from coverage. McEnroe argues that his interaction with Schneider, although occurring in the midst of a tennis match, is an activity "ordinarily incident to non-business pursuits," and is therefore embraced by the exclusion.

In interpreting an insurance policy, it is a well-settled principle that "[w]hen the terms used are clear and unambiguous, they are generally to be taken and understood in their plain, ordinary and proper sense." McGrail v. Equitable Life Assur. Soc., 292 N.Y. 419, 424, 55 N.E.2d 483, 486 (1944). Reading McEnroe's homeowner's policy "as a layman would read it and not as it might be analyzed by an attorney or insurance expert," 13 Appleman, Insurance Law and Practice, § 7384 at 99 (1976), it is indisputable that the tennis match on August 30, 1983 was a "business pursuit" with regard to McEnroe and that any injury suffered by Schneider during the match "arose out of" this pursuit. As to the first point, there is simply no question that McEnroe is a professional tennis player who participated in the 1983 U.S. Open to compete for prize money and to advance his career. Indeed, in his answer, McEnroe concedes that "he played the August 30 match for the purpose of engaging in a business pursuit." Answer of Defendant McEnroe ¶ 15.

As to the second point, however, McEnroe denies that "the incident * * * arose out of a business pursuit within the meaning of the insurance policy." Id. McEnroe argues that non-business activities do not become business pursuits, nor may they be said to arise out of such pursuits, simply because they occur in a business setting. See, e.g., Farmers Insurance Exchange v. Sipple, 255 N.W.2d 373, 375 (Minn. 1977) ("Personal acts * * * do not become part of a business pursuit * * * merely because [they are] performed during business hours and on business property.") Yet McEnroe's own rendition of the facts belies the assertion that his altercation with Schneider was merely coincidental to the tennis match. The observation that "Schneider was pulling for McEnroe's opponent" and the admission that McEnroe approached Schneider "*in response to* [his] repeated heckling" (emphasis added) make plain that, in ordinary parlance, the altercation did "arise out of" the tennis match. Put another way, "but for this business pursuit, the [altercation] would not have occurred." Kermans v. Pendleton, 62 Mich.App. 576, 233 N.W.2d 658, 660 (1975).

The factual setting of this case also undermines McEnroe's reliance on the clause excepting "activities which are ordinarily incident to non-business pursuits" from the reach of the "business pursuits" exclusion. McEnroe contends that his altercation with Schneider should be considered a non-business activity because it was a "frolic and detour" from the tennis match, not in furtherance of any business pursuit. Citing a line of cases involving various pranks and practical jokes, McEnroe asserts that a "momentary deviation from * * * 'business pursuits'— * * * horseplay * * *—should be classified as an activity ordinarily incident to non-business pursuits * * *." State Farm Fire & Cas. Co. v. National Union Fire Ins. Co., 87 Ill.App.2d 15, 230 N.E.2d 513, 515 (1967). Whether or not these cases are correctly decided, they are simply inapposite to the facts at issue. McEnroe can claim a "momentary deviation" from his business pursuit only by defining that pursuit far too narrowly. Unlike the occupations involved in the "horseplay" cases—State Farm, supra (elevator repairman), Morrill v. Gallagher, 370 Mich. 578, 122 N.W.2d 687 (1963) (general manager), Jackson v. Lajaunie, 270 So.2d 859 (La.1972) (service station operator)—professional tennis is a form of entertainment whose very existence depends on the participation of third parties, its fans. McEnroe's attempt to describe his business pursuit as including only the course of play, and excluding all interaction with spectators, is unrealistic. The attitude of the fans, whether hushed in a close match, or effusive in their support of a local favorite, is integral to the business of professional tennis. Likewise, like a baseball player doffing his cap after a home run, or a wide receiver dancing in the end zone after a touchdown, a tennis player plies his trade and gains an audience not only by gracefully executing lobs and passing shots, but also by graciously accepting the cheers of the crowd after a hard-fought victory.

The understanding that the business of tennis is not confined solely to the game of tennis is not lost on those who promote that business. The Tournament Regulations of the Men's International Professional Tennis Council provide, for example, that "[a] player participating in the finals of a tournament * * * must attend and participate in the final ceremonies after the match * * * " Art. V, § I. Perhaps more to the point are rules directing that players shall not verbally or physically "abuse any * * * spectator * * * within the precincts of the tournament site." Art. V, §§ Q, R. Violations of these latter rules during a match may subject the player to penalties ranging from a warning to a default of the entire match. Art. V, §§ Q, R, V. Because the incident with Schneider could have had an immediate and substantial effect on McEnroe's business pursuit, i.e., the tennis match in which he was participating, it defies common sense to argue that this business pursuit was somehow suspended for the "several moments" during which the incident took place. Instead, the only reasonable conclusion is that, in the unambiguous language of the policy at issue, any injury that Schneider may have suffered did arise out of McEnroe's business pursuit.

For the reasons stated herein, plaintiff's motion for summary judgment is granted.

## *Note*

## The "Business Pursuit" Exclusion in H.O. Policies

Commercial enterprises and providers of professional services can obtain (at some cost perhaps) coverage for damage to others arising out of their activities. Homeowner insurers quite naturally do not wish to either defend or indemnify for such damages. Just as with damages arising out of the use etc. of automobiles the homeowner insurers have inserted an exclusion as to the insureds' "business pursuits" or "business enterprises" or "professional services." In doing so they have encountered parallel perils of interpretation; as for example, in Pacific Indemnity Co. v. Linn, 766 F.2d 754 (3d Cir.1985):

Robert Linn, D.O., a specialist in nutritional and family medicine, was well insured by four policies—two professional liability policies; one generalized personal injury policy (excluding injury "due to rendering or failure to render any professional service"); and a H.O. policy insuring against negligent personal acts (excluding "activities in connection with a business solely owned by the insured.")

In 1976, Dr. Linn wrote *The Last Chance Diet,* a program for a protein-sparing fast diet. Soon after publication, numerous actions for personal injury or death began to be filed by readers (or survivors of readers) of the book, none of whom had been patients of the doctor. The various insurers raised questions of coverage and the duty to defend. For purposes of brevity it may be stated that these issues were resolved against the professional liability insurers in all cases where medical malpractice was alleged in the underlying actions. As to the C.G.L. policy, it was decided that the "professional services" exclusion was not effective since it applied only to office visits. (It was also held that neither the "products hazard" nor the "completed operations" exclusion of the C.G.L. applied).

As regards the H.O. policy exclusion, it might at first seem highly improbable that coverage could be extended to the untoward consequences of a highly profitable venture of an osteopath cum author, and as to those bookreader plaintiffs alleging only professional negligence, the decision agreed. However the court concluded that the H.O. insurer had the duty to defend all the suits alleging that Dr. Linn was negligent in writing the book (a negligent personal act "which falls outside the ambiguous personal services exemption"). Nor was Dr. Linn engaged in a "business," said the court, in authoring a diet book.

*Query:* Is not the pleading of the "negligent writing of a book" to evade the "business pursuits" exclusion the same as pleading the "negligent entrustment" of an auto to evade the "use, operation or maintenance" exclusion in a H.O. policy?

## AMERICAN STATES INSURANCE COMPANY v. ALLSTATE INSURANCE COMPANY

District Court of Appeal of Florida, Fifth District, 1986.
484 So.2d 1363.

ORFINGER, JUDGE.

When a dog which is riding in the back of a pickup truck bites a passenger who has just exited from it, does the injury to the passenger arise "out of the use, operation or maintenance" of the truck? The trial court held that under the facts of this case it did not. We affirm.

William C. Connor drove his mother's pickup truck to a store to make a purchase. Accompanying him in the truck was a friend, William J. Sullivan. In the back of the pickup, which was equipped with a topper and rear window, was William Connor's pit bull dog, Lila, just along for the ride. When they reached the store, Connor stopped the truck and both men got out. As Sullivan passed the open rear window, Lila bit him, causing serious injury.

Sullivan made a claim against William's mother, June V. Connor, who referred the claim to American States Insurance Company, her homeowner's insurance carrier. American States settled the claim with Sullivan, took an assignment of June Connor's rights, then in turn filed this action for reimbursement against Allstate Insurance Company, June Connor's automobile insurance carrier. Allstate denied liability, asserting lack of coverage because the incident did not arise "out of the ownership, maintenance or use" of the motor vehicle, as required by the policy of insurance.

This court has previously held that where a motor vehicle is merely the *situs* of an injury that could have happened anywhere, the injuries do not arise out of the "ownership, maintenance or use" of the motor vehicle. *Reynolds v. Allstate Insurance Company,* 400 So.2d 496 (Fla. 5th DCA 1981). Other courts have applied the same principle in various factual situations. *See Doyle v. State Farm Mutual Automobile Insurance Company,* 464 So.2d 1277 (Fla. 3d DCA 1985) (injuries suffered at the hands of a robber who shot the insured as he exited his automobile, held not to have arisen out of ownership or use of automobile); *Allstate Insurance Company v. Famigletti,* 459 So.2d 1149 (Fla. 4th DCA 1984) (injury to insureds who were shot by a neighbor when they passed by in their automobile, did not arise out of the ownership or use of the automobile); *Hutchins v. Mills,* 363 So.2d 818 (Fla. 1st DCA 1978), *cert. denied,* 368 So.2d 1368 (Fla.1979) (accidental shooting of decedent by insured while using the flatbed of his truck as a deer stand, held not "arising out of the use" of the truck); *Watson v. Watson,* 326 So.2d 48 (Fla. 2d DCA 1976) (death of the son who was killed when the pistol discharged as he was removing it from his father's car at the scene of an accident so that the car could be taken to a garage for repairs, held not to have arisen out of the ownership, maintenance or use of the car).

The appellant relies primarily on *Government Employees Insurance Company v. Novak,* 453 So.2d 1116 (Fla.1984) and *National Indemnity Company v. Corbo,* 248 So.2d 238 (Fla. 3d DCA 1971), but these cases are clearly distinguishable on their facts. In *Novak,* while noting that the phrase "arising out of the use of a motor vehicle" is a comprehensive term which should be liberally construed to extend coverage broadly, the supreme court held that there must be some nexus between the motor vehicle and the injury. In *Novak,* the majority of the court found the nexus in the fact that the person who attacked and injured the insured wanted to use the vehicle because he shot the insured, pulled her out of the car and drove off in it after he had been refused a ride. Thus, the use of the car was the reason for the attack, and a sufficient nexus. While *Corbo* is closer, the dog which bit the plaintiff in that case was a guard dog owned by the insured and being transported to the insured's place of business at the time of the incident. Thus, the transportation of the dog was the sole reason for the vehicle's use at that time, thereby providing the nexus between the use of the automobile and the injury.

Here, the only purpose of the trip was to go to the store, and the dog was merely along for the ride, as was the passenger. The accident occurred at the vehicle, but it did not arise out of the use of the vehicle.

Affirmed.

### *Note*

### *Arising out of "use, maintenance or operation" of car*

Issues of fact, issues of causation, and imaginative interpretation tinged with a bit of the "reasonable expectation" approach, characterize the surprisingly large number of cases which turn upon this bit of phraseology. Consistency, is not to be expected; but, in general, it may be safely pointed that the average owner's or permittee's expectancy would envision the automobile's use as limited to its use as a vehicle. (Indeed policies may be so worded). Parents with even a limited recall of their own escapades might well cringe at the implications of full liability for all that may take place in the family auto. A sampling of recent cases may give a sense as to how things are going. (For another dog case similar to main decision see Duvigneaud v. Government Employees Insurance Co., 363 So.2d 1292 (La. App.1978).) The seeming gist of the court's opinion are given at the conclusion of the exercise.

*The vehicle as a helpful appliance or tool*

1. The insured, under first party insurance (no fault) saw ripe plums along highway. Unable to reach them from bed of the truck, he stood with both feet on top of the side panel, and fell off. Leverette v. Aetna Casualty and Surety Co., 157 Ga.App. 175, 276 S.E.2d 859 (1981).

2. Insured (auto liability policy) also owned an airplane (not covered) with a dead battery. He was charging the plane's battery with jumper wires from the car when the plane took off down runway damaging other aircraft. Associated Indemnity Corp. v. Warner, 143 Ariz. 567, 694 P.2d 1181 (1985).

3. Named insured utilized the top of a car as a gun rest. A deflected bullet tore through top of car injuring occupant. National Farmer's Union Property & Casualty Co. v. Gibbons, 338 F.Supp. 430 (D.C.N.D.1972).

4. Suppose the insured broke bottle on his automobile to fashion a weapon which was used on a victim. Cf. Farmer's Insurance Exchange v. Hansel, 12 Cal.App.3d 570, 90 Cal.Rptr. 654 (1970) (a similar question arising in context of an uninsured motorist provision).

5. Individuals were sitting in the car loading rifles preparatory to target shooting. One of rifles accidentally discharges injuring a member of

party. Aetna Casualty & Surety Co. v. Safeco Insurance Co., 103 Cal.App.3d 694, 163 Cal.Rptr. 219 (1980).

6. Father (the insured) drove his intoxicated son in his (father's) car over to son's own car. Son then ran own car into plaintiff. Interinsurance Exchange of Auto Club v. Macias, 116 Cal.App.3d 935, 172 Cal.Rptr. 385 (1981).

*A towing case*

7. Perry and his two sons had an antique Model A Ford which was inoperable, without license plates, and uninsured. To move it the trio hooked it to a van which was insured under a "no fault" plan. The sons drove the van and Perry was steering the Model A when the procession was stopped by a police officer. When Perry was getting out of the Model A, he was fatally shot by the officer. Did his death arise out of the use of the van? Perry v. State Farm Mutual Automobile Insurance Co., 506 F.Supp. 130 (D.Minn.1980).

*A most common occurrence*

8. An auto collision. The enraged participants engage in a fist fight injuring each other. Do their auto policies apply? Cf. Day v. State Farm Mutual Insurance Co., 261 Pa.Super. 216, 396 A.2d 3 (1978) (case arising out of uninsured motorist provision).

*Projectile cases*

9. An ongoing fight between youngsters on way to rendezvous for a rumble led to beer mug being thrown from insured vehicle resulting in death of one of youths. Valdes v. Smalley, 303 So.2d 342 (Fla.App.1974), petition for certiorari discharged 341 So.2d 975 (1976).

10. Boy threw egg from moving car thereby putting out eye of pedestrian. National America Insurance Co. v. Insurance Co. of North America, 74 Cal.App.3d 565, 140 Cal.Rptr. 828 (1977).

*"Maintenance" cases*

11. Insured vehicle stalled while insured's spouse was driving it. Neighbors attempted to restart the vehicle by priming the carburetor with gas. An explosion injured the insured's son. Liberty Mutual Insurance Co. v. O'Rourke, 122 N.J.Super. 68, 298 A.2d 725 (1973).

12. Insured under a homeowner's as well as an auto policy ran out of gas. After obtaining a can full at a gas station, the insured was joined by two "good samaritans" giving assistance. Insured negligently stepped out of the assembled group onto highway and was killed. (Eichelberger v. Warner, 290 Pa.Super. 269, 434 A.2d 747 (1981).

13. Insured (under no fault policy) could not get truck started in cold weather. He decided to heat the oil pan by putting charcoal in an old tire rim, lighting it and shoving the whole thing under the pan. He seeks P.I.P. benefits. Wagner v. Michigan Mut. Liab. Ins. Co., 135 Mich.App. 767, 356 N.W.2d 262 (1984).

*"Operating" cases*

14. Thomas, age 19, was shifting gears on his VW when Diane, age 18, grabbed the steering wheel in an attempt to make Thomas stop the car. A

wreck ensued. West Bend Mut. Ins. Co. v. Milwaukee Mut. Ins. Co., 384 N.W.2d 877 (Minn.1986)

15. A 7 year old child left in car disengages the brakes. The car runs over his mother. Tucker v. State Farm Mutual Automobile Insurance Co., 154 So.2d 226 (La.App.1963).

*Concurrent Contributing Causes*

16. Insured (both auto liability and H.O.'s) shoveled some hot ashes into uncovered barrels, put the barrels into a pick-up truck and headed for the dump at 35 miles per hour. The breeze fanned the embers into flame and set the countryside afire. Waseca Mut. Ins. Co. v. Noska, 331 N.W.2d 917 (Minn.1983)

What the courts seem to have held:

1. For insurer. "The injury need not be the proximate result of 'use' in the strict sense, but it cannot be extended to something distinctly remote. Each case turns on its precise individual facts. The question to be answered is whether the injury 'originated from' or 'had its origin in' or 'grew out of' or 'flowed from' the use of the motor vehicle as a vehicle." The injury in this case resulted "neither from an accident peculiar to the motor vehicle nor was it intrinsically related to the vehicle itself."

*Query:* Suppose the plum picking activity of the pick-up was as a moving carrier for pickers along orchard rows?

2. For the insurer. But cf. with Hedlund v. Milwaukee Mutual Ins. Co., 373 N.W.2d 823 (Minn.App.1985) where owner of pick-up truck insured under a no fault policy, was injured in trying to jump start his tractor.

3. For insurer.

4. For insurer. Not "use" of car within meaning of policy.

5. No action by driver related to accident. Note the fact that the action is between insurance companies. Very frequently the car owner also has general liability protection under his H.O. policy for the consequences of actions taking place in or around autos but not arising from their use.

*Query:* If the movement of the car caused the firearm to discharge would the holding be different? Yes, according to State Farm Mutual Auto Insurance Co. v. Partridge, 10 Cal.3d 94, 109 Cal.Rptr. 811, 514 P.2d 123 (1973), wherein the offending pistol had been modified to a hair trigger condition so that it went off when car turned off paved highway onto rough trail. Accord. Southeastern Fidelity Insurance Co. v. Stevens, 142 Ga.App. 562, 236 S.E.2d 550 (1977).

6. For insurer. Liability did not arise out of "use" of father's auto. Chain of causation broken when son left father's car and got into own.

7. For beneficiary. A causal connection between the death and the use of the van.

8. No.

9. Coverage. Speed of vehicle also contributed to extraordinary velocity of the missile.

But compare with # 8 above.

10. Auto policy covered rather than H.O.'s. "Only minimal causal connection is necessary." "Need not be proximate cause." There is little uniformity here. The throwing of bottles was considered as connected with the use of car in Wyoming Farm Bureau Mutual Insurance Co. v. State Farm Mutual Auto Insurance Co., 467 F.2d 990 (10th Cir.1972), and Government Employees Insurance Co. v. Melton, 357 F.Supp. 416 (D.C.S.C.1972), affirmed 473 F.2d 909 (4th Cir.1973). Coverage was denied, however, in some of the cherry bomb cases. McDonald v. Great American Insurance Co., 224 F.Supp. 369 (D.C.R.I.1963), and Wirth v. Maryland Casualty Co., 368 F.Supp. 789 (D.C.Ky.1973), affirmed 497 F.2d 925 (6th Cir.1974). See also, Farm Bureau Mutual Insurance Co., Inc. v. Evans, 7 Kan.App.2d 60, 637 P.2d 491 (1981), where car was not in motion.

Does visualizing the auto as a launching pad help in the analysis?

11. Held to be a "use" within meaning of standard omnibus clause. Repairs were necessary to the continuation of the journey.

12. Held: both the auto and H.O.'s covered.

13. For insured. The procedure constituted "maintenance."

14. Diane was covered under parents' H.O.'s policy, not the auto insurance.

15. For insurer. No purposeful use or operation of car.

16. *Held:* the H.O.'s policy covered the negligent act of putting hot ashes into barrels as non automobile related; the auto policy also applied as its use was a contributing cause. Reliance was placed on State Farm Mut. Auto. Ins. Co. v. Partridge, 10 Cal.3d 94, 109 Cal.Rptr. 811, 514 P.2d 123 (1973) cited in example 5 above.

### *Problems*

1. Suppose a terrorist borrows car from an innocent insured, turns it into a dynamite chamber and explodes it in a crowded market place? Does an omnibus provision cover? Cf. Kraus v. Allstate Insurance Co., 258 F.Supp. 407 (D.C.Pa.1966), affirmed 379 F.2d 443 (3d Cir.1967). Would owner be liable under provisions such as § 17150 and § 17151 of the California Vehicle Code?

2. Suppose an insured car owner comes across road repairs. A flagman negligently motions him into a hidden ditch so that a third party is injured. Is the flagman an insured under an omnibus clause in the policy?

3. Insured has a no fault policy covering injuries arising out of use, etc. of an automobile. He steps on the starter of his car and is killed by an explosive device attached to ignition. Does the policy cover?

4. Suppose X is sleeping in the bed of a motorhome and falls out when it is moving. When it is parked for the night. Coverage under H.O.'s or auto no fault policy?

5. Reflect on example 16 above. Assume insured has a H.O.'s policy with the use or operation of an auto exclusion. Her daughter, driving with permission but with only rudimentary instruction, causes an accident. Can the exclusion be overridden by alleging that the insured "negligently entrusted" the car to the daughter as a contributing cause of the accident?

Numerous decisions have dealt with this ploy. An exhaustive list may be found in Southeastern Fire Ins. Co. v. Heard, 626 F.Supp. 476 (N.D.Ga.1985) together with Huggins v. Tri–County Bonding Co., 175 W.Va. 643, 337 S.E.2d 12 (W.Va.1985).

### *Note*

### *Loading and Unloading Provisions*

Closely associated with the policy clauses covering liability arising out of the "use" of a vehicle are provisions extending the coverage to include accidents during the loading and unloading period. A typical fact situation which triggers the wealth of litigation interpreting such clauses is presented in Estes Co. of Bettendorf v. Employers Mutual Casualty Co., 79 Ill.2d 228, 37 Ill.Dec. 611, 402 N.E.2d 613, 6 A.L.R.4th 679 (1980). Here Ready–Mix concrete was being delivered to a building construction site where the contractor had the forms ready. The concrete was poured by the Ready–Mix driver into a bucket connected to an overhead crane which lifted the concrete into the forms. This operation was performed by the contractor's workmen. As one filled bucket was being swung from the concrete truck over to the forms, the crane hit a high tension wire injuring the contractor's employees. The basic issue becomes whether the insurance policy of the concrete supplier covered. Said the court:

> "Loading and unloading clauses have been a feature of insurance policies for many years. A substantial body of case law has developed to assist in the construction of these clauses in particular situations. As the appellate court has noted, the decisions construing unloading clauses have utilized one of two theories to determine when unloading is complete, the 'coming to rest' doctrine or the 'complete operations' doctrine. Under the 'coming to rest' approach, the unloading process includes only the actual moving of the article from the motor vehicle until it first comes to rest. When the article has begun to move toward its final destination, independent of the motor vehicle, the vehicle is no longer connected with the process of unloading. (See American Automobile Insurance Co. v. American Fidelity & Casualty Co. (1951), 106 Cal.App.2d 630, 235 P.2d 645.) Unloading under the 'complete operations' doctrine, however, includes all the operations necessary to effect a completed delivery. (See Entz v. Fidelity & Casualty Co. of New York (1966), 64 Cal.2d 379, 412 P.2d 382, 50 Cal.Rptr. 190.) We agree with the appellate court that the 'complete operations' doctrine, which embraces all of the operations necessary to effect a completed delivery of the article, is the preferred view. See Magarick, Loading and Unloading Under the Standard Automobile Policy, 67 Dick.L.Rev. 257, 258–59 (1963); Risjord, Loading and Unloading, 13 Vand.L.Rev. 903, 904 (1960); Annot., 95 A.L.R.2d 1122, 1129 (1964).
>
> "The mere assertion of the 'complete operations' doctrine, however, will not serve to resolve this case. Those courts which have adopted this doctrine have arrived at inconsistent conclusions in resolving substantially similar controversies. Some courts following this rule have held that 'unloading' is not completed until the material has been delivered to its ultimate destination, in the present case, the concrete forms. (See St. Paul Mercury Insurance Co. v. Huitt (6th Cir.1964), 336

F.2d 37, 42; Employers' Liability Assurance Corp. v. Travelers Insurance Co. (D.Conn.1968), 293 F.Supp. 604, 607.) Other courts, applying the same doctrine, have held that loading is completed when commercial delivery has been accomplished. See Galloway Crane & Trucking Co. v. Truck Insurance Exchange (1977), 67 Cal.App.3d 386, 391, 136 Cal.Rptr. 645, 648; Liberty Mutual Insurance Co. v. Johnson, Drake & Piper, Inc. (8th Cir.1968), 390 F.2d 410, 416.

"Although it is true that the loading and unloading clause expands the scope of activities included within the use of the vehicle, we do not believe that the parties intended to extend coverage to an accident occurring after the concrete has been placed in a receptacle furnished by or on behalf of the purchaser. (Galloway Crane & Trucking Co. v. Truck Insurance Exchange (1977), 67 Cal.App.3d 386, 390, 136 Cal.Rptr. 645, 646.) We believe it more reasonable to hold that 'unloading' has been completed when, subsequent to removal of the material from the vehicle, the deliverer has finished his handling of it, and the material has been placed in the hands of the receiver at the designated reception point, despite the fact that it is necessary to transport the material thereafter to another point. * * *

"In the present case, it is unrebutted that the custom in the industry is that delivery of the premixed concrete to the purchaser is complete when placed in the first receptacle provided at the construction site. The injuries to Cosper and Jones occurred subsequent to delivery of the cement to Anderson Construction Company. The truck was unloaded so far as the concrete deposited in the bucket was concerned. At that point the concrete had been placed in the hands of the receiver at the designated reception point. Ready Mixed exercised no control over the cement, the bucket, or the crane. We therefore hold that the injuries to Cosper and Jones did not arise out of the unloading of the vehicle.

"* * * The fact that there remained additional material to be delivered will not serve to bring these subsequent injuries within the scope of the unloading clauses." * * *

## B. PROBLEMS WITH "PERMITTED" DRIVERS

___ **effect of financial responsibility laws**

___ **permission—scope, comparison with agency rules**

___ **the "omnibus clause"—regulation by statute**

___ **the "family exclusion" problem**

### *Note*

Many states require vehicle owners or operators to show the ability to satisfy a minimum financial liability arising from ownership or use of the vehicle. As an example, a portion of the California Financial Responsibility Law, West's Ann.California Vehicle Code §§ 16000ff, is reproduced below with some of the basic provisions relating to civil liability found in West's Ann.California Vehicle Code §§ 17000ff. However, the "total public policy" of the State is set forth in the West's Ann.California Insurance Code, see § 11580.05, quoted at p. 669.

CALIFORNIA VEHICLE CODE

### § 16020. Evidence of financial responsibility

(a) Every driver and every owner of a motor vehicle shall at all times be able to establish financial responsibility pursuant to Section 16021, and shall at all times carry in the vehicle evidence of the form of financial responsibility in effect for the vehicle.

(b) "Evidence of financial responsibility" means any of the following:

(1) The name of the insurance or surety company that issued a policy or bond for the vehicle that meets the requirements of Section 16056 and is currently in effect, and the number of the insurance policy or surety bond.

(2) If the owner is a self-insurer, as provided in Section 16052 or a depositor, as provided in Section 16054.2, the certificate or deposit number issued by the department.

(3) An insurance covering note, as specified in Section 382 of the INSURANCE CODE.

(4) A showing that the vehicle is owned or leased by, or under the direction of, the United States or any public entity, as defined in Section 811.2 of the Government Code.

(c) For purposes of this section, "evidence of financial responsibility" also includes the identifying symbol issued to a highway carrier by the Public Utilities Commission pursuant to Section 3543 of the Public Utilities Code and displayed on the motor vehicle.

(d) For purposes of this section, "evidence of financial responsibility" shall be in writing, and established by writing the name of the insurance company or surety company and the policy number on the vehicle registration card issued by the department.

### § 16021. Establishing financial responsibility

Financial responsibility of the driver or owner is established if the driver or owner of the vehicle involved in an accident described in Section 16000 is:

(a) A self-insurer under the provisions of this division.

(b) An insured or obligee under a form of insurance or bond which complies with the requirements of this division and which covers the driver for the vehicle involved in the accident.

(c) The United States of America, this state, any municipality or subdivision thereof, or the lawful agent thereof.

(d) A depositor in compliance with subdivision (a) of Section 16054.2.

(e) In compliance with the requirements authorized by the department by any other manner which effectuates the purposes of this chapter.

### § 16025. Accidents; exchange of information; fines and penalties

(a) Every driver involved in the accident shall, unless rendered incapable, exchange with any other driver or property owner involved in the accident and present at the scene, all of the following information:

(1) Driver's name and current residence address, driver's license number, vehicle identification number, and current residence address of registered owner.

(2) Evidence of financial responsibility, as specified in Section 16020. If the financial responsibility of a person is a form of insurance, then that person shall supply the name and address of the insurance company.

(b) Any person failing to comply with all of the requirements of this section is guilty of an infraction punishable by a fine not to exceed two hundred fifty dollars ($250).

### § 17150. Liability of private owners

Every owner of a motor vehicle is liable and responsible for death or injury to person or property resulting from a negligent or wrongful act or omission in the operation of the motor vehicle, in the business of the owner or otherwise, by any person using or operating the same with the permission, express or implied, of the owner.

### § 17151. Limitation of liability

(a) The liability of an owner, bailee of an owner, or personal representative of a decedent imposed by this chapter and not arising through the relationship of principal and agent or master and servant is limited to the amount of fifteen thousand dollars ($15,000) for the death of or injury to one person in any one accident and, subject to the limit as to one person, is limited to the amount of thirty thousand dollars ($30,000) for the death of or injury to more than one person in any one accident and is limited to the amount of five thousand dollars ($5,000) for damage to property of others in any one accident.

(b) An owner, bailee of an owner, or personal representative of a decedent is not liable under this chapter for damages imposed for the sake of example and by way of punishing the operator of the vehicle. Nothing in this subdivision makes an owner, bailee, or personal representative immune from liability for damages imposed for the sake of example and by way of punishing him for his own wrongful conduct.

### § 17152. Liability of operator

In any action against an owner, bailee of an owner, or personal representative of a decedent on account of liability imposed by Sections 17150, 17154, or 17159 for the negligent or wrongful act or omission of the operator of a vehicle, the operator shall be made a part defendant if service of process can be made in a manner sufficient to secure personal jurisdiction over the operator. Upon recovery of judgment, recourse shall first be had against the property of the operator so served.

### § 17153. Subrogation of owner

If there is recovery under this chapter against an owner, bailee of an owner, or personal representative of a decedent, the owner, bailee of an owner, or personal representative of a decedent is subrogated to all the rights of the person injured or whose property has been injured and may recover from the operator the total amount of any judgment and costs recovered against the owner, bailee of an owner, or personal representative of a decedent.

### § 17154. Bailee as operator

If the bailee of an owner with the permission, express or implied, of the owner permits another to operate the motor vehicle of the owner, then the bailee and the driver shall both be deemed operators of the vehicle of the owner within the meaning of Sections 17152 and 17153.

Every bailee of a motor vehicle is liable and responsible for death or injury to person or property resulting from a negligent or wrongful act or omission in the operation of the motor vehicle, in the business of the bailee or otherwise, by any person using or operating the same with the permission, express or implied, of the bailee.

### § 17155. Settlement of claims

Where two or more persons are injured or killed in one accident, the owner, bailee of an owner, or personal representative of a decedent may settle and pay any bona fide claims for damages arising out of personal injuries or death, whether reduced to judgment or not, and the payments shall diminish to the extent thereof such person's total liability on account of the accident. Payments aggregating the full sum of thirty thousand dollars ($30,000) shall extinguish all liability of the owner, bailee of an owner, or personal representative of a decedent for death or personal injury arising out of the accident which exists pursuant to this chapter, and did not arise through the negligent or wrongful act or omission of the owner, bailee of an owner, or personal representative of a decedent nor through the relationship of principal and agent or master and servant.

### § 17158. Owner as passenger; liability

No person riding in or occupying a vehicle owned by him and driven by another person with his permission has any right of action for civil damages against the driver of the vehicle or against any other person legally liable for the conduct of the driver on account of personal injury to or the death of the owner during the ride, unless the plaintiff in any such action establishes that the injury or death proximately resulted from the intoxication or willful misconduct of the driver.

## CURTIS v. STATE FARM MUTUAL AUTOMOBILE INSURANCE CO.

United States Court of Appeals, Tenth Circuit, 1979.
591 F.2d 572.

HOLLOWAY, CIRCUIT JUDGE.

Defendant State Farm Mutual Automobile Insurance Company appeals from a declaratory judgment, entered on a jury verdict, declaring that a liability insurance policy issued by State Farm to Robert E. Ahrens and JoAnn Ahrens extended coverage to one Joseph Wallace, the driver of the Ahrens vehicle at the time of the accident involved herein. Jurisdiction is founded upon diversity. The primary question before us is whether Wallace comes within the definition of "insured" contained in the policy's omnibus clause, as "any * * * *person* while using the *owned motor vehicle,* PROVIDED THE OPERATION AND THE ACTUAL USE OF SUCH VEHICLE ARE WITH THE PERMISSION OF THE NAMED INSURED * * * AND ARE WITHIN THE SCOPE OF SUCH PERMISSION * * *."[26]

The Ahrens family had three cars—an Oldsmobile, a Volkswagen owned by Mr. and Mrs. Ahrens, and a pickup. The older Ahrens girls, Beth and Shawnna, mainly used the Oldsmobile and Volkswagen, and Mr. Ahrens used the pickup to drive to work.

The accident in question occurred in the early morning of July 5, 1973, outside of Cheyenne, Wyoming. During the previous afternoon, Deborah Ahrens, the 14-year-old daughter of Robert and JoAnn Ahrens, had made arrangements with her friend Helen Curtis and with Brian Tottenhoff and Joseph Wallace to meet at the local ballpark between 1:00 and 2:00 a.m. to shoot off some fireworks. * * * Helen was spending the night of July 4 with Deborah at her home. Sometime between 1:30 and 2:00 a.m., Deborah and Helen left the Ahrens home—after Deborah's parents had gone to bed—and proceeded to drive the family Volkswagen to the chosen meeting place.

Deborah was not licensed to drive. She had taken the car keys from their customary location on top of the television set without her parents' knowledge. * * * On their way out of the Ahrens' neighborhood, the girls encountered Deborah's older sister, Beth, driving home in the family Oldsmobile. The two sisters stopped and talked for five or ten minutes, but Deborah's use of the Volkswagen was never discussed. * * * Before she left home, Deborah had also told Shawnna what they were going to do that night; Shawnna knew the girls were going out and made no comment either to forbid or consent to their going. However, Deborah did not tell Beth or Shawnna that she and Helen were going to pick up the boys.

**26.** The omnibus clause constitutes only one part of the five-part definition of "insured" contained in the policy. The definition as a whole states that the unqualified word "insured" includes:

(1) the named insured, and

(2) if the named insured is a *person* or *persons,* also includes his or their spouse(s), if a *resident* of the same household, and

(3) if *residents* of the same household, the relatives of the first *person* named in the declarations, or of his spouse, and

(4) any other *person* while using the *owned motor vehicle,* PROVIDED THE OPERATION AND THE ACTUAL USE OF SUCH VEHICLE ARE WITH THE PERMISSION OF THE NAMED INSURED OR SUCH SPOUSE AND ARE WITHIN THE SCOPE OF SUCH PERMISSION, and

(5) under coverages A and B any other *person* or organization, but only with respect to his or its liability for the use of such *owned motor vehicle* by an *insured* as defined in the four subsections above.

(Plaintiff's Ex. No. 1). It is evident that Wallace can fit—if at all—only within the omnibus clause (4), since he is unrelated to the named insureds, Robert E. Ahrens and JoAnn Ahrens.

Deborah and Helen picked up the boys and went to shoot off the fireworks. The four then started home around 3:30 a.m. Deborah had been driving all along, but at this point Joe Wallace asked if he could drive, and she agreed. * * * Wallace, like Deborah, was unlicensed. According to Deborah, the accident occurred about five minutes after Wallace took the wheel: "He was going too fast, and he went airbound with the car, and it went over on to the embankment."

Helen Curtis suffered extensive injuries in the accident, and her father incurred about $15,000 in medical expenses for her treatment. When State Farm disclaimed coverage as to Wallace, Helen's father brought this suit on her behalf for a determination that the defendant State Farm was obligated to defend and indemnify Wallace under the company's policy issued to Mr. and Mrs. Ahrens. As noted, a verdict and declaratory judgment adverse to the company resulted. This appeal followed.

I

The company's primary contention on appeal is that the evidence is clear that Wallace did not have permission to drive the vehicle under the terms of the omnibus clause of the policy, so that coverage did not extend to him. The company says that the district court therefore erred in its denial of a motion for a directed verdict made at the conclusion of plaintiff's case and again at the end of defendant's case, as well as in its denial of a motion for judgment n.o.v.

Wallace was not covered by the policy unless his operation and actual use of the Volkswagen were with the permission of a named insured. The district court instructed the jury that Robert Ahrens and his wife JoAnn were the named insureds under the policy and that neither named insured gave Wallace actual permission to drive the car. * * * Thus, the controlling question is whether Wallace had implied permission for use of the car so as to bring him within the coverage of the policy.

In United Services Automobile Association v. Preferred Accident Insurance Co., 190 F.2d 404, 406 (10th Cir.), we stated that:

> The necessary permission may be in the form of implied affirmative consent. It may result by implication from the relationship of the parties and their course of conduct in which they mutually acquiesced. And it may arise from a course of conduct pursued with knowledge of the facts for such time and in such manner as to signify clearly and convincingly an understanding consent which amounts in law to a grant of the privilege involved.

The question of implied permission is thus one of fact. Phoenix Assurance Co. v. Latta, 373 P.2d 146, 149 (Wyo.). Plaintiff points to much in the record which, it is said, supports the jury's implicit finding of implied permission. In view of such evidence, plaintiff argues that it would have been improper for the trial court to direct a verdict or grant judgment n.o.v. for defendant, because the evidence did not point "all one way" in favor of the moving party. Bertot v. School District No. 1, 522 F.2d 1171, 1178 (10th Cir.).

The foundation for a finding of implied permission, plaintiff argues, is the fact that JoAnn Ahrens, Deborah's mother and one of the named insureds, has been blind due to the effects of diabetes since before 1973. Because of this tragic fact, Mrs. Ahrens has had to rely on her three daughters to "take care of everything" around the house. * * * In July 1973, the two older daughters, Beth (then age 17) and Shawnna (age 16), were licensed drivers and had free use of the family cars, both for carrying out family-related responsibilities such as grocery shopping and for going to and from their part-time jobs. * * * As noted, the family custom was to keep the car keys on top of the television set; anyone who had used the car would lay the keys down on the set and anyone who wanted to use the car would take the keys off the set.

Around that time Beth also often took one of the cars out of town on recreational trips to Steamboat Springs and similar places, staying two or three days. Mrs. Ahrens knew that on such trips friends of Beth's went with her and drove the car. There was testimony that Beth's friends McCue and Fleming would sometimes drive the car on such trips and that, while neither JoAnn nor Robert Ahrens gave express permission to them to drive, both parents knew about such driving and neither objected to it. * * * Also, Shawnna was allowed to take the family cars around town frequently and drove one of the cars to work sometimes.

Thus, Beth and Shawnna were allowed to drive the cars "as they needed or liked"

—except when their father was using them. They bought gas "when they had money and they were out and they needed it"—though customarily their father would maintain the automobiles in working condition. * * * And with Beth at least, there was precedent for allowing other persons to drive the family automobiles without express permission from either parent.

With respect to Deborah, there was testimony that Mr. Ahrens had signed a statement that he had never given Deborah any restrictions as to her use of the car and that there had been no express prohibition to its use. The statement also said, however, that "Debbie was not supposed to drive this vehicle." * * * Mr. Ahrens testified that he thought his wife had been asked during the taking of earlier statements whether the parents had ever specifically told Deborah she could not take the car, that he had said they never specified she could not take it, but that it was "understood on down the line, that I think it probably started with Beth and then Shawnna and then Debbie." * * *. Both Mr. and Mrs. Ahrens testified that they had not given Deborah permission to use the car on the night of the accident and did not know that she had taken the car until they were notified about the accident.

Deborah testified that one time she had driven a family car with her father to a friend's house. She also said that once about a month before the accident she had driven the car without her father. * * * However, her parents both testified they had not known that Deborah had taken the Volkswagen out on any occasion before the accident. * * *

Plaintiff argues that because of the unusual circumstances relating to the blindness of Mrs. Ahrens, the mother and father had permitted the two older daughters to operate the family vehicles as if they had actually been owners, and that when the older daughters were aware of Deborah's going for the ride in the Volkswagen on the night of July 4, they had unqualified permission to allow Deborah to operate the car. * * * From Beth and Shawnna's implied consent that Deborah drive the car, and from Deborah's actual consent for Wallace to drive, plaintiff says there was implied consent by Mr. and Mrs. Ahrens that Wallace drive the Volkswagen at the time of the accident.[27]

We must hold that, on this record, the judgment in favor of coverage cannot stand. Plaintiff had the burden of proof to establish coverage. See Chronister v. State Farm Mutual Automobile Insurance Co., 72 N.M. 159, 381 P.2d 673, 675; 46 C.J.S. Insurance § 1641. Under the terms of the omnibus clause, permission of the named insureds, Mr. and Mrs. Ahrens, to the operation and actual use of the Volkswagen was required for coverage to apply. The only plausible theory in this case is that permission flowed from the parents to Beth and Shawnna, from them to Deborah, and from Deborah then to Wallace, the driver at the time of the accident. As noted, however, Beth and Shawnna were not told by Deborah that Wallace would even be accompanying Deborah and Helen the night of the accident and, of course, the parents did not even know that Deborah was going to use the car.

In view of the broad permission given by the parents to Beth and Shawnna for use of the family cars, an inference might be drawn that the older daughters as first permittees could permit Deborah to use the Volkswagen. See Gillen v. Globe Indemnity Co., 377 F.2d 328, 331 (8th Cir.); Krebsbach v. Miller, 22 Wis.2d 171, 125 N.W.2d 408, 411; Baesler v. Globe Indemnity Co., 33 N.J. 148, 162 A.2d 854, 857; Government Employees Insurance Co. v. Lammert, 483 S.W.2d 652 (Mo.Ct.App.). The trial judge apparently accepted such a view as valid under Wyoming law since he charged the jury that "the named insured's permission to a second permittee need not be express, *but may be implied from the broad nature of scope of the initial permission,* or from the conduct of the parties and from the attendant facts and circumstances."

The difficulty, however, is that here it is not the driving of Deborah as a second permittee which is in question, but that of Wallace as a *third* permittee. We note again that neither of the first permittees, Beth and Shawnna, were told by Deborah that Wallace was to be in the car with

**27.** There is no evidence which would support an inference that Deborah had direct permission to drive the Volkswagen from her parents. For this reason it cannot be said that Wallace had implied permission from Mr. and Mrs. Ahrens as the named insureds merely because he had Deborah's actual permission to drive. See Travelers Insurance Co. v. Weatherford, 520 S.W.2d 726 (Tenn.); State Farm Mutual Automobile Insurance Co. v. Strang, 27 Utah 2d 362, 496 P.2d 707; Bilsten v. Porter, 547 P.2d 255 (Colo.Ct.App.).

Deborah and Helen. We are convinced that implied permission cannot be stretched so far as to include the driving of Wallace on the night of the accident. See West v. McNamara, 159 Ohio St. 187, 111 N.E.2d 909; Bailey v. General Insurance Co., 265 N.C. 675, 144 S.E.2d 898; Novo v. Employers' Liability Assurance Corp., 295 Mass. 232, 3 N.E.2d 737, denying coverage as to third permittees.[28] A scintilla of evidence, such as the remote permission of the parents given to Beth and Shawnna to drive the family cars, was not enough to raise a jury question of implied permission for Wallace to drive the Volkswagen. We are convinced that the evidence points only one way and is not susceptible of a reasonable inference that Wallace had any implied permission of the parents to drive their car. Bertot v. School District No. 1, supra, 522 F.2d 1171, 1175–76.

* * *

Plaintiff Curtis further contends that if the company were to prevail here, then an undesirable situation would result, contrary to the public's understanding about insurance coverage. The argument is that if any children were riding in a vehicle driven and operated by a child of the owner, and that child were to permit another child to drive, then according to the company there would be no coverage, contrary to the public's expectation. This policy argument does not persuade us. We cannot impose liability contrary to the terms of the agreement and without justification in the facts of record. As the Supreme Court of Wyoming stated in Wyoming Farm Bureau Mutual Insurance Co. v. May, supra, 434 P.2d at 511–12, in rejecting a similar public policy argument:

> Granting that the need for better regulation of use of highways is a meritorious and even a necessary objective, to argue that liability coverage of one person should be extended to cover another simply because it is desirable that all drivers of motor vehicles should be covered, is whimsical and unsupported either in reason or by law. This contention is without merit.

For these reasons we conclude that the verdict and judgment cannot stand and that the defendant was entitled to judgment notwithstanding the verdict. Accordingly, the judgment is reversed and the cause is remanded for entry of judgment in accordance with this opinion.

**28.** We find only one case holding that a third permittee was covered under an omnibus clause and it is easily distinguished from this case, as well as from *West, Bailey* and *Novo.* In Boyer v. Massachusetts Bonding & Insurance Co., 277 Mass. 359, 178 N.E. 523, the named insured lent the vehicle to his son (the first permittee) who in turn permitted one Chester Carter (the second permittee) to take the car to Massachusetts and have use of it, and then leave it with his family to be sold. Chester Carter left the car with his father, who permitted Chester's brother Lloyd to use the car, and Lloyd's use resulted in the accident. It was found that the insured's son (the first permittee) had been given full use and custody of the car and that his acts were within his authority.

On appeal, the Massachusetts Court referred to the fact that the insured "knew what his son had done, and [that] it could be found that he assented to the use of the vehicle by the Carters, although the details of that use were not specifically authorized." Thus, *Boyer* is unlike the instant case where the named insureds had no knowledge that either Deborah or Wallace would use the car.

## UNIVERSAL UNDERWRITERS INSURANCE CO. v. TAYLOR

Supreme Court of Appeals of West Virginia, 1991.
185 W.Va. 606, 408 S.E.2d 358.

WORKMAN, J.

* * *

On November 22, 1986, Carl Taylor entered the premises of Harry Green in Clarksburg, West Virginia, for the ostensible purpose of purchasing an automobile. Mr. Taylor requested permission from a salesperson to take a black 1986 Camaro to the residence of a friend to ask if she approved of the vehicle prior to his purchase of it. The salesperson gave Mr. Taylor permission to take the vehicle at approximately 12:20 p.m., but informed Mr. Taylor that the vehicle was to be returned no later than 1:00 p.m. that same day.

When Mr. Taylor failed to return the vehicle to Harry Green at the appointed hour, Harry Green notified the West Virginia State Police between 3:00 p.m. and 3:30 p.m. that Mr. Taylor had stolen the Camaro. On December 7, 1986, sixteen days after Mr. Taylor had initially driven away from Harry Green in the dealership's vehicle, Mr. Taylor was involved in an automobile accident which resulted in the death of Robert F. Beafore.

On August 2, 1988, Robert J. Beafore brought suit against Mr. Taylor and Harry Green in the Circuit Court of Marion County, West Virginia, as administrator of the estate of Robert F. Beafore. That civil action was predicated on two counts of negligence: (1) Mr. Taylor was negligent in causing the death of Robert F. Beafore; and (2) Harry Green was negligent in allowing Mr. Taylor to steal its vehicle. Harry Green ultimately settled the negligence claim filed against it for the sum of $250,000 and Robert J. Beafore proceeded to trial against Mr. Taylor.

At the time Mr. Taylor stole the vehicle from Harry Green, the dealership was insured by a policy issued by Universal. Universal filed a declaratory judgment action in the Circuit Court of Marion County, West Virginia, against Mr. Taylor to resolve whether it owed coverage to Mr. Taylor under the policy. On January 18, 1990, the circuit court entered an order in favor of Universal, finding that the insurance policy Universal issued to Harry Green did not provide coverage to an individual who stole a vehicle from its insured. It is the circuit court's decision in the declaratory judgment action regarding lack of coverage that forms the basis for this appeal.

The sole question on appeal is whether Universal has a duty to provide coverage to Mr. Taylor under the policy which it issued to Harry Green. Appellant urges this Court to find coverage pursuant to the mandatory omnibus clause adopted by this state in 1967. The omnibus clause requires that all motor vehicle insurance policies "shall contain a provision insuring the named insured and any other person, except a bailee for hire and any persons specifically excluded by any restrictive endorsement attached to the policy, responsible for the use of or using the motor vehicle with the consent, expressed or implied, of the named insured or his spouse against liability for death or bodily injury sustained, or loss or damage occasioned within the coverage of the policy or contract as a result of negligence in the operation or use of such vehicle by the named insured or by such person: Provided, That in any such automobile liability insurance policy or contract, or endorsement thereto, if coverage resulting from the use of a non-owned automobile is conditioned upon the consent of the owner of such motor vehicle, the word 'owner' shall be construed to include the custodian of such non-owned motor vehicles." W.Va.Code § 33–6–31(a) (Supp.1991).

The purpose of an omnibus clause in an automobile insurance policy, as this Court recognized in syllabus point 1 of State Farm Mutual Automobile Insurance Co. v. Allstate Insurance Co., 154 W.Va. 448, 175 S.E.2d 478 (1970), is "to extend coverage, in proper circumstances, to any person using the insured vehicle, and to afford greater protection to the public generally. . . ." Consistent with that purpose, we have recognized that the omnibus clause "is remedial in nature and must be construed liberally so as to provide insurance coverage where possible." Burr v. Nationwide Mut. Ins. Co., ___ W.Va. ___, 359 S.E.2d 626, 632 (1987); see generally 7 Am.Jur.2d Automobile Insurance § 248 (1980) (recognizing liberalizing purpose of omnibus clause as protecting "any person injured . . . by giving him a cause of action against the insurer for injuries deemed by law to have been caused by the operation of the car").

Universal contends that, notwithstanding the state motor vehicle omnibus clause, the policy definition of an insured excepts Mr. Taylor from any category of individuals to which it owes coverage. The policy definition upon which Universal relies to support its position defines an insured with respect to an auto hazard as "[a]ny other person or organization required by law to be an INSURED while using an AUTO covered by this Coverage Part within the scope of YOUR permission." Universal maintains that Mr. Taylor's use of the vehicle at the time of the accident was outside the scope of the insured's permission based on his failure to return the vehicle by 1:00 p.m. on the same date on which he test-drove it, as the salesperson had directed. Relying solely on the policy language which conditions coverage on permission, appellee argues that coverage is precluded.

Issues of coverage involving application of an omnibus clause are resolved pursuant to one of three judicially-created tests. See Annotation, Automobile Liability Insurance: Permission or Consent to Employee's Use of Car Within Meaning of Omnibus Coverage Clause, 5 A.L.R.2d 600, 626–43 (1949 and Later Case Service 1985) (recognizing three theories for interpreting omnibus clauses: (1) the strict or conversion rule which requires use precisely within scope of permission granted, (2) the "minor deviation" rule, and (3) the liberal or "initial permission" rule); see also 6C J. Appleman, Insurance Law and Practice §§ 4366–4368 (1979 & Supp.1990). In this case, appellant advances the use of the "initial permission" rule whereas Universal argues that the "minor deviation" rule controls. Under the liberal or "initial permission" rule, "the bailee need only have received permission in the first instance, and any use while it remains in his possession is with permission though that use is for a purpose not contemplated by the bailor when he parted with possession of the vehicle. In other words, if the original taking was with the insured's consent, every act subsequent thereto while the bailee is driving the car is held to be with the insured's permission in order to permit a recovery under the omnibus clause. Under this rule a deviation from the permitted use is immaterial, the only essential thing being that permission be given for use in the first instance." 7 Am.Jur.2d, supra, at § 265 (footnote omitted).

The "minor deviation" rule provides that "if the use made by an employee or other bailee is not such a gross violation, even though it may have amounted to a deviation, protection is still afforded to the bailee under the omnibus clause." Id. at § 266. Application of the "minor deviation" theory has resulted in a denial of coverage when the operator of the vehicle violates instructions regarding (1) the time of operation; (2) the purpose of the operation; (3) the route the vehicle is to be driven; and (4) the person who is to operate the vehicle. See, e.g., Aetna Casualty & Sur. Co. v. Anderson, 200 Va. 385, 105 S.E.2d 869 (1958).

Universal argues that Mr. Taylor not only committed a "minor deviation" but in fact deviated grossly; (1) from the extent or scope of the initial permission; (2) as to the distance he was authorized to travel; (3) from the time limits of the initial permission; and (4) from the purpose of the initial permission. Appellee further argues that this Court in Collins v. New York Casualty Co., 140 W.Va. 1, 82 S.E.2d 288 (1954), specifically adopted the "minor deviation" standard and explicitly rejected the "initial permission" rule.

To support its position that West Virginia is an "initial permission" jurisdiction in operation, if not at law, appellant argues that once the omnibus clause was enacted in 1967, this Court's holding in Collins was no longer valid. Appellant argues that states that have a statutory insurance scheme similar to West Virginia, referring to the combination of an omnibus statute and a mandatory insurance statute, have been determined to be "initial permission" jurisdictions. Appellant further maintains that the circuit court's ruling runs counter to this state's public policy of requiring mandatory insurance coverage to make the owners of automobiles financially responsible for damages caused by their automobiles. Finally, appellant asserts that this Court has implicitly adopted the "initial permission" rule in recent decisions by virtue of its repeated recognition of the liberalizing purpose of omnibus clauses.

In Allstate Insurance Co. v. Jensen, 109 N.M. 584, 788 P.2d 340 (1990), the New Mexico Supreme Court squarely addressed the issue facing this Court: whether the enactment of an omnibus clause renders the state an "initial permission" jurisdiction which in turn requires an insurer to "provide coverage to any person using the insured vehicle with the owner's consent, without regard to any restrictions or understanding between the parties on the particular use for which the permission was given." Id. at 587, 788 P.2d at 343. Like West Virginia, New Mexico has in effect as a part of its Mandatory Financial Responsibility Act the standard omnibus language which requires that all motor vehicle liability policies "insure the person named in the policy and any other person, as insured, using any such motor vehicle with the express or implied permission of the named insured." N.M.Stat.Ann. § 66–5–221(A)(2) (1978); see W.Va.Code § 17D–4–12(b)(2).

The insurance policy at issue in the Jensen case, similar to the Harry Green policy, contained language which provided coverage in addition to the named insured to " '[a]ny other person with respect to the owned automobile, provided the use thereof is with the permission of the insured and within the scope of that permission.' " 788 P.2d at 341. Just as in this case, the insurer in Jensen sought to obtain a declaratory judgment ruling that the driver of the insured's vehicle was not a permissive driver within the meaning of the policy's omnibus clause based on the driver's excessive deviation from his announced purpose for using the vehicle. Id.

Recognizing that a "contract for liability insurance cannot be more restrictive than the statutory clause," the Jensen court articulated the following conflict between the New Mexico omnibus clause and the Allstate insurance policy provision: "While the Allstate policy clearly indicates that permission to use the vehicle is defined by the particular use being made of it at the time of the accident, we do not believe that the statutory provision is so qualified." 788 P.2d at 342–43. To resolve this conflict, the New Mexico court looked to the statement of legislative purpose accompanying the state's Mandatory Financial Responsibility Act: "The purpose of the Mandatory Financial Responsibility Act is to require and encourage residents of the state of New Mexico who own and operate motor vehicles upon the highways of the state to have the ability to respond in damages to accidents arising out of the use and operation of a motor vehicle. *It is the intent that the risks and financial burdens of motor vehicle accidents be equitably distributed among all owners and operators of motor vehicles within the state.*" Id. (quoting N.M.Stat. Ann. § 66–5–201.1 (1978) and emphasis supplied).

Based upon its conclusion that mandatory automobile liability insurance "is for the benefit of the public generally, innocent victims of automobile accidents, as well as the insured[,]" the Jensen court ruled that "[a]n owner may certainly impose restrictions on the particular use of a loaned vehicle, and we do not mean to discourage such agreements between individuals. However, we do not believe the legislature intended that the owner's liability coverage for the motor vehicle be affected by such understandings. * * * [w]e conclude that the omnibus clause of the Allstate liability policy must provide coverage to any person using the insured vehicle with the owner's consent, without regard to any restrictions or understanding between the parties on the particular use to which the permission was given. We wish to emphasize that we construe Section 66–5–221(A)(2) to adopt what may be called the initial permission rule because we believe the legislature intended to accomplish this result." 788 P.2d at 343.

We find the reasoning employed by the court in Jensen both instructive and persuasive on the issue of what we will refer to as the "legislative" enactment of the "initial permission" rule. Like the New Mexico court, we find a conflict between the policy provision which attempts to limit coverage for additional insureds based on whether the driver was within the scope of permitted use at the time of the accident. Continuing the Jensen analysis, this Court has also recognized that "[a]ny provision in an insurance policy which attempts to contravene W.Va.Code, 33–6–31(a) is of no effect." Syl.Pt. 2, Burr, 359 S.E.2d 626. Accordingly, if we determine that West Virginia is an "initial permission" jurisdiction based on the legislative intent underlying the omnibus clause, as did the Jensen court with regard to the New Mexico statute, then the policy provision at issue which conditions coverage for additional insureds on the scope of permission is unenforceable because it alters by contract what is intended by the statute.

In contrast to the New Mexico statute, we do not have a statement of legislative intent incorporated into either of the omnibus statutes. See W.Va.Code §§ 33–6–31(a), 17D–4–12(b)(2). The absence of such a statement, however, does not preclude application of the Jensen rationale because the legislative intent underlying enactment of omnibus statutes can arguably be said to be universal in nature. Moreover, this Court has had the opportunity previously to comment on the legislative intent underlying the motor vehicle omnibus clause and made the following observation: "The mandatory omnibus requirements imposed by W.Va.Code, 33–6–31(a), indicate that the legislature has demonstrated a clear intent to afford coverage to anyone using a vehicle with the owner's permission as a means of giving greater protection to those who are involved in automobile accidents. The statute should be liberally construed to effect coverage." Syl.Pt. 3, Burr, 359 S.E.2d 626.

Having concluded that the legislature's enactment of the omnibus clause evinces an unmistakable intent to maximize insurance coverage for the greater protection of the public and that effectuation of such intent requires a broad interpretation of the statute, it necessarily follows that the "initial permission" rule rather than the "minor deviation" rule best comports with and aids in the accomplishment of this "policy of liberalizing coverage." Id. at 632. We concur with the New Jersey Supreme Court in Matits v. Nationwide Mutual Insurance Co., 33

N.J. 488, 166 A.2d 345 (1960), that the "conversion" and "minor deviation"

> rules making coverage turn on the scope of permission given in the first instance, render coverage uncertain in many cases, foster litigation as to the existence or extent of any alleged deviations, and ultimately inhibit achievement of the legislative goal. *We think that the 'initial permission' rule best effectuates the legislative policy of providing certain and maximum coverage, and is consistent with the language of the standard omnibus clause automobile liability insurance policies.* Id. at 496, 166 A.2d at 349 (emphasis supplied).

Adoption of the "initial permission" rule as the controlling standard furthers the "important policy * * * of assuring that all persons wrongfully injured have financially responsible persons to look to for damages." Odolecki v. Hartford Accident & Indem. Co., 55 N.J. 542, 549, 264 A.2d 38, 42 (1970) (citation omitted). Based on our recognition that "a liability insurance contract is for the benefit of the public as well as for the benefit of the named or additional insured * * *," we hereby determine that the state motor vehicle omnibus clause requires an insurer to provide coverage when permission has been granted by the insured owner of the vehicle or its authorized agent to a driver who then causes injury or property damage during the permissive use. Given the remedial nature of the omnibus clause, insurance coverage is not affected by the fact that the driver's use of the vehicle may have exceeded or differed from the owner's or his agent's specifications. Id. We hereby overrule our previous decision in Collins to the extent that Collins designated West Virginia as a "minor deviation" rule state.

Unlike the insurance policy provision, neither of the omnibus statutes attempt to limit coverage based on the scope of permission. Since use, rather than scope of permission is the only relevant factor in this Court's interpretation of the omnibus statute, the policy provision must be viewed as contravening W.Va.Code § 33–6–31(a) and is therefore unenforceable under this Court's holding in Burr. See 359 S.E.2d at 626; cf. Jordan v. Consolidated Mut. Ins. Co., 59 Cal.App.3d 26, 130 Cal.Rptr. 446 (1976) (only after California legislature amended its omnibus clause such that use of the insured vehicle must be within scope of permission was coverage effected by parameters of restricted use). Although vehicle owners may certainly place restrictions on the use of their vehicles, we agree with the Jensen court that the legislature, by its enactment of the omnibus clauses, did not intend that the owner's liability coverage be affected by such restrictions. To suggest otherwise would clearly defeat the purpose of an omnibus clause and would invite a swearing contest regarding the existence of any purported restriction and its terms.

Universal argues alternatively that even if this state chooses to adopt the "initial permission" rule, Mr. Taylor's theft of the vehicle from Harry Green vitiates the permission granted by the dealership. Several courts that have adopted the "initial permission" rule have implemented a limitation which annuls coverage in cases of theft or the like. See Matits, 166 A.2d at 349 (following granting of permissive use of vehicle, "any subsequent use short of theft or the like while it remains in his possession, * * * is a permissive use"); accord Milbank Mut. Ins. Co. v. United States Fidelity and Guar. Co., 332 N.W.2d 160, 167 (Minn.1983). The cases adopting this "theft or the like" limitation have not expanded on the issue of whether theft by a permittee falls within this exception. Looking to the Matits language which refers to a theft which occurs while the insured vehicle is in the permittee's possession and the court's explanatory comment in Commercial Union Insurance Co. v. Johnson, 294 Ark. 444, 745 S.W.2d 589 (1988), where it stated that "we agree that an insurer should not be liable to a thief or a person who has no permission to use a vehicle and who converts it to his or her own use," we do not believe the theft exception applies to the facts of this case. Johnson, 745 S.W.2d at 594.

In this Court's opinion, the Matits court's intention was to protect the insurer from liability that arose from a theft occurring while the insured's vehicle was in the permittee's possession, but not a theft by the permittee. See 166 A.2d at 349. As the Johnson court suggested, the key to activating the exception is "a person who has no permission to use a vehicle." 745 S.W.2d at 594. Consistent with our rationale in declaring West Virginia an "initial permission" jurisdiction, we believe that because Harry Green did in fact voluntarily turn over the keys to its vehicle to Mr. Taylor, even a subsequent act of theft by Mr. Taylor does not vitiate that permission. If the legislature of this state wishes to amend the omnibus language found in W.Va.Code §§ 33–6–31(a) and 17D–4–12(b)(2) to except coverage under these facts, it of course may do so. However, as the language in both omnibus clauses clearly conditions coverage on use of the insured vehicle, we find it necessary to require coverage based on the initial permission granted by Harry Green to Mr. Taylor. Mr. Taylor's subsequent acts, which evidence an intent to steal the vehicle, have no bearing, in this Court's opinion, on the issue of coverage in an "initial permission" jurisdiction. But see Jensen, 788 P.2d at 344–45 (holding that wrongful intent to deprive owner of insured vehicle bars coverage).

One final argument advanced by Universal is that because Mr. Taylor provided the Harry Green salesperson with a false name, occupation, and address, the permission granted by the dealer to Mr. Taylor should be determined to be void. See Federal Kemper Ins. Co. v. Neary, 366 Pa.Super. 135, 530 A.2d 929 (1987) (permission held void where unlicensed minor fraudulently misrepresented his age and existence of valid learner's permit to obtain permission to operate motor vehicle).

We do not accept this argument because the record does not indicate that the salesperson relied on the name or personal history provided by Mr. Taylor in granting him permission to test-drive the dealership's vehicle. Had the salesperson requested that Mr. Taylor exhibit a valid driver's license as proof of his identity and as proof of his entitlement to legally operate a motor vehicle and Mr. Taylor had tendered false identification or an invalid operator's license, then Universal's argument on this issue might be more convincing. In this Court's opinion, the salesperson's decision to grant Mr. Taylor permission to test-drive a vehicle was motivated by his desire to sell a vehicle and not by any reliance on whatever personal information Mr. Taylor provided. Certainly an automobile dealer may take a number of steps to protect itself from an occurrence such as that which resulted in this case. As we suggested, the salesperson can be instructed to request proof of identity as well as inspection of an operator's license. Even more obvious, however, is that the salesperson can be required to accompany potential buyers on their test-drives. In this case, Harry Green and its agents did nothing to prevent the events which transpired and the death of an innocent third party was the result.

Based on the foregoing, we hereby reverse the decision of the Circuit Court of Marion County.

Reversed.

### *Note*

The requirement of *permission* as an integral part of the omnibus clause has been variously rephrased in the newer, "simplified," language policies. One version reads: *"with permission or reasonably believed to be with the permission of the owner."* Is the scope of coverage broader under the italicized language than that used in *Curtis,* supra? Government Employees Ins. Co. v. Kinyon, 119 Cal.App.3d 213, 173 Cal.Rptr. 805 (1981) reviews the decisions on this point. Are not insurers inviting litigation by making coverage depend upon the subjective perception of the potential insured?

Another version (see Appendix D) states that: "we do not provide Liability Coverage for any person using a vehicle without a reasonable belief that that person is entitled to do so." (Note that such a provision applies not only to the omnibus clause but also to the coverage of an insured who is driving someone else's automobile.) Could an unlicensed 14 year old, like Deborah in the *Curtis* case, supra, reasonably believe that she was "entitled" to drive the car? See Safeco Insurance Co. of America v. Davis, 44 Wash. App. 161, 721 P.2d 550 (1986) which held the word "entitled" was ambiguous, and therefore sustained coverage. Is the scope of the supposed permission an issue when such language is used? See United Pacific Ins. Co. v. Larsen, 44 Wn.App. 529, 723 P.2d 8 (1986).

### *Problem*

On the evening of May 6, 1960, Summers and Straus were present at a party at Snowcrest Inn outside of Hanover, New Hampshire, where both were attending Dartmouth College. Summers gave permission to one Haynesworth to borrow his automobile to drive to Hanover, and when he failed to return as expected, Summers and Miss Brandt went out into the parking lot where they discovered Straus' automobile with the keys in it. They took the car to drive to Hanover in search of Haynesworth and enroute met with an accident. Straus testified by deposition that if Summers had asked permission to use his car he would probably have granted it. There was evidence of a general custom at Dartmouth whereby students loaned their cars to one another, but Summers had neither driven Straus' car before nor asked permission to do so.

While Summers and Straus were classmates and acquainted with one another, they were not fraternity brothers, had no classes together, and did not participate in any common college activities.

The policy contained a provision extending coverage to persons using the automobile provided "the actual use thereof is with the permission of the named insured."

Concededly, there was no express permission given so the question becomes whether permission may be implied from the circumstances and the relationship of the parties.

Is the Insurance Company obliged to provide a defense for Summers in a personal injury action brought by Brandt? (See: Fireman's Fund Insurance Co. v. Brandt, 217 F.Supp. 893 (D.C.N.H.1962).)

## *Note*

## *Regulation of the Contents of the "Omnibus Clause" by Statute*

WEST'S ANN.CAL.INS.CODE

### § 11580. Required policy provisions

A policy insuring against losses set forth in subdivision (a) shall not be issued or delivered to any person in this state unless it contains the provisions set forth in subdivision (b). Such policy, whether or not actually containing such provisions, shall be construed as if such provisions were embodied therein.

(a) Unless it contains such provisions, the following policies of insurance shall not be thus issued or delivered:

(1) Against loss or damage resulting from liability for injury suffered by another person other than (i) a policy of workers' compensation insurance, or (ii) a policy issued by a nonadmitted Mexican insurer solely for use in the Republic of Mexico.

(2) Against loss of or damage to property caused by draught animals or any vehicle, and for which the insured is liable, other than a policy which provides insurance in the Republic of Mexico, issued or delivered in this state by a nonadmitted Mexican insurer.

(b) Such policy shall not be thus issued or delivered to any person in this state unless it contains all the following provisions:

(1) A provision that the insolvency or bankruptcy of the insured will not release the insurer from the payment of damages for injury sustained or loss occasioned during the life of such policy.

(2) A provision that whenever judgment is secured against the insured or the executor or administrator of a deceased insured in an action based upon bodily injury, death, or property damage, then an action may be brought against the insurer on the policy and subject to its terms and limitations, by such judgment creditor to recover on the judgment.

### § 11580.05. Legislative declaration

The Legislature declares that the public policy of this state in regard to provisions authorized or required to be included in policies affording automobile liability insurance or motor vehicle liability insurance issued or delivered in this state shall be as stated in this article, that this article expresses the total public policy of this state respecting the content of such policies, and that no provision of this article or of the Vehicle Code shall apply to policies affording automobile liability insurance or motor vehicle liability insurance in the Republic of Mexico issued or delivered in this state by a nonadmitted Mexican insurer. The Legislature further declares that it is the intent of the Legislature that the requirements set forth in Article 2 (commencing with Section 16450) of Chapter 3 of Division 7 of the Vehicle Code shall apply only to an owner's policy or operator's policy of liability insurance certified as provided in Section 16431 of the Vehicle Code as proof of ability to respond in damages, and that the requirements set forth in Article 4 (commencing with Section 11620) of Chapter 1 of Part 3 of Division 2 of the Insurance Code shall apply only to automobile liability insurance policies issued under the California Assigned Risk Plan. Except as provided above, any other policy issued or delivered in this state affording liability insurance with respect to ownership, maintenance, or use of a motor vehicle shall comply with the requirements set forth in Sections 11580, 11580.1, and 11580.2.

### § 11580.1. Automobile liability insurance; required and optional provisions

(a) No policy of automobile liability insurance described in Section 16054 of the Vehicle Code covering liability arising out of the ownership, maintenance, or use of any motor vehicle shall be issued or delivered in this state on or after the effective date of this section unless it contains the provisions set forth in subdivision (b). However, none of the requirements of subdivision (b) shall apply to the insurance afforded under any such policy (1) to the extent that such insurance exceeds the limits specified in subdivision (a) of Section 16056 of the Vehicle Code, or (2) if such policy contains an underlying insurance requirement, or provides for a retained limit of self-insurance, equal to or greater than the limits specified in subdivision (a) of Section 16056 of the Vehicle Code.

(b) Every policy of automobile liability insurance to which subdivision (a) applies shall contain all of the following provisions:

(1) Coverage limits not less than the limits specified in subdivision (a) of Section 16056 of the Vehicle Code.

(2) Designation by explicit description of, or appropriate reference to, the motor vehicles or class of motor vehicles to which coverage is specifically granted.

(3) Designation by explicit description of the purposes for which coverage for such motor vehicles is specifically excluded.

(4) Provision affording insurance to the named insured with respect to any motor vehicle covered by such policy, and to the same extent that insurance is afforded to the named insured, to any other person using, or legally responsible for the use of, such motor vehicle, provided such use is by the named insured or with his or her permission, express or implied, and within the scope of such permission, except that: (i) with regard to insurance afforded for the loading or unloading of any such motor vehicle, the insurance may be limited to apply only to the named insured, a relative of the named insured who is a resident of the named insured's household, a lessee or bailee of the motor vehicle, or an employee of any such person; and (ii) the insurance afforded to any person other than the named insured need not apply to: (A) any employee with respect to bodily injury sustained by a fellow employee injured in the scope and course of his or her employment, or (B) any person, or to any agent or employee thereof, employed or otherwise engaged in the business of selling, repairing, servicing, delivering, testing, road-testing, parking, or storing automobiles with respect to any accident arising out of the maintenance or use of a motor vehicle in connection therewith.

(c) In addition to any exclusion as provided in paragraph (3) of subdivision (b), the insurance afforded by any such policy of automobile liability insurance to which subdivision (a) applies, including the insurer's obligation to defend, may, by appropriate policy provision, be made inapplicable to any or all of the following:

(1) Liability assumed by the insured under contract.

(2) Liability for bodily injury or property damage caused intentionally by or at the direction of the insured.

(3) Liability imposed upon or assumed by the insured under any workers' compensation law.

(4) Liability for bodily injury to any employee of the insured arising out of and in the course of his employment.

(5) Liability for bodily injury to an insured or liability for bodily injury to an insured whenever the ultimate benefits of that indemnification accrue directly or indirectly to an insured.

(6) Liability for damage to property owned, rented to, transported by, or in the charge of, an insured. A motor vehicle operated by an insured shall be considered to be property in the charge of an insured.

(7) Liability for any bodily injury or property damage with respect to which insurance is or can be afforded under a nuclear energy liability policy.

(8) Any motor vehicle or class of motor vehicles, as described or designated in the policy, with respect to which coverage is explicitly excluded, in whole or in part.

The term "the insured" as used in paragraphs (1), (2), (3), and (4) shall mean only that insured under the policy against whom the particular claim is made or suit brought. The term "an insured" as used in paragraphs (5) and (6) shall mean any insured under the policy including those persons who would have otherwise been included within the policy's definition of an insured but, by agreement, are subject to the limitations of paragraph (1) of subdivision (d).

(d) Notwithstanding the provisions of paragraph (4) of subdivision (b), or the provisions of Article 2 (commencing with Section 16450) of Chapter 3 of Division 7, or Article 2 (commencing with Section 17150) of Chapter 1 of Division 9, of the Vehicle Code, the insurer and any named insured may, by the terms of any policy of automobile liability insurance to which subdivision (a) applies, or by a separate writing relating thereto, agree as to either or both of the following limitations, such agreement to be binding upon every insured to whom such policy applies and upon every third party claimant:

(1) That coverage and the insurer's obligation to defend under such policy shall not apply nor accrue to the benefit of any insured or any third party claimant while any motor vehicle is being used or operated by a natural person or persons designated by name. These limitations shall apply to any use or operation of a motor vehicle including the negligent or alleged negligent entrustment of a motor vehicle to such designated person or persons. The insurer shall have an obligation to defend the named insured when all of the following apply to such designated natural person:

1. He or she is a resident of the same household as the named insured.

2. As a result of operating the insured motor vehicle of the named insured, he or she is jointly sued with the named insured.

3. He or she is an insured under a separate automobile liability insurance policy issued to him or her as a named insured, which policy does not provide a defense to the named insured.

* * *

(2) That with regard to any such policy issued to a named insured engaged in the business of leasing vehicles for those vehicles which are leased for a term in excess of six months, or selling, repairing, servicing, delivering, testing, road-testing, parking, or storing automobiles, coverage shall not apply to any person other than the named insured or his or her agent or employee, except to the extent that the limits of liability of any other valid and collectible insurance available to such person are not equal to the limits of liability specified in subdivision (a) of Section 16056 of the Vehicle Code. If the policy is issued to a named insured engaged in the business of leasing vehicles, which business includes the lease of vehicles for a term in excess of six months, and the lessor includes in the lease automobile liability insurance, the terms and limits of which are not otherwise specified in the lease, the named insured shall incorporate a provision in each vehicle lease contract advising the lessee of the provisions of this subdivision and the fact that this limitation is applicable except as otherwise provided for by statute or federal law.

* * *

### § 11580.2. Uninsured motorist endorsement or coverage; underinsured motorist coverage

(a)(1) No policy of bodily injury liability insurance covering liability arising out of the ownership, maintenance, or use of any motor vehicle, except for policies which provide insurance in the Republic of Mexico issued or delivered in this state by nonadmitted Mexican insurers, shall be issued or delivered in this state to the owner or operator of a motor vehicle, or shall be issued or delivered by any insurer licensed in this state upon any motor vehicle then principally used or principally garaged in this state, unless the policy contains, or has added to it by endorsement, a provision with coverage limits at least equal to the limits specified in subdivision (m) and in no case less than the financial responsibility requirements specified in Section 16056 of the Vehicle Code insuring the insured, the insured's heirs or legal representative for all sums within the limits which he, she, or they, as the case may be, shall be legally entitled to recover as damages for bodily injury or wrongful death from the owner or operator of an uninsured motor vehicle. The insurer and any named insured, prior to or subsequent to the issuance or renewal of a policy, may, by agreement in writing, in the form specified in paragraph (2) or paragraph (3), (1) delete the provision covering damage caused by an uninsured motor vehicle completely, or (2) delete the coverage when a motor vehicle is operated by a natural person or persons designated by name, or (3) agree to provide the coverage in an amount less than that required by subdivision (m) but not less than the financial responsibility requirements specified in Section 16056 of the Vehicle Code. Any of these agreements by any named insured or agreement for the amount of coverage shall be binding upon every insured to whom the policy or endorsement provisions apply while the policy is in force, and shall continue to be so binding with respect to any continuation or renewal of the policy or with respect to any other policy which extends, changes, supersedes, or replaces the policy issued to the named insured by the same insurer, or with respect to reinstatement of the policy within 30 days of any lapse thereof.

* * *

(c) The insurance coverage provided for in this section does not apply either as primary or as excess coverage:

(1) To property damage sustained by the insured.

(2) To bodily injury of the insured while in or upon or while entering into or alighting from a motor vehicle other than the described motor vehicle if the owner thereof has insurance similar to that provided in this section.

(3) To bodily injury of the insured with respect to which the insured or his or her representative shall, without the written consent of the insurer, make any settlement with or prosecute to judgment any action against any person who may be legally liable therefor.

(4) In any instance where it would inure directly or indirectly to the benefit of any workers' compensation carrier or to any person qualified as a self-insurer under any workers' compensation law, or directly to the benefit of the United States, or any state or any political subdivision thereof.

(5) To establish proof of financial responsibility as provided in subdivisions (a), (b), and (c) of Section 16054 of the Vehicle Code.

(6) To bodily injury of the insured while occupying a motor vehicle owned by an insured or leased to an insured under a written contract for a period of six months or longer, unless the occupied vehicle is an insured motor vehicle. "Motor vehicle" as used in this paragraph means any self-propelled vehicle.

(7) To bodily injury of the insured when struck by a vehicle owned by an insured.

(8) To bodily injury of the insured while occupying a motor vehicle rented or leased to the insured for public or livery purposes.

(d) Subject to paragraph (2) of subdivision (c), the policy or endorsement may provide that if the insured has insurance available to the insured under more than one uninsured motorist coverage provision, any damages shall not be deemed to exceed the higher of the applicable limits of the respective coverages, and the damages shall be prorated between the applicable coverages as the limits of each coverage bear to the total of the limits.

(e) The policy or endorsement added thereto may provide that if the insured has valid and collectible automobile medical payment insurance available to him or her, the damages which the insured shall be entitled to recover from the owner or operator of an uninsured motor vehicle shall be reduced for purposes of uninsured motorist coverage by the amounts paid or due to be paid under the automobile medical payment insurance.

(f) The policy or an endorsement added thereto shall provide that the determination as to whether the insured shall be legally entitled to recover damages, and if so entitled, the amount thereof, shall be made by agreement between the insured and the insurer or, in the event of disagreement, by arbitration. The arbitration shall be conducted by a single neutral arbitrator. An award or a judgment confirming an award shall not be conclusive on any party in any action or proceeding between (i) the insured, his or her insurer, his or her legal representative, or his or her heirs and (ii) the uninsured motorist to recover damages arising out of the accident upon which the award is based.

* * *

(g) The insurer paying a claim under an uninsured motorist endorsement or coverage shall be entitled to be subrogated to the rights of the insured to whom the claim was paid against any person legally liable for the injury or death to the extent that payment was made. The action may be brought within three years from the date that payment was made hereunder.

(h) An insured entitled to recovery under the uninsured motorist endorsement or coverage shall be reimbursed within the conditions stated herein without being required to sign any release or waiver of rights to which he or she may be entitled under any other insurance coverage applicable; nor shall payment under this section to the insured be delayed or made contingent upon the decisions as to liability or distribution of loss costs under other bodily injury liability insurance or any bond applicable to the accident. Any loss payable under the terms of the uninsured motorist endorsement or coverage to or for any person may be reduced:

(1) By the amount paid and the present value of all amounts payable to him or her, his or her executor, administrator, heirs, or legal representative under any workers' compensation law, exclusive of nonoccupational disability benefits.

(2) By the amount the insured is entitled to recover from any other person insured under the underlying liability insurance policy of which the uninsured

motorist endorsement or coverage is a part, including any amounts tendered to the insured as advance payment on behalf of the other person by the insurer providing the underlying liability insurance.

(i) No cause of action shall accrue to the insured under any policy or endorsement provision issued pursuant to this section unless one of the following actions have been taken within one year from the date of the accident:

(1) Suit for bodily injury has been filed against the uninsured motorist, in a court of competent jurisdiction.

(2) Agreement as to the amount due under the policy has been concluded.

(3) The insured has formally instituted arbitration proceedings.

(j) Notwithstanding subdivisions (b) and (i), in the event the accident occurs in any other state or foreign jurisdiction to which coverage is extended under the policy and the insurer of the tortfeasor becomes insolvent, any action authorized pursuant to this section may be maintained within three months of the insolvency of the tortfeasor's insurer, but in no event later than the pertinent period of limitation of the jurisdiction in which the accident occurred.

(k) Notwithstanding subdivision (i), any insurer whose insured has made a claim under his or her uninsured motorist coverage, and the claim is pending, shall, at least 30 days before the expiration of the applicable statute of limitation, notify its insured in writing of the statute of limitation applicable to the injury or death. Failure of the insurer to provide the written notice shall operate to toll any applicable statute of limitation or other time limitation for a period of 30 days from the date the written notice is actually given. The notice shall not be required if the insurer has received notice that the insured is represented by an attorney.

* * *

(m) Coverage provided under an uninsured motorist endorsement or coverage shall be offered with coverage limits equal to the limits of liability for bodily injury in the underlying policy of insurance, but shall not be required to be offered with limits in excess of the following amounts:

(1) A limit of thirty thousand dollars ($30,000) because of bodily injury to or death of one person in any one accident.

(2) Subject to the limit for one person set forth in paragraph (1), a limit of sixty thousand dollars ($60,000) because of bodily injury to or death of two or more persons in any one accident.

(n) Underinsured motorist coverage shall be offered with limits equal to the limits of liability for the insured's uninsured motorist limits in the underlying policy, and may be offered with limits in excess of the uninsured motorist coverage. For the purposes of this section, uninsured and underinsured motorist coverage shall be offered as a single coverage. However, an insurer may offer coverage for damages for bodily injury or wrongful death from the owner or operator of an underinsured motor vehicle at greater limits than an uninsured motor vehicle.

* * *

## THE "FAMILY EXCLUSION" PROBLEM

On p. 654 above, California Vehicle Code § 17158 is quoted. Before 1973 this was also the "automobile guest" statute. It not only prohibited liability of the driver to "guests" (unless they paid compensation or unless the driver was intoxicated or guilty of wilful misconduct) but also prohibited liability of the driver to the owner of the car "riding in or occupying the vehicle" when it was driven by another person with his permission, unless the driver was intoxicated or guilty of wilful misconduct. In 1973, Brown v. Merlo, 8 Cal.3d 855, 106 Cal.Rptr. 388, 506 P.2d 212 (1973), held the section unconstitutional so far as the "guest" was concerned. The Legislature amended the section thereafter to drop the reference to the "guest" so that the bar against liability of the driver extended only to the owner. The constitutionality of this bar was upheld in Schwalbe v. Jones, 16 Cal.3d 514, 128 Cal.Rptr. 321, 546 P.2d 1033 (1976). Within a short time after Schwalbe v. Jones, the California Supreme Court reversed itself in Cooper v. Bray and struck down the bar (against the owner holding the driver liable) on Federal and State constitutional grounds, 21 Cal.3d 841, 148 Cal.Rptr. 148, 582 P.2d 604 (1978). This had the potential of serious implications for a common policy provision sometimes called the "family exclusion" which excluded from the policy coverage liability of an insured driver to the insured named in the policy or his relatives resident in the same household. What should be the result when the named insured drives his own car with his wife as passenger and she is injured?

## STATE FARM MUTUAL INSURANCE CO. v. SCHWARTZ

United States Court of Appeals, Tenth Circuit, 1991.
933 F.2d 848.

MOORE, CIRCUIT JUDGE.

State Farm filed this action in district court seeking a declaratory judgment that it is not obligated to defend or indemnify Glenda Schwartz in an Oklahoma state court action filed against her by her children. The children brought suit against their mother alleging that her negligent driving resulted in their injury. The district court granted summary judgment in favor of the Schwartz children, holding that the "household exclusion" in their parents' State Farm insurance policy, denying coverage for bodily injury to any insured or member of the insured's household, violated the public policy of Oklahoma under the state's compulsory automobile liability insurance law. The court held that State Farm is therefore liable to defend and indemnify Glenda Schwartz against her children's lawsuit. We affirm.

### I. BACKGROUND

The parties stipulated: 1) the insurance policy covering the automobile involved in the accident was in full force; 2) the policy excludes from coverage damages "[f]or any bodily injury to: ... c. any insured or any member of the insured's family residing in the insured's household" [the household exclusion at issue here]; 3) the policy defines "insured" as: "1. you [Charles Schwartz, in this case]; 2. your spouse; 3. the relatives of the first person named in the declarations [Charles Schwartz is the only named insured]; 4) the policy defines 'relative' as: 'a person related to you or your spouse by blood, marriage, or adoption who lives with you. It includes your unmarried and unemancipated child away at school;' and 5) the Schwartz children are relatives for the purposes of this policy. We review a summary judgment order de novo and apply the same legal standard used by the district court under Fed.R.Civ.P. 56(c)." Osgood v. State Farm Mut. Auto. Ins. Co., 848 F.2d 141, 143 (10th Cir.1988).

The issue in this case is straightforward: whether the district court erred in determining that the household exclusion in the Schwartz' insurance policy with State Farm contravenes the public policy established by Oklahoma's compulsory liability insurance law. In reviewing the district court's decision, we are faced with the difficult task of divining a coherent state policy from an ambiguous statute, directly conflicting positions announced in dicta in several state court opinions, and the persuasive authority of the public policies of other states with compulsory liability insurance laws.

## II. Conceptual Analysis

Conceptually, there are two ways to analyze this issue: 1) whether the policy definition of the children as "insureds" precludes recovery, or 2) whether the household exclusion in the policy offends Oklahoma public policy. First, taking notice of the fact that the Schwartz children are defined as "insureds" in the policy, and the fact that according to the policy "insureds" may not recover for bodily injury under the liability provisions, one could argue that under Looney v. Farmers Ins. Group, 616 P.2d 1138, 1141 (Okla.1980), the children, as "insureds," are not covered by the insurance policy. This resolution would avoid reaching the difficult public policy question of the validity of the household exclusion.

However, there are flaws in this rationale. First, the claimant in Looney, as the spouse of the policyholder, was defined in the policy as a "named insured." In the present case the children are defined within the class of the "insured." Id. at 1139 n. 2. While the linguistic distinction between a "named insured" and an "insured" may not be significant, it does point to a more serious problem. The spouse of the policyholder is much more likely than the children of the policyholder to be a true, consenting party to the contract. It is highly unlikely that household members such as minor, unemancipated children will have consented, or are legally able to consent, to the terms of the insurance contract.[1] In Young v. Mid-Continent Casualty Co., 743 P.2d 1084, 1088

1. See Mutual of Enumclaw Ins. Co. v. Wiscomb, 97 Wash.2d 203, 643 P.2d 441, 446 (1982) (citations omitted), distinguishing "named insureds" from children exclud-

(Okla.1987), the court distinguished parties to the contract from those "innocent victims" the Act intended to protect. Id. at 1087–88. The Young court noted that this conclusion was consistent with Looney because, in essence, a "named insured" is simply another name for a party to the contract.

In the present case, the district court properly pointed out that under Oklahoma law, Okla.Stat.Ann. tit. 15, § 11 (West 1983), children are incapable of contracting, and, in addition, simply because they are third party beneficiaries does not make them contracting parties. Okla. Stat.Ann. tit. 15, § 29 (West 1983). Logic supports this conclusion as well.

Adopting Young's division of the world into two populations: innocent victims and parties to the contract, and remembering that parental immunity has been abrogated in automobile injury cases in Oklahoma, Unah By and Through Unah v. Martin, 676 P.2d 1366 (Okla.1984), it would undermine Unah for parents and their insurance company to be able to prevent suits against the parents by their children by simply defining the children as "insureds."

Also, assuming for the moment that the household exclusion does contravene Oklahoma public policy, the contracting parties should not be able to accomplish the same results as would a household exclusion by simply defining all parties they would like to exclude from coverage as "insureds." For these reasons, we follow the second conceptual path. Our quest will therefore be to analyze whether the household exclusion violates Oklahoma public policy.

### III. Public Policy

Oklahoma's compulsory liability insurance law states in relevant part: "On and after January 1, 1983, every owner of a motor vehicle registered in this state, other than a licensed used motor vehicle dealer, shall, at all times, maintain in force with respect to such vehicle security for the payment of loss resulting from the liability imposed by law for bodily injury, death and property damage *sustained by any person* arising out of the ownership, maintenance, operation or use of the vehicle." Okla.Stat.Ann. tit. 47, § 7–601(B) (West 1988) (emphasis added). Also, as mentioned above, Oklahoma has abrogated parental immunity from suit to allow a child's action for negligence arising from an automobile accident to the extent of the parent's automobile insurance. Unah, 676 P.2d at 1369–70.

ed from coverage by a household exclusion, reasoning that: [t]hose named insureds could then intelligently choose to add the exclusion, with an adjustment in their premiums reflecting any decreased risks, or retain the coverage at the higher premium rate. Under any circumstances, exclusion clauses which purport to deny coverage to children of the insured or any person not a party to the insurance contract are violative of this state's public policy * * *. The family or household exclusion clause violates this state's public policy of assuring compensation to the victims of negligent and careless drivers.

Since passage of the Compulsory Liability Insurance Act (the Act) in 1976, Oklahoma courts have invalidated several insurance policy exclusions as contrary to the public policy established by the Act. In Young, 743 P.2d at 1087–88, the Oklahoma supreme court held an age exclusion (no liability coverage if the operator was under age twenty-five and not a relative of the insured) violated the public policy. The Young court reached this result by concluding the legislative intent underlying the Act was to mandate that "any vehicle operated on the highways of Oklahoma be secured against liability to innocent victims of the negligent operation or use of the insured vehicle." Id. at 1088. Young also cited that portion of the Act requiring coverage for loss "sustained by any person" as further support for its conclusion. Id. at 1087, 1088.

In Equity Mut. Ins. Co. v. Spring Valley Wholesale Nursery, Inc., 747 P.2d 947, 952 (Okla.1987), the Oklahoma supreme court held that a geographical exclusion (policy did not cover travel outside a two hundred mile radius) also contravened the public policy of the Act, holding that "when liability insurance is issued in compliance with compulsory insurance laws, statutory policy *at the very minimum* requires coverage for all actionable claims which may arise within the state." Id. (emphasis in original). The Equity court noted in dictum, mischaracterizing the holding of Looney, that, unlike the geographical exclusion, the household exclusion would comply with Oklahoma public policy under the Act because "[t]he purpose of the law is to shield the public, not members of the named insured's household." Id. 747 P.2d at 953.

The Young and Equity discussions of the household exclusion are at best persuasive dicta because they dealt with other types of exclusions. Looney is closer to the facts of the present case because it indirectly involved a household exclusion as well as an exclusion prohibiting recovery by one of the insured parties. Id. at 1139 n. 2. The Equity court stated that Looney determined the household exclusion did not violate public policy in Oklahoma. This is a questionable characterization of Looney because the court there based its decision in favor of the insurance company upon the fact that the claimant was a named insured. The court simply did not base its decision on the validity of the household exclusion; indeed, the court stated, "[t]he appellant was more than a mere member of the family of the *insured;* she was the *insured.* Her relationship with the defendant Looney surpasses mere household member status." Id. at 1141 (emphasis in original). However, the Looney court unfortunately obscured the exact basis for its holding by expressing agreement with this court's treatment of household exclusions in Farmers Ins. Co. v. McClain, 603 F.2d 821 (10th Cir.1979).

McClain was a declaratory judgment action filed to determine whether the insurance company was obligated to defend and indemnify the policyholder for torts committed in his automobile against a member of his family. The policy in question contained a household exclusion. The McClain court held that the explicit terms of the policy (i.e., the household exclusion) relieved the insurance company from its duty to defend and indemnify the policyholder. Id. at 823.

The court's reference to McClain is not helpful, however, because the McClain court did not consider the validity of the household exclusion in the context of the compulsory liability insurance law. This consideration undermines Looney as precedent for the question before us. We are constrained to conclude that the discussion of the household exclusion in Looney is also nonbinding dictum.

Finally, the Oklahoma supreme court in Unah, in the context of partially abrogating parental immunity, stated, "[w]e can no longer countenance the legal anomaly where two minor children, negligently injured in the operation of a motor vehicle, one of them a stranger, could recover compensation for his injuries and the other one, a minor child of the operator of the vehicle, could not. Today, where all other passengers in a car are mandatorily protected by liability coverage it is unfair and against public interest to deprive an unemancipated minor the benefit of recovery." Id. at 1370. As dictum, this discussion is also of scarce precedential value in determining the validity of the household exclusion in Oklahoma, but it nonetheless demonstrates clear public policy preferences that assist us in determining the scope of the comprehensive liability insurance law.

To summarize, Oklahoma courts have presented us with four opinions adopting contradictory positions in dicta bearing on the validity of the household exclusion. The Young and Unah opinions make a strong argument for affirming the district court in this case. The Equity and Looney opinions, however, appear to urge an opposite conclusion. Since Oklahoma case law is contradictory, we must look elsewhere for guidance.

Many states have addressed the issue of whether household exclusions are valid in the context of a compulsory liability insurance law. These states have almost uniformly held that the household exclusion is contrary to the public policy created by compulsory liability insurance laws.[4] Most state courts that have addressed this issue but which have not explicitly ruled that the household exclusion violates public policy,

4. See Beacon Ins. Co. of Am. v. State Farm Mut. Ins. Co., 795 S.W.2d 62, 64 (Ky.1990); Stepho v. Allstate Ins. Co., 259 Ga. 475, 383 S.E.2d 887, 888 (1989) (household exclusion invalid if broader than common law tort immunity); Government Employees Ins. Co. v. Ropka, 74 Md.App. 249, 536 A.2d 1214, 1218, cert. denied, 312 Md. 601, 541 A.2d 964 (1988) (household exclusion invalid only to extent of statutorily required minimum insurance amount); State Farm Mut. Auto Ins. Co. v. Mastbaum, 748 P.2d 1042, 1044 (Utah 1987) (household exclusion invalid only to extent of statutorily required minimum insurance amount); Farmers Ins. Group v. Reed, 109 Idaho 849, 712 P.2d 550, 552 (1985); Meyer v. State Farm Mut. Auto. Ins. Co., 689 P.2d 585, 589–90 (Colo.1984); Dowdy v. Allstate Ins. Co., 68 Or.App. 709, 685 P.2d 444, 449 (1984); Transamerica Ins. Co. v. Royle, 202 Mont. 173, 656 P.2d 820, 824 (1983); Allstate Ins. Co. v. Wyoming Ins. Dept., 672 P.2d 810, 813–16 (Wyo.1983); DeWitt v. Young, 229 Kan. 474, 625 P.2d 478, 482 (1981); Bishop v. Allstate Ins. Co., 623 S.W.2d 865, 866 (Ky.1981); State Farm Mut. Auto. Ins. Co. v. Traycik, 86 Mich. App. 285, 272 N.W.2d 629, 631 (1978); Estate of Neal v. Farmers Ins. Exchange, 93 Nev. 348, 566 P.2d 81, 83 (1977); Hughes v. State Farm Mut. Auto. Ins. Co., 236 N.W.2d 870, 885–86 (N.D.1975); Jordan v. Aetna Casualty and Sur. Co., 264 S.C. 294, 214 S.E.2d 818, 820 (1975).

are states without compulsory liability insurance laws.[5] Thus, our review leads us to conclude the overwhelming majority of states that have addressed this issue have determined, under various lines of reasoning, that the household exclusion violates public policy created by compulsory liability insurance laws.

One of the most common lines of reasoning in these cases leading to invalidation of the household exclusion, and the logic used by the Young and Unah courts in Oklahoma, holds that: "[compulsory liability insurance] legislation embodies a public policy that innocent victims of the negligent operation of motor vehicles should be compensated for their injuries. The perspective which this public policy adopts is that of the innocent victim rather than that of the insurer or the insured tortfeasor." Young, 743 P.2d at 1087 (footnotes omitted). Young noted that this interpretation of legislative intent is also consistent with the explicit statutory requirement of the Act that every driver have security to cover losses sustained by "any person." Id.

We believe that this position, combined with the passage we have quoted from Unah, best harmonizes the language of the Act, the legislative intent expressed by the Oklahoma courts, and the overwhelming trend among other jurisdictions in finding the household exclusion contrary to public policy in compulsory liability insurance states. Therefore, we hold the district court did not err in granting summary judgment in favor of the Schwartz children because the household exclusion in their parents' insurance policy contravened the public policy of Oklahoma under the Act.

AFFIRMED.

### *Notes*

1. There is little or no practical purpose in going through the laborious process of abolishing intra-family immunity to tort actions, unless there are extra familial sources of funds to pay for the consequences. Such a pragmatic consideration no doubt contributes to the hostility toward the "household exclusion." A representative list of decisions appears in notes 4 & 5 of the principal case.

Sometimes the shift in "public policy" (or who is making it) is difficult to keep up with. Consider Kansas. In 1980 the Kansas Supreme Court

5. See, e.g., Faraj v. Allstate Ins. Co., 486 A.2d 582, 585–86 (R.I.1984); State Farm Mut. Auto. Ins. Co. v. Suarez, 104 Ill.App.3d 556, 60 Ill.Dec. 305, 309, 432 N.E.2d 1204, 1208 (1982). Appellant cites Southern Guaranty Ins. Co. v. Preferred Risk Mut. Ins. Co., 257 Ga. 355, 359 S.E.2d 665 (1987), and various other cases in support of its assertion that the household exclusion has "long enjoyed judicial support." Appellant's Brief in Chief, at 15. However, each of these decisions have been either overturned or limited to their facts by subsequent decisions. See cases cited in footnote 4. Arizona and Indiana appear to be the only states which have upheld the household exclusion in the face of a compulsory liability insurance law. State Farm Mut. Auto. Ins. Co. v. Transport Indem. Co., 109 Ariz. 56, 505 P.2d 227, 230 (1973); Transamerica Ins. Co. v. Henry, 563 N.E.2d 1265 (Ind.1990). California has adopted a somewhat qualified acceptance of the household exclusion by allowing an insurer to exclude from coverage any person insured under the policy. Farmers Ins. Exch. v. Cocking, 29 Cal.3d 383, 173 Cal.Rptr. 846, 847–48, 628 P.2d 1, 2–3 (1981).

abolished parental immunity in auto accident cases. The following year it declared the "household exclusion" void. In 1982 the Kansas legislature expressly authorized the clauses, but in 1984 repealed that validation. However the Supreme Court declined to give the repeal retroactive effect. See Hilyard v. Estate of Clearwater, 240 Kan. 362, 729 P.2d 1195 (1986).

2. *What is given by statute may be taken away by contract interpretation (who is "family" anyway?)*

The family exclusion in the omnibus clause may be (oftentimes grudgingly) sanctioned, but as an exclusion it is, of course, subject to the close scrutiny for ambiguity given to insurance policies (Part A, Chap. 2A and a dozen other places in this book). Would the ordinary layman say that a young man living with his mother, brother, and his stepfather (the insured) who treated him as a natural son and fully supported him, was a member of the family? The California Supreme Court in Reserve Ins. Co. v. Pisciotta, 30 Cal.3d 800, 180 Cal.Rptr. 628, 640 P.2d 764 (1982) said he was not, thus allowing the young man, who was injured by his stepfather's boat the benefit of the stepfather's liability policy.

3. *The "family exclusion" clauses and uninsured motorist coverage.*

Assume a jurisdiction which sustains the validity of the "family exclusion," but has discarded the intra-family immunity doctrine as to tort liability. Father, insured under liability policy containing the "family exclusion" clause, negligently runs over an offspring. Child sues Father. Can Child collect judgment under the uninsured motorist's provisions of Father's policy? See Severs v. Country Mutual Insurance Co., 89 Ill.2d 515, 61 Ill.Dec. 137, 434 N.E.2d 290 (1982) and Faraj v. Allstate Ins. Co., 486 A.2d 582 (R.I.1984). But cf. Harrison v. Metropolitan Property and Liability Ins. Co., 475 So.2d 1370 (Fla.App.1985).

4. *The Named Driver Exclusion*

Statutory provisions such as West's Ann.Cal.Ins.Code 11580(d)(1) allowing named drivers (or sometimes drivers under a certain age) to be excluded from coverage have also been challenged on public policy grounds, usually without success. Garza v. Glen Falls Ins. Co., 105 N.M. 220, 731 P.2d 363 (1986). Some jurisdictions, however, have held the exclusion to have no force or effect up to the limits of the Financial Responsibility Law. Jones v. Motorists Mut. Ins. Co., 177 W.Va. 763, 356 S.E.2d 634 (1987).

## C. THE POLICY HAS BEEN RESCINDED OR CANCELLED

### BARRERA v. STATE FARM MUTUAL AUTOMOBILE INSURANCE CO.

Supreme Court of California, 1969.
71 Cal.2d 659, 79 Cal.Rptr. 106, 456 P.2d 674.

TOBRINER, JUSTICE.

Plaintiff sued State Farm Mutual Automobile Insurance Company (hereinafter "State Farm") to compel payment of a judgment obtained against Anthony and Sandra Alves. Plaintiff obtained the judgment against the Alveses on the ground that plaintiff, while a pedestrian, was injured by Mrs. Alves's negligent driving. Plaintiff alleged and urged the enforceability at the time of the accident of an automobile liability policy issued by State Farm to the Alveses. State Farm denied the validity of the policy, and filed a cross-complaint seeking a declaration that the policy was void *ab initio* because issued in reliance on a material misrepresentation by Mr. Alves. In opposition, plaintiff contended that State Farm was estopped to rescind the policy six months after the accident because State Farm led Mr. Alves to believe that he was insured and because State Farm negligently failed to discover within a reasonable time the misrepresentation in the application tendered 1½ years prior to the accident.

The trial court found that State Farm issued the automobile liability policy in reliance on a material misrepresentation, that rescission was therefore justified, and that State Farm acted promptly *upon discovery* of the misrepresentation. Accordingly, the court entered judgment for State Farm on both the complaint and the cross-complaint. Plaintiff moved for a new trial, urging that the public policy expressed in California's Financial Responsibility Law impelled a finding of laches by State Farm in its belated discovery of the misrepresentations; that its failure to act promptly worked to the detriment of an innocent member of the public, who should therefore recover against the carrier. The trial court denied the motion. Plaintiff appeals.[29]

We conclude that an automobile liability insurer must undertake a reasonable investigation of the insured's insurability within a reasonable period of time from the acceptance of the application and the issuance of a policy. This duty directly inures to the benefit of third persons injured by the insured. Such an injured party, who has obtained an unsatisfied judgment against the insured, may properly proceed against the insurer; the insurer cannot then successfully defend upon the ground of its own failure reasonably to investigate the application. On retrial, therefore, plaintiff, upon showing that State Farm did not, within a reasonable time, reasonably investigate the insured's insurability, may recover from State Farm, within the policy limits, the amount of the judgment she obtained against the Alveses.[30]

**29.** The Alveses are not a party to this appeal.

**30.** In addition to arguing that State Farm was estopped to rescind the policy because of negligent failure to discover the misrepresentation within a reasonable time, plaintiff also argued that section 651 of the Insurance Code applied to rescission as well as to prospective cancellation of automobile insurance policies, and that therefore the attempted rescission did not take effect until 10 days after notice of the rescission was sent to Mr. Alves. If termination of the policy did not occur until after notice, the policy remained in effect at the time of the accident.

Plaintiff's contention regarding section 651 runs counter to the statutory scheme for termination of insurance contracts and blurs the clear statutory distinction between "rescission" (retroactive termination) and "cancellation" (prospective termination) of insurance policies. Section 651 provides: "Notwithstanding any other provision of this code, no cancellation by an insurer of an auto liability insurance policy shall be effective prior to the mailing or delivery to the named insured at the address shown in the policy, of a written notice of the cancellation stating when, not less than ten (10) days after the date of

The parties stipulated to the following facts: On April 29, 1958, Mr. Alves signed an application for automobile insurance prepared by Mr. Pucci, State Farm's agent, and on that same date, State Farm issued a policy insuring Alves against public liability for $10,000, for any one person's injury. Alves paid premiums on the policy in April 1958, October 1958, and April 1959. On November 28, 1959, Mrs. Alves, while driving a Lincoln automobile, struck plaintiff. On December 4, 1959, plaintiff's attorneys notified State Farm of plaintiff's claim. On December 8, 1959, State Farm sent a reply letter to plaintiff's attorneys. On April 22, 1960, State Farm rescinded the insurance policy and returned all premiums paid. On July 26, 1960, plaintiff sued the Alveses, and Alves forwarded a copy of the summons and complaint to State Farm. On August 2, 1960, State Farm advised the Alveses that it would not defend the action. On November 3, 1960, judgment was entered in favor of plaintiff against the Alveses.

The parties further stipulated that plaintiff did not consent to, or concur in, any rescission or attempted rescission between State Farm and the Alveses. They further agreed that on September 6, 1958, five months after the issuance of the original policy, State Farm paid to, or on behalf of, Mr. Alves a claim arising out of the comprehensive coverage provisions of the policy in effect at that time.

The record discloses the following facts as to the application for insurance and the misrepresentations. In April 1958 Mr. Alves purchased a Chevrolet from one Roberti, a used-car salesman. Roberti

such mailing or delivery, the date the cancellation shall become effective."

The Legislature added section 651 in 1957. (Stats.1957, ch. 723, § 1, p. 1931.) In 1957, the Insurance Code did not contain a separate chapter on "Cancellation" (present ch. 10). Section 651 was incorporated into the "Rescission" chapter (ch. 9). The Legislature did not insert the section in the "Cancellation" chapter when that chapter was added by 1965 Statutes, chapter 1716, section 1, page 3850. The Insurance Code specifically provides, however, that "Division, part, chapter, article, and section headings contained herein shall not be deemed to govern, limit, modify or in any manner affect the scope, meaning, or intent of the provisions of any division, part, chapter, article or section hereof." (§ 6.)

The statutory scheme reflects a deliberate distinction between "rescission" and "cancellation." Sections 331, 338, and 359, which prescribe the grounds for rescission, all involve false statements or material omissions in the procurement of the policy. Section 660 (Stats.1965, ch. 1716, § 1, p. 3850), on the other hand, provided: "The commissioner, by regulation, shall prescribe the grounds upon which an insurer may cancel a policy of automobile insurance. No insurer shall cancel a policy of automobile insurance except upon such ground or grounds as have been prescribed by the commissioner." (Repealed, Stats.1968, ch. 137, p. 352, § 1, effective Jan. 1, 1969).

Unless we say that automobile liability insurance policies cannot be rescinded at all and that section 660 completely abrogated the rescission section for automobile liability insurance, we must hold that section 651, which specifically refers to "cancellation", does not control the procedure for "rescission" of automobile liability insurance. Instead, the general section governing rescission of insurance policies, section 650, applies. Section 650 provides: "Whenever a right to rescind a contract of insurance is given to the insurer by any provision of this part such right may be exercised at any time previous to the commencement of an action on the contract." The issue, then, turns on the validity of plaintiff's contention that the public policy of this state requires that an automobile liability insurer reasonably investigate within a reasonable time after issuance of the policy or otherwise be estopped to rescind the policy, at least in an action by an injured person who has obtained judgment from the insured.

arranged with Pucci, State Farm's agent, that he come to the agency in order to obtain insurance for Alves's car. Both Alves, who was 24 years old at the time, and Pucci testified that Alves did not read the application, and that Pucci filled in the answers to the questions.

Question 18 on the application stated: "Has your license to drive or registration been suspended, revoked or refused, to the applicant or any member of his household in the last five years?" Contrary to the Department of Motor Vehicles (hereinafter "DMV") report on Mr. Alves which evidenced one suspension and two probation orders within the five years preceding April 1958, a "No" answer appeared on the application in response to question 18.

* * * [W]e must therefore accept the trial court's finding of misrepresentation.[31]

* * *

Maurice Hammer, an insurance broker for the previous two years, and prior thereto an agent for Allstate Insurance for three years, testified that the general custom and practice of the insurance industry was to obtain DMV reports in connection with applications, either as a basis for determining rates or insurability of the risk.

With respect to State Farm's policy on initial applications, Pucci testified that State Farm always issued a policy when he gave a binding receipt to the applicant. The binding receipt provided for insurance coverage for 30 days from the date of the receipt, even if the company subsequently refused to approve the risk. Pucci handed Alves a binding receipt on April 28, 1958.

Daniel Priest, an underwriting superintendent of State Farm, testifying as to State Farm's investigative policies, stated that State Farm orders DMV reports and makes other inspections "on a judgment basis." In some cases State Farm does check on statements made by its applicants; but "in other cases the underwriting people just passed on the risk based on the statement on the application as submitted." In response to the question whether State Farm customarily checks the driving record of an insured when a claim is presented against him, Priest stated: "Again, it depends upon the nature of the claim, the type of claim situation, circumstances involved, things of this nature. * * * We don't have any fixed custom or practice." He further stated that

31. Alves's response to question 18 on the application constitutes "concealment" sufficient to justify rescission under Insurance Code, section 331. That section explicitly states, and the cases construing it so hold, that the misrepresentation involved need not be intentional in order to justify rescission. Furthermore, whether the insured misstated or concealed certain facts with the intention to deceive the insurer is irrelevant to the right to rescind. (See, Telford v. New York Life Ins. Co. (1937) 9 Cal.2d 103, 105, 69 P.2d 835.)

Indeed, the trial court in the present case found only that Alves materially misrepresented facts within his knowledge; there was no finding of *scienter,* that Alves fraudulently misrepresented the facts. Thus, under the present interpretation of the Insurance Code, an insurer may rescind the contract of insurance *ab initio* for a material misrepresentation—even though the insured's misstatements were the result of negligence, or, indeed, the product of innocence.

once a claim has occurred the claims, rather than the underwriting, department, determines whether the claim is sufficiently "significant" to warrant an investigation. Before any claim has been made against the insured, the underwriter handling the file exercises the discretion to decide whether to obtain a DMV report. Priest further testified that the cost of an entire investigation in 1958 was $3.35, and that the cost of a DMV check was only 25 cents.

Although at the time of his application in April 1958 Alves, then being under 25 years of age, fell within the class of applicants who received the greatest number of spot checks, State Farm did not begin its investigation until February 4, 1960, more than two months after plaintiff was injured, and almost two years after the initial application. After discovering that Alves's file did not contain a DMV report, the underwriting department requested one. On February 12, 1960, it received a reply from the department; on March 2, 1960, it obtained the report. Prior to obtaining the report, and in response to an underwriter's question whether to cancel Alves's policy, the claims department on February 16 responded that it was in the process of developing evidence for rescission. On April 22, State Farm notified Alves of the rescission of his policy.

The evidence suggests that State Farm, in failing to investigate Alves's insurability and to obtain a DMV report, pursued a policy of saving minor costs on its part at the expense and sacrifice of the interests of its insured and those of the general public who were the potential victims of the insured's negligence. If, at the time of an initial or transfer application, the underwriter handling the risk relies on the application and fails to order a DMV report, the claims department thereafter determines whether a claim by or against an insured is sufficiently "significant" to warrant investigation. Here, State Farm must have considered Mr. Alves's September 6, 1958, claim under the comprehensive provisions of his policy "insignificant," since State Farm apparently did not investigate but paid the claim. Not until plaintiff's attorneys notified State Farm of a $10,000 claim under the personal liability provision of the policy did State Farm attempt to check Alves's driving record.

State Farm's investigative practices may fail to conform to the standard of service which the public may reasonably expect of an insurance company and, more importantly here, may violate the public policy underlying California's Financial Responsibility Law. [T]he "quasi-public" nature of the insurance business and the public policy underlying the Financial Responsibility Law impose upon the automobile liability insurer a duty both to the insured and to the public to conduct a reasonable investigation of insurability within a reasonable time after issuance of an automobile liability policy. We may characterize this duty as one sounding either in tort or quasi-contract. The label is not important. We hold, however, that in order to avoid liability to an innocent victim of the insured an insurer cannot take advantage of a breach of its duty reasonably to check an application for automobile liability insurance within a reasonable time after acceptance of that application.

The requirement that the carrier act promptly to determine insurability after issuance of an automobile liability insurance policy inures primarily to the benefit of those members of the public who suffer injury from negligent motorists and seek recovery against the responsible tortfeasors. The duty arises from the public policy that protects the innocent victim of the careless use of automobiles from an inability to sue a financially responsible defendant. This duty, which the insurer incurs with the issuance of an automobile liability policy, therefore runs directly to the class of potential victims of the insured. Consequently, when the insurer breaches that duty, it may not defeat recovery by the injured person, who has recovered a judgment against the insured, by relying on an untimely attempt to rescind.

* * *

* * * After the injured person has obtained a judgment against the insured, therefore, he may compel the insurer to pay the judgment to the extent of the monetary limits set forth in the Financial Responsibility Law. (Veh.Code, § 16430.)

That the automobile liability insurer that fails to make such an investigation loses its right to rescind does not, however, necessarily mean that it forfeits all remedies *against the insured* for his misrepresentations. The insurer may still prosecute a cause of action against the insured for damages for wrongful misrepresentation, after satisfying the injured person's claim, or, in an action brought by the insured, after he has satisfied a judgment against him by the injured person, defend on the ground of misrepresentations in the application. (Cf., e.g., De Campos v. State Comp. Ins. Fund (1954) 122 Cal.App.2d 519, 528–529, 265 P.2d 617.) This recognition of the right of the insurer to rely on the insured's misrepresentations either as a basis for a damages suit against the insured or as a defense in an action by the insured does not conflict with the purpose of the Financial Responsibility Law, the assurance of a solvent defendant for those innocently injured by the use of automobiles.

*The question whether State Farm negligently breached a duty owed to plaintiff in the present action is a question of fact to be determined on remand*

* * * The trial court in the present case awarded judgment for State Farm without reference to this duty. Accordingly, the judgment must be reversed. On remand, the trial court will determine whether or not the insurer conducted such a reasonable investigation. If the court finds that State Farm acted reasonably in light of its duty to undertake a reasonable investigation of insurability, it may allow State Farm once again to assert the invalidity of its contract of insurance with the Alveses as a defense to the plaintiff's action. On the other hand, if the trial court concludes that State Farm breached its duty, as defined in this

opinion, the defense of the rescission *ab initio* will no longer be available to State Farm.

Factors to be taken into account by the trial court in assessing the reasonableness of State Farm's course of conduct in failing to investigate Alves's driving record are, inter alia: the cost of obtaining the information from the Department of Motor Vehicles, the availability of this information from the department or elsewhere (e.g., Alves claimed that his license suspensions appeared on the back of his driver's license), and the general administrative burden of making such an investigation. These factors must be weighed against the importance of the protection of innocent members of the public against the consequences of automobile owners driving with voidable liability policies.

The judgment on plaintiff Barrera's complaint and defendant State Farm's cross-complaint is reversed. The cause is remanded for proceedings consistent with this opinion.

### *Note*

Below is a statutory modification of the general California requirement of disclosure in insurance applications (see Sec. 332, West's Ann.Insurance Code) with regard to auto liability insurance:

**§ 11580.08 Motor vehicle insurance: Arrest record**

With respect to disclosure of the fact of an arrest for any violation of the Vehicle Code or of a city or county ordinance or resolution relating to vehicles or their operators or owner which did not result in a conviction, the issuer, or his agency or employee, of any policy of automobile liability insurance (as described in Section 16056 of the Vehicle Code), any motor vehicle liability policy (as described in Section 16450 of the Vehicle Code), or any policy or coverage described in Section 660, shall not inquire of an applicant whether he has been arrested under such circumstances or to condition the issuance of any such policy on the applicant's making such disclosure.

### *Questions*

a. Are incidents of arrest which do not result in convictions material facts within the meaning of § 334, West's Ann.California Insurance Code?

b. Is Sec. 11580.08 consistent with the public policy rationale of *Barrera?*

### *A STATUTORY SOLUTION*

1. Subsection F, Arizona Revised Statutes § 28–1170 reads:

Every motor vehicle liability policy shall be subject to the following provisions which need not be contained therein:

1. The liability of the insurance carrier with respect to the insurance required by this chapter shall become absolute when injury or damage covered by the motor vehicle liability policy occurs. The policy may not be cancelled or annulled as to such liability by an agreement between the insurance carrier and the insured after the occurrence of the injury or damage, and no

statement made by the insured or on his behalf and no violation of the policy shall defeat or void the policy.

The constitutionality of the above statute was challenged in Allstate Insurance Co. v. Dorr, 411 F.2d 198 (9th Cir.1969), wherein the insurer's practices followed the pattern revealed in the *Barrera* decision. In upholding the statute the Court observed:

> "We think that the economic burden placed by the Arizona statute upon companies which sell liability insurance of paying an occasional claim which they would not, but for the statute, have had to pay, falls easily within the power of a legislature to legislate. Insurance companies can alleviate their situation by exercising more care in selling their policies, by exerting more diligence in earlier discovery of their mistakes, and, of course, by increasing their insurance rates to spread the cost over larger numbers of the motoring public."

2. *An Important Addendum*

The above Arizona statute reads in part that "no statement made by the insured * * * *and no violation of the policy* shall defeat or void the policy" after an auto accident occurs. Does the italicized language mean that breaches of policy conditions by the insured as well as misrepresentations by him cannot be asserted by the insurer, when suit is brought by the victim upon the judgment obtained by the latter against the insured? An example would be the insureds' duty to co-operate with the insurer in the defense of the tort action, which is taken up in the next section. In Tibbs v. Johnson, 30 Wn.App. 107, 632 P.2d 904 (1981), the precise issue was raised under the Washington Financial Responsibility Law (R.C.W. 46.29.490) which uses the same language as the Arizona statute. The court held that the insurer could not assert the non-cooperation of the insured as a defense to the 3rd person's action on the policy, except to the extent the policy limits exceed the minimum established by the Financial Responsibility Law.

## STATUTORY LIMITATIONS WITH REGARD TO CANCELLATION AND RENEWAL OF AUTOMOBILE LIABILITY POLICIES. CAL.INS.CODE:

### § 661. Grounds for valid notice of cancellation

(a) A notice of cancellation of a policy shall be effective only if it is based on one or more of the following reasons:

(1) Nonpayment of premium.

(2) The driver's license or motor vehicle registration of the named insured or of any other operator who either resides in the same household or customarily operates an automobile insured under the policy has been under suspension or revocation during the policy period or, if the policy is a renewal, during its policy period or the 180 days immediately preceding its effective date.

(3) Discovery of fraud by the named insured in pursuing a claim under the policy provided the insurer does not rescind the policy.

(b) This section shall not apply to any policy or coverage which has been in effect less than 60 days at the time notice of cancellation is mailed or delivered by the insurer unless it is a renewal policy.

(c) Modification of automobile physical damage coverage by the inclusion of a deductible not exceeding one hundred dollars ($100) shall not be deemed a cancellation of the coverage or of the policy.

(d) This section shall not apply to nonrenewal.

### § 662. Mailing or delivery of notice of cancellation to named insured, lienholder, or additional interest; time; reasons for cancellation

No notice of cancellation of a policy to which Section 661 applies shall be effective unless mailed or delivered by the insurer to the named insured, lienholder, or additional interest at least 20 days prior to the effective date of cancellation; provided, however, that where cancellation is for nonpayment of premium, at least 10 days' notice of cancellation accompanied by the reason therefor shall be given. Unless the reason accompanies or is included in the notice of cancellation, the notice of cancellation shall state or be accompanied by a statement that upon written request of the named insured, mailed or delivered to the insurer not less than 15 days prior to the effective date of cancellation, the insurer will specify the reason for such cancellation.

This section shall not apply to nonrenewal.

### § 663. Policy expiration; delivery or mailing of renewal offer or notice of nonrenewal

At least 20 days prior to policy expiration, an insurer shall deliver to the named insured or mail to the named insured at the address shown in the policy, either of the following:

(a) A written or verbal offer of renewal of the policy contingent upon payment of premium as stated in the offer.

(b) A notice of nonrenewal of the policy. That notice shall contain or be accompanied by a statement that upon written request by the named insured, made not later than one month following the expiration of the policy period, or delivered to the insurer, the insurer will notify the insured in writing, within 20 days of his request, the reason or reasons for such nonrenewal.

* * *

### § 663.5. Nonrenewal based on insured's age

No insurer shall fail to renew a policy solely on the basis of the age of the insured.

### § 664. Proof of mailing of notice

Proof of mailing of notice of cancellation, or of intention not to renew or of reasons for cancellation, to the named insured at the address shown in the policy or to the named insured's latest known address, shall be sufficient proof of notice.

### § 664.5. Payment of cost of physical examinations

Any insurer who requires periodic physical examinations of an insured as a condition of renewal of a policy shall pay the cost of such physical examinations, except that an insurer shall not pay any cost if it elects to accept the certified written results of an insured's physical examination voluntarily conducted within 12 months preceding the policy expiration or renewal date.

### § 665. Notice of assigned risk plan

When a policy of automobile liability insurance is canceled, other than for nonpayment of premium, or in the event of failure to renew a policy of automobile liability insurance to which Section 663 applies, the insurer shall notify the named insured of his possible eligibility for automobile liability insurance through the automobile liability assigned risk plan. Such notice shall accompany or be included in the notice of cancellation or the notice of intent not to renew.

### § 666. Specification of reason for cancellation

Where the reason for cancellation does not accompany or is not included in the notice of cancellation, the insurer shall upon written request of the named insured, mailed or delivered to the insurer not less than 15 days prior to the effective date of cancellation, specify in writing the reason for such cancellation. Such reason shall be mailed or delivered to the named insured within five days after receipt of such request.

### § 669. Violation of § 663; penalty

Any insurer willfully violating any provisions of Section 663 is guilty of a misdemeanor and is punishable by a fine of not exceeding one thousand dollars ($1,000) for each violation thereof.

### § 1861.03. Unfair insurance practices; prohibition

* * *

(c)(1) Notwithstanding any other provision of law, a notice of cancellation or nonrenewal of a policy for automobile insurance shall be effective only if it is based on one or more of the following reasons: (A) nonpayment of premium; (B) fraud or material misrepresentation affecting the policy or insured; (C) a substantial increase in the hazard insured against. (2) This subdivision shall not prevent a reciprocal insurer, organized prior to November 8, 1988, by a motor club holding a certificate of authority under Chapter 2 (commencing with Section 12160) of Part 5 of Division 2, and which requires membership in the motor club as a condition precedent to applying for insurance, from issuing an effective notice of nonrenewal based solely on the failure of the insured to maintain membership in the motor club.

* * *

## SPINDLE v. TRAVELERS INSURANCE COMPANIES

Court of Appeal of California, Second Division, 1977.
66 Cal.App.3d 951, 136 Cal.Rptr. 404.

JEFFERSON, ASSOCIATE JUSTICE.

Plaintiff David K. Spindle, M.D., filed a first amended complaint for money damages (bad faith) against defendants Travelers Insurance

Companies, a corporation, and the Phoenix Insurance Co. [a subsidiary]. Defendants demurred to this complaint upon the ground that plaintiff had failed to state a cause of action. The demurrer was sustained by the trial court, without leave to amend, and a judgment of dismissal was accordingly entered. Plaintiff has appealed.

* * *

It appears from plaintiff's amended complaint that he is a physician and surgeon duly licensed to practice medicine in the State of California. More particularly, Dr. Spindle is a specialist in neurosurgery, and an employee and shareholder of the Southeast Neuro–Medical Group, Inc., a California professional corporation, located in Downey, California. * * *

Plaintiff Spindle is also a member of the Southern California Physicians Council, a nonprofit association of approximately 7,000 physicians and surgeons in Southern California. He alleges that in December 1973, defendant Phoenix entered into a "written Master Contract" with the council whereby Phoenix agreed to provide malpractice insurance coverage to council members. * * * Council members had previously been insured by Hartford Fire Insurance Company, but that contract expired December 31, 1973.

Pursuant to the "Master Contract," Dr. Spindle was issued a policy of malpractice insurance on or about January 1, 1974 * * *

Plaintiff alleges that during the period of negotiation between the council and defendant Phoenix for the master contract, he is informed and believes that defendant Phoenix represented to the council that if its members "complied with the conditions precedent" and did not have excessive claims filed against them, defendant Phoenix would keep the members' malpractice policies in full force and effect.

While Dr. Spindle had been insured by Hartford, a number of malpractice claims had been filed against him. However, defendant Phoenix accepted Dr. Spindle's premium—an annual premium of $7,452—and, upon defendant Phoenix' request, plaintiff advised defendant in writing of all claims that had previously been made against plaintiff of which he was aware.

From January 1974, until July 3, 1975, no malpractice claims were made against plaintiff. On that latter date, however, defendant Phoenix advised plaintiff in writing of its intention to cancel plaintiff's malpractice insurance as of August 3, 1975.

Plaintiff charges that by this action defendant Phoenix breached "its implied obligation to plaintiff [to act in good faith] * * * did not act in good faith and did not deal fairly with plaintiff," but cancelled his policy "willfully, with malice, and with the intent and purpose to hurt, harm and injure the plaintiff in the practice of his profession." Plaintiff further alleges that the act of cancellation was intended to coerce and intimidate other members of the council in their dispute with defendant Phoenix over the allowable rate of premium increases provided for in the master agreement.

It is plaintiff's contention that defendant was seeking a premium increase of 141 percent while members of the council were resisting this percentage increase and contending that the master contract between the council and defendant Phoenix limited such increase during the period from January 2, 1975 to January 1, 1976, to 15 percent. In effect, plaintiff alleges that his malpractice insurance policy was cancelled to serve as an example to other members so they would agree to the greater premium increase sought by defendant, the only insurer in a position to insure them.

Plaintiff alleges that he was informed by Norman Aronson, head of the professional claims department of defendant Travelers that his insurance would not have been cancelled had the council agreed to the 141 percent premium increase.

Plaintiff further alleges that, at the time of cancellation, defendant Phoenix was aware that plaintiff would be unable to practice medicine and surgery in hospitals without malpractice insurance. He also states that the wrongful cancellation of his insurance was "intended as a threat and a warning" to every member of the council, i.e., that the members could each expect similar treatment if they opposed the premium increase.

Plaintiff alleges that the cancelled insurance was not available at competitive rates from solvent, nonhazardous insurance carriers; that plaintiff has been forced to secure replacement malpractice insurance from a carrier that has been deemed "undercapitalized" by the Commissioner of Insurance of the State of California, at a premium 350 percent higher than that paid to defendant Phoenix. Plaintiff asserts that as a result of the cancellation by defendant Phoenix, plaintiff has been damaged in his professional reputation, and that he has suffered emotional distress. Plaintiff's amended complaint seeks damages for plaintiff's emotional distress in the amount of $10,000,000, punitive damages in the same amount, and special damages of $7,053.25, representing the difference in the premium plaintiff had to pay his new insurer for coverage from August 26, 1975 to January 1, 1976 as opposed to that which he would have been obligated to pay defendant Phoenix for the same period of time.

In asserting by their demurrer that plaintiff's amended complaint fails to state a cause of action, defendants rely on what they regard as their "absolute" right, set forth in the contract with the council and in the contract with plaintiff, to cancel the policy of insurance for any reason upon which they chose to act. We note that the master contract, exhibit A to the amended complaint, provides: "No provision of this Agreement [dealing with the circumstances under which the Council and the defendant Phoenix could terminate it] shall restrict the rights of cancellation specified in the policies of insurance issued pursuant to this Agreement." We note also that plaintiff's particular policy provides: "This policy may be cancelled by the *named insured* by surrender thereof to the Company or any of its authorized agents or by mailing to the Company written notice stating when thereafter the cancellation shall be effective. This policy may be cancelled by the *Company* by *mailing* to the *named insured* at the address shown in this policy, written *notice stating when,* not less than 30 days thereafter, such *cancellation shall be effective.* The mailing of notice as aforesaid shall be sufficient proof of notice. * * *

Plaintiff's contention below, and upon this appeal, is that, these cancellation provisions notwithstanding, his policy also included a good faith undertaking by defendant Phoenix not to cancel the policy for a malicious reason—a reason unrelated to his professional performance as a neurosurgeon. It is plaintiff's contention that public policy requires the rule of law that precludes an insurance carrier from possessing the right to cancel a policy for a malicious reason such as the wrongful objective of making an "example" of plaintiff, the insured, during the struggle between the council and its members and defendant Phoenix over the problem of premium increases. Defendants reject the notion that public policy requires, as plaintiff contends, that the legal principle of good faith and fair dealing between an insurer and its insured be extended to include a limitation on an insurer's right to cancel malpractice insurance policies issued to its insured.

We have not discovered any California decisional law authority expressing a rule of law relative to a bad faith cancellation of a policy of medical malpractice insurance. Plaintiff has formulated his theory of a right to recover damages on the principle that public policy does—or should—dictate a legal remedy when such a cancellation occurs. For this view, plaintiff relies on the federal case of L'Orange v. Medical Protective Company (6th Cir.1968) 394 F.2d 57. In this case, Dr. L'Orange, a dentist, had his malpractice insurance policy cancelled by defendant Medical Protective after 25 years of uninterrupted coverage, assertedly for revenge, because he testified for a plaintiff in a malpractice action brought against another dentist, who was also insured by Medical Protective. A substantial verdict was returned by the jury in the malpractice action in which L'Orange testified as a witness. The *L'Orange* court held that plaintiff L'Orange's complaint had alleged a good cause of action against the defendant insurer because cancellation of a policy to stifle testimony of witnesses was an act which violated the public policy of the State of Ohio.

Defendants argue that the *L'Orange* case is poorly reasoned and should not be regarded as a precedent in the case at bench.

Despite the absence of an expressed "public policy" basis pursuant to existing California decisional law, it is clear that the right of insurers to cancel insurance policies is not absolute in this state. Sections 660 through 679.73 of the Insurance Code deal with the subjects of cancellation and failure to renew particular kinds of insurance policies such as automobile liability policies and property loss policies. Section 661 sets forth and limits specifically the grounds upon which an automobile liability or collision policy may be cancelled, and section 676 specifies and limits the grounds for cancellation of property loss policies. In addition, section 679.71 declares that real or personal property loss insurance policies may not be cancelled because of the insured's marital status, sex, race, color, religion, national origin, or ancestry. These sections reflect legislative policy limiting the "absolute" right of insurance policy cancellation.

In addition, there is the area of developed case law in California which pertains to the matter of bad faith in carrying out the terms of a contract. While defendants term plaintiff's allegations of bad faith as "absurd," we note again that in a demurrer situation, we are compelled to accept plaintiff's allegation as true for the purpose of weighing the sufficiency of the amended complaint against a demurrer thereto, and need not concern ourselves with any problems of proof that plaintiff Spindle may encounter in a trial.

* * *

We are unable to discern any logical basis for distinguishing between an insurer's conduct in settling a claim made pursuant to the policy and that involved in an insurer's cancelling a policy if bad faith conduct is the basis for the cancellation. The situations are similar in that the ultimate result of the conduct of the insurer effectively deprives the insured of the benefit of his bargain, i.e., the coverage for the period for which he paid a premium. Cancellation provisions of a contract are subject to the covenant of good faith and fair dealing just as are other provisions of a contract. No plausible reason exists why cancellation provisions of a contract should be treated differently from other contractual provisions insofar as application of the implied covenant of good faith and fair dealing is concerned. It has been stated that "where a contract confers on one party a discretionary power affecting the rights of the other, a duty is imposed to exercise that discretion in good faith and in accordance with fair dealing." (Cal. Lettuce Growers v. Union Sugar Co. (1955) 45 Cal.2d 474, 484, 289 P.2d 785, 49 A.L.R.2d 496.)

In the instant case, the deprivation to the insured of the benefit of his bargain is greater than average due to the lack of competition in the field of malpractice insurance alleged in the amended complaint.

Conspiratorial conduct on the part of insurers to avoid the contractual liability they undertake is not countenanced in California (see Gruenberg v. Aetna Ins. Co. (1973) 9 Cal.3d 566, 108 Cal.Rptr. 480, 510 P.2d 1032), and the evolvement of the doctrine of the implied covenant of good faith and fair dealing *is* an expression of *public policy* in our state. We hold that this same doctrine is applicable to subject an insurer to liability to its insured for cancelling a malpractice insurance policy in accordance with permissible terms of the cancellation provisions of the policy, if the reasons for such cancellation are such as to make the cancellation a violation of the implied covenant of good faith and fair dealing. Plaintiff's amended complaint, therefore, has stated a cause of action against defendants.

The judgment (order of dismissal) appealed from is reversed.

* * *

### *Note*

See Murphy v. Seed–Roberts Agency, Inc., 79 Mich.App. 1, 261 N.W.2d 198, 99 A.L.R.3d 457 (1977), and Annotation: Wrongful Cancellation of Medical Malpractice Insurance, 99 A.L.R.3d 469 (1980).

# Chapter 14

# SPECIAL LITIGATION PROBLEMS OF LIABILITY INSURANCE

---

- **the insured's duty of co-operation**
- **the insurer's duty of defense**
- **waiver agreements and reservation of rights**
- **the insurer's duty to negotiate and to effect settlements**

## PRELIMINARY NOTE

The cases in this chapter highlight the difficulty of balancing the duties and relationships of insurance defense counsel. The insurance contract does not alter the primary attorney-client relationship. However, it does introduce potentially conflicting objectives between the insurer and the insured, especially where an insurer's "House" counsel is assigned. A defense attorney may lose the ability to objectively manage settlement and litigation when a long term relationship with an insurer is contrasted with a transitory claim file. As the cases show, there may be divergent interests when a claim rests on alternative theories, or when a claim is partially covered. Consider the effect on settlement and litigation strategy when defense expenses are included within the policy limits (Professional Liability–Appendix F) or are unlimited (Commercial GL–Appendix E).

The American Bar Association addressed the inherent conflict of the tripartite relationship the Model Rules of Professional Conduct. Rule 1.8(f) requires that the attorney assess any conflicts and explain them to the client as well as maintain confidentiality. Courts and counsel alike have been unable to formulate a satisfactory bright-line test.

For additional information on the ethical and malpractice considerations, See 2 Ronald E. Mallen and Jeffrey M. Smith, *Legal Malpractice* § 23 (3rd ed. 1989), Keeton and Widiss, *Insurance Law,* § 7.6(c) (1988), Robert E. O'Malley, *Ethics Principles for the Insurer, the Insured, and Defense Counsel: The Eternal Triangle Reformed,* 66 Tul.L.Rev. 511 (1991), William C. Carpenter, *Note: Reservation of Rights in Insurance Contracts,* 32 Ariz.L.Rev. 387 (1990).

### *Problems*

(A) Enrico Porsche–Ferrari has the ordinary auto liability policy with Maginot Auto Insurance Co. He is involved in an altercation wherein he uses the door of his car as a battering-ram against an assailant. He is sued by the assailant and Porsche–Ferrari notifies Maginot. After short reflection Maginot refuses to defend Porsche–Ferrari on the stated ground that the policy does not cover intentional wrongdoing (the policy says it does not apply to "bodily injury or property damage caused intentionally by the insured") and that therefore it has no duty to defend. Does it have the duty? See Gray v. Zurich, 65 Cal.2d 263, 54 Cal.Rptr. 104, 419 P.2d 168 (1966).

(B) If a court should conclude that Maginot Insurance Co. breached its duty by refusing to defend, is its liability confined to breach of contract damages (e.g. the costs of defense plus liability for any judgment up to the policy limits?) or is there some other measure of liability?

See: Maneikis v. St. Paul Insurance Co. of Illinois, 655 F.2d 818 (7th Cir.1981) (in this case the insured settled and assigned his cause of action to the plaintiff); Comunale v. Traders & General Insurance Co., 50 Cal.2d 654, 328 P.2d 198 (1958); Annotation: Consequences of Liability Insurer's Refusal to Assume Defense of Action Against Insured Upon Ground that Claim Upon Which the Action is Based is not Within Coverage or Policy, 49 A.L.R.2d 694 (1956); Smith v. American Family Mutual Insurance Co., 294 N.W.2d 751 (N.D.1980), reprinted *infra*.

(C) Assume the same facts except that Maginot after receiving notice of the claim against Porsche–Ferrari, immediately (without reserving any rights it had to contest coverage under the policy) sprang to his defense but lost the case. Can Maginot thereafter refuse to pay the judgment against Porsche–Ferrari on the grounds that intentional injury is not covered? [This line of conduct by the insurer is actually pretty improbable.]

See: Tomerlin v. Canadian Insurance Co., 61 Cal.2d 638, 39 Cal.Rptr. 731, 394 P.2d 571 (1964); Note: The Insurer's Duty to Defend Under a Liability Insurance Policy, 114 Pa.L.Rev. 734 (1966).

(D) Assume the same facts as in (B), except that, prior to assuming the defense, Maginot has obtained an agreement from Porsche–Ferrari that its defense of the case will not preclude it from asserting non-coverage, (a "non-waiver agreement"—meaning that Maginot does not waive its right to claim "no coverage" because it defends Porsche–Ferrari). After the case goes against Porsche–Ferrari, may Maginot assert that it has no liability under the policy to pay the judgment?

See: Norman v. Insurance Co. of North America, 218 Va. 718, 239 S.E.2d 902 (1978); Milbank Mutual Insurance Co. v. Wentz, 352 F.2d 592 (8th Cir.1965); Val's Painting & Drywall, Inc. v. Allstate Insurance Co., 53 Cal.App.3d 576, 126 Cal.Rptr. 267 (1975).

(E) Assume the same facts as in (D) except that when he is asked to sign a "non-waiver" agreement, Porsche–Ferrari refuses and Maginot then delivers a statement to him saying it reserves its rights to claim non-coverage and does not waive any of its policy defenses (a so-called "reservation of rights" letter). Porsche–Ferrari refused to consent to the reservation of rights. Maginot conducts the defense and loses. May it defend against liability on the policy on grounds injury involved was intentionally committed by the insured?

See: Crawford v. Ranger Insurance Co., 653 F.2d 1248 (9th Cir.1981), distinguishing Yuen v. London Guarantee & Accident Co., 40 Hawaii 213 (1953). For comment on the impact of the refusal to accept the reservation of rights, see Val's Painting & Drywall, Inc. v. Allstate Insurance Co., 53 Cal.App.3d 576, 588, 126 Cal.Rptr. 267, 273 (1975) (Dicta); Roos, The Obligation to Defend and Some Related Problems, 13 Hast.L.J. 206, 207 (1961).

(F) Assume that after the incident and notice to Maginot, Porsche–Ferrari fled the jurisdiction and was altogether unavailable to cooperate in his defense. Is Maginot thereby relieved of its duty to defend? * Assume that Porsche–Ferrari's absence cannot be regarded as prejudicial to the defense; there were many other witnesses available for both plaintiff and defense.

See: MFA Mutual Insurance Co. v. Sailors, 180 Neb. 201, 141 N.W.2d 846 (1966); State Farm Mutual Automobile Insurance Co. v. Commercial Union Insurance Co., 394 So.2d 890 (Miss.1981); Billington v. Interinsurance Exchange of Southern California, 71 Cal.2d 728, 79 Cal.Rptr. 326, 456 P.2d 982 (1969). Annotation: Liability Insurance: Failure or Refusal of Insured to Attend Trial or to Testify as Breach of Cooperation Clause, 9 A.L.R. 4th 218 (1981).

(G) Assume the facts in (A). Can Maginot base its refusal to defend the lawsuit brought against Porsche–Ferrari on the averments made in the complaint? In brief, the complaint sets out two counts both sounding in tort one of the counts alleges an assault and battery, the other count alleges negligence.

Cf. Sears Roebuck and Co. v. Reliance Insurance Co., 654 F.2d 494 (7th Cir.1981); Anno. Allegations in Third Person's Action Against Insured as Determining Liability Insurer's Duty to Defend, 50 A.L.R.2d 458 (1956); Mullen v. Glens Falls Insurance Co., 73 Cal.App.3d 163, 140 Cal.Rptr. 605 (1977).

(H) Assume the Maginot Ins. Co. had issued auto policies to both the plaintiff and Porsche–Ferrari. What are its duties to its two insureds?

See: Anno. "Liability Insurer's Rights and Duties as to Defense and Settlement as Affected by Its Having Issued Policies Covering Parties Who Have Conflicting Interests," 18 A.L.R.3d 482 (1968). See also: O'Morrow v. Borad, 27 Cal.2d 794, 167 P.2d 483, 163 A.L.R. 894 (1946); Allstate Insur-

* [Editors' Footnote] As to the possibility that the insurer may be limited by statute in asserting the non-cooperation defense in cases like this, see the note following the *Barrera* case, *supra*.

ance Co. v. Fisher, 31 Cal.App.3d 391, 107 Cal.Rptr. 251 (1973); Spindle v. Chubb/Pacific Indemnity Group, 89 Cal.App.3d 706, 152 Cal.Rptr. 776 (1979).

(I) Assume that before Porsche–Ferrari dealt with him, the assailant mentioned previously managed to inflict significant damage on Porsche–Ferrari's car. May the Maginot Ins. Co., if it decides to furnish counsel to defend Porsche–Ferrari, employ the same counsel in an action brought by Porsche–Ferrari against Maginot for the damage to his car?

See: Executive Aviation, Inc. v. National Insurance Underwriters, 16 Cal.App.3d 799, 94 Cal.Rptr. 347 (1971).

### *Note*

See Sharpe and Shaffer, The Parameters of the Insurer's Duty to Defend, XIX Forum 555 (1984); Dondanville, Defense Counsel Beware: The Perils of Conflicts of Interest, XVIII Forum 62 (1982); Revere and Chapman, Insurer's Duty to Defend, 13 Pac.L.J. 889 (1982). See also 7C Appleman, Insurance Law and Practice, secs. 4681–4715 (on insurers' duties with respect to defense and settlement); 8 id. secs. 4731–4810 (duties of the insured); Stanley, Can We Defend Both: A Defense Counsel's Dilemma, 22 Tort & Ins.L.J. 59 (Fall, 1986). See also the following annotations (among many others): 34 A.L.R.3d 533 (1970) ("Liability Insurer's Negligence or Bad Faith in Conducting Defense as Ground of Liability to Insured"); 20 A.L.R. 4th (1983) ("Insurer's Tort Liability for Consequential or Punitive Damages for Wrongful Failure or Refusal to Defend Insured").

## DARCY v. HARTFORD INSURANCE CO.

Supreme Judicial Court of Massachusetts, 1990.
407 Mass. 481, 554 N.E.2d 28.

GREANEY, J.

After trial, a judge in the Superior Court concluded that Lillian Darcy and Mary Iglesias (plaintiffs), and third-party plaintiff, The Hartford Insurance Company (Hartford), could recover the proceeds of a liability insurance policy issued by Royal Globe Insurance Company (Royal Globe). Royal Globe has appealed, claiming that the delay in notice of the plaintiffs' claims, and the failure of its insured to cooperate, permitted Royal Globe to disclaim coverage under the policy. We transferred the appeal to this court on our own motion. We agree with the judge that Royal Globe may not avoid coverage on either of its stated grounds. Consequently, we affirm the judgment of the Superior Court.

The facts found by the judge are as follows. In 1979, Aladdin Building Maintenance Company (Aladdin) was awarded a contract to provide janitorial services for the John F. Kennedy Federal Building in Boston. Aladdin subsequently entered into a subcontract assigning those duties to United Building Maintenance, Inc. (United). At all relevant times, Aladdin carried a comprehensive commercial liability insurance policy with personal injury coverage issued by Hartford, while United carried a similar policy issued by Royal Globe. On September 15,

1979, the plaintiffs were working in the Federal building at their desks, which were separated by a free-standing room partition or baffle. The baffle was accidentally knocked over by a United employee who was attempting to clean around it, and it fell on the plaintiffs, injuring them both severely.

The plaintiffs brought suit against United in the Superior Court on February 18, 1981, seeking damages for their personal injuries. United never filed an appearance, nor did it notify its insurer, Royal Globe, of either the accident or the lawsuit. On August 15, 1981, the plaintiffs filed suit against Aladdin, the main contractor, in the United States District Court for Massachusetts. This action was concluded on September 23, 1983, when the plaintiffs won judgments for $582,080.12, and $82,055.35, respectively.

On November 4, 1983, the plaintiffs sought to satisfy their Federal court judgments by suing Hartford in the Superior Court to reach and apply the proceeds of the Hartford policy issued to Aladdin. Hartford responded by filing a third-party complaint against Royal Globe, seeking recovery from Royal Globe as the liability insurer of United, Aladdin's subcontractor. Hartford's complaint, filed on January 8, 1985, reached Royal Globe nine days later, on January 17, 1985. This was the first notice Royal Globe had received of the accident, which had occurred on September 15, 1979.

At the time Royal Globe received notice of the plaintiffs' claims against its insured, the underlying tort action against United in the Superior Court had not been resolved. Accordingly, Royal Globe undertook an investigation of the claim. The claims adjuster assigned to the case examined Royal Globe's records and discovered reference to a previous claim involving United. The records indicated that United had not responded to Royal Globe's correspondence in that case. The claims adjuster thus assumed that any attempt to make contact with United's principals directly would be futile, and he hired an investigation bureau to locate them.

As found by the judge, the investigation authorized by Royal Globe was limited to the following efforts: An investigator was assigned to locate United's principals. To this end, the investigator examined the telephone directory and various public records, and wrote to the attorney listed on United's articles of incorporation. The investigator eventually located one Pasquale Verro, who was named as a principal of United. However, upon reaching this man, the investigator discovered that he was not the Pasquale Verro associated with United, but was a relative. The investigation went no further. The Royal Globe claims adjuster responded to this information by sending a letter to the Pasquale Verro located by the investigator, despite actual knowledge that this was not the right man, informing him that Royal Globe was disclaiming coverage due to lack of notice and cooperation from United. Subsequently, on

August 14, 1987, and October 19, 1987, respectively, default judgments entered against United in the pending State court actions. More than two years had elapsed between Royal Globe's first notice of the claim (January 8, 1985) and the eventual entry of the default judgments against United, Royal Globe's insured.

On October 19, 1987, Hartford and the plaintiffs entered into a settlement agreement pursuant to which the plaintiffs agreed to dismiss their claims against Hartford with prejudice in consideration of a $300,000 payment. The plaintiffs, in the meantime, had brought claims directly against Royal Globe. Hartford and the plaintiffs further agreed to pursue their respective claims against Royal Globe, and stipulated that any recovery on those claims would be divided equally between them.

A trial ensued on the issue whether the plaintiffs and Hartford could reach and recover the proceeds of Royal Globe's policy with United. Royal Globe defended on the basis that it had properly disclaimed coverage because United, its insured, had violated its policy obligations to provide seasonable notice of the claims and to cooperate in the defense thereof. The judge rejected both claims. Relying upon G.L. c. 175, § 112, and our decision in Johnson Controls, Inc. v. Bowes, 381 Mass. 278, 409 N.E.2d 185 (1980), the judge concluded that Royal Globe had not carried its burden of proving that the delay in giving notice had materially prejudiced its interests. Further, the judge determined that Royal Globe had not fulfilled its duty to exercise diligence and make a good faith effort to obtain United's cooperation. See Allen v. Atlantic Nat'l Ins. Co., 350 Mass. 181, 214 N.E.2d 28 (1966). Accordingly, the judge concluded that neither breach entitled Royal Globe to disclaim liability, and entered a judgment against Royal Globe (divided between the plaintiffs and Hartford) in the total amount of $300,000.

1. *The duty to provide seasonable notice.* The Royal Globe policy issued to United contains the notice provision set forth below.[3] As Royal Globe concedes, breach of that provision by an insured is not an independently sufficient basis for an insurer to disclaim liability. Rather, the insurer must prove that its interests have been prejudiced by the insured's failure to provide timely notice of the accident. See G.L. c. 175, § 112, as amended by St.1977, c. 437 ("An insurance company shall not deny insurance coverage to an insured because of failure of an insured to seasonably notify an insurance company of an occurrence, incident, claim or of a suit founded upon an occurrence, incident or claim, which may give rise to liability insured against unless the insurance company has been prejudiced thereby."); Johnson Controls, Inc. v. Bowes, supra, 381 Mass. at 282, 409 N.E.2d 185 (insurer bears the

3. "In the event of an occurrence, written notice containing particulars sufficient to identify the insured and also reasonably obtainable information with respect to the time, place and circumstances thereof, and the names and addresses of the injured and of available witnesses, shall be given by or

burden of proving prejudice).[4] See also MacInnis v. Aetna Life & Casualty Co., 403 Mass. 220, 223, 526 N.E.2d 1255 (1988).

Royal Globe urges that we adopt a rebuttable presumption of prejudice in cases where the delay in notifying an insurer of a claim or possible claim is "extreme." Such a rule, Royal Globe contends, "makes sense in light of the legitimate purposes served by the notice provisions and fairly balances the competing interests of the insurer, insured and third parties." Were we to adopt such a rule, argues Royal Globe, we should find (contrary to the judge) that the more than five-year delay in notifying Royal Globe in this case was "extreme," and thus entitles Royal Globe to the benefit of the presumption. We decline Royal Globe's request to modify existing law in this area.

Adopting the presumption Royal Globe seeks would, in effect, constitute a retreat to a mode of interpretation of insurance policies which invites technical forfeitures, and would conflict sharply with the view, previously expressed by both the Legislature and this court, that forfeitures should occur only upon a showing of actual prejudice to an insurer's interests. See G.L. c. 175, § 112 (1988 ed.); Johnson Controls, Inc. v. Bowes, supra. By its very nature, a presumption, in cases in which it applied, would tend to relieve an insurer of its burden to demonstrate actual harm to its interests. Such a rule could permit an insurer to avoid liability on the basis of the possibility, rather than on proof of actual prejudice. The proposed rule would tend to shift unfairly the burden of showing prejudice from the party in the best position, and with the most resources, to ascertain the existence of prejudice to the party who is least capable of investigating the likelihood that a claim, despite a delay in notice, can be adequately defended. In the process, the protections for which insurance was obtained and paid for, could be denied. Additionally, the Legislature's concern that an insurer attempting to disclaim coverage for lack of notice must show prejudice would be frustrated contrary to the directive of G.L. c. 175, § 112.

The length of delay, of course, in notice will always be a relevant factor to be considered in determining whether actual prejudice has been shown by an insurer, and the longer the delay, the more likely that prejudice exists. But, before a denial of coverage by an insurer is justified, the delay in notice must be accompanied by a showing of some other facts or circumstances (such as, for example, the loss of critical evidence, or testimony from material witnesses despite diligent good faith efforts on the part of the insurer to locate them) which demonstrates that the insurer's interests have been actually harmed. See Thompson v. Grange Ins. Ass'n, 34 Wash.App. 151, 163–164, 660 P.2d 307 (1983) (refusing to presume prejudice because of five-year delay in

for the insured to the company or any of its authorized agents as soon as practicable."

4. While the assignment of the burden of proof in the Johnson Controls case was made in connection with a legal malpractice insurance policy not covered by the statutory prejudice requirement of G.L. c. 175, § 112, the holding of the case applies to other types of policies such as the comprehensive commercial liability policy at issue here.

notice and requiring a showing of actual prejudice). We see no reason to absolve the insurer of the burden of identifying the precise manner in which its interests have suffered.

Royal Globe next contends that, even without the benefit of a presumption, it has demonstrated actual prejudice to its interests in this case by showing that it has been "placed in a substantially less favorable position than it would have been in had timely notice been provided." In support of his conclusion that actual prejudice had not been demonstrated, the judge relied primarily on the fact that Royal Globe learned of the claim against its insured more than two years before the default judgment entered. The judge also found that the accident had occurred less than one block from Royal Globe's offices, and that it was likely to have generated considerable documentation, including reports in connection with workers' compensation claims and Department of Labor records. Further, the judge found that Royal Globe would have had access to the documents compiled for the plaintiffs' Federal court suit against Aladdin, which was based on the same accident. The judge noted that Royal Globe made no meaningful attempt to identify employees of United, or to locate eyewitnesses to the accident. Royal Globe's efforts boil down to a torpid effort at finding United's principal without any corresponding effort to investigate the incident itself. Thus, the judge concluded that Royal Globe had "sufficient opportunity to investigate the circumstances surrounding the plaintiffs' injuries," even after its receipt of admittedly unseasonable notice; and, consequently, Royal Globe had not demonstrated at all that it had been placed in a substantially less favorable position than it would have been had it received earlier notice. Because this conclusion is amply supported by the evidence, we decline to disturb it on appeal.[5]

2. *The duty to cooperate.* The Royal Globe policy contains a provision obligating United to cooperate in the event of a lawsuit, including the duties of attending hearings and trials and assisting in the procurement of relevant evidence and witnesses. Royal Globe asserts that United's failure to cooperate justifies a denial of liability under the policy's terms. The plaintiffs, on the other hand, suggest that we extend the prejudice requirement, which we previously have applied in other

5. Most of the contrary arguments Royal Globe raises in its brief do not rise beyond the level of speculation. For example, Royal Globe claims that the "memories of any witnesses who might continue to be available can hardly be said to be fresh," that "it is reasonable to assume" that United's principals "may have had" valuable information, and that potential claims against third parties "would likely have been barred" by some unspecified statute of limitations. Royal Globe further claims prejudice resulting from the default judgment entered against United more than two years after Royal Globe received notice of the claim. The argument that Royal Globe was "powerless" to prevent the entry of the default judgment because it could not have drafted a responsive pleading in the case is specious. As the judge found, Royal Globe had ample time and opportunity to uncover sufficient facts to file a pleading which could have responded to the merits of the action. Had Royal Globe actually been unable to ascertain such facts, prejudice would have been shown. Any prejudice which resulted from the entry of the default judgment in this case is directly due to Royal Globe's inaction in its investigation rather than to United's failure to provide prompt notice.

insurance policy contexts, to the lack of cooperation context as well. If we make this extension, plaintiffs argue, Royal Globe cannot disclaim liability due to lack of cooperation because, as has been decided above, Royal Globe has not demonstrated that its interests have suffered actual prejudice.

Under current law, breach of the duty to cooperate on the part of an insured must be "substantial and material" before it permits an insurer to disclaim liability. See Morrison v. Lewis, 351 Mass. 386, 390, 221 N.E.2d 401 (1966). See also 14 G. Couch, Insurance, § 51.107, at 607 (2d ed. 1982). A showing of prejudice on the part of the insurer has not previously been expressly required. See Imperiali v. Pica, 338 Mass. 494, 498, 156 N.E.2d 44 (1959); Polito v. Galluzzo, 337 Mass. 360, 364–365, 149 N.E.2d 375 (1958). The vast majority of jurisdictions which have considered the issue have decided that actual prejudice to an insurer's interests due to lack of an insured's cooperation must be demonstrated before a denial of coverage will be permitted, and we conclude that that should be the rule here as well.[6]

We have previously modified the common law in this area by adding prejudice requirements in the contexts of notice provisions, see Johnson Controls, Inc. v. Bowes, 381 Mass. 278, 409 N.E.2d 185 (1980), and consent-to-settlement provisions, see MacInnis v. Aetna Life & Casualty Co., 403 Mass. 220, 526 N.E.2d 1255 (1988). Our rationale in both of those cases stemmed from a rejection of the strict contractual view of insurance policy interpretation, under which the failure of any policy provision, characterized as a condition precedent, automatically relieved an insurer of any obligation to pay on the policy. See, e.g., Rose v. Regan, 344 Mass. 223, 181 N.E.2d 796 (1962). In Johnson Controls, Inc. v. Bowes, supra, we expressed the view that this approach was no longer persuasive because it " 'fails to recognize the true nature of the relation-

6. The jurisdictions that have adopted this view are as follows: Clemmer v. Hartford Ins. Co., 22 Cal.3d 865, 881–882, 151 Cal.Rptr. 285, 587 P.2d 1098 (1978); Rochon v. Preferred Accident Ins. Co., 118 Conn. 190, 198, 171 A. 429 (1934); Brooks Transp. Co. v. Merchants Mut. Casualty Co., 36 Del. 40, 55, 171 A. 207 (1933); American Fire & Casualty Co. v. Vliet, 148 Fla. 568, 571, 4 So.2d 862 (1941); Farley v. Farmers Ins. Exch., 91 Idaho 37, 40, 415 P.2d 680 (1966); State Farm Mut. Auto. Ins. Co. v. McSpadden, 88 Ill.App.3d 1135, 1138, 44 Ill.Dec. 215, 411 N.E.2d 121 (1980); Miller v. Dilts, 463 N.E.2d 257, 261 (Ind.1984); Boone v. Lowry, 8 Kan.App.2d 293, 299, 657 P.2d 64 (1983); Metropolitan Casualty Ins. Co. v. Albritton, 214 Ky. 16, 19, 282 S.W. 187 (1926); Bourgeois v. Great Am. Ins. Co., 222 So.2d 70, 75 (La.Ct.App. 1969); Medico v. Employers Liab. Assurance Corp. 132 Me. 422, 427, 172 A. 1 (1934); Harleysville Ins. Co. v. Rosenbaum, 30 Md.App. 74, 83–84, 351 A.2d 197 (1975); Anderson v. Kemper Ins. Co., 128 Mich. App. 249, 340 N.W.2d 87, 90 (1983); White v. Boulton, 259 Minn. 325, 328–329, 107 N.W.2d 370 (1961); MFA Mut. Ins. Co. v. Sailors, 180 Neb. 201, 203–204, 141 N.W.2d 846 (1966); Solvents Recovery Serv. of New England v. Midland Ins. Co., 218 N.J.Super. 49, 55, 526 A.2d 1112 (1987); Foundation Reserve Ins. Co. v. Esquibel, 94 N.M. 132, 134, 607 P.2d 1150 (1980); Bailey v. Universal Underwriters Ins. Co., 258 Or. 201, 219, 474 P.2d 746 (1971); Cameron v. Berger, 336 Pa. 229, 233, 7 A.2d 293 (1939); Evans v. American Home Assurance Co., 252 S.C. 417, 420, 166 S.E.2d 811 (1969); Oberhansly v. Travelers Ins. Co., 5 Utah 2d 15, 19–20, 295 P.2d 1093 (1956); Francis v. London Guar. & Accident Co., 100 Vt. 425, 429, 138 A. 780 (1927); Oregon Auto. Ins. Co. v. Salzberg, 85 Wash.2d 372, 376–377, 535 P.2d 816 (1975); Dietz v. Hardware Dealers Mut. Fire Ins. Co., 88 Wis.2d 496, 503, 276 N.W.2d 808 (1979).

ship between insurance companies and their insureds. An insurance contract is not a negotiated agreement; rather its conditions are by and large dictated by the insurance company to the insured. The only aspect of the contract over which the insured can "bargain" is the monetary amount of coverage.' " Id. 381 Mass. at 281, 409 N.E.2d 185, quoting Brakeman v. Potomac Ins. Co., 472 Pa. 66, 72, 371 A.2d 193 (1977).

The better approach, we decided, was to determine whether the insured's breach of a policy requirement frustrated the underlying purpose of that requirement. Only in cases in which that question was answered affirmatively would an insurer be permitted to disclaim coverage. Both notice and consent-to-settlement provisions, we reasoned, exist to enable the insurer to protect its interests. See Johnson Controls, Inc. v. Bowes, supra, 381 Mass. at 281–282, 409 N.E.2d 185; MacInnis v. Aetna Life & Casualty Co., supra 403 Mass. at 223, 526 N.E.2d 1255. Accordingly, we held in those decisions that an insurer would be able to disclaim coverage because of an insured's breach of the notice or consent-to-settlement provisions in a policy only if the insurer could prove that any such breach actually prejudiced its position. Johnson Controls, Inc. v. Bowes, supra, 381 Mass. at 282, 409 N.E.2d 185; MacInnis v. Aetna Life & Casualty Co., supra 403 Mass. at 223, 526 N.E.2d 1255.

The foregoing reasoning applies with equal force to cooperation provisions. Like notice and consent-to-settlement clauses, cooperation clauses are designed primarily to protect the insurer's interest in avoiding payment on claims which it cannot adequately defend. When that interest has not been jeopardized by the insured's breach, in the sense that the insured's infraction does not seriously impair the insurer's investigation or defense of the action, there is no persuasive reason to permit the insurer to deny coverage under the policy. We now join the considerable authority throughout the country, see note 5, supra, which requires a showing of prejudice by the insurer. We do so "to afford to affected members of the public—frequently innocent third persons—the maximum protection possible consonant with fairness to the insurer." Oregon Auto. Ins. Co. v. Salzberg, 85 Wash.2d 372, 376–377, 535 P.2d 816 (1975). We hold that an insurer seeking to disclaim liability on the grounds of an insured's breach of a cooperation provision may do so only upon making an affirmative showing of actual prejudice resulting from that breach. However, because our holding constitutes a "drastic or radical incursion upon existing law," which could disturb preexisting contractual arrangements of the insurer and the insured, we limit its application to claims arising after the date of this opinion. Diaz v. Eli Lilly & Co., 364 Mass. 153, 167, 302 N.E.2d 555 (1973).[8]

In resolving the cooperation issue in this case, we rely, as did the judge, on the rule that an insurer may not disclaim liability due to lack of cooperation unless it has exercised "diligence and good faith" in

8. We need not consider the limited application of this new rule to this case because, as we conclude the judge correctly decided, under existing law, Royal Globe did not make adequate efforts to procure United's cooperation.

obtaining that cooperation. Imperiali v. Pica, supra 338 Mass. at 498–499, 156 N.E.2d 44. See DiMarzo v. American Mut. Ins. Co., 389 Mass. 85, 100, 449 N.E.2d 1189 (1983); Peters v. Saulinier, 351 Mass. 609, 613–614, 222 N.E.2d 871 (1967). The judge concluded, as we have noted above, that Royal Globe's efforts to locate United's principals were inadequate, and that no effort at all was made to investigate the circumstances surrounding the accident, despite nearby sources that might have disclosed useful information. This conclusion is amply supported by the facts found by the judge, and is not clearly erroneous as matter of law.[9] Accordingly, the judge correctly concluded that Royal Globe may not disclaim liability in this case due to United's failure to cooperate in the defense of the plaintiff's underlying tort action.

Judgment affirmed.

### *Note*

[The tactical side of cases involving claims for extra-contractual and punitive damages (e.g., claims against insurers for breach of the duty of good faith and fair dealing) ought not be ignored. Nor ought the difficulties of defense in such cases. Speaking for the defense (and revealing many of the tactical problems of the plaintiff's side) Guy O. Kornblum of San Francisco writes in For the Defense (August (p. 1–2) and September (p. 1–3), 1981 issues):] *

When posing a claim for extra-contractual damages, plaintiff's counsel usually pursues the claim with vigor. Defense counsel can expect the plaintiff's discovery to include an early request for the claim file. This is usually the first step that the plaintiff takes after a complaint has been filed. Plaintiff's counsel can then determine how the claim was processed, who was involved in the claim, and what position in the company each person held.

You can expect the plaintiff to take some depositions, at least of those witnesses whose depositions will be read at trial because they are outside the subpoena range of the court in which the action will be tried. The plaintiff may also take depositions of other company personnel, to clarify any uncertainties about the claim's handling and, possibly, to verify the claim decision which was adverse to him but helpful to his extra-contract action.

The plaintiff may also request production of company manuals, such as those outlining sales and claims procedures or policies of the company. He will investigate the company's structure, to locate a managerial employee who can testify that all of the conduct which occurred during the course of the claim's processing was either authorized or ratified by the company, thus proving the case against the company for punitive damages.

9. Royal Globe's arguments to the contrary—that the search for United's principals was adequate, and that the absence of any inquiry into the circumstances of the accident is irrelevant—lack both factual and legal support. The fact remains that cooperation was lacking in this case due in large part to Royal Globe's failure to exercise diligence in seeking it out. That being the case, it would be ironic to permit Royal Globe to deny liability based on a situation which resulted from its own inaction.

The plaintiff's pretrial and discovery strategy will probably be based on an aggressive effort to obtain the claim file at an early stage and to obtain early depositions at the home office, the goal being to catch the company off-guard, without sufficient preparation of key personnel. Typically, plaintiff's counsel will first, either formally or informally, request the company's underwriting and claims files pertaining to the insured. He may also request the pertinent company manuals. Whether these documents are discoverable depends upon local rules; however, before they are produced, they should be screened, to prevent discovery of those portions of the claims file which are privileged. In addition, any manuals outlining company procedures or policies should be reviewed prior to disclosure, so that only those which are relevant to the lawsuit are disclosed.

**Discovery of Objectives**

During the course of depositions of company personnel, plaintiff's counsel will generally try to accomplish several objectives. He will try to: (1) determine the facts pertaining to the claim's processing, and commit each witness to a version of the facts most favorable to the plaintiff; (2) establish that company personnel took an adversary and defensive posture and insinuate they did not give the insured equal consideration with the interests of the company; and (3) show that in handling the claim, company personnel were nonobjective, biased in the company's favor, and in fact, hostile, and that this was their usual course of conduct (which can help establish the punitive claim). He will also attempt to: (4) establish that the company should not have rejected the claim or terminated benefits; and (5) demonstrate that the company used its economic advantage and the plaintiff's financial disadvantage to force a settlement at a figure favorable to the company.

He will also try to show that the company did not completely investigate the file and that there was additional information it should have secured but did not. For example, plaintiff's counsel may allege that the company should have discussed the opinion of its own medical examiner with the insured's physician or consulted its own medical or legal staff before a claims decision was made. If there was some disagreement as to a claims decision, possibly a third, outside opinion (either legal or medical) should have been obtained.

During discovery, there are certain key areas into which plaintiff's counsel will be making inquiry. He will want to know whether company personnel followed company policy at all times in handling the claim and whether the claim would be handled the same way again. This inquiry is very important in establishing the case's punitive damages aspect, since the plaintiff will try to persuade the jury that a large punitive award is necessary to deter future similar conduct. He will want to know whether there is any additional information the company would normally request which it did not have at the time the claims decision was made. In this connection, he will ask: "What did the company have and what did it not have which has been uncovered during discovery? What could the company have gotten that it did not? Did it have the proper authorizations? On what facts did the company rely in making its claim decision? Did it ignore information favorable to the insured and isolate only that information which supported its position? Did it immediately decide the case upon receipt of a favorable medical examination by its examiner while ignoring plaintiff's own treating physician?"

Plaintiff's counsel will have each of these objectives in mind while pursuing discovery.

Counsel can use several techniques to defeat or limit the plaintiff's claim for extra-contractual or punitive damages. Removal to a federal court is one which should be considered. The decision to seek removal involves balancing the opportunity to get a more intelligent and possibly more conservative jury in the federal forum against differing requirements of jury unanimity. In some state courts, there is a right to a twelve-person jury, and a unanimous verdict is not required. In federal court, on the other hand, there is a six-person jury in civil cases and a unanimous verdict is required. Consequently, at least in some jurisdictions, removal to a federal forum may be desirable.

In some instances, plaintiff's counsel, in any effort to destroy diversity jurisdiction, may join local company personnel. If it can be shown that no claim can be stated against these defendants and that their joinder was for the ulterior motive of preventing removal, the case may be removed and an effort to remand successfully resisted. In addition, if a dismissal of all resident defendants can be obtained by a pre-trial motion, consideration should be given to a prompt removal.

Whether a change of venue can and should be obtained is a local question which each trial counsel must answer for himself, basing his decision on the types of juries and judges he is likely to get in the county in which the action is initially filed. Trial counsel must weigh those considerations against the effect of trying the case before courts in other counties to which the case can be removed.

### Attacking Complaints

An aggressive defense is extremely important in representing an insurer in these cases. The first line of defense may be an attack on the complaint in an effort to show that it fails to state precisely the facts upon which relief might be granted. For example, the plaintiff may not have pleaded specifically or fully the elements of his punitive claim. If not, then the sufficiency of his pleading as to the specific claim may be challenged. As a result, the plaintiff is forced to plead the precise facts upon which he seeks such relief.

If possible, attempts should be made to eliminate any nonmeritorious single cause of action or claim from the complaint at an early stage. As a practical matter, however, elimination usually cannot be accomplished until some discovery has been completed and a motion for summary judgment has been made.

Since the most important aspect of defending any extra-contract claim is to prevent the imposition of punitive damages, every effort must be made to challenge the grounds upon which the plaintiff bases this claim. In some cases the challenge may be accomplished by attacking the complaint by a motion to dismiss for failure to state a claim under Rule 12(b) of the Federal Rules of Civil Procedure, or a comparable state court motion. In other cases, the chances of a successful dismissal of the punitive damages claim may be enhanced by deferring the attack until most of the discovery has been completed, and the facts on which the punitive claim is based have been fairly well established by depositions and interrogatories.

The assault on the punitive damages claim should be launched at the earliest strategically advisable moment, however. If unsuccessful on the first effort, it should be pursued by subsequent motions, such as a motion for a nonsuit, directed verdict or other evidentiary motion seeking dismissal, both during and, if necessary, after trial.

The success of these motions will generally depend upon an argument that the facts simply do not provide a basis for concluding that the aggravated misconduct prerequisite to a punitive damages award is present. Therefore, in making such arguments to the court, counsel should emphasize that dismissal of the punitive claim does not mean that the plaintiff's entire claim is lost. Rather, a dismissal eliminates only the plaintiff's claim for windfall damages, leaving the court or jury to decide the extent to which the insured's actual injury warrants compensation.

### Early File Review

It is extremely important for trial counsel to meet with the corporate counsel and the company personnel involved in the case at an early stage. Group discussions of the case should be held with these persons so that each has a complete understanding of the issues involved, the basis for the underwriting and claim decisions, and the point upon which the plaintiff will be likely to focus. Often it will take at least a full day or two for trial counsel to completely and thoroughly explore the case in this fashion.

Either at or before this time, trial counsel should be provided with all pertinent documents, including claims files and their file jackets, which may contain important notations regarding the claim's handling or company decisions. These documents should be reviewed with company personnel at the home office.

Claim files are not easy to review. The forms are usually unfamiliar to counsel and difficult to interpret, particularly if they contain a mixture of forms completed by the insured, forms completed by doctors and hospital personnel, computer printouts, handwritten notes, field reports, and telephone messages. For this reason it is often quite helpful for someone at the company to prepare an outline or chronology of the claims handling process which defense counsel can use as a guide for reviewing the file with company personnel.

In addition to obtaining pertinent company documents when the case is referred to him, defense counsel should also request all relevant documents which the plaintiff has in his possession. Documents to be obtained include the original policy, to determine if the provisions or endorsements are the same as the specimen policy he should have obtained from the company; copies of cancelled premium checks; diaries containing notes regarding medical examinations and medications; and correspondence with company personnel.

### Discovery

It is advantageous, generally, to take the plaintiff's deposition at an early stage, in order to obtain the precise facts which form the plaintiff's version of the case. If possible this deposition should be taken before the first responsive pleading is filed. If counsel plans to challenge the sufficiency of the allegations of the complaint in this first responsive pleading, an early deposition will compel the plaintiff to state the facts supporting the complaint. Then, if the claims made in the complaint are found to be insufficient, the plaintiff, in preparing his amended complaint, will be limited to the facts described in his deposition; the possible result being that the plaintiff will be incapable of stating claims for extra-contract or punitive damages.

During discovery, there are a number of specific areas upon which defense counsel should focus. He should attempt to establish that the sales and claim handling processes at issue in the case were at all times courteous, prompt and cooperative, particularly the communications with the insured. He also should determine the precise facts upon which the plaintiff bases his claim for extra-contract benefits, by pinpointing the basis for misrepresentation charges and the conduct constituting the alleged bad faith or any other alleged improper handling.

If a claim for damages due to emotional distress is made, defense counsel should determine the medical history of the plaintiff, obtaining a complete list of all doctors treating him both before and after the claim was denied, the nature and extent of treatment, the type of any medication taken, whether it was taken with or without a prescription, and the frequency with which it was taken. Defense counsel should obtain copies of the records of any treating physicians, considering depositions of some or all of these doctors, as well as a medical examination of the plaintiff. Counsel should also carefully document the plaintiff's activity during the period of alleged emotional distress, seeking to ascertain the plaintiff's work history, travel and vacation activities, and social and family activities.

The plaintiff should be required to document all financial damages. This documentation, if in doubt, should be confirmed by obtaining pertinent records or depositions from the financial institutions involved.

Defense counsel should also carefully investigate benefits received from collateral sources—such as worker's compensation, Social Security, state disability, other private insurance and disability health plans (either group or individual) and pension and retirement plans—to mitigate any emotional distress claim based on financial hardship. He should also obtain the records pertaining to the plaintiff from each of these collateral sources, whether the claim was paid or denied.

It is critical to the case for each company witness to be thoroughly and completely prepared for his deposition and trial testimony. It is also important that each company witness understand the basic factual contentions which the plaintiff is making and why the plaintiff contends that the company, and the particular company witness, acted improperly.

Most important, however, is for counsel to ensure that the witnesses do not try to avoid blame by placing it on someone else, that they testify to facts and not speculate as to what action they took in processing the claim and why, and that they understand the basis for the claim rejection or the termination of benefits. Of course, in preparing the company witnesses, each anticipated area of inquiry by plaintiff's counsel should be reviewed with each witness.

Handling claims for extra-contract and punitive damages in the method suggested will put the defense in the best posture for trial or settlement. Defense counsel must carefully maneuver his case and, to the extent that he can, maintain control over plaintiff's counsel and his evidence. This will ensure that in the event the case goes to trial, the potential for jury outrage will be blocked. A careful marshalling of the evidence by defense counsel may mean that the court will refuse to submit the questions of punitive damages to the jury, leaving only the extra-contract compensatory claim to be resolved.

## GRAY v. GRAIN DEALERS MUTUAL INSURANCE CO.

United States Court of Appeals, D.C. Circuit, 1989.
276 U.S.App.D.C. 388, 871 F.2d 1128.

SILBERMAN, CIRCUIT JUDGE:

Following a personal injury claim filed against Windell Speed by Vernon Gray, a pedestrian Speed hit while driving his car, Grain Dealers Mutual Insurance Company breached its duty to settle on behalf of its insured, Speed. In doing so, Grain Dealers exposed itself to liability in excess of Speed's policy limits for consequential damages resulting from its breach. Speed assigned to Gray Speed's chose in action against Grain Dealers in exchange for Gray's release of Speed from liability to pay a default judgment of $334,000 entered against him. The district court awarded Gray $334,000, 684 F.Supp. 1108, and we affirm that result.

I.

This case comes to us primarily on stipulated facts. The district court, however, made certain findings, apparently not in dispute, which supplement the stipulations. In 1985, Grain Dealers Mutual Insurance Company, an Indiana corporation, issued an automobile liability insurance policy to Windell Speed, then a North Carolina resident. The contract, mailed to Speed at his North Carolina address, lists a North Carolina agent for Grain Dealers. Subsequently, Speed moved to Washington, D.C. and in August 1985, while driving his car in Washington, D.C., struck and seriously injured Vernon Gray, a pedestrian. Speed timely reported the accident to Grain Dealers, which referred Speed to its agent in Northern Virginia, R.W. Parker. In September 1985, Gray filed suit against Speed seeking $2 million in damages. The insurance contract included a standard "duty-to-defend clause" obligating the insurer to provide legal counsel to defend or settle on behalf of Speed in the event of a lawsuit arising out of an insured risk. Speed accordingly mailed the complaint to Parker who assured Speed that he would take care of the lawsuit. Gray's attorney made several attempts to contact Parker and discuss settlement of the case. In a letter dated January 7, 1986, Gray's attorney offered to settle the case for $25,000—the policy limit. Parker did not respond to the letter.

In light of Parker's silence, Gray's attorney sought and gained a default judgment against Speed at the end of January 1986. The next month, when the district court held a hearing to ascertain Gray's damages, no one appeared for Speed. After hearing evidence on Gray's injuries and medical expenses, the court awarded him $334,000. Several months later, in April 1986, Parker sent Gray's January 7 settlement offer to Grain Dealers.

In June, Speed agreed to assign his claim against the insurance company to Gray in exchange for Gray's releasing Speed of any obligation to pay the judgment. Shortly thereafter Gray sued Grain Dealers and R.W. Parker to recover the amount of the judgment. After Gray filed his suit against Grain Dealers and Parker, Grain Dealers filed, in its own name, a "motion for relief from judgment" in the previous suit that Gray had filed against Speed. The court granted Gray's responsive motion to strike Grain Dealers' motion, on the grounds that Grain Dealers was not a party to that suit, and that the assignment released Speed from any obligation under the suit. In response to the suit filed against it, Grain Dealers asserted that it was only liable under the policy to indemnify Speed and by reason of the assignment, Speed's liability to Gray—and any liability of Grain Dealers to Speed or Gray—was extinguished. Alternatively, the company claimed it could not be held liable under North Carolina law in excess of its policy limits for only negligence, to which the company had stipulated. On cross motions for summary judgment, the district court awarded Gray the full amount of the default judgment against Grain Dealers, notwithstanding its recognition that the result was "harsh."

II.

[part II of the opinion holding that North Carolina law applied to the case is omitted]

III.

We therefore examine first Grain Dealers' contention that under North Carolina law, it is not liable in excess of policy limits for ordinary negligence in handling Gray's claim against Speed. If appellant is correct, then Speed had no claim in excess of policy limits against the company that could have been assigned to Gray, and the assignment would be, at least in part, a nullity.

Although North Carolina law is by no means crystal clear on the point, we think appellee has the better argument. It may well be that in North Carolina, if the insurance company actively assumes the defense of an insured, it is not liable for mere negligence in failing to gain the best settlement for the insured. In that event, a showing of bad faith may be required to recover in excess of policy limits. Coca–Cola Bottling Co. v. Maryland Casualty Co., 325 F.Supp. 204, 206 (W.D.N.C.1971).

Still, the Supreme Court of North Carolina and lower courts have described the insurer's settlement duty as "to act diligently and in good faith." Alford v. Textile Ins. Co., 248 N.C. 224, 103 S.E.2d 8, 12 (1958) (emphasis added); Coca–Cola Bottling Co., 325 F.Supp. at 206; Abernethy v. Utica Mut. Ins. Co., 373 F.2d 565, 568 (4th Cir.1967). It is surely impossible to characterize the company's conduct in this case as diligent. Although the North Carolina courts may wish to insulate insurance companies from liability for "honest mistakes of judgment" Coca–Cola, 325 F.Supp. at 206 (which might be characterized as negligent), we detect no solicitude for the insurance company that negligently fails to exercise any judgment at all. Indeed, Grain Dealers' stipulated negligence in this case may even be indistinguishable from bad faith under North Carolina law. In Abernethy, the Fourth Circuit heard an appeal from summary judgment granted in "a case of a flat refusal to negotiate under circumstances that * * * gave rise to an obligation to engage with bona fides in settlement negotiations." 373 F.2d at 569. Deciding that a jury question was presented, the court found that "the flat refusal to negotiate, under the circumstances of substantial exposure to liability, a demonstrated receptive climate for settlement and limited insurance coverage, *could have been found to show lack of good faith* in [the insurer's] exercise of its exclusive power to settle." Id. at 570 (emphasis added).

Even assuming it could be liable in excess of policy limits as a result of its behavior, Grain Dealers further argues that it is not liable to Gray because the judgment against Speed was not paid or shown to be payable. Appellant contends that in order to recover against the insurance company, Gray must prove that Speed would have paid the judgment against Gray, otherwise the insurance company is liable for more than its insured's true damage. Grain Dealers argues that the value of Speed's claim against the insurance company should be modified by his ability to pay the judgment to Gray. If the modification is not made, then, through the assignment-release, a silk purse has been made out of a sow's ear. Although no direct evidence was presented by either party as to Speed's net worth, his earnings, or his intention to attempt to pay the judgment prior to the assignment and release, we could infer from the record that Speed was a man of modest means.

Under circumstances such as this, where the insured has not yet paid any of the judgment, there is a split of authority among the states as to the extent of an insurance company's liability to the assignee of its insured for a claim above the policy limit. The majority of jurisdictions adheres to the judgment rule:[2] "an entry of judgment in excess [of policy limits] alone is sufficient damage to sustain a recovery from an

2. Those states supporting the judgment rule are: Alabama, Arizona, Arkansas, California, Delaware, Florida, Georgia, Illinois, Indiana, Iowa, Kansas, Kentucky, Louisiana, Maryland, Massachusetts, Minnesota, Missouri, Montana, New Hampshire, New Mexico, Ohio, Oregon, Pennsylvania, South Carolina, Tennessee, Texas, and Utah. An-

insurer for its breach of duty." Carter v. Pioneer Mut. Casualty Co., 67 Ohio St.2d 146, 423 N.E.2d 188, 190 (1981). To be sure, not all of the states following the judgment rule have considered the case of an insolvent or bankrupt insured, which presents the most difficult challenge to the integrity of the judgment rule.[3] (But, of course, Speed was never found to be insolvent.)[4] The minority, concerned about collusion between the insured and the assignee, follows the payment rule and limits the insurance company's liability to that portion of the judgment that equals "the amount of [the insured's] assets not exempt from legal process."[5] Stockdale v. Jamison, 416 Mich. 217, 330 N.W.2d 389, 390–91 (1981). If the insurance company were to be obliged to pay more than the insured was capable of paying at the time of the assignment and release, the insurance company, it has been thought, would be charged punitive damages. Gordon v. Nationwide Mut. Ins. Co., 30 N.Y.2d 427, 334 N.Y.S.2d 601, 611, 285 N.E.2d 849 (1972) (Fuld, C.J., concurring), cert. denied, 410 U.S. 931, 93 S.Ct. 1374, 35 L.Ed.2d 593 (1973). Although it is never fully articulated, a somewhat different perception of normal behavior underlies these rules. The courts appear to be in fundamental disagreement over the issue of whether or not it is proper to presume that a person will attempt to pay his debts, and therefore that a judgment against an insured, in itself, can be assumed to be good for full value.

Unfortunately, North Carolina courts have not been obliged to choose which line of authority they prefer. A court of appeals has held

notation, Liability Insurer's Failure to Settle, 63 A.L.R.3d 630, 641–69 (1975 & Supp. 1986); Torrez v. State Farm Mut. Auto Ins. Co., 705 F.2d 1192, 1197–1201 (10th Cir. 1982).

**3.** The following states have applied the judgment rule where the insured (or his estate) was insolvent or even bankrupt: California, Florida, Indiana, Iowa, Kansas, Louisiana, Maryland, Minnesota, Montana, New Mexico, Ohio, South Carolina, and Tennessee; but see n. 8. Although not squarely presented with an insolvent or bankrupt insured, courts in Alabama, Delaware, Georgia, Illinois, Massachusetts, New Hampshire, Pennsylvania, Texas, and Utah have written dicta indicating that the judgment rule would be followed in those states under such circumstances. Arizona, Arkansas, Kentucky, Missouri, and Oregon endorse the judgment rule without discussing the solvency of the insured. Annotation, Liability Insurer's Failure to Settle, 63 A.L.R.3d 630, 641–69 (1975 & Supp.1986).

**4.** In any event, even if Speed were to have been found insolvent, Grain Dealers would be disadvantaged by the language of the contract: "Bankruptcy or insolvency of the *covered person* shall not relieve us of any obligations under this policy."

**5.** In addition to Michigan, California, Connecticut and New York have endorsed the payment rule noting that where an insured (or his estate) is insolvent or bankrupt no damage is shown to have harmed him. Annotation, Liability Insurer's Failure to Settle, 63 A.L.R.3d 630, 641–69 (1975). The California courts distinguish between the case of an insured who dies penniless and then has a judgment levied against his estate (payment rule applies) and an insured who is forced into bankruptcy by a judgment (judgment rule applies). In New York, the rule varies according to the circumstances in which it is applied: "1) where the assured pays part of the judgment or is solvent enough to do so at the time of the excess judgment, the judgment rule applies and he is entitled to the full amount of the excess as his damages; 2) where he was insolvent before the judgment and obtained a bankruptcy discharge after it, he is not damaged and may not recover for it; and 3) where he was insolvent or nearly insolvent prior to the judgment the jury must consider his past, his prospects, and other economic factors and assess his damages." Levantino v. Insurance Co. of N. Am., 102 Misc.2d 77, 422 N.Y.S.2d 995, 1002 (1979).

that an insurance company was not liable where an insured and a plaintiff (injured party) entered into a consent judgment which, by its terms, provided that it was not enforceable against the insured. Huffman v. Peerless Ins. Co., 17 N.C.App. 292, 193 S.E.2d 773, 774, cert. denied, 283 N.C. 257, 159 S.E.2d 689 (1973). The Supreme Court, however, in Alford v. Textile Ins. Co., 248 N.C. 224, 103 S.E.2d 8 (1958), said: "If the insurer had failed to make these settlements, and judgments for greater amounts had been obtained against its insured; it would * * * be liable to [the tortfeasor/insured] for such amounts as the judgments exceeded the amounts for which the insurer could have settled * * *. *The liability imposed on the insurer would not * * * be affected or diminished by the question of solvency or insolvency of its insured.*" Id. 103 S.E.2d at 12. (citations omitted and emphasis added). Although dictum, that passage suggests sympathy with the policies underlying the judgment rule. Therefore we think we would be safe in concluding that, under North Carolina law, introduction of the judgment is at least prima facie evidence that the insured was obligated, willing, and capable of paying the judgment. It may be open to the insurer to challenge that evidence or even to show collusion but Grain Dealers produced no such evidence here.

We note, moreover, that the insurance contract states that Grain Dealers "will pay damages for bodily injury or property damage for which any covered person becomes *legally responsible* because of an auto accident." It seems rather clear to us that after the judgment but before the assignment and release, Speed was legally responsible to pay the judgment, whether or not he ever intended to pay. So we conclude under North Carolina law Grain Dealers could be made liable for the whole judgment.

IV.

That brings us to question whether or not the assignment and release were self-contradicting. According to the insurance company, the release nullified the assignment of the claim because the release extinguished the basis for the assignment. If so, that which Speed assigned to Gray was worthless upon transfer. This somewhat metaphysical contention is to be tested first according to D.C. law because it depends on a construction of the agreement reached between the two parties in the District. We note somewhat ruefully that there are no cases in the District squarely on point. However, many other jurisdictions have considered similar transactions and the majority of them have allowed the transfer.[7] A few courts have taken the path urged by the

7. Steedly v. London & Lancashire Ins. Co., 416 F.2d 259, 262 (6th Cir.1969) (assignment/release did not free insurer from liability; if insured "had satisfied judgment by making full payment * * * in return for the release, [insurer] agrees that he could have then brought an action against it or have assigned this right"); LaRotunda v. Royal Globe Ins. Co., 87 Ill.App.3d 446, 42 Ill.Dec. 219, 408 N.E.2d 928 (1980) (agreement not to collect against insured given in exchange for assignment of rights against insurer evidenced no collusion); Metcalf v. Hartford Accident & Indem. Co., 176 Neb. 468, 126 N.W.2d 471, 475–76 (1964) (rejecting insurer's contention that consent judg-

appellant, and have held that a similar transaction was ineffective in passing the claim against the insurance company to the assignee. It is apparent that underlying the construction of the assignment and release made by those courts declining to uphold them is the concern—discussed in the previous portion of the opinion—about collusion between the insured and the assignee. See, e.g., Freeman v. Schmidt Real Estate & Ins., 755 F.2d 135, 138–39 (8th Cir.1985) (where insurer, like insured, is no longer "legally obligated to pay" court cites fear of collusion as policy rationale for declining to give effect to assignment/release); Bendall v. White, 511 F.Supp. 793, 794–95 (N.D.Ala.1981) (same).[8] That policy rationale arises not so much out of a construction of the assignment and release, but rather stems from an evaluation of the insurance company's liability under the insurance policy. As we have already concluded, North Carolina law determines liability under the insurance policy. We think it would be quite artificial therefore to allow these policy considerations to enter into our interpretation of the assignment and release. That would be so even if D.C. law reflected these anti-collusion considerations—which it does not—because the *effect* of the assignment on the insurance company must be governed by North Carolina law. See Fox–Greenwald Sheet Metal Co. v. Markowitz Bros., 452 F.2d 1346, 1354 (D.C.Cir.1971).

Accordingly, we see no reason why, under D.C. and North Carolina law, we should not construe the assignment and release to give full effect to its terms. After all, if the release of Speed extinguished the claim Speed had against the insurance company simultaneously with the assignment of the claim, that would also be true of that part of the claim Speed had against the insurance company within the policy limits. As appellee points out, appellant's argument reduces to an absurd conclusion: if the insured were to have paid the judgment in full and obtained a release from the injured party, he would have no right to proceed against the insurer for indemnification. We think appellant's self-

ment created no legal obligation to pay); Zander v. Casualty Ins. Co., 259 Cal.App.2d 793, 66 Cal.Rptr. 561, 568 (1968) (settlement with insured does not release insurer because to do so penalizes insured for attempt to minimize damages); Critz v. Farmers Ins. Group, 230 Cal.App.2d 788, 41 Cal.Rptr. 401, 404 (1964) (assignment of chose of action in exchange for release from liability before judgment entered against insured not void against public policy because assignment's value is determined by bad faith of insurer).

Covenants not to execute are different than releases, as the legal liability remains in force against those who have covenants, whereas a release represents total freedom from liability. However, courts have used much the same reasoning in upholding covenants/assignments as they have when considering release/assignments. Bishop v. Crowther, 101 Ill.App.3d 933, 57 Ill.Dec. 341, 344, 428 N.E.2d 1021, 1024 (1981) (insurer's argument that insured no longer "legally obligated to pay" judgments against him, and therefore insurer is released as well, fails because "[a]n agreement limiting execution to specific assets does not negate damages") appeal denied, 88 Ill.2d 549 (1982); State Farm Mut. Auto. Ins. Co. v. Paynter, 122 Ariz. 198, 593 P.2d 948, 950–51 (Ct.App.1979) (assignment of rights under policy and $500 in exchange for covenant not to execute future judgments against insured upheld as not "inherently fraudulent").

8. See also Steil v. Florida Physicians' Ins. Reciprocal, 448 So.2d 589, 592 (Fla. Dist.Ct.App.1984) (suspicion of collusion and fraud led court to deny effect to settlement agreement/assignment but, in dictum, court indicated that such an agreement may be upheld where free from taint).

destruct interpretation of the document can only be adopted for policy reasons quite apart from appropriate legal methods of document construction, and therefore the judgment of the district court is

Affirmed.

### *Notes*

1. See Annotation, Bankruptcy or insolvency of insured as affecting right of person injured to proceeds of indemnity insurance, in absence of provision in policy in that regard 59 A.L.R. 1123 (1929).

2. Michigan statutes provide that liability policies, with certain exemptions, contain "a provision that the insolvency or bankruptcy of the person insured shall not release the insurer from the payment of damages for injury sustained or loss occasioned * * *." M.C.L.A. §§ 500.3004, 500.3006. Upon the return unsatisfied of an execution on the insured, an action in the nature of a writ of garnishment may be maintained against the insurer "under the terms of the policy for the amount of the judgment in the said action not exceeding the amount of the policy." M.C.L.A. § 500.3006.

3. California has a statutory provision similar to the first of those quoted above: West's Ann.Cal.Insurance Code § 11580, which provides:

**§ 11580. Insolvency, bankruptcy, or death of insured**

A policy insuring against losses set forth in subdivision (a) shall not be issued or delivered to any person in this state unless it contains the provisions set forth in subdivision (b). * * *

(b) * * *

(1) A provision that the insolvency or bankruptcy of the insured will not release the insurer from the payment of damages for injury sustained or loss occasioned during the life of such policy.

(2) A provision that whenever judgment is secured against the insured or the executor or administrator of a deceased insured in an action based upon bodily injury, death, or property damage, then an action may be brought against the insurer on the policy and subject to its terms and limitations, by such judgment creditor to recover on the judgment.

Subsection 11580(b)(2) "makes the judgment creditor a third party beneficiary of the insurance contract between the insurer and the insured", Murphy v. Allstate Insurance Company, 17 Cal.3d 937, 943, 132 Cal.Rptr. 424, 428, 553 P.2d 584, 588 (1976).

## GRAY v. ZURICH INSURANCE CO.

Supreme Court of California, 1966.
65 Cal.2d 263, 54 Cal.Rptr. 104, 419 P.2d 168.

TOBRINER, JUSTICE.

This is an action by an insured against his insurer for failure to defend an action filed against him which stemmed from a complaint alleging that he had committed an assault. The main issue turns on the argument of the insurer that an exclusionary clause of the policy excuses its defense of an action in which a plaintiff alleges that the insured intentionally caused the bodily injury. Yet the language of the policy does not clearly define the application of the exclusionary clause to the duty to defend. Since in that event we test the meaning of the policy according to the insured's reasonable expectation of coverage and since the language of the policy would lead the insured here to expect defense of the third party suit, we cannot exonerate the carrier from the rendition of such protection.

Plaintiff, Dr. Vernon D. Gray, is the named insured under an insurance policy issued by defendant. A "Comprehensive Personal Liability Endorsement" in the policy states, under a paragraph designated "Coverage L," that the insurer agrees "(T)o pay on behalf of the insured all sums which the insured shall become legally obligated to pay as damages because of bodily injury or property damage, and the company shall defend any suit against the insured alleging such bodily injury or property damage and seeking damages which are payable under the terms of this endorsement, even if any of the allegations are groundless, false or fraudulent; but the company may make such investigation and settlement of any claim or suit as it deems expedient." The policy contains a provision that "(T)his endorsement does not apply" to a series of specified exclusions set forth under separate headings, including a paragraph (c) which reads, "under coverages L and M, to bodily injury or property damages caused intentionally by or at the direction of the insured."

The suit which Dr. Gray contends Zurich should have defended arose out of an altercation between him and a Mr. John R. Jones.[1] Jones filed a complaint in Missouri alleging that Dr. Gray "wilfully, maliciously, brutally and intentionally assaulted" him; he prayed for actual damages of $50,000 and punitive damages of $50,000. Dr. Gray notified defendant of the suit, stating that he had acted in self-defense, and requested that the company defend. Defendant refused on the ground that the complaint alleged an intentional tort which fell outside the coverage of the policy. Dr. Gray thereafter unsuccessfully defended on the theory of self-defense; he suffered a judgment of $6,000 actual damages although the jury refused to award punitive damages.

Dr. Gray then filed the instant action charging defendant with breach of its duty to defend. Defendant answered, admitting the execution of the policy but denying any such obligation. The record on appeal has been augmented to include an offer of proof, presented by plaintiff and rejected by the trial court, which detailed the circumstances surrounding the altercation. The augmented record also includes exhibits introduced at the trial, consisting of copies of the pleadings and verdict in the Missouri suit and a copy of the subject insurance policy. The

1. Immediately preceding the altercation Dr. Gray had been driving an automobile on a residential street when another automobile narrowly missed colliding with his car. Jones, the driver of the other car, left his vehicle, approached Dr. Gray's car in a menacing manner and jerked open the door. At that point Dr. Gray, fearing physical harm to himself and his passengers, rose from his seat and struck Jones.

parties waived written findings of fact and conclusions of law; the court rendered judgment in favor of defendant. We must decide whether or not defendant bore the obligation to defend plaintiff in the Missouri action.

Defendant argues that it need not defend an action in which the complaint reveals on its face that the claimed bodily injury does not fall within the indemnification coverage; that here the Jones complaint alleged that the insured committed an assault, which fell outside such coverage. Defendant urges, as a second answer to plaintiff's contention, that the contract, if construed to require defense of the insured, would violate the public policy of the state and that, indeed, the judgment in the third party suit upholding the claim of an intentional bodily injury operates to estop the insured from recovery. Defendant thirdly contends that any requirement that it defend the Jones suit would embroil it in a hopeless conflict of interest. Finally it submits that, even if it should have defended the third party suit, the damages against it should encompass only the insured's expenses of defense and not the judgment against him.

We shall explain our reasons for concluding that defendant was obligated to defend the Jones suit, and our grounds for rejecting defendant's remaining propositions. Since the policy sets forth the duty to defend as a primary one and since the insurer attempts to avoid it only by an unclear exclusionary clause, the insured would reasonably expect, and is legally entitled to, such protection. As an alternative but secondary ground for our ruling we accept, for purposes of argument, defendant's contention that the duty to defend arises only if the third party suit involves a liability for which the insurer would be required to indemnify the insured, and, even upon this basis, we find a duty to defend.

In interpreting an insurance policy we apply the general principle that doubts as to meaning must be resolved against the insurer and that any exception to the performance of the basic underlying obligation must be so stated as clearly to apprise the insured of its effect.

These principles of interpretation of insurance contracts have found new and vivid restatement in the doctrine of the adhesion contract. As this court has held, a contract entered into between two parties of unequal bargaining strength, expressed in the language of a standardized contract, written by the more powerful bargainer to meet its own needs, and offered to the weaker party on a "take it or leave it basis" carries some consequences that extend beyond orthodox implications. Obligations arising from such a contract inure not alone from the consensual transaction but from the relationship of the parties.

Although courts have long followed the basic precept that they would look to the words of the contract to find the meaning which the parties expected from them, they have also applied the doctrine of the adhesion contract to insurance policies, holding that in view of the disparate bargaining status of the parties we must ascertain that meaning of the contract which the insured would reasonably expect. Thus as Kessler stated in his classic article on adhesion contracts: "In dealing with standardized contracts courts have to determine what the weaker contracting party could legitimately expect by way of services according to the enterpriser's 'calling', and to what extent the stronger party disappointed reasonable expectations based on the typical life situation." (Kessler, Contracts of Adhesion (1943) 43 Colum.L.Rev. 629, 637.)

Professor Patterson, in describing one characteristic consequence of "the conception of adhesion, whether that term is used or not," writes: "The court interprets the form contract to mean what a reasonable buyer would expect it to mean, and thus protects the weaker party's expectation at the expense of the stronger's. This process of interpretation was used many years ago in interpreting (or construing) insurance contracts. * * *" (Fn. omitted; Patterson, The Interpretation and Construction of Contracts (1964) 64 Colum.L.Rev. 833, 858.)

Thus we held in Steven v. Fidelity & Casualty Co., 58 Cal.2d 862, 27 Cal.Rptr. 172, 377 P.2d 284, that we would not enforce an exclusionary clause in an insurance contract which was unclear, saying: "If (the insurer) deals with the public upon a mass basis, the notice of non-coverage of the policy, in a situation in which the public may reasonably expect coverage, must be conspicuous, plain and clear." P. 878, 27 Cal.Rptr. p. 182, 377 P.2d p. 294.)

When we test the instant policy by these principles we find that its provisions as to the obligation to defend are uncertain and undefined; in the light of the reasonable expectation of the insured, they require the performance of that duty. At the threshold we note that the nature of the obligation to defend is itself necessarily uncertain. Although insurers have often insisted that the duty arises only if the insurer is bound to indemnify the insured, this very contention creates a dilemma. No one can determine whether the third party suit does or does not fall within the indemnification coverage of the policy until that suit is resolved; in the instant case, the determination of whether the insured engaged in intentional, negligent or even wrongful conduct depended upon the judgment in the Jones suit, and, indeed, even after that judgment, no one could be positive whether it rested upon a finding of plaintiff's negligent or his intentional conduct. The carrier's obligation to indemnify inevitably will not be defined until the adjudication of the very action which it should have defended. Hence the policy contains its own seeds of uncertainty; the insurer has held out a promise that by its very nature is ambiguous.

Although this uncertainty in the performance of the duty to defend could have been clarified by the language of the policy we find no such specificity here. An examination of the policy discloses that the broadly stated promise to defend is not conspicuously or clearly conditioned solely on a nonintentional bodily injury; instead, the insured could reasonably expect such protection.

The policy is a "comprehensive personal liability" contract; the designation in itself connotes general protection for alleged bodily injury caused by the insured. The insurer makes two wide promises: "(1.) To pay on behalf of the insured all sums which the insured shall become legally obligated to pay as damages because of bodily injury or property damage, and (2.) the company shall defend any suit against the insured alleging such bodily injury or property damage and seeking damages which are payable under the terms of this endorsement, even if any of the allegations of the suit are groundless, false, or fraudulent": clearly these promises, without further clarification, would lead the insured reasonably to expect the insurer to defend him against suits seeking damages for bodily injury, whatever the alleged cause of the injury, whether intentional or inadvertent.

But the insurer argues that the third party suit must seek "damages which are *payable* under the terms of this endorsement"; it contends that this limitation *modifies* the general duty to defend by confining the duty only to actions seeking damages within the primary coverage of the policy. Under "Exclusions" the policy provides that it "does not apply * * * under coverage L and M to bodily injury * * * caused intentionally by * * * the insured."

The very first paragraph as to coverage, however, provides that "the company shall defend any such suit against the insured alleging such bodily injury" although the allegations of the suit are groundless, false or fraudulent. This language, in its broad sweep, would lead the insured reasonably to expect defense of *any* suit regardless of merit or cause. The relation of the exclusionary clause to this basic promise is anything but clear. The basic promise would support the insured's reasonable expectation that he had bought the rendition of legal services to defend against a suit for bodily injury which alleged he had caused it, negligently, nonintentionally, intentionally or in any other manner. The doctrines and cases we have set forth tell us that the exclusionary clause must be "conspicuous, plain and clear." (Steven v. Fidelity & Casualty Co., supra, 58 Cal.2d 862, 878, 27 Cal.Rptr. 172, 377 P.2d 284.) This clause is not "conspicuous" since it appears only after a long and complicated page of fine print, and is itself in fine print; its relation to the remaining clauses of the policy and its effect is surely not "plain and clear."

A further uncertainty lurks in the exclusionary clause itself. It alludes to damage caused "intentionally by or at the direction of the insured." Yet an act of the insured may carry out his "intention" and also cause unintended harm. When set next to the words "at the direction of the insured" the word "intentionally" might mean to the layman collusive, wilful or planned action beyond the classical notion of intentional tort. This built-in ambiguity has caused debate and refined definition in many courts; in any event, the word surely cannot be "plain and clear" to the layman.

The insured is unhappily surrounded by concentric circles of uncertainty: the first, the unascertainable nature of the insurer's duty to defend; the second, the unknown effect of the provision that the insurer must defend even a groundless, false or fraudulent claim; the third, the uncertain extent of the indemnification coverage. Since we must resolve uncertainties in favor of the insured and interpret the policy provisions according to the layman's reasonable expectations, and since the effect of the exclusionary clause is neither conspicuous, plain nor clear, we hold that in the present case the policy provides for an obligation to defend and that such obligation is independent of the indemnification coverage.

The insurer counters with the contention that this position would compel an insurer "issuing a policy covering liability of the insured for maintenance, use or operation of an automobile * * * to defend the insured in an action for damages for negligently maintaining a stairway and thereby allegedly causing injury to another—because the insured claims that the suit for damages was false or groundless." The "groundless, false, or fraudulent" clause, however, does not extend the obligation to defend without limits; it includes only defense to those actions of the nature and kind covered by the policy. Here the policy insures against "damages because of bodily injury." As we have pointed out, in view of the language of the policy, the insured would reasonably expect protection in an action involving alleged bodily injury. On the other hand the insured could not reasonably expect protection under an automobile insurance policy for injury which occurs from defect in a stairway. Similarly an insured would not expect a defense for an injury involving an automobile under a general comprehensive policy which excluded automobile coverage. We look to the nature and kind of risk covered by the policy as a limitation upon the duty to defend; we cannot absolve the carrier from the duty to defend an insured for loss of the nature and kind against which it insured.

Our holding that the insurer bore the obligation to defend because the policy led plaintiff reasonably to expect such defense, and because the insurer's exclusionary clause did not exonerate it, cuts across defendant's answering contention that the duty arises only if the pleadings disclose a cause of action for which the insurer must indemnify the insured. Defendant would equate the duty to defend with the complaint that pleaded a liability for which the insurer was bound to indemnify the insured. Yet even if we accept defendant's premises, and define the duty to defend by measuring the allegations in the Jones case against the carrier's liability to indemnify, defendant's position still fails. We proceed to discuss this alternative ground of liability of the insurer, accepting for such purpose the insurer's argument that we must test the third party suit against the indemnification coverage of the policy. We point out that the carrier must defend a suit which *potentially* seeks damages within the coverage of the policy; the Jones action was such a suit.

Defendant cannot construct a formal fortress of the third party's pleadings and retreat behind its walls. The pleadings are malleable, changeable and amendable. Although an earlier decision reads: "In determining whether or not the appellant was bound to defend * * * the language of its contract must first be looked to, and next the allegations of the complaints * * *" (Lamb v. Belt Casualty Co., 3 Cal.App.2d 624, 630, 40 P.2d 311, 314), courts do not examine only the pleaded word but the potential liability created by the suit. Since the instant action presented the potentiality of a judgment based upon nonintentional conduct, and since liability for such conduct would fall within the indemnification coverage, the duty to defend became manifest at the outset.

To restrict the defense obligation of the insurer to the precise language of the pleading would not only ignore the thrust of the cases but would create an anomaly for the insured. Obviously, as Ritchie v. Anchor Casualty Co., 135 Cal.App.2d 245, 286 P.2d 1000, points out, the complainant in the third party action drafts his complaint in the broadest terms; he may very well stretch the action which lies in only nonintentional conduct to the dramatic complaint that alleges intentional misconduct. In light of the likely overstatement of the complaint and of the plasticity of modern pleading, we should hardly designate the third party as the arbiter of the policy's coverage.

Since modern procedural rules focus on the facts of a case rather than the theory of recovery in the complaint, the duty to defend should be fixed by the facts which the insurer learns from the complaint, the insured, or other sources. An insurer, therefore, bears a duty to defend its insured whenever it ascertains facts which give rise to the potential of liability under the policy. In the instant case the complaint itself, as well as the facts known to the insurer, sufficiently apprised the insurer of these possibilities; hence we need not set out when and upon what other occasions the duty of the insurer to ascertain such possibilities otherwise arises.

Jones' complaint clearly presented the possibility that he might obtain damages that were covered by the indemnity provisions of the policy. Even conduct that is traditionally classified as "intentional" or "wilful" has been held to fall within indemnification coverage. Moreover, despite Jones' pleading of intentional and wilful conduct, he could have amended his complaint to allege merely negligent conduct. Further, plaintiff might have been able to show that in physically defending himself, even if he exceeded the reasonable bounds of self-defense, he did not commit wilful and intended injury, but engaged only in nonintentional tortious conduct. Thus, even accepting the insurer's premise that it had no obligation to defend actions seeking damages not within the indemnification coverage, we find, upon proper measurement of the third party action against the insurer's liability to indemnify, it should have defended because the loss could have fallen within that liability.

We turn to the insurer's second major contention that the contract cannot be read to require the insurer to defend an action seeking damages for an intentional wrong because such an obligation would violate public policy. In support of this argument it relies upon Insurance Code section 533, and Civil Code section 1668.[17]

The contention fails on two grounds. In the first place, the statutes forbid only contracts which indemnify for "*loss*" or "*responsibility*" resulting from wilful wrong-doing. Here we deal with a contract which provides for *legal defense* against an action charging such conduct; the contract does not call for indemnification of the insured if the third party plaintiff prevails. In the second place, as we pointed out in Tomerlin v. Canadian Indemnity Co. (1964) 61 Cal.2d 638, 648, 39 Cal.Rptr. 731, 737, 394 P.2d 571, 577, the statutes "establish a public policy to prevent insurance coverage from encouragement of wilful tort." Thus Tomerlin held that if an insurer's obligation to pay a judgment based on wilful conduct results from an estoppel *after* the conduct, the obligation could not have previously encouraged the conduct. Similarly, the present contract does not offend the statute; a contract to defend an assured upon mere accusation of a wilful tort does not encourage such wilful conduct.

Nor can we accept defendant's argument that the duty to defend dissolves simply because the insured is unsuccessful in his defense and because the injured party recovers on the basis of a finding of the assured's wilful conduct. Citing Abbott v. Western Nat. Indem. Co. (1958) 165 Cal.App.2d 302, 331 P.2d 997, the insurer urges that if the judgment in a third party suit goes against the insured it operates as "res judicata or collateral estoppel in the insured's action or proceeding against the insurer."

We have explained that the insured would reasonably expect a defense by the insurer in all personal injury actions against him. If he is to be required to finance his own defense and then, only if successful, hold the insurer to its promise by means of a second suit for reimbursement, we defeat the basic reason for the purchase of the insurance. In purchasing his insurance the insured would reasonably expect that he would stand a better chance of vindication if supported by the resources and expertise of his insurer than if compelled to handle and finance the presentation of his case. He would, moreover, expect to be able to avoid the time, uncertainty and capital outlay in finding and retaining an attorney of his own. "The courts will not sanction a construction of the insurer's language that will defeat the very purpose or object of the insurance." (Ritchie v. Anchor Casualty Co., supra, 135 Cal.App.2d 245, 257, 286 P.2d 1000, 1007.)

Similarly, we find no merit in the insurer's third contention that our holding will embroil it in a conflict of interests. According to the insurer

**17.** Insurance Code section 533 provides: "An insurer is not liable for a loss caused by the wilful act of the insured; but he is not exonerated by the negligence of the insured, or of the insured's agents or others."

Civil Code section 1668 provides, in relevant part: "All contracts which have for their object, directly or indirectly, to exempt anyone from responsibility for his own * * * willful injury to the person or property of another * * * are against the policy of the law."

our ruling will require defense of an action in which the interests of insurer and insured are so opposed as to nullify the insurer's fulfillment of its duty of defense and of the protection of its own interests. For example, the argument goes, if defendant had defended against the Jones suit it would have sought to establish either that the insured was free from any liability or that such liability rested on intentional conduct. The insured, of course, would also seek a verdict holding him not liable but, if found liable, would attempt to obtain a ruling that such liability emanated from the nonintentional conduct within his insurance coverage. Thus, defendant contends, an insurer, if obligated to defend in this situation, faces an insoluble ethical problem.

Since, however, the court in the third party suit does not adjudicate the issue of coverage, the insurer's argument collapses. The only question there litigated is the insured's *liability*. The alleged victim does not concern himself with the theory of *liability;* he desires only the largest possible judgment. Similarly, the insured and insurer seek only to avoid, or at least to minimize, the judgment. As we have noted, modern procedural rules focus on whether, on a given set of facts, the plaintiff, regardless of the theory, may recover. Thus the question of whether or not the insured engaged in intentional conduct does not normally formulate an issue which is resolved in that litigation.[18]

In any event, if the insurer adequately reserves its right to assert the noncoverage defense later, it will not be bound by the judgment. If the injured party prevails, that party or the insured will assert his claim against the insurer.[19] At this time the insurer can raise the noncoverage defense previously reserved. In this manner the interests of insured and insurer in defending against the injured party's primary suit will be identical; the insurer will not face the suggested dilemma.

Finally, defendant urges that our holding should require only the reimbursement of the insured's expenses in defending the third party action but not the payment of the judgment. Defendant acknowledges the general rule that an insurer that wrongfully refuses to defend is liable on the judgment against the insured. (Arenson v. Nat. Automobile & Cas. Ins. Co. (1955) 45 Cal.2d 81, 84, 286 P.2d 816; Civ.Code, § 2778.) Defendant argues, however, that the instant situation should be distinguished from that case because here the judgment has not necessarily been rendered on a theory within the policy coverage. Thus defendant would limit the insured's recovery to the expenses of the third party suit.

**18.** In rare cases the issue of punitive damages or a special verdict might present a potential conflict of interests, but such a possibility does not outweigh the advantages of the general rule. Even in such cases, however, the insurer will still be bound, ethically and legally, to litigate in the interests of the insured.

**19.** Insurance Code section 11580, subdivision (b)(2) provides that "whenever judgment is secured against the insured * * * in an action based upon bodily injury, death, or property damage, then an action may be brought against the insurer on the policy and subject to its terms and limitations, by such judgment creditor to recover on the judgment."

We rejected a similar proposal in Tomerlin v. Canadian Indemnity Co., supra, 61 Cal.2d 638, 649–650, 39 Cal.Rptr. 731, 394 P.2d 571. In that case, as we have noted, the insurer's obligation to defend arose out of estoppel. The insurer contended that we should apply a "tort" theory of damages to its wrongful refusal to defend. Such a theory, we explained, would impose upon the insured "the impossible burden" of proving the extent of the loss caused by the insurer's breach. As this court said in an analogous situation in Arenson v. National Auto. & Cas. Ins. Co. (1957) 48 Cal.2d 528, 539, 310 P.2d 961, 968: "Having defaulted such agreement the company is manifestly bound to reimburse its insured for the full amount of any obligation reasonably incurred by him. It will not be allowed to defeat or whittle down its obligation on the theory that plaintiff himself was of such limited financial ability that he could not afford to employ able counsel, or to present every reasonable defense, or to carry his cause to the highest court having jurisdiction, * * *. Sustaining such a theory * * * would tend * * * to encourage insurance companies to similar disavowals of responsibility with everything to gain and nothing to lose."

In summary, the individual consumer in the highly organized and integrated society of today must necessarily rely upon institutions devoted to the public service to perform the basic functions which they undertake. At the same time the consumer does not occupy a sufficiently strong economic position to bargain with such institutions as to specific clauses of their contracts of performance, and, in any event, piecemeal negotiation would sacrifice the advantage of uniformity. Hence the courts in the field of insurance contracts have tended to require that the insurer render the basic insurance protection which it has held out to the insured. This obligation becomes especially manifest in the case in which the insurer has attempted to limit the principal coverage by an unclear exclusionary clause. We test the alleged limitation in the light of the insured's reasonable expectation of coverage; that test compels the indicated outcome of the present litigation.

The judgment is reversed and the trial court instructed to take evidence solely on the issue of damages alleged in plaintiff's complaint including the amount of the judgment in the Jones suit, and the costs, expenses and attorney's fees incurred in defending such suit.

TRAYNOR, C.J., and PETERS, PEEK, MOSK and BURKE, JJ., concur. The dissenting opinion of MCCOMB, J. is omitted.

## SMITH v. AMERICAN FAMILY MUTUAL INSURANCE CO.

Supreme Court of North Dakota, 1980.
294 N.W.2d 751.

VANDE WALLE, JUSTICE.

American Family Mutual Insurance Company ("American Family") appeals from a judgment entered against it upon a jury verdict in favor of Kenneth A. Smith. It also appeals from the trial court's order denying its motions for judgment notwithstanding the verdict or, in the alternative, a new trial. We affirm.

In February 1976, American Family, through James Erickson as agent, sold an automobile insurance policy to Smith providing liability and collision coverage for Smith's 1970 automobile. At that time Smith was working as a contract deputy sheriff in Wildrose, North Dakota. There is some dispute in the testimony as to whether or not Erickson was informed that Smith used his automobile in his police work although Smith's automobile was specially equipped for police work. Subsequently, Smith accepted employment as chief of police at Pembina, North Dakota. On June 10, 1976, Smith, while off duty and driving his own automobile, answered an assistance call from a deputy sheriff in Cavalier County. The deputy was pursuing a van and, according to Smith's testimony, he asked the deputy if he (Smith) should set up a roadblock. Smith testified that the officer replied in the affirmative and Smith did drive his car crosswise on the two-laned highway, blocking the northbound lane. Smith placed a revolving red light on the top of his car and waited on the side of the road. The driver of the van which was being pursued did not stop and ran into Smith's car, demolishing it. Smith reported the loss to Erickson but Erickson told Smith the loss was not covered.

Smith and his wife, Joyce, lived in Langdon; Joyce worked in Cavalier and Smith also needed a car to drive to work in Pembina. Because they both needed automobiles to drive to work, Smith was anxious to have his claim settled. Smith asked Erickson on several occasions when an insurance adjuster would come to investigate the claim. Erickson told Smith the adjusters were busy. On June 24, an independent adjuster did investigate the accident. He agreed on the amount of the loss but requested that Smith sign a nonwaiver agreement, which the adjuster also executed on behalf of American Family, wherein Smith and American Family agreed that any action taken by American Family in investigating the accident would not operate to invalidate any of the provisions of the policy and that if a suit were filed as a result of the accident and American Family elected to defend the suit, such action would not be construed as a waiver of any of the conditions of the policy. The agreement further provided:

> "It is the intention of this agreement to preserve all the rights of the parties hereto and provide for an investigation of the said accident without in any way affecting, impairing or adding to the liability of the Company under said policy or under any statutes or the common law, and no act of the Company hereunder shall be construed as an admission of its liability or coverage."

Although Smith was asked to execute and did execute the agreement, he testified the agent told him that in his opinion the collision was covered and Smith should get a check in a week or two. When Smith contacted Erickson inquiring why the check was not forthcoming, Erickson told him the reason could be that the loss was not covered. Smith had another car he owned, which had motor problems, repaired for $770 in order that he and his wife would have cars to drive to their places of employment. American Family paid the claim for the loss of Smith's car some two months later. Prior to the time the check arrived, Erickson, when asked about the delay, gave various excuses including the response that there was no coverage under the policy. When the check did arrive, Erickson told Smith the only reason American Family paid the loss was that the adjusters had determined that a badly hurt passenger (Herzog) in the van which collided with Smith's automobile had decided not to sue Smith.

Herzog did sue Smith later. Smith immediately delivered the papers to Erickson. Erickson told Smith that American Family was not named in the lawsuit and therefore the company did not have to defend Smith, and that Smith must secure his own attorney to defend the suit because American Family was not liable. Smith became very upset and contacted an attorney (Sillers) who agreed to represent Smith for $50 per hour.

Sillers contacted Harrington, American Family's claim counsel, by telephone on September 29, 1976, inquiring as to what American Family was going to do on the defense of the Herzog lawsuit. Harrington informed Sillers he had called Herzog's attorney and asked for an extension to file an answer. He also told Sillers the matter was being forwarded to the Letnes & Marshall law firm in Grand Forks to commence a declaratory-judgment action to determine American Family's liability under the insurance contract. Harrington told Sillers it was American Family's position that when Smith agreed with the deputy sheriff of Pembina County to use Smith's car as a roadblock it came within the provision of the policy excluding liability assumed by the insured under any contract or agreement.

In October 1976, Sillers called American Family and asked for an immediate decision by American Family on the matter of defending Smith in the action brought against him by Herzog. Sillers spoke with Harrington, who told Sillers he would deny the claim. Harrington then wrote a letter on October 11, 1976, to Sillers denying coverage on the part of American Family. Sillers commenced this lawsuit against American Family on Smith's behalf on October 18, 1976. Subsequently, Sillers received a copy of a letter from American Family's claim counsel, Harrington, addressed to the Letnes & Marshall law firm of Grand Forks, requesting that firm to defend American Family and Erickson in the lawsuit filed by Smith against them. In that letter Harrington suggested filing a counterclaim against Sillers for abuse of process in the amount of $1,000,000. Because of that letter Sillers advised Smith there might be a conflict of interest if he were sued by American Family and continued to represent Smith in the lawsuit against American Family. Smith requested Sillers to continue in the lawsuit but, at Sillers's suggestion, another attorney was retained to work with Sillers in the matter.

In January 1977, Sillers told Smith that American Family had reversed its position and would take over Smith's defense in the action brought by the passenger in the van, but the company refused to pay Sillers the full $50 per hour. Sillers advised Smith that if he accepted American Family's offer, Smith would still owe him the difference between the $50 per hour agreed upon as his fee and the amount American Family agreed to pay. Smith told Sillers to use his best judgment. American Family did take over defense of the lawsuit against Smith but made no direct contact with Smith prior to the trial of this action. At the time this action was tried the action against Smith was still pending. The evidence at trial indicated that Smith was upset and worried over the pending action against him, whether or not American Family would defend the action, and whether or not, if a verdict was rendered against Smith, American Family would pay the judgment to the limits of the insurance policy.

In his action against American Family, Smith alleged breach of contract of his automobile liability insurance policy, tortious breach of the implied covenant of good faith and fair dealing, malice, oppression, and fraud, and intentional infliction of severe emotional distress on the part of American Family. After trial to a jury, the jury found that Smith failed to prove he suffered severe emotional distress caused by the conduct of American Family; the jury dismissed any claim against American Family's agent, James Erickson; but found against American Family in the sum of $4,120 for breach of contract, $3,000 for breach of an implied covenant of good faith and fair dealing, and $50,000 for exemplary damages. American Family moved for judgment notwithstanding the verdict or, in the alternative, a new trial. The motion was denied by the district court and American Family took this appeal. In its appeal American Family raises several issues, some of which we will consider separately and others together.

I

In its first issue American Family argues that the trial court erred in refusing to dismiss Smith's action in tort because it failed to state a claim upon which relief could be granted. American Family's position is that a failure to defend an insured as required by the insurance policy is a breach of contract on the part of the insurer and does not constitute a tort on the part of the insurer. In support of its position American Family cites Prince v. Universal Underwriters Insurance Co., 143 N.W.2d 708 (N.D.1966), in which this court held that a failure to defend was a breach of the insurer's obligation under the policy which renders the insurer liable to the insured to the extent of the insured's costs and expenses incurred in defending the action. The decision in *Prince* is not applicable to the issue raised by American Family. * * * In *Prince* the insured did not bring action against the insurer in tort nor did the court consider whether or not that action was permitted. Furthermore, since the decision in *Prince,* this court decided Corwin Chrysler–Plymouth v. Westchester Fire Insurance Company, 279 N.W.2d 638 (N.D.1979), wherein we quoted with approval the following statement of the Oklahoma Supreme Court in Christian v. American Home Assurance Company, 577 P.2d 899, 904–905 (Okl.1978):

> "We approve and adopt the rule that an insurer has an implied duty to deal fairly and act in good faith with its insured and that the violation of this duty gives rise to an action in tort for which consequential and, in a proper case, punitive, damages may be sought. We do not hold that an insurer who resists and litigates a claim made by its insured does so at its peril that if it loses the suit or suffers a judgment against it for a larger amount than it had offered in payment, it will be held to have breached its duty to act fairly and in good faith and thus will be liable in tort." 279 N.W.2d at 645.

In *Corwin Chrysler–Plymouth,* we also cited and relied upon Gruenberg v. Aetna Insurance Company, 9 Cal.3d 566, 108 Cal.Rptr. 480, 510 P.2d 1032 (1973), and Mustachio v. Ohio Farmers Insurance Company, 44 Cal.App.3d 358, 118 Cal.Rptr. 581 (1975), in affirming a decision of the district court that an insurer, which initially refused to pay a portion of an embezzlement claim representing funds taken subsequent to the expiration of its policy but which continued to refuse to pay after being informed that the embezzler had admitted the funds had been taken prior to the expiration of the policy, did, under the facts of that case, breach its obligation to deal with its insured in good faith.

American Family attempts to distinguish this holding on the basis that *Corwin Chrysler–Plymouth* and the California decisions upon which it relies give rise to tort liability only where the insurer fails to accept a reasonable settlement and not where, as here, there is only a wrongful refusal by an insurer to defend an insured. It points to Comunale v. Traders & General Insurance Company, 50 Cal.2d 654, 328 P.2d 198 (1958), and Hogan v. Midland National Insurance Co., 3 Cal.3d 553, 91 Cal.Rptr. 153, 476 P.2d 825 (1970), as supporting its position. *Comunale* involved an action against an insurer to recover the portion of a judgment which was in excess of policy limits. The California Supreme Court held that where the insurer wrongfully refused to defend the insured and refused a reasonable settlement within limits of the policy, the insurer's breach of its express obligation to defend did not release it from its implied duty to consider the insured's interest in settlement. The court held the insurer liable for the entire judgment rendered against the insured even though the judgment exceeded policy limits. The discussion by the California court noted that most of the cases dealing with the insurer's failure to settle involve an insurer which had assumed the defense of the action against the insured but further noted that the decisive factor in fixing the extent of the insurer's liability in the case before it was the refusal to accept an offer of settlement within the policy limits, not the refusal to defend. The insurer in *Comunale* never assumed the defense of the insured. As dictum the California court noted that where there is no opportunity to compromise the claim and the only wrongful act of the insurer is the refusal to defend, the liability of the insurer is ordinarily limited to the amount of the policy plus attorney fees and costs; the rationale being that if the insured has employed competent counsel to represent him, there is no ground for concluding that the judgment would have been for a lesser sum had the defense been conducted by the insurer's counsel and that the detriment suffered by the insured as a result of a judgment in excess of the policy limits was not proximately caused by the insurer's refusal to defend.

*Hogan* cited *Comunale* for the proposition that the insurer is liable for amounts over the policy limit because of its wrongful refusal to settle the underlying action and noted the *Comunale* opinion distinguished the consequences of a wrongful refusal to settle and a wrongful refusal to defend, pointing out that as to a wrongful refusal to defend the liability of the insurer is ordinarily limited to the amount of the policy plus attorney fees and costs.

Although we believe the statements of the California Supreme Court in *Comunale* and *Hogan* to be dicta as used in those opinions, we note both opinions were issued prior to the 1973 decision in Gruenberg v. Aetna Insurance Company, supra. Although *Gruenberg* did not involve a third party, but rather involved the failure of the insurer to pay the insured under a fire insurance policy for a fire loss incurred by the insured, the Court referred to the decisions in *Comunale* and Crisci v. Security Ins. Co., 66 Cal.2d 425, 58 Cal.Rptr. 13, 426 P.2d 173 (1967), and stated:

> "Thus in *Comunale* and *Crisci* we made it clear that '[l]iability is imposed [on the insurer] not for a bad faith breach of contract but for failure to meet the duty to accept reasonable settlements, a duty included within the implied covenant of good faith and fair dealing.' In those two cases, we considered the duty of the insurer to act in good faith and fairly in handling the claims of third persons against the insured, described as a 'duty to accept reasonable settlements'; in the case before us we consider the duty of an insurer to act in good faith and fairly in handling the claims of an insured, namely a duty not to withhold unreasonably payments due under a policy. These are merely two different aspects of the same duty. That responsibility is not the requirement mandated by the terms of the policy itself—to defend, settle, or pay. It is the obligation, deemed to be imposed by the law, under which the insurer must act fairly and in good faith in discharging its contractual responsibilities."

Significantly, the court in *Gruenberg,* relying upon its decision in *Crisci,* supra, upheld recovery for mental suffering and emotional distress because an action against an insurer for breach of its implied duty of good faith sounds in tort as well as contract. We cannot differentiate between a failure to pay, as in *Gruenberg,* and, here, a failure to defend, if the insurer breaches its covenant to act fairly and in good faith in discharging its contractual responsibilities. Insofar as claims for emotional distress and mental suffering are made, the failure of the insurer to defend the insured against a multithousand-dollar action filed by a third party against the insured may be significantly greater than the failure to pay a claim to the insured under a fire policy such as in *Gruenberg*. To limit the recovery by the insured and the liability of the insurer to the amount of the policy plus attorney fees and costs in instances in which the insured has breached its duty to act fairly and in good faith by failing to defend the insured would, in many instances, preclude recovery by the insured for damages for emotional distress.

In Farris v. U.S. Fidelity and Guaranty Co., 284 Or. 453, 587 P.2d 1015 (1978), the Oregon Supreme Court considered the issue of whether or not the failure of the insurer to defend the insured under a liability policy could give rise to a tort action. The majority of the Oregon court concluded that, in view of its previous decision in Santilli v. State Farm Life Ins. Co., 278 Or. 53, 562 P.2d 965 (1977), an insurer's failure to undertake representation of the insured could only have been a breach of contract for which no recovery for mental distress because of threat of pecuniary loss was available. In reaching its decision, the majority in *Farris* relied in part upon the unfair-trade-practices provisions of that State's Insurance Code (Or.Rev.Stat. Chapter 746) and the civil penalties provided for the violation of the Insurance Code (Or.Rev.Stat. Section 731.988). Similar provisions are found in our statutes. Secs. 26–30–04 and 26–30–11, N.D.C.C. The Oregon court also recognized a distinction between failure of the insurer to settle within the policy limits and failure to defend, concluding that in the case of failure to settle the insurer was acting in a fiduciary capacity which imposed a higher duty of good faith and fair dealing upon the insurer, but that failure to defend was merely a breach of contract for which no recovery for mental distress because of threat of pecuniary loss is recoverable.

[T]he Oregon court recognized that *Gruenberg* and related decisions would permit an action in tort for failure to defend but refused to adopt the rationale of those decisions.

* * *

An insurer's obligation to defend and an insurer's obligation to indemnify are separate and distinct contractual elements. Afcan v. Mutual Fire, Marine and Inland Ins. Co., 595 P.2d 638 (Alaska 1979). We agree with the trial court that the defense and vindication of an insured by his insurance carrier against third-party claims is one of the chief benefits of the insurance contract.

Smith's cause of action in this instance alleged tortious breach of the implied covenant of good faith and fair dealing, malice, oppression, and fraud against American Family. That allegation was predicated on American Family's failure to defend as required by its policy with Smith. To adopt a rationale that distinguishes between the insurer's failure to defend and the failure to accept a settlement would, as the trial court noted in its memorandum opinion denying American Family's post-trial motions, "encourage insurance companies to exert whatever coercion in whatever manner and under whatever circumstances as would serve their financial interest, and under the circumstances here present would leave the plaintiff without a remedy for damages for the failure to defend beyond attorney's fees and legal costs."

American Family also argues that even if there is an implied tort remedy for failure by the insurer to defend the insured, Smith's complaint should have been dismissed because it was brought prior to the resolution of the Herzog suit against him. In support of its argument, American Family refers us to the decision in Critz v. Farmers Insurance Group, 230 Cal.App.2d 788, 41 Cal.Rptr. 401 (1965), wherein the California Court of Appeals, in deciding whether or not an insured could assign to another party his right to maintain a bad-faith action against his insurer prior to the time he suffered adverse judgment in a personal-injury action, held the insured could make the assignment because the breach of the duty of good faith was complete when it occurred. That court also held, however, that the breach of the duty would not result in an immediately enforceable chose in action against the insurer because of the uncertainty as to the damages—which would be determined only when the insured incurred a binding judgment in excess of the policy limit.

In this instance Smith claimed damages of $4,900 for loss of employment as a result of American Family's failure to defend the action filed against him by Herzog; $300 in costs for repairing an automobile; traveling expenses in the amount of $125; medical expenses in the amount of $115 for treatment and evaluation of mental injury and depression resulting from American Family's failure to defend him; $50,000 for mental distress and emotional injury; and $3,861.89 for legal expenses incurred in defending the lawsuit brought against him by Herzog. In addition, Smith made a claim for future costs of defending the Herzog suit in an unspecified amount. Smith also asked that American Family be required to pay on Smith's behalf all sums for which Smith might be adjudged liable in the suit brought by Herzog and he requested $1,000,000, in exemplary damages. The jury awarded Smith $4,120 for breach of contract; $3,000 for American Family's breach of its obligation to deal fairly and in good faith with Smith; and $50,000 in punitive (exemplary) damages. It is apparent from an examination of the special jury verdict that the jury did not award Smith any speculative damages for a judgment which might be entered against him in the Herzog action. The actual damages which were awarded Smith were for injury he had already suffered. It is best explained by the trial court's memorandum opinion denying American Family's motions:

> "Smith's cause of action is not grounded upon the carrier's refusal to settle, but rather upon the company's refusal to defend, a cause of action complete under the facts of this case at the time of trial. Future refusal to defend is unlikely and should not be presumed. If the plaintiff wishes to chance a splitting of a cause of action then he takes the election made in this instance."

Because the limit of liability of American Family under the insurance policy was $50,000 and because the jury returned a verdict of

$50,000 in exemplary damages, American Family argues that the jury did speculate as to the outcome of the Herzog lawsuit inasmuch as the $50,000 exemplary damages awarded equals the liability limit of Smith's insurance policy. This is conjecture on the part of American Family and a theory we refuse to adopt.

* * *

[Parts II–VII of the Court's opinion are omitted]

The order denying American Family's motions for judgment notwithstanding the verdict or, in the alternative, a new trial and the judgment are affirmed.

* * *

## FITZPATRICK v. AMERICAN HONDA MOTOR CO., INC.

Court of Appeals of New York, 1991.
78 N.Y.2d 61, 571 N.Y.S.2d 672, 575 N.E.2d 90.

OPINION OF THE COURT, TITONE, J.

It is well established that a liability insurer has a duty to defend its insured in a pending lawsuit if the pleadings allege a covered occurrence, even though facts outside the four corners of those pleadings indicate that the claim may be meritless or not covered (see, e.g., Ruder & Finn v. Seaboard Sur. Co., 52 N.Y.2d 663, 669–670, 439 N.Y.S.2d 858, 422 N.E.2d 518). The issue in this appeal is whether the insurer has a duty to defend in the opposite circumstance, i.e., where the pleadings do not allege a covered occurrence but the insurer has actual knowledge of facts demonstrating that the lawsuit does involve such an occurrence. Under these facts, we hold that the insurer cannot use a third party's pleadings as a shield to avoid its contractual duty to defend its insured.

The plaintiff in the main action, Linda Fitzpatrick, sought recovery for the wrongful death of her husband, John Fitzpatrick, who died on October 31, 1985 while operating a three-wheel all-terrain vehicle. The complaint alleged that the vehicle in question was owned by defendant Frank Moramarco and that Moramarco had given Fitzpatrick permission to use it in connection with the performance of certain yardwork and household chores. According to the complaint, codefendant Cherrywood Property Owners Association (CPOA), the owner of the property on which the accident occurred, had retained Moramarco, and Moramarco, acting as CPOA's agent, had in turn hired Fitzpatrick as an "independent contractor."

In fact, Moramarco was an officer, shareholder and director of an independent concern called Cherrywood Landscaping, Inc. (CLI), which had been retained by CPOA to do landscaping work on CPOA's property. The vehicle involved in Fitzpatrick's accident had been purchased by Moramarco on behalf of CLI for use in its landscaping and gardening business. CLI had also purchased a liability insurance policy from

National Casualty Co. (National), which indemnified the corporation against having to pay damages for bodily injury and property damage arising out of its business. While the policy was not an "owner's policy" and Moramarco was not a specifically named insured, the terms of the policy included as "insured persons" "any executive officer, director or stockholder [of the named insured (i.e., CLI) ] while acting within the scope of his duties as such."

Shortly after Moramarco was served with papers in the main action, he notified National and requested that the insurer provide him with a defense. National, however, refused, stating that the policy it had issued to CLI did not appear to cover the claim against Moramarco. In subsequent correspondence, Moramarco advised the insurer that the vehicle involved in the Fitzpatrick accident was "owned for and * * * used exclusively for landscaping operations" and that the claims asserted against him in the main action all arose out of activities he undertook for CLI, the named insured. The same circumstances were brought to the insurer's attention in a letter from its own agent in which the company was urged to reconsider its prior decision. Nonetheless, National maintained that it was not required to provide a defense because the complaint did not name CLI, and Moramarco, the named defendant, was not insured as an individual.

Moramarco thereafter commenced a third-party action against National seeking payment of his legal fees in the main action, as well as "judgment over" for any judgment entered against him in the main action. National promptly moved, pursuant to CPLR 3211(a)(1) and (7), to dismiss the third-party complaint. Relying wholly on the absence of allegations in the Fitzpatrick complaint suggesting that the claim against Moramarco arose in connection with his activities as an officer, shareholder or director of the insured CLI, National argued that it had no duty to defend or indemnify Moramarco under the terms of the policy. In response, Moramarco submitted proof to show that, despite the complaint's inaccuracies, the Fitzpatrick claim actually did involve a covered event.

The Supreme Court denied National's dismissal motion, holding that the question of whether its policy covered the Fitzpatrick accident "must await a plenary trial." The Appellate Division, 159 A.D.2d 548, 552 N.Y.S.2d 413, however, reversed and dismissed the third-party complaint. The court held that the allegations in the complaint are the determinative factor in resolving whether the provisions of an insurance policy have been "activated" in a particular action. Since the Fitzpatrick complaint named Moramarco only in his individual capacity and the insured, CLI, was never even mentioned, the Appellate Division concluded that the existing documentary evidence, i.e., the Fitzpatrick complaint and the National policy, was sufficient to warrant dismissal of Moramarco's third-party claim (see, CPLR 3211[a][1] ). This Court granted Moramarco leave to appeal from the Appellate Division order. We now reverse.

This Court has repeatedly held that an insurer's duty to defend its insured arises whenever the allegations in a complaint state a cause of action that gives rise to the reasonable possibility of recovery under the policy (see, e.g., Technicon Elecs. Corp. v. American Home Assur. Co., 74 N.Y.2d 66, 73, 544 N.Y.S.2d 531, 542 N.E.2d 1048; Meyers & Sons Corp. v. Zurich Am. Ins. Group, 74 N.Y.2d 298, 302, 546 N.Y.S.2d 818, 545 N.E.2d 1206; see, Servidone Constr. Corp. v. Security Ins. Co., 64 N.Y.2d 419, 424, 488 N.Y.S.2d 139, 477 N.E.2d 441). In the present appeal, National asks this Court to hold that the converse is also true. According to National, the complaint allegations are, in all cases, the *sole* determining consideration and, consequently, an insurer is relieved of the duty to defend whenever the complaint allegations do not on their face set forth a covered cause of action. However, the position National advocates is neither compelled by our prior case law nor consistent with sound legal principles and policies. Accordingly, we reject it.

The rationale underlying the cases in which the "four corners of the complaint" rule was delineated and applied (see, e.g., Meyers & Sons Corp. v. Zurich Am. Ins. Group, supra; International Paper Co. v. Continental Cas. Co., 35 N.Y.2d 322, 361 N.Y.S.2d 873, 320 N.E.2d 619; Goldberg v. Lumber Mut. Cas. Ins. Co., 297 N.Y. 148, 77 N.E.2d 131), is based on the oft-stated principle that the duty to defend is broader than the duty to indemnify (see, e.g., Ruder & Finn v. Seaboard Sur. Co., 52 N.Y.2d 663, 669–670, 439 N.Y.S.2d 858, 422 N.E.2d 518, supra). In other words, as the rule has developed, an insurer may be contractually bound to defend even though it may not ultimately be bound to pay, either because its insured is not factually or legally liable or because the occurrence is later proven to be outside the policy's coverage.

It follows logically from this principle that an insurer's duty to defend is called into play whenever the pleadings allege an act or omission within the policy's coverage. Even where there exist extrinsic facts suggesting that the claim may ultimately prove meritless or outside the policy's coverage, the insurer cannot avoid its commitment to provide a defense, since "[a] complaint subject to defeat because of debatable theories * * * must [nevertheless] be defended by the insured." (International Paper Co. v. Continental Cas. Co., supra, 35 N.Y.2d at 326, 361 N.Y.S.2d 873, 320 N.E.2d 619.) Accordingly, the courts of this State have refused to permit insurers to look beyond the complaint's allegations to avoid their obligation to defend and have held that the duty to defend exists "[i]f the complaint contains any facts or allegations which bring the claim even potentially within the protection purchased" (Technicon Elecs. Corp. v. American Home Assur. Co., supra, 74 N.Y.2d at 73, 544 N.Y.S.2d 531, 542 N.E.2d 1048). The holdings thus clearly establish that an insurer's duty to defend is at least broad enough to apply when the "four corners of the complaint" suggest the reasonable possibility of coverage.

However, to say that the duty to defend is *at least* broad enough to apply to actions in which the complaint alleges a covered occurrence is a far cry from saying that the complaint allegations are the *sole* criteria for measuring the scope of that duty. Indeed, in these circumstances, where the insurer is attempting to shield itself from the responsibility to defend despite its actual knowledge that the lawsuit involves a covered event, wooden application of the "four corners of the complaint" rule would render the duty to defend narrower than the duty to indemnify—clearly an unacceptable result. For that reason, courts and commentators have indicated that the insurer must provide a defense if it has knowledge of facts which potentially bring the claim within the policy's indemnity coverage. [citations omitted]

We agree with these authorities and hold that, rather than mechanically applying only the "four corners of the complaint" rule in these circumstances, the sounder approach is to require the insurer to provide a defense when it has actual knowledge of facts establishing a reasonable possibility of coverage. This holding fits easily and appropriately within the existing rules governing coverage disputes, which certainly do not require us to extend the "four corners of the complaint" rule to a situation such as this one, where it has not been applied before and, in fact, has no apparent value. Although it has been argued that the "four corners of the complaint" rule has the advantage of certainty (see, dissenting opn., at 73, at 679 of 571 N.Y.S.2d, at 97 of 575 N.E.2d), there is no reason to believe that the rule we adopt here will engender any more litigation.

The conclusion we reach here flows naturally from the fact that the duty to defend derives, in the first instance, not from the complaint drafted by a third party, but rather from the insurer's own contract with the insured. While the allegations in the complaint may provide the significant and usual touchstone for determining whether the insurer is contractually bound to provide a defense, the contract itself must always remain a primary point of reference (see also, Technicon Elecs. Corp. v. American Home Assur. Co., supra, 74 N.Y.2d at 73, 544 N.Y.S.2d 531, 542 N.E.2d 1048 [duty to defend arises from complaint and insurance contract] ). Indeed, a contrary rule making the terms of the complaint controlling "would allow the insurer to construct a formal fortress of the third party's pleadings * * * thereby successfully ignoring true but unpleaded facts within its knowledge that require it * * * to conduct the * * * insured's defense" (Associated Indem. Co. v. Insurance Co., 68 Ill.App.3d 807, 816–817, 25 Ill.Dec. 258, 265, 386 N.E.2d 529, 536). Further, an insured's right to a defense should not depend solely on the allegations a third party chooses to put in the complaint. This is particularly so because the drafter of the pleading may be unaware of the true underlying facts or the nuances that may affect the defendant's coverage and it might not be in the insured's (or the insurer's) interest to reveal them.

The principle that an insurer may not rely on the pleadings to narrow the scope of its duty to defend also finds support in the practical realities that prevail under modern pleading rules. As one commentator has observed, "considering the plasticity of modern pleadings, in many cases no one can determine whether the third party suit does or does not fall within the indemnification coverage of the policy until the suit itself is resolved" (7C Appleman, op. cit., § 4684, at 83). This observation is particularly apt in the context of New York's liberal pleading rules, which permit the pleadings to be amended to conform to the proof *at any time,* provided that no prejudice is shown (see, CPLR 3025[a] ).

The facts in this case—where the complaint on its face did not state a covered claim but the underlying facts made known to the insurer by its insured unquestionably involved a covered event—present a clear example. The insurer here refused to defend Frank Moramarco because he was sued, albeit mistakenly, as an employee of CPOA and the owner of the injury-causing vehicle. Had the complaint correctly identified Moramarco as an officer and/or shareholder of the insured CLI, he would have unquestionably been covered for this lawsuit, since the policy provided that "any executive officer, director or stockholder [of CLI] while acting within the scope of his duties as such" was an additional "insured person" under the policy. Further, the insurer promised to "defend any suit against the insured seeking damages on account of * * * bodily injury or property damage" arising out of CLI's landscaping and gardening business—a condition plainly satisfied here. To deny Moramarco an insurance-company sponsored defense under these circumstances merely because the attorney for the plaintiff in the main action accidentally mischaracterized Moramarco's role would be to afford the insurer an undeserved windfall at the expense of its insured.

Indeed, relieving the insurer of its duty to defend is particularly imprudent and counterproductive where, as here, the inaccuracies in the plaintiff's pleadings are likely to become apparent when the true facts are developed on the record and the role of the insured in the incident is fully exposed. At that point, the trial court could well grant a request by the plaintiff to conform the pleadings to the proof (see, CPLR 3025[c] ), in which event the insurer's core policy obligation to defend Frank Moramarco as an additional insured would unquestionably be triggered. Moramarco should not be required to wait until that point is reached before obtaining an insurance-company sponsored defense, since a "provision for defense of suits is useless and meaningless unless it is offered when the suit arises" (7C Appleman, op. cit., § 4684, at 83).

In sum, application of the "four corners of the complaint" rule in these circumstances is not required by our prior cases and is not even supported by the rationale usually offered in support of the rule. Further, invocation of the rule here and in analogous cases leads to an unjust result, since it exalts form over substance and denies an insured party the benefit of the "litigation insurance" for which it has paid. These factors militate in favor of a rule requiring the insurer to provide a defense where, notwithstanding the complaint allegations, underlying facts made known to the insurer create a "reasonable possibility that the insured may be held liable for some act or omission covered by the policy" (Meyers & Sons Corp. v. Zurich Am. Ins. Group, supra, 74 N.Y.2d at 302, 546 N.Y.S.2d 818, 545 N.E.2d 1206). We therefore hold that National cannot ignore the facts made known to it by its insured and rely instead on the Fitzpatrick complaint alone to assess its duty to defend Moramarco. The third-party complaint by Moramarco seeking payment of his attorney's fees and indemnification in the event that a judgment was entered against him should not have been dismissed. Accordingly, the order of the Appellate Division should be reversed, with costs, and the motion to dismiss the third-party complaint denied.

ALEXANDER, JUDGE (dissenting).

Because the majority today discards a rule of long standing and, in my view, does so without justification and under circumstances not warranting such a drastic departure from settled precedent, I respectfully dissent.

It is axiomatic that the obligations of a liability insurance carrier to its insured are governed by the terms of the contract of insurance between them and it is only by examining the terms and conditions of that policy that those obligations can be determined with certainty. Obviously, where an insured has been found liable to a third party in respect to a risk covered by the policy, the carrier is obligated to indemnify its insured. Additionally, where the policy so provides, the carrier is obligated to defend its insured against claims asserting risks covered by the policy. Indeed the rule is firmly established that the duty to defend is broader than the duty to indemnify (Ruder & Finn v. Seaboard Sur. Co., 52 N.Y.2d 663, 669–670, 439 N.Y.S.2d 858, 422 N.E.2d 518; Servidone Constr. Corp. v. Security Ins. Co., 64 N.Y.2d 419, 424, 488 N.Y.S.2d 139, 477 N.E.2d 441). When the policy contains the insurer's promise to defend the insured, the "liability insurance" is in fact "litigation insurance" as well (Seaboard Sur. Co. v. Gillette Co., 64 N.Y.2d 304, 486 N.Y.S.2d 873, 476 N.E.2d 272; International Paper Co. v. Continental Cas. Co., 35 N.Y.2d 322, 326, 361 N.Y.S.2d 873, 320 N.E.2d 619).

However, this Court has repeatedly held, in a long line of cases, unbroken until now, that the duty of a liability insurer to defend an action brought against an insured is determined by the allegations in the complaint pursuant to which the insured's liability is asserted (see, Meyers & Sons Corp. v. Zurich Am. Ins. Group, 74 N.Y.2d 298, 546 N.Y.S.2d 818, 545 N.E.2d 1206; Technicon Elecs. Corp. v. American Home Assur. Co., 74 N.Y.2d 66, 544 N.Y.S.2d 531, 542 N.E.2d 1048; Servidone Constr. Corp. v. Security Ins. Co., 64 N.Y.2d 419, 488 N.Y.S.2d 139, 477 N.E.2d 441, supra; Seaboard Sur. Co. v. Gillette Co., 64 N.Y.2d 304, 486 N.Y.S.2d 873, 476 N.E.2d 272, supra; International Paper Co. v. Continental Cas. Co., 35 N.Y.2d 322, 361 N.Y.S.2d 873, 320 N.E.2d 619, supra; Goldberg v. Lumber Mut. Cas. Ins. Co., 297 N.Y. 148, 77 N.E.2d 131). "If the facts alleged [in the complaint] raise a reasonable possibility that the insured may be held liable for some act or omission covered by the policy, then the insurer must defend" (Meyers & Sons Corp. v. Zurich Am. Ins. Group, 74 N.Y.2d 298, 302, 546 N.Y.S.2d 818, 545 N.E.2d 1206, supra).

In determining whether there is a duty to defend however, the Court must compare the allegations of the complaint with the terms of the policy (see, Lionel Freedman, Inc. v. Glens Falls Ins. Co., 27 N.Y.2d 364, 367, 318 N.Y.S.2d 303, 267 N.E.2d 93). If those allegations, on their face, are within the compass of the risk covered by the insurance policy, the insurer is obligated to assume the defense of the action (Goldberg v. Lumber Mut. Cas. Ins. Co., supra; International Paper Co. v. Continental Cas. Co., 35 N.Y.2d 322, 361 N.Y.S.2d 873, 320 N.E.2d 619, supra). Conversely, it logically follows, that if that comparison demonstrates that those allegations are not within the coverage of the policy, the insurance company's duty to defend does not arise (see, Goldberg v. Lumber Mut. Cas. Ins. Co., 297 N.Y. 148, 77 N.E.2d 131). Indeed where it can be determined "that no basis for recovery within the coverage of the policy is stated in the complaint * * * defendant's refusal to defend [may be sustained]." (Lionel Freedman, Inc. v. Glens Falls Ins. Co., 27 N.Y.2d 364, 368, 318 N.Y.S.2d 303, 267 N.E.2d 93, rearg. denied 28 N.Y.2d 859, 322 N.Y.S.2d 1029, 271 N.E.2d 236; Sucrest Corp. v. Fisher Governor Co., 83 Misc.2d 394, 400, 371 N.Y.S.2d 927.)

* * *

Deviating from these settled rules, the majority concludes that notwithstanding that the Fitzpatrick complaint, when compared to the terms of the policy, fails to demonstrate the existence of a covered event, "the insurer must provide a defense if it has knowledge of facts which potentially bring the claim within the policy's indemnity coverage" (majority opn., at 66, at 674 of 571 N.Y.S.2d, at 92 of 575 N.E.2d). It should be noted that to support this proposition the majority relies upon cases from other jurisdictions which impose an obligation upon the insurance company to investigate the claim before declining to defend—a requirement that this Court has never before imposed.

The rule which until now has prevailed in this jurisdiction provides certainty in this area of law and is easily applied. By changing the rule, the majority has supplanted certainty with uncertainty; an insurer now will be less clear as to what, if any, investigation it must make into a demand to defend and when it is permissible to decline representation. Concomitantly, the new rule presumably will increase collateral proceedings such as this, to determine whether an insurer in fact has a duty to defend. These collateral proceedings will be made more complicated because courts now will be obligated to look beyond the allegations in the complaint to discover the "actual" facts, or at a minimum whether the insurer "knew" or perhaps even "should have known" of such "actual facts". The rule could also place the insured in the position of dictating the theory of the action, conceivably requiring the carrier to defend a claim the plaintiff has no intention of asserting merely because allegedly there are "facts" which support such a claim.

The majority posits this new rule as being corollary to the established rule that where the allegations of the complaint state a claim within the coverage of the policy, the "insurers [may not] look beyond the complaint's allegations to avoid their obligation to defend" (majority opn., at 66, at 674 of 571 N.Y.S.2d, at 92 of 575 N.E.2d). The fact is, however, that under the rule cited by the majority, "the insurance company's duty to defend came into being when it appeared from the allegations in the negligence action that the injury was within the coverage of the policy, and it persisted despite the advice [from the insured] pointing [to] a contrary conclusion" (Goldberg v. Lumber Mut. Cas. Ins. Co., 297 N.Y. 148, 154, 77 N.E.2d 131, supra).

Thus it is clear that under that established rule it is the allegations of the complaint, compared to the policy provisions, that trigger the duty to defend, a duty which persists notwithstanding that liability may ultimately be shown not to exist. This rule gives certainty to the inception of the carrier's duty to defend and is entirely consistent with its obligations under its policy. No satisfactory reason for altering this rule is shown to exist here; thus the order granting summary judgment to the third-party defendant National Casualty Co. should be affirmed.

WACHTLER, C.J., and KAYE and BELLACOSA, JJ., concur with TITONE, J.

ALEXANDER, J., dissents and votes to affirm in a separate opinion in which SIMONS and HANCOCK, JJ., concur.

Order reversed, etc.

### *Notes*

1. *Fitzpatrick v. American Honda* is being felt in the defense of environmental litigation in which insurers have been held to a duty to defend despite the uncertainty of pleadings and the difficulty of identifying defendants. See New York v. AMRO Realty Corp., 936 F.2d 1420 (2d Cir.1991); Continental Casualty Co. v. Rapid–American Corp., 80 N.Y.2d 640, 593 N.Y.S.2d 966, 609 N.E.2d 506 (1993).

2. *Civil procedure and the Duty to Defend.* The courts of California and other states have had difficulty defining the boundaries of the *Gray* doctrine. In a typical coverage dispute, the carrier or insured seeks a judicial determination of the duty to defend in a separate action for declaratory relief. What evidence should be available, and what should be the burden of proof for each party's routine motion for summary judgement? The California Supreme Court recently addressed this issue in the thorny context of a massive CERCLA litigation. *See* Montrose Chemical Corp. of California v. Superior Court, 6 Cal.4th 287, 24 Cal.Rptr.2d 467, 861 P.2d 1153 (1993). Montrose produced DDT at a Southern California location from 1947 to 1982. The federal government ordered Montrose to participate in the cleanup of the now infamous Stringfellow disposal site and the Los Angeles Harbor. Seven carriers who wrote CGL coverage for Montrose over the period refused or severely limited tender of defense for various reasons, among them that the dumpings were intentional acts. The court held that in proceedings for summary judgement: (1) both the insured and insurer could look to facts outside the third party's complaint to determine the coverage question, (2) the insured must make a *prima facia* showing of the *potential* for coverage, and (3) the insurer must show as a matter of law that

there is no coverage under the policy. The insurer, however, is limited to reliance on *undisputed or extrinsic facts* in making its showing so that the insured is not prejudiced by the prospect of having an adverse finding in the declaratory relief action. The court did not decide whether a carrier could demand reimbursement of defense costs under a prior reservation of rights if the third party action is later found to be outside the scope of coverage, but it seems unlikely in light of the continuing vitality of *Gray*. Montrose is involved in other court actions which bear watching by students of insurance and environmental law.

3. San Diego Navy Federal Credit Union v. Cumis Insurance Society, Inc., 162 Cal.App.3d 358, 208 Cal.Rptr. 494 (1984) has become an eponymous case spawning such expressions as "Cumis Counsel," "Cumis Provision" and the like. Essentially the case holds that whenever the insurer denies coverage (e.g. proceeds under a reservation of rights) or a conflict of interest exists (e.g. when insured is sued for damages above the liability coverage), the insured has the right to independent counsel paid by the insurer.

Bitter controversy ensued centering around such issues as:

1. Has not the insurer in effect lost control of the defense in the underlying tort case?

2. What is the proper standard of conduct for Cumis counsel? What has he or she to lose, since his or her bill will be paid in any event? Is not the Cumis attorney in a basic conflict of interest situation?

3. Excessive Costs? The Cumis lawyer is paid according to an essentially open-ended scale, not according to the fees established between insurance companies and the traditional defense firm specialists. Moreover in cases involving multiple victims, the courtroom may be filled with 25 attorneys of whom 18 or more may be "Cumis."

4. Qualifications? Insurers have complained of having to pay fees of "brothers-in-law who have only been doing drunk driving cases for years."

5. Does not protection of the interests of the victims of torts outweigh all other considerations?

The California Legislature responded to some of these concerns by enacting in 1987 the following provisions in the state's Civil Code

OBLIGATION TO DEFEND ACTION

### § 2860. Conflict of interest; duty to provide independent counsel; waiver; qualifications of independent counsel; fees; disclosure of information

(a) If the provisions of a policy of insurance impose a duty to defend upon an insurer and a conflict of interest arises which creates a duty on the part of the insurer to provide independent counsel to the insured, the insurer shall provide independent counsel to represent the insured unless, at the time the insured is informed that a possible conflict may arise or does exist, the insured expressly waives, in writing, the right to independent counsel. An insurance contract may contain a provision which sets forth the method of selecting that counsel consistent with this section.

(b) For purposes of this section, a conflict of interest does not exist as to allegations or facts in the litigation for which the insurer denies coverage; however, when an insurer reserves its rights on a given issue and the outcome of that coverage issue can be controlled by counsel first retained by the insurer for the defense of the claim, a conflict of interest may exist. No conflict of interest shall be deemed to exist as to allegations of punitive damages or be deemed to exist solely because an insured is sued for an amount in excess of the insurance policy limits.

(c) When the insured has selected independent counsel to represent him or her, the insurer may exercise its right to require that the counsel selected by the insured possess certain minimum qualifications which may include that the selected counsel have (1) at least five years of civil litigation practice which includes substantial defense experience in the subject at issue in the litigation, and (2) errors and omissions coverage. The insurer's obligation to pay fees to the independent counsel selected by the insured is limited to the rates which are actually paid by the insurer to attorneys retained by it in the ordinary course of business in the defense of similar actions in the community where the claim arose or is being defended. This subdivision does not invalidate other different or additional policy provisions pertaining to attorney's fees or providing for methods of settlement of disputes concerning those fees. Any dispute concerning attorney's fees not resolved by these methods shall be resolved by final and binding arbitration by a single neutral arbitrator selected by the parties to the dispute.

(d) When independent counsel has been selected by the insured, it shall be the duty of that counsel and the insured to disclose to the insurer all information concerning the action except privileged materials relevant to coverage disputes, and timely to inform and consult with the insurer on all matters relating to the action. Any claim of privilege asserted is subject to in camera review in the appropriate law and motion department of the superior court. Any information disclosed by the insured or by independent counsel is not a waiver of the privilege as to any other party.

(e) The insured may waive its right to select independent counsel by signing the following statement: "I have been advised and informed of my right to select independent counsel to represent me in this lawsuit. I have considered this matter fully and freely waive my right to select independent counsel at this time. I authorize my insurer to select a defense attorney to represent me in this lawsuit."

(f) Where the insured selects independent counsel pursuant to the provisions of this section, both the counsel provided by the insurer and independent counsel selected by the insured shall be allowed to participate in all aspects of the litigation. Counsel shall cooperate fully in the exchange of information that is consistent with each counsel's ethical and legal obligation to the insured. Nothing in this section shall relieve the insured of his or her duty to cooperate with the insurer under the terms of the insurance contract.

4. Section 2860 has been interpreted to require a finding of both a duty to defend and a conflict of interest as conditions precedent to application of the section's provisions regarding arbitration of counsel's fees. In addition, provision of a defense under a reservation of rights does not establish the

conditions. Rather, the conditions must be satisfied by stipulation or judicial determination. *Callahan & Gauntlett v. Superior Court,* 9 Cal.App. 4th 1140, 11 Cal.Rptr.2d 875 (1992).

## CHI OF ALASKA, INC. v. EMPLOYERS REINSURANCE CORP.

Supreme Court of Alaska, 1993.
844 P.2d 1113.

MATTHEWS, J.

A seaman aboard a vessel owned by Oceanic Research Services, Inc. (Oceanic) accidentally sustained serious injuries. Oceanic believed it was insured against the loss by a $500,000 bodily injury insurance policy it purchased through CHI of Alaska, Inc. (CHI). That policy, however, actually had a bodily injury limit of only $100,000. Oceanic sued CHI, asserting contract and negligent tort claims, as well as a claim that CHI had intentionally misrepresented that the policy coverage was $500,000. Oceanic sought compensatory and punitive damages.

CHI tendered the defense of this suit to its liability insurer, Employers Reinsurance Corporation (Employers). Employers agreed to defend CHI, conditional on reserving its rights to disclaim coverage with respect to Oceanic's claim of intentional misconduct. Employers claimed that intentional misconduct would be excluded under the policy if such misconduct was ratified by CHI.

CHI objected, noting that the reservation of rights created a conflict of interest between Employers and CHI, and demanded independent counsel paid for by Employers and selected by CHI. CHI stated that it wanted its personal attorney Brett von Gemmingen to defend it. Employers expressed reservations about von Gemmingen's experience in handling claims of this nature and suggested that CHI provide the names of other attorneys with more experience who might be retained by Employers to defend CHI. This was not acceptable to CHI. Next Employers offered to pay von Gemmingen to defend that portion of the lawsuit pertaining to the intentional misconduct claim while retaining the law firm of Hughes, Thorsness, Gantz, Powell & Brundin to act as co-counsel for CHI with responsibility for the defense of all claims. CHI declined this offer. CHI then brought the present action for declaratory relief, seeking vindication of its position that it is entitled to select independent counsel. In the meanwhile, the Oceanic case has been jointly defended by Hughes Thorsness and von Gemmingen.

CHI and Employers each moved for summary judgment in the present case. CHI contended that there was necessarily a conflict of interest between CHI and Employers respecting the defense of Oceanic's claim because Employers could win either by defeating all claims of liability or by establishing that CHI is liable for intentional misconduct. Given this conflict of interest, CHI contended that Employers should have no role in the selection of defense counsel because any attorney selected by an insurance company "will attempt to help his real client, the insurance company, at the expense of the insured." CHI argued that the retention of von Gemmingen "to defend claims as they are pushed outside the policy coverage does not resolve the conflict." Instead, dual representation, according to CHI, would still permit the attorney hired by the insurance company to work against the interests of the insured and in addition would cause confusion concerning who is to control various litigation decisions. In response and in support of its motion for summary judgment, Employers argued that potential conflicts were eliminated by allowing CHI to have its personal attorney handle the non-covered claim at Employers' expense.

The superior court granted Employers' motion for summary judgment. The court ruled that Employers' offer to allow CHI to retain counsel of its choice to defend it on the intentional tort claim adequately resolved potential conflicts of interest. In addition, the court stated that if CHI contends at the conclusion of the Oceanic lawsuit "that a conflict existed despite Employers' action in allowing it to retain its own counsel to defend uncovered claims, then it can raise this issue at the coverage trial." Following the order granting Employers' motion for summary judgment, a final judgment was entered which contained no explicit declaration. CHI has appealed from this judgment.

There are three issues on appeal: 1. Did Employers' reservation of rights to disclaim coverage give CHI a right to retain independent counsel? 2. Does the two-counsel scheme proposed by Employers and approved by the superior court satisfy CHI's right to independent counsel? 3. Does CHI have the unilateral right to select independent counsel? We turn to a discussion of these issues.

1. *Did Employers' reservation of rights to disclaim coverage give CHI a right to retain independent counsel?*

We answer this question in the affirmative.

Liability insurers have separate duties to defend and to indemnify their insureds. In order to discharge their duty to defend, insurers hire counsel to conduct the defense of their insureds. Often there is no conflict of interest between the interests of the insurers and the interests of the insureds. Both wish to successfully defend and, if that is not possible, minimize damages.

Sometimes, however, the insurer claims that the policy has been breached by the insured. These are so-called policy defenses of which the insured's failure to give notice or to cooperate are typical examples. The insurer may wish to preserve its policy defenses and still provide a defense to the insured. By doing so it may be able to avoid paying the underlying claim either by succeeding in its defense of the insured or, failing that, by successfully asserting its policy defense. The insurer can preserve these options by defending the insured under a reservation of rights to later disclaim coverage if the reservation of rights is acquiesced in by the insured. Continental Ins. Co. v. Bayless & Roberts, Inc., 608 P.2d 281, 288 (Alaska 1980).

Similarly, the insurer may claim that although no condition of the policy has been breached by the insured, a particular claim made by the plaintiff does not come within the coverage of the policy. Such defenses are called coverage defenses. The most typical example is the coverage defense in this case where alternative theories of negligent and intentional tort are plead and negligent acts are covered by the policy but intentional acts are not. In such cases the insurer's duty to defend may require it to defend even if the most likely theory of recovery is one for which there is no insurance coverage.[5] The insurer can preserve its coverage defense and fulfill its duty to defend by defending under a reservation of rights to later disclaim coverage if liability is attributable to the excluded theory.

In cases where an insurer asserts either policy or coverage defenses, and defends its insured under a reservation of rights, there are various conflicts of interest between the insurer and the insured. We identified three of these in Continental. First, if the insurer knows that it can later assert non-coverage, or if it thinks that the loss which it is defending will not be covered under the policy, it may only go through the motions of defending: "it may offer only a token defense * * *. [I]t may not be motivated to achieve the lowest possible settlement or in other ways treat the interests of the insured as its own." Id. at 289. Second, if there are several theories of recovery, at least one of which is not covered under the policy, the insurer might conduct the defense in such a manner as to make the likelihood of a plaintiff's verdict greater under the uninsured theory. Id. Third, the insurer might gain access to confidential or privileged information in the process of the defense which it might later use to its advantage in litigation concerning coverage. Id. at 291.

Merely because the insurer and the insured have divergent interests when the insurer seeks to defend under a reservation of rights does not necessarily mean that appointed counsel also has conflicting interests. If appointed counsel makes it clear at the outset of his engagement that he is going to be involved only in the defense of the liability claim, not in coverage issues, and that his client is the insured, not the insurer, conflicts should be rare. A number of authorities hold that this is the appropriate role of appointed counsel. For example, the Arizona Supreme Court held that appointed counsel who in the course of representing the insured gains access to information which may give rise to a policy defense is prohibited from communicating that information to the insurance company. Farmers Ins. Co. of Arizona v. Vagnozzi, 138 Ariz. 443, 448, 675 P.2d 703, 708 (1983): "We emphasize that the attorney who represents the insured owes him an undeviating allegiance whether compensated by the insurer or the insured and cannot act as an agent of

5. The duty to defend arises "if the complaint *on its face* alleges facts which, standing alone, give rise to a possible finding of liability covered by the policy," Afcan v. Mutual Fire, Marine & Inland Ins. Co., 595 P.2d 638, 645 (Alaska 1979); or, if the complaint does not contain such allegations, where "the true facts are within, or potentially within, the policy coverage and are known or reasonably ascertainable to the insurer." National Indem. Co. v. Flesher, 469 P.2d 360, 366 (Alaska 1970).

the insurance company by supplying information detrimental to the insured." Employers agrees with this view, noting that counsel has "an absolute duty of fidelity to the insured over the interests of the insurer."

Other authorities, however, take the view that appointed counsel represents both the insured and the insurer. A former president of the Defense Research Institute has written that appointed counsel has an obligation to disclose to the insurance company information detrimental to the insured. Thomas A. Ford, The Insurance Contract: The Conflicts of Interest it Breeds, Ins.Couns.J. 610, 620 (Oct. 1969): "In order for the attorney to perform his role properly, he must never lose sight of the fact that he is working for two different and distinct parties—the insured and the insurer. He must fully disclose to both parties the information he has obtained as a result of his unique relationship with them." See also Shafer v. Utica Mutual Ins. Co., 248 A.D. 279, 289 N.Y.S. 577, 587 (1936) (appointed attorney acted properly in disclosing to insurer information which enabled insurer to disclaim liability); Alaska Code of Professional Responsibility EC 5–17 (stating that one typically recurring situation involving potentially different interests is dual representation of insured and insurer).

Where there is a conflict between insurer and insured, appointed counsel may tend to favor the interests of the insurer primarily because of the prospect of future employment. United States Fidelity & Guar. Co. v. Lewis A. Roser Co., 585 F.2d 932, 938 n. 5 (8th Cir.1978) ("Even the most optimistic view of human nature requires us to realize that an attorney employed by an insurance company will slant his efforts, perhaps unconsciously, in the interest of his real client—the one who is paying his fee and from whom he hopes to receive future business—the insurance company."); San Diego Navy Fed. Credit Union v. Cumis Ins. Soc'y, Inc., 162 Cal.App.3d 358, 208 Cal.Rptr. 494, 498 (1984) ("'A lawyer who does not look out for the carrier's best interest may soon find himself out of work.'" (quoting the trial court)); Michael A. Berch and Rebecca W. Berch, Will the Real Counsel for the Insured Please Rise?, 19 Ariz.St.L.J. 27, 29–30 (1987) ("[T]he attorney's economic interests weigh heavily in favor of the insurer, which, after all, may retain his services in other cases; yet the rules of professional responsibility tip the scales toward the insured."); Arthur P. Berg, Losing Control of the Defense—The Insured's Right to Select His Own Counsel, 26 For the Defense 10, 15 (July 1984) ("Although [some] courts seem to trust the insurer and attorney to act in the best interests of the insured, the more common view is that the longstanding ties that defense counsel has with the insurer will inevitably influence his conduct of the case."); Sampson A. Brown and John L. Romaker, Cumis, Conflicts and the Civil Code: Section 2860 Changes Little, 25 Cal.W.L.Rev. 45, 54 (1988) ("The attorney, wishing to maintain the insurer's business, does not want to aggravate the company."); Mark A. Saxon, Conflicts of Interest: Insurers' Expanding Duty to Defend and the Impact of "Cumis" Counsel, 23 Idaho L.Rev. 351, 353 (1987) (Insurance counsel's "relationship with the insurer is contractual, usually ongoing, supported by strong financial interests, and often strengthened by sincere friendships."). In recognition of this, most courts hold that in conflict situations the insured has the right to independent counsel to conduct its defense and the insurance company has the obligation to pay the reasonable value of the defense conducted by independent counsel.

In dicta in National Indemnity Co. v. Flesher, 469 P.2d 360, 367 n. 22 (Alaska 1970), we recognized the right of the insured to independent counsel under circumstances involving a coverage defense: "In such circumstances, the insurer must provide the insured with independent counsel." Ten years later in Continental Insurance Co. v. Bayless & Roberts, Inc., 608 P.2d 281 (Alaska 1980), we recognized the right of the insured to independent counsel in cases involving policy defenses. However, we reserved the question whether the insured had the same right in coverage defense cases. Id. at 289.

In Continental the insurer claimed that the insured had breached the cooperation clause of the policy, but offered to defend the insured under a reservation of rights. Id. at 283. The insured rejected the insurer's offer of a conditional defense and demanded a defense without a reservation of rights. Id. at 286. This the insurer refused to do. Id. Subsequently, the insured's personal counsel took over the defense of the case and entered into a settlement which resulted in a consent judgment against the insured. Id. In the ensuing litigation between the insured and the insurer, the insurer contended that the insured had breached the insurance policy by refusing to accept the insurer's offer to defend under a reservation of rights. Id. at 288. We held that the insured did not breach the policy and that it was within its rights to require the insurer to defend unconditionally or withdraw from the defense. Id. at 291. We also affirmed the jury's award which included $4,000 expended by the insured as its defense costs. Id. at 296 n. 28.

In reaching this result, we expressed and adopted in policy defense cases the general rule that the insurer must surrender its right to control the defense to the insured if the insured refuses to accept a defense under a reservation of rights: "[T]he general rule is that, if an insured refuses to accede to the insurer's reservation of rights, the carrier must either accept liability under the policy and defend unconditionally or surrender control of the defense * * *." Id. at 288. We explained in some detail the types of conflicts of interests which arise when the insurer asserts a right to later contest its liability. Id. at 289–90. We noted that these conflicts might be avoided if the insured were offered the right to retain independent counsel: "The possibility of a conflict might be avoided in such cases if the insurance company were to offer its insured the right to retain independent counsel to conduct his defense, and agree to pay all the necessary costs of that defense. In that event, it would seem that the company should be entitled to reserve the right to later litigate an alleged policy defense." Id. at 291 n. 17. As already stated, the holding in Continental was limited to policy defenses; the question as to whether the same rules should apply where coverage defenses are involved was reserved. Id. at 289.

All three general types of conflicts of interests between insurer and insured which we identified in Continental—the insurer may offer mere token defense, the insurer may steer result to judgment under an uninsured theory of recovery, the insurer may gain access to confidential or privileged information which it may later use to its advantage—apply in coverage defense cases. However, the second reason does not apply in policy defense cases. Policy defenses, such as lack of notice or non-cooperation, involve facts which are generally irrelevant to the litigation between the plaintiff and the insured. Therefore, appointed counsel has no opportunity to "covertly frame [a] defense to achieve a verdict based upon [a theory under which no coverage would result] so that [the insurer] could later assert that the defense was not covered * * *." Id. at 289. Thus, the need for independent counsel is, if anything, greater in coverage than in policy defense cases. We conclude that the right to independent counsel recognized in Continental should also apply to cases involving coverage defenses.[10] We thus adhere to the dicta contained in National Indemnity, which we noted above.

2. *Does the two-counsel scheme proposed by Employers and approved by the superior court satisfy CHI's right to independent counsel?*

We answer this question in the negative.

The trial court was of the view that neither CHI nor Employers was bound by any determination of fact made in the underlying tort suit concerning whether CHI's conduct was negligent or intentional. From this the trial court concluded that Employers' two-counsel scheme would solve the conflict of interest between the insurer and the insured. The view that issues determined in the initial action as to which a conflict of interest exists between insurer and insured may be subsequently relitigated appears to be sensible and in accordance with a number of authorities. That view, however, does not resolve all conflicts of interest between insurer and insured. It does not alleviate the access of appointed counsel to information in possession of the insured which may be used against the insured in subsequent coverage litigation: "This solution overlooks the fact that, during the initial litigation, the insured may transmit information to counsel that the insurer could use in subsequent litigation to the insured's disadvantage. A heavy burden of silence falls on the attorney the insurer selects to defend the insured." Berch & Berch, supra, at 32 n. 23. The fact that personal counsel for CHI is acting as co-counsel with counsel appointed by the insurer also does not

10. We have recently recognized the application of the right to independent counsel expressed in Continental in the context of a coverage defense case in Sauer v. The Home Indemnity Co., 841 P.2d 176, 182, 183 (Alaska 1992), where we stated: However, if the insured does not consent to a non-waiver agreement, or to a defense under a reservation of rights, then the insurance company must choose whether it wishes to defend unconditionally or pursue other options. One such option is to permit the insured to exercise its right to reject the defense offered by the insurer and to obtain substitute counsel at the insurer's expense. In the event the defense is conducted by substitute counsel, the insurance company retains the right to later contest policy coverage. See Continental Ins. Co. v. Bayless & Roberts, Inc., 608 P.2d 281, 291 n. 17 (Alaska 1980).

eliminate this conflict. Appointed counsel has and should have full access to the client so that the defense may be effectively conducted.

Moreover, even where the facts in conflict may be relitigated, the opportunity to direct a case through witness selection, interrogation, and discovery may afford a dispositive advantage in subsequent litigation: "In such cases, the insured's attorney has the opportunity to develop the facts through discovery and to shape the case for, and present the evidence at, the trial. So even though the insured or the insurer may relitigate the coverage issue in a subsequent proceeding, controlling the defense in the main proceeding could be critical. Testifying under oath in the main proceeding may freeze in the witnesses' minds one version of the facts. Very little latitude may remain in subsequent proceedings to mold the evidence bearing upon coverage." Id. at 37–38.

We conclude therefore that the two-counsel solution does not satisfactorily resolve the conflicts which have given rise to the right to independent counsel.

3. *Does CHI have the unilateral right to select independent counsel?*

We answer this question in the affirmative.

Most cases which recognize the right to independent counsel express the view that the insured has the right to select independent counsel of its choice. American Family Life Assur. Co. v. United States Fire Co., 885 F.2d 826, 831 (11th Cir.1989) (if insured had rejected conflicted counsel, insurer "would have been obligated to pay" for defense conducted by insured) (interpreting Georgia law); Rhodes v. Chicago Ins. Co., 719 F.2d 116, 120–21 (5th Cir.1983) ("When a reservation of rights is made * * * the insured may * * * pursue his own defense [and the] insurer remains liable for attorneys' fees") (interpreting Texas law); Previews Inc. v. California Union Ins. Co., 640 F.2d 1026 (9th Cir.1981) ("the insurer's obligation to defend extends to paying the reasonable value of the legal services and costs performed by independent counsel selected by the insured") (interpreting California law); San Diego Navy Fed. Credit Union v. Cumis Ins. Soc'y, 162 Cal.App.3d 358, 208 Cal.Rptr. 494, 501–02 (1984) ("the insurer must pay the reasonable cost for hiring independent counsel by the insured"); Maryland Casualty Co. v. Peppers, 64 Ill.2d 187, 355 N.E.2d 24, 31 (1976) (The insured "has the right to be defended * * * by an attorney of his own choice who shall have the right to control the conduct of the case."); Illinois Masonic Medical Ctr. v. Turegum Ins. Co., 168 Ill.App.3d 158, 118 Ill.Dec. 941, 943, 522 N.E.2d 611, 613 (1988) ("where a conflict of interest exists the insured, rather than the insurer, is entitled to assume control of the defense of the underlying action; * * * the insurer must underwrite the reasonable costs incurred by the insured in defending the action with counsel of his own choosing."); Prashker v. United States Guar. Co., 1 N.Y.2d 584, 154 N.Y.S.2d 910, 915, 136 N.E.2d 871, 876 (1956) ("the selection of the attorneys to represent the assureds should be made by them rather than by the insurance company, which should remain liable for the reasonable value of the services"); Allstate Ins. Co. v. Noorhassan, 158 A.D.2d 638,

551 N.Y.S.2d 942, 944 (1990) (the insured "should be permitted to select their own attorney [and the insurer] is liable for the reasonable value of the services"); Gorman v. Pattengell, 145 A.D.2d 411, 535 N.Y.S.2d 402, 404 (1988) (the insured "is entitled to retain, at her insurer's expense, an attorney with no business connection to her insurance carrier and who will defend solely her interests"). Under this line of authority the insurance company is obligated to pay the "reasonable cost for hiring independent counsel by the insured." Cumis, 208 Cal.Rptr. at 506.

A recent California case, Center Foundation v. Chicago Insurance Co., 227 Cal.App.3d 547, 278 Cal.Rptr. 13 (1991), has noted that the insured's right to select independent counsel is subject to the implied covenant of good faith and fair dealing. In context, this means that the insured must act reasonably to select an attorney who is capable of presenting an effective defense and who will bill reasonably for his or her services. The court stated: "In our view, the duty of good faith imposed upon an insured includes the obligation to act reasonably in selecting as independent counsel an experienced attorney qualified to present a meaningful defense and willing to engage in ethical billing practices susceptible to review at a standard stricter than that of the marketplace. Conduct arguably acceptable in the ordinary attorney-client relationship where the latter pays the former from his own pocket is not necessarily appropriate in the tripartite context created when independent counsel undertakes to represent the insured at the expense of the insurer." Center Foundation, 278 Cal.Rptr. at 21 (footnote omitted).

A few cases support Employers' argument that it should have the right to approve of CHI's choice for independent counsel. In Employers' Fire Insurance Co. v. Beals, 103 R.I. 623, 240 A.2d 397, 404 (1968), the court approved of the solution suggested in Prashker, that the insured should be allowed to select independent counsel. However, the Beals court added the proviso that counsel selected by the insured should be approved by the insurer and that "[s]uch approval, however, should not be unreasonably withheld." Id. 240 A.2d at 404. Fireman's Fund Insurance Co. v. Waste Management of Wisconsin, 777 F.2d 366 (7th Cir.1985) (apparently interpreting Wisconsin law), involves an atypical fact pattern. The question whether the insurer should have approval rights for independent counsel was not the issue; however, the case does contain dicta which states that giving the insurer the right to approve or disapprove of independent counsel selected by the insured is "fair, sensible and reasonable." Id. at 370.

We conclude that the insured should have the unilateral right to select independent counsel and that this right should be subject to the implied covenant of good faith and fair dealing. In our view the covenant of good faith and fair dealing in this context requires that the insured select an attorney who is, by experience and training, reasonably thought to be competent to conduct the defense of the insured. Such a result, in our view, fairly balances the interest of the insured—being defended by competent counsel of undivided loyalty—with the interests of the insurer—having the defense of the insured conducted by competent counsel. The insurer is only required to pay the reasonable cost of the defense. See, e.g., Turegum, 118 Ill.Dec. at 943, 522 N.E.2d at 613 ("insurer must underwrite reasonable costs incurred by the insured in defending the action"); Noorhassan, 551 N.Y.S.2d at 944 (same). This provides a measure of protection for insurers against overbilling—and overlitigating—by independent counsel.

In the present case the record is unclear as to whether it is reasonable for CHI to select von Gemmingen as independent counsel. On remand, a hearing should be conducted promptly in order to determine this question. If the trial court finds that von Gemmingen is a reasonable selection, a declaration should be entered that he may conduct the defense of CHI as independent counsel. If the court finds that he is not a reasonable selection, the court should so declare and CHI should proceed to select qualified counsel.

For the above reasons the judgment of the superior court is REVERSED and this case is REMANDED for further proceedings and entry of a declaration in accordance with this opinion.

MOORE, J., concurring in part and dissenting in part.

In its decision today, the court holds that an insured has the right to reject the counsel appointed by the insurer and to unilaterally select replacement counsel whenever dual representation creates a potential conflict of interest. Under the guise of balancing the interests of the insured and the insurer, the court completely abrogates the insurer's right to participate in the insured's defense. Neither existing case law nor sound policy mandates such a drastic curtailment of the insurer's contract rights. Although I agree that the insured is entitled to select independent counsel in conflict of interest situations, I believe the insurer retains the right of reasonable approval. Such a rule accommodates both the important interest of the insured in controlling the litigation and the legitimate interest of the insurer in assuring that the defense will be competently handled by qualified counsel in a cost-effective manner.

Most courts agree that an insured may reject insurer-selected counsel when the insurer assumes the defense under a reservation of rights because of a coverage question. See Ronald E. Mallen, A New Definition of Insurance Defense Counsel, 53 Ins.Couns.J. 108, 113 (Jan. 1986). Most courts also conclude that the presence of a conflict of interest does not relieve an insurer of its obligation to pay defense costs under its duty to defend. See Babcock & Wilcox Co. v. Parsons Corp., 430 F.2d 531, 538 (8th Cir.1970). The critical issue, which few courts have identified, is whether, in this context, an insured has the unilateral right to select replacement counsel when the insurance agreement gives the insurer the right to defend the insured. This is a matter of first impression in Alaska. I would hold that the insurer has the right to approve the counsel selected by the insured, but that the insurer may not unreasonably withhold such approval.

The court simply fails to recognize that Employers has both a contractual right as well as the contractual duty to defend CHI. An insurer's right to control the defense is "a valuable one in that it reserves to the insurer the right to protect itself against unwarranted liability claims and is essential in protecting its financial interest in the outcome of litigation." 7C John A. Appleman, Insurance Law and Practice § 4681 (Walter F. Berdal ed., rev. ed. 1979). Such an important right should not be ignored in the analysis. Although the insurer's right to control the litigation must yield to the insured's right to independent representation when a conflict arises, this does not mean that the insurer's right to defend is completely extinguished.

* * *

Two cases cited by the court, while speaking of a "right to independent counsel," implicitly recognize the right of an insurer to participate in the defense of its insured. The courts in both American Family Life Assur. Co. v. U.S. Fire Co., 885 F.2d 826 (11th Cir.1989), and San Diego Navy Fed. Credit Union v. Cumis Ins. Soc'y, Inc., 162 Cal.App.3d 358, 208 Cal.Rptr. 494 (1984), required an insurer to pay the cost of "independent counsel" selected by the insured to act as co-counsel with an attorney selected by the insurer. Neither case stands for the proposition that an insured has a unilateral right to select exclusive defense counsel when a coverage dispute creates a conflict of interest. In fact, American Family Life includes a partial quote from Appleman which recognizes the right of an insured "to refuse to accept an offer of counsel appointed by the insurer," 885 F.2d at 831 (citing 7C Appleman, supra, § 4685.01), but omits that part of the sentence which recognizes the insurer's right to approve of substitute counsel.

Some courts and commentators recognize that cases permitting an insured to select "independent counsel" do not define what is meant by that term. See, e.g., Federal Ins. Co. v. X–Rite, Inc., 748 F.Supp. 1223, 1228 n. 1 (W.D.Mich.1990) (" 'Independent Counsel' is a term which has not been defined in the case law."); Allan D. Windt, Insurance Claims and Disputes—Representation of Insurance Companies and Insureds § 4.20 at 179 (2d ed. 1988). Courts have used the phrase in a variety of contexts, some of them diametrically opposed. Commentators have stated that "[t]he right to independent counsel means an attorney of the insured's choice." Ronald E. Mallen & Jeffrey M. Smith, Legal Malpractice § 23.16 at 418 (3d ed. 1989). On the other hand, courts have also recognized "a right in the insurer to determine whether to provide independent counsel of its choosing or to reimburse the insured for counsel of its choice." Federal Ins. Co., 748 F.Supp. at 1228 (citing nine cases for this proposition). Because there is disagreement as to what the right to independent counsel entails, and because many cases recognize the insurer's right to select replacement "independent counsel," or at a minimum, to participate in the defense of the insured alongside counsel selected by the insured, it is questionable whether the view espoused by the court represents a "majority view," statements by courts and commentators to that effect notwithstanding.

However, if, as the court apparently believes, an insured's interest in fair representation requires the complete abrogation of an insurer's right to participate in the defense, the insurer's right should at least be addressed in terms of established principles of contract law. In interpreting a contract, a court must give effect to the reasonable expectation of the parties. Peterson v. Wirum, 625 P.2d 866 (Alaska 1981); Fairbanks N. Star Borough v. Tundra Tours, Inc., 719 P.2d 1020 (Alaska 1986) (in order to give effect to the parties' reasonable expectations, a court should look to the contract language, relevant extrinsic evidence and case law interpreting similar provisions). Clearly, the insurance agreement here gave Employers a reasonable expectation that it would have some control over the defense. Even if the right to defend provision is deemed ambiguous and is therefore construed against the insurer, see Puritan Life Ins. Co. v. Guess, 598 P.2d 900 (Alaska 1979), it is not necessary to extinguish the right entirely. Rather, the right to defend provision can and should be interpreted in a way which balances the interests of both the insurer and the insured.

As one court has stated when considering the scope of an insurer's contractual right to defend in conflict situations: "Unless 'right to defend' is to be deemed mere surplusage, * * * it must be viewed as conferring upon [the insurer] some prerogative with respect to the defense beyond simply paying expenses. This prerogative cannot, in a conflict of interest situation, include an absolute right to control the litigation. On the other hand, [the insured's] apparent presumption that the conflict of interest, posing a potential of prejudice to its interests, automatically and completely negated all prerogative, is not reasonable. * * * [The] 'right to defend' can hardly be deemed to contemplate anything less than participation in selection of counsel, which contractual right ought to be enforced unless contrary to public policy." Federal Ins. Co., 748 F.Supp. at 1229; see also New York State Urban Dev. Corp. v. VSL Corp., 738 F.2d 61, 65–66 (2d Cir.1984). Here, Employers' right to participate in CHI's defense should encompass, at a minimum, the right to have a role in the selection of defense counsel.

Courts which have recognized the right of the insurer to participate in the selection of substitute counsel do not agree as to the latitude an insurer should have. In Federal Ins. Co., the court concluded that, under Michigan law, an insurer is entitled to select replacement counsel, but its selection must be made with the utmost of good faith. 748 F.Supp. at 1229. On the other hand, in Employers' Fire Ins. Co. v. Beals, 240 A.2d 397 (R.I.1968), the court held that an insured may elect to choose its own counsel, but that the insurer has a right to approve of the counsel selected by the insured. The Beals court stated: "Because the insurer has a legitimate interest in seeing that any recovery based on finding of negligence on the part of its insured is kept within reasonable bounds, and since the total expense of this defense is to be assumed by the insurer under its promise to defend, we believe that * * * the engagement of an independent counsel to represent the insured should be approved by the insurer. Such approval, however, should not be unreasonably withheld." 240 A.2d at 404; see Fireman's Fund Ins. Co. v. Waste Management of Wis. Inc., 777 F.2d 366, 370 (7th Cir.1985) (approving parties' agreement to allow insured to select replacement counsel subject to insurer's approval as the most "fair, sensible, and reasonable way for both parties to terminate [conflict of interest] dispute and to get on with trial of the [cases against insured] on their merits"). This approach is also recommended by a noted commentator on insurance law who stated: "[W]here a conflict of interest exists between the insurer and the insured in the conduct of the defense of the action brought against the insured, the insured has the right to refuse to accept an offer of the counsel appointed by the insurer and insurer's desire to control the defense must yield to its obligation to defend the policyholder; and where a conflict of interest exists the engagement of independent counsel to represent the insured should be approved by the insurer to assure the employment of competent counsel. Such approval should not be unreasonably withheld." 7C Appleman, supra, § 4685.01 (footnotes omitted).

The majority dismisses these authorities without analysis, summarily concluding that the insurer's interests are sufficiently protected by the implied covenant of good faith and fair dealing inherent in all contracts. Principally relying on a recent California court of appeals decision, Center Found. v. Chicago Ins. Co., 227 Cal.App.3d 547, 278 Cal.Rptr. 13 (1991), the majority observes that the covenant of good faith and fair dealing requires that the insured "select an attorney who is, by experience and training, *reasonably thought to be competent to conduct the defense of the insured.*" (emphasis added) The majority asserts that the implied covenant "provides a measure of protection for insurers against overbilling—and overlitigating—by independent counsel."

Unfortunately, the majority fails to specify by whose standards the competency of replacement counsel should be measured. In the absence of any objective criteria by which to judge whether replacement counsel is "reasonably competent," I believe that this "measure of protection" is both inadequate and unworkable.

* * *

When the insured has selected independent counsel to represent him or her, the insurer may exercise its right to require that the counsel selected by the insured possess certain minimum qualifications which may include that the selected counsel have (1) at least five years of civil litigation practice which includes substantial defense experience in the subject at issue in the litigation, and (2) errors and omissions coverage.* While I would not adopt this standard as a per se rule in Alaska, I believe that section 2860(c) provides reasonable guidance as to whether an insurer must approve of its insured's selection of substitute counsel.

* This is § 2860(c) text verbatim (ed.).

Here, it is undisputed that attorney von Gemmingen graduated from law school in May, 1985. When this dispute arose in late 1989, he had been practicing law for approximately four years. Nothing in the record indicates that he had substantial defense experience in the types of disputes at issue in the suit against CHI. For these reasons, I would hold that Employers did not unreasonably withhold its approval of CHI's choice of attorney.

Apparently, the court believes that any participation by the insurer in the appointment of independent counsel automatically taints the outcome. However, it is far from clear that the scope of the conflict of interest problem in the defense context is so broad and the frequency of harm to the insured so great as to warrant such a drastic curtailment of the insurer's contract rights. None of the authorities cited by the court address the prevalence of the problem in quantifiable terms, nor do they address effectiveness of malpractice actions, disciplinary actions, or insurance bad faith actions in remedying the problem. As one commentator has noted, "[t]he validity of the assumption that there exists a severe risk that an insurer will favor its coverage interests over the insured's liability has not been critically examined." Mallen, supra, at 108. The same can be said of the assumption that there is a severe risk that defense attorneys will favor the interests of the insurer over the insured. Assuming without conceding that these risks are great, conflict of interest concerns would be a compelling policy reason for permitting an insured to reject counsel selected by the insurer. They would also be a reason for allowing the insured to select a new attorney at the insurer's expense. But it goes too far to ignore the insurer's contractual right to defend and to hold that these perceived dangers warrant allowing an insured to unilaterally select substitute counsel regardless of the attorney's qualifications.

* * *

A potential conflict of interest between the insurer and the insured arises when, as in this case, a plaintiff brings an action against an insured which is based on both covered and uncovered theories of liability. When the complaint alleges both negligent conduct, which is covered under the policy, and intentional conduct, which is not covered, it would be in the best interest of the insurer if liability were ultimately found based on intentional conduct. In such a case, an attorney selected by the insurer to defend the insured would be under an ethical obligation to disclose the effect of this conflict "on the exercise of [the attorney's] independent professional judgment on behalf of each." Alaska Code of Professional Responsibility DR 5–105. Unless "it is obvious that [the attorney] can adequately represent the interest of each" and "each consents to the representation after full disclosure," the attorney would be required to decline the employment. Id. Whether the attorney declines, accepts, or withdraws from the employment, he would be obligated to preserve the confidences of the insured. Alaska Code of Professional Responsibility DR 4–101.

The conflict between the insured and the insurer is to be distinguished from that which arises between the insured and the attorney under these circumstances. As commentators have stated: "In this situation, * * * separate counsel retained by the insurance company is under the less-than-subtle influence of the insurance company. Insurance companies concentrate their legal representation into a few firms. The attorney, wishing to maintain the insurer's business, does not want to aggravate the company. Furthermore, the insurance counsel has close ties and a long-term relationship with the insurer, while he has only a transient relationship with the insured. These factors could, unconsciously, dilute the loyalty of the most honest attorney." Sampson A. Brown & John L. Romaker, Cumis, Conflicts and the Civil Code: Section 2860 Changes Little, 25 Cal.W.L.Rev. 45, 54 (1988) (footnotes omitted). Here again, the attorney's duties are clear. If the exercise of the attorney's professional judgment on behalf of the insured may be affected by these interests, an attorney can only accept the employment if the client consents after full disclosure. Alaska Code of Professional Responsibility DR 5–101(A). Furthermore, the attorney is prohibited from permitting the insurer to "direct or regulate his professional judgment" in representing the insured. Alaska Code of Professional Responsibility DR 5–107(B). A breach of these ethical obligations may subject an attorney to disciplinary actions and may serve as the basis for a legal malpractice action, thus serving as a deterrent to the kinds of abuses which concern the court. Absent a showing that the Code of Professional Responsibility and the threat of legal malpractice actions are ineffective in preventing such abuses, the broad prophylactic rule adopted by the court seems superfluous.

In further support of its conclusion, the majority voices its concern over the danger that an insurer might gain access to information not otherwise available to it which could be used to its advantage in the coverage dispute. In Continental we discussed this danger in the policy defense context. 608 P.2d at 291. However, in the context of a coverage dispute, I believe this danger to be more imagined than real. It is difficult to imagine a case or set of facts where information tending to defeat coverage would be unavailable to the insurer. Under most insurance agreements, the insured has a duty to cooperate with the insurer. "The duties of the insured have been held to require a fair, frank and truthful disclosure of information reasonably demanded by the insurer, for the purpose of enabling it to determine whether or not there is a genuine defense." 8 John A. Appleman & Jean Appleman, Insurance Law and Practice § 4774 (1981). In addition, facts tending to defeat coverage will most likely be developed in the liability trial and will be discoverable by the insurer in subsequent coverage litigation. Even confidential attorney-client communications may be discoverable by an insurer under certain circumstances. See, e.g., Glacier Gen. Assur. Co. v. Superior Court, 95 Cal.App.3d 836, 157 Cal.Rptr. 435 (1979). See generally John P. Ludington, Annotation, Insured–Insurer Communications As Privileged, 55 A.L.R.4th 336, 354–59 (1987).

Of course this does not mean the insured's attorney is free to share any confidential or privileged information with the insurer. Regardless of whether defense counsel is selected by the insured or the insurer, the attorney is bound by the same ethical duties regarding confidentiality. See Alaska Code of Professional Responsibility DR 4–101. In those rare cases where such a breach of confidentiality actually occurs, the law affords adequate protection and recourse to the insured. An attorney who breaches a client's confidentiality may be subject to discipline for a violation of his professional responsibility or to a suit by the insured for legal malpractice. Of more significance to the insured, an insurer who relies on breach of confidentiality by defense counsel to assert non-coverage may be subsequently estopped from denying coverage based on policy exclusion. See Parsons v. Continental Nat'l Am. Group, 113 Ariz. 223, 228, 550 P.2d 94, 99 (1976). Such remedies serve as adequate protection of the insured and as a strong disincentive to both insurers and defense counsel to compromise the insured's interest.

Other considerations prevent me from supporting the rule adopted today. First, "[t]ypically, the coverage issue [and resulting conflict of interest are] not created by the insurer but by the allegations of the claimant. Often those allegations bear little relationship to reality." Mallen & Smith, supra, § 23.16. In light of this, a rule which operates to deprive an insurer of its contractual right to participate in the defense whenever the insurer reserves its rights unnecessarily penalizes the insurer. Second, an insurer may be required to issue a reservation of rights letter or risk its right to later challenge coverage of the claim under the policy. See Continental Ins. Co. v. Bayless & Roberts, Inc., 608 P.2d 281, 289 n. 13 (Alaska 1980). The insurer should not be forced to sacrifice its right to participate in the selection of counsel in order to preserve its right to subsequently contest coverage. Third, because an insurer, under agency principles, may be subject to liability for the malpractice of the attorney which represents the insured, see Mallen & Smith, supra, § 23.6, it is fair and reasonable that the insurer should have a role in selection of counsel. Finally, the rule adopted by the court today presupposes that no counsel selected or approved of by an insurer can represent an insured without consciously or unconsciously compromising the insured's interests in favor of those of the insurer. My confidence in the integrity of the members of the Alaska Bar will not allow me to support the adoption of a rule of law based on such an assumption.

The dissent of COMPTON, J. is omitted.

## MERRIMACK MUTUAL FIRE INSURANCE CO. v. NONAKA

Supreme Judicial Court of Massachusetts, 1993.
414 Mass. 187, 606 N.E.2d 904.

WILKINS, J.

On June 11, 1990, Anthony J. D'Urso shot Keizo Nonaka wounding him seriously. The plaintiff (Merrimack) commenced this action seeking a declaratory judgment that a Merrimack homeowner's insurance policy covering D'Urso as an insured did not provide coverage of Nonaka's claim against D'Urso. That insurance policy excluded coverage for bodily injury "which is expected or intended by the insured." A jury in this action found that D'Urso intentionally shot Nonaka. Subsequently, a second jury awarded $900,000 to Nonaka in his action against D'Urso.

Nonaka does not argue that, by its terms, the Merrimack policy covers his claim against D'Urso. He argued below successfully that Merrimack must afford him coverage of that claim because of Merrimack's conduct in defending the Nonaka claim for approximately five months without giving D'Urso notice of a reservation of rights or a disclaimer of coverage. Because the trial judge found that D'Urso was in no way prejudiced by Merrimack's defense of the tort case, he rejected Nonaka's claim that Merrimack was estopped to deny coverage. His decision in favor of Nonaka was based on his conclusion that Merrimack's dominion over the case, before it commenced this action, "during most of the pretrial period, during which important events such as the deposition of the plaintiff [Nonaka] and the preliminary pretrial conference occurred" obligated it to cover the Nonaka claim. In the judge's view, Merrimack's delay was too great, even if there was no prejudice to D'Urso.

We granted Merrimack's application for direct appellate review. We vacate the judgment and order the entry of a declaration that Merrimack is not obliged to provide coverage of Nonaka's claim against D'Urso.

We recite the significant facts found by the judge or established in the pleadings. On July 30, 1990, Nonaka sued D'Urso alleging only negligent conduct. On August 24, counsel for D'Urso filed an answer. In September, D'Urso's counsel notified Merrimack of the claim. Early in October, counsel selected by Merrimack entered an appearance for D'Urso and original counsel for D'Urso withdrew his appearance. New counsel for D'Urso conducted a deposition of Nonaka in October. Early that month Merrimack retained coverage counsel. On November 19, Nonaka filed an amended complaint that alleged assault and battery as well as other claims, including negligence, and added D'Urso's son Anthony as a defendant. On January 25, 1991, the filing of a second amended complaint was allowed. That complaint alleged no intentional conduct. On February 21, the tort case was called for a preliminary pretrial conference, and an early trial date was set. On March 11, Merrimack filed this declaratory judgment action. Later that month counsel selected by the D'Ursos appeared for them in Nonaka's tort action (at Merrimack's expense), and counsel selected by Merrimack withdrew his appearance. On May 23, the jury in this action found that D'Urso intentionally shot Nonaka. On May 31, judgment was entered for Nonaka in his action against D'Urso.

Any claim that Merrimack's conduct bars it from disclaiming coverage must rest either on estoppel or on waiver. Sweeney v. Frew, 318 Mass. 595, 598, 63 N.E.2d 350 (1945). Estoppel is not involved here because D'Urso did not rely to his detriment on anything Merrimack did or did not do. See Royal–Globe Ins. Co. v. Craven, 411 Mass. 629, 635, 585 N.E.2d 315 (1992).[3] To succeed Nonaka must establish that Merrimack waived its right to disclaim coverage.

An insurance company is obliged to provide coverage to an insured who has violated a provision of the policy if the company has waived its right to assert the policy breach as a ground for denying liability. Waiver consists of the insurer's voluntary or intentional relinquishment of a known right. See Sheehan v. Commercial Travelers Mut. Accident Ass'n of Am., 283 Mass. 543, 186 N.E. 627 (1933); Powell v. Fireman's Fund Ins. Cos., 26 Mass.App.Ct. 508, 511, 529 N.E.2d 1228 (1988). An insurer's intention to waive a ground for not providing coverage may be inferred from the circumstances. Eaton v. Globe & Rutgers Fire Ins. Co., 227 Mass. 354, 364, 116 N.E. 536 (1917). See Hurley v. Metropolitan Life Ins. Co., 296 Mass. 130, 136, 5 N.E.2d 16 (1936). One class of waiver case involves a claimed breach of an insured's duty to the insurer, such as the failure promptly to notify the insurance company of a claim or the failure of an insured to cooperate with the insurance company. See, e.g., DiMarzo v. American Mut. Ins. Co., 389 Mass. 85, 99, 449 N.E.2d 1189 (1983); Rose v. Regan, 344 Mass. 223, 181 N.E.2d 796 (1962). Another class of waiver case involves claimed misrepresentations by the insured that led the insurer to provide insurance coverage. See, e.g., Employers' Liab. Assurance Corp., Ltd. v. Vella, 366 Mass. 651, 321 N.E.2d 910 (1975).[5]

Nonaka's argument rests on a claim that the entry of an appearance for D'Urso by an attorney selected by Merrimack in fulfilment of its duty to defend Nonaka's claim and the continuation of that appearance for approximately five months resulted, as a matter of law, in a waiver of Merrimack's right to disclaim coverage. The concept of waiver has had

3. By not earlier (a) disclaiming coverage, (b) withdrawing from the defense of the case, (c) tendering notice of a reservation of rights to D'Urso, or (d) commencing an action such as this, Merrimack ran the risk that D'Urso might be able to prove that Merrimack was estopped to deny coverage. In retrospect, it seems that Merrimack would have been well-advised to have acted sooner to protect its position.

5. In the Vella case, the insurer sought a determination that it could disclaim liability because of an intentional misrepresentation by its policyholder. We held that the policyholder had made no material misrepresentation (id., 366 Mass. at 656, 321 N.E.2d 910), and that, in any event, the insurer lost its right to disclaim liability "when it [knew] the facts, [failed] to disclaim within a reasonable time, and [acted] in a way inconsistent with an intention to disclaim" (id. at 658, 321 N.E.2d 910). There, the insurer did not raise the question of its right to disclaim until one year and a half after it had discovered the facts on which it relied. Although the word "waiver" does not appear in the opinion, the authorities cited in support of the principle just set forth deal with the loss of the power to avoid an agreement, with waiver, or with acts manifesting an election to affirm a transaction. Id. The delay was too great, and the insurer lost any right to disclaim. In such circumstances, the passage of an unreasonable length of time before disclaiming liability, after learning the facts and after undertaking a defense of a claim under the policy required a finding of waiver and, therefore, the insurer lost the right to disclaim liability.

Two courts may have treated the Vella case as an estoppel case. See Powell v. Fireman's Fund Ins. Cos., 26 Mass.App.Ct. 508, 512, 529 N.E.2d 1228 (1988); Whitney v. Continental Ins. Co., 595 F.Supp. 939, 943 (D.Mass.1984). There was no reliance in the Vella case. Estoppel was, therefore, not involved. It was a waiver case.

no part to play in the insurance law of the Commonwealth when an insured has argued that the insurance company has waived the limits of coverage defined in the insurance policy. In Palumbo v. Metropolitan Life Ins. Co., 293 Mass. 35, 199 N.E. 335 (1935), we said that "whatever may be the scope of waiver in the law of insurance, it does not extend to the broadening of the coverage, so as to make the policy cover a risk not within its terms. That would require a new contract, and cannot be accomplished by waiver." Id. at 37–38, 199 N.E. 335. See New England Gas & Elec. Ass'n v. Ocean Accident & Guar. Corp. Ltd., 330 Mass. 640, 665, 116 N.E.2d 671 (1953); Wedgwood v. Eastern Commercial Travelers Accident Ass'n, 308 Mass. 463, 467, 32 N.E.2d 687 (1941). This is the majority view in this country. See A.D. Windt, Insurance Claims and Disputes § 6.33 at 361 (2d ed. 1988) ("coverage under an insurance contract cannot be created or enlarged by waiver"). This principle, argued to us by Merrimack and not discussed in Nonaka's brief, is dispositive of this case. The waiver cases on which Nonaka relies are not applicable to this case.

Even if we were to reexamine the question whether an insurance company could be found to have waived the limits of coverage stated in its policy, this case would not support a waiver theory. There was, of course, no express waiver. An implication that Merrimack intended to waive the coverage question is not warranted. Because there were negligence counts in each successive complaint, it was reasonable for Merrimack to conclude that it had a duty to defend all aspects of the case. See Aetna Casualty & Sur. Co. v. Continental Casualty Co., 413 Mass. 730, 732 n. 1, 604 N.E.2d 30 (1992) (weight of authority imposes duty to defend all counts of complaint if insurer has duty to defend at least one count).[6] Merrimack retained coverage counsel shortly after it initially retained counsel to defend D'Urso. The trial judge noted that "presumably all of the attorneys were aware of a potential coverage issue."

The judgment is vacated. Judgment shall be entered declaring that Merrimack Mutual Fire Insurance Company is not obliged to afford coverage under its homeowner's policy to Anthony J. D'Urso, or Anthony A. D'Urso, with respect to claims arising out of the shooting of Keizo Nonaka on June 11, 1990.

So ordered.

### *Notes*

1. As noted in the *CHI* dissent, in many states the insured does not necessarily have the exclusive right to select its independent defense counsel where a conflict exists. The dissent cites *New York State Urban Develop-*

6. The purpose of reserving the right to disclaim is to permit an insurer to fulfil its duty to defend without forfeiting any subsequent right to disclaim. See Salonen v. Paanenen, 320 Mass. 568, 573, 71 N.E.2d 227 (1947). It seems that Merrimack should have availed itself of this option at least as early as when Nonaka filed a complaint alleging an intentional tort. Merrimack's failure to do so cannot alone support a finding of waiver.

*ment Corp. v. VSL Corp.,* 738 F.2d 61 (2d Cir.1984), in which VSL faced a claim for damages allegedly sustained as a result of its work on the Roosevelt Island tramway. In a separate trial, VSL's professional liability insurer, Northbrook, was ordered to provide a defense. When VSL refused to name or accept any counsel other than the firm which had represented it against Northbrook in the prior action, Northbrook made an appointment. VSL argued that this violated the order, but the court held that, despite the earlier conflict, Northbrook was still able to assert the policy term which called for payment of, "(1) fees charged by any attorney designated by [Northbrook] * * * (3) fees charged by any attorney designated by [VSL] with the written consent of [Northbrook]." By this term, the insurer would be justified in unilaterally selecting independent counsel provided the power was exercised in good faith. After reviewing the Northbrook's failed attempt to satisfy VSL, the qualifications of the appointed counsel and the insurer's impartial relationship and instructions to counsel, the court found the requisite good faith.

2. In some circumstances, the technique employed by insurers of seeking declaratory relief (a proceeding in which the insurer appears as a party plaintiff perhaps without a jury trial) while a tort action is progressing against its insured has been questioned. Recognizing the dilemma in which the insured is placed, the Colorado Supreme Court held that it was not an abuse of discretion for the trial court to postpone the declaratory suit until resolution of the tort litigation. Hartford Insurance Group v. District Court, 625 P.2d 1013 (Colo.1981).

### *Problem*

An injured person files a personal injury action against an insured. The liability insurer undertakes the defense under a reservation of rights letter, at the same time advising the insured that it unequivocally disclaims any coverage under the policy. The insured then files suit in another court for declaratory judgment as to whether there is coverage, and for an injunction against the injured party's proceeding with the tort action. Should the declaratory relief be granted? See: American Food Management v. Transamerica Insurance Co., 608 S.W.2d 552 (Mo.App.1980).

## GROSS v. LLOYDS OF LONDON INSURANCE COMPANY

Supreme Court of Wisconsin, 1984.
121 Wis.2d 78, 358 N.W.2d 266.

CALLOW, JUSTICE.

The issue presented for review is whether an insurer may terminate the defense of its insured by tendering its policy limit for settlement pursuant to the terms of the liability insurance policy.

On July 30, 1982, Dr. Ivan D. Frantz submitted an application to the Imperial Casualty and Indemnity Company (Imperial) for the renewal of a policy of aircraft bodily injury liability insurance. The application was in the form of a conditional insurance binder, and it stated that the limits of liability for bodily injury were $100,000 for each person and $300,000 for each occurrence. The policy itself was issued on August 11, 1982.

On August 5, 1982, at The Experimental Aircraft Association's annual fly-in at Oshkosh, Wisconsin, an unoccupied Piper aircraft, owned by Frantz, rolled into the tent occupied by Sandra Gross, seriously injuring her. Imperial investigated the accident and concluded that Gross's damages for injuries could greatly exceed the policy limits of $100,000. On October 5, 1982, Imperial forwarded a check for $100,000 along with a partial release and indemnification agreement to Gross's attorney in an attempt to settle the claim. The proposed release was a standard *Pierringer*-type release, *Pierringer v. Hoger,* 21 Wis.2d 182, 124 N.W.2d 106 (1963), which would have released both Imperial and Frantz from any liability resulting from the accident. Gross rejected payment of the policy limits and refused to execute the release. On October 18, 1982, Gross commenced an action in Milwaukee county circuit court seeking damages of $11,000,000 against Imperial, Frantz, The Experimental Aircraft Association, and Lloyds of London (the EAA's insurer).

On December 3, 1982, Imperial filed a motion in the trial court seeking permission to pay its policy limit into court and seeking to be relieved from any further obligation to defend Frantz under the terms of the insurance policy. The policy issued to Frantz contained the following language: [4]

> "[T]he Company shall defend any suit * * * seeking damages which are payable under the terms of this policy, even if any of the allegations of the suit are groundless, false or fraudulent; but the Company may make such investigation and settlement of any claim or suit as it deems expedient, *but the Company shall not be obligated to pay any claim or judgment or to defend any suit after the applicable limit of the Company's liability has been exhausted by payment of judgments or settlements or after such limit of the Company's liability has been tendered for settlements.*" (Emphasis added.)

The trial court entered an order allowing Imperial to pay its policy limit into court and relieving it of any further obligation to defend Frantz in the litigation. The court of appeals affirmed the trial court's order, stating that the plain language of the policy envisioned that the company could be relieved of its obligation to defend its insured either upon payment of a judgment or settlement in the amount of the policy limit or upon tender of the policy limit to the court. 118 Wis.2d at 371–72, 347 N.W.2d 899. In addition, the court of appeals found that allowing the insurer to be relieved of its obligation to defend the insured upon payment of the policy limit into court was not contrary to public

4. The policy was not issued until August 11, 1982, four days after the accident. The binder which Dr. Frantz received at the time he made application for renewal of the policy contained no statement regarding Imperial's reserving the right to terminate its defense of the insured upon payment or tender of the policy limits.

policy. While the policy at issue was a renewal of a previously issued policy, the original policy of insurance was not made part of the record. The court of appeals did not comment on the fact that, at the time of the accident, Frantz had not yet received the policy and nothing in the record showed that Frantz had any notice of Imperial's right to terminate its defense upon tender of the policy limits for settlement. Frantz petitioned this court for review, and we granted the petition.

[Prior to 1966 policies of this type did not contain the above italicized language and] it was not clear whether the insurer's duty to defend the insured would be terminated once the policy limits had been paid out.

In 1966 the standard form liability policy was revised. The 1966 policy language directly defined the insurer's right to terminate the defense of its insured as follows:

> "The Company will pay on behalf of the insured all sums which the insured shall become legally obligated to pay * * * *but the Company shall not be obligated to pay any claim or judgment or to defend any suit after the applicable limit of the Company's liability has been exhausted by payment of judgments or settlements.*" (Emphasis added.)

The 1966 revisions were meant to clarify when the insurer's duty to defend the insured has been satisfied by providing that the duty to defend ceases after the policy limits are exhausted either by payment of judgments or settlements. 7C J. Appleman, *supra,* sec. 4682 at 29. Despite the clear policy language, Appleman cautions that the insurer's duty to defend the insured may continue even after the policy limits have been exhausted:

> "Despite the 1966 and subsequent revisions, the primary insurer may not walk away from the insured by paying relatively low limits into court and abandon the insured with a substantial judgment simply because the cost of appeal or other handling may be formidable. The insured's interests may demand continued protection despite threatened exhaustion of the primary limits." *Id.* at 36 (footnote omitted).

In its opinion, the court of appeals reasoned that Appleman's caveat spoke to policies lacking the "tendered for settlements" language present in the Imperial policy. The language contained in the Imperial policy permitting the insurer to terminate its duty to defend once the policy limits have been tendered for settlement (as well as when the limits have been exhausted by payment of judgments or settlements) is a further revision in the language of liability insurance policies which first appeared several years ago. We conclude the "payment of judgments or settlements" language in the 1966 policy form contemplates payment upon the conclusion of the litigation or termination of the claim by settlement. The "tendered for settlements" language added by the insurer contemplates payment prior to the conclusion of the litigation or settlement of the claim against the insured. The addition of the "tendered for settlements" language is persuasive evidence of a substantial change in the obligation of the insurer to defend. Not only is the enforceability of such a provision a matter of first impression in Wisconsin, but no reported cases from other jurisdictions have yet construed a like provision.

While numerous cases have dealt with the language contained in the older policy forms, there is a split of authority in those cases as to whether an insurer may be relieved of its obligation to defend the insured after the policy limits have been exhausted. 1 R.Long, *The Law of Liability Insurance*, sec. 5.12 at 5–69; Annot., 27 A.L.R.3d 1057 (1969). It has been stated that the insurer's duty to defend is broader than the duty to indemnify, and that regardless of the exhaustion of the policy limits, the insurer should not be permitted to withdraw from the defense in a manner that would prejudice the rights and interests of the insured. Alternatively, some courts have stated that insurers are only obligated to defend insureds up to the limits of coverage afforded by the policy and that exhaustion of the policy limits also terminates the duty to defend. *Denham v. La Salle–Madison Hotel Co.*, 168 F.2d 576, 584 (7th Cir.1948). "Defendant's theory (that the insurer's obligation to defend survives the payment of the policy limit) would produce the incongruous situation that plaintiff would have a continuing obligation to defend, notwithstanding its obligation to pay has been exhausted." *Id.*

When construing language covering an obligation such as the insurer's duty to defend the insured, courts must look to the reasonable expectations of the insured. *Kocse v. Liberty Mutual Insurance Co.*, 159 N.J.Super. 340, 345–46, 387 A.2d 1259 (1978). Both parties concede that the provision in the Imperial policy terminating the insurer's duty to defend once the policy limits have been tendered for settlement was a substantial deviation from the defense provisions contained in previous policy forms. The "tendered for settlements" language was a supplement at the end of the sentence contained in older policy forms which provided that "the Company shall not be obligated to pay any claim or judgment or to defend any suit after the applicable limit of the Company's liability has been exhausted by payment of judgments or settlements." The new language was not highlighted in any way so as to put insureds on notice that the standard form liability policy, which had been in use in the insurance industry since 1966, had been changed with respect to the insurer's duty to defend. We believe the reasonable expectations of insureds would be that the policy language in use by the industry since 1966 would be present in new policies unless they were specifically given notice of a change.

In order for an insurer to be relieved of its duty to defend upon tender of the policy limits, the "tendered for settlements" language must be highlighted in the policy and binder by means of conspicuous print, such as bold, italicized, or colored type, which gives clear notice to the insured that the insurer may be relieved of its duty to defend by tendering the policy limits for settlement. Provisions regarding the insurer's duty to defend are typically contained in liability insurance policies, and if insurers elect to adopt the "tendered for settlements" language, they must highlight it in the policy. Insurers may terminate their duty to defend insureds by tendering the policy limits, but they may only do so if the insureds receive adequate notice as outlined in this opinion.

The decision of the court of appeals is reversed, and the cause is remanded to the circuit court for further proceedings consistent with this opinion.

HEFFERNAN, CHIEF JUSTICE (concurring).

I do not join in the dicta concerning the public policy of allowing insurers to terminate their obligation to defend nor in the *sub silentio* implication that, had proper notice been given, the provision in question would be enforceable. These public policy issues were neither considered nor decided by this court and, under the rationale of the court, are not necessary for the disposition of the case.

I am authorized to state that JUSTICE WILLIAM A. BABLITCH joins in this concurrence.

[Other concurring opinions differ as to whether the public policy issue was actually decided in the majority opinion].

### *Notes*

1. The split of authority as to whether insurers using either the pre-'67 or post-'67 C.G.L. policy forms are relieved from the obligation to defend upon the exhaustion of policy limits further complicates the handling of the massive asbestos-related, and similar, litigation.

For example, consider the position of a company that insured an asbestos manufacturer against liability for one year in the early sixties under a pre-'67 C.G.L. policy. For some time it has shared in the defense of the manufacturer in a jurisdiction that adheres to the continuing exposure (or triple trigger) theory of liability. The jurisdiction also follows the line of cases holding that pre-'67 policies do not allow discharge from the duty to defend upon exhaustion of policy limits, whereas post-'67 policies do. The insurer would very much like to pay its policy limits and be done with it—as the insurers under the post-'67 policies are doing—but instead appears to be faced with the prospect of increasing defense costs. Cf. Zurich Ins. Co. v. Raymark Industries, Inc., 118 Ill.2d 23, 112 Ill.Dec. 684, 514 N.E.2d 150 (1987). In *Zurich* the court simplified the matter by holding that the wording of *both* pre-'67 and post-'67 policies allowed termination of the duty to defend when the policy limits are exhausted.

See the revised wording of the provision in question in Appendix B and Appendix D.

2. While California makes clear that an insurer cannot avoid its duty to defend an insured once trial has begun, it is also clear that an insurer may withdraw once an insured is otherwise free of liability. Heredia v. Farmers Insurance Exchange, 228 Cal.App.3d 1345, 279 Cal.Rptr. 511 (1991) (plaintiff wanted to force insurer to continue defense beyond release of insurer and

tender of limits to avoid an "empty chair defense" by remaining defendants); Johnson v. Continental Insurance Companies, 202 Cal.App.3d 477, 248 Cal.Rptr. 412 (1988) (claims against plaintiff insured had been settled at limits, insured named in cross-complaint in a later action).

### *Notes*

### *On Tort Liability*

1. It is usually said that joint tortfeasors are jointly liable, that is, that the injured person may sue both or either (in which case the injured person may recover all his damage against the one he sues), leaving the latter to whatever recourse against his joint tortfeasor the law allows and whatever is practicable. Suing the "deeper pocket" may have its practical aspects.

2. What may happen when the injured person sues the joint tortfeasors in a single action can get complicated. [We must reflect that, although an insurer will not be able to be sued directly *on the tort,* in many instances one or another tortfeasor may have applicable insurance.] Consider the following rather noted case and the note following it.

## BOOTH v. MARY CARTER PAINT CO.

District Court of Appeal of Florida, 1967.
202 So.2d 8.

PER CURIAM.

Appellant, J.D. Booth, in his complaint charged the defendants with the negligent operation of their motor vehicles which resulted in the death of his wife. Defendants' answer denied the charge of negligence. Trial was had and the jury returned a verdict in the amount of $15,000 for the plaintiff. The trial court denied appellant's motion for a new trial and he brings this appeal seeking a new trial primarily on the question of damages only.

This action at law was previously before this Court in the case styled Booth v. Mary Carter Paint Company, reported in 182 So.2d 292. The facts reported in the opinion of that case should be reviewed in order to more fully understand the facts established in the trial of the case sub judice.

* * *

The lower court, upon motion of the defendants, struck from the complaint subparagraph 9(a), i.e., "the loss of care and support of plaintiff and his and decedent's minor children." During the trial of the case plaintiff attempted to introduce evidence of the wife's earnings, etc., claimed under subparagraph 9(a) above mentioned, which the court refused to permit.

Based on the contents of the complaint at the time of trial, the court did not commit error in denying the proffered evidence since the complaint being tried had no provision for this specific damage. * * *

An agreement between William T. Keen of the firm of Shackleford, Farrior, Stallings, Glos & Evans, as counsel of record for the defendants, B.C. Willoughby and Harry Lee Sutton, and Mark R. Hawes, of the firm of Hawes and Hadden, counsel of record for the plaintiff, J.D. Booth, provides: "1. That the maximum liability, exposure or financial contribution of the defendants, B.C. Willoughby and Harry Lee Sutton, shall be $12,500.00." The agreement further provides:

> Second, that in the event of a joint verdict against Willoughby and the Mary Carter Paint Company exceeding $37,500.00, that the plaintiff will satisfy said judgment against Mary Carter Paint Company entirely, with no contribution from Willoughby and Sutton. Provided, however, that if the Mary Carter Paint Company is not financially responsible to the extent of $37,500.00, the defendant Willoughby will contribute an amount of money between Mary Carter Paint Company's actual responsibility and the figure of $37,500.00, but not to exceed $12,500.00.
>
> Third, Willoughby and Sutton agreed that in the event of a verdict for all the defendants, they would pay the plaintiff $12,500.00; and in the event of a verdict against Mary Carter Paint Company less than $37,500.00, that Willoughby and Sutton would contribute the sum of $12,500.00.
>
> Fourth, Willoughby and Sutton shall continue as active defendants in the active defense of said litigation until all questions of liability and damages are resolved between the plaintiff and the other defendants.
>
> Fifth, that should the conditions laid down in the agreement result in any financial responsibility on the part of Willoughby and Sutton, they will pay the plaintiff within five days after the questions of liability and damages between the plaintiff and the other defendants are settled or concluded.

In paragraph 6 we again find the provision that the financial responsibility, exposure or liability of Willoughby and Sutton shall not exceed the sum of $12,500.00.

> Seventh, it is stated: "It is the intention of the parties hereto that this agreement shall be construed as a conditional agreement between them as to financial responsibility only, and that it shall in no wise constitute, or be construed to constitute, a release, settlement, admission of liability, or otherwise, and shall have no effect upon the trial of this case as to liability or extent of damages, nor shall said agreement be revealed to the jury trying said case."
>
> Eighth, it was agreed that the contents of this agreement would be furnished to no one, unless so ordered by the court, and
>
> Ninth, that the terms and conditions specified in the agreement, which are dependent upon a jury verdict, should be equally applicable to and binding on the parties in the event plaintiff Booth

amicably settles the issues of liability and damages with Mary Carter Paint Company.

This instrument was signed by Mark R. Hawes of Hawes and Hadden, attorneys for the plaintiff Booth, and William T. Farrior of Shackleford, Farrior, Stallings, Glos & Evans, attorneys for B.C. Willoughby and Harry Lee Sutton.

The appellees, Mary Carter Paint Company, Hancock and Tompkins, in their brief (p. 7) state a Fourth Point as follows: "Whether or not the trial court erred in failing to construe the Agreement between William T. Keen as counsel of record for the Defendants Willoughby and Sutton, and Mark R. Hawes as counsel of record for the Plaintiff Booth, as a release, and in denying the ore tenus motion of Defendants Mary Carter Paint Company, Hancock and Tompkins to offset the $12,500.00 consideration being paid by Defendants Willoughby and Sutton to Plaintiff Booth under the terms of said Agreement, as provided by Section 54.28, Florida Statutes?"

We hold that the instrument hereinabove discussed was not a release and that the lower court did not err in denying the ore tenus motion of defendants Mary Carter Paint Company, Tompkins and Hancock to offset the $12,500.00 consideration being paid by the defendants Willoughby and Sutton to plaintiff Booth under the terms of said agreement, as provided by Section 54.28, Fla.Stats., F.S.A.

No cases on point were cited by the appellees and we have failed to find any. We think the instrument is what it purports to be, an agreement that would limit the liability of defendants Willoughby and Sutton to pay a sum not exceeding $12,500.00 and which would guarantee the plaintiff the sum of $12,500.00 if any verdict was secured for less than $37,500.00.

We do not think the errors raised by the parties need be discussed and we specifically deny each of the same and affirm the lower court.

Affirmed.

## *Notes*

1. Of course, rules on liability and settlements may be modified by statute. To illustrate the rules applicable in one jurisdiction—California—the following statutes are quoted in part.

West's Ann.Cal.Civil Code

**§ 1431. Joint liability**

An obligation imposed upon several persons, or a right created in favor of several persons, is presumed to be joint, and not several, except as provided in Section 1431.2, and except in the special cases mentioned in the title on the interpretation of contracts. This presumption, in the case of a right, can be overcome only by express words to the contrary.

**§ 1431.1. Findings and declaration of purpose**

The People of the State of California find and declare as follows:

(a) The legal doctrine of joint and several liability, also known as "the deep pocket rule", has resulted in a system of inequity and injustice that has threatened financial bankruptcy of local governments, other public agencies, private individuals and businesses and has resulted in higher prices for goods and services to the public and in higher taxes to the taxpayers.

(b) Some governmental and private defendants are perceived to have substantial financial resources or insurance coverage and have thus been included in lawsuits even though there was little or no basis for finding them at fault. Under joint and several liability, if they are found to share even a fraction of the fault, they often are held financially liable for all the damage. The People—taxpayers and consumers alike—ultimately pay for these lawsuits in the form of higher taxes, higher prices and higher insurance premiums.

(c) Local governments have been forced to curtail some essential police, fire and other protections because of the soaring costs of lawsuits and insurance premiums.

Therefore, the People of the State of California declare that to remedy these inequities, defendants in tort actions shall be held financially liable in closer proportion to their degree of fault. To treat them differently is unfair and inequitable.

The People of the State of California further declare that reforms in the liability laws in tort actions are necessary and proper to avoid catastrophic economic consequences for state and local governmental bodies as well as private individuals and businesses.

### § 1431.2. Several liability for non-economic damages

(a) In any action for personal injury, property damage, or wrongful death, based upon principles of comparative fault, the liability of each defendant for non-economic damages shall be several only and shall not be joint. Each defendant shall be liable only for the amount of non-economic damages allocated to that defendant in direct proportion to that defendant's percentage of fault, and a separate judgment shall be rendered against that defendant for that amount.

(b)(1) For purposes of this section, the term "economic damages" means objectively verifiable monetary losses including medical expenses, loss of earnings, burial costs, loss of use of property, costs of repair or replacement, costs of obtaining substitute domestic services, loss of employment and loss of business or employment opportunities.

(2) For the purposes of this section, the term "non-economic damages" means subjective, non-monetary losses including, but not limited to, pain, suffering, inconvenience, mental suffering, emotional distress, loss of society and companionship, loss of consortium, injury to reputation and humiliation.

### § 1432. Contribution among joint obligors

Except as provided in Section 877 of the Code of Civil Procedure, a party to a joint, or joint and several obligation, who satisfies more than his share of the claim against all, may require a proportionate contribution from all the parties joined with him.

§§ 1431.1 and 1431.2 above were enacted by one of California's "initiatives", Proposition 51 of 1986.

2. Nor are these the only statutes which may pertain in cases like the Mary Carter case set out above. Consider the following sections from the California Code of Civil Procedure:

**§ 877. Release of one or more joint tortfeasors or co-obligors; effect upon liability of others**

Where a release, dismissal with or without prejudice, or a covenant not to sue or not to enforce judgment is given in good faith before verdict or judgment to one or more of a number of tortfeasors claimed to be liable for the same tort, or to one or more other co-obligors mutually subject to contribution rights, it shall have the following effect:

(a) It shall not discharge any other such party from liability unless its terms so provide, but it shall reduce the claims against the others in the amount stipulated by the release, the dismissal or the covenant, or in the amount of the consideration paid for it whichever is the greater.

(b) It shall discharge the party to whom it is given from all liability for any contribution to any other parties.

(c) This section shall not apply to co-obligors who have expressly agreed in writing to an apportionment of liability for losses or claims among themselves.

(d) This section shall not apply to a release, dismissal with or without prejudice, or a covenant not to sue or not to enforce judgment given to a co-obligor on an alleged contract debt where the contract was made prior to January 1, 1988.

**§ 877.5. Sliding scale recovery agreement; disclosure to court and jury; service of notice of intent to enter**

(a) Where an agreement or covenant is made which provides for a sliding scale recovery agreement between one or more, but not all, alleged defendant tortfeasors and the plaintiff or plaintiffs:

(1) The parties entering into any such agreement or covenant shall promptly inform the court in which the action is pending of the existence of the agreement or covenant and its terms and provisions.

(2) If the action is tried before a jury, and a defendant party to the agreement is called as a witness at trial, the court shall, upon motion of a party, disclose to the jury the existence and content of the agreement or covenant, unless the court finds that this disclosure will create substantial danger of undue prejudice, of confusing the issues, or of misleading the jury.

The jury disclosure herein required shall be no more than necessary to inform the jury of the possibility that the agreement may bias the testimony of the witness.

(b) As used in this section, a "sliding scale recovery agreement" means an agreement or covenant between a plaintiff or plaintiffs and one or more, but not all, alleged tortfeasor defendants, which limits the liability of the agreeing tortfeasor defendants to an amount which is dependent upon the amount of recovery which the plaintiff is able to recover from the nonagreeing defendant or defendants. This includes, but is not limited to, agreements within the scope of Section 877, and agreements in the form of a loan from the agreeing tortfeasor defendant or defendants to the plaintiff or plaintiffs which is repayable in whole or in part from the recovery against the nonagreeing tortfeasor defendant or defendants.

(c) No sliding scale recovery agreement is effective unless, at least 72 hours prior to entering into the agreement, a notice of intent to enter into an agreement has been served on all nonsignatory alleged defendant tortfeasors. However, upon a showing of good cause, the court or a judge thereof may allow a shorter time. The failure to comply with the notice requirements of this subdivision shall not constitute good cause to delay commencement of trial.

### § 877.6. Determination of good faith of settlement with one or more tortfeasors or co-obligors; review by writ of mandate; tolling of time limitations

(a)(1) Any party to an action wherein it is alleged that two or more parties are joint tortfeasors or co-obligors on a contract debt shall be entitled to a hearing on the issue of the good faith of a settlement entered into by the plaintiff or other claimant and one or more alleged tortfeasors or co-obligors, upon giving notice thereof in the manner provided in subdivision (b) of Section 1005. Upon a showing of good cause, the court may shorten the time for giving the required notice to permit the determination of the issue to be made before the commencement of the trial of the action, or before the verdict or judgment if settlement is made after the trial has commenced.

(2) In the alternative, a settling party may give notice of settlement to all parties and to the court, together with an application for determination of good faith settlement and a proposed order. The application shall indicate the settling parties, and the basis, terms, and amount of the settlement. The notice, application, and proposed order shall be given by certified mail, return receipt requested. Proof of service shall be filed with the court. Within 25 days of the mailing of the notice, application, and proposed order, a nonsettling party may file a notice of motion to contest the good faith of the settlement. If none of the nonsettling parties files a motion within 25 days of mailing of the notice, application, and proposed order, the court may approve the settlement. The notice by a nonsettling party shall be given in the manner provided in subdivision (b) of Section 1005. However, this paragraph shall not apply to settlements in which a confidentiality agreement has been entered into regarding the case or the terms of the settlement.

(b) The issue of the good faith of a settlement may be determined by the court on the basis of affidavits served with the notice of hearing, and any counteraffidavits filed in response thereto, or the court may, in its discretion, receive other evidence at the hearing.

(c) A determination by the court that the settlement was made in good faith shall bar any other joint tortfeasor or co-obligor from any further claims against the settling tortfeasor or co-obligor for equitable comparative contribution, or partial or comparative indemnity, based on comparative negligence or comparative fault.

(d) The party asserting the lack of good faith shall have the burden of proof on that issue.

(e) When a determination of the good faith or lack of good faith of a settlement is made, any party aggrieved by the determination may petition the proper court to review the determination by writ of mandate. * * *

3. The chief California case under § 877 et al. is Tech–Bilt, Inc. v. Woodward–Clyde & Associates, Inc., 38 Cal.3d 488, 213 Cal.Rptr. 256, 698 P.2d 159 (1985) in which Justice Grodin outlined some tests for the fairness of settlements under the cited sections. His tests were summarized in Yanez v. United States, 989 F.2d 323, 328 (9th Cir.1993):

> We agree that whether a settlement is in good faith under Cal.Civ. P.Code § 877 is a finding of fact for the trial court * * *. The district court is advised to apply all the factors enunciated in Tech–Bilt, Inc. v. Woodward–Clyde & Associates, 38 Cal.3d 488, 213 Cal.Rptr. 256, 698 P.2d 159 (1985). It appears that the district court overlooked several of these factors when determining the settlement was not in good faith. The factors are: 1. A rough approximation of plaintiffs' total recovery and the settlors' proportionate liability; 2. The amount paid in settlement; 3. The allocation of settlement proceeds among plaintiffs; 4. A recognition that a settlor should pay less in settlement than he would if he were found liable after trial; 5. The financial conditions and insurance policy limits of settling defendants; and, 6. The existence of collusion, fraud, or tortious conduct aimed to injure the interest of non-settling defendants. Tech–Bilt, 213 Cal.Rptr. at 262–63, 698 P.2d at 166–67.

# Chapter 15

# PROBLEMS OF MULTIPLE COVERAGE, INCLUDING "STACKING"

— **overlapping and conflicting liability insurance coverages**
— **primary and secondary coverages**
— **stacking of uninsured and similar first party coverages**

## PRELIMINARY NOTE

### Other Insurance

Where more than one insurer covers a loss or liability, difficult questions arise as to the distribution of the obligation to pay among the insurers.

If Policy A (Insurer A) and Policy B (Insurer B) apply to cover the same loss or liability and *neither* policy contains a provision indicating how losses or liabilities are to be shared with other insurers, presumably the insured can recover no more than the extent of his loss or liability in the light of the principle of indemnity. Double recovery should not be permitted and, if Insurer A pays the whole loss or liability, A ought somehow to receive contribution from Insurer B on the basis of a fair prorating of responsibility. And if the amount of the loss or liability is greater than the amount of Policies A and B, then the insured should receive the face amount of Policies A and B. See 16 Couch on Insurance, 2d, 62:1, 62:2.

But, of course, insurers have given thought to this problem and want to have their responsibilities as clearly delineated as they may be. For this reason, Policy A and Policy B may (especially if they are property or liability policies) contain provisions, referred to as "other insurance" provisions, to the following effect:

(a) Policy A and/or Policy B may state that it will only share proportionally in covering the loss or liability ("pro rata" clause); or

(b) Policy A and/or Policy B may state that if there is other valid insurance then Policy A or Policy B will be invalid ("escape" clause); or

(c) Policy A and/or Policy B may state that it will be "primary" or "excess" insurance. That is, if Policy A is primary it will pay up to its face value for any loss or liability incurred by the insured; if Policy B is excess it will cover only the amount of loss or liability over that paid by Insurer A and then only to B's face value. Obviously critical difficulties will arise if *both* Policy A and B say that they are "excess"; or

(d) Various combinations of (a), (b), or (c).

(e) In addition, we should take careful note, primary and excess provisions will be found in liability insurance where insurers may desire to arrange for a contingent sharing of the insured's liability. E.g., Insurer A may "cover" the first $1,000,000 and Insurer B may cover anything over that sum. This sort of planned "primary" and "excess" structure should be allowed to operate as planned.

Consult Keeton, Basic Insurance Text, pages 168–73 (West Publishing Co., 1971). See also Carriers Ins. Co. v. American Policyholders Ins. Co. infra p. 689.

It seems obvious that legislatures will be tempted or prompted to intervene. In California, Insurance Code 11580.9 provides a careful scheme for identifying "primary" and "excess" auto insurers depending on the type of vehicle, its use, and certain other factors. The section includes a "catch all" provision stating:

> "(d) Except * * *, where two or more policies affording and valid and collectible liability insurance apply to the same motor vehicle in an occurrence out of which a liability loss shall arise, it shall be conclusively presumed that the insurance afforded by that policy in which such motor vehicle is described or rated as an owned automobile shall be primary and the insurance afforded by any other policy or any other policies shall be excess."

The presumption stated in the subsection quoted, and presumptions in other subsections of Insurance Code 11580.9, are permitted by the statute to be modified or amended only by written agreement signed by all insurers who have issued a policy or policies applicable to the loss and all named insureds under such policies.

The problems of "primary" and "excess" as well as "escape" provisions reach throughout the field of insurance. It is certainly a substantial problem in property and casualty insurance, but the strikingly complicated illustrations seem today to be found in the area of automobile liability insurance. John P. Kurtock, Jr., in an article in 25 Federation of Insurance Counsel Quarterly 45 (Fall, 1974) comments extensively on the subject. Kurtock says:

> Duplication of coverage is common place. In automobile insurance it is not impossible for a person driving the automobile of another with permission to receive protection for the same loss under insurance contracts issued to:

(1) himself, on his personal automobile temporary substitute;

(2) the owner of the borrowed automobile (omnibus coverage);

(3) his employer, under a nonowned automobile cover; and

(4) his employer, under a general liability policy for an on premises automobile loss.

Overlapping coverages can result from a number of combinations of insurance contracts, such as:

(1) the omnibus coverage of an auto owner's personal automobile liability policy and the nonowned automobile coverage of the driver's automobile liability policy;

(2) the temporary substitute or nonowned automobile coverage of the driver's personal automobile policy and the omnibus or leased car coverage under a garage liability policy;

(3) an employee's personal automobile policy, and his employer's comprehensive general liability policy covering business use of the employee's automobile;

(4) two concurrent liability policies on the same automobile;

(5) a lessor's policy with provisions as to leased vehicles and a lessee's policy with provisions as to hired vehicles;

(6) a driver's nonowned automobile coverage of his personal automobile liability policy while using a leased vehicle and the omnibus coverage provided by the lessor;

(7) a comprehensive general liability policy covering an employee who is assisting in loading or unloading a motor vehicle and a motor vehicle liability policy.

8A Appleman, Insurance Law and Practice, 4906, suggests some additional overlapping coverages.

The impact (on the overlapping coverages described by Kurtock) of the three types of "other insurance" clauses described previously in this note (that is the "pro rata," the "excess" and the "escape" clauses) is obviously going to raise perplexing questions. What if Policy A contains an "excess" clause and Policy B contains a "pro rata" clause?

## RICHARDSON v. LUDWIG

Court of Appeals of Minnesota, 1993.
495 N.W.2d 869.

SCHUMACHER, J.

* * *

Appellant Jermike Corporation, a Domino's Pizza franchisee, operated two pizza delivery franchises. Jermike employed approximately 30 drivers, who delivered about 10,000 pizzas per month. Jermike required its drivers to have liability coverage on their delivery vehicles.

Respondent Debra L. Richardson commenced a negligence action as a result of injuries sustained in an October 21, 1988 automobile accident. Richardson's automobile was rear-ended by an automobile driven by respondent Richard Byron Ludwig and owned by respondent Elizabeth Couture, Ludwig's stepmother. At the time of the accident, Ludwig was returning from delivering a pizza for Jermike.

The vehicle Ludwig used for making pizza deliveries was owned by Couture and insured by State Farm, which provided liability coverage through a personal automobile policy. As a permissive user of Couture's vehicle and as a resident relative of the named insured, Ludwig was insured under the State Farm policy.

Jermike was insured under a business automobile policy issued by U.S. Fire. Under the U.S. Fire policy, liability coverage was afforded only for hired autos or non-owned autos. Non-owned autos were defined as: "Only those 'autos' you do not own, lease, hire, rent or borrow that are used in connection with your business. This includes 'autos' owned by your employees or partners or members of their households but only while used in your business or your personal affairs." Richardson sued Ludwig, Couture, Jermike, and Domino's Pizza. Ludwig and Couture cross-claimed against Jermike and Domino's; Jermike and Domino's cross-claimed against Ludwig and Couture.

U.S. Fire, through its insured, Jermike, moved for summary judgment, claiming Ludwig was not an insured under its policy and, even if he were, the State Farm policy was primary. State Farm, through its insureds, Ludwig and Couture, brought a cross motion for summary judgment, asserting the U.S. Fire policy was primary. The trial court denied U.S. Fire's motion and granted State Farm's motion, finding the U.S. Fire policy to be primary.

Subsequently, U.S. Fire settled Richardson's claims. The settlement agreement reserves U.S. Fire's right to seek indemnity from State Farm. After settling, U.S. Fire moved for reconsideration of the trial court's prior order. * * * Jermike appeals.

* * *

[The court concluded that Ludwig was not an insured within the meaning of the U.S. Fire policy.]

The Minnesota Supreme Court has stated, with respect to situations in which two or more insurance companies may be liable for the same loss:

> Often two or more companies would be fully liable for a loss but for their respective other insurance clauses, and many times those clauses conflict in their provisions. When it is clear that two or more companies are among themselves liable to the insured for his loss but the apportionment among the companies cannot be made without violating the other insurance clause of at least one company, then the courts must look outside the policies for rules of apportionment. One approach, known as the Lamb–Weston doctrine, is to

> require, when "other insurance" clauses conflict, that the loss be prorated among the insurers on the basis of their respective limits of liability. Lamb–Weston, Inc. v. Oregon Auto. Ins. Co., 219 Or. 110, 341 P.2d 110 (1959).
>
> The approach of the Minnesota court has traditionally been more complex than the Lamb–Weston doctrine. In Federal Ins. Co. v. Prestemon, 278 Minn. 218, 231, 153 N.W.2d 429, 437 (1967), we stated that the better approach is to allocate respective policy coverages in light of the total policy insuring intent, as determined by the primary policy risks upon which each policy's premiums were based and as determined by the primary function of each policy. * * *
>
> The nub of the Minnesota doctrine is that coverages of a given risk shall be "stacked" for payment in the order of their closeness to the risk. That is, the insurer whose coverage was effected for the primary purpose of insuring that risk will be liable first for payment, and the insurer whose coverage of the risk was the most incidental to the basic purpose of its insuring intent will be liable last. Integrity Mut. Ins. Co. v. State Auto. & Casualty Underwriters Ins. Co., 307 Minn. 173, 174–76, 239 N.W.2d 445, 446–47 (1976).

In Prestemon, the supreme court noted certain criteria for determining the primary and secondary liability of insurers of the same risk. Among the criteria noted were which policy was intended to cover the activity out of which the accident arose; which company specifically described the involved automobile in its policy; which company charged a premium reflecting a greater contemplated exposure; and which company apparently issued a policy designed to cover the particular car and the risks inherent in using that particular car. Prestemon, 278 Minn. at 229–30, 153 N.W.2d at 436–37, cited in Auto Owners Ins. Co. v. Northstar Mut. Ins. Co., 281 N.W.2d 700, 704 (Minn.1979).

Until 1988, the law in Minnesota was that, when two insurers insured against the same risk, the priority of applicability of coverage was to be determined by examining the total policy insuring intent of the policies; this intent was to be determined by using three or four nonexclusive criteria. It was essentially a balancing test, in which the court was to consider all of the circumstances surrounding the policies.

In 1988, indications began to appear that this singular test was, in fact, two separate tests. See Interstate Fire & Casualty Co. v. Auto-Owners Ins. Co., 433 N.W.2d 82, 86 (Minn.1988). In that case, the dispute was whether a homeowner's policy covering a student or an umbrella liability policy issued to a school district was primarily liable for injuries inflicted on another student occurring on school property. In determining that the umbrella policy issued to the school district was primarily liable, the Minnesota Supreme Court stated: "It appears to us that, in this case, rather than applying the three-part 'closest-to-the-risk' test, it is more helpful to use the broader approach set out in Integrity of allocating respective policy coverages in light of the total policy insuring intent, as determined by the primary policy risks and the primary function of each policy." Id. Subsequently, the Minnesota Supreme Court apparently reaffirmed the existence of two separate tests, the "broader" test of Integrity Mutual and the three-part test of Auto Owners. Garrick v. Northland Ins. Co., 469 N.W.2d 709, 712 (Minn. 1991).

This court has stated that the "broader" analysis of Interstate Fire and Garrick applies when the policies were intended to cover risks differing in kind and in size. Illinois Farmers Ins. Co. v. Depositors Ins. Co., 480 N.W.2d 657, 661 (Minn.App.1992). The analysis of Garrick and Interstate Fire, however, is "broader" only in the sense that it involves more than a mechanical application of the three factors set out in Auto Owners. The earlier cases, particularly Integrity Mutual and Prestemon, indicate that an analysis of all relevant factors must be made in every case involving overlapping coverage of the same risk.

U.S. Fire contends the other insurance clauses of the two policies can be reconciled and these clauses determine which policy is primary. The Minnesota Supreme Court has stated, however, that the language of the other insurance clauses—or even the existence of such a clause—is not dispositive. Garrick, 469 N.W.2d at 712. In addition, where, as in this case, one policy contains an excess clause and the other policy contains a pro rata clause, the clauses conflict. Integrity, 307 Minn. at 176–77, 239 N.W.2d at 447.

*Specific Description*

State Farm's policy covered the specific vehicle involved. State Farm agrees that its policy was intended to cover Couture and permissive drivers, including Ludwig, while using the car for business or pleasure. The U.S. Fire policy's declarations page does not specifically describe any vehicle; instead, it states that it covers nonowned autos.

*Premium*

Jermike paid a $46 annual premium for its business auto coverage. The premium paid for the State Farm policy is not in the record. The U.S. Fire policy provided only liability coverage; the State Farm policy also provided all the coverages required by the No–Fault Act.

*Primary/Incidental Coverage*

The State Farm policy was intended to cover Couture, Couture's vehicle, and permissive drivers of that vehicle. The U.S. Fire policy, on the other hand, provided liability coverage to Jermike for its vicarious liability arising out of automobiles it did not own. The State Farm policy provided coverage for business or pleasure use; the U.S. Fire policy provided coverage only for business use of nonowned autos.

*Other Relevant Factors*

Although Ludwig was using Couture's vehicle for business purposes, this is not a case similar to Garrick, in which an automobile insurer had been held primarily liable for an accident involving a commercial truck.

State Farm, in fact, specifically agreed to provide coverage for business use. By its very nature, pizza delivery is the sort of use of a personal automobile that an individual's insurer ought to anticipate.

We conclude the trial court erred in finding the U.S. Fire policy primary. The State Farm policy was intended to provide coverage for precisely what occurred in this case. The U.S. Fire policy was not intended to provide primary liability coverage for Jermike's driver employees.

DECISION

Ludwig was not an insured under the U.S. Fire policy and, even if the U.S. Fire policy provided coverage, it would be secondary to State Farm's coverage.

Reversed.

## EMPLOYERS REINSURANCE v. MISSION EQUITIES CORP.

Court of Appeal, First District, 1977.
74 Cal.App.3d 826, 141 Cal.Rptr. 727.

FEINBERG, ACTING PRESIDING JUSTICE.

We are asked in this appeal to decide which of two insurance companies must bear a loss occasioned by a claim of negligence on the part of an attorney.

There is no dispute as to the relevant facts. Mission Equities Corporation (hereinafter Mission) issued its malpractice policy to a firm of attorneys (hereinafter Attorneys) effective January 1, 1968 to January 1, 1969. Employers Reinsurance Corporation (hereinafter Employers) issued its policy to the Attorneys effective January 2, 1969 through January 2, 1970. On February 22, 1971, at which time the Employers' insurance policy was in effect through renewal, a malpractice action was filed against the Attorneys. The action alleged that the Attorneys filed an action on August 6, 1963, and that as a result of Attorneys' failure to prosecute the action in a timely fashion, the case was dismissed on September 20, 1968, pursuant to Code of Civil Procedure section 583. Employers defended the action and settled the case for $13,000. Mission was given notice of the suit by a letter from Attorneys but did not participate in the defense. On May 29, 1974, Employers filed suit against Mission, requesting a declaration that Mission afforded primary coverage for the alleged negligence and that Mission shall pay Employers $13,000 plus interest, attorney's fees and for costs of the suit. Both Employers and Mission filed motions for summary judgment. Employers' motion was granted on the issue of liability. A subsequent trial on the issue of damages resulted in a judgment against Mission in the amount of $15,580.17 plus costs. Mission appeals from that judgment.

> *Did Mission's policy cover the malpractice action where the cause of action for malpractice arose during the life of the policy but the action was not begun until after the policy had expired?*

The operative clause of the Mission policy at issue here has been interpreted in two previous California cases. The clause reads as follows: "This insurance is to indemnify * * * against any claim or claims for breach of professional duty as Lawyers *which may be made against them* during the period set forth in the Certificate by reason of any negligent act, error or omission * * *." (Emphasis added.) In Gyler v. Mission Ins. Co. (1973) 10 Cal.3d 216, 219, 110 Cal.Rptr. 139, 140, 514 P.2d 1219, 1220, the court considered identical language and held that the term "which may be made against them" should be construed to require indemnity "for claims maturing during the policy period whether or not the claim is actually asserted during that period." The court reached this result by first finding that the term "may" created an ambiguity. It then enunciated the rules that "(t)he meaning of an insurance policy is determined by the insured's reasonable expectation of coverage" and that "(a)ny uncertainty or ambiguity in the peril insured against will be resolved in favor of imposing liability." (Id.) (Parenthetically, we note that Gyler, too, involved a policy of legal malpractice insurance issued by the same company that is appellant herein.)

Appellant argues that the holding of Gyler is inapposite here because Gyler should apply only to disputes between an insurance company and the insured because the purpose of the holding was to protect the reasonable expectation of the insured. This same contention, however, was argued by this same appellant and decided adversely to appellant by Division Two of this court in Chamberlin v. Smith (1977) 72 Cal.App.3d 835, 140 Cal.Rptr. 493. We agree with the decision in Chamberlin.

*Who must provide primary coverage for the claim here?*

Both appellant's and respondent's policies have provisions concerning the effect of other insurance upon its coverage. The Mission policy provides: "There shall be no liability hereunder in respect of any claim for which the Firm are entitled to any indemnity under any other insurance." Employers' policy provides: "If, but for the insurance afforded by this policy, the assured would have other insurance against a loss otherwise covered hereby, the insurance afforded by this policy shall be excess over such other insurance."

The question arises how to reconcile Mission's escape clause with Employers' excess clause, which, on their faces, seem irreconcilable. The particular fact situation of a pure excess clause conflicting with a pure escape clause does not appear to have been addressed hitherto. This case does not involve a conflict between a composite excess-escape clause and a pro rata clause (Peerless Cas. Co. v. Continental Cas. Co. (1956) 144 Cal.App.2d 617, 301 P.2d 602), or an escape clause specifically authorized by statute (Argonaut Ins. Co. v. Transport Indem. Co. (1972) 6 Cal.3d 496, 99 Cal.Rptr. 617, 492 P.2d 673), or a composite escape and excess clause reconcilable with a pure excess clause (Underground Constr. Co. v. Pacific Indemnity Co. (1975) 49 Cal.App.3d 62, 122 Cal.Rptr. 330), or a conflict between an escape clause and a clause excepting certain acts, errors or omissions from coverage (Chamberlin v. Smith, supra, 72 Cal.App.3d 835, 140 Cal.Rptr. 493.) In addition to the absence of direct authority on the question whether an excess clause should be given preference over an escape clause, there exists no clear trend from other jurisdictions as to a resolution of this question.[1]

Absent direct authority from California cases and a clear trend from other jurisdictions, we must rest our decision here on analogy to related cases and considerations of policy. Both of these considerations dictate that the excess clause be given preference over the escape clause. California decisions demonstrate a preference for excess clauses. Where one policy contains a pro rata clause and the other contains an excess clause, for example, the excess clause will be given effect and the carrier with the pro rata clause will become the primary insurer. (See Firemen's Fund etc. Ins. Companies v. State Farm etc. Ins. Co. (1969) 273 Cal.App.2d 445, 78 Cal.Rptr. 38, followed in Donahue Constr. Co. v. Transport Indem. Co. (1970) 7 Cal.App.3d 291, 301–303, 86 Cal.Rptr. 632, and Owens Pacific Marine, Inc. v. Insurance Co. of North America (1970) 12 Cal.App.3d 661, 668–669, 90 Cal.Rptr. 826.) This is true even where it is clear that there will be no excess and the excess clause therefore operates much like an escape clause. (Owens Pacific Marine, Inc. v. Insurance Co. of North America, supra, at pp. 668–669, 90 Cal.Rptr. 826.) Consistency in the judicial interpretation of "other insurance" clause thus demands that the excess clause be preferred over the escape clause.

More importantly, it is well established that an escape clause is less favored under the law than a pro rata or excess clause. [citations omitted] The trial court, thus, correctly concluded that Mission's escape provision was disfavored because of its potential for leaving the insured without coverage.

The final argument on behalf of Mission is that the court here should follow the "Oregon rule," disregarding both of these irreconcilable provisions and mandating proration. This rule, however, is the minority rule and has not been adopted in California. (See Peerless Cas. Co. v. Continental Cas. Co., supra, at p. 623, 301 P.2d 602; Note, Conflicts Between "Other Insurance" Clauses in Automobile Liability Insurance Policies (1969) 20 Hastings L.J. 1292, 1305–1306.)

* * *

The judgment is affirmed.

1. Most courts have given effect to the "excess" provision and imposed full liability for the loss upon the other policy involved despite the "escape" (no liability) provision contained therein. [citations omitted] A number of courts, however, have given effect to the "escape" clause and imposed full liability for the loss upon the other policy involved despite the excess provision contained therein. [citations omitted] Other courts have refused to recognize either "other insurance" clause and have prorated the loss between the insurance companies. This position is known as the "Oregon rule" because the leading case espousing proration is Oregon Auto Insurance Co. v. United States Fidelity & Guar. Co. (9th Cir.1952) 195 F.2d 958.

### *Note*

In the case of conflicting excess coverages, the California courts have declined to follow the main case on the basis that the escape provisions are strongly disfavored while there is no basis for choice of one excess policy or another. Continental Casualty Co. v. Pacific Indemnity Co., 134 Cal.App.3d 389, 184 Cal.Rptr. 583 (1982).

## YORK MUTUAL INSURANCE CO. v. CONTINENTAL INSURANCE CO.

Supreme Judicial Court of Maine, 1989.
560 A.2d 571.

COLLINS, J.

This declaratory judgment action concerns insurance policies issued by the plaintiff, York Mutual Insurance Company (York), to Patricia Champagne, and by the defendant, Continental Insurance Company (Continental), to David Dubord, Esquire. The coverage issues stem from an automobile accident on May 31, 1985 involving Laurier Audet and Champagne, a legal secretary acting within the scope of her employment for Dubord. At the time of the accident Champagne owned and operated a 1984 Chevrolet insured by a policy containing liability limits of $100,000 issued by York. Dubord held a business insurance policy containing liability limits of $1,000,000 issued by Continental. An action brought by Audet against Champagne was settled for $185,000 and paid equally by York and Continental. York then initiated this action seeking a declaration that Champagne is an additional insured under Continental's policy; and that York is required to pay, after considering Continental's policy, only its proportional share (100,000/1,100,000 or 1/11) of the settlement. We affirm the portion of the Superior Court's (Androscoggin County, Alexander, J.) judgment finding Champagne covered by Continental's policy. We vacate that portion finding that York's policy affords primary coverage, and thus the judgment for Continental for $7,500.

I.

In the present case, Continental's policy contains the following coverage provision: "1. Liability Coverages * * * We will pay any amounts up to your Limit of Coverage for which you or anyone else covered under your *Liability Coverages* becomes liable as a result of bodily injury or property damage that is caused by an accident * * *." "Anyone else covered" includes Champagne as "an employee[ ] * * * acting within the scope of [her] duties." The next section entitled "Restrictions On Your Policy's Liability Coverages" limits the above coverage in the following provision: "Vehicles and aircraft. We will not cover liability for bodily injury or property damage which results from the ownership, maintenance, use, loading or unloading of any vehicle or aircraft:

* * *

* * * which is used by an employee of yours or of anyone else covered under your Liability Coverages in the course of that employment." Within the same section appears the following provision: "We will also cover private passenger vehicles that someone other than you uses in your business, as long as the private passenger vehicle is not owned, rented, borrowed, or furnished for regular use by you or one of your partners * * *." "You" is defined as "the person or organization named as the 'Insured' on the Coverage Data Page," in this case, David Dubord.

The first restriction excludes Champagne from coverage as Audet's injuries resulted from the use of a vehicle by an employee of Dubord acting in the course of her employment. The second, however, provides an exception to this exception and extends coverage to Champagne as she was using a private passenger vehicle in Dubord's business that was not owned, rented, borrowed, or furnished for regular use by Dubord or one of his partners. We thus hold that the Superior Court properly found Champagne an additional insured under Continental's policy. See Travelers Indem. Co. v. Dingwell, 414 A.2d 220, 223 (Me.1980) ("Unambiguous language in a contract must be given its plain meaning.").

II.

We have previously recognized the complexity and conflict that result in situations like the present case where more than one applicable insurance policy contains an "other insurance" clause.[1] Carriers Ins. Co. v. American Policyholders' Ins. Co., 404 A.2d 216, 218 (Me.1979). Inconsistent or repugnant other insurance clauses must be disregarded, thus rendering applicable the general coverage of each policy. Id. at 220.

In the present case, York's policy contains the following "pro rata" clause: "If there is other applicable similar insurance we will pay only our share of the loss. Our share is the proportion that our limit of liability bears to the total of all applicable limits. However, any insurance we provide with respect to a vehicle you do not own shall be excess over any other collectible insurance." (App. 31). In addition, Continental's policy contains an "excess" clause: "If You Have Other Insurance If you have other insurance available to you covering a Property or Business Income loss, or a liability or medical payments claim, or that would have covered the loss or claim if you did not have this policy, we will pay the amount of your loss or the liability that is left after you have collected the full amount available under the other policy. We will not, however, pay more than the applicable Limits of Coverage under this policy." Because these two clauses are repugnant, we must disregard them and consider the general coverage of each policy. Carriers, 404 A.2d at 220; cf. Royal Globe Ins. Co. v. Hartford Accident and Indemnity

1. There are three basic types of other insurance clauses that regulate how liability is to be divided when multiple coverage exists. The first, a "pro-rata" clause, limits the liability of any insurer to a proportion of the total loss. The second, an "escape" clause, seeks to avoid all liability. The third, an "excess" clause, provides that the insurance will only be excess. Carriers Ins. Co. v. American Policyholders' Ins. Co., 404 A.2d 216, 218 (Me.1979).

Co., 485 A.2d 242, 243 (Me.1984) (finding "excess" and "pro rata" other insurance clauses not repugnant where "excess" clause specifically made its coverage "excess coverage" and "pro rata" clause was silent). In the case at bar, neither clause expressly makes its policy's coverage "primary" or "excess;" thus, we consider both policies' coverage to be primary. Id. at 244.

III.

Because we find that York and Continental's policies both provide primary coverage in the present case, we must determine how liability should be prorated. In Carriers we recognized that "on equitable principles the loss should be shared among the insurers," 404 A.2d at 221, and thus adopted a "minority rule" requiring each company to contribute equally until the limit of the smaller policy is exhausted, with any remaining portion of the loss then being paid from the larger policy up to its limits. Id. Applying this rule to the case at hand, York and Continental are each responsible for one-half of the settlement judgment, or $92,500. We thus vacate the Superior Court's judgment for Continental in the amount of $7,500.

The entry is:

Judgment affirmed in part and vacated in part. Remanded to the Superior Court for further proceedings consistent with the opinion herein.

## CARRIERS INSURANCE CO. v. AMERICAN POLICYHOLDERS INSURANCE CO.

Supreme Judicial Court of Maine, 1979.
404 A.2d 216.

DELAHANTY, JUSTICE.

This action was brought in the Superior Court, Kennebec County, by the plaintiff, Carriers Insurance Company (Carriers), seeking contribution from the defendant, American Policyholders' Insurance Co. (American). The parties joined issue upon whether and to what extent American was required to contribute to a settlement made by the plaintiff. Upon an agreed statement of facts, the presiding Justice found for Carriers, and American has appealed. We deny the appeal.

During April of 1963, Cummings Bros. (Cummings) entered into a contractual agreement with Merrill's Rental Service, Inc. (Merrill's) whereby it leased certain motor vehicles from Merrill's. Pursuant to the lease and for Cummings' benefit, Merrill's agreed to provide insurance coverage—both personal injury and property damage—for its vehicles while they were being operated by Cummings' employees. In 1971, this personal injury liability coverage which Merrill's obtained through Carriers stood at approximately $3,000,000 with $500,000 of property damage coverage. In the meantime, Cummings independently procured $250,000 of liability insurance through the defendant, American.

In March of 1972, one of Cummings' employees, while negligently driving a vehicle leased from Merrill's, collided with a Lincoln Continental killing the driver and extensively damaging his automobile. Carriers, acting in good faith and in the best interests of its insured, settled a wrongful death claim for $200,000 and a property damage claim for approximately $8,000. Both prior and subsequent to the settlement, American refused Carriers' demand for contribution. Thereafter, Carriers instituted the present action and received a judgment against the defendant for approximately $104,000. Both Carriers and American had "other insurance" clauses in their insurance policies. Carriers' contract stated:

> OTHER INSURANCE
>
> If there is other insurance against an occurrence covered by this policy, the insurance afforded by this policy shall be deemed *excess insurance* over and above the applicable limits of all such other insurance. (emphasis supplied.)

American's policy contained an endorsement specifically covering "hired automobiles" which provided:

> OTHER INSURANCE
>
> This insurance shall be *excess insurance* over any other valid and collectible insurance for Bodily Injury Liability, for Property Damage Liability and for Automobile Medical Payments. (emphasis supplied.)

Faced with these competing clauses, the presiding Justice disregarded them as "mutually repugnant." American assigns this as error and insists that its clause should be given preference over Carriers'.

I

We begin our discussion by acknowledging the utter confusion that pervades the entire realm of "other insurance" clauses. See Insurance Company of Texas v. Employers Liability Assurance Corp., 163 F.Supp. 143, 145 (S.D.Cal.1958). Originating in the property insurance field, these clauses were designed to prevent fraudulent claims induced by overinsuring. With automobiles, however, the fear of death or injury was in itself sufficient to deter specious accidents. The original purpose of other insurance clauses has little relevance, therefore, to automobile liability insurance other than to limit, reduce, or avoid an insurer's loss in those cases where there is multiple coverage. See Comment, "Other Insurance" Clauses: The Lamb–Weston Doctrine, 47 Or.L.Rev. 430 (1968); Note, Concurrent Coverage in Automobile Liability Insurance, 65 Colum.L.Rev. 319 (1965). However, these clauses violate no public policy and in the absence of a statute to the contrary they will be given effect, even if the insured is unaware of the existence of the other insurance. 8 D. Blashfield, Automobile Law and Practice § 345.10 (3rd ed. 1966).

There are three basic types of other insurance clauses which regulate how liability is to be divided when multiple coverage exists. The first, a "pro-rata" clause, limits the liability of an insurer to a proportion of the total loss. The second, an "escape" clause, seeks to avoid all liability. The third, an "excess" clause, the provision used in the present case, provides that the insurance will only be excess. See 8 J. Appleman, Insurance Law and Practice § 4911 (Cum.Supp.1973); 7 Am.Jur.2d *Automobile Insurance* §§ 200–202 (2d ed. 1963).

No problems arise as long as only one policy contains an other insurance clause since the particular provision can be given effect as written. Complications and conflicts occur where more than one applicable policy contains an other insurance clause. In that situation, the court is faced with a battle of the clauses.[59]

In the case at bar, each policy, in virtually identical language, states that it will be excess over any other valid and collectible insurance. Any attempt at a literal reconciliation of the clauses involves hopeless circular reasoning. One clause cannot be given effect as "excess" unless the other is considered "primary." Since both claim to be excess, neither could operate as primary and hence neither could take effect as excess. Taken to its *reductio ad absurdum* conclusion, even though each insurer concedes that its policy would have covered the loss in the absence of the other, where there is double coverage both would escape liability, a result which neither party advocates. As well stated in State Farm Mutual Insurance Co. v. Travelers Insurance Co., 184 So.2d 750, 753–54 (La.App.1966) (Tate, J., concurring),

> [i]ndeed, there is actually no way by logic or word-sense to reconcile two such clauses, where each policy by itself can apply as a primary insurer, but where the clause in each policy nevertheless attempts to make its own liability secondary to that of any other policy issued by a similar primary insurer: For then the primary and (attempted) secondary liability of each policy chase the other through infinity, something like trying to answer the question: Which came first, the chicken or the egg?

Faced with this logical logjam, a number of different and conflicting methods have at various times been used to determine which policy is primary and hence which should bear the brunt of the loss. Thus, it has been stated that the primary policy is the one: covering the tortfeasor, Employers Mutual Liability Insurance Company of Wisconsin v. Pacific Indemnity Company, 167 Cal.App.2d 369, 334 P.2d 658 (1959); issued prior in time, Automobile Insurance Company of Hartford v. Springfield Dyeing Company, 109 F.2d 533 (3rd Cir.1940); insuring the vehicle's owner, Farm Bureau Mut. Automobile Ins. Co. v. Preferred Acc. Ins. Co., 78 F.Supp. 561 (W.D.Va.1948); whose policy covered the particular loss more specifically, Trinity Universal Insurance Co. v. General Accident,

**59.** Some of the more common interchanges have been commented upon: excess clause v. pro-rata clause, see Annot., 76 A.L.R.2d 502 (1961); escape clause v. pro-rata clause, see Annot., 46 A.L.R.2d 1163, 1167 (1956); excess clause v. excess clause, see Annot., 69 A.L.R.2d 1122 (1960); excess clause v. escape clause, see 46 A.L.R.2d, supra at 1165. See Union Ins. Co. (Mut.) v. Iowa Hardware Mut. Ins. Co., 175 N.W.2d 413, 415 (Iowa 1970).

Fire & Life Assurance Corp., 138 Ohio St. 488, 35 N.E.2d 836 (1941); or whose other insurance clause is written in more general terms, Zurich General Accident & Liability Insurance Co. v. Clamor, 124 F.2d 717 (7th Cir.1941).

Seizing on one of these approaches, American argues that Carriers' policy should be construed as primary based upon minute differences in the language of the excess insurance clauses. We prefer not to engage in such semantic microscopy. "It [merely] encourages the continuing draftsmanship battle by which insurers seek still more specific policy terms, and the end is not in sight." Note, Concurrent Coverage in Automobile Liability Insurance, supra at 322. Fairly read, each insurer, through its excess clause, seeks to place the initial loss on any other applicable insurance, saving for itself a role as secondary insurer.

As an alternative argument, American asserts that the intent of the underlying parties should be given effect. Merrill's, for valuable consideration, contractually agreed to insure Cummings.[60] Merrill's insurance should therefore be considered primary.

We disagree.

American's argument would be well taken were this suit simply one for breach of contract between Cummings and Merrill's. We fail, however, to see the relevance in this case of the lease agreement to which the insurers were neither parties nor beneficiaries. The only appropriate considerations are the two insurance policies through which the respective insurers and insureds manifested their contractual intent. See Farm Bureau Mutual Insurance Co. v. Waugh, 159 Me. 115, 188 A.2d 889 (1963). An examination of the policies issued is the single criteria for analyzing an insurer's obligations which can neither be enlarged nor diminished beyond the terms employed. Limberis v. Aetna Casualty & Surety Co., Me., 263 A.2d 83 (1970). A determination of the primary insurer must turn, therefore, upon a construction of the insurance contracts and not upon a collateral agreement between an insured and a third party.

**60.** In pertinent part, the lease provided:

F. INSURANCE COVERAGE AND LIABILITY

Subject to the following conditions, MERRILL shall provide, at its expense, insurance coverage for its benefit and the benefit of CUMMINGS and the drivers and/or operators of CUMMINGS.

1. All rental units described in Schedule A including any emergency spares or other vehicles or trailers of MERRILL's used by CUMMINGS under the terms hereof will be covered, for the benefit of CUMMINGS and its operating and driving personnel:

(a) Personal injury, [$2,990,000.00].

(b) Property damage, $500,000.00.

2. CUMMINGS shall not be liable to MERRILL for any damages or injuries sustained to the rental units described in Schedule A while being used by CUMMINGS under the terms hereof if occasioned by:

(a) The negligent operation of CUMMINGS' drivers or operators while operating or driving said rental units in the scope of their employment with CUMMINGS.

We perceive no methodology which is neither arbitrary nor utterly mechanical by which we could rationally resolve the enigma of which policy should be given effect over the other. Both clauses attempt to occupy the same legal status. Any construction this Court renders should attempt to maintain this status quo. This goal can be achieved only by abandoning the search for the mythical "primary" insurer and insisting instead that both insurers share in the loss. Such an approach best carries out the intent of the insurers which was to reduce or limit their liability.

There are additional benefits to adopting this rule. It would introduce certainty and uniformity into the insurance industry, discourage litigation between insurers, and enable underwriters to predict the losses of the insurers more accurately. Note, Conflicts Between "Other Insurance" Clauses in Automobile Liability Insurance Policies, 20 Hastings L.J. 1292, 1304 (1969). We hold that where there are conflicting excess insurance clause provisions they are to be disregarded as mutually repugnant thus rendering applicable the general coverage of each policy. This, we note, is the clear majority rule [citations].

II

Having found that both policies are to be considered "primary," we are brought to the question of how should the liability be prorated where the total loss does not exceed the limits of either policy. American argues that the loss should be prorated according to the policy limits. Because Carriers provided $2,990,000 of coverage compared to only $250,000 for American, appellant contends that Carriers should bear close to ninety percent of the settlement cost. Carriers, on the other hand, argues that the loss should be shared equally between the insurers, the approach adopted by the presiding Justice.

There are three basic methods of proration. The majority rule, the one urged upon by appellant, prorates liability according to the limits contained in each policy.[62] The next, which is seldom followed, prorates on the basis of the premiums paid to each insurer.[63] Finally, there is a minority but growing number of courts which prorate the loss equally up to the limits of the lower policy,[64] the approach adopted by the court below.

Each method is grounded on the premises, often unarticulated, that on equitable principles the loss should be shared among the insurers either on the basis of the risk that they have undertaken or the benefit

**62.** See, e.g., State Farm Mut. Auto. Ins. Co. v. General Mut. Ins. Co., 282 Ala. 212, 210 So.2d 688 (1968); Buckeye Union Ins. Co. v. State Auto. Mut. Ins. Co., supra note 4; Lamb–Weston, Inc. v. Oregon Auto. Ins. Co., 219 Or. 110, 346 P.2d 643 (1959); Pacific Indem. Co. v. Federated Am. Ins. Co., 82 Wash.2d 412, 511 P.2d 56 (1973).

**63.** Insurance Co. of Tex. v. Employers Liab. Assur. Corp., [163 F.Supp. 143 (S.D.Cal.1958) ].

**64.** See, e.g., Ruan Transport Corp. v. Truck Rentals, Inc., 278 F.Supp. 692 (D.Colo.1968); Ryder Truck Rental, Inc. v. Schapiro & Whitehouse, Inc., 259 Md. 354, 269 A.2d 826 (1970); Cosmopolitan Mut. Ins. Co. v. Continental Cas. Co., [28 N.J. 554, 147 A.2d 529 (1959) ].

they have received. In its clearest expression, the majority rule has been justified on the theory that

> the burden imposed on each insurer is generally proportional to the benefit which he received, since the size of the premium is most always directly related to the size of the policy. Lamb–Weston, Inc. v. Oregon Automobile Insurance Company, [219 Or.] at 137, 346 P.2d at 647.

On precisely these grounds, the majority rule has been criticized since "[i]t is commonly known that the cost of liability insurance does not increase proportionately with the policy limits." Cosmopolitan Mutual Insurance Company v. Continental Casualty Co., [28 N.J.] at 564, 147 A.2d at 534. Once minimum coverage has been obtained, significant supplemental coverage can be provided at only a modest increase in cost.

On the other hand, if the majority rule is less equitable than that minority approach which apportions on the basis of premiums received, it has the advantage of facile application. Unless the multiple policies cover the identical risks, there would be too many variables affecting the premiums to permit them to serve as a benchmark for an equitable adjustment. Nationwide Mutual Insurance Company v. State Farm Mutual Automobile Insurance Company, 209 F.Supp. 83 (N.D.W.Va. 1962).

The minority rule adopted by the presiding Justice utilizes the best aspects of both approaches without limitations. Like the majority rule, it is easy to administer. It would simply require each company to contribute equally until the limits of the smaller policy were exhausted, with any remaining portion of the loss then being paid from the larger policy up to its limits. Nationwide Mutual Insurance Company v. State Farm Mutual Automobile Insurance Company, supra; Dairyland Insurance Company v. Drum, 568 P.2d 459, 464 (Colo.1977) (Carrigan, J., dissenting in part).

Unlike the majority rule, this Solomon-like approach comports with a most basic sense of justice. See Exodus, ch. 21, par. 35 ("When one man's ox hurts another's ox so badly that it dies, they shall sell the live ox and divide this money as well as the dead animal they shall divide equally between them.") Moreover, the majority rule unfairly discriminates against the larger policy by apportioning the loss in proportion to the respective policy limits, utterly forgetting that both insurers, by their contracts, have in fact agreed to cover a loss up to the limits of the lesser policy. Until that point is reached, the majority rule amounts to no more than an unacceptable subsidy from the high-coverage to the low-coverage carrier. We are in complete accord with the presiding Justice when he adopted the persuasive opinion of Judge Doyle in Ruan Transport Corp. v. Truck Rentals, Inc., supra note 7 at 696.

> The majority method of prorating operates inequitably in its differentiating treatment of the high-loss and low-loss insurer. In return for a greater premium the insurer providing higher coverage has undertaken to protect the insured against accidents involving high

losses. Yet because of this undertaking to protect against high loss the larger insurer is in an unfavorable position vis-a-vis the other insurer even in cases of low loss, since under the majority method of prorating the insurer affording the greater maximum coverage pays the greater segment of any loss incurred, regardless of the amount of the loss. This seems inequitable since both insurers have equally undertaken to insure against the low-loss accident.

The majority rule would hardly encourage an insurer from increasing its coverage where it is aware that there is a lesser policy. It would increase the insurer's potential liability not only in the high-risk situation which the additional premiums are presumably meant to recompense, but it would have the untoward effect of increasing liability in the more likely to occur low-risk situation. Carried to its extreme, it would further increase the cost of additional insurance thereby reducing the likelihood that an insured would choose such coverage. * * * The Court would be reluctant to adopt a rule which would seemingly have little social utility.

* * *

Judgment affirmed.

### *Note*

The Washington Supreme Court has overruled Pacific Indemnity Co. v. Federated American Insurance Co., 82 Wn.2d 412, 511 P.2d 56 (1973) (the majority rule) to adopt the "minority" rule of apportionment as espoused in the principal case. Mission Insurance Co. v. Allendale Mutual Insurance Co., 95 Wn.2d 464, 626 P.2d 505 (1981).

### *Problem*

The "majority" method of apportionment calls for prorating "according to the limits in each policy". Suppose two auto policies with irreconcilable or mutually repugnant "other insurance" clauses. Policy A (issued by company Y) states a single limit of $50,000 per occurrence; Policy B (issued by company Z) states a limit of $15,000, per person, $30,000 (that is for all persons injured in one occurrence) and $5,000 for property damages. This is usually referred to as "15/30/5". Both policies A and B cover Jones in an accident in which Jones is responsible for injuries to two persons in the total amount of $29,000 and for property damage of $2,500. How would you pro rate between the insurers? See Forest Industries Ins. Exchange v. Viking Ins. Co., 82 Or.App. 615, 728 P.2d 943 (1986).

## AMERICAN CENTENNIAL INSURANCE CO. v. CANAL INSURANCE CO.

Supreme Court of Texas, 1992.
843 S.W.2d 480.

DOGGETT, J.

We consider whether an excess insurance carrier has a cause of action against a primary carrier and trial counsel for mishandling a claim. We extend this court's holding in G.A. Stowers Furniture Co. v. American Indemnity Co., 15 S.W.2d 544 (Tex.Comm'n App.1929, holding approved), to permit such an action.

General Rent-A-Car International, Inc. was sued for injuries and death allegedly resulting from a blowout of a defective tire on one of its rental cars. At the time of the accident, General was insured by three companies. Canal Insurance Co., the primary carrier, provided coverage to $100,000; First State Insurance Co. insured from $100,000 to $1 million; and American Centennial Insurance Co. was responsible for $1 million to $4 million. Canal investigated and defended the suit, hiring an outside law firm. Because of alleged mishandling by trial counsel of the litigation, the insurers were forced to settle for $3.7 million.

The two excess carriers, First State and American Centennial brought suit against Canal, the law firm handling the defense and two of the firm's attorneys for negligence, gross negligence, breach of the duty of good faith and fair dealing and violations of the Texas Deceptive Trade Practices—Consumer Protection Act, Tex.Bus. & Com.Code §§ 17.41–.63, and article 21.21 of the Texas Insurance Code. The trial court granted summary judgment, denying all claims as barred by the statute of limitations, determining that the primary insurer and its counsel owed no duties to the excess carriers and finding that no genuine issue of material fact existed. The court of appeals reversed the judgment as to Canal, but affirmed as to defense counsel on the basis of the statute of limitations. 810 S.W.2d 246. Because we hold that the excess carrier may bring an equitable subrogation action against both the primary insurer and defense counsel and that a fact issue was raised in the summary judgment record as to whether the claim was properly handled, we affirm in part and reverse in part.

Texas law vests a clear right in the insured to sue the primary carrier for a wrongful refusal to settle a claim within the limits of the policy. G.A. Stowers Furniture Co. v. American Indemnity Co., 15 S.W.2d 544. The insurer's duty to act as an ordinarily prudent person in business management extends to claim investigation, trial defense and settlement negotiations. Ranger County Mut. Ins. Co. v. Guin, 723 S.W.2d 656, 659 (Tex.1987). We have not previously considered whether a similar duty is imposed upon the primary insurer in protecting the excess carrier from damages for wrongful handling of a claim.

Although a question of first impression in Texas, many other states have considered whether the doctrine of equitable subrogation permits actions between carriers. Under this theory, the insurer paying a loss under a policy becomes equitably subrogated to any cause of action the insured may have against a third party responsible for the loss. The excess insurer would thus be able to maintain any action that the insured may have against the primary carrier for mishandling of the claim. Equitable subrogation has been recognized in Texas, although not in this particular context. See, e.g., Employers Casualty Co. v. Transport Ins. Co., 444 S.W.2d 606, 610 (Tex.1969); Interfirst Bank

Dallas, N.A. v. United States Fidelity and Guar. Co., 774 S.W.2d 391, 397 (Tex.App.—Dallas 1989, writ denied); International Ins. Co. v. Medical–Professional Bldg. of Corpus Christi, 405 S.W.2d 867, 869 (Tex.Civ. App.—Corpus Christi 1966, writ ref'd n.r.e.).

While many states recognize an action by an excess carrier against a primary insurer, a majority of those permitting suit do so on grounds of equitable subrogation. In recognizing a cause of action for equitable subrogation, these courts have sought to encourage fair and reasonable settlement of lawsuits. See Northwestern Mut. Ins. Co. v. Farmers Ins. Group, 76 Cal.App.3d 1031, 1050–51, 143 Cal.Rptr. 415, 427 (1978); Ranger Ins. Co. v. Travelers Indem. Co., 389 So.2d 272, 275 (Fla.Dist.Ct. App.1980). If the excess carrier had no remedy, the primary insurer would have less incentive to settle within the policy limits. Hartford Accident & Indem. Co. v. Aetna Casualty & Sur. Co., 164 Ariz. 286, 792 P.2d 749, 757 (1990); Commercial Union Ins. Co. v. Medical Protective Co., 426 Mich. 109, 393 N.W.2d 479, 483 (1986) ("[A]llowing the excess insurer to enforce the primary insurer's duty to settle in good faith serves the public and judicial interests in fair and reasonable settlements of lawsuits by discouraging primary carriers from 'gambling' with the excess carrier's money when potential judgments approach the primary insurer's policy limits."). Additionally, the wrongful failure to settle would likely result in increased premiums by excess carriers. See id.; Peter v. Travelers Ins. Co., 375 F.Supp. 1347, 1350–51 (C.D.Cal.1974).

These courts have also employed equitable subrogation "to prevent an unfair distribution of losses among primary and excess insurers." Hartford Accident & Indem. Co. v. Aetna Casualty & Sur. Co., 792 P.2d at 757; see Continental Casualty Co. v. Reserve Ins. Co., 238 N.W.2d at 865.

Because we find the reasoning of these cases persuasive, we hold that an excess carrier may bring an equitable subrogation action against the primary carrier. This does not, however, impose new or additional burdens on the primary carrier, since our prior decisions in Stowers and Ranger County imposed clear duties on the primary carrier to protect the interests of the insured. The primary carrier should not be relieved of these obligations simply because the insured has separately contracted for excess coverage. See Peter v. Travelers Ins. Co., 375 F.Supp. at 1350; Commercial Union Ins. Co. v. Medical Protective Co., 393 N.W.2d at 483. In this situation, where the insured has little incentive to enforce the primary carrier's duties, the excess carrier should be permitted to do so through equitable subrogation.

American Centennial and First State urge the court to recognize a direct duty running from the primary to the excess insurer. Only a few jurisdictions have permitted a direct action, rather than limiting the excess carrier to an equitable subrogation claim. Excess insurers prefer a direct action because, under the theory of equitable subrogation, they are subject to any defenses assertable against an insured, including the refusal to settle and the failure to cooperate. Because none of these circumstances is present in the case before us, however, and the excess insurers appear to have an adequate remedy using equitable subrogation, we decline at this time to permit a direct action. See Twin City Fire Ins. Co. v. Superior Court, 164 Ariz. 295, 792 P.2d 758, 759 (1990).

The court of appeals correctly held that the equitable subrogation claim against Canal was not time-barred. Since the applicable statute of limitations parallels that of a traditional Stowers action, this action was timely brought. We also agree that any claims against Canal for negligence, gross negligence and violations of the DTPA and Insurance Code were barred by the applicable statutes of limitations. Thus we need not, and do not, decide whether the doctrine of equitable subrogation would extend to permit such actions by an excess carrier against the primary insurer.

The court of appeals held the action against the attorneys was barred by the statute of limitations, finding the excess insurers' cause of action accrued at the time of the alleged malpractice. This conflicts with our recent writing in Hughes v. Mahaney & Higgins, 821 S.W.2d 154, 157 (Tex.1991), that "when an attorney commits malpractice in the prosecution or defense of a claim that results in litigation, the statute of limitations is tolled until all appeals on the underlying claim are exhausted." The court of appeals' holding is thus in error.

Because the malpractice suit is not time-barred, we must consider whether an excess carrier may bring such a cause of action. Under Texas law, attorneys are not ordinarily liable for damages to a nonclient, because privity of contract is absent. See, e.g., Parker v. Carnahan, 772 S.W.2d 151, 156 (Tex.App.—Texarkana 1989, writ denied); First Mun. Leasing Corp. v. Blankenship, Potts, Aikman, Hagin and Stewart, 648 S.W.2d 410, 413 (Tex.App.—Dallas 1983, writ ref'd n.r.e.); Bell v. Manning, 613 S.W.2d 335, 339 (Tex.Civ.App.—Tyler 1981, writ ref'd n.r.e.). Texas courts have been understandably reluctant to permit a malpractice action by a nonclient because of the potential interference with the duties an attorney owes to the client. See, e.g., Supreme Court of Texas, State Bar Rules art. X, § 9 (Texas Disciplinary Rules of Professional Conduct), Rule 2.01 (1990) (requiring exercise of independent professional judgment on behalf of client). None of these prior cases, however, have considered whether an excess carrier may be equitably subrogated to an insured's action against counsel.

The few jurisdictions to have considered this question are divided on whether to permit suit. The single Texas decision to consider this issue held that the excess carrier may bring a malpractice action. Stonewall Surplus Lines Ins. Co. v. Drabek, 835 S.W.2d 708 (Tex.App.—Corpus Christi 1992, writ denied) (en banc).

Although in the context of insurance defense, the insurance company pays the legal fees, the attorney "owes the insured the same type of unqualified loyalty as if he had been originally employed by the insured." Employers Casualty Co. v. Tilley, 496 S.W.2d 552, 558 (Tex. 1973); see also 16A Appleman, Insurance Law and Practice § 8839.35, at 108 & n. 9.5 (1981). Defense counsel must be particularly sensitive to the varying interests of the insured and the insurer which produce complex and often conflicting relationships.

Recognizing an equitable subrogation action by the excess carrier against defense counsel would not, however, interfere with the relationship between the attorney and the client nor result in additional conflicts of interest. Subrogation permits the insurer only to enforce existing duties of defense counsel to the insured.

Further, the concerns of the excess and primary carriers and the insured generally overlap in ensuring that the merits of the defense are not precluded from being heard because of attorney malpractice. "The best interests of both insurer and insured converge in expectations of competent representation." Atlanta Int'l Ins. Co. v. Bell, 438 Mich. 512, 475 N.W.2d 294, 298 (1991). While in some circumstances these interests may diverge, presenting a different situation, here the excess insurers do not predicate liability on tactical decisions by trial counsel implicating conflicting interests between the insured and the insurer.

Those considerations that have resulted in our recognizing an excess carrier's right to bring an equitable subrogation action against the primary insurer offer similar support for an action by the excess carrier against defense counsel.[6] No new or additional burdens are imposed on the attorney, who already has the duty to represent the insured previously described in Employers Casualty Co. Defense counsel should not be relieved of these obligations merely because the insurer, rather than the client, must pay the claim. If the asserted malpractice has resulted in payment of a judgment or settlement within the excess carrier's policy limits, the insured has little incentive to enforce its right to competent representation. Refusal to permit the excess carrier to vindicate that right would burden the insurer with a loss caused by the attorney's negligence while relieving the attorney from the consequences of legal malpractice. Such an inequitable result should not arise simply because the insured has contracted for excess coverage.[7]

The court of appeals correctly remanded for further proceedings as to the cause of action of First State and American against Canal for wrongful handling of a claim but erred in failing to allow the insurers to pursue their malpractice action against defense counsel. The judgment of the court of appeals is affirmed in part and reversed in part.

**6.** The question of whether a malpractice claim may be assigned is not presented today; our inquiry is limited solely to whether the doctrine of equitable subrogation permits an excess insurer to sue in the stead of the insured.

**7.** In permitting the primary carrier to bring a malpractice action against the insured's defense counsel, one court concluded: "[T]o completely absolve a negligent defense counsel from malpractice liability would not rationally advance the attorney-client relationship. Moreover, defense counsel's immunity from suit by the insurer would place the loss for the attorney's misconduct on the insurer. *The only winner produced by an analysis precluding liability would be the malpracticing attorney.* Equity cries out for application [of equitable subrogation] under such circumstances." Atlanta Int'l Ins. Co. v. Bell, 438 Mich. 512, 475 N.W.2d 294, 298 (1991) (emphasis added).

Concurring opinion by HECHT, J., joined by PHILLIPS, C.J., and GONZALEZ, COOK and CORNYN, JJ.

HECHT, JUSTICE, concurring.

I agree that if an excess insurance carrier is required to pay a portion of a judgment rendered against its insured in favor of a third party, it is equitably subrogated to its insured's rights against a primary insurance carrier under G.A. Stowers Furniture Co. v. American Indem. Co., 15 S.W.2d 544 (Tex.Comm'n App.1929, holding approved), and Ranger County Mut. Ins. Co. v. Guin, 723 S.W.2d 656 (Tex.1987), for negligently investigating, preparing to defend, trying or settling the third party action. As the Court notes, this is already the rule in many jurisdictions. Ante at 482 & n. 3; see also North River Ins. Co. v. St. Paul Fire & Marine Ins. Co., 600 F.2d 721, 723 n. 3 (8th Cir.1979); Fireman's Fund Ins. Co. v. Continental Ins. Co., 308 Md. 315, 519 A.2d 202, 204–205 (1987); see generally Annotation, Excess Carrier's Right to Maintain Action Against Primary Liability Insurer for Wrongful Failure to Settle Claim Against Insured, 10 A.L.R.4th 879, 881–87 (1981); Jane M. Draper, Liability Insurance: Excess Carrier's Right of Action Against Primary Carrier for Improper or Inadequate Defense of Claim, 49 A.L.R.4th 304, 305 (1986); Cherry D. Williams, A New Twist in Insurance Litigation: Stowers Suits by Excess Carriers Against Primary Carriers, 33 S.Tex.L.Rev. 1 (1992); Anthony M. Lanzone & Stephen G. Ringel, Duties of a Primary Insurer to an Excess Insurer, 61 Neb.L.Rev. 259 (1982). As a general rule, "[s]ubrogation gives indemnity and no more." Phipps v. Fuqua, 32 S.W.2d 660, 663 (Tex.Civ.App.—Amarillo 1930, writ ref'd) (citation omitted). Thus, an excess carrier may recover only the difference between what it was required to pay and what it would have paid but for the primary carrier's negligent handling of the action, plus interest. It is not entitled to damages in its own right, or statutory or punitive damages. See InterFirst Bank Dallas v. United States Fidelity & Guar. Co., 774 S.W.2d 391, 399 (Tex.App.—Dallas 1989, writ denied) (subrogee limited to recovery of amount paid); McAllen State Bank v. Linbeck Constr. Corp., 695 S.W.2d 10, 24 n. 5 (Tex.App.—Corpus Christi 1985, writ ref'd n.r.e.) (subrogee not entitled to statutory damages under Texas Deceptive Trade Practices—Consumer Protection Act). The primary carrier is entitled to assert any defense available against either the insured or the excess carrier.

The excess carriers in this case assert claims against the primary carrier based upon negligence, gross negligence, breach of a duty of good faith and fair dealing, and violations of the Texas Deceptive Trade Practices—Consumer Protection Act, Tex.Bus. & Com.Code §§ 17.41–.63, and article 21.21 of the Texas Insurance Code. Although the Court does not expressly consider which of these theories is available to the excess carriers by subrogation, I assume from its reliance on the Stowers and Ranger County cases, and would so hold, that the excess carriers' only cause of action is for negligence. I agree with the Court that the primary carrier failed to establish as a matter of law that such an action is barred by limitations.

I also agree that an excess carrier in the circumstances described above is equitably subrogated to its insured's rights against his attorney for negligent handling of the defense of the third party action. Ante at 484 n. 5; see generally Ronald E. Mallen & Jeffrey M. Smith, Legal Malpractice §§ 7.7, 23.11 (1989). Like the primary carrier, the attorney would have any defense available against either the insured or the excess carrier, including the excess carrier's unreasonable refusal to cooperate in the defense and settlement of the action. Thus, the attorney should not be exposed to any greater liability to the excess carrier than to his client, the insured. Again, the excess carrier is limited to an action for negligence, which, on the record before us, is not as a matter of law barred by limitations. By allowing the excess carrier an action against its insured's attorney through equitable subrogation, the Court's holding does not suggest that a client's rights against his attorney may be assigned. See id.; Charles F. Herring, Jr., Texas Legal Malpractice & Lawyer Discipline § 3.28 (1991).

With this understanding of the Court's opinion, I join in the judgment.

PHILLIPS, C.J., and GONZALEZ, COOK and CORNYN, JJ., join in this concurring opinion.

### *Note*

Can an excess surety be subrogated to the insured's claim against the primary insurer for breach of the duty of good faith? See Continental Casualty Co. v. Reserve Insurance Co., 307 Minn. 5, 238 N.W.2d 862 (1976) (holding "yes").

## WAGNER v. STATE FARM MUTUAL AUTOMOBILE INSURANCE COMPANY

Supreme Court of California, 1985.
40 Cal.3d 460, 220 Cal.Rptr. 659, 709 P.2d 462.

KAUS, JUSTICE.

Section 11580.2 of the Insurance Code [1] provides for quasi-compulsory uninsured motorists (UM) coverage for most kinds of automobile liability policies. Among others, UM coverage protects as insureds the named insured, as well as family members living in the same household. (§ 11580.2, subd. (b).) Subdivision (d) of section 11580.2 (subdivision (d)) permits UM policies to provide "that if the insured has insurance available to him under more than one uninsured motorist coverage provision, any damages shall not be deemed to exceed the higher of the applicable limits of the respective coverages, and such damages shall be prorated between the applicable coverages as the limits of each coverage bears to the total of such limits." [2]

1. Unless otherwise specified, all statutory references are to the Insurance Code.

2. Translated into insurance jargon, subdivision (d) permits UM coverage to contain a provision to avoid "stacking."

In the case at bar the insured was covered by two UM coverages contained in identical, but separate policies issued by the same insurer. Each contained the following as part of condition 9: "* * * [Under UM coverage] if the insured has other similar insurance available to him against a loss covered by this coverage, then the damages shall be deemed not to exceed the higher of the applicable limits of liability of this insurance and such other insurance, and the company shall not be liable under this coverage for a greater proportion of the applicable limit of liability of this coverage than such limit bears to the sum of the applicable limits of liability of this insurance and such other insurance."

The issues on this appeal are: (1) whether condition 9 complies with subdivision (d); (2) whether the fact that the two policies were issued by the same insurer nullifies its effect. * * *

I

Plaintiff Susan K. Welch is the step-daughter of plaintiff Lee A. Wagner and the daughter of plaintiff Barbara W. Wagner. She lived with the Wagners who had in effect two liability policies issued by State Farm: (1) a policy on an International Travelall, first issued in 1973, and (2) a policy on a Porsche, first issued in 1975. Each policy provided for UM coverage, but contained condition 9, the anti-stacking clause. Each policy charged a semi-annual premium of $4.50 for UM coverage. Each policy's applicable limit of UM coverage was $15,000.

On April 24, 1977, Susan was seriously injured in a collision between an uninsured automobile and an uninsured motorcycle on which she was riding as a passenger. Liability under State Farm's UM coverage is conceded. It is also undisputed that Susan's damages exceed $15,000. She demanded that State Farm pay her damages up to the policy limits of both policies—$30,000. State Farm refused, but did pay $15,000. Any additional liability was left to litigation.

Plaintiffs later filed the present action in which they assert State Farm's liability in excess of $15,000. Summary judgment in State Farm's favor was eventually entered. [Plaintiff appeals].

II

Attempting to avoid the impact of subdivision (d) altogether, plaintiffs attack condition 9. They claim, in wholly conclusory fashion, that it is uncertain, ambiguous, "all but incomprehensible" and "contractual gobbledygook." When one examines plaintiffs' argument, however, the real complaint coincides with their argument that subdivision (d) and,

"Stacking" is sometimes defined to mean the recovery by a claimant several times over for his injuries. (*Langston v. Allstate Ins. Co.* (1978), 40 Md.App. 414, 392 A.2d 561, 569.) It has also been held to refer to "the ability of the insured, when covered by more than one insurance policy, to obtain benefits from a second policy on the same claim when recovery from the first policy would alone be inadequate" to compensate for the actual damages suffered. (*Nationwide Ins. Co. v. Gode* (1982) 187 Conn. 386, 446 A.2d 1059, 1060, fn. 2.) The term is used in its latter sense in this opinion; plaintiffs do not seek recovery in excess of their actual damages.

hence, condition 9, do not apply where both policies are issued by the same insurer. As such it will be dealt with in part III of this opinion.

In any event it appears to us that the policy condition is as clear as subdivision (d) allows.[4] The statute limits the damages to the higher of the applicable limits. The policy condition does the same, using almost identical language. The statute then provides for prorating among the applicable coverages "as the limits of each coverage bears to the total of such limits." The policy condition expresses precisely the same formula from the point of view of the carrier. While condition 9 uses a few more words than the statute, that is inherent in the nature of the problem and hardly turns a quite clearly expressed formula into "gobbledygook."

III

We now turn to the central problem of this appeal: the applicability of subdivision (d) to multiple policies issued by the same insurer. As background to our discussion we note that anti-stacking clauses in UM coverages have spawned a surprising number of reported cases.[5] These, in turn, have provoked a certain amount of scholarly comment.[6] As may be expected, the various courts' attitudes toward anti-stacking clauses vary all the way from ready acceptance to open hostility. No useful purpose would be served in surveying the field in detail, since we are confronted with an almost [7] unique situation: the effect of anti-stacking

4. The statutory language is, perhaps, more ponderous than necessary. Compare a similar Ohio statute quoted in *Karabin v. State Auto. Mut. Ins. Co.* (1984) 10 Ohio St.3d 163, 462 N.E.2d 403, 405: "Any automobile liability * * * policy of insurance that includes uninsured motorist coverage may include terms and conditions that preclude stacking of uninsured motor vehicle coverages." It must be noted, however, that the quoted portion of this Ohio statute does not deal with the problem most difficult to express: the prorating among the affected coverages.

5. Numerous annotations in American Law Reports have collected the decisions of various jurisdictions in particular factual situations relating to uninsured motorist coverage, the "other insurance" clause, and stacking. (Annots., Combining or "Stacking" Uninsured Motorist Coverages Provided in Policies Issued by Different Insurers to Different Insureds, 28 A.L.R.4th 362; Combining or "Stacking" Uninsured Motorist Coverages Provided in Separate Policies Issued by Same Insurer to Different Insureds, 23 A.L.R.4th 108; Combining or "Stacking" Uninsured Motorist Coverages Provided in Single Policy Applicable to Different Vehicles of Individual Insured, 23 A.L.R.4th 12; Uninsured Motorist Insurance: Validity and Construction of "Other Insurance" Provisions, 28 A.L.R.3d 551; Combining or "Stacking" Uninsured Motorist Coverages Provided in *Separate Policies* Issued by *Same Insurer* to *Same Insured,* 25 A.L.R.4th 6.) (Italics added.) We are concerned in this case only with the situation described in the last of these annotations.

6. See, e.g., Note, *Contractual Attempts to Limit Liability Under Uninsured Motorist Coverage* (1978) 47 Cin.U.L.Rev. 245, 255–258; Davis, *Uninsured Motorist Coverage: Some Significant Problems and Developments* (1977) 42 Mo.L.Rev. 1, 17–23; York, *"Stacking" Uninsured Motorist Protection, Medical Payments, and Personal Injury Protection Coverages in Texas* (1976) 7 St. Mary's L.J. 837, 838–842.

7. Almost, but not quite. While we have not made a thorough state-by-state check, it appears that at least three states—Florida, Maryland and Louisiana—have statutes which actually prohibit stacking. (See discussions in *Dewberry v. Auto-Owners Ins. Co.* (Fla.1978) 363 So.2d 1077, *Rafferty v. Allstate Ins. Co.* (1985) 303 Md. 63, 492 A.2d 290 and *Sciple v. Cosse-Hickey Co. Inc.* (La.App.1985) 468 So.2d 15.) Iowa and Tennessee, as well as Ohio (see fn. 4, *ante*) have statutes which expressly permit anti-stacking clauses. (See *Davenport v. Aid Ins. Co. (Mutual)* (Iowa 1983) 334 N.W.2d 711 and *Jones v. Mulkey* (Tenn.App.1981) 620 S.W.2d 498.) Ohio passed the statute from which we quote in footnote 4, *ante,* in

clauses in separate policies issued by the same insurer to the same insured, where a state statute expressly authorizes such clauses.

Actually there is a surprising dearth of California cases involving subdivision (d) and policy conditions written pursuant thereto. We count precisely two.[8]

The first is *Mid–Century Ins. Co. v. Koch* (1970) 11 Cal.App.3d 1019, 90 Cal.Rptr. 280, a case identical with ours, except that two different companies were involved. Without extended discussion the court denied the insured's claim that he was entitled to UM benefits under both policies. Even brisker was the same division of the same Court of Appeal in *Rudder v. Farmers Ins. Exchange* (1980) 107 Cal.App.3d 158, 165 Cal.Rptr. 562, which involved four policies, with limits totalling $60,000. Each policy contained the condition permitted by subdivision (d). The cumulative liability was held to be limited to $15,000.[9]

Thus we finally reach the issue presented by this appeal: whether subdivision (d) and policy conditions written pursuant thereto are of no effect where the policies are issued by the same company. Two arguments in favor of this proposition are advanced: (1) Application of the anti-stacking condition is unfair where both policies are written by the same company, because the insured pays two premiums but receives nothing for the second which he does not already have by virtue of the first; and (2) subdivision (d) which provides for prorating between insurers is not applicable where, because of the identity of carriers, there is nothing to prorate.

In support of the first argument plaintiffs look myopically at the injured plaintiff Susan K. Welch. They point out that each of the two UM coverages involved was obtained for an identical premium payment of $4.50. If only the first policy had issued and, therefore, only one premium had been paid, she would have received $15,000. State Farm contends, of course, that she should get no more than that even though it issued two policies and received two premiums. Why, ask plaintiffs, should State Farm get a windfall of, possibly, as much as $15,000? What did plaintiffs get for the second premium? The answer is simple: additional protection for additional risks. While this additional protection does not increase the maximum payable to any particular member of plaintiffs' family, the reason why two premiums were paid was that

1980. With respect to losses incurred before the statute went into effect, the Ohio Supreme Court had held that in view of the remedial purpose of UM legislation, anti-stacking clauses were simply not to be given effect. The accident involved in *Karabin v. State Auto. Mut. Ins. Co., supra,* however, took place in 1981. The Ohio Supreme court did not hesitate to apply the statute to the insured who had two policies, issued, incidentally, *by the same company.*

**8.** For present purposes we ignore *Allstate Ins. Co. v. Shmitka* (1970) 12 Cal.App.3d 59, 90 Cal.Rptr. 399 which involved not just two, but five UM coverages, all written by the same carrier. *Shmitka* did not permit stacking without even referring to subdivision (d) or relying on the "other insurance" clause. (*Id.* p. 69, 90 Cal.Rptr. 399.)

**9.** It so happens that two of the four policies were issued by the same insurer, Farmers. The point at issue in this case was, however, not argued.

two cars were being operated with a correspondingly greater risk of injury to more persons on a greater number of occasions. The issue is beautifully laid to rest by a leading writer in the field: "If there were but a single insured, and only he ever drove an automobile, obviously he can drive only one vehicle at a time and the reasoning of such courts might then be logical. But, in considering basic underwriting and the actuarial computation of rate structures, we must take into consideration the customary procedures of mankind. Automobile policies are now written so as to afford liability protection not only to the named insured, who is usually the owner, but to members of his family, perhaps persons residing in the same household and—with a few exceptions—anyone operating with the permission of the named insured or adult members of his household. When it comes to UM coverages, we have a like multiplication of exposure, since we have classes of risk, including all of the persons stated above, and pedestrians as well, with benefits granted in many circumstances when one may be in another vehicle or even upon the highway. [¶] When the insured then owns more than a single vehicle, almost always it is with the contemplation that the second, or third, vehicles will be operated by others. And those others may, also, if injured by an uninsured motorist, expose the insurer to loss under that aspect of the contract." (8C Appleman, Insurance Law and Practice (1981) § 5101, pp. 449–450.) [10]

Common sense also tells us that plaintiff's point proves too much. Plaintiffs must concede that if the second policy had been written by, say, Travelers, the $15,000 limit would apply. Yet under the prorating provision of the statute, State Farm would be entitled to a contribution of $7,500 from Travelers. Thus State Farm's exposure would have been halved without it having received any consideration therefor. A windfall is a windfall. It will not do to say that the halving of the loss in the State Farm–Travelers situation is an unexpected lucky break, unavoidable if subdivision (d) is to be given any effect, while the possible involvement of two State Farm policies is precisely what the insurer should have foreseen when it collected two premiums. The answer is that "breaks"—good or bad—are what premium calculations are all about. If California did not permit anti-stacking clauses and State Farm could not assume decreased exposure per policy because of the occasional contribution by another applicable policy—whether written by itself or another carrier—plaintiffs simply would have been unable to purchase UM coverage for $4.50.

The other reason advanced for not applying subdivision (d) where but a single carrier is involved, is that in such a case the prorating provisions of the subdivision could not take effect. With all respect, that argument permits the solution to wag the problem. It seems likely that

**10.** Precisely the same point is made in *Allstate Ins. Co. v. Shmitka, supra,* 12 Cal. App.3d at pages 64–66, 90 Cal.Rptr. 399, even without relying on an anti-stacking clause. As noted that case involved coverages on five vehicles issued by the same insurer. Plaintiffs seek to distinguish the case, because the opinion stated that the insured paid $7 for the UM coverage on the first car and only $6 for such coverage on each of the others. The opinion, however, makes nothing of that fact.

the Legislature called for prorating of all applicable coverages for two reasons: first, to avoid endless squabbles based on the relationship between the named insured, the vehicles involved in the accident, and the injured claimant, and, second, to forestall a legal game of scissors-paper-stone, triggered by anti-stacking provisions being couched as "escape," "excess" or "proration" clauses. (See *Prieto v. State Farm Mut. Automobile Ins. Co.,* 268 Cal.App.2d 891, 74 Cal.Rptr. 472.) Of course none of those problems arises when only one insurer is involved.

Whatever may have been the problem which the Legislature tried to solve by calling for prorating across the board, it is safe to assume that it did not consider the arithmetical exercise involved in prorating as an end in itself. Subdivision (d) provides for coverage at the highest available limit. If more than one company is involved, prorating will have to take place. If all policies are issued by the same company, that step can be skipped, or becomes a paper exercise in the office of a single insurer. Certainly no one—insurer or insured—is worse off because after the insured has been paid the full limit called for by the statute and the policy, prorating can be avoided.[11] * * *

Affirmed.

MOSK, JUSTICE, dissenting.

I dissent.

By denying plaintiff the right to aggregate her uninsured motorist (UM) coverage, the majority have reached a harsh result. Plaintiff was injured by an uninsured motorist and her damages were in excess of $30,000. She was covered by two separate insurance policies with the same carrier, each providing for up to $15,000 in UM coverage. Yet, because of the majority's gratuitous reading of the "antistacking" clause of the Insurance Code (Ins.Code, § 11580.2, subd. (d)), she will receive only $15,000, less than half of her actual damages. In effect, plaintiff receives no benefit whatever from the second UM policy, although she paid, and State Farm received, a full premium for it.

There is a sharp division of authority among the jurisdictions as to whether clauses similar to that included in plaintiff's policy can be applied to limit damages so that the insured is not entitled to full recovery under the UM endorsement of more than one policy. (See Widiss, A Guide to Uninsured Motorist Coverage (1969) §§ 2.59, 2.60, 2.61, pp. 106–116 [hereinafter Widiss, Guide to UMC]; Glidden v. Farmers Automobile Insurance Ass'n (Ill.1974) 312 N.E.2d 247, 249–

11. In *Glidden v. Farmers Automobile Insurance Assn.* (1974) 57 Ill.2d 330, 312 N.E.2d 247, the Illinois court fell victim to the same confusion between purpose and effect. It said: "The apparent purpose of 'other insurance' clauses is to make certain that one company does not pay a disproportionate amount of a loss which is to be shared by another company. There is no purpose in proration unless the 'other insurance' is written by another company." The Arizona court was dead right when, in *State Farm Mutual Automobile Insurance Company v. Williams* (1979) 123 Ariz. 455, 600 P.2d 759, 763, it called this reasoning naive: "The sole purpose of the 'other insurance' clause *is to decrease the liability of the insurer under the policy.*" (Italics added.) If this purpose can be achieved without prorating, so much the better.

250.) A majority, however, refuse to enforce anti-stacking provisions in insurance policies. (Widiss, Guide to UMC (1981 Supp.) §§ 2.59, 2.60, 2.61, pp. 198–222.) These courts reason that to allow an insurer to prorate damages results in the issuance of a policy below the limits required by the uninsured motorist statute (e.g., *United Farm Bureau Mut. Ins. Co. v. Runnels* (1978) 178 Ind.App. 441, 382 N.E.2d 1015, 1016–1017), and that the insured is entitled to and reasonably expects to recover under each policy because he has paid separate premiums for such coverage. (E.g., *Glidden v. Farmers Automobile Insurance Ass'n,* supra, 312 N.E.2d 247, 250–251.) As a leading commentator on California uninsured motorist law queried, "Assume an insured pays for extra coverage, might it not be assumed that he wishes to be protected for *all* the damages he might suffer and not just be bound by the minimal limits of the financial responsibility law?" (Eisler, Cal. Uninsured Motorist Law Handbook (3d ed. 1979) § 8.7, p. 242.)

The majority here conclude that plaintiff has received something for the second premium: "additional protection for additional risks." This "added risk" apparently arises from the possibility that if both the insured cars were being driven at the same time they might be involved in simultaneous accidents with uninsured motorists. I submit that such added risk is as remote as being struck by Halley's comet and is not an element of second car UM coverage that the insured could reasonably have contemplated. Furthermore, such actuarial hypothesizing does not withstand scrutiny because of the peculiarities of UM coverage.

UM coverage is not tied to the use of a particular vehicle, or to the particular insured who pays the premiums. It covers—as in the present case—relatives living in the same household, when driving the insured's car, but also when driving in someone else's uninsured vehicle, and even when injured as pedestrians. Obviously, even with a single UM policy, it is already calculated into the premiums that two accidents could occur simultaneously. When a single carrier sells two policies with UM coverage, the risk it reasonably contemplates is not more accidents, but liability on both policies when one accident occurs. In no case does the added risk cited by the majority account for the full premium charged to plaintiff's father on the second of his two policies. Rather, by virtue of the majority's holding, State Farm will be unjustly enriched at plaintiff's expense.

The majority apply the code's proration clause (Ins.Code, § 11580.2, subd. (d)) to the present facts with the view that if prorating is avoidable, so much the better. I agree with the majority that the main purpose of the prorating clause is to avoid controversies among insurance companies. It assures that an insurer does not pay a disproportionate amount of the loss that is to be shared by another insurer. (See 8C Appleman, Insurance Law and Practice (1981) § 5102.45, p. 486.)

As the majority concede, the Legislature did not contemplate prorating by a single insurer where it would be a mere arithmetical exercise. I would conclude from this, however, not that the statute applies nonetheless to the present facts, but that it is meaningless where, as here, a single insurer is involved. [citations]

Nothing in the legislative history or case law supports the majority's assertion that the "other insurance" clause is aimed to protect insurance companies by minimizing their liability. So long as there is no recovery for a plaintiff beyond the amount of actual damages, the thrust of the UM statute is to protect injured parties, not to allow insurance companies to collect premiums for coverage they know they will not provide. Worse than prorating for its own sake would be paying premiums for their own sake, and I conclude that the Legislature contemplated neither. The policy in California has always been to encourage the purchase of insurance—that was why UM coverage was made quasi-mandatory by statute. Requiring multiple premiums for no more coverage than is provided by a single policy frustrates the legitimate expectations of the insured who paid for the UM policies.

In sum, the limitation on uninsured motorist coverage authorized by subdivision (d) should not apply where, as here, the policies are issued by the same insurer and there is no likelihood that the insured will recover more than his actual damage. Thus, I would conclude that the "other insurance" provision in State Farm's policy, which echoes subdivision (d), is also inapplicable and State Farm should be held liable for the payment of UM benefits under both policies.

Bird, C.J., concurs.

### *Note*

A further complicating factor is that some statutes refer to the uninsured *motorist* who caused the accident, while others refer to the uninsured *vehicle* that was involved. Suppose X, whose policy provides coverage if he is struck by an uninsured vehicle, is negligently injured in a collision with a vehicle driven by Y who is personally insured although the vehicle is not. The applicable state statute mandate that all auto policies contain coverage for damages from "operators of uninsured vehicles." X settles with Y personally and then seeks recovery from his own auto insurer. Is this possible? See State Farm Mutual Auto. Ins. Co. v. Taylor, 223 Mont. 215, 725 P.2d 821 (1986). (Held: yes).

## NORTH RIVER INSURANCE CO. v. TABOR

United States Court of Appeals, Third Circuit, 1991.
934 F.2d 461.

Greenberg, Circuit Judge.

In our opinion in West American Ins. Co. v. Park, 933 F.2d 1236 (3d Cir.1991), we have concluded that West American was estopped from challenging the legality of its own policy under Section 1736 of the Pennsylvania Motor Vehicle Responsibility Law ("MVFRL"), because the policy permitted the insured to stack *uninsured* motorist coverage to exceed her liability coverage. In this diversity of citizenship declaratory judgment action under Pennsylvania Law between appellant-plaintiff, North River Insurance Company, and appellee-defendant, the estate of Todd Tabor, dealing with *underinsured* motorist coverage rather than *uninsured* motorist coverage, essentially the same stacking issue is presented. Inasmuch as we find no meaningful difference between the two coverages with respect to stacking, and there being no factual differences to distinguish the cases so that the basis for estoppel present in Park is present here, we find our discussion in Park fully determinative of the stacking issue presented herein and thus we will affirm the judgment of the district court allowing stacking without further discussion.

In this case, however, an additional issue is raised, and we are called upon to predict whether the Supreme Court of Pennsylvania would rule invalid, as contrary to the public policy embodied in the MVFRL, an insurance contract clause providing for the set-off or reduction of underinsured motorist coverage benefits "by all sums paid * * * by or on behalf of persons or organizations who may be legally responsible." This issue cannot be decided on the estoppel rationale adopted in Park, as here North River obviously does not seek to contradict its policy. On cross-motions for summary judgment, the district court determined that Supreme Court of Pennsylvania would so rule and entered judgment for Tabor's estate. North River Ins. Co. v. Tabor, 744 F.Supp. 625 (M.D.Pa. 1990). The courts that have considered the issue are split. Compare, e.g., Lytle v. Allstate Ins. Co., 72 Erie L.J. 46 (Ct.C.P.Erie County 1989) (set-off provision enforceable); Nationwide Mut. Ins. Co. v. Hampton, 1990 WESTLAW 87276 (U.S.D.C., E.D.Pa. June 18, 1990) (set-off provision enforceable to extent statutorily-mandated floor for underinsured motorist coverage not affected), with, e.g., North River Ins. Co. v. Tabor, 744 F.Supp. 625 (set-off provision unenforceable); Conrad v. Progressive Cas. Ins. Co., 48 Pa.D. & C.3d 71 (Blair County 1987) (same).

I.

Factional Background and Contentions of the Parties

The district court's concise recitation of the undisputed facts in this case is as follows: "Defendant James E. Tabor is the administrator for the estate of Todd J. Tabor who was killed in an automobile accident. Aetna Life & Casualty Company insured the host vehicle in which the decedent, who was a passenger, was killed. That company paid to the estate $250,000 in liability coverage. The Tabors have a personal automobile policy [with North River Insurance Company] which provides coverage for three vehicles owned by them and $100,000 of underinsured motorist coverage for [each vehicle] per accident with bodily injury * * *." 744 F.Supp. at 626.

"The policy in question contains an express offset provision entitling [North River] to reduce the underinsured motorist benefits owing under its own policy by the liability coverage amounts already paid by other companies, in this case Aetna." Id. at 627.

As Tabor's estate is under Park entitled to stack the underinsured motorist coverage on the three Tabor vehicles to achieve a total of $300,000 coverage from North River, and as Tabor's estate has already received $250,000 from Aetna, the question of set-off arises. Tabor's estate claims that the set-off clause is unenforceable as contrary to public policy and accordingly the additional $300,000 in stacked coverage is available to satisfy its remaining damages which it asserts are at least $300,000. North River, however, argues that, pursuant to its contract with the Tabors, the $250,000 received from Aetna must be set-off against the $300,000 in stacked underinsured motorist coverage, so that its liability to Tabor's estate for underinsured benefits cannot exceed $50,000.[2] Under the view held by Tabor's estate, the combination of the tortfeasor's liability coverage with Aetna and the Tabors' underinsurance coverage will satisfy $550,000 of the damages it claims; North River's view, since we are allowing stacking, potentially leaves $250,000 of these damages unsatisfied. For the reasons that follow, we find the North River position untenable under the MVFRL.

As noted by Judge Smith in Conrad v. Progressive Cas. Ins. Co., 48 Pa.D. & C.3d 71, there are two types of underinsured motorist coverage. Under the first the coverage places the insured party in the same position that he would have been in had the tortfeasor carried liability insurance in the amount of the insured's underinsured motorist policy limit. See Higgins v. Fireman's Fund Ins. Co., 160 Ariz. 20, 22, 770 P.2d 324, 326 (1989). Under this "gap" theory of underinsured motorist coverage—so-called because the coverage merely fills the "gap" between the tortfeasor's liability coverage and the injured party's underinsured motorist coverage, Conrad, 48 Pa.D. & C.3d at 74, a driver is considered "underinsured" when his liability coverage does not at least equal *the uninsured/underinsured coverage carried* by the injured insured. See, e.g., Raggio v. Volkswagen Ins. Co., 327 So.2d 505, 511 (La.Ct.App.1976).

Under the second view, underinsured motorist coverage supplies a fund for full compensation to the injured insured and thus the insured is entitled to compensation from his insurer regardless of any recovery obtained from other sources. The insured may therefore recover underinsured motorist benefits until his policy limits are reached or he is fully compensated for his damages, whichever comes first. See Hamilton v. Farmers Ins. Co. of Washington, 107 Wash.2d 721, 727, 733 P.2d 213, 216 (1987). Under this "excess" theory of underinsured motorist coverage—i.e., the injured insured's coverage being reckoned as "excess" over and above the liability policy of the tortfeasor, Conrad, 48 Pa.D. & C.3d at 74, a tortfeasor is "underinsured" when his liability coverage does not at least equal the *damages suffered* by the injured insured.

Under 75 Pa.Cons.Stat.Ann. § 1731(a) (Purdon Supp. March 1990), every insurance policy issued in Pennsylvania must include "underinsured motorist coverage" unless it is rejected by the insured. Section

2. North River, of course, urges that stacking is not permitted but we reject that contention. It argues, however, that if stacking is allowed its maximum exposure would be $50,000, i.e., three times $100,000 or $300,000 less $250,000 paid by Aetna.

1731(c) defines "underinsured motorist coverage" so as to make clear that an insurer must provide coverage for all "persons who suffer injury * * * and are legally entitled to recover damages therefore from owners or operators of underinsured motor vehicles." Since section 1702 of the MVFRL defines any "underinsured motor vehicle" as any "motor vehicle for which the limits of available liability insurance * * * are insufficient to pay losses and damages," it follows that insurers must provide protection for all persons injured by a motor vehicle having less liability insurance than the loss and damages sustained. This would include, for example, a person who has purchased for herself $100,000 per person in underinsured motorist coverage and who suffers a $300,000 loss at the hands of a driver who has purchased $100,000 liability coverage. If an insurer were entitled to include a set-off provision such as that in the North River policy, a person so injured would have no underinsured motorist protection, a result clearly inconsistent with the statutory text. For this reason, we read the statute as reflecting a legislative choice in favor of "excess" underinsured motorist protection.

As the court in Conrad noted: "The legislative mandate to insurance carriers issuing motor vehicle insurance policies in Pennsylvania was to provide coverage to insureds for those cases when third party liability limits were inadequate or not enough to satisfy an injured parties' [sic] losses," and "[a] determination of inadequacy can only be made by reference to the injured party's losses and damages." 48 Pa.D. & C.3d at 79–80. A set-off provision preventing Pennsylvania's statutory scheme from having its desired effect—i.e., to require insurers to provide underinsured motorist coverage *in excess to* the tortfeasor's liability coverage—is therefore contrary to public policy and unenforceable.

Moreover, under the MVFRL as applicable to this case, as opposed to prior Pennsylvania law, insurers are *required* to offer underinsured coverage of at least $15,000 per person, $30,000 per accident. See 75 Pa.Cons.Stat.Ann. §§ 1702, 1715(c), 1731(a) (Purdon Supp.1990). This alone distinguishes the pre–MVFRL cases upholding set-off provisions with regard to underinsurance coverage, as in those cases the issue was one merely of construing a contract. See, e.g. Kovaleski v. Erie Ins. Group, 398 Pa.Super. 519, 530–31, 581 A.2d 585, 591 (1990); Sparler v. Fireman's Ins. Co. of Newark, 360 Pa.Super. 597, 521 A.2d 433 (1987); Votedian v. General Accident Fire & Life Assur. Corp., 330 Pa.Super. 13, 478 A.2d 1324 (1984). Thus, as noted by Votedian, underinsured motorist coverage not then being required, "[w]hen [it] is included [in an insurance contract], the terms and limitations thereof *are not controlled by statute or by public policy* but by agreement reached by the parties. That agreement, as expressed in the policy of insurance, *may place limitations* upon underinsured motorist coverage, *subject only to* the requirement that the limitation be clearly worded and conspicuously displayed." 330 Pa.Super. at 19, 478 A.2d at 1327 (emphasis added). Accordingly, under at least some of those pre–MVFRL cases, the insurance policy at issue contractually adopted the "gap" version of underinsured motorist coverage when defining the benefits to which the insured was entitled. [citations omitted]

The North River policy in this case also purports to define "underinsured motor vehicle" using the "gap" theory. But now, of course, the situation has changed. Under the MVFRL, insurers must offer underinsured motorist coverage, and that coverage is controlled by statute and by a public policy meant to foster the fullest possible, or "excess," coverage. The pre–MVFRL cases, then, are inapposite, and insurers may not by contract convert Pennsylvania's broad statutory scheme for underinsured motorist coverage into a narrow one merely providing "gap" coverage. North River's attempt to do this through its off-set provision and its definition of "underinsured motorist vehicle" is therefore unavailing. Indeed, the Superior Court in Davis v. Erie Ins. Group, 400 Pa.Super. 345, 583 A.2d 819 (1990), expressly rejected a contention that a policy liberalization clause which resulted in the addition to a policy of underinsured coverage after the adoption of the MVFRL provided for "gap" coverage. Thus, it affirmed a judgment of a common pleas court granting $15,000 in underinsured coverage even though the insured recovered $50,000 from the other driver.

We also observe that our determination is bolstered by reference to the policies and the rationales behind stacking. Throughout the several programs adopted by Pennsylvania for automobile insurance its courts have consistently seen a legislative intent to provide for the fullest coverage possible for injured insureds, not in excess of their damages,—and this intent has extended into the current MVFRL era, see Tallman v. Aetna Ca. & Sur. Co., 372 Pa.Super. 593, 598–99, 539 A.2d 1354, 1357, allocatur denied, 520 Pa. 607, 553 A.2d 969 (1988). Accordingly, in repeatedly striking down anti-stacking provisions, one reason cited by the Pennsylvania cases has been the insurer's improper attempt to cut back the coverage of insureds in violation of the statutes' intent. See, e.g., Utica Mut. Ins. Co. v. Contrisciane, 504 Pa. 328, 473 A.2d 1005 (1984); State Farm Mut. Auto Ins. Co. v. Williams, 481 Pa. 130, 392 A.2d 281 (1978); Harleysville Mut. Cas. Co. v. Blumling, 429 Pa. 389, 241 A.2d 112 (1968). Here, of course, the set-off provision attempts to limit the coverage of the insured but it was the Pennsylvania Legislature's intent in promulgating the MVFRL to provide insureds with the fullest coverage possible.

The other main reason cited by the Pennsylvania courts in striking down anti-stacking provisions is protection of the reasonable expectations of the insured. This reflects the concept that the insured, having paid multiple premiums, is entitled reasonably to believe that he has multiple coverage—e.g., having paid for a total of $300,000 worth of uninsured/underinsured motorist coverage ($100,000 on each of three vehicles), the insured is entitled to $300,000 worth of coverage. See, e.g., Williams, 481 Pa. at 143, 392 A.2d at 287. The facts of this case expose, in the set-off provision, the type of unfairness that has been condemned in anti-stacking provisions. Due to the set-off, the Tabors, while having purchased $300,000 worth of underinsured motorist coverage, are now told that Tabor's estate is entitled to only $50,000 in coverage. This state of affairs, we believe, would be repugnant to the Legislature of Pennsylvania and to its Supreme Court as well. In sum we believe that the Pennsylvania Supreme Court would not countenance policy provisions that would, in any situation, allow underinsured coverage to be obviated because of a partial recovery received from the negligent underinsured.[6]

Finally, even if the result we reach here were not mandated by statute, the recent Pennsylvania Supreme Court case of Bateman v. Motorists Mut. Ins. Co., ___ Pa. ___, 590 A.2d 281 (1991), rev'g 377 Pa.Super. 400, 547 A.2d 428 (1988), would direct us to the same conclusion as a matter of contractual interpretation. In Bateman, a pre-MVFRL case, the set-off provision contained in the uninsured/underinsured motorist portion of the insurance policy read: "Any amounts otherwise payable for damages under this coverage shall be reduced by all sums: 1. Paid because of the bodily injury by or on behalf of persons or organizations who may be responsible." 377 Pa.Super. at 403, 547 A.2d at 430.

Pursuant to the policy, the insured in Bateman had $50,000 worth of underinsured motorist coverage. After Bateman's fatal accident, his estate collected a total of $78,334 in settlement from three sources: the manufacturer of the vehicle, the owners of a tavern, and the driver of the other vehicle involved in the accident. Total damages, it was agreed, were in excess of $128,334. However, when the estate sought the additional $50,000 in underinsured motorist benefits, Motorists Mutual claimed its underinsurance liability was obviated by the set-off clause as the settlement figure exceeded underinsurance coverage. The majority of a panel of arbitrators agreed with Motorists Mutual. The arbitrators' decision was affirmed by the Court of Common Pleas which, in turn, was affirmed by the Superior Court.

The Supreme Court, however, reversed the determination of the Superior Court. The court held that the set-off clause was ambiguous and, construing it against the insurer, found that Bateman's estate was entitled to the $50,000 worth of underinsured motorist coverage provided by the policy:

> Appellee, the drafter of this policy, argues that the phrase "Any amounts otherwise payable for damages under this coverage * * *" refers to the limits of liability of its policy so that any sums that Appellant recovers from other persons reduces the amount available to Appellant under the under-insurance provision. Since Appellant

6. We therefore reject the approach taken by Nationwide Mut. Ins. Co. v. Hampton, 1990 WESTLAW 87276 (U.S.D.C., E.D.Pa. June 18, 1990), which approved a set-off provision to the extent that it did not reduce underinsured motorist coverage below the statutory floor. This approach has not been taken by the Pennsylvania courts in the stacking cases where the court has struck down anti-stacking provisions which, in the particular cases being considered, did not affect the minimum coverage required by law. Neither is this approach consistent with the primary basis for our determination here, i.e., Pennsylvania's legislative program of "excess" underinsured motorist coverage.

> recovered at least $50,000.00 from other parties, the limits of underinsurance coverage must be reduced to zero and her claim for under-insurance rejected.
>
> Appellee, however, neglects to take into account the word "otherwise" which has been inserted into the policy and its effect upon the meaning of this phrase. The word "otherwise" is defined as "in a different way or manner" and when inserted into this phrase reads, "Any amounts payable in a different way or manner for damages under this coverage * * *". The problem generated by this word when placed in this phrase is that under this policy the only damages payable are for under-insurance payments and there are no other payments payable in a different way or manner which are to be reduced by sums paid by others. Thus, the inclusion into this phrase of the word "otherwise" makes Appellee's interpretation that the clause refers to its under-insurance limits of liability an impossible one and renders the language ambiguous.
>
> Appellant, on the other hand, argues that the damages otherwise payable referred to are her decedent's total damages sustained (stipulated to be in excess of $128,334) minus the $78,334 recovered from other parties which must be deducted from her damages leaving $50,000 as damages which Appellee as under-insurer must pay.
>
> Since the provision of the policy is ambiguous it must be construed as Appellant suggests. ___ Pa. at ___, 590 A.2d at 293.

Thus, following Bateman, when we interpret the phrase "amounts *otherwise* payable for damages payable under this coverage" to mean Tabor's estate's *total* damages claimed to exceed $550,000, and reducing that amount by $250,000—i.e., by the "sums * * * [p]aid * * * on behalf of persons * * * who may be legally responsible"—, we find North River is liable to Tabor's estate for up to $300,000 underinsured motorist coverage, not to exceed actual damages.

### Conclusion

Per West American Ins. Co. v. Park, 933 F.2d 1236, (3d Cir.1991), the estate of Todd Tabor is entitled to stack underinsured motorist coverage in excess of liability coverage. Moreover, we determine that the Supreme Court of Pennsylvania would hold that set-off provisions of the type at issue herein are void and unenforceable as contrary to the public policy expressed in the MVFRL. Even if the Supreme Court would not so hold, however, per Bateman v. Motorists Mut. Ins. Co., ___ Pa. ___, 590 A.2d 281 (1991), we find that the provision at issue herein is ambiguous and is ineffective to work a set-off from underinsurance coverage of settlement monies received. Accordingly, we will affirm the judgment of the district court.

# WEST AMERICAN INSURANCE CO. v. PARK

United States Court of Appeals, Third Circuit, 1991.
933 F.2d 1236.

STAPLETON, CIRCUIT JUDGE.

In this diversity of citizenship, declaratory judgment action, appellee-plaintiff West American Insurance Company asks us to predict that the Supreme Court of Pennsylvania would not enforce the terms of a policy that West American wrote for appellant-defendant Suzanne Park. West American argues that section 1736 of the Pennsylvania Motor Vehicle Financial Responsibility Law ("MVFRL"), 75 Pa.Cons.Stat.Ann. § 1736 (Purdon Supp. 1990), prohibits the aggregation or "stacking" [1] of uninsured/underinsured motorist coverage to exceed the liability coverage carried by the insured, a proposition upon which Pennsylvania courts have not authoritatively ruled. On cross-motions for summary judgment, the district court determined that the Supreme Court of Pennsylvania would so hold and entered judgment for West American. The district courts that have considered the issue are split. Because we conclude that the Supreme Court of Pennsylvania would find West American estopped from challenging the legality of its own policy, we will reverse without considering whether the policy does in fact violate the MVFRL.

## I.

### FACTUAL BACKGROUND AND CONTENTIONS OF THE PARTIES

The following facts have been stipulated. On June 3, 1988, Suzanne Park was operating her husband's 1986 Mercury Topaz automobile when she was allegedly injured by an uninsured motorist. At that time the Mercury was insured under a West American policy which also covered her husband's 1983 Ford Escort. The policy had a limit of coverage for liability to third persons of $100,000 and also provided uninsured/underinsured motorist coverage of $100,000 for each vehicle. West American charged separate premiums for the uninsured/underinsured motorist coverage for each automobile.

After the accident, Suzanne Park initiated a claim against West American for uninsured motorist benefits. On February 22, 1990, West American, a California corporation with its principal place of business in California, commenced this action in the district court seeking a declaratory judgment against Park, a citizen of Pennsylvania, as to the limits of uninsured motorist coverage under the policy.

Park claims that she may stack the $100,000 worth of uninsured motorist coverage provided for each of the vehicles so that she may

1. "Stacking is where a claimant adds all available policies together to create a greater pool in order to satisfy his actual damages." 12A Couch on Insurance 2d § 45:651 at 207 (1981). It "permits the total amount of uninsured motorist coverage provided for all vehicles listed in an insurance policy to be applied to the damages resulting from an accident involving only one of the vehicles." Rhody v. State Farm Mut. Ins. Co., 771 F.2d 1416, 1418 (10th Cir.1985).

potentially recover up to $200,000 of uninsured motorist coverage benefits. West American asserts that section 1736 of the MVFRL prevents Park from stacking the uninsured motorist coverage benefits to exceed the maximum amount available to third parties under the liability portion of the policy, i.e., $100,000. Section 1736 states that: "The [uninsured/underinsured motorist] coverages provided under this subchapter may be offered by insurers in amounts higher than those required by this chapter but may not be greater than the limits of liability specified in the bodily injury liability provisions of the insured's policy." 75 Pa.Cons.Stat.Ann. § 1736 (Purdon Supp. 1990). West American contends that although stacking is authorized by the policy, "[i]n instances such as this case in which [the] stacking allowed by a policy would run afoul of the express statutory limitation of [section] 1736, the public policy behind the statute must prevail." Appellee's Brief at 17. Two intermediate Pennsylvania courts have indicated that section 1736 is intended to prevent "an insured from providing greater coverage, via uninsured/underinsured coverages, for himself and his additional insureds than the amount of coverage he provides for others injured through his negligence." Tallman v. Aetna Cas. & Sur. Co., 372 Pa.Super. 593, 539 A.2d 1354, 1358–59 allocatur denied, 520 Pa. 607, 553 A.2d 969 (1988) (quoting Wolgemuth v. Hurleysville Mut. Ins. Co., 370 Pa.Super. 51, 535 A.2d 1145, 1147 n. 3, allocatur denied, 520 Pa. 590, 551 A.2d 216 (1988)). The district court agreed with West American, and this appeal followed.

* * *

West American claims that Park should be denied recovery on public policy grounds because section 1736 prohibits insurers from offering uninsured/underinsured motorist coverage in excess of liability coverage. In other words, West American claims that it should be excused from fulfilling Park's reasonable expectations and its own obligations under the policy's plain language, because it violated the MVFRL. Assuming that West American did violate the MVFRL, as it contends, we conclude that the courts of Pennsylvania would find it estopped from denying the existence of uninsured motorist coverage it in fact issued.

Pennsylvania insurance law incorporates principles of equitable estoppel. As one Pennsylvania court expressed it, "reduced to its essence, equitable estoppel is a doctrine of fundamental fairness intended to preclude a party from depriving another of a reasonable expectation, when the party inducing the expectation knew or should have known that the other would rely to his detriment upon that conduct." Straup v. Times Herald, 283 Pa.Super. 58, 423 A.2d 713, 720 (1980). As the Supreme Court of Pennsylvania has cogently put it: "[t]he reasonable expectation of the insured is the focal point of the insurance transaction * * *. Courts should be concerned with assuring that the insurance public's reasonable expectations are fulfilled. Thus, regardless of the ambiguity, or lack thereof, inherent in a given set of insurance documents * * * the public has a right to expect that they will receive something of value in return for the premium paid." Collister v. Nationwide Life Ins. Co., 479 Pa. 579, 388 A.2d 1346, 1353 (1978), cert. denied, 439 U.S. 1089, 99 S.Ct. 871, 59 L.Ed.2d 55 (1979).[4]

In the Collister case, a life insurance applicant died after he sent in an application for life insurance and the first premium, but before the insurer had accepted or rejected the application. Disregarding plain language in the application that made coverage conditional on insurer receiving a completed medical exam, the Pennsylvania Supreme Court concluded that the reasonable expectations of the insured, specifically the expectation that he would receive something upon paying the first premium, controlled. It held that those expectations created a temporary insurance contract until the insurer either accepted or rejected the application. In essence, the principles of equitable estoppel were used to bar the insurer from both accepting the first premium and denying that coverage existed.

Collister and subsequent insurance cases expand traditional notions of equitable estoppel so that the insurer is bound not only by the expectations that it creates, but also by any other reasonable expectation of the insured. The insured's reasonable expectations control, even if they are contrary to the explicit terms of the policy. State Farm Mut. Auto Ins. Co. v. Williams, 481 Pa. 130, 392 A.2d 281, 286–87 (1978). If the insurer wishes to change the reasonable expectations of the insured, it must do more than insert the condition in the policy. Tonkovic v. State Farm Mut. Auto Ins. Co., 513 Pa. 445, 521 A.2d 920, 925 (1987).

Thus, the Supreme Court of Pennsylvania has consistently applied equitable estoppel to prevent an insurer from attempting to frustrate the reasonable expectations of the insured. We predict that it would apply that doctrine to achieve that objective in context of the facts of this case, even though the result may be to provide Park with more underinsured motorist protection than the legislature intended her to have, i.e., more underinsured motorist protection than the liability protection for which she had contracted. The Pennsylvania courts on more than one occasion have applied equitable estoppel to bar arguments supported by legislatively established public policy.

In Fraternal Order of Police, E.B. Jermyn Lodge # 2 v. Hickey, 499 Pa. 194, 452 A.2d 1005 (1982) (plurality), the Supreme Court found that the City of Scranton and its officers were estopped from claiming that a provision of its collective bargaining agreement with its policemen was illegal. The plurality applied equitable estoppel noting that the City had theretofore received the benefit of the agreement: "the statutorily

4. This rationale also underlies Pennsylvania courts' preference for stacking (even under policies which *expressly prohibit* stacking): "the intended beneficiary of an uninsured motorist policy is entitled to multiple coverage when multiple premiums have been paid. [This] rationale is grounded in the belief that a person has reasonable expectations when he pays separate premiums that he has obtained coverage under separate policies, and therefore is entitled to benefits under each." Utica Mut. Ins. Co. v. Contrisciane, 504 Pa. 328, 473 A.2d 1005, 1010 (1984) (citation omitted).

mandated obligation to bargain in good faith is not met by permitting the governmental employer to avoid the performance of a term by questioning its legality after having received the advantages that flowed from that term's acceptance." 452 A.2d at 1007–08. See also Scranton v. Local Union No. 669, 122 Pa.Cmwlth. 140, 551 A.2d 643, 646 (1988) ("where an employer voluntarily agrees to perform an act * * * it cannot later contend that the act is illegal and refuse to perform it; indeed it will be estopped from doing so.")

More recently, Pennsylvania's Commonwealth Court has applied equitable estoppel to bar a party from asserting that the position advocated by its opponent would violate the Health Care Facilities Act. In Laurel Mobile H. Serv. v. Health Department, 121 Pa.Cmwlth. 291, 550 A.2d 616 (1988), one health care provider attempted to argue that another provider was violating the Act by providing CT scanning services without proper state authorization. The court held that the first provider was estopped to so argue because it had benefitted from receiving CT services under the same arrangement it now sought to challenge: "[The hospital] never asserted the illegality or impropriety of the assignment of contracts, but instead accepted and paid for the [medical] services provided by the Laurel without objection. Having accepted the benefits, [the hospital] is now estopped from asserting that the arrangement was prohibited." 550 A.2d at 620–21.

We conclude that the courts of Pennsylvania would find this case a far more compelling one for application of the doctrine of equitable estoppel than Hickey or Laurel Mobile. West American wrote the policy that it now seeks to challenge and received premiums for the coverage it now tries to contest. Moreover, the Pennsylvania legislature has determined that the most effective means of securing the desired objective of this portion of the MVFRL is to impose a duty on all insurers not to issue uninsured/underinsured coverage above a prescribed amount. We would expect a Pennsylvania court fashioning an equitable remedy in a situation of this kind to take note of that legislative decision and to choose a result that will not reward an insurer for violating what the insurer claims to be the proper interpretation of § 1736.

## IV.

## Conclusion

Pennsylvania law will not allow an insurer to use the explicit language of an insurance policy to defeat the reasonable expectations of the insured. West American seeks to use a provision of Pennsylvania law, prohibiting certain conduct by insurers, to defeat both the reasonable expectations of the insured and the explicit terms of the policy it wrote. We are confident that the Pennsylvania Supreme Court would not allow an insurer to challenge the legality of a policy which it wrote, for which it collected premiums, and on which it gave the insured every reason to rely. Accordingly, we will reverse the order of June 19, 1990, of the district court and remand with instructions to enter a judgment declaring that West American is responsible for such damages as Park can establish up to a limit of $200,000.

CIRCUIT JUDGE GREENBERG's concurring opinion is omitted.

## KIRSCH v. NATIONWIDE INS. CO.

United States District Court, Eastern District of Pennsylvania, 1982.
532 F.Supp. 766.

WEBER, CHIEF JUDGE.

We have before us another case involving the intricacies of the Pennsylvania No–Fault Act.

Decedent, Kenneth Kirsch, died as a result of a two car collision in Northeast Township on November 30, 1980. At the time of his death, Kenneth was 19 years of age, and resided with his parents who, together with a sister, have survived him. Decedent's father, Urban J. Kirsch, plaintiff herein, was the owner of the vehicle driven by Kenneth at the time of his death.

* * *

The parties have filed cross-motions for summary judgment on two remaining issues. First, whether a parent of a dependent child is entitled to recover work loss benefits and second, whether the No–Fault Act allows the "stacking" of benefits where the plaintiff has a single insurance policy covering two vehicles. [The court held that work loss benefits are payable upon the death of an insured, and that the plaintiff, as administrator of the estate, may recover such work loss benefits without the necessity of showing dependency upon the deceased.]

The second issue involves the propriety of "stacking" of no-fault benefits. Plaintiff insured two separate vehicles under one insurance policy issued by the defendant. An additional premium was paid for the coverage of the second vehicle. Plaintiff alleges that since two vehicles were covered by this policy, plaintiff is allowed double recovery of no-fault benefits, amounting to $30,000 in work loss benefits. Although it has been stipulated that decedent's wage loss would exceed $30,000, defendant claims that the terms of the Act do not permit such "stacking" of no-fault benefits.

In support of its claim to cumulative benefits plaintiff draws an analogy to uninsured motorist coverage in which Pennsylvania courts have allowed stacking in cases where one policy covered two or more vehicles. Marchese v. Aetna Casualty Insurance Co., 284 Pa.Super. 579, 426 A.2d 646 (1981); Sones v. Aetna Casualty Insurance Co., 270 Pa.Super. 330, 411 A.2d 552 (1979). These cases have allowed stacking based upon public policy and legislative intent to provide protection to innocent victims from injuries caused by the negligence of irresponsible drivers. Harleysville Mutual Casualty Co. v. Blumling, 429 Pa. 389, 395, 241 A.2d 112 (1968). Plaintiff alleges that the public policy behind the Uninsured Motorist Act is the same as that underlying the No–Fault

Act. Therefore stacking of no-fault benefits should similarly be permitted.

This argument fails, however, because the analogy to the Uninsured Motorist Act is faulty. The Uninsured Motorist Act was enacted specifically to provide coverage to innocent victims of negligent acts of uninsured third parties. The Act was not intended to limit causes of action against tortfeasors, but to assure recovery where tortfeasors are financially unable to pay any judgment awarded. The Act does not place any statutory maximum on the amount of coverage any individual insured can obtain, only the minimum amount of coverage each insurance policy must provide.

The No–Fault Act, on the other hand, has an entirely different purpose. The No–Fault Act provides for a specific amount of possible recovery to be awarded to victims of motor vehicle accidents, *regardless of fault.* This arrangement allows for prompt compensation to victims. However, once the statutory ceilings are exceeded, the negligent party is still liable for any further damages caused by his actions. The cause of action against the faulty driver is not limited at this point. Furthermore, the very fact that, unlike the Uninsured Motorist Act, the No–Fault Act does contain statutory ceilings in the amount of recovery indicates an intent to limit the amount of no-fault recovery under the statute. In the *Harleysville* case, the Pennsylvania Supreme Court, in their decision to allow stacking of uninsured motorist benefits stated:

> The purpose of the uninsured motorist law is to provide protection to innocent victims of irresponsible drivers. The amount of the coverage to be afforded by the uninsured motorist feature of the policy is set by the statute, but *nowhere, explicitly or implicitly, does the act place a limit on the total amount a victim may recover if he suffers a loss resulting from the negligence of an uninsured motorist.* (emphasis added) 429 Pa. at 395, 241 A.2d 112.

In contrast to that feature in the uninsured motorist statute, the No–Fault Act does specifically place such a limit on the no-fault recovery available.

* * *

The legislature enacted the No–Fault Act [§ 1009.102] to "assure every victim * * * recovery of a *reasonable amount* of work loss, replacement services and survivor's loss." Since the legislature placed specific ceilings on those types of recovery, it can reasonably be inferred that these ceilings represent that "reasonable amount" of recovery to be provided by the Act. The legislature also found that this type of insurance law "eliminates the need to determine fault except when a victim is seriously injured." The ceilings on recovery thus represent that the legislature intended to be the demarcation between serious and minor injuries. In the case of serious injury, the tortfeasor is still intended to be the liable party.

Finally, the statute contains many inferences to the necessity of this insurance to be available to all insured parties at a low cost. We agree with the reasoning of Pontius v. United States Fidelity & Guaranty Co., 102 Dauphin Co. Rep. 432 (1981) which held that stacking is not permitted:

> Although the No–Fault Act declares essential the maximum feasible restoration of injured individuals and the compensation of economic losses, it also emphatically states and reiterates the need for its own purported design of a low cost insurance system.

The language of the legislative findings and purposes for the No–Fault Act, together with the fact that the legislature specifically included ceilings on recovery, leads this court to the conclusions that stacking is not permitted under the Pennsylvania No–Fault Act.

### *Note*

The Pennsylvania No Fault Act in place when the above opinion was written has been repealed as of October 1984 and replaced by an auto insurance system featuring certain mandatory first party benefits for accident victims with no restrictions on the right to sue. The cycle of changes in Pennsylvania revealed in the last few cases reflect part of the turmoil characteristic of the law of Insurance; as the kind (and patient) reader who has reached this point is all too well aware.

# Appendix A

# BASIC STANDARD FIRE POLICY

In Consideration of the Provisions and Stipulations Herein or Added Hereto and of the Premium Specified, this Company, for the Policy term specified in item 2 of the Declarations from inception date shown at 12:01 a.m. (Standard Time) to expiration date shown at 12:01 a.m. (Standard Time) at location of property involved, to an amount not exceeding the limit of liability specified, does insure the Insured named in item 1 of the Declarations and legal representatives, to the extent of the actual cash value of the property at the time of loss, but not exceeding the amount which it would cost to repair or replace the property with material of like kind and quality within a reasonable time after such loss, without allowance for any increased cost of repair or reconstruction by reason of any ordinance or law regulating construction or repair, and without compensation for loss resulting from interruption of business or manufacture, nor in any event for more than the interest of the Insured, against all LOSS BY FIRE, LIGHTNING AND OTHER PERILS INSURED AGAINST IN THIS POLICY INCLUDING REMOVAL FROM PREMISES ENDANGERED BY THE PERILS INSURED AGAINST IN THIS POLICY, EXCEPT AS HEREINAFTER PROVIDED, to the property described herein while located or contained as described in this policy, or pro rata for five days at each proper place to which any of the property shall necessarily be removed for preservation from the perils insured against in this policy, but not elsewhere.

Assignment of this policy shall not be valid except with the written consent of this Company.

This policy is made and accepted subject to the foregoing provisions and stipulations and those hereinafter stated, which are hereby made a part of this policy, together with such other provisions, stipulations and agreements as may be added hereto, as provided in this policy.

[C436*]

**Concealment, fraud.** This entire policy shall be void if, whether before or after a loss, the insured has wilfully concealed or misrepresented any material fact or circumstance concerning this insurance or the subject thereof, or the interest of the insured therein, or in case of any fraud or false swearing by the insured relating thereto.

**Uninsurable and excepted property.** This policy shall not cover accounts, bills, currency, deeds, evidences of debt, money or securities; nor, unless specifically named hereon in writing, bullion or manuscripts.

**Perils not included.** This Company shall not be liable for loss by fire or other perils insured against in this policy caused, directly or indirectly, by: (a) enemy attack by armed forces, including action taken by military, naval or air forces in resisting an actual or an immediately impending enemy attack; (b) invasion; (c) insurrection; (d) rebellion; (e) revolution; (f) civil war; (g) usurped power; (h) order of any civil authority except acts of destruction at the time of and for the purpose of preventing the spread of fire, provided that such fire did not originate from any of the perils excluded by this policy; (i) neglect of the insured to use all reasonable means to save and preserve the property at and after a loss, or when the property is endangered by fire in neighboring premises; (j) nor shall this Company be liable for loss by theft.

**Other insurance.** Other insurance may be prohibited or the amount of insurance may be limited by endorsement attached hereto.

**Conditions suspending or restricting insurance.** Unless otherwise provided in writing added hereto this Company shall not be liable for loss occurring (a) while the hazard is increased by any means within the control or knowledge of the insured; or (b) while a described building, whether intended for occupancy by owner or tenant, is vacant or unoccupied beyond a period of 60 consecutive days; or (c) as a result of explosion or riot, unless fire ensue, and in that event for loss by fire only.

**Other perils or subjects.** Any other peril to be insured against or subject of insurance to be covered in this policy shall be by endorsement in writing hereon or added hereto.

**Added provisions.** The extent of the application of insurance under this policy and of the contribution to be made by this Company in case of loss, and any other provision or agreement not inconsistent with the provisions of this policy, may be provided for in writing added hereto, but no provision may be waived except such as by the terms of this policy or by statute is subject to change.

**Waiver provisions.** No permission affecting this insurance shall exist, or waiver of any provision be valid, unless granted herein or expressed in writing added hereto. No provision, stipulation or forfeiture shall be held to be waived by any requirement or proceeding on the part of this Company relating to appraisal or to any examination provided for herein.

**Cancellation of policy.** This policy shall be canceled at any time at the request of the insured, in which case this Company shall, upon demand and surrender of this policy, refund the excess of paid premium above the customary short rates for the expired time. This policy may be canceled at any time by this Company by giving to the insured a five days' written notice of cancellation with or without tender of the excess of paid premium above the pro rata premium for the expired time, which excess, if not tendered, shall be refunded on demand. Notice of cancellation shall state that said excess premium (if not tendered) will be refunded on demand.

**Mortgagee interests and obligations.** If loss hereunder is made payable, in whole or in part, to a designated mortgagee not named herein as the insured, such interest in this policy may be canceled by giving to such mortgagee a 10 days' written notice of cancellation.

If the insured fails to render proof of loss such mortgagee, upon notice, shall render proof of loss in the form herein specified within sixty (60) days thereafter and shall be subject to the provisions hereof relating to appraisal and time of payment and of bringing suit. If this Company shall claim that no liability existed as to the mortgagor or owner, it shall, to the extent of payment of loss to the mortgagee, be subrogated to all the mortgagee's rights of recovery, but without impairing mortgagee's right to sue; or it may pay off the mortgage debt and require an assignment thereof and of the mortgage. Other provisions relating to the interests and obligations of such mortgagee may be added hereto by agreement in writing.

**Pro rata liability.** This Company shall not be liable for a greater proportion of any loss than the amount hereby insured shall bear to the whole insurance covering the property against the peril involved, whether collectible or not.

**Requirements in case loss occurs.** The insured shall give written notice to this Company of any loss without unnecessary delay, protect the property from further damage, forthwith separate the damaged and undamaged personal property, put it in the best possible order, furnish a complete inventory of the destroyed, damaged and undamaged property, showing in detail quantities, costs, actual cash value and amount of loss claimed; and within 60 days after the loss, unless such time is extended in writing by this Company, the insured shall render to this Company a proof of loss, signed and sworn to by the insured, stating the knowledge and belief of the insured as to the following: the time and origin of the loss, the interest of the insured and of all others in the property, the actual cash value of each item thereof and the amount of loss thereto, all encumbrances thereon, all other contracts of insurance, whether valid or not, covering any of said property, any changes in the title, use, occupation, location, possession or exposures of said property since the issuing of this policy, by whom and for what purpose any building herein described and the several parts thereof were occupied at the time of loss and whether or not it then stood on leased ground, and shall furnish a copy of all the descriptions and schedules in all policies and, if required and obtainable, verified plans and specifications of any building, fixtures or machinery destroyed or damaged. The insured, as often as may be reasonably required, shall exhibit to any person designated by this Company all that remains of any property herein described, and submit to examinations under oath by any person named by this Company, and subscribe the same; and, as often as may be reasonably required, shall produce for examination all books of account, bills, invoices and other vouchers, or certified copies thereof if originals be lost, at such reasonable time and place as may be designated by this Company or its representative, and shall permit extracts and copies thereof to be made.

**Appraisal.** In case the insured and this Company shall fail to agree as to the actual cash value or the amount of loss, then, on the written demand of either, each shall select a competent and disinterested appraiser and notify the other of the appraiser selected within 20 days of such demand. The appraisers shall first select a competent and disinterested umpire; and failing for 15 days to agree upon such umpire, then, on request of the insured or this Company, such umpire shall be selected by a judge of a court of record in the state in which the property covered is located. The appraisers shall then appraise the loss, stating separately actual cash value and loss to each item; and, failing to agree, shall submit their differences, only, to the umpire. An award in writing, so itemized, of any two when filed with this Company shall determine the amount of actual cash value and loss. Each appraiser shall be paid by the party selecting him and the expenses of appraisal and umpire shall be paid by the parties equally.

**Company's options.** It shall be optional with this Company to take all, or any part, of the property at the agreed or appraised value, and also to repair, rebuild or replace the property destroyed or damaged with other of like kind and quality within a reasonable time, on giving notice of its intention so to do within 30 days after the receipt of the proof of loss herein required.

**Abandonment.** There can be no abandonment to this Company of any property.

**When loss payable.** The amount of loss for which this Company may be liable shall be payable 60 days after proof of loss, as herein provided, is received by this Company and ascertainment of the loss is made either by agreement between the insured and this Company expressed in writing or by the filing with this Company of an award as herein provided.

**Suit.** No suit or action on this policy for the recovery of any claim shall be sustainable in any court of law or equity unless all the requirements of this policy shall have been complied with, and unless commenced within 12 months next after inception of the loss.

**Subrogation.** This Company may require from the insured an assignment of all right of recovery against any party for loss to the extent that payment therefor is made by this Company.

**In Witness Whereof,** this Company has executed and attested these presents; but this policy shall not be valid unless countersigned by the duly authorized Agent of this Company at the agency hereinbefore mentioned.

[C4362]

# Appendix B

# HOMEOWNER'S POLICY AGREEMENT

**Homeowners 3**
**Special Form**
**Ed. 4-84**

## AGREEMENT

We will provide the insurance described in this policy in return for the premium and compliance with all applicable provisions of this policy.

## DEFINITIONS

In this policy, "you" and "your" refer to the "named insured" shown in the Declarations and the spouse if a resident of the same household. "We," "us" and "our" refer to the Company providing this insurance. In addition, certain words and phrases are defined as follows:

1. **"bodily injury"** means bodily harm, sickness or disease, including required care, loss of services and death that results.
2. **"business"** includes trade, profession or occupation.
3. **"insured"** means you and residents of your household who are:
   a. your relatives; or
   b. other persons under the age of 21 and in the care of any person named above.

   Under Section II, **"insured"** also means:

   c. with respect to animals or watercraft to which this policy applies, any person or organization legally responsible for these animals or watercraft which are owned by you or any person included in 3a or 3b above. A person or organization using or having custody of these animals or watercraft in the course of any **business** or without consent of the owner is not an **insured;**

   d. with respect to any vehicle to which this policy applies:

   (1) persons while engaged in your employ or that of any person included in 3a or 3b above; or

   (2) other persons using the vehicle on an **insured location** with your consent.
4. **"insured location"** means:
   a. the **residence premises;**
   b. the part of other premises, other structures and grounds used by you as a residence and:

   (1) which is shown in the Declarations; or

   (2) which is acquired by you during the policy period for your use as a residence;

   c. any premises used by you in connection with a premises in 4a or 4b above;
   d. any part of a premises:

   (1) not owned by an **insured;** and

   (2) where an **insured** is temporarily residing;

   e. vacant land, other than farm land, owned by or rented to an **insured;**
   f. land owned by or rented to an **insured** on which a one or two family dwelling is being built as a residence for an **insured;**
   g. individual or family cemetery plots or burial vaults of an **insured**; or
   h. any part of a premises occasionally rented to an **insured** for other than **business** use.
5. **"occurrence"** means an accident, including exposure to conditions, which results, during the policy period, in:
   a. **bodily injury;** or
   b. **property damage.**
6. **"property damage"** means physical injury to, destruction of, or loss of use of tangible property.
7. **"residence employee"** means:
   a. an employee of an **insured** whose duties are related to the maintenance or use of the **residence premises,** including household or domestic services; or
   b. one who performs similar duties elsewhere not related to the **business** of an **insured.**

8. "**residence premises**" means:

   a. the one family dwelling, other structures, and grounds; or

   b. that part of any other building;

   where you reside and which is shown as the "**residence premises**" in the Declarations.

"**Residence premises**" also means a two family dwelling where you reside in at least one of the family units and which is shown as the "**residence premises**" in the Declarations.

# SECTION I—PROPERTY COVERAGES

**COVERAGE A—Dwelling**

We cover:

1. the dwelling on the **residence premises** shown in the Declarations, including structures attached to the dwelling; and
2. materials and supplies located on or next to the **residence premises** used to construct, alter or repair the dwelling or other structures on the **residence premises.**

This coverage does not apply to land, including land on which the dwelling is located.

**COVERAGE B—Other Structures**

We cover other structures on the **residence premises** set apart from the dwelling by clear space. This includes structures connected to the dwelling by only a fence, utility line, or similar connection.

This coverage does not apply to land, including land on which the other structures are located.

We do not cover other structures:

1. used in whole or in part for **business;** or
2. rented or held for rental to any person not a tenant of the dwelling, unless used solely as a private garage.

The limit of liability for this coverage will not be more than 10% of the limit of liability that applies to Coverage A. Use of this coverage does not reduce the Coverage A limit of liability.

**COVERAGE C—Personal Property**

We cover personal property owned or used by an **insured** while it is anywhere in the world. At your request, we will cover personal property owned by:

1. others while the property is on the part of the **residence premises** occupied by an **insured;**
2. a guest or a **residence employee,** while the property is in any residence occupied by an **insured.**

Our limit of liability for personal property usually located at an **insured's** residence, other than the **residence premises,** is 10% of the limit of liability for Coverage C, or $1000, whichever is greater. Personal property in a newly acquired principal residence is not subject to this limitation for the 30 days from the time you begin to move the property there.

**Special Limits of Liability.** These limits do not increase the Coverage C limit of liability. The special limit for each numbered category below is the total limit for each loss for all property in that category.

1. $200 on money, bank notes, bullion, gold other than goldware, silver other than silverware, platinum, coins and medals.
2. $1000 on securities, accounts, deeds, evidences of debt, letters of credit, notes other than bank notes, manuscripts, passports, tickets and stamps.
3. $1000 on watercraft, including their trailers, furnishings, equipment and outboard motors.
4. $1000 on trailers not used with watercraft.
5. $1000 on grave markers.
6. $1000 for loss by theft of jewelry, watches, furs, precious and semi-precious stones.
7. $2000 for loss by theft of firearms.
8. $2500 for loss by theft of silverware, silver-plated ware, goldware, gold-plated ware and pewterware. This includes flatware, hollowware, tea sets, trays and trophies made of or including silver, gold or pewter.
9. $2500 on property, on the **residence premises,** used at any time or in any manner for any **business** purpose.
10. $250 on property, away from the **residence premises,** used at any time or in any manner for any **business** purpose.

**Property Not Covered.** We do not cover:

1. articles separately described and specifically insured in this or other insurance;
2. animals, birds or fish;
3. motor vehicles or all other motorized land conveyances. This includes:
   a. equipment and accessories; or
   b. any device or instrument for the transmitting, recording, receiving or reproduction of sound or pictures which is operated by power from the electrical system of motor vehicles or all other motorized land conveyances, including:
      (1) accessories or antennas; or
      (2) tapes, wires, records, discs or other media for use with any such device or instrument;

   while in or upon the vehicle or conveyance.

   We do cover vehicles or conveyances not subject to motor vehicle registration which are:
   a. used to service an **insured's** residence; or
   b. designed for assisting the handicapped;
4. aircraft and parts. Aircraft means any contrivance used or designed for flight, except model or hobby aircraft not used or designed to carry people or cargo;
5. property of roomers, boarders and other tenants, except property of roomers and boarders related to an **insured;**
6. property in an apartment regularly rented or held for rental to others by an **insured;**
7. property rented or held for rental to others off the **residence premises;**
8. a. books of account, drawings or other paper records; or
   b. electronic data processing tapes, wires, records, discs or other software media;

   containing **business** data. But, we do cover the cost of blank or unexposed records and media;
9. credit cards or fund transfer cards except as provided in Additional Coverages 6.

**COVERAGE D—Loss Of Use**

The limit of liability for Coverage D is the total limit for all the coverages that follow.

1. If a loss covered under this Section makes that part of the **residence premises** where you reside not fit to live in, we cover, at your choice, either of the following. However, if the **residence premises** is not your principal place of residence, we will not provide the option under paragraph b. below.
   a. **Additional Living Expense,** meaning any necessary increase in living expenses incurred by you so that your household can maintain its normal standard of living; or
   b. **Fair Rental Value,** meaning the fair rental value of that part of the **residence premises** where you reside less any expenses that do not continue while the premises is not fit to live in.

   Payment under a. or b. will be for the shortest time required to repair or replace the damage or, if you permanently relocate, the shortest time required for your household to settle elsewhere.
2. If a loss covered under this Section makes that part of the **residence premises** rented to others or held for rental by you not fit to live in, we cover the:

   **Fair Rental Value,** meaning the fair rental value of that part of the **residence premises** rented to others or held for rental by you less any expenses that do not continue while the premises is not fit to live in.

   Payment will be for the shortest time required to repair or replace that part of the premises rented or held for rental.
3. If a civil authority prohibits you from use of the **residence premises** as a result of direct damage to neighboring premises by a Peril Insured Against in this policy, we cover the Additional Living Expense or Fair Rental Value loss as provided under 1 and 2 above for no more than two weeks.

The periods of time under 1, 2 and 3 above are not limited by expiration of this policy.

We do not cover loss or expense due to cancellation of a lease or agreement.

**ADDITIONAL COVERAGES**

1. **Debris Removal.** We will pay your reasonable expense for the removal of:
   a. debris of covered property if a Peril Insured Against causes the loss; or
   b. ash, dust or particles from a volcanic eruption that has caused direct loss to a building or property contained in a building.

   This expense is included in the limit of liability that applies to the damaged property. If the amount to be paid for the actual damage to the property plus the debris removal expense is more than the limit of liability for the damaged property, an additional 5% of that limit of liability is available for debris removal expense.

  

We will also pay your reasonable expense for the removal of fallen trees from the **residence premises** if:

a. coverage is not afforded under Additional Coverages 3. Trees, Shrubs and Other Plants for the peril causing the loss; or

b. the tree is not covered by this policy;

provided the tree damages covered property and a Peril Insured Against under Coverage C causes the tree to fall. Our limit of liability for this coverage will not be more than $500 in the aggregate for any one loss.

2. **Reasonable Repairs.** We will pay the reasonable cost incurred by you for necessary repairs made solely to protect covered property from further damage if a Peril Insured Against causes the loss. This coverage does not increase the limit of liability that applies to the property being repaired.

3. **Trees, Shrubs and Other Plants.** We cover trees, shrubs, plants or lawns, on the **residence premises,** for loss caused by the following Perils Insured Against: Fire or lightning, Explosion, Riot or civil commotion, Aircraft, Vehicles not owned or operated by a resident of the **residence premises,** Vandalism or malicious mischief or Theft.

The limit of liability for this coverage will not be more than 5% of the limit of liability that applies to the dwelling, or more than $500 for any one tree, shrub or plant. We do not cover property grown for **business** purposes.

This coverage is additional insurance.

4. **Fire Department Service Charge.** We will pay up to $500 for your liability assumed by contract or agreement for fire department charges incurred when the fire department is called to save or protect covered property from a Peril Insured Against. We do not cover fire department service charges if the property is located within the limits of the city, municipality or protection district furnishing the fire department response.

This coverage is additional insurance. No deductible applies to this coverage.

5. **Property Removed.** We insure covered property against direct loss from any cause while being removed from a premises endangered by a Peril Insured Against and for no more than 30 days while removed. This coverage does not change the limit of liability that applies to the property being removed.

6. **Credit Card, Fund Transfer Card, Forgery and Counterfeit Money.**

We will pay up to $500 for:

a. the legal obligation of an **insured** to pay because of the theft or unauthorized use of credit cards issued to or registered in an **insured's** name;

b. loss resulting from theft or unauthorized use of a fund transfer card used for deposit, withdrawal or transfer of funds, issued to or registered in an **insured's** name;

c. loss to an **insured** caused by forgery or alteration of any check or negotiable instrument; and

d. loss to an **insured** through acceptance in good faith of counterfeit United States or Canadian paper currency.

We do not cover use of a credit card or fund transfer card:

a. by a resident of your household;

b. by a person who has been entrusted with either type of card; or

c. if an **insured** has not complied with all terms and conditions under which the cards are issued.

All loss resulting from a series of acts committed by any one person or in which any one person is concerned or implicated is considered to be one loss.

We do not cover loss arising out of **business** use or dishonesty of an **insured.**

This coverage is additional insurance. No deductible applies to this coverage.

Defense:

a. We may investigate and settle any claim or suit that we decide is appropriate. Our duty to defend a claim or suit ends when the amount we pay for the loss equals our limit of liability.

b. If a suit is brought against an **insured** for liability under the Credit Card or Fund Transfer Card coverage, we will provide a defense at our expense by counsel of our choice.

c. We have the option to defend at our expense an **insured** or an **insured's** bank against any suit for the enforcement of payment under the Forgery coverage.

7. **Loss Assessment.** We will pay up to $1000 for your share of any loss assessment charged during the policy period against you by a corporation or association of property owners. This only applies when the assessment is made as a result of each direct loss to the property, owned by all members collectively, caused by a Peril Insured Against under Coverage A—Dwelling, other than earthquake or land shock waves or tremors before, during or after a volcanic eruption.

This coverage applies only to loss assessments charged against you as owner or tenant of the **residence premises.**

We do not cover loss assessments charged against you or a corporation or association of property owners by any governmental body.

  

**8. Collapse.** We insure for direct physical loss to covered property involving collapse of a building or any part of a building caused only by one or more of the following:

a. Perils Insured Against in Coverage C—Personal Property. These perils apply to covered building and personal property for loss insured by this additional coverage;

b. hidden decay;

c. hidden insect or vermin damage;

d. weight of contents, equipment, animals or people;

e. weight of rain which collects on a roof; or

f. use of defective material or methods in construction, remodeling or renovation if the collapse occurs during the course of the construction, remodeling or renovation.

Loss to an awning, fence, patio, pavement, swimming pool, underground pipe, flue, drain, cesspool, septic tank, foundation, retaining wall, bulkhead, pier, wharf or dock is not included under items b, c, d, e, and f unless the loss is a direct result of the collapse of a building.

Collapse does not include settling, cracking, shrinking, bulging or expansion.

This coverage does not increase the limit of liability applying to the damaged covered property.

# SECTION I—PERILS INSURED AGAINST

**COVERAGE A—DWELLING and**
**COVERAGE B—OTHER STRUCTURES**

We insure against risks of direct loss to property described in Coverages A and B only if that loss is a physical loss to property; however, we do not insure loss:

**1.** involving collapse, other than as provided in Additional Coverage 8;

**2.** caused by:

a. freezing of a plumbing, heating, air conditioning or automatic fire protective sprinkler system or of a household appliance, or by discharge, leakage or overflow from within the system or appliance caused by freezing. This exclusion applies only while the dwelling is vacant, unoccupied or being constructed unless you have used reasonable care to:

(1) maintain heat in the building; or

(2) shut off the water supply and drain the system and appliances of water;

b. freezing, thawing, pressure or weight of water or ice, whether driven by wind or not, to a:

(1) fence, pavement, patio or swimming pool;

(2) foundation, retaining wall or bulkhead; or

(3) pier, wharf or dock;

c. theft in or to a dwelling under construction, or of materials and supplies for use in the construction until the dwelling is finished and occupied;

d. vandalism and malicious mischief or breakage of glass and safety glazing materials if the dwelling has been vacant for more than 30 consecutive days immediately before the loss. A dwelling being constructed is not considered vacant;

e. constant or repeated seepage or leakage of water or steam over a period of weeks, months or years from within a plumbing, heating, air conditioning or automatic fire protective sprinkler system or from within a household appliance;

f. (1) wear and tear, marring, deterioration;

(2) inherent vice, latent defect, mechanical breakdown;

(3) smog, rust, mold, wet or dry rot;

(4) smoke from agricultural smudging or industrial operations;

(5) release, discharge or dispersal of contaminants or pollutants;

(6) settling, cracking, shrinking, bulging or expansion of pavements, patios, foundations, walls, floors, roofs or ceilings; or

(7) birds, vermin, rodents, insects or domestic animals.

If any of these cause water damage not otherwise excluded, from a plumbing, heating, air conditioning or automatic fire protective sprinkler system or household appliance, we cover loss caused by the water including the cost of tearing out and replacing any part of a building necessary to repair the system or appliance. We do not cover loss to the system or appliance from which this water escaped.

**3.** excluded under Section I—Exclusions.

Under items 1 and 2, any ensuing loss to property described in Coverages A and B not excluded or excepted in this policy is covered.

  

**COVERAGE C—PERSONAL PROPERTY**

We insure for direct physical loss to the property described in Coverage C caused by a peril listed below unless the loss is excluded in Section I—Exclusions.

1. **Fire or lightning.**
2. **Windstorm or hail.**

   This peril does not include loss to the property contained in a building caused by rain, snow, sleet, sand or dust unless the direct force of wind or hail damages the building causing an opening in a roof or wall and the rain, snow, sleet, sand or dust enters through this opening.

   This peril includes loss to watercraft and their trailers, furnishings, equipment, and outboard motors, only while inside a fully enclosed building.
3. **Explosion.**
4. **Riot or civil commotion.**
5. **Aircraft,** including self-propelled missiles and spacecraft.
6. **Vehicles.**
7. **Smoke,** meaning sudden and accidental damage from smoke.

   This peril does not include loss caused by smoke from agricultural smudging or industrial operations.
8. **Vandalism or malicious mischief.**
9. **Theft,** including attempted theft and loss of property from a known place when it is likely that the property has been stolen.

   This peril does not include loss caused by theft:

   a. committed by an **insured;**

   b. in or to a dwelling under construction, or of materials and supplies for use in the construction until the dwelling is finished and occupied; or

   c. from that part of a **residence premises** rented by an **insured** to other than an **insured.**

   This peril does not include loss caused by theft that occurs off the **residence premises** of:

   a. property while at any other residence owned by, rented to, or occupied by an **insured,** except while an **insured** is temporarily living there. Property of a student who is an **insured** is covered while at a residence away from home if the student has been there at any time during the 45 days immediately before the loss;

   b. watercraft, including their furnishings, equipment and outboard motors; or

   c. trailers and campers.
10. **Falling objects.**

    This peril does not include loss to property contained in a building unless the roof or an outside wall of the building is first damaged by a falling object. Damage to the falling object itself is not included.
11. **Weight of ice, snow or sleet** which causes damage to property contained in a building.
12. **Accidental discharge or overflow of water or steam** from within a plumbing, heating, air conditioning or automatic fire protective sprinkler system or from within a household appliance.

    This peril does not include loss:

    a. to the system or appliance from which the water or steam escaped;

    b. caused by or resulting from freezing except as provided in the peril of freezing below; or

    c. on the **residence premises** caused by accidental discharge or overflow which occurs off the **residence premises.**
13. **Sudden and accidental tearing apart, cracking, burning or bulging** of a steam or hot water heating system, an air conditioning or automatic fire protective sprinkler system, or an appliance for heating water.

    We do not cover loss caused by or resulting from freezing under this peril.
14. **Freezing** of a plumbing, heating, air conditioning or automatic fire protective sprinkler system or of a household appliance.

    This peril does not include loss on the **residence premises** while the dwelling is unoccupied, unless you have used reasonable care to:

    a. maintain heat in the building; or

    b. shut off the water supply and drain the system and appliances of water.
15. **Sudden and accidental damage from artificially generated electrical current.**

    This peril does not include loss to a tube, transistor or similar electronic component.
16. **Damage by glass or safety glazing material** which is part of a building, storm door or storm window.

    This peril does not include loss on the **residence premises** if the dwelling has been vacant for more than 30 consecutive days immediately before the loss. A dwelling being constructed is not considered vacant.
17. **Volcanic Eruption** other than loss caused by earthquake, land shock waves or tremors.

  

# SECTION I—EXCLUSIONS

1. We do not insure for loss caused directly or indirectly by any of the following. Such loss is excluded regardless of any other cause or event contributing concurrently or in any sequence to the loss.

   a. **Ordinance or Law,** meaning enforcement of any ordinance or law regulating the construction, repair, or demolition of a building or other structure, unless specifically provided under this policy.

   b. **Earth Movement,** meaning earthquake including land shock waves or tremors before, during or after a volcanic eruption; landslide; mudflow; earth sinking, rising or shifting; unless direct loss by:

      (1) fire;

      (2) explosion; or

      (3) breakage of glass or safety glazing material which is part of a building, storm door or storm window;

      ensues and then we will pay only for the ensuing loss.

      This exclusion does not apply to loss by theft.

   c. **Water Damage,** meaning:

      (1) flood, surface water, waves, tidal water, overflow of a body of water, or spray from any of these, whether or not driven by wind;

      (2) water which backs up through sewers or drains; or

      (3) water below the surface of the ground, including water which exerts pressure on or seeps or leaks through a building, sidewalk, driveway, foundation, swimming pool or other structure.

      Direct loss by fire, explosion or theft resulting from water damage is covered.

   d. **Power Failure,** meaning the failure of power or other utility service if the failure takes place off the **residence premises.** But, if a Peril Insured Against ensues on the **residence premises,** we will pay only for that ensuing loss.

   e. **Neglect,** meaning neglect of the **insured** to use all reasonable means to save and preserve property at and after the time of a loss.

   f. **War,** including undeclared war, civil war, insurrection, rebellion, revolution, warlike act by a military force or military personnel, destruction or seizure or use for a military purpose, and including any consequence of any of these. Discharge of a nuclear weapon will be deemed a warlike act even if accidental.

   g. **Nuclear Hazard,** to the extent set forth in the Nuclear Hazard Clause of Section I—Conditions.

   h. **Intentional Loss,** meaning any loss arising out of any act committed:

      (1) by or at the direction of an **insured;** and

      (2) with the intent to cause a loss.

2. We do not insure for loss to property described in Coverages A and B caused by any of the following. However, any ensuing loss to property described in Coverages A and B not excluded or excepted in this policy is covered.

   a. **Weather conditions.** However, this exclusion only applies if weather conditions contribute in any way with a cause or event excluded in paragraph 1. above to produce the loss;

   b. **Acts or decisions,** including the failure to act or decide, of any person, group, organization or governmental body;

   c. **Faulty, inadequate or defective:**

      (1) planning, zoning, development, surveying, siting;

      (2) design, specifications, workmanship, repair, construction, renovation, remodeling, grading, compaction;

      (3) materials used in repair, construction, renovation or remodeling; or

      (4) maintenance;

      of part or all of any property whether on or off the **residence premises.**

## SECTION I—CONDITIONS

1. **Insurable Interest and Limit of Liability.** Even if more than one person has an insurable interest in the property covered, we will not be liable in any one loss:

   a. to the **insured** for more than the amount of the **insured's** interest at the time of loss; or

   b. for more than the applicable limit of liability.

2. **Your Duties After Loss.** In case of a loss to covered property, you must see that the following are done:

   a. give prompt notice to us or our agent;

   b. notify the police in case of loss by theft;

   c. notify the credit card or fund transfer card company in case of loss under Credit Card or Fund Transfer Card coverage;

   d. (1) protect the property from further damage;

      (2) make reasonable and necessary repairs to protect the property; and

      (3) keep an accurate record of repair expenses;

   e. prepare an inventory of damaged personal property showing the quantity, description, actual cash value and amount of loss. Attach all bills, receipts and related documents that justify the figures in the inventory;

   f. as often as we reasonably require:

      (1) show the damaged property;

      (2) provide us with records and documents we request and permit us to make copies; and

      (3) submit to questions under oath and sign and swear to them;

   g. send to us, within 60 days after our request, your signed, sworn proof of loss which sets forth, to the best of your knowledge and belief:

      (1) the time and cause of loss;

      (2) the interest of the **insured** and all others in the property involved and all liens on the property;

      (3) other insurance which may cover the loss;

      (4) changes in title or occupancy of the property during the term of the policy;

      (5) specifications of damaged buildings and detailed repair estimates;

      (6) the inventory of damaged personal property described in 2e above;

      (7) receipts for additional living expenses incurred and records that support the fair rental value loss; and

      (8) evidence or affidavit that supports a claim under the Credit Card, Fund Transfer Card, Forgery and Counterfeit Money coverage, stating the amount and cause of loss.

3. **Loss Settlement.** Covered property losses are settled as follows:

   a. (1) Personal property;

      (2) Awnings, carpeting, household appliances, outdoor antennas and outdoor equipment, whether or not attached to buildings; and

      (3) Structures that are not buildings;

   at actual cash value at the time of loss but not more than the amount required to repair or replace.

   b. Buildings under Coverage A or B at replacement cost without deduction for depreciation, subject to the following:

      (1) If, at the time of loss, the amount of insurance in this policy on the damaged building is 80% or more of the full replacement cost of the building immediately before the loss, we will pay the cost to repair or replace, after application of deductible and without deduction for depreciation, but not more than the least of the following amounts:

         (a) the limit of liability under this policy that applies to the building;

         (b) the replacement cost of that part of the building damaged for like construction and use on the same premises; or

         (c) the necessary amount actually spent to repair or replace the damaged building.

  

(2) If, at the time of loss, the amount of insurance in this policy on the damaged building is less than 80% of the full replacement cost of the building immediately before the loss, we will pay the greater of the following amounts, but not more than the limit of liability under this policy that applies to the building:

(a) the actual cash value of that part of the building damaged; or

(b) that proportion of the cost to repair or replace, after application of deductible and without deduction for depreciation, that part of the building damaged, which the total amount of insurance in this policy on the damaged building bears to 80% of the replacement cost of the building.

(3) To determine the amount of insurance required to equal 80% of the full replacement cost of the building immediately before the loss, do not include the value of:

(a) excavations, foundations, piers or any supports which are below the undersurface of the lowest basement floor;

(b) those supports in (a) above which are below the surface of the ground inside the foundation walls, if there is no basement; and

(c) underground flues, pipes, wiring and drains.

(4) We will pay no more than the actual cash value of the damage unless:

(a) actual repair or replacement is complete; or

(b) the cost to repair or replace the damage is both:

(i) less than 5% of the amount of insurance in this policy on the building; and

(ii) less than $1000.

(5) You may disregard the replacement cost loss settlement provisions and make claim under this policy for loss or damage to buildings on an actual cash value basis. You may then make claim within 180 days after loss for any additional liability on a replacement cost basis.

4. **Loss to a Pair or Set.** In case of loss to a pair or set we may elect to:

a. repair or replace any part to restore the pair or set to its value before the loss; or

b. pay the difference between actual cash value of the property before and after the loss.

5. **Glass Replacement.** Loss for damage to glass caused by a Peril Insured Against will be settled on the basis of replacement with safety glazing materials when required by ordinance or law.

6. **Appraisal.** If you and we fail to agree on the amount of loss, either may demand an appraisal of the loss. In this event, each party will choose a competent appraiser within 20 days after receiving a written request from the other. The two appraisers will choose an umpire. If they cannot agree upon an umpire within 15 days, you or we may request that the choice be made by a judge of a court of record in the state where the **residence premises** is located. The appraisers will separately set the amount of loss. If the appraisers submit a written report of an agreement to us, the amount agreed upon will be the amount of loss. If they fail to agree, they will submit their differences to the umpire. A decision agreed to by any two will set the amount of loss.

Each party will:

a. pay its own appraiser; and

b. bear the other expenses of the appraisal and umpire equally.

7. **Other Insurance.** If a loss covered by this policy is also covered by other insurance, we will pay only the proportion of the loss that the limit of liability that applies under this policy bears to the total amount of insurance covering the loss.

8. **Suit Against Us.** No action can be brought unless the policy provisions have been complied with and the action is started within one year after the date of loss.

9. **Our Option.** If we give you written notice within 30 days after we receive your signed, sworn proof of loss, we may repair or replace any part of the damaged property with like property.

10. **Loss Payment.** We will adjust all losses with you. We will pay you unless some other person is named in the policy or is legally entitled to receive payment. Loss will be payable 60 days after we receive your proof of loss and:

a. reach an agreement with you;

b. there is an entry of a final judgment; or

c. there is a filing of an appraisal award with us.

11. **Abandonment of Property.** We need not accept any property abandoned by an **insured.**

  

**12. Mortgage Clause.**

The word "mortgagee" includes trustee.

If a mortgagee is named in this policy, any loss payable under Coverage A or B will be paid to the mortgagee and you, as interests appear. If more than one mortgagee is named, the order of payment will be the same as the order of precedence of the mortgages.

If we deny your claim, that denial will not apply to a valid claim of the mortgagee, if the mortgagee:

a. notifies us of any change in ownership, occupancy or substantial change in risk of which the mortgagee is aware;

b. pays any premium due under this policy on demand if you have neglected to pay the premium; and

c. submits a signed, sworn statement of loss within 60 days after receiving notice from us of your failure to do so. Policy conditions relating to Appraisal, Suit Against Us and Loss Payment apply to the mortgagee.

If the policy is cancelled or not renewed by us, the mortgagee will be notified at least 10 days before the date cancellation or nonrenewal takes effect.

If we pay the mortgagee for any loss and deny payment to you:

a. we are subrogated to all the rights of the mortgagee granted under the mortgage on the property; or

b. at our option, we may pay to the mortgagee the whole principal on the mortgage plus any accrued interest. In this event, we will receive a full assignment and transfer of the mortgage and all securities held as collateral to the mortgage debt.

Subrogation will not impair the right of the mortgagee to recover the full amount of the mortgagee's claim.

**13. No Benefit to Bailee.** We will not recognize any assignment or grant any coverage that benefits a person or organization holding, storing or moving property for a fee regardless of any other provision of this policy.

**14. Nuclear Hazard Clause.**

a. "Nuclear Hazard" means any nuclear reaction, radiation, or radioactive contamination, all whether controlled or uncontrolled or however caused, or any consequence of any of these.

b. Loss caused by the nuclear hazard will not be considered loss caused by fire, explosion, or smoke, whether these perils are specifically named in or otherwise included within the Perils Insured Against in Section I.

c. This policy does not apply under Section I to loss caused directly or indirectly by nuclear hazard, except that direct loss by fire resulting from the nuclear hazard is covered.

**15. Recovered Property.** If you or we recover any property for which we have made payment under this policy, you or we will notify the other of the recovery. At your option, the property will be returned to or retained by you or it will become our property. If the recovered property is returned to or retained by you, the loss payment will be adjusted based on the amount you received for the recovered property.

**16. Volcanic Eruption Period.** One or more volcanic eruptions that occur within a 72-hour period will be considered as one volcanic eruption.

## SECTION II—LIABILITY COVERAGES

**COVERAGE E — Personal Liability**

If a claim is made or a suit is brought against an **insured** for damages because of **bodily injury** or **property damage** caused by an **occurrence** to which this coverage applies, we will:

1. pay up to our limit of liability for the damages for which the **insured** is legally liable; and

2. provide a defense at our expense by counsel of our choice, even if the suit is groundless, false or fraudulent. We may investigate and settle any claim or suit that we decide is appropriate. Our duty to settle or defend ends when the amount we pay for damages resulting from the **occurrence** equals our limit of liability.

**COVERAGE F — Medical Payments To Others**

We will pay the necessary medical expenses that are incurred or medically ascertained within three years from the date of an accident causing **bodily injury.** Medical expenses means reasonable charges for medical, surgical, x-ray, dental, ambulance, hospital, professional nursing, prosthetic devices and funeral services. This coverage does not apply to you or regular residents of your household except **residence employees.** As to others, this coverage applies only:

1. to a person on the **insured location** with the permission of an **insured;** or

  

2. to a person off the **insured location,** if the **bodily injury:**
   a. arises out of a condition on the **insured location** or the ways immediately adjoining;
   b. is caused by the activities of an **insured;**
   c. is caused by a **residence employee** in the course of the **residence employee's** employment by an **insured;** or
   d. is caused by an animal owned by or in the care of an **insured.**

# SECTION II—EXCLUSIONS

1. **Coverage E — Personal Liability and Coverage F — Medical Payments to Others** do not apply to **bodily injury** or **property damage:**
   a. which is expected or intended by the **insured;**
   b. arising out of **business** pursuits of an **insured** or the rental or holding for rental of any part of any premises by an **insured.**

      This exclusion does not apply to:

      (1) activities which are usual to non-**business** pursuits; or

      (2) the rental or holding for rental of an **insured location:**

      (a) on an occasional basis if used only as a residence;

      (b) in part for use only as a residence, unless a single family unit is intended for use by the occupying family to lodge more than two roomers or boarders; or

      (c) in part, as an office, school, studio or private garage;
   c. arising out of the rendering of or failure to render professional services;
   d. arising out of a premises:

      (1) owned by an **insured;**

      (2) rented to an **insured;** or

      (3) rented to others by an **insured;**

      that is not an **insured location;**
   e. arising out of:

      (1) the ownership, maintenance, use, loading or unloading of motor vehicles or all other motorized land conveyances, including trailers, owned or operated by or rented or loaned to an **insured;**

      (2) the entrustment by an **insured** of a motor vehicle or any other motorized land conveyance to any person; or

      (3) statutorily imposed vicarious parental liability for the actions of a child or minor using a conveyance excluded in paragraph (1) or (2) above.

      This exclusion does not apply to:

      (1) a trailer not towed by or carried on a motorized land conveyance.

      (2) a motorized land conveyance designed for recreational use off public roads, not subject to motor vehicle registration and:

      (a) not owned by an **insured;** or

      (b) owned by an **insured** and on an **insured location.**

      (3) a motorized golf cart when used to play golf on a golf course.

      (4) a vehicle or conveyance not subject to motor vehicle registration which is:

      (a) used to service an **insured's** residence;

      (b) designed for assisting the handicapped; or

      (c) in dead storage on an **insured location.**
   f. arising out of:

      (1) the ownership, maintenance, use, loading or unloading of a watercraft described below;

      (2) the entrustment by an **insured** of a watercraft described below to any person; or

      (3) statutorily imposed vicarious parental liability for the actions of a child or minor using a watercraft described below.

      Watercraft:

      (1) with inboard or inboard-outdrive motor power owned by an **insured;**

      (2) with inboard or inboard-outdrive motor power of more than 50 horsepower rented to an **insured;**

(3) that is a sailing vessel, with or without auxiliary power, 26 feet or more in length owned by or rented to an **insured;** or

(4) powered by one or more outboard motors with more than 25 total horsepower if the outboard motor is owned by an **insured.** But, outboard motors of more than 25 total horsepower are covered for the policy period if:

(a) you acquire them prior to the policy period and:

(i) you declare them at policy inception; or

(ii) your intention to insure is reported to us in writing within 45 days after you acquire the outboard motors.

(b) you acquire them during the policy period.

This exclusion does not apply while the watercraft is stored.

g. arising out of:

(1) the ownership, maintenance, use, loading or unloading of an aircraft;

(2) the entrustment by an **insured** of an aircraft to any person; or

(3) statutorily imposed vicarious parental liability for the actions of a child or minor using an aircraft.

An aircraft means any contrivance used or designed for flight, except model or hobby aircraft not used or designed to carry people or cargo.

h. caused directly or indirectly by war, including undeclared war, civil war, insurrection, rebellion, revolution, warlike act by a military force or military personnel, destruction or seizure or use for a military purpose, and including any consequence of any of these. Discharge of a nuclear weapon will be deemed a warlike act even if accidental.

Exclusions d., e., f., and g. do not apply to **bodily injury** to a **residence employee** arising out of and in the course of the **residence employee's** employment by an **insured.**

2. **Coverage E — Personal Liability,** does not apply to:

a. liability:

(1) for your share of any loss assessment charged against all members of an association, corporation or community of property owners;

(2) under any contract or agreement. However, this exclusion does not apply to written contracts:

(a) that directly relate to the ownership, maintenance or use of an **insured location;** or

(b) where the liability of others is assumed by the **insured** prior to an **occurrence;**

unless excluded in (1) above or elsewhere in this policy;

b. **property damage** to property owned by the **insured;**

c. **property damage** to property rented to, occupied or used by or in the care of the **insured.** This exclusion does not apply to **property damage** caused by fire, smoke or explosion;

d. **bodily injury** to any person eligible to receive any benefits:

(1) voluntarily provided; or

(2) required to be provided;

by the **insured** under any:

(1) workers' compensation law;

(2) non-occupational disability law; or

(3) occupational disease law;

e. **bodily injury** or **property damage** for which an **insured** under this policy:

(1) is also an insured under a nuclear energy liability policy; or

(2) would be an insured under that policy but for the exhaustion of its limit of liability.

A nuclear energy liability policy is one issued by:

(1) American Nuclear Insurers;

(2) Mutual Atomic Energy Liability Underwriters;

(3) Nuclear Insurance Association of Canada;

or any of their successors; or

f. **bodily injury** to you or an **insured** within the meaning of part a. or b. of "**insured**" as defined.

  

3. **Coverage F—Medical Payments to Others,** does not apply to **bodily injury:**

   a. to a **residence employee** if the **bodily injury:**

      (1) occurs off the **insured location;** and

      (2) does not arise out of or in the course of the **residence employee's** employment by an **insured;**

   b. to any person eligible to receive benefits:

      (1) voluntarily provided; or

      (2) required to be provided;

      under any:

      (1) workers' compensation law;

      (2) non-occupational disability law; or

      (3) occupational disease law;

   c. from any:

      (1) nuclear reaction;

      (2) nuclear radiation; or

      (3) radioactive contamination;

      all whether controlled or uncontrolled or however caused; or

      (4) any consequence of any of these.

   d. to any person, other than a **residence employee** of an **insured**, regularly residing on any part of the **insured location.**

## SECTION II—ADDITIONAL COVERAGES

We cover the following in addition to the limits of liability:

1. **Claim Expenses.** We pay:

   a. expenses we incur and costs taxed against an **insured** in any suit we defend;

   b. premiums on bonds required in a suit we defend, but not for bond amounts more than the limit of liability for Coverage E. We need not apply for or furnish any bond;

   c. reasonable expenses incurred by an **insured** at our request, including actual loss of earnings (but not loss of other income) up to $50 per day, for assisting us in the investigation or defense of a claim or suit;

   d. interest on the entire judgment which accrues after entry of the judgment and before we pay or tender, or deposit in court that part of the judgment which does not exceed the limit of liability that applies;

   e. prejudgment interest awarded against the **insured** on that part of the judgment we pay. If we make an offer to pay the applicable limit of liability, we will not pay any prejudgment interest based on that period of time after the offer.

2. **First Aid Expenses.** We will pay expenses for first aid to others incurred by an **insured** for **bodily injury** covered under this policy. We will not pay for first aid to you or any other **insured.**

3. **Damage to Property of Others.** We will pay, at replacement cost, up to $500 per **occurrence** for **property damage** to property of others caused by an **insured.**

   We will not pay for **property damage:**

   a. to the extent of any amount recoverable under Section I of this policy;

   b. caused intentionally by an **insured** who is 13 years of age or older;

   c. to property owned by an **insured;**

   d. to property owned by or rented to a tenant of an **insured** or a resident in your household; or

   e. arising out of:

      (1) **business** pursuits;

      (2) any act or omission in connection with a premises owned, rented or controlled by an **insured,** other than the **insured location;** or

      (3) the ownership, maintenance, or use of aircraft, watercraft or motor vehicles or all other motorized land conveyances.

      This exclusion does not apply to a motorized land conveyance designed for recreational use off public roads, not subject to motor vehicle registration and not owned by an **insured.**

4. **Loss Assessment.** We will pay up to $1000 for your share of any loss assessment charged during the policy period against you by a corporation or association of property owners, when the assessment is made as a result of:

   a. each **occurrence** to which Section II of this policy would apply;

  

b. liability for each act of a director, officer or trustee in the capacity as a director, officer or trustee, provided:

(1) the director, officer or trustee is elected by the members of a corporation or association of property owners; and

(2) the director, officer or trustee serves without deriving any income from the exercise of duties which are solely on behalf of a corporation or association of property owners.

This coverage applies only to loss assessments charged against you as owner or tenant of the **residence premises.**

We do not cover loss assessments charged against you or a corporation or association of property owners by any governmental body.

Section II — Coverage E — Personal Liability Exclusion 2.a.(1) does not apply to this coverage.

# SECTION II—CONDITIONS

1. **Limit of Liability.** Our total liability under Coverage E for all damages resulting from any one **occurrence** will not be more than the limit of liability for Coverage E as shown in the Declarations. This limit is the same regardless of the number of **insureds,** claims made or persons injured.

   Our total liability under Coverage F for all medical expense payable for **bodily injury** to one person as the result of one accident will not be more than the limit of liability for Coverage F as shown in the Declarations.

2. **Severability of Insurance.** This insurance applies separately to each **insured.** This condition will not increase our limit of liability for any one **occurrence.**

3. **Duties After Loss.** In case of an accident or **occurrence,** the **insured** will perform the following duties that apply. You will help us by seeing that these duties are performed:

   a. give written notice to us or our agent as soon as is practical, which sets forth:

      (1) the identity of the policy and **insured;**

      (2) reasonably available information on the time, place and circumstances of the accident or **occurrence;** and

      (3) names and addresses of any claimants and witnesses;

   b. promptly forward to us every notice, demand, summons or other process relating to the accident or **occurrence;**

   c. at our request, help us:

      (1) to make settlement;

      (2) to enforce any right of contribution or indemnity against any person or organization who may be liable to an **insured;**

      (3) with the conduct of suits and attend hearings and trials;

      (4) to secure and give evidence and obtain the attendance of witnesses;

   d. under the coverage — Damage to Property of Others — submit to us within 60 days after the loss, a sworn statement of loss and show the damaged property, if in the **insured's** control;

   e. the **insured** will not, except at the **insured's** own cost, voluntarily make payment, assume obligation or incur expense other than for first aid to others at the time of the **bodily injury.**

4. **Duties of an Injured Person—Coverage F—Medical Payments to Others.**

   The injured person or someone acting for the injured person will:

   a. give us written proof of claim, under oath if required, as soon as is practical; and

   b. authorize us to obtain copies of medical reports and records.

   The injured person will submit to a physical exam by a doctor of our choice when and as often as we reasonably require.

5. **Payment of Claim—Coverage F—Medical Payments to Others.** Payment under this coverage is not an admission of liability by an **insured** or us.

6. **Suit Against Us.** No action can be brought against us unless there has been compliance with the policy provisions.

   No one will have the right to join us as a party to any action against an **insured.** Also, no action with respect to Coverage E can be brought against us until the obligation of the **insured** has been determined by final judgment or agreement signed by us.

7. **Bankruptcy of an Insured.** Bankruptcy or insolvency of an **insured** will not relieve us of our obligations under this policy.

8. **Other Insurance — Coverage E — Personal Liability.** This insurance is excess over other valid and collectible insurance except insurance written specifically to cover as excess over the limits of liability that apply in this policy.

  

## SECTIONS I AND II—CONDITIONS

1. **Policy Period.** This policy applies only to loss in Section I or **bodily injury** or **property damage** in Section II, which occurs during the policy period.

2. **Concealment or Fraud.** We do not provide coverage for an **insured** who has:

   a. intentionally concealed or misrepresented any material fact or circumstance; or

   b. made false statements or engaged in fraudulent conduct;

   relating to this insurance.

3. **Liberalization Clause.** If we adopt a revision which would broaden the coverage under this policy without additional premium within 60 days prior to or during the policy period, the broadened coverage will immediately apply to this policy.

4. **Waiver or Change of Policy Provisions.**

   A waiver or change of a provision of this policy must be in writing by us to be valid. Our request for an appraisal or examination will not waive any of our rights.

5. **Cancellation.**

   a. You may cancel this policy at any time by returning it to us or by letting us know in writing of the date cancellation is to take effect.

   b. We may cancel this policy only for the reasons stated below by letting you know in writing of the date cancellation takes effect. This cancellation notice may be delivered to you, or mailed to you at your mailing address shown in the Declarations.

   Proof of mailing will be sufficient proof of notice.

   (1) When you have not paid the premium, we may cancel at any time by letting you know at least 10 days before the date cancellation takes effect.

   (2) When this policy has been in effect for less than 60 days and is not a renewal with us, we may cancel for any reason by letting you know at least 10 days before the date cancellation takes effect.

   (3) When this policy has been in effect for 60 days or more, or at any time if it is a renewal with us, we may cancel:

   (a) if there has been a material misrepresentation of fact which if known to us would have caused us not to issue the policy; or

   (b) if the risk has changed substantially since the policy was issued.

   This can be done by letting you know at least 30 days before the date cancellation takes effect.

   (4) When this policy is written for a period of more than one year, we may cancel for any reason at anniversary by letting you know at least 30 days before the date cancellation takes effect.

   c. When this policy is cancelled, the premium for the period from the date of cancellation to the expiration date will be refunded pro rata.

   d. If the return premium is not refunded with the notice of cancellation or when this policy is returned to us, we will refund it within a reasonable time after the date cancellation takes effect.

6. **Non-Renewal.** We may elect not to renew this policy. We may do so by delivering to you, or mailing to you at your mailing address shown in the Declarations, written notice at least 30 days before the expiration date of this policy. Proof of mailing will be sufficient proof of notice.

7. **Assignment.** Assignment of this policy will not be valid unless we give our written consent.

8. **Subrogation.** An **insured** may waive in writing before a loss all rights of recovery against any person. If not waived, we may require an assignment of rights of recovery for a loss to the extent that payment is made by us.

   If an assignment is sought, an **insured** must sign and deliver all related papers and cooperate with us.

   Subrogation does not apply under Section II to Medical Payments to Others or Damage to Property of Others.

9. **Death.** If any person named in the Declarations or the spouse, if a resident of the same household, dies:

   a. we insure the legal representative of the deceased but only with respect to the premises and property of the deceased covered under the policy at the time of death;

   b. **insured** includes:

   (1) any member of your household who is an **insured** at the time of your death, but only while a resident of the **residence premises;** and

   (2) with respect to your property, the person having proper temporary custody of the property until appointment and qualification of a legal representative.

  

# Appendix C

# LIFE INSURANCE POLICY

## WHOLE LIFE INSURANCE POLICY WITH PREMIUM ADJUSTMENT PROVISION

*Whole Life Insurance payable in event of death. Premiums payable for life. Nonparticipating—no dividends. Schedule of Benefits and Premiums, and the Premium Class, are shown in Section 1, Policy Specifications.*


INA LIFE INSURANCE COMPANY

HOME OFFICE
4050 WILSHIRE BOULEVARD
LOS ANGELES
CALIFORNIA 90054

ADMINISTRATIVE OFFICE
1600 ARCH STREET
PHILADELPHIA
PENNSYLVANIA 19103


81 PLI 02

INA Life Insurance Company ("we", "us", "our" and "company") promises to pay the Face Amount to the Beneficiary upon receipt at our Administrative Office of due proof of the Insured's death. All benefits will be payable subject to the policy provisions. The Owner ("you", "your") is the Insured unless another person is named in the application or later becomes the Owner as allowed by this policy.

Signed for us at Philadelphia, Pennsylvania on the Date of Issue.

JAMES F. NAGLE Secretary — ROBERT F. RINK President

Attest: ______________________ *Countersigned*

**NOTICE OF YOUR RIGHT TO EXAMINE POLICY FOR 10 DAYS**

It is important to us that you are satisfied with this policy and that it meets the insurance goals you planned for it. If you are not satisfied, you may return the policy to us or the agent from whom you purchased it within ten days after it is delivered to you and receive a full refund of any premiums you have paid.

## 1. POLICY SPECIFICATIONS

| | |
|---|---|
| INSURED:<br>JAMES Q. PUBLIC | MALE AGE 35 |
| | EFFECTIVE DATE: MARCH 08, 1981 |
| POLICY NUMBER: SPECIMEN<br>FACE AMOUNT: $100,000 | DATE OF ISSUE: MARCH 08, 1981 |
| | PREMIUM CLASS: STANDARD |
| POLICY LOAN INTEREST RATE: 8% | |

SCHEDULE OF BENEFITS AND PREMIUMS

The premiums for each benefit below are payable for the period from the effective date to the date stated, or for the number of policy years stated, or as otherwise stated or until the prior death of the insured.

| Benefits | Annual Premium | Payable |
|---|---|---|
| WHOLE LIFE INSURANCE WITH PREMIUM ADJUSTMENT PROVISION | $1040.00<br>1369.00 | 3 YEARS<br>THEREAFTER |

**End of Schedule**

| | Annual | Semi-Annual | Quarterly |
|---|---|---|---|
| TOTAL INITIAL PREMIUM ON EFFECTIVE DATE | $1040.00 | $535.60 | $275.60 |

* After the third policy year we reserve the right to change the annual premium. It may be more or less than the initial premium shown for the first three years. It will never exceed the maximum annual premium of $1369.00. For further details please read the premium adjustments paragraph in the premiums and premium adjustments provision of your policy.

## 2. TABLE OF VALUES

This table lists the various guaranteed values available to you in your policy.

You will find a complete explanation of each of those options in sections 7 and 8.

[E5922]

INSURED: JAMES Q. PUBLIC MALE AGE 35

POLICY NUMBER: SPECIMEN FACE AMOUNT: $100,000

COVERAGE: WHOLE LIFE INSURANCE WITH
PREMIUUM ADJUSTMENT PROVISION

| END OF POLICY YEAR | CASH OR LOAN VALUE | REDUCED PAID-UP INSURANCE | EXTENDED TERM INSURANCE | |
|---|---|---|---|---|
| | | | YEARS | DAYS |
| 1 | $ 0 | $ 0 | 0 | 0 |
| 2 | 0 | 0 | 0 | 0 |
| 3 | 200 | 1,100 | 0 | 197 |
| 4 | 1,300 | 6,300 | 3 | 57 |
| 5 | 2,400 | 11,100 | 5 | 85 |
| 6 | 3,500 | 15,500 | 6 | 323 |
| 7 | 4,700 | 20,000 | 8 | 124 |
| 8 | 5,900 | 24,100 | 9 | 174 |
| 9 | 7,200 | 28,200 | 10 | 178 |
| 10 | 8,500 | 32,000 | 11 | 99 |
| 11 | 9,800 | 35,500 | 11 | 318 |
| 12 | 11,200 | 39,000 | 12 | 150 |
| 13 | 12,600 | 42,200 | 12 | 295 |
| 14 | 14,100 | 45,400 | 13 | 62 |
| 15 | 15,600 | 48,400 | 13 | 153 |
| 16 | 17,100 | 51,100 | 13 | 210 |
| 17 | 18,700 | 53,800 | 13 | 262 |
| 18 | 20,300 | 56,400 | 13 | 286 |
| 19 | 21,900 | 58,700 | 13 | 284 |
| 20 | 23,500 | 60,800 | 13 | 260 |
| AT AGE 65 | 41,200 | 78,100 | 12 | 16 |

## 3. GENERAL PROVISIONS

### The Contract

This is your policy. We issued it in consideration of your application and your payment of premiums. This policy and the application, a copy of which is attached to it, make up the entire contract. We agree not to use any statements other than those made in the application in challenging a claim or attempting to avoid liability under this policy. The statements made in the application will be treated as representations and not as warranties.

### Incontestability

This policy will be incontestable, unless you do not pay the premium, after it has been in force during the lifetime of the Insured for two years from its Date of Issue, except for any rider which has a separate incontestability clause. This means that we cannot use any misstatement to challenge a claim or avoid liability after that time.

### Change of Provisions

No agent or other person except our President, a Vice President, or our Secretary has authority to bind us, to extend the time in which you can pay your premiums or to agree to change this policy.

### Misstatement of age or Sex

If the Insured's age or sex is misstated, we will adjust any proceeds payable to the amounts which the premiums paid would have purchased at the correct age and sex.

## 4. EXCLUSIONS

### Suicide Exclusion

If the Insured commits suicide, while sane or insane, within two years from the Date of Issue, we will limit our payment to a refund of premiums paid, less any Indebtedness (money owed the Company).

## 5. OWNERSHIP AND BENEFICIARY

### Ownership

This policy belongs to you. The Owner ("you," "your") is the Insured unless otherwise designated in the application or unless changed as provided under the Change of Ownership or Beneficiary provision. Unless you provide otherwise, you may exercise all rights and privileges granted by this policy during the Insured's lifetime.

### Beneficiary

Unless you change the Beneficiary as provided under the Change of Ownership or Beneficiary provision, the Beneficiary will remain as designated on the application. Any reference to a Beneficiary living or surviving means that the person must be living on the earlier of:

1. the day that we receive due proof of the Insured's death; or
2. the 15th day after the Insured's death.

The legal rights of a Beneficiary are given consideration after the legal rights of any person to whom the policy has been assigned.

### Assignment

You may assign this policy. We assume no responsibility for the validity of any assignment, and we will not be considered to have knowledge of it unless it is filed in writing at our Administrative Office. When it is filed, your rights and those of any Beneficiary will be subject to it.

### Change of Ownership or Beneficiary

Unless you request otherwise, you may change the Owner or Beneficiary of this policy during the lifetime of the Insured. Changes must be requested in writing on a form satisfactory to us and sent to our Administrative Office. We may require the return of this policy for endorsement. No change is valid until it is received by us in our Administrative Office. Upon receipt, it is effective as of the date you signed the written request, subject to any payments made or other action taken by us before we received your written request.

You may also name an Owner's Designee in the same manner. The Owner's Designee is the person who will become the Owner if he or she is living and you are still the Owner at the time of your death. This designation may be changed or terminated in the same manner as it is made. Transfer to the new Owner is subject to any payment made or action taken by us before we are notified of the prior Owner's death. Notification must be received at our Administrative Office.

## 6. PREMIUMS AND PREMIUM ADJUSTMENTS

### Premium

The Effective Date is the date from which premium due dates, policy years and policy anniversaries are determined. The first premium is due on the Effective Date. To keep this policy in force during the Insured's lifetime, you must pay each premium for as long as is shown in the Policy Specifications. You may pay premiums under any mode of payment at the applicable premium rate for the method of payment requested, subject to our approval. All premiums, after the first, must be paid by the due date to us at our Administrative Office. Any premium paid for insurance beyond the month in which the Insured dies will be refunded.

### Grace Period

All premiums are payable by the due date. You do have thirty-one days after the due date to pay each premium (except the first). If you do not pay the premium within this time, your policy will lapse and all its benefits will end, unless the premium is paid under the Automatic Premium Loan provision. However, policy benefits may be continued under one of the options which are available if you quit paying premiums (see Section 7). If the Insured dies during the grace period, we will deduct one month's premium from the benefits.

### Reinstatement

If your policy lapses because you did not pay a premium, we will reinstate it if you ask us to, unless you have surrendered it for its Cash Value. We will reinstate your policy on four conditions:

1. your written request is received at our Administrative Office within 5 years of the due date of the first premium which you did not pay;
2. you show us that the Insured is still insurable according to our normal rules;
3. you pay all overdue premiums plus 6% compound interest on those premiums; and
4. you repay, or agree to continue in effect, any loan made to you under this policy before it lapsed and also pay any interest due on that loan.

### Premium Adjustments

In all policy years after the first three we reserve the right to change the Annual Premium. It may be more or less than the premium you paid for the prior policy year but, it will never be more than the maximum premium shown in the Policy Specifications. Before each policy year begins, we will send you written notice of the premium for that year. We will not change your premium more than once in a policy year.

Any change in premium will be due to a change in our future expectations with respect to one or more of the following factors:

1. Interest rates
2. Mortality
3. Persistency

Any change in premiums will be determined in accordance with any procedures and standards on file with the Insurance Supervisory Officials of the state in which this Policy is delivered.

Changes will be applied on a uniform basis to a class of insureds. Class will be determined by:

1. Issue age;
2. Sex;
3. Premium class at time of issue;
4. Amount of Insurance; and
5. The number of years the Policy has been in force.

No change in classification or premium will occur due to a change in the Insured's health.

Premium changes will not have any effect on the premiums for any riders attached to this Policy. They will also not alter the Cash Values and Paid-Up Insurance Values shown in the Table Of Values.

### 7. CASH VALUE AND PAID–UP INSURANCE OPTIONS

You may surrender, or turn in, this policy at any time in return for its Cash Value less any Indebtedness. You may request instead, within sixty days after the date your premium was due, to have any one of the Paid-Up Insurance Options take effect instead of paying the premium due.

If you do not choose an option within sixty days after the date your premium was due, or if the Insured dies after the thirty-one day grace period without having chosen an option, the Extended Term Insurance Option will automatically take effect if this policy is in the standard premium class. Otherwise, the Reduced Paid-Up Insurance Option will automatically take effect.

If your insurance is continued under one of the Paid-Up Insurance Options, it will not include any benefits other than the Face Amount of this policy. No additional benefits in any riders attached to the policy are included in the Paid-Up Insurance Options.

#### Cash Value

The Cash Values on policy anniversaries are shown in the Table of Values, assuming premiums due have been paid. The Cash Value at any other time will be determined by us with an allowance for the portion of the premiums paid and the time elapsed in the policy year. The basis for determining Cash Value is explained under Basis of Computation. We may delay the payment of the Cash Value for a period of no more than six months after you request payment.

[E5926]

If you do not pay a premium within sixty days of the date it is due, the Cash Value of the policy remains the same as it was on that date. After sixty days, the Cash Value will be used to purchase the appropriate paid-up benefits.

If the policy is being continued under one of the Paid-Up Options, you may surrender it for its Cash Value. That Cash Value may not be less than the Cash Value on the previous policy anniversary if the policy is surrendered within 31 days of that anniversary.

### Extended Term Insurance

This option is available only if this policy is in the standard premium class. This is shown in the Policy Specifications. The amount of insurance continued in force will be the Face Amount less any Indebtedness. The period of Extended Term Insurance will begin on the due date of the first premium which you did not pay. This period is calculated using the Cash Value less any Indebtedness as a net single premium for the Insured's sex and age nearest birthday. This period is shown in the Table of Values, based on the assumption that there is no Indebtedness.

### Reduced Paid-Up Insurance

Instead of having Extended Term Insurance, you may continue this policy as Reduced Paid-Up Insurance. It is payable at the death of the Insured and is effective from the date to which you have paid premiums. The amount of the Reduced Paid-Up Insurance is shown in the Table of Values, based on the assumption that there is no Indebtedness. It is calculated by using the Cash Value less any Indebtedness as a net single premium based on the Insured's sex and age nearest birthday. This option has Cash Value which may be used in the same manner as Cash Value while premiums were being paid.

### Basis of Computation of Cash Values

The Commissioners 1958 Standard Ordinary Mortality Table with interest at 5½% a year, on the basis of age of the Insured at his or her nearest birthday is used to compute all cash values, paid-up insurance benefits, net premiums and present values for this policy except those for Extended Term Insurance, which are computed using the Commissioners 1958 Extended Term Insurance Table with interest at 5½% a year. Cash values of the policy are shown in the Table of Values and are equal at each duration to the excess of the present value at that time per $1,000 face amount of future guaranteed benefits over the present value of non-forfeiture factors for the remainder of the premium paying period. Calculations for female lives are based on a three year setback for ages 10 and over, except that ages 11 and 12 are setback to age 10.

Values for years not shown in the Table of Values are available on request and will be calculated on the same basis as those shown. During any policy year the amount of cash value and paid-up insurance and the period of extended insurance will be calculated with due allowance for the lapse of time and the payment of any fractional premiums. The cash value at any time of any paid-up or extended insurance will be the present value at that time of future guaranteed paid-up benefits, except that within 31 days after a policy anniversary it will not be less than the cash value on that anniversary.

The cash value and paid-up insurance benefits of this policy are not less than the minimum values or benefits required by the law of the State in which this policy is delivered. A detailed statement of the method used for computing the benefits is on file with the insurance supervisory officials of the State in which this policy is delivered.

**Basis of Computation of Reserves**

The Commissioners 1958 Standard Ordinary Mortality Table with interest at $4^1/_2\%$ a year, on the basis of age of the Insured at his or her nearest birthday is used to compute all reserves for this policy except those for Extended Term Insurance, which are computed using the Commissioners 1958 Extended Term Insurance Table with interest at $4^1/_2\%$ a year. Calculations for female lives are based on a three year setback for age 10 and over, except that ages 11 and 12 are setback to age 10.

**8. POLICY LOANS**

**Cash Loans**

You may make a loan against this policy by requesting from us in writing the amount that you wish to borrow. You may borrow up to the amount of Cash Value available. The Cash Value available on a premium due date, or during a grace period, or on a policy anniversary date if the policy is on a Paid-Up Insurance Option, is the Cash Value of the policy less any Indebtedness. The Cash Value available at any other time is the amount which, together with loan interest, will equal the Cash Value available on the next premium due date or the next policy anniversary date if the policy is on a Paid-Up Insurance Option.

The annual rate of interest on your loan will be the maximum permissible under the law of the state of issue of the policy on its Effective Date, but in no case shall that interest rate exceed 8% per year, payable on each policy anniversary. The actual rate of interest is shown in the Policy Specifications. If you do not pay the interest when it is due, the amount of interest will be added to the loan.

You may repay all or any part of the loan at any time during the lifetime of the Insured. We will not terminate the policy if you do not repay the loan or loan interest unless the loan and the interest together are more than the Cash Value of the policy. In that case, we will terminate the policy thirty-one days after we mail a termination notice to the last known addresses of both you and any assignee of record.

We may delay making a loan for a period of no more than six months after you request the loan. However, we will not delay the making of loans to pay premiums for this policy.

**Indebtedness**

Indebtedness means that you owe money including any interest because of a loan on this policy. Any Indebtedness at time of settlement will reduce the proceeds. Indebtedness may be repaid in whole or in part at any time

[E5928]

before the policy matures. However, if you do not pay a premium within the grace period, any outstanding Indebtedness can be repaid only if the policy is reinstated. If at any time Indebtedness equals or exceeds the policy's value, the policy will terminate. We will give thirty-one days notice to you and any assignee. It will be mailed to your last known address and to the last known address of any assignee.

**Automatic Premium Loan**

You may request on the application or by writing to us at our Administrative Office that the Automatic Premium Loan provision be used to pay premiums. If this provision is used and your policy has enough Cash Value available, any premium you have not paid by the end of the thirty-one day grace period will be paid by an Automatic Premium Loan.

When two consecutive premiums have been paid by Automatic Premium Loans, the applicable Paid-Up Insurance Option will automatically take effect at the next premium due date.

## 9. CHANGE OF PLAN

[Omitted]

## 10. SETTLEMENT OPTIONS

[Omitted]

[E5929]

# Appendix D

# PERSONAL AUTO POLICY

## PERSONAL AUTO POLICY

### AGREEMENT

In return for payment of the premium and subject to all the terms of this policy, we agree with you as follows:

### DEFINITIONS

**A.** Throughout this policy, "you" and "your" refer to:

**1.** The "named insured" shown in the Declarations; and

**2.** The spouse if a resident of the same household.

**B.** "We," "us" and "our" refer to the Company providing this insurance.

**C.** For purposes of this policy, a private passenger type auto shall be deemed to be owned by a person if leased:

**1.** Under a written agreement to that person; and

**2.** For a continuous period of at least 6 months.

Other words and phrases are defined. They are in quotation marks when used.

**D.** "Bodily injury" means bodily harm, sickness or disease, including death that results.

**E.** "Business" includes trade, profession or occupation.

**F.** "Family member" means a person related to you by blood, marriage or adoption who is a resident of your household. This includes a ward or foster child.

**G.** "Occupying" means in, upon, getting in, on, out or off.

**H.** "Property damage" means physical injury to, destruction of or loss of use of tangible property.

**I.** "Trailer" means a vehicle designed to be pulled by a:

**1.** Private passenger auto; or

**2.** Pickup or van.

It also means a farm wagon or farm implement while towed by a vehicle listed in 1. or 2. above.

**J.** "Your covered auto" means:

**1.** Any vehicle shown in the Declarations.

**2.** Any of the following types of vehicles on the date you become the owner:

**a.** a private passenger auto; or

**b.** a pickup or van that:

**(1)** has a Gross Vehicle Weight of less than 10,000 lbs.; and

**(2)** is not used for the delivery or transportation of goods and materials unless such use is:

**(a)** incidental to your "business" of installing, maintaining or repairing furnishings or equipment; or

**(b)** for farming or ranching.

This provision (J.2.) applies only if:

**a.** you acquire the vehicle during the policy period;

**b.** you ask us to insure it within 30 days after you become the owner; and

**c.** with respect to a pickup or van, no other insurance policy provides coverage for that vehicle.

If the vehicle you acquire replaces one shown in the Declarations, it will have the same coverage as the vehicle it replaced. You must ask us to insure a replacement vehicle within 30 days only if you wish to add or continue Coverage for Damage to Your Auto.

If the vehicle you acquire is in addition to any shown in the Declarations, it will have the broadest coverage we now provide for any vehicle shown in the Declarations.

**3.** Any "trailer" you own.

**4.** Any auto or "trailer" you do not own while used as a temporary substitute for any other vehicle described in this definition which is out of normal use because of its:

**a.** breakdown;
**b.** repair;
**c.** servicing;
**d.** loss; or
**e.** destruction.

This provision (J.4.) does not apply to Coverage for Damage to Your Auto.

  

## PART A - LIABILITY COVERAGE

### INSURING AGREEMENT

**A.** We will pay damages for "bodily injury" or "property damage" for which any "insured" becomes legally responsible because of an auto accident. Damages include prejudgment interest awarded against the "insured." We will settle or defend, as we consider appropriate, any claim or suit asking for these damages. In addition to our limit of liability, we will pay all defense costs we incur. Our duty to settle or defend ends when our limit of liability for this coverage has been exhausted. We have no duty to defend any suit or settle any claim for "bodily injury" or "property damage" not covered under this policy.

**B.** "Insured" as used in this Part means:

1. You or any "family member" for the ownership, maintenance or use of any auto or "trailer."
2. Any person using "your covered auto."
3. For "your covered auto," any person or organization but only with respect to legal responsibility for acts or omissions of a person for whom coverage is afforded under this Part.
4. For any auto or "trailer," other than "your covered auto," any other person or organization but only with respect to legal responsibility for acts or omissions of you or any "family member" for whom coverage is afforded under this Part. This provision (B.4.) applies only if the person or organization does not own or hire the auto or "trailer."

### SUPPLEMENTARY PAYMENTS

In addition to our limit of liability, we will pay on behalf of an "insured:"

1. Up to $250 for the cost of bail bonds required because of an accident, including related traffic law violations. The accident must result in "bodily injury" or "property damage" covered under this policy.
2. Premiums on appeal bonds and bonds to release attachments in any suit we defend.
3. Interest accruing after a judgment is entered in any suit we defend. Our duty to pay interest ends when we offer to pay that part of the judgment which does not exceed our limit of liability for this coverage.
4. Up to $50 a day for loss of earnings, but not other income, because of attendance at hearings or trials at our request.
5. Other reasonable expenses incurred at our request.

### EXCLUSIONS

**A.** We do not provide Liability Coverage for any person:

1. Who intentionally causes "bodily injury" or "property damage."
2. For "property damage" to property owned or being transported by that person.
3. For "property damage" to property:
   a. rented to;
   b. used by; or
   c. in the care of;

   that person.

   This exclusion (A.3.) does not apply to "property damage" to a residence or private garage.
4. For "bodily injury" to an employee of that person during the course of employment. This exclusion (A.4.) does not apply to "bodily injury" to a domestic employee unless workers' compensation benefits are required or available for that domestic employee.
5. For that person's liability arising out of the ownership or operation of a vehicle while it is being used as a public or livery conveyance. This exclusion (A.5.) does not apply to a share-the-expense car pool.
6. While employed or otherwise engaged in the "business" of:
   a. selling;
   b. repairing;
   c. servicing;
   d. storing; or
   e. parking;

   vehicles designed for use mainly on public highways. This includes road testing and delivery. This exclusion (A.6.) does not apply to the ownership, maintenance or use of "your covered auto" by:
   a. you;
   b. any "family member;" or
   c. any partner, agent or employee of you or any "family member."

  

7. Maintaining or using any vehicle while that person is employed or otherwise engaged in any "business" (other than farming or ranching) not described in Exclusion A.6. This exclusion (A.7.) does not apply to the maintenance or use of a:
   a. private passenger auto;
   b. pickup or van that you own; or
   c. "trailer" used with a vehicle described in a. or b. above.
8. Using a vehicle without a reasonable belief that that person is entitled to do so.
9. For "bodily injury" or "property damage" for which that person:
   a. is an insured under a nuclear energy liability policy; or
   b. would be an insured under a nuclear energy liability policy but for its termination upon exhaustion of its limit of liability.

   A nuclear energy liability policy is a policy issued by any of the following or their successors:
   a. American Nuclear Insurers;
   b. Mutual Atomic Energy Liability Underwriters; or
   c. Nuclear Insurance Association of Canada.

B. We do not provide Liability Coverage for the ownership, maintenance or use of:
1. Any motorized vehicle having fewer than four wheels.
2. Any vehicle, other than "your covered auto," which is:
   a. owned by you; or
   b. furnished or available for your regular use.
3. Any vehicle, other than "your covered auto," which is:
   a. owned by any "family member;" or
   b. furnished or available for the regular use of any "family member."

   However, this exclusion (B.3.) does not apply to you while you are maintaining or "occupying" any vehicle which is:
   a. owned by a "family member;" or
   b. furnished or available for the regular use of a "family member."

**LIMIT OF LIABILITY**

A. The limit of liability shown in the Declarations for this coverage is our maximum limit of liability for all damages resulting from any one auto accident. This is the most we will pay regardless of the number of:
1. "Insureds;"
2. Claims made;
3. Vehicles or premiums shown in the Declarations; or
4. Vehicles involved in the auto accident.

B. We will apply the limit of liability to provide any separate limits required by law for bodily injury and property damage liability. However, this provision (B.) will not change our total limit of liability.

**OUT OF STATE COVERAGE**

If an auto accident to which this policy applies occurs in any state or province other than the one in which "your covered auto" is principally garaged, we will interpret your policy for that accident as follows:

A. If the state or province has:
1. A financial responsibility or similar law specifying limits of liability for "bodily injury" or "property damage" higher than the limit shown in the Declarations, your policy will provide the higher specified limit.
2. A compulsory insurance or similar law requiring a nonresident to maintain insurance whenever the nonresident uses a vehicle in that state or province, your policy will provide at least the required minimum amounts and types of coverage.

B. No one will be entitled to duplicate payments for the same elements of loss.

**FINANCIAL RESPONSIBILITY**

When this policy is certified as future proof of financial responsibility, this policy shall comply with the law to the extent required.

**OTHER INSURANCE**

If there is other applicable liability insurance we will pay only our share of the loss. Our share is the proportion that our limit of liability bears to the total of all applicable limits. However, any insurance we provide for a vehicle you do not own shall be excess over any other collectible insurance.

  

## PART B - MEDICAL PAYMENTS COVERAGE

### INSURING AGREEMENT

A. We will pay reasonable expenses incurred for necessary medical and funeral services because of "bodily injury:"

1. Caused by accident; and
2. Sustained by an "insured."

We will pay only those expenses incurred within 3 years from the date of the accident.

B. "Insured" as used in this Part means:

1. You or any "family member:"
   a. while "occupying;" or
   b. as a pedestrian when struck by;

   a motor vehicle designed for use mainly on public roads or a trailer of any type.
2. Any other person while "occupying" "your covered auto."

### EXCLUSIONS

We do not provide Medical Payments Coverage for any person for "bodily injury:"

1. Sustained while "occupying" any motorized vehicle having fewer than four wheels.
2. Sustained while "occupying" "your covered auto" when it is being used as a public or livery conveyance. This exclusion (2.) does not apply to a share-the-expense car pool.
3. Sustained while "occupying" any vehicle located for use as a residence or premises.
4. Occurring during the course of employment if workers' compensation benefits are required or available for the "bodily injury."
5. Sustained while "occupying," or when struck by, any vehicle (other than "your covered auto") which is:
   a. owned by you; or
   b. furnished or available for your regular use.
6. Sustained while "occupying," or when struck by, any vehicle (other than "your covered auto") which is:
   a. owned by any "family member;" or
   b. furnished or available for the regular use of any "family member."

   However, this exclusion (6.) does not apply to you.
7. Sustained while "occupying" a vehicle without a reasonable belief that that person is entitled to do so.
8. Sustained while "occupying" a vehicle when it is being used in the "business" of an "insured." This exclusion (8.) does not apply to "bodily injury" sustained while "occupying" a:
   a. private passenger auto;
   b. pickup or van that you own; or
   c. "trailer" used with a vehicle described in a. or b. above.
9. Caused by or as a consequence of:
   a. discharge of a nuclear weapon (even if accidental);
   b. war (declared or undeclared);
   c. civil war;
   d. insurrection; or
   e. rebellion or revolution.
10. From or as a consequence of the following, whether controlled or uncontrolled or however caused:
    a. nuclear reaction;
    b. radiation; or
    c. radioactive contamination.

### LIMIT OF LIABILITY

A. The limit of liability shown in the Declarations for this coverage is our maximum limit of liability for each person injured in any one accident. This is the most we will pay regardless of the number of:

1. "Insureds;"
2. Claims made;
3. Vehicles or premiums shown in the Declarations; or
4. Vehicles involved in the accident.

B. Any amounts otherwise payable for expenses under this coverage shall be reduced by any amounts paid or payable for the same expenses under Part A or Part C.

C. No payment will be made unless the injured person or that person's legal representative agrees in writing that any payment shall be applied toward any settlement or judgment that person receives under Part A or Part C.

### OTHER INSURANCE

If there is other applicable auto medical payments insurance we will pay only our share of the loss. Our share is the proportion that our limit of liability bears to the total of all applicable limits. However, any insurance we provide with respect to a vehicle you do not own shall be excess over any other collectible auto insurance providing payments for medical or funeral expenses.

  

## PART C - UNINSURED MOTORISTS COVERAGE

### INSURING AGREEMENT

**A.** We will pay compensatory damages which an "insured" is legally entitled to recover from the owner or operator of an "uninsured motor vehicle" because of "bodily injury:"

1. Sustained by an "insured;" and
2. Caused by an accident.

The owner's or operator's liability for these damages must arise out of the ownership, maintenance or use of the "uninsured motor vehicle."

Any judgment for damages arising out of a suit brought without our written consent is not binding on us.

**B.** "Insured" as used in this Part means:

1. You or any "family member."
2. Any other person "occupying" "your covered auto."
3. Any person for damages that person is entitled to recover because of "bodily injury" to which this coverage applies sustained by a person described in 1. or 2. above.

**C.** "Uninsured motor vehicle" means a land motor vehicle or trailer of any type:

1. To which no bodily injury liability bond or policy applies at the time of the accident.
2. To which a bodily injury liability bond or policy applies at the time of the accident. In this case its limit for bodily injury liability must be less than the minimum limit for bodily injury liability specified by the financial responsibility law of the state in which "your covered auto" is principally garaged.
3. Which is a hit-and-run vehicle whose operator or owner cannot be identified and which hits:
   a. you or any "family member;"
   b. a vehicle which you or any "family member" are "occupying;" or
   c. "your covered auto."
4. To which a bodily injury liability bond or policy applies at the time of the accident but the bonding or insuring company;
   a. denies coverage; or
   b. is or becomes insolvent.

However, "uninsured motor vehicle" does not include any vehicle or equipment:

1. Owned by or furnished or available for the regular use of you or any "family member."
2. Owned or operated by a self-insurer under any applicable motor vehicle law, except a self-insurer which is or becomes insolvent.
3. Owned by any governmental unit or agency.
4. Operated on rails or crawler treads.
5. Designed mainly for use off public roads while not on public roads.
6. While located for use as a residence or premises.

### EXCLUSIONS

**A.** We do not provide Uninsured Motorists Coverage for "bodily injury" sustained by any person:

1. While "occupying," or when struck by, any motor vehicle owned by you or any "family member" which is not insured for this coverage under this policy. This includes a trailer of any type used with that vehicle.
2. If that person or the legal representative settles the "bodily injury" claim without our consent.
3. While "occupying" "your covered auto" when it is being used as a public or livery conveyance. This exclusion (A.3.) does not apply to a share-the-expense car pool.
4. Using a vehicle without a reasonable belief that that person is entitled to do so.

**B.** This coverage shall not apply directly or indirectly to benefit any insurer or self-insurer under any of the following or similar law:

1. Workers' compensation law; or
2. Disability benefits law.

**C.** We do not provide Uninsured Motorists Coverage for punitive or exemplary damages.

### LIMIT OF LIABILITY

**A.** The limit of liability shown in the Declarations for this coverage is our maximum limit of liability for all damages resulting from any one accident. This is the most we will pay regardless of the number of:

1. "Insureds;"
2. Claims made;
3. Vehicles or premiums shown in the Declarations; or
4. Vehicles involved in the accident.

**B.** Any amounts otherwise payable for damages under this coverage shall be reduced by all sums:

1. Paid because of the "bodily injury" by or on behalf of persons or organizations who may be legally responsible. This includes all sums paid under Part A; and

  

2. Paid or payable because of the "bodily injury" under any of the following or similar law:
   a. workers' compensation law; or
   b. disability benefits law.

C. Any payment under this coverage will reduce any amount that person is entitled to recover for the same damages under Part A.

OTHER INSURANCE

If there is other applicable similar insurance we will pay only our share of the loss. Our share is the proportion that our limit of liability bears to the total of all applicable limits. However, any insurance we provide with respect to a vehicle you do not own shall be excess over any other collectible insurance.

ARBITRATION

A. If we and an "insured" do not agree:
   1. Whether that person is legally entitled to recover damages under this Part; or
   2. As to the amount of damages;

   either party may make a written demand for arbitration. In this event, each party will select an arbitrator. The two arbitrators will select a third. If they cannot agree within 30 days, either may request that selection be made by a judge of a court having jurisdiction.

B. Each party will:
   1. Pay the expenses it incurs; and
   2. Bear the expenses of the third arbitrator equally.

C. Unless both parties agree otherwise, arbitration will take place in the county in which the "insured" lives. Local rules of law as to procedure and evidence will apply. A decision agreed to by two of the arbitrators will be binding as to:
   1. Whether the "insured" is legally entitled to recover damages; and
   2. The amount of damages. This applies only if the amount does not exceed the minimum limit for bodily injury liability specified by the financial responsibility law of the state in which "your covered auto" is principally garaged. If the amount exceeds that limit, either party may demand the right to a trial. This demand must be made within 60 days of the arbitrators' decision. If this demand is not made, the amount of damages agreed to by the arbitrators will be binding.

## PART D - COVERAGE FOR DAMAGE TO YOUR AUTO

INSURING AGREEMENT

A. We will pay for direct and accidental loss to "your covered auto" or any "non-owned auto," including their equipment, minus any applicable deductible shown in the Declarations. We will pay for loss to "your covered auto" caused by:
   1. Other than "collision" only if the Declarations indicate that Other Than Collision Coverage is provided for that auto.
   2. "Collision" only if the Declarations indicate that Collision Coverage is provided for that auto.

   If there is a loss to a "non-owned auto," we will provide the broadest coverage applicable to any "your covered auto" shown in the Declarations.

B. "Collision" means the upset of "your covered auto" or a "non-owned auto" or their impact with another vehicle or object.

   Loss caused by the following is considered other than "collision:"
   1. Missiles or falling objects;
   2. Fire;
   3. Theft or larceny;
   4. Explosion or earthquake;
   5. Windstorm;
   6. Hail, water or flood;
   7. Malicious mischief or vandalism;
   8. Riot or civil commotion;
   9. Contact with bird or animal; or
   10. Breakage of glass

   If breakage of glass is caused by a "collision," you may elect to have it considered a loss caused by "collision."

C. "Non-owned auto" means:
   1. Any private passenger auto, pickup, van or "trailer" not owned by or furnished or available for the regular use of you or any "family member" while in the custody of or being operated by you or any "family member;" or
   2. Any auto or "trailer" you do not own while used as a temporary substitute for "your covered auto" which is out of normal use because of its:
      a. breakdown;
      b. repair;
      c. servicing;
      d. loss; or
      e. destruction.

  

**TRANSPORTATION EXPENSES**

In addition we will pay, without application of a deductible, up to $15 per day, to a maximum of $450, for:

1. Transportation expenses incurred by you in the event of the total theft of "your covered auto." This applies only if the Declarations indicate that Other Than Collision Coverage is provided for that auto.
2. Loss of use expenses for which you become legally responsible in the event of the total theft of a "non-owned auto." This applies only if the Declarations indicate that Other Than Collision Coverage is provided for any "your covered auto."

We will pay only expenses incurred during the period:

1. Beginning 48 hours after the theft; and
2. Ending when "your covered auto" or the "non-owned auto" is returned to use or we pay for its loss.

**EXCLUSIONS**

We will not pay for:

1. Loss to "your covered auto" or any "non-owned auto" which occurs while it is being used as a public or livery conveyance. This exclusion (1.) does not apply to a share-the-expense car pool.
2. Damage due and confined to:
   a. wear and tear;
   b. freezing;
   c. mechanical or electrical breakdown or failure; or
   d. road damage to tires.

   This exclusion (2.) does not apply if the damage results from the total theft of "your covered auto" or any "non-owned auto."
3. Loss due to or as a consequence of:
   a. radioactive contamination;
   b. discharge of any nuclear weapon (even if accidental);
   c. war (declared or undeclared);
   d. civil war;
   e. insurrection; or
   f. rebellion or revolution.
4. Loss to:
   a. any electronic equipment designed for the reproduction of sound, including, but not limited to:
      (1) radios and stereos;
      (2) tape decks; or
      (3) compact disc players;
   b. any other electronic equipment that receives or transmits audio, visual or data signals, including, but not limited to:
      (1) citizens band radios;
      (2) telephones;
      (3) two-way mobile radios;
      (4) scanning monitor receivers;
      (5) television monitor receivers;
      (6) video cassette recorders;
      (7) audio cassette recorders; or
      (8) personal computers;
   c. tapes, records, discs, or other media used with equipment described in a. or b.; or
   d. any other accessories used with equipment described in a. or b.

   This exclusion (4.) does not apply to:
   a. equipment designed solely for the re-pro- duction of sound and accessories used with such equipment, provided such equipment is permanently installed in "your covered auto" or any "non-owned auto;" or
   b. any other electronic equipment that is:
      (1) necessary for the normal operation of the auto or the monitoring of the auto's operating systems; or
      (2) an integral part of the same unit housing any sound reproducing equipment described in a. and per-manently installed in the opening of the dash or console of "your cov-ered auto" or any "non-owned auto" normally used by the manufacturer for installation of a radio.
5. Loss to "your covered auto" or any "non-owned auto" due to destruction or confiscation by governmental or civil au-thorities because you or any "family member:"
   a. engaged in illegal activities; or
   b. failed to comply with Environmental Protection Agency or Department of Transportation standards.

   This exclusion (5.) does not apply to the interests of Loss Payees in "your covered auto."
6. Loss to a camper body or "trailer" you own which is not shown in the Declara-tions. This exclusion (6.) does not apply to a camper body or "trailer" you:
   a. acquire during the policy period; and
   b. ask us to insure within 30 days after you become the owner.
7. Loss to any "non-owned auto" when used by you or any "family member" without a reasonable belief that you or that "family member" are entitled to do so.

  

**8.** Loss to:

**a.** awnings or cabanas; or

**b.** equipment designed to create additional living facilities.

**9.** Loss to equipment designed or used for the detection or location of radar.

**10.** Loss to any custom furnishings or equipment in or upon any pickup or van. Custom furnishings or equipment include but are not limited to:

**a.** special carpeting and insulation, furniture or bars;

**b.** facilities for cooking and sleeping;

**c.** height-extending roofs; or

**d.** custom murals, paintings or other decals or graphics.

**11.** Loss to any "non-owned auto" being maintained or used by any person while employed or otherwise engaged in the "business" of:

**a.** selling;
**b.** repairing;
**c.** servicing;
**d.** storing; or
**e.** parking;

vehicles designed for use on public highways. This includes road testing and delivery.

**12.** Loss to any "non-owned auto" being maintained or used by any person while employed or otherwise engaged in any "business" not described in exclusion 11. This exclusion (12.) does not apply to the maintenance or use by you or any "family member" of a "non-owned auto" which is a private passenger auto or "trailer."

**LIMIT OF LIABILITY**

**A.** Our limit of liability for loss will be the lesser of the:

**1.** Actual cash value of the stolen or damaged property; or

**2.** Amount necessary to repair or replace the property.

However, the most we will pay for loss to any "non-owned auto" which is a "trailer" is $500.

**B.** An adjustment for depreciation and physical condition will be made in determining actual cash value at the time of loss.

**PAYMENT OF LOSS**

We may pay for loss in money or repair or replace the damaged or stolen property. We may, at our expense, return any stolen property to:

**1.** You; or

**2.** The address shown in this policy.

If we return stolen property we will pay for any damage resulting from the theft. We may keep all or part of the property at an agreed or appraised value.

**NO BENEFIT TO BAILEE**

This insurance shall not directly or indirectly benefit any carrier or other bailee for hire.

**OTHER SOURCES OF RECOVERY**

If other sources of recovery also cover the loss, we will pay only our share of the loss. Our share is the proportion that our limit of liability bears to the total of all applicable limits. However, any insurance we provide with respect to a "non-owned auto" shall be excess over any other collectible source of recovery including, but not limited to:

**1.** Any coverage provided by the owner of the "non-owned auto;"

**2.** Any other applicable physical damage insurance;

**3.** Any other source of recovery applicable to the loss.

**APPRAISAL**

**A.** If we and you do not agree on the amount of loss, either may demand an appraisal of the loss. In this event, each party will select a competent appraiser. The two appraisers will select an umpire. The appraisers will state separately the actual cash value and the amount of loss. If they fail to agree, they will submit their differences to the umpire. A decision agreed to by any two will be binding. Each party will:

**1.** Pay its chosen appraiser; and

**2.** Bear the expenses of the appraisal and umpire equally.

**B.** We do not waive any of our rights under this policy by agreeing to an appraisal.

  

## PART E - DUTIES AFTER AN ACCIDENT OR LOSS

We have no duty to provide coverage under this policy unless there has been full compliance with the following duties:

**A.** We must be notified promptly of how, when and where the accident or loss happened. Notice should also include the names and addresses of any injured persons and of any witnesses.

**B.** A person seeking any coverage must:

1. Cooperate with us in the investigation, settlement or defense of any claim or suit.
2. Promptly send us copies of any notices or legal papers received in connection with the accident or loss.
3. Submit, as often as we reasonably require:
   a. to physical exams by physicians we select. We will pay for these exams.
   b. to examination under oath and subscribe the same.
4. Authorize us to obtain:
   a. medical reports; and
   b. other pertinent records.
5. Submit a proof of loss when required by us.

**C.** A person seeking Uninsured Motorists Coverage must also:

1. Promptly notify the police if a hit-and-run driver is involved.
2. Promptly send us copies of the legal papers if a suit is brought.

**D.** A person seeking Coverage for Damage to Your Auto must also:

1. Take reasonable steps after loss to protect "your covered auto" or any "non-owned auto" and their equipment from further loss. We will pay reasonable expenses incurred to do this.
2. Promptly notify the police if "your covered auto" or any "non-owned auto" is stolen.
3. Permit us to inspect and appraise the damaged property before its repair or disposal.

## PART F - GENERAL PROVISIONS

**BANKRUPTCY**

Bankruptcy or insolvency of the "insured" shall not relieve us of any obligations under this policy.

**CHANGES**

**A.** This policy contains all the agreements between you and us. Its terms may not be changed or waived except by endorsement issued by us.

**B.** If there is a change to the information used to develop the policy premium, we may adjust your premium. Changes during the policy term that may result in a premium increase or decrease include, but are not limited to, changes in:

1. The number, type or use classification of insured vehicles;
2. Operators using insured vehicles;
3. The place of principal garaging of insured vehicles;
4. Coverage, deductible or limits.

If a change resulting from A. or B. requires a premium adjustment, we will make the premium adjustment in accordance with our manual rules.

**C.** If we make a change which broadens coverage under this edition of your policy without additional premium charge, that change will automatically apply to your policy as of the date we implement the change in your state. This paragraph (C.) does not apply to changes implemented with a general program revision that includes both broadenings and restrictions in coverage, whether that general program revision is implemented through introduction of:

1. A subsequent edition of your policy; or
2. An Amendatory Endorsement.

**FRAUD**

We do not provide coverage for any "insured" who has made fraudulent statements or engaged in fraudulent conduct in connection with any accident or loss for which coverage is sought under this policy.

**LEGAL ACTION AGAINST US**

**A.** No legal action may be brought against us until there has been full compliance with all the terms of this policy. In addition, under Part A, no legal action may be brought against us until:

1. We agree in writing that the "insured" has an obligation to pay; or

  

2. The amount of that obligation has been finally determined by judgment after trial.

B. No person or organization has any right under this policy to bring us into any action to determine the liability of an "insured."

OUR RIGHT TO RECOVER PAYMENT

A. If we make a payment under this policy and the person to or for whom payment was made has a right to recover damages from another we shall be subrogated to that right. That person shall do:

1. Whatever is necessary to enable us to exercise our rights; and

2. Nothing after loss to prejudice them.

However, our rights in this paragraph (A.) do not apply under Part D, against any person using "your covered auto" with a reasonable belief that that person is entitled to do so.

B. If we make a payment under this policy and the person to or for whom payment is made recovers damages from another, that person shall:

1. Hold in trust for us the proceeds of the recovery; and

2. Reimburse us to the extent of our payment.

POLICY PERIOD AND TERRITORY

A. This policy applies only to accidents and losses which occur:

1. During the policy period as shown in the Declarations; and

2. Within the policy territory.

B. The policy territory is:

1. The United States of America, its territories or possessions;

2. Puerto Rico; or

3. Canada.

This policy also applies to loss to, or accidents involving, "your covered auto" while being transported between their ports.

TERMINATION

A. **Cancellation.** This policy may be cancelled during the policy period as follows:

1. The named insured shown in the Declarations may cancel by:

a. returning this policy to us; or

b. giving us advance written notice of the date cancellation is to take effect.

2. We may cancel by mailing to the named insured shown in the Declarations at the address shown in this policy:

a. at least 10 days notice:

(1) if cancellation is for nonpayment of premium; or

(2) if notice is mailed during the first 60 days this policy is in effect and this is not a renewal or continuation policy; or

b. at least 20 days notice in all other cases.

3. After this policy is in effect for 60 days, or if this is a renewal or continuation policy, we will cancel only:

a. for nonpayment of premium; or

b. if your driver's license or that of:

(1) any driver who lives with you; or

(2) any driver who customarily uses "your covered auto;"

has been suspended or revoked. This must have occurred:

(1) during the policy period; or

(2) since the last anniversary of the original effective date if the policy period is other than 1 year; or

c. if the policy was obtained through material misrepresentation.

B. **Nonrenewal.** If we decide not to renew or continue this policy, we will mail notice to the named insured shown in the Declarations at the address shown in this policy. Notice will be mailed at least 20 days before the end of the policy period. If the policy period is other than 1 year, we will have the right not to renew or continue it only at each anniversary of its original effective date.

C. **Automatic Termination.** If we offer to renew or continue and you or your representative do not accept, this policy will automatically terminate at the end of the current policy period. Failure to pay the required renewal or continuation premium when due shall mean that you have not accepted our offer.

If you obtain other insurance on "your covered auto," any similar insurance provided by this policy will terminate as to that auto on the effective date of the other insurance.

  

**D. Other Termination Provisions.**

1. If the law in effect in your state at the time this policy is issued, renewed or continued:
   a. requires a longer notice period;
   b. requires a special form of or procedure for giving notice; or
   c. modifies any of the stated termination reasons;

   we will comply with those requirements.
2. We may deliver any notice instead of mailing it. Proof of mailing of any notice shall be sufficient proof of notice.
3. If this policy is cancelled, you may be entitled to a premium refund. If so, we will send you the refund. The premium refund, if any, will be computed according to our manuals. However, making or offering to make the refund is not a condition of cancellation.
4. The effective date of cancellation stated in the notice shall become the end of the policy period.

**TRANSFER OF YOUR INTEREST IN THIS POLICY**

**A.** Your rights and duties under this policy may not be assigned without our written consent. However, if a named insured shown in the Declarations dies, coverage will be provided for:

1. The surviving spouse if resident in the same household at the time of death. Coverage applies to the spouse as if a named insured shown in the Declarations; and
2. The legal representative of the deceased person as if a named insured shown in the Declarations. This applies only with respect to the representative's legal responsibility to maintain or use "your covered auto."

**B.** Coverage will only be provided until the end of the policy period.

**TWO OR MORE AUTO POLICIES**

If this policy and any other auto insurance policy issued to you by us apply to the same accident, the maximum limit of our liability under all the policies shall not exceed the highest applicable limit of liability under any one policy.

  

# Appendix E

# COMMERCIAL GENERAL LIABILITY COVERAGE FORM

## COMMERCIAL GENERAL LIABILITY COVERAGE FORM

Various provisions in this policy restrict coverage. Read the entire policy carefully to determine rights, duties and what is and is not covered.

Throughout this policy the words "you" and "your" refer to the Named Insured shown in the Declarations, and any other person or organization qualifying as a Named Insured under this policy. The words "we," "us" and "our" refer to the company providing this insurance.

The word "insured" means any person or organization qualifying as such under WHO IS AN INSURED (SECTION II).

Other words and phrases that appear in quotation marks have special meaning. Refer to DEFINITIONS (SECTION V).

SECTION I - COVERAGES

COVERAGE A. BODILY INJURY AND PROPERTY DAMAGE LIABILITY

**1. Insuring Agreement.**

a. We will pay those sums that the insured becomes legally obligated to pay as damages because of "bodily injury" or "property damage" to which this insurance applies. We will have the right and duty to defend any "suit" seeking those damages. We may at our discretion investigate any "occurrence" and settle any claim or "suit" that may result. But:

(1) The amount we will pay for damages is limited as described in LIMITS OF INSURANCE (SECTION III); and

(2) Our right and duty to defend end when we have used up the applicable limit of insurance in the payment of judgments or settlements under Coverages A or B or medical expenses under Coverage C.

No other obligation or liability to pay sums or perform acts or services is covered unless explicitly provided for under SUPPLEMENTARY PAYMENTS - COVERAGES A AND B.

b. This insurance applies to "bodily injury" and "property damage" only if:

(1) The "bodily injury" or "property damage" is caused by an "occurrence" that takes place in the "coverage territory;" and

(2) The "bodily injury" or "property damage" occurs during the policy period.

c. Damages because of "bodily injury" include damages claimed by any person or organization for care, loss of services or death resulting at any time from the "bodily injury."

**2. Exclusions.**

This insurance does not apply to:

a. "Bodily injury" or "property damage" expected or intended from the standpoint of the insured. This exclusion does not apply to "bodily injury" resulting from the use of reasonable force to protect persons or property.

b. "Bodily injury" or "property damage" for which the insured is obligated to pay damages by reason of the assumption of liability in a contract or agreement. This exclusion does not apply to liability for damages:

(1) Assumed in a contract or agreement that is an "insured contract," provided the "bodily injury" or "property damage" occurs subsequent to the execution of the contract or agreement; or

(2) That the insured would have in the absence of the contract or agreement.

c. "Bodily injury" or "property damage" for which any insured may be held liable by reason of:

(1) Causing or contributing to the intoxication of any person;

(2) The furnishing of alcoholic beverages to a person under the legal drinking age or under the influence of alcohol; or

(3) Any statute, ordinance or regulation relating to the sale, gift, distribution or use of alcoholic beverages.

This exclusion applies only if you are in the business of manufacturing, distributing, selling, serving or furnishing alcoholic beverages.

  

**d.** Any obligation of the insured under a workers' compensation, disability benefits or unemployment compensation law or any similar law.

**e.** "Bodily injury" to:

**(1)** An employee of the insured arising out of and in the course of employment by the insured; or

**(2)** The spouse, child, parent, brother or sister of that employee as a consequence of (1) above.

This exclusion applies:

**(1)** Whether the insured may be liable as an employer or in any other capacity; and

**(2)** To any obligation to share damages with or repay someone else who must pay damages because of the injury.

This exclusion does not apply to liability assumed by the insured under an "insured contract."

**f.** **(1)** "Bodily injury" or "property damage" arising out of the actual, alleged or threatened discharge, dispersal, seepage, migration, release or escape of pollutants:

**(a)** At or from any premises, site or location which is or was at any time owned or occupied by, or rented or loaned to, any insured;

**(b)** At or from any premises, site or location which is or was at any time used by or for any insured or others for the handling, storage, disposal, processing or treatment of waste;

**(c)** Which are or were at any time transported, handled, stored, treated, disposed of, or processed as waste by or for any insured or any person or organization for whom you may be legally responsible; or

**(d)** At or from any premises, site or location on which any insured or any contractors or subcontractors working directly or indirectly on any insured's behalf are performing operations:

**(i)** if the pollutants are brought on or to the premises, site or location in connection with such operations by such insured, contractor or subcontractor; or

**(ii)** if the operations are to test for, monitor, clean up, remove, contain, treat, detoxify or neutralize, or in any way respond to, or assess the effects of pollutants.

Subparagraphs (a) and (d)(i) do not apply to "bodily injury" or "property damage" arising out of heat, smoke or fumes from a hostile fire.

As used in this exclusion, a hostile fire means one which becomes uncontrollable or breaks out from where it was intended to be.

**(2)** Any loss, cost or expense arising out of any:

**(a)** Request, demand or order that any insured or others test for, monitor, clean up, remove, contain, treat, detoxify or neutralize, or in any way respond to, or assess the effects of pollutants; or

**(b)** Claim or suit by or on behalf of a governmental authority for damages because of testing for, monitoring, cleaning up, removing, containing, treating, detoxifying or neutralizing, or in any way responding to, or assessing the effects of pollutants.

Pollutants means any solid, liquid, gaseous or thermal irritant or contaminant, including smoke, vapor, soot, fumes, acids, alkalis, chemicals and waste. Waste includes materials to be recycled, reconditioned or reclaimed.

**g.** "Bodily injury" or "property damage" arising out of the ownership, maintenance, use or entrustment to others of any aircraft, "auto" or watercraft owned or operated by or rented or loaned to any insured. Use includes operation and "loading or unloading."

  

This exclusion does not apply to:

(1) A watercraft while ashore on premises you own or rent;

(2) A watercraft you do not own that is:

(a) Less than 26 feet long; and

(b) Not being used to carry persons or property for a charge;

(3) Parking an "auto" on, or on the ways next to, premises you own or rent, provided the "auto" is not owned by or rented or loaned to you or the insured;

(4) Liability assumed under any "insured contract" for the ownership, maintenance or use of aircraft or watercraft; or

(5) "Bodily injury" or "property damage" arising out of the operation of any of the equipment listed in paragraph f.(2) or f.(3) of the definition of "mobile equipment" (Section V.8.).

h. "Bodily injury" or "property damage" arising out of:

(1) The transportation of "mobile equipment" by an "auto" owned or operated by or rented or loaned to any insured; or

(2) The use of "mobile equipment" in, or while in practice or preparation for, a prearranged racing, speed or demolition contest or in any stunting activity.

i. "Bodily injury" or "property damage" due to war, whether or not declared, or any act or condition incident to war. War includes civil war, insurrection, rebellion or revolution. This exclusion applies only to liability assumed under a contract or agreement.

j. "Property damage" to:

(1) Property you own, rent, or occupy;

(2) Premises you sell, give away or abandon, if the "property damage" arises out of any part of those premises;

(3) Property loaned to you;

(4) Personal property in the care, custody or control of the insured;

(5) That particular part of real property on which you or any contractors or subcontractors working directly or indirectly on your behalf are performing operations, if the "property damage" arises out of those operations; or

(6) That particular part of any property that must be restored, repaired or replaced because "your work" was incorrectly performed on it.

Paragraph (2) of this exclusion does not apply if the premises are "your work" and were never occupied, rented or held for rental by you.

Paragraphs (3), (4), (5) and (6) of this exclusion do not apply to liability assumed under a sidetrack agreement.

Paragraph (6) of this exclusion does not apply to "property damage" included in the "products-completed operations hazard."

k. "Property damage" to "your product" arising out of it or any part of it.

l. "Property damage" to "your work" arising out of it or any part of it and included in the "products-completed operations hazard."

This exclusion does not apply if the damaged work or the work out of which the damage arises was performed on your behalf by a subcontractor.

m. "Property damage" to "impaired property" or property that has not been physically injured, arising out of:

(1) A defect, deficiency, inadequacy or dangerous condition in "your product" or "your work;" or

(2) A delay or failure by you or anyone acting on your behalf to perform a contract or agreement in accordance with its terms.

This exclusion does not apply to the loss of use of other property arising out of sudden and accidental physical injury to "your product" or "your work" after it has been put to its intended use.

n. Damages claimed for any loss, cost or expense incurred by you or others for the loss of use, withdrawal, recall, inspection, repair, replacement, adjustment, removal or disposal of:

(1) "Your product;"

(2) "Your work;" or

(3) "Impaired property;"

if such product, work, or property is withdrawn or recalled from the market or from use by any person or organization because of a known or suspected defect, deficiency, inadequacy or dangerous condition in it.

Exclusions c. through n. do not apply to damage by fire to premises rented to you. A separate limit of insurance applies to this coverage as described in LIMITS OF INSURANCE (SECTION III).

**COVERAGE B. PERSONAL AND ADVERTISING INJURY LIABILITY**

**1. Insuring Agreement.**

**a.** We will pay those sums that the insured becomes legally obligated to pay as damages because of "personal injury" or "advertising injury" to which this coverage part applies. We will have the right and duty to defend any "suit" seeking those damages. We may at our discretion investigate any "occurrence" or offense and settle any claim or "suit" that may result. But:

(1) The amount we will pay for damages is limited as described in LIMITS OF INSURANCE (SECTION III); and

(2) Our right and duty to defend end when we have used up the applicable limit of insurance in the payment of judgments or settlements under Coverage A or B or medical expenses under Coverage C.

No other obligation or liability to pay sums or perform acts or services is covered unless explicitly provided for under SUPPLEMENTARY PAYMENTS – COVERAGES A AND B.

**b.** This insurance applies to:

(1) "Personal injury" caused by an offense arising out of your business, excluding advertising, publishing, broadcasting or telecasting done by or for you;

(2) "Advertising injury" caused by an offense committed in the course of advertising your goods, products or services;

but only if the offense was committed in the "coverage territory" during the policy period.

**2. Exclusions.**

This insurance does not apply to:

**a.** "Personal injury" or "advertising injury:"

(1) Arising out of oral or written publication of material, if done by or at the direction of the insured with knowledge of its falsity;

(2) Arising out of oral or written publication of material whose first publication took place before the beginning of the policy period;

(3) Arising out of the willful violation of a penal statute or ordinance committed by or with the consent of the insured; or

(4) For which the insured has assumed liability in a contract or agreement. This exclusion does not apply to liability for damages that the insured would have in the absence of the contract or agreement.

**b.** "Advertising injury" arising out of:

(1) Breach of contract, other than misappropriation of advertising ideas under an implied contract;

  

(2) The failure of goods, products or services to conform with advertised quality or performance;

(3) The wrong description of the price of goods, products or services; or

(4) An offense committed by an insured whose business is advertising, broadcasting, publishing or telecasting.

COVERAGE C. MEDICAL PAYMENTS

1. **Insuring Agreement.**

a. We will pay medical expenses as described below for "bodily injury" caused by an accident:

(1) On premises you own or rent;

(2) On ways next to premises you own or rent; or

(3) Because of your operations;

provided that:

(1) The accident takes place in the "coverage territory" and during the policy period;

(2) The expenses are incurred and reported to us within one year of the date of the accident; and

(3) The injured person submits to examination, at our expense, by physicians of our choice as often as we reasonably require.

b. We will make these payments regardless of fault. These payments will not exceed the applicable limit of insurance. We will pay reasonable expenses for:

(1) First aid at the time of an accident;

(2) Necessary medical, surgical, x-ray and dental services, including prosthetic devices; and

(3) Necessary ambulance, hospital, professional nursing and funeral services.

2. **Exclusions.**

We will not pay expenses for "bodily injury:"

a. To any insured.

b. To a person hired to do work for or on behalf of any insured or a tenant of any insured.

c. To a person injured on that part of premises you own or rent that the person normally occupies.

d. To a person, whether or not an employee of any insured, if benefits for the "bodily injury" are payable or must be provided under a workers' compensation or disability benefits law or a similar law.

e. To a person injured while taking part in athletics.

f. Included within the "products-completed operations hazard."

g. Excluded under Coverage A.

h. Due to war, whether or not declared, or any act or condition incident to war. War includes civil war, insurrection, rebellion or revolution.

SUPPLEMENTARY PAYMENTS - COVERAGES A AND B

We will pay, with respect to any claim or "suit" we defend:

1. All expenses we incur.

2. Up to $250 for cost of bail bonds required because of accidents or traffic law violations arising out of the use of any vehicle to which the Bodily Injury Liability Coverage applies. We do not have to furnish these bonds.

3. The cost of bonds to release attachments, but only for bond amounts within the applicable limit of insurance. We do not have to furnish these bonds.

  

4. All reasonable expenses incurred by the insured at our request to assist us in the investigation or defense of the claim or "suit," including actual loss of earnings up to $100 a day because of time off from work.
5. All costs taxed against the insured in the "suit."
6. Prejudgment interest awarded against the insured on that part of the judgment we pay. If we make an offer to pay the applicable limit of insurance, we will not pay any prejudgment interest based on that period of time after the offer.
7. All interest on the full amount of any judgment that accrues after entry of the judgment and before we have paid, offered to pay, or deposited in court the part of the judgment that is within the applicable limit of insurance.

These payments will not reduce the limits of insurance.

SECTION II - WHO IS AN INSURED

1. If you are designated in the Declarations as:
   a. An individual, you and your spouse are insureds, but only with respect to the conduct of a business of which you are the sole owner.
   b. A partnership or joint venture, you are an insured. Your members, your partners, and their spouses are also insureds, but only with respect to the conduct of your business.
   c. An organization other than a partnership or joint venture, you are an insured. Your executive officers and directors are insureds, but only with respect to their duties as your officers or directors. Your stockholders are also insureds, but only with respect to their liability as stockholders.
2. Each of the following is also an insured:
   a. Your employees, other than your executive officers, but only for acts within the scope of their employment by you. However, no employee is an insured for:
      (1) "Bodily injury" or "personal injury" to you or to a co-employee while in the course of his or her employment, or the spouse, child, parent, brother or sister of that co-employee as a consequence of such "bodily injury" or "personal injury," or for any obligation to share damages with or repay someone else who must pay damages because of the injury; or
      (2) "Bodily injury" or "personal injury" arising out of his or her providing or failing to provide professional health care services; or
      (3) "Property damage" to property owned or occupied by or rented or loaned to that employee, any of your other employees, or any of your partners or members (if you are a partnership or joint venture).
   b. Any person (other than your employee), or any organization while acting as your real estate manager.
   c. Any person or organization having proper temporary custody of your property if you die, but only:
      (1) With respect to liability arising out of the maintenance or use of that property; and
      (2) Until your legal representative has been appointed.
   d. Your legal representative if you die, but only with respect to duties as such. That representative will have all your rights and duties under this Coverage Part.
3. With respect to "mobile equipment" registered in your name under any motor vehicle registration law, any person is an insured while driving such equipment along a public highway with your permission. Any other person or organization responsible for the conduct of such person is also an insured, but only with respect to liability arising out of the operation of the equipment, and only if no other insurance of any kind is available to that person or organization for this liability. However, no person or organization is an insured with respect to:
   a. "Bodily injury" to a co-employee of the person driving the equipment; or
   b. "Property damage" to property owned by, rented to, in the charge of or occupied by you or the employer of any person who is an insured under this provision.
4. Any organization you newly acquire or form, other than a partnership or joint venture, and over which you maintain ownership or majority interest, will qualify as a Named Insured if there is no other similar insurance available to that organization. However:
   a. Coverage under this provision is afforded only until the 90th day after you acquire or form the organization or the end of the policy period, whichever is earlier;

  

b. Coverage A does not apply to "bodily injury" or "property damage" that occurred before you acquired or formed the organization; and

c. Coverage B does not apply to "personal injury" or "advertising injury" arising out of an offense committed before you acquired or formed the organization.

No person or organization is an insured with respect to the conduct of any current or past partnership or joint venture that is not shown as a Named Insured in the Declarations.

SECTION III - LIMITS OF INSURANCE

1. The Limits of Insurance shown in the Declarations and the rules below fix the most we will pay regardless of the number of:

   a. Insureds;

   b. Claims made or "suits" brought; or

   c. Persons or organizations making claims or bringing "suits."

2. The General Aggregate Limit is the most we will pay for the sum of:

   a. Medical expenses under Coverage C;

   b. Damages under Coverage A, except damages because of "bodily injury" or "property damage" included in the "products-completed operations hazard;" and

   c. Damages under Coverage B.

3. The Products-Completed Operations Aggregate Limit is the most we will pay under Coverage A for damages because of "bodily injury" and "property damage" included in the "products-completed operations hazard."

4. Subject to 2. above, the Personal and Advertising Injury Limit is the most we will pay under Coverage B for the sum of all damages because of all "personal injury" and all "advertising injury" sustained by any one person or organization.

5. Subject to 2. or 3. above, whichever applies, the Each Occurrence Limit is the most we will pay for the sum of:

   a. Damages under Coverage A; and

   b. Medical expenses under Coverage C

   because of all "bodily injury" and "property damage" arising out of any one "occurrence."

6. Subject to 5. above, the Fire Damage Limit is the most we will pay under Coverage A for damages because of "property damage" to premises rented to you arising out of any one fire.

7. Subject to 5. above, the Medical Expense Limit is the most we will pay under Coverage C for all medical expenses because of "bodily injury" sustained by any one person.

The limits of this Coverage Part apply separately to each consecutive annual period and to any remaining period of less than 12 months, starting with the beginning of the policy period shown in the Declarations, unless the policy period is extended after issuance for an additional period of less than 12 months. In that case, the additional period will be deemed part of the last preceding period for purposes of determining the Limits of Insurance.

SECTION IV - COMMERCIAL GENERAL LIABILITY CONDITIONS

1. **Bankruptcy.**

   Bankruptcy or insolvency of the insured or of the insured's estate will not relieve us of our obligations under this Coverage Part.

2. **Duties In The Event Of Occurrence, Claim Or Suit.**

   a. You must see to it that we are notified as soon as practicable of an "occurrence" or an offense which may result in a claim. To the extent possible, notice should include:

      (1) How, when and where the "occurrence" or offense took place;

      (2) The names and addresses of any injured persons and witnesses; and

      (3) The nature and location of any injury or damage arising out of the "occurrence" or offense.

   b. If a claim is made or "suit" is brought against any insured, you must:

      (1) Immediately record the specifics of the claim or "suit" and the date received; and

      (2) Notify us as soon as practicable.

      You must see to it that we receive written notice of the claim or "suit" as soon as practicable.

  

c. You and any other involved insured must:

(1) Immediately send us copies of any demands, notices, summonses or legal papers received in connection with the claim or "suit;"

(2) Authorize us to obtain records and other information;

(3) Cooperate with us in the investigation, settlement or defense of the claim or "suit;" and

(4) Assist us, upon our request, in the enforcement of any right against any person or organization which may be liable to the insured because of injury or damage to which this insurance may also apply.

d. No insureds will, except at their own cost, voluntarily make a payment, assume any obligation, or incur any expense, other than for first aid, without our consent.

**3. Legal Action Against Us.**

No person or organization has a right under this Coverage Part:

a. To join us as a party or otherwise bring us into a "suit" asking for damages from an insured; or

b. To sue us on this Coverage Part unless all of its terms have been fully complied with.

A person or organization may sue us to recover on an agreed settlement or on a final judgment against an insured obtained after an actual trial; but we will not be liable for damages that are not payable under the terms of this Coverage Part or that are in excess of the applicable limit of insurance. An agreed settlement means a settlement and release of liability signed by us, the insured and the claimant or the claimant's legal representative.

**4. Other Insurance.**

If other valid and collectible insurance is available to the insured for a loss we cover under Coverages A or B of this Coverage Part, our obligations are limited as follows:

a. Primary Insurance

This insurance is primary except when b. below applies. If this insurance is primary, our obligations are not affected unless any of the other insurance is also primary. Then, we will share with all that other insurance by the method described in c. below.

b. Excess Insurance

This insurance is excess over any of the other insurance, whether primary, excess, contingent or on any other basis:

(1) That is Fire, Extended Coverage, Builder's Risk, Installation Risk or similar coverage for "your work;"

(2) That is Fire insurance for premises rented to you; or

(3) If the loss arises out of the maintenance or use of aircraft, "autos" or watercraft to the extent not subject to Exclusion g. of Coverage A (Section I).

When this insurance is excess, we will have no duty under Coverage A or B to defend any claim or "suit" that any other insurer has a duty to defend. If no other insurer defends, we will undertake to do so, but we will be entitled to the insured's rights against all those other insurers.

When this insurance is excess over other insurance, we will pay only our share of the amount of the loss, if any, that exceeds the sum of:

(1) The total amount that all such other insurance would pay for the loss in the absence of this insurance; and

(2) The total of all deductible and self-insured amounts under all that other insurance.

We will share the remaining loss, if any, with any other insurance that is not described in this Excess Insurance provision and was not bought specifically to apply in excess of the Limits of Insurance shown in the Declarations of this Coverage Part.

c. Method of Sharing

If all of the other insurance permits contribution by equal shares, we will follow this method also. Under this approach each insurer contributes equal amounts until it has paid its applicable limit of insurance or none of the loss remains, whichever comes first.

  

If any of the other insurance does not permit contribution by equal shares, we will contribute by limits. Under this method, each insurer's share is based on the ratio of its applicable limit of insurance to the total applicable limits of insurance of all insurers.

5. **Premium Audit.**
   a. We will compute all premiums for this Coverage Part in accordance with our rules and rates.
   b. Premium shown in this Coverage Part as advance premium is a deposit premium only. At the close of each audit period we will compute the earned premium for that period. Audit premiums are due and payable on notice to the first Named Insured. If the sum of the advance and audit premiums paid for the policy term is greater than the earned premium, we will return the excess to the first Named Insured.
   c. The first Named Insured must keep records of the information we need for premium computation, and send us copies at such times as we may request.
6. **Representations.**

   By accepting this policy, you agree:
   a. The statements in the Declarations are accurate and complete;
   b. Those statements are based upon representations you made to us; and
   c. We have issued this policy in reliance upon your representations.
7. **Separation Of Insureds.**

   Except with respect to the Limits of Insurance, and any rights or duties specifically assigned in this Coverage Part to the first Named Insured, this insurance applies:
   a. As if each Named Insured were the only Named Insured; and
   b. Separately to each insured against whom claim is made or "suit" is brought.
8. **Transfer Of Rights Of Recovery Against Others To Us.**

   If the insured has rights to recover all or part of any payment we have made under this Coverage Part, those rights are transferred to us. The insured must do nothing after loss to impair them. At our request, the insured will bring "suit" or transfer those rights to us and help us enforce them.
9. **When We Do Not Renew.**

   If we decide not to renew this Coverage Part, we will mail or deliver to the first Named Insured shown in the Declarations written notice of the nonrenewal not less than 30 days before the expiration date.

   If notice is mailed, proof of mailing will be sufficient proof of notice.

SECTION V - DEFINITIONS

1. "Advertising injury" means injury arising out of one or more of the following offenses:
   a. Oral or written publication of material that slanders or libels a person or organization or disparages a person's or organization's goods, products or services;
   b. Oral or written publication of material that violates a person's right of privacy;
   c. Misappropriation of advertising ideas or style of doing business; or
   d. Infringement of copyright, title or slogan.
2. "Auto" means a land motor vehicle, trailer or semitrailer designed for travel on public roads, including any attached machinery or equipment. But "auto" does not include "mobile equipment."
3. "Bodily injury" means bodily injury, sickness or disease sustained by a person, including death resulting from any of these at any time.
4. "Coverage territory" means:
   a. The United States of America (including its territories and possessions), Puerto Rico and Canada;
   b. International waters or airspace, provided the injury or damage does not occur in the course of travel or transportation to or from any place not included in a. above; or
   c. All parts of the world if:
      (1) The injury or damage arises out of:
         (a) Goods or products made or sold by you in the territory described in a. above, or

  

(b) The activities of a person whose home is in the territory described in a. above, but is away for a short time on your business; and

(2) The insured's responsibility to pay damages is determined in a "suit" on the merits, in the territory described in a. above or in a settlement we agree to.

5. "Impaired property" means tangible property, other than "your product" or "your work," that cannot be used or is less useful because:

a. It incorporates "your product" or "your work" that is known or thought to be defective, deficient, inadequate or dangerous; or

b. You have failed to fulfill the terms of a contract or agreement;

if such property can be restored to use by:

a. The repair, replacement, adjustment or removal of "your product" or "your work;" or

b. Your fulfilling the terms of the contract or agreement.

6. "Insured contract" means:

a. A lease of premises;

b. A sidetrack agreement;

c. Any easement or license agreement, except in connection with construction or demolition operations on or within 50 feet of a railroad;

d. An obligation, as required by ordinance, to indemnify a municipality, except in connection with work for a municipality;

e. An elevator maintenance agreement;

f. That part of any other contract or agreement pertaining to your business (including an indemnification of a municipality in connection with work performed for a municipality) under which you assume the tort liability of another party to pay for "bodily injury" or "property damage" to a third person or organization. Tort liability means a liability that would be imposed by law in the absence of any contract or agreement.

An "insured contract" does not include that part of any contract or agreement:

a. That indemnifies any person or organization for "bodily injury" or "property damage" arising out of construction or demolition operations, within 50 feet of any railroad property and affecting any railroad bridge or trestle, tracks, road-beds, tunnel, underpass or crossing;

b. That indemnifies an architect, engineer or surveyor for injury or damage arising out of:

(1) Preparing, approving or failing to prepare or approve maps, drawings, opinions, reports, surveys, change orders, designs or specifications; or

(2) Giving directions or instructions, or failing to give them, if that is the primary cause of the injury or damage;

c. Under which the insured, if an architect, engineer or surveyor, assumes liability for an injury or damage arising out of the insured's rendering or failure to render professional services, including those listed in b. above and supervisory, inspection or engineering services; or

d. That indemnifies any person or organization for damage by fire to premises rented or loaned to you.

7. "Loading or unloading" means the handling of property:

a. After it is moved from the place where it is accepted for movement into or onto an aircraft, watercraft or "auto;"

b. While it is in or on an aircraft, watercraft or "auto;" or

c. While it is being moved from an aircraft, watercraft or "auto" to the place where it is finally delivered;

but "loading or unloading" does not include the movement of property by means of a mechanical device, other than a hand truck, that is not attached to the aircraft, watercraft or "auto."

8. "Mobile equipment" means any of the following types of land vehicles, including any attached machinery or equipment:

  

a. Bulldozers, farm machinery, forklifts and other vehicles designed for use principally off public roads;

b. Vehicles maintained for use solely on or next to premises you own or rent;

c. Vehicles that travel on crawler treads;

d. Vehicles, whether self-propelled or not, maintained primarily to provide mobility to permanently mounted:

(1) Power cranes, shovels, loaders, diggers or drills; or

(2) Road construction or resurfacing equipment such as graders, scrapers or rollers;

e. Vehicles not described in a., b., c. or d. above that are not self-propelled and are maintained primarily to provide mobility to permanently attached equipment of the following types:

(1) Air compressors, pumps and generators, including spraying, welding, building cleaning, geophysical exploration, lighting and well servicing equipment; or

(2) Cherry pickers and similar devices used to raise or lower workers;

f. Vehicles not described in a., b., c. or d. above maintained primarily for purposes other than the transportation of persons or cargo.

However, self-propelled vehicles with the following types of permanently attached equipment are not "mobile equipment" but will be considered "autos:"

(1) Equipment designed primarily for:

(a) Snow removal;

(b) Road maintenance, but not construction or resurfacing;

(c) Street cleaning;

(2) Cherry pickers and similar devices mounted on automobile or truck chassis and used to raise or lower workers; and

(3) Air compressors, pumps and generators, including spraying, welding, building cleaning, geophysical exploration, lighting and well servicing equipment.

9. "Occurrence" means an accident, including continuous or repeated exposure to substantially the same general harmful conditions.

10. "Personal injury" means injury, other than "bodily injury," arising out of one or more of the following offenses:

a. False arrest, detention or imprisonment;

b. Malicious prosecution;

c. The wrongful eviction from, wrongful entry into, or invasion of the right of private occupancy of a room, dwelling or premises that a person occupies by or on behalf of its owner, landlord or lessor;

d. Oral or written publication of material that slanders or libels a person or organization or disparages a person's or organization's goods, products or services; or

e. Oral or written publication of material that violates a person's right of privacy.

11.a. "Products-completed operations hazard" includes all "bodily injury" and "property damage" occurring away from premises you own or rent and arising out of "your product" or "your work" except:

(1) Products that are still in your physical possession; or

(2) Work that has not yet been completed or abandoned.

b. "Your work" will be deemed completed at the earliest of the following times:

(1) When all of the work called for in your contract has been completed.

(2) When all of the work to be done at the site has been completed if your contract calls for work at more than one site.

(3) When that part of the work done at a job site has been put to its intended use by any person or organization other than another contractor or subcontractor working on the same project.

Work that may need service, maintenance, correction, repair or replacement, but which is otherwise complete, will be treated as completed.

c. This hazard does not include "bodily injury" or "property damage" arising out of:

  

(1) The transportation of property, unless the injury or damage arises out of a condition in or on a vehicle created by the "loading or unloading" of it;

(2) The existence of tools, uninstalled equipment or abandoned or unused materials;

(3) Products or operations for which the classification in this Coverage Part or in our manual of rules includes products or completed operations.

12. "Property damage" means:

a. Physical injury to tangible property, including all resulting loss of use of that property. All such loss of use shall be deemed to occur at the time of the physical injury that caused it; or

b. Loss of use of tangible property that is not physically injured. All such loss shall be deemed to occur at the time of the "occurrence" that caused it.

13. "Suit" means a civil proceeding in which damage because of "bodily injury," "property damage," "personal injury" or "advertising injury" to which this insurance applies are alleged. "Suit" includes:

a. An arbitration proceeding in which such damages are claimed and to which you must submit or do submit with our consent; or

b. Any other alternative dispute resolution proceeding in which such damages are claimed and to which you submit with our consent.

14. "Your product" means:

a. Any goods or products, other than real property, manufactured, sold, handled, distributed or disposed of by:

(1) You;

(2) Others trading under your name; or

(3) A person or organization whose business or assets you have acquired; and

b. Containers (other than vehicles), materials, parts or equipment furnished in connection with such goods or products.

"Your product" includes:

a. Warranties or representations made at any time with respect to the fitness, quality, durability, performance or use of "your product;" and

b. The providing of or failure to provide warnings or instructions.

"Your product" does not include vending machines or other property rented to or located for the use of others but not sold.

15. "Your work" means:

a. Work or operations performed by you or on your behalf; and

b. Materials, parts or equipment furnished in connection with such work or operations.

"Your work" includes:

a. Warranties or representations made at any time with respect to the fitness, quality, durability, performance or use of "your work;" and

b. The providing of or failure to provide warnings or instructions.

  

# Appendix F

## LAWYERS' MUTUAL INSURANCE COMPANY



## LAWYERS' MUTUAL INSURANCE COMPANY

### IMPORTANT

The policy contained herein does not become effective unless a DECLARATIONS insert is issued to form a part hereof.

### NOTICE

THIS IS A CLAIMS-MADE POLICY

This is a "Claims-Made" policy. The coverage afforded by this policy is limited to Claims arising from the performance of Professional Services which are first made against the Insured and reported in writing to the Company while the policy is in force. Please review the policy carefully and discuss the coverage thereunder with your insurance agent, broker or other representative.

This policy excludes prior acts. Unless otherwise provided in an endorsement attached to this policy, this policy provides no coverage or defense for acts, errors, omissions or personal injuries which occur prior to the effective date of the first policy issued to the Named Insured or any predecessor thereof by the Company and continuously renewed thereafter.



Form 1 Revised 6-87

In consideration of the undertaking of the Named Insured to pay, when due, the premium, the Deductible, and other amounts to the Company as described herein and in reliance upon the statements in the application made a part hereof and subject to all the terms and conditions of this policy, Lawyers' Mutual Insurance Company ("Company") agrees with the Named Insured as follows:

**ARTICLE 1.**

# The Definitions

Whenever used in this policy the term

1.1 "Claim" means:

a demand including service of suit or institution of arbitration proceedings, for money against an Insured. A Multiple Claim shall constitute one Claim for purposes of this policy.

1.2 "Claim Expenses" means:

(a) Except as provided in Section 1.2 (b) below:

(i) fees charged by any Lawyer designated by the Company;

(ii) all other fees, costs and expenses incurred by the Company resulting from the investigation, adjustment, defense and appeal of a Claim;

(iii) reasonable fees, at hourly rates and in the aggregate per comparable Claim not to exceed those customarily charged by the panel of defense counsel designated by the Company, charged by any Lawyer designated by the Insured with the prior written consent of the Company.

(b) Claim Expenses does not include salaried charges of regular employees or officials of the Company, nor does Claim Expenses include any fees or costs incurred by the Insured without the prior written consent of the Company, including but not limited to any fees and costs incurred prior to the date the Claim out of which such fees and costs arise is first reported to the Company. The Company shall have no obligation to apply for or furnish, or provide collateral for, attachment or appeal bonds. However, premiums for such bonds shall constitute Claim Expenses. Claim Expenses shall not include fees charged by any Lawyer designated by the Insured with the prior written consent of the Company in excess of amounts specified in Section 1.2(a)(iii).

1.3 "Claim Expense Allowance" means:

a $50,000 allowance for Claim Expenses, in excess of the Deductible, and aggregate for all Claims, as provided for in Section 4.4 of this policy entitled "Damages and Excess Claim Expenses Included in Policy Limits".

1.4 "Damages" means:

a monetary judgment, award or settlement but does not include:

(a) any fine, sanction, penalty, or punitive or exemplary damages;

(b) Claim Expenses including, but not limited to, legal fees, costs or expenses in connection with a monetary judgment, award or settlement; or

(c) restitution of legal fees previously paid to any Insured.

1.5 "Deductible" means:

the deductible applicable to each Claim under the policy as set forth in Section 4.5 of this policy.

1.6 "Excess Claim Expenses" means:

any Claim Expenses in excess of the Claim Expense Allowance. Excess Claim Expenses are included in policy limits and reduce amounts available to pay Damages.

1.7 "Extended Reporting Period" means:

the period provided for in an endorsement issued pursuant to Section 2.6 of this policy entitled "Extended Reporting Option."

1.8 "Incidental Interest in Publicly Traded Securities" means:

beneficial ownership of securities of a class registered under Section 12 of the Securities Exchange Act of 1934 or exempted from registration by Section 12(g)(2)(A) thereof, if, taking into account the beneficial ownership interest of each and every Insured and the beneficial ownership interest of their respective Related Individuals as a group, such group does not beneficially own more than 1% of the outstanding securities of such class.

1.9 "Insured" means:

(a) the Named Insured, defined as the partnership, professional corporation or individual named in Item 1 of the Declarations;

(b) any Lawyer who is a partner of, stockholder in, or employee of the Named Insured at the effective date of this policy, for so long as such Lawyer remains a partner of, stockholder in, or employee of the Named Insured and solely with respect to acts on behalf of the Named Insured or Predecessor Firm. The individuals listed in Item 2 of the Declarations will be conclusively presumed to constitute all such individuals at the effective date of this policy;

[E5095]

(c) any Lawyer who becomes a stockholder in, partner of, or employee of the Named Insured during the policy period, who was not an Insured at the effective date of this policy, for so long as such Lawyer remains a stockholder in, partner of, or an employee of the Named Insured and solely with respect to acts on behalf of the Named Insured. A Lawyer shall be an Insured pursuant to this subsection 1.9(c), if and only if the Named Insured has given notice of the name of such Lawyer to the Company in writing within 30 days after the date of such Lawyer's becoming a stockholder in, partner of, or an employee of the Named Insured and such Lawyer has submitted appropriate underwriting information promptly upon request therefore by the Company;

(d) any Lawyer who was formerly a stockholder in, partner of, or employee of the Named Insured solely with respect to acts on behalf of the Named Insured or Predecessor Firm;

(e) any employee of the Named Insured who is not a Lawyer, solely with respect to acts on behalf of the Named Insured or Predecessor Firm within the course and scope of his employment;

(f) any Predecessor or Successor Firm;

(g) any Lawyer who acts Of Counsel to the Named Insured or Predecessor Firm, but only with respect to acts on behalf of the Named Insured or Predecessor Firm, and under the name of the Named Insured or Predecessor Firm. The individuals listed in Item 2 of the Declarations will be conclusively presumed to constitute all such individuals as of the effective date of this policy. Any Lawyer who is designated "Of Counsel" on the letterhead of the Named Insured subsequent to the effective date of this policy shall be an Insured pursuant to this subsection 1.9(g) if and only if the Named Insured has given notice of the name of such Lawyer to the Company in writing within 30 days after such designation, and such Lawyer has submitted appropriate underwriting information promptly upon request therefore by the Company.

1.10 "Lawyer" means:

a lawyer or professional corporation owned by a lawyer or lawyers.

1.11 "Limit of Liability — Each Claim" means:

the limit of liability for each Claim as set forth in Section 4.1 of this policy.

1.12 "Limit of Liability — Policy Aggregate" means:

the limit of liability for all Claims under the policy as set forth in Section 4.2 of this policy.

1.13 "Multiple Claim" means:

two or more demands received by the Insured for money, including service of suit or institution of arbitration proceedings against the Insured, arising out of a single act, error or omission or Personal Injury or a series of related acts, errors, omissions or Personal Injuries, whether such demands are made against one or more Insureds or whether such demands are made by one or more persons or organizations. Without limitation on the foregoing, a shareholder derivative or class action suit brought against the Insured for acts, errors, omissions or Personal Injuries or a related series of acts, errors, omissions or Personal Injuries shall constitute a Multiple Claim.

1.14 "Of Counsel" means:

a Lawyer who is designated "Of Counsel" on the letterhead of the Named Insured.

1.15 "Personal Injury" means:

(a) false arrest, detention or imprisonment, wrongful entry or eviction; or

(b) the publication or utterance of a libel or slander or other defamatory or disparaging material or a publication or utterance in violation of an individual's right of privacy.

1.16 "Policy Period" means:

the period from the effective date and time of this policy, as set forth in the Declarations, to the policy expiration date and time, as set forth in the Declarations, unless the policy is terminated earlier, in which event the Policy Period shall end on the date of such earlier Termination. The Extended Reporting Period, if any, is excluded from the Policy Period.

1.17 "Predecessor Firm" means:

a partnership or professional corporation which has undergone a dissolution and which is listed in Item 3 of the Declarations, if and only if at least two-thirds of the Lawyers who were shareholders in, partners of, or employees of such firm at the time of its dissolution were at any subsequent time partners of, shareholders in, or employees of the Named Insured.

1.18 "Professional Services" means:

(a) legal services performed for others as a Lawyer or notary public;

(b) legal services performed for others, as an administrator, conservator, receiver, executor, guardian, or trustee of an express trust.

1.19 "Related Individual" means:

the spouse, former spouse, children, grandchildren, parents and siblings of an Insured, and any trust or estate of which any of them is a beneficiary. With respect to a professional corporation which is an Insured, "Related Individual" includes a Related Individual of each owner of such professional corporation.

1.20 "Successor Firm" means:

a professional corporation or partnership which is created upon the dissolution of the Named Insured subsequent to the date of this policy, if immediately subsequent to the dissolution of the Named Insured:

[E5096]

(a) at least two-thirds of the Lawyers who are shareholders in, partners of, or employees of such firm are individuals listed in Item 2 of the Declarations; and

(b) at least one-half of the Lawyers listed in Item 2 of the Declarations are shareholders in, partners of, or employees of such firm.

1.21 "Termination" with respect to the policy means:

cancellation or nonrenewal by either the Named Insured or the Company.

**ARTICLE 2.**

# The Coverage

2.1 **Coverage for Professional Liability.**

Subject to the terms and conditions of this policy, including, but not limited to Article 4 of this policy entitled "Limits of Liability" and Section 2.5 of this policy entitled "Reduction of Claim Payment", and in reliance upon the representations made in the Application attached to and made a part hereof, the Company agrees to pay on behalf of the Insured all sums in excess of the Deductible stated in the Declarations which the Insured shall become legally obligated to pay as Damages as a result of CLAIMS FIRST MADE AGAINST THE INSURED DURING THE POLICY PERIOD AND REPORTED IN WRITING TO THE COMPANY DURING THE POLICY PERIOD:

(a) By reason of any act, error, omission or Personal Injury arising out of Professional Services rendered or that should have been rendered by the Insured or by any person whose Professional Services were performed solely at the direction of the Insured and for whose acts, errors, omissions or Personal Injuries the Insured is legally responsible;

(b) By reason of any act, error, omission or Personal Injury committed by any non-Lawyer employee of the Named Insured but solely if arising out of services rendered within the scope of such person's employment by the Named Insured and arising out of the Named Insured's Professional Services.

PROVIDED THAT such act, error or omission or such Personal Injury happens on or subsequent to the effective date of the first policy issued to the Named Insured or any Predecessor Firm by the Company and continuously renewed and maintained in effect to the inception of this Policy Period.

2.2 **Defense and Settlement.**

For any Claim seeking Damages with respect to such insurance as is afforded by the policy, the Company shall have the right to appoint counsel and shall have the duty to defend such Claim even if any or all of the allegations of the Claim are groundless, false or fraudulent. It is further agreed that the Company may make such investigation, undertake such negotiations and with the written consent of the Insured, such settlement of any Claim as it deems expedient. If the Insured shall refuse to consent to any settlement or compromise recommended by the Company and acceptable to the claimant and shall elect to continue to contest the Claim, then the Company's liability shall not exceed the amount for which the Company would have been liable for Damages and Claim Expenses at the time the Claim could have been settled or compromised.

It is further provided that the Company shall not be obligated to pay any Damages or Claim Expenses, or continue to undertake defense of any Claim after the Limit of Liability — Each Claim or the Limit of Liability — Policy Aggregate have been exhausted by payments of Damages and Claim Expenses, and that, in such a case, the Company shall have the right to withdraw from further defense thereof, by tendering control of the defense to the Named Insured and the Named Insured agrees, as a condition to the issuance of this policy to accept such tender. The Company shall have no obligation to apply for or furnish, or provide collateral for, attachment or appeal bonds.

2.3 **Payment of Claim Expenses.**

Subject to Article 4 of this policy entitled "Limits of Liability," including, without limitation, Sections 4.1, 4.2, 4.4 and 4.5 thereof entitled respectively "Limit of Liability — Each Claim", "Limit of Liability — Policy Aggregate", "Damages and Claim Expenses Included in Limits of Liability", and "Deductible", the Company shall pay Claim Expenses.

2.4 **Policy Territory.**

This policy applies to acts, errors or omissions occurring anywhere in the world, provided that the Company shall have no obligation to pay any amount as Damages pursuant to a judgment or award made in any suit or proceeding brought in a jurisdiction outside of the United States (including its territories and possessions) or Canada, or defend the Insured pursuant to Section 2.2 of this policy entitled "Defense and Settlement" in such suit or proceeding. However, the Company may, at its option, assume the defense of such a suit or proceeding. Even if the Company defends such a suit or proceeding, it shall have no obligation to pay any amount on behalf of the Insured with respect to any judgment or award of Damages in such proceeding.

2.5 **Reduction of Claim Payment.**

The Company shall reduce any sum otherwise payable on behalf of the Insured as Damages with respect to a Claim by an amount equal to any amount (a) received by the Insured on or after the date such Claim is first made against the Insured for any Professional Services rendered to the claimant, plus (b) any amount claimed, as of the date payment is made on behalf of an Insured by the Company as Damages, by the Insured for Professional Services rendered to the claimant.

[E5097]

2.6 **Extended Reporting Option.**

In case of Termination by either the Named Insured or the Company, the Named Insured shall have the right, upon payment of an additional premium, within 30 days of the Termination, to have issued a policy providing an Extended Reporting Period covering Claims first reported during the Extended Reporting Period on acts, errors or omissions occurring prior to the Termination date and on or subsequent to the effective date of the first policy issued to the Named Insured or any Predecessor Firm by the Company and continuously renewed and maintained in effect to the inception of this Policy Period (or such earlier date or dates as provided in a prior acts endorsement to this policy). The price and terms of such policy and the duration of the Extended Reporting Period shall be solely within the discretion of the Company. Issuance of such policy shall not increase the Limit of Liability — Each Claim or the Limit of Liability — Policy Aggregate.

If, on the date of Termination, the Named Insured has failed to pay a premium due or has failed, after demand, to reimburse the Company such amounts as the Company has paid as Damages or for Claim Expenses in excess of the applicable Limits of Liability, or within the amount of the applicable Deductible, or has otherwise failed to pay other amounts due the Company, the Named Insured shall not have the right to have such Extended Reporting Period policy issued.

**ARTICLE 3.**

# The Exclusions

THIS POLICY DOES NOT APPLY:

3.1 To any Claim based on or arising out of any criminal act, error, omission or Personal Injury committed by an Insured or any dishonest, fraudulent or malicious acts, errors, omissions or Personal Injuries committed by an Insured with actual, dishonest or fraudulent purpose or intent or with Malice. As used herein, "Malice" means conduct which is intended by the Insured to cause injury or conduct which is carried on by the Insured with conscious disregard of the rights or safety of others.

3.2 To any Claim made by any Insured or a present, former or prospective employer, partner, officer, director, owner, stockholder or employee or Related Individual of any Insured.

3.3 To any Claim, or any portion of a Claim, for emotional distress, mental illness, humiliation, bodily injury, sickness, disease, or death of any person or injury to, conversion of, or destruction of, any tangible property or to the loss of use thereof.

3.4 To any loss sustained by any Insured as the beneficiary or distributee of any trust or estate.

3.5 To Damages arising out of any and all Claims made under this policy to the extent Damages for any such Claim or for all such Claims in the aggregate are in excess of $50,000 and are based on liability under:

(a) Statutes of the United States or any rules or regulations promulgated thereunder relating to the issuance, offering, sale or distribution of securities, including, without limitation:

(i) The Securities Act of 1933, as amended;

(ii) The Securities Exchange Act of 1934, as amended;

(iii) The Public Utility Holding Company Act of 1935, as amended;

(iv) The Trust Indenture Act of 1939, as amended;

(v) The Investment Advisors Act of 1940, as amended;

(vi) The Investment Company Act of 1940, as amended;

(b) Statutes of California or any rules or regulations promulgated thereunder relating to the issuance, offering, sale or distribution of securities, including, without limitation:

(i) The Corporate Securities Law of 1968, as amended, except those transactions arising solely under the provisions of Sections 25102(f) or 25102(h), as amended, of the California Corporations Code;

(ii) Comparable provisions of California law relating to the jurisdiction of the Real Estate Commissioner, the Insurance Commissioner or other state regulatory authority over the issuance, offering, sale or distribution of securities;

(c) Statutes or rules or regulations promulgated thereunder, of any other jurisdiction, United States or foreign, which are comparable in purpose or scope to the statutes encompassed in (a) and/or (b) above.

3.6 To any Claim made against or by any business enterprise (other than the Named Insured), not-for profit organization (including a charity), or pension, welfare, profit sharing, mutual or investment plan or trust not named in the Declarations in which any Insured or Related Individual is a director, officer, employee, trustee, administrator, partner, manager or with respect to which any Insured or Related Individual has any ownership interest (whether through ownership of stock, partnership shares or otherwise), unless such interest consists solely of an Incidental Interest in Publicly Traded Securities.

3.7 To any Claim based on or arising out of any Insured's services and/or capacity as:

(a) an officer, director, partner, trustee, or employee of a business enterprise or charitable organization or pension, welfare, profit sharing, mutual or investment fund or trust;

(b) a public official, or an employee of a governmental body, subdivision, or agency;

[E5098]

(c) a fiduciary under the Employee Retirement Income Security Act of 1974 and its amendments or any regulation or order issued pursuant thereto, except if the Insured is deemed to be a fiduciary solely by reason of legal advice rendered with respect to an employee benefit plan.

3.8 To any Claim based on or arising out of discrimination of any kind by any Insured including, but not limited to, discrimination on the basis of race, national origin, creed, religion, age, sex or marital status.

3.9 To any Claim based on or arising out of the certification or acknowledgment of a signature by any Insured acting in the capacity of a notary public if such certification or acknowledgment was made without the contemporaneous physical presence of the individual whose act of signature was certified or acknowledged.

3.10 To any Claim based on or arising out of a contract for, or other right relating to, division of fees or fee apportionment between any Insured and any other Lawyer or Lawyers.

3.11 To any Claim, proceeding or suit brought by any governmental or quasi-governmental regulatory agency (including, but not limited to, the State Bar of California) partly or wholly seeking to impose disciplinary action, including but not limited to reprimand, suspension or disbarment, injunctive relief, criminal sanctions, statutory fines or incidental damages.

3.12 To any Claim based on or arising out of an obligation assumed by contract other than an obligation to perform Professional Services.

3.13 To any Claim based on or arising out of the rendering of investment advice by any Insured to any person in connection with the purchase or sale of any investment or property, including but not limited to, securities, real property, commodities or franchises, or based on or arising out of any Insured's services or capacity as a broker, dealer, investment advisor, accountant, real estate broker, or real estate agent.

3.14 To any Claim based on or arising out of deprivation by any Insured of any rights, privileges or immunities secured by the Constitution and laws of the United States of America or the States thereof, including but not limited to, Federal Civil Rights Act of 1964, Federal Civil Rights Act of 1957, Federal Civil Rights Act of 1968, California Unruh Civil Rights Act (California Civil Code § 51 et seq.), California Fair Employment and Housing Act (California Government Code § 12900 et seq.), the California Rumford Act (Health & Safety Code § 3500 et seq.) and other similar statutes.

**ARTICLE 4.**

# Limits of Liability

4.1 **Limit of Liability — Each Claim.**

The Liability of the Company for each Claim FIRST MADE AGAINST THE INSURED DURING THE POLICY PERIOD AND REPORTED IN WRITING TO THE COMPANY DURING THE POLICY PERIOD shall not exceed the amount stated in the Declarations for each Claim, subject to the $50,000 limitation on Damages with respect to each Claim to which Section 3.5 of this policy is applicable.

4.2 **Limit of Liability — Policy Aggregate.**

Subject to the Limit of Liability — Each Claim, and subject to the $50,000 limitation on Damages with respect to all Claims to which Section 3.5 of this policy is applicable, liability of the Company shall not exceed the amount stated in the Declarations as "Aggregate" as a result of all Claims FIRST MADE AGAINST THE INSURED DURING THE POLICY PERIOD AND REPORTED IN WRITING TO THE COMPANY DURING THE POLICY PERIOD.

4.3 **Multiple Insureds, Claims and Claimants.**

A Multiple Claim shall be one Claim for all purposes of this policy. The inclusion in a Claim of more than one Insured or the making of demands by more than one person or organization shall not operate to increase the Company's limit of liability.

4.4 **Damages and Excess Claim Expenses Included in Limits of Liability.**

There shall be a Claim Expense Allowance of $50,000 for aggregate Claim Expenses incurred with respect to all Claims FIRST MADE AGAINST THE INSURED DURING THE POLICY PERIOD AND REPORTED IN WRITING TO THE COMPANY DURING THE POLICY PERIOD. Claim Expenses included within the Deductible shall not be charged against the Claim Expense Allowance. Claim Expenses which exceed the Claim Expense Allowance are referred to in this policy as Excess Claim Expenses. Excess Claim Expenses shall be paid and applied first against and shall reduce the Limit of Liability — Each Claim and the Limit of Liability — Policy Aggregate. The difference between applicable Limits and Excess Claim Expenses, if any, shall be the amount available to pay Damages.

4.5 **Deductible.**

The Deductible stated in the Declarations shall be applicable to Damages and Claim Expenses with respect to Each Claim first made during the Policy Period, and the Company shall not be liable for the Deductible. The Deductible shall first be applied to Claim Expenses and then to Damages.

4.6 **Reimbursement.**

If the Company has paid any amounts as Damages or Claim Expenses in excess of the applicable Limit of Liability — Each Claim or Limit of Liability — Policy Aggregate or within the amount of the applicable Deductible, the Named Insured shall be liable to the Company for any and all such amounts and upon written demand, shall pay such amounts within 30 days to the Company. [E5099]

ARTICLE 5.

# Claims

5.1 **Notice of Claim or Suit.**

As a condition precedent to the Insured's right to the protection afforded by this insurance, the Insured shall, as soon as practicable during the Policy Period, give to the Company written notice of any Claim made against the Insured directed to Lawyers' Mutual Insurance Company, 134 Kenwood Street, Burbank, California, 91505-4201, Attention: Claims Representative.

In the event suit is brought against the Insured, the Insured shall IMMEDIATELY forward to the Company, directed to the attention of the Company's Claims Representative, every demand, notice, summons or other process received by him or by his representatives.

Even though it does not qualify as a Claim under this policy, the Insured shall, as soon as practicable during the Policy Period, give to the Company similar written notice of any demand by another for remedial services and of any required participation in hearings or proceedings before governmental agencies or entities with regard to his activities as a Lawyer.

5.2 **Assistance and Cooperation of the Insured.**

The Insured shall cooperate with the Company and upon the Company's request shall submit to examination and interrogation by a representative of the Company under oath, if required, and shall attend hearings, depositions and trials and shall assist in effecting settlement, securing and giving evidence, obtaining the attendance of witnesses and in the conduct of suits, as well as in the giving of a written statement or statements to the Company's representatives and meeting with such representatives for the purpose of investigation and/or defense all without charge to the Company. The Insured shall further cooperate with the Company and do whatever is necessary to secure and effect any rights of indemnity, contribution or apportionment which the Insured may have, and the Company may exercise those rights in the name of the Insured.

The insured shall notify the Company of the Insured's right to demand arbitration of a Claim and shall exercise the Insured's right to demand or to reject the arbitration of any Claim made against the Insured in accordance with the written instructions of the Company. The Insured shall not make any payments, admit any liability, settle any Claims, assume any obligation, or incur any expense without the prior written consent of the Company.

5.3 **Date Claim Made.**

No Claim (including a Multiple Claim) shall be deemed first made against the Insured during the Policy Period if such Claim or any act, error or omission or Personal Injury giving rise to such Claim was reported by the Insured prior to the effective date of this policy to the Company or other professional liability insurer, or was known to the Insured prior to the effective date of this policy. If during the Policy Period the Named Insured shall first become aware that an Insured has committed an act, error or omission or Personal Injury with respect to which no Claim has been made and if the Company shall be given written notice of:

(a) the specific act, error, omission or Personal Injury;

(b) the injury or damage which has or may result from such act, error, omission or Personal Injury; and

(c) the circumstances by which the Insured first became aware of such act, error, omission, or Personal Injury,

then any Claim that may subsequently be made against the Insured arising out of such act, error, omission or Personal Injury shall be deemed for the purpose of this insurance to have been made and reported in writing on the date such notice is received by the Company.

5.4 **Date of Reporting.**

A Claim shall be considered reported to the Company on the date when it was first reported in writing to the Company. A Multiple Claim shall be considered to be reported in writing to the Company on the date the first of the demands for money which is one of the demands constituting the Multiple Claim is reported in writing to the Company.

5.5 **Subrogation.**

In the event of any payment under this policy, the Company shall be subrogated to all the Insured's rights of recovery therefore, against any person or organization, and the Insured shall execute and deliver instruments and papers and do whatever else is necessary to secure such rights. The Insured shall do nothing after loss to prejudice such rights. The Company shall have the right to pursue subrogation in the name of the Insured or in its own name.

The Company shall not exercise any such rights against any persons, firms or corporations included in the definition of "Insured". Notwithstanding the foregoing, however, the Company reserves the right to exercise any rights of subrogation against an Insured in respect of any Claim brought about or contributed to by the dishonest, fraudulent, criminal, malicious or knowingly wrongful acts, errors or omissions committed by or at the direction of, or ratified by, the Insured or where the Insured intended to inflict the harm out of which the Claim arises or acted with a conscious disregard of the rights of others. And notwithstanding the foregoing, the Company may pursue any subrogation rights or coverage Claims which may exist as against any other coverage possessed by an Insured.

[E5100]

Any amount recovered pursuant to subrogation shall be apportioned as follows:

Any recovery shall first be used for the repayment of expenses incurred toward subrogation; second, to Damages and/or Claim Expenses paid by the Company; third, to any loss and expense payment by the Insured in excess of any Deductible(s); fourth, to any loss and expense payments by an excess carrier on behalf of the Insured; fifth, to any loss and expense payments by any primary carrier on behalf of the Insured; and last, to repayment of the Insured's Deductible.

5.6 **Arbitration.**

In the event that a dispute arises between an Insured and the Company with respect to (1) coverage; (2) liability for premiums, deductibles, or other amounts; or (3) any term or condition of the Policy, the matter shall be resolved by arbitration and such arbitration shall be governed by the provisions of the California Arbitration Act, Sections 1280 through 1294.2 of the Code of Civil Procedure. If a dispute subject to arbitration hereunder should arise, either party may make a demand for arbitration by filing a demand in writing with the other. There shall be three arbitrators, one named in writing by each of the parties within ten (10) days after demand for arbitration is given and a third chosen by the two appointed. Should either party refuse or neglect to join in the appointment of the arbitrator(s) or to furnish the arbitrator(s) with any papers or information demanded, the arbitrator(s) are empowered by both parties to proceed ex parte. Arbitration shall take place in the City of Burbank, County of Los Angeles, State of California, and the hearing before the arbitrator(s) of the matter to be arbitrated shall be at the time and place within said city as is selected by the arbitrator(s). The arbitrator(s) shall select such time and place promptly after his (or their) appointment and shall give written notice thereof to each party at least 20 days prior to the date so fixed. At the hearing any relevant evidence may be presented by either party, and the formal rules of evidence applicable to judicial proceedings shall not govern. Evidence may be admitted or excluded in the sole discretion of the arbitrator(s). Said arbitrator(s) shall hear and determine the matter and shall execute and acknowledge their award in writing and cause a copy thereof to be delivered to each of the parties. The decision of any two arbitrators shall be final, binding and conclusive. The submission of a dispute to the arbitrator(s) may be rendered by any Superior Court having jurisdiction; or such Court may vacate, modify, or correct the award in accordance with the prevailing sections of the California Arbitration Act. If three arbitrators are selected under the foregoing procedure but two of the three fail to reach an agreement in the determination of the matter in question, the matter shall be decided by three new arbitrators who shall be appointed and shall proceed in the same manner, and the process shall be repeated until a decision is finally reached by two of the three arbitrators selected. The costs of such arbitration shall be borne equally by the parties or in such proportions as the arbitrator(s) shall determine.

Each party shall appoint and pay for any counsel appointed to represent it in such arbitration, unless otherwise provided by law.

This Section 5.6 is not to be construed to give a direct right of action against the Company by a claimant not otherwise provided by law.

5.7 **Action Against the Company.**

No action shall lie against the Company unless, as a condition precedent thereto, the Insured shall have fully complied with all the terms of this policy, nor until the amount of the Insured's obligations to pay shall have been fully and finally determined either by judgment against the Insured after actual trial or by written agreement of the claimant and the Company.

Nothing contained in this policy shall give any person or organization any right to join the Company as a co-defendant in any action against the Insured to determine the Insured's liability. Bankruptcy or insolvency of the Insured or the Insured's estate shall not relieve the Company of any of its obligations hereunder.

5.8 **False or Fraudulent Claims.**

If any Insured shall commit fraud in proffering any Claims as to amount or otherwise, this insurance shall become void as to such Insured from the date such fraudulent Claim is proffered.

**ARTICLE 6.**

# Other Conditions

6.1 **Application.**

By acceptance of this policy, the Insured agrees that the statements in the application are his representations, that they shall be deemed material, that this policy is issued in reliance upon the truth of such representations and that this policy embodies all agreements existing between himself and the Company, or any of its agents, relating to this insurance.

6.2 **Other Insurance.**

This insurance shall be in excess of any other valid and collectible insurance available to the Insured whether such other insurance is stated to be primary, contributory, excess, contingent or otherwise, unless such other insurance is written only as a specific excess insurance over the limits of liability provided in this policy. With regard to any other insurance which is listed in the Declarations, the insurance shall be deemed to be written only as specific excess insurance over the limits of liability provided by said other insurance.

[E5101]

6.3 **Policy Changes.**

Notice to any agent or knowledge possessed by any agent or other person acting on behalf of the Company shall not effect a waiver or a change in any part of this policy or estop the Company from asserting any right under the terms of this policy, nor shall the terms of this policy be waived or changed except by endorsement issued to form a part of this policy.

6.4 **Assignment.**

Assignment of interest under this Policy shall not bind the Company unless its consent is endorsed herein.

6.5 **Cancellations.**

This policy may be cancelled for any reason consistent with Section 676.2 of the California Insurance Code, as now in effect or hereafter amended.

This policy may be cancelled by the Named Insured by surrender thereof to the Company or to any of its authorized agents or by mailing to the aforementioned written notice stating when thereafter such cancellation shall be effective. If cancelled by the Named Insured, the Company shall return to the Named Insured a proportion of the premium determined in accordance with the Company's standard practices which may include use of a customary "short rate" table. The Company may offset the return premium against sums otherwise due and owing to the Company by the Named Insured.

This policy may be cancelled by the Company by mailing to the Named Insured, and to the producer of record, if any, at the mailing address shown on the Declarations, written notice stating when, not less than thirty (30) days thereafter, such cancellation shall be effective. However, if the Company cancels the policy because the Insured has failed to pay premium when due, or for fraud, this policy may be cancelled by the Company by mailing a written notice of cancellation to the Named Insured and his producer of record, if any, stating when not less than ten (10) days thereafter, such cancellation shall be effective. The mailing of notice as aforementioned shall be sufficient notice and the effective date of cancellation stated in the notice shall become the end of the Policy Period. Delivery of such written notice by the Named Insured, the Company, or the authorized agent of the Company shall be equivalent to mailing. If cancelled by the Company, returned premium shall be computed pro rata. The Company may offset the return premium against sums otherwise due and owing to the Company by the Named Insured. Premium adjustment may be made at the time cancellation is effected or as soon as practicable thereafter. Without limiting the generality of the foregoing, the Company may cancel this policy if the Named Insured is subject to dissolution and there is no successor firm. Any such cancellation shall not affect the liability of the Named Insured for premiums then due.

6.6 **Premium.**

The premium for this policy is as set forth in the Declarations. Should a person become an Insured pursuant to Section 1.9 of this Policy entitled "Insured," during the Policy Period, the Company may assess a reasonable extra premium for the coverage afforded to such person. Any such additional premium is immediately due and owing upon assessment.

6.7 **Death or Incompetency of Insured.**

If an Insured dies or is adjudged incompetent or bankrupt, this policy shall inure to the benefit of the legal representative of such Insured.

6.8 **Notices.**

Except as specified in Article 5 of this policy entitled "Claims", all notices to the Company required hereunder shall be sent to Lawyers' Mutual Insurance Company, 134 Kenwood Street, Burbank, California, 91505, Attention: Policy Notices.

6.9 **Mutual Policy Condition: Dividends.**

The Named Insured is a member of the Company and shall participate to the extent and upon the conditions fixed and determined by the Board of Directors in accordance with the provisions of law, in the distribution of dividends so fixed and determined.

6.10 **Mutual Policy Condition: Voting.**

The Named Insured is a member of the Company and is entitled to vote, either in person or by proxy, at any and all meetings of the Company, pursuant to the Bylaws and Articles of Incorporation thereof.

6.11 **Mutual Policy Condition: Nonassessable Policy.**

This policy is not assessable

IN WITNESS WHEREOF, LAWYERS' MUTUAL INSURANCE COMPANY has caused this policy to be signed by its President and Secretary at Burbank, California, but the same shall not be binding except in conjunction with a completed Declarations insert issued to the Named Insured to form a part of this policy by a duly authorized representative of the Company.

RICHARDS D. BARGER
Secretary

JAMES D. HADFIELD
President

[E5102]

# Appendix G

# PERSONAL LIABILITY CATASTROPHE POLICY

*This is your policy.*
*Keep it in a safe place.*

## *Personal Liability Catastrophe Policy*

This insurance policy is designed to give you and your family protection against many liabilities not covered by your other policies. We've written it in plain, easy-to-understand English. We hope you'll read it and familiarize yourself with what it says. If you've any questions about what risks are covered or what persons your policy insures, call or write your agent or us and we'll be glad to answer them. As you read the policy, remember that the words **you, your** and **yours** mean the person named on the attached declarations page or his or her wife or husband who lives in the same household. The words **we, us, our** and **ours** mean St. Paul Fire and Marine Insurance Company.

**Where To Find It** **Page**




ST. PAUL FIRE AND MARINE INSURANCE COMPANY
St. Paul, Minnesota 55102
*(A stock insurance company)*
(C4381)

**How This Policy Protects You and Your Family**

We've designed this policy to give you and your family extra liability protection above and beyond the coverage of your present auto, homeowners and other policies listed on the attached declarations page. It doesn't matter whether you bought these other policies from us or other insurance companies.

This policy gives you two types of extra protection. First, it adds to the liability limits of your other policies. Say you have a standard auto policy that covers you up to a $300, 000 liability limit for bodily injury for each accident. With this policy you're covered even if a jury says you have to pay $1,300,000.

Second, there are liabilities your other policies don't cover. Different companies have different policies, but none of them cover the full range of all possible claims. This policy is designed to protect you against some unusual claims that aren't covered by your standard policies. **And its coverage is worldwide – you're protected wherever you happen to be.**

*You have an auto accident while on vacation in Italy. Your auto policy probably covers you only for accidents in the U.S.A. and Canada. This policy has no such limitation.*

We'll give you this extra protection up to the limit listed on the attached declarations page for each accident or incident happening during the policy period. There's no limit to the number of accidents or incidents covered during that period. But we won't pay more than the limit for any one accident or incident, no matter how many claims are made against one or more of those insured. We'll pay the full amount payable under a court decision or out-of-court settlement we agreed to, minus whatever can be collected as recovery or salvage.

But remember, this is a liability policy. It covers only somebody else's claim against you. It doesn't cover damages to your own property, your car, your house or your valuables.

---

**Extra Insurance on Top of Your Other Policies**

Now let's explain the basic conditions of the first type of extra protection that adds to the liability limits of your other policies.

If a liability covered by this policy is also covered by one or more of your other insurance policies, we'll pay only the outstanding balance after all your other insurance and that of all those insured for the same accident is used up. We'll do this up to the limit of this policy. If your other insurance coverage at the time of the accident has lapsed or is less than the limit listed on the attached declarations page, we'll pay only the difference between the coverage you said you had and your total liability. **So remember, you're responsible for the amount of damages to be paid below the limit where this policy applies.**

Also, if your other insurance company becomes insolvent or you broke your contract with them, for instance, you didn't give proper notice of the accident, we'll pay only the difference between the listed minimum limit and your total liability.

If you're covered or should've been covered by other insurance policies listed on the attached declarations page, we won't be responsible for any defense, investigation, negotiation or settlement that should've been made by your other insurance company. And we won't pay for legal expenses such as lawyers' fees, court costs, interest on judgments, salaries or office expenses. But we have the right to enter any such suit if we want to.

---

**Broader Coverage Than Your Other Policies**

Now let's turn to the basic conditions of the **second** type of extra protection when you're **not** covered by another policy. This may happen because of

(C4362)

gaps in your coverage or because a claim against you is so unusual that it isn't covered by standard policies.

*Your son is driving a friend's motorcycle and has an accident. Chances are your auto policy will not provide liability protection for this accident.*

To give you this type of extra protection, we give you broader coverage than you're likely to have in any of your other policies. Our definitions of accident or incident, property damage and personal injury are unusually broad.

*You damage a rented piano or a borrowed car or boat. Most liability policies exclude damage to rented or borrowed property.*

What do we mean by an accident or incident? **Anything that causes property damage, personal injury or death without your expecting or intending it.** If you could've expected the result, you're not covered except for assault and battery committed to save life or property.

If the accident or incident is covered under this policy, we'll pay claims you may legally have to pay because of someone's property damage, personal injury or death.

What do we mean by property damage? **Any damage to tangible property or its loss or destruction. Also the loss of its use** – for instance, the cost of having to rent a substitute car to go to work while the damaged car is being repaired.

What do we mean by personal injury? **Bodily injury, of course. But also injuries to a person's feelings or reputation.** Like mental injury. Mental anguish. Shock. Wrongful eviction. Libel. Slander. Defamation of character. Invasion of privacy. False arrest.

**If a liability covered by this policy is not covered by another policy of yours or anyone else insured, we'll pay claims you legally have to pay up to the limit listed on the attached declarations page. However, you'll have to pay a small deductible of 50% up to the first $500 -- in other words, no more than $250.**

*You've boarded your neighbors' poodle while they're away on vacation. You're careless and the poodle runs away and gets lost. Your neighbors insist on your paying for the loss. If he was an ordinary poodle worth say $400, you pay $200 and we pay $200. But if he was a prize-winning show dog worth $4,000, you pay $250 and we pay $3,750.*

We'll be responsible for your defense and related investigation, negotiation or settlement. And we'll pay all legal expenses and court costs on top of the liability limits of this policy. The details of this are spelled out in **"What Else We Will Do For You."**

**Five Types of Claims Not Covered By This Policy**

This policy does not cover five types of claims:

1. We won't cover any liability connected with the business, profession or occupation of anyone insured, such as malpractice claims against a doctor. Nor will we cover accidents happening on an insured person's business property. But we will cover accidents in and around a one, two- or three-family house held for rental, or on a farm.

2. We won't cover any liability that's payable or has to be provided for under a worker's compensation, occupational disease, unemployment compensation or disability benefits law.

3. We won't cover any liability connected with a nuclear energy incident that's covered by one of the specialized nuclear energy insurance groups. Or would've been covered if the insurance liability limit hadn't been used up.

[C4383]

4. We won't cover liability of any one in his or her capacity as a corporate officer or a member of the board of directors of any corporation except a religious, charitable or civic non-profit corporation.
5. We won't cover uninsured motorists or no-fault auto insurance claims.

**A Closer Look at Your Coverage**

Now that we've given you a bird's-eye view of how this policy will protect you and your family, let's go into details. In the following sections we'll show you how this policy covers your auto, homeowners and other liability.

If you've any doubts whether a specific claim is covered or not, go back to these opening sections to make sure.

Scattered through this policy you'll find examples printed in green ink. Of course these examples are just a handful of illustrations out of many possible situations.

**Your Extra Auto Liability Insurance**

If you have an accident covered by your auto insurance, we'll pay the difference between what's payable under that policy and the sum total of what you legally have to pay, up to the liability limit shown on the attached declarations page.

*You miss a stop sign and crash into a motorcycle. Its 28-year-old married driver is paralyzed from the waist down and will spend the rest of his life in a wheelchair. A jury says you have to pay him $1,300,000. Your standard insurance liability limit is $300,000 for each person. We'll pay the balance of $1,000,000.*

This policy covers any kind of private motor vehicle – cars, trucks, station wagons, jeeps, motorcycles, trailers, semitrailers and so on. **It covers private cars even if they're used for business or carpooling.** But it doesn't cover private cars used as taxis or for hire or any other motor vehicles, such as trucks, used for business.

If you're a farmer, this policy covers any kind of motor vehicle used for your farm, such as trucks and tractors. Coverage for recreational motor vehicles such as golf carts and snowmobiles is explained under "**Your Extra Golf Cart and Snowmobile Insurance.**"

**Broad Auto Coverage for You And Others**

You're covered for any accident involving an auto you own, borrow, rent or use as a temporary substitute. We'll also cover accidents during maintenance, loading and unloading. **And we'll cover your liability to the owner for damage to an auto you borrow or rent.**

We'll also cover anyone else who uses a covered car with your permission provided it's used for the purpose you intended.

*You're transferred from New York to California. You and your family go by plane, so you hire Mike, a college student, to drive the family car west. Mike has an accident in which a passenger of the other car loses his right arm. Mike is sued for $500,000. Mike has no insurance, but he's covered by your automobile policy up to $300,000. We cover him too, and negotiate a settlement for $100,000 for our part of the coverage.*

Under this section we'll cover all relatives living with you and anyone under 21 in your or their care. They're covered for any accidents involving an auto they own, rent, or use as a temporary substitute. But if they borrow a car, they're covered only if they drive or use it with the owner's permission. Even then they have to use it for the purpose intended by the owner.

*Your teenage daughter borrows a car belonging to her friend's father with the understanding that she's to drive to the airport. She's covered if she goes to the airport but not if she goes on a 400-mile trip.*

[C4384]

We'll cover anyone using a car owned by a relative living with you if they have your relative's permission and use it for the purpose intended.

We'll also cover any person or organization legally responsible for the use of a car, if it's used by you or with your permission. But again, the use has to be for the intended purpose.

*You loan your station wagon to a teacher to drive a group of children to the zoo. She and the school are covered by this policy if she actually drives to the zoo, but not if she lets the children off at the zoo and drives to her ' parents' farm 30 miles away.*

*But if you yourself use your station wagon to drive a group of school-children to the zoo, the school is covered whether you drive to the zoo or anywhere else.*

We will **not** cover the owner of a borrowed or rented car or his agents or employees. Nor will we cover sales agencies, repair shops, service stations, storage garages or public parking lots and their agents and employees.

---

**Your Extra Boat Liability Insurance**

If you have an accident covered by your boat liability insurance, we'll make up the difference between what's payable under that policy and the sum total of what you legally have to pay, up to your own limit.

*You own a boat and cause an accident in which someone drowns. A jury says you have to pay $150,000. Your boat liability covers you only up to $100,000. We'll pay the other $50,000.*

If you or a relative living with you own a boat that's 26 feet long or longer we'll pay for extra liability only if it's covered by a boat liability policy listed on the attached declarations page. If such a boat is bought during the policy period you'll have to give us notice within 30 days and pay an added premium if you want it covered.

If you or a relative living with you have or buy a boat that's under 26 feet long, you and they are covered even if you don't have a boat liability policy listed on the attached declarations page.

You're covered for accidents that happen while using a boat you borrow or rent regardless of size. So are your relatives who live with you. But if they borrow a boat they're covered only if they use it with the owner's permission. Even then they have to use it for the purpose intended by the owner. We'll also cover accidents happening during maintenance, loading. or unloading. And your liability to the owner for damage to a boat you borrow or rent.

We'll cover any person or organization legally responsible for the use of a boat if it's used by you or with permission. But that's only true, as with a car, if the boat is used for the purpose you intended.

*Your grownup son, with your permission, takes out your boat for an after-noon on the lake. He's covered if he's just cruising around, but not if he uses the boat, against your instructions, for waterskiing.*

Shipyards, boat repair yards, marinas, yacht clubs, boat sales agencies, boat service stations and the like are **not** covered. Nor are their owners, agents or employees.

---

**Your Extra Golf Cart and Snowmobile Insurance**

Golf carts and snowmobiles are the chief examples of recreational motor vehicles, vehicles designed for use off public roads.

[C4385]

For recreational motor vehicles **owned** by you or by relatives living with you, we'll cover you only if you have coverage for them under a policy listed on the attached declarations page. If there's an accident involving an owned recreational motor vehicle that's not covered by your other liability insurance, we won't cover it either. We'll only make up the difference between what's payable under your other policy and the total of what you legally have to pay up to the liability limit shown on the attached declarations page.

If you or your relative living with you buys a recreational motor vehicle during the policy period, you'll have to give us notice within 30 days and pay an added premium if you want it covered.

You're covered for accidents involving a recreational vehicle you borrow or rent. So are your relatives who live with you. But if they borrow one they're covered only if it's used with the owner's permission -- and then only for the purpose intended by the owner.

We'll also cover your liability for damage to a recreational motor vehicle you borrow or rent.

---

**Your Extra Airplane Insurance**

For any accident involving airplanes, we'll only make up the difference between what's payable under an aircraft liability policy listed on the attached declarations page and the total of what you legally have to pay, up to the liability limit shown on the attached declarations page.

This policy does not give you any coverage for liability resulting from airplane accidents not covered by your other policies.

In no case will we cover your liability for damage to an aircraft you borrow or rent or that's entrusted to you.

---

**Your Extra Personal Liability Insurance**

Under this section we cover accidents or incidents that don't involve autos, boats, recreational vehicles or airplanes.

If an accident is covered by the liability section of your homeowners or comprehensive personal liability insurance, we'll make up the difference between what's payable under that policy and the sum total of what you legally have to pay, up to the liability limit shown on the attached declarations page.

*Your guest falls down your slippery, uncarpeted stairs and suffers permanent injuries. A jury awards her $150,000. Your homeowners policy has a limit of $100,000 for each occurrence. We'll pay the remaining $50,000.*

For this kind of liability we cover you, your relatives living with you, and anyone under 21 in your or their care.

We cover any person or organization legally responsible for an animal owned by anyone insured. But this doesn't apply to vets, pet groomers and the like, and their employees.

*You've boarded your cat with a friend and the cat severely injures someone. We'll protect not only you but also your friend beyond whatever liability insurance he carries.*

We also cover many types of personal injury or property damage that are probably not covered by your homeowners or comprehensive personal liability policy. We cover the personal injuries mentioned on page 4 -- mental anguish, defamation of character, libel, and so on. The coverage we give you is worldwide. And we cover loss or damage to tangible property that's entrusted to anyone insured under this policy.

[C4386]

**What Else We Will Do for You**

In those cases where this policy protects you against claims not covered in any of your other policies, we'll do much more for you than just pay for legal liabilities.

We'll defend any suit for damages against you or anyone else insured even if it's groundless or fraudulent. And we'll investigate, negotiate and settle on your behalf any claim or suit if that seems to us proper and wise.

*You own a two-family house and rent the second-floor apartment to the Miller family. The Millers don't pay the rent and you finally have to evict them. Out of sheer spite, they sue you for wrongful eviction. You're clearly in the right, but the defense of the suit costs $750. Under this policy we defend you and win the case in court. The whole business doesn't cost you a penny.*

We'll pay premiums for bonds to release attachments up to the limit of this policy. We'll also pay premiums on appeal bonds and the cost of bail bonds. But we won't apply for those bonds or furnish them ourselves.

We'll pay all our own expenses of your suit and all court costs owed by you or anyone insured. And we'll pay interest on the part of the judgment we owe.

**We'll pay for all these extra expenses on top of the liability limit of this policy.**

If there's a verdict against you that's higher than your other insurance liability limits and neither you nor your other insurance company decides to appeal, we may appeal. **At our own expense.**

*Returning from a party on a rainy night, you skid off the road and run into a brick wall. A passenger in your car is seriously hurt. A jury awards him $310,000, on the grounds that you caused the accident because you were drunk. Your auto insurance company feels it's hopeless to appeal. We believe your protestations that you were **not** drunk, appeal, and win a second trial. The second jury hears more evidence about your behavior at the party and decides in your favor.*

We'll also reimburse you and your family members for earnings lost at our request, such as while testifying in court. We'll pay up to $100 a day and $5,000 total.

We'll pay the extra insurance amount directly to the claimants after there's a final verdict or a settlement signed by the claimants, you and us. If you've made a settlement we've agreed to and you've paid the claimants personally, we'll reimburse you for what we owe you.

In countries where we can't handle your case ourselves, we'll pay for someone else to handle the case if we've given our written consent.

---

**What You Must Do for Us**

Here are a few things you'll have to do for us. Not only you, but anyone who's insured under this policy.

**If there's an accident or incident that may be covered by this policy, notify us in writing as soon as possible.** You can give this notice to any of our authorized agents. Include all the information you have or can get.

If anyone makes any claim against you, notify us as soon as possible. If you're sued, send us copies of all suit papers, reports and documents. If we decide to enter the negotiations or suit, help us in any way you can.

**We're not obligated to pay for your loss unless you do all this.**

[C4387]

**Other Conditions of This Policy**

Neither you nor anyone else covered can assign or turn over the interest under this policy without our written consent. Nor can you or anyone else bring us into any action against you or anyone insured.

You must do everything you can to preserve your rights of recovery. These rights will belong to us up to the amount we've paid for the loss.

If you go bankrupt or become insolvent, this doesn't free us of our obligations under this policy. If you die or are declared bankrupt or insolvent within the policy period, your legal representative will still be covered until the end of the policy period.

Waivers or changes of your coverage or our rights are valid only with a written endorsement to this policy.

If any of the terms of this policy should conflict with state or local law, you can enforce them as if they'd been changed to conform.

**Can This Policy Be Canceled?**

Yes it can. Both by you and by us.

If you want to cancel the policy, hand or send your cancellation notice to us or our authorized agent. Or mail us a written notice with the date when you want the policy canceled. We'll send you a check for the unearned premium, figured by the short rate table – that is, pro rata minus a service charge.

If we decide to cancel the policy, we'll mail or deliver to you a cancellation notice effective after at least 30 days. As soon as we can, we'll send you a check for the unearned premium, figured pro rata.

**A Final Word**

We hope for your sake that you'll never have occasion to use this policy. But if you do, be sure to call your agent at once. He'll do everything he can to help you.

Thank you for taking out this policy with us.

PROVISIONS REQUIRED BY LAW TO BE STATED IN THIS POLICY:–"This Policy is issued under and in pursuance of the laws of the State of Minnesota, relating to Guaranty Surplus and Special Reserve Funds." Chapter 437, General Laws of 1909.

This policy is signed here by the President and Secretary of the St. Paul Fire and Marine Insurance Company and countersigned on the declarations page by its authorized representative.

Secretary. President

[C4388]

*

# Index

(References are normally to the beginning page of cases or other materials which bear upon the topic indexed. On occasion, references have also been made to items deserving special attention which are found within the text of a case, a note, etc.)

†